HOLT McDOUGAL

Algebra 1

Edward B. Burger

David J. Chard

Paul A. Kennedy

Steven J. Leinwand

Freddie L. Renfro

Tom W. Roby

Bert K. Waits

HOLT McDOUGAL

HOUGHTON MIFFLIN HARCOURT

COMMON CORE EDITION

Printed in the U.S.A.

ISBN   978-0-547-64703-6

6 7 8 9 10 0868 20 19 18 17 16 15 14

4500453060   C D E F G

Cover photo: © James L. Amos/Corbis

AUTHORS

Edward B. Burger, Ph.D., is Professor of Mathematics at Williams College and is the author of numerous articles, books, and videos. He has won several of the most prestigious writing and teaching awards offered by the Mathematical Association of America. Dr. Burger has made numerous television and radio appearances and has given countless mathematical presentations around the world.

David J. Chard, Ph.D., is the Leon Simmons Dean of the School of Education and Human Development at Southern Methodist University. He is a past president of the Divison of Research at the Council for Exceptional Children, a member of the International Academy for Research on Learning Disabilities, and has been the Principal Investigator on numerous research projects for the U.S. Department of Education.

Paul A. Kennedy, Ph.D., is a professor and Distinguished University Teaching Scholar in the Department of Mathematics at Colorado State University. Dr. Kennedy is a leader in mathematics education. His research focuses on developing algebraic thinking by using multiple representations and technology. He is the author of numerous publications.

Steven J. Leinwand is a Principal Research Analyst at the American Institutes for Research in Washington, D.C. He was previously, for 22 years, the Mathematics Supervisor with the Connecticut Department of Education.

Freddie L. Renfro, MA, has 35 years of experience in Texas education as a classroom teacher and director/coordinator of Mathematics PreK-12 for school districts in the Houston area. She has served as a reviewer and TXTEAM trainer for Texas Math Institutes and has presented at numerous math workshops.

Tom W. Roby, Ph.D., is Associate Professor of Mathematics and Director of the Quantitative Learning Center at the University of Connecticut. He founded and directed the Bay Area-based ACCLAIM professional development program. He also chaired the advisory board of the California Mathematics Project and reviewed content for the California Standards Tests.

Bert K. Waits, Ph.D., is a Professor Emeritus of Mathematics at The Ohio State University and cofounder of T^3 (Teachers Teaching with Technology), a national professional development program. Dr. Waits is also a former board member of the NCTM and an author of the original NCTM Standards.

REVIEWERS

John Bakelaar
Assistant Principal
Whitten Middle School
Jackson, MS

Jennifer Bauer
Mathematics Instructional Leader
East Haven High School
East Haven, CT

Doug Becker
Mathematics Teacher
Gaylord High School
Gaylord, MI

Joe Brady
Mathematics Department Chair
Ensworth High School
Nashville, TN

Sharon Butler
Adjunct Faculty
Montgomery College of The Woodlands
Spring, TX

Kathy Dean Davis
Mathematics Department Chair, retired
Bowling Green Junior High
Bowling Green, KY

Maureen "Willie" DiLaura
Middle School Math Specialist, retired
Lockerman Middle School
Denton, MD

Arlane Frederick
Curriculum & Learning Specialist in
   Mathematics, retired
Kenmore-Town of Tonawanda UFSD
Buffalo, NY

Marieta W. Harris
Mathematics Specialist
Memphis, TN

Connie Johnsen
Mathematics Teacher
Harker Heights High School
Harker Heights, TX

Mary Jones
Mathematics Supervisor/Teacher
Grand Rapids Public Schools
Grand Rapids, MI

Lendy Jones
Algebra Teacher
Liberty Hill Middle School
Killeen, TX

Mary Joy
Algebra Teacher
Mayfield High School
Las Cruces, NM

Vilma Martinez
Algebra Teacher
Nikki Rowe High School
McAllen, TX

Mende Mays
Algebra Teacher
Crockett Junior High
Odessa, TX

Rebecca Newburn
Lead Math Teacher
Davidson Middle School
San Rafael, CA

Vicki Petty
Mathematics Teacher
Central Middle School
Murfreesboro, TN

Susan Pippen
Mathematics Department Chair
Hinsdale South High School
Darien, IL

Elaine Rafferty
Mathematics Learning Specialist
Charleston County SD
Charleston, SC

Susan Rash
Manager of Secondary Curriculum
Red Clay CSD
Wilmington, DE

John Remensky
Mathematics Department Chair
South Park High School
South Park, PA

Raymond Seymour
Mathematics Department Head, retired
Kirby Middle School
San Antonio, TX

Jennifer J. Southers
Mathematics Teacher
Hillcrest High School
Simpsonville, SC

Jill Springer
Mathematics Teacher
Henderson County High School
Henderson, KY

Dr. Katherine Staltare
Mathematics Consultant & Graduate Level
 Course Developer
NYSUT, Effective Teaching Program
New York State

Pam Walker
Curriculum Teacher Specialist
Nacogdoches ISD
Nacogdoches, TX

Larry Ward
Mathematics Supervisor, retired
Carrollton-Farmers Branch ISD
Carrollton, TX

Carmen Whitman
Director, Mathematics for All Consulting
Pflugerville, TX

CONTRIBUTING AUTHORS

Carmen Whitman
Pflugerville, TX

Linda Antinone
Fort Worth, TX

FIELD TEST PARTICIPANTS

Len Zigment
Mesa Ridge High School
Colorado Springs, CO

John Bakelaar
Peebles Middle School
Jackson, MS

Vicky Petty
Central Middle School
Murfreesboro, TN

Carey Carter
Alvarado High School
Alvarado, TX

Equations

Inequalities

Learn It Online
Online Resources **my.hrw.com**

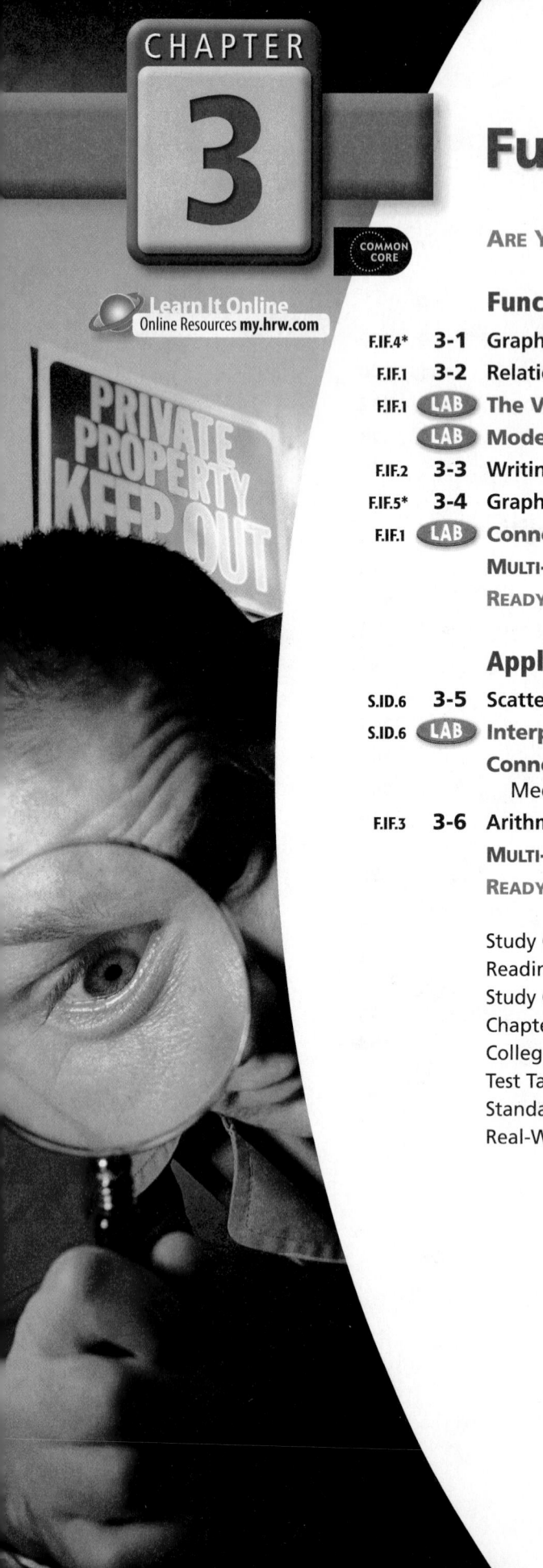

CHAPTER 3

COMMON CORE

Learn It Online
Online Resources **my.hrw.com**

Functions

CHAPTER 4

Linear Functions

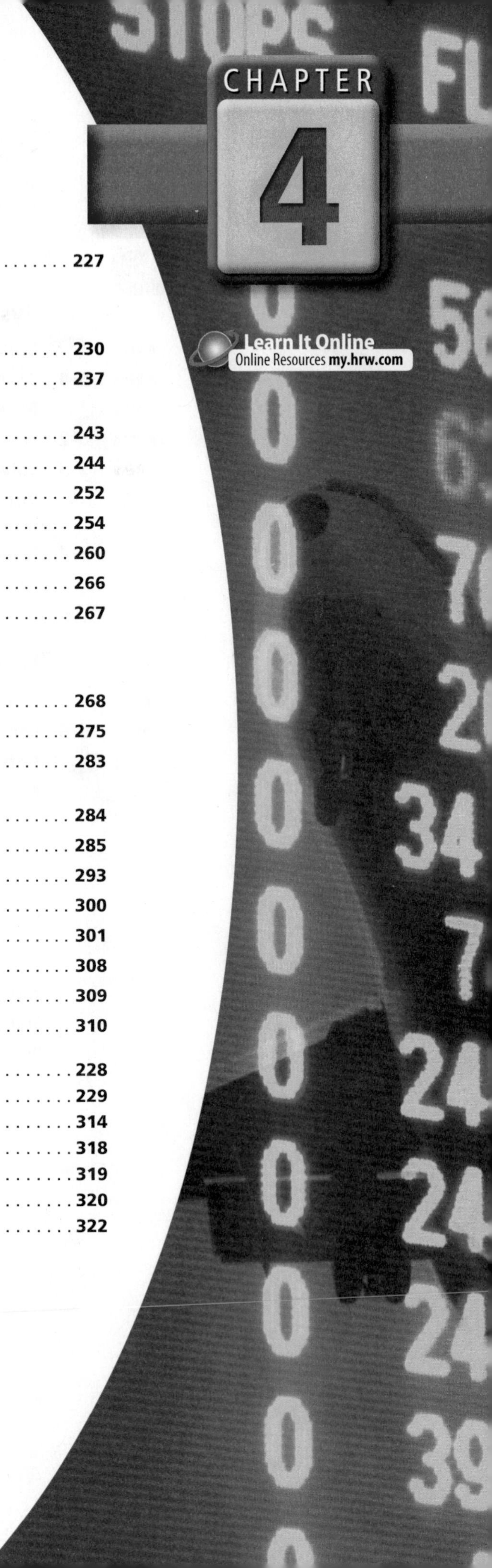

Learn It Online
Online Resources my.hrw.com

COMMON CORE

Dennis Hallinan/Alamy Photos

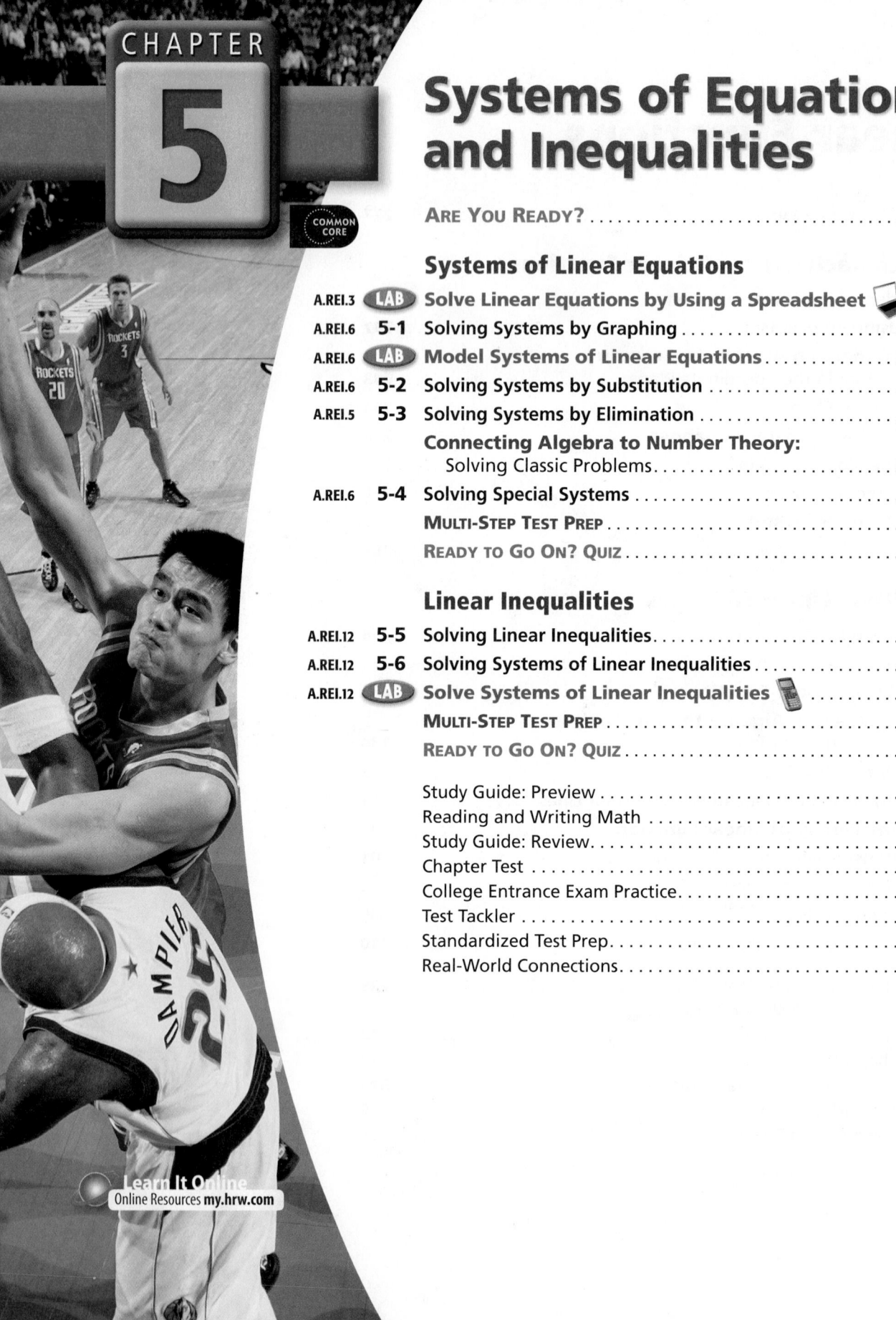

Systems of Equations and Inequalities

Learn It Online
Online Resources **my.hrw.com**

Glenn James/NBAE/Getty Images

Exponents and Polynomials

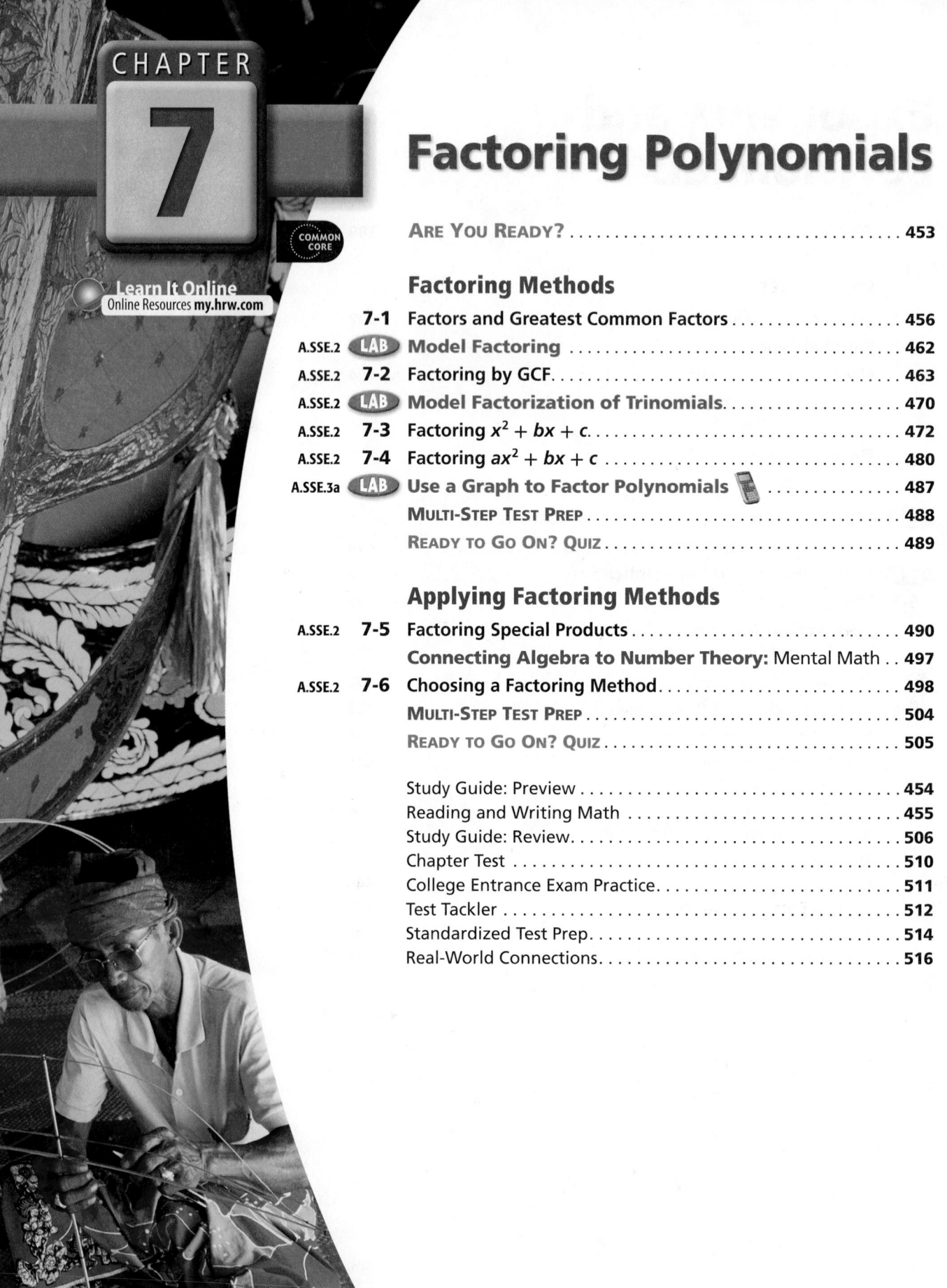

CHAPTER 7

Factoring Polynomials

COMMON CORE

Learn It Online
Online Resources **my.hrw.com**

Quadratic Functions and Equations

COMMON CORE

Learn It Online
Online Resources **my.hrw.com**

James Randklev/CORBIS

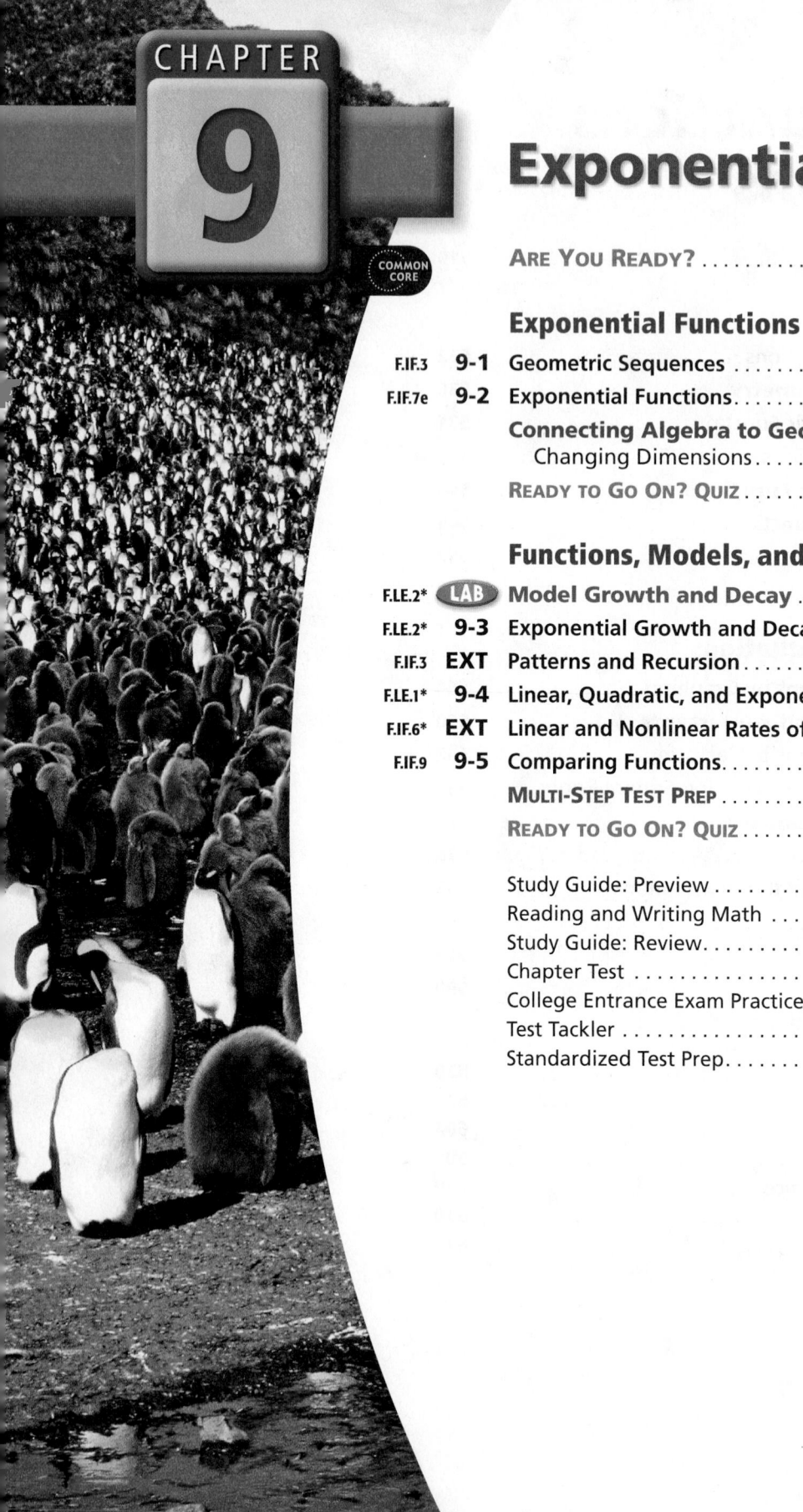

Exponential Functions

Data Analysis and Probability

COMMON CORE

Learn It Online
Online Resources **my.hrw.com**

Standards for Mathematical Content
Correlation for Holt McDougal Algebra 1, Geometry, and Algebra 2

Standards	Descriptor	Algebra 1	Geometry	Algebra 2
Standards for Mathematical Content				
(+ = advanced; * = also a Modeling Standard)				
Number and Quantity				
CC.9-12.N.RN.1	Explain how the definition of the meaning of rational exponents follows from extending the properties of integer exponents to those values, allowing for a notation for radicals in terms of rational exponents.	SE: 392–393, 398–402		SE: 358–360, 395
CC.9-12.N.RN.2	Rewrite expressions involving radicals and rational exponents using the properties of exponents.	SE: 400–402	SE: 358	SE: 358–365, 392, 394, 398
CC.9-12.N.RN.3	Explain why the sum or product of two rational numbers is rational; that the sum of a rational number and an irrational number is irrational; and that the product of a nonzero rational number and an irrational number is irrational.	SE: 431–432		
CC.9-12.N.Q.1	Use units as a way to understand problems and to guide the solution of multi-step problems; choose and interpret units consistently in formulas; choose and interpret the scale and the origin in graphs and data displays.*	SE: 10, 26–30, 43–45, 53, 56–58, 59, 61, 62–68, 70–74, 83, 85–86, 88, 93, 108, 110, 115, 118, 122–124, 144, 159, 176, 184–185, 189–191, 194, 202, 208–209, 212, 213, 223, 265, 271–273, 279–281, 284, 488, 534, 536–537, 539–542, 549–550, 553, 556–558, 564–566, 572, 577–578, 598, 603, 628, 639–641	SE: 105, 108, 140, 186, 193–195, 197, 200, 211, 273, 445, 461, 528, 586, 593, 657, 671, 684–685, 695, 697–698, 703, 708, 713, 715, 727, 750, 753–756, 777, 786, 800, 865	SE: 12, 39, 90, 122, 229, 265, 293–294, 325, 340, 345–348, 363–364, 373, 381, 383, 437, 506, 650, 713, 732

SE = Student Edition

Standards	Descriptor	Algebra 1	Geometry	Algebra 2
Standards for Mathematical Content				
(+ = advanced; * = also a Modeling Standard)				
Number and Quantity				
CC.9-12.N.Q.2	Define appropriate quantities for the purpose of descriptive modeling.*	SE: 62–68, 75–81, 686–694, 695–701		
CC.9-12.N.Q.3	Choose a level of accuracy appropriate to limitations on measurement when reporting quantities.*	SE: 75–81		
CC.9-12.N.CN.1	Know there is a complex number i such that $i^2 = -1$, and every complex number has the form $a + bi$ with a and b real.			SE: 94–95, 138
CC.9-12.N.CN.2	Use the relation $i^2 = -1$ and the commutative, associative, and distributive properties to add, subtract, and multiply complex numbers.			SE: 128–131, 139, 141, 477
CC.9-12.N.CN.3	(+) Find the conjugate of a complex number; use conjugates to find moduli and quotients of complex numbers.			SE: 96–99, 126–133, 138, 145, 226
CC.9-12.N.CN.4	(+) Represent complex numbers on the complex plane in rectangular and polar form (including real and imaginary numbers), and explain why the rectangular and polar forms of a given complex number represent the same number.			*Opportunities to address this standard can be found on the following pages:* SE: 126–128, 139
CC.9-12.N.CN.5	(+) Represent addition, subtraction, multiplication, and conjugation of complex numbers geometrically on the complex plane; use properties of this representation for computation.			*Opportunities to address this standard can be found on the following pages:* SE: 126–133

SE = Student Edition

Standards	Descriptor	Algebra 1	Geometry	Algebra 2
Standards for Mathematical Content				
(+ = advanced; * = also a Modeling Standard)				
Number and Quantity				
CC.9-12.N.CN.6	(+) Calculate the distance between numbers in the complex plane as the modulus of the difference, and the midpoint of a segment as the average of the numbers at its endpoints.	*This standard is outside the scope of the Holt McDougal AGA series.*		
CC.9-12.N.CN.7	Solve quadratic equations with real coefficients that have complex solutions.			SE: 96–99, 101–107, 109, 138, 140, 190–195, 221
CC.9-12.N.CN.8	(+) Extend polynomial identities to the complex numbers.			SE: 189–195, 221
CC.9-12.N.CN.9	(+) Know the Fundamental Theorem of Algebra; show that it is true for quadratic polynomials.			SE: 189–195, 221, 222
CC.9-12.N.VM.1	(+) Recognize vector quantities as having both magnitude and direction. Represent vector quantities by directed line segments, and use appropriate symbols for vectors and their magnitudes (e.g., v, $|v|$, $\|v\|$, v).		SE: 577–585	
CC.9-12.N.VM.2	(+) Find the components of a vector by subtracting the coordinates of an initial point from the coordinates of a terminal point.		SE: 577	
CC.9-12.N.VM.3	(+) Solve problems involving velocity and other quantities that can be represented by vectors.		SE: 577–585, 586, 587, 591, 592, 593, 595	

SE = Student Edition

Standards	Descriptor	Algebra 1	Geometry	Algebra 2
Standards for Mathematical Content				
(+ = advanced; * = also a Modeling Standard)				
Number and Quantity				
CC.9-12.N.VM.4	(+) Add and subtract vectors. a. Add vectors end-to-end, component-wise, and by the parallelogram rule. Understand that the magnitude of a sum of two vectors is typically not the sum of the magnitudes. b. Given two vectors in magnitude and direction form, determine the magnitude and direction of their sum. c. Understand vector subtraction $v - w$ as $v + (-w)$, where $-w$ is the additive inverse of w, with the same magnitude as w and pointing in the opposite direction. Represent vector subtraction graphically by connecting the tips in the appropriate order, and perform vector subtraction component-wise.		SE: 577–585, 586, 587, 591, 596, 785	
CC.9-12.N.VM.5	(+) Multiply a vector by a scalar. a. Represent scalar multiplication graphically by scaling vectors and possibly reversing their direction; perform scalar multiplication component-wise, e.g., as $c(v_x, v_y) = (cv_x, cv_y)$. b. Compute the magnitude of a scalar multiple cv using $\|cv\| = |c|v$. Compute the direction of cv knowing that when $|c|v \neq 0$, the direction of cv is either along v (for $c > 0$) or against v (for $c < 0$).		SE: 577–585	
CC.9-12.N.VM.6	(+) Use matrices to represent and manipulate data, e.g., to represent payoffs or incidence relationships in a network.	*This standard is outside the scope of the Holt McDougal AGA series.*		

SE = Student Edition

Standards	Descriptor	Algebra 1	Geometry	Algebra 2
Standards for Mathematical Content				
(+ = advanced; * = also a Modeling Standard)				
Number and Quantity				
CC.9-12.N.VM.7	(+) Multiply matrices by scalars to produce new matrices, e.g., as when all of the payoffs in a game are doubled.	*This standard is outside the scope of the Holt McDougal AGA series.*		
CC.9-12.N.VM.8	(+) Add, subtract, and multiply matrices of appropriate dimensions.			SE: 144
CC.9-12.N.VM.9	(+) Understand that, unlike multiplication of numbers, matrix multiplication for square matrices is not a commutative operation, but still satisfies the associative and distributive properties.	*This standard is outside the scope of the Holt McDougal AGA series.*		
CC.9-12.N.VM.10	(+) Understand that the zero and identity matrices play a role in matrix addition and multiplication similar to the role of 0 and 1 in the real numbers. The determinant of a square matrix is nonzero if and only if the matrix has a multiplicative inverse.	*This standard is outside the scope of the Holt McDougal AGA series.*		
CC.9-12.N.VM.11	(+) Multiply a vector (regarded as a matrix with one column) by a matrix of suitable dimensions to produce another vector. Work with matrices as transformations of vectors.	*This standard is outside the scope of the Holt McDougal AGA series.*		
CC.9-12.N.VM.12	(+) Work with 2×2 matrices as a transformations of the plane, and interpret the absolute value of the determinant in terms of area.	*This standard is outside the scope of the Holt McDougal AGA series.*		

SE = Student Edition

Standards	Descriptor	Algebra 1	Geometry	Algebra 2
Standards for Mathematical Content				
(+ = advanced; * = also a Modeling Standard)				
Algebra				
CC.9-12.A.SSE.1	Interpret expressions that represent a quantity in terms of its context.* a. Interpret parts of an expression, such as terms, factors, and coefficients. b. Interpret complicated expressions by viewing one or more of their parts as a single entity.	SE: 10–11, 512, 514	SE: 36–41, 312–318, 689, 751, 757, 759	SE: 75, 234–240
CC.9-12.A.SSE.2	Use the structure of an expression to identify ways to rewrite it.	SE: 462, 463–469, 470–471, 472–479, 480–486, 487, 488, 489, 490–496, 498–503, 504, 505, 507–509, 510, 511, 514–515, 739	SE: 13–19	SE: 75, 141, 174–179, 219
CC.9-12.A.SSE.3	Choose and produce an equivalent form of an expression to reveal and explain properties of the quantity represented by the expression. a. Factor a quadratic expression to reveal the zeros of the function it defines. b. Complete the square in a quadratic expression to reveal the maximum or minimum value of the function it defines. c. Use the properties of exponents to transform expressions for exponential functions.	SE: a. & b.) 470–471, 472–479, 480–486, 487, 488, 489, 490–496, 499–503, 504, 505, 508–509, 510, 511, 514, 739 a.) 562–563, 636–641		SE: a. & b.) 75, 76, 77–84, 86–93, 137, 307 c.) 239
CC.9-12.A.SSE.4	Derive the formula for the sum of a finite geometric series (when the common ratio is not 1), and use the formula to solve problems.			SE: 658, 660–661, 678, 680

SE = Student Edition

Standards	Descriptor	Algebra 1	Geometry	Algebra 2
Standards for Mathematical Content				
(+ = advanced; * = also a Modeling Standard)				
Algebra				
CC.9-12.A.APR.1	Understand that polynomials form a system analogous to the integers, namely, they are closed under the operations of addition, subtraction, and multiplication; add, subtract, and multiply polynomials.	SE: 414–419, 422–429, 433–439		SE: 150–156, 158–164, 181, 218, 219, 222, 223, 224, 227, 307, 309, 335–338, 399, 403, 751
CC.9-12.A.APR.2	Know and apply the Remainder Theorem: For a polynomial $p(x)$ and a number a, the remainder on division by $x - a$ is $p(a)$, so $p(a) = 0$ if and only if $(x - a)$ is a factor of $p(x)$.			SE: 166–172, 174–179, 189–195, 220, 222
CC.9-12.A.APR.3	Identify zeros of polynomials when suitable factorizations are available, and use the zeros to construct a rough graph of the function defined by the polynomial.	SE: 562–567, 600–601		SE: 176–179, 181, 182–188, 219, 220, 223, 880
CC.9-12.A.APR.4	Prove polynomial identities and use them to describe numerical relationships.	SE: 433–439, 490–496, 497		SE: 158–161, 174–179
CC.9-12.A.APR.5	(+) Know and apply the Binomial Theorem for the expansion of $(x + y)^n$ in powers of x and y for a positive integer n, where x and y are any numbers, with coefficients determined for example by Pascal's Triangle. (The Binomial Theorem can be proved by mathematical induction or by a combinatorial argument.)			SE: 157, 158–164, 531, 532, 587, 590, 684
CC.9-12.A.APR.6	Rewrite simple rational expressions in different forms; write $a(x)/b(x)$ in the form $q(x) + r(x)/b(x)$, where $a(x)$, $b(x)$, $q(x)$, and $r(x)$ are polynomials with the degree of $r(x)$ less than the degree of $b(x)$, using inspection, long division, or, for the more complicated examples, a computer algebra system.		SE: 682, 685	SE: 166–172, 219, 222, 224, 537

SE = Student Edition

Standards	Descriptor	Algebra 1	Geometry	Algebra 2
Standards for Mathematical Content				
(+ = advanced; * = also a Modeling Standard)				
Algebra				
CC.9-12.A.APR.7	(+) Understand that rational expressions form a system analogous to the rational numbers, closed under addition, subtraction, multiplication, and division by a nonzero rational expression; add, subtract, multiply, and divide rational expressions.			SE: 321–326, 327–334, 335–338, 357, 391, 394, 395, 881
CC.9-12.A.CED.1	Create equations and inequalities in one variable and use them to solve problems. Include equations arising from linear and quadratic functions, and simple rational and exponential functions.*	SE: 19–22, 26–29, 34–38, 42–46, 54–59, 100–105, 107–111, 114–117, 118, 119, 122–125, 127–132, 144–147, 148, 149, 150–153, 154, 156–157, 158–159, 562–567, 568–573, 575–581, 582–589, 624–630		SE: 42, 46, 77–84, 85–92, 94–99, 100–107, 110–117, 144, 182–188, 189–195, 266–272, 348–355, 376–383, 474, 785–797
CC.9-12.A.CED.2	Create equations in two or more variables to represent relationships between quantities; graph equations on coordinate axes with labels and scales.*	SE: 179–185, 186–192, 230–236, 237–242, 244–251, 254–259, 260–265, 268–274, 275–282, 293–299, 301–307, 329–334, 336–342, 343–349, 352–357, 538–543, 545–551, 554–559, 582–589, 635–642, 649–655	SE: 182–187, 190–197, 201, 205, 206, 517	SE: 15–21, 24–30, 32–39, 44, 46, 59–66, 67–74, 118–125, 150–156, 197–203, 204–209, 210–215, 226, 234–240, 242–248, 249–255, 275–280, 281–288, 289–295, 313–320, 340–347, 367–375, 422–429, 432–439, 442–448, 450–456, 458–465, 536, 749, 754–761, 767

SE = Student Edition

Standards	Descriptor	Algebra 1	Geometry	Algebra 2
Standards for Mathematical Content				
(+ = advanced; * = also a Modeling Standard)				
Algebra				
CC.9-12.A.CED.3	Represent constraints by equations or inequalities, and by systems of equations and/or inequalities, and interpret solutions as viable or nonviable options in a modeling context.*	SE: 179–185, 230–236, 237–242, 260–265, 268–274, 275–282, 301–307, 331–334, 339–342, 346–349, 350–351, 354–356, 358, 359, 369–371, 374, 375, 376–378, 380, 381, 384–385, 451, 538–543, 554–559, 562–567, 568–573, 575–581, 582–589, 613, 635–642, 649–655		SE: 15–21, 24–30, 32–39, 59–66, 67–74, 110–117, 118–125, 150–156, 197–203, 204–209, 210–215, 234–240, 242–248, 249–255, 275–280, 281–288, 289–295, 313–320, 340–347, 367–375, 422–429, 432–439, 442–448, 450–456, 458–465, 749, 754–761, 762–767
CC.9-12.A.CED.4	Rearrange formulas to highlight a quantity of interest, using the same reasoning as in solving equations.*	SE: 49–53, 59, 68, 85, 88, 161	SE: 41, 673, 674, 676, 685	SE: 449
CC.9-12.A.REI.1	Explain each step in solving a simple equation as following from the equality of numbers asserted at the previous step, starting from the assumption that the original equation has a solution. Construct a viable argument to justify a solution method.	SE: 17–22, 24–30, 32–38, 40–46, 54–59, 61, 84–85	SE: 104–109, 127, 132, 134	SE: 77–84, 85–92, 100–107, 182–188, 266–272, 348–355, 376–383
CC.9-12.A.REI.2	Solve simple rational and radical equations in one variable, and give examples showing how extraneous solutions may arise.	SE: 669, 673, 674	SE: 466–471, 482–489, 493, 495–501, 520	SE: 348–355, 357, 376–383, 388, 389, 392, 393, 394, 395, 398, 399, 476, 809

SE = Student Edition

Standards	Descriptor	Algebra 1	Geometry	Algebra 2
Standards for Mathematical Content				
(+ = advanced; * = also a Modeling Standard)				
Algebra				
CC.9-12.A.REI.3	Solve linear equations and inequalities in one variable, including equations with coefficients represented by letters.	SE: 16, 17–22, 24–30, 31, 32–38, 39, 40–46, 53, 59, 60, 61, 68, 84–85, 88, 89, 92–93, 97, 106–111, 112–117, 118, 119, 120–125, 126–132, 140, 147, 148, 149, 151–152, 154, 155, 158–159, 161, 169, 185, 192, 203, 211, 222, 223, 236, 274, 299, 325, 334, 397, 403, 419, 450, 469, 519, 612, 623, 630, 679, 701, 721, 760		SE: 43, 46, 47, 48
CC.9-12.A.REI.4	Solve quadratic equations in one variable. a. Use the method of completing the square to transform any quadratic equation in x into an equation of the form $(x - p)^2 = q$ that has the same solutions. Derive the quadratic formula from this form. b. Solve quadratic equations by inspection (e.g., for $x^2 = 49$), taking square roots, completing the square, the quadratic formula and factoring, as appropriate to the initial form of the equation. Recognize when the quadratic formula gives complex solutions and write them as $a \pm bi$ for real numbers a and b.	SE: 554–559, 560–561, 562–567, 568–573, 576–581, 582–583, 585–589, 598, 599, 606–607, 608, 609, 613, 655	SE: 27, 45, 47–48, 55, 59, 63, 243, 245, 289, 338, 361–367, 377, 381, 382, 400, 427, 442, 444–446, 508, 798, 842, 844–846	SE: 77–84, 85–92, 96–99, 100–107, 108, 109, 137, 140, 143, 145, 307, 309, 684, 749
CC.9-12.A.REI.5	Prove that, given a system of two equations in two variables, replacing one equation by the sum of that equation and a multiple of the other produces a system with the same solutions.	SE: 343–349		

SE = Student Edition

Standards	Descriptor	Algebra 1	Geometry	Algebra 2
Standards for Mathematical Content				
(+ = advanced; * = also a Modeling Standard)				
Algebra				
CC.9-12.A.REI.6	Solve systems of linear equations exactly and approximately (e.g., with graphs), focusing on pairs of linear equations in two variables.	SE: 329–334, 336–342, 343–349, 350–351, 352–357, 358, 359, 376–378, 380, 381, 383, 384	SE: 152–153, 158–160, 161, 176, 194, 195, 328, 329–330	SE: 684
CC.9-12.A.REI.7	Solve a simple system consisting of a linear equation and a quadratic equation in two variables algebraically and graphically.	SE: 590–597	SE: 853	SE: 809, 862–869, 871, 872, 876, 877
CC.9-12.A.REI.8	(+) Represent a system of linear equations as a single matrix equation in a vector variable.	*This standard is outside the scope of the Holt McDougal AGA series.*		
CC.9-12.A.REI.9	(+) Find the inverse of a matrix if it exists and use it to solve systems of linear equations (using technology for matrices of dimension 3 × 3 or greater).	*This standard is outside the scope of the Holt McDougal AGA series.*		
CC.9-12.A.REI.10	Understand that the graph of an equation in two variables is the set of all its solutions plotted in the coordinate plane, often forming a curve (which could be a line).	SE: 186–192, 193, 216		SE: 43, 46
CC.9-12.A.REI.11	Explain why the x-coordinates of the points where the graphs of the equations $y = f(x)$ and $y = g(x)$ intersect are the solutions of the equation $f(x) = g(x)$; find the solutions approximately, e.g., using technology to graph the functions, make tables of values, or find successive approximations. Include cases where $f(x)$ and/or $g(x)$ are linear, polynomial, rational, absolute value, exponential, and logarithmic functions.*	SE: 47–48, 554–559, 560–561, 628, 629		SE: 79–80, 182–186, 191–192, 268–269, 351–352, 384–387

SE = Student Edition

Standards	Descriptor	Algebra 1	Geometry	Algebra 2
Standards for Mathematical Content				
(+ = advanced; * = also a Modeling Standard)				
Algebra				
CC.9-12.A.REI.12	Graph the solutions to a linear inequality in two variables as a half-plane (excluding the boundary in the case of a strict inequality), and graph the solution set to a system of linear inequalities in two variables as the intersection of the corresponding half-planes.	SE: 360–366, 368–372, 373, 374, 375, 379, 380, 381, 486		SE: 44, 46, 47, 50, 307, 880
CC.9-12.F.IF.1	Understand that a function from one set (called the domain) to another set (called the range) assigns to each element of the domain exactly one element of the range. If f is a function and x is an element of its domain, then $f(x)$ denotes the output of f corresponding to the input x. The graph of f is the graph of the equation $y = f(x)$.	SE: 170–176, 177, 179–186, 187–192, 193, 195, 215, 219, 222		
CC.9-12.F.IF.2	Use function notation, evaluate functions for inputs in their domains, and interpret statements that use function notation in terms of a context.	SE: 180–185, 192, 195, 216, 218, 219, 223, 322, 397, 629		SE: 50
CC.9-12.F.IF.3	Recognize that sequences are functions, sometimes defined recursively, whose domain is a subset of the integers.	SE: 206–211, 618–623		SE: 626–632
CC.9-12.F.IF.4	For a function that models a relationship between two quantities, interpret key features of graphs and tables in terms of the quantities, and sketch graphs showing key features given a verbal description of the relationship. Key features include: intercepts; intervals where the function is increasing, decreasing, positive, or negative; relative maximums and minimums; symmetries; end behavior; and periodicity.*	SE: 165, 167–168, 195, 214, 230, 234–235, 237–238, 240–242, 266, 267, 271–273, 309, 310–313, 315, 318, 531–532, 535–537, 541–543, 545–551, 552, 553, 554–559, 600–601, 603, 604–605, 608, 613, 630, 641, 644–647, 649–655, 565–659		SE: 7–14, 24–30, 43, 59–66, 67–74, 77–84, 109, 137, 140, 153–156, 183–188, 197–203, 204–209, 218, 220, 221, 222, 223, 236–240, 251–255, 275–280, 281–288, 313–320, 340–347, 367–375, 399, 406–413, 422–429, 432–439, 457, 476, 754–761, 762–767

SE = Student Edition

Standards	Descriptor	Algebra 1	Geometry	Algebra 2
Standards for Mathematical Content				
(+ = advanced; * = also a Modeling Standard)				
Functions				
CC.9-12.F.IF.5	Relate the domain of a function to its graph and, where applicable, to the quantitative relationship it describes.*	SE: 170–176, 182–184, 186–192, 194, 195, 218, 223, 233–235, 241, 260–265, 310–311, 313, 314, 323, 486, 525–529, 542–543, 545–551, 553, 600–601, 603, 669, 672, 674, 675	SE: 401, 685	SE: 14, 19–21, 65, 70, 72–73, 134, 172, 196, 226, 240, 241, 242, 245, 247, 253, 263, 280, 285–286, 288, 299, 302, 341, 345, 367–368, 371–372, 375, 388, 389, 392–393, 394, 413, 428–429, 439, 441, 453–454, 467, 470, 472, 685, 713, 719, 749, 754–761, 767, 851
CC.9-12.F.IF.6	Calculate and interpret the average rate of change of a function (presented symbolically or as a table) over a specified interval. Estimate the rate of change from a graph.*	SE: 244–245, 248–251, 254–259, 267, 268–274, 308, 315, 318, 323, 469, 656–659, 660–667, 739		SE: 44, 210–215, 408–413, 414–421, 468

SE = Student Edition

Standards	Descriptor	Algebra 1	Geometry	Algebra 2
Standards for Mathematical Content				
(+ = advanced; * = also a Modeling Standard)				
Functions				
CC.9-12.F.IF.7	Graph functions expressed symbolically and show key features of the graph, by hand in simple cases and using technology for more complicated cases.* a. Graph linear and quadratic functions and show intercepts, maxima, and minima. b. Graph square root, cube root, and piecewise-defined functions, including step functions and absolute value functions. c. Graph polynomial functions, identifying zeros when suitable factorizations are available, and showing end behavior. d. (+) Graph rational functions, identifying zeros and asymptotes when suitable factorizations are available, and showing end behavior. e. Graph exponential and logarithmic functions, showing intercepts and end behavior, and trigonometric functions, showing period, midline, and amplitude.	SE: a.) 186–192, 193, 195, 216, 218, 219, 220, 230–236, 237–242, 260–265, 266, 267, 268–274, 275–282, 283, 301–307, 309, 314–317, 318, 320, 321, 522–529, 531–537, 538–543, 553, 554–559, 605, 608, 609, 649–655 b.) 310–313 c.) 544, 545–551, 600–603 e.) 624–630		SE: a.) 24–30, 43, 46, 59–66, 67–74, 76, 77–84, 109, 137, 140, 144, 226, 476 b.) 45, 46, 367–375, 388, 389, 393, 394, 398, 422–429, 430–431, 441, 469, 685 c.) 153–156, 182–188, 196, 197–203, 204–209, 218, 220, 221 d.) 339, 340–347, 357, 392, 395, 399 e.) 234–240, 251–255, 275–280, 297, 298, 302, 754–755, 762–767, 768, 769, 800, 801, 804, 807
CC.9–12.F.IF.8	Write a function defined by an expression in different but equivalent forms to reveal and explain different properties of the function. a. Use the process of factoring and completing the square in a quadratic function to show zeros, extreme values, and symmetry of the graph, and interpret these in terms of a context. b. Use the properties of exponents to interpret expressions for exponential functions.	SE: 530, 533–534, 536–537, 541, 543, 553, 605, 608, 624–630		SE: a.) 67–74, 77–84, 85–92, 109, 881 b.) 234–240, 265, 302, 684

SE = Student Edition

Standards	Descriptor	Algebra 1	Geometry	Algebra 2
Standards for Mathematical Content				
(+ = advanced; * = also a Modeling Standard)				
Functions				
CC.9-12.F.IF.9	Compare properties of two functions each represented in a different way (algebraically, graphically, numerically in tables, or by verbal descriptions).	SE: 230–236, 310–313, 531–537, 538–543, 600–601, 624–630, 660–667		SE: 414–421
CC.9-12.F.BF.1	Write a function that describes a relationship between two quantities.* a. Determine an explicit expression, a recursive process, or steps for calculation from a context. b. Combine standard function types using arithmetic operations. c. (+) Compose functions.	SE: 179–185, 230–236, 268–274, 275–282, 545–551, 568–573, 635–642, 644–647, 649–655		SE: 32–39, 118–125, 159–163, 169–171, 180, 181, 206–209, 210–215, 219, 221, 222, 278, 289–295, 425–429, 434–438, 442–448, 450–456, 458–465, 470, 472, 475, 476, 881
CC.9-12.F.BF.2	Write arithmetic and geometric sequences both recursively and with an explicit formula, use them to model situations, and translate between the two forms.*	SE: 206–210, 622–623, 644–647		SE: 626–632, 647–650, 653, 654–663, 676, 677, 678, 680, 681, 684, 685, 749
CC.9-12.F.BF.3	Identify the effect on the graph of replacing $f(x)$ by $f(x) + k$, $k f(x)$, $f(kx)$, and $f(x + k)$ for specific values of k (both positive and negative); find the value of k given the graphs. Experiment with cases and illustrate an explanation of the effects on the graph using technology. Include recognizing even and odd functions from their graphs and algebraic expressions for them.	SE: 300, 301–307, 309, 310–313, 317, 318, 544, 545–551, 553, 559, 606, 608, 732, 747	SE: 101, 374, 618, 638, 640, 748	SE: 7–14, 15–21, 22, 23, 24–30, 44, 46, 51, 59–66, 109, 136, 204–209, 221, 222, 223, 225, 227, 281–288, 301, 302, 306, 368–375, 388, 389, 432–439, 469, 472, 473, 684, 748, 756–761, 762–767

SE = Student Edition

Standards	Descriptor	Algebra 1	Geometry	Algebra 2
Standards for Mathematical Content				
(+ = advanced; * = also a Modeling Standard)				
Functions				
CC.9-12.F.BF.4	Find inverse functions. a. Solve an equation of the form $f(x) = c$ for a simple function f that has an inverse and write an expression for the inverse. b. (+) Verify by composition that one function is the inverse of another. c. (+) Read values of an inverse function from a graph or a table, given that the function has an inverse. d. (+) Produce an invertible function from a non-invertible function by restricting the domain.		SE: 551, 558	SE: a.–c.) 241, 242–248, 251–255, 265, 299, 302, 303, 306, 450–456, 470, 472, 473, 684, 881 c.) 367
CC.9-12.F.BF.5	(+) Understand the inverse relationship between exponents and logarithms and use this relationship to solve problems involving logarithms and exponents.			SE: 249–255, 256–263, 264, 265, 266–272, 275–280, 297, 300, 302, 303, 306, 399, 881
CC.9-12.F.LE.1	Distinguish between situations that can be modeled with linear functions and with exponential functions.* a. Prove that linear functions grow by equal differences over equal intervals, and that exponential functions grow by equal factors over equal intervals. b. Recognize situations in which one quantity changes at a constant rate per unit interval relative to another. c. Recognize situations in which a quantity grows or decays by a constant percent rate per unit interval relative to another.	SE: 625–628, 649–655		SE: a.) 210–215, 406–413, 458–465 b.) 406–413, 441, 458–465, 471, 472 c.) 234–240, 458–465, 471, 472

SE = Student Edition

Standards	Descriptor	Algebra 1	Geometry	Algebra 2
Standards for Mathematical Content				
(+ = advanced; * = also a Modeling Standard)				
Functions				
CC.9-12.F.LE.2	Construct linear and exponential functions, including arithmetic and geometric sequences, given a graph, a description of a relationship, or two input-output pairs (include reading these from a table).*	SE: 206–211, 213, 216–217, 218, 219, 220, 230–236, 237–242, 260–265, 268–274, 275–282, 309, 314–317, 318, 320, 321, 618–623, 633, 635–642, 644–647, 649–655		SE: 44, 46, 234–240, 305, 398, 406–413, 441, 458–465, 468, 471, 472, 537, 643–651, 654–753, 880
CC.9-12.F.LE.3	Observe using graphs and tables that a quantity increasing exponentially eventually exceeds a quantity increasing linearly, quadratically, or (more generally) as a polynomial function.*	SE: 630, 660–667		SE: 234–240, 458–465
CC.9-12.F.LE.4	For exponential models, express as a logarithm the solution to $ab^{ct} = d$ where a, c, and d are numbers and the base b is 2, 10, or e; evaluate the logarithm using technology.*			SE: 249–255, 268–272, 274, 275–280
CC.9-12.F.LE.5	Interpret the parameters in a linear or exponential function in terms of a context.*	SE: 268–274, 635–642		SE: 234–240, 299
CC.9-12.F.TF.1	Understand radian measure of an angle as the length of the arc on the unit circle subtended by the angle.			SE: 707–713
CC.9-12.F.TF.2	Explain how the unit circle in the coordinate plane enables the extension of trigonometric functions to all real numbers, interpreted as radian measures of angles traversed counterclockwise around the unit circle.			SE: 700–702, 706–709

SE = Student Edition

Standards	Descriptor	Algebra 1	Geometry	Algebra 2
Standards for Mathematical Content				
(+ = advanced; * = also a Modeling Standard)				
Functions				
CC.9-12.F.TF.3	(+) Use special triangles to determine geometrically the values of sine, cosine, tangent for $\pi/3$, $\pi/4$ and $\pi/6$, and use the unit circle to express the values of sine, cosines, and tangent for x, $\pi + x$, and $2\pi - x$ in terms of their values for x, where x is any real number.			SE: 693–699, 706–713, 721, 741, 744, 745
CC.9-12.F.TF.4	(+) Use the unit circle to explain symmetry (odd and even) and periodicity of trigonometric functions.			*Opportunities to address this standard can be found on the following pages:* SE: 707–713, 754–761
CC.9-12.F.TF.5	Choose trigonometric functions to model periodic phenomena with specified amplitude, frequency, and midline.*			SE: 756–760, 762–767
CC.9-12.F.TF.6	(+) Understand that restricting a trigonometric function to a domain on which it is always increasing or always decreasing allows its inverse to be constructed.			SE: 714–719
CC.9-12.F.TF.7	(+) Use inverse functions to solve trigonometric equations that arise in modeling contexts; evaluate the solutions using technology, and interpret them in terms of the context.*		SE: 551, 552–559	SE: 716–719, 721, 742, 744, 745, 748, 791–797
CC.9-12.F.TF.8	Prove the Pythagorean identity $sin^2(\theta) + cos^2(\theta) = 1$ and use it to calculate trigonometric ratios.			SE: 772–777, 801, 804, 807
CC.9-12.F.TF.9	(+) Prove the addition and subtraction formulas for sine, cosine, and tangent and use them to solve problems.			SE: 778–783, 799, 802, 804, 805, 808

SE = Student Edition

Standards	Descriptor	Algebra 1	Geometry	Algebra 2
Standards for Mathematical Content				
(+ = advanced; * = also a Modeling Standard)				
Geometry				
CC.9-12.G.CO.1	Know precise definitions of angle, circle, perpendicular line, parallel line, and line segment, based on the undefined notions of point, line, distance along a line, and distance around a circular arc.		SE: 6–11, 20–27, 35, 64, 68, 69, 146–151, 688–693	SE: 700–705, 707–713
CC.9-12.G.CO.2	Represent transformations in the plane using, e.g., transparencies and geometry software; describe transformations as functions that take points in the plane as inputs and give other points as outputs. Compare transformations that preserve distance and angle to those that do not (e.g., translation versus horizontal stretch).		SE: 50–55, 56–57, 509–514, 523, 529, 596, 604–610, 611–617, 619–625, 626–631, 633, 650–657, 660–663, 664, 668, 669, 785	
CC.9-12.G.CO.3	Given a rectangle, parallelogram, trapezoid, or regular polygon, describe the rotations and reflections that carry it onto itself.		SE: 604–610, 611–617, 619–625, 626–631, 633, 634–640, 660–663, 664, 665	
CC.9-12.G.CO.4	Develop definitions of rotations, reflections, and translations in terms of angles, circles, perpendicular lines, parallel lines, and line segments.		SE: 50–55, 604–610, 611–617, 619–625, 633, 660, 661, 664	
CC.9-12.G.CO.5	Given a geometric figure and a rotation, reflection, or translation, draw the transformed figure using, e.g., graph paper, tracing paper, or geometry software. Specify a sequence of transformations that will carry a given figure onto another.		SE: 50–55, 56–57, 59, 63, 64, 604–610, 611–617, 619–625, 626–631, 633, 660–663, 664, 665, 668, 669, 785	

SE = Student Edition

Standards	Descriptor	Algebra 1	Geometry	Algebra 2
Standards for Mathematical Content				
(+ = advanced; * = also a Modeling Standard)				
Geometry				
CC.9-12.G.CO.6	Use geometric descriptions of rigid motions to transform figures and to predict the effect of a given rigid motion on a given figure; given two figures, use the definition of congruence in terms of rigid motions to decide if they are congruent.		SE: 220–223, 258–267, 274–277, 293, 298, 300, 604–610, 611–617, 619–625	
CC.9-12.G.CO.7	Use the definition of congruence in terms of rigid motions to show that two triangles are congruent if and only if corresponding pairs of sides and corresponding pairs of angles are congruent.	SE: 69–74	SE: 220–223, 268–273, 274–277, 293, 294–295, 298, 300	
CC.9-12.G.CO.8	Explain how the criteria for triangle congruence (ASA, SAS, and SSS) follow from the definition of congruence in terms of rigid motions.		SE: 248–249, 250–257, 260–267, 293, 297, 300, 302, 304, 387	
CC.9-12.G.CO.9	Prove geometric theorems about lines and angles. Theorems include: vertical angles are congruent; when a transversal crosses parallel lines, alternate interior angles are congruent and corresponding angles are congruent; points on a perpendicular bisector of a line segment are exactly those equidistant from the segment's endpoints.		SE: 118–125, 155–159, 162, 169, 181, 203–204, 206, 312–318	

SE = Student Edition

Standards	Descriptor	Algebra 1	Geometry	Algebra 2
Standards for Mathematical Content				
(+ = advanced; * = also a Modeling Standard)				
Geometry				
CC.9-12.G.CO.10	Prove theorems about triangles. Theorems include: measures of interior angles of a triangle sum to 180°; base angles of isosceles triangles are congruent; the segment joining midpoints of two sides of a triangle is parallel to the third side and half the length; the medians of a triangle meet at a point.		SE: 231–238, 247, 285–291, 293, 296, 299, 300, 326–331, 334–339, 341, 379, 380	
CC.9-12.G.CO.11	Prove theorems about parallelograms. Theorems include: opposite sides are congruent, the diagonals of a parallelogram bisect each other, and conversely, rectangles are parallelograms with congruent diagonals.	SE: 294, 297, 299	SE: 403–404, 419, 420–427, 451, 454	
CC.9-12.G.CO.12	Make formal geometric constructions with a variety of tools and methods (compass and straightedge, string, reflective devices, paper folding, dynamic geometry software, etc.). Copying a segment; copying an angle; bisecting a segment; bisecting an angle; constructing perpendicular lines, including the perpendicular bisector of a line segment; and constructing a line parallel to a given line through a point not on the line.		SE: 14, 16, 17-18, 22–27, 35, 61, 170–171, 172, 177, 179	
CC.9-12.G.CO.13	Construct an equilateral triangle, a square, and a regular hexagon inscribed in a circle.		SE: 392–393, 826	

SE = Student Edition

Standards	Descriptor	Algebra 1	Geometry	Algebra 2
Standards for Mathematical Content				
(+ = advanced; * = also a Modeling Standard)				
Geometry				
CC.9-12.G.SRT.1	Verify experimentally the properties of dilations given by a center and a scale factor: a. A dilation takes a line not passing through the center of the dilation to a parallel line, and leaves a line passing through the center unchanged. b. The dilation of a line segment is longer or shorter in the ratio given by the scale factor.		SE: 472–479, 509–514, 650–657, 659, 663, 664	
CC.9-12.G.SRT.2	Given two figures, use the definition of similarity in terms of similarity transformations to decide if they are similar; explain using similarity transformations the meaning of similarity for triangles as the equality of all corresponding angles and the proportionality of all corresponding pairs of sides.		SE: 466–471, 472–479, 480–481, 482–489, 493, 495–501, 519, 521, 524, 525, 526, 527, 531, 597	
CC.9-12.G.SRT.3	Use the properties of similarity transformations to establish the AA criterion for two triangles to be similar.		SE: 482–489, 521, 524	
CC.9-12.G.SRT.4	Prove theorems about triangles. Theorems include: a line parallel to one side of a triangle divides the other two proportionally, and conversely; the Pythagorean Theorem proved using triangle similarity.	SE: 69–70, 72–74, 83, 86, 88, 89, 185, 236, 323	SE: 312–318, 341, 359, 360–367, 377, 378, 490–491, 495, 501, 522, 696	
CC.9-12.G.SRT.5	Use congruence and similarity criteria for triangles to solve problems and prove relationships in geometric figures.		SE: 250–257, 258–267, 268–273, 293, 297–298, 300, 302, 304, 482–489, 493, 495–501, 519, 521, 524	

SE = Student Edition

Standards	Descriptor	Algebra 1	Geometry	Algebra 2
Standards for Mathematical Content				
(+ = advanced; * = also a Modeling Standard)				
Geometry				
CC.9-12.G.SRT.6	Understand that by similarity, side ratios in right triangles are properties of the angles in the triangle, leading to definitions of trigonometric ratios for acute angles.		SE: 534–539, 540, 541–548, 561, 588, 589, 592	SE: 693
CC.9-12.G.SRT.7	Explain and use the relationship between the sine and cosine of complementary angles.		SE: 549–550	
CC.9-12.G.SRT.8	Use trigonometric ratios and the Pythagorean Theorem to solve right triangles in applied problems.		SE: 360–371, 377, 381, 382, 383, 385, 552–559, 560, 561, 562–567, 568, 587, 589, 590, 592, 594, 596, 865	SE: 689, 693–699, 721, 740, 744, 745, 749, 809
CC.9-12.G.SRT.9	(+) Derive the formula $A = \frac{1}{2} ab \sin(C)$ for the area of a triangle by drawing an auxiliary line from a vertex perpendicular to the opposite side.		SE: 701	SE: 722
CC.9-12.G.SRT.10	(+) Prove the Laws of Sines and Cosines and use them to solve problems.		SE: 569–576, 587, 590, 592, 593	SE: 722–729, 730–737, 739, 742–743, 744, 745, 748
CC.9-12.G.SRT.11	(+) Understand and apply the Law of Sines and the Law of Cosines to find unknown measurements in right and non-right triangles (e.g., surveying problems, resultant forces).		SE: 569–576, 587, 590, 592, 593	SE: 725–729, 733–737, 739, 742–743, 744
CC.9-12.G.C.1	Prove that all circles are similar.		SE: 472–479	

SE = Student Edition

Standards	Descriptor	Algebra 1	Geometry	Algebra 2
Standards for Mathematical Content				
(+ = advanced; * = also a Modeling Standard)				
Geometry				
CC.9-12.G.C.2	Identify and describe relationships among inscribed angles, radii, and chords. Include the relationship between central, inscribed, and circumscribed angles; inscribed angles on a diameter are right angles; the radius of a circle is perpendicular to the tangent where the radius intersects the circle.		SE: 820–827, 830–837, 840–846, 855, 856, 860, 863, 864	
CC.9-12.G.C.3	Construct the inscribed and circumscribed circles of a triangle, and prove properties of angles for a quadrilateral inscribed in a circle.		SE: 319, 325, 823–827, 855, 858, 865	
CC.9-12.G.C.4	(+) Construct a tangent line from a point outside a given circle to the circle.		SE: 827	
CC.9-12.G.C.5	Derive using similarity the fact that the length of the arc intercepted by an angle is proportional to the radius, and define the radian measure of the angle as the constant of proportionality; derive the formula for the area of a sector.		SE: 810–815, 816–817	SE: 707–713
CC.9-12.G.GPE.1	Derive the equation of a circle of given center and radius using the Pythagorean Theorem; complete the square to find the center and radius of a circle given by an equation.		SE: 847–853, 859, 860	SE: 823–828, 858–860, 870, 871
CC.9-12.G.GPE.2	Derive the equation of a parabola given a focus and directrix.			SE: 845–851, 853, 871, 874, 876, 880

SE = Student Edition

Standards	Descriptor	Algebra 1	Geometry	Algebra 2
Standards for Mathematical Content				
(+ = advanced; * = also a Modeling Standard)				
Geometry				
CC.9–12.G.GPE.3	(+) Derive the equations of ellipses and hyperbolas given foci and directrices.			SE: 748, 830–836, 837, 838–844, 852, 853, 871, 873–874, 876, 881
CC.9-12.G.GPE.4	Use coordinates to prove simple geometric theorems algebraically.		SE: 279–284	SE: 820, 821
CC.9-12.G.GPE.5	Prove the slope criteria for parallel and perpendicular lines and use them to solve geometric problems (e.g., find the equation of line parallel or perpendicular to a given line that passes through a given point).	SE: 293–299, 307, 309, 317, 318, 323, 384, 450, 573, 761	SE: 190–197, 216–219, 412–417, 419, 426–427, 452, 454, 669	
CC.9-12.G.GPE.6	Find the point on a directed line segment between two given points that partitions the segment in a given ratio.	SE: 267, 316	SE: 515–516, 704–709	
CC.9-12.G.GPE.7	Use coordinates to compute perimeters of polygons and areas of triangles and rectangles, e.g., using the distance formula.*		SE: 704–705, 706–709, 727, 730, 732, 737	
CC.9-12.G.GMD.1	Give an informal argument for the formulas for the circumference of a circle, area of a circle, volume of a cylinder, pyramid, and cone. Use dissection arguments, Cavalieri's principle, and informal limit arguments.		SE: 688–693, 749–751, 757	
CC.9-12.G.GMD.2	(+) Give an informal argument using Cavalieri's principle for the formulas for the volume of a sphere and other solid figures.		SE: 749–756, 757–763, 765–772	

SE = Student Edition

Standards	Descriptor	Algebra 1	Geometry	Algebra 2
Standards for Mathematical Content				
(+ = advanced; * = also a Modeling Standard)				
Geometry				
CC.9-12.G.GMD.3	Use volume formulas for cylinders, pyramids, cones, and spheres to solve problems.*	SE: 402–403, 429, 430, 503, 573, 631	SE: 668, 749–756, 757–764, 766–773, 777, 779, 781, 784, 785, 864	SE: 172, 191–192, 325, 366, 816, 829
CC.9-12.G.GMD.4	Identify the shapes of two-dimensional cross-sections of three-dimensional objects, and identify three-dimensional objects generated by rotations of two-dimensional objects.		SE: 742–748, 778	
CC.9-12.G.MG.1	Use geometric shapes, their measures, and their properties to describe objects (e.g., modeling a tree trunk or a human torso as a cylinder).*	SE: 365, 410, 417, 428, 441, 477, 479, 485, 495, 577–578, 580	SE: 226–228, 235–237, 243–244, 253, 256, 266, 290, 291, 300, 316–317, 322–323, 336–337, 440, 444–446, 448, 449, 453, 544–547, 560, 750, 753–755, 758, 761–763, 797–799, 808, 813–814, 841, 843–845	
CC.9-12.G.MG.2	Apply concepts of density based on area and volume in modeling situations (e.g., persons per square mile, BTUs per cubic foot).*	SE: 68	SE: 750, 753, 755, 777	
CC.9-12.G.MG.3	Apply geometric methods to solve design problems (e.g., designing an object or structure to satisfy physical constraints or minimize cost; working with typographic grid systems based on ratios).*		SE: 105, 264, 268, 283, 323, 325, 329–330, 348, 372, 415, 445, 460–461, 471, 512–513, 605, 627, 695, 724, 748	

SE = Student Edition

Standards	Descriptor	Algebra 1	Geometry	Algebra 2
Standards for Mathematical Content				
(+ = advanced; * = also a Modeling Standard)				
Statistics and Probability				
CC.9-12.S.ID.1	Represent data with plots on the real number line (dot plots, histograms, and box plots).*	SE: 686–694, 695–701, 704–709, 710–713, 752, 753, 756		SE: 531, 532, 543–544, 547–548, 749
CC.9-12.S.ID.2	Use statistics appropriate to the shape of the data distribution to compare center (median, mean) and spread (interquartile range, standard deviation) of two or more different data sets.*	SE: 702–709		SE: 548, 576
CC.9-12.S.ID.3	Interpret differences in shape, center, and spread in the context of the data sets, accounting for possible effects of extreme data points (outliers).*	SE: 702–709, 710–713		SE: 527, 543–548
CC.9-12.S.ID.4	Use the mean and standard deviation of a data set to fit it to a normal distribution and to estimate population percentages. Recognize that there are data sets for which such a procedure is not appropriate. Use calculators, spreadsheets, and tables to estimate areas under the normal curve.*			SE: 594–595, 596–603
CC.9-12.S.ID.5	Summarize categorical data for two categories in two-way frequency tables. Interpret relative frequencies in the context of the data (including joint, marginal, and conditional relative frequencies). Recognize possible associations and trends in the data.*			SE: 501, 503–506, 509, 511–518, 530, 536

SE = Student Edition

Standards	Descriptor	Algebra 1	Geometry	Algebra 2
Standards for Mathematical Content				
(+ = advanced; * = also a Modeling Standard)				
Statistics and Probability				
CC.9-12.S.ID.6	Represent data on two quantitative variables on a scatter plot, and describe how the variables are related.* a. Fit a function to the data; use functions fitted to data to solve problems in the context of the data. Use given functions or choose a function suggested by the context. Emphasize linear and exponential models. b. Informally assess the fit of a function by plotting and analyzing residuals. c. Fit a linear function for a scatter plot that suggests a linear association.	SE: 196–198, 200–203, 204, 205, 211, 212, 213, 217, 218, 284, 285–292, 551, 649–655		SE: 32–39, 45, 46, 120–125, 135, 140, 210–215, 289–295, 296, 297, 301, 307, 458–465
CC.9-12.S.ID.7	Interpret the slope (rate of change) and the intercept (constant term) of a linear model in the context of the data.*	SE: 284, 285–292	SE: 183, 186, 193, 194, 195	SE: 32–39, 45
CC.9-12.S.ID.8	Compute (using technology) and interpret the correlation coefficient of a linear fit.*	SE: 285–292		SE: 32–39, 45, 46, 306
CC.9-12.S.ID.9	Distinguish between correlation and causation.*	SE: 285–292		
CC.9-12.S.IC.1	Understand statistics as a process for making inferences about population parameters based on a random sample from that population.*	SE: 716–721		SE: 551–558
CC.9-12.S.IC.2	Decide if a specified model is consistent with results from a given data-generating process, e.g., using simulation.*			SE: 505

SE = Student Edition

Standards	Descriptor	Algebra 1	Geometry	Algebra 2
Standards for Mathematical Content				
(+ = advanced; * = also a Modeling Standard)				
Statistics and Probability				
CC.9-12.S.IC.3	Recognize the purposes of and differences among sample surveys, experiments, and observational studies; explain how randomization relates to each.*	SE: 722–723		SE: 559–566
CC.9-12.S.IC.4	Use data from a sample survey to estimate a population mean or proportion; develop a margin of error through the use of simulation models for random sampling.*			SE: 579–586
CC.9-12.S.IC.5	Use data from a randomized experiment to compare two treatments; use simulations to decide if differences between parameters are significant.*			SE: 567–574
CC.9-12.S.IC.6	Evaluate reports based on data.*	SE: 716–721, 725, 754, 756		SE: 579–586
CC.9-12.S.CP.1	Describe events as subsets of a sample space (the set of outcomes) using characteristics (or categories) of the outcomes, or as unions, intersections, or complements of other events ("or," "and," "not").*	SE: 727–732, 734–739, 740–747		SE: 490–497, 509, 519–525, 530, 533, 534
CC.9-12.S.CP.2	Understand that two events A and B are independent if the probability of A and B occurring together is the product of their probabilities, and use this characterization to determine if they are independent.*	SE: 741–746, 755, 756	SE: 238	SE: 499–506, 509, 530, 532, 533

SE = Student Edition

Standards	Descriptor	Algebra 1	Geometry	Algebra 2
Standards for Mathematical Content				
(+ = advanced; * = also a Modeling Standard)				
Statistics and Probability				
CC.9-12.S.CP.3	Understand the conditional probability of A given B as P(A and B)/P(B), and interpret independence of A and B as saying that the conditional probability of A given B is the same as the probability of A, and the conditional probability of B given A is the same as the probability of B.*	SE: 740–747	SE: 351, 583	SE: 499–506, 530, 685
CC.9-12.S.CP.4	Construct and interpret two-way frequency tables of data when two categories are associated with each object being classified. Use the two-way table as a sample space to decide if events are independent and to approximate conditional probabilities.*			SE: 493–500, 511–518
CC.9-12.S.CP.5	Recognize and explain the concepts of conditional probability and independence in everyday language and everyday situations.*	SE: 740–741, 744–746		SE: 511–518
CC.9-12.S.CP.6	Find the conditional probability of A given B as the fraction of B's outcomes that also belong to A, and interpret the answer in terms of the model.*	SE: 740–747		SE: 499–506, 530
CC.9-12.S.CP.7	Apply the Addition Rule, P(A or B) = P(A) + P(B) − P(A and B), and interpret the answer in terms of the model.*	SE: 748–749		SE: 509, 519–525, 530, 535

SE = Student Edition

Standards	Descriptor	Algebra 1	Geometry	Algebra 2
Standards for Mathematical Content				
(+ = advanced; * = also a Modeling Standard)				
Statistics and Probability				
CC.9-12.S.CP.8	(+) Apply the general Multiplication Rule in a uniform probability model, $P(A \text{ and } B) = P(A)P(B\|A) = P(B)P(A\|B)$, and interpret the answer in terms of the model.*	SE: 740–747		SE: 499–506, 509, 530, 533
CC.9-12.S.CP.9	(+) Use permutations and combinations to compute probabilities of compound events and solve problems.*			SE: 482–488, 490–497, 509, 519–525, 528, 532, 534, 536, 809
CC.9-12.S.MD.1	(+) Define a random variable for a quantity of interest by assigning a numerical value to each event in a sample space; graph the corresponding probability distribution using the same graphical displays as for data distributions.*			SE: 592, 594
CC.9-12.S.MD.2	(+) Calculate the expected value of a random variable; interpret it as the mean of the probability distribution.*			SE: 527, 531, 532, 533, 545, 547
CC.9-12.S.MD.3	(+) Develop a probability distribution for a random variable defined for a sample space in which theoretical probabilities can be calculated; find the expected value. *			SE: 550

SE = Student Edition

Standards	Descriptor	Algebra 1	Geometry	Algebra 2
Standards for Mathematical Content				
(+ = advanced; * = also a Modeling Standard)				
Statistics and Probability				
CC.9-12.S.MD.4	(+) Develop a probability distribution for a random variable defined for a sample space in which probabilities are assigned empirically; find the expected value.*			SE: 527, 531, 532, 588–593
CC.9-12.S.MD.5	(+) Weigh the possible outcomes of a decision by assigning probabilities to payoff values and finding expected values.* a. Find the expected payoff for a game of chance. b. Evaluate and compare strategies on the basis of expected values.			SE: 509, 522–526
CC.9-12.S.MD.6	(+) Use probabilities to make fair decisions (e.g., drawing by lots, using a random number generator).*			SE: 551–558
CC.9-12.S.MD.7	(+) Analyze decisions and strategies using probability concepts (e.g., product testing, medical testing, pulling a hockey goalie at the end of a game).*	SE: 729, 731, 746, 748–749, 750, 754, 756		SE: 495–496, 504, 524, 526, 604–609

SE = Student Edition

Mastering the *Standards*

for Mathematical Practice

The topics described in the Standards for Mathematical Content will vary from year to year. However, the *way* in which you learn, study, and think about mathematics will not. The Standards for Mathematical Practice describe skills that you will use in all of your math courses. These pages show some features of your book that will help you gain these skills and use them to master this year's topics.

① Make sense of problems and persevere in solving them.

Mathematically proficient students start by explaining to themselves the meaning of a problem... They analyze givens, constraints, relationships, and goals. They make conjectures about the form... of the solution and plan a solution pathway...

In your book

Focus on Problem Solving describes a four-step plan for problem solving. The plan is introduced at the beginning of your book, and practice appears throughout.

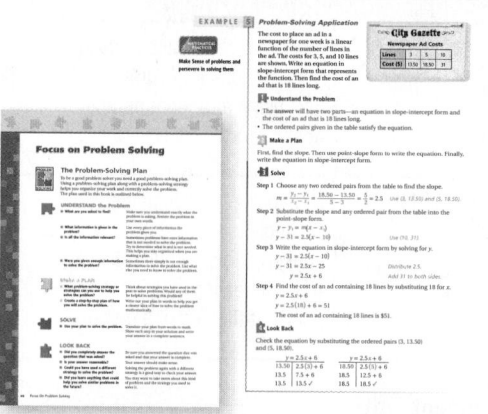

② Reason abstractly and quantitatively.
③ Construct viable arguments and critique the reasoning of others.

Mathematically proficient students... justify their conclusions, [and]... distinguish correct... reasoning from that which is flawed.

In your book

Think and Discuss asks you to evaluate statements, explain relationships, apply mathematical principles, and justify your reasoning.

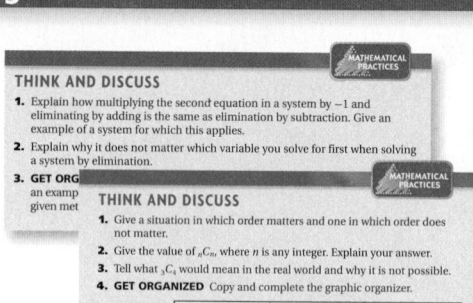

④ Model with mathematics.

Mathematically proficient students can apply... mathematics... to... problems... in everyday life, society, and the workplace...

In your book

Multi-Step Test Prep and **Real-World Connections** apply mathematics to other disciplines and in real-world scenarios.

⑤ Use appropriate tools strategically.

Mathematically proficient students consider the available tools when solving a... problem... [and] are... able to use technological tools to explore and deepen their understanding...

In your book

Algebra Labs and **Technology Labs** use concrete and technological tools to explore mathematical concepts.

⑥ Attend to precision.

Mathematically proficient students... communicate precisely... with others and in their own reasoning... [They] give carefully formulated explanations...

In your book

Reading and Writing Math and **Write About It** help you learn and use the language of math to communicate mathematics precisely.

⑦ Look for and make use of structure.
⑧ Look for and express regularity in repeated reasoning.

Mathematically proficient students... look both for general methods and for shortcuts...

In your book

Lesson examples group similar types of problems together, and the solutions are carefully stepped out. This allows you to make generalizations about— and notice variations in—the underlying structures.

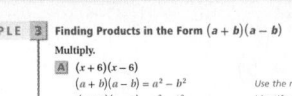

EXAMPLE 3   **Finding Products in the Form** $(a + b)(a - b)$

Multiply.

A $(x + 6)(x - 6)$
   $(a + b)(a - b) = a^2 - b^2$ *Use the rule for $(a + b)(a - b)$.*
   $(x + 6)(x - 6) = x^2 - 6^2$ *Identify a and b: a = x and b = 6.*
                  $= x^2 - 36$ *Simplify.*

B $(x^2 + 2y)(x^2 - 2y)$
   $(a + b)(a - b) = a^2 - b^2$ *Use the rule for $(a + b)(a - b)$.*
   $(x^2 + 2y)(x^2 - 2y) = (x^2)^2 - (2y)^2$ *Identify a and b: a = x^2 and b = 2y.*
                       $= x^4 - 4y^2$ *Simplify.*

C $(7 + n)(7 - n)$
   $(a + b)(a - b) = a^2 - b^2$ *Use the rule for $(a + b)(a - b)$.*
   $(7 + n)(7 - n) = 7^2 - n^2$ *Identify a and b: a = 7 and b = n.*
                  $= 49 - n^2$ *Simplify.*

Countdown to Mastery

DAY 1

Which expression always represents an odd number when n is a natural number?

- Ⓐ $n^2 + 1$
- Ⓑ $2n + 1$
- Ⓒ n^2
- Ⓓ $n + 1$

DAY 2

Cell phone bills are based on a flat monthly fee and the number of minutes used. In the equation $c = 0.07m + 29.99$, what does the variable m represent?

- Ⓕ The number of months billed
- Ⓖ The total amount of the bill
- Ⓗ The number of minutes used
- Ⓙ The phone number

DAY 3

Which equation best describes the relationship between the number of students and the number of tables in the cafeteria?

Students (n)	Tables (t)
720	18
600	15
960	24

- Ⓐ $n = 40t$
- Ⓒ $t = 40n$
- Ⓑ $n = 35t + 90$
- Ⓓ $n = 45t - 90$

DAY 4

Which expression represents the verbal phrase "the sum of three times a number and five"?

- Ⓕ $3(n + 5)$
- Ⓖ $3 + n \cdot 5$
- Ⓗ $3n + 5$
- Ⓙ $3 + (n + 5)$

DAY 5

What is the next term in the pattern?

$$-3, 6, -12, 24, \underline{\quad}, \ldots$$

- Ⓐ 36
- Ⓑ 30
- Ⓒ -32
- Ⓓ -48

Countdown to Mastery

WEEK 2

DAY 1

What is the next term in the pattern?

$$-1, \frac{1}{2}, -\frac{1}{4}, \frac{1}{8}, ___, \ldots$$

Ⓐ $-\frac{1}{10}$

Ⓑ $-\frac{1}{16}$

Ⓒ $\frac{1}{16}$

Ⓓ $\frac{1}{10}$

DAY 2

Which expression is equivalent to $2(3x - 4) - 8x + 3$?

Ⓕ $2x + 11$

Ⓖ $-2x - 5$

Ⓗ $2x - 5$

Ⓙ $-2x - 11$

DAY 3

Based on the table, which inequality correctly shows the relationship between *x* and *y*?

x	2	3	5	6
y	−3	−8	−10	−9

Ⓐ $x > -y$

Ⓑ $2x < -y$

Ⓒ $x < -y$

Ⓓ $2x > -y$

DAY 4

The sum of three consecutive even numbers is 42. The sum can be represented by the equation $n + (n + 2) + (n + 4) = 42$. What does n represent?

Ⓕ The greatest number

Ⓖ The average of the numbers

Ⓗ The middle number

Ⓙ The least number

DAY 5

A job advertisement states that the position pays $12 an hour. Which equation represents the relationship between the salary *s* and the number of hours *h* worked?

Ⓐ $s = 12 + h$

Ⓑ $s = 12h$

Ⓒ $h = 12s$

Ⓓ $h = 12 + s$

Countdown to Mastery

DAY 1

Which expression is equivalent to 2^3?

(A) $2 \cdot 3$

(B) $3 + 3$

(C) $2 + 2 + 2$

(D) $2 \cdot 2 \cdot 2$

DAY 2

Which number is not a solution of $-7y + 19 < 75$?

(F) 13

(G) 0

(H) -2

(J) -8

DAY 3

Lydia received a gift card for $25.00 worth of smoothies from the Smoothie Spot. If the cost of each smoothie is $3.25, which table best describes b, the balance remaining on the gift card after she buys n smoothies?

(A)

n	b
1	$21.75
3	$15.25
4	$12.00
7	$2.25

(C)

n	b
1	$21.75
2	$18.50
5	$15.25
7	$12.00

(B)

n	b
2	$18.50
4	$12.00
6	$6.50
8	$0

(D)

n	b
2	$18.50
3	$15.25
5	$7.75
6	$4.50

DAY 4

The band is trying to raise money to take a field trip to the Rock and Roll Hall of Fame. They decide to sell sweatshirts. The equation for the amount of money a that they will make for selling t sweatshirts is $a = 22t - 350$. In order to make at least $2100, how many sweatshirts do the band members need to sell?

(F) 112

(G) 111

(H) 80

(J) 79

DAY 5

What is the solution to the equation $8x - 10 = 54$?

(A) 5.5

(B) 6.75

(C) 8

(D) 12

CC38   *Countdown to Mastery*

DAY 1

Which expression is equivalent to
$2x(3x + 5) - x^2 + 8$?

Ⓐ $-x^2 + 6x + 18$

Ⓑ $5x^2 + 10x + 8$

Ⓒ $10x + 14$

Ⓓ $-x^2 + 16x + 8$

DAY 2

What is the value of $3x^2 - 5x + 2$ when
$x = -4$?

Ⓕ -66

Ⓖ -26

Ⓗ 30

Ⓙ 70

DAY 3

Which graph matches the values from the table?

x	−3	−1	2	4
y	6	2	−4	−8

Ⓐ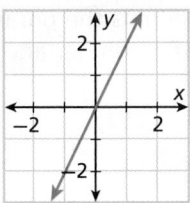

Ⓒ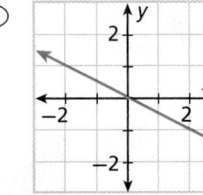

Ⓑ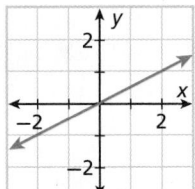

Ⓓ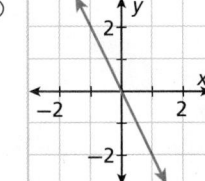

DAY 4

A rectangle has a length of 8 m and a
width of 3 m. If a similar rectangle has a
length of 22 m, what is its width?

Ⓕ 58.67 m

Ⓖ 17 m

Ⓗ 8.25 m

Ⓙ 9 m

DAY 5

Simplify the algebraic expression
$4(x + 5) - 2(x + 5)$.

Ⓐ $2x + 10$

Ⓑ $2x + 30$

Ⓒ $6x + 30$

Ⓓ $-8x^2 - 200$

Countdown to Mastery

WEEK 5

DAY 1

Which description of the relationship between x and y best represents the table below?

x	9	0	−6	1
y	3	0	−2	$\frac{1}{3}$

(A) The value of y is three times the value of x.

(B) The value of x is three more than the value of y.

(C) The value of x is three less than the value of y.

(D) The value of x is three times the value of y.

DAY 2

Claire's father is 6 years more than 3 times her age. If her father is 39 years old, how old is Claire?

(F) 15 years old

(G) 11 years old

(H) 7 years old

(J) 6 years old

DAY 3

Which expression represents the phrase "four times the sum of a number and 2"?

(A) $4n + 2$

(B) $4(2n)$

(C) $4(n + 2)$

(D) $4 \cdot n + 2$

DAY 4

What is the solution to $-8x - 3 = -4x + 5$?

(F) −4

(G) −2

(H) 2

(J) 4

DAY 5

The cheerleaders are selling tickets to a pasta dinner to raise money for new competition outfits. They plan to charge $6 per person, and their total expenses for dinner are $135. Which value for the number of tickets sold would result in the cheerleaders not making a profit?

(A) 46

(B) 45

(C) 23

(D) 22

Countdown to Mastery

WEEK 6

DAY 1

Which equation matches the data in the table?

x	3	1	−2	6
y	2	4	7	−1

Ⓐ $y = -x + 5$

Ⓑ $y = 2x - 1$

Ⓒ $y = x + 3$

Ⓓ $y = -3x + 11$

DAY 2

The drama club charges $3 admission to the one-act play festival. Their expenses are $115. In order for the club to make exactly $110 after expenses, how many people must attend the festival?

Ⓕ 39

Ⓖ 75

Ⓗ 114

Ⓙ 152

DAY 3

Melissa's brother is 6 years less than twice her age. The sum of her age and her brother's age is 27. Which equation best shows this information?

Ⓐ $x + (6 - 2x) = 27$

Ⓑ $x + (2x - 6) = 27$

Ⓒ $2x - 6 = 27$

Ⓓ $x = 2x - 6$

DAY 4

A rectangle has a length of 5 inches and a width of 3 inches. If a similar rectangle has a width of 15 inches, what is its length?

Ⓕ 5 inches

Ⓖ 9 inches

Ⓗ 15 inches

Ⓙ 25 inches

DAY 5

A bus company sells an annual bus pass for $8.50, and then charges a rider $0.25 per ride. Use the equation $c = 0.25b + 8.5$ to answer the following question: How much will it cost for someone to ride the bus 38 times?

Ⓐ $118.00

Ⓑ $20.00

Ⓒ $18.00

Ⓓ $9.50

DAY 1

Daniel's recipe for 24 cookies calls for $2\frac{1}{2}$ cups of flour. How much flour will Daniel need to make 60 cookies?

A 1 cup

B $6\frac{1}{4}$ cups

C $6\frac{1}{2}$ cups

D $7\frac{1}{2}$ cups

DAY 2

What is the value of $2x^2 + 3x - 5$ when $x = -2$?

F -7

G -3

H 5

J 9

DAY 3

Which graph shows a line where each value of y is three more than half of x?

A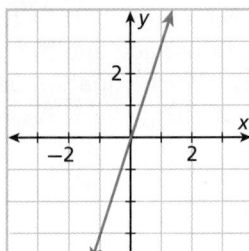

C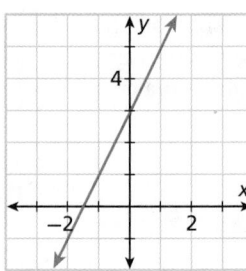

B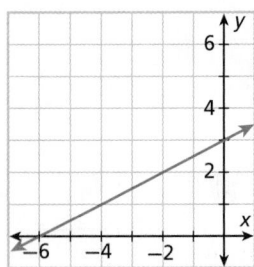

D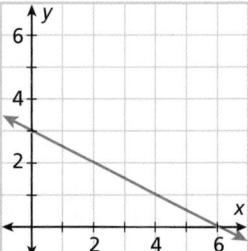

DAY 4

What is the solution to $2x + 8 < 3x - 4$?

F $x < 12$

G $x > \frac{12}{5}$

H $x > 12$

J $x < \frac{12}{5}$

DAY 5

Simplify the expression $3(5x - 8) + 2(4x - 1)$.

A $23x + 26$

B $23x + 22$

C $23x - 22$

D $23x - 26$

Countdown to Mastery

DAY 1

A swimming pool charges an annual $75 membership fee, and it costs $1.50 each time a member brings a guest. Which equation shows the yearly cost y in terms of the number of guests g?

(A) $y = 75g + 1.5$

(B) $y = -1.5g + 75$

(C) $y = 1.5g + 75$

(D) $y = 1.5g + 75g$

DAY 2

On a certain standardized test, the equation $s = 9q + 218$ is used to determine a student's score. In this equation, s is the score and q is the number of questions answered correctly. If the maximum score on the test is 650, how many questions are on the test?

(F) 96 questions

(G) 72 questions

(H) 48 questions

(J) 24 questions

DAY 3

If you belong to Lowell's Gym and plan to work out 82 times in a year, what is your total cost for the year?

Lowell's Gym

Membership fee $75

Workout fee (per visit) $2

(A) $89   (B) $157   (C) $164   (D) $239

DAY 4

A publishing company must ship boxes of a particular book to bookstores around the country. The boxes used for shipping can hold a maximum of 35 pounds. If the company wants to ship at least 10 books per box, what is the maximum weight of a book that can be put in the box?

(F) 3 pounds

(G) $3\frac{1}{2}$ pounds

(H) 4 pounds

(J) 25 pounds

DAY 5

Which verbal description does not match the function $f(x) = -\frac{1}{3}x - 5$?

(A) The function value is the difference between x times $-\frac{1}{3}$ and 5.

(B) The function value is 5 less than the product of x and $-\frac{1}{3}$.

(C) The function value is $-\frac{1}{3}$ of x subtracted from 5.

(D) The function value is $-\frac{1}{3}$ of x decreased by 5.

DAY 1

Brian calculates the charge for each lawn he mows by using the function $f(t) = 10t + 5.5$, where t is the number of hours spent mowing the lawn. He always works for at least one full hour. Which statement cannot be inferred from this information?

(A) Brian's hourly rate is $10.

(B) Brian includes a charge of $5.50 for all lawns.

(C) Brian uses $5.50 worth of gas for each job.

(D) The minimum that Brian will make for each lawn is $15.50.

DAY 2

Which of the following relationships has a negative correlation?

(F) A person's height and weight

(G) The number of minutes spent studying and a test grade

(H) The outside temperature and the number of layers of clothes a person wears

(J) The number of years a person spent in school and the person's salary

DAY 3

The graph shows the value of a car over a period of years. Which of the following statements cannot be concluded from the graph?

(A) The car started at a value of approximately $8400.

(B) The car's value depreciates more quickly at the beginning, and then less quickly as time goes on.

(C) The car is worth approximately $3000 when it is 5 years old.

(D) The car should be sold before its worth drops below $2000.

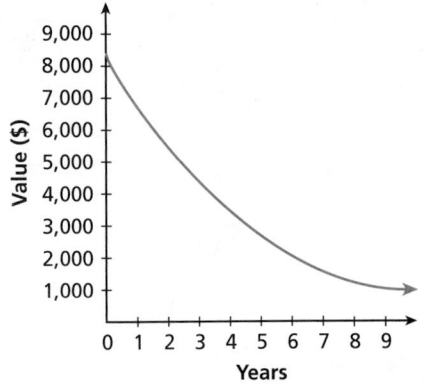

DAY 4

Which function best matches the table?

x	−3	0	3	6
y	2	4	6	8

(F) $y = -\frac{2}{3}x$

(G) $y = 2x + 4$

(H) $y = \frac{2}{3}x + 4$

(J) $y = \frac{1}{3}x + 3$

DAY 5

To change from degrees Celsius to degrees Fahrenheit, you can use the equation $f = \frac{9}{5}c + 32$. If the temperature is at least 55 degrees Fahrenheit, what inequality can you use to find the temperature in Celsius?

(A) $55 \geq \frac{9}{5}c + 32$

(B) $f \geq \frac{9}{5} \cdot 55 + 32$

(C) $55 \leq \frac{9}{5}c + 32$

(D) $f \leq \frac{9}{5} \cdot 55 + 32$

DAY 1

A function relating two quantities is $f(x) = \frac{1}{5}x + 6$. What will always be true based on this function?

(A) $f(x)$ will be less than x.

(B) If x is positive, then $f(x)$ will be positive.

(C) If x is negative, then $f(x)$ will be negative.

(D) $f(x)$ will be greater than x.

DAY 2

In the equation $p = -40q + 163$, which relationship between p and q is true?

(F) You cannot determine the relationship based on this information.

(G) q is dependent on p.

(H) p and q are independent of each other.

(J) p is dependent on q.

DAY 3

What is the equation of the line shown?

(A) $y = 2x$

(B) $y = -2x$

(C) $y = \frac{1}{2}x$

(D) $y = -\frac{1}{2}x$

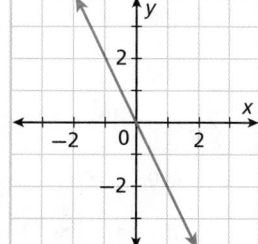

DAY 4

What is the solution to $-8x - 3 \geq -4x + 5$?

(F) $x \leq -2$

(G) $x \geq 2$

(H) $x \leq 2$

(J) $x \geq -2$

DAY 5

The sum of three consecutive integers is 54. What is the greatest of the three integers?

(A) 17

(B) 18

(C) 19

(D) 20

DAY 1

Darian has a picture that is 4 inches wide and 6 inches long. He wants to enlarge the picture so that it has a width of 18 inches. What is the length of the enlarged picture?

Ⓐ 27 inches

Ⓑ 24 inches

Ⓒ 20 inches

Ⓓ 12 inches

DAY 2

At a computer repair shop, the function $f(t) = 40t + 35$ is used to calculate fees, where t is the number of hours technicians spend working on the computer. If you pay $315 to get your computer repaired, how long did the technician work on repairing your computer?

Ⓕ 8.75 hours

Ⓖ 7.875 hours

Ⓗ 7.5 hours

Ⓙ 7 hours

DAY 3

The scatter plot shows the relationship between the size of a diamond in Carats and its retail price. What is the approximate retail price of a 0.30 Carat diamond?

Ⓐ $400

Ⓑ $600

Ⓒ $800

Ⓓ $1000

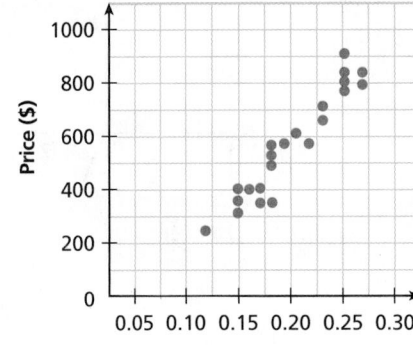

DAY 4

What is the next term in the pattern?

50, 10, 2, $\frac{2}{5}$, ___, ...

Ⓕ $\frac{1}{25}$

Ⓖ $\frac{2}{25}$

Ⓗ $\frac{2}{10}$

Ⓙ $\frac{1}{5}$

DAY 5

Which expression is equivalent to $5x - 35$?

Ⓐ $5(x - 35)$

Ⓑ $5(x - 7)$

Ⓒ $5(x + 35)$

Ⓓ $5(x + 7)$

DAY 1

Based on the information in the table, what is the relationship between the weight of the object and its volume?

Weight (lb)	2	5	8	12
Volume (in³)	0.5	1.25	2	3

Ⓐ The weight is 1.5 more than the volume.

Ⓑ The volume is 4 times the weight.

Ⓒ The weight is 4 times the volume.

Ⓓ The volume is 6 less than the weight.

DAY 2

What is the range of the function shown in the table?

x	1	3	5	8
f(x)	2	−2	0	2

Ⓕ {1, 3, 5, 8}

Ⓖ {4}

Ⓗ {−2, 0, 2}

Ⓙ {7}

DAY 3

Which graph shows a linear function?

Ⓐ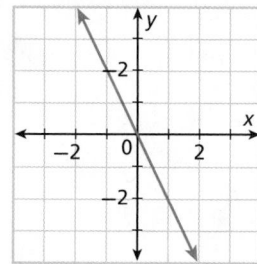

Ⓒ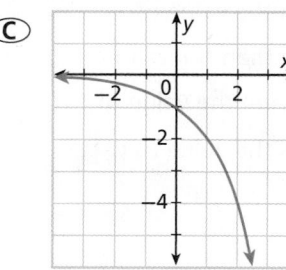

Ⓑ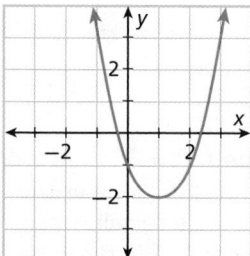

Ⓓ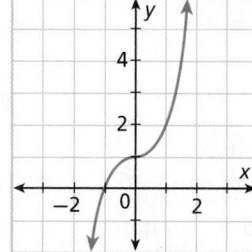

DAY 4

What is the solution to the equation $6(x - 9) = -12x + 36$?

Ⓕ $x = 5$

Ⓖ $x = 2.5$

Ⓗ $x = -1$

Ⓙ $x = -5$

DAY 5

Simplify the algebraic expression $5x - 2(4x - 3) + 7$.

Ⓐ $-3x + 1$

Ⓑ $13x + 13$

Ⓒ $-3x + 13$

Ⓓ $3x + 1$

DAY 1

The slope of a line is $-\frac{1}{4}$, and the y-intercept is –3. What is the equation of the line?

(A) $x + y = -3$

(B) $y = -\frac{1}{4}x + 1$

(C) $y = -\frac{1}{4}x - 3$

(D) $x - 4y = -3$

DAY 2

A taxi company charges a $2.50 fee per ride plus an additional $2.10 per mile traveled. If the taxi fee increases to $2.75, which characteristic of this function would change?

(F) The slope

(G) The x-intercept

(H) The y-intercept

(J) There would be no changes

DAY 3

Which description of the relationship between x and y best matches the graph below?

(A) The value of y is 3 times the value of x.

(B) The value of x is 2 more than the value of y.

(C) The value of x is 2 less than the value of y.

(D) The value of x is 3 times the value of y.

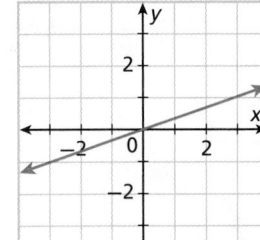

DAY 4

In which relationship are the two quantities independent of one another?

(F) The amount of tax paid for an item and the price of the item

(G) The number of snacks bought from a snack machine and the amount of money in the machine

(H) The number of hours worked at $6.50 per hour and the amount of money earned

(J) The age of a person and the number of televisions in his or her home

DAY 5

The linear function $f(x) = 3x + 15$ models the cost of renting x movies over the course of a year from a certain store. What range restrictions will there be if you graph this function?

(A) $f(x) \geq 0$

(B) $f(x) \geq 15$

(C) $f(x) > 0$

(D) $0 \leq f(x) \leq 15$

DAY 1

Which function matches the data in the table?

x	−3	2	5
$f(x)$	15	0	15

Ⓐ $f(x) = -3x + 6$

Ⓑ $f(x) = -5x$

Ⓒ $f(x) = x^2 - 2x$

Ⓓ $f(x) = 3x^2 - 12$

DAY 2

A consultant charges her clients for her services based on an equation relating the total bill $f(h)$ to the number of hours worked h. The best interpretation of this function $f(h) = 125h + 150$ is:

Ⓕ She charges $150 per hour plus a $125 flat fee.

Ⓖ She charges $125 per hour plus a $150 flat fee.

Ⓗ She charges $275 per hour.

Ⓙ Her hourly charges vary from $125 to $150 depending on the job.

DAY 3

A rectangle has the dimensions shown. Which value for the area has the correct number of significant digits?

Ⓐ 55.728 square centimeters

Ⓑ 55.73 square centimeters

Ⓒ 55.7 square centimeters

Ⓓ 56 square centimeters

8.6 cm

6.48 cm

DAY 4

What is the range of the function $f(x) = 2x + 3$?

Ⓕ All real numbers

Ⓖ $f(x) \geq 3$

Ⓗ $f(x) \geq 0$

Ⓙ $f(x) \geq -3$

DAY 5

At Terry's TVs, profit is calculated using the equation $p = 0.4c - 125$, where p is the profit and c is the wholesale cost. If the company makes a profit of $375 on one TV, what is the wholesale cost of the TV?

Ⓐ $25

Ⓑ $937.50

Ⓒ $1250

Ⓓ $1062.50

DAY 1

Which graph shows a linear function?

Ⓐ
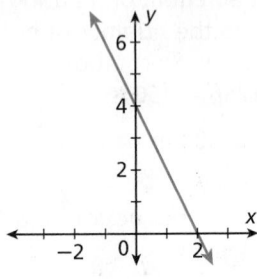

Ⓒ
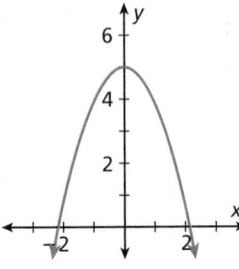

Ⓑ
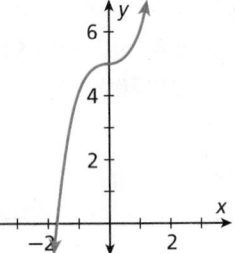

Ⓓ
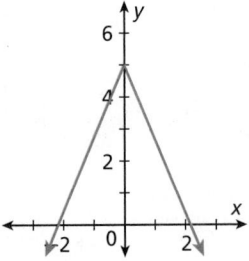

DAY 2

The relationship between which two quantities can be represented by a linear function?

Ⓕ The volume of a cube and its side length

Ⓖ The perimeter of a rectangle and its area

Ⓗ The perimeter of an equilateral triangle and its side length

Ⓙ The area of a square and its side length

DAY 3

Which equation represents a linear function with a slope of $\frac{2}{3}$?

Ⓐ $y = \frac{3}{2}x$

Ⓑ $y = \frac{2}{3}x + 4$

Ⓒ $y = x + \frac{2}{3}$

Ⓓ $y = \frac{2}{3}$

DAY 4

What are the x- and y-intercepts of $y = \frac{2}{5}x - 2$?

Ⓕ x-intercept: –2; y-intercept: 5

Ⓖ x-intercept: $\frac{2}{5}$; y-intercept: –2

Ⓗ x-intercept: 0; y-intercept: –2

Ⓙ x-intercept: 5; y-intercept: –2

DAY 5

A system of equations is set up to determine how many pounds of hazelnut coffee and how many pounds of Colombian coffee were mixed together to make a blend. The total mixture was 20 pounds of coffee. Which of the following is not a possible solution to the system?

Ⓐ (7, 13)　　　Ⓒ (11, 9)

Ⓑ (32, –12)　　Ⓓ (1, 19)

DAY 1

If a graph shows the relationship between the amount of sand in the top of an hourglass y over time x, what quantity does the x-intercept represent?

(A) The amount of sand that is in the top of the hourglass originally

(B) The speed at which the sand passes to the bottom of the hourglass

(C) The height of the hourglass

(D) The amount of time it takes for all of the sand to pass to the bottom of the hourglass

DAY 2

Which equation represents a line parallel to the one shown?

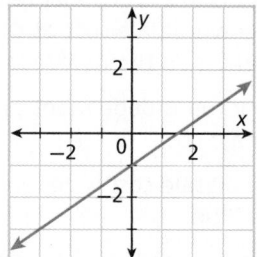

(F) $y = \frac{3}{2}x + 1$ (H) $y = \frac{2}{3}x + 1$

(G) $y = -\frac{3}{2}x - 1$ (J) $y = -\frac{2}{3}x$

DAY 3

The Whartons are planting a rectangular vegetable garden. Suppose the width of the garden is x feet and the length of the garden is $5 - x$ feet. Which type of function can you use to model the area y of the garden in terms of its width?

(A) linear

(B) quadratic

(C) exponential decay

(D) exponential growth

DAY 4

Your school is selling candles to raise money. If profit y is related to the number of items sold x, what are reasonable restrictions on the domain?

(F) $y \geq 0$

(G) No restrictions

(H) $x \geq 0$

(J) $0 \leq y \leq 2000$

DAY 5

What is the solution to the system of equations graphed below?

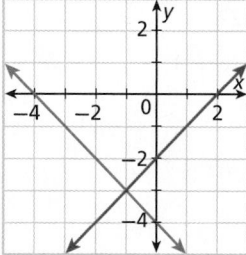

(A) $(-1, 3)$ (C) $(-3, -1)$

(B) $(-1, -3)$ (D) $(3, -1)$

DAY 1

A store manager increases the wholesale cost of an item by 35%. Which statement best represents the functional relationship between the wholesale cost of the item and the markup on the item?

(A) The markup is dependent on the wholesale cost.

(B) The wholesale cost is dependent on the markup.

(C) The markup and the wholesale cost are independent of each other.

(D) The relationship cannot be determined.

DAY 2

Which situation can best be represented by a linear function?

(F) The distance that an airplane is away from the airport as it comes in for a landing and time

(G) The distance traveled by a car moving at a constant speed and time

(H) The number of apples on a tree and the number of trees in the orchard

(J) The height from the ground of a person riding a roller coaster and time

DAY 3

The scatter plot shows the percent of households that own a car versus the household income. What is a reasonable estimate for the percent of households that own a car if the household income is $50,000?

(A) 50%

(B) 65%

(C) 77%

(D) 85%

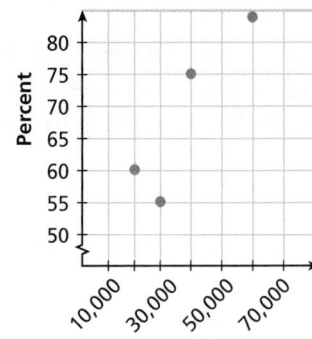

DAY 4

What is the slope of the line with equation $3x - 5y = 12$?

(F) -3

(G) $-\dfrac{3}{5}$

(H) $\dfrac{3}{5}$

(J) 3

DAY 5

Joy and a friend start a business. What linear function relates the total income and each partner's share of the profit based on the data in the table?

Total Income (t)	Profit Share (p)
$350.00	$50.00
$425.00	$87.50
$500.00	$125.00

(A) $p = \dfrac{1}{2}t - 125$ (C) $p = t - 300$

(B) $p = \dfrac{1}{4}t - 37.5$ (D) $p = \dfrac{1}{7}t$

DAY 1

What is the range of the function
$f(x) = 2x^2 + 1$ if the domain is $\{-2, 0, 3\}$?

Ⓐ $\{1, 9, 19\}$ Ⓒ $\{-9, 1, 19\}$

Ⓑ $\{0, 8, 18\}$ Ⓓ $\{-2, 0, 3\}$

DAY 2

Which function has a y-intercept of -2
and a graph whose slope is $\frac{5}{4}$?

Ⓕ $5x + 4y = 2$ Ⓗ $y = -\frac{5}{4}x + 2$

Ⓖ $y = \frac{5}{4}x + 2$ Ⓙ $y = \frac{5}{4}x - 2$

DAY 3

The graph represents a residual plot for a data set and a linear model. Based on
the residual plot, which statement best describes the goodness of fit of the linear
model?

Ⓐ The line is a good fit for the data.

Ⓑ The line is in the wrong place.

Ⓒ The data are not linear.

Ⓓ The data may have relatively no
correlation.

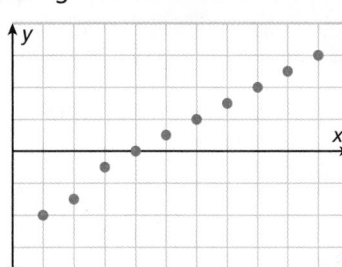

DAY 4

Which of the following cannot be
represented by a linear function?

Ⓕ The amount of water w coming out
of a dripping faucet over m minutes

Ⓖ The height h of a person over t years

Ⓗ The gross sales s made from the sale
of c CDs priced at $14 each

Ⓙ The amount of sales tax on a
purchase of d dollars if the rate is 6%

DAY 5

The graph shows the distance that a
person is from home while driving at
a constant speed. What quantity is
represented by the y-intercept?

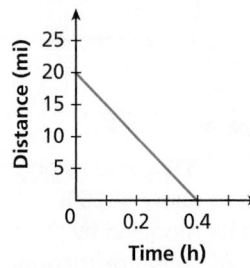

Ⓐ The speed at which the person is driving

Ⓑ The distance from home at the start

Ⓒ The amount of time it takes to get home

Ⓓ The distance from home at the end

DAY 1

Assuming that the graph below has the same x- and y-scale, which is the best estimate for the solution to the system?

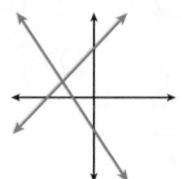

A $(-5, 10)$ **C** $(3, -6)$

B $(-4, 2)$ **D** $(8, -4)$

DAY 2

What is the y-intercept of the function whose graph has a slope of $-\frac{1}{3}$ and passes through the point $(-6, 4)$?

F 6

G 2

H -2

J -6

DAY 3

Which graph shows a function from the family $f(x) = x^2$?

A

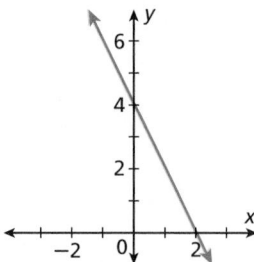

C

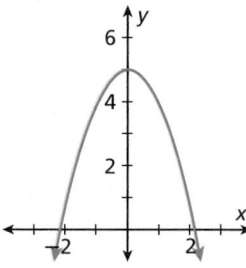

B

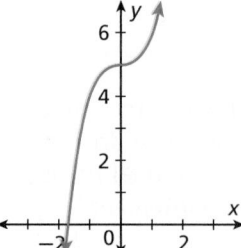

D

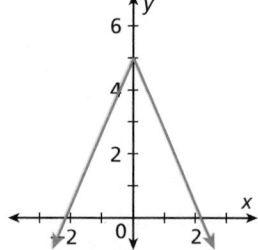

DAY 4

Miguel earns a 15% commission on his sales in addition to a salary of $500 a week. His earnings can be modeled by the equation $p = 0.15s + 500$. What restrictions on the values of p and s best fit this situation?

F $p \geq 0$, s can be any value.

G $s \geq 0$, p can be any value.

H $s \geq 500$, $p \geq 0$

J $s \geq 0$, $p \geq 500$

DAY 5

If $f(x) = \frac{1}{2}x$, what best describes the relationship between x and $f(x)$?

A As the value of x increases by 1, the value of $f(x)$ will increase by 2.

B As the value of x increases by 1, the value of $f(x)$ will remain the same.

C As the value of x increases by 1, the value of $f(x)$ will increase by $\frac{1}{2}$.

D The value of x will not affect the value of $f(x)$.

DAY 1

On Saturday, Suzie's Pretzel Stand sells a total of 12 items. Suzie charges $3 for a pretzel and $2 for a milkshake. If she took in $32 on Saturday, which system of equations can be used to determine how many pretzels and how many milkshakes were sold?

(A) $\begin{cases} 3x + 2y = 12 \\ x + y = 32 \end{cases}$ (C) $\begin{cases} 3x - 2y = 12 \\ x + y = 32 \end{cases}$

(B) $\begin{cases} 3x - 2y = 32 \\ x + y = 12 \end{cases}$ (D) $\begin{cases} x + y = 12 \\ 3x + 2y = 32 \end{cases}$

DAY 2

What is the slope of the line shown?

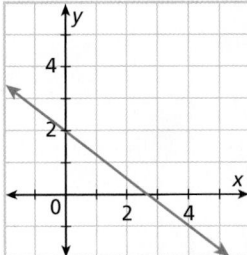

(F) $-\dfrac{4}{3}$ (H) $\dfrac{3}{4}$

(G) $-\dfrac{3}{4}$ (J) $\dfrac{4}{3}$

DAY 3

If the x-intercept of the function graphed below were to stay the same and the slope of the line decreased, what impact would that have on the y-intercept?

(A) The y-intercept will decrease.

(B) The y-intercept will remain the same.

(C) The y-intercept will increase.

(D) The y-intercept will double.

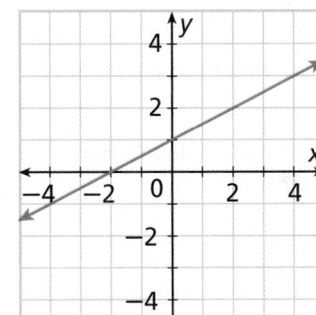

DAY 4

A system of equations is set up to determine the number of nickels and the number of quarters that Elissa has. Which ordered pair does not represent a valid solution to this system?

(F) (0, 15)

(G) (12, −5)

(H) (31, 4)

(J) (7, 0)

DAY 5

A gym membership costs $25 a month plus $3 per visit. This is modeled by the function $c = 3v + 25$, where c is the cost per month and v is the number of visits. If the slope of this function's graph were to increase, what would that mean about the prices that the gym charges?

(A) The gym raised its monthly fee.

(B) The gym lowered the cost per visit.

(C) The gym raised the cost per visit.

(D) The gym lowered its monthly fee.

DAY 1

Which of the functions, when graphed, will result in the most narrow parabola?

(A) $y = 5x^2$

(B) $y = \frac{1}{5}x^2$

(C) $y = x^2$

(D) $y = \frac{1}{2}x^2$

DAY 2

How do the graphs of the functions $f(x) = x^2 - 5$ and $g(x) = x^2 + 4$ relate to each other?

(F) The graph of $f(x)$ is 9 units to the left of the graph of $g(x)$.

(G) The graph of $f(x)$ is 1 unit below the graph of $g(x)$.

(H) The graph of $f(x)$ is 9 units below the graph of $g(x)$.

(J) The graph of $f(x)$ is 1 unit to the left of the graph of $g(x)$.

DAY 3

The graph shows the proposed balance in Jake's bank account if Jake saves an average of $15 a week. Which statement would not be true if the slope of the line were to increase?

(A) Jake is saving more money per week.

(B) Jake started with more money in his bank account.

(C) It will take less time for Jake's bank balance to reach $120.

(D) After 6 weeks Jake will have more than $90 in his bank account.

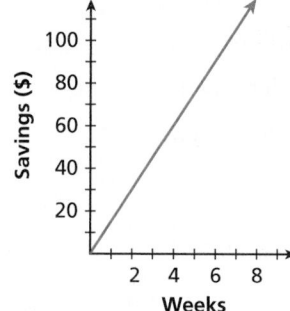

DAY 4

What are the roots of the function $f(x) = (2x - 1)(x + 5)$?

(F) $\frac{1}{2}$ and -5

(G) -1 and 5

(H) 1 and -5

(J) $-\frac{1}{2}$ and 5

DAY 5

For a typical shot in basketball, the ball's height in feet will be a function of time in seconds, modeled by an equation such as $h = -16t^2 + 25t + 6$. Which inequality shows the restrictions that should be put on the domain of this function?

(A) $t \leq 0$

(B) $h \leq 0$

(C) $h \geq 0$

(D) $t \geq 0$

DAY 1

What are the roots of the graphed function?

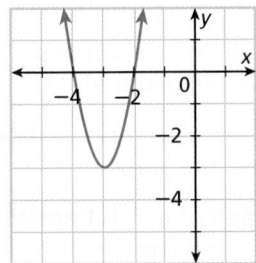

(A) 2 and 4

(C) −2 and 4

(B) −2 and −4

(D) 2 and −4

DAY 2

What is the range of the function shown?

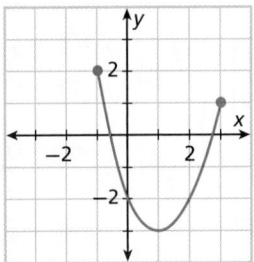

(F) $-2 < y < 3$

(H) $-3 \leq y \leq 2$

(G) $-3 < y \leq 2$

(J) $-2 \leq y \leq 3$

DAY 3

The graph shows the height of a baseball from the time it is thrown until the time it hits the ground. What value is not shown on the graph?

(A) The amount of time that the ball was in the air

(B) The height at which the ball started

(C) The maximum height that the ball reached

(D) The speed at which the ball was thrown

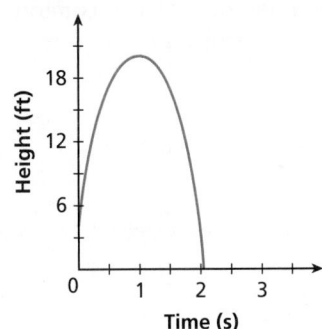

DAY 4

What are the solution(s) of the equation $x^2 - 10x - 24 = 0$?

(F) $x = -4, 6$

(G) $x = 2, -12$

(H) $x = -2, 12$

(J) $x = 4, -6$

DAY 5

What is the solution to the system of equations?

$$\begin{cases} 3x - 4y = 19 \\ y = 2x - 11 \end{cases}$$

(A) $(5, -1)$

(B) $(-5, -21)$

(C) $(5, 1)$

(D) $(-5, -8.5)$

DAY 1

Which graph shows a function $y = ax^2$ when $a > 1$?

(A)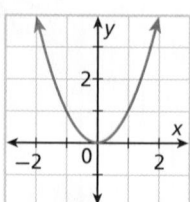

(C)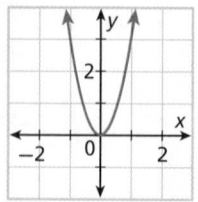

(B)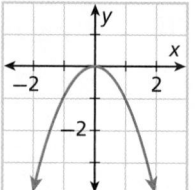

(D)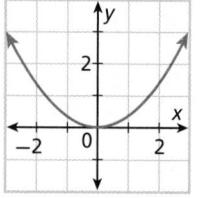

DAY 2

Which best describes the difference between the graphs of $f(x) = x^2$ and $g(x) = x^2 - 3$?

(F) The graph of $g(x)$ is translated 3 units up from the graph of $f(x)$.

(G) The graph of $g(x)$ is translated 3 units left from the graph of $f(x)$.

(H) The graph of $g(x)$ is translated 3 units right from the graph of $f(x)$.

(J) The graph of $g(x)$ is translated 3 units down from the graph of $f(x)$.

DAY 3

The graph shows the height of water coming out of a fountain over time. How many seconds pass before the water reaches the ground?

(A) 0

(B) 2

(C) 4

(D) 18

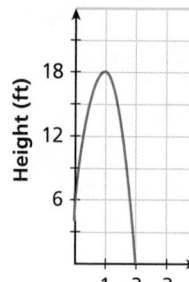

DAY 4

What is one solution to the equation $2x^2 + 7x + 3 = 0$?

(F) $x = 3$

(G) $x = \frac{1}{2}$

(H) $x = -\frac{1}{2}$

(J) $x = -1$

DAY 5

What is the solution to the system of equations $4x + 2y = -8$ and $x - 2y = 13$?

(A) $(25, 6)$

(B) $(1, 6)$

(C) $(-1, -6)$

(D) $(1, -6)$

DAY 1

Which is the parent function of the graph shown?

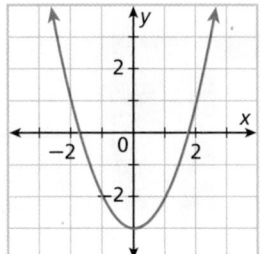

Ⓐ $y = x$

Ⓑ $y = |x|$

Ⓒ $y = x^2$

Ⓓ $y = x^3$

DAY 2

What is the x-intercept of the function shown?

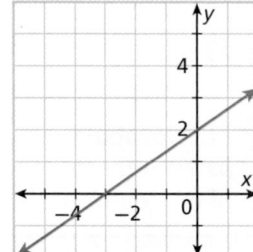

Ⓕ $x = -3$

Ⓖ $x = -2$

Ⓗ $x = 2$

Ⓙ $x = 3$

DAY 3

Which situation cannot be described by a linear function?

Ⓐ The amount of commission earned on a sale if the commission rate is 12%

Ⓑ The area of a square given its side length

Ⓒ The cost of renting a car if the charge is $25 plus $0.15 per mile

Ⓓ The amount paid for babysitting h hours if you charge $8.25 per hour

DAY 4

What is the equation of the line that passes through the points $(-4, 2)$ and $(-8, 8)$?

Ⓕ $y = -\frac{3}{2}x - 4$

Ⓖ $y = -\frac{3}{2}x - 20$

Ⓗ $y = -\frac{3}{2}x - 8$

Ⓙ $y = -\frac{3}{2}x + 4$

DAY 5

What is the slope of the line given the equation $3x - 4y = -8$?

Ⓐ $m = 3$

Ⓑ $m = 2$

Ⓒ $m = \frac{3}{4}$

Ⓓ $m = -3$

HOW TO STUDY ALGEBRA 1

This book has many features designed to help you learn and study effectively. Becoming familiar with these features will prepare you for greater success on your exams.

Learn

The **vocabulary** is listed at the beginning of every lesson.

Look for the **Know-It-Note** icons to identify important information.

Study the **examples** to apply new concepts and skills. Examples include stepped out solutions.

Test your understanding of examples by trying the **Check It Out** problems. Check your work in the Selected Answers.

Practice

Use a **graphic organizer** to summarize each lesson.

Refer to the examples from the lesson to solve the **Guided Practice** exercises.

If you get stuck, use the internet for **Homework Help Online.**

Review

Study and review **vocabulary** from the entire chapter.

Test yourself with **practice problems** from every lesson in the chapter.

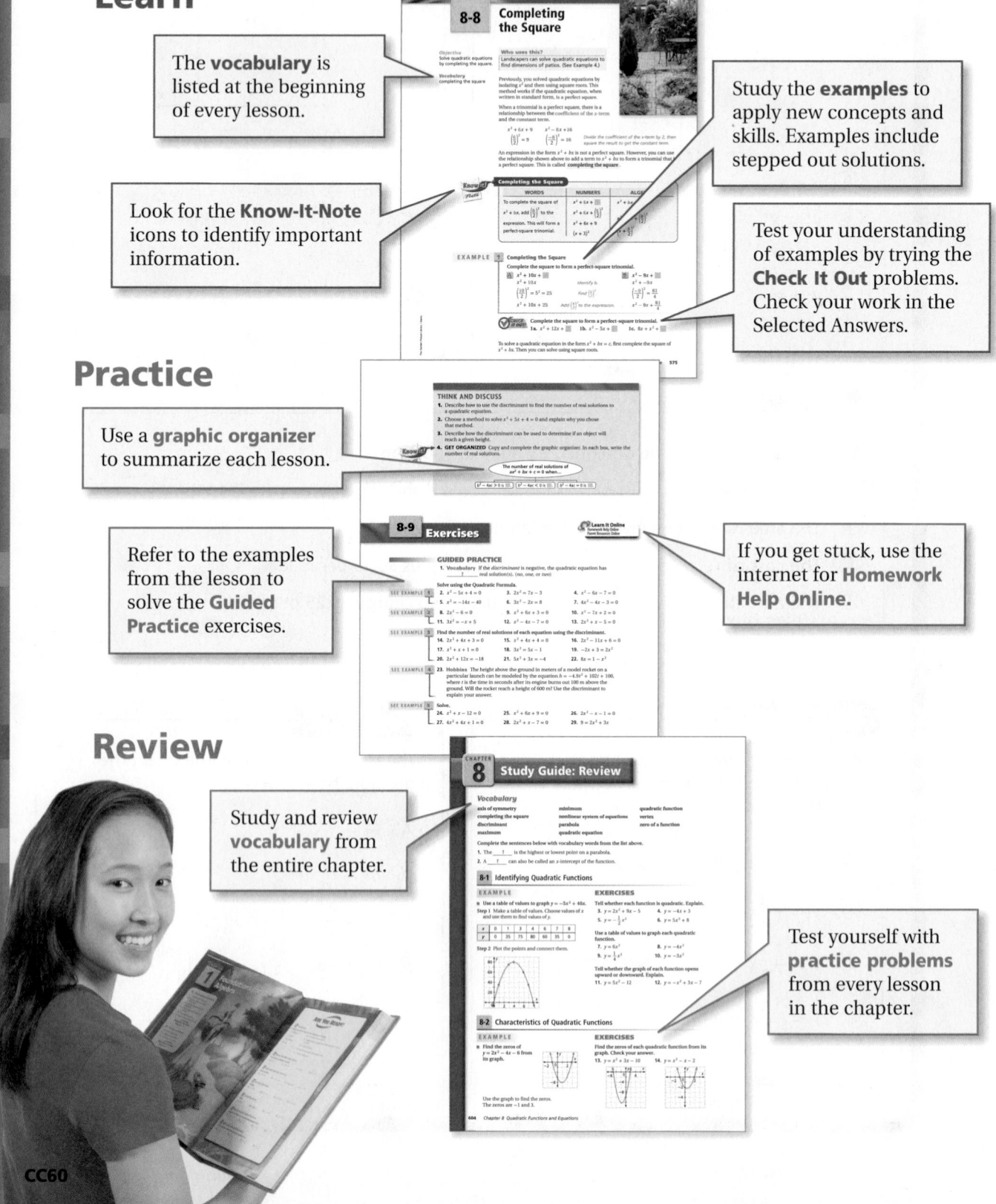

Focus on Problem Solving

The Problem Solving Plan

Mathematical problems are a part of daily life. You need to use a good problem-solving plan to be a good problem solver. The plan used in this textbook is outlined below.

UNDERSTAND the Problem

First make sure you understand the problem you are asked to solve.

■ **What are you asked to find?**	Restate the question in your own words.
■ **What information is given?**	Identify the key facts given in the problem.
■ **What information do you need?**	Determine what information you need to solve the problem.
■ **Do you have all the information needed?**	Determine if you need more information.
■ **Do you have too much information?**	Determine if there is unnecessary information and eliminate it from your list of important facts.

Make a PLAN

Plan how to use the information you are given.

■ **Have you solved similar problems?**	Think about similar problems you have solved successfully.
■ **What problem solving strategy or strategies could you use to solve this problem?**	Choose an appropriate problem solving strategy and decide how you will use it.

SOLVE

Use your plan to solve the problem. Show the steps in the solution, and write a final statement that gives the solution to the problem.

LOOK BACK

Check your answer against the original problem.

■ **Have you answered the question?**	Make sure you have answered the original question.
■ **Is the answer reasonable?**	The answer must make sense in relation to the question.
■ **Are your calculations correct?**	Check to make sure your calculations are accurate.
■ **Can you use another strategy or solve the problem in another way?**	Using another strategy is a good way to check your answer.
■ **Did you learn anyting that could help you solve similar problems in the future?**	Try to remember the types of problems you have solved and the strategies you applied.

ARE YOU READY?

Pre-Course Test

Whole Number Operations

Add, subtract, multiply, or divide.

1. $623 - 432$ **2.** 8×23

3. $882 \div 14$ **4.** $178 + 842$

Add and Subtract Decimals

Add or subtract.

5. $43.21 + 16.8$ **6.** $16.3 - 9.11$

Multiply Decimals

Multiply.

7. 2.3×0.6 **8.** 6.4×3.2

Divide Decimals

Divide.

9. $25.6 \div 8$ **10.** $0.84 \div 0.6$

Multiply and Divide Fractions

Multiply or divide. Give your answer in simplest form.

11. $\frac{2}{9} \times \frac{3}{4}$ **12.** $\frac{5}{9} \div 5$

Add and Subtract Fractions

Add or subtract. Give your answer in simplest form.

13. $\frac{3}{4} + \frac{5}{12}$ **14.** $1\frac{2}{9} - \frac{4}{9}$

Add and Subtract Integers

Add or subtract.

15. $-54 + 35$ **16.** $-18 - (-30)$

Multiply and Divide Integers

Multiply or divide.

17. $15(-4)$ **18.** $-30 \div (-6)$

Fractions, Decimals, and Percents

Write the equivalent decimal and the equivalent percent.

19. $\frac{4}{25}$ **20.** $\frac{9}{8}$

Order of Operations

Evaluate each expression.

21. $12 + 3 \div 3$ **22.** $3 + 2 \times 4^2$

23. $4 + 6 \times 10 - 2$ **24.** $25 \times (4 + 5)$

Distributive Property

Simplify each expression.

25. $5(12 + g)$ **26.** $(r - 6)9$

Rates and Unit Rates

Find each unit rate.

27. $30 for 8 students

28. 96 packages in 6 days

Connect Words and Algebra

29. Mario has saved $165. At the end of each week he saves an additional $15. Write an equation representing the total amount S he has saved at the end of any given week w.

Graph Numbers on a Number Line

Identify the point on the number line that matches each number.

30. -0.5

31. 2.5

32. -3

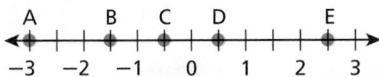

Compare and Order Real Numbers

Compare. Write $<$, $>$, or $=$.

33. $\frac{5}{12}$ ▨ $\frac{3}{4}$

34. $\frac{4}{20}$ ▨ 20%

Evaluate Expressions

Evaluate each expression for the given value of the variable.

35. $5w - 16$ for $w = 6$

36. $-8 - \frac{2}{3}h$ for $h = 6$

Solve One-Step Equations

Solve each equation.

37. $5g = 135$

38. $x - 16 = 8$

Combine Like Terms

Simply each expression by combining like terms.

39. $3b - 32 + 4b$

40. $-3f + 4t - 3t + 6f$

Solve Multi-Step Equations

Solve each equation.

41. $4x + 16 = 40$

42. $\frac{x}{5} - 9 = 1$

Solve Proportions

Solve each proportion.

43. $\frac{3}{4} = \frac{z}{12}$

44. $\frac{10}{30} = \frac{6}{t}$

Function Tables

45. Generate ordered pairs for the function for $x = -2, -1, 0, 1, 2$.

$$y = 5x + 3$$

x	y
-2	▨
-1	▨
0	▨
1	▨
2	▨

Ordered Pairs

Graph each point on the same coordinate grid.

46. $A(-3, -4)$

47. $B(2, 0)$

Graph Linear Functions

48. Graph the function $y = 2x + 1$.

Solve and Graph Inequalities

Solve and graph each inequality.

49. $b - 8 \geq -11$

50. $-\frac{3}{4}x > 3$

CHAPTER 1

Equations

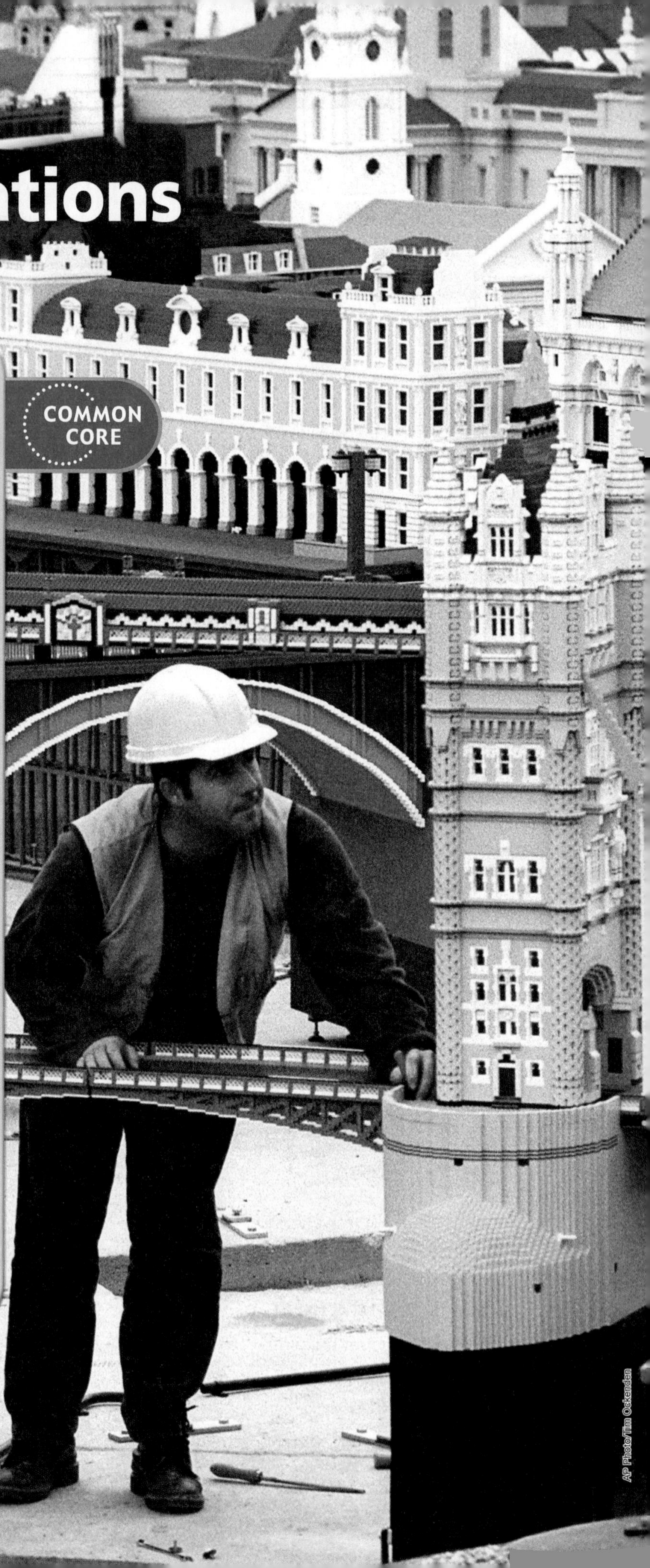

AP Photo/Tim Ockenden

COMMON CORE

Chapter Focus

- Choose procedures to solve equations efficiently.
- Differentiate between accuracy and precision.

All in *Proportion*

A common use of equations and proportional relationships is the construction of scale models.

Learn It Online
Chapter Project Online

ARE YOU READY?

✅ Vocabulary

Match each term on the left with a definition on the right.

1. constant

2. expression

3. order of operations

4. variable

A. a mathematical phrase that contains operations, numbers, and/or variables

B. a mathematical statement that two expressions are equivalent

C. a process for evaluating expressions

D. a symbol used to represent a quantity that can change

E. a value that does not change

✅ Order of Operations

Simplify each expression.

5. $(7 - 3) \div 2$

6. $4 \cdot 6 \div 3$

7. $12 - 3 + 1$

8. $2 \cdot 10 \div 5$

9. $125 \div 5^2$

10. $7 \cdot 6 + 5 \cdot 4$

✅ Add and Subtract Integers

Add or subtract.

11. $-15 + 19$

12. $-6 - (-18)$

13. $6 + (-8)$

14. $-12 + (-3)$

✅ Add and Subtract Fractions

Perform each indicated operation. Give your answer in the simplest form.

15. $\frac{1}{4} + \frac{2}{3}$

16. $1\frac{1}{2} - \frac{3}{4}$

17. $\frac{3}{8} + \frac{2}{3}$

18. $\frac{3}{2} - \frac{2}{3}$

✅ Evaluate Expressions

Evaluate each expression for the given value of the variable.

19. $2x + 3$ for $x = 7$

20. $3n - 5$ for $n = 7$

21. $13 - 4a$ for $a = 2$

22. $3y + 5$ for $y = 5$

✅ Connect Words and Algebra

23. Janie bought 4 apples and 6 bananas. Each apple cost $0.75, and each banana cost $0.60. Write an expression representing the total cost.

24. A rectangle has a width of 13 inches and a length of ℓ inches. Write an expression representing the area of the rectangle.

25. Write a phrase that could be modeled by the expression $n + 2n$.

1 Study Guide: Preview

Where You've Been

Previously, you
- practiced using operations in algebra.
- used variables to represent quantities.
- wrote expressions to represent situations.
- simplified and evaluated expressions.

In This Chapter

You will study
- how to use inverse operations to solve equations containing variables.
- writing equations to represent situations.
- simplifying equations before solving.

Where You're Going

You can use the skills in this chapter
- to compare unit prices for consumer products.
- to create or interpret scale models and drawings.
- To make measurements within an acceptable range of values.
- to solve problems in science courses and all future math courses.

Key Vocabulary/Vocabulario

accuracy	veracidad
equation	ecuación
formula	fórmula
identity	identidad
indirect measurement	medición indirecta
literal equation	ecuación literal
precision	precisión
proportion	proporción
ratio	razón
tolerance	tolerancia
unit rate	tasa unitaria

Vocabulary Connections

To become familiar with some of the vocabulary terms in the chapter, consider the following. You may refer to the chapter, the glossary, or a dictionary if you like.

1. The word **equation** begins with the root *equa-*. List some other words that begin with *equa-*. What do all these words have in common?

2. The word *literal* means "of letters." How might a **literal equation** be different from an equation like $3 + 5 = 8$?

3. One definition of **identity** is "exact sameness." An equation consists of two expressions. If an equation is an *identity*, what do you think is true about the expressions?

4. The word *tolerate* means "to put up with" or "accept." How can this meaning help to understand the term **tolerance**?

Chapter 1

Reading Strategy: Use Your Book for Success

Understanding how your textbook is organized will help you locate and use helpful information.

Pay attention to the **margin notes.** Know-It Note icons point out key information. Writing Math notes, Helpful Hints, and Caution notes help you understand concepts and avoid common mistakes.

Writing Math

These expressions mean "2 times y": $2y$ $2(y)$

Helpful Hint

A replacement set a set of numbers t can be substituted

Caution!

In the expression -5^2, 5 is the base because the nega

The **Glossary** is found in the back of your textbook. Use it as a resource when you need the definition of an unfamiliar word or property.

The **Index** is located at the end of your textbook. Use it to locate the page where a particular concept is taught.

The **Problem-Solving Handbook** is found in the back of your textbook. These pages review strategies that can help you solve real-world problems.

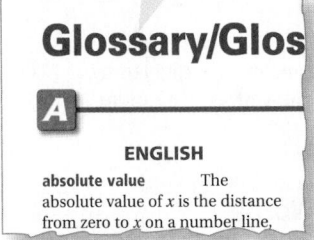

Glossary/Glos

A

ENGLISH

absolute value The absolute value of x is the distance from zero to x on a number line,

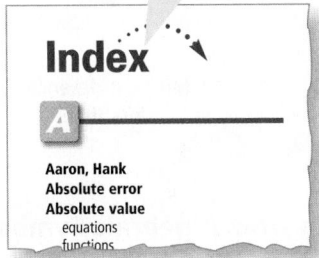

Index

A

Aaron, Hank
Absolute error
Absolute value
   equations
   functions

Problem Sol

Draw a Diagra

You can **draw a diagram** the words of a problem are

Use your textbook for the following problems.

1. Use the index to find the page where a term from this chapter is defined.

2. Describe how a strategy from the Problem Solving Workbook can be used in this chapter.

3. Use the glossary to find the definition of a term from this chapter.

Variables and Expressions

CC.9-12.A.SSE.1 Interpret expressions that represent a quantity in terms of its context.* *Also* CC.9-12.N.Q.1*

Objectives
Translate between words and algebra.

Evaluate algebraic expressions.

Vocabulary
variable
constant
numerical expression
algebraic expression
evaluate

Why learn this?
Variables and expressions can be used to determine how many plastic drink bottles must be recycled to make enough carpet for a house.

Container City, in East London, UK, is a development of buildings made from recycled shipping containers.

A home that is "green built" uses many recycled products, including carpet made from recycled plastic drink bottles. You can determine how many square feet of carpet can be made from a certain number of plastic drink bottles by using *variables, constants,* and *expressions.*

A **variable** is a letter or symbol used to represent a value that can change.

A **constant** is a value that does not change.

A **numerical expression** may contain only constants and/or operations.

An **algebraic expression** may contain variables, constants, and/or operations.

You will need to translate between algebraic expressions and words to be successful in math. The diagram below shows some of the ways to write mathematical operations with words.

    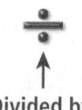

| Plus, sum, increased by | Minus, difference, less than | Times, product, equal groups of | Divided by, quotient |

EXAMPLE 1 **Translating from Algebraic Symbols to Words**

Give two ways to write each algebraic expression in words.

Writing Math

These expressions all mean "2 times y":
$2y$ $2(y)$
$2 \cdot y$ $(2)(y)$
$2 \times y$ $(2)y$

A $x + 3$
the sum of x and 3
x increased by 3

B $m - 7$
the difference of m and 7
7 less than m

C $2 \cdot y$
2 times y
the product of 2 and y

D $k \div 5$
k divided by 5
the quotient of k and 5

 Give two ways to write each algebraic expression in words.

1a. $4 - n$ **1b.** $\dfrac{t}{5}$ **1c.** $9 + q$ **1d.** $3(h)$

Ray Roberts/Alamy Photos; (sky), PhotoDisc/Getty Images

To translate words into algebraic expressions, look for words that indicate the action that is taking place.

Add   **Subtract**   **Multiply**   **Divide**

↑   ↑   ↑   ↑

Put together,   Find how much   Put together   Separate into
combine   more or less   equal groups   equal groups

EXAMPLE 2   **Translating from Words to Algebraic Symbols**

A   Eve reads 25 pages per hour. Write an expression for the number of pages she reads in h hours.

h represents the number of hours that Eve reads.

$25 \cdot h$ or $25h$ *Think: h groups of 25 pages.*

B   Sam is 2 years younger than Sue, who is y years old. Write an expression for Sam's age.

y represents Sue's age.

$y - 2$ *Think: "younger than" means "less than."*

C   William runs a mile in 12 minutes. Write an expression for the number of miles that William runs in m minutes.

m represents the total time William runs.

$\dfrac{m}{12}$ *Think: How many groups of 12 are in m?*

2a. Lou drives at 65 mi/h. Write an expression for the number of miles that Lou drives in t hours.

2b. Miriam is 5 cm taller than her sister, who is m cm tall. Write an expression for Miriam's height in centimeters.

2c. Elaine earns \$32 per day. Write an expression for the amount that she earns in d days.

To **evaluate** an expression is to find its value. To evaluate an algebraic expression, substitute numbers for the variables in the expression and then simplify the expression.

EXAMPLE 3   **Evaluating Algebraic Expressions**

Evaluate each expression for $x = 8$, $y = 5$, and $z = 4$.

A $x + y$

$x + y = 8 + 5$ *Substitute 8 for x and 5 for y.*

$ = 13$ *Simplify.*

B $\dfrac{x}{z}$

$\dfrac{x}{z} = \dfrac{8}{4}$ *Substitute 8 for x and 4 for z.*

$\phantom{\dfrac{x}{z}} = 2$ *Simplify.*

Evaluate each expression for $m = 3$, $n = 2$, and $p = 9$.

3a. mn **3b.** $p - n$ **3c.** $p \div m$

EXAMPLE 4 | *Recycling Application*

Approximately fourteen 20-ounce plastic drink bottles must be recycled to produce 1 square foot of carpet.

a. Write an expression for the number of bottles needed to make *c* square feet of carpet.

The expression $14c$ models the number of bottles needed to make *c* square feet of carpet.

b. Find the number of bottles needed to make 40, 120, and 224 square feet of carpet.

Evaluate $14c$ for $c = 40$, 120, and 224.

c	**14*c***
40	$14(40) = 560$
120	$14(120) = 1680$
224	$14(224) = 3136$

To make 40 ft^2 of carpet, 560 bottles are needed.
To make 120 ft^2 of carpet, 1680 bottles are needed.
To make 224 ft^2 of carpet, 3136 bottles are needed.

Helpful Hint

A *replacement set* is a set of numbers that can be substituted for a variable. The replacement set in Example 4 is {40, 120, 224}.

4. To make one sweater, sixty-three 20-ounce plastic drink bottles must be recycled.

   a. Write an expression for the number of bottles needed to make *s* sweaters.

   b. Find the number of bottles needed to make 12, 25, and 50 sweaters.

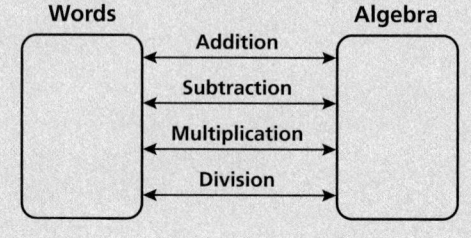

THINK AND DISCUSS

1. Write two ways to suggest each of the following, using words or phrases: addition, subtraction, multiplication, division.

2. Explain the difference between a numerical expression and an algebraic expression.

3. GET ORGANIZED Copy and complete the graphic organizer. Next to each operation, write a word phrase in the left box and its corresponding algebraic expression in the right box.

Words		Algebra
	Addition	
	Subtraction	
	Multiplication	
	Division	

(tc), Sam Dudgeon/HMH; (tr), Thinkstock/Getty

GUIDED PRACTICE

1. **Vocabulary** A(n) ___?___ is a value that can change. (*algebraic expression*, *constant*, or *variable*)

SEE EXAMPLE 1 Give two ways to write each algebraic expression in words.

2. $n - 5$ 3. $\dfrac{f}{3}$ 4. $c + 15$ 5. $9 - y$

6. $\dfrac{x}{12}$ 7. $t + 12$ 8. $8x$ 9. $x - 3$

SEE EXAMPLE 2
10. George drives at 45 mi/h. Write an expression for the number of miles George travels in h hours.

11. The length of a rectangle is 4 units greater than its width w. Write an expression for the length of the rectangle.

SEE EXAMPLE 3 Evaluate each expression for $a = 3$, $b = 4$, and $c = 2$.

12. $a - c$ 13. ab 14. $b \div c$ 15. ac

SEE EXAMPLE 4
16. Brianna practices the piano 30 minutes each day.
   a. Write an expression for the number of hours she practices in d days.
   b. Find the number of hours Brianna practices in 2, 4, and 10 days.

PRACTICE AND PROBLEM SOLVING

Independent Practice

For Exercises	See Example
17–24	1
25–26	2
27–30	3
31	4

Extra Practice
See Extra Practice for more Skills Practice and Applications Practice exercises.

Give two ways to write each algebraic expression in words.

17. $5p$ 18. $4 - y$ 19. $3 + x$ 20. $3y$

21. $-3s$ 22. $r \div 5$ 23. $14 - t$ 24. $x + 0.5$

25. Friday's temperature was 20° warmer than Monday's temperature t. Write an expression for Friday's temperature.

26. Ann sleeps 8 hours per night. Write an expression for the number of hours Ann sleeps in n nights.

Evaluate each expression for $r = 6$, $s = 5$, and $t = 3$.

27. $r - s$ 28. $s + t$ 29. $r \div t$ 30. sr

31. Jim is paid for overtime when he works more than 40 hours per week.
   a. Write an expression for the number of hours he works overtime when he works h hours.
   b. Find the number of hours Jim works overtime when he works 40, 44, 48, and 52 hours.

 32. **Write About It** Write a paragraph that explains to another student how to evaluate an expression.

Write an algebraic expression for each verbal expression. Then write a real-world situation that could be modeled by the expression.

33. the product of 2 and x 34. b less than 17   35. 10 more than y

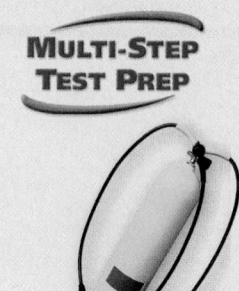

MULTI-STEP TEST PREP

36. The air around you puts pressure on your body equal to 14.7 pounds per square inch (psi). When you are underwater, the water exerts additional pressure on your body. For each foot you are below the surface of the water, the pressure increases by 0.445 psi.

  a. What does 14.7 represent in the expression $14.7 + 0.445d$?

  b. What does d represent in the expression?

  c. What is the total pressure exerted on a person's body when $d = 8$ ft?

37. Geometry The length of a rectangle is 9 inches. Write an expression for the area of the rectangle if the width is w inches. Find the area of the rectangle when the width is 1, 8, 9, and 11 inches.

38. Geometry The perimeter of any rectangle is the sum of its lengths and widths. The area of any rectangle is the length ℓ times the width w.

  a. Write an expression for the perimeter of a rectangle.

  b. Find the perimeter of the rectangle shown.

  c. Write an expression for the area of a rectangle.

  d. Find the area of the rectangle shown.

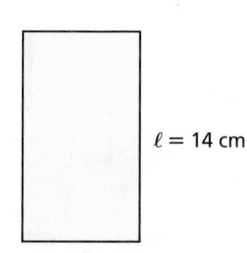

$\ell = 14$ cm

$w = 8$ cm

Complete each table. Evaluate the expression for each value of x.

39.

x	$x + 12$
1	
2	
3	
4	

40.

x	$10x$
1	
5	
10	
15	

41.

x	$x \div 2$
12	
20	
26	
30	

Astronomy

A crater on Canada's Devon Island is geologically similar to the surface of Mars. However, the temperature on Devon Island is about 37 °F in summer, and the average summer temperature on Mars is −85 °F.

42. Astronomy An object's weight on Mars can be found by multiplying 0.38 by the object's weight on Earth.

  a. An object weighs p pounds on Earth. Write an expression for its weight on Mars.

  b. Dana weighs 120 pounds, and her bicycle weighs 44 pounds. How much would Dana and her bicycle together weigh on Mars?

43. Meteorology Use the bar graph to write an expression for the average annual precipitation in New York, New York.

  a. The average annual precipitation in New York is m inches more than the average annual precipitation in Houston, Texas.

  b. The average annual precipitation in New York is s inches less than the average annual precipitation in Miami, Florida.

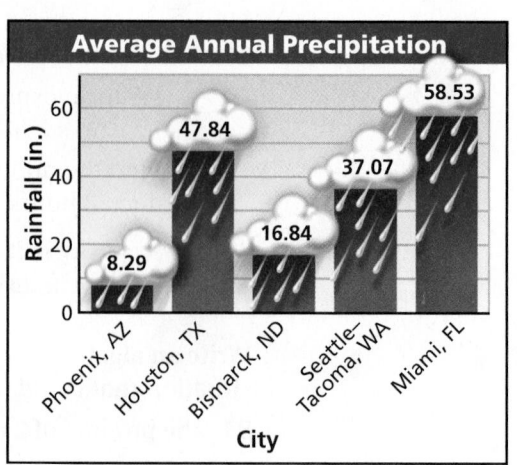

Average Annual Precipitation

Rainfall (in.)

58.53
47.84
37.07
16.84
8.29

Phoenix, AZ · Houston, TX · Bismarck, ND · Seattle–Tacoma, WA · Miami, FL

City

44. **Critical Thinking** Compare algebraic expressions and numerical expressions. Give examples of each.

Write an algebraic expression for each verbal expression. Then evaluate the algebraic expression for the given values of x.

	Verbal	Algebraic	$x = 12$	$x = 14$
	x reduced by 5	$x - 5$	$12 - 5 = 7$	$14 - 5 = 9$
45.	7 more than x	▨	▨	▨
46.	The quotient of x and 2	▨	▨	▨
47.	The sum of x and 3	▨	▨	▨

48. Claire has had her driver's license for 3 years. Bill has had his license for b fewer years than Claire. Which expression can be used to show the number of years Bill has had his driver's license?

 Ⓐ $3 + b$ Ⓑ $b + 3$ Ⓒ $3 - b$ Ⓓ $b - 3$

49. Which expression represents x?

 Ⓕ $12 - 5$ Ⓗ $12(5)$

 Ⓖ $12 + 5$ Ⓙ $12 \div 5$

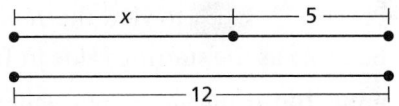

50. Which situation is best modeled by the expression $25 - x$?

 Ⓐ George places x more video games on a shelf with 25 games.

 Ⓑ Sarah has driven x miles of a 25-mile trip.

 Ⓒ Amelia paid 25 dollars of an x dollar lunch that she shared with Ariel.

 Ⓓ Jorge has 25 boxes full of x baseball cards each.

CHALLENGE AND EXTEND

Evaluate each expression for the given values of the variables.

51. $2ab$; $a = 6$, $b = 3$ 52. $2x + y$; $x = 4$, $y = 5$ 53. $3x \div 6y$; $x = 6$, $y = 3$

54. **Multi-Step** An Internet service provider charges \$9.95/month for the first 20 hours and \$0.50 for each additional hour. Write an expression representing the charges for h hours of use in one month when h is more than 20 hours. What is the charge for 35 hours?

1-1

Technology LAB

Create a Table to Evaluate Expressions

You can use a graphing calculator to quickly evaluate expressions for many values of the variable.

Use with Variables and Expressions

Learn It Online
Lab Resources Online

MATHEMATICAL PRACTICES

Use appropriate tools strategically.

Activity 1

Evaluate $2x + 7$ for $x = 25, 125, 225, 325,$ and 425.

1 Press **Y=** and enter **2X+7** for **Y1**.

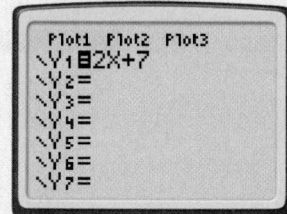

2 Determine a pattern for the values of x.
The x-values start with 25 and increase by 100.

3 Press **2nd** **WINDOW** (TBLSET) to view the *Table Setup* window.
Enter **25** as the starting value in **TblStart=**.

Enter **100** as the amount by which x changes in **△Tbl=**.

4 Press **2nd** **GRAPH** (TABLE) to create a table of values.
The first column shows values of x starting with 25 and increasing by 100.

The second column shows values of the expression $2x + 7$ when x is equal to the value in the first column.

You can use the arrow keys to view the table when x is greater than 625.

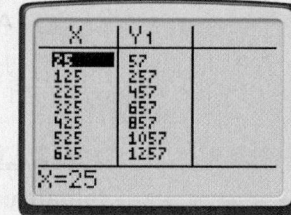

Try This

1. Use the table feature of a graphing calculator to evaluate $5x - 7$ for $x = 4, 6, 8, 10,$ and 12.

   a. What value did you enter in **TblStart=**?

   b. What value did you enter in **△Tbl=**?

2. Use the table feature of a graphing calculator to evaluate $3x + 4$ for $x = -5, -1, 3, 7,$ and 11.

   a. What value did you enter in **TblStart=**?

   b. What value did you enter in **△Tbl=**?

You can also use a spreadsheet program to evaluate expressions.

Activity 2

Evaluate $2x + 7$ for $x = 3, 5, 7, 9,$ and 11.

① In the first column, enter the values 3, 5, 7, 9, and 11.

	A	B	C	D	E	F	G
	126		f_x				
1	3						
2	5						
3	7						
4	9						
5	11						
6							

② Enter the expression in cell B1.

To do this, type the following:
= 2 * A1 + 7

	A	B	C	D	E	F	G
	SUM	▾ ✕ ✓	f_x =2*A1+7				
1	3	=2*A1+7					
2	5						
3	7						
4	9						
5	11						
6							

③ Press Enter.

The value of $2x + 7$ when $x = 3$ appears in cell B1.

	A	B	C	D	E	F	G
	B1	▾	f_x =2*A1+7				
1	3	13					
2	5						
3	7						
4	9						
5	11						
6							

④ Copy the formula into cells B2, B3, B4, and B5.

Use the mouse to click on the lower right corner of cell B1. Hold down the mouse button and drag the cursor through cell B5.

	A	B	C	D	E	F	G
	B1	▾	f_x =2*A1+7				
1	3	13					
2	5	17					
3	7	21					
4	9	25					
5	11	29					
6							

For each row in column B, the number that is substituted for x is the value in the same row of column A.

	A	B	C	D	E	F	G
	B2	▾	f_x =2(A2)+7				
1	3	13					
2	5	17					
3	7	21					
4	9	25					
5	11	29					
6							

You can continue the table by entering more values in column A and copying the formula from B1 into more cells in column B.

Try This

3. Use a spreadsheet program to evaluate $-2x + 9$ for $x = -5, -2, 1, 4,$ and 7.

    a. What values did you enter in column A?

    b. What did you type in cell B1?

4. Use a spreadsheet program to evaluate $7x - 10$ for $x = 2, 7, 12, 17,$ and 22.

    a. What values did you enter in column A?

    b. What did you type in cell B1?

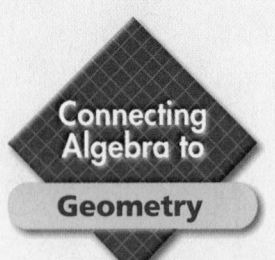

Perimeter

The distance around a geometric figure is called the *perimeter*. You can use what you have learned about combining like terms to simplify expressions for perimeter.

A closed figure with straight sides is called a *polygon*. To find the perimeter of a polygon, add the lengths of the sides.

Example 1

A **Write an expression for the perimeter of the quadrilateral.**

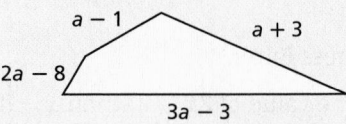

Add the lengths of the four sides.

$$P = (a + 3) + (2a - 8) + (3a - 3) + (a - 1)$$

Combine like terms to simplify.

$$P = (a + 2a + 3a + a) + (3 - 8 - 3 - 1)$$

$$= 7a - 9 \qquad \textit{This is a general expression for the perimeter.}$$

B **Find the perimeter of this quadrilateral for $a = 5$.**

Substitute 5 for a.

$$P = 7(5) - 9 \qquad \textit{Multiply; then subtract.}$$

$$= 35 - 9$$

$$= 26 \qquad \textit{This is the perimeter when a = 5.}$$

Try This

Write and simplify an expression for the perimeter of each figure.

1.
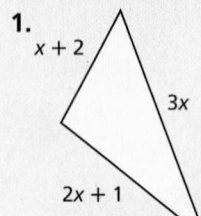

2.
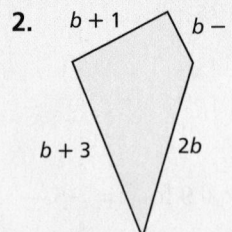

3.
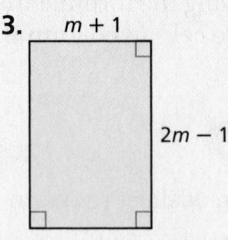

Find the perimeter of each figure for the given value of the variable.

4. $k = 3$
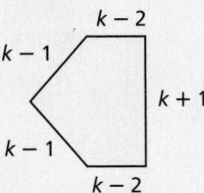

5. $n = 10$
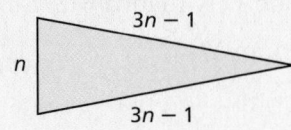

6. $y = 4$
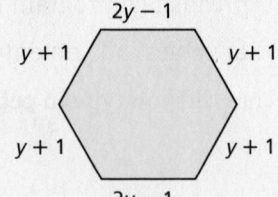

Combining like terms is one way to explore what happens to the perimeter when you double the sides of a triangle or other polygon.

Example 2

What happens to the perimeter of this triangle when you double the length of each side?

Write an expression for the perimeter of the smaller triangle.
Combine like terms to simplify the expression.

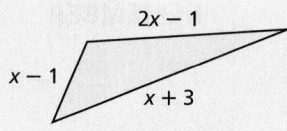

$(x-1) + (2x-1) + (x+3)$

$(x + 2x + x) + (-1 -1 + 3)$

$4x + 1$ *Perimeter of small triangle*

Double the length of each side of the triangle.

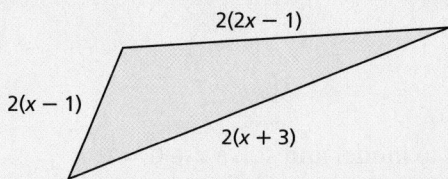

$2(x-1) = 2x - 2$

$2(2x-1) = 4x - 2$

$2(x+3) = 2x + 6$

Find the perimeter of the larger triangle.
Combine like terms to simplify.

$(2x-2) + (4x-2) + (2x+6)$ *Add the lengths of the sides.*

$(2x + 4x + 2x) + (-2 - 2 + 6)$ *Use the Associative and Commutative Properties of Addition and combine like terms.*

$8x + 2$ *Perimeter of large triangle*

Use the Distributive Property to show that the new perimeter is twice the original perimeter.

$8x + 2 = 2(4x + 1)$

Try This

Each set of expressions represents the side lengths of a triangle. Use the Distributive Property to show that doubling the side lengths doubles the perimeter.

7. $2p + 1$	**8.** $c - 1$	**9.** $w + 5$	**10.** $h - 2$
$3p + 2$	$2c + 1$	$w + 5$	$3h$
$5p$	$3c - 1$	$3w - 1$	$2h + 3$

Solve each problem.

11. Use the triangles in Example 2. Find the side lengths and perimeters for $x = 5$.

12. The sides of a quadrilateral are $2x - 1$, $x + 3$, $3x + 1$, and $x - 1$. Double the length of each side. Then find an expression for the perimeter of the new figure.

13. What happens to the perimeter of this trapezoid when you triple the length of each side? Use the variables a, b, b, and c for the lengths of the sides. Explain your answer using the Distributive Property.

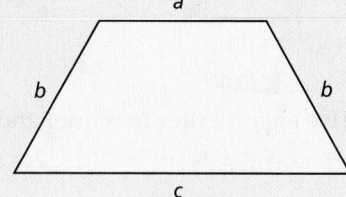

Model One-Step Equations

You can use algebra tiles and an equation mat to model and solve equations. To find the value of the variable, place or remove tiles to get the x-tile by itself on one side of the mat. You must place or remove the same number of yellow tiles or the same number of red tiles on both sides.

Use with Solving Equations by Adding or Subtracting

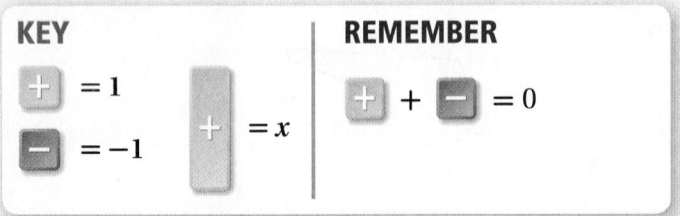

KEY

$\boxed{+} = 1$

$\boxed{-} = -1$

$\boxed{+} = x$

REMEMBER

$\boxed{+} + \boxed{-} = 0$

Learn It Online
Lab Resources Online

MATHEMATICAL PRACTICES **Use appropriate tools strategically.**

CC.9-12.A.REI.1 Explain each step in solving a simple equation as following from the equality of numbers asserted at the previous step, starting from the assumption that the original equation has a solution. Construct a viable argument to justify a solution method. *Also* **CC.9-12.A.REI.3**

Activity

Use algebra tiles to model and solve $x + 6 = 2$.

MODEL		ALGEBRA
	Model $x + 6$ on the left side of the mat and 2 on the right side of the mat.	$x + 6 = 2$
	Place 6 red tiles on both sides of the mat. This represents adding -6 to both sides of the equation.	$x + 6 + (-6) = 2 + (-6)$
	Remove zero pairs from both sides of the mat.	$x + 0 = 0 + (-4)$
	One x-tile is equivalent to 4 red tiles.	$x = -4$

Try This

Use algebra tiles to model and solve each equation.

1. $x + 2 = 5$ **2.** $x - 7 = 8$ **3.** $x - 5 = 9$ **4.** $x + 4 = 7$

1-2 Solving Equations by Adding or Subtracting

CC.9-12.A.REI.1 Explain each step in solving a simple equation as following from the equality of numbers asserted at the previous step, starting from the assumption that the original equation has a solution. ... *Also* **CC.9-12.A.REI.3, CC.9-12.A.CED.1***

Objective
Solve one-step equations in one variable by using addition or subtraction.

Vocabulary
equation
solution of an equation

Who uses this?
Athletes can use an equation to estimate their maximum heart rates. (See Example 4.)

An **equation** is a mathematical statement that two expressions are equal. A **solution of an equation** is a value of the variable that makes the equation true.

To find solutions, *isolate the variable*. A variable is isolated when it appears by itself on one side of an equation, and not at all on the other side. Isolate a variable by using inverse operations, which "undo" operations on the variable.

An equation is like a balanced scale. To keep the balance, perform the same operation on both sides.

Inverse Operations
Add x. $\longleftrightarrow$ Subtract x.

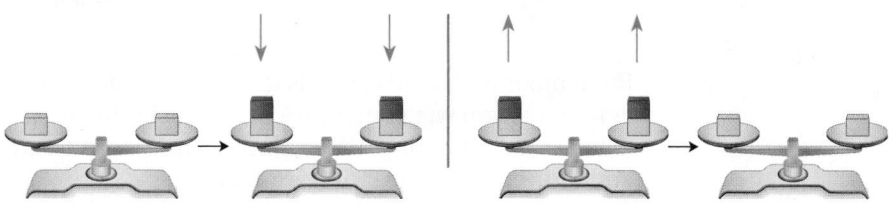

EXAMPLE 1 Solving Equations by Using Addition

Solve each equation.

A $x - 10 = 4$

$$\begin{array}{rl} x - 10 = & 4 \\ \underline{+\ 10} & \underline{+\ 10} \\ x\ \ \ = & 14 \end{array}$$

Since 10 is subtracted from x, add 10 to both sides to undo the subtraction.

Writing Math

Solutions are sometimes written in a *solution set*. For Example 1A, the solution set is {14}. For Example 1B, the solution set is $\left\{\frac{3}{5}\right\}$.

Check
$$\begin{array}{r|l} x - 10 = 4 \\ \hline 14 - 10 & 4 \\ 4 & 4\ \checkmark \end{array}$$

To check your solution, substitute 14 for x in the original equation.

B $\dfrac{2}{5} = m - \dfrac{1}{5}$

$$\dfrac{2}{5} = m - \dfrac{1}{5}$$

$$\underline{+\dfrac{1}{5} \qquad\qquad +\dfrac{1}{5}}$$

$$\dfrac{3}{5} = m$$

Since $\frac{1}{5}$ is subtracted from m, add $\frac{1}{5}$ to both sides to undo the subtraction.

CHECK IT OUT!

Solve each equation. Check your answer.

1a. $n - 3.2 = 5.6$ **1b.** $-6 = k - 6$ **1c.** $16 = m - 9$

EXAMPLE `2` **Solving Equations by Using Subtraction**

Solve each equation. Check your answer.

A $x + 7 = 9$

$$\begin{array}{rcl} x + 7 &=& 9 \\ \underline{-7} & & \underline{-7} \\ x &=& 2 \end{array}$$

Since 7 is added to x, subtract 7 from both sides to undo the addition.

Check $\begin{array}{c|c} x + 7 = 9 \\ \hline 2 + 7 & 9 \\ 9 & 9 \checkmark \end{array}$

To check your solution, substitute 2 for x in the original equation.

B $0.7 = r + 0.4$

$$\begin{array}{rcl} 0.7 &=& r + 0.4 \\ \underline{-0.4} & & \underline{-0.4} \\ 0.3 &=& r \end{array}$$

Since 0.4 is added to r, subtract 0.4 from both sides to undo the addition.

Check $\begin{array}{c|c} 0.7 = r + 0.4 \\ \hline 0.7 & 0.3 + 0.4 \\ 0.7 & 0.7 \checkmark \end{array}$

To check your solution, substitute 0.3 for r in the original equation.

 Solve each equation. Check your answer.

2a. $d + \dfrac{1}{2} = 1$ **2b.** $-5 = k + 5$ **2c.** $6 + t = 14$

Remember that subtracting is the same as adding the opposite. When solving equations, you will sometimes find it easier to add an opposite to both sides instead of subtracting. For example, this method may be useful when the equation contains negative numbers.

EXAMPLE `3` **Solving Equations by Adding the Opposite**

Solve $-8 + b = 2$.

$$\begin{array}{rcl} -8 + b &=& 2 \\ \underline{+8} & & \underline{+8} \\ b &=& 10 \end{array}$$

Since −8 is added to b, add 8 to both sides.

 Solve each equation. Check your answer.

3a. $-2.3 + m = 7$ **3b.** $-\dfrac{3}{4} + z = \dfrac{5}{4}$ **3c.** $-11 + x = 33$

Student to Student *Zero As a Solution*

Ama Walker
Carson High School

I used to get confused when I got a solution of 0. But my teacher reminded me that 0 is a number just like any other number, so it can be a solution of an equation. Just check your answer and see if it works.

$$\begin{array}{rcl} x + 6 &=& 6 \\ \underline{-6} & & \underline{-6} \\ x &=& 0 \end{array}$$

Check $\begin{array}{c|c} x + 6 = 6 \\ \hline 0 + 6 & 6 \\ 6 & 6 \checkmark \end{array}$

EXAMPLE 4 *Fitness Application*

A person's maximum heart rate is the highest rate, in beats per minute, that the person's heart should reach. One method to estimate maximum heart rate states that your age added to your maximum heart rate is 220. Using this method, write and solve an equation to find the maximum heart rate of a 15-year-old.

Age	added to	maximum heart rate	is	220.
a	$+$	r	$=$	220

$a + r = 220$ Write an equation to represent the relationship.

$15 + r = 220$ Substitute 15 for a. Since 15 is added to r,

$\underline{-15 \qquad -15}$ subtract 15 from both sides to undo the

$r = 205$ addition.

The maximum heart rate for a 15-year-old is 205 beats per minute. Since age added to maximum heart rate is 220, the answer should be less than 220. So 205 is a reasonable answer.

CHECK IT OUT!

4. **What if...?** Use the method above to find a person's age if the person's maximum heart rate is 185 beats per minute.

The properties of equality allow you to perform inverse operations, as in the previous examples. These properties say that you can perform the same operation on both sides of an equation.

Properties of Equality

WORDS	NUMBERS	ALGEBRA
Addition Property of Equality You can add the same number to both sides of an equation, and the statement will still be true.	$3 = 3$ $3 + 2 = 3 + 2$ $5 = 5$	$a = b$ $a + c = b + c$
Subtraction Property of Equality You can subtract the same number from both sides of an equation, and the statement will still be true.	$7 = 7$ $7 - 5 = 7 - 5$ $2 = 2$	$a = b$ $a - c = b - c$

THINK AND DISCUSS

1. Describe how the Addition and Subtraction Properties of Equality are like a balanced scale.

2. **GET ORGANIZED** Copy and complete the graphic organizer. In each box, write an example of an equation that can be solved by using the given property, and solve it.

Exercises

GUIDED PRACTICE

1. Vocabulary Will the *solution of an equation* such as $x - 3 = 9$ be a variable or a number? Explain.

Solve each equation. Check your answer.

SEE EXAMPLE **1**

2. $s - 5 = 3$

3. $17 = w - 4$

4. $k - 8 = -7$

5. $x - 3.9 = 12.4$

6. $8.4 = y - 4.6$

7. $\frac{3}{8} = t - \frac{1}{8}$

SEE EXAMPLE **2**

8. $t + 5 = -25$

9. $9 = s + 9$

10. $42 = m + 36$

11. $2.8 = z + 0.5$

12. $b + \frac{2}{3} = 2$

13. $n + 1.8 = 3$

SEE EXAMPLE **3**

14. $-10 + d = 7$

15. $20 = -12 + v$

16. $-46 + q = 5$

17. $2.8 = -0.9 + y$

18. $-\frac{2}{3} + c = \frac{2}{3}$

19. $-\frac{5}{6} + p = 2$

SEE EXAMPLE **4**

20. Geology In 1673, the Hope diamond was reduced from its original weight by about 45 carats, resulting in a diamond weighing about 67 carats. Write and solve an equation to find how many carats the original diamond weighed. Show that your answer is reasonable.

PRACTICE AND PROBLEM SOLVING

Independent Practice

For Exercises	See Example
21–30	1
31–40	2
41–48	3
49	4

Extra Practice

See Extra Practice for more Skills Practice and Applications Practice exercises.

Solve each equation. Check your answer.

21. $1 = k - 8$

22. $u - 15 = -8$

23. $x - 7 = 10$

24. $-9 = p - 2$

25. $\frac{3}{7} = p - \frac{1}{7}$

26. $q - 0.5 = 1.5$

27. $6 = t - 4.5$

28. $4\frac{2}{3} = r - \frac{1}{3}$

29. $6 = x - 3$

30. $1.75 = k - 0.75$

31. $19 + a = 19$

32. $4 = 3.1 + y$

33. $m + 20 = 3$

34. $-12 = c + 3$

35. $v + 2300 = -800$

36. $b + 42 = 300$

37. $3.5 = n + 4$

38. $b + \frac{1}{2} = \frac{1}{2}$

39. $x + 5.34 = 5.39$

40. $2 = d + \frac{1}{4}$

41. $-12 + f = 3$

42. $-9 = -4 + g$

43. $-1200 + j = 345$

44. $90 = -22 + a$

45. $26 = -4 + y$

46. $1\frac{3}{4} = -\frac{1}{4} + w$

47. $-\frac{1}{6} + h = \frac{1}{6}$

48. $-5.2 + a = -8$

49. Finance Luis deposited $500 into his bank account. He now has $4732. Write and solve an equation to find how much was in his account before the deposit. Show that your answer is reasonable.

50. ///ERROR ANALYSIS/// Below are two possible solutions to $x + 12.5 = 21.6$. Which is incorrect? Explain the error.

A
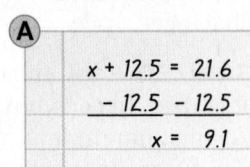

$$\begin{array}{r} x + 12.5 = 21.6 \\ -12.5 \quad -12.5 \\ \hline x = 9.1 \end{array}$$

B
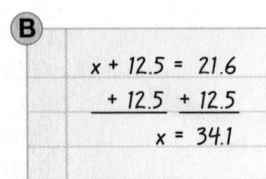

$$\begin{array}{r} x + 12.5 = 21.6 \\ +12.5 \quad +12.5 \\ \hline x = 34.1 \end{array}$$

Write an equation to represent each relationship. Then solve the equation.

51. Ten less than a number is equal to 12.

52. A number decreased by 13 is equal to 7.

53. Eight more than a number is 16.

54. A number minus 3 is −8.

55. The sum of 5 and a number is 6.

56. Two less than a number is −5.

57. The difference of a number and 4 is 9.

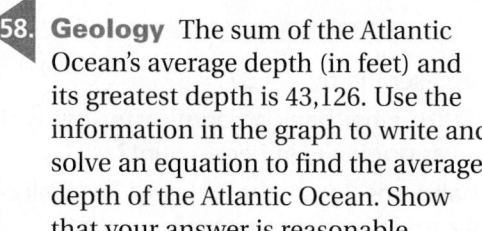
58. Geology The sum of the Atlantic Ocean's average depth (in feet) and its greatest depth is 43,126. Use the information in the graph to write and solve an equation to find the average depth of the Atlantic Ocean. Show that your answer is reasonable.

59. School Helene's marching band needs money to travel to a competition. Band members have raised $560. They need to raise a total of $1680. Write and solve an equation to find how much more they need. Show that your answer is reasonable.

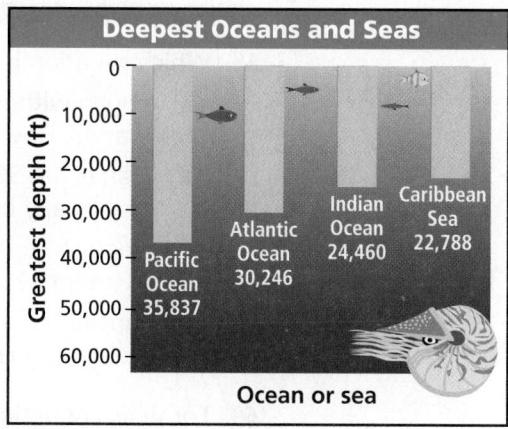

Deepest Oceans and Seas

60. Economics When you receive a loan to make a purchase, you often must make a down payment in cash. The amount of the loan is the purchase cost minus the down payment. Riva made a down payment of $1500 on a used car. She received a loan of $2600. Write and solve an equation to find the cost of the car. Show that your answer is reasonable.

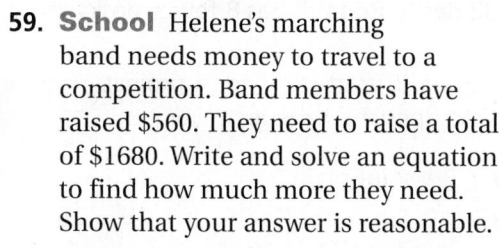 **Geometry** The angles in each pair are complementary. Write and solve an equation to find each value of *x*. (*Hint:* The measures of complementary angles add to 90°.)

61.

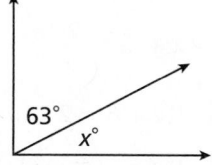

63°
x°

62.

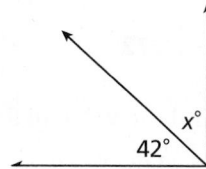

x°
42°

63.

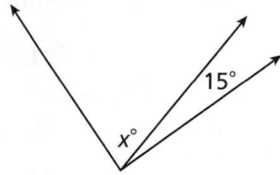

15°
x°

64. *Rates* are often used to describe how quickly something is moving or changing.

   a. A wildfire spreads at a rate of 1000 acres per day. How many acres will the fire cover in 2 days? Show that your answer is reasonable.

   b. How many acres will the fire cover in 5 days? Explain how you found your answer.

   c. Another wildfire spread for 7 days and covered a total of 780 square miles. How can you estimate the number of square miles the fire covered per day?

65. **Statistics** The range of a set of scores is 28, and the lowest score is 47. Write and solve an equation to find the highest score. (*Hint:* In a data set, the range is the difference between the highest and the lowest values.) Show that your answer is reasonable.

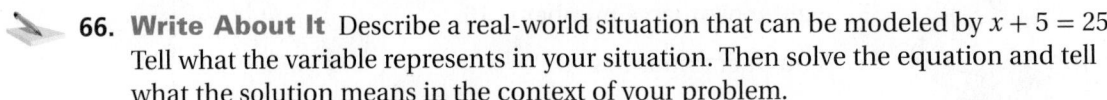

66. **Write About It** Describe a real-world situation that can be modeled by $x + 5 = 25$. Tell what the variable represents in your situation. Then solve the equation and tell what the solution means in the context of your problem.

67. **Critical Thinking** Without solving, tell whether the solution of $-3 + z = 10$ will be greater than 10 or less than 10. Explain.

68. Which situation is best represented by $x - 32 = 8$?
    (A) Logan withdrew $32 from her bank account. After her withdrawal, her balance was $8. How much was originally in her account?
    (B) Daniel has 32 baseball cards. Joseph has 8 fewer baseball cards than Daniel. How many baseball cards does Joseph have?
    (C) Room A contains 32 desks. Room B has 8 fewer desks. How many desks are in Room B?
    (D) Janelle bought a bag of 32 craft sticks for a project. She used 8 craft sticks. How many craft sticks does she have left?

69. For which equation is $a = 8$ a solution?
    (F) $15 - a = 10$ (G) $10 + a = 23$ (H) $a - 18 = 26$ (J) $a + 8 = 16$

70. **Short Response** Julianna used a gift card to pay for an $18 haircut. The remaining balance on the card was $22.
    a. Write an equation that can be used to determine the original value of the card.
    b. Solve your equation to find the original value of the card.

CHALLENGE AND EXTEND

Solve each equation. Check your answer.

71. $3\frac{1}{5} + b = \frac{4}{5}$ 72. $x - \frac{7}{4} = \frac{2}{3}$ 73. $x + \frac{7}{4} = \frac{2}{3}$ 74. $x - \frac{4}{9} = \frac{4}{9}$

75. If $p - 4 = 2$, find the value of $5p - 20$.   76. If $t + 6 = 21$, find the value of $-2t$.

77. If $x + 3 = 15$, find the value of $18 + 6x$.   78. If $2 + n = -11$, find the value of $6n$.

Area of Composite Figures

Review the area formulas for squares, rectangles, and triangles in the table below.

Squares	Rectangles	Triangles
![square with side s]	![rectangle with length ℓ and width w]	![triangle with height h and base b]
$A = s^2$	$A = \ell w$	$A = \dfrac{1}{2}bh$

A *composite figure* is a figure that is composed of basic shapes. You can divide composite figures into combinations of squares, rectangles, and triangles to find their areas.

Example

Find the area of the figure shown.

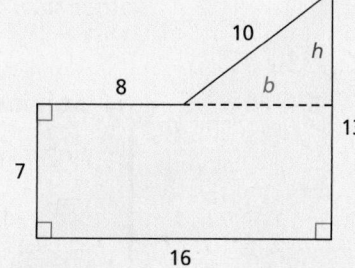

Divide the figure into a rectangle and a right triangle. Notice that you do not know the base or the height of the triangle. Use b and h to represent these lengths.

The bottom of the rectangle is 16 units long; the top of the rectangle is 8 units long plus the base of the triangle. Use this information to write and solve an equation.

$$\begin{aligned} b + 8 &= 16 \\ -8 \quad &\ \ -8 \\ \hline b \ \ &= 8 \end{aligned}$$

The right side of the figure is 13 units long: 7 units from the rectangle plus the height of the triangle. Use this information to write and solve an equation.

$$\begin{aligned} h + 7 &= 13 \\ -7 \quad &\ \ -7 \\ \hline h \ \ &= 6 \end{aligned}$$

The area of the figure is the sum of the areas of the rectangle and the triangle.

Area of rectangle
Area of triangle

$$A = \ell w + \frac{1}{2}bh$$
$$A = \mathbf{16}(\mathbf{7}) + \frac{1}{2}(\mathbf{8})(\mathbf{6})$$
$$A = 112 + 24$$
$$A = 136 \text{ square units}$$

Try This

Find the area of each composite figure.

1.

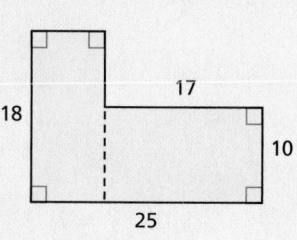

2.

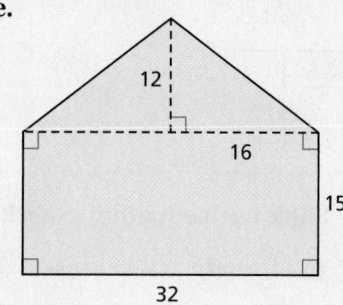

3.

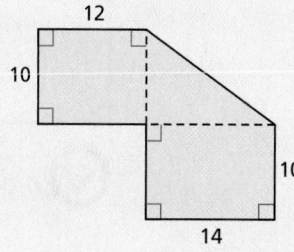

CC.9-12.A.REI.1 Explain each step in solving a simple equation as following from the equality of numbers asserted at the previous step, starting from the assumption that the original equation has a solution.... *Also* CC.9-12.A.REI.3, CC.9-12.A.CED.1*

1-3 Solving Equations by Multiplying or Dividing

Objective
Solve one-step equations in one variable by using multiplication or division.

Who uses this?
Pilots can make quick calculations by solving one-step equations. (See Example 4.)

Solving an equation that contains multiplication or division is similar to solving an equation that contains addition or subtraction. Use inverse operations to undo the operations on the variable.

Remember that an equation is like a balanced scale. To keep the balance, whatever you do on one side of the equation, you must also do on the other side.

Inverse Operations
Multiply by *x*. ←→ Divide by *x*.

EXAMPLE 1 **Solving Equations by Using Multiplication**

Solve each equation. Check your answer.

A $-4 = \dfrac{k}{-5}$

$(-5)(-4) = (-5)\left(\dfrac{k}{-5}\right)$ *Since k is divided by −5, multiply both sides by −5 to undo the division.*

$20 = k$

Check $-4 = \dfrac{k}{-5}$ *To check your solution, substitute 20 for k in the original equation.*

$$\begin{array}{c|c} -4 & \dfrac{20}{-5} \\ \hline -4 & -4 \checkmark \end{array}$$

B $\dfrac{m}{3} = 1.5$

$(3)\left(\dfrac{m}{3}\right) = (3)(1.5)$ *Since m is divided by 3, multiply both sides by 3 to undo the division.*

$m = 4.5$

Check $\dfrac{m}{3} = 1.5$ *To check your solution, substitute 1.5 for m in the original equation.*

$$\begin{array}{c|c} \dfrac{4.5}{3} & 1.5 \\ \hline 1.5 & 1.5 \checkmark \end{array}$$

 Solve each equation. Check your answer.

1a. $\dfrac{p}{5} = 10$ **1b.** $-13 = \dfrac{y}{3}$ **1c.** $\dfrac{c}{8} = 7$

EXAMPLE 2 | **Solving Equations by Using Division**

Solve each equation. Check your answers.

A $7x = 56$

$$\frac{7x}{7} = \frac{56}{7}$$

$$x = 8$$

Since x is multiplied by 7, divide both sides by 7 to undo the multiplication.

Check $7x = 56$

$$\frac{7(8)}{} \bigg| \frac{56}{}$$

$$56 \bigg| 56 \checkmark$$

To check your solution, substitute 8 for x in the original equation.

B $13 = -2w$

$$\frac{13}{-2} = \frac{-2w}{-2}$$

$$-6.5 = w$$

Since w is multiplied by −2, divide both sides by −2 to undo the multiplication.

Check $13 = -2w$

$$13 \bigg| -2(-6.5)$$

$$13 \bigg| 13 \checkmark$$

To check your solution, substitute −6.5 for w in the original equation.

 Solve each equation. Check your answer.

2a. $16 = 4c$ **2b.** $0.5y = -10$ **2c.** $15k = 75$

Remember that dividing is the same as multiplying by the reciprocal. When solving equations, you will sometimes find it easier to multiply by a reciprocal instead of dividing. This is often true when an equation contains fractions.

EXAMPLE 3 | **Solving Equations That Contain Fractions**

Solve each equation.

A $\frac{5}{9}v = 35$

$$\left(\frac{9}{5}\right)\frac{5}{9}v = \left(\frac{9}{5}\right)35$$

$$v = 63$$

The reciprocal of $\frac{5}{9}$ is $\frac{9}{5}$. Since v is multiplied by $\frac{5}{9}$, multiply both sides by $\frac{9}{5}$.

B $\frac{5}{2} = \frac{4y}{3}$

$$\frac{5}{2} = \frac{4y}{3}$$

$$\frac{5}{2} = \frac{4}{3}y$$

$\frac{4y}{3}$ is the same as $\frac{4}{3}y$.

$$\left(\frac{3}{4}\right)\frac{5}{2} = \left(\frac{3}{4}\right)\frac{4}{3}y$$

$$\frac{15}{8} = y$$

The reciprocal of $\frac{4}{3}$ is $\frac{3}{4}$. Since y is multiplied by $\frac{4}{3}$, multiply both sides by $\frac{3}{4}$.

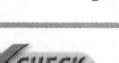 Solve each equation. Check your answer.

3a. $-\frac{1}{4} = \frac{1}{5}b$ **3b.** $\frac{4j}{6} = \frac{2}{3}$ **3c.** $\frac{1}{6}w = 102$

EXAMPLE 4 | *Aviation Application*

The distance in miles from the airport that a plane should begin descending, divided by 3, equals the plane's height above the ground in thousands of feet. If a plane is 10,000 feet above the ground, write and solve an equation to find the distance at which the pilot should begin descending.

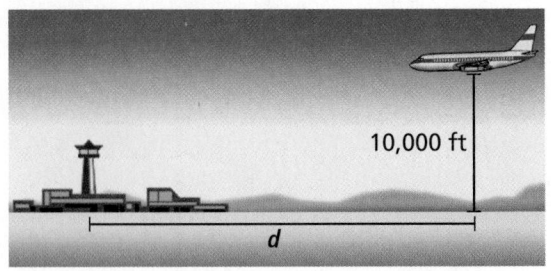

10,000 ft

d

Distance	divided by 3	equals	height in thousands of feet.

$$\frac{d}{3} = h \qquad \text{*Write an equation to represent the relationship.*}$$

$$\frac{d}{3} = 10 \qquad \text{*Substitute 10 for h. Since d is divided by 3, multiply both sides by 3 to undo the division.*}$$

$$(3)\frac{d}{3} = (3)10$$

$$d = 30$$

The pilot should begin descending 30 miles from the airport.

4. What if...? A plane began descending 45 miles from the airport. Use the equation above to find how high the plane was flying when the descent began.

> **Caution!**
>
> The equation uses the plane's height above the ground in *thousands* of feet. So substitute 10 for *h*, not 10,000.

You have now used four properties of equality to solve equations. These properties are summarized in the box below.

Properties of Equality

WORDS	NUMBERS	ALGEBRA
Addition Property of Equality You can add the same number to both sides of an equation, and the statement will still be true.	$3 = 3$ $3 + 2 = 3 + 2$ $5 = 5$	$a = b$ $a + c = b + c$
Subtraction Property of Equality You can subtract the same number from both sides of an equation, and the statement will still be true.	$7 = 7$ $7 - 5 = 7 - 5$ $2 = 2$	$a = b$ $a - c = b - c$
Multiplication Property of Equality You can multiply both sides of an equation by the same number, and the statement will still be true.	$6 = 6$ $6(3) = 6(3)$ $18 = 18$	$a = b$ $ac = bc$
Division Property of Equality You can divide both sides of an equation by the same nonzero number, and the statement will still be true.	$8 = 8$ $\frac{8}{4} = \frac{8}{4}$ $2 = 2$	$a = b$ $(c \neq 0)$ $\frac{a}{c} = \frac{b}{c}$

THINK AND DISCUSS

1. Tell how the Multiplication and Division Properties of Equality are similar to the Addition and Subtraction Properties of Equality.

2. GET ORGANIZED Copy and complete the graphic organizer. In each box, write an example of an equation that can be solved by using the given property, and solve it.

1-3

Exercises

Learn It Online
Homework Help Online
Parent Resources Online

GUIDED PRACTICE

Solve each equation. Check your answer.

SEE EXAMPLE 1

1. $\frac{k}{4} = 8$

2. $\frac{z}{3} = -9$

3. $-2 = \frac{w}{-7}$

4. $6 = \frac{t}{-5}$

5. $\frac{g}{1.9} = 10$

6. $2.4 = \frac{b}{5}$

SEE EXAMPLE 2

7. $4x = 28$

8. $-64 = 8c$

9. $-9j = -45$

10. $84 = -12a$

11. $4m = 10$

12. $2.8 = -2h$

SEE EXAMPLE 3

13. $\frac{1}{2}d = 7$

14. $15 = \frac{5}{6}f$

15. $\frac{2}{3}s = -6$

16. $9 = -\frac{3}{8}r$

17. $\frac{1}{10} = \frac{4}{5}y$

18. $\frac{1}{4}v = -\frac{3}{4}$

SEE EXAMPLE 4

19. Recreation The Baseball Birthday Batter Package at a minor league ballpark costs $192. The package includes tickets, drinks, and cake for a group of 16 children. Write and solve an equation to find the cost per child.

20. Nutrition An orange contains about 80 milligrams of vitamin C, which is 10 times as much as an apple contains. Write and solve an equation to find the amount of vitamin C in an apple.

PRACTICE AND PROBLEM SOLVING

Solve each equation. Check your answer.

21. $\frac{x}{2} = 12$

22. $-40 = \frac{b}{5}$

23. $-\frac{j}{6} = 6$

24. $-\frac{n}{3} = -4$

25. $-\frac{q}{5} = 30$

26. $1.6 = \frac{d}{3}$

27. $\frac{v}{10} = 5.5$

28. $\frac{h}{8.1} = -4$

29. $5t = -15$

30. $49 = 7c$

31. $-12 = -12u$

32. $-7m = 63$

33. $-52 = -4c$

34. $11 = -2z$

35. $5f = 1.5$

36. $-8.4 = -4n$

Independent Practice		
For Exercises		See Example
21–28		1
29–36		2
37–44		3
45		4

Solve each equation. Check your answer.

37. $\frac{5}{2}k = 5$
38. $-9 = \frac{3}{4}d$
39. $-\frac{5}{8}b = 10$
40. $-\frac{4}{5}g = -12$

41. $\frac{4}{7}t = -2$
42. $-\frac{4}{5}p = \frac{2}{3}$
43. $\frac{2}{3} = -\frac{1}{3}q$
44. $-\frac{5}{8} = -\frac{3}{4}a$

Extra Practice

See Extra Practice for more Skills Practice and Applications Practice exercises.

45. Finance After taxes, Alexandra's take-home pay is $\frac{7}{10}$ of her salary before taxes. Write and solve an equation to find Alexandra's salary before taxes for the pay period that resulted in $392 of take-home pay.

46. Earth Science Your weight on the Moon is about $\frac{1}{6}$ of your weight on Earth. Write and solve an equation to show how much a person weighs on Earth if he weighs 16 pounds on the Moon. How could you check that your answer is reasonable?

47. ///ERROR ANALYSIS/// For the equation $\frac{x}{3} = 15$, a student found the value of x to be 5. Explain the error. What is the correct answer?

 Geometry The perimeter of a square is given. Write and solve an equation to find the length of each side of the square.

48. $P = 36$ in.
49. $P = 84$ in.
50. $P = 100$ yd
51. $P = 16.4$ cm

Statistics

American Robert P. Wadlow (1918–1940) holds the record for world's tallest man— 8 ft 11.1 in. He also holds world records for the largest feet and hands.

Source: Guinness World Records 2005

Write an equation to represent each relationship. Then solve the equation.

52. Five times a number is 45.

53. A number multiplied by negative 3 is 12.

54. A number divided by 4 is equal to 10.

55. The quotient of a number and 3 is negative 8.

56. Statistics The mean height of the students in Marta's class is 60 in. There are 18 students in her class. Write and solve an equation to find the total measure of all students' heights. (*Hint:* The mean is found by dividing the sum of all data values by the number of data values.)

57. Finance Lisa earned $6.25 per hour at her after-school job. Each week she earned $50. Write and solve an equation to show how many hours she worked each week.

58. Critical Thinking Will the solution of $\frac{x}{2.1} = 4$ be greater than 4 or less than 4? Explain.

59. Consumer Economics Dion's long-distance phone bill was $13.80. His long-distance calls cost $0.05 per minute. Write and solve an equation to find the number of minutes he was charged for. Show that your answer is reasonable.

60. Nutrition An 8 oz cup of coffee has about 184 mg of caffeine. This is 5 times as much caffeine as in a 12 oz soft drink. Write and solve an equation to find about how much caffeine is in a 12 oz caffeinated soft drink. Round your answer to the nearest whole number. Show that your answer is reasonable.

Use the equation $8y = 4x$ to find y for each value of x.

	x	$4x$	$8y = 4x$	y
61.	−4	$4(-4) = -16$	$8y = -16$	
62.	−2			
63.	0			
64.	2			

65. a. The formula for the mean of a data set is $\text{mean} = \frac{\text{sum of data values}}{\text{number of data values}}$. One summer, there were 1926 wildfires in Arizona. Which value does this number represent in the formula?

b. The mean number of acres burned by each wildfire was 96.21. Which value does this number represent in the formula?

c. Use the formula and information given to find how many acres were burned by wildfires in Arizona that summer. Round your answer to the nearest acre. Show that your answer is reasonable.

Solve each equation. Check your answer.

66. $\dfrac{m}{6} = 1$ **67.** $4x = 28$ **68.** $1.2h = 14.4$ **69.** $\dfrac{1}{5}x = 121$

70. $2w = 26$ **71.** $4b = \dfrac{3}{4}$ **72.** $5y = 11$ **73.** $\dfrac{n}{1.9} = 3$

Biology Use the table for Exercises 74 and 75.

Average Weight			
Animal	**At Birth (g)**	**Adult Female (g)**	**Adult Male (g)**
Hamster	2	130	110
Guinea pig	85	800	1050
Rat	5	275	480

74. The mean weight of an adult male rat is 16 times the mean weight of an adult male mouse. Write and solve an equation to find the mean weight of an adult male mouse. Show that your answer is reasonable.

75. On average, a hamster at birth weighs $\frac{2}{3}$ the weight of a gerbil at birth. Write and solve an equation to find the average weight of a gerbil at birth. Show that your answer is reasonable.

 76. Write About It Describe a real-world situation that can be modeled by $3x = 42$. Solve the equation and tell what the solution means in the context of your problem.

77. Which situation does NOT represent the equation $\frac{d}{2} = 10$?

  Ⓐ Leo bought a box of pencils. He gave half of them to his brother. They each got 10 pencils. How many pencils were in the box Leo bought?

  Ⓑ Kasey evenly divided her money from baby-sitting into two bank accounts. She put $10 in each account. How much did Kasey earn?

  Ⓒ Gilbert cut a piece of ribbon into 2-inch strips. When he was done, he had ten 2-inch strips. How long was the ribbon to start?

  Ⓓ Mattie had 2 more CDs than her sister Leona. If Leona had 10 CDs, how many CDs did Mattie have?

78. Which equation below shows a correct first step for solving $3x = -12$?

  Ⓕ $3x + 3 = -12 + 3$ Ⓗ $3(3x) = 3(-12)$

  Ⓖ $3x - 3 = -12 - 3$ Ⓙ $\dfrac{3x}{3} = \dfrac{-12}{3}$

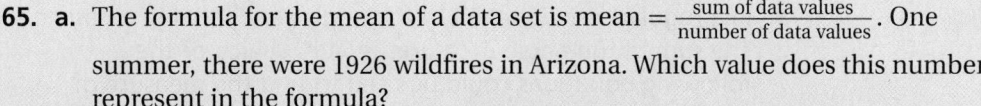
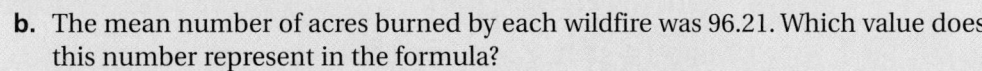

(tl), ©Index Stock/Alamy; (cr), PhotoDisc/gettyimages

79. In a regular pentagon, all of the angles are equal in measure. The sum of the angle measures is 540°. Which of the following equations could be used to find the measure of each angle?

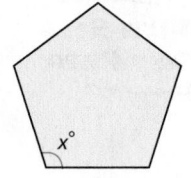

   (A) $\dfrac{x}{540} = 5$　　　(C) $540x = 5$

   (B) $5x = 540$　　　(D) $\dfrac{x}{5} = 540$

80. For which equation is $m = 10$ a solution?

   (F) $5 = 2m$　　(G) $5m = 2$　　(H) $\dfrac{m}{2} = 5$　　(J) $\dfrac{m}{10} = 2$

81. **Short Response** Luisa bought 6 cans of cat food that each cost the same amount. She spent a total of $4.80.

   a. Write an equation to determine the cost of one can of cat food. Tell what each part of your equation represents.

   b. Solve your equation to find the cost of one can of cat food. Show each step.

CHALLENGE AND EXTEND

Solve each equation. Check your answer.

82. $\left(3\dfrac{1}{5}\right)b = \dfrac{4}{5}$　　　83. $\left(1\dfrac{1}{3}\right)x = 2\dfrac{2}{3}$　　　84. $\left(5\dfrac{4}{5}\right)x = -52\dfrac{1}{5}$

85. $\left(-2\dfrac{9}{10}\right)k = -26\dfrac{1}{10}$　　　86. $\left(1\dfrac{2}{3}\right)w = 15\dfrac{1}{3}$　　　87. $\left(2\dfrac{1}{4}\right)d = 4\dfrac{1}{2}$

Find each indicated value.

88. If $2p = 4$, find the value of $6p + 10$.　　　89. If $6t = 24$, find the value of $-5t$.

90. If $3x = 15$, find the value of $12 - 4x$.　　　91. If $\dfrac{n}{2} = -11$, find the value of $6n$.

92. To isolate x in $ax = b$, what should you divide both sides by?

93. To isolate x in $\dfrac{x}{a} = b$, what operation should you perform on both sides of the equation?

94. **Travel** The formula $d = rt$ gives the distance d that is traveled at a rate r in time t.

   a. If $d = 400$ and $r = 25$, what is the value of t?

   b. If $d = 400$ and $r = 50$, what is the value of t?

   c. **What if...?** How did t change when r increased from 25 to 50?

   d. **What if...?** If r is doubled while d remains the same, what is the effect on t?

1-4 Technology LAB

Solve Equations by Graphing

You can use graphs to solve equations. As you complete this activity, you will learn some of the connections between graphs and equations.

Use with Solving Two-Step and Multi-Step Equations

Use appropriate tools strategically.

CC.9-12.A.REI.3 Solve linear equations and inequalities in one variable, including equations with coefficients represented by letters.

Learn It Online
Lab Resources Online

Activity

Solve $3x - 4 = 5$.

1 Press [Y=]. In Y_1, enter the left side of the equation, $3x - 4$.

In Y_2, enter the right side of the equation, 5.

2 Press [GRAPH]. Press [TRACE]. The display will show the x- and y-values of a point on the first line. Press the right arrow key several times. Notice that the x- and y-values change.

3 Continue to trace as close as possible to the intersection of the two lines. The x-value of this point 2.9787…, is an approximation of the solution. The solution is about 3.

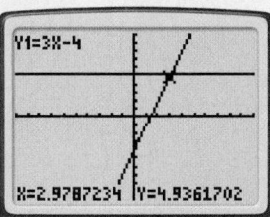

4 While still in trace mode, to check, press **3** [ENTER]. The display will show the y-value when $x = 3$. When $x = 3$, $y = 5$. So 3 is the solution. You can also check this solution by substituting 3 for x in the equation:

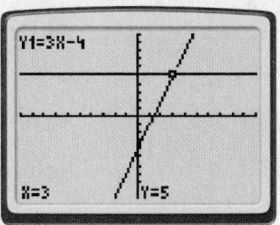

$$\textit{Check} \quad \begin{array}{r|l} 3x - 4 = 5 \\ \hline 3(3) - 4 & 5 \\ 9 - 4 & 5 \\ 5 & 5 \checkmark \end{array}$$

Try This

1. Solve $3x - 4 = 2$, $3x - 4 = 17$, and $3x - 4 = -7$ by graphing.

2. What does each line represent?

3. Describe a procedure for finding the solution of $3x - 4 = y$ for any value of y.

4. Solve $\frac{1}{2}x - 7 = -4$, $\frac{1}{2}x - 7 = 0$, and $\frac{1}{2}x - 7 = 2$ by graphing.

1-4 Solving Two-Step and Multi-Step Equations

CC.9-12.A.REI.1 Explain each step in solving a simple equation as following from the equality of numbers asserted at the previous step, starting from the assumption that the original equation has a solution.... *Also* **CC.9-12.A.REI.3, CC.9-12.A.CED.1***

Objective
Solve equations in one variable that contain more than one operation.

Why learn this?

Equations containing more than one operation can model real-world situations, such as the cost of a music club membership.

Alex belongs to a music club. In this club, students can buy a student discount card for $19.95. This card allows them to buy CDs for $3.95 each. After one year, Alex has spent $63.40.

To find the number of CDs c that Alex bought, you can solve an equation.

Cost of discount card
↓
Cost per CD → $3.95c + 19.95 = 63.40$ ← Total cost

Notice that this equation contains multiplication and addition. Equations that contain more than one operation require more than one step to solve. Identify the operations in the equation and the order in which they are applied to the variable. Then use inverse operations and work backward to undo them one at a time.

$$3.95c + 19.95 = 63.40$$

Operations in the Equation	To Solve
❶ First c is multiplied by 3.95.	❶ Subtract 19.95 from both sides of the equation.
❷ Then 19.95 is added.	❷ Then divide both sides by 3.95.

Work Backward

EXAMPLE **1** **Solving Two-Step Equations**

Solve $10 = 6 - 2x$. Check your answer.

$$
\begin{array}{ll}
10 = 6 - 2x & \textit{First x is multiplied by } -2. \textit{ Then 6 is added.}\\
\underline{-6 \quad -6} & \textit{Work backward: Subtract 6 from both sides.}\\
4 = \quad -2x & \textit{Since x is multiplied by } -2, \textit{ divide both sides}\\
\dfrac{4}{-2} = \dfrac{-2x}{-2} & \textit{by } -2 \textit{ to undo the multiplication.}\\
-2 = 1x\\
-2 = x
\end{array}
$$

Check

$10 = 6 - 2x$	
10	$6 - 2(-2)$
10	$6 - (-4)$
10	$10 \checkmark$

CHECK IT OUT!

Solve each equation. Check your answer.

1a. $-4 + 7x = 3$ **1b.** $1.5 = 1.2y - 5.7$ **1c.** $\dfrac{n}{7} + 2 = 2$

Solving Two-Step Equations That Contain Fractions

Solve $\dfrac{q}{15} - \dfrac{1}{5} = \dfrac{3}{5}$.

Method 1 Use fraction operations.

$$\dfrac{q}{15} - \dfrac{1}{5} = \dfrac{3}{5}$$

$$\underline{+ \dfrac{1}{5} \quad + \dfrac{1}{5}}$$

Since $\dfrac{1}{5}$ is subtracted from $\dfrac{q}{15}$, add $\dfrac{1}{5}$ to both sides to undo the subtraction.

$$\dfrac{q}{15} = \dfrac{4}{5}$$

Since q is divided by 15, multiply both sides by 15 to undo the division.

$$15\left(\dfrac{q}{15}\right) = 15\left(\dfrac{4}{5}\right)$$

$$q = \dfrac{15 \cdot 4}{5}$$ *Simplify.*

$$q = \dfrac{60}{5}$$

$$q = 12$$

Method 2 Multiply by the least common denominator (LCD) to clear the fractions.

$$\dfrac{q}{15} - \dfrac{1}{5} = \dfrac{3}{5}$$

$$15\left(\dfrac{q}{15} - \dfrac{1}{5}\right) = 15\left(\dfrac{3}{5}\right)$$ *Multiply both sides by 15, the LCD of the fractions.*

$$15\left(\dfrac{q}{15}\right) - 15\left(\dfrac{1}{5}\right) = 15\left(\dfrac{3}{5}\right)$$ *Distribute 15 on the left side.*

$$q - 3 = 9$$ *Simplify.*

$$\underline{+3 \quad +3}$$ *Since 3 is subtracted from q, add 3 to*

$$q = 12$$ *both sides to undo the subtraction.*

 **Solve each equation. Check your answer.**

2a. $\dfrac{2x}{5} - \dfrac{1}{2} = 5$ **2b.** $\dfrac{3}{4}u + \dfrac{1}{2} = \dfrac{7}{8}$ **2c.** $\dfrac{1}{5}n - \dfrac{1}{3} = \dfrac{8}{3}$

Equations that are more complicated may have to be simplified before they can be solved. You may have to use the Distributive Property or combine like terms before you begin using inverse operations.

Simplifying Before Solving Equations

Solve each equation.

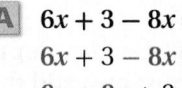 $6x + 3 - 8x = 13$

$$6x + 3 - 8x = 13$$

$$6x - 8x + 3 = 13$$ *Use the Commutative Property of Addition.*

$$-2x + 3 = 13$$ *Combine like terms.*

$$\underline{-3 \quad -3}$$ *Since 3 is added to −2x, subtract 3 from both sides to undo the addition.*

$$-2x = 10$$

$$\dfrac{-2x}{-2} = \dfrac{10}{-2}$$ *Since x is multiplied by −2, divide both sides by −2 to undo the multiplication.*

$$x = -5$$

Solve each equation.

B $9 = 6 - (x + 2)$

$9 = 6 + (-1)(x + 2)$ *Write subtraction as addition of the opposite.*

$9 = 6 + (-1)(x) + (-1)(2)$ *Distribute −1 on the right side.*

Simplify.

$9 = 6 - x - 2$

Use the Commutative Property of Addition.

$9 = 6 - 2 - x$ *Combine like terms.*

$9 = \quad 4 - x$

$\underline{-4 \quad -4}$ *Since 4 is added to −x, subtract 4 from both sides to undo the addition.*

$5 = \qquad -x$

$\dfrac{5}{-1} = \dfrac{-x}{-1}$ *Since x is multiplied by −1, divide both sides by −1 to undo the multiplication.*

$-5 = x$

 Solve each equation. Check your answer.

3a. $2a + 3 - 8a = 8$

3b. $-2(3 - d) = 4$

3c. $4(x - 2) + 2x = 40$

 **4** **Problem-Solving Application**

Alex belongs to a music club. In this club, students can buy a student discount card for $19.95. This card allows them to buy CDs for $3.95 each. After one year, Alex has spent $63.40. Write and solve an equation to find how many CDs Alex bought during the year.

Make sense of problems and persevere in solving them.

 Understand the Problem

The **answer** will be the number of CDs that Alex bought during the year.

List the important information:

• Alex paid $19.95 for a student discount card.

• Alex pays $3.95 for each CD purchased.

• After one year, Alex has spent $63.40.

 Make a Plan

Let c represent the number of CDs that Alex purchased. That means Alex has spent $3.95c$. However, Alex must also add the amount spent on the card. Write an equation to represent this situation.

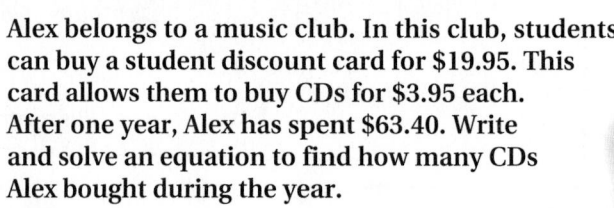

total cost	=	cost of compact discs	+	cost of discount card
63.40	=	3.95c	+	19.95

Solve

$$63.40 = 3.95c + 19.95$$
$$\underline{-19.95 \qquad\quad -19.95}$$
$$43.45 = 3.95c$$
$$\frac{43.45}{3.95} = \frac{3.95c}{3.95}$$
$$11 = c$$

Since 19.95 is added to 3.95c, subtract 19.95 from both sides to undo the addition.

Since c is multiplied by 3.95, divide both sides by 3.95 to undo the multiplication.

Alex bought 11 CDs during the year.

 **Look Back**

Check that the answer is reasonable. The cost per CD is about $4, so if Alex bought 11 CDs, this amount is about $11(4) = \$44$.

Add the cost of the discount card, which is about $20: $44 + 20 = 64$. So the total cost was about $64, which is close to the amount given in the problem, $63.40.

CHECK IT OUT!

4. Sara paid $15.95 to become a member at a gym. She then paid a monthly membership fee. Her total cost for 12 months was $735.95. How much was the monthly fee?

EXAMPLE **5** **Solving Equations to Find an Indicated Value**

If $3a + 12 = 30$, find the value of $a + 4$.

Step 1 Find the value of a.

$$3a + 12 = 30$$
$$\underline{\quad -12 \quad -12}$$
$$3a \quad\;\; = 18$$
$$\frac{3a}{3} = \frac{18}{3}$$
$$a = 6$$

Since 12 is added to 3a, subtract 12 from both sides to undo the addition.

Since a is multiplied by 3, divide both sides by 3 to undo the multiplication.

Step 2 Find the value of $a + 4$.

$$a + 4$$
$$6 + 4$$
$$10$$

To find the value of a + 4, substitute 6 for a.

Simplify.

CHECK IT OUT!

5. If $2x + 4 = -24$, find the value of $3x$.

THINK AND DISCUSS

1. Explain the steps you would follow to solve $2x + 1 = 7$. How is this procedure different from the one you would follow to solve $2x - 1 = 7$?

2. GET ORGANIZED Copy and complete the graphic organizer. In each box, write and solve a multi-step equation. Use addition, subtraction, multiplication, and division at least one time each.

Solving Multi-Step Equations	

GUIDED PRACTICE

Solve each equation. Check your answer.

SEE EXAMPLE **1**

1. $4a + 3 = 11$

2. $8 = 3r - 1$

3. $42 = -2d + 6$

4. $x + 0.3 = 3.3$

5. $15y + 31 = 61$

6. $9 - c = -13$

SEE EXAMPLE **2**

7. $\dfrac{x}{6} + 4 = 15$

8. $\dfrac{1}{3}y + \dfrac{1}{4} = \dfrac{5}{12}$

9. $\dfrac{2}{7}j - \dfrac{1}{7} = \dfrac{3}{14}$

10. $15 = \dfrac{a}{3} - 2$

11. $4 - \dfrac{m}{2} = 10$

12. $\dfrac{x}{8} - \dfrac{1}{2} = 6$

SEE EXAMPLE **3**

13. $28 = 8x + 12 - 7x$

14. $2y - 7 + 5y = 0$

15. $2.4 = 3(m + 4)$

16. $3(x - 4) = 48$

17. $4t + 7 - t = 19$

18. $5(1 - 2w) + 8w = 15$

SEE EXAMPLE **4**

19. **Transportation** Paul bought a student discount card for the bus. The card cost $7 and allows him to buy daily bus passes for $1.50. After one month, Paul spent $29.50. How many daily bus passes did Paul buy?

SEE EXAMPLE **5**

20. If $3x - 13 = 8$, find the value of $x - 4$.

21. If $3(x + 1) = 7$, find the value of $3x$.

22. If $-3(y - 1) = 9$, find the value of $\dfrac{1}{2}y$.

23. If $4 - 7x = 39$, find the value of $x + 1$.

PRACTICE AND PROBLEM SOLVING

Independent Practice

For Exercises	See Example
24–29	1
30–35	2
36–41	3
42	4
43–46	5

Extra Practice

See Extra Practice for more Skills Practice and Applications Practice exercises.

Solve each equation. Check your answer.

24. $5 = 2g + 1$

25. $6h - 7 = 17$

26. $0.6v + 2.1 = 4.5$

27. $3x + 3 = 18$

28. $0.6g + 11 = 5$

29. $32 = 5 - 3t$

30. $2d + \dfrac{1}{5} = \dfrac{3}{5}$

31. $1 = 2x + \dfrac{1}{2}$

32. $\dfrac{z}{2} + 1 = \dfrac{3}{2}$

33. $\dfrac{2}{3} = \dfrac{4j}{6}$

34. $\dfrac{3}{4} = \dfrac{3}{8}x - \dfrac{3}{2}$

35. $\dfrac{1}{5} - \dfrac{x}{5} = -\dfrac{2}{5}$

36. $6 = -2(7 - c)$

37. $5(h - 4) = 8$

38. $-3x - 8 + 4x = 17$

39. $4x + 6x = 30$

40. $2(x + 3) = 10$

41. $17 = 3(p - 5) + 8$

42. **Consumer Economics** Jennifer is saving money to buy a bike. The bike costs $245. She has $125 saved, and each week she adds $15 to her savings. How long will it take her to save enough money to buy the bike?

43. If $2x + 13 = 17$, find the value of $3x + 1$.

44. If $-(x - 1) = 5$, find the value of $-4x$.

45. If $5(y + 10) = 40$, find the value of $\dfrac{1}{4}y$.

46. If $9 - 6x = 45$, find the value of $x - 4$.

Geometry Write and solve an equation to find the value of x for each triangle. (*Hint:* The sum of the angle measures in any triangle is 180°.)

47.

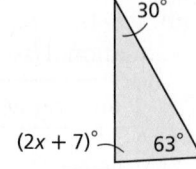

30°

$(2x + 7)°$ 63°

48.

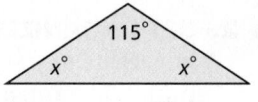

115°

$x°$ $x°$

49.

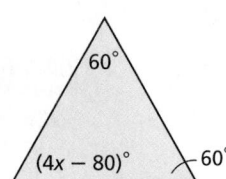

60°

$(4x - 80)°$ 60°

Write an equation to represent each relationship. Solve each equation.

50. Seven less than twice a number equals 19.

51. Eight decreased by 3 times a number equals 2.

52. The sum of two times a number and 5 is 11.

53. **History** In 1963, Dr. Martin Luther King Jr. began his famous "I have a dream" speech with the words "Five score years ago, a great American, in whose symbolic shadow we stand, signed the Emancipation Proclamation." The proclamation was signed by President Abraham Lincoln in 1863.

  a. Using the dates given, write and solve an equation that can be used to find the number of years in a score.

  b. How many score would represent 60?

History

Martin Luther King Jr. entered college at age 15. During his life he earned 3 degrees and was awarded 20 honorary degrees.

Source: lib.lsu.edu

Solve each equation. Check your answer.

54. $3t + 44 = 50$

55. $3(x - 2) = 18$

56. $15 = \dfrac{c}{3} - 2$

57. $2x + 6.5 = 15.5$

58. $3.9w - 17.9 = -2.3$

59. $17 = x - 3(x + 1)$

60. $5x + 9 = 39$

61. $15 + 5.5m = 70$

Biology Use the graph for Exercises 62 and 63.

62. The height of an ostrich is 20 inches more than 4 times the height of a kiwi. Write and solve an equation to find the height of a kiwi. Show that your answer is reasonable.

63. Five times the height of a kakapo minus 70 equals the height of an emu. Write and solve an equation to find the height of a kakapo. Show that your answer is reasonable.

64. The sum of two consecutive whole numbers is 57. What are the two numbers? (*Hint:* Let n represent the first number. Then $n + 1$ is the next consecutive whole number.)

65. Stan's, Mark's, and Wayne's ages are consecutive whole numbers. Stan is the youngest, and Wayne is the oldest. The sum of their ages is 111. Find their ages.

66. The sum of two consecutive even whole numbers is 206. What are the two numbers? (*Hint:* Let n represent the first number. What expression can you use to represent the second number?)

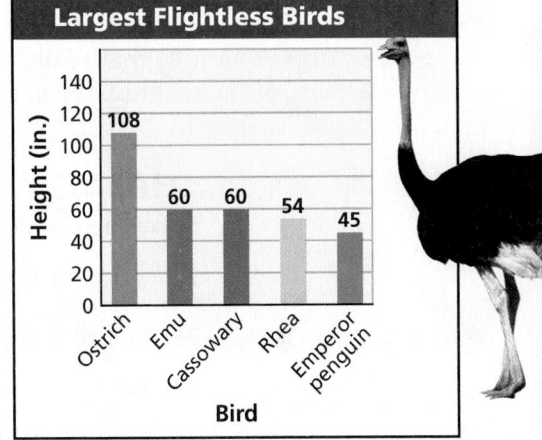

Largest Flightless Birds

Height (in.) vs. Bird: Ostrich 108, Emu 60, Cassowary 60, Rhea 54, Emperor penguin 45

Source: The Top Ten of Everything

MULTI-STEP TEST PREP

67. a. The cost of fighting a certain forest fire is $225 per acre. Complete the table.

  b. Write an equation for the relationship between the cost c of fighting the fire and the number of acres n.

Cost of Fighting Fire	
Acres	**Cost ($)**
100	22,500
200	
500	
1000	
1500	
n	

(tl), © Robert W. Kelley/Time Life Pictures/Getty Images; (bl), ©Index Stock/Alamy; (cr),Photodisc/Getty Images

68. Critical Thinking The equation $2(m - 8) + 3 = 17$ has more than one solution method. Give at least two different "first steps" to solve this equation.

 69. Write About It Write a series of steps that you can use to solve any multi-step equation.

70. Lin sold 4 more shirts than Greg. Fran sold 3 times as many shirts as Lin. In total, the three sold 51 shirts. Which represents the number of shirts Greg sold?

    Ⓐ $3g = 51$ Ⓑ $3 + g = 51$ Ⓒ $8 + 5g = 51$ Ⓓ $16 + 5g = 51$

71. If $\frac{4m - 3}{7} = 3$, what is the value of $7m - 5$?

    Ⓕ 6   Ⓖ 10.5   Ⓗ 37   Ⓙ 68.5

72. The equation $c = 48 + 0.06m$ represents the cost c of renting a car and driving m miles. Which statement best describes this cost?

    Ⓐ The cost is a flat rate of $0.06 per mile.

    Ⓑ The cost is $0.48 for the first mile and $0.06 for each additional mile.

    Ⓒ The cost is a $48 fee plus $0.06 per mile.

    Ⓓ The cost is a $6 fee plus $0.48 per mile.

73. Gridded Response A telemarketer earns $150 a week plus $2 for each call that results in a sale. Last week she earned a total of $204. How many of her calls resulted in sales?

CHALLENGE AND EXTEND

Solve each equation. Check your answer.

74. $\frac{9}{2}x + 18 + 3x = \frac{11}{2}$ **75.** $\frac{15}{4}x - 15 = \frac{33}{4}$

76. $(x + 6) - (2x + 7) - 3x = -9$ **77.** $(4x + 2) - (12x + 8) + 2(5x - 3) = 6 + 11$

78. Find a value for b so that the solution of $4x + 3b = -1$ is $x = 2$.

79. Find a value for b so that the solution of $2x - 3b = 0$ is $x = -9$.

80. Business The formula $p = nc - e$ gives the profit p when a number of items n are each sold at a cost c and expenses e are subtracted.

    a. If $p = 2500$, $n = 2000$, and $e = 800$, what is the value of c?

    b. If $p = 2500$, $n = 1000$, and $e = 800$, what is the value of c?

    c. What if...? If n is divided in half while p and e remain the same, what is the effect on c?

Algebra LAB

Model Equations with Variables on Both Sides

Algebra tile models can help you understand how to solve equations with variables on both sides.

Use with Solving Equations with Variables on Both Sides

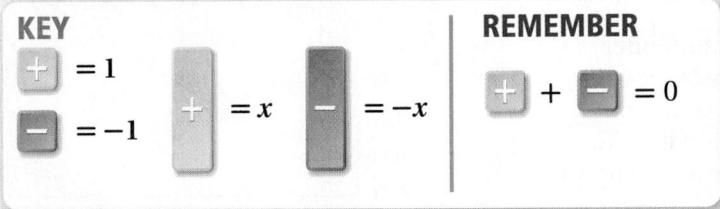

KEY

$\boxed{+}$ = 1

$\boxed{-}$ = −1

$\boxed{+}$ = x $\boxed{-}$ = −x

REMEMBER

$\boxed{+}$ + $\boxed{-}$ = 0

Learn It Online
Lab Resources Online

Use appropriate tools strategically.

CC.9-12.A.REI.1 Explain each step in solving a simple equation as following from the equality of numbers asserted at the previous step, starting from the assumption that the original equation has a solution. Construct a viable argument to justify a solution method. *Also* **CC.9-12.A.REI.3**

Activity

Use algebra tiles to model and solve $5x - 2 = 2x + 10$.

MODEL		ALGEBRA
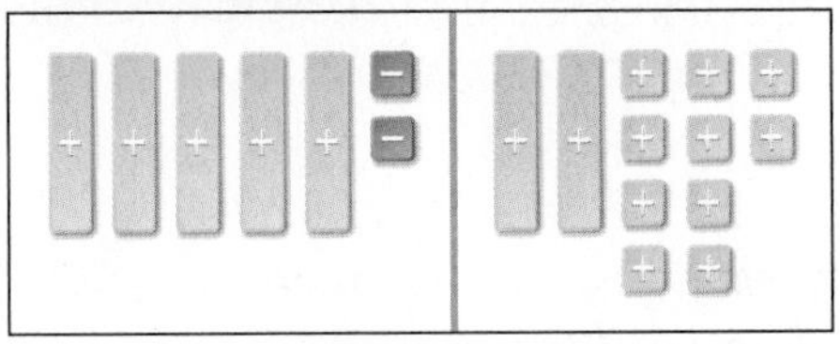	Model $5x - 2$ on the left side of the mat and $2x + 10$ on the right side. Remember that $5x - 2$ is the same as $5x + (-2)$.	$5x - 2 = 2x + 10$
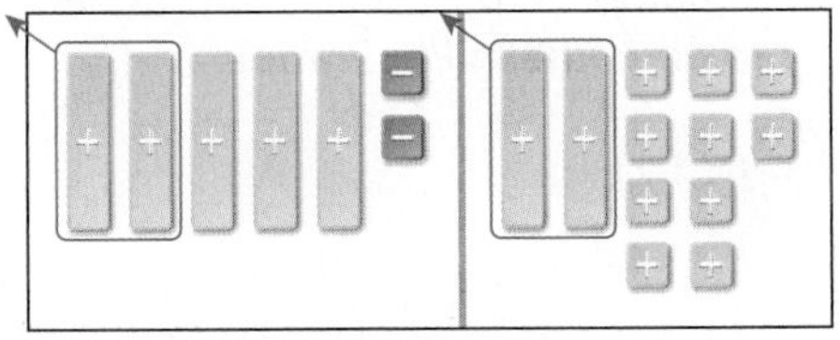	Remove 2 x-tiles from both sides. This represents subtracting $2x$ from both sides of the equation.	$5x - 2 - 2x = 2x - 2x + 10$ $3x - 2 = 10$
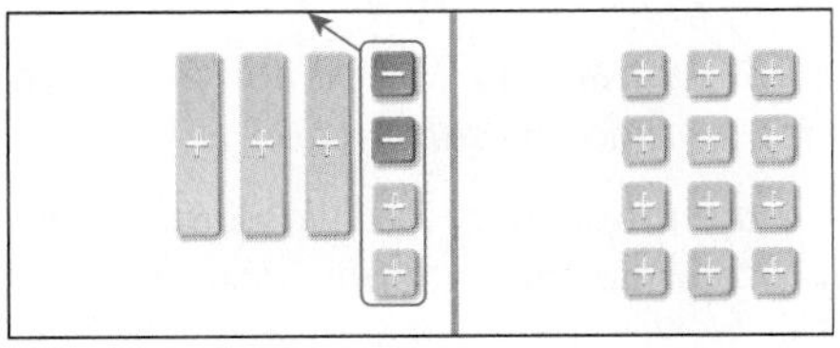	Place 2 yellow tiles on both sides. This represents adding 2 to both sides of the equation. Remove zero pairs.	$3x - 2 + 2 = 10 + 2$ $3x = 12$
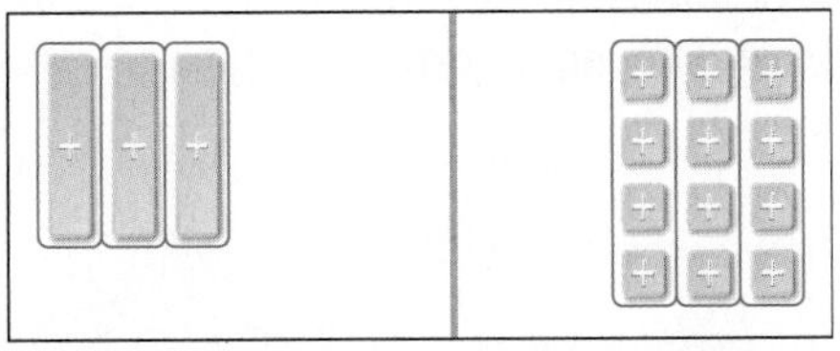	Separate each side into 3 equal groups. Each group is $\frac{1}{3}$ of the side. One x-tile is equivalent to 4 yellow tiles.	$\frac{1}{3}(3x) = \frac{1}{3}(12)$ $x = 4$

Try This

Use algebra tiles to model and solve each equation.

1. $3x + 2 = 2x + 5$ **2.** $5x + 12 = 2x + 3$ **3.** $9x - 5 = 6x + 13$ **4.** $x = -2x + 9$

COMMON CORE

1-5 Solving Equations with Variables on Both Sides

CC.9-12.A.REI.1 Explain each step in solving a simple equation as following from the equality of numbers asserted at the previous step, starting from the assumption that the original equation has a solution.... *Also* **CC.9-12.A.REI.3, CC.9-12.A.CED.1***

Objective
Solve equations in one variable that contain variable terms on both sides.

Vocabulary
identity

Why learn this?
You can compare prices and find the best value.

Many phone companies offer low rates for long-distance calls without requiring customers to sign up for their services. To compare rates, solve an equation with variables on both sides.

To solve an equation like this, use inverse operations to "collect" variable terms on one side of the equation.

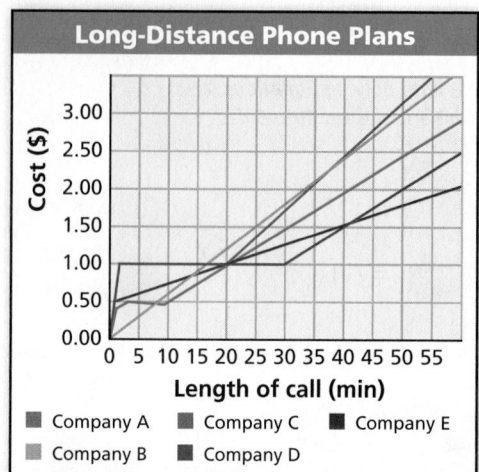

Long-Distance Phone Plans

Cost ($) vs. Length of call (min)

■ Company A ■ Company C ■ Company E
■ Company B ■ Company D

EXAMPLE 1 **Solving Equations with Variables on Both Sides**

Solve each equation.

A $7k = 4k + 15$

$$7k = 4k + 15$$
$$\underline{-4k \quad -4k}$$
$$3k = \qquad 15$$
$$\frac{3k}{3} = \frac{15}{3}$$
$$k = 5$$

To collect the variable terms on one side, subtract 4k from both sides.

Since k is multiplied by 3, divide both sides by 3 to undo the multiplication.

B $5x - 2 = 3x + 4$

$$5x - 2 = 3x + 4$$
$$\underline{-3x \qquad -3x}$$
$$2x - 2 = \qquad 4$$
$$\underline{+2 \qquad +2}$$
$$2x \quad = \qquad 6$$
$$\frac{2x}{2} = \frac{6}{2}$$
$$x = 3$$

To collect the variable terms on one side, subtract 3x from both sides.

Since 2 is subtracted from 2x, add 2 to both sides to undo the subtraction.

Since x is multiplied by 2, divide both sides by 2 to undo the multiplication.

Check $\quad 5x - 2 = 3x + 4$

$5(3) - 2$	$3(3) + 4$
$15 - 2$	$9 + 4$
13	13 ✓

To check your solution, substitute 3 for x in the original equation.

> **Helpful Hint**
>
> Equations are often easier to solve when the variable has a positive coefficient. Keep this in mind when deciding on which side to "collect" variable terms.

 **Solve each equation. Check your answer.**

1a. $4b + 2 = 3b$

1b. $0.5 + 0.3y = 0.7y - 0.3$

To solve more complicated equations, you may need to first simplify by using the Distributive Property or combining like terms.

EXAMPLE 2 **Simplifying Each Side Before Solving Equations**

Solve each equation.

A $2(y + 6) = 3y$

$$2(y + 6) = 3y$$
$$2(y) + 2(6) = 3y$$
$$2y + 12 = 3y$$
$$\underline{-2y \qquad -2y}$$
$$12 = y$$

Distribute 2 to the expression in parentheses.

To collect the variable terms on one side, subtract 2y from both sides.

Check $2(y + 6) = 3y$

$$\begin{array}{c|c} 2(12 + 6) & 3(12) \\ 2(18) & 36 \\ 36 & 36 \checkmark \end{array}$$

To check your solution, substitute 12 for y in the original equation.

B $2k - 5 = 3(1 - 2k)$

$$2k - 5 = 3(1 - 2k)$$
$$2k - 5 = 3(1) - 3(2k)$$
$$2k - 5 = 3 - 6k$$
$$\underline{+6k \qquad\qquad +6k}$$
$$8k - 5 = 3$$
$$\underline{\quad +5 \qquad +5}$$
$$8k = 8$$
$$\frac{8k}{8} = \frac{8}{8}$$
$$k = 1$$

Distribute 3 to the expression in parentheses.

To collect the variable terms on one side, add 6k to both sides.

Since 5 is subtracted from 8k, add 5 to both sides.

Since k is multiplied by 8, divide both sides by 8.

C $3 - 5b + 2b = -2 - 2(1 - b)$

$$3 - 5b + 2b = -2 - 2(1 - b)$$
$$3 - 5b + 2b = -2 - 2(1) - 2(-b)$$
$$3 - 5b + 2b = -2 - 2 + 2b$$
$$3 - 3b = -4 + 2b$$
$$\underline{\quad +3b \qquad\quad +3b}$$
$$3 = -4 + 5b$$
$$\underline{+4 \qquad +4}$$
$$7 = 5b$$
$$\frac{7}{5} = \frac{5b}{5}$$
$$1.4 = b$$

Distribute −2 to the expression in parentheses.

Combine like terms.

Add 3b to both sides.

Since −4 is added to 5b, add 4 to both sides.

Since b is multiplied by 5, divide both sides by 5.

Solve each equation. Check your answer.

2a. $\frac{1}{2}(b + 6) = \frac{3}{2}b - 1$ **2b.** $3x + 15 - 9 = 2(x + 2)$

An **identity** is an equation that is always true, no matter what value is substituted for the variable. The solutions of an identity are all real numbers. Some equations are always false. These equations have no solutions.

EXAMPLE 3 **Infinitely Many Solutions or No Solutions**

Solve each equation.

A $x + 4 - 6x = 6 - 5x - 2$

$x + 4 - 6x = 6 - 5x - 2$	*Identify like terms.*
$4 - 5x = 4 - 5x$	*Combine like terms on the left and the right.*
$\underline{+5x \qquad +5x}$	*Add 5x to both sides.*
$4 \quad = 4 \checkmark$	*True statement*

The equation $x + 4 - 6x = 6 - 5x - 2$ is an identity. All values of x will make the equation true. All real numbers are solutions.

Writing Math

The solution set for Example 3B is an empty set—it contains no elements. The empty set can be written as $\varnothing$ or {}.

B $-8x + 6 + 9x = -17 + x$

$-8x + 6 + 9x = -17 + x$	*Identify like terms.*
$x + 6 = -17 + x$	*Combine like terms.*
$\underline{-x \qquad\qquad -x}$	*Subtract x from both sides.*
$6 = -17 \: ✗$	*False statement*

The equation $-8x + 6 + 9x = -17 + x$ is always false. There is no value of x that will make the equation true. There are no solutions.

 Solve each equation.

3a. $4y + 7 - y = 10 + 3y$ **3b.** $2c + 7 + c = -14 + 3c + 21$

EXAMPLE 4 *Consumer Application*

The long-distance rates of two phone companies are shown in the table. How long is a call that costs the same amount no matter which company is used? What is the cost of that call?

Phone Company	Charges
Company A	36¢ plus 3¢ per minute
Company B	6¢ per minute

Let m represent minutes, and write expressions for each company's cost.

When is	36¢	plus	3¢ per minute	times number of minutes	the same as	6¢ per minute	times number of minutes	?
	36	+	3	(m)	=	6	(m)	

$36 + 3m = 6m$	
$\underline{-3m \quad -3m}$	*To collect the variable terms on one side,*
$36 \quad = 3m$	*subtract 3m from both sides.*
$\dfrac{36}{3} = \dfrac{3m}{3}$	*Since m is multiplied by 3, divide both sides by 3 to undo the multiplication.*
$12 = m$	

The charges will be the same for a 12-minute call using either phone service. To find the cost of this call, evaluate either expression for $m = 12$:

$$36 + 3m = 36 + 3(12) = 36 + 36 = 72 \qquad 6m = 6(12) = 72$$

The cost of a 12-minute call through either company is 72¢.

 **4.** Four times Greg's age, decreased by 3 is equal to 3 times Greg's age, increased by 7. How old is Greg?

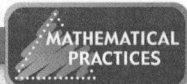

THINK AND DISCUSS

1. Tell which of the following is an identity. Explain your answer.

    a. $4(a+3) - 6 = 3(a+3) - 6$ **b.** $8.3x - 9 + 0.7x = 2 + 9x - 11$

2. GET ORGANIZED Copy and complete the graphic organizer. In each box, write an example of an equation that has the indicated number of solutions.

An equation with variables on both sides can have…

one solution:	many solutions:	no solution:

1-5 Exercises

Learn It Online
Homework Help Online
Parent Resources Online

GUIDED PRACTICE

1. Vocabulary How can you recognize an identity?

Solve each equation. Check your answer.

SEE EXAMPLE **1**

  2. $2c - 5 = c + 4$ **3.** $8r + 4 = 10 + 2r$

  4. $2x - 1 = x + 11$ **5.** $28 - 0.3y = 0.7y - 12$

SEE EXAMPLE **2**

  6. $-2(x + 3) = 4x - 3$ **7.** $3c - 4c + 1 = 5c + 2 + 3$

  8. $5 + 3(q - 4) = 2(q + 1)$ **9.** $5 - (t + 3) = -1 + 2(t - 3)$

SEE EXAMPLE **3**

 10. $7x - 4 = -2x + 1 + 9x - 5$ **11.** $8x + 6 - 9x = 2 - x - 15$

 12. $6y = 8 - 9 + 6y$ **13.** $6 - 2x - 1 = 4x + 8 - 6x - 3$

SEE EXAMPLE **4**

 14. Consumer Economics A house-painting company charges $376 plus $12 per hour. Another painting company charges $280 plus $15 per hour.

    a. How long is a job for which both companies will charge the same amount?

    b. What will that cost be?

PRACTICE AND PROBLEM SOLVING

Solve each equation. Check your answer.

15. $7a - 17 = 4a + 1$ **16.** $2b - 5 = 8b + 1$ **17.** $4x - 2 = 3x + 4$

18. $2x - 5 = 4x - 1$ **19.** $8x - 2 = 3x + 12.25$ **20.** $5x + 2 = 3x$

21. $3c - 5 = 2c + 5$ **22.** $-17 - 2x = 6 - x$ **23.** $3(t - 1) = 9 + t$

24. $5 - x - 2 = 3 + 4x + 5$ **25.** $2(x + 4) = 3(x - 2)$ **26.** $3m - 10 = 2(4m - 5)$

27. $5 - (n - 4) = 3(n + 2)$ **28.** $6(x + 7) - 20 = 6x$ **29.** $8(x + 1) = 4x - 8$

30. $x - 4 - 3x = -2x - 3 - 1$ **31.** $-2(x + 2) = -2x + 1$ **32.** $2(x + 4) - 5 = 2x + 3$

Independent Practice	
For Exercises	See Example
15–22	1
23–29	2
30–32	3
33	4

Extra Practice

See Extra Practice for more Skills Practice and Applications Practice exercises.

33. Sports Justin and Tyson are beginning an exercise program to train for football season. Justin weighs 150 lb and hopes to gain 2 lb per week. Tyson weighs 195 lb and hopes to lose 1 lb per week.

   a. If the plan works, in how many weeks will the boys weigh the same amount?

   b. What will that weight be?

Write an equation to represent each relationship. Then solve the equation.

34. Three times the sum of a number and 4 is the same as 18 more than the number.

35. A number decreased by 30 is the same as 14 minus 3 times the number.

36. Two less than 2 times a number is the same as the number plus 64.

Solve each equation. Check your answer.

37. $2x - 2 = 4x + 6$

38. $3x + 5 = 2x + 2$

39. $4x + 3 = 5x - 4$

40. $-\frac{2}{5}p + 2 = \frac{1}{5}p + 11$

41. $5x + 24 = 2x + 15$

42. $5x - 10 = 14 - 3x$

43. $12 - 6x = 10 - 5x$

44. $5x - 7 = -6x - 29$

45. $1.8x + 2.8 = 2.5x + 2.1$

46. $2.6x + 18 = 2.4x + 22$

47. $1 - 3x = 2x + 8$

48. $\frac{1}{2}(8 - 6h) = h$

49. $3(x + 1) = 2x + 7$

50. $9x - 8 + 4x = 7x + 16$

51. $3(2x - 1) + 5 = 6(x + 1)$

52. Travel Rapid Rental Car company charges a $40 rental fee, $15 for gas, and $0.25 per mile driven. For the same car, Capital Cars charges $45 for rental and gas and $0.35 per mile.

   a. Find the number of miles for which the companies' charges will be the same. Then find that charge. Show that your answers are reasonable.

   b. The Barre family estimates that they will drive about 95 miles during their vacation to Hershey, Pennsylvania. Which company should they rent their car from? Explain.

   c. What if...? The Barres have extended their vacation and now estimate that they will drive about 120 miles. Should they still rent from the same company as in part **b**? Why or why not?

   d. Give a general rule for deciding which company to rent from.

53. Geometry The triangles shown have the same perimeter. What is the value of *x*?

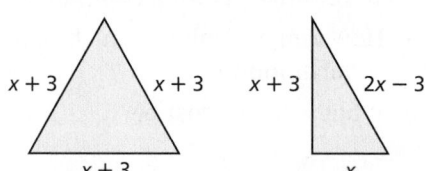

MULTI-STEP TEST PREP

54. a. A fire currently covers 420 acres and continues to spread at a rate of 60 acres per day. How many total acres will be covered in the next 2 days? Show that your answer is reasonable.

   b. Write an expression for the total area covered by the fire in *d* days.

   c. The firefighters estimate that they can put out the fire at a rate of 80 acres per day. Write an expression for the total area that the firefighters can put out in *d* days.

   d. Set the expressions in parts **b** and **c** equal. Solve for *d*. What does *d* represent?

© Index Stock /Alamy

55. **Critical Thinking** Write an equation with variables on both sides that has no solution.

56. **Biology** The graph shows the maximum recorded speeds of the four fastest mammals.

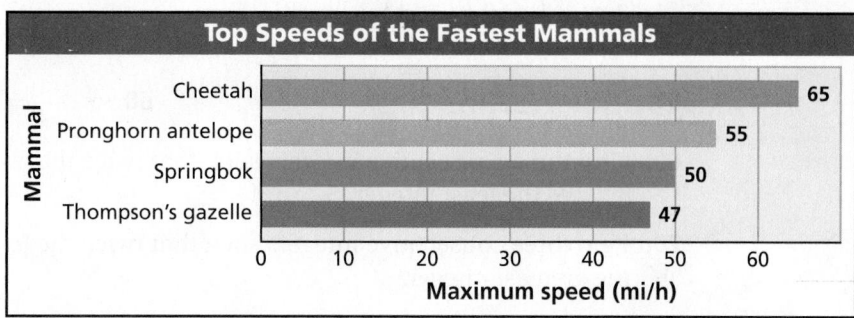

Source: The Top 10 of Everything

a. Write an expression for the distance in miles that a Thompson's gazelle can run at top speed in *x* hours.

b. Write an expression for the distance in miles that a cheetah can run at top speed in *x* hours.

c. A cheetah and a Thompson's gazelle are running at their top speeds. The cheetah is one mile behind the gazelle. Write an expression for the distance the cheetah must run to catch up with the gazelle.

d. Write and solve an equation that represents how long the cheetah will have to run at top speed to catch up with the gazelle.

e. A cheetah can maintain its top speed for only 300 yards. Will the cheetah be able to catch the gazelle? Explain.

57. **Write About It** Write a series of steps that you can use to solve any equation with variables on both sides.

 **TEST PREP**

58. Lindsey's monthly magazine subscription costs $1.25 per issue. Kenzie's monthly subscription costs $1.50 per issue, but she received her first 2 issues free. Which equation can be used to find the number of months after which the girls will have paid the same amount?

Ⓐ $1.25m = 1.50m - 2$ Ⓒ $1.25m = 1.50(m - 2)$

Ⓑ $1.25m = 1.50m - 2m$ Ⓓ $1.25m = 3m - 1.50$

59. What is the numerical solution of the equation *7 times a number equals 3 less than 5 times that number*?

Ⓕ -1.5 Ⓖ 0.25 Ⓗ $\frac{2}{3}$ Ⓙ 4

60. Three packs of markers cost $9.00 less than 5 packs of markers. Which equation best represents this situation?

Ⓐ $5x + 9 = 3x$ Ⓑ $3x + 9 = 5x$ Ⓒ $3x - 9 = 5x$ Ⓓ $9 - 3x = 5x$

61. Nicole has $120. If she saves $20 per week, in how many days will she have $500?

Ⓕ 19 Ⓖ 25 Ⓗ 133 Ⓙ 175

62. **Gridded Response** Solve $-2(x - 1) + 5x = 2(2x - 1)$.

CHALLENGE AND EXTEND

Solve each equation.

63. $4x + 2\big[4 - 2(x + 2)\big] = 2x - 4$

64. $\dfrac{x + 5}{2} + \dfrac{x - 1}{2} = \dfrac{x - 1}{3}$

65. $\dfrac{2}{3}w - \dfrac{1}{4} = \dfrac{2}{3}\left(w - \dfrac{1}{4}\right)$

66. $-5 - 7 - 3f = -f - 2(f + 6)$

67. $\dfrac{2}{3}x + \dfrac{1}{2} = \dfrac{3}{5}x - \dfrac{5}{6}$

68. $x - \dfrac{1}{4} = \dfrac{x}{3} + 7\dfrac{3}{4}$

69. Find three consecutive integers such that twice the greatest integer is 2 less than 3 times the least integer.

70. Find three consecutive integers such that twice the least integer is 12 more than the greatest integer.

71. Rob had twice as much money as Sam. Then Sam gave Rob 1 quarter, 2 nickels, and 3 pennies. Rob then gave Sam 8 dimes. If they now have the same amount of money, how much money did Rob originally have? Check your answer.

Career Path

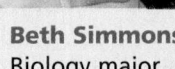

Beth Simmons
Biology major

Q: What math classes did you take in high school?

A: Algebra 1 and 2, Geometry, and Precalculus

Q: What math classes have you taken in college?

A: Two calculus classes and a calculus-based physics class

Q: How do you use math?

A: I use math a lot in physics. Sometimes I would think a calculus topic was totally useless, and then we would use it in physics class! In biology, I use math to understand populations.

Q: What career options are you considering?

A: When I graduate, I could teach, or I could go to graduate school and do more research. I have a lot of options.

1-5 Technology LAB

Solve Equations Graphically

You can use graphs to solve equations. As you complete this activity, you will explore connections between graphs and equations.

Use with Lesson Solving Equations with Variables on Both Sides

Activity 1

MATHEMATICAL PRACTICES
Use appropriate tools strategically.

Use a graphing calculator to solve $x + 1 = 3x - 5$.

CC.9-12.A.REI.11 Explain why the *x*-coordinates of the points where the graphs of the equations $y = f(x)$ and $y = g(x)$ intersect are the solutions of the equation $f(x) = g(x)$; find the solutions approximately, e.g., using technology to graph the functions, make tables of values, ….*

1 Write the equation $x + 1 = 3x - 5$ as two separate equations:

$$y = x + 1$$
$$y = 3x - 5$$

2 Press **Y=** . Enter the first equation, $y = x + 1$, in Y_1 and the second equation, $y = 3x - 5$, in Y_2.

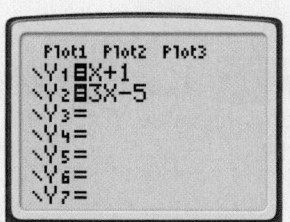

3 Press **2nd** **GRAPH** (TABLE) to use the **TABLE** function.

4 Scroll through the values using ▲ and ▼ . Look for values where Y_1 and Y_2 are equal, and then find the corresponding *x*-value. This *x*-value is the solution of the equation.

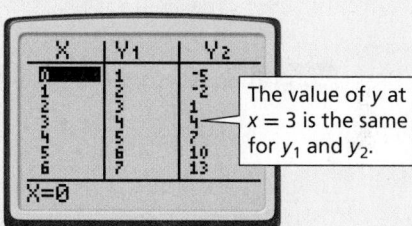

The value of *y* at $x = 3$ is the same for y_1 and y_2.

5 Press **GRAPH** and verify where the lines intersect.

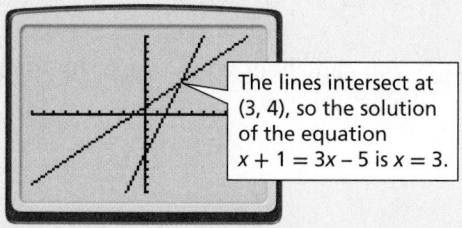

The lines intersect at (3, 4), so the solution of the equation $x + 1 = 3x - 5$ is $x = 3$.

6 You can check your answer by solving the equation algebraically.

$$x + 1 = 3x - 5$$
$$x - x + 1 = 3x - x - 5$$
$$1 = 2x - 5$$
$$1 + 5 = 2x - 5 + 5$$
$$6 = 2x$$
$$\frac{6}{2} = \frac{2x}{2}$$
$$3 = x \checkmark$$

Try This

Solve each equation by graphing.

1. $2x + 1 = x + 8$ **2.** $4x - 3 = 2x + 9$ **3.** $2x - 5 = x - 9$

4. $-x + 3 = 5 - 2x$ **5.** $x - 10 = -3x + 2$ **6.** $-6x + 5 = -x$

Activity 2

Use a graphing calculator to solve $1 - 4x + 3x = -1 - 3(2 - x)$.

1 Press **Y=** and enter each side of the equation into Y_1 and Y_2. You do not need to simplify first.

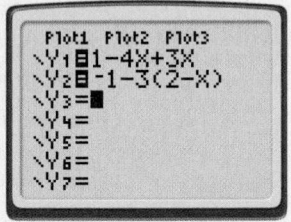

2 Press **2nd** **GRAPH** to use the **TABLE** function. Scroll until you find the value of x for which the y-values are the same.

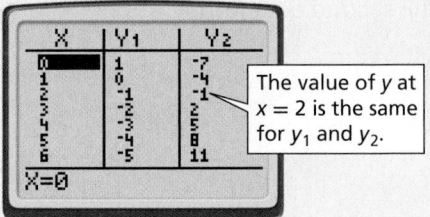

The value of y at $x = 2$ is the same for y_1 and y_2.

3 Press **GRAPH** and verify where the lines intersect.

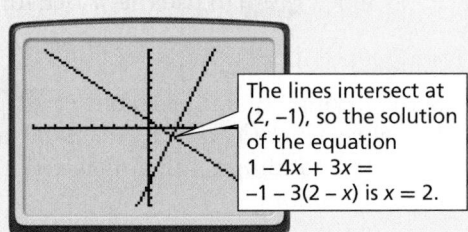

The lines intersect at $(2, -1)$, so the solution of the equation $1 - 4x + 3x = -1 - 3(2 - x)$ is $x = 2$.

4 You can check your answer by solving the equation algebraically.

$$1 - 4x + 3x = -1 - 3(2 - x)$$
$$1 - x = -1 - 6 + 3x$$
$$1 - x - 3x = -7 + 3x - 3x$$
$$1 - 4x = -7$$
$$1 - 1 - 4x = -7 - 1$$
$$-4x = -8$$
$$\frac{-4x}{-4} = \frac{-8}{-4}$$
$$x = 2 \checkmark$$

Try This

Solve each equation by graphing.

7. $-5x + 2(x - 2) = 5x + 4$ **8.** $3(x + 2) = -x + 18$ **9.** $2x - 5x + 4 = 2(x - 1) + 16$

1-6 Solving for a Variable

CC.9-12.A.CED.4 Rearrange formulas to highlight a quantity of interest, using the same reasoning as in solving equations.*
Also **CC.9-12.A.REI.3, CC.9-12.N.Q.1***

Objectives
Solve a formula for a given variable.

Solve an equation in two or more variables for one of the variables.

Vocabulary
formula
literal equation

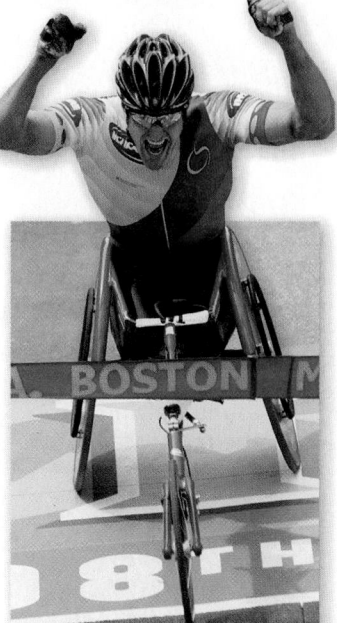

Who uses this?
Athletes can "rearrange" the distance formula to calculate their average speed.

Many wheelchair athletes compete in marathons, which cover about 26.2 miles. Using the time t it took to complete the race, the distance d, and the *formula* $d = rt$, racers can find their average speed r.

A **formula** is an equation that states a rule for a relationship among quantities.

In the formula $d = rt$, d is isolated. You can "rearrange" a formula to isolate any variable by using inverse operations. This is called *solving for a variable*.

Solving for a Variable
Step 1 Locate the variable you are asked to solve for in the equation.
Step 2 Identify the operations on this variable and the order in which they are applied.
Step 3 Use inverse operations to undo operations and isolate the variable.

EXAMPLE 1 *Sports Application*

In 2004, Ernst Van Dyk won the wheelchair race of the Boston Marathon with a time of about 1.3 hours. The race was about 26.2 miles. What was his average speed? Use the formula $d = rt$ and round your answer to the nearest tenth.

The question asks for speed, so first solve the formula $d = rt$ for r.

$d = \mathbf{r}t$ *Locate r in the equation.*

$\dfrac{d}{t} = \dfrac{rt}{t}$ *Since r is multiplied by t, divide both sides by t to undo the multiplication.*

$\dfrac{d}{t} = r$, or $r = \dfrac{d}{t}$

Now use this formula and the information given in the problem.

$r = \dfrac{d}{t} \approx \dfrac{26.2}{1.3}$

≈ 20.2

Van Dyk's average speed was about 20.2 miles per hour.

Helpful Hint

A number divided by itself equals 1. For $t \neq 0$, $\dfrac{t}{t} = 1$.

1. Solve the formula $d = rt$ for t. Find the time in hours that it would take Van Dyk to travel 26.2 miles if his average speed was 18 miles per hour. Round to the nearest hundredth.

EXAMPLE 2 **Solving Formulas for a Variable**

A The formula for a Fahrenheit temperature in terms of degrees Celsius is $F = \frac{9}{5}C + 32$. Solve for C.

$$F = \frac{9}{5}C + 32$$ *Locate C in the equation.*

$$\underline{\quad -32 \qquad\qquad -32\quad}$$ *Since 32 is added to $\frac{9}{5}C$, subtract 32 from both sides to undo the addition.*

$$F - 32 = \frac{9}{5}C$$

$$\left(\frac{5}{9}\right)(F - 32) = \left(\frac{5}{9}\right)\frac{9}{5}C$$ *Since C is multiplied by $\frac{9}{5}$, divide both sides by $\frac{9}{5}$ (multiply by $\frac{5}{9}$) to undo the*

$$\frac{5}{9}(F - 32) = C$$ *multiplication.*

Remember!

Dividing by a fraction is the same as multiplying by the reciprocal.

B The formula for a person's typing speed is $s = \frac{w - 10e}{m}$, where s is speed in words per minute, w is number of words typed, e is number of errors, and m is number of minutes typing. Solve for w.

$$s = \frac{w - 10e}{m}$$ *Locate w in the equation.*

$$m(s) = m\left(\frac{w - 10e}{m}\right)$$ *Since $w - 10e$ is divided by m, multiply both sides by m to undo the division.*

$$ms = w - 10e$$

$$\underline{\quad +10e \qquad\qquad +10e\quad}$$ *Since 10e is subtracted from w, add 10e to*

$$ms + 10e = w$$ *both sides to undo the subtraction.*

CHECK IT OUT! **2.** The formula for an object's final velocity f is $f = i - gt$, where i is the object's initial velocity, g is acceleration due to gravity, and t is time. Solve for i.

A formula is a type of *literal equation*. A **literal equation** is an equation with two or more variables. To solve for one of the variables, use inverse operations.

EXAMPLE 3 **Solving Literal Equations for a Variable**

A Solve $m - n = 5$ for m.

$$m - n = \quad 5$$ *Locate m in the equation.*

$$\underline{\quad +n \quad +n\quad}$$ *Since n is subtracted from m, add n to both sides to*

$$m = 5 + n$$ *undo the subtraction.*

B Solve $\frac{m}{k} = x$ for k.

$$\frac{m}{k} = x$$ *Locate k in the equation.*

$$k\left(\frac{m}{k}\right) = kx$$ *Since k appears in the denominator, multiply both sides by k.*

$$m = kx$$

$$\frac{m}{x} = \frac{kx}{x}$$ *Since k is multiplied by x, divide both sides by x to undo the multiplication.*

$$\frac{m}{x} = k$$

CHECK IT OUT! **3a.** Solve $5 - b = 2t$ for t. **3b.** Solve $D = \frac{m}{V}$ for V.

THINK AND DISCUSS

1. Describe a situation in which a formula could be used more easily if it were "rearranged." Include the formula in your description.

2. Explain how to solve $P = 2\ell + 2w$ for w.

3. **GET ORGANIZED** Copy and complete the graphic organizer. Write a formula that is used in each subject. Then solve the formula for each of its variables.

Common Formulas	
Subject	**Formula**
Geometry	
Physical science	
Earth science	

1-6 Exercises

Learn It Online
Homework Help Online
Parent Resources Online

GUIDED PRACTICE

1. **Vocabulary** Explain why a *formula* is a type of *literal equation*.

SEE EXAMPLE 1

2. **Construction** The formula $a = 46c$ gives the floor area a in square meters that can be wired using c circuits.

   a. Solve $a = 46c$ for c.

   b. If a room is 322 square meters, how many circuits are required to wire this room?

SEE EXAMPLE 2

3. The formula for the volume of a rectangular prism with length ℓ, width w, and height h is $V = \ell w h$. Solve this formula for w.

SEE EXAMPLE 3

4. Solve $st + 3t = 6$ for s.

5. Solve $m - 4n = 8$ for m.

6. Solve $\dfrac{f + 4}{g} = 6$ for f.

7. Solve $b + c = \dfrac{10}{a}$ for a.

PRACTICE AND PROBLEM SOLVING

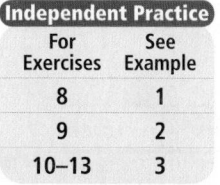

Independent Practice	
For Exercises	**See Example**
8	1
9	2
10–13	3

Extra Practice

See Extra Practice for more Skills Practice and Applications Practice exercises.

8. **Geometry** The formula $C = 2\pi r$ relates the circumference C of a circle to its radius r. (Recall that π is the constant ratio of circumference to diameter.)

   a. Solve $C = 2\pi r$ for r.

   b. If a circle's circumference is 15 inches, what is its radius? Leave the symbol π in your answer.

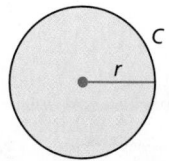

C is the distance around the circle.

r is the distance from the center of the circle to any point on the circle.

9. **Finance** The formula $A = P + I$ shows that the total amount of money A received from an investment equals the principal P (the original amount of money invested) plus the interest I. Solve this formula for I.

10. Solve $-2 = 4r + s$ for s.

11. Solve $xy - 5 = k$ for x.

12. Solve $\dfrac{m}{n} = p - 6$ for n.

13. Solve $\dfrac{x - 2}{y} = z$ for y.

Solve for the indicated variable.

14. $S = 180n - 360$ for n **15.** $\frac{x}{5} - g = a$ for x **16.** $A = \frac{1}{2}bh$ for b

17. $y = mx + b$ for x **18.** $a = 3n + 1$ for n **19.** $PV = nRT$ for T

20. $T + M = R$ for T **21.** $M = T - R$ for T **22.** $PV = nRT$ for R

23. $2a + 2b = c$ for b **24.** $5p + 9c = p$ for c **25.** $ax + r = 7$ for r

26. $3x + 7y = 2$ for y **27.** $4y + 3x = 5$ for x **28.** $y = 3x + 3b$ for b

29. Estimation The table shows the flying time and distance traveled for five flights on a certain airplane.

Flying Times		
Flight	**Time (h)**	**Distance (mi)**
A	2	1018
B	3	1485
C	4	2103
D	5	2516
E	6	2886

   a. Use the data in the table to write a rule that *estimates* the relationship between flying time t and distance traveled d.

   b. Use your rule from part **a** to estimate the time that it takes the airplane to fly 1300 miles.

   c. Solve your rule for d.

   d. Use your rule from part **c** to estimate the distance the airplane can fly in 8 hours.

30. Sports To find a baseball pitcher's earned run average (ERA), you can use the formula $Ei = 9r$, where E represents ERA, i represents number of innings pitched, and r represents number of earned runs allowed. Solve the equation for E. What is a pitcher's ERA if he allows 5 earned runs in 18 innings pitched?

31. Meteorology For altitudes up to 36,000 feet, the relationship between temperature and altitude can be described by the formula $t = -0.0035a + g$, where t is the temperature in degrees Fahrenheit, a is the altitude in feet, and g is the ground temperature in degrees Fahrenheit. Solve this formula for a.

32. Write About It In your own words, explain how to solve a literal equation for one of the variables.

33. Critical Thinking How is solving $a - ab = c$ for a different from the problems in this lesson? How might you solve this equation for a?

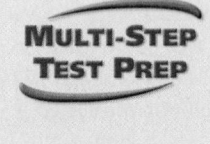
MULTI-STEP TEST PREP

34. a. Suppose firefighters can extinguish a wildfire at a rate of 60 acres per day. Use this information to complete the table.

   b. Use the last row in the table to write an equation for acres A extinguished in terms of the number of days d.

   c. Graph the points in the table with *Days* on the horizontal axis and *Acres* on the vertical axis. Describe the graph.

Days	Acres
1	60
2	
3	180
4	
5	
d	

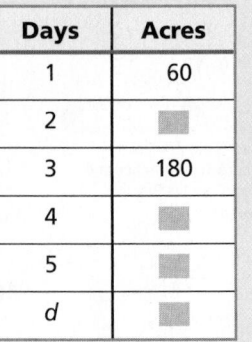

35. Which equation is the result of solving $9 + 3x = 2y$ for x?

    Ⓐ $\dfrac{9 + 3y}{2} = x$ Ⓑ $\dfrac{2}{3}y - 9 = x$ Ⓒ $x = \dfrac{2}{3}y - 3$ Ⓓ $x = 2y - 3$

36. Which of the following is a correct method for solving $2a - 5b = 10$ for b?

    Ⓕ Add $5b$ to both sides, then divide both sides by 2.

    Ⓖ Subtract $5b$ from both sides, then divide both sides by 2.

    Ⓗ Divide both sides by 5, then add $2a$ to both sides.

    Ⓙ Subtract $2a$ from both sides, then divide both sides by -5.

37. The formula for the volume of a rectangular prism is $V = \ell wh$. Anna wants to make a cardboard box with a length of 7 inches, a width of 5 inches, and a volume of 210 cubic inches. Which variable does Anna need to solve for in order to build her box?

    Ⓐ V Ⓑ ℓ Ⓒ w Ⓓ h

CHALLENGE AND EXTEND

Solve for the indicated variable.

38. $3.3x + r = 23.1$ for x **39.** $\dfrac{2}{5}a - \dfrac{3}{4}b = c$ for a **40.** $\dfrac{3}{5}x + 1.4y = \dfrac{2}{5}$ for y

41. $t = \dfrac{d}{500} + \dfrac{1}{2}$ for d **42.** $s = \dfrac{1}{2}gt^2$ for g **43.** $v^2 = u^2 + 2as$ for s

44. Solve $y = mx + 6$ for m. What can you say about y if $m = 0$?

45. **Entertainment** The formula $S = \dfrac{h \cdot w \cdot f \cdot t}{35,000}$ gives the approximate size in kilobytes (Kb) of a compressed video. The variables h and w represent the height and width of the frame measured in pixels, f is the number of frames per second (fps) the video plays, and t is the time the video plays in seconds. Estimate the time a movie trailer will play if it has a frame height of 320 pixels, has a frame width of 144 pixels, plays at 15 fps, and has a size of 2370 Kb.

1-7 Solving Absolute-Value Equations

CC.9-12.A.CED.1 Create equations and inequalities in one variable and use them to solve problems.* *Also* CC.9-12.A.REI.3

Objective
Solve equations in one variable that contain absolute-value expressions.

Why learn this?
Engineers can solve absolute-value equations to calculate the length of the deck of a bridge. (See Example 3.)

Recall that the absolute value of a number is that number's distance from zero on a number line. For example, $|-5| = 5$ and $|5| = 5$.

For any nonzero absolute value, there are exactly two numbers with that absolute value. For example, both 5 and −5 have an absolute value of 5.

To write this statement using algebra, you would write $|x| = 5$. This equation asks, "What values of x have an absolute value of 5?" The solutions are 5 and −5. Notice that this equation has two solutions.

Know it!
·Note

Absolute-Value Equations

WORDS	NUMBERS
The equation $|x| = a$ asks, "What values of x have an absolute value of a?" The solutions are a and the opposite of a.	$|x| = 5$ $x = 5$ or $x = -5$

GRAPH	ALGEBRA
←a units→←a units→ ◄————●——————|——————●————► −a 0 a	$|x| = a$ $x = a$ or $x = -a$ $(a \geq 0)$

To solve absolute-value equations, perform inverse operations to isolate the absolute-value expression on one side of the equation. Then you must consider two cases.

EXAMPLE 1 **Solving Absolute-Value Equations**

Solve each equation.

Helpful Hint

Be sure to check both solutions when you solve an absolute-value equation.

$|x| = 4$	$|x| = 4$
$|-4|$ 4	$|4|$ 4
4 4 ✓	4 4 ✓

 $|x| = 4$

$|x| = 4$ *Think: What numbers are 4 units from 0?*

←— 4 units —→←— 4 units —→
◄—+——+——+——+——+——+——+——+——+——+——►
−5 −4 −3 −2 −1   0   1   2   3   4   5

Case 1	**Case 2**	*Rewrite the equation as two cases.*
$x = -4$	$x = 4$	

The solutions are −4 and 4.

Solve each equation.

B $4|x + 2| = 24$

$$\frac{4|x + 2|}{4} = \frac{24}{4}$$

Since $|x + 2|$ is multiplied by 4, divide both sides by 4 to undo the multiplication.

$$|x + 2| = 6$$

Think: What numbers are 6 units from 0?

Case 1	**Case 2**
$x + 2 = -6$	$x + 2 = 6$
$\underline{ -2 -2}$	$\underline{ -2 -2}$
$x = -8$	$x = 4$

Rewrite the equation as two cases. Since 2 is added to x, subtract 2 from both sides of the equation.

The solutions are –8 and 4.

 Solve each equation. Check your answer.

1a. $|x| - 3 = 4$ **1b.** $8 = |x - 2.5|$

The table summarizes the steps for solving absolute-value equations.

Solving an Absolute-Value Equation
1. Use inverse operations to isolate the absolute-value expression.
2. Rewrite the resulting equation as two cases that do not involve absolute values.
3. Solve the equation in each of the two cases.

Not all absolute-value equations have two solutions. If the absolute-value expression equals 0, there is one solution. If an equation states that an absolute value is negative, there are no solutions.

EXAMPLE 2 **Special Cases of Absolute-Value Equations**

Solve each equation.

A $|x + 3| + 4 = 4$

$$|x + 3| + 4 = 4$$
$$\underline{ -4 -4}$$
$$|x + 3| = 0$$

Since 4 is added to $|x + 3|$, subtract 4 from both sides to undo the addition.

$$x + 3 = 0$$
$$\underline{ -3 -3}$$
$$x = -3$$

There is only one case. Since 3 is added to x, subtract 3 from both sides to undo the addition.

B $5 = |x + 2| + 8$

$$5 = |x + 2| + 8$$
$$\underline{-8 -8}$$
$$-3 = |x + 2| \; ✗$$

Since 8 is added to $|x + 2|$, subtract 8 from both sides to undo the addition.

Absolute value cannot be negative.

This equation has no solution.

Remember!

Absolute value must be nonnegative because it represents a distance.

 Solve each equation.

2a. $2 - |2x - 5| = 7$ **2b.** $-6 + |x - 4| = -6$

EXAMPLE 3 *Engineering Application*

Sydney Harbour Bridge in Australia is 1149 meters long. Because of changes in temperature, the bridge can expand or contract by as much as 420 millimeters. Write and solve an absolute-value equation to find the minimum and maximum lengths of the bridge.

First convert millimeters to meters.

420 mm = 0.4 2 0 m *Move the decimal point three places to the left.*

The length of the bridge can vary by 0.42 m, so find two numbers that are 0.42 units away from 1149 on a number line.

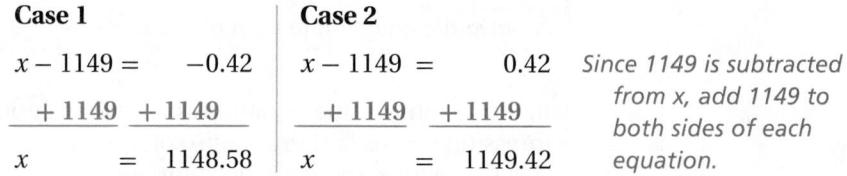

0.42 0.42
units units

1147   1148   1149   1150   1151

You can find these numbers by using the absolute-value equation $|x - 1149| = 0.42$. Solve the equation by rewriting it as two cases.

Case 1

$$x - 1149 = -0.42$$
$$+1149 \quad +1149$$
$$x \qquad = 1148.58$$

Case 2

$$x - 1149 = 0.42$$
$$+1149 \quad +1149$$
$$x \qquad = 1149.42$$

Since 1149 is subtracted from x, add 1149 to both sides of each equation.

The minimum length of the bridge is 1148.58 m, and the maximum length is 1149.42 m.

 **3.** Sydney Harbour Bridge is 134 meters tall. The height of the bridge can rise or fall by 180 millimeters because of changes in temperature. Write and solve an absolute-value equation to find the minimum and maximum heights of the bridge.

MATHEMATICAL PRACTICES

THINK AND DISCUSS

1. Explain the steps you would use to solve the equation $\frac{1}{5}|x - 3| = 2$.

2. GET ORGANIZED Copy and complete the graphic organizer. In each box, write an example of an absolute-value equation that has the indicated number of solutions, and then solve.

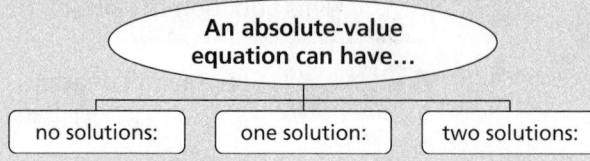

An absolute-value equation can have...

no solutions: one solution: two solutions:

GUIDED PRACTICE

Solve each equation.

SEE EXAMPLE 1

1. $|x| = 6$

2. $9 = |x + 5|$

3. $|3x| + 2 = 8$

4. $2|x| = 18$

5. $\left|x + \dfrac{1}{2}\right| = 1$

6. $|x - 3| - 6 = 2$

SEE EXAMPLE 2

7. $-8 = |x|$

8. $|x| = 0$

9. $|x + 4| = -7$

10. $7 = |3x + 9| + 7$

11. $|2.8 - x| + 1.5 = 1.5$

12. $5|x + 7| + 14 = 8$

SEE EXAMPLE 3

13. Communication Barry's walkie-talkie has a range of 2 mi. Barry is traveling on a straight highway and is at mile marker 207. Write and solve an absolute-value equation to find the minimum and maximum mile marker from 207 that Barry's walkie-talkie will reach.

PRACTICE AND PROBLEM SOLVING

Independent Practice

For Exercises	See Example
14–22	1
23–28	2
29	3

Extra Practice

See Extra Practice for more Skills Practice and Applications Practice exercises.

Solve each equation.

14. $|x| = \dfrac{1}{5}$

15. $|2x - 4| = 22$

16. $18 = 3|x - 1|$

17. $-2|x| = -4$

18. $3|x| - 12 = 18$

19. $|x - 42.04| = 23.24$

20. $\left|\dfrac{2}{3}x - \dfrac{2}{3}\right| = \dfrac{2}{3}$

21. $|3x + 1| = 13$

22. $|-2x + 3| = 5.8$

23. $|4x| + 9 = 9$

24. $8 = 7 - |x|$

25. $|x| + 6 = 12 - 6$

26. $|x - 3| + 14 = 5$

27. $0 = \left|\dfrac{2}{3} - x\right|$

28. $3 + |x - 1| = 3$

29. Space Shuttle The diameter of a valve for the space shuttle must be within 0.001 mm of 5 mm. Write and solve an absolute-value equation to find the boundary values for the acceptable diameters of the valve.

5 mm

30. The two numbers that are 5 units from 3 on the number line are represented by the equation $|n - 3| = 5$. What are these two numbers? Graph the solutions.

31. Write and solve an absolute-value equation that represents two numbers x that are 2 units from 7 on a number line. Graph the solutions.

32. Manufacturing A quality control inspector at a bolt factory examines random bolts that come off the assembly line. Any bolt whose diameter differs by more than 0.04 mm from 6.5 mm is sent back. Write and solve an absolute-value equation to find the maximum and minimum diameters of an acceptable bolt.

33. Construction A brick company guarantees to fill a contractor's order to within 5% accuracy. A contractor orders 1500 bricks. Write and solve an absolute-value equation to find the maximum and minimum number of bricks guaranteed.

34. Multi-Step A machine prints posters and then trims them to the correct size. The equation $|\ell - 65.1| = 0.2$ gives the maximum and minimum acceptable lengths for the posters in inches. Does a poster with a length of 64.8 inches fall within the acceptable range? Why or why not?

Write an absolute-value equation whose solutions are graphed on the number line.

35.
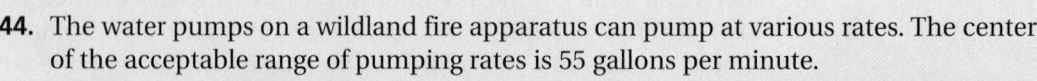
```
← | | ● | | | | | ● | | → 
 -5 -4 -3 -2 -1 0 1 2 3 4 5
```

36.
```
← | | | | | ● | ● | | | → 
 -5 -4 -3 -2 -1 0 1 2 3 4 5
```

37.
```
← | | | | ● | | | | | ● → 
 -5 -4 -3 -2 -1 0 1 2 3 4 5
```

38.
```
← | ● | | | | | | ● | | → 
 -5 -4 -3 -2 -1 0 1 2 3 4 5
```

Tell whether each statement is sometimes, always, or never true. Explain.

39. An absolute-value equation has two solutions.

40. The value of $|x + 4|$ is equal to the value of $|x| + 4$.

41. The absolute value of a number is nonnegative.

42. Temperature A thermostat is set so that the temperature in a laboratory freezer stays within 2.5 °F of 2 °F. Write and solve an absolute-value equation to find the maximum and minimum temperatures in the freezer.

43. Recreation To ensure safety, boaters must be aware of wind conditions while they are on the water. A particular anemometer gives a measurement of wind speed within a certain amount of the true wind speed, as shown in the table.

Measured Wind Speed (mi/h)	True Wind Speed (mi/h)
20	15–25
22	17–27
24	19–29
26	21–31
28	23–33
30	25–35

 a. Use the table to write an absolute-value equation for the minimum and maximum possible true wind speeds *t* for the measured wind speed shown on the anemometer.

 b. Solve your equation from part **a.** Check that the solution is correct by comparing it to the values given in the table when the measured wind speed is 24 mi/h.

 c. Will your equation work for all of the values in the table? Explain.

 d. Explain what your equation says about the instrument's measurements.

MULTI-STEP TEST PREP

44. The water pumps on a wildland fire apparatus can pump at various rates. The center of the acceptable range of pumping rates is 55 gallons per minute.

 a. Write an absolute-value expression that gives the distance on the number line of a pump's rate *r* from 55.

 b. The smallest and largest pumps have rates that differ by 45 gallons per minute from the rate at the center of the range. Write an absolute-value equation for the rates of these pumps.

 c. Find the least and greatest rates that are acceptable for a wildland fire apparatus.

45. **Write About It** Do you agree with the following statement: "To solve an absolute-value equation, you need to solve two equations." Why or why not?

46. **Critical Thinking** Is there a value of a for which the equation $|x - a| = 1$ has exactly one solution? Explain.

47. Which situation could be modeled by the equation $|x - 65| = 3$?

   Ⓐ Two numbers on the number line are 65 units away from 3.

   Ⓑ The length of a carpet is 3 inches less than 65 inches.

   Ⓒ The maximum and minimum weights of wrestlers on the team are within 3 kg of 65 kg.

   Ⓓ The members of an exercise club for seniors are all between 63 and 67 years old.

48. For which of the following is $n = -3$ a solution?

   Ⓕ $|n - 1| = 2$ Ⓖ $|n + 2| = -1$ Ⓗ $|n - 2| = 1$ Ⓙ $|n + 1| = 2$

49. The minimum and maximum sound levels at a rock concert are 90 decibels and 95 decibels. Which equation models this situation?

   Ⓐ $|x - 90| = 5$ Ⓑ $|x - 92.5| = 2.5$ Ⓒ $|x - 92.5| = 5$ Ⓓ $|x - 95| = 2.5$

CHALLENGE AND EXTEND

50. The perimeter of a rectangle is 100 inches. The length of the rectangle is $|2x - 4|$ inches, and the width is x inches. What are the possible values of x? Explain.

51. Fill in the missing reasons to justify each step in solving the equation $3|2x + 1| = 21$.

Statements	Reasons
1. $3|2x + 1| = 21$	1. Given
2. $|2x + 1| = 7$	2. _____?_____
3. $2x + 1 = -7$ or $2x + 1 = 7$	3. Definition of absolute value
4. $2x = -8$ or $2x = 6$	4. _____?_____
5. $x = -4$ or $x = 3$	5. _____?_____

52. Solve $|x| = |x + 1|$. (*Hint:* Consider two cases: $x \geq 0$ and $x < 0$.)

MULTI-STEP TEST PREP

MATHEMATICAL PRACTICES

Make sense of problems and persevere in solving them.

Equations and Formulas

All Fired Up A large forest fire in the western United States burns for 14 days, spreading to cover approximately 3850 acres. Firefighters do their best to contain the fire, but hot temperatures and high winds may prompt them to request additional support.

1. The fire spreads at an average rate of how many acres per day?

2. Officials estimate that the fire will spread to cover 9075 acres before it is contained. At this rate, how many more days will it take for the fire to cover an area of 9075 acres? Answer this question using at least two different methods.

3. Additional help arrives, and the firefighters contain the fire in 7 more days. In total, how many acres does the fire cover before it is contained?

4. If the fire had spread to cover an area of 7000 acres, it would have reached Bowman Valley. Explain how the graph shows that firefighters stopped the spread of the fire before it reached Bowman Valley.

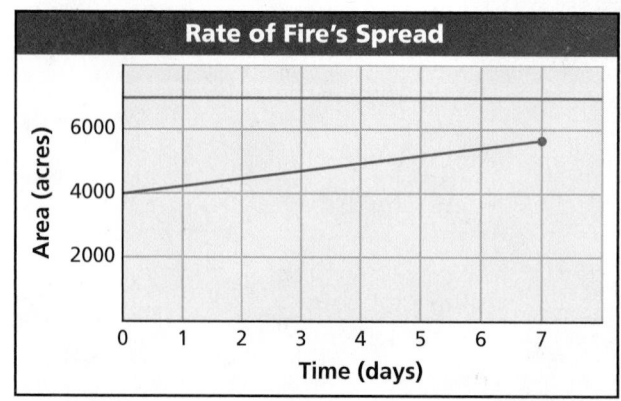

5. The total cost of fighting the fire for 21 days was approximately $1,440,000. What was the approximate cost per acre of fighting the fire?

(tl),©Index Stock/Alamy; (cr),© Francis Specker/Corbis

Quiz for Lessons 1-1 Through 1-7

1-1 Variables and Expressions

Give two ways to write each algebraic expression in words.

1. $4 + n$

2. $m - 9$

3. $\dfrac{g}{2}$

4. $4z$

1-2 Solving Equations by Adding or Subtracting

Solve each equation.

5. $x - 32 = -18$

6. $1.1 = m - 0.9$

7. $j + 4 = -17$

8. $\dfrac{9}{8} = g + \dfrac{1}{2}$

9. When she first purchased it, Soledad's computer had 400 GB of hard drive space. After six months, there were only 313 GB available. Write and solve an equation to find the amount of hard drive space that Soledad used in the first six months.

1-3 Solving Equations by Multiplying or Dividing

Solve each equation.

10. $\dfrac{h}{3} = -12$

11. $-2.8 = \dfrac{w}{-3}$

12. $42 = 3c$

13. $-0.1b = 3.7$

14. A fund-raiser raised $2400, which was $\dfrac{3}{5}$ of the goal. Write and solve an equation to find the amount of the goal.

1-4 Solving Two-Step and Multi-Step Equations

Solve each equation.

15. $2r + 20 = 200$

16. $\dfrac{3}{5}k + 5 = 7$

17. $5n + 6 - 3n = -12$

18. $4(x - 7) = 2$

19. A taxicab company charges $2.10 plus $0.80 per mile. Carmen paid a fare of $11.70. Write and solve an equation to find the number of miles she traveled.

1-5 Solving Equations with Variables on Both Sides

Solve each equation.

20. $4x - 3 = 2x + 5$

21. $3(2x - 5) = 2(3x - 2)$

22. $2(2t - 3) = 6(t + 2)$

23. $7(x + 5) = -7(x + 5)$

1-6 Solving for a Variable

24. Solve $2x + 3y = 12$ for x.

25. Solve $\dfrac{x}{r} = v$ for x.

26. Solve $5j + s = t - 2$ for t.

27. Solve $h + p = 3(k - 8)$ for k.

1-7 Solving Absolute-Value Equations

Solve each equation.

28. $|r| = 7$

29. $|h + 4| = 11$

30. $|2x + 4| = 0$

31. $16 = 7|p + 3| + 30$

1-8 Rates, Ratios, and Proportions

CC.9-12.N.Q.1 Use units as a way to understand problems and to guide the solution of multi-step problems; choose and interpret units consistently in formulas….* *Also* **CC.9-12.A.CED.1*, CC.9-12.A.REI.3**

Objectives
Write and use ratios, rates, and unit rates.

Write and solve proportions.

Vocabulary
ratio   proportion
rate   cross products
scale   scale drawing
unit rate   scale model
conversion   dimensional
   factor   analysis

Why learn this?
Ratios and proportions are used to draw accurate maps. (See Example 5.)

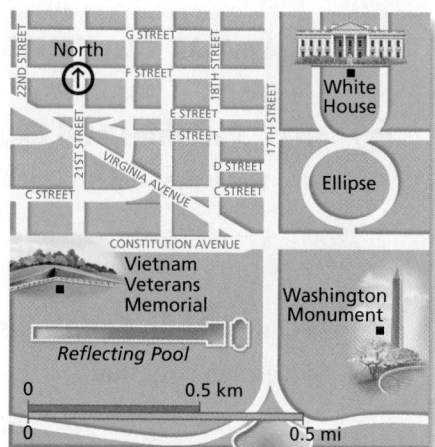

A **ratio** is a comparison of two quantities by division. The ratio of a to b can be written $a{:}b$ or $\frac{a}{b}$, where $b \neq 0$. Ratios that name the same comparison are said to be *equivalent*.

A statement that two ratios are equivalent, such as $\frac{1}{12} = \frac{2}{24}$, is called a **proportion**.

EXAMPLE 1   Using Ratios

The ratio of faculty members to students at a college is 1:15. There are 675 students. How many faculty members are there?

$$\frac{\text{faculty}}{\text{students}} \rightarrow \frac{1}{15}$$ *Write a ratio comparing faculty to students.*

$$\frac{1}{15} = \frac{x}{675}$$ *Write a proportion. Let x be the number of faculty members.*

$$675\left(\frac{x}{675}\right) = 675\left(\frac{1}{15}\right)$$ *Since x is divided by 675, multiply both sides of the equation by 675.*

$$x = 45$$

There are 45 faculty members.

Reading Math

Read the proportion $\frac{1}{15} = \frac{x}{675}$ as "1 is to 15 as x is to 675."

> **CHECK IT OUT!** **1.** The ratio of games won to games lost for a baseball team is $3{:}2$. The team won 18 games. How many games did the team lose?

A **rate** is a ratio of two quantities with different units, such as $\frac{34 \text{ mi}}{2 \text{ gal}}$. Rates are usually written as *unit rates*. A **unit rate** is a rate with a second quantity of 1 unit, such as $\frac{17 \text{ mi}}{1 \text{ gal}}$, or 17 mi/gal. You can convert any rate to a unit rate.

EXAMPLE 2   Finding Unit Rates

Takeru Kobayashi of Japan ate 53.5 hot dogs in 12 minutes to win a contest. Find the unit rate in hot dogs per minute. Round to the nearest hundredth.

$$\frac{53.5}{12} = \frac{x}{1}$$ *Write a proportion to find an equivalent ratio with a second quantity of 1.*

$$4.46 \approx x$$ *Divide on the left side to find x.*

The unit rate is approximately 4.46 hot dogs per minute.

> **CHECK IT OUT!** **2.** Cory earns $52.50 in 7 hours. Find the unit rate in dollars per hour.

Dimensional analysis is a process that uses rates to convert measurements from one unit to another. A rate such as $\frac{12 \text{ in.}}{1 \text{ ft}}$, in which the two quantities are equal but use different units, is called a **conversion factor**. To convert from one set of units to another, multiply by a conversion factor.

EXAMPLE **3** **Using Dimensional Analysis**

A **A large adult male human has about 12 pints of blood. Use dimensional analysis to convert this quantity to gallons.**

Step 1 Convert pints to quarts.

$12 \text{ pt} \cdot \dfrac{1 \text{ qt}}{2 \text{ pt}}$ *Multiply by a conversion factor whose first quantity is quarts and whose second quantity is pints.*

6 qt

12 pints is 6 quarts.

Step 2 Convert quarts to gallons.

$6 \text{ qt} \cdot \dfrac{1 \text{ gal}}{4 \text{ qt}}$ *Multiply by a conversion factor whose first quantity is gallons and whose second quantity is quarts.*

$\dfrac{6}{4} \text{ gal} = 1\dfrac{1}{2} \text{ gal}$

A large adult male human has about $1\frac{1}{2}$ gallons of blood.

B **The dwarf sea horse *Hippocampus zosterae* swims at a rate of 52.68 feet per hour. Use dimensional analysis to convert this speed to inches per minute.**

Use the conversion factor $\frac{12 \text{ in.}}{1 \text{ ft}}$ to convert feet to inches, and use the conversion factor $\frac{1 \text{ h}}{60 \text{ min}}$ to convert hours to minutes.

$$\frac{52.68 \text{ ft}}{1 \text{ h}} \cdot \frac{12 \text{ in.}}{1 \text{ ft}} \cdot \frac{1 \text{ h}}{60 \text{ min}} = \frac{10.536 \text{ in.}}{1 \text{ min}}$$

The speed is 10.536 inches per minute.

Check that the answer is reasonable. The answer is about 10 in./min.

- There are 60 min in 1 h, so 10 in./min is $60(10) = 600$ in./h.

- There are 12 in. in 1 ft, so 600 in./h is $\frac{600}{12} = 50$ ft/h. This is close to the rate given in the problem, 52.68 ft/h.

CHECK IT OUT! **3.** A cyclist travels 56 miles in 4 hours. Use dimensional analysis to convert the cyclist's speed to feet per second. Round your answer to the nearest tenth, and show that your answer is reasonable.

In the proportion $\frac{a}{b} = \frac{c}{d}$, the products $a \cdot d$ and $b \cdot c$ are called **cross products**. You can solve a proportion for a missing value by using the Cross Products Property.

Cross Products Property

WORDS	NUMBERS	ALGEBRA
In a proportion, cross products are equal.	$\dfrac{2}{3} \diagdown\!\!\!\!\diagup \dfrac{4}{6}$ $2 \cdot 6 = 3 \cdot 4$	If $\dfrac{a}{b} \diagdown\!\!\!\!\diagup \dfrac{c}{d}$ and $b \neq 0$ and $d \neq 0$, then $ad = bc$.

Hippocampus zosterae

EXAMPLE **4** **Solving Proportions**

Solve each proportion.

A $\dfrac{5}{9} = \dfrac{3}{w}$

$\dfrac{5}{9} \bowtie \dfrac{3}{w}$

$5(w) = 9(3)$ *Use cross*
                    products.

$5w = 27$

$\dfrac{5w}{5} = \dfrac{27}{5}$ *Divide both sides*
                 by 5.

$w = \dfrac{27}{5}$

B $\dfrac{8}{x+10} = \dfrac{1}{12}$

$\dfrac{8}{x+10} \bowtie \dfrac{1}{12}$

$8(12) = 1(x+10)$ *Use cross*
                     products.

$96 = x + 10$

$\underline{-10 \quad\quad -10}$ *Subtract 10 from*
                    both sides.

$86 = x$

 **CHECK IT OUT!** Solve each proportion.

4a. $\dfrac{-5}{2} = \dfrac{y}{8}$

4b. $\dfrac{g+3}{5} = \dfrac{7}{4}$

A **scale** is a ratio between two sets of measurements, such as 1 in:5 mi. A **scale drawing** or **scale model** uses a scale to represent an object as smaller or larger than the actual object. A map is an example of a scale drawing.

EXAMPLE **5** **Scale Drawings and Scale Models**

A On the map, the distance from Chicago to Evanston is 0.625 in. What is the actual distance?

$\dfrac{\text{map}}{\text{actual}} \rightarrow \dfrac{1\text{ in.}}{18\text{ mi}}$ *Write the scale as a fraction.*

$\dfrac{1}{18} \bowtie \dfrac{0.625}{x}$ *Let x be the actual distance.*

$x \cdot 1 = 18(0.625)$ *Use cross products to solve.*

$x = 11.25$

The actual distance is 11.25 mi.

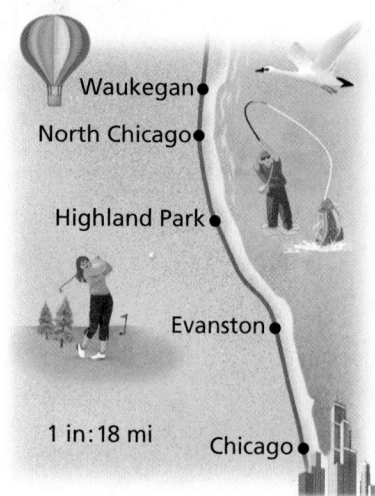

Waukegan
North Chicago
Highland Park
Evanston
1 in:18 mi
Chicago

B The actual distance between North Chicago and Waukegan is 4 mi. What is this distance on the map? Round to the nearest tenth.

$\dfrac{\text{map}}{\text{actual}} \rightarrow \dfrac{1\text{ in.}}{18\text{ mi}}$ *Write the scale as a fraction.*

$\dfrac{1}{18} \bowtie \dfrac{x}{4}$ *Let x be the distance on the map.*

$4 = 18x$ *Use cross products to solve the proportion.*

$\dfrac{4}{18} = \dfrac{18x}{18}$ *Since x is multiplied by 18, divide both sides by 18 to undo the multiplication.*

$0.2 \approx x$ *Round to the nearest tenth.*

The distance on the map is about 0.2 in.

Reading Math

A scale written without units, such as 32:1, means that 32 units of any measure correspond to 1 unit of that same measure.

 **CHECK IT OUT!** **5.** A scale model of a human heart is 16 ft long. The scale is 32:1. How many inches long is the actual heart it represents?

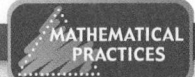
THINK AND DISCUSS

1. Explain two ways to solve the proportion $\frac{t}{4} = \frac{3}{5}$.

2. How could you show that the answer to Example 5A is reasonable?

3. GET ORGANIZED Copy and complete the graphic organizer. In each box, write an example of each use of ratios.

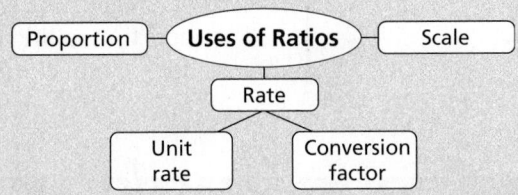

1-8 Exercises

GUIDED PRACTICE

1. Vocabulary What does it mean when two ratios form a *proportion*?

SEE EXAMPLE **1**

2. The ratio of the sale price of a jacket to the original price is $3:4$. The original price is 64. What is the sale price?

3. Chemistry The ratio of hydrogen atoms to oxygen atoms in water is $2:1$. If an amount of water contains 341 trillion atoms of oxygen, how many hydrogen atoms are there?

SEE EXAMPLE **2**

4. A computer's fan rotates 2000 times in 40 seconds. Find the unit rate in rotations per second.

5. Twelve cows produce 224,988 pounds of milk. Find the unit rate in pounds per cow.

6. A yellow jacket can fly 4.5 meters in 9 seconds. Find the unit rate in meters per second.

SEE EXAMPLE **3**

7. Lydia wrote $4\frac{1}{2}$ pages of her science report in one hour. What was her writing rate in pages per minute?

8. A model airplane flies 18 feet in 2 seconds. What is the airplane's speed in miles per hour? Round your answer to the nearest hundredth.

9. A vehicle uses 1 tablespoon of gasoline to drive 125 yards. How many miles can the vehicle travel per gallon? Round your answer to the nearest mile. (*Hint:* There are 256 tablespoons in a gallon.)

SEE EXAMPLE **4**   Solve each proportion.

10. $\frac{3}{z} = \frac{1}{8}$

11. $\frac{x}{3} = \frac{1}{5}$

12. $\frac{b}{4} = \frac{3}{2}$

13. $\frac{f+3}{12} = \frac{7}{2}$

14. $\frac{-1}{5} = \frac{3}{2d}$

15. $\frac{3}{14} = \frac{s-2}{21}$

16. $\frac{-4}{9} = \frac{7}{x}$

17. $\frac{3}{s-2} = \frac{1}{7}$

18. $\frac{10}{h} = \frac{52}{13}$

19. Archaeology Stonehenge II in Hunt, Texas, is a scale model of the ancient construction in Wiltshire, England. The scale of the model to the original is 3:5. The Altar Stone of the original construction is 4.9 meters tall. Write and solve a proportion to find the height of the model of the Altar Stone.

Alfred Sheppard, one of the builders of Stonehenge II.

PRACTICE AND PROBLEM SOLVING

Independent Practice

For Exercises	See Example
20–21	1
22–23	2
24–25	3
26–37	4
38	5

Extra Practice
See Extra Practice for more Skills Practice and Applications Practice exercises.

20. Gardening The ratio of the height of a bonsai ficus tree to the height of a full-size ficus tree is 1:9. The bonsai ficus is 6 inches tall. What is the height of a full-size ficus?

21. Manufacturing At one factory, the ratio of defective light bulbs produced to total light bulbs produced is about 3:500. How many light bulbs are expected to be defective when 12,000 are produced?

22. Four gallons of gasoline weigh 25 pounds. Find the unit rate in pounds per gallon.

23. Fifteen ounces of gold cost $6058.50. Find the unit rate in dollars per ounce.

24. Biology The tropical giant bamboo can grow 11.9 feet in 3 days. What is this rate of growth in inches per hour? Round your answer to the nearest hundredth, and show that your answer is reasonable.

25. Transportation The maximum speed of the Tupolev Tu-144 airliner is 694 m/s. What is this speed in kilometers per hour?

Solve each proportion.

26. $\dfrac{v}{6} = \dfrac{1}{2}$ **27.** $\dfrac{2}{5} = \dfrac{4}{y}$ **28.** $\dfrac{2}{h} = \dfrac{-5}{6}$ **29.** $\dfrac{3}{10} = \dfrac{b+7}{20}$

30. $\dfrac{5t}{9} = \dfrac{1}{2}$ **31.** $\dfrac{2}{3} = \dfrac{6}{q-4}$ **32.** $\dfrac{x}{8} = \dfrac{7.5}{20}$ **33.** $\dfrac{3}{k} = \dfrac{45}{18}$

34. $\dfrac{6}{a} = \dfrac{15}{17}$ **35.** $\dfrac{9}{2} = \dfrac{5}{x+1}$ **36.** $\dfrac{3}{5} = \dfrac{x}{100}$ **37.** $\dfrac{38}{19} = \dfrac{n-5}{20}$

38. Science The image shows a dust mite as seen under a microscope. The scale of the drawing to the dust mite is 100:1. Use a ruler to measure the length of the dust mite in the image in millimeters. What is the actual length of the dust mite?

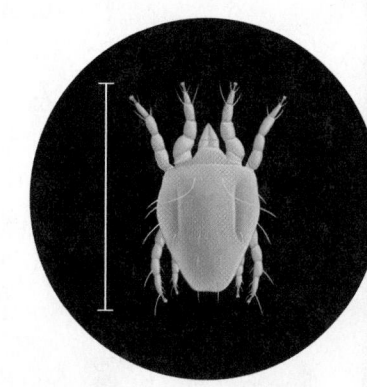

39. Finance On a certain day, the exchange rate was 60 U.S. dollars for 50 euro. How many U.S. dollars were 70 euro worth that day? Show that your answer is reasonable.

40. Environmental Science An environmental scientist wants to estimate the number of carp in a pond. He captures 100 carp, tags all of them, and releases them. A week later, he captures 85 carp and records how many have tags. His results are shown in the table. Write and solve a proportion to estimate the number of carp in the pond.

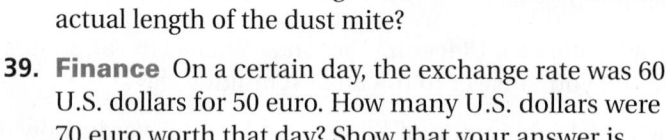

Status	Number Captured
Tagged	20
Not tagged	65

41. ///**ERROR ANALYSIS**/// Below is a bonus question that appeared on an algebra test and a student's response.

> The ratio of junior varsity members to varsity members on the track team is 3:5. There are 24 members on the team. Write a proportion to find the number of junior varsity members.
>
> $\dfrac{3}{5} = \dfrac{x}{24}$

The student did not receive the bonus points. Why is this proportion incorrect?

Sports

42. **Sports** The table shows world record times for women's races of different distances.

a. Find the speed in meters per second for each race. Round your answers to the nearest hundredth.

b. Which race has the fastest speed? the slowest?

c. **Critical Thinking** Give a possible reason why the speeds are different.

World Records (Women)	
Distance (m)	Time (s)
100	10.5
200	21.3
800	113.3
5000	864.7

43. **Entertainment** Lynn, Faith, and Jeremy are film animators. In one 8-hour day, Lynn rendered 203 frames, Faith rendered 216 frames, and Jeremy rendered 227 frames. How many more frames per hour did Faith render than Lynn did?

The records for the women's 100-meter dash and the women's 200-meter dash were set by Florence Griffith-Joyner, known as "Flo Jo." She is still referred to as the world's fastest woman.

Solve each proportion.

44. $\dfrac{x-1}{3} = \dfrac{x+1}{5}$ **45.** $\dfrac{m}{3} = \dfrac{m+4}{7}$ **46.** $\dfrac{1}{x-3} = \dfrac{3}{x-5}$ **47.** $\dfrac{a}{2} = \dfrac{a-4}{30}$

48. $\dfrac{3}{2y} = \dfrac{16}{y+2}$ **49.** $\dfrac{n+3}{5} = \dfrac{n-1}{2}$ **50.** $\dfrac{1}{y} = \dfrac{1}{6y-1}$ **51.** $\dfrac{2}{n} = \dfrac{4}{n+3}$

52. $\dfrac{5t-3}{-2} = \dfrac{t+3}{2}$ **53.** $\dfrac{3}{d+3} = \dfrac{4}{d+12}$ **54.** $\dfrac{3x+5}{14} = \dfrac{x}{3}$ **55.** $\dfrac{5}{2n} = \dfrac{8}{3n-24}$

56. **Decorating** A particular shade of paint is made by mixing 5 parts red paint with 7 parts blue paint. To make this shade, Shannon mixed 12 quarts of blue paint with 8 quarts of red paint. Did Shannon mix the correct shade? Explain.

 57. **Write About It** Give three examples of proportions. How do you know they are proportions? Then give three nonexamples of proportions. How do you know they are not proportions?

MULTI-STEP TEST PREP

58. a. Marcus is shopping for a new jacket. He finds one with a price tag of $120. Above the rack is a sign that says that he can take off $\frac{1}{5}$. Find out how much Marcus can deduct from the price of the jacket.

b. What price will Marcus pay for the jacket?

c. Copy the model below. Complete it by placing numerical values on top and the corresponding fractional parts below.

$0	?	$48	?	?	$120
0	$\frac{1}{5}$	?	?	$\frac{4}{5}$	1

d. Explain how this model shows proportional relationships.

SALE PRICE 50% OFF

59. One day the U.S. dollar was worth approximately 100 yen. An exchange of 2500 yen was made that day. What was the value of the exchange in dollars?

Ⓐ $25   Ⓑ $400   Ⓒ $2500   Ⓓ $40,000

60. Brett walks at a speed of 4 miles per hour. He walks for 20 minutes in a straight line at this rate. Approximately what distance does Brett walk?

Ⓕ 0.06 miles   Ⓖ 1.3 miles   Ⓗ 5 miles   Ⓙ 80 miles

61. A shampoo company conducted a survey and found that 3 out of 8 people use their brand of shampoo. Which proportion could be used to find the expected number of users n in a city of 75,000 people?

Ⓐ $\dfrac{3}{8} = \dfrac{75,000}{n}$ Ⓑ $\dfrac{3}{75,000} = \dfrac{n}{8}$ Ⓒ $\dfrac{8}{3} = \dfrac{n}{75,000}$ Ⓓ $\dfrac{3}{8} = \dfrac{n}{75,000}$

62. A statue is 3 feet tall. The display case for a model of the statue can fit a model that is no more than 9 inches tall. Which of the scales below allows for the tallest model of the statue that will fit in the display case?

Ⓕ 2:1   Ⓖ 1:1   Ⓗ 1:3   Ⓙ 1:4

CHALLENGE AND EXTEND

63. Geometry Complementary angles are two angles whose measures add up to 90°. The ratio of the measures of two complementary angles is 4:5. What are the measures of the angles?

64. A customer wanted 24 feet of rope. The clerk at the hardware store used what she thought was a yardstick to measure the rope, but the yardstick was actually 2 inches too short. How many inches were missing from the customer's piece of rope?

65. Population The population density of Jackson, Mississippi, is 672.2 people per square kilometer. What is the population density in people per square meter? Show that your answer is reasonable. (*Hint:* There are 1000 meters in 1 kilometer. How many square meters are in 1 square kilometer?)

1-9 Applications of Proportions

CC.9-12.N.Q.1 Use units as a way to understand problems and to guide the solution of multi-step problems; choose and interpret units consistently in formulas....* *Also* **CC.9-12.A.CED.1***, **CC.9-12.A.REI.3**

Objectives

Use proportions to solve problems involving geometric figures.

Use proportions and similar figures to measure objects indirectly.

Vocabulary

similar
corresponding sides
corresponding angles
indirect measurement
scale factor

Why learn this?

Proportions can be used to find the heights of tall objects, such as totem poles, that would otherwise be difficult to measure. (See Example 2.)

Similar figures have exactly the same shape but not necessarily the same size.

Corresponding sides of two figures are in the same relative position, and **corresponding angles** are in the same relative position. Two figures are similar if and only if the lengths of corresponding sides are proportional and all pairs of corresponding angles have equal measures.

Reading Math

- $\overline{AB}$ means segment AB. AB means the length of $\overline{AB}$.
- $\angle A$ means angle A. $m\angle A$ means the measure of angle A.

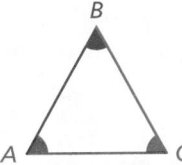
$$\frac{AB}{DE} = \frac{BC}{EF} = \frac{AC}{DF}$$
$$m\angle A = m\angle D$$
$$m\angle B = m\angle E$$
$$m\angle C = m\angle F$$

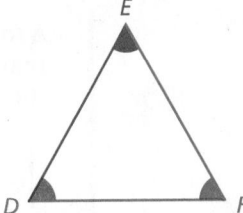

When stating that two figures are similar, use the symbol ~. For the triangles above, you can write $\triangle ABC \sim \triangle DEF$. Make sure corresponding vertices are in the same order. It would be incorrect to write $\triangle ABC \sim \triangle EFD$.

You can use proportions to find missing lengths in similar figures.

EXAMPLE 1 **Finding Missing Measures in Similar Figures**

Find the value of x in each diagram.

A $\triangle RST \sim \triangle BCD$

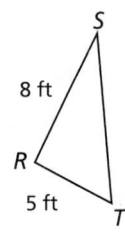
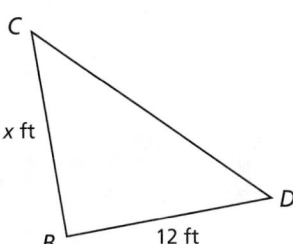

R corresponds to B, S corresponds to C, and T corresponds to D.

$$\frac{5}{12} = \frac{8}{x}$$

$$\frac{RT}{BD} = \frac{RS}{BC}$$

Use cross products.

$$5x = 96$$

Since x is multiplied by 5, divide both sides by 5 to undo the multiplication.

$$\frac{5x}{5} = \frac{96}{5}$$

$$x = 19.2$$

The length of $\overline{BC}$ is 19.2 ft.

Find the value of _x_ in each diagram.

  FGHJKL ~ MNPQRS

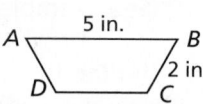

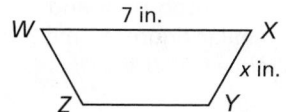

$$\frac{6}{4} = \frac{x}{2}$$ $\frac{NP}{GH} = \frac{RQ}{KJ}$

$4x = 12$ *Use cross products.*

$\frac{4x}{4} = \frac{12}{4}$ *Since x is multiplied by 4, divide both sides by 4 to*

$x = 3$ *undo the multiplication.*

The length of $\overline{QR}$ is 3 cm.

CHECK IT OUT! **1.** Find the value of _x_ in the diagram if *ABCD ~ WXYZ*.

A 5 in. B   W 7 in. X
2 in. x in.
D C   Z Y

You can solve a proportion involving similar triangles to find a length that is not easily measured. This method of measurement is called **indirect measurement**. If two objects form right angles with the ground, you can apply indirect measurement using their shadows.

EXAMPLE 2 *Measurement Application*

A totem pole casts a shadow 45 feet long at the same time that a 6-foot-tall man casts a shadow that is 3 feet long. Write and solve a proportion to find the height of the totem pole.

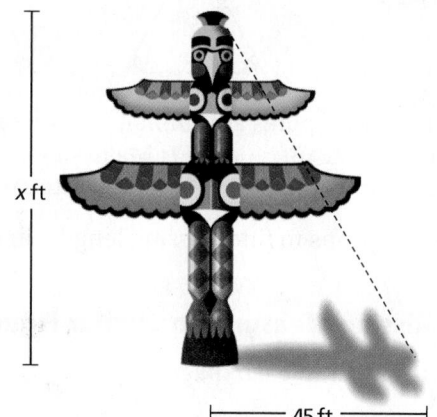

x ft

⊢—— 45 ft ——⊣

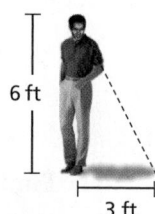

6 ft

3 ft

Both the man and the totem pole form right angles with the ground, and their shadows are cast at the same angle. You can form two similar right triangles.

$$\frac{6}{x} = \frac{3}{45}$$

$3x = 270$

$\frac{3x}{3} = \frac{270}{3}$

$x = 90$

$\dfrac{\text{man's height}}{\text{pole's height}} = \dfrac{\text{man's shadow}}{\text{pole's shadow}}$

Use cross products. Since x is multiplied by 3, divide both sides by 3 to undo the multiplication.

The totem pole is 90 feet tall.

CHECK IT OUT! **2a.** A forest ranger who is 150 cm tall casts a shadow 45 cm long. At the same time, a nearby tree casts a shadow 195 cm long. Write and solve a proportion to find the height of the tree.

2b. A woman who is 5.5 feet tall casts a shadow 3.5 feet long. At the same time, a building casts a shadow 28 feet long. Write and solve a proportion to find the height of the building.

If every dimension of a figure is multiplied by the same number, the result is a similar figure. The multiplier is called a **scale factor** .

EXAMPLE 3 **Changing Dimensions**

A Every dimension of a 2-by-4-inch rectangle is multiplied by 1.5 to form a similar rectangle. How is the ratio of the perimeters related to the ratio of corresponding sides? How is the ratio of the areas related to the ratio of corresponding sides?

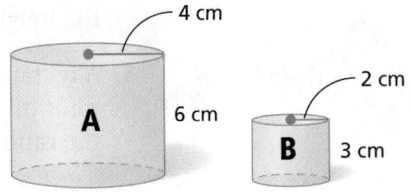

	Rectangle A	Rectangle B
$P = 2\ell + 2w$	$2(2) + 2(4) = 12$	$2(6) + 2(3) = 18$
$A = \ell w$	$4(2) = 8$	$6(3) = 18$

Sides: $\dfrac{4}{6} = \dfrac{2}{3}$ Perimeters: $\dfrac{12}{18} = \dfrac{2}{3}$ Areas: $\dfrac{8}{18} = \dfrac{4}{9} = \left(\dfrac{2}{3}\right)^2$

The ratio of the perimeters is equal to the ratio of corresponding sides. The ratio of the areas is the square of the ratio of corresponding sides.

Helpful Hint

A scale factor between 0 and 1 reduces a figure. A scale factor greater than 1 enlarges it.

B Every dimension of a cylinder with radius 4 cm and height 6 cm is multiplied by $\frac{1}{2}$ to form a similar cylinder. How is the ratio of the volumes related to the ratio of corresponding dimensions?

	Cylinder A	Cylinder B
$V = \pi r^2 h$	$\pi(4)^2(6) = 96\pi$	$\pi(2)^2(3) = 12\pi$

Radii: $\dfrac{4}{2} = \dfrac{2}{1} = 2$ Heights: $\dfrac{6}{3} = \dfrac{2}{1} = 2$ Volumes: $\dfrac{96\pi}{12\pi} = \dfrac{8}{1} = 8 = 2^3$

The ratio of the volumes is the cube of the ratio of corresponding dimensions.

CHECK IT OUT!

3. A rectangle has width 12 inches and length 3 inches. Every dimension of the rectangle is multiplied by $\frac{1}{3}$ to form a similar rectangle. How is the ratio of the perimeters related to the ratio of the corresponding sides?

THINK AND DISCUSS

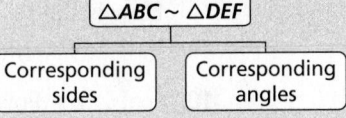

1. Name some pairs of real-world items that appear to be similar figures.

2. GET ORGANIZED Copy and complete the graphic organizer. In the top box, sketch and label two similar triangles. Then list the corresponding sides and angles in the bottom boxes.

GUIDED PRACTICE

1. Vocabulary What does it mean for two figures to be *similar*?

SEE EXAMPLE **1** **Find the value of *x* in each diagram.**

2. $\triangle ABC \sim \triangle DEF$

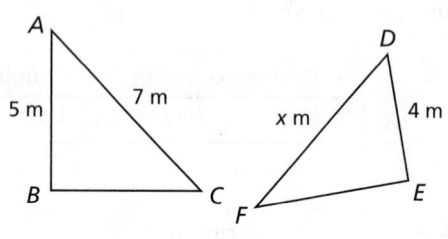

3. $RSTV \sim WXYZ$

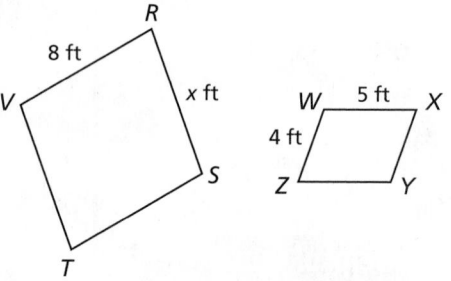

SEE EXAMPLE **2** **4.** Roger is 5 feet tall and casts a shadow 3.5 feet long. At the same time, the flagpole outside his school casts a shadow 14 feet long. Write and solve a proportion to find the height of the flagpole.

SEE EXAMPLE **3** **5.** A rectangle has length 12 feet and width 8 feet. Every dimension of the rectangle is multiplied by $\frac{3}{4}$ to form a similar rectangle. How is the ratio of the areas related to the ratio of corresponding sides?

PRACTICE AND PROBLEM SOLVING

Independent Practice

For Exercises	See Example
6–7	1
8	2
9	3

Extra Practice
See Extra Practice for more Skills Practice and Applications Practice exercises.

Find the value of *x* in each diagram.

6. $\triangle LMN \sim \triangle RST$

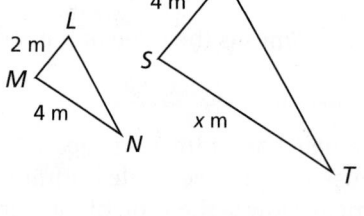

7. prism $A \sim$ prism B

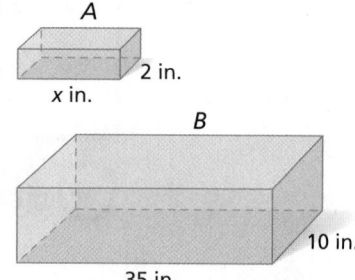

8. Write and solve a proportion to find the height of the taller tree in the diagram at right.

9. A triangle has side lengths of 5 inches, 12 inches, and 15 inches. Every dimension is multiplied by $\frac{1}{5}$ to form a new triangle. How is the ratio of the perimeters related to the ratio of corresponding sides?

10. Hobbies For a baby shower gift, Heather crocheted a baby blanket whose length was $2\frac{1}{2}$ feet and whose width was 2 feet. She plans to crochet a proportionally larger similar blanket for the baby's mother. If she wants the length of the mother's blanket to be $6\frac{1}{4}$ feet, what should the width be? Show that your answer is reasonable.

11. **Real Estate** Refer to the home builder's advertisement. The family rooms in both models are rectangular. How much carpeting is needed to carpet the family room in the Weston model?

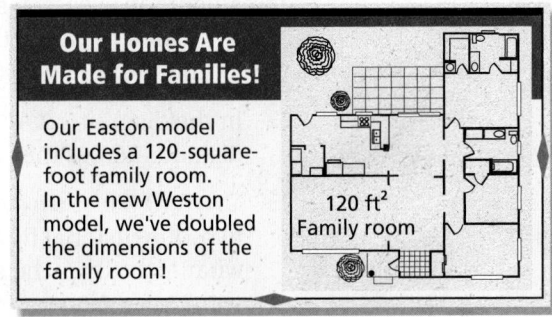

Our Homes Are Made for Families!

Our Easton model includes a 120-square-foot family room. In the new Weston model, we've doubled the dimensions of the family room!

120 ft² Family room

12. A rectangle has an area of 16 ft². Every dimension is multiplied by a scale factor, and the new rectangle has an area of 64 ft². What was the scale factor?

13. A cone has a volume of 98π cm³. Every dimension is multiplied by a scale factor, and the new cone has a volume of 6272π cm³. What was the scale factor?

Find the value of x in each diagram.

14. $FGHJK \sim MNPQR$

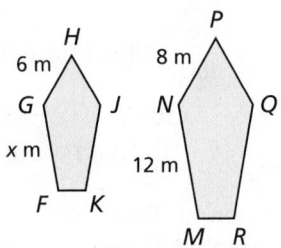

15. cylinder $A \sim$ cylinder B

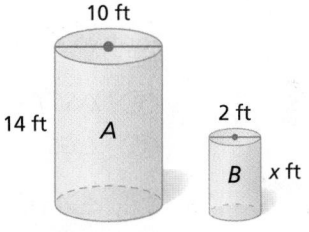

16. $\triangle BCD \sim \triangle FGD$

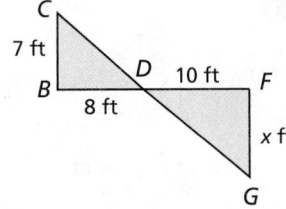

17. $\triangle RST \sim \triangle QSV$

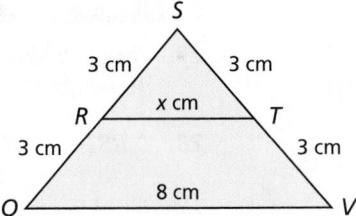

18. A tower casts a 450 ft shadow at the same time that a 4 ft child casts a 6 ft shadow. Write and solve a proportion to find the height of the tower.

19. **Write About It** At Pizza Palace, a pizza with a diameter of 8 inches costs $6.00. The restaurant manager says that a 16-inch pizza should be priced at $12.00 because it is twice as large. Do you agree? Explain why or why not.

MULTI-STEP TEST PREP

20. Another common application of proportion is *percents*. A percent is a ratio of a number to 100. For example, $80\% = \frac{80}{100}$.

   a. Write 12%, 18%, 25%, 67%, and 98% as ratios.

   b. Percents can also be written as decimals. Write each of your ratios from part **a** as a decimal.

   c. What do you notice about a percent and its decimal equivalent?

21. A lighthouse casts a shadow that is 36 meters long. At the same time, a person who is 1.5 meters tall casts a shadow that is 4.5 meters long. Write and solve a proportion to find the height of the lighthouse.

22. In the diagram, $\triangle ABC \sim \triangle DEC$. What is the distance across the river from A to B?

23. Critical Thinking If every dimension of a two-dimensional figure is multiplied by k, by what quantity is the area multiplied?

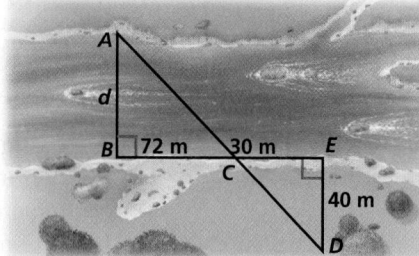

24. A beach ball holds 800 cubic inches of air. Another beach ball has a radius that is half that of the larger ball. How much air does the smaller ball hold?

- (A) 400 cubic inches
- (C) 100 cubic inches
- (B) 200 cubic inches
- (D) 80 cubic inches

25. For two similar triangles, $\dfrac{SG}{MW} = \dfrac{GT}{WR} = \dfrac{TS}{RM}$. Which statement below is NOT correct?

- (F) $\triangle SGT \sim \triangle MWR$
- (H) $\triangle TGS \sim \triangle RWM$
- (G) $\triangle GST \sim \triangle MRW$
- (J) $\triangle GTS \sim \triangle WRM$

26. Gridded Response A rectangle has length 5 centimeters and width 3 centimeters. A similar rectangle has length 7.25 centimeters. What is the width in centimeters of this rectangle?

CHALLENGE AND EXTEND

27. Find the values of w, x, and y given that $\triangle ABC \sim \triangle DEF \sim \triangle GHJ$.

28. $\triangle RST \sim \triangle VWX$ and $\dfrac{RT}{VX} = b$.

What is $\dfrac{\text{area of } \triangle RST}{\text{area of } \triangle VWX}$?

29. Multi-Step Rectangles A and B are similar. The area of A is 30.195 cm². The length of B is 6.1 cm. Each dimension of B is $\frac{2}{3}$ the corresponding dimension of A. What is the perimeter of B?

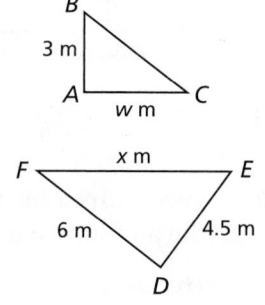

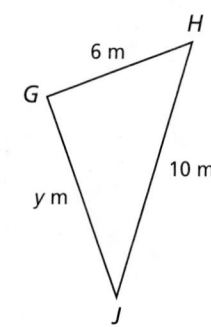

1-10 Precision and Accuracy

COMMON CORE

CC.9-12.N.Q.3 Choose a level of accuracy appropriate to limitations on measurement when reporting quantities.*
Also **CC.9-12.N.Q.2***

Objectives
Analyze and compare measurements for precision and accuracy.

Choose an appropriate level of accuracy when reporting measurements.

Vocabulary
precision
accuracy
tolerance

Who uses this?

Chemists must understand precision and accuracy when weighing or mixing specific amounts of chemicals. (See Example 2.)

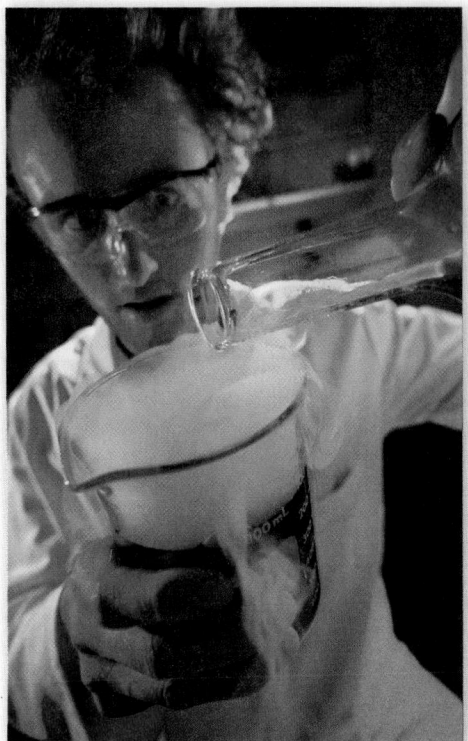

When you measure an object, you must use an instrument that will give an appropriate measurement. A scale to measure the mass of a person may show mass to the nearest kilogram. A scale to measure chemicals in a lab may show mass to the nearest milligram.

Precision is the level of detail in a measurement and is determined by the smallest unit or fraction of a unit that you can reasonably measure. Sometimes, the instrument determines the precision of a measurement. At other times, measurements are rounded to a specified precision.

A scale that shows the mass of an object to the nearest milligram is more precise than a scale that shows the mass of an object to the nearest kilogram, because a milligram is a smaller unit of measure than a kilogram. Likewise, a scale that shows the mass of an object as 24.23 grams is more precise than a scale that shows the mass of the same object as 24.2 grams.

EXAMPLE 1 **Comparing Precision of Measurements**

Choose the more precise measurement in each pair.

A **3.4 kg; 3421 g**

| 3.4 kg | *Nearest tenth of a kilogram* |
| 3421 g | *Nearest gram* |

A gram is smaller than a tenth of a kilogram, so 3421 g is more precise.

B **3.4 cm; 3.43 cm**

| 3.4 cm | *Nearest tenth of a centimeter* |
| 3.43 cm | *Nearest hundredth of a centimeter* |

A hundredth of a centimeter is smaller than a tenth of a centimeter, so 3.43 cm is more precise.

C **3 ft; 36 in.**

| 3 ft | *Nearest foot* |
| 36 in. | *Nearest inch* |

An inch is smaller than a foot, so 36 in. is more precise.

 **Choose the more precise measurement in each pair.**

1a. 2 lb; 17 oz   **1b.** 7.85 m; 7.8 m   **1c.** 6 kg; 6000 g

A precise measurement is only useful if the measurement is also *accurate*. The **accuracy** of a measurement is the closeness of a measured value to the actual or true value. Two measurement tools may measure to the same precision, but not have the same accuracy. Similarly, using a more precise measuring instrument will not necessarily give a more accurate measurement.

EXAMPLE 2 **Comparing Precision and Accuracy**

Sam is a technician in a pharmaceutical lab. Each week, she must test the scales in the lab to make sure they are accurate. She uses a standard mass that is *exactly* 5.000 grams and gets the following results:

Scale 1 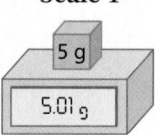   Scale 2 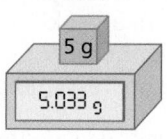   Scale 3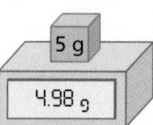

a. Which scale is the most precise?

Scales 1 and 3 measure to the nearest hundredth of a gram.

Scale 2 measures to the nearest thousandth of a gram.

Because a thousandth of a gram is smaller than a hundredth of a gram, Scale 2 is the most precise.

b. Which scale is the most accurate?

For each scale, find the absolute value of the difference of the standard mass and the scale reading.

Scale 1: $|5.000 - 5.01| = 0.01$

Scale 2: $|5.000 - 5.033| = 0.033$

Scale 3: $|5.000 - 4.98| = 0.02$

Because $0.01 < 0.02 < 0.033$, Scale 1 is the most accurate.

 **2.** A standard mass of 16 ounces is used to test three postal scales. The results are shown below.

Scale A   Scale B   Scale C

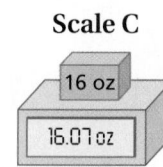

a. Which scale is the most precise?

b. Which scale is the most accurate?

When you measure a group of objects that are expected to be similar, you may find that there are variations from the expected value. **Tolerance** describes the amount by which a measurement is permitted to vary from a specified value. Tolerance is often expressed as a range of values, such as 5 mm ± 0.3 mm, which is equivalent to 4.7 mm–5.3 mm.

EXAMPLE 3 Using a Specified Tolerance

Acme Nuts & Bolts is manufacturing a bolt to use in an airplane. The length of the bolt should be 50 mm, with a tolerance of 0.5 mm (50 mm ± 0.5 mm). A batch of bolts had the lengths shown in the table. Do all of the bolts measure within the specified tolerance? If not, which bolt(s) are not within the specified tolerance?

Bolt	Length (mm)
A	49.8
B	50.4
C	49.5
D	50.1
E	49.4
F	50.0

$50 - 0.5 = 49.5$ *50 mm ± 0.5 mm means that the*
$50 + 0.5 = 50.5$ *bolts must be between 49.5 and 50.5 mm.*

Bolt E measures 49.4 mm, so it is not within the specified tolerance.

CHECK IT OUT!

3. A lacrosse ball must weigh 5.25 oz ± 0.25 oz. The weights of the lacrosse balls in one box are given in the table. Do all of the lacrosse balls weigh within the specified tolerance? If not, which lacrosse ball(s) are not within the specified tolerance?

Ball	Weight (oz)
A	5.41
B	5.23
C	5.54
D	5.33
E	5.21

Tolerance can also be expressed as a percent. A measurement written as 5 mm ± 5% means that the measurement can be greater or less than 5 mm by an amount equal to 5% of 5 mm, or 0.25 mm. Therefore, the measurement can have a range of 4.75 mm–5.25 mm.

EXAMPLE 4 Using Tolerance Expressed as a Percent

Write the possible range of each measurement. Round to the nearest hundredth if necessary.

A 50 kg ± 2%
$50(0.02) = 1$ *Find 2% of 50.*
50 kg ± 1 kg   *Write the measurement and tolerance.*
49 kg–51 kg   *Write the measurement as a range.*

B 125 lb ± 1.5%
$125(0.015) = 1.875$ *Find 1.5% of 125.*
125 lb ± 1.88 lb   *Write the measurement and tolerance. Round to the nearest hundredth.*
123.12 lb–126.88 lb   *Write the measurement as a range.*

C 45 mm ± 0.3%
$45(0.003) = 0.135$ *Find 0.3% of 45.*
45 mm ± 0.14 mm   *Write the measurement and tolerance. Round to the nearest hundredth.*
44.86 mm–45.14 mm *Write the measurement as a range.*

CHECK IT OUT!

Write the possible range of each measurement. Round to the nearest hundredth if necessary.

4a. 4.1 in. ± 5%   **4b.** 475 m ± 2.5%   **4c.** 85 mg ± 0.5%

THINK AND DISCUSS

1. Explain the difference between precision and accuracy.

2. Describe a situation where the expected size of an object might be specified as 10 in. ± 0.5 in.

3. **GET ORGANIZED** Copy and complete the graphic organizer. In each box, write an example of when that characteristic of measurement would be important.

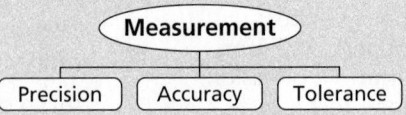

Measurement
Precision | Accuracy | Tolerance

1-10 Exercises

GUIDED PRACTICE

Vocabulary Apply the vocabulary from this lesson to answer each question.

1. A ruler that can measure length to a smaller unit than another ruler is said to be more ____?____. (*precise* or *acurate*)

2. A scale that gives a mass closer to the true mass of an object than another scale of the exact same type is said to be more ____?____. (*precise* or *accurate*)

SEE EXAMPLE 1

Choose the more precise measurement in each pair.

3. 4 mL; 4.3 mL
4. 7 m; 6.8 m
5. 2.4 mg; 2.37 mg
6. 7 lb; 6.5 lb
7. 47 ft; 47.3 ft
8. 14 oz; 13.9 oz

SEE EXAMPLE 2

9. Sarah is comparing five different scales using a standard mass that is exactly 10 grams. Her results are shown below.

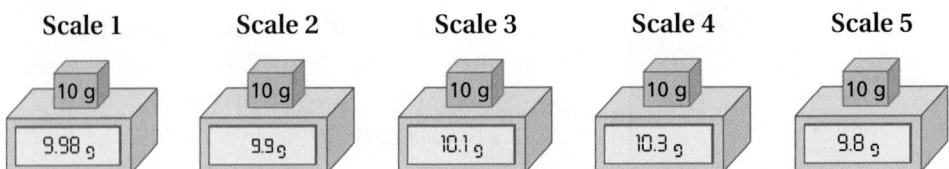

Scale 1   Scale 2   Scale 3   Scale 4   Scale 5
10 g   10 g   10 g   10 g   10 g
9.98 g   9.9 g   10.1 g   10.3 g   9.8 g

a. Which scale is the most precise?

b. Which scale is the most accurate?

10. A group of students compare the odometer readings on their bicycle computers after riding their bikes on a one-mile track. Their odometer readings are shown in the table. Whose odometer is the most precise? Whose is the most accurate?

Student	Distance (mi)
Jen	1.01
Bill	0.97
Rasheed	0.989
Sasha	1.02

11. Sports A basketball for men's college games must have a mass of 595.5 ± 28.5 grams. Several basketballs are tested. Their masses are shown in the table. Do all of the basketballs fall within the specified tolerance? If not, which basketball(s) do not fall within the specified tolerance?

Basketball	1	2	3	4	5
Mass (g)	617.5	567.5	608	624.5	593.5

12. Sports A basketball for men's college games must bounce 51.5 ± 2.5 in. when dropped from a height of 6 feet. The bounce heights of several basketballs when dropped from a height of 6 feet are shown in the graph. Do all of the basketballs fall within the specified tolerance? If not, which basketball(s) do not have a bounce height within the specified tolerance?

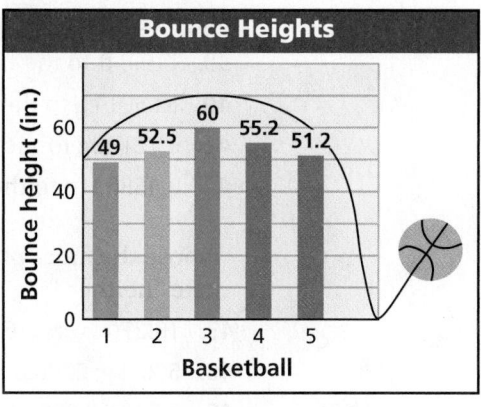

Write the possible range of each measurement. Round to the nearest hundredth if necessary.

13. 50 lb ± 2%

14. 100 yd ± 0.5%

15. 25 cm ± 4%

16. 400 L ± 6%

17. 250 mm ± 4%

18. 70 kg ± 3%

PRACTICE AND PROBLEM SOLVING

Choose the more precise measurement in each pair.

For Exercises	See Example
19–26	1
27	2
28	3
29–36	4

Independent Practice

19. 4.33 g; 4337 mg   **20.** 11 ft; 122 in.   **21.** 6 tons; 11,000 lb   **22.** 3 c; 2 pt

23. 67 mm; 6.83 cm   **24.** 4.5 km; 3 mi   **25.** 12 cm; 0.0127 m   **26.** 7.23 lb; 115 oz

27. Maria is trying to beat the school record for the 400-meter dash. Her friends timed her using the stopwatch functions in their cell phones. The official track timer, which is highly accurate, reported that she ran the race in 51.12 seconds. Her friends recorded the times shown in the table.

Name	Time (s)
Lucy	51.1
Juan	52.23
Chandra	51.769
Pei	50.97

  a. Who recorded the most precise time?

  b. Who recorded the most accurate time?

28. Anael cut several boards to build a deck. The boards must be 100 in. ± 0.25 in. Her measurements of the boards after cutting them are shown in the graph. Which boards, if any, can she not use?

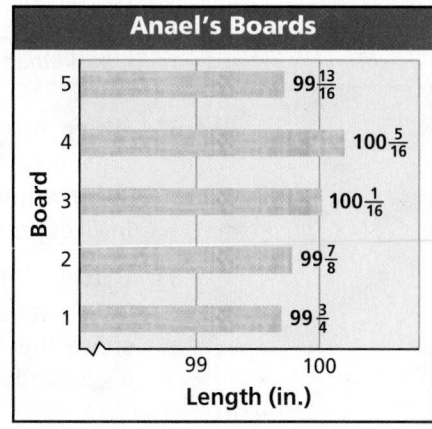

Write the possible range of each measurement. Round to the nearest hundredth if necessary.

29. 45 lb ± 2%   **30.** 3 m ± 5%   **31.** 37 °C ± 1.5%   **32.** 750 kg ± 3%

33. 30 ft ± 4%   **34.** 550 mL ± 8%   **35.** 0.2 cm ± 5%   **36.** 0.25 kg ± 10%

Round each measurement to the specified precision.

37. 5456.3 mi to the nearest mile

38. 3.627 m to the nearest hundredth of a meter

39. 119.8 ft to the nearest ten feet

40. 62.301 cg to the nearest tenth of a centigram

41. 5,721 mg to the nearest kilogram

42. 0.4586 km to the nearest meter

Choose the more precise measurement in each pair. If they are equally precise, write "neither."

43. 16.270 liters; 16,453.2 mL   **44.** 437 cm; 437 mm   **45.** 0.265 cm; 260 mm

46. 5.20 kg; 5200.0 mg   **47.** 55 yd; 165 ft   **48.** 67 min; 1.1 h

49. 33 mg; 0.033 g   **50.** 42.7 cm; 427.0 mm   **51.** 475.0 mL; 0.475 L

Technology

Rewrite each specified tolerance as a percent.

52. 100 m ± 2 m   **53.** 50 g ± 2 g   **54.** 240 ft ± 12 ft   **55.** 750 kg ± 15 kg

56. 25 in. ± 0.25 in.   **57.** 425 lb ± 8.5 lb   **58.** 60 oz ± 1.5 oz   **59.** 175 km ± 5.25 km

60. **Technology** Postcards that do not fit in the U.S. Postal Service's automatic sorting machines require additional postage for mailing. The machine will accept postcards whose length is between 5 and 6 inches and whose width is between $3\frac{1}{2}$ and $4\frac{1}{4}$ inches. Write these requirements as tolerances.

61. Sports For women's collegiate competition, a basketball's circumference, mass, and bounce height must fall within given tolerance levels of regulation measurements. The table shows these tolerance levels as well as measurements taken on five different basketballs. Which basketball meets all of the specified tolerances?

Automated equipment plays a large role in processing the approximately 584 million pieces of mail that the U.S. Postal Service delivers each day. Machines sort mail, cancel stamps, scan barcodes, and even "read" handwritten addresses.

Source: Postal Facts 2010, USPS

	Circumference (mm)	Mass (g)	Bounce Height (mm)
Tolerance	730.56 ± 6.5	538.5 ± 28.5	1358.5 ± 63.5
Basketball #1	729.8	509.3	1343.4
Basketball #2	723.5	529.8	1299.8
Basketball #3	734.2	542.6	1293.5
Basketball #4	725.5	528.0	1364.5
Basketball #5	740.0	555.9	1407.4

62. Write About It Linda wants to purchase a new sofa. Before buying the sofa, Linda must measure her doorway to make sure that the sofa will fit through the door. The sofa manufacturer says that the sofa measures 39 inches from front to back. What level of precision would you recommend Linda measure to? Explain.

63. Critical Thinking Yusuf measured a board and determined that it was 125.5 centimeters long. He then cut the board into eight equal pieces. His calculator shows that 125.5 ÷ 8 = 15.6875. Is it reasonable for Yusuf to record the length of the 8 smaller boards as 15.6875 centimeters? Explain why or why not.

64. The mass of a crystal is 0.9728 grams. What is the mass of the crystal to the nearest milligram?

(A) 1 milligram

(B) 9.73 milligrams

(C) 973 milligrams

(D) 972.8 milligrams

65. A piece used to assemble a computer must be 1.4 millimeters ± 0.02 millimeters in diameter. Which of the following measurements does NOT meet the specified tolerance?

(F) 1.420 millimeters

(G) 1.402 millimeters

(H) 1.382 millimeters

(J) 1.378 millimeters

66. Which measurement is most precise?

(A) 475.3 milliliters

(B) 475 milliliters

(C) 0.475 liter

(D) 0.5 liter

CHALLENGE AND EXTEND

Percent accuracy or *percent error* indicates how far a measurement is from the true value. An instrument that has 1.5% accuracy means that the measured value is within 1.5% of the true value.

67. A scale shows that a standard mass of exactly 5.000 grams has a mass of 5.002 grams. What is the percent accuracy of the scale?

68. A car odometer is accurate to within 0.5%. The odometer records the distance from Charlotte, North Carolina, to Orlando, Florida, as 525.3 miles. What is the range of possible values for the actual mileage?

69. Astronomy A scientist measures the distance to the moon using a method that has a percent error of 0.02%. He finds that the distance at a particular time is 384,403 kilometers. What is the range of possible values for the actual distance?

MULTI-STEP TEST PREP

MATHEMATICAL PRACTICES

Make sense of problems and persevere in solving them.

Percentages

Bargain Hunters Maria is on her high school's lacrosse team, and her friend Paula is on the softball team. The girls notice an advertisement in the newspaper for a clearance sale at their favorite sporting goods store. The ad shows an additional $\frac{1}{4}$ off the already reduced prices of 60% off. Maria and Paula head to the store to shop for bargains.

1. Maria finds a lacrosse stick with a regular price of $65. Find the sale price of the lacrosse stick prior to the additional $\frac{1}{4}$ off.

2. Find the sale price of Maria's lacrosse stick with the additional $\frac{1}{4}$ off.

3. Paula says that with the extra $\frac{1}{4}$ off, the total discount is 85% off. Maria thinks the discount is less than that. Who is correct? Explain your reasoning.

4. Paula finds a softball glove with a price tag that is not readable. The sales clerk scans the bar code and says the sale price, including the extra $\frac{1}{4}$ off, is $16.50. What was the original price of the softball glove? Show your reasoning.

5. Sales tax is 7.8%. Find the total amount that the girls will pay for the lacrosse stick and the softball glove together, including tax.

READY TO GO ON?

Quiz for Lessons 1-8 Through 1-10

☑ **1-8 Rates, Ratios, and Proportions**

1. Last week, the ratio of laptops to desktops sold at a computer store was 2:3. Eighteen desktop models were sold. How many laptop models were sold?

2. Anita read 150 pages in 5 hours. What is her reading rate in pages per minute?

3. Twenty-six crackers contain 156 Calories. Find the unit rate in Calories per cracker.

4. A store developed 1024 photographs in 8 hours. Find the unit rate in photographs per hour.

Solve each proportion.

5. $\dfrac{-18}{n} = \dfrac{9}{2}$

6. $\dfrac{d}{5} = \dfrac{2}{4}$

7. $\dfrac{4}{12} = \dfrac{r+2}{16}$

8. $\dfrac{-3}{7} = \dfrac{6}{x+6}$

☑ **1-9 Applications of Proportions**

Find the value of n in each diagram.

9. $\triangle RST \sim \triangle XYZ$

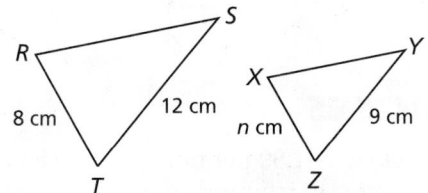

10. $ABCD \sim FGHJ$

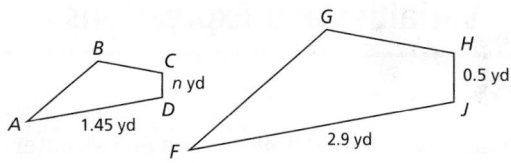

☑ **1-10 Precision and Accuracy**

Choose the more precise measurement in each pair.

11. 2.5 ft; 2 ft

12. 1 yd; 3 ft

13. 5910 g; 5.9 kg

14. 16 oz; 16.0 oz

Write the possible range of each measurement. Round to the nearest hundredth if necessary.

15. 300 m ± 1%

16. 150 lb ± 6%

17. 60 L ± 0.5%

18. 220 kg ± 1.5%

Study Guide: Review

Vocabulary

accuracy	formula	scale drawing
algebraic expression	identity	scale factor
constant	indirect measurement	scale model
conversion factor	literal equation	similar
corresponding angles	numerical expression	solution of an equation
corresponding sides	precision	tolerance
cross products	proportion	unit rate
dimensional analysis	rate	variable
equation	ratio	
evaluate	scale	

Complete the sentences below with vocabulary words from the list above.

1. A formula is a type of a(n) ____?____ .

2. A(n) ____?____ is used to compare two quantities by division.

3. A(n) ____?____ is a value that does not change.

1-1 Variables and Expressions

EXAMPLES

- Barbara has saved d dollars for a $65 sweater. Write an expression for the amount of money she still needs to buy the sweater.

  $65 - d$ *Think: d dollars less than the price of the sweater.*

- Evaluate $b - a$ for $a = 7$ and $b = 15$.

  $b - a = 15 - 7$ *Substitute the values for*
  $= 8$ *the variables.*

EXERCISES

4. Grapes cost $1.99 per pound. Write an expression for the cost of g pounds of grapes.

5. Today's temperature is 3 degrees warmer than yesterday's temperature t. Write an expression for today's temperature.

Evaluate each expression for $p = 5$ and $q = 1$.

6. qp **7.** $p \div q$ **8.** $q + p$

9. Each member of the art club will make the same number of posters to advertise their club. They will make 150 posters total. Write an expression for how many posters each member will make if there are m members. Find how many posters each member will make if there are 5, 6, and 10 members.

1-2 Solving Equations by Adding or Subtracting

EXAMPLES

Solve each equation. Check your answer.

■ $x - 12 = -8.3$

$\quad \dfrac{+ 12 \quad + 12}{x \quad = \quad 3.7}$

■ $-7.8 = 5 + t$

$\quad \dfrac{-5 \quad -5}{-12.8 = \quad t}$

Check $\dfrac{x - 12 = -8.3}{\begin{array}{c|c} 3.7 - 12 & -8.3 \\ -8.3 & -8.3 \checkmark \end{array}}$

Check $\dfrac{-7.8 = 5 + t}{\begin{array}{c|c} -7.8 & 5 + (-12.8) \\ -7.8 & -7.8 \checkmark \end{array}}$

EXERCISES

Solve each equation. Check your answer.

10. $b - 16 = 20$ **11.** $4 + x = 2$

12. $9 + a = -12$ **13.** $-7 + y = 11$

14. $z - \dfrac{1}{4} = \dfrac{7}{8}$ **15.** $w + \dfrac{2}{3} = 3$

16. Robin needs 108 signatures for her petition. So far, she has 27. Write and solve an equation to determine how many more signatures she needs.

1-3 Solving Equations by Multiplying or Dividing

EXAMPLES

Solve each equation.

■ $\dfrac{z}{2.4} = 12$

$\quad (2.4)\dfrac{z}{2.4} = (2.4)\,12$

$\quad\quad z = 28.8$

■ $-8x = 148$

$\quad \dfrac{-8x}{-8} = \dfrac{148}{-8}$

$\quad\quad x = -18.5$

EXERCISES

Solve each equation. Check your answer.

17. $35 = 5x$ **18.** $-3n = 10$

19. $-30 = \dfrac{n}{3}$ **20.** $\dfrac{x}{-5} = -2.6$

21. $5y = 0$ **22.** $-4.6r = 9.2$

1-4 Solving Two-Step and Multi-Step Equations

EXAMPLE

■ Solve $\dfrac{3x}{5} - \dfrac{x}{4} + \dfrac{1}{2} = \dfrac{6}{5}$.

$\dfrac{3x}{5} - \dfrac{x}{4} + \dfrac{1}{2} = \dfrac{6}{5}$

$20\left(\dfrac{3x}{5} - \dfrac{x}{4} + \dfrac{1}{2}\right) = 20\left(\dfrac{6}{5}\right)$ *Multiply by the LCD.*

$12x - 5x + 10 = 24$

$7x + 10 = 24$ *Combine like terms.*

$\quad \dfrac{-10 \quad\quad -10}{7x \quad\quad = \quad 14}$

$\dfrac{7x}{7} = \dfrac{14}{7}$

$x = 2$

EXERCISES

Solve each equation. Check your answer.

23. $4t - 13 = 57$ **24.** $5 - 2y = 15$

25. $\dfrac{k}{5} - 6 = 2$ **26.** $\dfrac{5}{6}f - \dfrac{3}{4}f + \dfrac{3}{4} = \dfrac{1}{2}$

27. $7x - 19x = 6$ **28.** $4 + 3a - 6 = 43$

29. If $8n + 22 = 70$, find the value of $3n$.

30. If $0 = 6n - 36$, find the value of $n - 5$.

31. The sum of the measures of two angles is 180°. One angle measures $3a$ and the other angle measures $2a - 25$ Find a. Then find the measure of each angle.

1-5 Solving Equations with Variables on Both Sides

EXAMPLE

■ Solve $x + 7 = 12 + 3x - 7x$.

$$x + 7 = 12 + 3x - 7x$$
$$x + 7 = 12 - 4x \qquad \textit{Combine like terms.}$$

$$\underline{+4x \qquad\qquad +4x}$$
$$5x + 7 = 12$$

$$\underline{-7 \quad -7}$$
$$5x \quad = 5$$

$$\frac{5x}{5} = \frac{5}{5}$$

$$x = 1$$

EXERCISES

Solve each equation. Check your answer.

32. $4x + 2 = 3x$ **33.** $-3r - 8 = -5r - 12$

34. $-a - 3 + 7 = 3a$ **35.** $-(x - 4) = 2x + 6$

36. $\frac{2}{3}n = 4n - \frac{10}{3}n - \frac{1}{2}$ **37.** $0.2(7 + 2t) = 0.4t + 1.4$

38. One photo shop charges $0.36 per print. Another photo shop charges $2.52 plus $0.08 per print. Juan finds that the cost of printing his photos is the same at either shop. How many photos does Juan have to print?

1-6 Solving for a Variable

EXAMPLE

■ Solve $A = P + Prt$ for r.

$$A = \quad P + Prt$$
$$\underline{-P \quad -P}$$
$$A - P = \qquad Prt$$

$$\frac{A - P}{Pt} = \frac{Prt}{Pt}$$

$$\frac{A - P}{Pt} = r$$

EXERCISES

Solve for the indicated variable.

39. $C = \dfrac{360}{n}$ for n **40.** $S = \dfrac{n}{2}(a + \ell)$ for a

41. The formula $a = \frac{d}{g}$ gives the average gas mileage a of a vehicle that uses g gallons of gas to travel d miles. Use the formula to find how many gallons of gas a vehicle with an average gas mileage of 20.2 miles per gallon will use to travel 75 miles. Round your answer to the nearest tenth.

1-7 Solving Absolute-Value Equations

EXAMPLES

■ Solve $3|y + 4| = 30$.

$$\frac{3|y + 4|}{3} = \frac{|30|}{3} \qquad \textit{Divide both sides by 3.}$$
$$|y + 4| = 10$$

Case 1

$$y + 4 = 10$$
$$\underline{-4 \quad -4}$$
$$y \quad = 6$$

Case 2

$$y + 4 = -10$$
$$\underline{-4 \qquad -4}$$
$$y \quad = -14$$

EXERCISES

Solve each equation. Check your answer.

42. $|x + 6| = 21$ **43.** $7|y - 5| = 14$

44. $3|y| + 4 = 31$ **45.** $12 = |x - 5.4|$

46. $|g + 6| + 12 = 14$ **47.** $|x| = \frac{5}{7}$

48. Jason is driving his car at 55 mi/h. He needs to keep his car within 5 mi/h of his current speed. Write and solve an absolute-value equation to find Jason's maximum and minimum speeds.

1-8 Rates, Ratios, and Proportions

■ The ratio of skateboarders to bikers in an extreme sports contest is 7 : 2. There are 91 skateboarders. How many bikers are there?

$$\dfrac{\text{skateboarders}}{\text{bikers}} \longrightarrow \dfrac{7}{2} \quad \textit{Write a proportion.}$$

$$\dfrac{7}{2} \diagup\!\!\!\!\diagdown \dfrac{91}{x} \qquad \textit{Let x be the number of bikers.}$$

$$7 \cdot x = 2 \cdot 91 \quad \textit{Use cross products.}$$

$$7x = 182$$

$$\dfrac{7x}{7} = \dfrac{182}{7} \qquad \textit{Solve for x.}$$

$$x = 26$$

There are 26 bikers.

49. A recipe for a casserole calls for 2 cups of rice. The recipe makes 6 servings of casserole. How many cups of rice will you need to make 10 servings of casserole?

Use dimensional analysis to convert each rate. Round your answer to the nearest hundredth if necessary.

50. 30 cm/s to m/h

51. 75 ft/s to mi/min

Solve each proportion. Check your answer.

52. $\dfrac{n}{8} = \dfrac{2}{10}$

53. $\dfrac{2}{9} = \dfrac{12}{x}$

54. $\dfrac{3}{k} = \dfrac{9}{15}$

55. $\dfrac{1}{3} = \dfrac{x}{x-6}$

1-9 Applications of Proportions

■ When Janelle stood next to the Washington Monument, she cast a 1.2-foot-long shadow, and the monument cast a 111-foot-long shadow. Janelle is 6 feet tall. How tall is the monument?

$$\dfrac{x}{111} = \dfrac{6}{1.2} \qquad \textit{Write a proportion.}$$

$$1.2x = 666 \qquad \textit{Use cross products.}$$

$$\dfrac{1.2x}{1.2} = \dfrac{666}{1.2} \qquad \textit{Solve for x.}$$

The monument is 555 feet tall.

56. Find the value of x in the diagram.

$$\triangle ABC \sim \triangle DEF$$

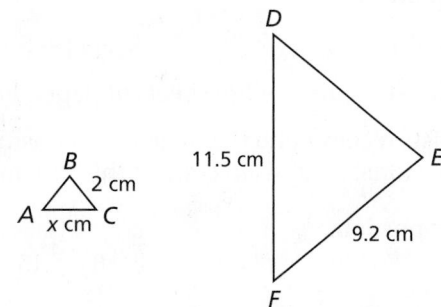

57. A tree casts a shadow that is 14 ft long at the same time that a nearby 2-foot-tall pole casts a shadow that is 1.75 ft long. How tall is the tree?

58. A circle has a radius of 9 inches. The radius is multiplied by $\frac{2}{3}$ to form a second circle. How is the ratio of the areas related to the ratio of the radii?

1-10 Precision and Accuracy

■ Choose the more precise measurement in the pair: 45.1 cm; 45.18 cm.

45.1 cm   *Nearest tenth of a centimeter*

45.18 cm   *Nearest hundredth of a centimeter*

A hundredth of a centimeter is smaller than a tenth of a centimeter, so 45.18 cm is more precise.

EXERCISES

Choose the more precise measurement in each pair.

59. 1 ft; 12 in.

60. 37 g; 37.0 g

61. 550 cm; 5.5 km

62. 1.5 L; 1 L

Write the possible range of each measurement. Round to the nearest hundredth if necessary.

63. 500 lb ± 4%

64. 20 oz ± 0.5%

65. 75 kg ± 3%

66. 1035 mm ± 10%

Evaluate each expression for $a = 2$, $b = 3$, and $c = 6$.

1. $c - a$ **2.** ab **3.** $c \div a$ **4.** $\dfrac{c}{b}$ **5.** $b - a$

6. Give two ways write $n - 5$ in words.

7. Nate runs 8 miles each week. Write an expression for the number of miles he runs in n weeks. Find the number of miles Nate runs in 5 weeks.

Solve each equation.

8. $y - 7 = 2$ **9.** $x + 12 = 19$ **10.** $-5 + z = 8$

11. $9x = 72$ **12.** $\dfrac{m}{-8} = -2.5$ **13.** $\dfrac{7}{8}a = 42$

14. $15 = 3 - 4x$ **15.** $\dfrac{2a}{3} + \dfrac{1}{5} = \dfrac{7}{6}$ **16.** $8 - (b - 2) = 11$

17. $-2x + 4 = 5 - 3x$ **18.** $3(q - 2) + 2 = 5q - 7 - 2q$ **19.** $5z = -3(z + 7)$

Solve for the indicated variable.

20. $r - 2s = 14$ for s **21.** $V = \dfrac{1}{3}bh$ for b **22.** $P = 2(\ell + w)$ for ℓ

Solve each equation.

23. $|x - 14| = 21$ **24.** $3|x| + 5 = 8$ **25.** $|2v| = 6$

26. Twenty-five students use 120 sheets of paper. Find the unit rate in sheets per student.

27. Nutritionists recommend that teenagers consume 1300 milligrams of calcium per day. Use dimensional analysis to convert this rate to grams per year.

Solve each proportion.

28. $\dfrac{5}{4} = \dfrac{x}{12}$ **29.** $\dfrac{8}{2z} = \dfrac{15}{60}$ **30.** $\dfrac{x + 10}{10} = \dfrac{18}{12}$

31. The scale on a map is 1 inch : 500 miles. If two cities are 875 miles apart, how far apart are they on the map?

Find the value of x in each diagram. Round your answer to the nearest tenth.

32. $\triangle EFG \sim \triangle RTS$

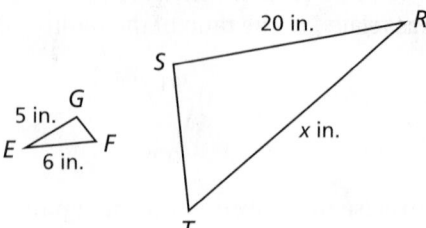

33. $HJKL \sim WXYZ$

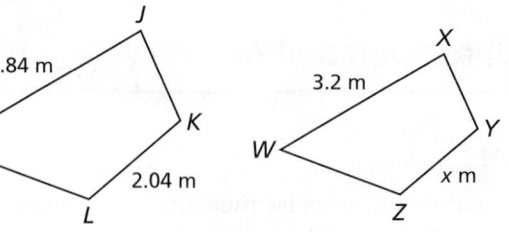

Choose the more precise measurement in each pair.

34. 6.5 oz; 6 oz   **35.** 16 oz; 1 lb   **36.** 3525 m; 3.5 km

Write the possible range of each measurement.

37. 25 ft $\pm$ 1%   **38.** 400 lb $\pm$ 4%   **39.** 250 cm $\pm$ 0.5%

COLLEGE ENTRANCE EXAM PRACTICE

FOCUS ON SAT*

The SAT is often used to predict academic success at the college level. SAT scores are used to compare the math and verbal reasoning skills of students from all over the world.

You may want to time yourself as you take this practice test. It should take you about 8 minutes to complete.

In each section of SAT questions, the easier questions are at the beginning of the section and harder questions come later. Answer as many of the easy questions as you can first, and then move on to the more challenging questions.

---

1. If $x - 3 = 4 - 2(x + 5)$, then $x = ?$

  (A) -3

  (B) -1

  (C) 1

  (D) $\dfrac{3}{2}$

  (E) $\dfrac{11}{3}$

---

2. A clothing store opens with 75 pairs of jeans on a sale table. By noon, 10 pairs have been sold. As of 2:00, another 8 pairs have been sold. A clerk then restocks with 12 pairs. Receipts show that 18 pairs of jeans were sold after 2:00. How many pairs of jeans are left at the end of the day?

  (A) 23

  (B) 27

  (C) 36

  (D) 51

  (E) 123

---

3. Which of the following is equal to -3^4?

  (A) 81

  (B) 12

  (C) -12

  (D) -64

  (E) -81

---

4. If Jack is three times as old as his sister Judy, which of the following expressions represents Jack's age if Judy is j years old?

  (A) $3 \div j$

  (B) $3j$

  (C) $j + 3$

  (D) $3 - j$

  (E) $\dfrac{1}{3}j$

---

5. If $\triangle ABC \sim \triangle DEF$, what is the length of $\overline{AC}$?

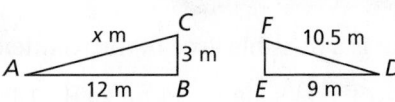

  (A) 2.6 meters

  (B) 3.5 meters

  (C) 7 meters

  (D) 14 meters

  (E) 15 meters

---

6. Which expression is equivalent to $8(6 + x)$?

  (A) $48x$

  (B) $8x + 14$

  (C) $8x + 48$

  (D) $x + 14$

  (E) $x + 48$

---

*SAT is a registered trademark of the College Board, which was not involved in the production of, and does not endorse, this product.

TEST TACKLER

Multiple Choice: Eliminate Answer Choices

You can answer some problems without doing many calculations. Use logic to eliminate answer choices and save time.

EXAMPLE 1

Which number is the square of 123,765?

(A) 15,317,775,225   (C) 15,317,775,230

(B) 15,317,775,233   (D) 15,317,775,227

Your calculator will not help you on this question. Due to rounding, any of the answer choices are possible.

But you can use this fact to eliminate three of the answer choices:

The square of any number ending in 5 is also a number ending in 5.

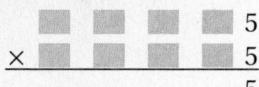

The only answer choice that ends in 5 is A, 15,317,775,225.

EXAMPLE 2

What is a possible area of the wooden triangle shown?

(F) 11 square feet   (H) 14 square feet

(G) 20 square feet   (J) 24 square feet

The triangle is inside a rectangle with an area of 7 × 4 = 28 square feet.

If the triangle had the same base and height as the rectangle, its area would be half the area of the rectangle, 14 square feet.

However, the triangle fits inside the rectangle, so its area must be less than 14 square feet.

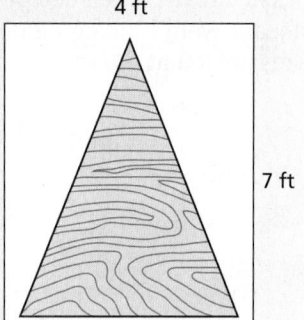

The only answer choice that is less than 14 square feet is F, 11 square feet.

Try to eliminate unreasonable answer choices. Some choices may be too great or too small, have incorrect units, or not be divisible by a necessary number.

Read each test item and answer the questions that follow.

Item A
The top speed of a three-toed sloth is 0.12 miles per hour. About how many feet can a sloth travel in an hour?

(A) 0.12 feet

(C) 2.27 feet

(B) 600 feet

(D) 7500 inches

1. Are there any answer choices you can eliminate immediately? If so, which choices and why?

2. Describe how you can use estimation to find the correct answer.

Item B
A city park is shaped like a triangle. The Liberty Street side of the park is 120 feet long, and the First Avenue side is 50 feet long.

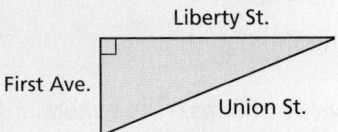

What is the approximate length of the side of the park that faces Union Street?

(F) 25 feet

(H) 65 feet

(G) 110 inches

(J) 130 feet

3. Can any of the answer choices be eliminated immediately? If so, which choices and why?

4. Are there any properties you can use to solve this problem? If so, what are they?

5. Describe how to find the correct answer without doing any calculations.

Item C
Approximately how long will the average 18-year-old have slept in his lifetime?

(A) 6 weeks

(C) 6 years

(B) 6 months

(D) 6 decades

6. Which answer choice can be eliminated immediately? Why?

7. Explain how to use mental math to solve this problem.

Item D
Sheila's paychecks for February and March were equal. If she worked every day during both months, for which month was her daily pay lower?

(F) February

(G) March

(H) Her daily pay did not change.

(J) Cannot be determined

8. What do you need to know to solve this problem?

9. Describe how you can find the correct answer.

Item E
Greg tripled the number of baseball cards he had last week. Which of these could be the number of cards Greg has now?

(A) 100

(C) 150

(B) 200

(D) 250

10. The number of cards that Greg has now must be divisible by what number? How can you tell if a number is divisible by this number?

11. Describe how to find the answer to this problem.

CUMULATIVE ASSESSMENT

Multiple Choice

1. What operation does $\Diamond$ represent if $x \Diamond 2.2 = 4.5$ when $x = 9.9$?

    A Addition

    B Subtraction

    C Multiplication

    D Division

2. Every dimension of cylinder A is multiplied by 4 to make cylinder B. What is the ratio of the volume of cylinder A to the volume of cylinder B?

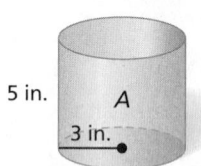

    F $\frac{1}{64}$ **H** $\frac{1}{4}$

    G $\frac{1}{16}$ **J** $\frac{1}{3}$

3. A clock loses 5 minutes every day. How much time will it lose in 2 hours?

    A 0.417 second

    B 25 seconds

    C 240 seconds

    D 600 seconds

4. A statue is 8 feet tall. The display case for a model of the statue is 18 inches tall. Which scale allows for the tallest model of the statue that will fit in the display case?

    F 1 inch : 2 inches

    G 1 inch : 7 inches

    H 1 inch : 5 inches

    J 1 inch : 10 inches

5. What is the value of $-\left|6^2\right|$?

    A -36 **C** -8

    B -12 **D** -3

6. Mr. Phillips wants to install hardwood flooring in his den. The flooring costs \$25.86 per square yard. The blueprint below shows his house. What other information do you need in order to find the total cost of the flooring?

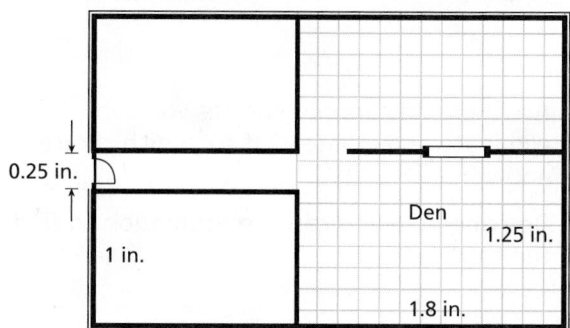

    F The lengths and widths of the adjoining rooms in the blueprint

    G The total area of the blueprint

    H The scale of inches in the blueprint to yards in the house

    J The width of the den

7. What value of n makes the equation below have no solution?
$$2x + 2 = nx - 3$$

    A -2

    B 0

    C 2

    D 3

8. Which of the equations below represents the second step of the solution process?

    Step 1: $3(5x - 2) + 27 = -24$
    Step 2:
    Step 3: $15x + 21 = -24$
    Step 4: $15x = -45$
    Step 5: $x = -3$

    F $3(5x + 27) - 2 = -24$

    G $3(5x + 25) = -24$

    H $15x - 2 + 27 = -24$

    J $15x - 6 + 27 = -24$

If you are stuck on a problem, skip it and come back later. Another problem might remind you of something that will help. If you feel yourself become tense, take a few deep breaths to relax.

9. Cass drove 3 miles to school, and then she drove *m* miles to a friend's house. The total mileage for these two trips was 8 miles. Which equation CANNOT be used to determine the number of miles Cass drove?

- Ⓐ $3 + m = 8$
- Ⓑ $3 - m = 8$
- Ⓒ $8 - 3 = m$
- Ⓓ $8 - m = 3$

10. If $\frac{20}{x} = \frac{4}{x-5}$, which of the following is a true statement?

- Ⓕ $x(x - 5) = 80$
- Ⓖ $20x = 4(x - 5)$
- Ⓗ $20(x - 5) = 4x$
- Ⓙ $24 = 2x - 5$

Gridded Response

11. Four times a number is two less than six times the same number minus ten. What is the number?

12. Melissa invested her savings in a retirement account that pays simple interest. A portion of her account record is shown below. What is the interest rate on Melissa's account? Write your answer as a decimal.

Date	Transaction	Amount	Balance
8/1	Beginning deposit	$6000.00	$6000.00
8/31	Interest payment	$192.00	$6192.00
9/1	Withdrawal	$1000.00	$5192.00
9/30	Interest payment	$166.14	$5358.14

13. At 2:45 P.M. you are 112 miles from Dallas. You want to be in Dallas at 4:30 P.M. What is the average number of miles per hour you must travel to be on time?

14. A cyclist travels 45 miles in 4 hours. How many feet does she travel in one second?

15. A bike rental shop charges a one-time charge of $8 plus an hourly fee to rent a bike. Dan paid $24.50 to rent a bike for $5\frac{1}{2}$ hours. Find the bike shop's hourly fee in dollars.

Short Response

16. Alex buys 5 calendars to give as gifts. Each calendar has the same price. When the cashier rings up Alex's calendars, the total cost before tax is $58.75.

- **a.** Write and solve an equation to find the cost of each calendar.
- **b.** The total cost of Alex's calendars after tax is $63.45. Find the percent sales tax. Show your work and explain in words how you found your answer.

17. Fatima enrolled in a traveler rewards program. She begins with 10,000 bonus points. For every trip she takes, she collects 3000 bonus points.

- **a.** Write a rule for the number of bonus points Fatima has after *x* trips.
- **b.** Make a table showing the number of bonus points Fatima has after 0, 1, 2, 3, 4, and 5 trips.
- **c.** When Fatima has collected 20,000 bonus points, she gets a free vacation. How many trips does Fatima need to take to get a free vacation?

Extended Response

18. Korena is putting a decorative border around her rectangular flower garden. The total perimeter of the garden is 200 feet.

- **a.** Draw three different rectangles that could represent Korena's flower garden. Label the dimensions of your rectangles.
- **b.** Use the table to show the lengths and widths of five different rectangles that could represent Korena's flower garden. Do not use any of your rectangles from part **a**.

Possible Dimensions of Korena's Garden		
Length (ℓ)	Width (w)	Perimeter (P)
▪	▪	▪
▪	▪	▪
▪	▪	▪
▪	▪	▪
▪	▪	▪

- **c.** The length of Korena's garden is 4 times its width. Explain how to use the perimeter formula $P = 2\ell + 2w$ to find the dimensions of Korena's garden.
- **d.** Find the dimensions of Korena's garden.

Real-World CONNECTIONS

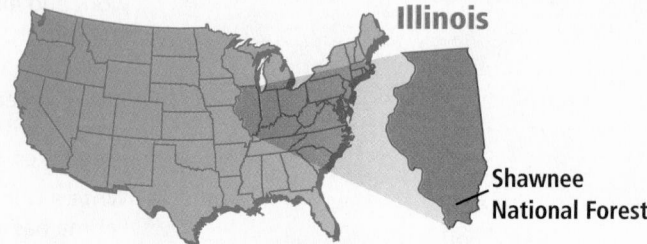

Illinois

Shawnee
National Forest

 **Bullfrogs**

The bullfrog is the largest frog in Illinois. Adult bullfrogs are usually between $3\frac{1}{2}$ and 6 inches in length, but some have been known to grow even larger. The largest recorded bullfrog found in Illinois was 8 inches long and weighed more than a pound!

Choose one or more strategies to solve each problem.

1. A bullfrog jumping up a hill is 8 feet from the top. Each time it jumps, it moves forward 18 inches. However, mud on the hill causes it to slide backward 2 inches after each jump. How many jumps will it take the frog to reach the top of the hill?

2. A certain pond is home to 120 bullfrog tadpoles. This is 90 more than 3 times the number of adult bullfrogs that live in a second pond. How many adult bullfrogs live in the second pond?

For 3–5, use the table.

3. How far could the largest recorded bullfrog in Illinois jump?

4. If a bullfrog is $4\frac{1}{2}$ inches long, what is its maximum jumping distance?

5. A certain adult bullfrog can jump $8\frac{3}{4}$ feet. This bullfrog must be at least how long?

Jumping Distances of Bullfrogs	
Length of Bullfrog (in.)	Maximum Jumping Distance (in.)
4	60
5	75
6	90

(all)Dan Suzio/Photo Researchers, Inc.

⭐ The Great Snake Migration

When temperatures drop, large numbers of snakes leave the swamps of southern Illinois. Some travel just a few hundred feet, while others travel several miles, to Snake Road, a 3-mile-long road on the western edge of the Shawnee Forest. In this area, you can see as many as 40 to 50 snakes in a day, including cottonmouth water moccasins, rattlesnakes, and copperheads.

Choose one or more strategies to solve each problem.

1. In one hour, a researcher saw six snakes crossing Snake Road— three moccasins, a rattlesnake, a garter snake, and a diamondback water snake, though not in that order. The second snake to cross was a moccasin, and the other two moccasins crossed one after the other. The diamondback crossed before the garter snake. The first snake to cross was not the garter snake or the diamondback. A moccasin crossed last. In what order did the snakes cross Snake Road?

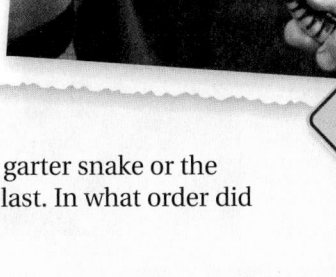

For 2, use the table.

In 2001–2002, several Illinois hospitals were asked how many vials of antivenom they had available to treat snake bites. The results are shown in the table. For example, 37 hospitals reported that they had between 1 and 4 vials of antivenom available.

Antivenom Survey Results						
Vials	0	1–4	5–9	10–14	15–19	20+
Hospitals		37	14	6	0	10

2. The number of hospitals with no antivenom available to treat snake bites was 6 less than 3 times the number of hospitals that had 1–4 vials. How many hospitals had no antivenom with which to treat snake bites? What percent of the total number of hospitals surveyed does this represent? Round your answer to the nearest percent.

COMMON CORE

Chapter Focus

- Solve multi-step inequalities.
- Write and solve inequalities to solve problems.

For a *Good* Cause

You can use the concepts in this chapter to plan for a fund-raising event. Inequalities help you determine how to reach your fund-raising goals.

Learn It Online
Chapter Project Online

Sam Dudgeon/HMH

ARE YOU READY?

✓ Vocabulary

Match each term on the left with a definition on the right.

1. equation
2. evaluate
3. inverse operations
4. like terms
5. solution of an equation

   A. mathematical phrase that contains operations, numbers, and/or variables

   B. mathematical statement that two expressions are equivalent

   C. value of a variable that makes a statement true

   D. terms that contain the same variables raised to the same powers

   E. to find the value of an expression

   F. operations that undo each other

✓ Evaluate Expressions

Evaluate each expression for $a = 2$ and $b = 6$.

6. $b - a$
7. ab
8. $b \div a$
9. $a + b$

✓ Compare and Order Real Numbers

Compare. Write $<$, $>$, or $=$.

10. $10 \;\blacksquare\; 21$
11. $5.27 \;\blacksquare\; 5.23$
12. $20\% \;\blacksquare\; 0.2$
13. $\dfrac{1}{3} \;\blacksquare\; \dfrac{2}{5}$

✓ Combine Like Terms

Simplify each expression by combining like terms.

14. $6x + x$
15. $-8a + 3a$
16. $9x^2 - 15x^2$
17. $2.1x + 4.3x$

✓ Distributive Property

Simplify each expression.

18. $2(x + 3)$
19. $(3 - d)5$
20. $4(r - 1)$
21. $3(4 + m)$

✓ Solve One-Step Equations

Solve.

22. $s - 3 = 8$
23. $-7x = 21$
24. $y + 11 = 2$
25. $\dfrac{h}{2} = 6$
26. $t + 2 = -2$
27. $6x = 42$
28. $r - 8 = -13$
29. $\dfrac{y}{3} = -12$

Study Guide: Preview

Where You've Been

Previously, you

- learned the properties of equality.
- solved equations by using inverse operations.
- solved equations with variables on both sides.

In This Chapter

You will study

- the properties of inequality.
- how to solve inequalities by using inverse operations.
- how to solve inequalities with variables on both sides.
- how to solve compound inequalities.

Where You're Going

You can use the skills in this chapter

- in all your future math classes, including Geometry.
- in other classes, such as Health, Chemistry, Physics, and Economics.
- in the real world to plan a budget, to find cost-efficient services, and to set financial goals.

Key Vocabulary/Vocabulario

compound inequality	desigualdad compuesta
inequality	desigualdad
intersection	intersección
solution of an inequality	solución de una desigualdad
union	unión

Vocabulary Connections

To become familiar with some of the vocabulary terms in the chapter, consider the following. You may refer to the chapter, the glossary, or a dictionary if you like.

1. The prefix *in-* means "not." An *equality* states that two things are equal. Use these meanings to write your own definition for the word **inequality**.

2. The word *compound* means "consisting of two or more parts." What do you think a **compound inequality** might be?

3. The **intersection** of two roads is the place where the two roads overlap. What do you think the *intersection* of two graphs would be?

4. The word **union** begins with the root *uni-*. List some other words that begin with *uni-*. What do all of these words have in common?

Reading and Writing Math

Study Strategy: Use Your Notes Effectively

Taking notes helps you arrange, organize, and process information from your textbook and class lectures. In addition to taking notes, you need to use your notes before and after class effectively.

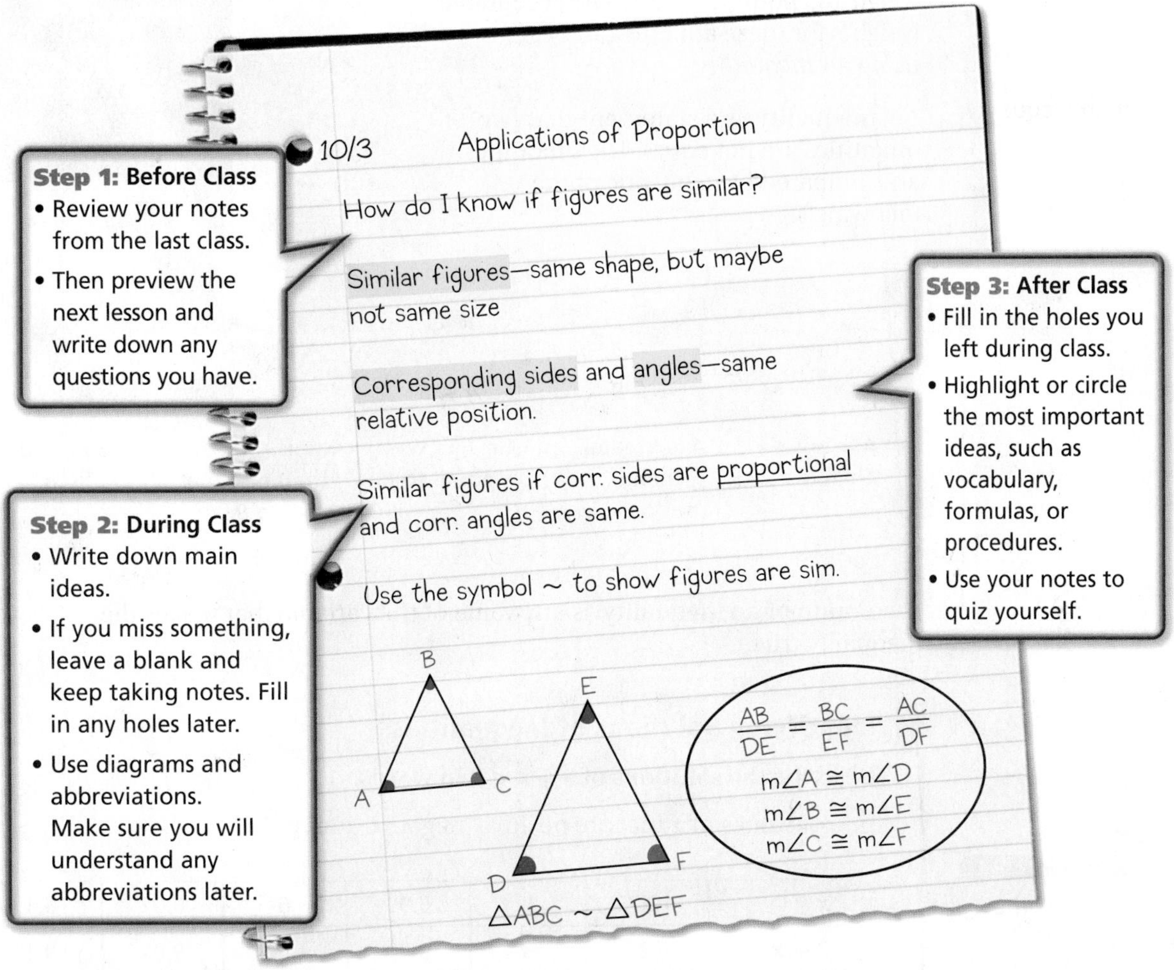

Step 1: Before Class
- Review your notes from the last class.
- Then preview the next lesson and write down any questions you have.

Step 2: During Class
- Write down main ideas.
- If you miss something, leave a blank and keep taking notes. Fill in any holes later.
- Use diagrams and abbreviations. Make sure you will understand any abbreviations later.

Step 3: After Class
- Fill in the holes you left during class.
- Highlight or circle the most important ideas, such as vocabulary, formulas, or procedures.
- Use your notes to quiz yourself.

10/3   Applications of Proportion

How do I know if figures are similar?

Similar figures—same shape, but maybe not same size

Corresponding sides and angles—same relative position.

Similar figures if corr. sides are proportional and corr. angles are same.

Use the symbol ~ to show figures are sim.

$$\frac{AB}{DE} = \frac{BC}{EF} = \frac{AC}{DF}$$

$$m\angle A \cong m\angle D$$
$$m\angle B \cong m\angle E$$
$$m\angle C \cong m\angle F$$

$\triangle ABC \sim \triangle DEF$

Try This

1. Look at the next lesson in your textbook. Write down some questions you have about the material in that lesson. Leave space between each question so that you can write the answers during the next class.

2. Look at the notes you took during the last class. List three ways you can improve your note-taking skills.

2-1 Graphing and Writing Inequalities

CC.9-12.A.REI.3 Solve linear equations and inequalities in one variable, including equations with coefficients represented by letters.

Objectives
Identify solutions of inequalities in one variable.

Write and graph inequalities in one variable.

Vocabulary
inequality
solution of an inequality

Who uses this?
Members of a crew team can use inequalities to be sure they fall within a range of weights. (See Example 4.)

The athletes on a lightweight crew team must weigh 165 pounds or less. The acceptable weights for these athletes can be described using an *inequality*.

An **inequality** is a statement that two quantities are not equal. The quantities are compared by using one of the following signs:

$A < B$

A is less than B.

$A > B$

A is greater than B.

$A \leq B$

A is less than or equal to B.

$A \geq B$

A is greater than or equal to B.

$A \neq B$

A is not equal to B.

A **solution of an inequality** is any value of the variable that makes the inequality true.

EXAMPLE 1 **Identifying Solutions of Inequalities**

Describe the solutions of $3 + x < 9$ in words.

Test values of x that are positive, negative, and 0.

x	−2.75	0	5.99	6	6.01	6.1
$3 + x$	0.25	3	8.99	9	9.01	9.1
$3 + x \overset{?}{<} 9$	$0.25 \overset{?}{<} 9$	$3 \overset{?}{<} 9$	$8.99 \overset{?}{<} 9$	$9 \overset{?}{<} 9$	$9.01 \overset{?}{<} 9$	$9.1 \overset{?}{<} 9$
Solution?	Yes	Yes	Yes	No	No	No

When the value of x is a number less than 6, the value of $3 + x$ is less than 9.
When the value of x is 6, the value of $3 + x$ is equal to 9.
When the value of x is a number greater than 6, the value of $3 + x$ is greater than 9.

The solutions of $3 + x < 9$ are numbers less than 6.

Writing Math

The solutions of the inequality in Example 1 can be written in *set-builder notation* as $\{x | x < 6\}$, which is read as "the set of all real numbers x such that x is less than 6."

1. Describe the solutions of $2p > 8$ in words.

© Charles Crust

An inequality like $3 + x < 9$ has too many solutions to list. You can use a graph on a number line to show all the solutions.

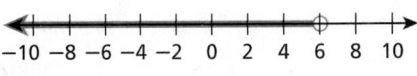

The solutions are shaded and an arrow shows that the solutions continue past those shown on the graph. To show that an endpoint is a solution, draw a solid circle at the number. To show that an endpoint is not a solution, draw an empty circle.

Graphing Inequalities

WORDS	ALGEBRA	GRAPH
All real numbers less than 5	$x < 5$	![number line -4 to 6, open circle at 5, shaded left]
All real numbers greater than -1	$x > -1$	![number line -4 to 6, open circle at -1, shaded right]
All real numbers less than or equal to $\frac{1}{2}$	$x \le \frac{1}{2}$	![number line -2 to 1, solid circle at 1/2, shaded left]
All real numbers greater than or equal to 0	$x \ge 0$	![number line -4 to 6, solid circle at 0, shaded right]

EXAMPLE **2** **Graphing Inequalities**

Graph each inequality.

A $b < -1.5$

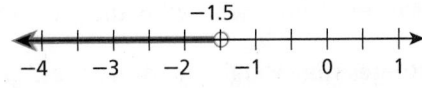

Draw an empty circle at -1.5.
Shade all the numbers less than -1.5 and draw an arrow pointing to the left.

B $r \ge 2$

number line -4 to 6, solid circle at 2, shaded right

Draw a solid circle at 2.
Shade all the numbers greater than 2 and draw an arrow pointing to the right.

 **CHECK IT OUT!** Graph each inequality.

2a. $c > 2.5$ **2b.** $2^2 - 4 \ge w$ **2c.** $m \le -3$

Student to Student

Graphing Inequalities

Victor Solomos
Palmer High School

To know which direction to shade a graph, I write inequalities with the variable on the left side of the inequality symbol. I know that the symbol has to point to the same number after I rewrite the inequality.

For example, I write $4 < y$ as $y > 4$.

Now the inequality symbol points in the direction that I should draw the shaded arrow on my graph.

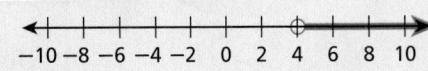

Digital Vision/gettyImages

EXAMPLE **3**

Writing an Inequality from a Graph

Write the inequality shown by each graph.

A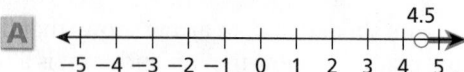

> *Use any variable. The arrow points to the right, so use either > or ≥.*
> *The empty circle at 4.5 means that 4.5 is not a solution, so use >.*

$h > 4.5$

B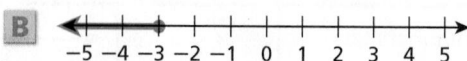

> *Use any variable. The arrow points to the left, so use either < or ≤.*
> *The solid circle at −3 means that −3 is a solution, so use ≤.*

$m \le -3$

 **3.** Write the inequality shown by the graph.

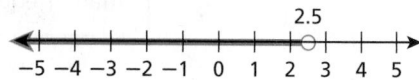

EXAMPLE **4**

Sports Application

The members of a lightweight crew team can weigh no more than 165 pounds each. Define a variable and write an inequality for the acceptable weights of the team members. Graph the solutions.

Let *w* represent the weights that are allowed.

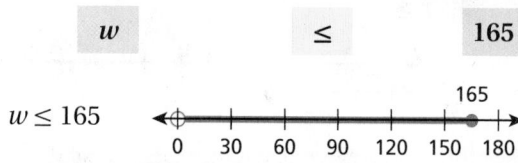

Athletes may weigh	no more than	165 pounds.
w	≤	165

$w \le 165$

Stop the graph at 0 because a person's weight must be a positive number.

Reading Math

"No more than" means "less than or equal to."

"At least" means "greater than or equal to."

 **4.** A store's employees earn at least $8.25 per hour. Define a variable and write an inequality for the amount the employees may earn per hour. Graph the solutions.

MATHEMATICAL PRACTICES

THINK AND DISCUSS

1. Compare the solutions of $x > 2$ and $x \ge 2$.

 **2. GET ORGANIZED** Copy and complete the graphic organizer. Draw a graph in the first row and write the correct inequality in the second row.

Inequality	Graph
$x > 1$	
	(graph: ←●—+—+—+—+—+→ −5 −4 −3 −2 −1 0 1)

Exercises

Learn It Online
Homework Help Online
Parent Resources Online

GUIDED PRACTICE

1. **Vocabulary** How is a *solution of an inequality* like a solution of an equation?

SEE EXAMPLE 1 Describe the solutions of each inequality in words.

2. $g - 5 \geq 6$
3. $-2 < h + 1$
4. $20 > 5t$
5. $5 - x \leq 2$

SEE EXAMPLE 2 Graph each inequality.

6. $x < -5$
7. $c \geq 3\frac{1}{2}$
8. $(4 - 2)^3 > m$
9. $p \geq \sqrt{17 + 8}$

SEE EXAMPLE 3 Write the inequality shown by each graph.

10.
```
←+——+——+——●——+——+——+——+——+——+——+→
 −6 −5 −4 −3 −2 −1  0  1  2  3  4
```

11.
```
        −8½
←+○——+——+——+——+——+——+——+——+——+→
−9 −8 −7 −6 −5 −4 −3 −2 −1  0  1
```

12.
```
                              5.5
←+——+——+——+——+——+——+——+——+——○——+→
−4 −3 −2 −1  0  1  2  3  4  5  6
```

13.
```
              −7
←+——+——+——+●——+——+——+——+——+→
−12  −10  −8  −6  −4  −2   0
```

14.
```
←+——+——+——+——+——+——●——+——+——+——+→
−4 −3 −2 −1  0  1  2  3  4  5  6
```

15.
```
←+——+——+——+——+——+——+——+——+——+——+→
−2  0  2  4  6  8  10  12  14  16  18
```

SEE EXAMPLE 4 Define a variable and write an inequality for each situation. Graph the solutions.

16. There must be at least 20 club members present in order to hold a meeting.

17. A trainer advises an athlete to keep his heart rate under 140 beats per minute.

PRACTICE AND PROBLEM SOLVING

Independent Practice

For Exercises	See Example
18–21	1
22–25	2
26–31	3
32–33	4

Extra Practice

See Extra Practice for more Skills Practice and Applications Practice exercises.

Describe the solutions of each inequality in words.

18. $-2t > -8$
19. $0 > w - 2$
20. $3k > 9$
21. $\frac{1}{2}b \leq 6$

Graph each inequality.

22. $7 < x$
23. $t \leq -\frac{1}{2}$
24. $d > 4(5 - 8)$
25. $t \leq 3^2 - 2^2$

Write the inequality shown by each graph.

26.
```
←+——+——+——+——+——+——+——+——●——+→
−4 −3 −2 −1  0  1  2  3  4  5  6
```

27.
```
                    −11
←+——+——+——+——○——+——+——+——+→
−16  −14  −12  −10  −8  −6  −4
```

28.
```
          −3.5
←+——+——○——+——+——+——+——+——+——+→
−6 −5 −4 −3 −2 −1  0  1  2  3  4
```

29.
```
      −3.3
←+——+——○——+——+——+——+——+——+——+→
−5 −4 −3 −2 −1  0  1  2  3  4  5
```

30.
```
←+——+——+——+——+——+——+——+——+——◇——+→
−5 −4 −3 −2 −1  0  1  2  3  4  5
```

31.
```
                    9
←+——+——+——+——+——+——●——+——+——+——+→
−2  0  2  4  6  8  10  12  14  16  18
```

Define a variable and write an inequality for each situation. Graph the solutions.

32. The maximum speed allowed on Main Street is 25 miles per hour.

33. Applicants must have at least 5 years of experience.

Write each inequality in words.

34. $x > 7$ **35.** $h < -5$ **36.** $d \leq 23$ **37.** $r \geq -2$

Write each inequality with the variable on the left. Graph the solutions.

38. $19 < g$ **39.** $17 \geq p$ **40.** $10 < e$ **41.** $0 < f$

Define a variable and write an inequality for each situation. Graph the solutions.

42. The highest temperature ever recorded on Earth was 135.9 °F at Al Aziziyah, Libya, on September 13, 1922.

43. Businesses with profits less than $10,000 per year will be shut down.

44. You must be at least 46 inches tall to ride a roller coaster at an amusement park.

45. Due to a medical condition, a hiker can hike only in areas with an elevation no more than 5000 feet above sea level.

Write a real-world situation that could be described by each inequality.

46. $x \geq 0$ **47.** $x < 10$ **48.** $x \leq 12$ **49.** $x > 8.5$

Match each inequality with its graph.

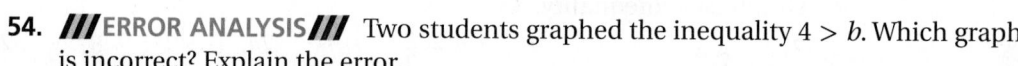

50. $x \geq 5$ **A.**

51. $x < 5$ **B.**

52. $x > 5$ **C.**

53. $x \leq 5$ **D.**

54. ///**ERROR ANALYSIS**/// Two students graphed the inequality $4 > b$. Which graph is incorrect? Explain the error.

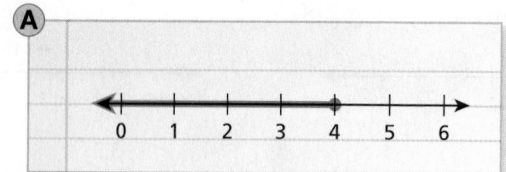
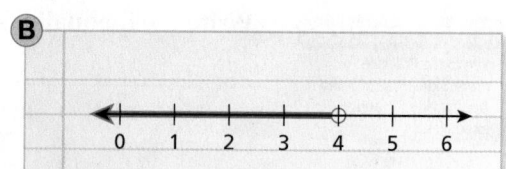

MULTI-STEP TEST PREP

55. a. Mirna earned $125 baby-sitting during the spring break. She needs to save $90 for the German Club trip. She wants to spend the remainder of the money shopping. Write an inequality to show how much she can spend.

   b. Graph the inequality you wrote in part **a.**

   c. Mirna spends $15 on a bracelet. Write an inequality to show how much money she has left to spend.

56. Critical Thinking Graph all positive integer solutions of the inequality $x < 5$.

57. Write About It Explain how to write an inequality that is modeled by a graph. What characteristics do you look for in the graph?

58. Write About It You were told in the lesson that the phrase "no more than" means "less than or equal to" and the phrase "at least" means "greater than or equal to."

   a. What does the phrase "at most" mean?

   b. What does the phrase "no less than" mean?

59. Which is NOT a solution of the inequality $5 - 2x \geq -3$?

   Ⓐ 0   Ⓑ 2   Ⓒ 4   Ⓓ 5

60. Which is NOT a solution of the inequality $3 - x < 2$?

   Ⓕ 1   Ⓖ 2   Ⓗ 3   Ⓙ 4

61. Which graph represents the solutions of $-2 \leq 1 - t$?

Ⓐ 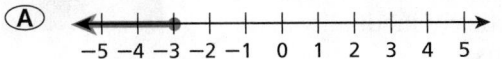   Ⓒ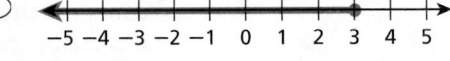

Ⓑ 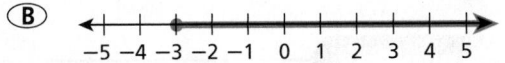   Ⓓ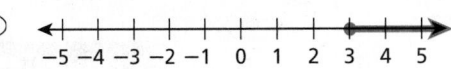

CHALLENGE AND EXTEND

Describe the values for x and y that make each inequality true.

62. $x + y \leq |x + y|$ **63.** $x^2 < xy$ **64.** $x - y \geq y - x$

Complete each statement. Write $<$ or $>$.

65. If $a > b$, then b ▮ a.   **66.** If $x > y$ and $y > z$, then x ▮ z.

67. Name a value of x that makes the statement $0.35 < x < 1.27$ true.

68. Is $\frac{5}{6}$ a solution of $x < 1$? How many solutions of $x < 1$ are between 0 and 1?

69. Write About It Explain how to graph all the solutions of $x \neq 5$.

2-2 Solving Inequalities by Adding or Subtracting

CC.9-12.A.REI.3 Solve linear equations and inequalities in one variable, including equations with coefficients represented by letters.

Objectives
Solve one-step inequalities by using addition.

Solve one-step inequalities by using subtraction.

Who uses this?
You can use inequalities to determine how many more photos you can take. (See Example 2.)

Tenea has a cell phone that also takes pictures. After taking some photos, Tenea can use a one-step inequality to determine how many more photos she can take.

Solving one-step inequalities is much like solving one-step equations. To solve an inequality, you need to isolate the variable using the properties of inequality and inverse operations.

Properties of Inequality

Addition and Subtraction

WORDS	NUMBERS	ALGEBRA
Addition You can add the same number to both sides of an inequality, and the statement will still be true.	$3 < 8$ $3 + 2 < 8 + 2$ $5 < 10$	$a < b$ $a + c < b + c$
Subtraction You can subtract the same number from both sides of an inequality, and the statement will still be true.	$9 < 12$ $9 - 5 < 12 - 5$ $4 < 7$	$a < b$ $a - c < b - c$

These properties are also true for inequalities that use the symbols $>$, $\geq$, and $\leq$.

EXAMPLE 1 Using Addition and Subtraction to Solve Inequalities

Solve each inequality and graph the solutions.

Helpful Hint

Use an inverse operation to "undo" the operation in an inequality. If the inequality contains addition, use subtraction to undo the addition.

A $x + 9 < 15$

$$x + 9 < 15$$
$$\underline{-9 \quad -9}$$
$$x \quad < 6$$

Since 9 is added to x, subtract 9 from both sides to undo the addition.

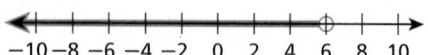

B $d - 3 > -6$

$$d - 3 > -6$$
$$\underline{+3 \quad +3}$$
$$d \quad > -3$$

Since 3 is subtracted from d, add 3 to both sides to undo the subtraction.

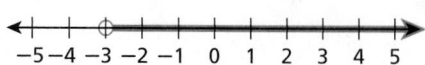

Solve each inequality and graph the solutions.

 C $\quad 0.7 \geq n - 0.4$

$\qquad 0.7 \geq n - 0.4$ *Since 0.4 is subtracted from n, add 0.4 to both sides to*

$\qquad \underline{+\,0.4 \qquad +\,0.4}$ *undo the subtraction.*

$\qquad\quad 1.1 \geq n$

$\qquad\quad\; n \leq 1.1$

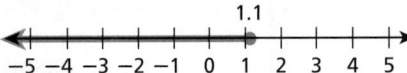 Solve each inequality and graph the solutions.

  1a. $s + 1 \leq 10$ **1b.** $2\frac{1}{2} > -3 + t$ **1c.** $q - 3.5 < 7.5$

Since there can be an infinite number of solutions to an inequality, it is not possible to check all the solutions. You can check the endpoint and the direction of the inequality symbol.

The solutions of $x + 9 < 15$ are given by $x < 6$.

Step 1 Check the endpoint.

Substitute 6 for x in the related equation $x + 9 = 15$. The endpoint should be a solution of the equation.

$$
\begin{array}{r|l}
\multicolumn{2}{l}{x + 9 = 15}\\
\hline
6 + 9 & 15\\
15 & 15 \;\checkmark
\end{array}
$$

Step 2 Check the inequality symbol.

Substitute a number less than 6 for x in the original inequality. The number you choose should be a solution of the inequality.

$$
\begin{array}{r|c|l}
\multicolumn{3}{l}{x + 9 < 15}\\
\hline
4 + 9 & < & 15\\
13 & < & 15 \;\checkmark
\end{array}
$$

Make sense of problems and persevere in solving them.

Problem Solving Application

The memory in Tenea's camera phone allows her to take up to 20 pictures. Tenea has already taken 16 pictures. Write, solve, and graph an inequality to show how many more pictures Tenea could take.

1 **Understand the Problem**

The **answer** will be an inequality and a graph that show all the possible numbers of pictures that Tenea can take.

  List the important information:
- Tenea can take up to, or *at most*, 20 pictures.
- Tenea has taken 16 pictures already.

2 **Make a Plan**

Write an inequality.
Let p represent the remaining number of pictures Tenea can take.

Number taken	plus	number remaining	is at most	20 pictures.
16	+	p	$\leq$	20

2-2 Solving Inequalities by Adding or Subtracting   **107**

Solve

$$16 + p \le 20$$ *Since 16 is added to p, subtract 16 from both sides to undo the addition.*
$$\underline{-16 \qquad -16}$$
$$p \le 4$$

It is not reasonable for Tenea to take a negative or fractional number of pictures, so graph the nonnegative integers less than or equal to 4.

Tenea could take 0, 1, 2, 3, or 4 more pictures.

 **Look Back**

Check Check the endpoint, 4.

$$16 + p = 20$$
$$\frac{16 + 4 \;\big|\; 20}{20 \;\big|\; 20 \checkmark}$$

Check a number less than 4.

$$16 + p \le 20$$
$$\frac{16 + 2 \;\big|{\le}\big|\; 20}{18 \;\big|{\le}\big|\; 20 \checkmark}$$

Adding 0, 1, 2, 3, or 4 more pictures will not exceed 20.

 **2.** The Recommended Dietary Allowance (RDA) of iron for a female in Sarah's age group (14–18 years) is 15 mg per day. Sarah has consumed 11 mg of iron today. Write and solve an inequality to show how many more milligrams of iron Sarah can consume without exceeding the RDA.

EXAMPLE 3 *Sports Application*

Josh can bench press 220 pounds. He wants to bench press at least 250 pounds. Write and solve an inequality to determine how many more pounds Josh must lift to reach his goal. Check your answer.

Let p represent the number of additional pounds Josh must lift.

220 pounds	plus	additional pounds	is at least	250 pounds.
220	+	p	$\ge$	250

$$220 + p \ge 250$$ *Since 220 is added to p, subtract 220 from both sides to undo the addition.*
$$\underline{-220 \qquad -220}$$
$$p \ge 30$$

Check Check the endpoint, 30.

$$220 + p = 250$$
$$\frac{220 + 30 \;\big|\; 250}{250 \;\big|\; 250 \checkmark}$$

Check a number greater than 30.

$$220 + p \ge 250$$
$$\frac{220 + 40 \;\big|{\ge}\big|\; 250}{260 \;\big|{\ge}\big|\; 250 \checkmark}$$

Josh must lift at least 30 additional pounds to reach his goal.

 **3. What if...?** Josh has reached his goal of 250 pounds and now wants to try to break the school record of 282 pounds. Write and solve an inequality to determine how many more pounds Josh needs to break the school record. Check your answer.

THINK AND DISCUSS

1. Show how to check your solution to Example 1B.

2. Explain how the Addition and Subtraction Properties of Inequality are like the Addition and Subtraction Properties of Equality.

3. GET ORGANIZED Copy and complete the graphic organizer. In each box, write an inequality that you must use the specified property to solve. Then solve and graph the inequality.

```
          Properties of Inequality
          ┌──────┴──────┐
     Addition        Subtraction
```

2-2 Exercises

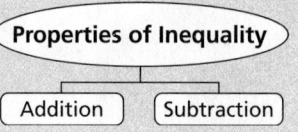
GUIDED PRACTICE

SEE EXAMPLE **1**   **Solve each inequality and graph the solutions.**

1. $12 < p + 6$ **2.** $w + 3 \geq 4$ **3.** $-5 + x \leq -20$ **4.** $z - 2 > -11$

SEE EXAMPLE **2**   **5. Health** For adults, the maximum safe water temperature in a spa is 104 °F. The water temperature in Bill's spa is 102 °F. The temperature is increased by t °F. Write, solve, and graph an inequality to show the values of t for which the water temperature is still safe.

SEE EXAMPLE **3**   **6. Consumer Economics** A local restaurant will deliver food to your house if the purchase amount of your order is at least $25.00. The total for part of your order is $17.95. Write and solve an inequality to determine how much more you must spend for the restaurant to deliver your order.

PRACTICE AND PROBLEM SOLVING

Independent Practice	
For Exercises	See Example
7–10	1
11	2
12	3

Extra Practice

See Extra Practice for more Skills Practice and Applications Practice exercises.

Solve each inequality and graph the solutions.

7. $a - 3 \geq 2$ **8.** $2.5 > q - 0.8$ **9.** $-45 + x < -30$ **10.** $r + \frac{1}{4} \leq \frac{3}{4}$

11. Engineering The maximum load for a certain elevator is 2000 pounds. The total weight of the passengers on the elevator is 1400 pounds. A delivery man who weighs 243 pounds enters the elevator with a crate of weight w. Write, solve, and graph an inequality to show the values of w that will not exceed the weight limit of the elevator.

12. Transportation The gas tank in Mindy's car holds at most 15 gallons. She has already filled the tank with 7 gallons of gas. She will continue to fill the tank with g gallons more. Write and solve an inequality that shows all values of g that Mindy can add to the car's tank.

Write an inequality to represent each statement. Solve the inequality and graph the solutions.

13. Ten less than a number x is greater than 32.

14. A number n increased by 6 is less than or equal to 4.

15. A number r decreased by 13 is at most 15.

Solve each inequality and graph the solutions.

16. $x + 4 \leq 2$

17. $-12 + q > 39$

18. $x + \frac{3}{5} < 7$

19. $4.8 \geq p + 4$

20. $-12 \leq x - 12$

21. $4 < 206 + c$

22. $y - \frac{1}{3} > \frac{2}{3}$

23. $x + 1.4 \geq 1.4$

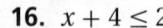

24. Use the inequality $s + 12 \geq 20$ to fill in the missing numbers.

    a. $s \geq$ ▇

    b. $s +$ ▇ ≥ 30

    c. $s - 8 \geq$ ▇

25. **Health** A particular type of contact lens can be worn up to 30 days in a row. Alex has been wearing these contact lenses for 21 days. Write, solve, and graph an inequality to show how many more days Alex could wear his contact lenses.

Solve each inequality and match the solutions to the correct graph.

26. $1 \leq x - 2$

    A.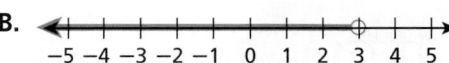

27. $8 > x - (-5)$

    B.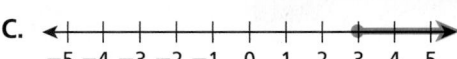

28. $x + 6 > 9$

    C.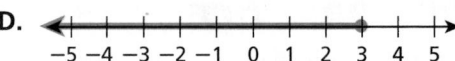

29. $-4 \geq x - 7$

    D.

30. **Estimation** Is $x < 10$ a reasonable estimate for the solutions to the inequality $11.879 + x < 21.709$? Explain your answer.

31. **Sports** At the Seattle Mariners baseball team's home games, there are 45,611 seats in the four areas listed in the table. Suppose all the suite level and club level seats during a game are filled. Write and solve an inequality to determine how many people p could be sitting in the other types of seats.

Mariners Home Game Seating	
Type of Seat	**Number of Seats**
Main bowl	24,399
Upper bowl	16,022
Club level	4,254
Suite level	936

32. **Critical Thinking** Recall that a balance scale was used to model solving equations. Describe how a balance scale could model solving inequalities.

33. **Critical Thinking** Explain why $x + 4 \geq 6$ and $x - 4 \geq -2$ have the same solutions.

34. **Write About It** How do the solutions of $x + 2 \geq 3$ differ from the solutions of $x + 2 > 3$? How do the graphs of the solutions differ?

MULTI-STEP TEST PREP

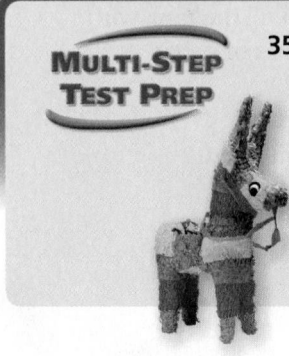

35. **a.** Daryl finds that the distance from Columbus, Ohio, to Washington, D.C., is 411 miles. What is the round-trip distance?

    b. Daryl can afford to drive a total of 1000 miles. Write an inequality to show the number of miles m he can drive while in Washington, D.C.

    c. Solve the inequality and graph the solutions on a number line. Show that your answer is reasonable.

36. Which is a reasonable solution of $4.7367 + p < 20.1784$?

    (A) 15   (B) 16   (C) 24   (D) 25

37. Which statement can be modeled by $x + 3 \leq 12$?

    (F) Sam has 3 bottles of water. Together, Sam and Dave have at most 12 bottles of water.

    (G) Jennie sold 3 cookbooks. To earn a prize, Jennie must sell at least 12 cookbooks.

    (H) Peter has 3 baseball hats. Peter and his brothers have fewer than 12 baseball hats.

    (J) Kathy swam 3 laps in the pool this week. She must swim more than 12 laps.

38. Which graph represents the solutions of $p + 3 < 1$?

    (A) 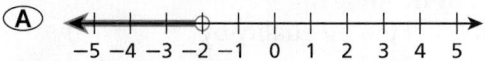   (C)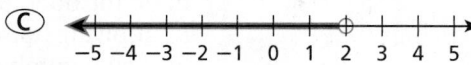

    (B) 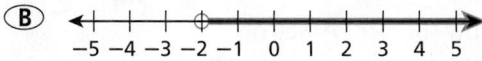   (D)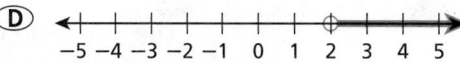

39. Which inequality does NOT have the same solutions as $n + 12 \leq 26$?

    (F) $n \leq 14$ (G) $n + 6 \leq 20$ (H) $10 \geq n - 4$ (J) $n - 12 \leq 14$

CHALLENGE AND EXTEND

Solve each inequality and graph the solutions.

40. $6\frac{9}{10} \geq 4\frac{4}{5} + x$ **41.** $r - 1\frac{2}{5} \leq 3\frac{7}{10}$ **42.** $6\frac{2}{3} + m > 7\frac{1}{6}$

Determine whether each statement is sometimes, always, or never true. Explain.

43. $a + b > a - b$

44. If $a > c$, then $a + b > c + b$.

45. If $a > b$ and $c > d$, then $a + c > b + d$.

46. If $x + b > c$ and $x > 0$ have the same solutions, what is the relationship between b and c?

2-3 Solving Inequalities by Multiplying or Dividing

CC.9-12.A.REI.3 Solve linear equations and inequalities in one variable, including equations with coefficients represented by letters.
Also **CC.9-12.A.CED.1***

Objectives
Solve one-step inequalities by using multiplication.

Solve one-step inequalities by using division.

Who uses this?
You can solve an inequality to determine how much you can buy with a certain amount of money. (See Example 3.)

Remember, solving inequalities is similar to solving equations. To solve an inequality that contains multiplication or division, undo the operation by dividing or multiplying both sides of the inequality by the same number.

The rules below show the properties of inequality for multiplying or dividing by a positive number. The rules for multiplying or dividing by a negative number appear later in this lesson.

"This is all I have, so I'll take 3 pencils, 3 notebooks, a binder, and 0.9 calculators."

Know it!
Note

Properties of Inequality

Multiplication and Division by Positive Numbers

WORDS	NUMBERS	ALGEBRA
Multiplication You can multiply both sides of an inequality by the same *positive* number, and the statement will still be true.	$7 < 12$ $7(3) < 12(3)$ $21 < 36$	If $a < b$ and $c > 0$, then $ac < bc$.
Division You can divide both sides of an inequality by the same *positive* number, and the statement will still be true.	$15 < 35$ $\dfrac{15}{5} < \dfrac{35}{5}$ $3 < 7$	If $a < b$ and $c > 0$, then $\dfrac{a}{c} < \dfrac{b}{c}$.

These properties are also true for inequalities that use the symbols $>$, $\geq$, and $\leq$.

EXAMPLE 1 **Multiplying or Dividing by a Positive Number**

Solve each inequality and graph the solutions.

A $3x > -27$

$3x > -27$ *Since x is multiplied by 3, divide both sides by 3 to*
$\dfrac{3x}{3} > \dfrac{-27}{3}$ *undo the multiplication.*

$x > -9$

Solve each inequality and graph the solutions.

B $\frac{2}{3}r < 6$

$$\frac{2}{3}r < 6$$

Since r is multiplied by $\frac{2}{3}$, multiply both sides by the reciprocal of $\frac{2}{3}$.

$$\frac{3}{2}\left(\frac{2}{3}r\right) < \frac{3}{2}(6)$$

$$r < 9$$

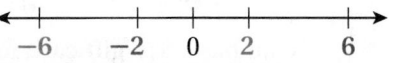

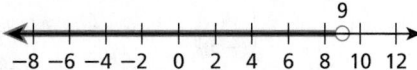Solve each inequality and graph the solutions.

1a. $4k > 24$ **1b.** $-50 \geq 5q$ **1c.** $\frac{3}{4}g > 27$

What happens when you multiply or divide both sides of an inequality by a negative number?

Look at the number line below.

2 < 6	6 > -2
-2 ■ -6 *Multiply both sides by -1.*	-6 ■ 2 *Multiply both sides by -1.*
-2 > -6 *Use the number line to determine the direction of the inequality.*	-6 < 2 *Use the number line to determine the direction of the inequality.*

Notice that when you multiply (or divide) both sides of an inequality by a negative number, you must reverse the inequality symbol. This means there is another set of properties of inequality for multiplying or dividing by a negative number.

Properties of Inequality

Multiplication and Division by Negative Numbers

WORDS	NUMBERS	ALGEBRA
Multiplication If you multiply both sides of an inequality by the same *negative* number, you must reverse the inequality symbol for the statement to still be true.	$8 > 4$ $8(-2) < 4(-2)$ $-16 < -8$	If $a > b$ and $c < 0$, then $ac < bc$.
Division If you divide both sides of an inequality by the same *negative* number, you must reverse the inequality symbol for the statement to still be true.	$12 > 4$ $\dfrac{12}{-4} < \dfrac{4}{-4}$ $-3 < -1$	If $a > b$ and $c < 0$, then $\dfrac{a}{c} < \dfrac{b}{c}$.

These properties are also true for inequalities that use the symbols <, ≥, and ≤.

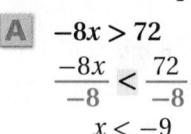

Multiplying or Dividing by a Negative Number

Solve each inequality and graph the solutions.

 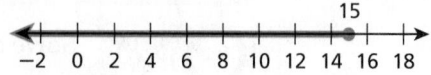
A $-8x > 72$

$\dfrac{-8x}{-8} < \dfrac{72}{-8}$ *Since x is multiplied by −8, divide both sides by −8.*
Change > to <.

$x < -9$

B $-3 \le \dfrac{x}{-5}$

$-5(-3) \ge -5\left(\dfrac{x}{-5}\right)$ *Since x is divided by −5, multiply both sides by −5.*
Change ≤ to ≥.

$15 \ge x \,(\text{or } x \le 15)$

CHECK IT OUT! Solve each inequality and graph the solutions.

2a. $10 \ge -x$ **2b.** $4.25 > -0.25h$

EXAMPLE 3 Consumer Application

Ryan has a $16 gift card for a health store where a smoothie costs $2.50 with tax. What are the possible numbers of smoothies that Ryan can buy?

Let s represent the number of smoothies Ryan can buy.

$2.50	times	number of smoothies	is at most	$16.00.
2.50	•	s	$\le$	16.00

$2.50s \le 16.00$

$\dfrac{2.50s}{2.50} \le \dfrac{16.00}{2.50}$ *Since s is multiplied by 2.50, divide both sides by 2.50.*
The symbol does not change.

$s \le 6.4$ *Ryan can buy only a whole number of smoothies.*

Ryan can buy 0, 1, 2, 3, 4, 5, or 6 smoothies.

CHECK IT OUT! **3.** A pitcher holds 128 ounces of juice. What are the possible numbers of 10-ounce servings that one pitcher can fill?

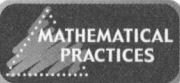

THINK AND DISCUSS

1. Compare the Multiplication and Division Properties of Inequality and the Multiplication and Division Properties of Equality.

2. GET ORGANIZED Copy and complete the graphic organizer. In each cell, write and solve an inequality.

Solving Inequalities by Using Multiplication and Division		
	By a Positive Number	**By a Negative Number**
Divide		
Multiply		

Exercises

GUIDED PRACTICE

Solve each inequality and graph the solutions.

SEE EXAMPLE 1

1. $3b > 27$
2. $-40 \geq 8b$
3. $\dfrac{d}{3} > 6$
4. $24d \leq 6$
5. $1.1m \leq 1.21$
6. $\dfrac{2}{3}k > 6$
7. $9s > -18$
8. $\dfrac{4}{5} \geq \dfrac{r}{2}$

SEE EXAMPLE 2

9. $-2x < -10$
10. $\dfrac{b}{-2} \geq 8$
11. $-3.5n < 1.4$
12. $4 > -8g$
13. $\dfrac{d}{-6} < \dfrac{1}{2}$
14. $-10h \geq -6$
15. $12 > \dfrac{t}{-6}$
16. $-\dfrac{1}{2}m \geq -7$

SEE EXAMPLE 3

17. **Travel** Tom saved $550 to go on a school trip. The cost for a hotel room, including tax, is $80 per night. What are the possible numbers of nights Tom can stay at the hotel?

PRACTICE AND PROBLEM SOLVING

Independent Practice

For Exercises	See Example
18–29	1
30–41	2
42	3

Extra Practice

See Extra Practice for more Skills Practice and Applications Practice exercises.

Solve each inequality and graph the solutions.

18. $10 < 2t$
19. $\dfrac{1}{3}j \leq 4$
20. $-80 < 8c$
21. $21 > 3d$
22. $\dfrac{w}{4} \geq -2$
23. $\dfrac{h}{4} \leq \dfrac{2}{7}$
24. $6y < 4.2$
25. $12c \leq -144$
26. $\dfrac{4}{5}x \geq \dfrac{2}{5}$
27. $6b \geq \dfrac{3}{5}$
28. $-25 > 10p$
29. $\dfrac{b}{8} \leq -2$
30. $-9a > 81$
31. $\dfrac{1}{2} < \dfrac{r}{-3}$
32. $-6p > 0.6$
33. $\dfrac{y}{-4} > -\dfrac{1}{2}$
34. $-\dfrac{1}{6}f < 5$
35. $-2.25t < -9$
36. $24 \leq -10w$
37. $-11z > 121$
38. $\dfrac{3}{5} < \dfrac{f}{-5}$
39. $-k \geq 7$
40. $-2.2b < -7.7$
41. $16 \geq -\dfrac{4}{3}p$

42. **Camping** The rope Roz brought with her camping gear is 54 inches long. Roz needs to cut shorter pieces of rope that are each 18 inches long. What are the possible number of pieces Roz can cut?

Solve each inequality and graph the solutions.

43. $-8x < 24$
44. $3t \leq 24$
45. $\dfrac{1}{4}x < 5$
46. $\dfrac{4}{5}p \geq -24$
47. $54 \leq -9p$
48. $3t > -\dfrac{1}{2}$
49. $-\dfrac{3}{4}b > -\dfrac{3}{2}$
50. $216 > 3.6r$

Write an inequality for each statement. Solve the inequality and graph the solutions.

51. The product of a number and 7 is not less than 21.

52. The quotient of h and -6 is at least 5.

53. The product of $-\dfrac{4}{5}$ and b is at most -16.

54. Ten is no more than the quotient of t and 4.

55. **Write About It** Explain how you know whether to reverse the inequality symbol when solving an inequality.

56. **Geometry** The area of a rectangle is at most 21 square inches. The width of the rectangle is 3.5 inches. What are the possible measurements for the length of the rectangle?

Solve each inequality and match the solution to the correct graph.

57. $-0.5t \geq 1.5$

A.
```
←─┼──┼──┼──┼──┼──┼──┼──┼──●──┼──┼→
 -5 -4 -3 -2 -1  0  1  2  3  4  5
```

58. $\frac{1}{9}t \leq -3$

B.
```
←─┼──┼──┼──┼──┼──┼──┼──┼──●━━┼→
 -5 -4 -3 -2 -1  0  1  2  3  4  5
```

59. $-13.5 \leq -4.5t$

C.
```
←━━●──┼──┼──┼──┼──┼──┼──┼──┼──┼→
 -5 -4 -3 -2 -1  0  1  2  3  4  5
```

60. $\frac{t}{-6} \leq -\frac{1}{2}$

D.
```
←─┼──┼──┼──●──┼──┼──┼──┼──┼→
-45 -36 -27 -18 -9   0   9
```

61. Animals A wildlife shelter is home to birds, mammals, and reptiles. If cat chow is sold in 20 lb bags, what is the least number of bags of cat chow needed for one year at this shelter?

Food Consumed at a Wildlife Shelter per Week	
Type of Food	**Amount of Food (lb)**
Grapes	4
Mixed seed	10
Peanuts	5
Cat chow	10
Kitten chow	5

62. Education In order to earn an A in a college math class, a student must score no less than 90% of all possible points. One semester, a student with 567 points earned an A in the class. Write an inequality to show the numbers of points possible.

63. Critical Thinking Explain why you cannot solve an inequality by multiplying both sides by zero.

64. ///**ERROR ANALYSIS**/// Two students have different answers for a homework problem. Which answer is incorrect? Explain the error.

A
$$9m \geq -27$$
$$\frac{9m}{9} \geq \frac{-27}{9}$$
$$m \leq -3$$

B
$$9m \geq -27$$
$$\frac{9m}{9} \geq \frac{-27}{9}$$
$$m \geq -3$$

65. Jan has a budget of $800 for catering. The catering company charges $12.50 per guest. Write and solve an inequality to show the numbers of guests Jan can invite.

MULTI-STEP TEST PREP

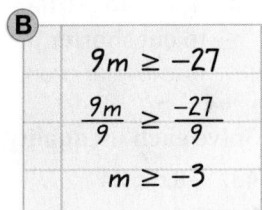

66. a. The Swimming Club can spend a total of $250 for hotel rooms for its spring trip. One hotel costs $75 per night. Write an inequality to find the number of rooms the club can reserve at this hotel. Let n be the number of rooms.

b. Solve the inequality you wrote in part **a.** Graph the solutions on a number line. Make sure your answer is reasonable.

c. Another hotel offers a rate of $65 per night. Does this allow the club to reserve more rooms? Explain your reasoning.

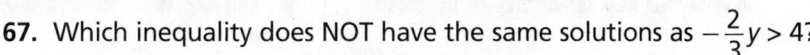

67. Which inequality does NOT have the same solutions as $-\frac{2}{3}y > 4$?

    Ⓐ $12 < -2y$

    Ⓑ $\frac{y}{2} < -12$

    Ⓒ $-\frac{3}{4}y > \frac{9}{2}$

    Ⓓ $-3y > 18$

68. The solutions of which inequality are NOT represented by the following graph?

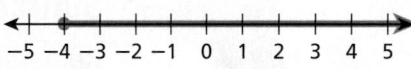

    Ⓕ $\frac{x}{2} \geq -2$

    Ⓖ $-5x \geq 20$

    Ⓗ $3x \geq -12$

    Ⓙ $-7x \leq 28$

69. Which inequality can be used to find the number of 39-cent stamps you can purchase for $4.00?

    Ⓐ $0.39s \geq 4.00$

    Ⓑ $0.39s \leq 4.00$

    Ⓒ $\frac{s}{0.39} \leq 4.00$

    Ⓓ $\frac{4.00}{0.39} \leq s$

70. Short Response Write three different inequalities that have the same solutions as $x > 4$. Show your work and explain each step.

CHALLENGE AND EXTEND

Solve each inequality.

71. $2\frac{1}{3} \leq -\frac{5}{6}g$

72. $\frac{2x}{3} < 8.25$

73. $2\frac{5}{8}m > \frac{7}{10}$

74. $3\frac{3}{5}f \geq 14\frac{2}{5}$

75. Estimation What is the greatest possible integer solution of the inequality $3.806x < 19.902$?

76. Critical Thinking The Transitive Property of Equality states that if $a = b$ and $b = c$, then $a = c$. Is there a Transitive Property of Inequality using the symbol $<$? Give an example to support your answer.

77. Critical Thinking The Symmetric Property of Equality states that if $a = b$, then $b = a$. Is there a Symmetric Property of Inequality? Give an example to support your answer.

MULTI-STEP TEST PREP

MATHEMATICAL PRACTICES

Make sense of
problems and
persevere in
solving them.

Simple Inequalities

Remember the Alamo! The Spanish Club is planning a trip
for next summer. They plan to travel from Fort Worth, Texas, to
San Antonio, Texas. They can spend only $550 for the entire trip.

1. The treasurer of the club budgets $60 for gasoline. The current gas
   price is $1.95/gallon. The school van gets an average of 20 miles
   per gallon of gasoline. Determine how many miles they can drive
   on this budget. Round your answer to the nearest mile.

2. The distance from Fort Worth to San Antonio is 266 miles. Write
   an inequality that can be used to solve for the number of miles
   m that they can drive while in San Antonio. Solve your inequality
   and graph the solutions.

3. The treasurer budgeted $200 for hotel rooms for one night. The club
   chose a hotel that charges $58 per night. Write an inequality that can
   be used to solve for the number of rooms they can reserve n. What is
   the maximum number of rooms that they can reserve in the hotel?

4. Use the maximum number of rooms you found in part **3.** How much
   will the club spend on hotel rooms?

5. The club members plan to
   spend $80 on food. They
   also want to see attractions
   in San Antonio, such as
   SeaWorld and the Alamo.

   Write an inequality that
   can be solved to find the
   amount of money available
   for seeing attractions. What
   is the maximum amount
   the club can spend seeing
   attractions?

6. Write a summary of the
   budget for the Spanish
   Club trip. Include
   the amount they plan to
   spend on gasoline, hotel
   rooms, food,
   and attractions.

Sara Karen Aimee
Janet Nancy Jaime
Loni :) Ron Diana

READY TO GO ON?

Quiz for Lessons 2-1 Through 2-3

2-1 Graphing and Writing Inequalities

Describe the solutions of each inequality in words.

1. $-2 < r$ **2.** $t - 1 \leq 7$ **3.** $2s \geq 6$ **4.** $4 > 5 - x$

Graph each inequality.

5. $x > -2$ **6.** $m \leq 1\frac{1}{2}$ **7.** $g < \sqrt{8+1}$ **8.** $h \geq 2^3$

Write the inequality shown by each graph.

9.

10.

11.

Write an inequality for each situation and graph the solutions.

12. You must purchase at least 5 tickets to receive a discount.

13. Children under 13 are not admitted to certain movies without an adult.

14. A cell phone plan allows up to 250 free minutes per month.

2-2 Solving One-Step Inequalities by Adding or Subtracting

Solve each inequality and graph the solutions.

15. $k + 5 \leq 7$ **16.** $4 > p - 3$ **17.** $r - 8 \geq -12$ **18.** $-3 + p < -6$

19. Allie must sell at least 50 gift baskets for the band fund-raiser. She already sold 36 baskets. Write and solve an inequality to determine how many more baskets Allie must sell for the fund-raiser.

20. Dante has at most $12 to spend on entertainment each week. So far this week, he spent $7.50. Write and solve an inequality to determine how much money Dante can spend on entertainment the rest of the week.

2-3 Solving One-Step Inequalities by Multiplying or Dividing

Solve each inequality and graph the solutions.

21. $-4x < 8$ **22.** $\frac{d}{3} \geq -3$ **23.** $\frac{3}{4}t \leq 12$ **24.** $8 > -16c$

25. A spool of ribbon is 80 inches long. Riley needs to cut strips of ribbon that are 14 inches long. What are the possible numbers of strips that Riley can cut?

Solving Two-Step and Multi-Step Inequalities

CC.9-12.A.REI.3 Solve linear equations and inequalities in one variable, including equations with coefficients represented by letters.
Also **CC.9-12.A.CED.1***

Objective
Solve inequalities that contain more than one operation.

Who uses this?

Contestants at a county fair can solve an inequality to find how many pounds a prize-winning pumpkin must weigh. (See Example 3.)

At the county fair, contestants can enter contests that judge animals, recipes, crops, art projects, and more. Sometimes an average score or average weight is used to determine the winner of the blue ribbon. A contestant can use a multi-step inequality to determine what score or weight is needed in order to win.

Inequalities that contain more than one operation require more than one step to solve. Use inverse operations to undo the operations in the inequality one at a time.

EXAMPLE **1** **Solving Multi-Step Inequalities**

Solve each inequality and graph the solutions.

A $160 + 4f \leq 500$

$$160 + 4f \leq 500$$
$$-160 \qquad -160$$
$$4f \leq 340$$

Since 160 is added to 4f, subtract 160 from both sides to undo the addition.

Since f is multiplied by 4, divide both sides by 4 to undo the multiplication.

$$\frac{4f}{4} \leq \frac{340}{4}$$
$$f \leq 85$$

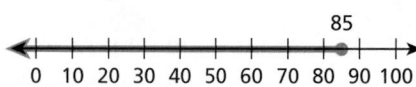

B $7 - 2t \leq 21$

$$7 - 2t \leq 21$$
$$-7 \qquad -7$$
$$-2t \leq 14$$

Since 7 is added to −2t, subtract 7 from both sides to undo the addition.

$$\frac{-2t}{-2} \geq \frac{14}{-2}$$
$$t \geq -7$$

Since t is multiplied by −2, divide both sides by −2 to undo the multiplication. Change ≤ to ≥.

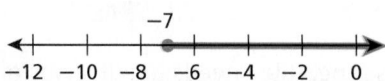

 **CHECK IT OUT!**

Solve each inequality and graph the solutions.

1a. $-12 \geq 3x + 6$ **1b.** $\dfrac{x+5}{-2} > 3$ **1c.** $\dfrac{1-2n}{3} \geq 7$

To solve more complicated inequalities, you may first need to simplify the expressions on one or both sides by using the order of operations, combining like terms, or using the Distributive Property.

EXAMPLE 2 **Simplifying Before Solving Inequalities**

Solve each inequality and graph the solutions.

A $-4 + (-8) < -5c - 2$

$$-12 < -5c - 2$$

Combine like terms. Since 2 is subtracted from $-5c$, add 2 to both sides to undo the subtraction.

$$\underline{+2 \qquad\quad +2}$$
$$-10 < -5c$$

$$\frac{-10}{-5} > \frac{-5c}{-5}$$

Since c is multiplied by -5, divide both sides by -5 to undo the multiplication. Change $<$ to $>$.

$$2 > c \,(\text{or } c < 2)$$

A number line from -5 to 5 with an open circle at 2 and shading to the left.

B $-3(3 - x) < 4^2$

$$-3(3 - x) < 4^2$$

Distribute -3 on the left side.

$$-3(3) - (-3)x < 4^2$$
$$-9 + 3x < 4^2$$

$$-9 + 3x < 16$$

Simplify the right side.

$$-9 + 3x < 16$$

Since -9 is added to $3x$, add 9 to both sides to undo the addition.

$$\underline{+9 \qquad\quad +9}$$
$$3x < 25$$

Since x is multiplied by 3, divide both sides by 3 to undo the multiplication.

$$\frac{3x}{3} < \frac{25}{3}$$

$$x < 8\frac{1}{3}$$

A number line from 0 to 10 with an open circle at $8\frac{1}{3}$ and shading to the left.

C $\frac{4}{5}x + \frac{1}{2} > \frac{3}{5}$

$$10\left(\frac{4}{5}x + \frac{1}{2}\right) > 10\left(\frac{3}{5}\right)$$

Multiply both sides by 10, the LCD of the fractions.

$$10\left(\frac{4}{5}x\right) + 10\left(\frac{1}{2}\right) > 10\left(\frac{3}{5}\right)$$

Distribute 10 on the left side.

$$8x + 5 > 6$$

Since 5 is added to 8x, subtract 5 from both sides to undo the addition.

$$\underline{-5 \quad -5}$$
$$8x \qquad > 1$$

$$\frac{8x}{8} > \frac{1}{8}$$

Since x is multiplied by 8, divide both sides by 8 to undo the multiplication.

$$x > \frac{1}{8}$$

A number line from $-\frac{1}{2}$ to $\frac{3}{4}$ with an open circle at $\frac{1}{8}$ and shading to the right.

Solve each inequality and graph the solutions.

2a. $2m + 5 > 5^2$ **2b.** $3 + 2(x + 4) > 3$ **2c.** $\frac{5}{8} < \frac{3}{8}x - \frac{1}{4}$

EXAMPLE **3** *Gardening Application*

To win the blue ribbon for the Heaviest Pumpkin Crop at the county fair, the average weight of John's two pumpkins must be greater than 819 lb. One of his pumpkins weighs 887 lb. What is the least number of pounds the second pumpkin could weigh in order for John to win the blue ribbon?

Let p represent the weight of the second pumpkin. The average weight of the pumpkins is the sum of each weight divided by 2.

(887	plus	p)	divided by	2	must be greater than	819.
(887	+	p)	÷	2	>	819

$\dfrac{887 + p}{2} > 819$ *Since 887 + p is divided by 2, multiply both sides by 2 to undo the division.*

$2\left(\dfrac{887 + p}{2}\right) > 2(819)$

$887 + p > 1638$ *Since 887 is added to p, subtract 887 from both sides to undo the addition.*

$\underline{-887 \qquad\quad -887\quad}$

$\qquad\qquad p > \ 751$

The second pumpkin must weigh more than 751 pounds.

Check   Check the endpoint, 751.   Check a number greater than 751.

$$\dfrac{887 + p}{2} = 819 \qquad\qquad\qquad \dfrac{887 + p}{2} > 819$$

$\dfrac{887 + 751}{2}$	819		$\dfrac{887 + 755}{2}$	>	819
$\dfrac{1638}{2}$	819		$\dfrac{1642}{2}$	>	819
819	819 ✓		821	>	819 ✓

 **3.** The average of Jim's two test scores must be at least 90 to make an A in the class. Jim got a 95 on his first test. What scores can Jim get on his second test to make an A in the class?

MATHEMATICAL PRACTICES

THINK AND DISCUSS

1. The inequality $v \geq 25$ states that 25 is the ___?___. (*value of v, minimum value of v,* or *maximum value of v*)

2. Describe two sets of steps for solving the inequality $\frac{x+5}{3} > 7$.

3. GET ORGANIZED Copy and complete the graphic organizer.

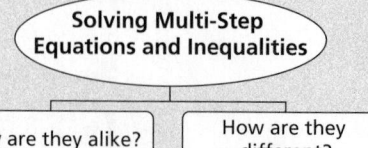

Solving Multi-Step Equations and Inequalities

How are they alike?	How are they different?

Paul Sakuma/AP/Wide World Photos

GUIDED PRACTICE

Solve each inequality and graph the solutions.

SEE EXAMPLE 1

1. $2m + 1 > 13$

2. $2d + 21 \leq 11$

3. $6 \leq -2x + 2$

4. $4c - 7 > 5$

5. $\dfrac{4 + x}{3} > -4$

6. $1 < 0.2x - 0.7$

7. $\dfrac{3 - 2x}{3} \leq 7$

8. $2x + 5 \geq 2$

SEE EXAMPLE 2

9. $4(x + 2) > 6$

10. $\dfrac{1}{4}x + \dfrac{2}{3} < \dfrac{3}{4}$

11. $4 - x + 6^2 \geq 21$

12. $4 - x > 3(4 - 2)$

13. $0.2(x - 10) > -1.8$

14. $3(j + 41) \leq 35$

SEE EXAMPLE 3

15. Business A sales representative is given a choice of two paycheck plans. One choice includes a monthly base pay of $300 plus 10% commission on his sales. The second choice is a monthly salary of $1200. For what amount of sales would the representative make more money with the first plan?

PRACTICE AND PROBLEM SOLVING

Independent Practice

For Exercises	See Example
16–27	1
28–36	2
37	3

Extra Practice

See Extra Practice for more Skills Practice and Applications Practice exercises.

Solve each inequality and graph the solutions.

16. $4r - 9 > 7$

17. $3 \leq 5 - 2x$

18. $\dfrac{w + 3}{2} > 6$

19. $11w + 99 < 77$

20. $9 \geq \dfrac{1}{2}v + 3$

21. $-4x - 8 > 16$

22. $8 - \dfrac{2}{3}z \leq 2$

23. $f + 2\dfrac{1}{2} < -2$

24. $\dfrac{3n - 8}{5} \geq 2$

25. $-5 > -5 - 3w$

26. $10 > \dfrac{5 - 3p}{2}$

27. $2v + 1 > 2\dfrac{1}{3}$

28. $4(x + 3) > -24$

29. $4 > x - 3(x + 2)$

30. $-18 \geq 33 - 3h$

31. $-2 > 7x - 2(x - 4)$

32. $9 - (9)^2 > 10x - x$

33. $2a - (-3)^2 \geq 13$

34. $6 - \dfrac{x}{3} + 1 > \dfrac{2}{3}$

35. $12(x - 3) + 2x > 6$

36. $15 \geq 19 + 2(q - 18)$

37. Communications One cell phone company offers a plan that costs $29.99 and includes unlimited night and weekend minutes. Another company offers a plan that costs $19.99 and charges $0.35 per minute during nights and weekends. For what numbers of night and weekend minutes does the second company's plan cost more than the first company's plan?

Solve each inequality and graph the solutions.

38. $-12 > -4x - 8$

39. $5x + 4 \leq 14$

40. $\dfrac{2}{3}x - 5 > 7$

41. $x - 3x > 2 - 10$

42. $5 - x - 2 > 3$

43. $3 < 2x - 5(x + 3)$

44. $\dfrac{1}{6} - \dfrac{2}{3}m \geq \dfrac{1}{4}$

45. $4 - (r - 2) > 3 - 5$

46. $0.3 - 0.5n + 1 \geq 0.4$

47. $6^2 > 4(x + 2)$

48. $-4 - 2n + 4n > 7 - 2^2$

49. $\dfrac{1}{4}(p - 10) \geq 6 - 4$

50. Use the inequality $-4t - 8 \leq 12$ to fill in the missing numbers.

a. $t \geq \blacksquare$

b. $t + 4 \geq \blacksquare$

c. $t - \blacksquare \geq 0$

d. $t + 10 \geq \blacksquare$

e. $3t \geq \blacksquare$

f. $\dfrac{t}{\blacksquare} \geq -5$

Write an inequality for each statement. Solve the inequality and graph the solutions.

51. One-half of a number, increased by 9, is less than 33.

52. Six is less than or equal to the sum of 4 and $-2x$.

53. The product of 4 and the sum of a number and 12 is at most 16.

54. The sum of half a number and two-thirds of the number is less than 14.

Solve each inequality and match the solution to the correct graph.

55. $4x - 9 \geq 7$

A.
```
←+——+——+——+——+——+——+——+——+——+——+——+——→
 -5 -4 -3 -2 -1  0  1  2  3  4  5
```

56. $-6 \geq 3(x - 2)$

B.
```
←+——+——+——+——+——+——+——+——+——+——+——+——→
 -5 -4 -3 -2 -1  0  1  2  3  4  5
```

57. $-2x - 6 \geq -4 + 2$

C.
```
                    $-\frac{3}{2}$
←+——+——+——+——+——+——+——+——+——+——+——+——→
 -5 -4 -3 -2 -1  0  1  2  3  4  5
```

58. $\frac{1}{2} - \frac{1}{3}x \leq \left(\frac{2}{3} + \frac{1}{3}\right)^2$

D.
```
←+——+——+——+——+——+——+——+——+——+——+——+——→
 -5 -4 -3 -2 -1  0  1  2  3  4  5
```

59. Entertainment A digital video recorder (DVR) records television shows on an internal hard drive. To use a DVR, you need a subscription with a DVR service company. Two companies advertise their charges for a DVR machine and subscription service.

EASY ELECTRONICS

$225 for DVR machine

$400 for lifetime subscription

CABLE SOLUTIONS

$275 for DVR machine

$15 per month for service

For what numbers of months will a consumer pay less for the machine and subscription at Easy Electronics than at Cable Solutions?

60. Geometry The area of the triangle shown is less than 55 square inches.

a. Write an inequality that can be used to find x.

b. Solve the inequality you wrote in part **a**.

c. What is the maximum height of the triangle?

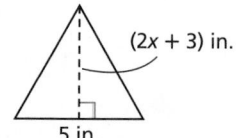

$(2x + 3)$ in.

5 in.

MULTI-STEP TEST PREP

61. a. A band wants to create a CD of their last concert. They received a donation of $500 to cover the cost. The total cost is $350 plus $3 per CD. Complete the table to find a relationship between the number of CDs and the total cost.

b. Write an equation for the cost c of the CDs based on the number of CDs n.

c. Write an inequality that can be used to determine how many CDs can be made with the $500 donation. Solve the inequality and determine how many CDs the band can have made from the $500 donation.

Number	Process	Cost
1	350 + 3	353
2		
3		
10		
n		

62. Critical Thinking What is the least whole number that is a solution of $4r - 4.9 > 14.95$?

63. Write About It Describe two sets of steps to solve $2(x + 3) > 10$.

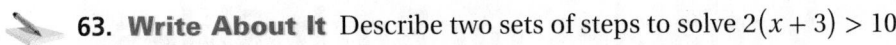

64. What are the solutions of $3y > 2x + 4$ when $y = 6$?

Ⓐ $7 > x$ Ⓑ $x > 7$ Ⓒ $x > 11$ Ⓓ $11 > x$

65. Cecilia has $30 to spend at a carnival. Admission costs $5.00, lunch will cost $6.00, and each ride ticket costs $1.25. Which inequality represents the number of ride tickets x that Cecilia can buy?

Ⓕ $30 - (5 - 6) + 1.25x \leq 30$ Ⓗ $30 - (5 + 6) \leq 1.25x$

Ⓖ $5 + 6 + 1.25x \leq 30$ Ⓙ $30 + 1.25x \leq 5 + 6$

66. Which statement is modeled by $2p + 5 < 11$?

Ⓐ The sum of 5 and 2 times p is at least 11.

Ⓑ Five added to the product of 2 and p is less than 11.

Ⓒ Two times p plus 5 is at most 11.

Ⓓ The product of 2 and p added to 5 is 11.

67. Gridded Response A basketball team scored 8 points more in its second game than in its first. In its third game, the team scored 42 points. The total number of points scored in the three games was more than 150. What is the least number of points the team might have scored in its *second* game?

CHALLENGE AND EXTEND

Solve each inequality and graph the solutions.

68. $3(x + 2) - 6x + 6 \leq 0$ **69.** $-18 > -(2x + 9) - 4 + x$ **70.** $\dfrac{2 + x}{2} - (x - 1) > 1$

Write an inequality for each statement. Graph the solutions.

71. x is a positive number.   **72.** x is a negative number.

73. x is a nonnegative number.   **74.** x is not a positive number.

75. x times negative 3 is positive.   **76.** The opposite of x is greater than 2.

2-5 Solving Inequalities with Variables on Both Sides

CC.9-12.A.REI.3 Solve linear equations and inequalities in one variable, including equations with coefficients represented by letters. *Also* **CC.9-12.A.CED.1***

Objective
Solve inequalities that contain variable terms on both sides.

Who uses this?
Business owners can use inequalities to find the most cost-efficient services. (See Example 2.)

Some inequalities have variable terms on both sides of the inequality symbol. You can solve these inequalities like you solved equations with variables on both sides.

Use the properties of inequality to "collect" all the variable terms on one side and all the constant terms on the other side.

EXAMPLE **Solving Inequalities with Variables on Both Sides**

Solve each inequality and graph the solutions.

A $x < 3x + 8$

$$
\begin{aligned}
x &< 3x + 8 \\
\underline{-x} \quad &\underline{-x} \\
0 &< 2x + 8 \\
\underline{-8} \quad &\underline{-8} \\
-8 &< 2x
\end{aligned}
$$

To collect the variable terms on one side, subtract x from both sides.

Since 8 is added to 2x, subtract 8 from both sides to undo the addition.

$$\frac{-8}{2} < \frac{2x}{2}$$

Since x is multiplied by 2, divide both sides by 2 to undo the multiplication.

$-4 < x \,(\text{or } x > -4)$

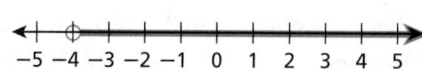

Helpful Hint

Your first step can also be to subtract $3x$ from both sides to get $-2x < 8$. When you divide by a negative number, remember to reverse the inequality symbol.

B $6x - 1 \le 3.5x + 4$

$$
\begin{aligned}
6x - 1 &\le 3.5x + 4 \\
\underline{-6x} \quad &\underline{-6x} \\
-1 &\le -2.5x + 4 \\
\underline{-4} \quad &\underline{-4} \\
-5 &\le -2.5x
\end{aligned}
$$

Subtract 6x from both sides.

Since 4 is added to −2.5x, subtract 4 from both sides to undo the addition.

$$\frac{-5}{-2.5} \ge \frac{-2.5x}{-2.5}$$

$2 \ge x$

Since x is multiplied by −2.5, divide both sides by −2.5 to undo the multiplication. Reverse the inequality symbol.

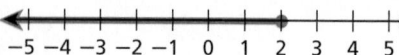

 **CHECK IT OUT!**

Solve each inequality and graph the solutions.

1a. $4x \ge 7x + 6$ **1b.** $5t + 1 < -2t - 6$

© Ariel Skelley/CORBIS

EXAMPLE 2 *Business Application*

The *Daily Info* charges a fee of $650 plus $80 per week to run an ad. The *People's Paper* charges $145 per week. For how many weeks will the total cost at *Daily Info* be less expensive than the cost at *People's Paper*?

Let w be the number of weeks the ad runs in the paper.

Daily Info fee	plus	$80 per week	times	number of weeks	is less expensive than	People's Paper charge per week	times	number of weeks.
$650	+	$80	·	w	<	$145	·	w

$$650 + 80w < 145w$$

$$\underline{\quad -80w \quad\quad -80w \quad}$$ *Subtract 80w from both sides.*

$$650 \quad\quad < \quad 65w$$ *Since w is multiplied by 65, divide both sides by 65 to undo the multiplication.*

$$\frac{650}{65} < \frac{65w}{65}$$

$$10 < w$$

The total cost at *Daily Info* is less than the cost at *People's Paper* if the ad runs for more than 10 weeks.

CHECK IT OUT! **2.** A-Plus Advertising charges a fee of $24 plus $0.10 per flyer to print and deliver flyers. Print and More charges $0.25 per flyer. For how many flyers is the cost at A-Plus Advertising less than the cost at Print and More?

You may need to simplify one or both sides of an inequality before solving it. Look for like terms to combine and places to use Distributive Property.

EXAMPLE 3 **Simplifying Each Side Before Solving**

Solve each inequality and graph the solutions.

A $6(1 - x) < 3x$

$$6(1 - x) < 3x$$ *Distribute 6 on the left side of the inequality.*

$$6(1) - 6(x) < 3x$$

$$6 - 6x < 3x$$ *Add 6x to both sides so that the coefficient of x is positive.*

$$\underline{\quad +6x \quad\quad +6x \quad}$$

$$6 \quad\quad < \quad 9x$$

$$\frac{6}{9} < \frac{9x}{9}$$ *Since x is multiplied by 9, divide both sides by 9 to undo the multiplication.*

$$\frac{2}{3} < x$$

$$-\frac{1}{3} \quad 0 \quad \frac{1}{3} \quad \frac{2}{3} \quad 1 \quad 1\frac{1}{3} \quad 1\frac{2}{3} \quad 2 \quad 2\frac{1}{3} \quad 2\frac{2}{3} \quad 3$$

Helpful Hint

In Example 3B, you can also multiply each term in the inequality by the same power of 10 to clear the decimals.
$10(1.6x) \leq 10(-0.2x)$
$\qquad + 10(0.9)$
$16x \leq -2x + 9$

Solve each inequality and graph the solutions.

B $\quad 1.6x \leq -0.2x + 0.9$

$$1.6x \leq -0.2x + 0.9$$
$$\underline{+\,0.2x \qquad +\,0.2x}$$
$$1.8x \leq \qquad\quad 0.9$$

Since $-0.2x$ is added to 0.9, subtract $-0.2x$ from both sides. Subtracting $-0.2x$ is the same as adding $0.2x$.

$$\frac{1.8x}{1.8} \leq \frac{0.9}{1.8}$$

Since x is multiplied by 1.8, divide both sides by 1.8 to undo the multiplication.

$$x \leq \frac{1}{2}$$

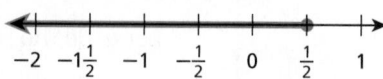

CHECK IT OUT! Solve each inequality and graph the solutions. Check your answer.

3a. $5(2 - r) \geq 3(r - 2)$ **3b.** $0.5x - 0.3 + 1.9x < 0.3x + 6$

Some inequalities are true no matter what value is substituted for the variable. For these inequalities, all real numbers are solutions.

Some inequalities are false no matter what value is substituted for the variable. These inequalities have no solutions.

If both sides of an inequality are fully simplified and the same variable term appears on both sides, then the inequality has all real numbers as solutions or it has no solutions. Look at the other terms in the inequality to decide which is the case.

EXAMPLE 4 **All Real Numbers as Solutions or No Solutions**

Solve each inequality.

A $x + 5 \geq x + 3$

$\qquad x + 5 \geq x + 3$

The same variable term (x) appears on both sides. Look at the other terms.

For any number x, adding 5 will always result in a greater number than adding 3.

All values of x make the inequality true.
All real numbers are solutions.

B $2(x + 3) < 5 + 2x$

$\qquad 2x + 6 < 5 + 2x \qquad$ *Distribute 2 on the left side.*

The same variable term ($2x$) appears on both sides. Look at the other terms.

For any number $2x$, adding 6 will never result in a lesser number than adding 5.

No values of x make the inequality true.
There are no solutions.

CHECK IT OUT! Solve each inequality.

4a. $4(y - 1) \geq 4y + 2$ **4b.** $x - 2 < x + 1$

THINK AND DISCUSS

1. Explain how you would collect the variable terms to solve the inequality $5c - 4 > 8c + 2$.

2. **GET ORGANIZED** Copy and complete the graphic organizer. In each box, give an example of an inequality of the indicated type.

Solutions of Inequalities with Variables on Both Sides

| All real numbers | | No solutions |

2-5 Exercises

Learn It Online
Homework Help Online
Parent Resources Online

GUIDED PRACTICE

SEE EXAMPLE **1**

Solve each inequality and graph the solutions.

1. $2x > 4x - 6$
2. $7y + 1 \leq y - 5$
3. $27x + 33 > 58x - 29$
4. $-3r < 10 - r$
5. $5c - 4 > 8c + 2$
6. $4.5x - 3.8 \geq 1.5x - 2.3$

SEE EXAMPLE **2**

7. **School** The school band will sell pizzas to raise money for new uniforms. The supplier charges $100 plus $4 per pizza. If the band members sell the pizzas for $7 each, how many pizzas will they have to sell to make a profit?

SEE EXAMPLE **3**

Solve each inequality and graph the solutions.

8. $5(4 + x) \leq 3(2 + x)$
9. $-4(3 - p) > 5(p + 1)$
10. $2(6 - x) < 4x$
11. $4x > 3(7 - x)$
12. $\frac{1}{2}f + \frac{3}{4} \geq \frac{1}{4}f$
13. $-36.72 + 5.65t < 0.25t$

SEE EXAMPLE **4**

Solve each inequality.

14. $2(x - 2) \leq -2(1 - x)$
15. $4(y + 1) < 4y + 2$
16. $4v + 1 < 4v - 7$
17. $b - 4 \geq b - 6$
18. $3(x - 5) > 3x$
19. $2k + 7 \geq 2(k + 14)$

PRACTICE AND PROBLEM SOLVING

Solve each inequality and graph the solutions.

20. $3x \leq 5x + 8$
21. $9y + 3 > 4y - 7$
22. $1.5x - 1.2 < 3.1x - 2.8$
23. $7 + 4b \geq 3b$
24. $7 - 5t < 4t - 2$
25. $2.8m - 5.2 > 0.8m + 4.8$

26. **Geometry** For what values of x is the area of the rectangle greater than the area of the triangle?

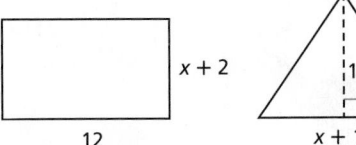

For Exercises	See Example
20–25	1
26	2
27–32	3
33–38	4

Independent Practice

Extra Practice

See Extra Practice for more Skills Practice and Applications Practice exercises.

Solve each inequality and graph the solutions.

27. $4(2 - x) \leq 5(x - 2)$

28. $-3(n + 4) < 6(1 - n)$

29. $9(w + 2) \leq 12w$

30. $4.5 + 1.3t > 3.8t - 3$

31. $\frac{1}{2}r + \frac{2}{3} \geq \frac{1}{3}r$

32. $2(4 - n) < 3n - 7$

Solve each inequality.

33. $3(2 - x) < -3(x - 1)$

34. $7 - y > 5 - y$

35. $3(10 + z) \leq 3z + 36$

36. $-5(k - 1) \geq 5(2 - k)$

37. $4(x - 1) \leq 4x$

38. $3(v - 9) \geq 15 + 3v$

Solve each inequality and graph the solutions.

39. $3t - 12 > 5t + 2$

40. $-5(y + 3) - 6 < y + 3$

41. $3x + 9 - 5x < x$

42. $18 + 9p > 12p - 31$

43. $2(x - 5) < -3x$

44. $-\frac{2}{5}x \leq \frac{4}{5} - \frac{3}{5}x$

45. $-2(x - 7) - 4 - x < 8x + 32$

46. $-3(2r - 4) \geq 2(5 - 3r)$

47. $-7x - 10 + 5x \geq 3(x + 4) + 8$

48. $-\frac{1}{3}(n + 8) + \frac{1}{3}n \leq 1 - n$

Recreation

The American Kitefliers Association has over 4000 members in 35 countries. Kitefliers participate in festivals, competitions, and kite-making workshops.

49. Recreation A red kite is 100 feet off the ground and is rising at 8 feet per second. A blue kite is 180 feet off the ground and is rising at 5 feet per second. How long will it take for the red kite to be higher than the blue kite? Round your answer to the nearest second.

50. Education The table shows the enrollment in Howard High School and Phillips High School for three school years.

School Enrollment	Year 1	Year 2	Year 3
Howard High School	1192	1188	1184
Phillips High School	921	941	961

  a. How much did the enrollment change each year at Howard?

  b. Use the enrollment in year 1 and your answer from part **a** to write an expression for the enrollment at Howard in any year x.

  c. How much did the enrollment change each year at Phillips?

  d. Use the enrollment in year 1 and your answer from part **c** to write an expression for the enrollment at Phillips in any year x.

  e. Assume that the pattern in the table continues. Use your expressions from parts **b** and **d** to write an inequality that can be solved to find the year in which the enrollment at Phillips High School will be greater than the enrollment at Howard High School. Solve your inequality and graph the solutions.

MULTI-STEP TEST PREP

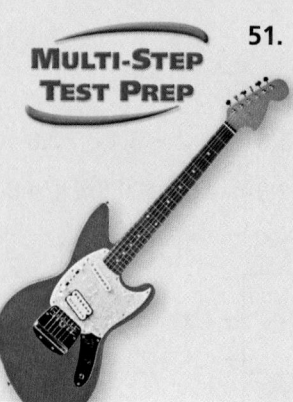

51. a. The school orchestra is creating a CD of their last concert. The total cost is $400 + 4.50 per CD. Write an expression for the cost of creating the CDs based on the number of CDs n.

  b. The orchestra plans to sell the CDs for $12. Write an expression for the amount the orchestra earns from the sale of n CDs.

  c. In order for the orchestra to make a profit, the amount they make selling the CDs must be greater than the cost of creating the CDs. Write an inequality that can be solved to find the number of CDs the orchestra must sell in order to make a profit. Solve your inequality.

(bl), © Brand X Pictures; (cl), HMH

Write an inequality to represent each relationship. Solve your inequality.

52. Four more than twice a number is greater than two-thirds of the number.

53. Ten less than five times a number is less than six times the number decreased by eight.

54. The sum of a number and twenty is less than four times the number decreased by one.

55. Three-fourths of a number is greater than or equal to five less than the number.

56. **Entertainment** Use the table to determine how many movies you would have to rent for Video View to be less expensive than Movie Place.

	Membership Fee ($)	Cost per Rental ($)
Movie Place	None	2.99
Video View	19.99	1.99

57. **Geometry** In an acute triangle, all angles measure less than 90°. Also, the sum of the measures of any two angles is greater than the measure of the third angle. Can the measures of an acute triangle be x, $x - 1$, and $2x$? Explain.

58. **Write About It** Compare the steps you would follow to solve an inequality to the steps you would follow to solve an equation.

59. **Critical Thinking** How can you tell just by looking at the inequality $x > x + 1$ that it has no solutions?

60. /// ERROR ANALYSIS /// Two students solved the inequality $5x < 3 - 4x$. Which is incorrect? Explain the error.

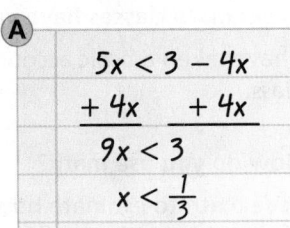

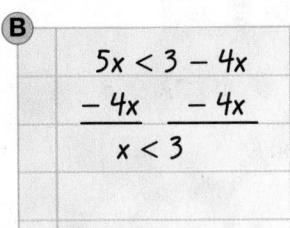

61. If $a - b > a + b$, which statement is true?

(A) The value of a is positive.

(B) The value of b is positive.

(C) The value of a is negative.

(D) The value of b is negative.

62. If $-a < b$, which statement is always true?

(F) $a < b$ (G) $a > b$ (H) $a < -b$ (J) $a > -b$

63. Which is a solution of the inequality $7(2 - x) > 4(x - 2)$?

(A) -2 (B) 2   (C) 4   (D) 7

64. Which is the graph of $-5x < -2x - 6$?

(F)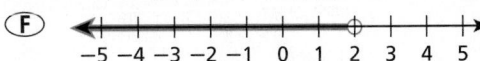

(H)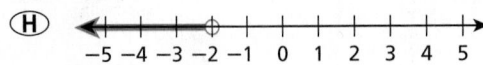

(G)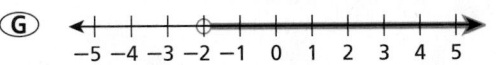

(J)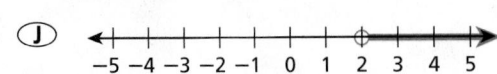

65. Short Response Write a real-world situation that could be modeled by the inequality $7x + 4 > 4x + 13$. Explain how the inequality relates to your situation.

CHALLENGE AND EXTEND

Solve each inequality.

66. $2\frac{1}{2} + 2x \geq 5\frac{1}{2} + 2\frac{1}{2}x$

67. $1.6x - 20.7 > 6.3x - (-2.2x)$

68. $1.3x - 7.5x < 8.5x - 29.4$

69. $-4w + \dfrac{-8 - 37}{9} \leq \dfrac{75 - 3}{9} + 3w$

70. Replace the square and circle with numbers so that the inequality has all real numbers as solutions. $\square - 2x < \bigcirc - 2x$

71. Replace the square and circle with numbers so that the inequality has no solutions. $\square - 2x < \bigcirc - 2x$

72. Critical Thinking Explain whether there are any numbers that can replace the square and circle so that the inequality has all real numbers as solutions. $\square + 2x < \bigcirc + x$

Career Path

Katie Flannigan
Culinary Arts program

Learn It Online
Career Resources Online

Q: What math classes did you take in high school?

A: Algebra 1, Geometry, and Algebra 2

Q: What math classes have you taken since high school?

A: I have taken a basic accounting class and a business math class.

Q: How do you use math?

A: I use math to estimate how much food I need to buy. I also use math when adjusting recipe amounts to feed large groups of people.

Q: What are your future plans?

A: I plan to start my own catering business. The math classes I took will help me manage the financial aspects of my business.

2-6 Algebra LAB

Truth Tables and Compound Statements

A compound statement is formed by combining two or more simple statements. A compound statement is either true or false depending on whether its simple statements are true or false.

Use with Solving Compound Inequalities

 **MATHEMATICAL PRACTICES**

Look for and express regularity in repeated reasoning.

CC.9-12.A.REI.3 Solve linear equations and inequalities in one variable, including equations with coefficients represented by letters.

Activity 1

- Let *P* be "Cindy is at least 17 years old."
- Let *Q* be "Cindy has a driver's license."

If...	then *P* is	and *Q* is	so *P* AND *Q* is
Cindy is 18 years old. Cindy has a driver's license.	True	True	True
Cindy is 17 years old. Cindy does not have a driver's license.	True	False	False
Cindy is 16 years old. Cindy has a driver's license.	False	True	False
Cindy is 15 years old. Cindy does not have a driver's license.	False	False	False

P AND *Q* is true when _____?_____.

Try This

For each pair of simple statements, tell whether *P* AND *Q* is true or false.

1. *P:* Many birds can fly; *Q:* A zebra is an animal.

Activity 2

- Let *P* be "Paul plays tennis."
- Let *Q* be "Paul has brown eyes."

If...	then *P* is	and *Q* is	so *P* OR *Q* is
Paul plays tennis. Paul has brown eyes.	True	True	True
Paul plays tennis. Paul has green eyes.	True	False	True
Paul does not play tennis. Paul has brown eyes.	False	True	True
Paul does not play tennis. Paul has green eyes.	False	False	False

P OR *Q* is true when _____?_____.

Try This

For each pair of simple statements, tell whether *P* OR *Q* is true or false.

2. *P:* The number 12 is even; *Q:* The number 12 is a composite number.

2-6 Solving Compound Inequalities

CC.9-12.A.REI.3 Solve linear equations and inequalities in one variable, including equations with coefficients represented by letters.

Objectives
Solve compound inequalities in one variable.

Graph solution sets of compound inequalities in one variable.

Vocabulary
compound inequality
intersection
union

Who uses this?
A lifeguard can use compound inequalities to describe the safe pH levels in a swimming pool. (See Example 1.)

The inequalities you have seen so far are simple inequalities. When two simple inequalities are combined into one statement by the words AND or OR, the result is called a **compound inequality**.

Know it! Note

Compound Inequalities

WORDS	ALGEBRA	GRAPH
All real numbers greater than 2 AND less than 6	$x > 2$ AND $x < 6$ $2 < x < 6$	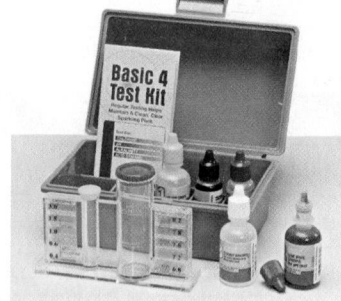 0 2 4 6 8
All real numbers greater than or equal to 2 AND less than or equal to 6	$x \geq 2$ AND $x \leq 6$ $2 \leq x \leq 6$	0 2 4 6 8
All real numbers less than 2 OR greater than 6	$x < 2$ OR $x > 6$	0 2 4 6 8
All real numbers less than or equal to 2 OR greater than or equal to 6	$x \leq 2$ OR $x \geq 6$	0 2 4 6 8

EXAMPLE 1   Chemistry Application

A water analyst recommends that the pH level of swimming pool water be between 7.2 and 7.6 inclusive. Write a compound inequality to show the pH levels that are within the recommended range. Graph the solutions.

Let p be the pH level of swimming pool water.

Helpful Hint

The phrase "between 7.2 and 7.6 *inclusive*" means that the numbers 7.2 and 7.6 are included in the solutions. Use a solid circle for endpoints that are solutions.

7.2	is less than or equal to	pH level	is less than or equal to	7.6
7.2	$\leq$	p	$\leq$	7.6

$7.2 \leq p \leq 7.6$

7.1 7.2 7.3 7.4 7.5 7.6 7.7

1. The free chlorine level in a pool should be between 1.0 and 3.0 parts per million inclusive. Write a compound inequality to show the levels that are within this range. Graph the solutions.

In this diagram, oval A represents some integer solutions of $x < 10$, and oval B represents some integer solutions of $x > 0$. The overlapping region represents numbers that belong in both ovals. Those numbers are solutions of *both* $x < 10$ *and* $x > 0$.

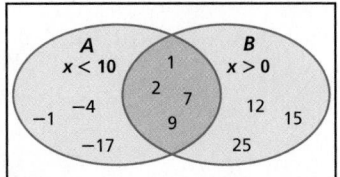

You can graph the solutions of a compound inequality involving AND by using the idea of an overlapping region. The overlapping region is called the **intersection** and shows the numbers that are solutions of both inequalities.

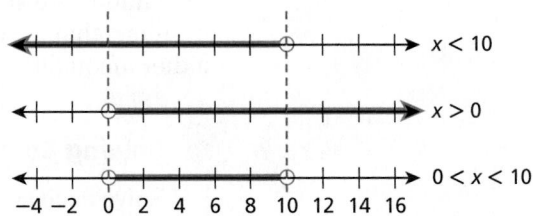

EXAMPLE **2** **Solving Compound Inequalities Involving AND**

Solve each compound inequality and graph the solutions.

 $4 \le x + 2 \le 8$

$$4 \le x + 2 \ \text{AND} \ x + 2 \le 8 \qquad \textit{Write the compound inequality using AND.}$$
$$\underline{-2 \quad -2} \qquad \qquad \underline{-2 \ -2} \qquad \textit{Solve each simple inequality.}$$
$$2 \le x \qquad \text{AND} \ x \qquad \le 6$$

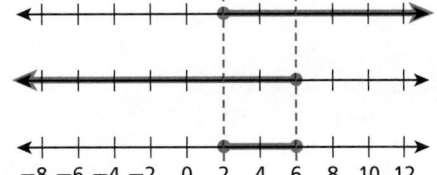

Graph $2 \le x$.

Graph $x \le 6$.

Graph the intersection by finding where the two graphs overlap.

B $-5 \le 2x + 3 < 9$

$$-5 \le 2x + 3 < 9 \qquad \textit{Since 3 is added to 2x, subtract 3 from each part}$$
$$\underline{-3 \qquad -3 \ -3} \qquad \textit{of the inequality.}$$
$$-8 \le 2x \qquad < 6$$

$$\frac{-8}{2} \le \frac{2x}{2} < \frac{6}{2} \qquad \textit{Since x is multiplied by 2, divide each part of the}$$
$$-4 \le x < 3 \qquad \textit{inequality by 2.}$$

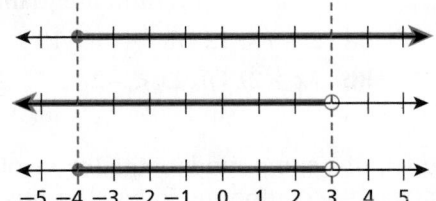

Graph $-4 \le x$.

Graph $x < 3$.

Graph the intersection by finding where the two graphs overlap.

Remember!

The statement $-5 \le 2x + 3 \le 9$ consists of two inequalities connected by AND. Example 2B shows a "shorthand" method for solving this type of inequality.

 Solve each compound inequality and graph the solutions.

2a. $-9 < x - 10 < -5$ **2b.** $-4 \le 3n + 5 < 11$

In this diagram, circle *A* represents some integer solutions of $x < 0$, and circle *B* represents some integer solutions of $x > 10$. The combined shaded regions represent numbers that are solutions of *either $x < 0$ or $x > 10$*.

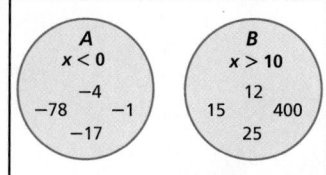

You can graph the solutions of a compound inequality involving OR by using the idea of combining regions. The combined regions are called the **union** and show the numbers that are solutions of either inequality.

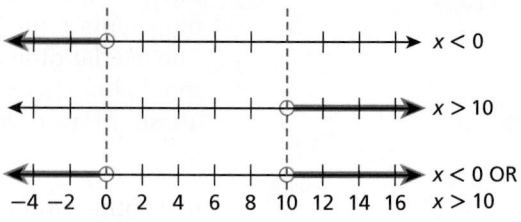

EXAMPLE **3** **Solving Compound Inequalities Involving OR**

Solve each compound inequality and graph the solutions.

A $-4 + a > 1$ OR $-4 + a < -3$

$$-4 + a > \quad 1 \text{ OR } -4 + a < -3$$
$$\underline{+4 \qquad +4 \quad +4 \qquad +4}$$
$$a > \quad 5 \text{ OR } \qquad a < \quad 1$$

Solve each simple inequality.

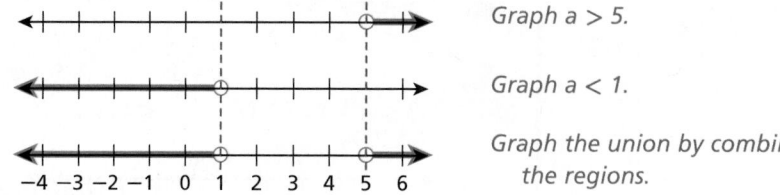

Graph a > 5.

Graph a < 1.

Graph the union by combining the regions.

B $2x \le 6$ OR $3x > 12$

$$2x \le 6 \text{ OR } 3x > 12$$
$$\frac{2x}{2} \le \frac{6}{2} \qquad \frac{3x}{3} > \frac{12}{3}$$
$$x \le 3 \text{ OR } \quad x > \quad 4$$

Solve each simple inequality.

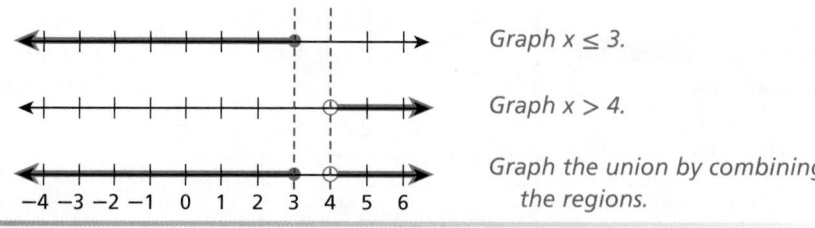

Graph x ≤ 3.

Graph x > 4.

Graph the union by combining the regions.

Solve each compound inequality and graph the solutions.

3a. $2 + r < 12$ OR $r + 5 > 19$

3b. $7x \ge 21$ OR $2x < -2$

Every solution of a compound inequality involving AND must be a solution of both parts of the compound inequality. If no numbers are solutions of *both* simple inequalities, then the compound inequality has no solutions.

The solutions of a compound inequality involving OR are not always two separate sets of numbers. There may be numbers that are solutions of both parts of the compound inequality.

EXAMPLE 4 **Writing a Compound Inequality from a Graph**

Write the compound inequality shown by each graph.

A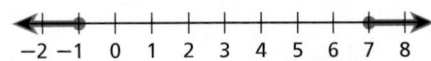

The shaded portion of the graph is not between two values, so the compound inequality involves OR.

> *On the left, the graph shows an arrow pointing left, so use either < or ≤. The solid circle at −1 means −1 is a solution, so use ≤.*

$x \le -1$

> *On the right, the graph shows an arrow pointing right, so use either > or ≥. The solid circle at 7 means 7 is a solution, so use ≥.*

$x \ge 7$

The compound inequality is $x \le -1$ OR $x \ge 7$.

B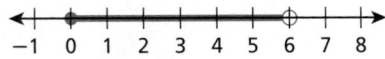

The shaded portion of the graph is between the values 0 and 6, so the compound inequality involves AND.

> *The shaded values are to the right of 0, so use > or ≥. The solid circle at 0 means 0 is a solution, so use ≥.*

$x \ge 0$

> *The shaded values are to the left of 6, so use < or ≤. The empty circle at 6 means 6 is not a solution, so use <.*

$x < 6$

The compound inequality is $x \ge 0$ AND $x < 6$.

Writing Math

The compound inequality in Example 4B can also be written with the variable between the two endpoints.
$0 \le x < 6$

 Write the compound inequality shown by the graph.

4a.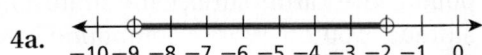

4b. (graph from −5 to 5)

THINK AND DISCUSS

1. Describe how to write the compound inequality $y > 4$ AND $y \le 12$ without using the joining word AND.

2. GET ORGANIZED Copy and complete the graphic organizers. Write three solutions in each of the three sections of the diagram. Then write each of your nine solutions in the appropriate column or columns of the table.

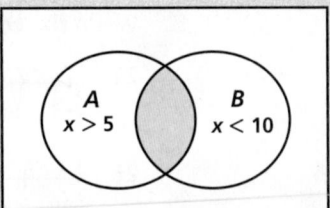

$x > 5$ AND $x < 10$	$x > 5$ OR $x < 10$

GUIDED PRACTICE

1. **Vocabulary** The graph of a(n) ___?___ shows all values that are solutions to both simple inequalities that make a compound inequality. (*union* or *intersection*)

SEE EXAMPLE 1

2. **Biology** An iguana needs to live in a warm environment. The temperature in a pet iguana's cage should be between 70 °F and 95 °F inclusive. Write a compound inequality to show the temperatures that are within the recommended range. Graph the solutions.

Solve each compound inequality and graph the solutions.

SEE EXAMPLE 2

3. $-3 < x + 2 < 7$

4. $5 \le 4x + 1 \le 13$

5. $2 < x + 2 < 5$

6. $11 < 2x + 3 < 21$

SEE EXAMPLE 3

7. $x + 2 < -6$ OR $x + 2 > 6$

8. $r - 1 < 0$ OR $r - 1 > 4$

9. $n + 2 < 3$ OR $n + 3 > 7$

10. $x - 1 < -1$ OR $x - 5 > -1$

SEE EXAMPLE 4

Write the compound inequality shown by each graph.

11.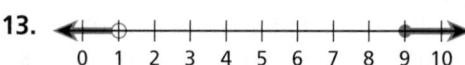

12.

13.

14.

PRACTICE AND PROBLEM SOLVING

Independent Practice

For Exercises	See Example
15	1
16–19	2
20–23	3
24–27	4

Extra Practice

See Extra Practice for more Skills Practice and Applications Practice exercises.

15. **Meteorology** One layer of Earth's atmosphere is called the stratosphere. At one point above Earth's surface the stratosphere extends from an altitude of 16 km to an altitude of 50 km. Write a compound inequality to show the altitudes that are within the range of the stratosphere. Graph the solutions.

Solve each compound inequality and graph the solutions.

16. $-1 < x + 1 < 1$

17. $1 \le 2n - 5 \le 7$

18. $-2 < x - 2 < 2$

19. $5 < 3x - 1 < 17$

20. $x - 4 < -7$ OR $x + 3 > 4$

21. $2x + 1 < 1$ OR $x + 5 > 8$

22. $x + 1 < 2$ OR $x + 5 > 8$

23. $x + 3 < 0$ OR $x - 2 > 0$

Write the compound inequality shown by each graph.

24.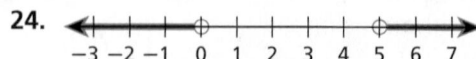

25.

26.

27.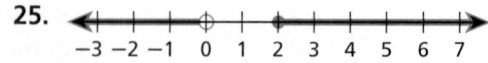

28. **Music** A typical acoustic guitar has a range of three octaves. When the guitar is tuned to "concert pitch," the range of frequencies for those three octaves is between 82.4 Hz and 659.2 Hz inclusive. Write a compound inequality to show the frequencies that are within the range of a typical acoustic guitar. Graph the solutions.

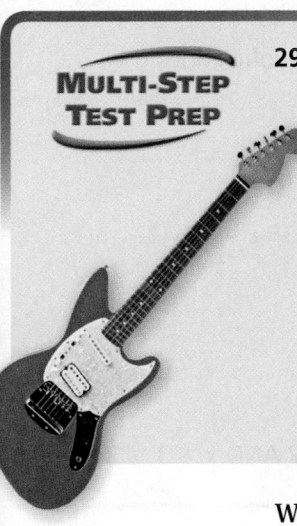

MULTI-STEP TEST PREP

29. Jenna's band is going to record a CD at a recording studio. They will pay $225 to use the studio for one day and $80 per hour for sound technicians. Jenna has $200 and can reasonably expect to raise up to an additional $350 by taking pre-orders for the CDs.

   a. Explain how the inequality $200 \leq 225 + 80n \leq 550$ can be used to find the number of hours Jenna and her band can afford to use the studio and sound technicians.

   b. Solve the inequality. Are there any numbers in the solution set that are not reasonable in this situation?

   c. Suppose Jenna raises $350 in pre-orders. How much more money would she need to raise if she wanted to use the studio and sound technicians for 6 hours?

Write and graph a compound inequality for the numbers described.

30. all real numbers between -6 and 6

31. all real numbers less than or equal to 2 and greater than or equal to 1

32. all real numbers greater than 0 and less than 15

33. all real numbers between -10 and 10 inclusive

Chemistry

The element gallium is in a solid state at room temperature but becomes a liquid at about 30 °C. Gallium stays in a liquid state until it reaches a temperature of about 2204 °C.

34. **Transportation** The cruise-control function on Georgina's car should keep the speed of the car within 3 mi/h of the set speed. Write a compound inequality to show the acceptable speeds s if the set speed is 55 mi/h. Graph the solutions.

35. **Chemistry** Water is not a liquid if its temperature is above 100 °C or below 0 °C. Write a compound inequality for the temperatures t when water is not a liquid.

Solve each compound inequality and graph the solutions.

36. $5 \leq 4b - 3 \leq 9$

37. $-3 < x - 1 < 4$

38. $r + 2 < -2$ OR $r - 2 > 2$

39. $2a - 5 < -5$ OR $3a - 2 > 1$

40. $x - 4 \geq 5$ AND $x - 4 \leq 5$

41. $n - 4 < -2$ OR $n + 1 > 6$

42. **Sports** The ball used in a soccer game may not weigh more than 16 ounces or less than 14 ounces at the start of the match. After $1\frac{1}{2}$ ounces of air was added to a ball, the ball was approved for use in a game. Write and solve a compound inequality to show how much the ball might have weighed before the air was added.

43. **Meteorology** Tornado damage is rated using the Fujita scale shown in the table. A tornado has a wind speed of 200 miles per hour. Write and solve a compound inequality to show how many miles per hour the wind speed would need to increase for the tornado to be rated "devastating" but not "incredible."

Fujita Tornado Scale		
Category	Type	Wind Speed (mi/h)
F0	Weak	40 to 72
F1	Moderate	73 to 112
F2	Significant	113 to 157
F3	Severe	158 to 206
F4	Devastating	207 to 260
F5	Incredible	261 to 318

44. Give a real-world situation that can be described by a compound inequality. Write the inequality that describes your situation.

45. **Write About It** How are the graphs of the compound inequality $x < 3$ AND $x < 7$ and the compound inequality $x < 3$ OR $x < 7$ different? How are the graphs alike? Explain.

46. Critical Thinking If there is no solution to a compound inequality, does the compound inequality involve OR or AND? Explain.

47. Which of the following describes the solutions of $-x + 1 > 2$ OR $x - 1 > 2$?

    Ⓐ all real numbers greater than 1 or less than 3

    Ⓑ all real numbers greater than 3 or less than 1

    Ⓒ all real numbers greater than −1 or less than 3

    Ⓓ all real numbers greater than 3 or less than −1

48. Which of the following is a graph of the solutions of $x - 3 < 2$ AND $x + 3 > 2$?

    Ⓕ 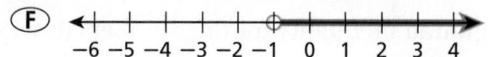   Ⓗ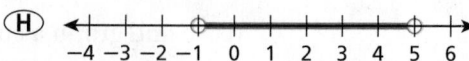

    Ⓖ 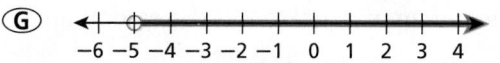   Ⓙ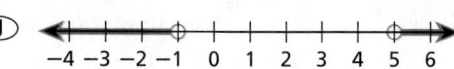

49. Which compound inequality is shown by the graph?

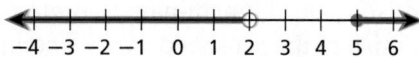

    Ⓐ $x \le 2$ OR $x > 5$ Ⓒ $x \le 2$ OR $x \ge 5$

    Ⓑ $x < 2$ OR $x \ge 5$ Ⓓ $x \ge 2$ OR $x > 5$

50. Which of the following is a solution of $x + 1 \ge 3$ AND $x + 1 \le 3$?

    Ⓕ 0   Ⓖ 1   Ⓗ 2   Ⓙ 3

CHALLENGE AND EXTEND

Solve and graph each compound inequality.

51. $2c - 10 < 5 - 3c < 7c$

52. $5p - 10 < p + 6 < 3p$

53. $2s \le 18 - s$ OR $5s \ge s + 36$

54. $9 - x \ge 5x$ OR $20 - 3x \le 17$

55. Write a compound inequality that represents all values of x that are NOT solutions to $x < -1$ OR $x > 3$.

56. For the compound inequality $x + 2 \ge a$ AND $x - 7 \le b$, find values of a and b for which the only solution is $x = 1$.

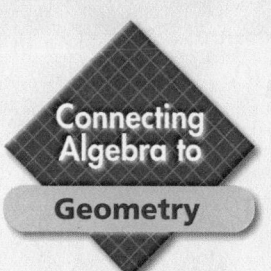

Triangle Inequality

Connecting Algebra to Geometry

For any triangle, the sum of the lengths of any two sides is greater than the length of the third side.

The sides of this triangle are labeled a, b, and c. You can use the Triangle Inequality to write three statements about the triangle.

$$a + b > c \qquad a + c > b \qquad b + c > a$$

Unless all three of the inequalities are true, the lengths a, b, and c cannot form a triangle.

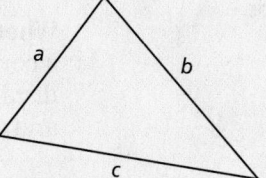

Example 1

Can three side lengths of 25 cm, 15 cm, and 5 cm form a triangle?

a. $25 + 15 > 5$
    $40 > 5$ *True*

b. $25 + 5 > 15$
    $30 > 15$ *True*

c. $15 + 5 > 25$
    $20 > 25$ *False*

One of the inequalities is false, so the three lengths will not make a triangle. The situation is shown in the figure to the right.

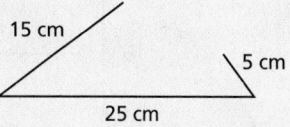

Example 2

Two sides of a triangle measure 8 ft and 10 ft. What is the range of lengths of the third side?

Start by writing three statements about the triangle. Use x for the unknown side length.

a. $8 + 10 > x$
    $18 > x$

The third side must be shorter than 18 ft.

b. $8 + x > 10$
    $8 + x - 8 > 10 - 8$
    $x > 2$

The third side must be longer than 2 ft.

c. $x + 10 > 8$
    $x + 10 - 10 > 8 - 10$
    $x > -2$

This provides no new useful information.

From part **a**, the third side must be shorter than 18 ft. And from part **b**, it must be longer than 2 ft. An inequality showing this is $2 < x < 18$.

Try This

Decide whether the three lengths given can form a triangle. If not, explain.

1. 14 ft, 30 ft, 10 ft

2. 11 cm, 8 cm, 17 cm

3. $6\frac{1}{2}$ yd, 3 yd, $2\frac{3}{4}$ yd

Write a compound inequality for the range of lengths of the third side of each triangle.

4.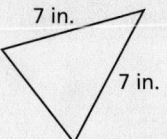

5.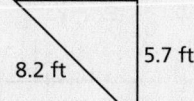

6.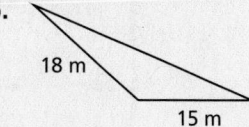

2-7 Solving Absolute-Value Inequalities

CC.9-12.A.REI.3 Solve linear equations and inequalities in one variable, including equations with coefficients represented by letters. *Also* **CC.9-12.A.CED.1***

Objective
Solve inequalities in one variable involving absolute-value expressions.

Why learn this?

You can solve an absolute-value inequality to determine the safe range for the pressure of a fire extinguisher. (See Example 3.)

When an inequality contains an absolute-value expression, it can be rewritten as a compound inequality. The inequality $|x| < 5$ describes all real numbers whose distance from 0 is less than 5 units. The solutions are all numbers between -5 and 5, so $|x| < 5$ can be rewritten as $-5 < x < 5$ or as $x > -5$ AND $x < 5$.

Know it! Note

Absolute-Value Inequalities Involving <

WORDS	NUMBERS
The inequality $|x| < a$ (when $a > 0$) asks, "What values of x have an absolute value less than a?" The solutions are numbers between $-a$ and a.	$|x| < 5$ $-5 < x < 5$ $x > -5$ AND $x < 5$

GRAPH	ALGEBRA
$\xleftarrow{\;a \text{ units}\;}\xrightarrow{\;a \text{ units}\;}$ ⊕————+————⊕ $-a$ $\quad$ 0 $\quad$ a	$|x| < a$ (when $a > 0$) $-a < x < a$ $x > -a$ AND $x < a$

The same properties are true for inequalities that use the symbol $\leq$.

EXAMPLE 1 Solving Absolute-Value Inequalities Involving <

Solve each inequality and graph the solutions.

Helpful Hint

Just as you do when solving absolute-value equations, you first isolate the absolute-value expression when solving absolute-value inequalities.

A $|x| + 3 < 12$

$$|x| + 3 < 12$$
$$\underline{\quad -3 \quad \quad -3 \quad}$$
$$|x| \quad < \quad 9$$

Since 3 is added to $|x|$, subtract 3 from both sides to undo the addition.

$$x > -9 \text{ AND } x < 9$$ *Write as a compound inequality.*

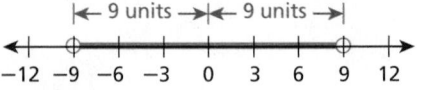

$\xleftarrow{\;9 \text{ units}\;}\xrightarrow{\;9 \text{ units}\;}$
```
←+——⊕——+——+——+——+——⊕——+→
 -12 -9  -6  -3   0   3   6   9   12
```

B $|x + 4| \leq 2$

$$x + 4 \geq -2 \text{ AND } x + 4 \leq 2$$ *Write as a compound inequality.*
$$\underline{\;-4 \quad -4 \quad} \quad \underline{\;-4 \quad -4\;}$$ *Solve each inequality.*
$$x \quad \geq -6 \text{ AND } x \quad \leq -2$$ *Write as a compound inequality.*

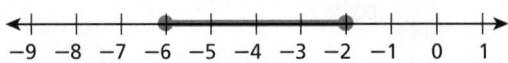
```
←+——+——+——●——+——+——+——●——+——+——+→
 -9 -8 -7 -6 -5 -4 -3 -2 -1  0  1
```

 **Solve each inequality and graph the solutions.**

1a. $2|x| \le 6$ **1b.** $|x + 3| - 4.5 \le 7.5$

The inequality $|x| > 5$ describes all real numbers whose distance from 0 is greater than 5 units. The solutions are all numbers less than -5 or greater than 5. The inequality $|x| > 5$ can be rewritten as the compound inequality $x < -5$ OR $x > 5$.

Absolute-Value Inequalities Involving >

WORDS	NUMBERS
The inequality $|x| > a$ (when $a > 0$) asks, "What values of x have an absolute value greater than a?" The solutions are numbers less than $-a$ or greater than a.	$|x| > 5$ $x < -5$ OR $x > 5$

GRAPH	ALGEBRA
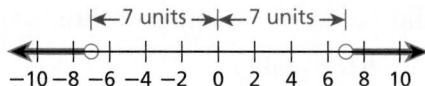	$|x| > a$ (when $a > 0$) $x < -a$ OR $x > a$

The same properties are true for inequalities that use the symbol $\ge$.

EXAMPLE 2 **Solving Absolute-Value Inequalities Involving >**

Solve each inequality and graph the solutions.

A $|x| - 20 > -13$

$|x| - 20 > -13$

$\dfrac{+20 \quad\quad +20}{|x| \quad > \quad 7}$ *Since 20 is subtracted from $|x|$, add 20 to both sides to undo the subtraction.*

$x < -7$ OR $x > 7$ *Write as a compound inequality.*

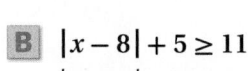

B $|x - 8| + 5 \ge 11$

$|x - 8| + 5 \ge 11$

$\dfrac{\quad -5 \quad -5}{|x - 8| \quad \ge \quad 6}$ *Since 5 is added to $|x - 8|$, subtract 5 from both sides to undo the addition.*

$x - 8 \le -6$ OR $x - 8 \ge 6$ *Write as a compound inequality.*

$\dfrac{+8 \quad +8 \quad\quad +8 \quad +8}{x \quad \le 2 \text{ OR } x \quad \ge 14}$ *Solve each inequality.*
 Write as a compound inequality.

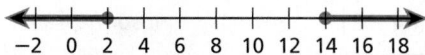

 **Solve each inequality and graph the solutions.**

2a. $|x| + 10 \ge 12$ **2b.** $\left| x + 2\frac{1}{2} \right| + \frac{1}{2} \ge 4$

EXAMPLE 3 *Safety Application*

Some fire extinguishers contain pressurized water. The water pressure should be 162.5 psi (pounds per square inch), but it is acceptable for the pressure to differ from this value by at most 12.5 psi. Write and solve an absolute-value inequality to find the range of acceptable pressures. Graph the solutions.

Let p represent the actual water pressure of a fire extinguisher.

The difference between p and the ideal pressure	is at most	12.5 psi.
$\lvert p - 162.5 \rvert$	$\leq$	12.5

$\lvert p - 162.5 \rvert \leq 12.5$

$p - 162.5 \geq -12.5$ AND $p - 162.5 \leq 12.5$ *Solve the two inequalities.*

$\underline{+\ 162.5 \qquad +\ 162.5} \qquad\qquad \underline{+\ 162.5 \qquad +\ 162.5}$

$p \qquad \geq \qquad 150$ AND $p \qquad\quad \leq \qquad 175$

140 145 150 155 160 165 170 175 180 185 190

The range of acceptable pressures is $150 \leq p \leq 175$.

 CHECK IT OUT!   **3.** A dry-chemical fire extinguisher should be pressurized to 125 psi, but it is acceptable for the pressure to differ from this value by at most 75 psi. Write and solve an absolute-value inequality to find the range of acceptable pressures. Graph the solutions.

When solving an absolute-value inequality, you may get a statement that is true for all values of the variable. In this case, all real numbers are solutions of the original inequality. If you get a false statement when solving an absolute-value inequality, the original inequality has no solutions.

EXAMPLE 4 **Special Cases of Absolute-Value Inequalities**

Solve each inequality.

A $\lvert x - 6 \rvert + 7 > 2$

$\lvert x - 6 \rvert + 7 > \quad 2$

$\underline{\qquad\ -7 \quad -7} \qquad$ *Subtract 7 from both sides.*

$\lvert x - 6 \rvert \quad > -5 \qquad$ *Absolute-value expressions are always nonnegative. Therefore, the statement is true for all values of x.*

All real numbers are solutions.

B $\lvert x + 12 \rvert - 5 \leq -6$

$\lvert x + 12 \rvert - 5 \leq \ -6$

$\underline{\qquad\ +5 \quad +5} \qquad$ *Add 5 to both sides.*

$\lvert x + 12 \rvert \quad \leq -1 \qquad$ *Absolute-value expressions are always nonnegative. Therefore, the statement is false for all values of x.*

The inequality has no solutions.

> **Remember!**
>
> An absolute value represents a distance, and distance cannot be less than 0.

 **CHECK IT OUT!**   Solve each inequality.

4a. $\lvert x \rvert - 9 \geq -11$ **4b.** $4 \lvert x - 3.5 \rvert \leq -8$

THINK AND DISCUSS

1. Describe how the solutions of $7|x| \leq 21$ are different from the solutions of $7|x| < 21$.

2. GET ORGANIZED Copy and complete the graphic organizer. In each box, write an example of the indicated type of absolute-value inequality and then solve.

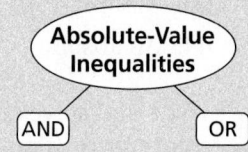

2-7 Exercises

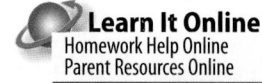

GUIDED PRACTICE

Solve each inequality and graph the solutions.

SEE EXAMPLE **1**

1. $|x| - 5 \leq -2$

2. $|x + 1| - 7.8 < 6.2$

3. $|3x| + 2 < 8$

4. $4|x| \leq 20$

5. $|x - 5| + 1 < 2$

6. $\left| x + \frac{1}{2} \right| - \frac{1}{2} \leq 3\frac{1}{2}$

SEE EXAMPLE **2**

7. $|x| - 6 > 16$

8. $|x| + 2.9 > 8.6$

9. $2|x| \geq 8$

10. $|x + 2| > 7$

11. $|x - 3| + 2 \geq 4$

12. $|x + 5| - 4\frac{1}{2} \geq 7\frac{1}{2}$

SEE EXAMPLE **3**

13. Nutrition A nutritionist recommends that an adult male consume 55 grams of fat per day. It is acceptable for the fat intake to differ from this amount by at most 25 grams. Write and solve an absolute-value inequality to find the range of fat intake that is acceptable. Graph the solutions.

SEE EXAMPLE **4**

Solve each inequality.

14. $|x| + 8 \leq 2$

15. $|x + 3| < -5$

16. $|x + 4| \geq -8$

17. $|x - 5| + \frac{1}{3} > -1$

18. $|3x| + 7 > 2$

19. $|x - 7| + 3.5 \leq 2$

PRACTICE AND PROBLEM SOLVING

Independent Practice	
For Exercises	See Example
20–25	1
26–31	2
32	3
33–38	4

Extra Practice

See Extra Practice for more Skills Practice and Applications Practice exercises.

Solve each inequality and graph the solutions.

20. $|x| + 6 \leq 10$

21. $|x - 3| < 1$

22. $|x - 2| - 8 \leq -3$

23. $|5x| < 15$

24. $|x - 2.4| + 4 \leq 6.4$

25. $4 + |x + 3| < 7$

26. $|x - 1| > 2$

27. $6|x| \geq 60$

28. $|x - 4| + 3 > 8$

29. $2|x + 2| \geq 16$

30. $3 + |x - 4| > 4$

31. $\left| x - \frac{1}{2} \right| + 9 > 10\frac{1}{2}$

32. The thermostat for a sauna is set to 175 °F, but the actual temperature of the sauna may vary by as much as 12 °F. Write and solve an absolute-value inequality to find the range of possible temperatures. Graph the solutions.

Solve each inequality.

33. $12 + |x| \leq 10$

34. $\left| x + \frac{3}{5} \right| - 2 > -4$

35. $|x + 1| + 5 \geq 4$

36. $|4x| - 3 < -6$

37. $3|x - 4| \leq -9$

38. $|2x| + 9 \geq 9$

Tell whether each statement is sometimes, always, or never true. Explain.

39. The value of $|x + 1|$ is greater than -5.

40. The value of $|x - 7|$ is less than 0.

41. An absolute-value inequality has all real numbers as solutions.

Write and solve an absolute-value inequality for each expression. Graph the solutions on a number line.

42. All numbers whose absolute value is less than or equal to 15

43. All numbers less than or equal to 3 units from 2 on the number line

44. All numbers at least 2 units from 8 on the number line

Write an absolute-value inequality for each graph.

45.

$\xleftarrow{\hspace{0.5em}}$ -5 -4 -3 -2 -1 0 1 2 3 4 5 $\xrightarrow{\hspace{0.5em}}$

46.

$\xleftarrow{\hspace{0.5em}}$ -5 -4 -3 -2 -1 0 1 2 3 4 5 $\xrightarrow{\hspace{0.5em}}$

47.

$-6\frac{1}{2}$ $\qquad\qquad$ $6\frac{1}{2}$

$\xleftarrow{\hspace{0.5em}}$ $-10\ -8\ -6\ -4\ -2\ \ 0\ \ 2\ \ 4\ \ 6\ \ 8\ \ 10$ $\xrightarrow{\hspace{0.5em}}$

48.

-7 $\qquad\qquad$ 7

$\xleftarrow{\hspace{0.5em}}$ $-10\ -8\ -6\ -4\ -2\ \ 0\ \ 2\ \ 4\ \ 6\ \ 8\ \ 10$ $\xrightarrow{\hspace{0.5em}}$

49. Multi-Step The frequency of a sound wave determines its pitch. The human ear can detect a wide range of frequencies, from 20 Hz (very low notes) to 20,000 Hz (very high notes).

   a. What frequency is at the middle of the range?

   b. Write an absolute-value inequality for the range of frequencies the human ear can detect.

50. Biology The diagram shows the temperature range at which several fish species can survive. For each species, write an absolute-value inequality that gives the range of temperatures at which it can survive.

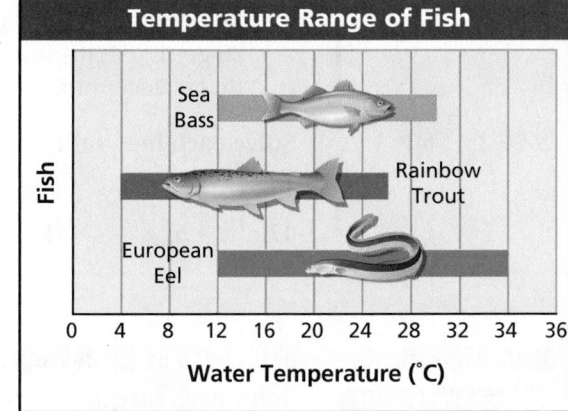

51. Entertainment On a game show, a contestant must guess a secret two-digit number. The secret number is 23. Write an absolute-value inequality that shows that the contestant's guess is more than 12 numbers away from the secret number.

MULTI-STEP TEST PREP

52. The manager of a band recommends that the band sell its CDs for $8.75. The band decides to sell the CDs for p dollars.

   a. Write an absolute-value expression that tells how far the band's price is from the recommended price.

   b. The band wants the price of its CD to be no more than $1.25 from the recommended price. Write an absolute-value inequality that gives the range of possible prices for the CD.

   c. Solve the inequality. Write the solution as a compound inequality.

53. Critical Thinking For which values of k does the inequality $|x| + 1 < k$ have no solutions? Explain.

54. Write About It Describe how to use an absolute-value inequality to find all the values on a number line that are within 5 units of -6.

55. What is the solution of the inequality $3 + |x + 4| < 6$?

   Ⓐ $-13 < x < 5$ Ⓒ $-6 < x < -2$

   Ⓑ $-7 < x < -1$ Ⓓ $1 < x < 7$

56. A thermometer gives temperature readings that may be inaccurate by at most 2 °F. The actual temperature is 75 °F. Which absolute-value inequality describes the range of temperatures that may be shown on the thermometer?

   Ⓕ $|x - 75| \leq 2$ Ⓖ $|x + 75| \leq 2$ Ⓗ $|x - 75| \geq 2$ Ⓙ $|x + 75| \geq 2$

57. The inequality $|w - 156| \leq 3$ describes the weights of members of a wrestling team. Which statement is NOT true?

   Ⓐ All of the team members weigh no more than 159 pounds.

   Ⓑ A team member may weigh 152 pounds.

   Ⓒ Every member of the team is at most 3 pounds away from 156 pounds.

   Ⓓ There are no team members who weigh 160 pounds.

CHALLENGE AND EXTEND

Write an absolute-value inequality for each graph.

58.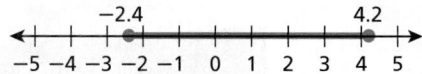
59.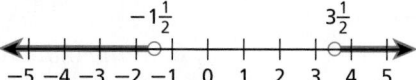

60. Critical Thinking Fill in the missing reasons to justify each step in solving $|2x - 6| + 5 \leq 7$.

Statements	Reasons
1. $|2x - 6| + 5 \leq 7$	Given
2. $|2x - 6| \leq 2$	_____?_____
3. $2x - 6 \geq -2$ AND $2x - 6 \leq 2$	Definition of absolute value
4. $2x \geq 4$ AND $2x \leq 8$	_____?_____
5. $x \geq 2$ AND $x \leq 4$	_____?_____

MULTI-STEP TEST PREP

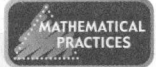

Make sense of problems and persevere in solving them.

Multi-Step and Compound Inequalities

Guitar Picks Cullen and his band are interested in recording a CD of their music. The recording studio charges $450 to record the music and then charges $5 for each CD. The band is required to spend at least $1000 for the total of the recording and CD charges.

1. Write an equation for the cost c of the CDs based on the number of CDs n.

2. Write an inequality that can be used to determine the minimum number of CDs that must be burned at this studio to meet the $1000 total.

3. Solve your inequality from Problem 2.

4. The band orders the minimum number of CDs found in Problem 3. They want to sell the CDs and make at least as much money as they spent for the recording studio and making the CDs. Write an inequality that can be solved to determine the minimum amount the band should charge for their CDs.

5. Solve your inequality from Problem 4.

6. If the band has 30 more CDs made than the minimum number found in Problem 3 and charges the minimum price found in Problem 5, will they make a profit? If so, how much profit will the band make?

Quiz for Lessons 2-4 Through 2-7

2-4 Solving Two-Step and Multi-Step Inequalities

Solve each inequality and graph the solutions.

1. $2x + 3 < 9$

2. $3t - 2 > 10$

3. $7 \geq 1 - 6r$

Solve each inequality.

4. $2(x - 3) > -1$

5. $\frac{1}{3}a + \frac{1}{2} > \frac{2}{3}$

6. $15 < 5(m - 7)$

7. $2 + (-6) > 0.8p$

8. The average of Mindy's two test scores must be at least 92 to make an A in the class. Mindy got an 88 on her first test. What scores can she get on her second test to make an A in the class?

2-5 Solving Inequalities with Variables on Both Sides

Solve each inequality and graph the solutions.

9. $5x < 3x + 8$

10. $6p - 3 > 9p$

11. $r - 8 \geq 3r - 12$

Solve each inequality.

12. $3(y + 6) > 2(y + 4)$

13. $4(5 - g) \geq g$

14. $4x < 4(x - 1)$

15. $3(1 - x) \geq -3(x + 2)$

16. Phillip has $100 in the bank and deposits $18 per month. Gil has $145 in the bank and deposits $15 per month. For how many months will Gil have a larger bank balance than Phillip?

2-6 Solving Compound Inequalities

Solve each compound inequality and graph the solutions.

17. $-2 \leq x + 3 < 9$

18. $m + 2 < -1$ OR $m - 2 > 6$

19. $-3 \geq x - 1 > 2$

20. $-2 > r + 2$ OR $r + 4 < 5$

21. It is recommended that a certain medicine be stored in temperatures above 32 °F and below 70 °F. Write a compound inequality to show the acceptable storage temperatures for this medicine.

2-7 Solving Absolute-Value Inequalities

Solve each inequality and graph the solutions.

22. $|x| + 9 \leq 12$

23. $|x + 7| - 15 < 6$

24. $4.5|x| \geq 31.5$

Solve each inequality.

25. $|x - 2| \leq 14$

26. $|x| - 9.2 < -5.7$

27. $\frac{1}{2} + 2|x| > -4$

28. $7 + |3x| > 13$

29. Eli attended a concert. The decibel level of the music averaged 110 decibels but varied by 22 decibels from the average. Write and solve an absolute-value inequality to find the decibel range. Graph the solutions.

Study Guide: Review

Vocabulary

compound inequality   intersection   union

inequality   solution of an inequality

Complete the sentences below with vocabulary words from the list above.

1. A(n) ____?____ is a mathematical statement that two quantities are not equal.

2. The numbers that are solutions to either inequality of a compound inequality is the ____?____ .

3. A statement formed by combining two simple inequalities with the words AND or OR is a(n) ____?____ .

4. The numbers that are solutions to both inequalities of a compound inequality is the ____?____ .

5. Any value that makes the inequality true is a(n) ____?____ .

2-1 Graphing and Writing Inequalities

EXAMPLES

■ Graph the inequality $y > -1$.

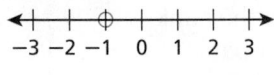

Draw an empty circle at -1.

Shade all the numbers greater than -1.

■ Write the inequality shown by the graph.

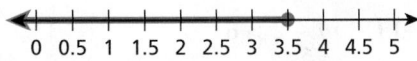

$n \leq 3.5$ Use the variable n.
The arrow points left, so use either $<$ or $\leq$. The solid circle means 3.5 is a solution, so use $\leq$.

■ Write an inequality for the situation and graph the solutions.

Applicants for a driver's permit must be at least 16 years old.

age	must be at least	16 years
a	$\geq$	16

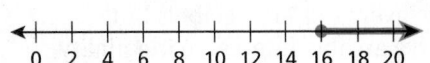

EXERCISES

Graph each inequality.

6. $x > -3$

7. $p \leq 4$

8. $-1 > t$

9. $r \geq 9.5$

10. $2(3 - 5) < k$

11. $w < 3$

Write the inequality shown by each graph.

12.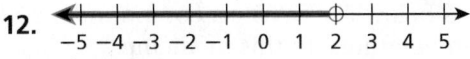

13.
```
        -3.5
◄──┼──●──┼──┼──┼──┼──┼──┼──┼──►
  -4    -3    -2    -1    0     1
```

14.
```
◄──┼──○──┼──┼──┼──┼──┼──►
 -12  -10  -8   -6   -4   -2    0
```

Define a variable and write an inequality for each situation. Graph the solutions.

15. The temperature must be at least 72 °F.

16. No more than 12 students were present.

17. It takes less than 30 minutes to complete the lab activity.

2-2 Solving Inequalities by Adding or Subtracting

EXAMPLES

Solve each inequality and graph the solutions.

■ $x + 6 > 2$

$$\begin{array}{rl} x + 6 > & 2 \\ \underline{-6 \quad -6} & \\ x \quad > & -4 \end{array}$$
Since 6 is added to x, subtract 6 from both sides.

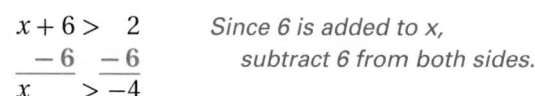

■ $n - 1.3 < 3.2$

$$\begin{array}{rl} n - 1.3 < & 3.2 \\ \underline{+1.3 \quad +1.3} & \\ n \quad < & 4.5 \end{array}$$
Since 1.3 is subtracted from x, add 1.3 to both sides.

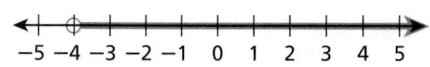

EXERCISES

Solve each inequality and graph the solutions.

18. $t + 3 < 10$

19. $k - 7 \leq -5$

20. $-1 < m + 4$

21. $x + 2.3 \geq 6.8$

22. $w - 3 < 6.5$

23. $4 > a - 1$

24. $h - \frac{1}{4} < \frac{3}{4}$

25. $5 > 7 + v$

26. Tammy wants to run at least 10 miles per week. So far this week, she ran 4.5 miles. Write and solve an inequality to determine how many more miles Tammy must run this week to reach her goal.

27. Rob has a gift card for $50. So far, he has selected a shirt that costs $32. Write and solve an inequality to determine the additional amount Rob could spend without exceeding the gift card limit.

2-3 Solving Inequalities by Multiplying or Dividing

EXAMPLES

■ Solve $\frac{p}{-3} \leq 6$ and graph the solutions.

$$\frac{p}{-3} \leq 6$$
Since p is divided by −3, multiply both sides by −3.

$$-3 \cdot \frac{p}{-3} \geq -3 \cdot 6$$

$$p \geq -18$$
Change ≤ to ≥.

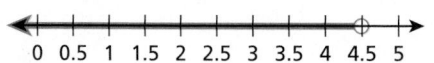

■ **Pizzas cost $5.50 each. What are the possible numbers of pizzas that can be purchased with $30?**

Let *n* represent the number of pizzas that can be purchased.

$5.50	times	number of pizzas	is at most	$30.
5.50	•	n	≤	30

$$5.50n \leq 30$$

$$\frac{5.50n}{5.50} \leq \frac{30}{5.50}$$
Since n is multiplied by 5.50, divide both sides by 5.50.

$$n \leq 5\frac{5}{11}$$

Only a whole number of pizzas can be purchased, so 0, 1, 2, 3, 4, or 5 pizzas can be purchased.

EXERCISES

Solve each inequality and graph the solutions.

28. $3a \leq 15$

29. $-18 < 6t$

30. $\frac{p}{4} > 2$

31. $\frac{2}{5}x \leq -10$

32. $-3n < -18$

33. $\frac{g}{-2} > 6$

34. $-2k < 14$

35. $-3 > \frac{1}{3}r$

36. $27 < -9h$

37. $-0.4g > -1$

38. Notebooks cost $1.39 each. What are the possible numbers of notebooks that can be purchased with $10?

39. A senior class is selling lanyards as a fundraiser. The profit for each lanyard is $0.75. Write and solve an inequality to determine the number of lanyards the class must sell to make a profit of at least $250.

2-4 Solving Two-Step and Multi-Step Inequalities

EXAMPLES

Solve each inequality and graph the solutions.

- $18 + 3t > -12$

$$
\begin{array}{ll}
18 + 3t > -12 & \textit{Since 18 is added to 3t,} \\
\underline{-18 \qquad -18} & \textit{subtract 18 from both} \\
3t > -30 & \textit{sides.} \\
\dfrac{3t}{3} > \dfrac{-30}{3} & \textit{Since t is multiplied by 3,} \\
& \textit{divide both sides by 3.} \\
t > -10 &
\end{array}
$$

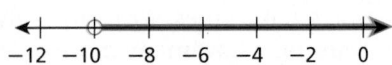

- $3^2 - 5 \leq 2(1 + x)$

$$
\begin{array}{ll}
3^2 - 5 \leq 2(1 + x) & \textit{Simplify the left side using} \\
9 - 5 \leq 2(1 + x) & \textit{order of operations.} \\
4 \leq 2(1 + x) & \textit{Distribute 2 on the right} \\
4 \leq 2(1) + 2(x) & \textit{side.} \\
4 \leq \quad 2 + 2x & \textit{Since 2 is added to 2x,} \\
\underline{-2 \quad -2} & \textit{subtract 2 from both} \\
2 \leq \qquad 2x & \textit{sides} \\
\dfrac{2}{2} \leq \dfrac{2x}{2} & \textit{Since x is multiplied by 2,} \\
1 \leq x & \textit{divide both sides by 2.}
\end{array}
$$

EXERCISES

Solve each inequality and graph the solutions.

40. $3x + 4 < 19$

41. $7 \leq 2t - 5$

42. $\dfrac{m + 3}{2} > -4$

43. $2(x + 5) < 8$

44. $-4(2 - 5) > (-3)^2 - h$

45. $\dfrac{1}{5}x + \dfrac{1}{2} > \dfrac{4}{5}$

46. $0.5(b - 2) \leq 4$

47. $\dfrac{1}{3}y - \dfrac{1}{2} > \dfrac{2}{3}$

48. $6 - 0.2n < 9$

49. Carl's Cable Company charges $55 for monthly service plus $4 for each pay-per-view movie. Teleview Cable Company charges $110 per month with no fee for movies. For what number of movies is the cost of Carl's Cable Company less than the cost of Teleview?

2-5 Solving Inequalities with Variables on Both Sides

EXAMPLES

- Solve $b + 16 < 3b$ and graph the solutions.

$$
\begin{array}{ll}
b + 16 > 3b & \textit{Subtract b from both sides so} \\
\underline{-b \qquad -b} & \textit{that the coefficient of b is} \\
16 > 2b & \textit{positive.} \\
\dfrac{16}{2} > \dfrac{2b}{2} & \textit{Since b is multiplied by 2,} \\
8 > b & \textit{divide both sides by 2.}
\end{array}
$$

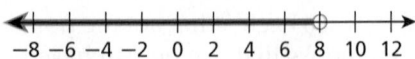

- Solve the inequality $3(1 + k) > 4 + 3k$.

$3 + 3k > 4 + 3k$ *Distribute 3 on the left side.*

The same variable term ($3k$) appears on both sides.

For any number $3k$, adding 3 will never result in a greater number than adding 4.

There are no solutions.

EXERCISES

Solve each inequality and graph the solutions.

50. $5 + 2m < -3m$ **51.** $y \leq 6 + 4y$

52. $4c - 7 > 9c + 8$ **53.** $-3(2 - q) \geq 6(q + 1)$

54. $2(5 - x) < 3x$ **55.** $3.5t - 1.8 < 1.6t + 3.9$

Solve each inequality.

56. $d - 2 < d - 4$ **57.** $2(1 - x) > -2(1 + x)$

58. $4(1 - p) < 4(2 + p)$ **59.** $3w + 1 > 3(w - 1)$

60. $5(4 - k) < 5k$ **61.** $3(c + 1) > 3c + 5$

62. Hanna has a savings account with a balance of $210 and deposits $16 per month. Faith has a savings account with a balance of $175 and deposits $20 per month. Write and solve an inequality to determine the number of months Hanna's account balance will be greater than Faith's account balance.

2-6 Solving Compound Inequalities

EXAMPLES

Solve each compound inequality and graph the solutions.

■ $-3 < c + 5 \le 11$ Since 5 is added to c, subtract
$\underline{-5 \qquad -5 \quad -5}$ 5 from each part of the
$-8 < c \qquad \le 6$ inequality.

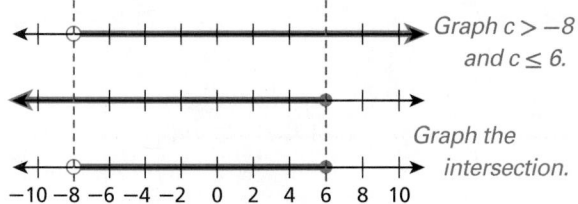

Graph $c > -8$
and $c \le 6$.

Graph the
intersection.

■ $-2 + t \ge 2$ OR $t + 3 < 1$
$\underline{+2 \qquad +2 \qquad -3 \quad -3}$ Solve the simple
$t \ge 4$ OR $t < -2$ inequalities.

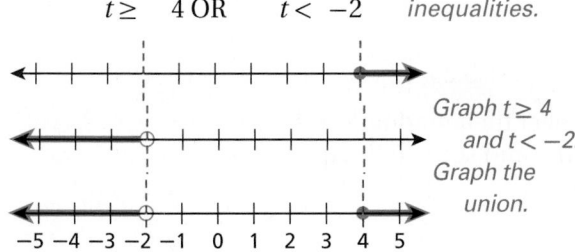

Graph $t \ge 4$
and $t < -2$.
Graph the
union.

EXERCISES

Solve each compound inequality and graph the solutions.

63. $-4 < t + 6 < 10$ **64.** $-8 < k - 2 \le 5$

65. $-3 + r > 4$ OR $r + 1 < -1$

66. $2 > n + 3 > 5$

67. $12 \ge p + 7 > 5$

68. $3 < s + 9$ OR $1 > s - 4$

69. One day, the high temperature was 84 °F and the low temperature was 68 °F. Write a compound inequality to represent the day's temperatures.

70. The table shows formulas for the recommended heart rates during exercise for a person who is a years old. Write and solve a compound inequality to determine the heart rate range for a 16-year-old person.

Recommended Heart Rate Range	
Lower Limit	$0.5 \times (220 - a)$
Upper Limit	$0.9 \times (220 - a)$

2-7 Solving Absolute-Value Inequalities

EXAMPLES

Solve each inequality and graph the solutions.

■ $|x| + 4 < 9$
$|x| + 4 < 9$
$\underline{\quad -4 \quad -4}$ Subtract 4 from both sides.
$|x| \qquad < 5$

$x > -5$ AND $x < 5$ Write as a compound
    inequality.

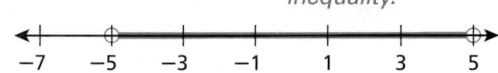

■ $|x - 3| + 7 \ge 13$
$\underline{\qquad -7 \quad -7}$ Subtract 7 from both sides.
$|x - 3| \qquad \ge 6$
$x - 3 \le -6$ OR $x - 3 \ge 6$ Solve the two
$\underline{+3 \quad +3 \qquad +3 \quad +3}$ inequalities.
$x \qquad \le -3$ OR $x \qquad \ge 9$

EXERCISES

Solve each inequality and graph the solutions.

71. $|x| - 7 \le 15$ **72.** $|x + 4| > 8$

73. $6|x| \le 24$ **74.** $|x + 9| + 11 < 20$

75. $3|x| \ge 9$ **76.** $4|2x| < 24$

Solve the inequality.

77. $|x| - 5.4 > 8.5$ **78.** $|5.2 + x| < 7.3$

79. $|x - 7| + 10 \ge 12$ **80.** $14|x| - 15 \ge 41$

81. $\left|x - \dfrac{1}{2}\right| + 4 \le \dfrac{5}{2}$ **82.** $|x + 5.5| - 6.4 \le 4.9$

83. The water depth for a pool is set to 6 ft, but the actual depth of the pool may vary by as much as 4 in. Write and solve an absolute-value inequality to find the range of possible water depths in inches. Graph the solutions.

CHAPTER TEST

Describe the solutions of each inequality in words.

1. $-6 \leq m$ **2.** $3t > 12$ **3.** $-x \geq 2$ **4.** $2 + b \leq 10$

Graph each inequality.

5. $b > -3$ **6.** $2.5 < c$ **7.** $y \leq -\sqrt{25}$ **8.** $3 - (4 + 7) \geq h$

Write the inequality shown by each graph.

9.
$$\xleftarrow{\quad}\overset{\substack{\\-5\;-4\;-3\;-2\;-1\;\;0\;\;1\;\;2\;\;3\;\;4\;\;5}}{+\!\!+\!\!+\!\!+\!\!+\!\!+\!\!+\!\!\circ\!\!+\!\!+\!\!+\!\!+}\xrightarrow{\quad}$$

10.
$$\overset{-4.5}{\xleftarrow{\quad}\underset{-5\quad-4\quad-3\quad-2\quad-1\quad0}{+\!\!\bullet\!\!+\!\!+\!\!+\!\!+\!\!+\!\!+\!\!+\!\!+}}\xrightarrow{\quad}$$

Write an inequality for the situation and graph the solutions.

11. Madison must run a mile in no more than 9 minutes to qualify for the race.

Solve each inequality and graph the solutions.

12. $d - 5 > -7$ **13.** $f + 4 < -3$ **14.** $4.5 \geq s + 3.2$ **15.** $g + (-2) \leq 9$

16. Students need at least 75 hours of volunteer service to meet their graduation requirement. Samir has already completed 48 hours. Write and solve an inequality to determine how many more hours he needs to complete.

Solve each inequality and graph the solutions.

17. $-2c \leq 2$ **18.** $3 > \dfrac{k}{2}$ **19.** $\dfrac{4}{5}x \leq -8$ **20.** $\dfrac{b}{3} > -7$

21. Marco needs to buy premium gasoline for his car. He has \$20 in his wallet. Write and solve an inequality to determine how many gallons of gas Marco can buy.

Gasoline Prices (\$)		
Regular	Plus	Premium
2.05	2.12	2.25

Solve each inequality and graph the solutions.

22. $3x - 8 < 4$ **23.** $-2(c - 3) > 4$ **24.** $5 \leq \dfrac{3}{4}n - 2^4$ **25.** $3 - 2a \leq -15 + (-9)$

Solve each inequality.

26. $2k - 6 > 3k + 2$ **27.** $2(5 - f) \leq f + 12$ **28.** $\dfrac{3}{2}d \leq -\dfrac{1}{2}d + 6$

Solve each compound inequality and graph the solutions.

29. $-1 \leq x - 3 < 3$ **30.** $t + 7 < 3 \text{ OR } t - 1 > 4$ **31.** $4 \leq d - 2 < 5$

32. The driving school instructor has asked Lina to stay within 2 miles of the posted speed limits. The current road has a speed limit of 45 mi/h. Write a compound inequality to show Lina's acceptable speeds s.

Solve each inequality.

33. $|x - 3| + 7 < 17$ **34.** $6|x| + 4 \geq 16$ **35.** $|x + 12| \leq 23$

COLLEGE ENTRANCE EXAM PRACTICE

FOCUS ON SAT STUDENT-PRODUCED RESPONSES

Ten questions on the SAT require you to enter your answer in a special grid like the one shown. You do not have to write your answer in the boxes at the top of the grid, but doing this may help you avoid errors when filling in the grid. The circles must be filled in correctly for you to receive credit.

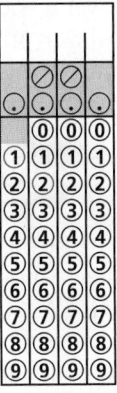

You cannot enter a zero in the first column of the grid. This is to encourage you to give a more accurate answer when you need to round. For example, $\frac{1}{16}$ written as a decimal is 0.0625. This should be entered in the grid as .063 instead of 0.06.

You may want to time yourself as you take this practice test. It should take you about 9 minutes to complete.

---

1. Mailing a standard-sized letter in 2005 by first-class mail cost $0.37 for a letter weighing 1 ounce or less and $0.23 for each additional ounce. How much did it cost, in dollars, to send a standard-sized letter that weighed 3 ounces?

---

2. If $p = q - 2$ and $\frac{q}{3} = 9$, what is the value of p?

---

3. Give the maximum value of x if $12 - 3(x + 1) \geq \frac{1}{2}(3 - 5)$.

---

4. Give the minimum value of x if $2x + y \leq 7x - 9$ and $y = -3$.

---

5. For what integer value of x is $2x - 9 < 5$ and $x - 1 > 4$?

---

6. What is the minimum value of z that satisfies the inequality $z - 7.3 \geq 4.1$?

---

7. To be eligible for financial aid, Alisa must work at least 15 hours per week in a work-study program. She wants to spend at least 5 more hours studying than working each week. What is the minimum number of hours per day (Monday through Friday) that she must study to meet this goal and be eligible for financial aid?

---

8. For all real numbers a and b, define the operation # as follows:
$$a \# b = 2a - b$$
Given $a = 3$ and $a \# b = 1$, what is the value of b?

TEST TACKLER

Standardized Test Strategies

Short Response: Understand Short Response Scores

To answer a short-response question completely, you must show how you solved the problem and explain your answer. Short response questions are scored using a 2-point scoring rubric. A sample scoring rubric is provided below.

EXAMPLE 1

Short Response An online company offers free shipping if the cost of the order is at least $35. Your order currently totals $26.50. Write an inequality to show how much more you need to spend to qualify for free shipping. Solve the inequality and explain what your answer means.

2-point response:

Let c be the amount I must add to my order.
c plus the amount I already ordered must be at least $35.
$$c + \quad\quad 26.50 \quad\quad\quad \geq \quad\quad 35$$

$$c + 26.50 \geq 35$$
$$c + 26.50 - 26.50 \geq 35 - 26.50$$
$$c \geq 8.50$$
Check:
$$8.50 + 26.50 \geq 35 \checkmark$$

To get free shipping on the order, I must spend at least $8.50 more since $8.50 + $26.50 is at least $35.

The student wrote and solved an inequality correctly. The student showed all work and explained the meaning of the solution to the inequality.

1-point response:

$$c + 26.50 > 35$$
$$c > 8.50$$

$$\$8.50$$

The student gave a correct answer, but the inequality symbol shown in the student's work is incorrect. No explanation was given.

0-point response:

$$\$9.25$$

The student gave an answer that satisfies the problem but did not show any work or give an explanation.

Scoring Rubric:

2 points: The student writes and correctly solves an inequality, showing all work. Student defines the variable, answers the question in a complete sentence, and provides an explanation.

1 point: The student writes and correctly solves an inequality but does not show all work, does not define the variable, or does not provide an explanation.

1 point: The student writes and solves an inequality but gives an incorrect answer. The student shows all work and provides an explanation for the answer.

0 points: The student gives no response or provides a solution without showing any work or explanation.

 Read short-response test items carefully. If you are allowed to write in the test booklet, underline or circle the parts of the question that tell you what your answer must include. Be sure to explain how you get your answer in complete sentences.

Read each sample and answer the questions that follow by using the scoring rubric below.

Scoring Rubric:

2 points: The student demonstrates a thorough understanding of the concept, correctly answers the question, and provides a complete explanation.

1 point: The student correctly answers the question but does not show all work or does not provide an explanation.

1 point: The student makes minor errors resulting in an incorrect solution but shows and explains understanding of the concept.

0 points: The student gives a response but shows no work or explanation, or the student gives no response.

Sample A
Short Response Write a real-world situation that can be modeled by the inequality $25s - 75 \geq 250$. Solve for s and explain how the value of s relates to your situation.

Student's Answer

A painter rents a booth at the county fair for $75. The artist sells his paintings for $25 each. If he makes at least $250 in profit, he can buy a new easel.

The artist has to sell at least 13 paintings.

1. What score should the student's answer receive? Explain your reasoning.

2. What additional information, if any, should the student's answer include in order to receive full credit?

Sample B
Short Response How do the solutions of $3s - 10 < 15 - 2s$ and $-34 + 9s \leq 4s - 9$ differ? How are the solutions alike? Include a graph in your explanation.

Student's Answer

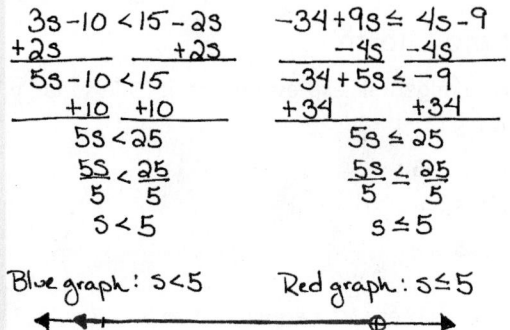

Solve both inequalities.

$$3s - 10 < 15 - 2s \qquad -34 + 9s \leq 4s - 9$$
$$+2s \qquad +2s \qquad\qquad -4s \quad -4s$$
$$5s - 10 < 15 \qquad\qquad -34 + 5s \leq -9$$
$$+10 \quad +10 \qquad\qquad +34 \qquad +34$$
$$5s < 25 \qquad\qquad 5s \leq 25$$
$$\frac{5s}{5} < \frac{25}{5} \qquad\qquad \frac{5s}{5} \leq \frac{25}{5}$$
$$s < 5 \qquad\qquad\qquad s \leq 5$$

Blue graph: $s < 5$ Red graph: $s \leq 5$

3. What score should the student's answer receive? Explain your reasoning.

4. What additional information, if any, should the student's answer include in order to receive full credit?

Sample C
Short Response Explain the difference between the solution of the equation $x - 6 = 2x + 9$ and the solutions of the inequality $x - 6 < 2x + 9$.

Student's Answer

The equation has a solution of x = −15, and the inequality has a solution of x > −15. The equation is true only when x equals −15. The inequality is true for all values greater than −15.

5. What score should the student's answer receive? Explain your reasoning.

6. What additional information, if any, should the student's answer include in order to receive full credit?

CUMULATIVE ASSESSMENT

Multiple Choice

1. Which algebraic expression means "5 less than y"?

(A) $5 - y$

(B) $y - 5$

(C) $5 < y$

(D) $5 \div y$

2. Which expression is equivalent to $5 + 2(x - 5)$?

(F) $2x$

(G) $2x + 5$

(H) $2x - 5$

(J) $7x - 35$

3. If $t + 8 = 2$, find the value of $2t$.

(A) -12

(B) -6

(C) 12

(D) 20

4. The length of the rectangle is $2(x + 1)$ meters and the perimeter is 60 meters. What is the length of the rectangle?

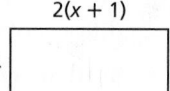

(F) 12 meters

(G) 26 meters

(H) 28 meters

(J) 56 meters

5. Samantha opened a bank account in June and deposited some money. She deposited twice that amount in August. At the end of August, Samantha had less than $600 in her account. If she made no other withdrawals or deposits, which inequality could be used to determine the maximum amount Samantha could have deposited in June?

(A) $2x < 600$

(B) $2x > 600$

(C) $3x < 600$

(D) $3x > 600$

6. Which proportion could be used to determine the ratio of the areas of these similar rectangles?

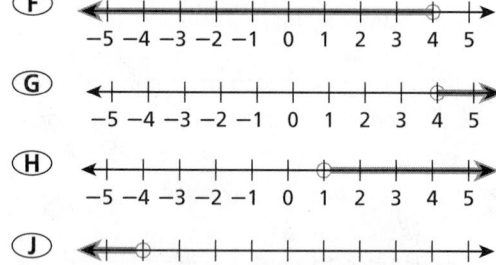

(F) $\dfrac{2}{3}$

(G) $\dfrac{2}{5}$

(H) $\dfrac{4}{9}$

(J) $\dfrac{4}{25}$

7. For which inequality is -2 a solution?

(A) $2x < -4$

(B) $-2x < 4$

(C) $-2x > -4$

(D) $-2x < -4$

8. Which graph shows the solutions of $-2(1 - x) < 3(x - 2)$?

(F)
```
←—+—+—+—+—+—+—+—+—+—○—+→
 −5 −4 −3 −2 −1  0  1  2  3  4  5
```

(G)
```
←—+—+—+—+—+—+—+—○—+—+—+→
 −5 −4 −3 −2 −1  0  1  2  3  4  5
```

(H)
```
←—+—+—+—+—+—+—○—+—+—+—+→
 −5 −4 −3 −2 −1  0  1  2  3  4  5
```

(J)
```
←—+—○—+—+—+—+—+—+—+—+—+→
 −5 −4 −3 −2 −1  0  1  2  3  4  5
```

9. Which compound inequality has no solution?

(A) $x > 1$ OR $x < -2$

(B) $x < 1$ AND $x > -2$

(C) $x < 1$ OR $x < -2$

(D) $x > 1$ AND $x < -2$

To check your answer, use a different method to solve the problem from the one you originally used. If you made a mistake the first time, you are unlikely to make the same mistake when you solve the problem a different way.

10. Which inequality has the same solutions as $p < -2$?

Ⓕ $p + 1 < -2$

Ⓖ $p + 4 < 2$

Ⓗ $2p + 1 < -4$

Ⓙ $3p < -12$

11. What is the greatest integer solution of $5 - 3m > 11$?

Ⓐ 0

Ⓑ -1

Ⓒ -2

Ⓓ -3

Gridded Response

12. The sum of the measures of any two sides of a triangle must be greater than the measure of the third side. What is the greatest possible integer value for x?

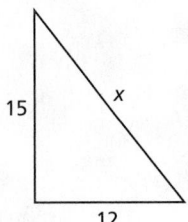

13. After 2 years, the simple interest paid on an investment of $2500 was $175. What percent was the interest rate?

14. Amy's bowling score in her third game was 10 points less than her score in the first game and 5 points more than her score in the second game. The total points for all three games was no more than 275. What is the greatest number of points Amy could have scored in her first game?

15. Trevor needs a 93 on his second quiz to have a quiz average of 90. What score did Trevor receive on his first quiz?

16. The radius of a circle can be determined by the formula $r = \sqrt{\frac{A}{\pi}}$. What is the length in meters of the radius of a circle that has an area of 314 square meters? (Use 3.14 for π.)

Short Response

17. Write 2 different inequalities that have the same solution as $n > 3$ such that

a. the first inequality uses the symbol $>$ and requires addition or subtraction to solve.

b. the second inequality uses the symbol $<$ and requires multiplication or division to solve.

18. Alison has twice as many video games as Kyle. Maurice has 5 more video games than Alison. The total number of video games is less than 40.

a. Write an inequality to represent this situation.

b. Solve the inequality to determine the greatest number of video games Maurice could have. Justify each step in your solution.

19. Donna's Deli delivers lunches for $7 per person plus a $35 delivery fee. Larry's Lunches delivers lunches for $11 per person.

a. Write an expression to represent the cost of x lunches from Donna's Deli. Write an expression to represent the cost of ordering x lunches from Larry's Lunches.

b. Write an inequality to determine the number of lunches for which the cost of Larry's Lunches is less than the cost of Donna's Deli.

c. Solve the inequality and explain what the answer means. Which restaurant charges less for an order of 10 lunches?

Extended Response

20. Aleya has two employment opportunities. Company A offered her a yearly salary of $31,000. Company B offered her a similar position with a yearly salary of $27,000 plus 2.5% commission on her total sales for the year.

a. Let x represent Aleya's total sales for the year at company B. Write an expression to represent the total income after one year at company B.

b. Use your expression from part **a** to write an inequality that could be solved to determine the amount of sales for which the yearly income at company A would be greater than that at company B.

c. Solve the inequality from part **b** and explain the meaning of the solution in relation to Aleya's decision to work for company A or company B.

d. How much more than the salary at company A would Aleya make after one year at company B if her total sales for the year were $200,000?

COMMON CORE

Chapter Focus

- Use tables, diagrams, graphs, and equations to describe functions.
- Translate among representations of functions.
- Use functions to represent, analyze, and solve problems.

Is That *Your* Foot?

Criminologists use measurements, such as the size of footprints, and functions to help them identify criminals.

Learn It Online
Chapter Project Online

© David McGlynn/Taxi/Getty Images

ARE YOU READY?

✓ Vocabulary

Match each term on the left with a definition on the right.

1. absolute value
2. algebraic expression
3. input
4. output
5. x-axis

A. a letter used to represent a value that can change

B. the value generated for y

C. a group of numbers, symbols, and variables with one or more operations

D. the distance of a number from zero on the number line

E. the horizontal number line in the coordinate plane

F. a value substituted for x

✓ Ordered Pairs

Graph each point on the same coordinate plane.

6. $(-2, 4)$ **7.** $(0, -5)$ **8.** $(1, -3)$ **9.** $(4, 2)$

10. $(3, -2)$ **11.** $(-1, -2)$ **12.** $(-1, 3)$ **13.** $(-4, 0)$

✓ Function Tables

Generate ordered pairs for each function for $x = -2, -1, 0, 1, 2$.

14. $y = -2x - 1$ **15.** $y = x + 1$ **16.** $y = -x^2$

17. $y = \frac{1}{2}x + 2$ **18.** $y = (x + 1)^2$ **19.** $y = (x - 1)^2$

✓ Solve Multi-Step Equations

Solve each equation. Check your answer.

20. $17x - 15 = 12$ **21.** $-7 + 2t = 7$ **22.** $-6 = \frac{p}{3} + 9$

23. $5n - 10 = 35$ **24.** $3r - 14 = 7$ **25.** $9 = \frac{x}{2} + 1$

26. $-2.4 + 1.6g = 5.6$ **27.** $34 - 2x = 12$ **28.** $2(x + 5) = -8$

✓ Solve for a Variable

Solve each equation for the indicated variable.

29. $A = \ell w$ for w **30.** $V = \ell w h$ for w **31.** $A = bh$ for h

32. $C = 2\pi r$ for r **33.** $I = Prt$ for P **34.** $V = \frac{1}{3}\ell w h$ for h

Study Guide: Preview

Where You've Been

Previously, you

- were introduced to functions when you generated and graphed ordered pairs.
- stated rules for relationships among values.
- represented and interpreted data using bar graphs and circle graphs.

In This Chapter

You will study

- relationships between variables and determine whether a relation is a function.
- relationships in function notation.
- how trend lines on scatter plots can help you make predictions.

Where You're Going

You can use the skills in this chapter

- to find values of a function from a graph.
- to analyze data and make predictions in other courses, such as Chemistry.
- to calculate total earnings for a certain hourly rate.

Key Vocabulary/Vocabulario

arithmetic sequence	sucesión aritmética
common difference	diferencia común
correlation	correlación
dependent variable	variable dependiente
domain	dominio
function	función
function notation	notación de función
independent variable	variable independiente
no correlation	sin correlación
range	rango
relation	relación
scatter plot	diagrama de dispersión
sequence	sucesión

Vocabulary Connections

To become familiar with some of the vocabulary terms in the chapter, consider the following. You may refer to the chapter, the glossary, or a dictionary if you like.

1. What does the word *dependent* mean? What do you think is true about the value of a **dependent variable**?

2. A *function* is a special type of relation and *notation* is a method of writing. What do you suppose is meant by **function notation**?

3. The word *correlation* means "relationship." What might it mean if two sets of data have **no correlation**?

4. What does it mean when someone says that two people have something in *common*? If *difference* is the answer to a subtraction problem, what might it mean for a list of numbers to have a **common difference**?

Reading and Writing Math

Reading Strategy: Read and Interpret Math Symbols

It is essential that as you read through each lesson of the textbook, you can interpret mathematical symbols.

Common Math Symbols

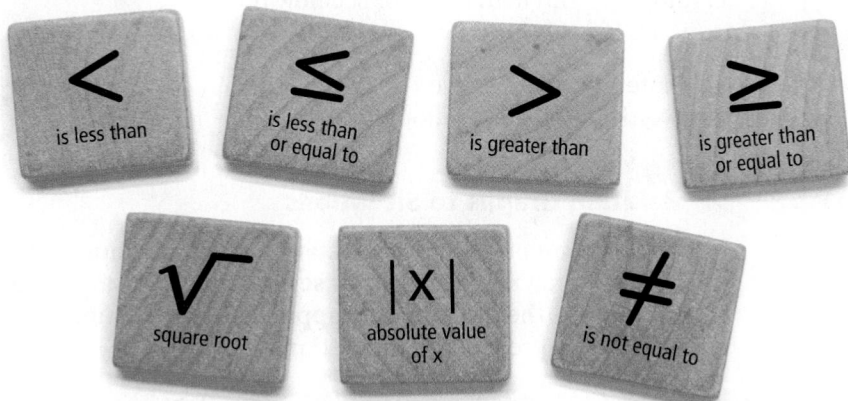

You must be able to translate symbols into words . . .

Using Symbols	Using Words
$3\left(\dfrac{x}{12}\right) - 1 = 21$	Three times the quotient of x and 12, minus 1 equals 21.
$25x + 6 \geq 17$	Twenty-five times x plus 6 is greater than or equal to 17.
$|x| > 14$	The absolute value of x is greater than 14.
$\sqrt{60 + x} \leq 40$	The square root of the sum of 60 and x is less than or equal to 40.

. . . and words into symbols.

Using Words	Using Symbols
The height of the shed is at least 9 feet.	$h \geq 9$ ft
The distance is at most one tenth of a mile.	$d \leq 0.1$ mi
The silo contains more than 600 cubic feet of corn.	$c > 600$ ft^3

Try This

Translate the symbols into words.

1. $x \leq \sqrt{10}$
2. $|x| + 2 > 45$
3. $-5 \leq x < 8$
4. $-6 - \dfrac{1}{5}x = -32$

Translate the words into symbols.

5. There are less than 15 seconds remaining.
6. The tax rate is 8.25 percent of the cost.

7. Ann counted over 100 pennies.
8. Joe can spend at least $22 but no more than $30.

Graphing Relationships

CC.9-12.F.IF.4 For a function that models a relationship between two quantities, interpret key features of graphs..., and sketch graphs showing key features given a verbal description of the relationship.* *Also* CC.9-12.N.Q.2*

Objectives
Match simple graphs with situations.

Graph a relationship.

Vocabulary
continuous graph
discrete graph

Who uses this?
Cardiologists can use graphs to analyze their patients' heartbeats. (See Example 2.)

Graphs can be used to illustrate many different situations. For example, trends shown on a cardiograph can help a doctor see how the patient's heart is functioning.

To relate a graph to a given situation, use key words in the description.

EXAMPLE 1 **Relating Graphs to Situations**

The air temperature was constant for several hours at the beginning of the day and then rose steadily for several hours. It stayed the same temperature for most of the day before dropping sharply at sundown. Choose the graph that best represents this situation.

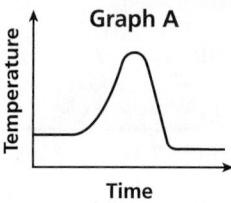
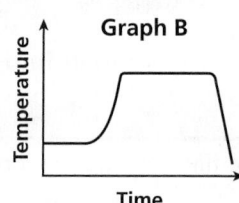
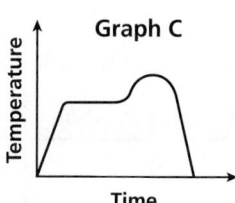

Step 1 Read the graphs from left to right to show time passing.

Step 2 List key words in order and decide which graph shows them.

Key Words	Segment Description	Graphs
Was constant	Horizontal	Graphs A and B
Rose steadily	Slanting upward	Graphs A and B
Stayed the same	Horizontal	Graph B
Dropped sharply	Slanting downward	Graph B

Step 3 Pick the graph that shows all the key phrases in order.

horizontal, **slanting upward,** horizontal, **slanting downward**

The correct graph is B.

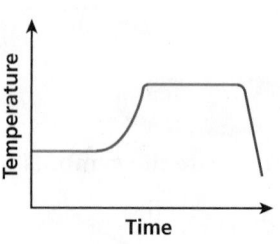

1. The air temperature increased steadily for several hours and then remained constant. At the end of the day, the temperature increased slightly again before dropping sharply. Choose the graph above that best represents this situation.

As seen in Example 1, some graphs are connected lines or curves called **continuous graphs**. Some graphs are only distinct points. These are called **discrete graphs**.

The graph on theme-park attendance is an example of a discrete graph. It consists of distinct points because each year is distinct and people are counted in whole numbers only. The values between the whole numbers are not included, since they have no meaning for the situation.

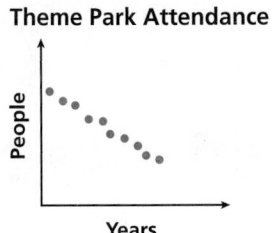

Theme Park Attendance

EXAMPLE 2 | **Sketching Graphs for Situations**

Sketch a graph for each situation. Tell whether the graph is continuous or discrete.

A Simon is selling candles to raise money for the school dance. For each candle he sells, the school will get $2.50. He has 10 candles that he can sell.

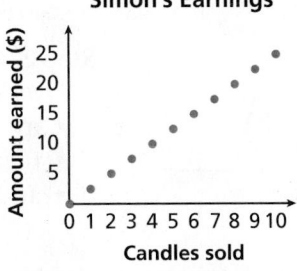

Simon's Earnings

The amount earned (y-axis) increases by $2.50 for each candle Simon sells (x-axis).

Since Simon can only sell whole numbers of candles, the graph is 11 distinct points.

The graph is discrete.

B Angelique's heart rate is being monitored while she exercises on a treadmill. While walking, her heart rate remains the same. As she increases her pace, her heart rate rises at a steady rate. When she begins to run, her heart rate increases more rapidly and then remains high while she runs. As she decreases her pace, her heart rate slows down and returns to her normal rate.

As time passes during her workout (moving left to right along the *x*-axis), her heart rate (*y*-axis) does the following:

- remains the same,
- rises at a steady rate,
- increases **more rapidly** (**steeper** than previous segment),
- remains high,
- slows down,
- and then returns to her normal rate.

Angelique's Heart Rate

The graph is continuous.

Sketch a graph for each situation. Tell whether the graph is continuous or discrete.

2a. Jamie is taking an 8-week keyboarding class. At the end of each week, she takes a test to find the number of words she can type per minute. She improves each week.

2b. Henry begins to drain a water tank by opening a valve. Then he opens another valve. Then he closes the first valve. He leaves the second valve open until the tank is empty.

When sketching or interpreting a graph, pay close attention to the labels on each axis. Both graphs below show a relationship about a child going down a slide. **Graph A** represents the child's *distance from the ground* over time. **Graph B** represents the child's *speed* over time.

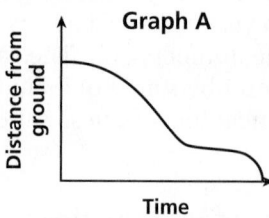

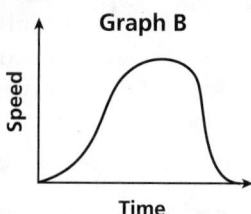

EXAMPLE 3 **Writing Situations for Graphs**

Write a possible situation for the given graph.

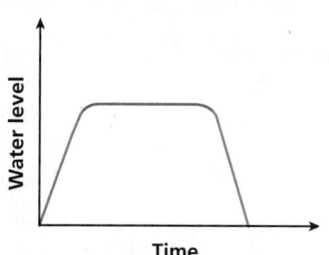

Step 1 Identify labels.
    x-axis: time   *y*-axis: water level

Step 2 Analyze sections.
    Over time, the water level
    • increases steadily,
    • remains unchanged,
    • and then decreases steadily.

Possible Situation: A watering can is filled with water. It sits for a while until some flowers are planted. The water is then emptied on top of the planted flowers.

3. Write a possible situation for the given graph.

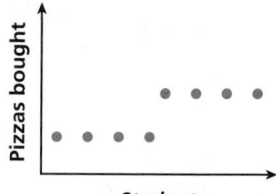

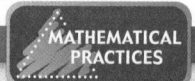

THINK AND DISCUSS

1. Should a graph of age related to height be a continuous graph or a discrete graph? Explain.

2. Give an example of a situation that, when graphed, would include a horizontal segment.

3. GET ORGANIZED Copy and complete the graphic organizer. Write an example of key words that suggest the given segments on a graph. One example for each segment is given for you.

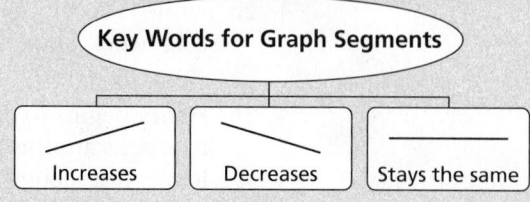

GUIDED PRACTICE

Vocabulary Apply the vocabulary from this lesson to answer each question.

1. A ___?___ graph is made of connected lines or curves. (*continuous* or *discrete*)

2. A ___?___ graph is made of only distinct points. (*continuous* or *discrete*)

SEE EXAMPLE 1 Choose the graph that best represents each situation.

3. A person alternates between running and walking.

4. A person gradually speeds up to a constant running pace.

5. A person walks, gradually speeds up to a run, and then slows back down to a walk.

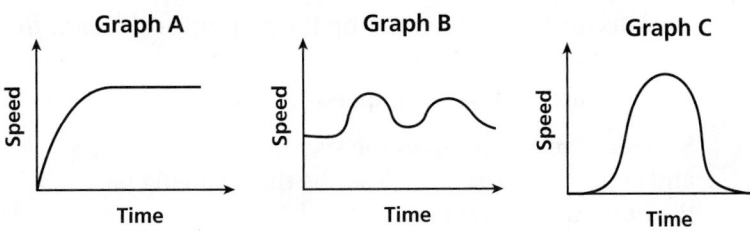

Graph A   Graph B   Graph C

SEE EXAMPLE 2

6. Maxine is buying extra pages for her photo album. Each page holds exactly 8 photos. Sketch a graph to show the maximum number of photos she can add to her album if she buys 1, 2, 3, or 4 extra pages. Tell whether the graph is continuous or discrete.

SEE EXAMPLE 3 Write a possible situation for each graph.

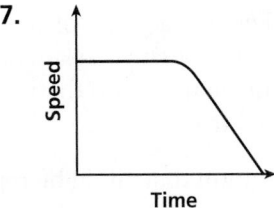 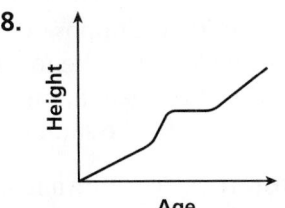 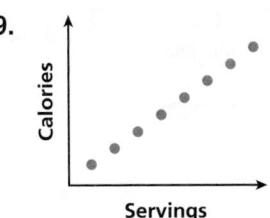

7.   8.   9.

PRACTICE AND PROBLEM SOLVING

Independent Practice	
For Exercises	See Example
10–12	1
13	2
14–16	3

Extra Practice

See Extra Practice for more Skills Practice and Applications Practice exercises.

Choose the graph that best represents each situation.

10. A flag is raised up a flagpole quickly at the beginning and then more slowly near the top.

11. A flag is raised up a flagpole in a jerky motion, using a hand-over-hand method.

12. A flag is raised up a flagpole at a constant rate of speed.

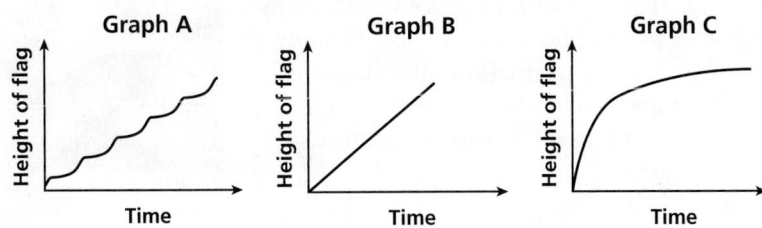

Graph A   Graph B   Graph C

13. For six months, a puppy gained weight at a steady rate. Sketch a graph to illustrate the weight of the puppy during that time period. Tell whether the graph is continuous or discrete.

Write a possible situation for each graph.

14.
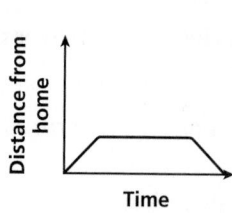

15.
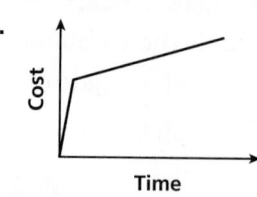

16.
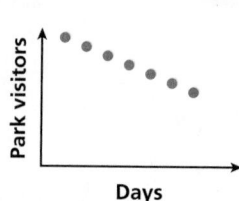

17. Data Collection Use a graphing calculator and motion detector for the following.

  a. On a coordinate plane, draw a graph relating distance from a starting point walking at various speeds and time.

  b. Using the motion detector as the starting point, walk away from the motion detector to make a graph on the graphing calculator that matches the one you drew.

  c. Compare your walking speeds to each change in steepness on the graph.

18. Sports The graph shows the speed of a horse during and after a race. Use it to describe the changing pace of the horse during the race.

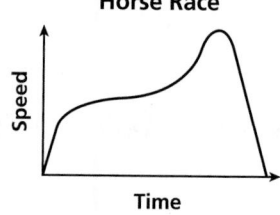

Horse Race

19. Recreation You hike up a mountain path starting at 10 A.M. You camp overnight and then walk back down the same path at the same pace at 10 A.M. the next morning. On the same set of axes, graph the relationship between distance from the top of the mountain and the time of day for both the hike up and the hike down. What does the point of intersection of the graphs represent?

20. Critical Thinking Suppose that you sketched a graph of speed related to time for a brick that fell from the top of a building. Then you sketched a graph for speed related to time for a ball that was rolled down a hill and then came to rest. How would the graphs be the same? How would they be different?

21. Write About It Describe a real-life situation that could be represented by a distinct graph. Then describe a real-life situation that could be represented by a continuous graph.

MULTI-STEP TEST PREP

22. A rectangular pool that is 4 feet deep at all places is being filled at a constant rate.

  a. Sketch a graph to show the depth of the water as it increases over time.

  b. The side view of another swimming pool is shown. If the pool is being filled at a constant rate, sketch a graph to show the depth of the water as it increases over time.

23. Which situation would NOT be represented by a discrete graph?

    Ⓐ Amount of money earned based on the number of cereal bars sold

    Ⓑ Number of visitors to a grocery store per day for one week

    Ⓒ The amount of iced tea in a pitcher at a restaurant during the lunch hour

    Ⓓ The total cost of buying 1, 2, or 3 CDs at the music store

24. Which situation is best represented by the graph?

    Ⓕ A snowboarder starts at the bottom of the hill and takes a ski lift to the top.

    Ⓖ A cruise boat travels at a steady pace from the port to its destination.

    Ⓗ An object falls from the top of a building and gains speed at a rapid pace before hitting the ground.

    Ⓙ A marathon runner starts at a steady pace and then runs faster at the end of the race before stopping at the finish line.

25. Short Response Marla participates in a triathlon consisting of swimming, biking, and running. Would a graph of Marla's speed during the triathlon be a continuous graph or a distinct graph? Explain.

CHALLENGE AND EXTEND

Pictured are three vases and graphs representing the height of water as it is poured into each of the vases at a constant rate. Match each vase with the correct graph.

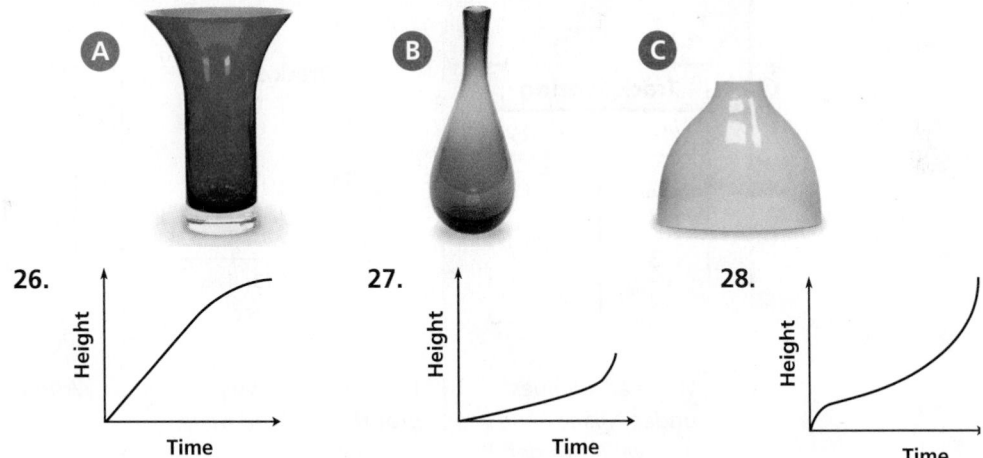

A   **B**   **C**

26.   **27.**   **28.**

3-2 Relations and Functions

CC.9-12.F.IF.1 Understand that a function from one set (called the domain) to another set (called the range) assigns to each element of the domain exactly one element of the range.... *Also* **CC.9-12.F.IF.5***

Objectives
Identify functions.

Find the domain and range of relations and functions.

Vocabulary
relation
domain
range
function

Why learn this?
You can use a relation to show finishing positions and scores in a track meet.

Previously, you saw relationships represented by graphs. Relationships can also be represented by a set of ordered pairs, called a **relation** .

In the scoring system of some track meets, **first place** is worth 5 points, **second place** is worth 3 points, **third place** is worth 2 points, and **fourth place** is worth 1 point. This scoring system is a relation, so it can be shown as ordered pairs, $\{(1, 5), (2, 3), (3, 2), (4, 1)\}$. You can also show relations in other ways, such as tables, graphs, or *mapping diagrams.*

EXAMPLE **1** **Showing Multiple Representations of Relations**

Express the relation for the track meet scoring system, $\{(1, 5), (2, 3), (3, 2), (4, 1)\}$, as a table, as a graph, and as a mapping diagram.

Table	Graph	Mapping Diagram

Table

Track Scoring

Place	Points
1	5
2	3
3	2
4	1

Write all x-values under "Place" and all y-values under "Points."

Graph

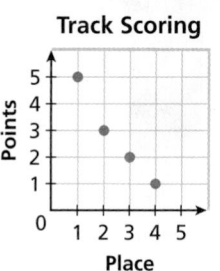

Track Scoring

Use the x- and y-values to plot the ordered pairs.

Mapping Diagram

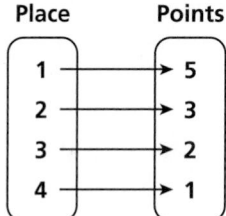

Write all x-values under "Place" and all y-values under "Points." Draw an arrow from each x-value to its corresponding y-value.

CHECK IT OUT!   **1.** Express the relation $\{(1, 3)\ (2, 4), (3, 5)\}$ as a table, as a graph, and as a mapping diagram.

The **domain** of a relation is the set of first coordinates (or *x*-values) of the ordered pairs. The **range** of a relation is the set of second coordinates (or *y*-values) of the ordered pairs. The domain of the track meet scoring system is {1, 2, 3, 4}. The range is {5, 3, 2, 1}.

EXAMPLE 2 **Finding the Domain and Range of a Relation**

Give the domain and range of the relation.

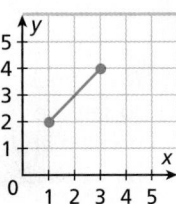

The domain is all *x*-values from 1 through 3, inclusive.

The range is all *y*-values from 2 through 4, inclusive.

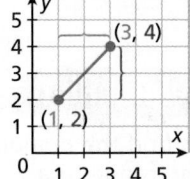

D: $1 \leq x \leq 3$ R: $2 \leq y \leq 4$

CHECK IT OUT! Give the domain and range of each relation.

2a.
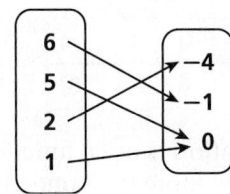

2b.

x	y
1	1
4	4
8	1

A **function** is a special type of relation that pairs each domain value with exactly one range value.

EXAMPLE 3 **Identifying Functions**

Give the domain and range of each relation. Tell whether the relation is a function. Explain.

A

Field Trip	
Students *x*	Buses *y*
75	2
68	2
125	3

D: $\{75, 68, 125\}$ *Even though 2 appears twice in the table, it is written only once when writing the range.*

R: $\{2, 3\}$

This relation is a function. Each domain value is paired with exactly one range value.

B

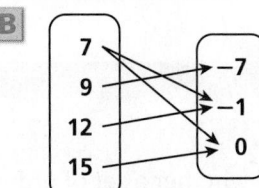

Use the arrows to determine which domain values correspond to each range value.

D: $\{7, 9, 12, 15\}$

R: $\{-7, -1, 0\}$

This relation is not a function. Each domain value does not have exactly one range value. The domain value 7 is paired with the range values −1 and 0.

Give the domain and range of each relation. Tell whether the relation is a function. Explain.

 C

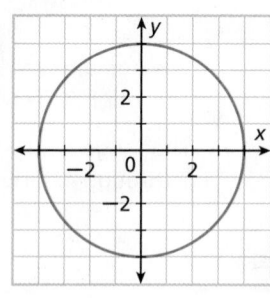

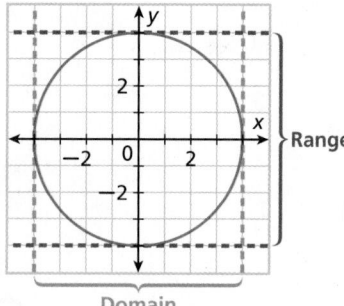

Draw lines to see the domain and range values.

Range

Domain

D: $-4 \leq x \leq 4$ R: $-4 \leq y \leq 4$

x	4	0	0	−4
y	0	4	−4	0

To compare domain and range values, make a table using points from the graph.

This relation is not a function because there are several domain values that have more than one range value. For example, the domain value 0 is paired with both 4 and −4.

CHECK IT OUT! Give the domain and range of each relation. Tell whether the relation is a function. Explain.

3a. $\{(8, 2), (-4, 1), (-6, 2), (1, 9)\}$ 3b.

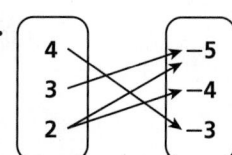

Student to Student   *Functions*

I decide whether a list of ordered pairs is a function by looking at the x-values. If they're all different, then it's a function.

(1, 6), (2, 5), (6, 5), (0, 8)	*(5, 6), (7, 2), (5, 8), (6, 3)*
All different x-values	*Same x-value* (with different *y*-values)
Function	*Not a function*

Eric Dawson
Boone High School

MATHEMATICAL PRACTICES

THINK AND DISCUSS

1. Describe how to tell whether a set of ordered pairs is a function.

2. Can the graph of a vertical line segment represent a function? Explain.

3. **GET ORGANIZED** Copy and complete the graphic organizer by explaining when a relation is a function and when it is not a function.

Know it!
Note

A relation is...	
A function if...	Not a function if...

GUIDED PRACTICE

Vocabulary Apply the vocabulary from this lesson to answer each question.

1. Use a mapping diagram to show a relation that is not a *function*.

2. The set of *x*-values for a relation is also called the ___?___. (*domain* or *range*)

SEE EXAMPLE **1** Express each relation as a table, as a graph, and as a mapping diagram.

3. $\{(1, 1), (1, 2)\}$

4. $\left\{(-1, 1), \left(-2, \frac{1}{2}\right), \left(-3, \frac{1}{3}\right), \left(-4, \frac{1}{4}\right)\right\}$

5. $\{(-1, 1), (-3, 3), (5, -5), (-7, 7)\}$

6. $\{(0, 0), (2, -4), (2, -2)\}$

SEE EXAMPLE **2** Give the domain and range of each relation.

7. $\{(-5, 7), (0, 0), (2, -8), (5, -20)\}$

8. $\{(1, 2), (2, 4), (3, 6), (4, 8), (5, 10)\}$

9.

x	3	5	2	8	6
y	9	25	4	81	36

10.

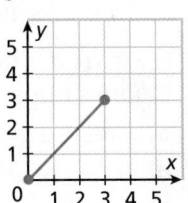

SEE EXAMPLE **3** **Multi-Step** Give the domain and range of each relation. Tell whether the relation is a function. Explain.

11. $\{(1, 3), (1, 0), (1, -2), (1, 8)\}$

12. $\{(-2, 1), (-1, 2), (0, 3), (1, 4)\}$

13.

x	−2	−1	0	1	2
y	1	1	1	1	1

14.

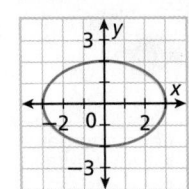

PRACTICE AND PROBLEM SOLVING

For Exercises	See Example
15–16	1
17–18	2
19–20	3

Independent Practice

Express each relation as a table, as a graph, and as a mapping diagram.

15. $\{(-2, -4), (-1, -1), (0, 0), (1, -1), (2, -4)\}$

16. $\left\{(2, 1), \left(2, \frac{1}{2}\right), (2, 2), \left(2, 2\frac{1}{2}\right)\right\}$

Extra Practice

See Extra Practice for more Skills Practice and Applications Practice exercises.

Give the domain and range of each relation.

17.

18.

x	*y*
4	4
5	5
6	6
7	7
8	8

Multi-Step Give the domain and range of each relation. Tell whether the relation is a function. Explain.

19.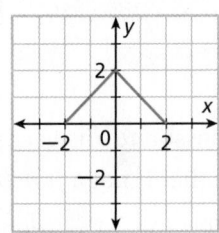

20.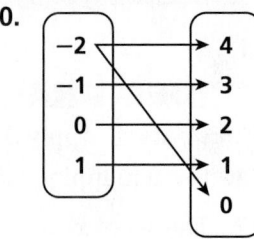

21. Consumer Application An electrician charges a base fee of $75 plus $50 for each hour of work. Create a table that shows the amount the electrician charges for 1, 2, 3, and 4 hours of work. Let x represent the number of hours and y represent the amount charged for x hours. Is this relation a function? Explain.

22. Geometry Write a relation as a set of ordered pairs in which the x-value represents the side length of a square and the y-value represents the area of that square. Use a domain of 2, 4, 6, 9, and 11.

23. Multi-Step Create a mapping diagram to display the numbers of days in 1, 2, 3, and 4 weeks. Is this relation a function? Explain.

24. Nutrition The illustrations list the number of grams of fat and the number of Calories from fat for selected foods.

   a. Create a graph for the relation between grams of fat and Calories from fat.

   b. Is this relation a function? Explain.

Hamburger
Fat (g):   14
Fat (Cal): 126

Cheeseburger
Fat (g):   18
Fat (Cal): 162

Grilled chicken filet
Fat (g):   3.5
Fat (Cal): 31.5

Breaded chicken filet
Fat (g):   11
Fat (Cal): 99

Taco salad
Fat (g):   19
Fat (Cal): 171

25. Recreation A shop rents canoes for a $7 equipment fee plus $2 per hour, with a maximum cost of $15 per day. Express the number of hours x and the cost y as a relation in table form, and find the cost to rent a canoe for 1, 2, 3, 4, and 5 hours. Is this relation a function? Explain.

26. Health You can burn about 6 Calories per minute bicycling. Let x represent the number of minutes bicycled, and let y represent the number of Calories burned.

   a. Write ordered pairs to show the number of Calories burned by bicycling for 60, 120, 180, 240, or 300 minutes. Graph the ordered pairs.

   b. Find the domain and range of the relation.

   c. Does this graph represent a function? Explain.

27. Critical Thinking For a function, can the number of elements in the range be greater than the number of elements in the domain? Explain.

28. Critical Thinking Tell whether each statement is true or false. If false, explain why.

   a. All relations are functions.   **b.** All functions are relations.

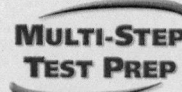
29. **a.** The graph shows the amount of water being pumped into a pool over a 5-hour time period. Find the domain and range.

b. Does the graph represent a function? Explain.

c. Give the time and volume as ordered pairs at 2 hours and at 3 hours 30 minutes.

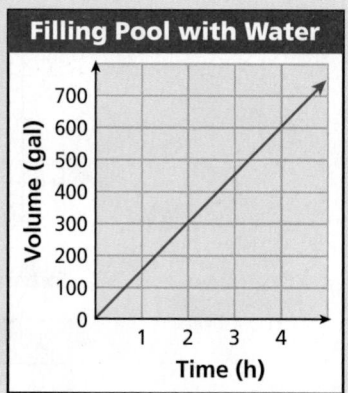

Filling Pool with Water

30. 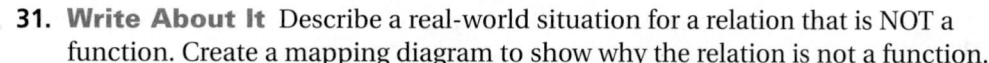ERROR ANALYSIS When asked whether the relation $\{(-4, 16), (-2, 4), (0, 0), (2, 4)\}$ is a function, a student stated that the relation is not a function because 4 appears twice. What error did the student make? How would you explain to the student why this relation is a function?

31. **Write About It** Describe a real-world situation for a relation that is NOT a function. Create a mapping diagram to show why the relation is not a function.

32. Which of the following relations is NOT a function?

Ⓐ $\{(6, 2), (-1, 2), (-3, 2), (-5, 2)\}$

Ⓒ

x	3	5	7
y	1	15	30

Ⓑ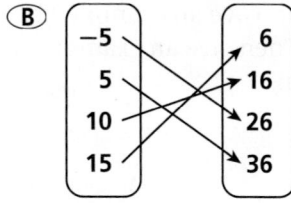

Ⓓ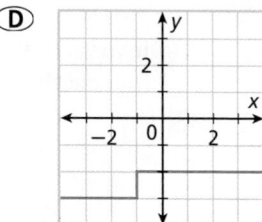

33. Which is NOT a correct way to describe the function $\{(-3, 2), (1, 8), (-1, 5), (3, 11)\}$?

Ⓕ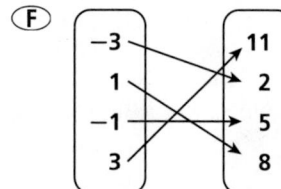

Ⓗ Domain: $\{-3, 1, -1, 3\}$

   Range: $\{2, 8, 5, 11\}$

Ⓖ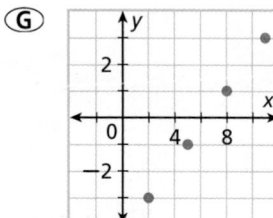

Ⓙ

x	y
−3	2
−1	5
1	8
3	11

34. Which graph represents a function?

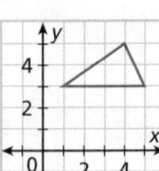 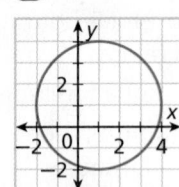 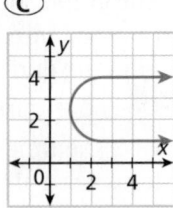 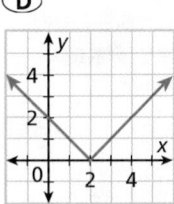

35. Extended Response Use the table for the following.

x	−3	−1	0	1	3
y	5	7	9	11	13

   a. Express the relation as ordered pairs.

   b. Give the domain and range of the relation.

   c. Does the relation represent a function? Explain your answer.

CHALLENGE AND EXTEND

36. What values of a make the relation $\{(a, 1), (2, 3), (4, 5)\}$ a function? Explain.

37. What values of b make the relation $\{(5, 6), (7, 8), (9, b)\}$ a function? Explain.

38. The *inverse* of a relation is created by interchanging the x- and y- coordinates of each ordered pair in the relation.

   a. Find the inverse of the following relation: $\{(-2, 5), (0, 4), (3, -8), (7, 5)\}$.

   b. Is the original relation a function? Why or why not? Is the inverse of the relation a function? Why or why not?

   c. The statement "If a relation is a function, then the inverse of the relation is also a function" is sometimes true. Give an example of a relation and its inverse that are both functions. Then give an example of a relation and its inverse that are both not functions.

3-2 Algebra LAB

The Vertical-Line Test

The *vertical-line test* can be used to visually determine whether a graphed relation is a function.

Use with Relations and Functions

Look for and express regularity in repeated reasoning.

CC.9-12.F.IF.1 Understand that a function from one set (called the domain) to another set (called the range) assigns to each element of the domain exactly one element of the range....

Activity

1. Look at the values in Table 1. Is every *x*-value paired with exactly one *y*-value? If not, what *x*-value(s) are paired with more than one *y*-value?

2. Is the relation a function? Explain.

3. Graph the points from the Table 1. Draw a vertical line through each point of the graph. Does any vertical line touch more than one point?

Table 1	
x	**y**
−2	−5
−1	−3
0	−1
1	1
2	3
3	5

4. Look at the values in Table 2. Is every *x*-value paired with exactly one *y*-value? If not, what *x*-value(s) are paired with more than one *y*-value?

5. Is the relation a function? Explain.

6. Graph the points from the Table 2. Draw a vertical line through each point of the graph. Does any vertical line touch more than one point?

7. What is the *x*-value of the two points that are on the same vertical line? Is that *x*-value paired with more than one *y*-value?

Table 2	
x	**y**
−2	−3
1	4
0	5
1	2
2	3
3	5

8. Write a statement describing how to use a vertical line to tell if a relation is a function. This is called the vertical-line test.

9. Why does the vertical-line test work?

Try This

Use the vertical-line test to determine whether each relation is a function. If a relation is not a function, list two ordered pairs that show the same *x*-value with two different *y*-values.

1.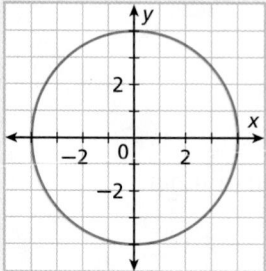

2.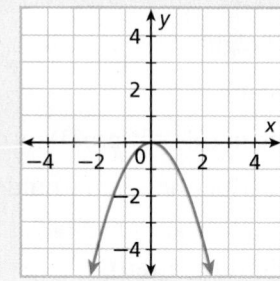

3.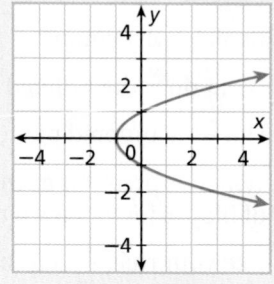

3-3 Algebra LAB

Use with Writing Functions

Model Variable Relationships

You can use models to represent an algebraic relationship. Using these models, you can write an algebraic expression to help describe and extend patterns.

The diagrams below represent the side views of tables. Each has a tabletop and a base. Copy and complete the chart using the pattern shown in the diagrams.

Tabletop →
Base →

MATHEMATICAL PRACTICES

Look for and express regularity in repeated reasoning.

TERM NUMBER	FIGURE	DESCRIPTION OF FIGURE	EXPRESSION FOR NUMBER OF BLOCKS	VALUE OF TERM (NUMBER OF BLOCKS)	ORDERED PAIR
1		length of tabletop = 4 height of base = 1	$4 + (2)1$	6	$(1, 6)$
2		length of tabletop = 4 height of base = 2	■	8	■
3		length of tabletop = 4 height of base = 3	■	10	■
4	■	■	■	■	■
5	■	■	■	■	■
n	✕	■	■	✕	■

Try This

1. Explain why you must multiply the height of the base by 2.

2. What does the ordered pair (1, 6) mean?

3. Does the ordered pair (10, 24) belong in this pattern? Why or why not?

4. Which expression from the table describes how you would find the total number of blocks for any term number n?

5. Use your rule to find the 25th term in this pattern.

COMMON CORE

3-3 Writing Functions

CC.9-12.F.IF.2 Use function notation, evaluate functions for inputs in their domains, and interpret statements that use function notation in terms of a context. *Also* **CC.9-12.F.IF.1, CC.9-12.F.IF.5*, CC.9-12.A.CED.3*, CC.9-12.F.BF.1*, CC.9-12.F.LE.2***

Objectives
Identify independent and dependent variables.

Write an equation in function notation and evaluate a function for given input values.

Vocabulary
independent variable
dependent variable
function rule
function notation

Why learn this?

You can use a function rule to calculate how much money you will earn for working specific amounts of time.

Suppose Tasha baby-sits and charges $5 per hour.

Time Worked (h) *x*	1	2	3	4
Amount Earned ($) *y*	5	10	15	20

The amount of money Tasha earns is $5 times the number of hours she works. Write an equation using two different variables to show this relationship.

Amount earned is $5 times the number of hours worked.

$$y = 5 \cdot x$$

Tasha can use this equation to find how much money she will earn for any number of hours she works.

EXAMPLE 1 **Using a Table to Write an Equation**

Determine a relationship between the *x*- and *y*-values. Write an equation.

x	1	2	3	4
y	−2	−1	0	1

Step 1 List possible relationships between the first *x*- and *y*-values.

$1 - 3 = -2$ or $1(-2) = -2$

Step 2 Determine if one relationship works for the remaining values.

$2 - 3 = -1$ ✓ $2(-2) \neq -1$ ✗

$3 - 3 = 0$ ✓ $3(-2) \neq 0$ ✗

$4 - 3 = 1$ ✓ $4(-2) \neq 1$ ✗

The first relationship works. The value of *y* is 3 less than *x*.

Step 3 Write an equation.

$y = x - 3$ *The value of y is 3 less than x.*

1. Determine a relationship between the *x*- and *y*-values in the relation $\{(1, 3), (2, 6), (3, 9), (4, 12)\}$. Write an equation.

The equation in Example 1 describes a function because for each *x*-value (input), there is only one *y*-value (output).

The **input** of a function is the **independent variable** . The **output** of a function is the **dependent variable** . The value of the dependent variable *depends* on, or is a function of, the value of the independent variable. For Tasha, the amount she earns depends on, or is a function of, the amount of time she works.

EXAMPLE **2** **Identifying Independent and Dependent Variables**

Identify the independent and dependent variables in each situation.

A In the winter, more electricity is used when the temperature goes down, and less is used when the temperature rises.

> The amount of electricity used *depends on* the temperature.
> Dependent: amount of electricity   Independent: temperature

B The cost of shipping a package is based on its weight.

> The cost of shipping a package *depends on* its weight.
> Dependent: cost   Independent: weight

C The faster Ron walks, the quicker he gets home.

> The time it takes Ron to get home *depends on* the speed he walks.
> Dependent: time   Independent: speed

CHECK IT OUT! Identify the independent and dependent variables in each situation.

2a. A company charges $10 per hour to rent a jackhammer.

2b. Apples cost $0.99 per pound.

An algebraic expression that defines a function is a **function rule** . 5 · *x* in the equation about Tasha's earnings is a function rule.

If *x* is the independent variable and *y* is the dependent variable, then **function notation** for *y* is *f*(*x*), read "*f* of *x*," where *f* names the function. When an equation in two variables describes a function, you can use function notation to write it.

The dependent variable	is	a function of	the independent variable .
y	is	a function of	*x* .
y	=	*f*	(*x*)

Since *y* = *f*(*x*), Tasha's earnings, *y* = 5*x*, can be rewritten in function notation by substituting *f*(*x*) for *y*: *f*(*x*) = 5*x*. Sometimes functions are written using *y*, and sometimes functions are written using *f*(*x*).

EXAMPLE **3** **Writing Functions**

Identify the independent and dependent variables. Write an equation in function notation for each situation.

A A lawyer's fee is $200 per hour for her services.

> The fee for the lawyer depends on how many hours she works.
> Dependent: fee   Independent: hours
> Let *h* represent the number of hours the lawyer works.
> The function for the lawyer's fee is $f(h) = 200h$.

Identify the independent and dependent variables. Write an equation in function notation for each situation.

B   The admission fee to a local carnival is $8. Each ride costs $1.50.

The **total cost** depends on the number of rides ridden, plus $8.

Dependent: **total cost**   Independent: number of rides

Let *r* represent the number of rides ridden.

The function for the total cost of the carnival is $f(r) = 1.50r + 8$.

 Identify the independent and dependent variables. Write an equation in function notation for each situation.

3a. Steven buys lettuce that costs $1.69/lb.

3b. An amusement park charges a $6.00 parking fee plus $29.99 per person.

You can think of a function as an **input-output machine**. For Tasha's earnings, $f(x) = 5x$, if you input a value *x*, the output is $5x$.

If Tasha wanted to know how much money she would earn by working 6 hours, she could input 6 for *x* and find the output. This is called *evaluating the function*.

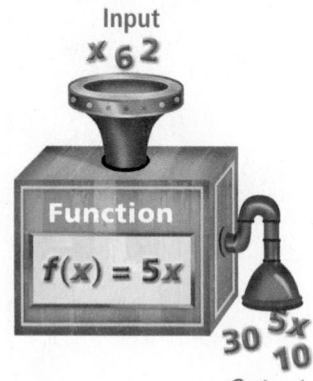

Input
x 6 2

Function

$f(x) = 5x$

30 5x
    10

Output

EXAMPLE 4   **Evaluating Functions**

Evaluate each function for the given input values.

A   For $f(x) = 5x$, find $f(x)$ when $x = 6$ and when $x = 7.5$.

$f(x) = 5x$ $f(x) = 5x$

$f(6) = 5(6)$ *Substitute 6 for x.* $f(7.5) = 5(7.5)$ *Substitute 7.5 for x.*

$= 30$ *Simplify.* $= 37.5$ *Simplify.*

Functions can be named with any letter; *f*, *g*, and *h* are the most common. You read $f(6)$ as "*f* of 6," and $g(2)$ as "*g* of 2."

B   For $g(t) = 2.30t + 10$, find $g(t)$ when $t = 2$ and when $t = -5$.

$g(t) = 2.30t + 10$ $g(t) = 2.30t + 10$

$g(2) = 2.30(2) + 10$ $g(-5) = 2.30(-5) + 10$

$= 4.6 + 10$ $= -11.5 + 10$

$= 14.6$ $= -1.5$

C   For $h(x) = \frac{1}{2}x - 3$, find $h(x)$ when $x = 12$ and when $x = -8$.

$h(x) = \frac{1}{2}x - 3$ $h(x) = \frac{1}{2}x - 3$

$h(12) = \frac{1}{2}(12) - 3$ $h(-8) = \frac{1}{2}(-8) - 3$

$= 6 - 3$ $= -4 - 3$

$= 3$ $= -7$

 Evaluate each function for the given input values.

4a. For $h(c) = 2c - 1$, find $h(c)$ when $c = 1$ and $c = -3$.

4b. For $g(t) = \frac{1}{4}t + 1$, find $g(t)$ when $t = -24$ and $t = 400$.

When a function describes a real-world situation, every real number is not always reasonable for the domain and range. For example, a number representing the length of an object cannot be negative, and only whole numbers can represent a number of people.

EXAMPLE 5 **Finding the Reasonable Domain and Range of a Function**

Manuel has already sold $20 worth of tickets to the school play. He has 4 tickets left to sell at $2.50 per ticket. Write a function to describe how much money Manuel can collect from selling tickets. Find the reasonable domain and range for the function.

Money collected from ticket sales	is	$2.50	per	ticket	plus	the $20 already sold.
$f(x)$	=	$2.50	·	x	+	20

If he sells x more tickets, he will have collected $f(x) = 2.50x + 20$ dollars.

Manuel has only 4 tickets left to sell, so he could sell 0, 1, 2, 3, or 4 tickets. A reasonable domain is {0, 1, 2, 3, 4}.

Substitute these values into the function rule to find the range values.

x	0	1	2	3	4
f (x)	$2.50(0) + 20$ $= 20$	$2.50(1) + 20$ $= 22.50$	$2.50(2) + 20$ $= 25$	$2.50(3) + 20$ $= 27.50$	$2.50(4) + 20$ $= 30$

The reasonable range for this situation is {$20, $22.50, $25, $27.50, $30}.

5. The settings on a space heater are the whole numbers from 0 to 3. The total number of watts used for each setting is 500 times the setting number. Write a function to describe the number of watts used for each setting. Find the reasonable domain and range for the function.

THINK AND DISCUSS

1. When you input water into an ice machine, the output is ice cubes. Name another real-world object that has an input and an output.

2. How do you identify the independent and dependent variables in a situation?

3. Explain how to find reasonable domain values for a function.

4. GET ORGANIZED Copy and complete the graphic organizer. Use the function $y = x + 3$ and the domain {−2, −1, 0, 1, 2}.

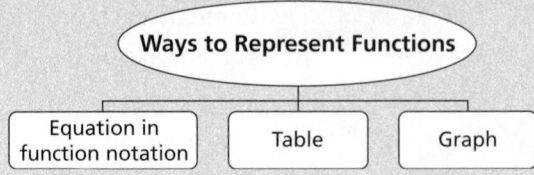

GUIDED PRACTICE

Vocabulary Apply the vocabulary from this lesson to answer each question.

1. The output of a function is the ___?___ variable. (*independent* or *dependent*)

2. An algebraic expression that defines a function is a ___?___. (*function rule* or *function notation*)

SEE EXAMPLE **1**

Determine a relationship between the *x*- and *y*-values. Write an equation.

3.

x	1	2	3	4
y	−1	0	1	2

4. $\{(1, 4), (2, 7), (3, 10), (4, 13)\}$

SEE EXAMPLE **2**

Identify the independent and dependent variables in each situation.

5. A small-size bottle of water costs $1.99 and a large-size bottle of water costs $3.49.

6. An employee receives 2 vacation days for every month worked.

SEE EXAMPLE **3**

Identify the independent and dependent variables. Write an equation in function notation for each situation.

7. An air-conditioning technician charges customers $75 per hour.

8. An ice rink charges $3.50 for skates and $1.25 per hour.

SEE EXAMPLE **4**

Evaluate each function for the given input values.

9. For $f(x) = 7x + 2$, find $f(x)$ when $x = 0$ and when $x = 1$.

10. For $g(x) = 4x − 9$, find $g(x)$ when $x = 3$ and when $x = 5$.

11. For $h(t) = \frac{1}{3}t − 10$, find $h(t)$ when $t = 27$ and when $t = −15$.

SEE EXAMPLE **5**

12. A construction company uses beams that are 2, 3, or 4 meters long. The measure of each beam must be converted to centimeters. Write a function to describe the situation. Find the reasonable domain and range for the function. (*Hint*: 1 m = 100 cm)

PRACTICE AND PROBLEM SOLVING

Independent Practice

For Exercises	See Example
13–14	1
15–16	2
17–19	3
20–22	4
23	5

Extra Practice

See Extra Practice for more Skills Practice and Applications Practice exercises.

Determine a relationship between the *x*- and *y*-values. Write an equation.

13.

x	1	2	3	4
y	−2	−4	−6	−8

14. $\{(1, −1), (2, −2), (3, −3), (4, −4)\}$

Identify the independent and dependent variables in each situation.

15. Gardeners buy fertilizer according to the size of a lawn.

16. The cost to gift wrap an order is $3 plus $1 per item wrapped.

Identify the independent and dependent variables. Write an equation in function notation for each situation.

17. To rent a DVD, a customer must pay $3.99 plus $0.99 for every day that it is late.

18. Stephen charges $25 for each lawn he mows.

19. A car can travel 28 miles per gallon of gas.

Evaluate each function for the given input values.

20. For $f(x) = x^2 - 5$, find $f(x)$ when $x = 0$ and when $x = 3$.

21. For $g(x) = x^2 + 6$, find $g(x)$ when $x = 1$ and when $x = 2$.

22. For $f(x) = \frac{2}{3}x + 3$, find $f(x)$ when $x = 9$ and when $x = -3$.

23. A mail-order company charges $5 per order plus $2 per item in the order, up to a maximum of 4 items. Write a function to describe the situation. Find the reasonable domain and range for the function.

24. **Transportation** Air Force One can travel 630 miles per hour. Let h be the number of hours traveled. The function $d = 630h$ gives the distance d in miles that Air Force One travels in h hours.

    a. Identify the independent and dependent variables. Write $d = 630h$ using function notation.

    b. What are reasonable values for the domain and range in the situation described?

    c. How far can Air Force One travel in 12 hours?

25. Complete the table for $g(z) = 2z - 5$.

z	1	2	3	4
$g(z)$				

26. Complete the table for $h(x) = x^2 + x$.

x	0	1	2	3
$h(x)$				

27. **Estimation** For $f(x) = 3x + 5$, estimate the output when $x = -6.89$, $x = 1.01$, and $x = 4.67$.

28. **Transportation** A car can travel 30 miles on a gallon of gas and has a 20-gallon gas tank. Let g be the number of gallons of gas the car has in its tank. The function $d = 30g$ gives the distance d in miles that the car travels on g gallons.

    a. What are reasonable values for the domain and range in the situation described?

    b. How far can the car travel on 12 gallons of gas?

29. **Critical Thinking** Give an example of a real-life situation for which the reasonable domain consists of 1, 2, 3, and 4 and the reasonable range consists of 2, 4, 6, and 8.

30. **///ERROR ANALYSIS///** Rashid saves $150 each month. He wants to know how much he will have saved in 2 years. He writes the rule $s = m + 150$ to help him figure out how much he will save, where s is the amount saved and m is the number of months he saves. Explain why his rule is incorrect.

31. **Write About It** Give a real-life situation that can be described by a function. Identify the independent variable and the dependent variable.

MULTI-STEP TEST PREP

32. The table shows the volume v of water pumped into a pool after t hours.

    a. Determine a relationship between the time and the volume of water and write an equation.

    b. Identify the independent and dependent variables.

    c. If the pool holds 10,000 gallons, how long will it take to fill?

Amount of Water in Pool	
Time (h)	Volume (gal)
0	0
1	1250
2	2500
3	3750
4	5000

(tl), © Bettmann/CORBIS; (bl), Sam Dudgeon/HMH

33. Marsha buys x pens at \$0.70 per pen and one pencil for \$0.10. Which function gives the total amount Marsha spends?

   (A) $c(x) = 0.70x + 0.10x$ (C) $c(x) = (0.70 + 0.10)x$

   (B) $c(x) = 0.70x + 1$ (D) $c(x) = 0.70x + 0.10$

34. Belle is buying pizzas for her daughter's birthday party, using the prices in the table. Which equation best describes the relationship between the total cost c and the number of pizzas p?

Pizzas	Total Cost ($)
5	26.25
10	52.50
15	78.75

   (F) $c = 26.25p$ (H) $c = p + 26.25$

   (G) $c = 5.25p$ (J) $c = 6p - 3.75$

35. Gridded Response What is the value of $f(x) = 5 - \frac{1}{2}x$ when $x = 3$?

CHALLENGE AND EXTEND

36. The formula to convert a temperature that is in degrees Celsius x to degrees Fahrenheit $f(x)$ is $f(x) = \frac{9}{5}x + 32$. What are reasonable values for the domain and range when you convert to Fahrenheit the temperature of water as it rises from 0° to 100° Celsius?

37. Math History In his studies of the motion of free-falling objects, Galileo Galilei found that regardless of its mass, an object will fall a distance d that is related to the square of its travel time t in seconds. The modern formula that describes free-fall motion is $d = \frac{1}{2}gt^2$, where g is the acceleration due to gravity and t is the length of time in seconds the object falls. Find the distance an object falls in 3 seconds. (*Hint:* Research to find acceleration due to gravity in meters per second squared.)

3-4 Graphing Functions

CC.9-12.F.IF.5 Relate the domain of a function to its graph and, where applicable, to the quantitative relationship it describes.* *Also* **CC.9-12.F.IF.1, CC.9-12.F.IF.2, CC.9-12.F.IF.7*, CC.9-12.A.REI.10**

Objectives
Graph functions given a limited domain.

Graph functions given a domain of all real numbers.

Who uses this?

Scientists can use a function to make conclusions about rising sea level.

Sea level is rising at an approximate rate of 2.5 millimeters per year. If this rate continues, the function $y = 2.5x$ can describe how many millimeters y sea level will rise in the next x years.

One way to understand functions such as the one above is to graph them. You can graph a function by finding ordered pairs that satisfy the function.

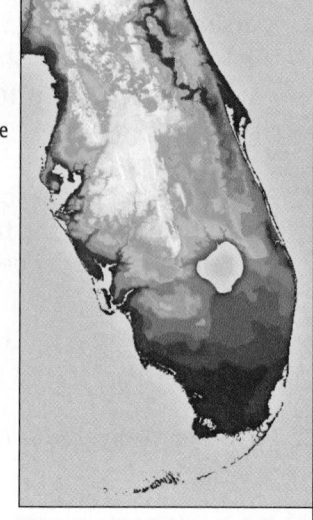

Current Florida coastline.

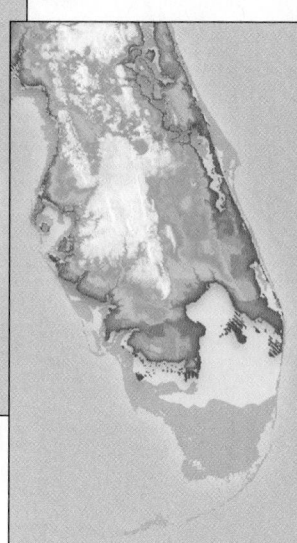

Possible Florida coastline in 2400 years.

EXAMPLE 1 Graphing Solutions Given a Domain

Graph each function for the given domain.

A $-x + 2y = 6$; D: {−4, −2, 0, 2}

Step 1 Solve for y since you are given values of the domain, or x.

$$-x + 2y = 6$$

$$\underline{+x \qquad\qquad +x} \qquad \text{Add } x \text{ to both sides.}$$

$$2y = x + 6$$

$$\frac{2y}{2} = \frac{x + 6}{2} \qquad \text{Since } y \text{ is multiplied by 2, divide both sides by 2.}$$

$$y = \frac{x}{2} + \frac{6}{2} \qquad \text{Rewrite } \frac{x+6}{2} \text{ as two separate fractions.}$$

$$y = \frac{1}{2}x + 3 \qquad \text{Simplify.}$$

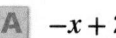

Helpful Hint

Sometimes solving for y first makes it easier to substitute values of x and find an ordered pair.

Step 2 Substitute the given values of the domain for x and find values of y.

Step 3 Graph the ordered pairs.

x	$y = \frac{1}{2}x + 3$	(x, y)
−4	$y = \frac{1}{2}(−4) + 3 = 1$	$(−4, 1)$
−2	$y = \frac{1}{2}(−2) + 3 = 2$	$(−2, 2)$
0	$y = \frac{1}{2}(0) + 3 = 3$	$(0, 3)$
2	$y = \frac{1}{2}(2) + 3 = 4$	$(2, 4)$

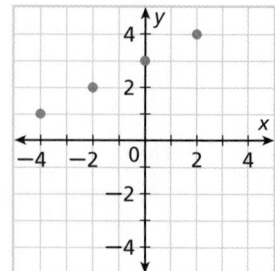

Graph each function for the given domain.

B $f(x) = |x|$; D: $\{-2, -1, 0, 1, 2\}$

Step 1 Use the given values of the domain to find values of $f(x)$.

x	$f(x) = |x|$	$(x, f(x))$
-2	$f(x) = |-2| = 2$	$(-2, 2)$
-1	$f(x) = |-1| = 1$	$(-1, 1)$
0	$f(x) = |0| = 0$	$(0, 0)$
1	$f(x) = |1| = 1$	$(1, 1)$
2	$f(x) = |2| = 2$	$(2, 2)$

Step 2 Graph the ordered pairs.

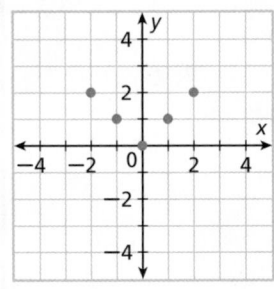

 Graph each function for the given domain.

1a. $-2x + y = 3$; D: $\{-5, -3, 1, 4\}$

1b. $f(x) = x^2 + 2$; D: $\{-3, -1, 0, 1, 3\}$

If the domain of a function is all real numbers, any number can be used as an input value. This process will produce an infinite number of ordered pairs that satisfy the function. Therefore, arrowheads are drawn at both "ends" of a smooth line or curve to represent the infinite number of ordered pairs. If a domain is not given, assume that the domain is all real numbers.

Graphing Functions Using a Domain of All Real Numbers	
Step 1	Use the function to generate ordered pairs by choosing several values for x.
Step 2	Plot enough points to see a pattern for the graph.
Step 3	Connect the points with a line or smooth curve.

EXAMPLE 2 **Graphing Functions**

Graph each function.

A $2x + 1 = y$

Step 1 Choose several values of x and generate ordered pairs.

Helpful Hint

When choosing values of x, be sure to choose both positive and negative values. You may not need to graph all the points to see the pattern.

x	$2x + 1 = y$	(x, y)
-3	$2(-3) + 1 = -5$	$(-3, -5)$
-2	$2(-2) + 1 = -3$	$(-2, -3)$
-1	$2(-1) + 1 = -1$	$(-1, -1)$
0	$2(0) + 1 = 1$	$(0, 1)$
1	$2(1) + 1 = 3$	$(1, 3)$
2	$2(2) + 1 = 5$	$(2, 5)$
3	$2(3) + 1 = 7$	$(3, 7)$

Step 2 Plot enough points to see a pattern.

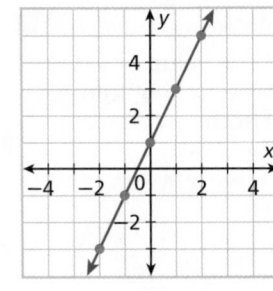

Step 3 The ordered pairs appear to form a line. **Draw a line** through all the points to show all the ordered pairs that satisfy the function. Draw arrowheads on both "ends" of the line.

Graph each function.

B $y = x^2$

Step 1 Choose several values of x and generate ordered pairs.

Step 2 Plot enough points to see a pattern.

x	y = x²	(x, y)
−3	$y = (−3)^2 = 9$	(−3, 9)
−2	$y = (−2)^2 = 4$	(−2, 4)
−1	$y = (−1)^2 = 1$	(−1, 1)
0	$y = (0)^2 = 0$	(0, 0)
1	$y = (1)^2 = 1$	(1, 1)
2	$y = (2)^2 = 4$	(2, 4)

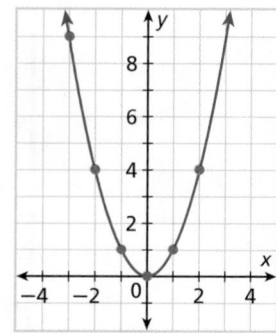

Step 3 The ordered pairs appear to form an almost U-shaped graph. **Draw a smooth curve** through the points to show all the ordered pairs that satisfy the function. Draw arrowheads on the "ends" of the curve.

Check If the graph is correct, any point on it will satisfy the function. Choose an ordered pair on the graph that was not in your table, such as (3, 9). Check whether it satisfies $y = x^2$.

$$\frac{y = x^2}{9 \mid 3^2}$$
$$9 \mid 9 \checkmark$$

Substitute the values for x and y into the function. Simplify.

The ordered pair (3, 9) satisfies the function.

CHECK IT OUT! **Graph each function.**

2a. $f(x) = 3x − 2$ **2b.** $y = |x − 1|$

EXAMPLE 3 **Finding Values Using Graphs**

Use a graph of the function $f(x) = \frac{1}{3}x + 2$ to find the value of $f(x)$ when $x = 6$. Check your answer.

Locate 6 on the x-axis. Move **up** to the graph of the function. Then move **left** to the y-axis to find the corresponding value of y.

$f(x) = 4$

Check Use substitution.

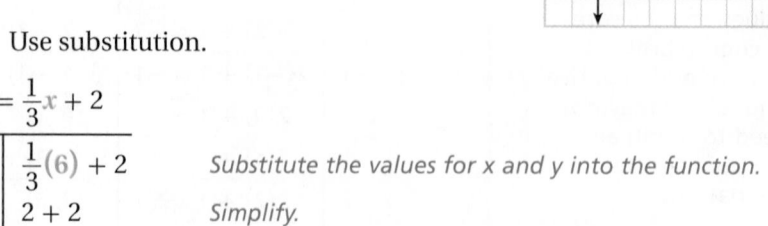

$$f(x) = \frac{1}{3}x + 2$$

4	$\frac{1}{3}(6) + 2$	*Substitute the values for x and y into the function.*
4	$2 + 2$	*Simplify.*
4	$4 \checkmark$	*The ordered pair (4, 6) satisfies the function.*

Writing Math

"The value of y is 4 when $x = 6$" can also be written as $f(6) = 4$.

CHECK IT OUT!  **3.** Use the graph above to find the value of x when $f(x) = 3$. Check your answer.

Recall that in real-world situations you may have to limit the domain to make answers reasonable. For example, quantities such as time, distance, and number of people can be represented using only nonnegative values. When both the domain and the range are limited to nonnegative values, the function is graphed only in Quadrant I.

EXAMPLE 4 **Problem-Solving Application**

Make sense of problems and persevere in solving them.

The function $y = 2.5x$ describes how many millimeters sea level y rises in x years. Graph the function. Use the graph to estimate how many millimeters sea level will rise in 3.5 years.

 Understand the Problem

The **answer** is a graph that can be used to find the value of y when x is 3.5.

List the important information:
• The function $y = 2.5x$ describes how many millimeters sea level rises.

2 Make a Plan

Think: What values should I use to graph this function? Both, the number of years sea level has risen and the distance sea level rises, cannot be negative. Use only nonnegative values for both the domain and the range. The function will be graphed in Quadrant I.

3 Solve

Choose several nonnegative values of x to find values of y. Then graph the ordered pairs.

x	$y = 2.5x$	(x, y)
0	$y = 2.5(0) = 0$	$(0, 0)$
1	$y = 2.5(1) = 2.5$	$(1, 2.5)$
2	$y = 2.5(2) = 5$	$(2, 5)$
3	$y = 2.5(3) = 7.5$	$(3, 7.5)$
4	$y = 2.5(4) = 10$	$(4, 10)$

Draw a line through the points to show all the ordered pairs that satisfy this function.

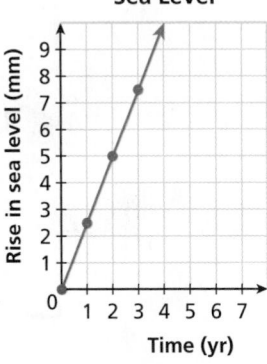

Use the graph to estimate the y-value when x is 3.5.
Sea level will rise about 8.75 millimeters in 3.5 years.

 Look Back

As the number of years increases, sea level also increases, so the graph is reasonable. When x is between 3 and 4, y is between 7.5 and 10. Since 3.5 is between 3 and 4, it is reasonable to estimate y to be 8.75 when x is 3.5.

 4. The fastest recorded Hawaiian lava flow moved at an average speed of 6 miles per hour. The function $y = 6x$ describes the distance y the lava moved on average in x hours. Graph the function. Use the graph to estimate how many miles the lava moved after 5.5 hours.

THINK AND DISCUSS

1. How do you find the range of a function if the domain is all real numbers?

2. Explain how to use a graph to find the value of a function for a given value of x.

 3. **GET ORGANIZED** Copy and complete the graphic organizer. Explain how to graph a function for each situation.

```
         Graphing a Function
        ┌──────────┴──────────┐
  Not a real-world        Real-world
    situation             situation
```

3-4 Exercises

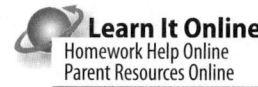

GUIDED PRACTICE

SEE EXAMPLE 1 Graph each function for the given domain.

1. $3x - y = 1$; D: $\{-3, -1, 0, 4\}$

2. $f(x) = -|x|$; D: $\{-5, -3, 0, 3, 5\}$

3. $f(x) = x + 4$; D: $\{-5, -3, 0, 4\}$

4. $y = x^2 - 1$; D: $\{-3, -1, 0, 1, 3\}$

SEE EXAMPLE 2 Graph each function.

5. $f(x) = 6x + 4$

6. $y = \frac{1}{2}x + 4$

7. $x + y = 0$

8. $y = |x| - 4$

9. $f(x) = 2x^2 - 7$

10. $y = -x^2 + 5$

SEE EXAMPLE 3 11. Use a graph of the function $f(x) = \frac{1}{2}x - 2$ to find the value of y when $x = 2$. Check your answer.

SEE EXAMPLE 4 12. **Oceanography** The floor of the Atlantic Ocean is spreading at an average rate of 1 inch per year. The function $y = x$ describes the number of inches y the ocean floor spreads in x years. Graph the function. Use the graph to estimate the number of inches the ocean floor will spread in $10\frac{1}{2}$ years.

PRACTICE AND PROBLEM SOLVING

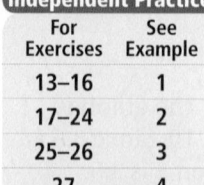

Independent Practice

For Exercises	See Example
13–16	1
17–24	2
25–26	3
27	4

Graph each function for the given domain.

13. $2x + y = 4$; D: $\{-3, -1, 4, 7\}$

14. $y = |x| - 1$; D: $\{-4, -2, 0, 2, 4\}$

15. $f(x) = -7x$; D: $\{-2, -1, 0, 1\}$

16. $y = (x + 1)^2$; D: $\{-2, -1, 0, 1, 2\}$

Extra Practice

See Extra Practice for more Skills Practice and Applications Practice exercises.

Graph each function.

17. $y = -3x + 5$

18. $f(x) = 3x$

19. $x + y = 8$

20. $f(x) = 2x + 2$

21. $y = -|x| + 10$

22. $f(x) = -5 + x^2$

23. $y = |x + 1| + 1$

24. $y = (x - 2)^2 - 1$

25. Use a graph of the function $f(x) = -2x - 3$ to find the value of y when $x = -4$. Check your answer.

26. Use a graph of the function $f(x) = \frac{1}{3}x + 1$ to find the value of y when $x = 6$. Check your answer.

27. Transportation An electric motor scooter can travel at 0.25 miles per minute. The function $y = 0.25x$ describes the number of miles y the scooter can travel in x minutes. Graph the function. Use the graph to estimate the number of miles an electric motor scooter travels in 15 minutes.

Graph each function.

28. $f(x) = x - 1$

29. $12 - x - 2y = 0$

30. $3x - y = 13$

31. $y = x^2 - 2$

32. $x^2 - y = -4$

33. $2x^2 = f(x)$

34. $f(x) = |2x| - 2$

35. $y = |-x|$

36. $-|2x + 1| = y$

37. Find the value of x so that $(x, 12)$ satisfies $y = 4x + 8$.

38. Find the value of x so that $(x, 6)$ satisfies $y = -x - 4$.

39. Find the value of y so that $(-2, y)$ satisfies $y = -2x^2$.

For each function, determine whether the given points are on the graph.

40. $y = 7x - 2$; $(1, 5)$ and $(2, 10)$

41. $y = |x| + 2$; $(3, 5)$ and $(-1, 3)$

42. $y = x^2$; $(1, 1)$ and $(-3, -9)$

43. $y = \frac{1}{4}x - 2$; $\left(1, -\frac{3}{4}\right)$ and $(4, -1)$

44. ///ERROR ANALYSIS/// Student A says that $(3, 2)$ is on the graph of $y = 4x - 5$, but student B says that it is not. Who is incorrect? Explain the error.

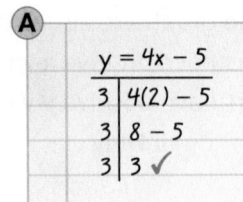 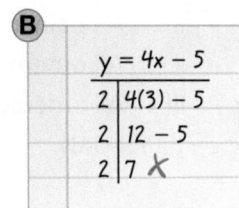

Determine whether $(0, -7)$, $\left(-6, -\frac{5}{3}\right)$, **and** $(-2, -3)$ **lie on the graph of each function.**

45. $x + 3y = -11$

46. $y + |x| = -1$

47. $x^2 - y = 7$

For each function, find three ordered pairs that lie on the graph of the function.

48. $-6 = 3x + 2y$

49. $y = 1.1x + 2$

50. $y = \frac{4}{5}x$

51. $y = 3x - 1$

52. $y = |x| + 6$

53. $y = x^2 - 5$

54. Critical Thinking Graph the functions $y = |x|$ and $y = -|x|$. Describe how they are alike. How are they different?

55. A pool containing 10,000 gallons of water is being drained. Every hour, the volume of the water in the pool decreases by 1500 gallons.

  a. Write an equation to describe the volume v of water in the pool after h hours.

  b. How much water is in the pool after 1 hour?

  c. Create a table of values showing the volume of the water in gallons in the pool as a function of the time in hours and graph the function.

56. **Estimation** Use the graph to estimate the value of y when $x = 2.117$.

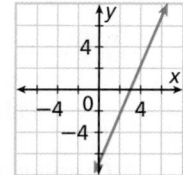

57. **Write About It** Why is a graph a convenient way to show the ordered pairs that satisfy a function?

58. Which function is graphed?

   Ⓐ $2y - 3x = 2$ Ⓒ $y = 2x - 1$
   Ⓑ $5x + y = 1$ Ⓓ $y = 5x + 8$

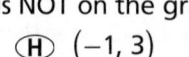

59. Which ordered pair is NOT on the graph of $y = 4 - |x|$?

   Ⓕ $(0, 4)$ Ⓗ $(-1, 3)$
   Ⓖ $(4, 0)$ Ⓙ $(3, -1)$

60. Which function has $(3, 2)$ on its graph?

   Ⓐ $2x - 3y = 12$ Ⓒ $y = -\dfrac{2}{3}x + 4$

   Ⓑ $-2x - 3y = 12$ Ⓓ $y = -\dfrac{3}{2}x + 4$

61. Which statement(s) is true about the function $y = x^2 + 1$?

   I.   All points on the graph are above the origin.
   II.   All ordered pairs have positive x-values.
   III. All ordered pairs have positive y-values.

   Ⓕ I Only   Ⓖ II Only   Ⓗ I and II   Ⓙ I and III

CHALLENGE AND EXTEND

62. Graph the function $y = x^3$. Make sure you have enough ordered pairs to see the shape of the graph.

63. The temperature of a liquid that started at 64 °F is increasing by 4 °F per hour. Write a function that describes the temperature of the liquid over time. Graph the function to show the temperatures over the first 10 hours.

3-4 Technology LAB

Connect Function Rules, Tables, and Graphs

You can use a graphing calculator to understand the connections among function rules, tables, and graphs.

CC.9-12.F.IF.1 Understand that a function … assigns to each element of the domain exactly one element of the range.… The graph of *f* is the graph of the equation *y* = *f*(*x*).

Activity

Use appropriate tools strategically.

Make a table of values for the function $f(x) = 4x + 3$. Then graph the function.

1 Press **Y=** and enter the function rule **4x + 3**.

2 Press **2nd** **WINDOW** (TBLSET). Make sure **Indpnt: Auto** and **Depend: Auto** are selected.

3 To view the table, press **2nd** **GRAPH** (TABLE). The *x*-values and the corresponding *y*-values appear in table form. Use the up and down arrow keys to scroll through the table.

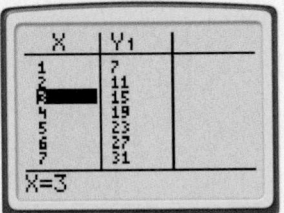

4 To view the table with the graph, press **MODE** and select **G-T** view. Press **ENTER**. Be sure to use the standard window.

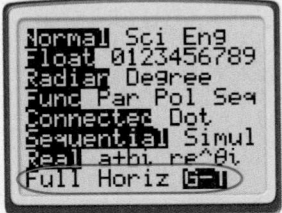

5 Press **TRACE** to see both the graph and a table of values.

6 Press the left arrow key several times to move the cursor. Notice that the point on the graph and the values in the table correspond.

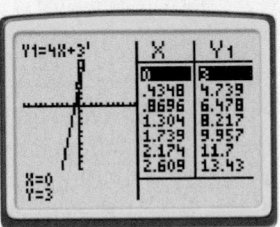

Try This

Make a table of values for each function. Then graph the function.

1. $f(x) = 2x - 1$

2. $f(x) = 1.5x$

3. $f(x) = \frac{1}{2}x + 2$

4. Explain the relationship between a function, its table of values, and the graph of the function.

MULTI-STEP TEST PREP

Make sense of problems and persevere in solving them.

Function Concepts

Down the Drain The graph shows the relationship between the number of hours that have passed since a pool began to drain and the amount of water in the pool.

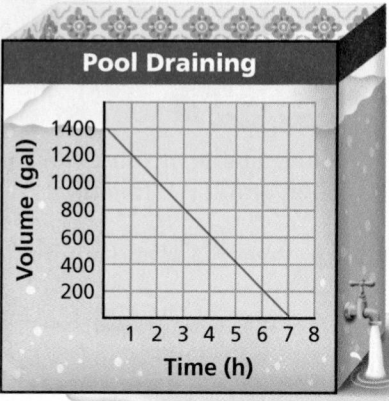

Pool Draining

1. Describe in words the relationship between the amount of water in the pool and the number of hours that have passed since the pool began to drain.

2. What are the domain and range for the graph?

3. Use the graph to determine how much water is in the pool after 3 hours. How much water is in the pool after $4\frac{1}{2}$ hours?

4. Copy and complete the table.

Draining Pool	
Time (h)	**Volume (gal)**
0	1400
1	
2	
3	
4	
5	
6	
7	

5. Write an equation to describe the relationship between the volume v and the time t. Use the equation to find how much water is in the pool after 5.2 hours.

READY TO GO ON?

Quiz for Lessons 3-1 Through 3-4

3-1 Graphing Relationships

Choose the graph that best represents each situation.

1. A person bungee jumps from a high platform.

2. A person jumps on a trampoline in a steady motion.

3. Xander takes a quiz worth 100 points. Each question is worth 20 points. Sketch a graph to show his score if he misses 1, 2, 3, 4, or 5 questions.

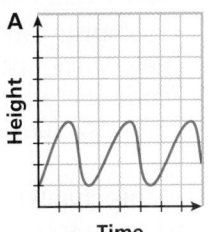

A

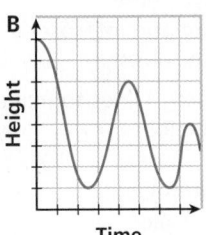

B

3-2 Relations and Functions

Give the domain and range of each relation. Tell whether the relation is a function. Explain.

4.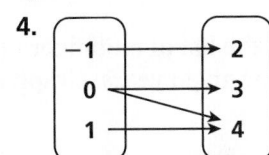

5.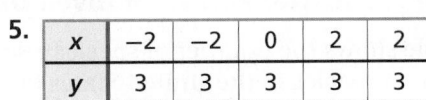

x	−2	−2	0	2	2
y	3	3	3	3	3

6.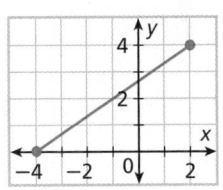

3-3 Writing Functions

Determine a relationship between the x- and y-values. Write an equation.

7.

x	1	2	3	4
y	−6	−5	−4	−3

8.

x	1	2	3	4
y	−3	−6	−9	−12

9. A printer can print 8 pages per minute. Identify the dependent and independent variables for the situation. Write an equation in function notation.

Evaluate each function for the given input values.

10. For $f(x) = 3x - 1$, find $f(x)$ when $x = 2$.

11. For $g(x) = x^2 - x$, find $g(x)$ when $x = -2$.

12. A photographer charges a sitting fee of $15 plus $3 for each pose. Write a function to describe the situation. Find a reasonable domain and range for up to 5 poses.

3-4 Graphing Functions

Graph each function for the given domain.

13. $2x - y = 3$; D: $\{-2, 0, 1, 3\}$ 14. $y = 4 - x^2$; D: $\{-1, 0, 1, 2\}$ 15. $y = 3 - 2x$; D: $\{-1, 0, 1, 3\}$

Graph each function.

16. $x + y = 6$

17. $y = |x| - 3$

18. $y = x^2 + 1$

19. The function $y = 8x$ represents how many miles y a certain storm travels in x hours. Graph the function and estimate the number of miles the storm travels in 10.5 h.

CC.9-12.S.ID.6 Represent data on two quantitative variables on a scatter plot, and describe how the variables are related. *Also* **CC.9-12.NQ.1***

Scatter Plots and Trend Lines

Objectives
Create and interpret scatter plots.

Use trend lines to make predictions.

Vocabulary
scatter plot
correlation
positive correlation
negative correlation
no correlation
trend line

Who uses this?

Ecologists can use scatter plots to help them analyze data about endangered species, such as ocelots. (See Example 1.)

In this chapter, you have examined relationships between sets of ordered pairs, or data. Displaying data visually can help you see relationships.

A **scatter plot** is a graph with points plotted to show a possible relationship between two sets of data. A scatter plot is an effective way to display some types of data.

EXAMPLE **1** **Graphing a Scatter Plot from Given Data**

The table shows the number of species added to the list of endangered and threatened species in the United States during the given years. Graph a scatter plot using the given data.

Increase in List							
Calendar Year	1996	1997	1998	1999	2000	2001	2002
Species	91	79	62	11	39	10	9

Source: U.S. Fish and Wildlife Service

Helpful Hint

The point (2000, 39) tells you that in the year 2000, the list increased by 39 species.

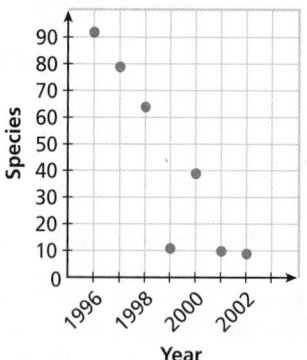

Use the table to make ordered pairs for the scatter plot.

The x-value represents the calendar year and the y-value represents the number of species added.

Plot the ordered pairs.

 **1.** The table shows the number of points scored by a high school football team in the first four games of a season. Graph a scatter plot using the given data.

Game	1	2	3	4
Score	6	21	46	34

A **correlation** describes a relationship between two data sets. A graph may show the correlation between data. The correlation can help you analyze trends and make predictions. There are three types of correlations between data.

Correlations

Positive Correlation	Negative Correlation	No Correlation
Both sets of data values increase.	One set of data values increases as the other set decreases.	There is no relationship between the data sets.
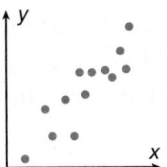	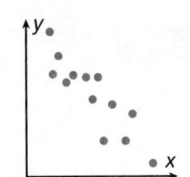	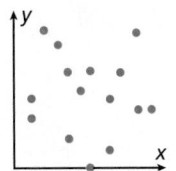

In the endangered species graph, as time increases, the number of new species added decreases. So the correlation between the data is negative.

EXAMPLE **2** **Describing Correlations from Scatter Plots**

Describe the correlation illustrated by the scatter plot.

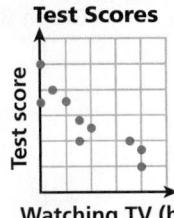

As the number of hours spent watching TV increased, test scores decreased.

There is a negative correlation between the two data sets.

 **2.** Describe the correlation illustrated by the scatter plot.

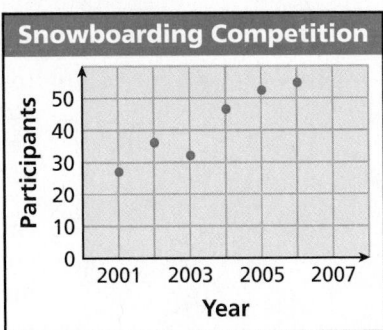

EXAMPLE **3** **Identifying Correlations**

Identify the correlation you would expect to see between each pair of data sets. Explain.

A **the number of empty seats in a classroom and the number of students seated in the class**

You would expect to see a negative correlation. As the number of students increases, the number of empty seats decreases.

B **the number of pets a person owns and the number of books that person read last year**

You would expect to see no correlation. The number of pets a person owns has nothing to do with how many books the person has read.

Identify the correlation you would expect to see between each pair of data sets. Explain.

 C the monthly rainfall and the depth of water in a reservoir

You would expect to see a positive correlation. As more rain falls, there is more water in the reservoir.

 Identify the correlation you would expect to see between each pair of data sets. Explain.

3a. the temperature in Houston and the number of cars sold in Boston

3b. the number of members in a family and the size of the family's grocery bill

3c. the number of times you sharpen your pencil and the length of your pencil

---

EXAMPLE 4 **Matching Scatter Plots to Situations**

Choose the scatter plot that best represents the relationship between the number of days since a sunflower seed was planted and the height of the plant. Explain.

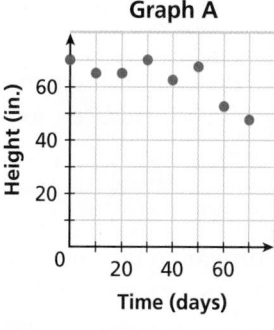

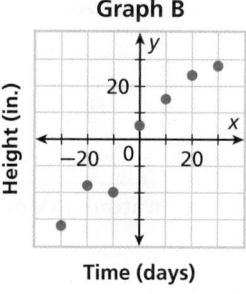

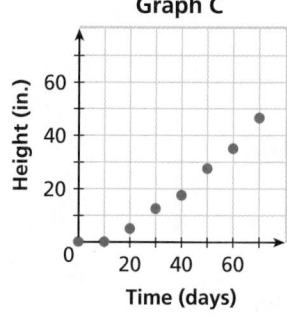

There will be a positive correlation between the number of days and the height because the plant will grow each day.

Graph A has a negative correlation, so it is incorrect.

Neither the number of days nor the plant heights can be negative.

Graph B shows negative values, so it is incorrect.

This graph shows all positive coordinates and a positive correlation, so it could represent the data sets.

Graph C is the correct scatter plot.

 **4.** Choose the scatter plot that best represents the relationship between the number of minutes since a pie has been taken out of the oven and the temperature of the oven. Explain.

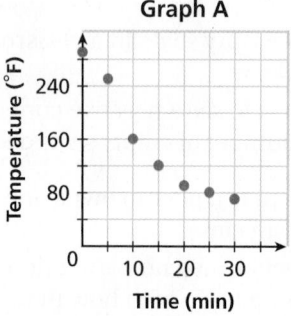

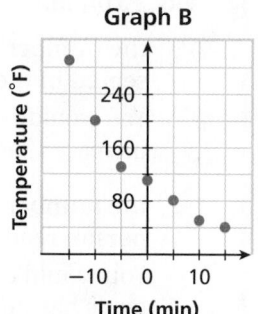

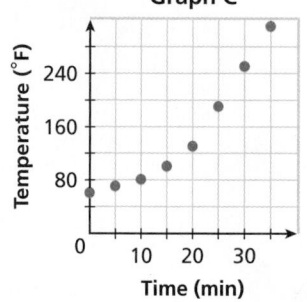

You can graph a line on a scatter plot to help show a relationship in the data. This line, called a **trend line,** helps show the correlation between data sets more clearly. It can also be helpful when making predictions based on the data.

EXAMPLE 5 *Fund-raising Application*

The scatter plot shows a relationship between the total amount of money collected and the total number of rolls of wrapping paper sold as a school fund-raiser. Based on this relationship, predict how much money will be collected when 175 rolls have been sold.

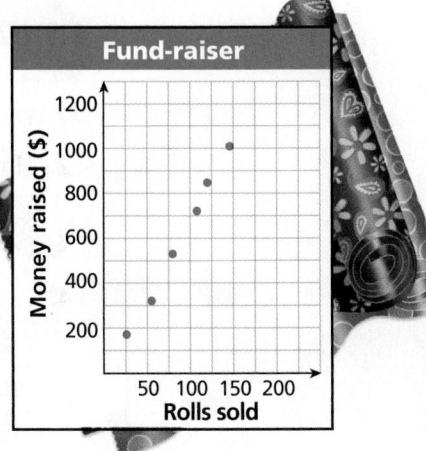

Draw a trend line and use it to make a prediction.

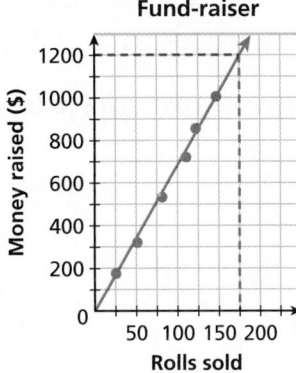

Draw a line that has about the same number of points above and below it. Your line may or may not go through data points.

Find the point on the line whose x-value is 175. The corresponding y-value is 1200.

Based on the data, $1200 is a reasonable prediction of how much money will be collected when 175 rolls have been sold.

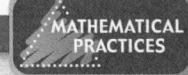 **5.** Based on the trend line above, predict how many wrapping paper rolls need to be sold to raise $500.

THINK AND DISCUSS

1. Is it possible to make a prediction based on a scatter plot with no correlation? Explain your answer.

2. GET ORGANIZED Copy and complete the graphic organizer with either a scatter plot, a real-world example, or both.

	Graph	Example
Positive Correlation		
Negative Correlation		The amount of water in a watering can and the number of flowers watered
No Correlation		

GUIDED PRACTICE

Vocabulary Apply the vocabulary from this lesson to answer each question.

1. Give an example of a graph that is not a *scatter plot*.

2. How is a scatter plot that shows *no correlation* different from a scatter plot that shows a *negative correlation*?

3. Does a *trend line* always pass through every point on a scatter plot? Explain.

SEE EXAMPLE **1**

4. Graph a scatter plot using the given data.

Garden Statue	Cupid	Gnome	Lion	Flamingo	Wishing well
Height (in.)	32	18	35	28	40
Price ($)	50	25	80	15	75

SEE EXAMPLE **2**

Describe the correlation illustrated by each scatter plot.

5.

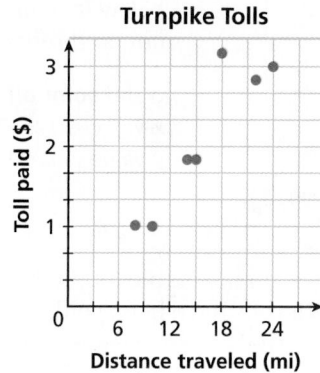

Turnpike Tolls

6.

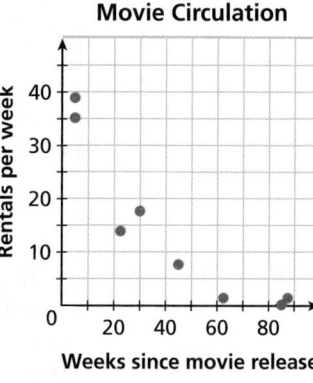

Movie Circulation

SEE EXAMPLE **3**

Identify the correlation you would expect to see between each pair of data sets. Explain.

7. the volume of water poured into a container and the amount of empty space left in the container

8. a person's shoe size and the length of the person's hair

9. the outside temperature and the number of people at the beach

SEE EXAMPLE **4**

Choose the scatter plot that best represents the described relationship. Explain.

10. age of car and number of miles traveled

11. age of car and sales price of car

12. age of car and number of states traveled to

Graph A

Graph B

Graph C

13. Transportation The scatter plot shows the total number of miles passengers flew on U.S. domestic flights in the month of April for the years 1997–2004. Based on this relationship, predict how many miles passengers flew in April 2008.

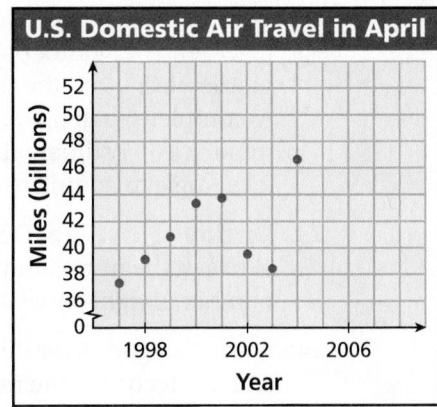

U.S. Domestic Air Travel in April

PRACTICE AND PROBLEM SOLVING

Independent Practice	
For Exercises	See Example
14	1
15–16	2
17–18	3
19–20	4
21	5

Extra Practice

See Extra Practice for more Skills Practice and Applications Practice exercises.

14. Graph a scatter plot using the given data.

Train Arrival Time	6:45 A.M.	7:30 A.M.	8:15 A.M.	9:45 A.M.	10:30 A.M.
Passengers	160	148	194	152	64

Describe the correlation illustrated by each scatter plot.

15.

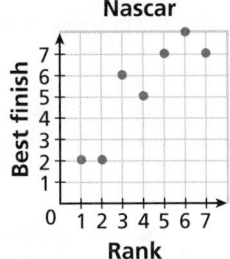

Nascar

16. Concert Ticket Costs

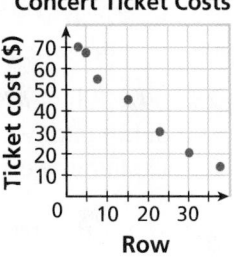

Identify the correlation you would expect to see between each pair of data sets. Explain.

17. the speed of a runner and the distance she can cover in 10 minutes

18. the year a car was made and the total mileage

Choose the scatter plot that best represents the described relationship. Explain.

19. the number of college classes taken and the number of roommates

20. the number of college classes taken and the hours of free time.

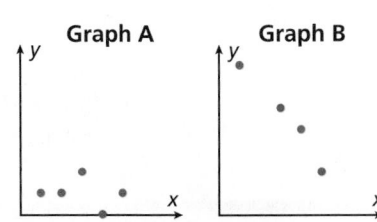

Graph A Graph B

21. Ecology The scatter plot shows a projection of the average ocelot population living in Laguna Atascosa National Wildlife Refuge near Brownsville, Texas. Based on this relationship, predict the number of ocelots living at the wildlife refuge in 2014 if nothing is done to help manage the ocelot population.

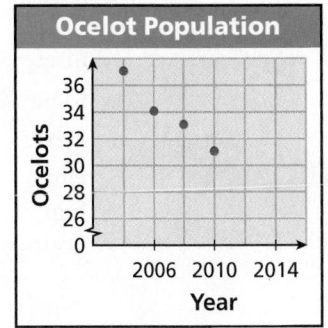

Ocelot Population

Ecology

The ocelot population in Texas is dwindling due in part to their habitat being destroyed. The ocelot population at Laguna Atascosa National Wildlife Refuge is monitored by following 5–10 ocelots yearly by radio telemetry.

22. Estimation Angie enjoys putting jigsaw puzzles together. The scatter plot shows the number of puzzle pieces and the time in minutes it took her to complete each of her last six puzzles. Use the trend line to estimate the time in minutes it will take Angie to complete a 1200-piece puzzle.

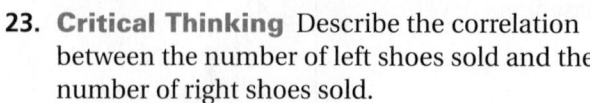

Puzzle Completion

23. Critical Thinking Describe the correlation between the number of left shoes sold and the number of right shoes sold.

24. Roma had guests for dinner at her house eight times and has recorded the number of guests and the total cost for each meal in the table.

Guests	3	4	4	6	6	7	8	8
Cost ($)	30	65	88	90	115	160	150	162

 a. Graph a scatter plot of the data.

 b. Describe the correlation.

 c. Draw a trend line.

 d. Based on the trend line you drew, predict the cost of dinner for 11 guests.

 e. **What if...?** Suppose that each cost in the table increased by $5. How will this affect the cost of dinner for 11 guests?

25. ///**ERROR ANALYSIS**/// Students graphed a scatter plot for the temperature of hot bath water and time if no new water is added. Which graph is incorrect? Explain the error.

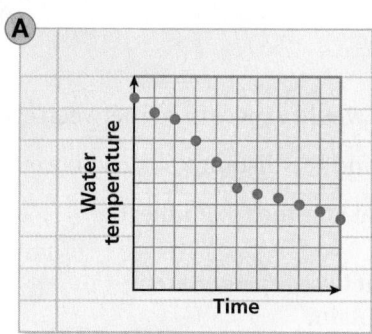

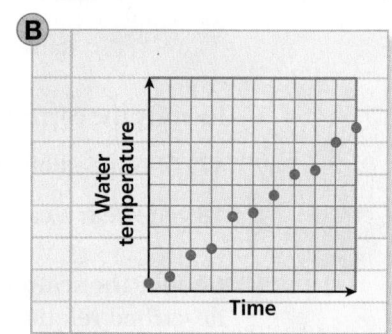

26. Critical Thinking Will more people or fewer people buy an item if the price goes up? Explain the relationship and describe the correlation.

MULTI-STEP TEST PREP

27. Juan and his parents are visiting a university 205 miles from their home. As they travel, Juan uses the car odometer and his watch to keep track of the distance.

 a. Make a scatter plot for this data set.

 b. Describe the correlation. Explain.

 c. Draw a trend line for the data and predict the distance Juan would have traveled going to a university 4 hours away.

Time (min)	Distance (mi)
0	0
30	28
60	58
90	87
120	117
150	148
180	178
210	205

28. **Write About It** Conduct a survey of your classmates to find the number of siblings they have and the number of pets they have. Predict whether there will be a positive, negative, or no correlation. Then graph the data in a scatter plot. What is the relationship between the two data sets? Was your prediction correct?

29. Which graph is the best example of a negative correlation?

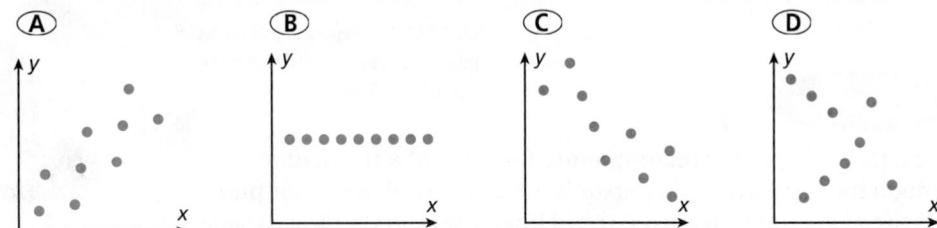

Ⓐ   Ⓑ   Ⓒ   Ⓓ

30. Which situation best describes a positive correlation?
   Ⓕ The amount of rainfall on Fridays
   Ⓖ The height of a candle and the amount of time it stays lit
   Ⓗ The price of a pizza and the number of toppings added
   Ⓙ The temperature of a cup of hot chocolate and the length of time it sits

31. **Short Response** Write a real-world situation for the graph. Explain your answer.

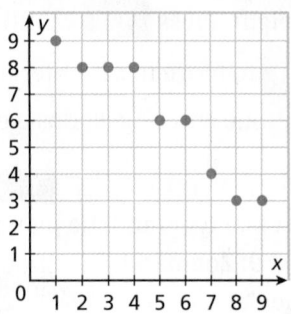

CHALLENGE AND EXTEND

32. Describe a situation that involves a positive correlation. Gather data on the situation. Make a scatter plot showing the correlation. Use the scatter plot to make a prediction. Repeat for a negative correlation and for no correlation.

33. Research an endangered or threatened species in your state. Gather information on its population for several years. Make a scatter plot using the data you gather. Is there a positive or negative correlation? Explain. Draw a trend line and make a prediction about the species population over the next 5 years.

Interpret Scatter Plots and Trend Lines

You can use a graphing calculator to graph a trend line on a scatter plot.

Use with Scatter Plots and Trend Lines

CC.9-12.S.ID.6 Represent data on two quantitative variables on a scatter plot, ...
Also CC.9-12.S.ID.6a, CC.9-12.S.ID.6c

Learn It Online
Lab Resources Online

Activity

Use appropriate tools strategically.

The table shows the recommended dosage of a particular medicine as related to a person's weight. Graph a scatter plot of the given data. Draw the trend line. Then predict the dosage for a person weighing 240 pounds.

Weight (lb)	90	100	110	125	140	155	170	180	200
Dosage (mg)	20	25	30	35	40	53	60	66	75

1 First enter the data. Press **STAT** and select **1: Edit**. In **L1**, enter the first weight. Press **ENTER**. Continue entering all weights. Use ▶ to move to **L2**. Enter the first dosage. Press **ENTER**. Continue entering all dosages.

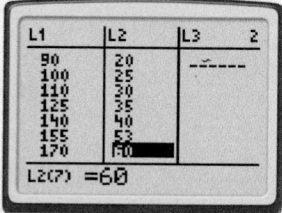

2 To view the scatter plot, press **2nd** **Y=**. Select **Plot 1**. Select **On**, the first plot type, and the plot mark +. Press **ZOOM**. Select **9: ZoomStat**. You should see a scatter plot of the data.

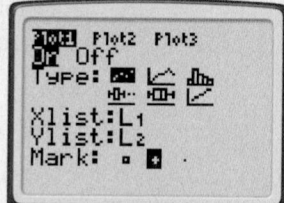

3 To find the trend line, press **STAT** and select the **CALC** menu. Select **LinReg (ax+b)**. Press **ENTER**. This gives you the values of *a* and *b* in the trend line.

4 To enter the equation for the trend line, press **Y=**, and then input **.5079441502x − 26.78767453**. Press **GRAPH**.

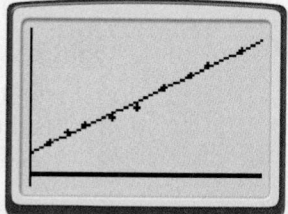

5 Now predict the dosage for a weight of 240 pounds. Press **VARS**. Select **Y-VARS** menu and select **1:Function**. Select **1:Y1**. Enter **(240)**. Press **ENTER**. The dosage is about 95 milligrams.

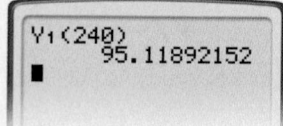

Try This

1. The table shows the price of a stock over an 8-month period. Graph a scatter plot of the given data. Draw the trend line. Then predict what the price of one share of stock will be in the twelfth month.

Month	1	2	3	4	5	6	7	8
Price ($)	32	35	37	41	46	50	54	59

Median-Fit Line

You have learned about trend lines. Now you will learn about another line of fit called the *median-fit line*.

Example

At a water raft rental shop, a group of up to four people can rent a single raft. The table shows the number of rafts rented to different groups of people one morning. Graph the median-fit line for the data.

People x	1	2	4	5	5	5	7	9	10	11	12	15
Rafts Rented y	1	1	1	3	4	5	4	7	5	3	4	6

1 Plot the points on a coordinate plane.

2 Divide the data into three sections of equal size. Find the medians of the x-values and the y-values for each section. Plot the three median points with an X.

1	2	4	5	5	5	7	9	10	11	12	15
1	1	1	3	4	5	4	7	5	3	4	6

Median point: (3, 1)   Median point: (6, 4.5)   Median point: (11.5, 4.5)

3 Connect the outside, or first and third, median points with a line.

4 Lightly draw a dashed line straight down from the middle median point to the line just drawn. Mark the dashed line to create three equal segments.

5 Keeping your ruler parallel to the first line you drew, move your ruler to the mark closest to the line. Draw the line. This is the median-fit line.

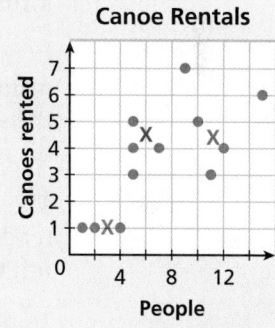

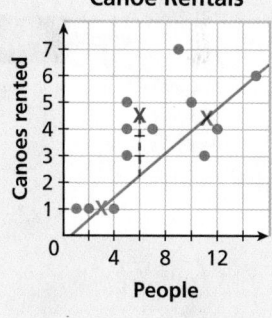

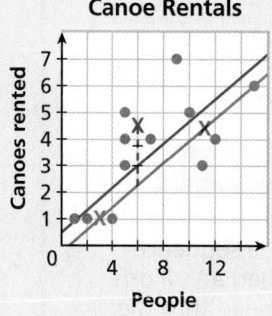

Try This

1. A manager at a restaurant kept track one afternoon of the number of people in a party and the time it took to seat them. Graph the median-fit line for the data.

2. Use your median-fit line to predict the time it would take to seat a party of 6.

People x	3	7	8	8	10	12
Wait Time y (min)	1	5	3	9	6	6

Arithmetic Sequences

CC.9-12.F.IF.3 Recognize that sequences are functions, sometimes defined recursively, whose domain is a subset of the integers. *Also* **CC.9-12.F.BF.2*, CC.9-12.F.LE.2***

Objectives
Recognize and extend an arithmetic sequence.

Find a given term of an arithmetic sequence.

Vocabulary
sequence
term
arithmetic sequence
common difference

Why learn this?
The distance between you and a lightning strike can be approximated by using an arithmetic sequence.

During a thunderstorm, you can estimate your distance from a lightning strike by counting the number of seconds from the time you see the lightning until the time you hear the thunder.

Time (s)	Distance (mi)	
1	0.2	+ 0.2
2	0.4	+ 0.2
3	0.6	+ 0.2
4	0.8	+ 0.2
5	1.0	+ 0.2
6	1.2	+ 0.2
7	1.4	+ 0.2
8	1.6	+ 0.2

When you list the times and distances in order, each list forms a *sequence*. A **sequence** is a list of numbers that may form a pattern. Each number in a sequence is a **term**.

In the distance sequence, each distance is 0.2 mi greater than the previous distance. When the terms of a sequence differ by the same nonzero number d, the sequence is an **arithmetic sequence** and d is the **common difference**. The distances in the table form an arithmetic sequence with $d = 0.2$.

The variable a is often used to represent terms in a sequence. The variable a_9, read "a sub 9," is the ninth term in a sequence. To designate any term, or the nth term, in a sequence, you write a_n, where n can be any number.

To find a term in an arithmetic sequence, add d to the previous term.

 **Know it! Note**

> ### Finding a Term of an Arithmetic Sequence
>
> The nth term of an arithmetic sequence with **common difference** d is
> $$a_n = a_{n-1} + d.$$

EXAMPLE **1** | **Identifying Arithmetic Sequences**

Determine whether each sequence appears to be an arithmetic sequence. If so, find the common difference and the next three terms in the sequence.

A 12, 8, 4, 0, …

Step 1 Find the difference between successive terms.

12, 8, 4, 0, …   *Add −4 to each term to find the next term.*
−4 −4 −4   *The common difference is −4.*

Step 2 Use the common difference to find the next 3 terms.

12, 8, 4, 0, −4, −8, −12
       −4 −4 −4 $a_n = a_{n-1} + d$

The sequence appears to be an arithmetic sequence with a common difference of −4. The next 3 terms are −4, −8, −12.

 Reading Math

The three dots at the end of a sequence are called an ellipsis. They mean that the sequence continues and can be read as "and so on."

B 1, 4, 9, 16, ...

Find the difference between successive terms.

1, 4, 9, 16, ...   *The difference between successive terms is*
+3 +5 +7   *not the same.*

This sequence is not an arithmetic sequence.

CHECK IT OUT! **Determine whether each sequence appears to be an arithmetic sequence. If so, find the common difference and the next three terms.**

1a. $-\dfrac{3}{4}, -\dfrac{1}{4}, \dfrac{1}{4}, \dfrac{3}{4}, \ldots$ **1b.** $-4, -2, 1, 5, \ldots$

To find the nth term of an arithmetic sequence when n is a large number, you need an equation or rule. Look for a pattern to find a rule for the sequence below.

1	2	3	4...	n	← Position
↓	↓	↓	↓		
3,	5,	7,	9...		← Term
a_1	a_2	a_3	a_4	a_n	

The sequence starts with 3. The common difference d is 2. You can use the first term and the common difference to write a rule for finding a_n.

Words	Numbers	Algebra
1st term	3	a_1
2nd term = 1st term plus common difference	$3 + (1)2 = 5$	$a_1 + 1d$
3nd term = 1st term plus 2 common differences	$3 + (2)2 = 7$	$a_1 + 2d$
4th term = 1st term plus 3 common differences	$3 + (3)2 = 9$	$a_1 + 3d$
$\vdots$	$\vdots$	$\vdots$
nth term = 1st term plus $(n-1)$ common differences	$3 + (n-1)2$	$a_1 + (n-1)d$

The pattern in the table shows that to find the nth term, add the **first term** to the product of $(n-1)$ and the **common difference**.

Know it!
Note

Finding the nth Term of an Arithmetic Sequence

The nth term of an arithmetic sequence with **common difference** d and **first term** a_1 is

$$a_n = a_1 + (n - 1)d.$$

EXAMPLE 2   **Finding the nth Term of an Arithmetic Sequence**

Find the indicated term of each arithmetic sequence.

A 22nd term: 5, 2, −1, −4, ...

Step 1 Find the common difference.

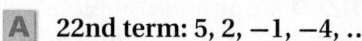

5, 2, −1, −4, ...   *The common difference is −3.*
−3 −3 −3

Step 2 Find the 22nd term.

$$a_n = a_1 + (n - 1)d \qquad \text{\textit{Write the rule to find the nth term.}}$$
$$a_{22} = 5 + (22 - 1)(-3) \qquad \text{\textit{Substitute 5 for a\textsubscript{1}, 22 for n, and −3 for d.}}$$
$$= 5 + (21)(-3) \qquad \text{\textit{Simplify the expression in parentheses.}}$$
$$= 5 - 63 \qquad \text{\textit{Multiply.}}$$
$$= -58 \qquad \text{\textit{Subtract.}}$$

B 15th term: $a_1 = 7$; $d = 3$

$$a_n = a_1 + (n - 1)d \qquad \text{\textit{Write the rule to find the nth term.}}$$
$$a_{15} = 7 + (15 - 1)3 \qquad \text{\textit{Substitute 7 for a\textsubscript{1}, 15 for n, and 3 for d.}}$$
$$= 7 + (14)3 \qquad \text{\textit{Simplify the expression in parentheses.}}$$
$$= 7 + 42 \qquad \text{\textit{Multiply.}}$$
$$= 49 \qquad \text{\textit{Add.}}$$

 **Find the indicated term of each arithmetic sequence.**
2a. 60th term: $11, 5, -1, -7, \dots$ **2b.** 12th term: $a_1 = 4.2$; $d = 1.4$

EXAMPLE 3 *Travel Application*

The odometer on a car reads 60,473 on day 1. Every day, the car is driven 54 miles. If this pattern continues, what is the odometer reading on day 20?

Notice that the sequence for the situation is arithmetic with $d = 54$ because the odometer reading will increase by 54 miles per day.

Since the odometer reading on day 1 is 60,473 miles, $a_1 = 60,473$.

Since you want to find the odometer reading on day 20, you will need to find the **20th term** of the sequence, so $n = 20$.

$$a_n = a_1 + (n - 1)d \qquad \text{\textit{Write the rule to find the nth term.}}$$
$$a_{20} = 60,473 + (20 - 1)54 \qquad \text{\textit{Substitute 60,473 for a\textsubscript{1}, 54 for d, and 21 for n.}}$$
$$= 60,473 + (19)54 \qquad \text{\textit{Simplify the expression in parentheses.}}$$
$$= 60,473 + 1026 \qquad \text{\textit{Multiply.}}$$
$$= 61,499 \qquad \text{\textit{Add.}}$$

The odometer will read 61,499 miles on day 20.

 **3.** Each time a truck stops, it drops off 250 pounds of cargo. After stop 1, its cargo weighed 2000 pounds. How much does the load weigh after stop 6?

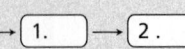
MATHEMATICAL PRACTICES

THINK AND DISCUSS

1. Explain how to determine if a sequence appears to be arithmetic.

2. GET ORGANIZED Copy and complete the graphic organizer with steps for finding the *n*th term of an arithmetic sequence.

> Finding the *n*th Term of an Arithmetic Sequence → 1. → 2.

GUIDED PRACTICE

1. **Vocabulary** When trying to find the *n*th term of an arithmetic sequence you must first know the _____?_____. (*common difference* or *sequence*)

SEE EXAMPLE **1** **Multi-Step** Determine whether each sequence appears to be an arithmetic sequence. If so, find the common difference and the next three terms.

2. 2, 8, 14, 20, ...

3. 2.1, 1.4, 0.7, 0, ...

4. 1, 1, 2, 3, ...

5. 0.1, 0.3, 0.9, 2.7, ...

SEE EXAMPLE **2** Find the indicated term of each arithmetic sequence.

6. 21st term: 3, 8, 13, 18, ...

7. 18th term: $a_1 = -2$; $d = -3$

SEE EXAMPLE **3** 8. **Shipping** To package and ship an item, it costs $5.75 for the first pound and $0.75 for each additional pound. What is the cost of shipping a 12-pound package?

PRACTICE AND PROBLEM SOLVING

Independent Practice	
For Exercises	See Example
9–12	1
13–14	2
15	3

Extra Practice
See Extra Practice for more Skills Practice and Applications Practice exercises.

Multi-Step Determine whether each sequence appears to be an arithmetic sequence. If so, find the common difference and the next three terms.

9. −1, 10, −100, 1,100, ...

10. 0, −2, −4, −6, ...

11. −22, −31, −40, −49, ...

12. 0.2, 0.5, 0.9, 1.1, ...

Find the indicated term of each arithmetic sequence.

13. 31st term: 1.40, 1.55, 1.70, ...

14. 50th term: $a_1 = 2.2$; $d = 1.1$

15. **Travel** Rachel signed up for a frequent-flier program. She receives 4300 frequent-flier miles for her first round trip and 1300 frequent-flier miles for each additional round-trip. How many frequent-flier miles will she have after 5 round-trips?

Find the common difference for each arithmetic sequence.

16. 0, 6, 12, 18, ...

17. $\frac{1}{2}, \frac{3}{4}, 1, \frac{5}{4}, \ldots$

18. 107, 105, 103, 101, ...

19. 7.9, 5.7, 3.5, 1.3, ...

20. $\frac{1}{5}, \frac{2}{5}, \frac{3}{5}, \frac{4}{5}, \ldots$

21. 4.25, 4.32, 4.39, 4.46, ...

Find the next four terms in each arithmetic sequence.

22. −4, −7, −10, −13, ...

23. $\frac{1}{8}, 0, -\frac{1}{8}, -\frac{1}{4}, \ldots$

24. 505, 512, 519, 526, ...

25. 1.8, 1.3, 0.8, 0.3, ...

26. $\frac{2}{3}, \frac{4}{3}, 2, \frac{8}{3}, \ldots$

27. −1.1, −0.9, −0.7, −0.5

Find the given term of each arithmetic sequence.

28. 5, 10, 15, 20, ...; 17th term

29. 121, 110, 99, 88, ...; 10th term

30. −2, −5, −8, −11, ...; 41st term

31. −30, −22, −14, −6, ...; 20th term

32. **Critical Thinking** Is the sequence $5a - 1, 3a - 1, a - 1, -a - 1, \ldots$ arithmetic? If not, explain why not. If so, find the common difference and the next three terms.

33. Recreation The rates for a go-cart course are shown.

    a. Explain why the relationship described on the flyer could be represented by an arithmetic sequence.

    b. Find the cost for 1, 2, 3, and 4 laps. Write a rule to find the nth term of the sequence.

    c. How much would 15 laps cost?

    d. What if...? After 9 laps, you get the 10th one free. Will the sequence still be arithmetic? Explain.

JESSIKA'S SPEEDWAY
License: **$7**
Per Lap: **$2**

Find the given term of each arithmetic sequence.

34. 2.5, 8.5, 14.5, 20.5, …; 30th term

35. 189.6, 172.3, 155, 137.7, …; 18th term

36. $\frac{1}{4}, \frac{3}{4}, \frac{5}{4}, \frac{7}{4}, …$; 15th term

37. $\frac{2}{3}, \frac{11}{12}, \frac{7}{6}, \frac{17}{12}, …$; 25th term

Number Theory

Fibonacci numbers occur frequently throughout nature. The number of petals on many flowers are numbers of the Fibonacci sequence. Two petals on a flower are rare but 3, 5, and even 34 petals are common.

38. Number Theory The sequence 1, 1, 2, 3, 5, 8, 13, … is a famous sequence called the Fibonacci sequence. After the first two terms, each term is the sum of the previous two terms.

    a. Write the first 10 terms of the Fibonacci sequence. Is the Fibonacci sequence arithmetic? Explain.

    b. Notice that the third term is divisible by 2. Are the 6th and 9th terms also divisible by 2? What conclusion can you draw about every third term? Why is this true?

    c. Can you find any other patterns? (*Hint:* Look at every 4th and 5th term.)

39. Entertainment Seats in a concert hall are arranged in the pattern shown.

    a. The numbers of seats in the rows form an arithmetic sequence. Write a rule for the arithmetic sequence.

    b. How many seats are in the 15th row?

    c. A ticket costs $40. Suppose every seat in the first 10 rows is filled. What is the total revenue from those seats?

    d. What if...? An extra chair is added to each row. Write the new rule for the arithmetic sequence and find the new total revenue from the first 10 rows.

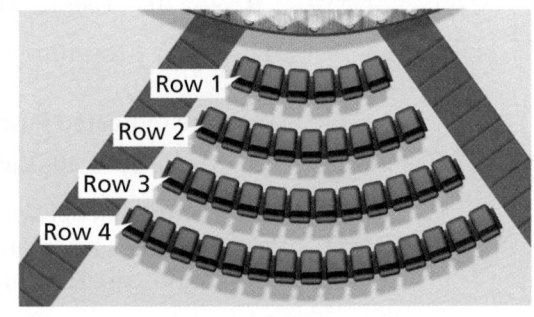

Row 1
Row 2
Row 3
Row 4

40. Write About It Explain how to find the common difference of an arithmetic sequence. How can you determine whether the arithmetic sequence has a positive common difference or a negative common difference?

MULTI-STEP TEST PREP

41. Juan is traveling to visit universities. He notices mile markers along the road. He records the mile marker every 10 minutes. His father is driving at a constant speed.

    a. Copy and complete the table.

    b. Write the rule for the sequence.

    c. What does the common difference represent?

    d. If this sequence continues, find the mile marker for time interval 10.

Time Interval	Mile Marker
1	520
2	509
3	498
4	■
5	■
6	■

42. What are the next three terms in the arithmetic sequence −21, −12, −3, 6, … ?

Ⓐ 9, 12, 15 Ⓑ 15, 24, 33 Ⓒ 12, 21, 27 Ⓓ 13, 20, 27

43. What is the common difference for the data listed in the second column?

Ⓕ −1.8 Ⓗ 2.8

Ⓖ 1.8 Ⓙ −3.6

Altitude (ft)	Boiling Point of Water (°F)
1000	210.2
2000	208.4
3000	206.6

44. Which of the following sequences is NOT arithmetic?

Ⓐ −4, 2, 8, 14, … Ⓑ 9, 4, −1, −6, … Ⓒ 2, 4, 8, 16, … Ⓓ $\frac{1}{3}$, $1\frac{1}{3}$, $2\frac{1}{3}$, $3\frac{1}{3}$, …

CHALLENGE AND EXTEND

45. The first term of an arithmetic sequence is 2, and the common difference is 9. Find two consecutive terms of the sequence that have a sum of 355. What positions in the sequence are the terms?

46. The 60th term of an arithmetic sequence is 106.5, and the common difference is 1.5. What is the first term of the sequence?

47. Athletics Verona is training for a marathon. The first part of her training schedule is shown below.

Session	1	2	3	4	5	6
Distance Run (mi)	3.5	5	6.5	8	9.5	11

a. If Verona continues this pattern, during which training session will she run 26 miles? Is her training schedule an arithmetic sequence? Explain.

b. If Verona's training schedule starts on a Monday and she runs every third day, on which day will she run 26 miles?

MULTI-STEP TEST PREP

Make sense of problems and persevere in solving them.

Applying Functions

College Knowledge Myra is helping her brother plan a college visit 10 hours away from their home. She creates a table listing approximate travel times and distances from their home.

1. Create a scatter plot for the data.

2. Draw a trend line through the data.

3. Based on the trend line, how many miles will they have traveled after 5 hours?

4. If Myra's brother decided to visit a college 13 hours away from their home, approximately how many miles will they travel?

5. To find the average speed for the entire trip, find $\frac{\text{change in distance}}{\text{change in time}}$ between the initial ordered pair and the final ordered pair. Include the units.

Time (h)	Distance (mi)
0	0
2	123
3	190
4	207
6	355
8	472
10	657

Quiz for Lessons 3-5 Through 3-6

✓ 3-5 Scatter Plots and Trend Lines

The table shows the time it takes different people to read a given number of pages.

Pages Read	2	6	6	8	8	10	10
Time (min)	10	15	20	15	30	25	30

1. Graph a scatter plot using the given data.

2. Describe the correlation illustrated by the scatter plot.

Choose the scatter plot that best represents the described relationship. Explain.

3. number of movie tickets sold and number of available seats

4. number of movie tickets sold and amount of concession sales

5. number of movie tickets sold and length of movie

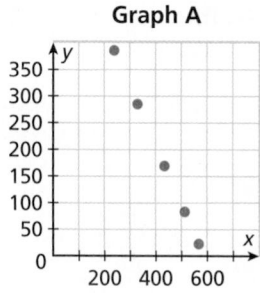

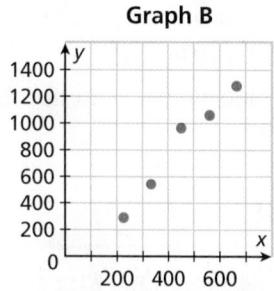

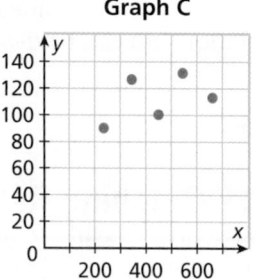

6. The scatter plot shows the estimated annual sales for an electronics and appliance chain of stores for the years 2004–2009. Based on this relationship, predict the annual sales in 2012.

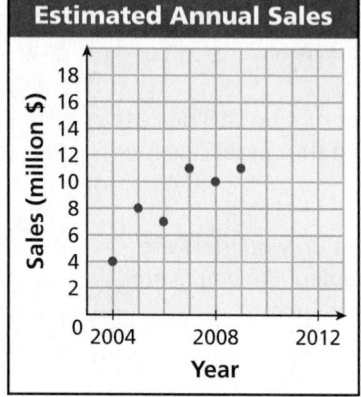

✓ 3-6 Arithmetic Sequences

Determine whether each sequence appears to be an arithmetic sequence. If so, find the common difference and the next three terms.

7. $7, 3, -1, -5, \ldots$ 8. $3, 6, 12, 24, \ldots$ 9. $-3.5, -2, -0.5, 1, \ldots$

Find the indicated term of the arithmetic sequence.

10. 31st term: $12, 7, 2, -3, \ldots$ 11. 22nd term: $a_1 = 6$; $d = 4$

12. With no air resistance, an object would fall 16 feet during the first second, 48 feet during the second second, 80 feet during the third second, 112 feet during the fourth second, and so on. How many feet will the object fall during the ninth second?

Study Guide: Review

Vocabulary

arithmetic sequence	function	range
common difference	function notation	relation
continuous graph	function rule	scatter plot
correlation	independent variable	sequence
dependent variable	negative correlation	term
discrete graph	no correlation	trend line
domain	positive correlation	

Complete the sentences below with vocabulary words from the list above.

1. The set of *x*-coordinates of the ordered pairs of a relation is called the ____?____ .

2. If one set of data values increases as another set of data values decreases, the relationship can be described as having a(n) ____?____ .

3. A sequence is an ordered list of numbers where each number is a(n) ____?____ .

3-1 Graphing Relationships

EXAMPLES

Sketch a graph for each situation. Tell whether the graph is continuous or discrete.

■ A parking meter has a limit of 1 hour. The cost is $0.25 per 15 minutes and the meter accepts quarters only.

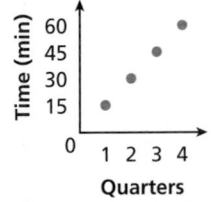

Since only quarters are accepted, the points are not connected.

The graph is discrete.

■ Ian bought a cup of coffee. At first, he sipped slowly. As it cooled, he drank more quickly. The last bit was cold, and he dumped it out.

As time passes the coffee was **sipped slowly,** **drank more quickly,** and then **dumped out.**

The graph is continuous.

EXERCISES

Sketch a graph for each situation. Tell whether the graph is continuous or discrete.

4. A girl was walking home at a steady pace. Then she stopped to talk to a friend. After her friend left, she jogged the rest of the way home.

5. A ball is dropped from a second story window and bounces to a stop on the patio below.

6. Jason was on the second floor when he got a call to attend a meeting on the sixth floor. He took the stairs. After the meeting, he took the elevator to the first floor.

Write a possible situation for each graph.

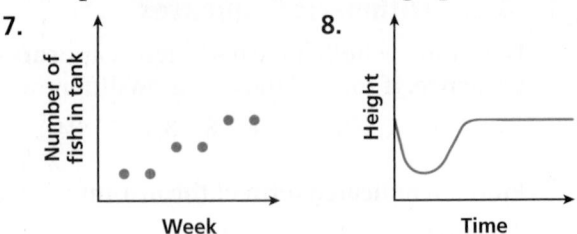

7.

8.

3-2 Relations and Functions

■ Express the relation $\{(2, 15), (4, 12), (5, 7), (7, 2)\}$ as a table, as a graph, and as a mapping diagram.

Table

x	y
2	15
4	12
5	7
7	2

Graph

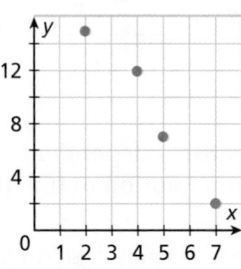

Mapping Diagram

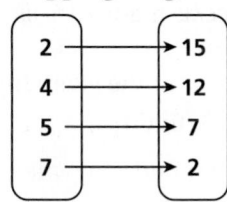

Give the domain and range of each relation. Tell whether the relation is a function. Explain.

■

x	y
−3	0
−2	0
−1	1

D: $\{-3, -2, -1\}$

R: $\{0, 1\}$

The relation is a function because each domain value is paired with exactly one range value.

■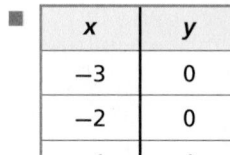

D: $\{1, 2\}$

R: $\{-5, -4, 4\}$

The relation is not a function because one domain value is paired with two range values.

■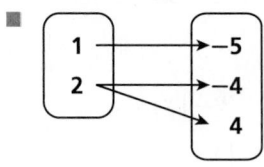

D: $-4 \leq x \leq 4$

R: $-2 \leq y \leq 6$

The relation is a function because every x-value is paired with exactly one y-value.

Express each relation as a table, as a graph, and as a mapping diagram.

9. $\{(-1, 0), (0, 1), (2, 1)\}$

10. $\{(-2, -1), (-1, 1), (2, 3), (3, 4)\}$

Give the domain and range of each relation.

11. $\{(-4, 5), (-2, 3), (0, 1), (2, -1)\}$

12. $\{(-2, -1) (-1, 0), (0, -1), (1, 0), (2, -1)\}$

13.

x	0	1	4	1	4
y	0	−1	−2	1	2

14.

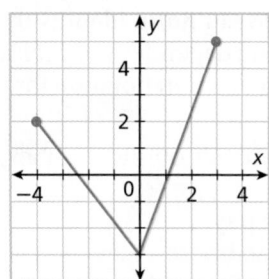

Give the domain and range of each relation. Tell whether the relation is a function. Explain.

15. $\{(-5, -3), (-3, -2), (-1, -1), (1, 0)\}$

16.

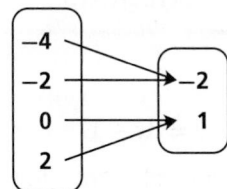

17.

x	1	2	3	4	1
y	3	2	1	0	−1

18. A local parking garage charges $5.00 for the first hour plus $1.50 for each additional hour or part of an hour. Write a relation as a set of ordered pairs in which the x-value represents the number of hours and the y-value represents the cost for x hours. Use a domain of 1, 2, 3, 4, 5. Is this relation a function? Explain.

19. A baseball coach is taking the team for ice cream. Four students can ride in each car. Create a mapping diagram to show the number of cars needed to transport 8, 10, 14, and 16 students. Is this relation a function? Explain.

3-3 Writing Functions

EXAMPLES

■ **Determine a relationship between the *x*- and *y*-values in the table. Write an equation.**

x	1	2	3	4
y	−3	−6	−9	−12

What are possible relationships between the x-values and the y-values?

$1 - 4 = -3$ $1(-3) = -3$

$2 - 4 \neq -6$ ✗ $2(-3) = -6$ ✓

     $3(-3) = -9$ ✓

     $4(-3) = -12$ ✓

$y = -3x$ *Write an equation.*

■ **Nia earns $5.25 per hour. Identify the independent and dependent variables. Write an equation in function notation for the situation.**

Nia's **pay** depends on the **number of hours** she works.
Dependent: **pay**
Independent: **hours**
Let *h* represent the number of hours Nia works.
The function for Nia's pay is $f(h) = 5.25h$.

EXERCISES

Determine the relationship between the *x*- and *y*-values. Write an equation.

20.

x	1	2	3	4
y	−6	−5	−4	−3

21. $\{(1, 9), (2, 18), (3, 27), (4, 36)\}$

Identify the independent and dependent variables. Write an equation in function notation for the situation.

22. A baker spends $6 on ingredients for each cake he bakes.

23. Tim will buy twice as many CDs as Raul.

Evaluate each function for the given input values.

24. For $f(x) = -2x + 4$, find $f(x)$ when $x = -5$.

25. For $g(n) = -n^2 - 2$, find $g(n)$ when $n = -3$.

26. For $h(t) = 7 - |t + 3|$, find $h(t)$ when $t = -4$ and when $t = 5$.

3-4 Graphing Functions

EXAMPLE

■ **Graph the function $y = 3x - 1$.**

Step 1 Choose several values of *x* to generate ordered pairs.

x	y = 3x − 1	y
−1	$y = 3(-1) - 1 = -4$	−4
0	$y = 3(0) - 1 = -1$	−1
1	$y = 3(1) - 1 = 2$	2
2	$y = 3(2) - 1 = 5$	5

Step 2 Plot enough points to see a pattern.

Step 3 Draw a line through the points to show all the ordered pairs that satisfy this function.

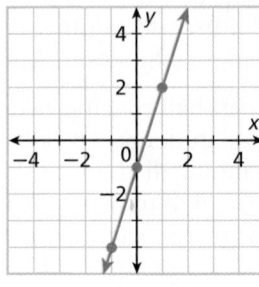

EXERCISES

Graph each function for the domain $\{-2, -1, 1, 2\}$.

27. $4x + y = 2$ **28.** $y = (1 - x)^2$

Graph each function.

29. $3x - y = 1$ **30.** $y = 2 - |x|$

31. $y = x^2 - 6$ **32.** $y = |x + 5| + 1$

33. The function $y = 6.25x$ describes the amount of money *y* Peter gets paid after *x* hours. Graph the function. Use the graph to estimate how much money Peter gets paid after 7 hours.

3-5 Scatter Plots and Trend Lines

EXAMPLE

■ **The graph shows the amount of money in a savings account. Based on this relationship, predict how much money will be in the account in month 7.**

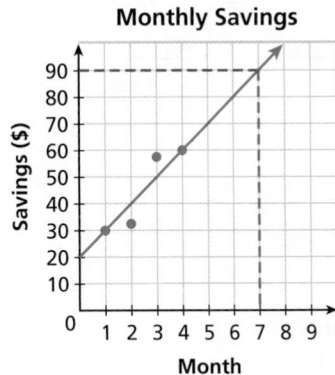

Monthly Savings

Draw a line that has about the same number of points above and below it. Your line may or may not go through data points.

Find the point on the line whose x-value is 7.

Based on the data, $90 is a reasonable prediction.

EXERCISES

34. The table shows the value of a car for the given years. Graph a scatter plot using the given data. Describe the correlation illustrated by the scatter plot.

Year	2000	2001	2002	2003
Value (thousand $)	28	25	23	20

35. The graph shows the results of a 2003–2004 survey on class size at the given grade levels. Based on this relationship, predict the class size for the 9th grade.

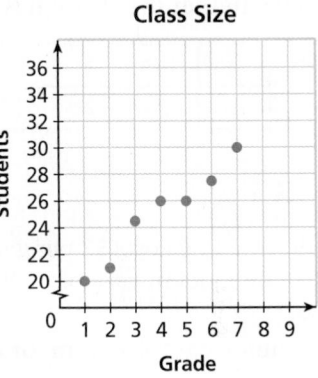

Class Size

3-6 Arithmetic Sequences

EXAMPLES

■ **Determine whether the sequence appears to be arithmetic. If so, find the common difference and the next three terms.**

−8, −5 ,−2 , 1,...

Step 1 Find the difference between successive terms.

−8, −5, −2, 1,...   *The common difference is 3.*
  +3 +3 +3

Step 2 Use the common difference to find the next 3 terms.

−8, −5, −2, 1, 4, 7, 10
           +3 +3 +3

■ **Find the 18th term of the arithmetic sequence for which $a_1 = -4$ and $d = 6$.**

$a_n = a_1 + (n-1)d$ *Write the rule.*
$a_{18} = -4 + (18-1)6$ *Substitute.*
$= -4 + (17)6$ *Simplify.*
$= -4 + 102$ *Simplify.*
$= 98$

The 18th term is 98.

EXERCISES

Determine whether each sequence appears to be arithmetic. If so, find the common difference and the next three terms.

36. 20, 14, 8, 2,...

37. −15, −12, −9, −4,...

38. 5, 4, 2, −1,...

39. −8, −5.5, −3, −0.5,...

Find the indicated term of each arithmetic sequence.

40. 31st term: −15, −11, −7, −3,...

41. 24th term: $a_1 = 7$; $d = -3$

42. 17th term: $a_1 = -20$; $d = 2.5$

43. Marie has $180 in a savings account in week 1. She plans to deposit $12 each following week. Assuming that she does not withdraw any money from her account, what will her balance be in week 20?

44. The table shows the temperature at the given heights above sea level. Use an arithmetic sequence to find the temperature at 8000 feet above sea level.

Height Above Sea Level (thousand feet)	1	2	3	4
Temperature (°C)	30	23.5	17	10.5

CHAPTER TEST

Choose the graph that best represents each situation.

1. A person walks leisurely, stops, and then continues walking.

2. A person jogs, then runs, and then jogs again.

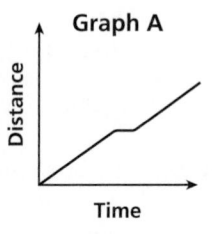

Graph A

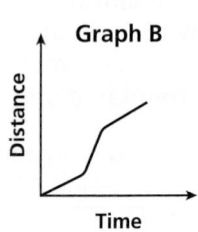

Graph B

Give the domain and range for each relation.
Tell whether the relation is a function. Explain.

3.

x	−2	1	0	1	3
y	3	2	1	0	−1

4.

5. Bowling costs $3 per game plus $2.50 for shoe rental. Identify the independent and dependent variables. Write an equation in function notation for the situation.

Evaluate each function for the given input values.

6. For $f(x) = -3x + 4$, find $f(x)$ when $x = -2$.   **7.** For $f(x) = 2x^2$, find $f(x)$ when $x = -3$.

8. An engraver charges a $10 fee plus $6 for each line of engraving. Write a function to describe the situation. Find a reasonable domain and range for the function for up to 8 lines.

Graph each function for the given domain.

9. $3x + y = 4$; D: $\{-2, -1, 0, 1, 2\}$ **10.** $y = |x - 1|$; D: $\{-3, 0, 1, 3, 5\}$ **11.** $y = x^2 - 1$; D: $\{-2, -1, 0, 1, 2\}$

Graph each function.

12. $y = x - 5$ **13.** $y = x^2 - 5$ **14.** $y = |x| + 3$

15. The function $y = 30x$ describes the amount of interest y earned in a savings account in x years. Graph the function. Use the graph to estimate the total amount of interest earned in 7 years.

The table shows possible recommendations for the amount of sleep that children should get every day.

16. Graph a scatter plot of the given data.

17. Describe the correlation illustrated by the scatter plot.

Age (yr)	1	2	3	4	5	14
Sleep Needed (h)	14	13	12	12	11	9

18. Predict how many hours of sleep a 16-year-old needs.

Determine whether each sequence appears to be an arithmetic sequence. If so, find the common difference and the next three terms.

19. 11, 6, 1, −4,…   **20.** −4, −3, −1, 2,…   **21.** 7, 21, 30, 45,…

Find the indicated term of the arithmetic sequence.

22. 32nd term: 18, 11, 4, −3,…   **23.** 24th term: $a_1 = 4$; $d = 6$

24. Mandy's new job has a starting salary of $16,000 and annual increases of $800. How much will she earn during her fifth year?

COLLEGE ENTRANCE EXAM PRACTICE

CHAPTER

3

FOCUS ON ACT

Questions on the ACT Mathematics Test do not require the use of a calculator, but you may bring one to use with the test. Make sure that it is a calculator that is on the approved list for the ACT.

You may want to time yourself as you take this practice test. It should take you about 6 minutes to complete.

When taking the test, you will be more comfortable using a calculator that you are used to. If you already have a calculator, make sure it is one of the permitted calculators. If you plan to use a new one, make sure to practice using it before the test.

---

1. The soccer team is ordering new uniforms. There is a one-time setup charge of $50.00, and each uniform costs $23.50. Which of the following best describes the total cost C for ordering uniforms for p players?

(A) $C = 23.50p$

(B) $C = 50p$

(C) $C = 73.50p$

(D) $C = 23.50p + 50$

(E) $C = 50p + 23.50$

---

2. In the given relation, what domain value corresponds to the range value -2?
$\{(-1, 2), (-2, 4), (2, 5), (0, -2), (2, 0)\}$

(F) -2

(G) 0

(H) 2

(J) 4

(K) 5

---

3. Evaluate $h(x) = \frac{1}{2}(5 - 6x) + 9x$ when $x = \frac{2}{3}$.

(A) $\frac{9}{2}$

(B) $\frac{13}{2}$

(C) 7

(D) $\frac{19}{2}$

(E) $\frac{23}{2}$

---

4. What is the seventh term of the arithmetic sequence $-4, -1, 2 \dots$?

(F) 5

(G) 10

(H) 11

(J) 14

(K) 17

---

5. The graph of which function is shown below?

(A) $y = -3x - 5$

(B) $y = -\frac{1}{3}x - \frac{5}{3}$

(C) $y = -5x - 3$

(D) $y = 3x - 5$

(E) $y = 5x + 3$

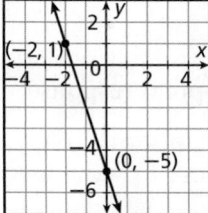

---

6. Which of the following relations is NOT a function?

(F) $\{(0, 1), (1, 2), (2, 3), (3, 4)\}$

(G) $\{(1, 2), (2, 2), (3, 3), (4, 3)\}$

(H) $\{(0, 2), (2, 4), (4, 1), (1, 3)\}$

(J) $\{(1, 3), (4, 2), (2, 0), (3, 4)\}$

(K) $\{(0, 2), (1, 3), (4 ,3), (1, 2)\}$

Extended Response: Understand the Scores

Extended response test items are typically multipart questions that require a high level of thinking. The responses are scored using a 4-point rubric. To receive full credit, you must correctly answer all parts of the question and provide a clear explanation. A partial answer is worth 2 or 3 points, an incorrect solution is worth 1 point, and no response is worth 0 points.

EXAMPLE 1

Extended Response A train traveling from Boston, Massachusetts, to Richmond, Virginia, averages about 55 miles per hour. Define variables, write an equation, make a table, and draw a graph to show the distance the train travels in 5 hours.

Here are examples of four different responses and their scores using the rubric shown.

4-point response:

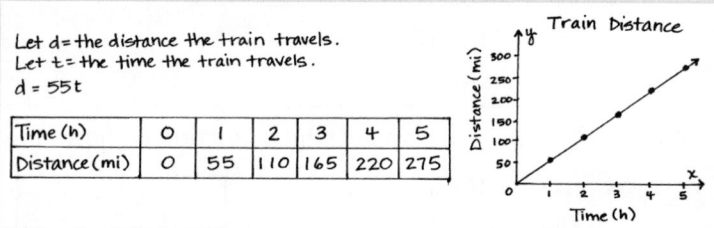

Let d = the distance the train travels.
Let t = the time the train travels.

$d = 55t$

Time (h)	0	1	2	3	4	5
Distance (mi)	0	55	110	165	220	275

3-point response:

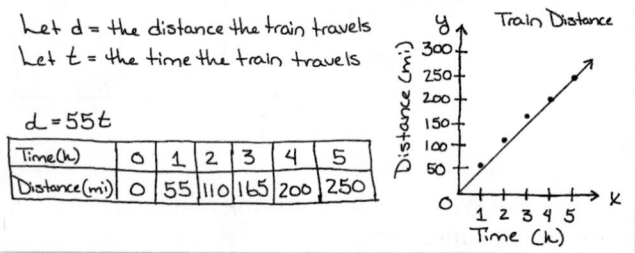

Let d = the distance the train travels
Let t = the time the train travels

$d = 55t$

Time (h)	0	1	2	3	4	5
Distance (mi)	0	55	110	165	200	250

The student shows all of the work, but there are two minor computation errors when t = 4 and t = 5.

2-point response:

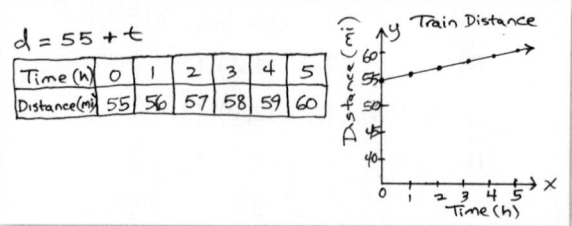

$d = 55 + t$

Time (h)	0	1	2	3	4	5
Distance (mi)	55	56	57	58	59	60

The student writes an incorrect equation and uses it to create an incorrect table and graph.

1-point response:

$d = 55t$

The student does not answer two parts of the question.

Read each test item and answer the questions that follow using the rubric below.

Scoring Rubric:

4 points: The student shows all of the work, correctly answers all parts of the question, and provides a clear explanation.

3 points: The student shows most of the work and provides a clear explanation but has a minor computation error, or the student shows all of the work and arrives at a correct solution but does not provide a clear explanation.

2 points: The student makes major errors resulting in an incorrect solution, or the student gives a correct solution but does not show any work nor provide an explanation.

1 point: The student shows no work and gives an incorrect solution.

0 points: The student gives no response.

Item A

Extended Response Draw a graph that is a function. Explain why it is a function. Then draw a graph that is NOT a function. Explain why it is not a function.

1. What should be included in a 4-point response?

2. Explain how would you score the response below.

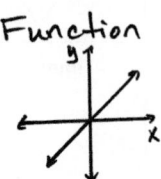

The first graph is a function because each x-value has exactly one y-value. When x=1, y=1. The second graph is not a function because there is more than one y-value for each x-value. When x=1, y=1, and y=-1. Therefore, the second graph is not a function.

Item B

Extended Response A car travels at a steady rate of 60 miles per hour. Identify the independent and dependent variables. Describe the domain and range. Write an equation to describe the situation.

3. Ana wrote the response below.

The equation is y = 60x. The independent variable is time and the dependent variable is distance. The domain and range are all real numbers.

Explain how would you score Ana's response.

4. If you did not give Ana full credit, what should be added to Ana's response, if anything, so that it receives full credit?

Item C

Extended Response Lara bought 8 notebooks and 4 binders. She spent $14 total without tax. How much did each notebook cost if each binder cost $2.50? Write an equation and find the solution.

5. Explain how would you score the response below.

Let s = the cost of each notebook.
Let b = the cost of each binder.
$8s + 4b = 14$
$8s + 4(2.50) = 14$
$8s + 10 = 14$
$8s = 4$
$s = 2$ The notebooks cost $2 each

6. If you did not give the response full credit, what should be added to the response, if anything, so that it receives full credit?

CUMULATIVE ASSESSMENT

Multiple Choice

1. Find the value of $|a| - b^2$ when $a = -3$ and $b = -5$.

  (A) -28 (C) -7

  (B) -22 (D) 4

2. Benito has x apples. He cuts each apple in half and gives each half to a different horse. Which expression represents the number of horses Benito feeds?

  (F) $x \cdot \frac{1}{2}$ (H) $x \cdot 1\frac{1}{2}$

  (G) $x \div \frac{1}{2}$ (J) $x \div 1\frac{1}{2}$

3. If the value of a^5 is positive, then which is true?

  (A) a is positive.

  (B) a is negative.

  (C) a^5 is odd.

  (D) a^5 is even.

4. Find the value of $\frac{2a}{a^3}$ if $4 - a = -6$.

  (F) $\frac{1}{50}$ (H) 8

  (G) $\frac{1}{2}$ (J) 10

5. There are 36 flowers in a bouquet. Two-thirds of the flowers are roses. One-fourth of the roses are red. What percent of the bouquet is made up of red roses?

  (A) 9% (C) 25%

  (B) $16\frac{2}{3}\%$ (D) $66\frac{2}{3}\%$

6. A large tree should be planted at least 70 feet away from a power line. Which inequality shows the acceptable number of feet x between a large tree and a power line?

  (F) $x < 70$ (H) $x > 70$

  (G) $x \leq 70$ (J) $x \geq 70$

7. Which statement is modeled by $3f + 2 > -16$?

  (A) Two added to 3 times f is at least -16.

  (B) Three times the sum of f and 2 is at most -16.

  (C) The sum of 2 and 3 times f is more than -16.

  (D) The product of $3f$ and 2 is no more than -16.

8. Jo Ann needs at least 3 pounds of peaches for a recipe. At the market, she calculates that she has enough money to buy 5 pounds at most. Which graph shows all possible numbers of pounds of peaches Jo Ann can buy so that she has enough for the recipe?

  (F)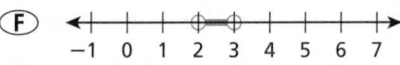

  (G)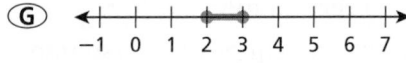

  (H)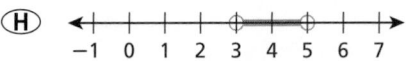

  (J)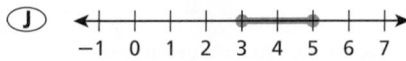

9. A bird flies from the ground to the top of a tree, sits there and sings for a while, flies down to the top of a picnic table to eat crumbs, and then flies back to the top of the tree to sing some more. Which graph best represents this situation?

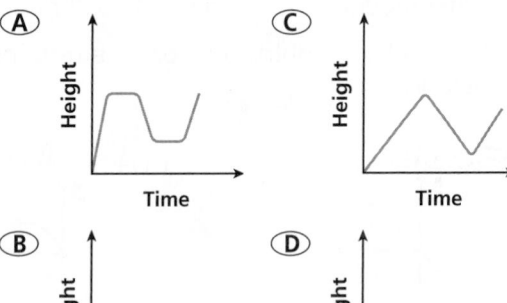

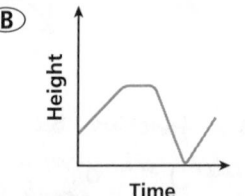

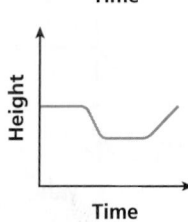

10. Which relation is NOT a function?

  (F) $\{(1, -5), (3, 1), (-5, 4), (4, -2)\}$

  (G) $\{(2, 7), (3, 7), (4, 7), (5, 8)\}$

  (H) $\{(1, -5), (-1, 6), (1, 5), (6, -3)\}$

  (J) $\{(3, -2), (5, -6), (7, 7), (8, 8)\}$

11. The graph below shows a function.

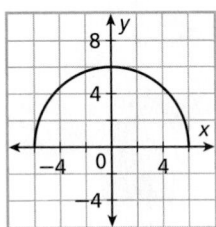

What is the domain of the function?

Ⓐ $x \geq 0$

Ⓑ $x \geq -6$

Ⓒ $0 \leq x \leq 6$

Ⓓ $-6 \leq x \leq 6$

12. Which situation best describes a negative correlation?

Ⓕ The speed of a runner and the time it takes to run a race

Ⓖ The number of apples in a bag and the weight of the bag of apples

Ⓗ The time it takes to repair a car and the amount of the bill

Ⓙ The number of people in a household and the amount of mail in their mailbox

13. Which of the following is a solution of $x + 1 \leq \frac{3}{2}$ AND $x - 1 \geq -\frac{5}{4}$?

Ⓐ $\frac{3}{2}$ Ⓒ $-\frac{1}{3}$

Ⓑ $\frac{1}{3}$ Ⓓ $-\frac{3}{2}$

Gridded Response

14. What is the value of x when $3(x + 7) - 6x = 4 - (x + 1)$?

15. For $h(x) = x^3 + 2x$, find $h(4)$.

16. WalkieTalkie phone company charges $18.00 for basic phone service per month and $0.15 per minute for long distance calls. Arena Calls charges $80.00 per month with no fee for long distance calls. What is the minimum number of minutes of long distance calls for which the cost of WalkieTalkie is more than the cost of Arena Calls?

Short Response

17. A function is graphed below.

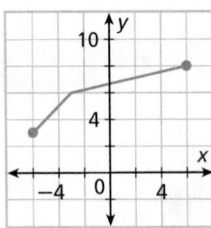

What is the domain and range of the function?

18. Rory made a pentagon by cutting two triangles from a square piece of cardboard as shown.

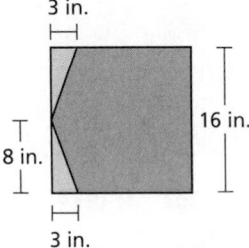

What is the area of the pentagon? Show your work or explain how you got your answer.

19. The manager of a new restaurant needs at most 12 servers. He has already hired 7 servers.

a. Write and solve an inequality to determine how many more servers the manager could hire.

b. Graph the solutions to the inequality you solved in part **a.**

20. Study the sequence below.

18, 24.5, 31, 37.5, 44,...

a. Could this sequence be arithmetic? Explain.

b. Find the 100th term of the sequence. Show your work.

Extended Response

21. A relation is shown in the table.

a. Express the relation as a mapping diagram.

b. Is the relation a function? Explain why or why not.

c. Write a possible real-life situation for the relation.

x	y
2	12
3	15
3	18
5	40
6	64

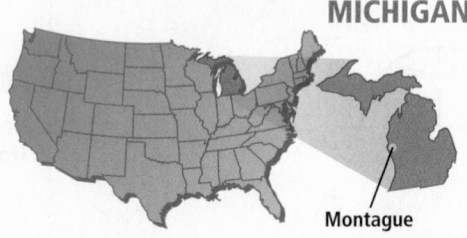

MICHIGAN

Montague

The World's Largest Weather Vane

The world's largest working weather vane weighs approximately 4300 pounds and is located in Montague, Michigan. Weather vanes are used to indicate the direction of the wind. When the wind blows, the vane points in the direction from which the wind is coming.

Choose one or more strategies to solve each problem.

1. The arrow on the world's largest weather vane has a length of 26 feet. The height of the weather vane is 4 feet shorter than twice its length. What is the height of the world's largest weather vane?

At the base of the weather vane is a working weather station. Weather stations include instruments such as thermometers, rain gauges, and wind gauges that measure different characteristics of the weather. The data gathered from weather stations are used to make predictions about future weather.

For 2 and 3, use the graph.

2. The data in the graph represent the average snowfall for each month, measured over a 30-year time period. The average amount of snowfall received in April is less than $\frac{1}{4}$ of the average snowfall in March. What is the greatest possible average snowfall for April? Round to the nearest tenth of an inch.

3. Which month do you predict will get the most snowfall next year? Explain your reasoning.

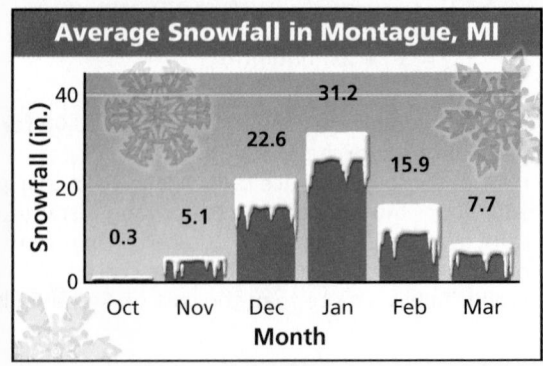

Maple Syrup

Michigan produces about 90,000 gallons of maple syrup each year. This places the state among the top ten states in U.S. production of maple syrup. Maple syrup is made from the sap of maple trees, but only about 1% of Michigan's maple trees are used in maple syrup production.

Choose one or more strategies to solve each problem.

1. The standard sugar concentration level of maple syrup is 66%. At certain levels above 66%, the product develops into maple cream, soft maple sugar, or hard maple sugar. The sugar concentration never reaches 100%, even in hard maple sugar. What is the range of sugar concentration levels in the various maple products? Show your answer on a number line.

For 2 and 3, use the table.

2. How many Calories are in 1 cup of maple syrup? (*Hint:* 4 tbsp = $\frac{1}{4}$ c)

3. Approximately how many tablespoons of maple syrup would you need to have the same number of Calories that are in 7 tablespoons of honey? Round to the nearest tablespoon.

4. It takes 40 gallons of maple sap to make 1 gallon of maple syrup. Each tap hole in a maple tree will produce about 10 gallons of sap in an average year. How many gallons of maple syrup could be made with the sap from 20 tap holes?

Sweetener	Calories (per tbsp)
Blackstrap molasses	43
Granulated sugar	46
Maple syrup	50
Corn syrup	57
Honey	64

5. It is recommended that maple trees be at least 10 inches in diameter before they are tapped. Only one tap should be placed in trees that are 10 to 18 inches in diameter, while 2 taps can be placed in trees greater than 18 inches in diameter. An orchard has 130 trees that are less than 10 inches in diameter, 104 trees that are 10–18 inches in diameter, and 48 trees that are greater than 18 inches in diameter. What is the maximum number of tap holes this orchard should have?

Linear Functions

COMMON CORE

Chapter Focus

- Translate among different representations of linear functions.
- Find and interpret slopes and intercepts of linear equations that model real-world problems
- Solve real-world problems involving linear equations.

Take *Flight*

You can use linear functions to describe patterns and relationships in flight times.

Learn It Online
Chapter Project Online

STOPS FLT GATE

0   560   72
632   85
0   760   77
0   200   73
0   3411   60
0   740.   78
0   2454   93
0   2464   94
0   2460   92
0   3977   60

ARE YOU READY?

✓ Vocabulary

Match each term on the left with a definition on the right.

1. coefficient
2. coordinate plane
3. transformation
4. perpendicular

A. a change in the size or position of a figure

B. forming right angles

C. a two-dimensional system formed by the intersection of a horizontal number line and a vertical number line

D. an ordered pair of numbers that gives the location of a point

E. a number that is multiplied by a variable

✓ Ordered Pairs

Graph each point on the same coordinate plane.

5. $A(2, 5)$
6. $B(-1, -3)$
7. $C(-5, 2)$
8. $D(4, -4)$
9. $E(-2, 0)$
10. $F(0, 3)$
11. $G(8, 7)$
12. $H(-8, -7)$

✓ Solve for a Variable

Solve each equation for the indicated variable.

13. $2x + y = 8; y$
14. $5y = 5x - 10; y$
15. $2y = 6x - 8; y$
16. $10x + 25 = 5y; y$

✓ Evaluate Expressions

Evaluate each expression for the given value of the variable.

17. $4g - 3; g = -2$
18. $8p - 12; p = 4$
19. $4x + 8; x = -2$
20. $-5t - 15; t = 1$

✓ Connect Words and Algebra

21. The value of a stock begins at $0.05 and increases by $0.01 each month. Write an equation representing the value of the stock v in any month m.

22. Write a situation that could be modeled by the equation $b = 100 - s$.

✓ Rates and Unit Rates

Find each unit rate.

23. 322 miles on 14 gallons of gas
24. $14.25 for 3 pounds of deli meat
25. 32 grams of fat in 4 servings
26. 120 pictures on 5 rolls of film

Study Guide: Preview

Where You've Been

Previously, you
- wrote equations in function notation.
- graphed functions.
- identified the domain and range of functions.
- identified independent and dependent variables.

In This Chapter

You will study
- writing and graphing linear functions.
- identifying and interpreting the components of linear graphs, including the *x*-intercept, *y*-intercept, and slope.
- graphing and analyzing families of functions.

Where You're Going

You can use the skills in this chapter
- to solve systems of linear equations in Chapter 5.
- to identify rates of change in linear data in biology and economics.
- to make calculations and comparisons in your personal finances.

Key Vocabulary/Vocabulario

constant of variation	constante de variación
direct variation	variación directa
family of functions	familia de funciones
linear function	función lineal
parallel lines	líneas paralelas
perpendicular lines	líneas perpendiculares
slope	pendiente
transformation	transformación
x-intercept	intersección con el eje *x*
y-intercept	intersección con el eje *y*

Vocabulary Connections

To become familiar with some of the vocabulary terms in the chapter, consider the following. You may refer to the chapter, the glossary, or a dictionary if you like.

1. What shape do you think is formed when a **linear function** is graphed on a coordinate plane?

2. The meaning of *intercept* is similar to the meaning of *intersection*. What do you think an **x-intercept** might be?

3. **Slope** is a word used in everyday life, as well as in mathematics. What is your understanding of the word *slope*?

4. A family is a group of related people. Use this concept to define **family of functions**.

Study Strategy: Use Multiple Representations

Representing a math concept in more than one way can help you understand it more clearly. As you read the explanations and example problems in your text, note the use of tables, lists, graphs, diagrams, and symbols, as well as words to explain a concept.

In this example, the given function is described using an equation, a table, ordered pairs, and a graph.

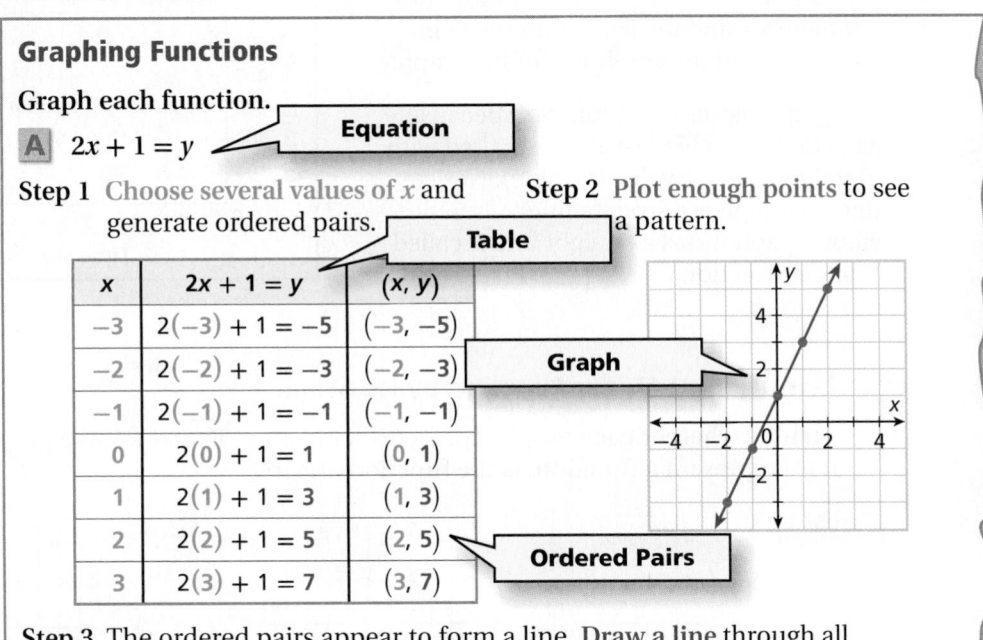

Graphing Functions

Graph each function.

A $2x + 1 = y$ — **Equation**

Step 1 Choose several values of x and generate ordered pairs. **Table**

Step 2 Plot enough points to see a pattern.

x	$2x + 1 = y$	(x, y)
-3	$2(-3) + 1 = -5$	$(-3, -5)$
-2	$2(-2) + 1 = -3$	$(-2, -3)$
-1	$2(-1) + 1 = -1$	$(-1, -1)$
0	$2(0) + 1 = 1$	$(0, 1)$
1	$2(1) + 1 = 3$	$(1, 3)$
2	$2(2) + 1 = 5$	$(2, 5)$
3	$2(3) + 1 = 7$	$(3, 7)$

Graph

Ordered Pairs

Step 3 The ordered pairs appear to form a line. Draw a line through all the points to show all the ordered pairs that satisfy the function. Draw arrowheads on both "ends" of the line.

Try This

1. If an employee earns $8.00 an hour, $y = 8x$ gives the total pay y the employee will earn for working x hours. For this equation, make a table of ordered pairs and a graph. Explain the relationships between the equation, the table, and the graph. How does each one describe the situation?

2. What situations might make one representation more useful than another?

4-1 Identifying Linear Functions

CC.9-12.A.REI.10 Understand that the graph of an equation in two variables is the set of all its solutions plotted in the coordinate plane.... *Also* **CC.9-12.F.IF.7***, **CC.9-12.A.CED.2***, **CC.9-12.F.IF.5***, **CC.9-12.F.LE.2***

Objectives
Identify linear functions and linear equations.

Graph linear functions that represent real-world situations and give their domain and range.

Vocabulary
linear function
linear equation

Why learn this?

Linear functions can describe many real-world situations, such as distances traveled at a constant speed.

Most people believe that there is no speed limit on the German autobahn. However, many stretches have a speed limit of 120 km/h. If a car travels continuously at this speed, $y = 120x$ gives the number of kilometers y that the car would travel in x hours. Solutions are shown in the graph.

The graph represents a function because each domain value (*x*-value) is paired with exactly one range value (*y*-value). Notice that the graph is a straight line. A function whose graph forms a straight line is called a **linear function**.

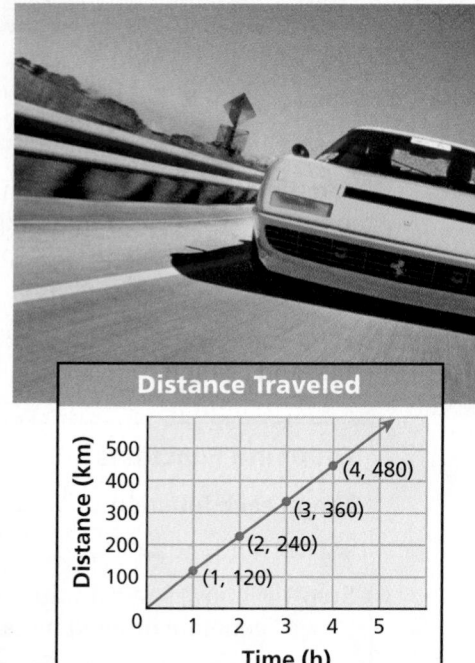

Distance Traveled

(4, 480)
(3, 360)
(2, 240)
(1, 120)

Distance (km) — Time (h)

EXAMPLE 1 Identifying a Linear Function by Its Graph

Identify whether each graph represents a function. Explain. If the graph does represent a function, is the function linear?

A

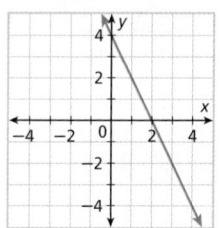

Each domain value is paired with exactly one range value. The graph forms a line.

linear function

B

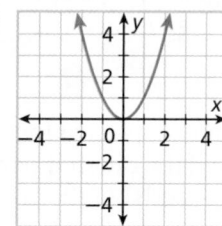

Each domain value is paired with exactly one range value. The graph is not a line.

not a linear function

C

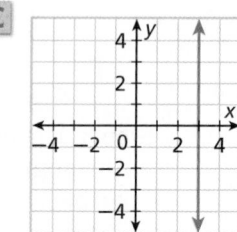

The only domain value, 3, is paired with many different range values.

not a function

CHECK IT OUT!

Identify whether each graph represents a function. Explain. If the graph does represent a function, is the function linear?

1a.
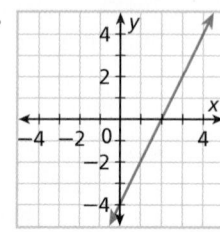

1b.
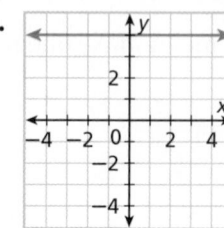

1c.
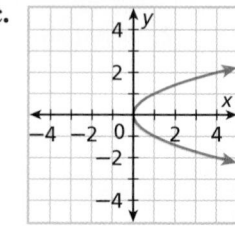

You can sometimes identify a linear function by looking at a table or a list of ordered pairs. In a linear function, a constant change in x corresponds to a constant change in y.

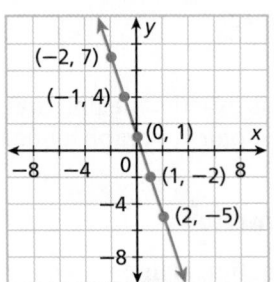

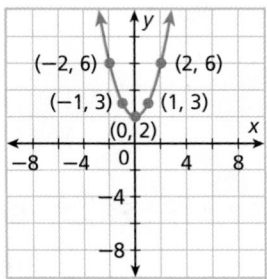

Caution!

If you find a constant change in the y-values, check for a constant change in the x-values. Both need to be constant for the function to be linear.

In this table, a constant change of +1 in x corresponds to a constant change of −3 in y. These points satisfy a linear function.

The points from this table lie on a line.

In this table, a constant change of +1 in x does *not* correspond to a constant change in y. These points do *not* satisfy a linear function.

The points from this table do not lie on a line.

EXAMPLE 2 **Identifying a Linear Function by Using Ordered Pairs**

Tell whether each set of ordered pairs satisfies a linear function. Explain.

A $\{(2, 4), (5, 3), (8, 2), (11, 1)\}$

x	y
2	4
5	3
8	2
11	1

+3 ... −1
+3 ... −1
+3 ... −1

Write the ordered pairs in a table. Look for a pattern.

A constant change of +3 in x corresponds to a constant change of −1 in y.

These points satisfy a linear function.

B $\{(-10, 10), (-5, 4), (0, 2), (5, 0)\}$

x	y
−10	10
−5	4
0	2
5	0

+5 ... −6
+5 ... −2
+5 ... −2

Write the ordered pairs in a table. Look for a pattern.

A constant change of +5 in x corresponds to different changes in y.

These points do not satisfy a linear function.

2. Tell whether the set of ordered pairs $\{(3, 5), (5, 4), (7, 3), (9, 2), (11, 1)\}$ satisfies a linear function. Explain.

Another way to determine whether a function is linear is to look at its equation. A function is linear if it is described by a *linear equation*. A **linear equation** is any equation that can be written in the *standard form* shown below.

Standard Form of a Linear Equation

$Ax + By = C$ where A, B, and C are real numbers and A and B are not both 0

Notice that when a linear equation is written in standard form
- x and y both have exponents of 1.
- x and y are not multiplied together.
- x and y do not appear in denominators, exponents, or radical signs.

Linear		Not Linear	
$3x + 2y = 10$	*Standard form*	$3xy + x = 1$	*x and y are multiplied.*
$y - 2 = 3x$	*Can be written as* $3x - y = -2$	$x^3 + y = -1$	*x has an exponent other than 1.*
$-y = 5x$	*Can be written as* $5x + y = 0$	$x + \dfrac{6}{y} = 12$	*y is in a denominator.*

For any two points, there is exactly one line that contains them both. This means you need only two ordered pairs to graph a line.

EXAMPLE 3 **Graphing Linear Functions**

Tell whether each function is linear. If so, graph the function.

A $y = x + 3$

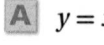

$$
\begin{array}{rl}
y = & x + 3 \quad \text{\textit{Write the equation in standard form.}} \\
\underline{-x \quad -x} & \quad \text{\textit{Subtraction Property of Equality}} \\
y - x = & \quad 3 \\
-x + y = & \quad 3 \quad \text{\textit{The equation is in standard form }} (A = -1, B = 1, C = 3).
\end{array}
$$

The equation can be written in standard form, so the function is linear.

To graph, choose three values of x, and use them to generate ordered pairs. (You only need two, but graphing three points is a good check.)

Plot the points and connect them with a straight line.

x	$y = x + 3$	(x, y)
0	$y = 0 + 3 = 3$	$(0, 3)$
1	$y = 1 + 3 = 4$	$(1, 4)$
2	$y = 2 + 3 = 5$	$(2, 5)$

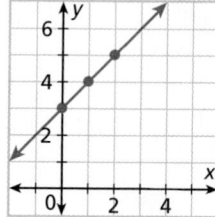

B $y = x^2$

This is not linear, because x has an exponent other than 1.

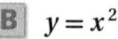  Tell whether each function is linear. If so, graph the function.

3a. $y = 5x - 9$ **3b.** $y = 12$ **3c.** $y = 2^x$

For linear functions whose graphs are not horizontal, the domain and range are all real numbers. However, in many real-world situations, the domain and range must be restricted. For example, some quantities cannot be negative, such as time.

Sometimes domain and range are restricted even further to a set of points. For example, a quantity such as number of people can only be whole numbers. When this happens, the graph is not actually connected because every point on the line is not a solution. However, you may see these graphs shown connected to indicate that the linear pattern, or trend, continues.

EXAMPLE 4

Career Application

Sue rents a manicure station in a salon and pays the salon owner $5.50 for each manicure she gives. The amount Sue pays each day is given by $f(x) = 5.50x$, where x is the number of manicures. Graph this function and give its domain and range.

Choose several values of x and make a table of ordered pairs.

Graph the ordered pairs.

x	$f(x) = 5.50x$
0	$f(0) = 5.50(0) = 0$
1	$f(1) = 5.50(1) = 5.50$
2	$f(2) = 5.50(2) = 11.00$
3	$f(3) = 5.50(3) = 16.50$
4	$f(4) = 5.50(4) = 22.00$
5	$f(5) = 5.50(5) = 27.50$

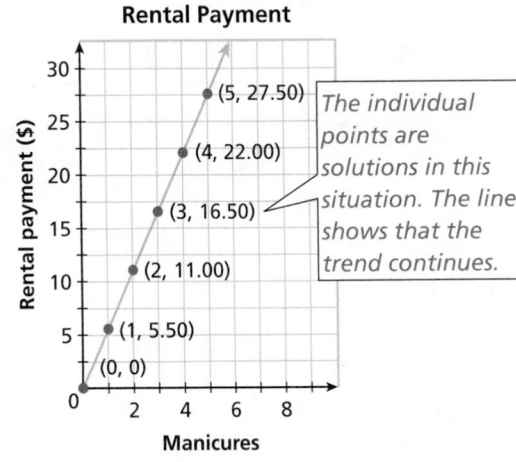

The individual points are solutions in this situation. The line shows that the trend continues.

The number of manicures must be a whole number, so the domain is $\{0, 1, 2, 3, ...\}$. The range is $\{0, 5.50, 11.00, 16.50, ...\}$.

 **4. What if...?** At another salon, Sue can rent a station for $10.00 per day plus $3.00 per manicure. The amount she would pay each day is given by $f(x) = 3x + 10$, where x is the number of manicures. Graph this function and give its domain and range.

THINK AND DISCUSS

1. Suppose you are given five ordered pairs that satisfy a function. When you graph them, four lie on a straight line, but the fifth does not. Is the function linear? Why or why not?

2. In Example 4, why is every point on the line not a solution?

3. GET ORGANIZED Copy and complete the graphic organizer. In each box, describe how to use the information to identify a linear function. Include an example.

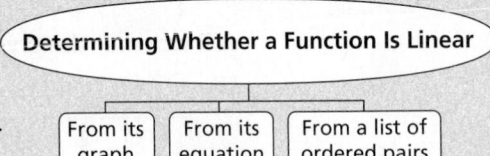

GUIDED PRACTICE

1. **Vocabulary** Is the *linear equation* $3x - 2 = y$ in standard form? Explain.

SEE EXAMPLE 1 Identify whether each graph represents a function. Explain. If the graph does represent a function, is the function linear?

2.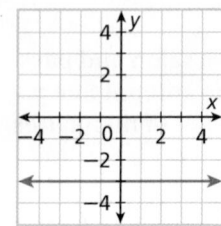

3.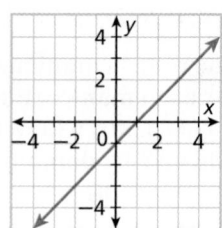

4.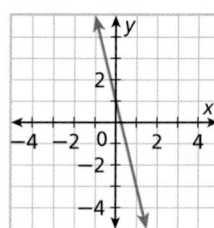

SEE EXAMPLE 2 Tell whether the given ordered pairs satisfy a linear function. Explain.

5.

x	5	4	3	2	1
y	0	2	4	6	8

6.

x	1	4	9	16	25
y	1	2	3	4	5

7. $\{(0, 5), (-2, 3), (-4, 1), (-6, -1), (-8, -3)\}$

8. $\{(2, -2), (-1, 0), (-4, 1), (-7, 3), (-10, 6)\}$

SEE EXAMPLE 3 Tell whether each function is linear. If so, graph the function.

9. $2x + 3y = 5$ 10. $2y = 8$ 11. $\dfrac{x^2 + 3}{5} = y$ 12. $\dfrac{x}{5} = \dfrac{y}{3}$

SEE EXAMPLE 4

13. **Transportation** A train travels at a constant speed of 75 mi/h. The function $f(x) = 75x$ gives the distance that the train travels in x hours. Graph this function and give its domain and range.

14. **Entertainment** A movie rental store charges a $6.00 membership fee plus $2.50 for each movie rented. The function $f(x) = 2.50x + 6$ gives the cost of renting x movies. Graph this function and give its domain and range.

PRACTICE AND PROBLEM SOLVING

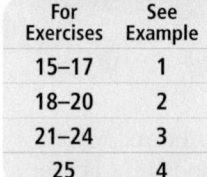
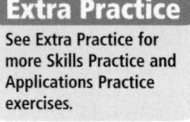

For Exercises	See Example
15–17	1
18–20	2
21–24	3
25	4

Extra Practice
See Extra Practice for more Skills Practice and Applications Practice exercises.

Identify whether each graph represents a function. Explain. If the graph does represent a function, is the function linear?

15.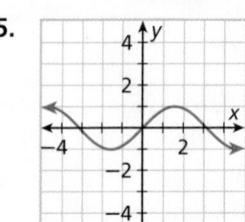

16.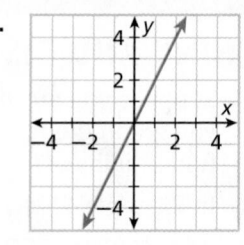

17.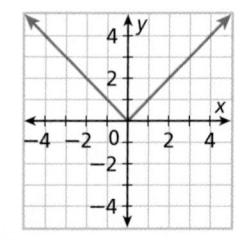

Tell whether the given ordered pairs satisfy a linear function. Explain.

18.

x	-3	0	3	6	9
y	-2	-1	0	2	4

19.

x	-1	0	1	2	3
y	-3	-2	-1	0	1

20. $\{(3, 4), (0, 2), (-3, 0), (-6, -2), (-9, -4)\}$

Tell whether each function is linear. If so, graph the function.

21. $y = 5$ **22.** $4y - 2x = 0$ **23.** $\frac{3}{x} + 4y = 10$ **24.** $5 + 3y = 8$

25. Transportation The gas tank in Tony's car holds 15 gallons, and the car can travel 25 miles for each gallon of gas. When Tony begins with a full tank of gas, the function $f(x) = -\frac{1}{25}x + 15$ gives the amount of gas $f(x)$ that will be left in the tank after traveling x miles (if he does not buy more gas). Graph this function and give its domain and range.

Tell whether the given ordered pairs satisfy a function. If so, is it a linear function?

26. $\{(2, 5), (2, 4), (2, 3), (2, 2), (2, 1)\}$ **27.** $\{(-8, 2), (-6, 0), (-4, -2), (-2, -4), (0, -6)\}$

28.

x	-10	-6	-2	2	4
y	0	0.25	0.50	0.75	1

29.

x	-5	-1	3	7	11
y	1	1	1	1	1

Tell whether each equation is linear. If so, write the equation in standard form and give the values of A, B, and C.

30. $2x - 8y = 16$ **31.** $y = 4x + 2$ **32.** $2x = \frac{y}{3} - 4$ **33.** $\frac{4}{x} = y$

34. $\frac{x + 4}{2} = \frac{y - 4}{3}$ **35.** $x = 7$ **36.** $xy = 6$ **37.** $3x - 5 + y = 2y - 4$

38. $y = -x + 2$ **39.** $5x = 2y - 3$ **40.** $2y = -6$ **41.** $y = \sqrt{x}$

Graph each linear function.

42. $y = 3x + 7$ **43.** $y = x + 25$ **44.** $y = 8 - x$ **45.** $y = 2x$

46. $-2y = -3x + 6$ **47.** $y - x = 4$ **48.** $y - 2x = -3$ **49.** $x = 5 + y$

50. Measurement One inch is equal to approximately 2.5 centimeters. Let x represent inches and y represent centimeters. Write an equation in standard form relating x and y. Give the values of A, B, and C.

51. Wages Molly earns \$8.00 an hour at her job.

    a. Let x represent the number of hours that Molly works. Write a function using x and $f(x)$ that describes Molly's pay for working x hours.

    b. Graph this function and give its domain and range.

 52. Write About It For $y = 2x - 1$, make a table of ordered pairs and a graph. Describe the relationships between the equation, the table, and the graph.

53. Critical Thinking Describe a real-world situation that can be represented by a linear function whose domain and range must be limited. Give your function and its domain and range.

MULTI-STEP TEST PREP

54. a. Juan is running on a treadmill. The table shows the number of Calories Juan burns as a function of time. Explain how you can tell that this relationship is linear by using the table.

    b. Create a graph of the data.

    c. How can you tell from the graph that the relationship is linear?

Time (min)	Calories
3	27
6	54
9	81
12	108
15	135
18	162
21	189

55. **Physical Science** A ball was dropped from a height of 100 meters. Its height above the ground in meters at different times after its release is given in the table. Do these ordered pairs satisfy a linear function? Explain.

Time (s)	0	1	2	3
Height (m)	100	90.2	60.8	11.8

56. **Critical Thinking** Is the equation $x = 9$ a linear equation? Does it describe a linear function? Explain.

57. Which is NOT a linear function?

    (A) $y = 8x$ (B) $y = x + 8$ (C) $y = \dfrac{8}{x}$ (D) $y = 8 - x$

58. The speed of sound in 0 °C air is about 331 feet per second. Which function could be used to describe the distance in feet d that sound will travel in air in s seconds?

    (F) $d = s + 331$ (G) $d = 331s$ (H) $s = 331d$ (J) $s = 331 - d$

59. **Extended Response** Write your own linear function. Show that it is a linear function in at least three different ways. Explain any connections you see between your three methods.

CHALLENGE AND EXTEND

60. What equation describes the x-axis? the y-axis? Do these equations represent linear functions?

Geometry Copy and complete each table below. Then tell whether the table shows a linear relationship.

61.

Perimeter of a Square	
Side Length	Perimeter
1	�
2	▪
3	▪
4	▪

62.

Area of a Square	
Side Length	Area
1	▪
2	▪
3	▪
4	▪

63.

Volume of a Cube	
Side Length	Volume
1	▪
2	▪
3	▪
4	▪

4-2 Using Intercepts

CC.9-12.F.IF.7 Graph functions expressed symbolically and show key features of the graph, by hand in simple cases....*
a. Graph linear ... functions and show intercepts, ... *Also* CC.9-12.A.CED.2*, CC.9-12.A.CED.3*, CC.9-12.F.IF.2, CC.9-12.F.IF.4*, CC.9-12.F.IF.5*

Objectives
Find *x*- and *y*-intercepts and interpret their meanings in real-world situations.

Use *x*- and *y*-intercepts to graph lines.

Vocabulary
y-intercept
x-intercept

Who uses this?

Divers can use intercepts to determine the time a safe ascent will take.

A diver explored the ocean floor 120 feet below the surface and then ascended at a rate of 30 feet per minute. The graph shows the diver's elevation below sea level during the ascent.

The **y-intercept** is the *y*-coordinate of the point where the graph intersects the *y*-axis. The *x*-coordinate of this point is always 0.

The **x-intercept** is the *x*-coordinate of the point where the graph intersects the *x*-axis. The *y*-coordinate of this point is always 0.

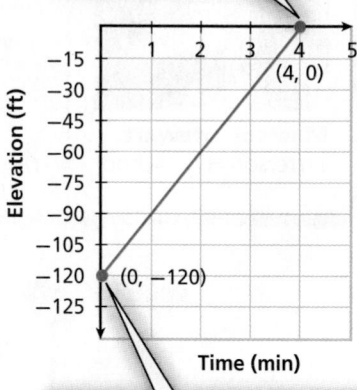

The *x*-intercept is 4. It represents the time that the diver reaches the surface, or when depth = 0.

The *y*-intercept is -120. It represents the diver's elevation at the start of the ascent, when time = 0.

EXAMPLE 1 **Finding Intercepts**

Find the *x*- and *y*-intercepts.

A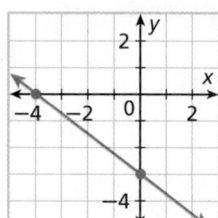

The graph intersects the *x*-axis at $(-4, 0)$.
The *x*-intercept is -4.

The graph intersects the *y*-axis at $(0, -3)$.
The *y*-intercept is -3.

B $3x - 2y = 12$

To find the *x*-intercept, replace *y* with 0 and solve for *x*.	To find the *y*-intercept, replace *x* with 0 and solve for *y*.
$3x - 2y = 12$	$3x - 2y = 12$
$3x - 2(0) = 12$	$3(0) - 2y = 12$
$3x - 0 = 12$	$0 - 2y = 12$
$3x = 12$	$-2y = 12$
$\dfrac{3x}{3} = \dfrac{12}{3}$	$\dfrac{-2y}{-2} = \dfrac{12}{-2}$
$x = 4$	$y = -6$
The *x*-intercept is 4.	The *y*-intercept is -6.

 Find the *x*- and *y*-intercepts.

1a.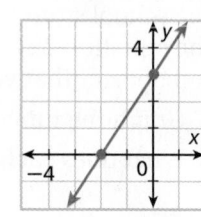

1b. $-3x + 5y = 30$

1c. $4x + 2y = 16$

Finding Intercepts

Madison Stewart
Jefferson High School

I use the "cover-up" method to find intercepts. To use this method, make sure the equation is in standard form first.

If I have $4x - 3y = 12$:

First, I cover $4x$ with my finger and solve the equation I can still see.

$$\text{✋} - 3y = 12$$
$$y = -4$$

The y-intercept is −4.

Then I cover $-3y$ with my finger and do the same thing.

$$4x \,\text{✋} = 12$$
$$x = 3$$

The x-intercept is 3.

EXAMPLE 2 **Travel Application**

The Sandia Peak Tramway in Albuquerque, New Mexico, travels a distance of about 4500 meters to the top of Sandia Peak. Its speed is 300 meters per minute. The function $f(x) = 4500 - 300x$ gives the tram's distance in meters from the top of the peak after x minutes. Graph this function and find the intercepts. What does each intercept represent?

Neither time nor distance can be negative, so choose several nonnegative values for x. Use the function to generate ordered pairs.

x	0	2	5	10	15
$f(x) = 4500 - 300x$	4500	3900	3000	1500	0

Graph the ordered pairs. Connect the points with a line.

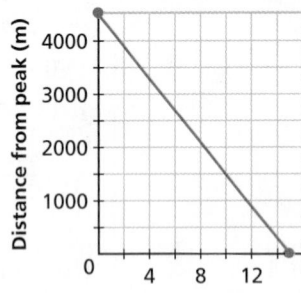

Sandia Peak Tramway

Caution!

The graph is not the path of the tram. Even though the line is descending, the graph describes the distance from the peak as the tram goes *up* the mountain.

- y-intercept: 4500. This is the starting distance from the top (time = 0).
- x-intercept: 15. This the time when the tram reaches the peak (distance = 0).

CHECK IT OUT!

2. The school store sells pens for $2.00 and notebooks for $3.00. The equation $2x + 3y = 60$ describes the number of pens x and notebooks y that you can buy for $60.

   a. Graph the function and find its intercepts.

   b. What does each intercept represent?

Remember, to graph a linear function, you need to plot only two ordered pairs. It is often simplest to find the ordered pairs that contain the intercepts.

EXAMPLE 3 **Graphing Linear Equations by Using Intercepts**

Use intercepts to graph the line described by each equation.

A $2x - 4y = 8$

Step 1 Find the intercepts.

x-intercept:

$2x - 4y = 8$
$2x - 4(0) = 8$
$2x = 8$
$\dfrac{2x}{2} = \dfrac{8}{2}$
$x = 4$

y-intercept:

$2x - 4y = 8$
$2(0) - 4y = 8$
$-4y = 8$
$\dfrac{-4y}{-4} = \dfrac{8}{-4}$
$y = -2$

Step 2 Graph the line.

Plot (4, 0) and (0, −2).
Connect with a straight line.

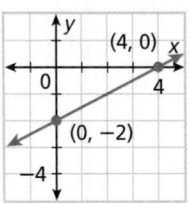

Helpful Hint

You can use a third point to check your line. Either choose a point from your graph and check it in the equation, or use the equation to generate a point and check that it is on your graph.

B $\dfrac{2}{3}y = 4 - \dfrac{1}{2}x$

Step 1 Write the equation in standard form.

$6\left(\dfrac{2}{3}y\right) = 6\left(4 - \dfrac{1}{2}x\right)$ *Multiply both sides by 6, the LCD of the fractions, to clear the fractions.*

$4y = 24 - 3x$

$3x + 4y = 24$ *Write the equation in standard form.*

Step 2 Find the intercepts.

x-intercept:

$3x + 4y = 24$
$3x + 4(0) = 24$
$3x = 24$
$\dfrac{3x}{3} = \dfrac{24}{3}$
$x = 8$

y-intercept:

$3x + 4y = 24$
$3(0) + 4y = 24$
$4y = 24$
$\dfrac{4y}{4} = \dfrac{24}{4}$
$y = 6$

Step 3 Graph the line.

Plot (8, 0) and (0, 6).
Connect with a straight line.

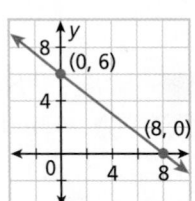

 Use intercepts to graph the line described by each equation.

3a. $-3x + 4y = -12$

3b. $y = \dfrac{1}{3}x - 2$

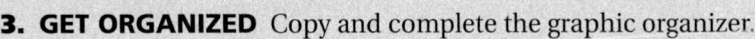

MATHEMATICAL PRACTICES

THINK AND DISCUSS

1. A function has x-intercept 4 and y-intercept 2. Name two points on the graph of this function.

2. What is the y-intercept of $2.304x + y = 4.318$? What is the x-intercept of $x - 92.4920y = -21.5489$?

3. GET ORGANIZED Copy and complete the graphic organizer.

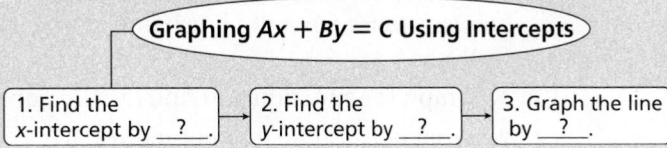

Graphing $Ax + By = C$ Using Intercepts

| 1. Find the x-intercept by ? . | 2. Find the y-intercept by ? . | 3. Graph the line by ? . |

GUIDED PRACTICE

1. **Vocabulary** The ____?____ is the y-coordinate of the point where a graph crosses the y-axis. (*x-intercept* or *y-intercept*)

SEE EXAMPLE 1 · Find the x- and y-intercepts.

2.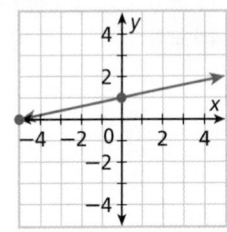

3.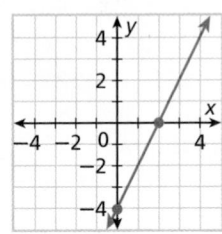

4.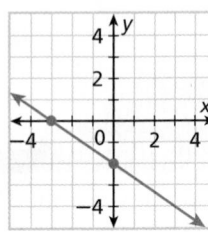

5. $2x - 4y = 4$

6. $-2y = 3x - 6$

7. $4y + 5x = 2y - 3x + 16$

SEE EXAMPLE 2 · 8. **Biology** To thaw a specimen stored at $-25\ °C$, the temperature of a refrigeration tank is raised $5\ °C$ every hour. The temperature in the tank after x hours can be described by the function $f(x) = -25 + 5x$.

   a. Graph the function and find its intercepts.

   b. What does each intercept represent?

SEE EXAMPLE 3 · Use intercepts to graph the line described by each equation.

9. $4x - 5y = 20$

10. $y = 2x + 4$

11. $\frac{1}{3}x - \frac{1}{4}y = 2$

12. $-5y + 2x = -10$

PRACTICE AND PROBLEM SOLVING

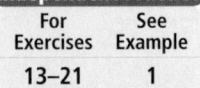

For Exercises	See Example
13–21	1
22–23	2
24–29	3

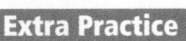
Extra Practice
See Extra Practice for more Skills Practice and Applications Practice exercises.

Find the x- and y-intercepts.

13.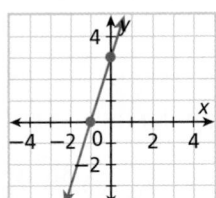

14.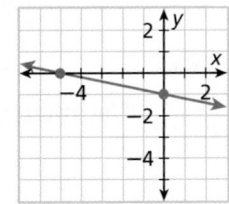

15.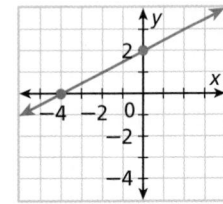

16. $6x + 3y = 12$

17. $4y - 8 = 2x$

18. $-2y + x = 2y - 8$

19. $4x + y = 8$

20. $y - 3x = -15$

21. $2x + y = 10x - 1$

22. **Environmental Science** A fishing lake was stocked with 300 bass. Each year, the population decreases by 25. The population of bass in the lake after x years is represented by the function $f(x) = 300 - 25x$.

   a. Graph the function and find its intercepts.

   b. What does each intercept represent?

23. **Sports** Julie is running a 5-kilometer race. She runs 1 kilometer every 5 minutes. Julie's distance from the finish line after x minutes is represented by the function $f(x) = 5 - \frac{1}{5}x$.

   a. Graph the function and find its intercepts.

   b. What does each intercept represent?

Use intercepts to graph the line described by each equation.

24. $4x - 6y = 12$

25. $2x + 3y = 18$

26. $\frac{1}{2}x - 4y = 4$

27. $y - x = -1$

28. $5x + 3y = 15$

29. $x - 3y = -1$

30. **Biology** A bamboo plant is growing 1 foot per day. When you first measure it, it is 4 feet tall.

   a. Write an equation to describe the height y, in feet, of the bamboo plant x days after you measure it.

   b. What is the y-intercept?

   c. What is the meaning of the y-intercept in this problem?

31. **Estimation** Look at the scatter plot and trend line.

   a. Estimate the x- and y-intercepts.

   b. What is the real-world meaning of each intercept?

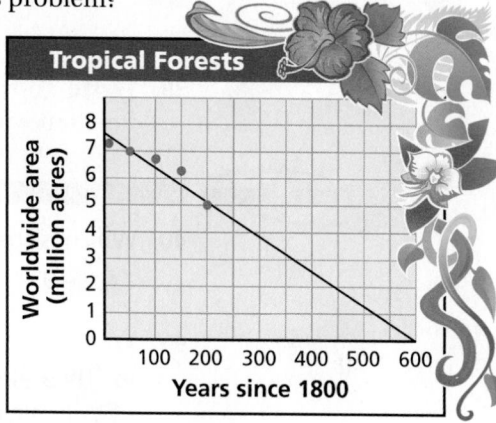

32. **Personal Finance** A bank employee notices an abandoned checking account with a balance of \$412. If the bank charges a \$4 monthly fee for the account, the function $b = 412 - 4m$ shows the balance b in the account after m months.

   a. Graph the function and give its domain and range. (*Hint:* The bank will keep charging the monthly fee even after the account is empty.)

   b. Find the intercepts. What does each intercept represent?

   c. When will the bank account balance be 0?

33. **Critical Thinking** Complete the following to learn about intercepts and horizontal and vertical lines.

   a. Graph $x = -6$, $x = 1$, and $x = 5$. Find the intercepts.

   b. Graph $y = -3$, $y = 2$, and $y = 7$. Find the intercepts.

   c. Write a rule describing the intercepts of linear equations whose graphs are horizontal and vertical lines.

Match each equation with a graph.

34. $-2x - y = 4$

35. $y = 4 - 2x$

36. $2y + 4x = 8$

37. $4x - 2y = 8$

A.

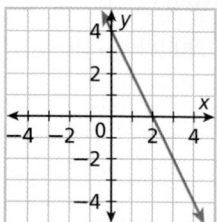

B.

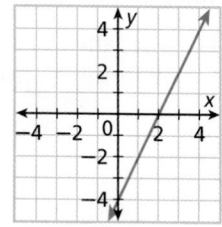

C.

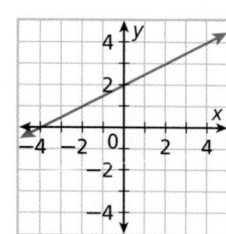

D.

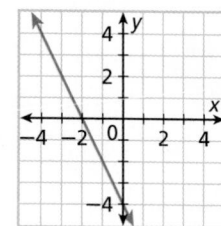

MULTI-STEP TEST PREP

38. Kristyn rode a stationary bike at the gym. She programmed the timer for 20 minutes. The display counted backward to show how much time remained in her workout. It also showed her mileage.

a. What are the intercepts?

b. What do the intercepts represent?

Time Remaining (min)	Distance Covered (mi)
20	0
16	0.35
12	0.70
8	1.05
4	1.40
0	1.75

39. Write About It Write a real-world problem that could be modeled by a linear function whose x-intercept is 5 and whose y-intercept is 60.

TEST PREP

40. Which is the x-intercept of $-2x = 9y - 18$?

Ⓐ -9 Ⓑ -2 Ⓒ 2 Ⓓ 9

41. Which of the following situations could be represented by the graph?

Ⓕ Jamie owed her uncle $200. Each week for 40 weeks she paid him $5.

Ⓖ Jamie owed her uncle $200. Each week for 5 weeks she paid him $40.

Ⓗ Jamie owed her uncle $40. Each week for 5 weeks she paid him $200.

Ⓙ Jamie owed her uncle $40. Each week for 200 weeks she paid him $5.

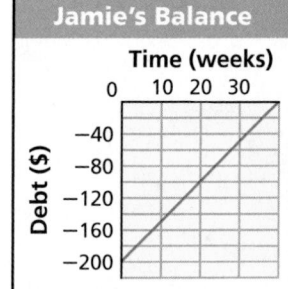

42. Gridded Response What is the y-intercept of $60x + 55y = 660$?

CHALLENGE AND EXTEND

Use intercepts to graph the line described by each equation.

43. $\frac{1}{2}x + \frac{1}{5}y = 1$ **44.** $0.5x - 0.2y = 0.75$ **45.** $y = \frac{3}{8}x + 6$

46. For any linear equation $Ax + By = C$, what are the intercepts?

47. Find the intercepts of $22x - 380y = 20,900$. Explain how to use the intercepts to determine appropriate scales for the graph.

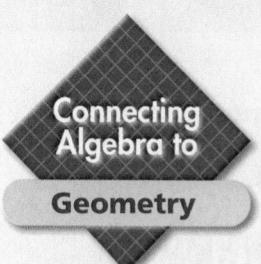

Connecting Algebra to Geometry

Area in the Coordinate Plane

Lines in the coordinate plane can form the sides of polygons. You can use points on these lines to help you find the areas of these polygons.

Example

Find the area of the triangle formed by the x-axis, the y-axis, and the line described by $3x + 2y = 18$.

Step 1 Find the intercepts of $3x + 2y = 18$.

x-intercept: y-intercept:

$$3x + 2y = 18 \qquad 3x + 2y = 18$$
$$3x + 2(0) = 18 \qquad 3(0) + 2y = 18$$
$$3x = 18 \qquad\qquad 2y = 18$$
$$x = 6 \qquad\qquad\quad y = 9$$

Step 2 Use the intercepts to graph the line. The x-intercept is 6, so plot $(6, 0)$. The y-intercept is 9, so plot $(0, 9)$. Connect with a straight line. Then shade the triangle formed by the line and the axes, as described.

Step 3 Recall that the area of a triangle is given by $A = \frac{1}{2}bh$.

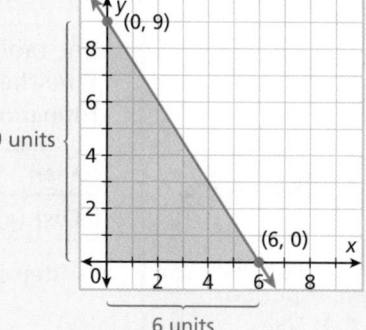

- The length of the base is **6**.
- The height is **9**.

Step 4 Substitute these values into the formula.

$$A = \frac{1}{2}bh$$

$$A = \frac{1}{2}(6)(9) \qquad \textit{Substitute into the area formula.}$$

$$= \frac{1}{2}(54) \qquad \textit{Simplify.}$$

$$= 27$$

The area of the triangle is 27 square units.

Try This

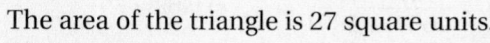

1. Find the area of the triangle formed by the x-axis, the y-axis, and the line described by $3x + 2y = 12$.

2. Find the area of the triangle formed by the x-axis, the y-axis, and the line described by $y = 6 - x$.

3. Find the area of the polygon formed by the x-axis, the y-axis, the line described by $y = 6$, and the line described by $x = 4$.

CC.9-12.F.IF.6 Calculate and interpret the average rate of change of a function (presented symbolically or as a table) over a specified interval. Estimate the rate of change from a graph.*

4-3 Rate of Change and Slope

Objectives
Find rates of change and slopes.

Relate a constant rate of change to the slope of a line.

Vocabulary
rate of change
rise
run
slope

Why learn this?
Rates of change can be used to find how quickly costs have increased.

In 1985, the cost of sending a 1-ounce letter was 22 cents. In 1988, the cost was 25 cents. How fast did the cost change from 1985 to 1988? In other words, at what *rate* did the cost change?

A **rate of change** is a ratio that compares the amount of change in a dependent variable to the amount of change in an independent variable.

$$\text{rate of change} = \frac{\text{change in dependent variable}}{\text{change in independent variable}}$$

EXAMPLE 1 *Consumer Application*

The table shows the cost of mailing a 1-ounce letter in different years. Find the rate of change in cost for each time interval. During which time interval did the cost increase at the greatest rate?

Year	1988	1990	1991	2004	2008
Cost (¢)	25	25	29	37	42

Step 1 Identify the dependent and independent variables.

   dependent: cost   independent: year

Step 2 Find the rates of change.

1988 to 1990 $\dfrac{\text{change in cost}}{\text{change in years}} = \dfrac{25 - 25}{1990 - 1988} = \dfrac{0}{2} = 0$ $\dfrac{0 \text{ cents}}{\text{year}}$

1990 to 1991 $\dfrac{\text{change in cost}}{\text{change in years}} = \dfrac{29 - 25}{1991 - 1990} = \dfrac{4}{1} = 4$ $\dfrac{4 \text{ cents}}{\text{year}}$

1991 to 2004 $\dfrac{\text{change in cost}}{\text{change in years}} = \dfrac{37 - 29}{2004 - 1991} = \dfrac{8}{13} \approx 0.62 \approx \dfrac{0.62 \text{ cents}}{\text{year}}$

2004 to 2008 $\dfrac{\text{change in cost}}{\text{change in years}} = \dfrac{42 - 37}{2008 - 2004} = \dfrac{5}{4} = 1.25$ $\dfrac{1.25 \text{ cents}}{\text{year}}$

The cost increased at the greatest rate from 1990 to 1991.

Caution!

A rate of change of 1.25 cents per year for a 4-year period means that the *average* change was 1.25 cents per year. The *actual* change in each year may have been different.

1. The table shows the balance of a bank account on different days of the month. Find the rate of change for each time interval. During which time interval did the balance decrease at the greatest rate?

Day	1	6	16	22	30
Balance ($)	550	285	210	210	175

EXAMPLE 2 **Finding Rates of Change from a Graph**

Graph the data from Example 1 and show the rates of change.

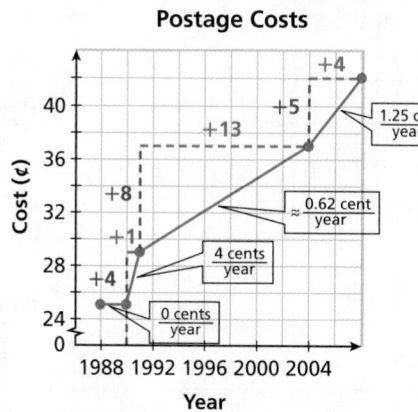

Postage Costs

Graph the ordered pairs. The vertical blue segments show the changes in the dependent variable, and the horizontal green segments show the changes in the independent variable.

Notice that the greatest rate of change is represented by the steepest of the red line segments.

Also notice that between 1988 and 1990, when the cost did not change, the red line segment is horizontal.

CHECK IT OUT! **2.** Graph the data from Check It Out Problem 1 and show the rates of change.

If all of the connected segments have the same rate of change, then they all have the same steepness and together form a straight line. The constant rate of change of a nonvertical line is called the *slope* of the line.

Slope of a Line

The **rise** is the difference in the *y*-values of two points on a line.

The **run** is the difference in the *x*-values of two points on a line.

The **slope** of a line is the ratio of rise to run for any two points on the line.

$$\text{slope} = \frac{\text{rise}}{\text{run}} = \frac{\text{change in } y}{\text{change in } x}$$

(Remember that *y* is the **dependent variable** and *x* is the **independent variable**.)

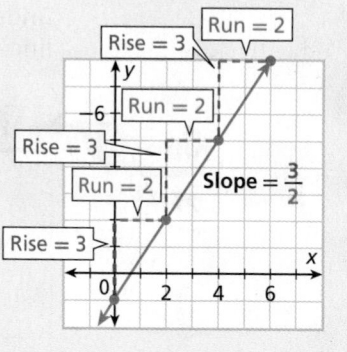

EXAMPLE 3 **Finding Slope**

Find the slope of the line.

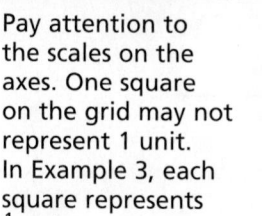

Caution!

Pay attention to the scales on the axes. One square on the grid may not represent 1 unit. In Example 3, each square represents $\frac{1}{2}$ unit.

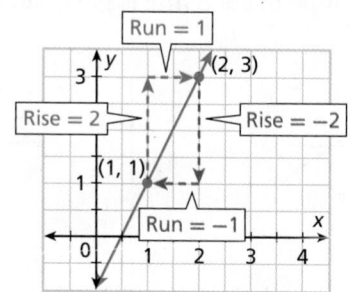

Begin at one point and count vertically to find the rise.

Then count horizontally to the second point to find the run.

It does not matter which point you start with. The slope is the same.

$$\text{slope} = \frac{2}{1} = 2$$

$$\text{slope} = \frac{-2}{-1} = 2$$

CHECK IT OUT! **3.** Find the slope of the line that contains $(0, -3)$ and $(5, -5)$.

EXAMPLE 4 **Finding Slopes of Horizontal and Vertical Lines**

Find the slope of each line.

 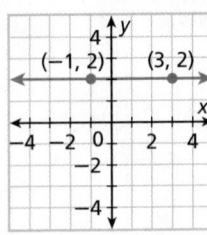

 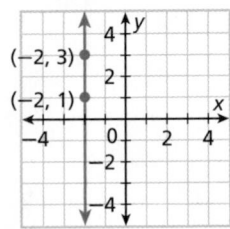

$$\frac{\text{rise}}{\text{run}} = \frac{0}{4} = 0$$

The slope is 0.

$$\frac{\text{rise}}{\text{run}} = \frac{2}{0}$$ *You cannot divide by 0.*

The slope is undefined.

 Find the slope of each line.

4a.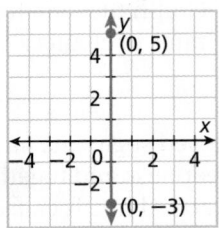

4b.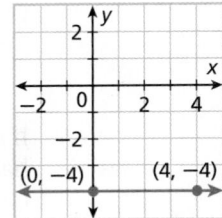

As shown in the previous examples, slope can be positive, negative, zero, or undefined. You can tell which of these is the case by looking at the graph of a line—you do not need to calculate the slope.

Positive Slope	Negative Slope	Zero Slope	Undefined Slope
Line rises from left to right.	Line falls from left to right.	Horizontal line	Vertical line

EXAMPLE 5 **Describing Slope**

Tell whether the slope of each line is positive, negative, zero, or undefined.

 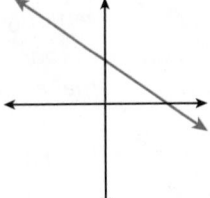

 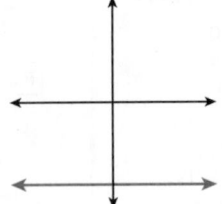

The line falls from left to right.

The slope is negative.

The line is horizontal.

The slope is 0.

Tell whether the slope of each line is positive, negative, zero, or undefined.

5a.

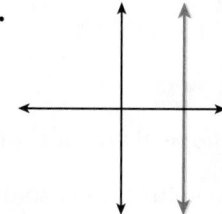

5b.

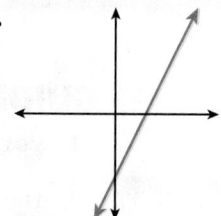

A line's slope is a measure of its steepness. Some lines are steeper than others. As the absolute value of the slope increases, the line becomes steeper.
As the absolute value of the slope decreases, the line becomes less steep.

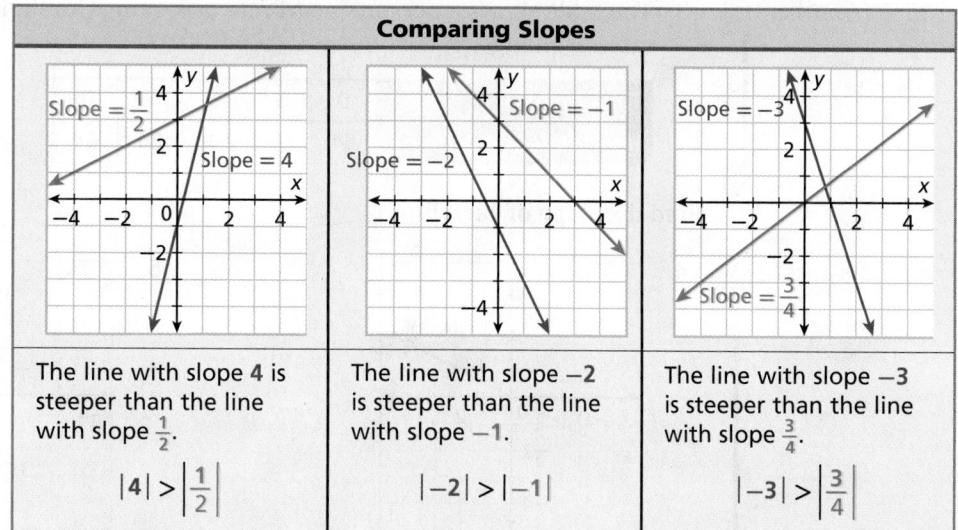

Comparing Slopes		
The line with slope **4** is steeper than the line with slope $\frac{1}{2}$.	The line with slope **−2** is steeper than the line with slope **−1**.	The line with slope **−3** is steeper than the line with slope $\frac{3}{4}$.
$\lvert 4 \rvert > \left\lvert \frac{1}{2} \right\rvert$	$\lvert -2 \rvert > \lvert -1 \rvert$	$\lvert -3 \rvert > \left\lvert \frac{3}{4} \right\rvert$

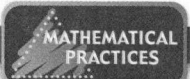

THINK AND DISCUSS

1. What is the rise shown in the graph? What is the run? What is the slope?

2. The rate of change of the profits of a company over one year is negative. How have the profits of the company changed over that year?

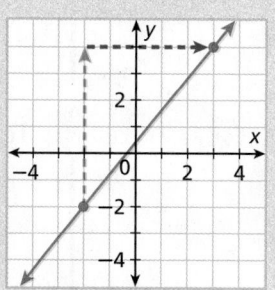

3. Would you rather climb a hill with a slope of 4 or a hill with a slope of $\frac{5}{2}$? Explain your answer.

4. GET ORGANIZED Copy and complete the graphic organizer. In each box, sketch a line whose slope matches the given description.

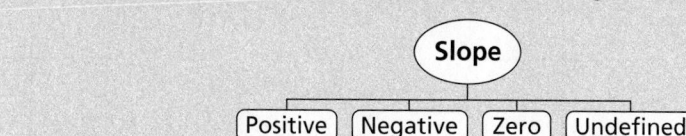

GUIDED PRACTICE

1. **Vocabulary** The *slope* of any nonvertical line is ___?___. (*positive* or *constant*)

SEE EXAMPLE 1

2. The table shows the volume of gasoline in a gas tank at different times. Find the rate of change for each time interval. During which time interval did the volume decrease at the greatest rate?

Time (h)	0	1	3	6	7
Volume (gal)	12	9	5	1	1

SEE EXAMPLE 2

3. The table shows a person's heart rate over time. Graph the data and show the rates of change.

Time (min)	0	2	5	7	10
Heart Rate (beats/min)	64	92	146	84	64

Find the slope of each line.

SEE EXAMPLE 3

4.

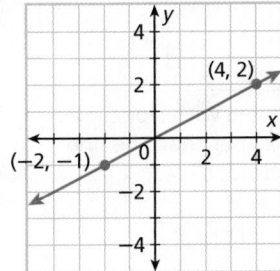

5.

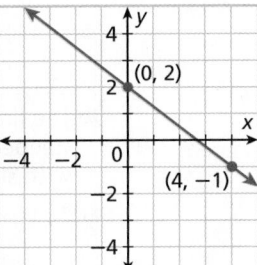

SEE EXAMPLE 4

6.

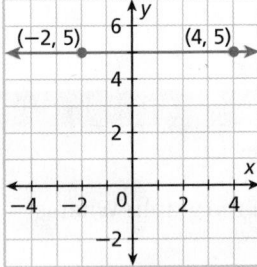

7.

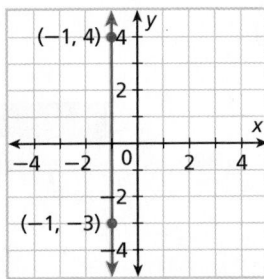

SEE EXAMPLE 5

Tell whether the slope of each line is positive, negative, zero, or undefined.

8.

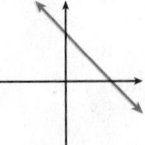

9.

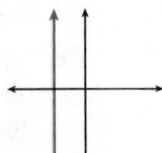

10.

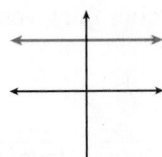

11.

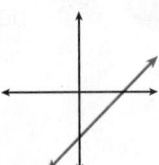

PRACTICE AND PROBLEM SOLVING

Independent Practice

For Exercises	See Example
12	1
13	2
14–15	3
16–17	4
18–19	5

Extra Practice

See Extra Practice for more Skills Practice and Applications Practice exercises.

12. The table shows the length of a baby at different ages. Find the rate of change for each time interval. Round your answers to the nearest tenth. During which time interval did the baby have the greatest growth rate?

Age (mo)	3	9	18	26	33
Length (in.)	23.5	27.5	31.6	34.5	36.7

13. The table shows the distance of an elevator from the ground floor at different times. Graph the data and show the rates of change.

Time (s)	0	15	23	30	35
Distance (m)	30	70	0	45	60

Find the slope of each line.

14.

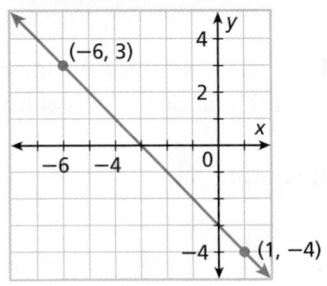

15.

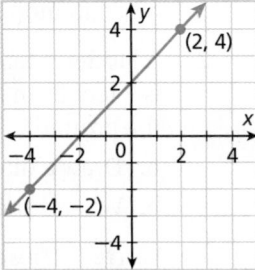

16.

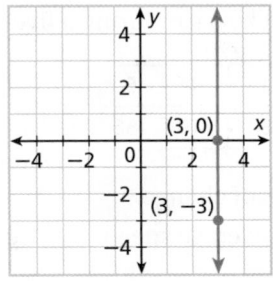

17.

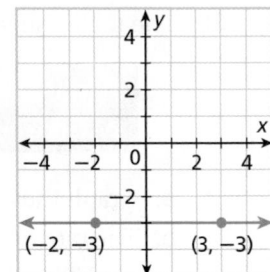

Tell whether the slope of each line is positive, negative, zero, or undefined.

18.

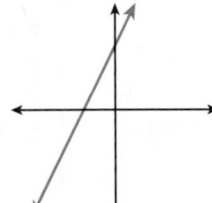

19.

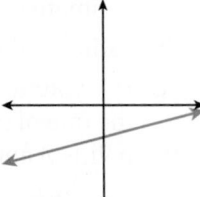

Travel

The Incline Railway's climb up Lookout Mountain has been called "America's Most Amazing Mile." A round-trip on the railway lasts about 1.5 hours.

20. Travel The Lookout Mountain Incline Railway in Chattanooga, Tennessee, is the steepest passenger railway in the world. A section of the railway has a slope of about 0.73. In this section, a vertical change of 1 unit corresponds to a horizontal change of what length? Round your answer to the nearest hundredth.

21. Critical Thinking Previously you learned that in a linear function, a constant change in x corresponds to a constant change in y. How is this related to slope?

22. **a.** The graph shows a relationship between a person's age and his or her estimated maximum heart rate in beats per minute. Find the slope.

   b. Describe the rate of change in this situation.

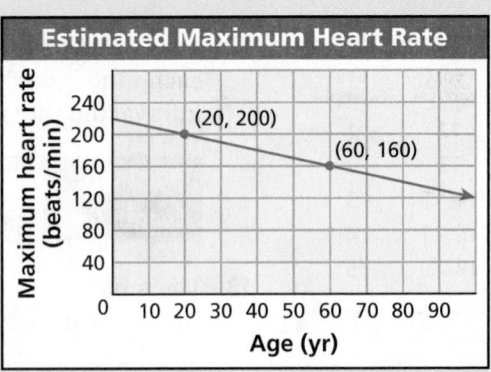

Estimated Maximum Heart Rate

(20, 200)

(60, 160)

Maximum heart rate (beats/min)

240
200
160
120
80
40
0

10 20 30 40 50 60 70 80 90

Age (yr)

23. **Construction** Most staircases in use today have 9-inch treads and $8\frac{1}{2}$-inch risers. What is the slope of a staircase with these measurements?

24. A ladder is leaned against a building. The bottom of the ladder is 9 feet from the building. The top of the ladder is 16 feet above the ground.

   a. Draw a diagram to represent this situation.

   b. What is the slope of the ladder?

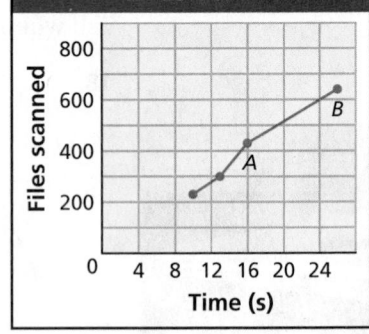

Tread

Riser

25. **Write About It** Why will the slope of any horizontal line be 0? Why will the slope of any vertical line be undefined?

26. The table shows the distance traveled by a car during a five-hour road trip.

Time (h)	0	1	2	3	4	5
Distance (mi)	0	40	80	80	110	160

   a. Graph the data and show the rates of change.

   b. The rate of change represents the average speed. During which hour was the car's average speed the greatest?

27. **Estimation** The graph shows the number of files scanned by a computer virus detection program over time.

   a. Estimate the coordinates of point A.

   b. Estimate the coordinates of point B.

   c. Use your answers from parts **a** and **b** to estimate the rate of change (in files per second) between points A and B.

Virus Scan

Files scanned

800
600
400
200
0

B

A

4   8   12 16 20 24

Time (s)

28. **Data Collection** Use a graphing calculator and a motion detector for the following. Set the equipment so that the graph shows distance on the y-axis and time on the x-axis.

   a. Experiment with walking in front of the motion detector. How must you walk to graph a straight line? Explain.

   b. Describe what you must do differently to graph a line with a positive slope vs. a line with a negative slope.

   c. How can you graph a line with slope 0? Explain.

29. The slope of which line has the greatest absolute value?

    Ⓐ line *A*   Ⓒ line *C*

    Ⓑ line *B*   Ⓓ line *D*

30. For which line is the run equal to 0?

    Ⓐ line *A*   Ⓒ line *C*

    Ⓑ line *B*   Ⓓ line *D*

31. Which line has a slope of 4?

Ⓕ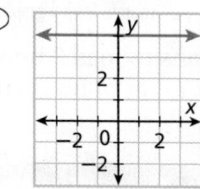

Ⓗ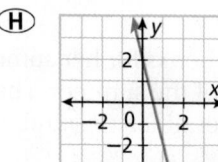

Ⓖ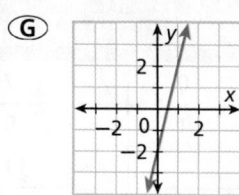

Ⓙ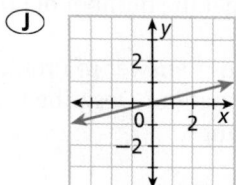

CHALLENGE AND EXTEND

32. Recreation Tara and Jade are hiking up a hill. Each has a different stride. The run for Tara's stride is 32 inches, and the rise is 8 inches. The run for Jade's stride is 36 inches. What is the rise of Jade's stride?

33. Economics The table shows cost in dollars charged by an electric company for various amounts of energy in kilowatt-hours.

Energy (kWh)	0	200	400	600	1000	2000
Cost ($)	3	3	31	59	115	150

    a. Graph the data and show the rates of change.

    b. Compare the rates of change for each interval. Are they all the same? Explain.

    c. What do the rates of change represent?

    d. Describe in words the electric company's billing plan.

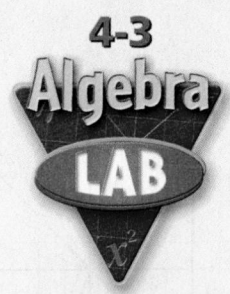

4-3 Algebra LAB

Explore Constant Changes

There are many real-life situations in which the amount of change is constant. In these activities, you will explore what happens when

- a quantity increases by a constant amount.

- a quantity decreases by a constant amount.

Use with Rate of Change and Slope

 **MATHEMATICAL PRACTICES**

Look for and express regularity in repeated reasoning.

CC.9-12.F.IF.6 Calculate and interpret the average rate of change of a function (presented symbolically or as a table) over a specified interval. Estimate the rate of change from a graph.*

Activity 1

Janice has read 7 books for her summer reading club. She plans to read 2 books each week for the rest of the summer. The table shows the total number of books that Janice will have read after different numbers of weeks have passed.

1 What number is added to the number of books in each row to get the number of books in the next row?

2 What does your answer to Problem 1 represent in Janice's situation? Describe the meaning of the constant change.

3 Graph the ordered pairs from the table. Describe how the points are related.

4 Look again at your answer to Problem 1. Explain how this number affects your graph.

Janice's Summer Reading	
Week	**Total Books Read**
0	7
1	9
2	11
3	13
4	15
5	17

Try This

At a particular college, a full-time student must take at least 12 credit hours per semester and may take up to 18 credit hours per semester. Tuition costs $200 per credit hour.

1. Copy and complete the table by using the information above.

2. What number is added to the cost in each row to get the cost in the next row?

3. What does your answer to Problem 2 above represent in the situation? Describe the meaning of the constant change.

4. Graph the ordered pairs from the table. Describe how the points are related.

5. Look again at your answer to Problem 2. Explain how this number affects your graph.

6. Compare your graphs from Activity 1 and Problem 4. How are they alike? How are they different?

7. Make a Conjecture Describe the graph of any situation that involves repeated addition of a positive number. Why do you think your description is correct?

Tuition Costs	
Credit Hours	**Cost ($)**
12	▨
13	▨
14	▨
15	▨
16	▨
17	▨
18	▨

Activity 2

An airplane is 3000 miles from its destination. The plane is traveling at a rate of 540 miles per hour. The table shows how far the plane is from its destination after various amounts of time have passed.

① What number is subtracted from the distance in each row to get the distance in the next row?

② What does your answer to Problem 1 represent in the situation? Describe the meaning of the constant change.

③ Graph the ordered pairs from the table. Describe how the points are related.

④ Look again at your answer to Problem 1. Explain how this number affects your graph.

Airplane's Distance	
Time (h)	Distance to Destination (mi)
0	3000
1	2460
2	1920
3	1380
4	840

Try This

A television game show begins with 20 contestants. Each week, the players vote 2 contestants off the show.

8. Copy and complete the table by using the information above.

9. What number is subtracted from the number of contestants in each row to get the number of contestants in the next row?

10. What does your answer to Problem 9 represent in the situation? Describe the meaning of the constant change.

11. Graph the ordered pairs from the table. Describe how the points are related.

12. Look again at your answer to Problem 9. Explain how this number affects your graph.

13. Compare your graphs from Activity 2 and Problem 11. How are they alike? How are they different?

14. Make a Conjecture Describe the graph of any situation that involves repeated subtraction of a positive number. Why do you think your description is correct?

15. Compare your two graphs from Activity 1 with your two graphs from Activity 2. How are they alike? How are they different?

16. Make a Conjecture How are graphs of situations involving repeated subtraction different from graphs of situations involving repeated addition? Explain your answer.

Game Show	
Week	Contestants Remaining
0	20
1	
2	
3	
4	
5	
6	

4-4 The Slope Formula

CC.9-12.F.IF.6 Calculate and interpret the average rate of change of a function (presented symbolically or as a table) over a specified interval. Estimate the rate of change from a graph.*

Objective
Find slope by using the slope formula.

Why learn this?
You can use the slope formula to find how quickly a quantity, such as the amount of water in a reservoir, is changing. (See Example 3.)

In a previous lesson, slope was described as the constant rate of change of a line. You saw how to find the slope of a line by using its graph.

There is also a formula you can use to find the slope of a line, which is usually represented by the letter m. To use this formula, you need the coordinates of two different points on the line.

Know it!
Note

Slope Formula

WORDS	FORMULA	EXAMPLE
The slope of a line is the ratio of the difference in y-values to the difference in x-values between any two different points on the line.	If (x_1, y_1) and (x_2, y_2) are any two different points on a line, the slope of the line is $m = \frac{y_2 - y_1}{x_2 - x_1}$.	If $(2, -3)$ and $(1, 4)$ are two points on a line, the slope of the line is $m = \frac{4 - (-3)}{1 - 2} = \frac{7}{-1} = -7$.

EXAMPLE 1 Finding Slope by Using the Slope Formula

Find the slope of the line that contains $(4, -2)$ and $(-1, 2)$.

$$m = \frac{y_2 - y_1}{x_2 - x_1}$$ *Use the slope formula.*

$$= \frac{2 - (-2)}{-1 - 4}$$ *Substitute $(4, -2)$ for (x_1, y_1) and $(-1, 2)$ for (x_2, y_2).*

$$= \frac{4}{-5}$$ *Simplify.*

$$= -\frac{4}{5}$$

The slope of the line that contains $(4, -2)$ and $(-1, 2)$ is $-\frac{4}{5}$.

CHECK IT OUT!

1a. Find the slope of the line that contains $(-2, -2)$ and $(7, -2)$.

1b. Find the slope of the line that contains $(5, -7)$ and $(6, -4)$.

1c. Find the slope of the line that contains $\left(\frac{3}{4}, \frac{7}{5}\right)$ and $\left(\frac{1}{4}, \frac{2}{5}\right)$.

Reading Math

The small numbers to the bottom right of the variables are called subscripts. Read x_1 as "x sub one" and y_2 as "y sub two."

Sometimes you are not given two points to use in the formula. You might have to choose two points from a graph or a table.

 Finding Slope from Graphs and Tables

Each graph or table shows a linear relationship. Find the slope.

A

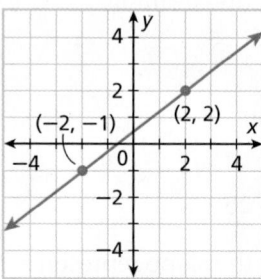

Let $(2, 2)$ be (x_1, y_1) and $(-2, -1)$ be (x_2, y_2).

$m = \dfrac{y_2 - y_1}{x_2 - x_1}$ *Use the slope formula.*

$= \dfrac{-1 - 2}{-2 - 2}$ *Substitute $(2, 2)$ for (x_1, y_1) and $(-2, -1)$ for (x_2, y_2).*

$= \dfrac{-3}{-4}$ *Simplify.*

$= \dfrac{3}{4}$

B

x	2	2	2	2
y	0	1	3	5

Step 1 Choose any two points from the table. Let $(2, 0)$ be (x_1, y_1) and $(2, 3)$ be (x_2, y_2).

Step 2 Use the slope formula.

$m = \dfrac{y_2 - y_1}{x_2 - x_1}$ *Use the slope formula.*

$= \dfrac{3 - 0}{2 - 2}$ *Substitute $(2, 0)$ for (x_1, y_1) and $(2, 3)$ for (x_2, y_2).*

$= \dfrac{3}{0}$ *Simplify.*

The slope is undefined.

 Each graph or table shows a linear relationship. Find the slope.

2a.

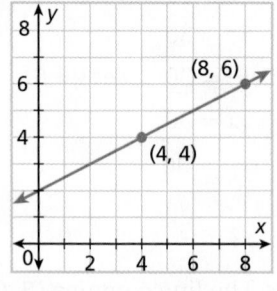

2b.

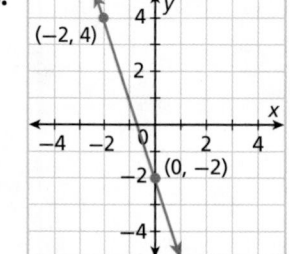

2c.

x	0	2	5	6
y	1	5	11	13

2d.

x	-2	0	2	4
y	3	0	-3	-6

Remember that slope is a rate of change. In real-world problems, finding the slope can give you information about how a quantity is changing.

EXAMPLE 3 · *Environmental Science Application*

The graph shows how much water is in a reservoir at different times. Find the slope of the line. Then tell what the slope represents.

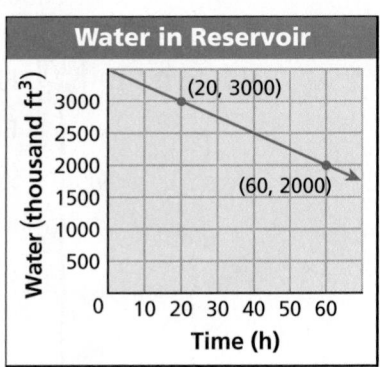

Step 1 Use the slope formula.

$$m = \frac{y_2 - y_1}{x_2 - x_1}$$

$$= \frac{2000 - 3000}{60 - 20}$$

$$= \frac{-1000}{40} = -25$$

Step 2 Tell what the slope represents.

In this situation, y represents **volume of water** and x represents **time**.

So slope represents $\dfrac{\text{change in volume}}{\text{change in time}}$ in units of $\dfrac{\text{thousands of cubic feet}}{\text{hours}}$.

A slope of -25 means the amount of water in the reservoir is decreasing (negative change) at a rate of 25 thousand cubic feet each hour.

 **3.** The graph shows the height of a plant over a period of days. Find the slope of the line. Then tell what the slope represents.

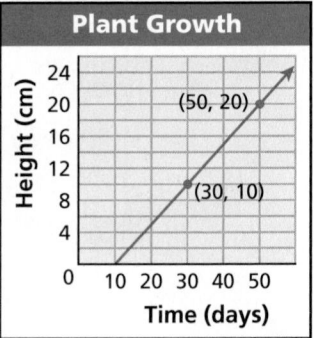

If you know the equation that describes a line, you can find its slope by using any two ordered-pair solutions. It is often easiest to use the ordered pairs that contain the intercepts.

EXAMPLE 4 · **Finding Slope from an Equation**

Find the slope of the line described by $6x - 5y = 30$.

Step 1 Find the x-intercept.

$6x - 5y = 30$

$6x - 5(0) = 30$ *Let y = 0.*

$6x = 30$

$\dfrac{6x}{6} = \dfrac{30}{6}$

$x = 5$

Step 2 Find the y-intercept.

$6x - 5y = 30$

$6(0) - 5y = 30$ *Let x = 0.*

$-5y = 30$

$\dfrac{-5y}{-5} = \dfrac{30}{-5}$

$y = -6$

Step 3 The line contains $(5, 0)$ and $(0, -6)$. Use the slope formula.

$$m = \frac{y_2 - y_1}{x_2 - x_1} = \frac{-6 - 0}{0 - 5} = \frac{-6}{-5} = \frac{6}{5}$$

 **4.** Find the slope of the line described by $2x + 3y = 12$.

THINK AND DISCUSS

1. The slope of a line is the difference of the ___?___ divided by the difference of the ___?___ for any two points on the line.

2. Two points lie on a line. When you substitute their coordinates into the slope formula, the value of the denominator is 0. Describe this line.

3. **GET ORGANIZED** Copy and complete the graphic organizer. In each box, describe how to find slope using the given method.

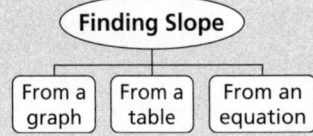

4-4 Exercises

Learn It Online
Homework Help Online
Parent Resources Online

GUIDED PRACTICE

SEE EXAMPLE **1**

Find the slope of the line that contains each pair of points.

1. $(3, 6)$ and $(6, 9)$ **2.** $(2, 7)$ and $(4, 4)$ **3.** $(-1, -5)$ and $(-9, -1)$

SEE EXAMPLE **2**

Each graph or table shows a linear relationship. Find the slope.

4.

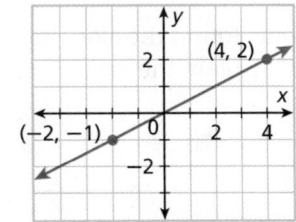

5.

x	y
0	25
2	45
4	65
6	85

SEE EXAMPLE **3**

Find the slope of each line. Then tell what the slope represents.

6.

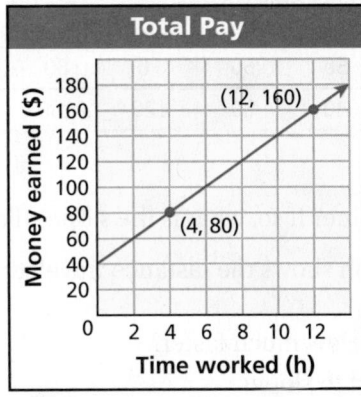

7.

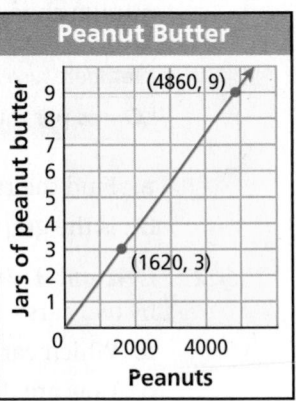

SEE EXAMPLE **4**

Find the slope of the line described by each equation.

8. $8x + 2y = 96$ **9.** $5x = 90 - 9y$ **10.** $5y = 160 + 9x$

4-4 The Slope Formula   **257**

PRACTICE AND PROBLEM SOLVING

Find the slope of the line that contains each pair of points.

Independent Practice

For Exercises	See Example
11–13	1
14–15	2
16–17	3
18–20	4

Extra Practice

See Extra Practice for more Skills Practice and Applications Practice exercises.

11. (2, 5) and (3, 1)   **12.** (−9, −5) and (6, −5)   **13.** (3, 4) and (3, −1)

Each graph or table shows a linear relationship. Find the slope.

14.

x	y
1	18.5
2	22
3	25.5
4	29

15.

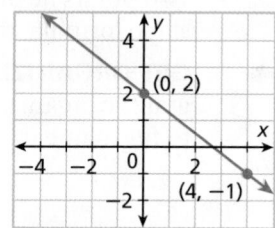

Find the slope of each line. Then tell what the slope represents.

16.

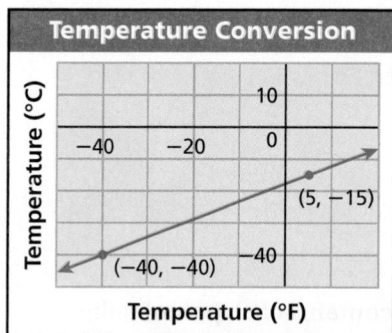

17.

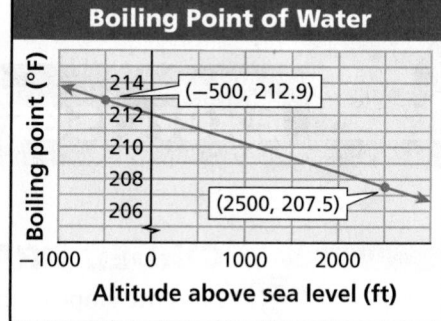

Find the slope of the line described by each equation.

18. $7x + 13y = 91$ **19.** $5y = 130 - 13x$ **20.** $7 - 3y = 9x$

21. ///ERROR ANALYSIS/// Two students found the slope of the line that contains $(-6, 3)$ and $(2, -1)$. Who is incorrect? Explain the error.

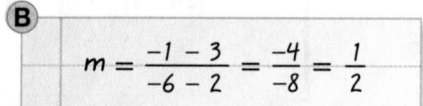

A
$$m = \frac{-1 - 3}{2 - (-6)} = \frac{-4}{8} = -\frac{1}{2}$$

B
$$m = \frac{-1 - 3}{-6 - 2} = \frac{-4}{-8} = \frac{1}{2}$$

22. Environmental Science The table shows how the number of cricket chirps per minute changes with the air temperature.

Temperature (°F)	40	50	60	70	80	90
Chirps per minute	0	40	80	120	160	200

  a. Find the rates of change.

  b. Is the graph of the data a line? If so, what is the slope? If not, explain why not.

23. Critical Thinking The graph shows the distance traveled by two cars.

  a. Which car is going faster? How much faster?

  b. How are the speeds related to slope?

  c. At what rate is the distance between the cars changing?

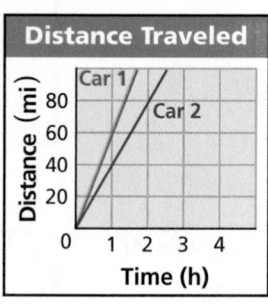

24. Write About It You are given the coordinates of two points on a line. Describe two different ways to find the slope of that line.

25. a. One way to estimate your maximum heart rate is to subtract your age from 220. Write a function to describe the relationship between maximum heart rate y and age x.

b. The graph of this function is a line. Find its slope. Then tell what the slope represents.

TEST PREP

26. The equation $2y + 3x = -6$ describes a line with what slope?

　ⓐ $\dfrac{3}{2}$ 　　　　ⓑ 0 　　　　ⓒ $\dfrac{1}{2}$ 　　　　ⓓ $-\dfrac{3}{2}$

27. A line with slope $-\dfrac{1}{3}$ could pass through which of the following pairs of points?

　Ⓕ $\left(0, -\dfrac{1}{3}\right)$ and $(1, 1)$ 　　　　Ⓗ $(0, 0)$ and $\left(-\dfrac{1}{3}, -\dfrac{1}{3}\right)$

　Ⓖ $(-6, 5)$ and $(-3, 4)$ 　　　　Ⓙ $(5, -6)$ and $(4, 3)$

28. Gridded Response Find the slope of the line that contains $(-1, 2)$ and $(5, 5)$.

CHALLENGE AND EXTEND

Find the slope of the line that contains each pair of points.

29. $(a, 0)$ and $(0, b)$ 　　　　**30.** $(2x, y)$ and $(x, 3y)$ 　　　　**31.** (x, y) and $(x + 2, 3 - y)$

Find the value of x so that the points lie on a line with the given slope.

32. $(x, 2)$ and $(-5, 8)$, $m = -1$ 　　　　**33.** $(4, x)$ and $(6, 3x)$, $m = \dfrac{1}{2}$

34. $(1, -3)$ and $(3, x)$, $m = -1$ 　　　　**35.** $(-10, -4)$ and (x, x), $m = \dfrac{1}{7}$

36. A line contains the point $(1, 2)$ and has a slope of $\dfrac{1}{2}$. Use the slope formula to find another point on this line.

37. The points $(-2, 4)$, $(0, 2)$, and $(3, x - 1)$ all lie on the same line. What is the value of x? (*Hint:* Remember that the slope of a line is constant for any two points on the line.)

4-5 Direct Variation

CC.9-12.A.CED.2 Create equations in two or more variables to represent relationships between quantities; graph equations on coordinate axes with labels and scales.* *Also* **CC.9-12.F.LE.1*, CC.9-12.F.LE.2*, CC.9-12.A.CED.3*, CC.9-12.F.IF.5*, CC.9-12.F.IF.7***

Objective
Identify, write, and graph direct variation.

Vocabulary
direct variation
constant of variation

Who uses this?
Chefs can use direct variation to determine ingredients needed for a certain number of servings.

A recipe for paella calls for 1 cup of rice to make 5 servings. In other words, a chef needs 1 cup of rice for every 5 servings.

Paella is a rice dish that originated in Valencia, Spain.

Rice (c) *x*	1	2	3	4
Servings *y*	5	10	15	20

The equation $y = 5x$ describes this relationship. In this relationship, the number of servings *varies directly* with the number of cups of rice.

A **direct variation** is a special type of linear relationship that can be written in the form $y = kx$, where k is a nonzero constant called the **constant of variation**.

EXAMPLE **1** **Identifying Direct Variations from Equations**

Tell whether each equation represents a direct variation. If so, identify the constant of variation.

A $y = 4x$

This equation represents a direct variation because it is in the form $y = kx$. The constant of variation is 4.

B $-3x + 5y = 0$

$$-3x + 5y = 0 \qquad \text{Solve the equation for y.}$$
$$\underline{+\,3x +\,3x} \qquad \text{Since } -3x \text{ is added to 5y, add 3x to both sides.}$$
$$5y = 3x$$
$$\frac{5y}{5} = \frac{3x}{5} \qquad \text{Since y is multiplied by 5, divide both sides by 5.}$$
$$y = \frac{3}{5}x$$

This equation represents a direct variation because it can be written in the form $y = kx$. The constant of variation is $\frac{3}{5}$.

C $2x + y = 10$

$$2x + y = 10 \qquad \text{Solve the equation for y.}$$
$$\underline{-\,2x -\,2x} \qquad \text{Since 2x is added to y, subtract 2x from both sides.}$$
$$y = -2x + 10$$

This equation does not represent a direct variation because it cannot be written in the form $y = kx$.

CHECK IT OUT!

Tell whether each equation represents a direct variation. If so, identify the constant of variation.

1a. $3y = 4x + 1$ **1b.** $3x = -4y$ **1c.** $y + 3x = 0$

What happens if you solve $y = kx$ for k?

$$y = kx$$

$$\frac{y}{x} = \frac{kx}{x} \qquad \textit{Divide both sides by x (x ≠ 0).}$$

$$\frac{y}{x} = k$$

So, in a direct variation, the ratio $\frac{y}{x}$ is equal to the constant of variation. Another way to identify a direct variation is to check whether $\frac{y}{x}$ is the same for each ordered pair (except where $x = 0$).

EXAMPLE 2 Identifying Direct Variations from Ordered Pairs

Tell whether each relationship is a direct variation. Explain.

x	1	3	5
y	6	18	30

Method 1 Write an equation.

$$y = 6x \qquad \textit{Each y-value is 6 times the corresponding x-value.}$$

This is a direct variation because it can be written as $y = kx$, where $k = 6$.

Method 2 Find $\frac{y}{x}$ for each ordered pair.

$$\frac{6}{1} = 6 \qquad\qquad \frac{18}{3} = 6 \qquad\qquad \frac{30}{5} = 6$$

This is a direct variation because $\frac{y}{x}$ is the same for each ordered pair.

x	2	4	8
y	−2	0	4

Method 1 Write an equation.

$$y = x - 4 \qquad \textit{Each y-value is 4 less than the corresponding x-value.}$$

This is not a direct variation because it cannot be written as $y = kx$.

Method 2 Find $\frac{y}{x}$ for each ordered pair.

$$\frac{-2}{2} = -1 \qquad\qquad \frac{0}{4} = 0 \qquad\qquad \frac{4}{8} = \frac{1}{2}$$

This is not a direct variation because $\frac{y}{x}$ is not the same for all ordered pairs.

 Tell whether each relationship is a direct variation. Explain.

2a.

x	y
−3	0
1	3
3	6

2b.

x	y
2.5	−10
5	−20
7.5	−30

2c.

x	y
−2	5
1	3
4	1

If you know one ordered pair that satisfies a direct variation, you can write the equation. You can also find other ordered pairs that satisfy the direct variation.

EXAMPLE 3 **Writing and Solving Direct Variation Equations**

The value of y varies directly with x, and $y = 6$ when $x = 12$.
Find y when $x = 27$.

Method 1 Find the value of k and then write the equation.

$y = kx$ *Write the equation for a direct variation.*

$6 = k(12)$ *Substitute 6 for y and 12 for x. Solve for k.*

$\dfrac{1}{2} = k$ *Since k is multiplied by 12, divide both sides by 12.*

The equation is $y = \dfrac{1}{2}x$. When $x = 27$, $y = \dfrac{1}{2}(27) = 13.5$.

Method 2 Use a proportion.

$\dfrac{6}{12} \diagdown \dfrac{y}{27}$ *In a direct variation, $\dfrac{y}{x}$ is the same for all values of x and y.*

$12y = 162$ *Use cross products.*

$y = 13.5$ *Since y is multiplied by 12, divide both sides by 12.*

CHECK IT OUT!   **3.** The value of y varies directly with x, and $y = 4.5$ when $x = 0.5$.
Find y when $x = 10$.

EXAMPLE 4 **Graphing Direct Variations**

The three-toed sloth is an extremely slow animal. On the ground, it travels at a speed of about 6 feet per minute. Write a direct variation equation for the distance y a sloth will travel in x minutes. Then graph.

Step 1 Write a direct variation equation.

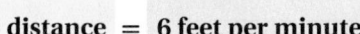

distance	=	6 feet per minute	times	number of minutes
y	=	6	$\cdot$	x

Step 2 Choose values of x and generate ordered pairs.

Step 3 Graph the points and connect.

x	$y = 6x$	(x, y)
0	$y = 6(0) = 0$	$(0, 0)$
1	$y = 6(1) = 6$	$(1, 6)$
2	$y = 6(2) = 12$	$(2, 12)$

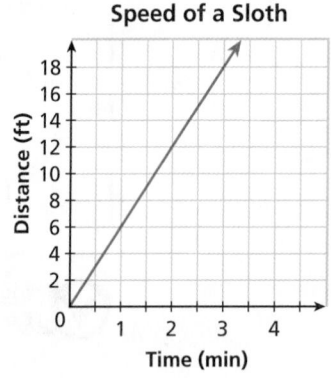

CHECK IT OUT!   **4.** The perimeter y of a square varies directly with its side length x.
Write a direct variation equation for this relationship. Then graph.

Look at the graph in Example 4. It passes through $(0, 0)$ and has a slope of 6.
The graph of any direct variation $y = kx$
  • is a line through $(0, 0)$.   • has a slope of k.

THINK AND DISCUSS

1. How do you know that a direct variation is linear?

2. How does the graph of a direct variation differ from the graphs of other types of linear relationships?

3. **GET ORGANIZED** Copy and complete the graphic organizer. In each box, describe how you can use the given information to identify a direct variation.

Recognizing a Direct Variation		
From an Equation	From Ordered Pairs	From a Graph

4-5 Exercises

Learn It Online
Homework Help Online
Parent Resources Online

GUIDED PRACTICE

1. **Vocabulary** If x varies directly with y, then the relationship between the two variables is said to be a ___?___. (*direct variation* or *constant of variation*)

SEE EXAMPLE 1 — Tell whether each equation represents a direct variation. If so, identify the constant of variation.

2. $y = 4x + 9$ 3. $2y = -8x$ 4. $x + y = 0$

SEE EXAMPLE 2 — Tell whether each relationship is a direct variation. Explain.

5.
x	10	5	2
y	12	7	4

6.
x	3	−1	−4
y	−6	2	8

SEE EXAMPLE 3

7. The value of y varies directly with x, and $y = -3$ when $x = 1$. Find y when $x = -6$.

8. The value of y varies directly with x, and $y = 6$ when $x = 18$. Find y when $x = 12$.

SEE EXAMPLE 4

9. **Wages** Cameron earns $7 per hour at her after-school job. The total amount of her paycheck varies directly with the amount of time she works. Write a direct variation equation for the amount of money y that she earns for working x hours. Then graph.

PRACTICE AND PROBLEM SOLVING

Tell whether each equation represents a direct variation. If so, identify the constant of variation.

10. $y = \frac{1}{6}x$ 11. $4y = x$ 12. $x = 2y - 12$

Tell whether each relationship is a direct variation. Explain.

13.
x	6	9	17
y	13.2	19.8	37.4

14.
x	−6	3	12
y	4	−2	−8

Independent Practice

For Exercises	See Example
10–12	1
13–14	2
15–16	3
17	4

Extra Practice

See Extra Practice for more Skills Practice and Applications Practice exercises.

15. The value of y varies directly with x, and $y = 8$ when $x = -32$. Find y when $x = 64$.

16. The value of y varies directly with x, and $y = \frac{1}{2}$ when $x = 3$. Find y when $x = 1$.

17. While on his way to school, Norman saw that the cost of gasoline was $2.50 per gallon. Write a direct variation equation to describe the cost y of x gallons of gas. Then graph.

Tell whether each relationship is a direct variation. Explain your answer.

18. The equation $-15x + 4y = 0$ relates the length of a videotape in inches x to its approximate playing time in seconds y.

19. The equation $y - 2.00x = 2.50$ relates the cost y of a taxicab ride to distance x of the cab ride in miles.

Each ordered pair is a solution of a direct variation. Write the equation of direct variation. Then graph your equation and show that the slope of the line is equal to the constant of variation.

20. $(2, 10)$ **21.** $(-3, 9)$ **22.** $(8, 2)$ **23.** $(1.5, 6)$

24. $(7, 21)$ **25.** $(1, 2)$ **26.** $(2, -16)$ **27.** $\left(\frac{1}{7}, 1\right)$

28. $(-2, 9)$ **29.** $(9, -2)$ **30.** $(4, 6)$ **31.** $(3, 4)$

32. $(5, 1)$ **33.** $(1, -6)$ **34.** $\left(-1, \frac{1}{2}\right)$ **35.** $(7, 2)$

Astronomy

36. **Astronomy** Weight varies directly with gravity. A Mars lander weighed 767 pounds on Earth but only 291 pounds on Mars. Its accompanying Mars rover weighed 155 pounds on Mars. How much did it weigh on Earth? Round your answer to the nearest pound.

37. **Environment** Mischa bought an energy-efficient washing machine. She will save about 15 gallons of water per wash load.

a. Write an equation of direct variation to describe how many gallons of water y Mischa saves for x loads of laundry she washes.

b. Graph your direct variation from part **a**. Is every point on the graph a solution in this situation? Why or why not?

The Mars rover *Spirit* landed on Mars in January 2004 and immediately began sending photos of the planet's surface back to Earth.

c. If Mischa does 2 loads of laundry per week, how many gallons of water will she have saved at the end of a year?

38. **Critical Thinking** If you double an x-value in a direct variation, will the corresponding y-value double? Explain.

39. **Write About It** In a direct variation $y = kx$, k is sometimes called the "constant of proportionality." How are proportions related to direct variations?

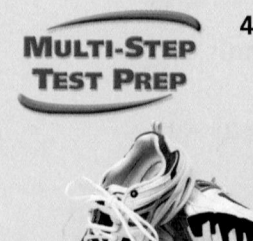

MULTI-STEP TEST PREP

40. Rhea exercised on a treadmill at the gym. When she was finished, the display showed that she had walked at an average speed of 3 miles per hour.

a. Write an equation that gives the number of miles y that Rhea would cover in x hours if she walked at this speed.

b. Explain why this is a direct variation and find the value of k. What does this value represent in Rhea's situation?

41. Which equation does NOT represent a direct variation?

(A) $y = \frac{1}{3}x$ (B) $y = -2x$ (C) $y = 4x + 1$ (D) $6x - y = 0$

42. Identify which set of data represents a direct variation.

(F)

x	1	2	3
y	1	2	3

(H)

x	1	2	3
y	3	5	7

(G)

x	1	2	3
y	0	1	2

(J)

x	1	2	3
y	3	4	5

43. Two yards of fabric cost $13, and 5 yards of fabric cost $32.50. Which equation relates the cost of the fabric c to its length ℓ?

(A) $c = 2.6\ell$ (B) $c = 6.5\ell$ (C) $c = 13\ell$ (D) $c = 32.5\ell$

44. Gridded Response A car is traveling at a constant speed. After 3 hours, the car has traveled 180 miles. If the car continues to travel at the same constant speed, how many hours will it take to travel a total of 270 miles?

CHALLENGE AND EXTEND

45. Transportation The function $y = 20x$ gives the number of miles y that a sport-utility vehicle (SUV) can travel on x gallons of gas. The function $y = 60x$ gives the number of miles y that a hybrid car can travel on x gallons of gas.

    a. If you drive 120 miles, how much gas will you save by driving the hybrid instead of the SUV?

    b. Graph both functions on the same coordinate plane. Will the lines ever meet other than at the origin? Explain.

    c. What if...? Shannon drives 15,000 miles in one year. How many gallons of gas will she use if she drives the SUV? the hybrid?

46. Suppose the equation $ax + by = c$, where a, b, and c are real numbers, describes a direct variation. What do you know about the value of c?

MULTI-STEP TEST PREP

Make sense of problems and persevere in solving them.

Characteristics of Linear Functions

Heart Health People who exercise need to be aware of their maximum heart rate.

1. One way to estimate your maximum heart rate m is to subtract 85% of your age in years from 217. Create a table of values that shows the maximum heart rates for people ages 13 to 18. Then write an equation to describe the data in the table.

2. Use your table from Problem 1 to graph the relationship between age and maximum heart rate. What are the intercepts? What is the slope?

3. What do the intercepts represent in this situation?

4. What does the slope represent? Explain why the slope is negative.

5. Another formula for estimating maximum heart rate is $m = 206.3 - 0.711a$, where a represents age in years. Describe how this equation is different from your equation in Problem 1. Include slope and intercepts in your description.

6. Which equation gives a higher maximum heart rate for people ages 75 and younger?

7. To be exercising in your *aerobic training zone* means that your heart rate is 70% to 80% of your maximum heart rate. Write two equations that someone could use to estimate the range of heart rates that are within his or her aerobic training zone. Use your equation for maximum heart rate from Problem 1.

READY TO GO ON?

4

SECTION 4A

Quiz for Lessons 4-1 Through 4-5

4-1 Identifying Linear Functions

Tell whether the given ordered pairs satisfy a linear function. Explain.

1.

x	−2	−1	0	1	2
y	1	0	1	4	9

2. $\{(-3, 8), (-2, 6), (-1, 4), (0, 2), (1, 0)\}$

4-2 Using Intercepts

Use intercepts to graph the line described by each equation.

3. $2x - 4y = 16$ **4.** $-3y + 6x = -18$ **5.** $y = -3x + 3$

4-3 Rate of Change and Slope

6. The chart gives the amount of water in a rain gauge in inches at various times. Graph the data and show the rates of change.

Time (h)	1	2	3	4	5
Rain (in.)	0.2	0.4	0.7	0.8	1.0

4-4 The Slope Formula

Find the slope of each line. Then tell what the slope represents.

7.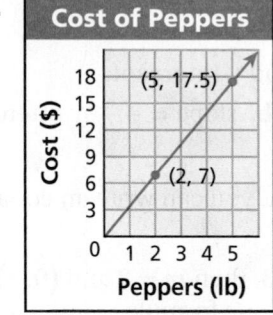

8.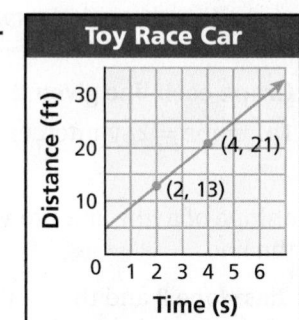

9.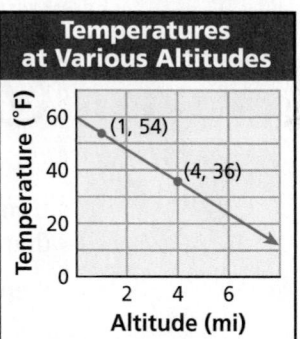

4-5 Direct Variation

Tell whether each relationship is a direct variation. If so, identify the constant of variation.

10.

x	1	4	8	12
y	3	6	10	14

11.

x	−6	−2	0	3
y	−3	−1	0	1.5

Ready to Go On?   **267**

COMMON CORE

4-6 Slope-Intercept Form

CC.9-12.A.CED.2 Create equations in two or more variables to represent relationships between quantities...* *Also* **CC.9-12.A.CED.3*, CC.9-12.F.IF.7*, CC.9-12.F.IF.6*, CC.9-12.F.BF.1*, CC.9-12.F.LE.2***

Objectives
Write a linear equation in slope-intercept form.

Graph a line using slope-intercept form.

Who uses this?
Consumers can use slope-intercept form to model and calculate costs, such as the cost of renting a moving van. (See Example 4.)

You have seen that you can graph a line if you know two points on the line. Another way is to use the slope of the line and the point that contains the *y*-intercept.

EXAMPLE 1 **Graphing by Using Slope and *y*-intercept**

Graph the line with slope −2 and *y*-intercept 4.

Step 1 The *y*-intercept is 4, so the line contains (0, 4). Plot (0, 4).

Step 2 Slope $= \dfrac{\text{change in } y}{\text{change in } x} = \dfrac{-2}{1}$

Count 2 units down and 1 unit right from (0, 4) and plot another point.

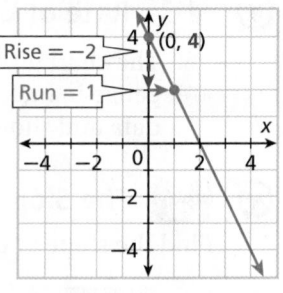

Step 3 Draw the line through the two points.

> **Writing Math**
>
> Any integer can be written as a fraction with 1 in the denominator.
>
> $-2 = \dfrac{-2}{1}$

 **CHECK IT OUT!** **Graph each line given the slope and *y*-intercept.**
1a. slope = 2, *y*-intercept = −3 **1b.** slope $= -\dfrac{2}{3}$, *y*-intercept = 1

If you know the slope of a line and the *y*-intercept, you can write an equation that describes the line.

Step 1 If a line has slope 2 and the *y*-intercept is 3, then $m = 2$ and $(0, 3)$ is on the line. Substitute these values into the slope formula.

Slope formula → $m = \dfrac{y_2 - y_1}{x_2 - x_1}$ $2 = \dfrac{y - 3}{x - 0}$ ←Since you don't know (x_2, y_2), use (x, y).

Step 2 Solve for *y*: $2 = \dfrac{y - 3}{x - 0}$

$2 = \dfrac{y - 3}{x}$ *Simplify the denominator.*

$2 \cdot x = \left(\dfrac{y - 3}{x}\right) \cdot x$ *Multiply both sides by x.*

$2x = y - 3$

$\underline{+3 \qquad +3}$ *Add 3 to both sides.*

$2x + 3 = y$, or $y = 2x + 3$

 **Know it! Note**

Slope-Intercept Form of a Linear Equation

> If a line has **slope** m and the **y-intercept** is b, then the line is described by the equation $y = mx + b$.

Any linear equation can be written in slope-intercept form by solving for y and simplifying. In this form, you can immediately see the slope and y-intercept. Also, you can quickly graph a line when the equation is written in slope-intercept form.

EXAMPLE 2 **Writing Linear Equations in Slope-Intercept Form**

Write the equation that describes each line in slope-intercept form.

A slope $= \dfrac{1}{3}$, y-intercept $= 6$

$y = mx + b$ *Substitute the given values for m and b.*

$y = \dfrac{1}{3}x + 6$ *Simplify if necessary.*

B slope $= 0$, y-intercept $= -5$

$y = mx + b$

$y = 0x + (-5)$

$y = -5$

C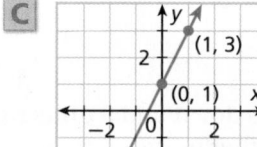

Step 1 Find the y-intercept. The graph crosses the y-axis at $(0, 1)$, so $b = 1$.

Step 2 Find the slope. The line contains the points $(0, 1)$ and $(1, 3)$.

$m = \dfrac{y_2 - y_1}{x_2 - x_1}$ *Use the slope formula.*

$m = \dfrac{3 - 1}{1 - 0} = \dfrac{2}{1} = 2$ *Substitute $(0, 1)$ for (x_1, y_1) and $(1, 3)$ for (x_2, y_2).*

Step 3 Write the equation.

$y = mx + b$ *Write the slope-intercept form.*

$y = 2x + 1$ *Substitute 2 for m and 1 for b.*

D slope $= 4$, $(2, 5)$ is on the line

Step 1 Find the y-intercept.

$y = mx + b$ *Write the slope-intercept form.*

$5 = 4(2) + b$ *Substitute 4 for m, 2 for x, and 5 for y.*

$5 = 8 + b$ *Solve for b. Since 8 is added to b, subtract 8 from both sides to undo the addition.*

$\underline{-8 -8}$

$-3 = b$

Step 2 Write the equation.

$y = mx + b$ *Write the slope-intercept form.*

$y = 4x + (-3)$ *Substitute 4 for m and −3 for b.*

$y = 4x - 3$

 **CHECK IT OUT!** Write the equation that describes each line in slope-intercept form.

2a. slope $= -12$, y-intercept $= -\dfrac{1}{2}$

2b. slope $= 1$, y-intercept $= 0$

2c. slope $= 8$, $(-3, 1)$ is on the line.

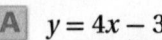 **E X A M P L E 3** **Using Slope-Intercept Form to Graph**

Write each equation in slope-intercept form. Then graph the line described by the equation.

A $y = 4x - 3$

$y = 4x - 3$ is in the form $y = mx + b$.

slope: $m = 4 = \dfrac{4}{1}$

y-intercept: $b = -3$

Step 1 Plot $(0, -3)$.

Step 2 Count **4 units up** and **1 unit right** and plot another point.

Step 3 Draw the line connecting the two points.

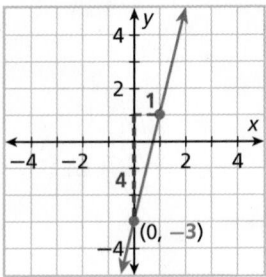

B $y = -\dfrac{2}{3}x + 2$

$y = -\dfrac{2}{3}x + 2$ is in the form $y = mx + b$.

slope: $m = -\dfrac{2}{3} = \dfrac{-2}{3}$

y-intercept: $b = 2$

Step 1 Plot $(0, 2)$

Step 2 Count **2 units down** and **3 units right** and plot another point.

Step 3 Draw the line connecting the two points.

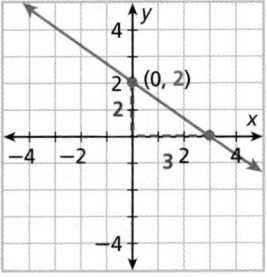

C $3x + 2y = 8$

Step 1 Write the equation in slope-intercept form by solving for y.

$$3x + 2y = 8$$
$$\underline{-3x \qquad\quad -3x} \qquad\qquad \text{Subtract } 3x \text{ from both sides.}$$
$$2y = 8 - 3x$$
$$\dfrac{2y}{2} = \dfrac{8 - 3x}{2} \qquad \text{\textit{Since y is multiplied by 2, divide both sides by 2.}}$$
$$y = 4 - \dfrac{3}{2}x \qquad\qquad \dfrac{3x}{2} = \dfrac{3}{2}x$$
$$y = -\dfrac{3}{2}x + 4 \qquad \text{\textit{Write the equation in the form } } y = mx + b.$$

Step 2 Graph the line.

$y = -\dfrac{3}{2}x + 4$ is in the form $y = mx + b$.

slope: $m = -\dfrac{3}{2} = \dfrac{-3}{2}$

y-intercept: $b = 4$

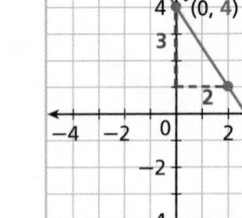

• Plot $(0, 4)$.

• Then count **3 units down** and **2 units right** and plot another point.

• Draw the line connecting the two points.

 **CHECK IT OUT!** Write each equation in slope-intercept form. Then graph the line described by the equation.

3a. $y = \dfrac{2}{3}x$ **3b.** $6x + 2y = 10$ **3c.** $y = -4$

> **Helpful Hint**
>
> To divide $(8 - 3x)$ by 2, you can multiply by $\dfrac{1}{2}$ and use the Distributive Property.
>
> $$\dfrac{8 - 3x}{2} = \dfrac{1}{2}(8 - 3x)$$
> $$= \dfrac{1}{2}(8) + \dfrac{1}{2}(-3x)$$
> $$= 4 - \dfrac{3}{2}x$$

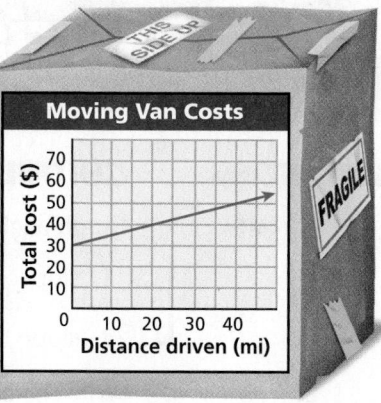

EXAMPLE 4 *Consumer Application*

To rent a van, a moving company charges $30.00 plus $0.50 per mile. The cost as a function of the number of miles driven is shown in the graph.

Moving Van Costs

a. Write an equation that represents the cost as a function of the number of miles.

Cost	is	$0.50 per mile	times	miles	plus	$30.00
y	=	0.5	•	x	+	30

An equation is $y = 0.5x + 30$.

b. Identify the slope and y-intercept and describe their meanings.

The y-intercept is 30. This is the cost for 0 miles, or the initial fee of $30.00.

The slope is 0.5. This is the rate of change of the cost: $0.50 per mile.

c. Find the cost of the van for 150 miles.

$y = 0.5x + 30$

$\quad = 0.5(150) + 30 = 105$ *Substitute 150 for x in the equation.*

The cost of the van for 150 miles is $105.

4. A caterer charges a $200 fee plus $18 per person served. The cost as a function of the number of guests is shown in the graph.

a. Write an equation that represents the cost as a function of the number of guests.

b. Identify the slope and y-intercept and describe their meanings.

c. Find the cost of catering an event for 200 guests.

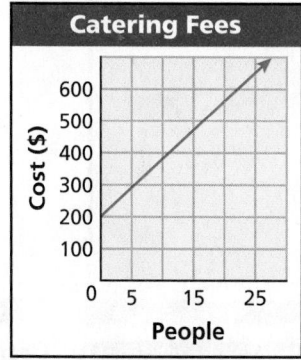

MATHEMATICAL PRACTICES

THINK AND DISCUSS

1. If a linear function has a y-intercept of b, at what point does its graph cross the y-axis?

2. Where does the line described by $y = 4.395x - 23.75$ cross the y-axis?

3. GET ORGANIZED Copy and complete the graphic organizer.

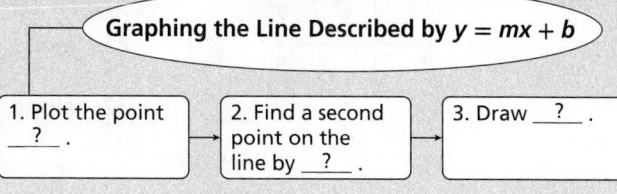

Graphing the Line Described by $y = mx + b$

| 1. Plot the point __?__ . | 2. Find a second point on the line by __?__ . | 3. Draw __?__ . |

GUIDED PRACTICE

SEE EXAMPLE 1 | **Graph each line given the slope and y-intercept.**

1. slope $= \frac{1}{3}$, y-intercept $= -3$ **2.** slope $= 0.5$, y-intercept $= 3.5$

3. slope $= 5$, y-intercept $= -1$ **4.** slope $= -2$, y-intercept $= 2$

SEE EXAMPLE 2 | **Write the equation that describes each line in slope-intercept form.**

5. 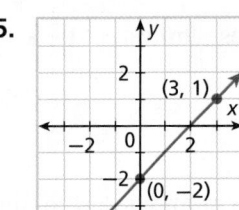   **6.** slope $= 8$, y-intercept $= 2$

7. slope $= 0$, y-intercept $= -3$

8. slope $= 5$, $(2, 7)$ is on the line.

9. slope $= -2$, $(1, -3)$ is on the line.

SEE EXAMPLE 3 | **Write each equation in slope-intercept form. Then graph the line described by the equation.**

10. $y = \frac{2}{5}x - 6$ **11.** $3x - y = 1$ **12.** $2x + y = 4$

SEE EXAMPLE 4 | **13.** Helen is in a bicycle race. She has already biked 10 miles and is now biking at a rate of 18 miles per hour. Her distance as a function of time is shown in the graph.

   a. Write an equation that represents the distance Helen has biked as a function of time.

   b. Identify the slope and y-intercept and describe their meanings.

   c. How far will Helen have biked after 2 hours?

Distance Biked

(graph: Distance (mi) vs. Time (h))

PRACTICE AND PROBLEM SOLVING

Independent Practice

For Exercises	See Example
14–17	1
19–22	2
23–25	3
26	4

Graph each line given the slope and y-intercept.

14. slope $= \frac{1}{4}$, y-intercept $= 7$ **15.** slope $= -6$, y-intercept $= -3$

16. slope $= 1$, y-intercept $= -4$ **17.** slope $= -\frac{4}{5}$, y-intercept $= 6$

Write the equation that describes each line in slope-intercept form.

Extra Practice

See Extra Practice for more Skills Practice and Applications Practice exercises.

18. 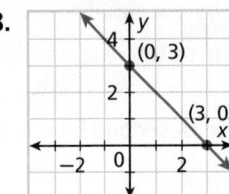   **19.** slope $= 5$, y-intercept $= -9$

20. slope $= -\frac{2}{3}$, y-intercept $= 2$

21. slope $= -\frac{1}{2}$, $(6, 4)$ is on the line.

22. slope $= 0$, $(6, -8)$ is on the line.

Write each equation in slope-intercept form. Then graph the line described by the equation.

23. $-\frac{1}{2}x + y = 4$

24. $\frac{2}{3}x + y = 2$

25. $2x + y = 8$

26. Fitness Pauline's health club has an enrollment fee of $175 and costs $35 per month. Total cost as a function of number of membership months is shown in the graph.

    a. Write an equation that represents the total cost as a function of months.

    b. Identify the slope and y-intercept and describe their meanings.

    c. Find the cost of one year of membership.

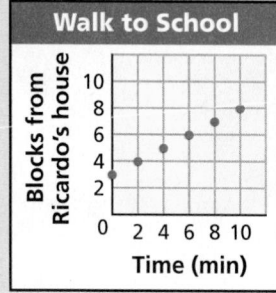

Health Club Membership Costs

27. A company rents video games. The table shows the linear relationship between the number of games a customer can rent at one time and the monthly cost of the service.

    a. Graph the relationship.

    b. Write an equation that represents the monthly cost as a function of games rented at one time.

Games Rented at One Time	1	2	3
Monthly Cost ($)	14	18	22

Critical Thinking Tell whether each situation is possible or impossible. If possible, draw a sketch of the graphs. If impossible, explain.

28. Two different lines have the same slope.

29. Two different linear functions have the same y-intercept.

30. Two intersecting lines have the same slope.

31. A linear function does not have a y-intercept.

Match each equation with its corresponding graph.

32.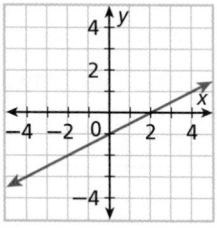

33.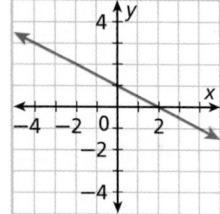

34.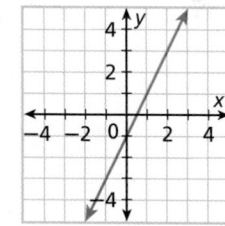

  A. $y = 2x - 1$

  B. $y = \frac{1}{2}x - 1$

  C. $y = -\frac{1}{2}x + 1$

 35. Write About It Write an equation that describes a vertical line. Can you write this equation in slope-intercept form? Why or why not?

MULTI-STEP TEST PREP

36. a. Ricardo and Sam walk from Sam's house to school. Sam lives 3 blocks from Ricardo's house. The graph shows their distance from Ricardo's house as they walk to school. Create a table of these values.

    b. Find an equation for the distance as a function of time.

    c. What are the slope and y-intercept? What do they represent in this situation?

Walk to School

37. Which function has the same y-intercept as $y = \frac{1}{2}x - 2$?

(A) $2x + 3y = 6$ (B) $x + 4y = -8$ (C) $-\frac{1}{2}x + y = 4$ (D) $\frac{1}{2}x - 2y = -2$

38. What is the slope-intercept form of $x - y = -8$?

(F) $y = -x - 8$ (G) $y = x - 8$ (H) $y = -x + 8$ (J) $y = x + 8$

39. Which function has a y-intercept of 3?

(A) $2x - y = 3$ (B) $2x + y = 3$ (C) $2x + y = 6$ (D) $y = 3x$

40. **Gridded Response** What is the slope of the line described by $-6x = -2y + 5$?

41. **Short Response** Write a function whose graph has the same slope as the line described by $3x - 9y = 9$ and the same y-intercept as $8x - 2y = 6$. Show your work.

CHALLENGE AND EXTEND

42. The standard form of a linear equation is $Ax + By = C$. Rewrite this equation in slope-intercept form. What is the slope? What is the y-intercept?

43. What value of n in the equation $nx + 5 = 3y$ would give a line with slope -2?

44. If b is the y-intercept of a linear function whose graph has slope m, then $y = mx + b$ describes the line. Below is an incomplete justification of this statement. Fill in the missing information.

Statements	Reasons
1. $m = \dfrac{y_2 - y_1}{x_2 - x_1}$	1. Slope formula
2. $m = \dfrac{y - b}{x - 0}$	2. By definition, if b is the y-intercept, then $\left(\blacksquare, b\right)$ is a point on the line. (x, y) is any other point on the line.
3. $m = \dfrac{y - b}{x}$	3. _____ ?
4. $m\ \blacksquare = y - b$	4. Multiplication Property of Equality (Multiply both sides of the equation by x.)
5. $mx + b = y$, or $y = mx + b$	5. _____ ?

4-7 Point-Slope Form

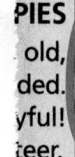

CC.9-12.A.CED.2 Create equations in two or more variables to represent relationships between quantities; graph equations on coordinate axes with labels and scales.* *Also* **CC.9-12.A.CED.3*, CC.9-12.F.IF.7*, CC.9-12.F.BF.1*, CC.9-12.F.LE.2***

Objectives
Graph a line and write a linear equation using point-slope form.

Write a linear equation given two points.

Why learn this?
You can use point-slope form to represent a cost function, such as the cost of placing a newspaper ad. (See Example 5.)

If you know the slope and any point on the line, you can write an equation of the line by using the slope formula. For example, suppose a line has a slope of 3 and contains $(2, 1)$. Let (x, y) be any other point on the line.

PIES	KITTENS AVAILABLE
old,	to good home. 2 mo.
ded.	old, litter trained. Very
yful!	cute and playful! $10
teer.	adoption fee.

DOG
8 mo.
shotsi
Very c
happy

$$m = \frac{y_2 - y_1}{x_2 - x_1} \longrightarrow 3 = \frac{y - 1}{x - 2}$$ *Substitute into the slope formula.*

Slope formula

$$3(x - 2) = \left(\frac{y - 1}{x - 2}\right)(x - 2)$$ *Multiplication Property of Equality*

$$3(x - 2) = y - 1$$ *Simplify.*

$$y - 1 = 3(x - 2)$$

Know it!
Note

> ### Point-Slope Form of a Linear Equation
>
> The line with slope m that contains the point (x_1, y_1) can be described by the equation $y - y_1 = m(x - x_1)$.

EXAMPLE **1**   **Writing Linear Equations in Point-Slope Form**

Write an equation in point-slope form for the line with the given slope that contains the given point.

A slope $= \frac{5}{2}$; $(-3, 0)$

$y - y_1 = m(x - x_1)$ *Write the point-slope form.*

$y - 0 = \frac{5}{2}[x - (-3)]$ *Substitute $\frac{5}{2}$ for m, −3 for x_1, and 0 for y_1.*

$y - 0 = \frac{5}{2}(x + 3)$ *Rewrite subtraction of negative numbers as addition.*

B slope $= -7$; $(4, 2)$

$y - y_1 = m(x - x_1)$

$y - 2 = -7(x - 4)$

C slope $= 0$; $(-2, -3)$

$y - y_1 = m(x - x_1)$

$y - (-3) = 0[x - (-2)]$

$y + 3 = 0(x + 2)$

CHECK IT OUT!   Write an equation in point-slope form for the line with the given slope that contains the given point.

1a. slope $= 2$; $\left(\frac{1}{2}, 1\right)$

1b. slope $= 0$; $(3, -4)$

Previously, you graphed a line given its equation in slope-intercept form. You can also graph a line when given its equation in point-slope form. Start by using the equation to identify a point on the line. Then use the slope of the line to identify a second point.

EXAMPLE **2** **Using Point-Slope Form to Graph**

Graph the line described by each equation.

A $y - 1 = 3(x - 1)$

$y - 1 = 3(x - 1)$ is in the form $y - y_1 = m(x - x_1)$.

The line contains the point $(1, 1)$.

slope: $m = 3 = \dfrac{3}{1}$

Step 1 Plot $(1, 1)$.

Step 2 Count **3 units up** and **1 unit right** and plot another point.

Step 3 Draw the line connecting the two points.

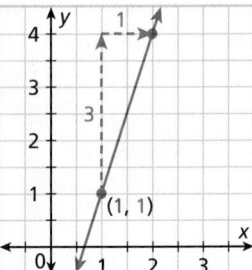

B $y + 2 = -\dfrac{1}{2}(x - 3)$

Step 1 Write the equation in point-slope form: $y - y_1 = m(x - x_1)$.

$y - (-2) = -\dfrac{1}{2}(x - 3)$ *Rewrite addition of 2 as subtraction of −2.*

Step 2 Graph the line.

The line contains the point $(3, -2)$.

slope: $m = -\dfrac{1}{2} = \dfrac{1}{-2}$

• Plot $(3, -2)$.

• Count **1 unit up** and **2 units left** and plot another point.

• Draw the line connecting the two points.

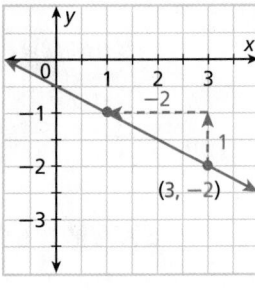

Helpful Hint

For a negative fraction, you can write the negative sign in one of three places.

$-\dfrac{1}{2} = \dfrac{-1}{2} = \dfrac{1}{-2}$

 Graph the line described by each equation.

2a. $y + 2 = -(x - 2)$ **2b.** $y + 3 = -2(x - 1)$

EXAMPLE **3** **Writing Linear Equations in Slope-Intercept Form**

Write the equation that describes each line in slope-intercept form.

A slope $= -4$, $(-1, -2)$ is on the line.

Step 1 Write the equation in point-slope form: $y - y_1 = m(x - x_1)$.

$y - (-2) = -4[x - (-1)]$

Step 2 Write the equation in slope-intercept form by solving for y.

$y - (-2) = -4[x - (-1)]$

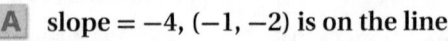

$y + 2 = -4(x + 1)$ *Rewrite subtraction of negative numbers as*
$y + 2 = -4x - 4$ *addition. Distribute −4 on the right side.*

$\underline{ -2 \qquad\quad -2}$ *Subtract 2 from both sides.*

$y \qquad = -4x - 6$

B $(1, -4)$ **and** $(3, 2)$ **are on the line.**

Step 1 Find the slope.

$$m = \frac{y_2 - y_1}{x_2 - x_1} = \frac{2 - (-4)}{3 - 1} = \frac{6}{2} = 3$$

Step 2 Substitute the slope and one of the points into the point-slope form. Then write the equation in slope-intercept form.

$y - y_1 = m(x - x_1)$

$y - 2 = 3(x - 3)$ *Use (3, 2).*

$y - 2 = 3x - 9$ *Distribute 3 on the right side.*

$y = 3x - 7$ *Add 2 to both sides.*

C *x*-intercept = –2, *y*-intercept = 4

Step 1 Use the intercepts to find two points: $(-2, 0)$ and $(0, 4)$.

Step 2 Find the slope.

$$m = \frac{y_2 - y_1}{x_2 - x_1} = \frac{4 - 0}{0 - (-2)} = \frac{4}{2} = 2$$

Step 3 Write the equation in slope-intercept form.

$y = mx + b$ *Write the slope-intercept form.*

$y = 2x + 4$ *Substitute 2 for m and 4 for b.*

 **Write the equation that describes each line in slope-intercept form.**

3a. slope $= \frac{1}{3}$, $(-3, 1)$ is on the line.

3b. $(1, -2)$ and $(3, 10)$ are on the line.

EXAMPLE **4** **Using Two Points to Find Intercepts**

The points $(4, 8)$ and $(-1, -12)$ are on a line. Find the intercepts.

Step 1 Find the slope.

$$m = \frac{y_2 - y_1}{x_2 - x_1} = \frac{-12 - 8}{-1 - 4} = \frac{-20}{-5} = 4$$

Step 2 Write the equation in slope-intercept form.

$y - y_1 = m(x - x_1)$ *Write the point-slope form.*

$y - 8 = 4(x - 4)$ *Substitute (4, 8) for (x_1, y_1) and 4 for m.*

$y - 8 = 4x - 16$ *Distribute 4 on the right side.*

$y = 4x - 8$ *Add 8 to both sides.*

Step 3 Find the intercepts.

x-intercept:

$y = 4x - 8$ *Replace y with*

$0 = 4x - 8$ *0 and solve*

$8 = 4x$ *for x.*

$2 = x$

y-intercept:

$y = 4x - 8$ *Use the slope-*

$b = -8$ *intercept form to identify the y-intercept.*

The *x*-intercept is 2, and the *y*-intercept is –8.

 **4.** The points $(2, 15)$ and $(-4, -3)$ are on a line. Find the intercepts.

EXAMPLE 5

MATHEMATICAL PRACTICES

Make sense of problems and persevere in solving them.

Problem-Solving Application

The cost to place an ad in a newspaper for one week is a linear function of the number of lines in the ad. The costs for 3, 5, and 10 lines are shown. Write an equation in slope-intercept form that represents the function. Then find the cost of an ad that is 18 lines long.

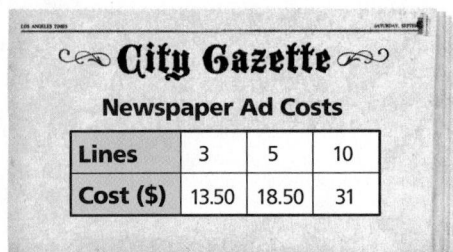

City Gazette

Newspaper Ad Costs

Lines	3	5	10
Cost ($)	13.50	18.50	31

1. Understand the Problem

- The **answer** will have two parts—an equation in slope-intercept form and the cost of an ad that is 18 lines long.
- The ordered pairs given in the table satisfy the equation.

2. Make a Plan

First, find the slope. Then use point-slope form to write the equation. Finally, write the equation in slope-intercept form.

3. Solve

Step 1 Choose any two ordered pairs from the table to find the slope.

$$m = \frac{y_2 - y_1}{x_2 - x_1} = \frac{18.50 - 13.50}{5 - 3} = \frac{5}{2} = 2.5 \quad \textit{Use (3, 13.50) and (5, 18.50).}$$

Step 2 Substitute the slope and any ordered pair from the table into the point-slope form.

$$y - y_1 = m(x - x_1)$$
$$y - 31 = 2.5(x - 10) \qquad\qquad \textit{Use (10, 31).}$$

Step 3 Write the equation in slope-intercept form by solving for y.

$$y - 31 = 2.5(x - 10)$$
$$y - 31 = 2.5x - 25 \qquad\qquad \textit{Distribute 2.5.}$$
$$y = 2.5x + 6 \qquad\qquad\quad \textit{Add 31 to both sides.}$$

Step 4 Find the cost of an ad containing 18 lines by substituting 18 for x.

$$y = 2.5x + 6$$
$$y = 2.5(18) + 6 = 51$$

The cost of an ad containing 18 lines is $51.

4. Look Back

Check the equation by substituting the ordered pairs (3, 13.50) and (5, 18.50).

$y = 2.5x + 6$	
13.50	2.5(3) + 6
13.5	7.5 + 6
13.5	13.5 ✓

$y = 2.5x + 6$	
18.50	2.5(5) + 6
18.5	12.5 + 6
18.5	18.5 ✓

CHECK IT OUT!

5. What if...? At a different newspaper, the costs to place an ad for one week are shown. Write an equation in slope-intercept form that represents this linear function. Then find the cost of an ad that is 21 lines long.

Lines	Cost ($)
3	12.75
5	17.25
10	28.50

THINK AND DISCUSS

1. How are point-slope form and slope-intercept form alike? different?

2. When is point-slope form useful? When is slope-intercept form useful?

3. GET ORGANIZED Copy and complete the graphic organizer. In each box, describe how to find the equation of a line by using the given method.

> Writing the Equation of a Line

If you know two points on the line	If you know the slope and y-intercept	If you know the slope and a point on the line

---

4-7 Exercises

Learn It Online
Homework Help Online
Parent Resources Online

GUIDED PRACTICE

SEE EXAMPLE 1 Write an equation in point-slope form for the line with the given slope that contains the given point.

1. slope = $\frac{1}{5}$; $(2, -6)$ **2.** slope = -4; $(1, 5)$ **3.** slope = 0; $(3, -7)$

SEE EXAMPLE 2 Graph the line described by each equation.

4. $y - 1 = -(x - 3)$ **5.** $y + 2 = -2(x + 4)$ **6.** $y + 1 = -\frac{1}{2}(x + 4)$

SEE EXAMPLE 3 Write the equation that describes each line in slope-intercept form.

7. slope = $-\frac{1}{3}$, $(-3, 8)$ is on the line.   **8.** slope = 2; $(1, 1)$ is on the line.

9. $(-2, 2)$ and $(2, -2)$ are on the line.   **10.** $(1, 1)$ and $(-5, 3)$ are on the line.

11. x-intercept = 8, y-intercept = 4   **12.** x-intercept = -2, y-intercept = 3

SEE EXAMPLE 4 Each pair of points is on a line. Find the intercepts.

13. $(5, 2)$ and $(7, 4)$ **14.** $(-1, 5)$ and $(-3, -5)$ **15.** $(2, 9)$ and $(-4, -9)$

SEE EXAMPLE 5   **16. Measurement** An oil tank is being filled at a constant rate. The depth of the oil is a function of the number of minutes the tank has been filling, as shown in the table. Write an equation in slope-intercept form that represents this linear function. Then find the depth of the oil after one-half hour.

Time (min)	Depth (ft)
0	3
10	5
15	6

PRACTICE AND PROBLEM SOLVING

Write an equation in point-slope form for the line with the given slope that contains the given point.

17. slope = $\frac{2}{9}$; $(-1, 5)$ **18.** slope = 0; $(4, -2)$ **19.** slope = 8; $(1, 8)$

For Exercises	See Example
17–19	1
20–22	2
23–30	3
31–33	4
34	5

Independent Practice

Extra Practice
See Extra Practice for more Skills Practice and Applications Practice exercises.

Graph the line described by each equation.

20. $y - 4 = -\frac{1}{2}(x + 3)$ **21.** $y + 2 = \frac{3}{5}(x - 1)$ **22.** $y - 0 = 4(x - 1)$

Write the equation that describes each line in slope-intercept form.

23. slope $= -\frac{2}{7}$, $(14, -3)$ is on the line.   **24.** slope $= \frac{4}{5}$, $(-15, 1)$ is on the line.

25. slope $= -6$, $(9, 3)$ is on the line.   **26.** $(7, 8)$ and $(-7, 6)$ are on the line.

27. $(2, 7)$ and $(4, -4)$ are on the line.   **28.** $(-1, 2)$ and $(4, -23)$ are on the line.

29. x-intercept $= 3$, y-intercept $= -6$ **30.** x-intercept $= 4$, y-intercept $= -1$

Each pair of points is on a line. Find the intercepts.

31. $(-1, -4)$ and $(6, 10)$ **32.** $(3, 4)$ and $(-6, 16)$ **33.** $(4, 15)$ and $(-2, 6)$

34. History The amount of fresh water left in the tanks of a 19th-century clipper ship is a linear function of the time since the ship left port, as shown in the table. Write an equation in slope-intercept form that represents the function. Then find the amount of water that will be left in the ship's tanks 50 days after leaving port.

Fresh Water Aboard Ship	
Time (days)	Amount (gal)
1	3555
8	3240
15	2925

35. Science At higher altitudes, water boils at lower temperatures. This relationship between altitude and boiling point is linear. At an altitude of 1000 feet, water boils at 210 °F. At an altitude of 3000 feet, water boils at 206 °F. Write an equation in slope-intercept form that represents this linear function. Then find the boiling point at 6000 feet.

36. Consumer Economics Lora has a gift card from an online music store where all downloads cost the same amount. After downloading 2 songs, the balance on her card was $18.10. After downloading a total of 5 songs, the balance was $15.25.

  a. Write an equation in slope-intercept form that represents the amount in dollars remaining on the card as a function of songs downloaded.

  b. Identify the slope of the line and tell what the slope represents.

  c. Identify the y-intercept of the line and tell what it represents.

  d. How many additional songs can Lora download when there is $15.25 left on the card?

Science

As altitude increases, the amount of breathable oxygen decreases. At elevations above 8000 feet, this can cause altitude sickness. To prevent this, mountain climbers often use tanks containing a mixture of air and pure oxygen.

Graph the line with the given slope that contains the given point.

37. slope $= -3$; $(2, 4)$ **38.** slope $= -\frac{1}{4}$; $(0, 0)$ **39.** slope $= \frac{1}{2}$; $(-2, -1)$

Tell whether each statement is sometimes, always, or never true.

40. A line described by the equation $y = mx + b$ contains the point $(0, b)$.

41. The slope of the line that contains the points $(0, 0)$ and (c, d) is negative if both c and d are negative.

42. The y-intercept of the graph of $y - y_1 = m(x - x_1)$ is negative if y_1 is negative.

43. Meteorology Snowfall accumulates at an average rate of 2.5 inches per hour during a snowstorm. Two hours after the snowstorm begins, the average depth of snow on the ground is 11 inches.

  a. Write an equation in point-slope form that represents the depth of the snow in inches as a function of hours since the snowstorm began.

  b. How much snow is on the ground when the snowstorm starts?

  c. The snowstorm begins at 2:15 P.M. and continues until 6:30 P.M. How much snow is on the ground at the end of the storm?

Write an equation in point-slope form that describes each graph.

44.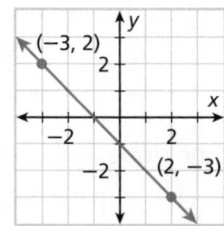

45.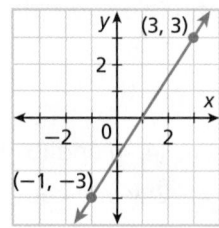

46.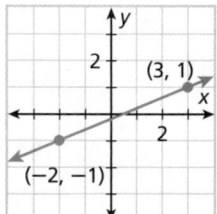

The tables show linear relationships between *x* and *y*. Copy and complete the tables.

47.

x	−2	0		7
y	−18		12	27

48.

x	−4	1	0	
y	14	4		−6

49. ///**ERROR ANALYSIS**/// Two students used point-slope form to find an equation that describes the line with slope −3 through $(-5, 2)$. Who is incorrect? Explain the error.

A
$$y - y_1 = m(x - x_1)$$
$$y - 2 = -3(x - 5)$$

B
$$y - y_1 = m(x - x_1)$$
$$y - 2 = -3[x - (-5)]$$
$$y - 2 = -3(x + 5)$$

50. Critical Thinking Compare the methods for finding the equation that describes a line when you know
   • a point on the line and the slope of the line.
   • two points on the line.

   How are the methods alike? How are they different?

51. Write About It Explain why the first statement is false but the second is true.
   • All linear equations can be written in point-slope form.
   • All linear equations that describe functions can be written in point-slope form.

52. Multi-Step The table shows the mean scores on a standardized test for several different years.

Years Since 1985	0	5	10	17	21
Mean Combined Score	994	1009	1001	1016	1020

   a. Make a scatter plot of the data and add a trend line to your graph.
   b. Use your trend line to estimate the slope and *y*-intercept, and write an equation in slope-intercept form.
   c. What do the slope and *y*-intercept represent in this situation?

53. a. Stephen is walking from his house to his friend Sharon's house. When he is 12 blocks away, he looks at his watch. He looks again when he is 8 blocks away and finds that 6 minutes have passed. Write two ordered pairs for these data in the form (time, blocks).

   b. Write a linear equation for these two points.

   c. What is the total amount of time it takes Stephen to reach Sharon's house? Explain how you found your answer.

54. Which equation describes the line through $(-5, 1)$ with slope of 1?

   Ⓐ $y + 1 = x - 5$ Ⓒ $y - 1 = -5(x - 1)$

   Ⓑ $y + 5 = x - 1$ Ⓓ $y - 1 = x + 5$

55. A line contains $(4, 4)$ and $(5, 2)$. What are the slope and y-intercept?

   Ⓕ slope $= -2$; y-intercept $= 2$ Ⓗ slope $= -2$; y-intercept $= 12$

   Ⓖ slope $= 1.2$; y-intercept $= -2$ Ⓙ slope $= 12$; y-intercept $= 1.2$

CHALLENGE AND EXTEND

56. A linear function has the same y-intercept as $x + 4y = 8$ and its graph contains the point $(2, 7)$. Find the slope and y-intercept.

57. Write the equation of a line in slope-intercept form that contains $\left(\frac{3}{4}, \frac{1}{2}\right)$ and has the same slope as the line described by $y + 3x = 6$.

58. Write the equation of a line in slope-intercept form that contains $\left(-\frac{1}{2}, -\frac{1}{3}\right)$ and $\left(1\frac{1}{2}, 1\right)$.

Career Path

 **Learn It Online**
Career Resources Online

Q: **What math classes did you take in high school?**

A: Algebra 1 and 2, Geometry, and Statistics

Q: **What math classes have you taken in college?**

A: Applied Statistics, Data Mining Methods, Web Mining, and Artificial Intelligence

Q: **How do you use math?**

A: Once for a class, I used software to analyze basketball statistics. What I learned helped me develop strategies for our school team.

Michael Raynor
Data mining major

Q: **What are your future plans?**

A: There are many options for people with data mining skills. I could work in banking, pharmaceuticals, or even the military. But my dream job is to develop game strategies for an NBA team.

4-7 Technology LAB

Graph Linear Functions

You can use a graphing calculator to quickly graph lines whose equations are in point-slope form. To enter an equation into your calculator, it must be solved for *y*, but it does not necessarily have to be in slope-intercept form.

Use with Point-Slope Form

Activity

Graph the line with slope 2 that contains the point $(2, 6.09)$.

1 Use point-slope form.
$$y - y_1 = m(x - x_1)$$
$$y - 6.09 = 2(x - 2)$$

2 Solve for *y* by adding 6.09 to both sides of the equation.
$$y - 6.09 = 2(x - 2)$$

$$y = 2(x - 2) + 6.09$$

3 Enter this equation into your calculator.

Plot1 Plot2 Plot3
\Y₁■2(X-2)+6.09
\Y₂=■

4 Graph in the *standard viewing window* by pressing ZOOM and selecting **6:ZStandard**. In this window, both the *x*- and *y*-axes go from −10 to 10.

5 Notice that the scale on the *y*-axis is smaller than the scale on the *x*-axis. This is because the width of the calculator screen is about 50% greater than its height. To see a more accurate graph of this line, use the *square viewing window*. Press ZOOM and select **5:ZSquare**.

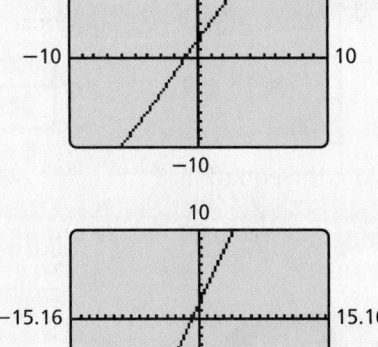

Try This

1. Graph the function represented by the line with slope −1.5 that contains the point $(2.25, -3)$. View the graph in the standard viewing window.

2. Now view the graph in the square viewing window. Press WINDOW and write down the minimum and maximum values on the *x*- and *y*-axes.

3. In which graph does the line appear steeper? Why?

4. Explain why it might sometimes be useful to look at a graph in a square window.

Interpreting Trend Lines

Previously, you learned how to draw trend lines on scatter plots. Now you will learn how to find the equations of trend lines and write them in slope-intercept form.

Example

Write an equation for the trend line on the scatter plot.

Two points on the trend line are (30, 75) and (60, 90).

To find the slope of the line that contains (**30**, **75**) and (**60**, **90**), use the slope formula.

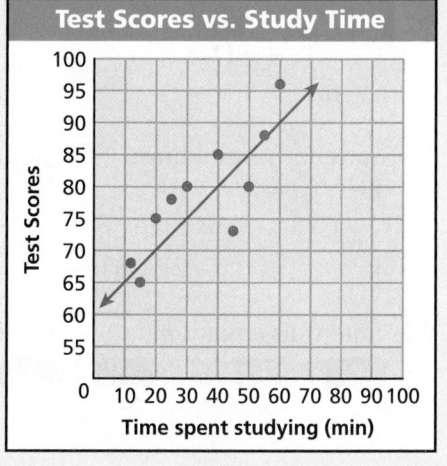

Test Scores vs. Study Time

$$m = \frac{y_2 - y_1}{x_2 - x_1}$$ *Use the slope formula.*

$$m = \frac{90 - 75}{60 - 30}$$ *Substitute (30, 75) for (x₁, y₁) and (60, 90) for (x₂, y₂).*

$$m = \frac{15}{30}$$ *Simplify.*

$$m = \frac{1}{2}$$

Use the slope and the point (30, 75) to find the *y*-intercept of the line.

$$y = mx + b$$ *Slope-intercept form*

$$75 = \frac{1}{2}(30) + b$$ *Substitute $\frac{1}{2}$ for m, 30 for x, and 75 for y.*

$$75 = 15 + b$$ *Solve for b.*

$$60 = b$$

Write the equation.

$$y = \frac{1}{2}x + 60$$ *Substitute $\frac{1}{2}$ for m and 60 for b.*

Try This

1. In the example above, what is the meaning of the slope?

2. What does the *y*-intercept represent?

3. Use the equation to predict the test score of a student who spent 25 minutes studying.

4. Use the table to create a scatter plot. Draw a trend line and find the equation of your trend line. Tell the meaning of the slope and *y*-intercept. Then use your equation to predict the race time of a runner who ran 40 miles in training.

Distance Run in Training (mi)	12	15	16	18	21	23	24	25	33
Race Time (min)	65	64	55	58	55	50	50	47	36

4-8 Line of Best Fit

CC.9-12.S.ID.6 Represent data on two quantitative variables on a scatter plot, and describe how the variables are related. *Also* CC.9-12.S.ID.6b, CC.9-12.S.ID.7, CC.9-12.S.ID.8, CC.9-12.S.ID.9

Objectives
Determine a line of best fit for a set of linear data.

Determine and interpret the correlation coefficient.

Vocabulary
residual
least-squares line
line of best fit
linear regression
correlation coefficient

Who uses this?
Climate scientists can use a least-squares line to study temperature-latitude relationships. (See Example 2.)

Recall that a scatter plot shows two data sets as one set of ordered pairs. A trend line, or line of fit, is a model for the data.

Some trend lines will fit a data set better than others. One way to evaluate how well a line fits a data set is to use *residuals*. A **residual** is the signed vertical distance between a data point and a line of fit. The closer the sum of the squared residuals is to 0, the better the line fits the data.

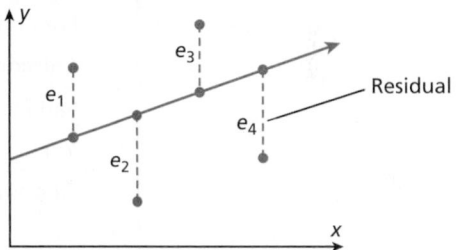

EXAMPLE 1 Calculating Residuals

The data in the table are graphed along with two lines of fit. For each line, find the sum of the squares of the residuals. Which line is a better fit?

x	2	4	6	8
y	6	3	7	5

$y = \frac{1}{2}x + 3$

$y = \frac{1}{2}x + 2$

Find the residuals.

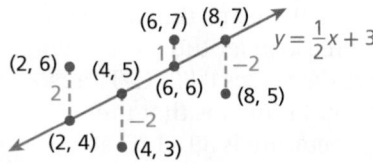

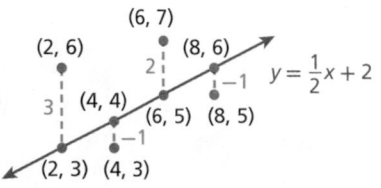

Sum of squared residuals:

$(2)^2 + (-2)^2 + (1)^2 + (-2)^2$

$4 + 4 + 1 + 4 = 13$

Sum of squared residuals:

$(3)^2 + (-1)^2 + (2)^2 + (-1)^2$

$9 + 1 + 4 + 1 = 15$

The line $y = \frac{1}{2}x + 3$ is a better fit for the data.

Helpful Hint

By using *squares* of residuals, positive and negative residuals do not "cancel out," and residuals with squares greater than 1 have a magnified effect on the sum.

CHECK IT OUT!

1. Two lines of fit for this data are $y = -\frac{1}{2}x + 6$ and $y = -x + 8$. For each line, find the sum of the squares of the residuals. Which line is a better fit?

x	2	4	6	8
y	3	6	1	4

The **least-squares line** for a data set is the line of fit for which the sum of the squares of the residuals is as small as possible. So, the least-squares line is a *line of best fit*. A **line of best fit** is the line that comes closest to all of the points in the data set, using a given process. **Linear regression** is a process of finding the least-squares line.

EXAMPLE 2   **Finding the Least-Squares Line**

The table shows the latitudes and average temperatures of several cities.

City	Latitude	Average Temperature (°C)
Barrow, Alaska, USA	71.2° N	−12.7
Yakutsk, Russia	62.1° N	−10.1
London, England	51.3° N	10.4
Chicago, Illinois, USA	41.9° N	10.3
San Francisco, California, USA	37.5° N	13.8
Yuma, Arizona, USA	32.7° N	22.8
Tindouf, Algeria	27.7° N	22.8
Dakar, Senegal	14.0° N	24.5
Mangalore, India	12.5° N	27.1

A   **Find an equation for a line of best fit.**

Use your calculator. To enter the data, press **STAT** and select **1:Edit**. Enter the latitudes in the **L1** column and the average temperatures in the **L2** column.

Then press **STAT** and choose **CALC**.

Choose **4:LinReg(ax+b)** and press **ENTER**. An equation for a line of best fit is $y \approx -0.69x + 39.11$.

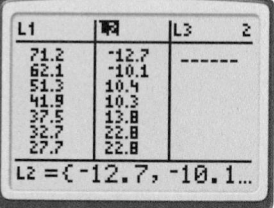

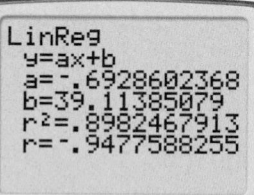

B   **Interpret the meaning of the slope and y-intercept.**

The slope, −0.69, means that for each 1-degree increase in latitude, the average temperature decreases 0.69 °C. The y-intercept, 39.11, means that the average temperature is 39.11 °C at 0° N latitude.

C   **The approximate latitude of Vancouver, Canada, is 49.1° N. Use your equation to predict Vancouver's average temperature.**

$y \approx -0.69x + 39.11$

$y \approx -0.69(49.1) + 39.11 \approx 5.23$

The average temperature of Vancouver should be close to 5 °C.

2. The table shows the prices and the lengths in yards of several balls of yarn at Knit Mart.

Length (yd)	1680	100	153	99	109	109	176	100	1440	61
Price ($)	65.85	7.85	9.80	10.85	8.35	7.85	19.85	5.35	65.85	14.85

    a. Find an equation for a line of best fit.

    b. Interpret the meaning of the slope and *y*-intercept.

    c. Knit Mart also sells yarn in a 1000-yard ball. Use your equation to predict the cost of this yarn.

In Example 2, you may have noticed the last value the calculator gave you, *r*. This is the *correlation coefficient.* The **correlation coefficient** is a number *r*, where $-1 \le r \le 1$, that describes how closely the points in a scatter plot cluster around a line of best fit.

Properties of the Correlation Coefficient *r*

r is a value in the range $-1 \le r \le 1$.

If $r = 1$, the data set forms a straight line with a positive slope.

If $r = 0$, the data set has no correlation.

If $r = -1$, the data set forms a straight line with a negative slope.

Helpful Hint

r-values close to 1 or –1 indicate a very strong correlation. The closer *r* is to 0, the weaker the correlation.

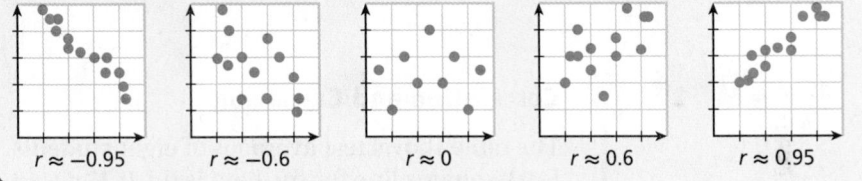

$r \approx -0.95$ $r \approx -0.6$ $r \approx 0$ $r \approx 0.6$ $r \approx 0.95$

EXAMPLE 3   Correlation Coefficient

The table shows a relationship between a city's population and the average time the city's citizens spend commuting to work each day.

City	Population (thousands)	Average Commute Time (min)
Albuquerque, NM	505	21.5
Atlanta, GA	486	31.1
Austin, TX	710	23.2
Charlotte, NC	630	25.1
Chicago, IL	2833	30.6
Eugene, OR	146	17.9
Houston, TX	2144	27.7
Las Vegas, NV	553	25.2
New York, NY	8496	34.0
New Orleans, LA	223	24.2

Find an equation for a line of best fit. How well does the line represent the data?

Use your calculator.

Enter the data into the lists **L1** and **L2**.

Then press **STAT** and choose **CALC**. Choose **4:LinReg(ax+b)** and press **ENTER** . An equation for a line of best fit is $y \approx 0.001x + 23.8$. The value of r is about 0.71, which indicates a moderate positive correlation.

LinReg
y=ax+b
a=.0013555626
b=23.78268592
r²=.5068914082
r=.7119630666

3. Kylie and Marcus designed a quiz to measure how much information adults retain after leaving school. The table below shows the quiz scores of several adults, matched with the number of years each person had been out of school. Find an equation for a line of best fit. How well does the line represent the data?

Time Out of School (yr)	1	1	1	2	2	3	5	7	10	10	14	25
Quiz Score	85	94	98	75	80	77	63	56	45	50	34	33

Causation refers to cause-and-effect. If a change in one variable directly causes a change in the other variable, then there is a cause-and-effect relationship between the variables. There is often correlation without causation.

EXAMPLE 4 **Correlation and Causation**

The table shows test averages of eight students. The equation of the least-squares line for the data is $y \approx 0.77x + 18.12$ and $r \approx 0.87$. Discuss correlation and causation for the data set.

U.S. History Test Average	90	70	75	100	90	85	80	90
Science Test Average	80	75	72	95	92	82	80	92

Caution!

Notice in Example 4, there is a strong correlation, but no causation. Two variables can be strongly correlated without having a direct cause-and-effect relationship.

There is a strong positive correlation between the U.S. history test average and the science test average for these students. There is *not* a likely cause-and-effect relationship because there is no apparent reason why test scores in one subject would directly affect test scores in the other subject.

4. Eight adults were surveyed about their education and earnings. The table shows the survey results. The equation of the least-squares line for the data is $y \approx 5.59x - 30.28$ and $r \approx 0.86$. Discuss correlation and causation for the data set.

Years of Education	12	16	20	14	18	16	16	18
Earnings Last Year (thousand $)	40	65	75	44	70	50	54	86

THINK AND DISCUSS

1. What is the residual for a data point that lies on the line of best fit?

2. GET ORGANIZED Copy and complete the graphic organizer. For each *r*-value, sketch a possible scatter plot and describe the correlation, choosing from the following: strong positive, weak positive, none, strong negative, weak negative.

r-value	−0.9	−0.4	0	0.4	0.9
Scatter Plot					
Description of Correlation					

4-8 Exercises

GUIDED PRACTICE

Vocabulary Apply the vocabulary from this lesson to answer each question.

1. A signed vertical distance between a data point and its corresponding model point is called a _____?_____ (*residual* or *correlation coefficient*)

2. A _____?_____ (*least squares line* or *correlation coefficient*) is a measure of how well a line of best fit models a data set.

SEE EXAMPLE 1

3. The data in the table are graphed along with two lines of fit. For each line, find the sum of the squares of the residuals. Which line is a better fit for the data?

x	2	3	4	5
y	2	5	6	2

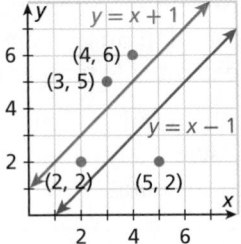

SEE EXAMPLE 2

4. The table shows numbers of books read by students in an English class over a summer and the students' grades for the following semester.

Books	0	0	0	0	1	1	1	2	3	5	6	8	10	12	20
Grade	65	69	70	73	70	75	78	77	86	85	89	90	95	99	98

a. Find an equation for a line of best fit.

b. Interpret the meaning of the slope and *y*-intercept.

c. Use your equation to predict the grade of a student who reads 15 books.

SEE EXAMPLE 3

5. A negative correlation exists between the time Shawnda spends on homework during an evening and the amount of sleep she gets that night. The table shows data for several nights. Find an equation for a line of best fit. How well does the line represent the data?

Homework (h)	0.5	0.5	1	1	1.5	2	2	2.5	3	3	3	4	4.5	5
Sleep (h)	8	9	8	8.5	8	7.5	8	7.5	7	7	8	6.5	6.5	6

SEE EXAMPLE 4

6. Some students were surveyed about how much time they spent playing video games last week and their overall test average. The equation of the least-squares line for the data is $y \approx -2.93x + 89.70$ and $r \approx -0.92$. Discuss correlation and causation for the data set.

Hours Playing Video Games	1	3	3	6	2	1	9	10
Test Average for all Subjects	80	85	78	70	86	92	60	64

PRACTICE AND PROBLEM SOLVING

Independent Practice

For Exercise	See Example
7	1
8	2
9	3
10	4

7. The data in the table are graphed along with two lines of fit. For each line, find the sum of the squares of the residuals. Which line is a better fit for the data?

x	2	4	6	8
y	5	6	1	1

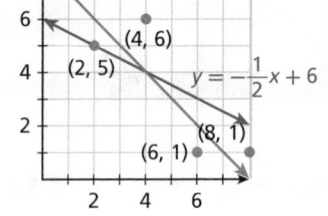

8. The table shows the mean outside temperature for each of six months and the amount of heating oil used by a family for each of those months.

Mean Outside Temperature (°F)	30	28	44	56	62	76
Heating Oil Used (gal)	112	115	94	60	35	12

a. Find an equation for a line of best fit.
b. Interpret the meaning of the slope and y-intercept.
c. Use your equation to predict the amount of heating oil used in a month in which the mean outside temperature is 20 °F.

9. The table shows the number of customers at a coffee shop and the number of cookies sold for several days. Find an equation for a line of best fit. How well does the line represent the data?

Customers	10	12	25	27	40	55	67	109
Cookies Sold	2	6	5	9	10	11	20	22

10. Some students were surveyed about how much time they spent watching television one week and how much time they spent playing video games the next week. The equation of the least-squares line for the data is $y \approx 0.76x + 1.63$ and $r \approx 0.77$. Discuss correlation and causation for the data set.

Week 1: Hours Watching Television	4	2	0	1	3	1	8	10
Week 2: Hours Playing Video Games	1	3	3	6	2	1	9	10

11. **Write About It** Tell which correlation coefficient, $r = 0.65$ or $r = -0.78$, indicates a stronger linear relationship between two variables. Explain your answer.

12. **Critical Thinking** What can you conclude if the sum of the squared residuals is 0? Explain why the same conclusion might not apply when the sum of the residuals is 0.

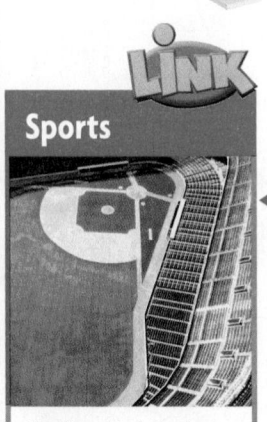

Sports

The New York Yankees opened a new stadium in 2009. Although the new stadium seats fewer fans than the old stadium (50,287 versus 56,886), the seats in the new stadium are wider, and there is more legroom between rows.

13. **Sports** The table shows hits and runs scored by eight New York Yankees in the 2009 baseball season.

a. Find the equation of the least-squares line.

b. Interpret the meaning of the slope.

c. Interpret the meaning of the y-intercept mathematically.

d. Describe any possible correlation for the data set. Use the correlation coefficient to support your answer.

e. Use the equation of the least-squares line from part **a** to predict how many runs a player will score if he gets 100 hits.

Player	Hits	Runs
Jorge Posada	109	55
Mark Teixeira	178	103
Robinson Cano	204	103
Derek Jeter	212	107
Johnny Damon	155	107
Melky Cabrera	133	66
Nick Swisher	124	84
Hideki Matsui	125	62

14. **Community** The table shows data about temperature and how much bottled water was sold at an annual summer festival in past years. The high temperature for the day of this year's festival is predicted to be 89 °F. The festival organizer must order bottled water in cases of 100. Find the equation of the least-squares line. Use the equation to decide how many cases the organizer should order.

Midtown Summer Fest						
Year	1	2	3	4	5	6
Daily High Temperature (°F)	75	82	95	92	80	84
Bottled Waters Sold	465	517	1052	940	611	625

Use the table for Exercises 15 and 16.

Regional Historical Museum						
Year	0	2	4	6	8	10
Visitors	980	1,251	1,667	1,785	2,110	2,056
Gift Shop Sales ($)	8,890	12,365	15,100	18,060	20,650	22,600

15. Complete parts **a–d** for the relationship between the year and the number of visitors.

a. Find the equation of the least-squares line and the correlation coefficient.

b. Interpret the meaning of the slope and the y-intercept.

c. Is it reasonable to use your equation to make predictions? Explain.

d. Is it reasonable to say there is a cause-and-effect relationship? Explain.

16. Complete parts **a–d** above for the relationship between the number of visitors and the gift shop sales.

17. Which could be the correlation coefficient of this graph?

    Ⓐ −1.00

    Ⓑ −0.93

    Ⓒ 0.93

    Ⓓ 1.00

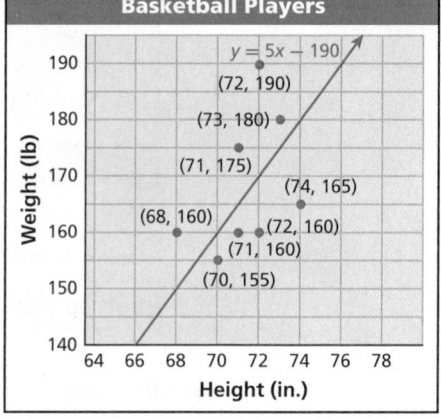

18. The table shows how much time five students studied for a test and their test scores. The equation of a line of fit for the data is $y = 5x + 60$. What is the sum of the squares of the residuals for the line of fit?

Hours Studying	0	2	4	6	8
Test Score	60	70	90	80	100

    Ⓕ 0   Ⓖ 20   Ⓗ 40   Ⓙ 200

CHALLENGE AND EXTEND

19. The heights and weights of eight basketball players are graphed along with a line of fit.

    a. Find the sum of the squares of the residuals.

    b. Find the *mean absolute deviation.* (The mean absolute deviation is the mean of the absolute values of the residuals.) Explain why the mean absolute deviation might be more useful than the sum of the squares of the residuals in some cases.

    Heights and Weights of Basketball Players

    $y = 5x - 190$

    (72, 190)
    (73, 180)
    (71, 175)
    (74, 165)
    (68, 160)
    (72, 160)
    (71, 160)
    (70, 155)

    Weight (lb)
    Height (in.)

20. Use these facts to complete the data table:
    The equation of a line of fit is $y = 2x - 3$.
    The sum of the residuals is 0.
    The sum of the squares of the residuals is 14.

x	1	3	4	5
y	1	▧	▧	8

4-9 Slopes of Parallel and Perpendicular Lines

CC.9-12.G.GPE.5 Prove the slope criteria for parallel and perpendicular lines and use them to solve geometric problems (e.g., find the equation of a line parallel or perpendicular to a given line that passes through a given point).
Also **CC.9-12.F.IF.7***

Objectives
Identify and graph parallel and perpendicular lines.

Write equations to describe lines parallel or perpendicular to a given line.

Vocabulary
parallel lines
perpendicular lines

Why learn this?

Parallel lines and their equations can be used to model costs, such as the cost of a booth at a farmers' market.

To sell at a particular farmers' market for a year, there is a $100 membership fee. Then you pay $3 for each hour that you sell at the market. However, if you were a member the previous year, the membership fee is reduced to $50.

- The red line shows the total cost if you are a new member.

- The blue line shows the total cost if you are a returning member.

These two lines are *parallel*. **Parallel lines** are lines in the same plane that have no points in common. In other words, they do not intersect.

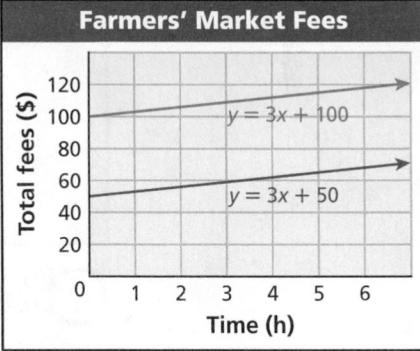

Farmers' Market Fees

Know it!
Note

Parallel Lines		
WORDS	Two different nonvertical lines are parallel if and only if they have the same slope.	All different vertical lines are parallel.
GRAPH	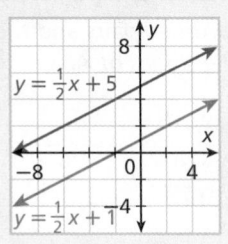	

E X A M P L E **1** **Identifying Parallel Lines**

Identify which lines are parallel.

A $y = \frac{4}{3}x + 3$; $y = 2$; $y = \frac{4}{3}x - 5$; $y = -3$

The lines described by $y = \frac{4}{3}x + 3$ and $y = \frac{4}{3}x - 5$ both have slope $\frac{4}{3}$. These lines are parallel. The lines described by $y = 2$ and $y = -3$ both have slope 0. These lines are parallel.

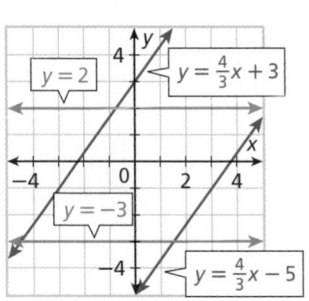

Identify which lines are parallel.

B $y = 3x + 2$; $y = -\frac{1}{2}x + 4$; $x + 2y = -4$; $y - 5 = 3(x - 1)$

Write all equations in slope-intercept form to determine the slopes.

$y = 3x + 2$	$y = -\frac{1}{2}x + 4$
slope-intercept form ✓	slope-intercept form ✓

$$
\begin{array}{ll}
x + 2y = -4 \\
\underline{-x \qquad\quad -x} \\
 2y = -x - 4 \\
 \dfrac{2y}{2} = \dfrac{-x - 4}{2} \\
 y = -\dfrac{1}{2}x - 2
\end{array}
\qquad
\begin{array}{l}
y - 5 = 3(x - 1) \\
y - 5 = 3x - 3 \\
\underline{+5 \qquad +5} \\
y = 3x + 2
\end{array}
$$

The lines described by $y = 3x + 2$ and $y - 5 = 3(x - 1)$ have the same slope, but they are not parallel lines. They are the same line.

The lines described by $y = -\frac{1}{2}x + 4$ and $x + 2y = -4$ represent parallel lines. They each have slope $-\frac{1}{2}$.

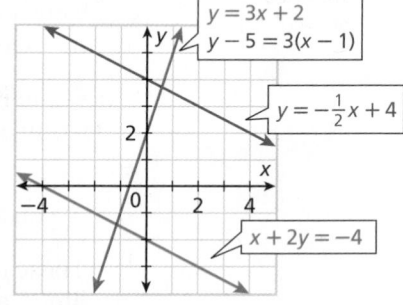

CHECK IT OUT! Identify which lines are parallel.

1a. $y = 2x + 2$; $y = 2x + 1$; $y = -4$; $x = 1$

1b. $y = \frac{3}{4}x + 8$; $-3x + 4y = 32$; $y = 3x$; $y - 1 = 3(x + 2)$

EXAMPLE  *Geometry Application*

Geometry

Show that ABCD is a parallelogram.

Use the ordered pairs and the slope formula to find the slopes of $\overline{AB}$ and $\overline{CD}$.

slope of $\overline{AB} = \dfrac{7 - 5}{4 - (-1)} = \dfrac{2}{5}$

slope of $\overline{CD} = \dfrac{3 - 1}{4 - (-1)} = \dfrac{2}{5}$

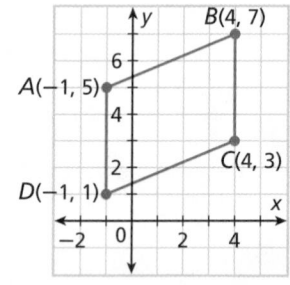

Remember!

In a parallelogram, opposite sides are parallel.

$\overline{AB}$ is parallel to $\overline{CD}$ because they have the same slope.

$\overline{AD}$ is parallel to $\overline{BC}$ because they are both vertical.

Therefore, $ABCD$ is a parallelogram because both pairs of opposite sides are parallel.

CHECK IT OUT!  **2.** Show that the points $A(0, 2)$, $B(4, 2)$, $C(1, -3)$, and $D(-3, -3)$ are the vertices of a parallelogram.

Perpendicular lines are lines that intersect to form right angles (90°).

Perpendicular Lines

WORDS	Two nonvertical lines are perpendicular if and only if the product of their slopes is −1.	Vertical lines are perpendicular to horizontal lines.
GRAPH	$y = -\frac{2}{3}x + 3$ $y = \frac{3}{2}x - 2$	$y = 3$ $x = 2$

EXAMPLE 3   Identifying Perpendicular Lines

Identify which lines are perpendicular: $x = -2; y = 1; y = -4x;$ $y + 2 = \frac{1}{4}(x + 1)$.

The graph described by $x = -2$ is a vertical line, and the graph described by $y = 1$ is a horizontal line. These lines are perpendicular.

The slope of the line described by $y = -4x$ is -4. The slope of the line described by $y + 2 = \frac{1}{4}(x - 1)$ is $\frac{1}{4}$.

$$(-4)\left(\frac{1}{4}\right) = -1$$

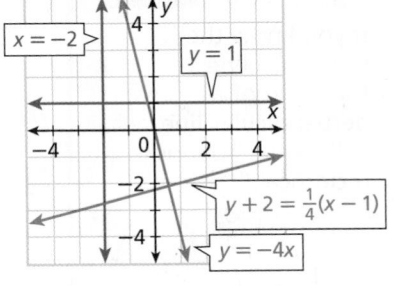

These lines are perpendicular because the product of their slopes is −1.

CHECK IT OUT! **3.** Identify which lines are perpendicular: $y = -4; y - 6 = 5(x + 4);$ $x = 3; y = -\frac{1}{5}x + 2$.

EXAMPLE 4   *Geometry Application*

🖥️ Geometry

Show that *PQR* **is a right triangle.**

If *PQR* is a right triangle, $\overline{PQ}$ will be perpendicular to $\overline{QR}$.

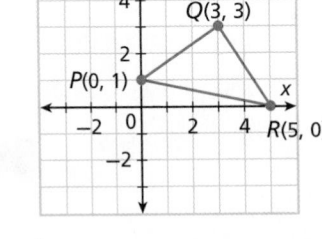

slope of $\overline{PQ} = \dfrac{3 - 1}{3 - 0} = \dfrac{2}{3}$

slope of $\overline{QR} = \dfrac{3 - 0}{3 - 5} = \dfrac{3}{-2} = -\dfrac{3}{2}$

$\overline{PQ}$ is perpendicular to $\overline{QR}$ because $\dfrac{2}{3}\left(-\dfrac{3}{2}\right) = -1$.

Therefore, *PQR* is a right triangle because it contains a right angle.

Helpful Hint

A right triangle contains one right angle. In Example 4, ∠*P* and ∠*R* are clearly not right angles, so the only possibility is ∠*Q*.

CHECK IT OUT! **4.** Show that $P(1, 4)$, $Q(2, 6)$, and $R(7, 1)$ are the vertices of a right triangle.

EXAMPLE 5 **Writing Equations of Parallel and Perpendicular Lines**

A Write an equation in slope-intercept form for the line that passes through $(4, 5)$ and is parallel to the line described by $y = 5x + 10$.

Step 1 Find the slope of the line.

$y = 5x + 10$ *The slope is 5.*

The parallel line also has a slope of 5.

Step 2 Write the equation in point-slope form.

$y - y_1 = m(x - x_1)$ *Use point-slope form.*

$y - 5 = 5(x - 4)$ *Substitute 5 for m, 4 for x_1, and 5 for y_1.*

Step 3 Write the equation in slope-intercept form.

$y - 5 = 5(x - 4)$

$y - 5 = 5x - 20$ *Distributive Property*

$y = 5x - 15$ *Addition Property of Equality*

B Write an equation in slope-intercept form for the line that passes through $(3, 2)$ and is perpendicular to the line described by $y = 3x - 1$.

Step 1 Find the slope of the line.

$y = 3x - 1$ *The slope is 3.*

The perpendicular line has a slope of $-\frac{1}{3}$, because $3\left(-\frac{1}{3}\right) = -1$.

Step 2 Write the equation in point-slope form.

$y - y_1 = m(x - x_1)$ *Use point-slope form.*

$y - 2 = -\frac{1}{3}(x - 3)$ *Substitute $-\frac{1}{3}$ for m, 3 for x_1, and 2 for y_1.*

Step 3 Write the equation in slope-intercept form.

$y - 2 = -\frac{1}{3}(x - 3)$

$y - 2 = -\frac{1}{3}x + 1$ *Distributive Property*

$y = -\frac{1}{3}x + 3$ *Addition Property of Equality*

Helpful Hint

If you know the slope of a line, the slope of a perpendicular line will be the "opposite reciprocal."

$\frac{2}{3} \rightarrow -\frac{3}{2}$

$\frac{1}{5} \rightarrow -5$

$-7 \rightarrow \frac{1}{7}$

 **CHECK IT OUT!**

5a. Write an equation in slope-intercept form for the line that passes through $(5, 7)$ and is parallel to the line described by $y = \frac{4}{5}x - 6$.

5b. Write an equation in slope-intercept form for the line that passes through $(-5, 3)$ and is perpendicular to the line described by $y = 5x$.

MATHEMATICAL PRACTICES

THINK AND DISCUSS

1. Are the lines described by $y = \frac{1}{2}x$ and $y = 2x$ perpendicular? Explain.

2. Describe the slopes and y-intercepts when two nonvertical lines are parallel.

3. GET ORGANIZED Copy and complete the graphic organizer. In each box, sketch an example and describe the slopes.

Parallel lines	Perpendicular lines

Exercises

GUIDED PRACTICE

1. **Vocabulary** ____?____ lines have the same slope. (*Parallel* or *Perpendicular*)

SEE EXAMPLE 1

Identify which lines are parallel.

2. $y = 6$; $y = 6x + 5$; $y = 6x - 7$; $y = -8$

3. $y = \frac{3}{4}x - 1$; $y = -2x$; $y - 3 = \frac{3}{4}(x - 5)$; $y - 4 = -2(x + 2)$

SEE EXAMPLE 2

4. **Geometry** Show that $ABCD$ is a trapezoid. (*Hint:* In a trapezoid, exactly one pair of opposite sides is parallel.)

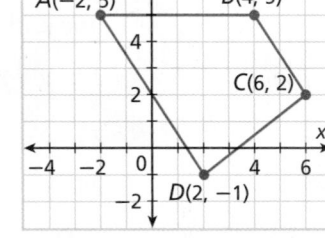

SEE EXAMPLE 3

Identify which lines are perpendicular.

5. $y = \frac{2}{3}x - 4$; $y = -\frac{3}{2}x + 2$; $y = -1$; $x = 3$

6. $y = -\frac{3}{7}x - 4$; $y - 4 = -7(x + 2)$;

   $y - 1 = \frac{1}{7}(x - 4)$; $y - 7 = \frac{7}{3}(x - 3)$

SEE EXAMPLE 4

7. **Geometry** Show that $PQRS$ is a rectangle. (*Hint:* In a rectangle, all four angles are right angles.)

SEE EXAMPLE 5

8. Write an equation in slope-intercept form for the line that passes through (5, 0) and is perpendicular to the line described by $y = -\frac{5}{2}x + 6$.

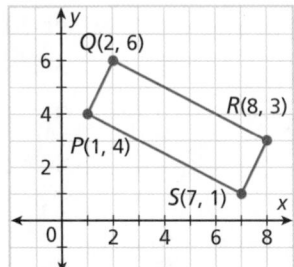

PRACTICE AND PROBLEM SOLVING

Independent Practice

For Exercises	See Example
9–11	1
12	2
13–15	3
16	4
17	5

Extra Practice

See Extra Practice for more Skills Practice and Applications Practice exercises.

Identify which lines are parallel.

9. $x = 7$; $y = -\frac{5}{6}x + 8$; $y = -\frac{5}{6}x - 4$; $x = -9$

10. $y = -x$; $y - 3 = -1(x + 9)$; $y - 6 = \frac{1}{2}(x - 14)$; $y + 1 = \frac{1}{2}x$

11. $y = -3x + 2$; $y = \frac{1}{2}x - 1$; $-x + 2y = 17$; $3x + y = 27$

12. **Geometry** Show that $LMNP$ is a parallelogram.

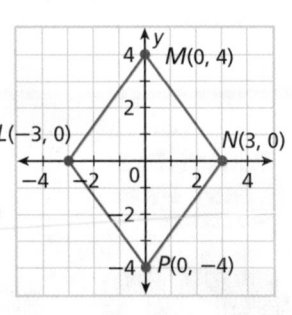

Identify which lines are perpendicular.

13. $y = 6x$; $y = \frac{1}{6}x$; $y = -\frac{1}{6}x$; $y = -6x$

14. $y - 9 = 3(x + 1)$; $y = -\frac{1}{3}x + 5$; $y = 0$; $x = 6$

15. $x - 6y = 15$; $y = 3x - 2$; $y = -3x - 3$; $y = -6x - 8$; $3y = -x - 11$

16. Geometry Show that *ABC* is a right triangle.

17. Write an equation in slope-intercept form for the line that passes through $(0, 0)$ and is parallel to the line described by $y = -\frac{6}{7}x + 1$.

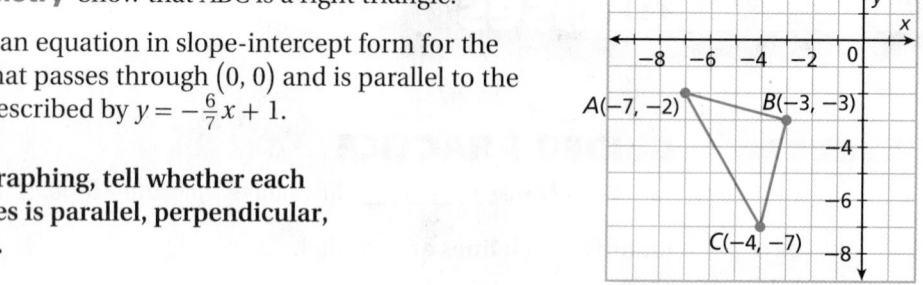
A(−7, −2) B(−3, −3)
C(−4, −7)

Without graphing, tell whether each pair of lines is parallel, perpendicular, or neither.

18. $x = 2$ and $y = -5$

19. $y = 7x$ and $y - 28 = 7(x - 4)$

20. $y = 2x - 1$ and $y = \frac{1}{2}x + 2$

21. $y - 3 = \frac{1}{4}(x - 3)$ and $y + 13 = \frac{1}{4}(x + 1)$

Write an equation in slope-intercept form for the line that is parallel to the given line and that passes through the given point.

22. $y = 3x - 7$; $(0, 4)$

23. $y = \frac{1}{2}x + 5$; $(4, -3)$

24. $4y = x$; $(4, 0)$

25. $y = 2x + 3$; $(1, 7)$

26. $5x - 2y = 10$; $(3, -5)$

27. $y = 3x - 4$; $(-2, 7)$

28. $y = 7$; $(2, 4)$

29. $x + y = 1$; $(2, 3)$

30. $2x + 3y = 7$; $(4, 5)$

31. $y = 4x + 2$; $(5, -3)$

32. $y = \frac{1}{2}x - 1$; $(0, -4)$

33. $3x + 4y = 8$; $(4, -3)$

Write an equation in slope-intercept form for the line that is perpendicular to the given line and that passes through the given point.

34. $y = -3x + 4$; $(6, -2)$

35. $y = x - 6$; $(-1, 2)$

36. $3x - 4y = 8$; $(-6, 5)$

37. $5x + 2y = 10$; $(3, -5)$

38. $y = 5 - 3x$; $(2, -4)$

39. $-10x + 2y = 8$; $(4, -3)$

40. $2x + 3y = 7$; $(4, 5)$

41. $4x - 2y = -6$; $(3, -2)$

42. $-2x - 8y = 16$; $(4, 5)$

43. $y = -2x + 4$; $(-2, 5)$

44. $y = x - 5$; $(0, 5)$

45. $x + y = 2$; $(8, 5)$

46. Write an equation describing the line that is parallel to the *y*-axis and that is 6 units to the right of the *y*-axis.

47. Write an equation describing the line that is perpendicular to the *y*-axis and that is 4 units below the *x*-axis.

48. Critical Thinking Is it possible for two linear functions whose graphs are parallel lines to have the same *y*-intercept? Explain.

49. Estimation Estimate the slope of a line that is perpendicular to the line through $(2.07, 8.95)$ and $(-1.9, 25.07)$.

50. Write About It Explain in words how to write an equation in slope-intercept form that describes a line parallel to $y - 3 = -6(x - 3)$.

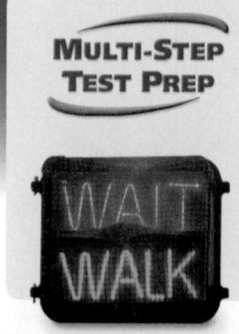
MULTI-STEP
TEST PREP

51. a. Flora walks from her home to the bus stop at a rate of 50 steps per minute. Write a rule that gives her distance from home (in steps) as a function of time.

b. Flora's neighbor Dan lives 30 steps closer to the bus stop. He begins walking at the same time and at the same pace as Flora. Write a rule that gives Dan's distance from *Flora's* house as a function of time.

c. Will Flora meet Dan along the walk? Use a graph to help explain your answer.

52. Which describes a line parallel to the line described by $y = -3x + 2$?

    Ⓐ $y = -3x$ Ⓑ $y = \frac{1}{3}x$ Ⓒ $y = 2 - 3x$ Ⓓ $y = \frac{1}{3}x + 2$

53. Which describes a line passing through $(3, 3)$ that is perpendicular to the line described by $y = \frac{3}{5}x + 2$?

    Ⓕ 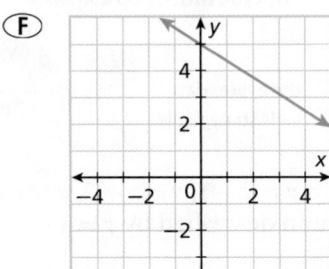   Ⓗ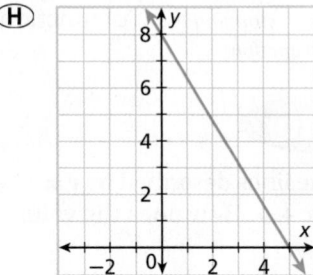

    Ⓖ $y = \frac{5}{3}x - 2$ Ⓙ $y = \frac{3}{5}x + \frac{6}{5}$

54. Gridded Response The graph of a linear function $f(x)$ is parallel to the line described by $2x + y = 5$ and contains the point $(6, -2)$. What is the y-intercept of $f(x)$?

CHALLENGE AND EXTEND

55. Three or more points that lie on the same line are called *collinear points*. Explain why the points *A*, *B*, and *C* must be collinear if the line containing *A* and *B* has the same slope as the line containing *B* and *C*.

56. The lines described by $y = (a + 12)x + 3$ and $y = 4ax$ are parallel. What is the value of *a*?

57. The lines described by $y = (5a + 3)x$ and $y = -\frac{1}{2}x$ are perpendicular. What is the value of *a*?

58. Geometry The diagram shows a square in the coordinate plane. Use the diagram to show that the diagonals of a square are perpendicular.

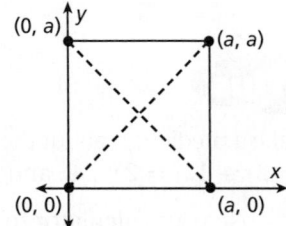

4-10
Technology LAB

Use with Transforming Linear Functions

The Family of Linear Functions

A *family of functions* is a set of functions whose graphs have basic characteristics in common. For example, all linear functions form a family. You can use a graphing calculator to explore families of functions.

 **Use appropriate tools strategically.**

Activity

Graph the lines described by $y = x - 2$, $y = x - 1$, $y = x$, $y = x + 1$, $y = x + 2$, $y = x + 3$, and $y = x + 4$. How does the value of b affect the graph described by $y = x + b$?

1 All of the functions are in the form $y = x + b$. Enter them into the **Y=** editor.

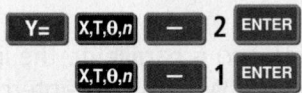

and so on.

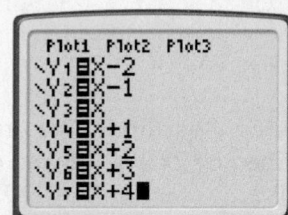

CC.9-12.F.BF.3 Identify the effect on the graph of replacing $f(x)$ by $f(x) + k$, $kf(x)$, $f(kx)$, and $f(x + k)$ for specific values of k. . . .

2 Press **ZOOM** and select **6:Zstandard.** Think about the different values of b as you watch the graphs being drawn. Notice that the lines are all parallel.

3 It appears that the value of b in $y = x + b$ shifts the graph up or down—up if b is positive and down if b is negative.

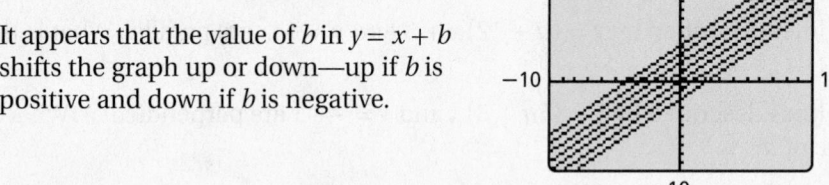

Try This

1. Make a prediction about the lines described by $y = 2x - 3$, $y = 2x - 2$, $y = 2x - 1$, $y = 2x$, $y = 2x + 1$, $y = 2x + 2$, and $y = 2x + 3$. Then graph. Was your prediction correct?

2. Now use your calculator to explore what happens to the graph of $y = mx$ when you change the value of m.

   a. Make a Prediction How do you think the lines described by $y = -2x$, $y = -x$, $y = x$, and $y = 2x$ will be related? How will they be alike? How will they be different?

   b. Graph the functions given in part **a**. Was your prediction correct?

   c. How is the effect of m different when m is positive from when m is negative?

4-10 Transforming Linear Functions

CC.9-12.F.BF.3 Identify the effect on the graph of replacing $f(x)$ by $f(x) + k$, $kf(x)$, $f(kx)$, and $f(x + k)$ for specific values of k (both positive and negative); ....

Objective
Describe how changing slope and *y*-intercept affect the graph of a linear function.

Vocabulary
family of functions
parent function
transformation
translation
rotation
reflection

Who uses this?
Business owners can use transformations to show the effects of price changes, such as the price of trophy engraving. (See Example 5.)

A **family of functions** is a set of functions whose graphs have basic characteristics in common. For example, all linear functions form a family because all of their graphs are the same basic shape.

A **parent function** is the most basic function in a family. For linear functions, the parent function is $f(x) = x$.

The graphs of all other linear functions are *transformations* of the graph of the parent function, $f(x) = x$. A **transformation** is a change in position or size of a figure.

There are three types of transformations—*translations, rotations,* and *reflections.*

Look at the four functions and their graphs below.

> **Remember!**
> Function notation—
> $f(x)$, $g(x)$, and so on—can be used in place of *y*.
> $y = f(x)$

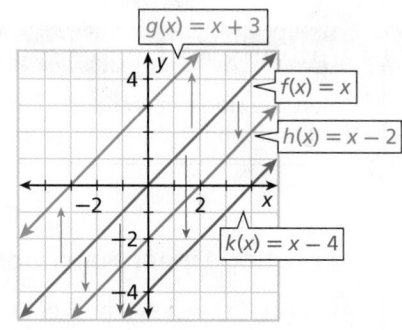

Notice that all of the lines above are parallel. The slopes are the same but the *y*-intercepts are different.

The graphs of $g(x) = x + 3$, $h(x) = x - 2$, and $k(x) = x - 4$ are vertical *translations* of the graph of the parent function, $f(x) = x$. A **translation** is a type of transformation that moves every point the same distance in the same direction. You can think of a translation as a "slide."

Vertical Translation of a Linear Function

When the *y*-intercept *b* is changed in the function $f(x) = mx + b$, the graph is translated vertically.

- If *b* increases, the graph is translated up.
- If *b* decreases, the graph is translated down.

4-10 Transforming Linear Functions **301**

EXAMPLE 1 **Translating Linear Functions**

Graph $f(x) = x$ and $g(x) = x - 5$. Then describe the transformation from the graph of $f(x)$ to the graph of $g(x)$.

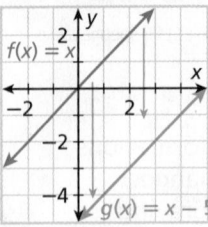 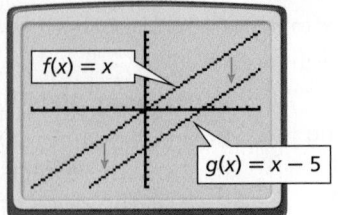

The graph of $g(x) = x - 5$ is the result of translating the graph of $f(x) = x$ 5 units down.

 **1.** Graph $f(x) = x + 4$ and $g(x) = x - 2$. Then describe the transformation from the graph of $f(x)$ to the graph of $g(x)$.

The graphs of $g(x) = 3x$, $h(x) = 5x$, and $k(x) = \frac{1}{2}x$ are *rotations* of the graph of $f(x) = x$. A **rotation** is a transformation about a point. You can think of a rotation as a "turn." The y-intercepts are the same, but the slopes are different.

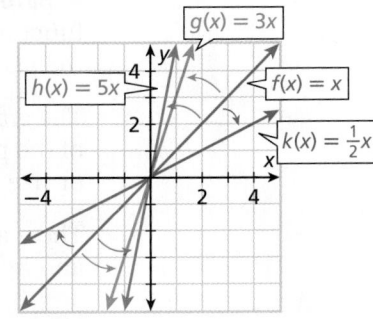

> **Know it!**
> **Note**

Rotation of a Linear Function

When the slope m is changed in the function $f(x) = mx + b$ it causes a rotation of the graph about the point $(0, b)$, which changes the line's steepness.

EXAMPLE 2 **Rotating Linear Functions**

Graph $f(x) = x + 2$ and $g(x) = 2x + 2$. Then describe the transformation from the graph of $f(x)$ to the graph of $g(x)$.

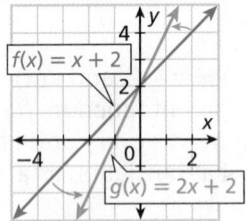 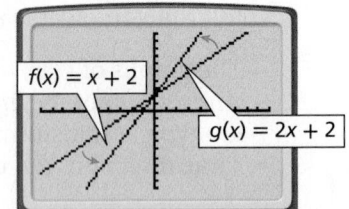

The graph of $g(x) = 2x + 2$ is the result of rotating the graph of $f(x) = x + 2$ about $(0, 2)$. The graph of $g(x)$ is steeper than the graph of $f(x)$.

 **2.** Graph $f(x) = 3x - 1$ and $g(x) = \frac{1}{2}x - 1$. Then describe the transformation from the graph of $f(x)$ to the graph of $g(x)$.

The diagram shows the *reflection* of the graph of $f(x) = 2x$ across the y-axis, producing the graph of $g(x) = -2x$. A **reflection** is a transformation across a line that produces a mirror image. You can think of a reflection as a "flip" over a line.

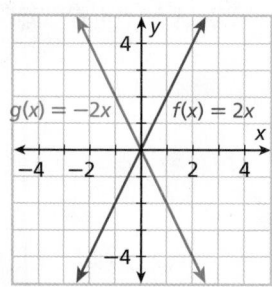

Reflection of a Linear Function

When the slope m is multiplied by -1 in $f(x) = mx + b$, the graph is reflected across the y-axis.

EXAMPLE 3

Reflecting Linear Functions

Graph $f(x)$. Then reflect the graph of $f(x)$ across the y-axis. Write a function $g(x)$ to describe the new graph.

A $f(x) = x$

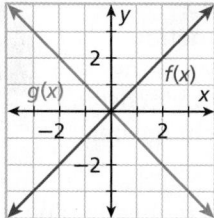
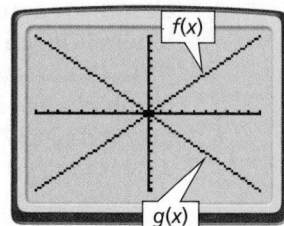

To find $g(x)$, multiply the value of m by -1.
In $f(x) = x$, $m = 1$.
$1(-1) = -1$ *This is the value of m for g(x).*
$g(x) = -x$

B $f(x) = -4x - 1$

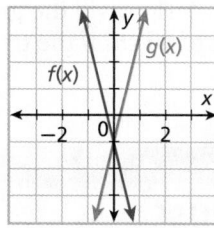
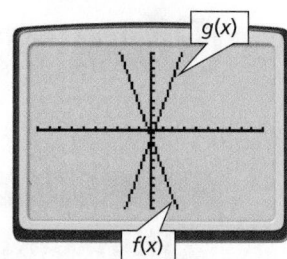

To find $g(x)$, multiply the value of m by -1.
In $f(x) = -4x - 1$, $m = -4$.
$-4(-1) = 4$ *This is the value of m for g(x).*
$g(x) = 4x - 1$

3. Graph $f(x) = \frac{2}{3}x + 2$. Then reflect the graph of $f(x)$ across the y-axis. Write a function $g(x)$ to describe the new graph.

EXAMPLE 4 Multiple Transformations of Linear Functions

Graph $f(x) = x$ and $g(x) = 3x + 1$. Then describe the transformations from the graph of $f(x)$ to the graph of $g(x)$.

Find transformations of $f(x) = x$ that will result in $g(x) = 3x + 1$:

- Multiply $f(x)$ by 3 to get $h(x) = 3x$. This rotates the graph about $(0, 0)$ and makes it steeper.

- Then add 1 to $h(x)$ to get $g(x) = 3x + 1$. This translates the graph 1 unit up.

The transformations are a rotation and a translation.

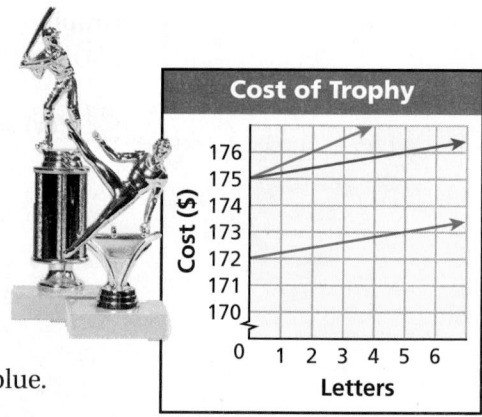

CHECK IT OUT! 4. Graph $f(x) = x$ and $g(x) = -x + 2$. Then describe the transformations from the graph of $f(x)$ to the graph of $g(x)$.

EXAMPLE 5 Business Application

A trophy company charges $175 for a trophy plus $0.20 per letter for the engraving. The total charge for a trophy with x letters is given by the function $f(x) = 0.20x + 175$. How will the graph change if the trophy's cost is lowered to $172? if the charge per letter is raised to $0.50?

Cost of Trophy

$f(x) = 0.20x + 175$ is graphed in blue.

If the trophy's cost is lowered to $172, the new function is $g(x) = 0.20x + 172$. The original graph will be translated 3 units down.

If the charge per letter is raised to $0.50, the new function is $h(x) = 0.50x + 175$. The original graph will be rotated about $(0, 175)$ and become steeper.

CHECK IT OUT! 5. **What if...?** How will the graph change if the charge per letter is lowered to $0.15? if the trophy's cost is raised to $180?

THINK AND DISCUSS

MATHEMATICAL PRACTICES

1. Describe the graph of $f(x) = x + 3.45$

2. Look at the graphs in Example 5. For each line, is every point on the line a solution in this situation? Explain.

3. **GET ORGANIZED** Copy and complete the graphic organizer. In each box, sketch a graph of the given transformation of $f(x) = x$, and label it with a possible equation.

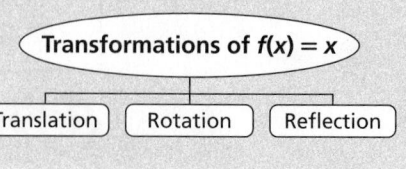

GUIDED PRACTICE

Vocabulary Apply the vocabulary from this lesson to answer each question.

1. Changing the value of b in $f(x) = mx + b$ results in a ___?___ of the graph. (*translation* or *reflection*)

2. Changing the value of m in $f(x) = mx + b$ results in a ___?___ of the graph. (*translation* or *rotation*)

Graph $f(x)$ and $g(x)$. Then describe the transformation from the graph of $f(x)$ to the graph of $g(x)$.

SEE EXAMPLE **1**

3. $f(x) = x$, $g(x) = x - 4$ **4.** $f(x) = x$, $g(x) = x + 1$

5. $f(x) = x$, $g(x) = x + 2$ **6.** $f(x) = x$, $g(x) = x - 6.5$

SEE EXAMPLE **2**

7. $f(x) = x$, $g(x) = \frac{1}{4}x$ **8.** $f(x) = \frac{1}{5}x + 3$, $g(x) = x + 3$

9. $f(x) = 2x - 2$, $g(x) = 4x - 2$ **10.** $f(x) = x + 1$, $g(x) = \frac{1}{2}x + 1$

Graph $f(x)$. Then reflect the graph of $f(x)$ across the y-axis. Write a function $g(x)$ to describe the new graph.

SEE EXAMPLE **3**

11. $f(x) = -\frac{1}{5}x$ **12.** $f(x) = 2x + 4$

13. $f(x) = \frac{1}{3}x - 6$ **14.** $f(x) = 5x - 1$

Graph $f(x)$ and $g(x)$. Then describe the transformations from the graph of $f(x)$ to the graph of $g(x)$.

SEE EXAMPLE **4**

15. $f(x) = x$, $g(x) = 2x - 2$ **16.** $f(x) = x$, $g(x) = \frac{1}{3}x + 1$

17. $f(x) = -x - 1$, $g(x) = -4x$ **18.** $f(x) = -x$, $g(x) = -\frac{1}{2}x - 3$

SEE EXAMPLE **5**

19. Entertainment For large parties, a restaurant charges a reservation fee of $25, plus $15 per person. The total charge for a party of x people is $f(x) = 15x + 25$. How will the graph of this function change if the reservation fee is raised to $50? if the per-person charge is lowered to $12?

PRACTICE AND PROBLEM SOLVING

Independent Practice

For Exercises	See Example
20–21	1
22–23	2
24–25	3
26–27	4
28	5

Extra Practice

See Extra Practice for more Skills Practice and Applications Practice exercises.

Graph $f(x)$ and $g(x)$. Then describe the transformation(s) from the graph of $f(x)$ to the graph of $g(x)$.

20. $f(x) = x$, $g(x) = x + \frac{1}{2}$ **21.** $f(x) = x$, $g(x) = x - 4$

22. $f(x) = \frac{1}{5}x - 1$, $g(x) = \frac{1}{10}x - 1$ **23.** $f(x) = x + 2$, $g(x) = \frac{2}{3}x + 2$

Graph $f(x)$. Then reflect the graph of $f(x)$ across the y-axis. Write a function $g(x)$ to describe the new graph.

24. $f(x) = 6x$ **25.** $f(x) = -3x - 2$

Graph $f(x)$ and $g(x)$. Then describe the transformations from the graph of $f(x)$ to the graph of $g(x)$.

26. $f(x) = 2x$, $g(x) = 4x - 1$ **27.** $f(x) = -7x + 5$, $g(x) = -14x$

28. **School** The number of chaperones on a field trip must include 1 teacher for every 4 students, plus 2 parents total. The function describing the number of chaperones for a trip of x students is $f(x) = \frac{1}{4}x + 2$. How will the graph change if the number of parents is reduced to 0? if the number of teachers is raised to 1 for every 3 students?

Describe the transformation(s) on the graph of $f(x) = x$ that result in the graph of $g(x)$. Graph $f(x)$ and $g(x)$, and compare the slopes and intercepts.

29. $g(x) = -x$

30. $g(x) = x + 8$

31. $g(x) = 3x$

32. $g(x) = -\frac{2}{7}x$

33. $g(x) = 6x - 3$

34. $g(x) = -2x + 1$

Sketch the transformed graph. Then write a function to describe your graph.

35. Rotate the graph of $f(x) = -x + 2$ until it has the same steepness in the opposite direction.

36. Reflect the graph of $f(x) = x - 1$ across the y-axis, and then translate it 4 units down.

37. Translate the graph of $f(x) = \frac{1}{6}x - 10$ six units up.

38. **Hobbies** A book club charges a membership fee of $20 and then $12 for each book purchased.

a. Write and graph a function to represent the cost y of membership in the club based on the number of books purchased x.

b. **What if...?** Write and graph a second function to represent the cost of membership if the club raises its membership fee to $30.

c. Describe the relationship between your graphs from parts **a** and **b**.

Describe the transformation(s) on the graph of $f(x) = x$ that result in the graph of $g(x)$.

39. $g(x) = x - 9$

40. $g(x) = -x$

41. $g(x) = 5x$

42. $g(x) = -\frac{2}{3}x + 1$

43. $g(x) = -2x$

44. $g(x) = \frac{1}{5}x$

45. **Careers** Kelly works as a salesperson. She earns a weekly base salary plus a commission that is a percent of her total sales. Her total weekly pay is described by $f(x) = 0.20x + 300$, where x is total sales in dollars.

a. What is Kelly's weekly base salary?

b. What percent of total sales does Kelly receive as commission?

c. **What if...?** What is the change in Kelly's salary plan if the weekly pay function changes to $g(x) = 0.25x + 300$? to $h(x) = 0.2x + 400$?

46. **Critical Thinking** To transform the graph of $f(x) = x$ into the graph of $g(x) = -x$, you can reflect the graph of $f(x)$ across the y-axis. Find another transformation that will have the same result.

47. **Write About It** Describe how a reflection across the y-axis affects each point on a graph. Give an example to illustrate your answer.

48. a. Maria is walking from school to the softball field at a rate of 3 feet per second. Write a rule that gives her distance from school (in feet) as a function of time (in seconds). Then graph.

b. Give a real-world situation that could be described by a line parallel to the one in part **a**.

c. What does the y-intercept represent in each of these situations?

Hobbies

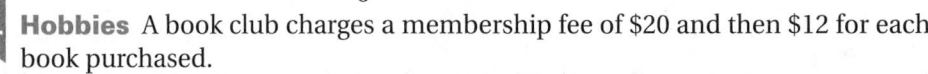

Seattle librarian Nancy Pearl started the first citywide reading program, "If All Seattle Reads the Same Book," in 1998. Many cities have since emulated this program, attempting to unite communities by having everyone read the same book at the same time.

49. Which best describes the effect on $f(x) = 2x - 5$ if the slope changes to 10?

    Ⓐ Its graph becomes less steep.

    Ⓑ Its graph moves 15 units up.

    Ⓒ Its graph makes 10 complete rotations.

    Ⓓ The x-intercept becomes $\frac{1}{2}$.

50. Given $f(x) = 22x - 182$, which does NOT describe the effect of increasing the y-intercept by 182?

    Ⓕ The new line passes through the origin.

    Ⓖ The new x-intercept is 0.

    Ⓗ The new line is parallel to the original.

    Ⓙ The new line is steeper than the original.

CHALLENGE AND EXTEND

51. You have seen that the graph of $g(x) = x + 3$ is the result of translating the graph of $f(x) = x$ three units up. However, you can also think of this as a *horizontal* translation—that is, a translation left or right. Graph $g(x) = x + 3$. Describe the horizontal translation of the graph of $f(x) = x$ to get the graph of $g(x) = x + 3$.

52. If $c > 0$, how can you describe the translation that transforms the graph of $f(x) = x$ into the graph of $g(x) = x + c$ as a horizontal translation? $g(x) = x - c$ as a horizontal translation?

MULTI-STEP TEST PREP

MATHEMATICAL PRACTICES

Make sense of problems and persevere in solving them.

Using Linear Functions

Take a Walk! All intersections in Durango, Colorado, have crossing signals with timers. Once the signal changes to walk, the timer begins at 28 seconds and counts down to show how much time pedestrians have to cross the street.

1. Pauline counted her steps as she crossed the street. She counted 15 steps with 19 seconds remaining. When she reached the opposite side of the street, she had counted a total of 30 steps and had 10 seconds remaining. Copy and complete the table below using these values.

Time Remaining (s)	28		
Steps	0		

2. Find the average rate of change for Pauline's walk.

3. Sketch a graph of the points in the table, or plot them on your graphing calculator.

4. Find an equation that describes the line through the points.

5. How would the graph change if Pauline increased her speed? What if she decreased her speed?

READY TO GO ON?

Quiz for Lessons 4-6 Through 4-10

4-6 Slope-Intercept Form

Write each equation in slope-intercept form. Then graph the line described by the equation.

1. $2x + y = 5$

2. $2x - 6y = 6$

3. $3x + y = 3x - 4$

4. Entertainment At a chili cook-off, people pay a $3.00 entrance fee and $0.50 for each bowl of chili they taste. The graph shows the total cost per person as a function of the number of bowls of chili tasted.

   a. Write an equation that represents the total cost per person as a function of the number of bowls of chili tasted.

   b. Identify the slope and y-intercept and describe their meanings.

Chili Cook-off

4-7 Point-Slope Form

Graph the line with the given slope that contains the given point.

5. slope $= -3$; $(0, 3)$

6. slope $= -\dfrac{2}{3}$; $(-3, 5)$

7. slope $= 2$; $(-3, -1)$

Write an equation in slope-intercept form for the line through the two points.

8. $(3, 1)$ and $(4, 3)$

9. $(-1, -1)$ and $(1, 7)$

10. $(1, -4)$ and $(-2, 5)$

4-8 Line of Best Fit

11. A street vendor noted the daily high temperature and the number of ice cream cones she sold each day for one week. Find an equation for a line of best fit. How well does the line represent the data?

Temperature (°F)	80	73	65	90	96	100	82
Ice Cream Cones Sold	32	27	22	38	45	48	35

4-9 Slopes of Parallel and Perpendicular Lines

Identify which lines are parallel.

12. $y = -2x$; $y = 2x + 1$; $y = 2x$; $y = 2(x + 5)$

13. $-3y = x$; $y = -\dfrac{1}{3}x + 1$; $y = -3x$; $y + 2 = x + 4$

Identify which lines are perpendicular.

14. $y = -4x - 1$; $y = \dfrac{1}{4}x$; $y = 4x - 6$; $x = -4$

15. $y = -\dfrac{3}{4}x$; $y = \dfrac{3}{4}x - 3$; $y = \dfrac{4}{3}x$; $y = 4$; $x = 3$

4-10 Transforming Linear Functions

Graph $f(x)$ and $g(x)$. Then describe the transformation(s) from the graph of $f(x)$ to the graph of $g(x)$.

16. $f(x) = 5x$, $g(x) = -5x$

17. $f(x) = \dfrac{1}{2}x - 1$, $g(x) = \dfrac{1}{2}x + 4$

EXTENSION Absolute-Value Functions

CC.9-12.F.BF.3 Identify the effect on the graph of replacing $f(x)$ by $f(x) + k$, $kf(x)$, $f(kx)$, and $f(x + k)$ for specific values of k (both positive and negative); find the value of k given the graphs.... *Also* **CC.9-12.F.IF.7***

Objectives
Graph absolute-value functions.

Identify characteristics of absolute-value functions and their graphs.

Vocabulary
absolute-value function
axis of symmetry
vertex

An **absolute-value function** is a function whose rule contains an absolute-value expression. To graph an absolute-value function, choose several values of x and generate some ordered pairs.

x	$f(x) = |x|$
-2	2
-1	1
0	0
1	1
2	2

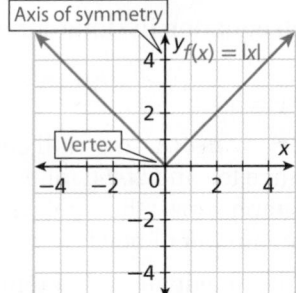

Absolute-value graphs are composed of two linear pieces. The **axis of symmetry** is the line that divides the graph into two congruent halves. The **vertex** is the "corner" point on the graph.

From the table and the graph of $f(x) = |x|$, you can tell that

- the **axis of symmetry** is the y-axis $(x = 0)$.
- the **vertex** is $(0, 0)$.
- the domain $(x$-values$)$ is the set of all real numbers.
- the range $(y$-values$)$ is described by $y \geq 0$.
- the x-intercept and the y-intercept are both 0.
- the slope of the left linear piece is -1 and the slope of the right linear piece is 1.

EXAMPLE **1** **Absolute-Value Functions**

Graph $f(x) = |2x| - 1$ and label the axis of symmetry and the vertex. Identify the intercepts, give the domain and range, and find the slope of each piece.

Choose positive, negative, and zero values for x, and find ordered pairs.

x	-2	-1	0	1	2
$f(x) = |2x| - 1$	3	1	-1	1	3

Plot the ordered pairs and connect them.

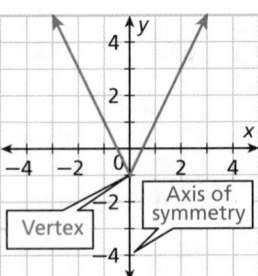

From the table and the graph, you can tell that

- the axis of symmetry is the y-axis $(x = 0)$.
- the vertex is $(0, -1)$.
- the x-intercepts are $\dfrac{1}{2}$ and $-\dfrac{1}{2}$.
- the y-intercept is -1.
- the domain is all real numbers.
- the range is described by $y \geq -1$.
- the slope of the left piece is -2 and the slope of the right piece is 2.

310 *Chapter 4 Linear Functions*

 **1.** Graph $f(x) = 3|x|$ and label the axis of symmetry and the vertex. Identify the intercepts, give the domain and range, and find the slope of each piece.

The parent function for absolute-value functions is $f(x) = |x|$. The graphs of all other absolute-value functions are transformations of the graph of $f(x) = |x|$.

For $f(x) = a|x - b| + c$

WORDS	EXAMPLES	WORDS	EXAMPLES
Opening Direction • If $a > 0$, the graph opens upward. • If $a < 0$, the graph opens downward.	$f(x) = |x|$ $g(x) = -|x|$	**Horizontal Translation** • If $b > 0$, the graph is translated b units right from $f(x) = |x|$. • If $b < 0$, the graph is translated b units left from $f(x) = |x|$.	$h(x) = |x + 2|$ $f(x) = |x|$ $g(x) = |x - 2|$
Width • If $|a| > 1$, the graph is narrower than the graph of $f(x) = |x|$. • If $|a| < 1$, the graph is wider than the graph of $f(x) = |x|$. The slopes of the two linear pieces are a and $-a$.	$g(x) = 3|x|$ $f(x) = |x|$ $h(x) = \frac{1}{2}|x|$	**Vertical Translation** • If $c > 0$, the graph is translated c units up from $f(x) = |x|$. • If $c < 0$, the graph is translated c units down from $f(x) = |x|$.	$g(x) = |x| + 2$ $f(x) = |x|$ $h(x) = |x| - 2$

EXAMPLE 2 Transforming Absolute-Value Functions

Describe the transformations from the graph of $f(x) = |x|$ to the graph of $g(x)$. Then graph both functions.

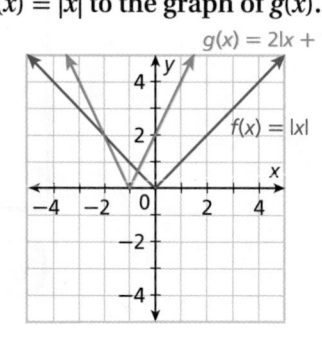
$g(x) = 2|x + 1|$

A $g(x) = 2|x + 1|$

Identify a, b, and c.

$g(x) = 2|x + 1| = 2|x - (-1)| + 0$

- $a = 2$: graph is narrower
- $b = -1$: translated 1 unit left
- $c = 0$: no vertical translation

Describe the transformations from the graph of $f(x) = |x|$ to the graph of $g(x)$. Then graph both functions.

B $g(x) = -|x - 3| + 2$

Identify a, b, and c.

$g(x) = -|x - 3| + 2 = -1|x - 3| + 2$

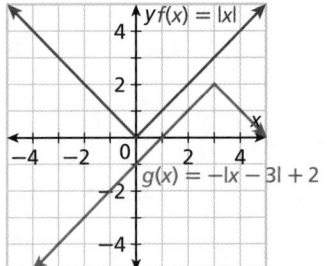

- $a = -1$: graph opens downward and width is unchanged
- $b = 3$: translated 3 units right
- $c = 2$: translated 2 units up

 Describe the transformations from the graph of $f(x) = |x|$ to the graph of $g(x)$. Then graph both functions.

2a. $g(x) = |x - 4| - 2$ **2b.** $g(x) = \frac{1}{3}|x| + 1$

Minimum and Maximum Values of Absolute-Value Functions

WORDS	If the graph of an absolute-value function opens upward, the *y*-value of the vertex is the **minimum** value of the function.	If the graph of an absolute-value function opens downward, the *y*-value of the vertex is the **maximum** value of the function.
EXAMPLES	$f(x) = 2|x| - 2$ Vertex: (0, −2) Minimum: −2	$f(x) = -|x - 1|$ Vertex: (1, 0) Maximum: 0

EXAMPLE 3 **Identifying the Minimum or Maximum**

Graph $f(x) = |x + 3| - 5$. Identify the vertex and give the minimum or maximum value of the function.

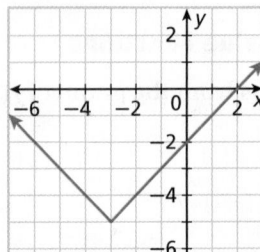

The vertex is (−3, −5).

The graph opens upward, so the function has a minimum.

The minimum is −5.

 Graph each absolute-value function. Identify the vertex and give the minimum or maximum value of the function.

3a. $f(x) = -|x| + 5$ **3b.** $f(x) = |x + 1| - 6$

EXAMPLE *Sports Application*

In a charity race, a water stand for the runners is halfway between the start and finish lines. The function $y = \left| \frac{x}{8} - 3 \right|$ models Riley's distance y in miles from the water stand x minutes into the race.

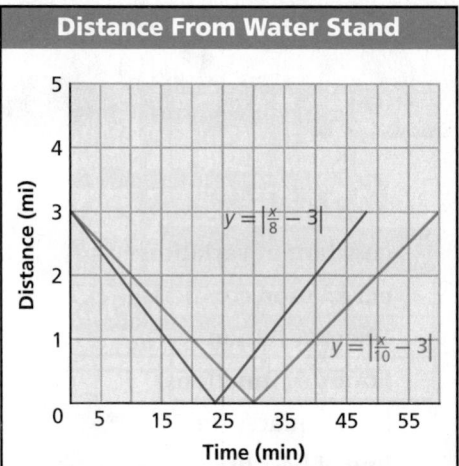

Distance From Water Stand

A How long is the race?

$y = \left| \frac{x}{8} - 3 \right|$ is graphed in blue.

At the start of the race ($x = 0$), Riley is 3 mi from the water stand. The water stand is halfway between the start and finish lines, so the race is 6 mi.

B How much time does it take Riley to reach the water stand?

When Riley reaches the water stand, $y = 0$. This happens when $x = 24$. It takes Riley 24 min to reach the water stand.

C The function $y = \left| \frac{x}{10} - 3 \right|$ models Dean's distance from the water stand during the same race. Compare Dean's graph to Riley's graph. What can you conclude about Dean's speed?

$y = \left| \frac{x}{10} - 3 \right|$ is graphed in red. Both graphs start at the same point, but Dean's graph is translated to the right. It takes him more time to reach the water stand and to finish the race. Therefore, he is running more slowly than Riley.

CHECK IT OUT! **4.** How would the graph be different for someone who runs faster than Riley?

EXTENSION

Exercises

Graph each absolute-value function and label the axis of symmetry and the vertex. Identify the intercepts, give the domain and range, and find the slope of each piece. Identify the maximum or minimum.

1. $f(x) = |x| + 3$ **2.** $f(x) = |x + 3|$ **3.** $f(x) = \frac{1}{2}|x|$ **4.** $f(x) = |x - 3|$

Tell whether each statement is sometimes, always, or never true.

5. The absolute value of a number is negative.

6. An absolute-value function has an x-intercept.

7. An absolute-value function has two y-intercepts.

Write a function to describe each of the following.

8. The graph of $f(x) = |x|$ is translated 2 units right.

9. The graph of $f(x) = |x|$ is narrowed and reflected across the x-axis.

10. Critical Thinking Suppose that an absolute-value function has no x-intercepts. What can you say about the function rule?

Study Guide: Review

Vocabulary

constant of variation	linear regression	rotation
correlation coefficient	parallel lines	run
direct variation	parent function	slope
family of functions	perpendicular lines	transformation
least-squares line	rate of change	translation
line of best fit	reflection	*x*-intercept
linear equation	residual	*y*-intercept
linear function	rise	

Complete the sentences below with vocabulary words from the list above. Words may be used more than once.

1. A(n) ___?___ is a "slide," a(n) ___?___ is a "turn," and a(n) ___?___ is a "flip."

2. The *x*-coordinate of the point that contains the ___?___ is always 0.

3. In the equation $y = mx + b$, the value of *m* is the ___?___, and the value of *b* is the ___?___.

4-1 Identifying Linear Functions

EXAMPLES

Tell whether each function is linear. If so, graph the function.

■ $y = -3x + 2$

$$
\begin{array}{ll}
y = -3x + 2 & \textit{Write the equation in} \\
\underline{+\,3x \quad +\,3x} & \textit{standard form.} \\
3x + y = \qquad 2 & \textit{This is a linear function.}
\end{array}
$$

Generate ordered pairs.

x	$y = -3x + 2$	*(x, y)*
−2	$y = -3(-2) + 2 = 8$	(−2, 8)
x	$y = -3(0) + 2 = 2$	(0, 2)
x	$y = -3(2) + 2 = -4$	(2, −4)

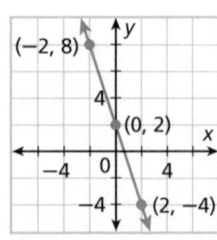

Plot the points and connect them with a straight line.

■ $y = 2x^3$

This is not a linear function because *x* has an exponent other than 1.

EXERCISES

Tell whether the given ordered pairs satisfy a linear function. Explain.

4.

x	*y*
−3	3
−1	1
1	1
3	3

5.

x	*y*
0	−3
1	−1
2	1
3	3

6. $\{(-2, 5), (-1, 3), (0, 1), (1, -1), (2, -3)\}$

7. $\{(1, 7), (3, 6), (6, 5), (9, 4), (13, 3)\}$

Each equation below is linear. Write each equation in standard form and give the values of *A*, *B*, and *C*.

8. $y = -5x + 1$

9. $\dfrac{x + 2}{2} = -3y$

10. $4y = 7x$

11. $9 = y$

12. Helene is selling cupcakes for $0.50 each. The function $f(x) = 0.5x$ gives the total amount of money Helene makes after selling *x* cupcakes. Graph this function and give its domain and range.

4-2 Using Intercepts

EXAMPLE

■ Find the *x*- and *y*-intercepts of $2x + 5y = 10$.

Let $y = 0$.

$2x + 5(0) = 10$
$2x + 0 = 10$
$2x = 10$
$\dfrac{2x}{2} = \dfrac{10}{2}$
$x = 5$

Let $x = 0$.

$2(0) + 5y = 10$
$0 + 5y = 10$
$5y = 10$
$\dfrac{5y}{5} = \dfrac{10}{5}$
$y = 2$

The *x*-intercept is 5.   The *y*-intercept is 2.

EXERCISES

Find the *x*- and *y*-intercepts.

13.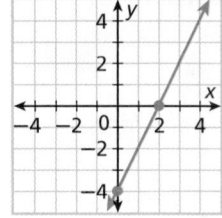

14.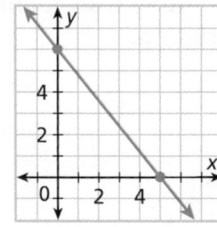

15. $3x - y = 9$

16. $-2x + y = 1$

17. $-x + 6y = 18$

18. $3x - 4y = 1$

4-3 Rate of Change and Slope

EXAMPLE

■ Find the slope of the line.

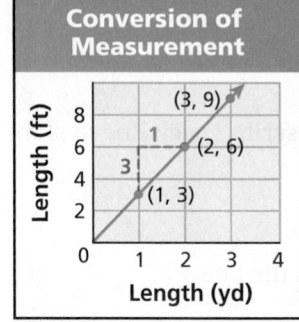

$$\text{slope} = \frac{\text{change in } y}{\text{change in } x}$$

$$= \frac{3}{1} = 3$$

EXERCISES

19. Graph the data and show the rates of change.

Time (s)	Distance (ft)
0	0
1	16
2	64
3	144
4	256

20. Find the slope of the line graphed below.

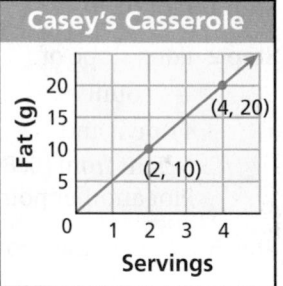

4-4 The Slope Formula

EXAMPLE

■ Find the slope of the line described by $2x - 3y = 6$.

Step 1 Find the *x*- and *y*-intercepts.

Let $y = 0$.

$2x - 3(0) = 6$
$2x = 6$
$x = 3$

Let $x = 0$.

$2(0) - 3y = 6$
$-3y = 6$
$y = -2$

The line contains $(3, 0)$ and $(0, -2)$.

Step 2 Use the slope formula.

$$m = \frac{y_2 - y_1}{x_2 - x_1} = \frac{-2 - 0}{0 - 3} = \frac{-2}{-3} = \frac{2}{3}$$

EXERCISES

Find the slope of the line described by each equation.

21. $4x + 3y = 24$

22. $y = -3x + 6$

23. $x + 2y = 10$

24. $3x = y + 3$

25. $y + 2 = 7x$

26. $16x = 4y + 1$

Find the slope of the line that contains each pair of points.

27. $(1, 2)$ and $(2, -3)$

28. $(4, -2)$ and $(-5, 7)$

29. $(-3, -6)$ and $(4, 1)$

30. $\left(\dfrac{1}{2}, 2\right)$ and $\left(\dfrac{3}{4}, \dfrac{5}{2}\right)$

31. $(2, 2)$ and $(2, 7)$

32. $(1, -3)$ and $(5, -3)$

4-5 Direct Variation

EXAMPLE

- Tell whether $6x = -4y$ represents a direct variation. If so, identify the constant of variation.

$$6x = -4y$$

$$\frac{6x}{-4} = \frac{-4y}{-4} \qquad \textit{Solve the equation for y.}$$

$$-\frac{6}{4}x = y$$

$$y = -\frac{3}{2}x \qquad \textit{Simplify.}$$

This equation represents a direct variation because it can be written in the form $y = kx$, where $k = -\frac{3}{2}$.

EXERCISES

Tell whether each equation is a direct variation. If so, identify the constant of variation.

33. $y = -6x$ **34.** $x - y = 0$

35. $y + 4x = 3$ **36.** $2x = -4y$

37. The value of y varies directly with x, and $y = -8$ when $x = 2$. Find y when $x = 3$.

38. Maleka charges \$8 per hour for baby-sitting. The amount of money she makes varies directly with the number of hours she baby-sits. Write a direct variation equation for the amount y Maleka earns for baby-sitting x hours. Then graph.

4-6 Slope-Intercept Form

EXAMPLE

- Graph the line with slope $= -\frac{4}{5}$ and y-intercept $= 8$.

  Step 1 Plot $(0, 8)$.

  Step 2 For a slope of $\frac{-4}{5}$, count **4 down** and **5 right** from $(0, 8)$. Plot another point.

  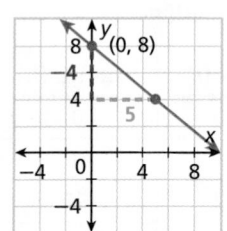

  Step 3 Connect the two points with a line.

EXERCISES

Graph each line given the slope and y-intercept.

39. slope $= -\frac{1}{2}$; y-intercept $= 4$

40. slope $= 3$; y-intercept $= -7$

Write the equation that describes each line in slope-intercept form.

41. slope $= \frac{1}{3}$, y-intercept $= 5$

42. slope $= 4$, $(1, -5)$ is on the line.

4-7 Point-Slope Form

EXAMPLE

- Write an equation in slope-intercept form for the line through $(4, -1)$ and $(-2, 8)$.

  Step 1 Find the slope.

  $$m = \frac{y_2 - y_1}{x_2 - x_1} = \frac{8 - (-1)}{-2 - 4} = \frac{9}{-6} = -\frac{3}{2}$$

  Step 2 Write the point-slope form.

  $$y - 8 = -\frac{3}{2}[x - (-2)] \qquad \textit{Substitute into the point-slope form.}$$

  $$y - 8 = -\frac{3}{2}(x + 2)$$

  Step 3 Write the slope-intercept form.

  $$y = -\frac{3}{2}x + 5 \qquad \textit{Solve for y.}$$

EXERCISES

Graph the line described by each equation.

43. $y + 3 = \frac{1}{2}(x - 4)$ **44.** $y - 1 = -(x + 3)$

Write the equation that describes each line in slope-intercept form.

45. slope $= 2$, $(1, 3)$ is on the line.

46. slope $= -5$, $(-6, 4)$ is on the line.

47. $(1, 4)$ and $(3, 8)$ are on the line.

48. $(-2, 4)$ and $(-1, 6)$ are on the line.

4-8 Line of Best Fit

EXAMPLE

■ Two lines of fit for the data in the table are $y = -x + 5$ and $y = -0.5x + 4$. For each line, find the sum of the squares of the residuals. Which line is a better fit?

x	1	2	4	5
y	3	4	2	1

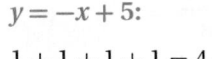

$y = -x + 5$:

$1 + 1 + 1 + 1 = 4$

$y = -0.5x + 4$:

$\frac{1}{4} + 1 + 0 + \frac{1}{4} = 2\frac{1}{2}$

$y = -0.5x + 4$ is a better fit.

EXERCISES

49. Two lines of fit for the data in the table are $y = 0.5x$ and $y = x - 1$. For each line, find the sum of the squares of the residuals. Which line is a better fit?

x	1	2	4	5
y	2	0	1	3

50. The lengths and weights of 6 koi in a pond are shown in the table. Find an equation of a line of best fit. How well does the line fit the data?

Length (in.)	9	12	11	15	8	10
Weight (oz)	5	11	9	20	4	7

4-9 Slopes of Parallel and Perpendicular Lines

EXAMPLE

■ Write an equation in slope-intercept form for the line that passes through $(4, -2)$ and is perpendicular to the line described by $y = -4x + 3$.

The slope of $y = -4x + 3$ is -4.

The perpendicular line has a slope of $\frac{1}{4}$ and contains $(4, -2)$.

$y + 2 = \frac{1}{4}(x - 4)$ *Substitute into the point-slope form.*

$y = \frac{1}{4}x - 3$ *Solve for y.*

EXERCISES

Identify which lines are parallel.

51. $y = -\frac{1}{3}x$; $y = 3x + 2$; $y = -\frac{1}{3}x - 6$; $y = 3$

52. $y - 2 = -4(x - 1)$; $y = 4x - 4$; $y = \frac{1}{4}x$; $y = -4x - 2$

Identify which lines are perpendicular.

53. $y - 1 = -5(x - 6)$; $y = \frac{1}{5}x + 2$; $y = 5$; $y = 5x + 8$

54. $y = 2x$; $y - 2 = 3(x + 1)$; $y = \frac{2}{3}x - 4$; $y = -\frac{1}{3}x$

55. Write an equation in slope-intercept form for the line that passes through $(1, -1)$ and is parallel to the line described by $y = 2x - 4$.

4-10 Transforming Linear Functions

EXAMPLE

■ Graph $f(x) = \frac{1}{2}x$ and $g(x) = 4x + 2$. Then describe the transformation(s) from the graph of $f(x)$ to the graph of $g(x)$.

• Multiply $f(x) = \frac{1}{2}x$ by 8 to get $h(x) = 4x$. This rotates the graph about $(0, 0)$, making it steeper.

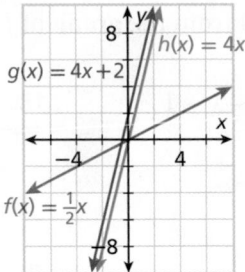

• Then add 2 to $h(x) = 4x$ to get $g(x) = 4x + 2$. This translates the graph 2 units up.

EXERCISES

Graph $f(x)$ and $g(x)$. Then describe the transformation(s) from the graph of $f(x)$ to the graph of $g(x)$.

56. $f(x) = x$, $g(x) = x + 4$

57. $f(x) = 4x$, $g(x) = -4x$

58. $f(x) = \frac{1}{3}x - 2$, $g(x) = -\frac{1}{3}x - 2$

59. The entrance fee at a carnival is $3 and each ride costs $1. The total cost for x rides is $f(x) = x + 3$. How will the graph of this function change if the entrance fee is increased to $5? if the cost per ride is increased to $2?

CHAPTER TEST

Tell whether each function is linear. If so, graph the function.

1. $3y = 2x + 3$

2. $y = x(4 + x)$

3. Lily plans to volunteer at the tutoring center for 45 hours. She can tutor 3 hours per week. The function $f(x) = 45 - 3x$ gives the number of hours she will have left to tutor after x weeks. Graph the function and find its intercepts. What does each intercept represent?

4. The table shows the number of guppies in an aquarium over time. Graph the data and show the rates of change.

Time (mo)	0	1	2	5	8
Guppies	4	4	10	25	31

Find the slope of each line. Then tell what the slope represents.

5.

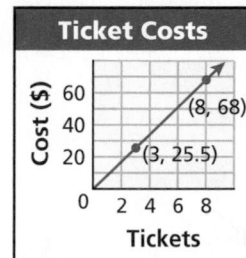

6.

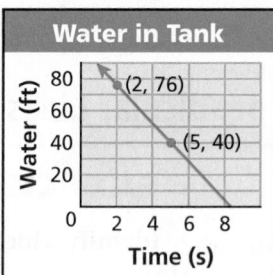

7.

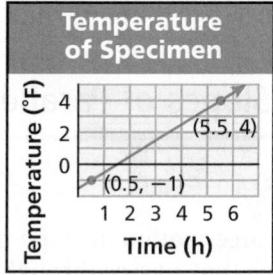

8. A space shuttle travels at a speed of about 5 miles per second. Write a direct variation equation for the distance y the space shuttle will travel in x seconds. Then graph.

9. Write the equation $2x - 2y = 4$ in slope-intercept form. Then graph the line described by the equation.

Write the equation that describes each line in slope-intercept form.

10. slope = 4, (–3, 3) is on the line.

11. x-intercept = 3, y-intercept = –3

Write an equation in point-slope form for the line with the given slope that contains the given point.

12. slope = –1; (1, 3)

13. slope = 5; (–3, 2)

14. Four friends recorded the numbers of CDs and video games their families purchased in the last month, as shown in the table. Find an equation of a line of best fit. How well does the line fit the data?

CDs	2	3	5	6
Games	2	5	4	6

15. Write an equation in slope-intercept form for the line that passes through (0, 6) and is parallel to the line described by $y = 2x + 3$.

Graph $f(x)$ and $g(x)$. Then describe the transformation(s) from the graph of $f(x)$ to the graph of $g(x)$.

16. $f(x) = 8x$, $g(x) = 4x$

17. $f(x) = -x + 2$, $g(x) = -x - 1$

18. $f(x) = 3x$, $g(x) = 6x - 1$

FOCUS ON SAT

SAT scores are based on the total number of items answered correctly minus a fraction of the number of multiple-choice questions answered incorrectly. No points are subtracted for questions unanswered.

On the SAT, there is a penalty for incorrect answers on multiple-choice items. Guess only when you can eliminate at least one of the answer choices.

You may want to time yourself as you take this practice test. It should take you about 7 minutes to complete.

---

1. The line through $A(1, -3)$ and $B(-2, d)$ has slope -2. What is the value of d?

(A) $-\dfrac{3}{2}$

(B) -1

(C) $\dfrac{1}{2}$

(D) 3

(E) 5

---

2. The ordered pairs $\{(0, -3), (4, -1), (6, 0),$ $(10, 2)\}$ satisfy a pattern. Which is NOT true?

(A) The pattern is linear.

(B) The pattern can be described by $2x - 4y = 12$.

(C) The ordered pairs lie on a line.

(D) $(-4, 1)$ satisfies the same pattern.

(E) The set of ordered pairs is a function.

---

3. If y varies directly as x, what is the value of x when $y = 72$?

x	7	12	
y	28	48	72

(A) 17

(B) 18

(C) 24

(D) 28

(E) 36

---

4. The line segment between the points $(4, 0)$ and $(2, -2)$ forms one side of a rectangle. Which of the following coordinates could determine another vertex of that rectangle?

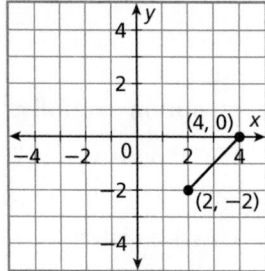

(A) $(-2, 6)$

(B) $(-2, -2)$

(C) $(0, 6)$

(D) $(1, 2)$

(E) $(4, 6)$

---

5. Which of the following has the same slope as the line described by $2x - 3y = 3$?

(A) $3x - 2y = 2$

(B) $\dfrac{2}{3}x - y = -2$

(C) $2x - 2y = 3$

(D) $\dfrac{1}{3}x - 2y = -2$

(E) $-2x - 3y = 2$

CHAPTER 4

TEST TACKLER

Standardized Test Strategies

Multiple Choice: Recognize Distracters

In multiple-choice items, the options that are incorrect are called *distracters*. This is an appropriate name, because these incorrect options can distract you from the correct answer.

Test writers create distracters by using common student errors. Beware! Even if the answer you get when you work the problem is one of the options, it may not be the correct answer.

EXAMPLE 1

What is the y-intercept of $4x + 10 = -2y$?

(A) 10

(B) 5

(C) -2.5

(D) -5

Look at each option carefully.

(A) This is a distracter. The y-intercept would be 10 if the function was $4x + 10 = y$. A common error is to ignore the coefficient of y.

(B) This is a distracter. Another common error is to divide by 2 instead of -2 when solving for y.

(C) This is a distracter. One of the most common errors students make is confusing the x-intercept and the y-intercept. This distracter is actually the *x-intercept* of the given line.

(D) This is the correct answer.

EXAMPLE 2

What is the equation of a line with a slope of -4 that contains $(2, -3)$?

(F) $y - 3 = -4(x - 2)$

(G) $y - 2 = -4(x + 3)$

(H) $y + 3 = -4(x - 2)$

(J) $y + 4 = -3(x - 2)$

Look at each option carefully.

(F) This is a distracter. Students often make errors with positive and negative signs. You would get this answer if you simplified $y - (-3)$ as $y - 3$.

(G) This is a distracter. You would get this answer if you switched the x-coordinate and the y-coordinate.

(H) This is the correct answer.

(J) This is a distracter. You would get this answer if you substituted the given values incorrectly in the point-slope equation.

When you calculate an answer to a multiple-choice test item, try to solve the problem again with a different method to make sure your answer is correct.

Read each test item and answer the questions that follow.

Item A
A line contains $(1, 2)$ and $(-2, 14)$. What are the slope and y-intercept?

(A) Slope $= -4$; y-intercept $= -2$

(B) Slope $= 4$; y-intercept $= 6$

(C) Slope $= -\frac{1}{4}$; y-intercept $= 1$

(D) Slope $= -4$; y-intercept $= 6$

1. What common error does the slope in choice B represent?

2. The slope given in choice A is correct, but the y-intercept is not. What error was made when finding the y-intercept?

3. What formula can you use to find the slope of a line? How was this formula used incorrectly to get the slope in choice C?

Item B
Which of these functions has a graph that is NOT parallel to the line described by $y = \frac{1}{2}x + 4$?

(F) $y = 6 - \frac{1}{2}x$

(G) $y = \frac{1}{2}x + 6$

(H) $-2y = -x + 1$

(J) $2y = x$

4. When given two linear functions, describe how to determine whether their graphs are parallel.

5. Which is the correct answer? Describe the errors a student might make to get each of the distracters.

Item C
Which of these lines has a slope of -3?

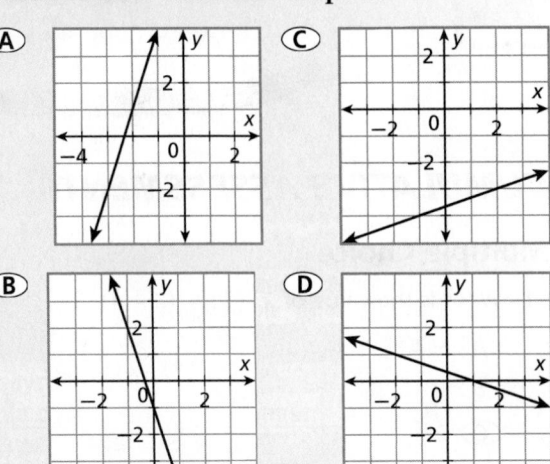

6. Which two answer choices can be eliminated immediately? Why?

7. Describe how to find the slope of a line from its graph.

8. What common error does choice A represent?

9. What common error does choice D represent?

10. Which is the correct answer?

Item D
Which is NOT a linear function?

(F) $f(x) = 4 + x$

(G) $f(x) = -x - 4$

(H) $f(x) = 4x^2$

(J) $f(x) = \frac{1}{4}x$

11. When given a function rule, how can you tell if the function is linear?

12. What part of the function given in choice G might make someone think it is not linear?

13. What part of the function given in choice J might make someone think it is not linear?

14. What part of the function given in choice H makes it NOT linear?

STANDARDIZED TEST PREP

CUMULATIVE ASSESSMENT

Multiple Choice

1. What is the value of $2 - \left[1 - (2 - 1)\right]$?

- (A) −2
- (B) 0
- (C) 2
- (D) 4

2. Frank borrowed $5000 with an annual simple interest rate. The amount of interest he owed after 6 months was $300. What is the interest rate of the loan?

- (F) 1%
- (G) 6%
- (H) 10%
- (J) 12%

3. Patty's Pizza charges $5.50 for a large pizza plus $0.30 for each topping. Pizza Town charges $5.00 for a large pizza plus $0.40 for each topping. Which inequality can you use to find the number of toppings x so that the cost of a pizza at Pizza Town is greater than the cost of a pizza at Patty's Pizza?

- (A) $(5 + 0.4)x > (5.5 + 0.3)x$
- (B) $5.5x + 0.3 > 5x + 0.4$
- (C) $5.5 + 0.3x > 5 + 0.4x$
- (D) $5 + 0.4x > 5.5 + 0.3x$

4. The side length of a square s can be determined by the formula $s = \sqrt{A}$ where A represents the area of the square. What is the side length of a square with area 0.09 square meter?

- (F) 0.0081 meters
- (G) 0.81 meters
- (H) 0.03 meters
- (J) 0.3 meters

5. What is the value of $f(x) = -3 - x$ when $x = -7$?

- (A) −10
- (B) −4
- (C) 4
- (D) 10

6. Which relationship is a direct variation?

(F)

x	1	2	3	4
y	−1	0	1	2

(G)

x	1	2	3	4
y	0	−1	−2	−3

(H)

x	1	2	3	4
y	3	5	7	9

(J)

x	1	2	3	4
y	3	6	9	12

7. Which function has x-intercept −2 and y-intercept 4?

- (A) $2x - y = 4$
- (B) $2y - x = 4$
- (C) $y - 2x = 4$
- (D) $x - 2y = 4$

8. Which equation describes the relationship between x and y in the table below?

x	−8	−4	0	4	8
y	2	1	0	−1	−2

- (F) $y = -4x$
- (G) $y = -\frac{1}{4}x$
- (H) $y = 4x$
- (J) $y = \frac{1}{4}x$

9. Which graph is described by $x - 3y = -3$?

(A)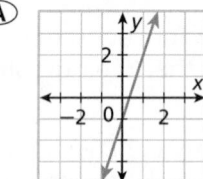

(C)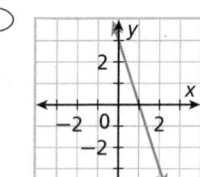

(B)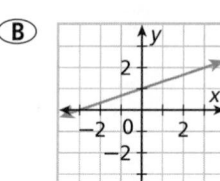

(D)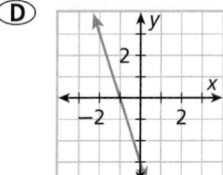

When answering multiple-choice test items, check that the test item number matches the number on your answer sheet, especially if you skip test items that you plan to come back to.

10. Which steps could you use to graph the line that has slope 2 and contains the point $(-1, 3)$?

(F) Plot $(-1, 3)$. Move 1 unit up and 2 units right and plot another point.

(G) Plot $(-1, 3)$. Move 2 units up and 1 unit right and plot another point.

(H) Plot $(-1, 3)$. Move 1 unit up and 2 units left and plot another point.

(J) Plot $(-1, 3)$. Move 2 units up and 1 unit left and plot another point.

11. Which line is parallel to the line described by $2x + 3y = 6$?

(A) $3x + 2y = 6$ (C) $2x + 3y = -6$

(B) $3x - 2y = -6$ (D) $2x - 3y = 6$

12. Which function's graph is NOT perpendicular to the line described by $4x - y = -2$?

(F) $y + \frac{1}{4}x = 0$ (H) $3y = \frac{3}{4}x + 3$

(G) $\frac{1}{2}x = 10 - 2y$ (J) $y = -\frac{1}{4}x + \frac{3}{2}$

13. Company A charges $30 plus $0.40 per mile for a car rental. The total charge for m miles is given by $f(m) = 30 + 0.4m$. For a similar car, company B charges $30 plus $0.30 per mile. The total charge for m miles is given by $g(m) = 30 + 0.3m$. Which best describes the transformation from the graph of $f(m)$ to the graph of $g(m)$?

(A) Translation up

(B) Translation down

(C) Rotation

(D) Reflection

Gridded Response

14. What is the value of x in the diagram below?

$$\triangle ABC \sim \triangle DEF$$

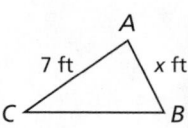 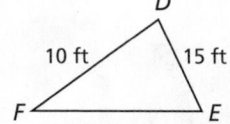

15. What is the 46th term in the arithmetic sequence $-1.5, -1.3, -1.1, -0.9, \ldots$?

16. What is the y-intercept of $y - 2 = 3(x + 4)$?

Short Response

17. A video store charges a $10 membership fee plus $2 for each movie rental. The total cost for x movie rentals is given by $f(x) = 2x + 10$.

a. Graph this function.

b. Give a reasonable domain and range.

18. The table below shows the federal minimum wage in different years.

Year	1960	1970	1980	1990	2000
Minimum Wage ($)	1.00	1.60	3.10	3.80	5.15

a. Find the rate of change for each ten-year time period. Show your work.

b. During which time period did the minimum wage increase the fastest? Explain what the rate of change for this time period means.

19. a. Find the slope of the line below.

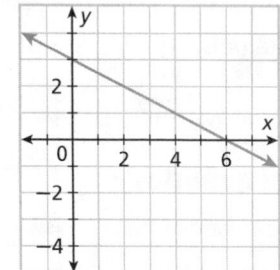

b. Write an equation in slope-intercept form for a line that is perpendicular to the line in part **a** and has the same y-intercept as the function in part **a**. Show your work and explain how you found your answer.

Extended Response

20. The relationship between the wind speed at a given temperature and the apparent temperature is approximately linear. The table shows the apparent temperature at various wind speeds when the actual temperature is t °F.

Wind Speed (mi/h)	5	10	15
Apparent Temperature (°F)	36	34	32

a. Write an equation in slope-intercept form that describes the data in the table. Explain how you found your answer.

b. What does the slope mean in this situation?

c. What is the actual temperature t? Explain.

d. Determine the apparent temperature when the wind speed is 12 miles per hour. Show your work.

CHAPTER 5

Systems of Equations and Inequalities

COMMON CORE

Chapter Focus

- Solve real-world problems involving systems of linear equations and inequalities.

Where's *the Money?*

You can solve a system of equations to determine how many basketball game tickets you can buy at different price levels.

Learn It Online
Chapter Project Online

ARE YOU READY?

✅ Vocabulary

Match each term on the left with a definition on the right.

1. inequality
2. linear equation
3. ordered pair
4. slope
5. solution of an equation

A. a pair of numbers (x, y) that represent the coordinates of a point

B. a statement that two quantities are not equal

C. the y-value of the point at which the graph of an equation crosses the y-axis

D. a value of the variable that makes the equation true

E. the ratio of the vertical change to the horizontal change for a nonvertical line

F. an equation whose graph is a straight line

✅ Graph Linear Functions

Graph each function.

6. $y = \frac{3}{4}x + 1$
7. $y = -3x + 5$
8. $y = x - 6$
9. $x + y = 4$
10. $y = -\frac{2}{3}x + 4$
11. $y = -5$

✅ Solve Multi-Step Equations

Solve each equation.

12. $-7x - 18 = 3$
13. $12 = -3n + 6$
14. $\frac{1}{2}d + 30 = 32$
15. $-2p + 9 = -3$
16. $33 = 5y + 8$
17. $-3 + 3x = 27$

✅ Solve for a Variable

Solve each equation for y.

18. $7x + y = 4$
19. $y + 2 = -4x$
20. $8 = x - y$
21. $x + 2 = y - 5$
22. $2y - 3 = 12x$
23. $y + \frac{3}{4}x = 4$

✅ Evaluate Expressions

Evaluate each expression for the given value of the variable.

24. $t - 5$ for $t = 7$
25. $9 - 2a$ for $a = 4$
26. $\frac{1}{2}x - 2$ for $x = 14$
27. $n + 15$ for $n = 37$
28. $9c + 4$ for $c = \frac{1}{3}$
29. $16 + 3d$ for $d = 5$

✅ Solve and Graph Inequalities

Solve and graph each inequality.

30. $b - 9 \geq 1$
31. $-2x < 10$
32. $3y \leq -3$
33. $\frac{1}{3}y \leq 5$

Study Guide: Preview

Previously, you

- solved one-step and multi-step equations.
- solved one-step and multi-step inequalities.
- graphed linear equations on a coordinate plane.

In This Chapter

You will study

- how to find a solution that satisfies two linear equations.
- how to find solutions that satisfy two linear inequalities.
- how to graph one or more linear inequalities on a coordinate plane.

Where You're Going

You can use the skills in this chapter

- to determine which purchases are better deals.
- in other classes, such as Economics and Chemistry.
- to solve linear equations that involve three or more variables in future math classes.

Key Vocabulary/Vocabulario

consistent system	sistema consistente
dependent system	sistema dependiente
inconsistent system	sistema inconsistente
independent system	sistema independiente
linear inequality	desigualdad lineal
solution of a linear inequality	solución de una desigualdad lineal
system of linear equations	sistema de ecuaciones lineales

Vocabulary Connections

To become familiar with some of the vocabulary terms in the chapter, consider the following. You may refer to the chapter, the glossary, or a dictionary if you like.

1. The word *system* means "a group." How do you think a **system of linear equations** is different from a linear equation?

2. A **consistent system** has *at least one* solution. How many solutions do you think an **inconsistent system** has?

3. A **dependent system** has infinitely many solutions. Which vocabulary term above means a system with *exactly one* solution?

4. A solution of a linear equation is an ordered pair that makes the equation true. Modify this to define **solution of a linear inequality**.

Reading *and* Writing Math

Writing Strategy: Write a Convincing Argument/Explanation

The Write About It icon appears throughout the book. These icons identify questions that require you to write a complete argument or explanation. Writing a convincing argument or explanation shows that you have a solid understanding of a concept.

To be effective, an argument or explanation should include

- evidence, work, or facts.
- a complete response that will answer or explain.

> **23. Write About It** Lewis invested $1000 at 3% simple interest for 4 years. Lisa invested $1000 at 4% simple interest for 3 years. Explain why Lewis and Lisa earned the same amount of interest.

Step 1 **Identify what you need to answer or explain.**
Explain why Lewis and Lisa earned the same amount of interest.

Step 2 **Give evidence, work, or facts that are needed to answer the question.**
Use the formula for simple interest to find the amount of interest earned: $I = Prt$.

Lewis: $P = 1000$, $r = 0.03$, $t = 4$ **Lisa:** $P = 1000$, $r = 0.04$, $t = 3$

$$I = Prt = 1000(0.03)(4) = 120 \qquad I = Prt = 1000(0.04)(3) = 120$$

$$I = 1000(0.12) = \$120 \qquad\qquad I = 1000(0.12) = \$120$$

Step 3 **Write a complete response that answers or explains.**
Lewis and Lisa both invested the same amount of money, $1000. They earned the same amount of interest because 0.04×3 and 0.03×4 both equal 0.12. They both earned $0.12 \times \$1000$, or $120.

Try This

Write a convincing argument or explanation.

1. What is the least whole number that is a solution of $12x + 15.4 > 118.92$? Explain.

2. Which equation has an error? Explain the error.

   A. $4(6 \cdot 5) = (4)6 \cdot (4)5$ **B.** $4(6 \cdot 5) = (4 \cdot 6)5$

Solve Linear Equations by Using a Spreadsheet

You can use a spreadsheet to answer "What if...?" questions. By changing one or more values, you can quickly model different scenarios.

Use with Solving Systems by Graphing

Learn It Online
Lab Resources Online

Activity

Company Z makes DVD players. The company's costs are $400 per week plus $20 per DVD player. Each DVD player sells for $45. How many DVD players must company Z sell in one week to make a profit?

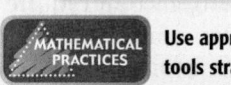
MATHEMATICAL PRACTICES

Use appropriate tools strategically.

CC.9-12.A.REI.3 Solve linear equations and inequalities in one variable, including equations with coefficients represented by letters.

Let n represent the number of DVD players company Z sells in one week.

$c = 400 + 20n$ *The total cost is $400 plus $20 times the number of DVD players made.*

$s = 45n$ *The total sales income is $45 times the number of DVD players sold.*

$p = s - c$ *The total profit is the sales income minus the total cost.*

1 Set up your spreadsheet with columns for number of DVD players, total cost, total income, and profit.

2 Under Number of DVD Players, enter 1 in cell A2.

Company Z Profit

	A	B	C	D
1	Number of DVD Players	Total Cost ($)	Total Income ($)	Profit ($)
2	1	420	45	-375

= 400 + 20*A2   = 45*A2   = C2 – B2

3 Use the equations above to enter the formulas for total cost, total sales, and total profit in row 2.

 • In cell B2, enter the formula for total cost.

 • In cell C2, enter the formula for total sales income.

 • In cell D2, enter the formula for total profit.

4 Fill columns A, B, C, and D by selecting cells A1 through D1, clicking the small box at the bottom right corner of cell D2, and dragging the box down through several rows.

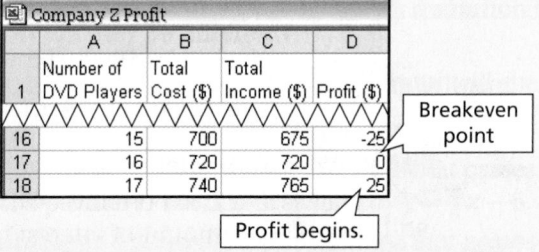

Company Z Profit

	A	B	C	D
1	Number of DVD Players	Total Cost ($)	Total Income ($)	Profit ($)
16	15	700	675	-25
17	16	720	720	0
18	17	740	765	25

Breakeven point

Profit begins.

5 Find the point where the profit is $0. This is known as the breakeven point, where total cost and total income are the same.

Company Z must sell 17 DVD players to make a profit. The profit is $25.

Try This

For Exercises 1 and 2, use the spreadsheet from the activity.

1. If company Z sells 10 DVD players, will they make a profit? Explain. What if they sell 16?

2. Company Z makes a profit of $225 dollars. How many DVD players did they sell?

For Exercise 3, make a spreadsheet.

3. Company Y's costs are $400 per week plus $20 per DVD player. They want the breakeven point to occur with sales of 8 DVD players. What should the sales price be?

COMMON CORE

5-1 Solving Systems by Graphing

CC.9-12.A.REI.6 Solve systems of linear equations exactly and approximately (e.g., with graphs), focusing on pairs of linear equations in two variables. *Also* **CC.9-12.A.REI.11*, CC.9-12.A.CED.2*, CC.9-12.A.CED.3***

Objectives
Identify solutions of systems of linear equations in two variables.

Solve systems of linear equations in two variables by graphing.

Vocabulary
system of linear equations
solution of a system of linear equations

Why learn this?
You can compare costs by graphing a system of linear equations. (See Example 3.)

Sometimes there are different charges for the same service or product at different places. For example, Bowl-o-Rama charges $2.50 per game plus $2 for shoe rental while Bowling Pinz charges $2 per game plus $4 for shoe rental. A *system of linear equations* can be used to compare these charges.

A **system of linear equations** is a set of two or more linear equations containing two or more variables. A **solution of a system of linear equations** with two variables is an ordered pair that satisfies each equation in the system. So, if an ordered pair is a solution, it will make both equations true.

EXAMPLE 1 | **Identifying Solutions of Systems**

Tell whether the ordered pair is a solution of the given system.

A $(4, 1)$; $\begin{cases} x + 2y = 6 \\ x - y = 3 \end{cases}$

$x + 2y = 6$	
$4 + 2(1)$	6
$4 + 2$	6
	6 | 6 ✓

$x - y = 3$	
$4 - 1$	3
	3 | 3 ✓

Substitute 4 for x and 1 for y in each equation in the system.

The ordered pair $(4, 1)$ makes both equations true.

$(4, 1)$ is a solution of the system.

> **Helpful Hint**
> If an ordered pair does not satisfy the first equation in the system, there is no need to check the other equations.

B $(-1, 2)$; $\begin{cases} 2x + 5y = 8 \\ 3x - 2y = 5 \end{cases}$

$2x + 5y = 8$	
$2(-1) + 5(2)$	8
$-2 + 10$	8
	8 | 8 ✓

$3x - 2y = 5$	
$3(-1) - 2(2)$	5
$-3 - 4$	5
	-7 | 5 ✗

Substitute −1 for x and 2 for y in each equation in the system.

The ordered pair $(-1, 2)$ makes one equation true, but not the other.

$(-1, 2)$ is not a solution of the system.

 **CHECK IT OUT!** Tell whether the ordered pair is a solution of the given system.

1a. $(1, 3)$; $\begin{cases} 2x + y = 5 \\ -2x + y = 1 \end{cases}$ **1b.** $(2, -1)$; $\begin{cases} x - 2y = 4 \\ 3x + y = 6 \end{cases}$

5-1 Solving Systems by Graphing **329**

All solutions of a linear equation are on its graph. To find a solution of a system of linear equations, you need a point that each line has in common. In other words, you need their point of intersection.

$$\begin{cases} y = 2x - 1 \\ y = -x + 5 \end{cases}$$

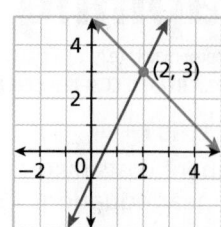

The point $(2, 3)$ is where the two lines intersect and is a solution of both equations, so $(2, 3)$ is the solution of the system.

EXAMPLE 2 **Solving a System of Linear Equations by Graphing**

Solve each system by graphing. Check your answer.

A $\begin{cases} y = x - 3 \\ y = -x - 1 \end{cases}$

Helpful Hint

Sometimes it is difficult to tell exactly where the lines cross when you solve by graphing. It is good to confirm your answer by substituting it into both equations.

Graph the system.

The solution appears to be at $(1, -2)$.

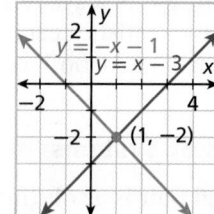

Check

Substitute $(1, -2)$ into the system.

$y = x - 3$	
-2	$1 - 3$
-2	$-2 \checkmark$

$y = -x - 1$	
-2	$-1 - 1$
-2	$-2 \checkmark$

The solution is $(1, -2)$.

B $\begin{cases} x + y = 0 \\ y = -\dfrac{1}{2}x + 1 \end{cases}$

$$\begin{aligned} x + y &= 0 \qquad \text{Rewrite the first equation in slope-intercept form.} \\ \underline{-x \; -x} & \\ y &= -x \end{aligned}$$

Graph using a calculator and then use the intersection command.

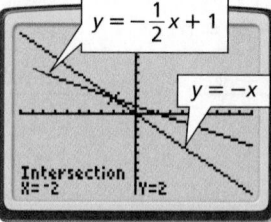

Check Substitute $(-2, 2)$ into the system.

$x + y = 0$	
$-2 + 2$	0
0	$0 \checkmark$

$y = -\dfrac{1}{2}x + 1$	
2	$-\dfrac{1}{2}(-2) + 1$
2	$1 + 1$
2	$2 \checkmark$

The solution is $(-2, 2)$.

 **Solve each system by graphing. Check your answer.**

2a. $\begin{cases} y = -2x - 1 \\ y = x + 5 \end{cases}$

2b. $\begin{cases} y = \dfrac{1}{3}x - 3 \\ 2x + y = 4 \end{cases}$

EXAMPLE **3** | *Problem-Solving Application*

MATHEMATICAL PRACTICES

Make sense of problems and persevere in solving them.

Bowl-o-Rama charges $2.50 per game plus $2 for shoe rental, and Bowling Pinz charges $2 per game plus $4 for shoe rental. For how many games will the cost to bowl be the same at both places? What is that cost?

1 **Understand the Problem**

The **answer** will be the number of games played for which the total cost is the same at both bowling alleys. **List the important information:**
• Game price: Bowl-o-Rama $2.50   Bowling Pinz: $2
• Shoe-rental fee: Bowl-o-Rama $2   Bowling Pinz: $4

2 **Make a Plan**

Write a system of equations, one equation to represent the price at each company. Let x be the number of games played and y be the total cost.

Total cost	is	price per game	times	games	plus	shoe rental.
Bowl-o-Rama y	=	2.5	•	x	+	2
Bowling Pinz y	=	2	•	x	+	4

3 **Solve**

Graph $y = 2.5x + 2$ and $y = 2x + 4$. The lines appear to intersect at $(4, 12)$. So, the cost at both places will be the same for 4 games bowled and that cost will be $12.

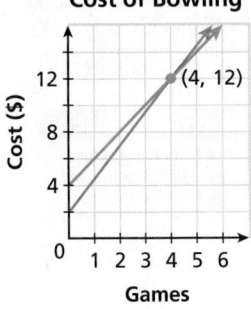

Cost of Bowling

4 **Look Back**

Check $(4, 12)$ using both equations.
Cost of bowling 4 games at Bowl-o-Rama:
$2.5(4) + $2 = 10 + 2 = 12 ✓
Cost of bowling 4 games at Bowling Pinz:
$2(4) + $4 = 8 + 4 = 12 ✓

3. Video club A charges $10 for membership and $3 per movie rental. Video club B charges $15 for membership and $2 per movie rental. For how many movie rentals will the cost be the same at both video clubs? What is that cost?

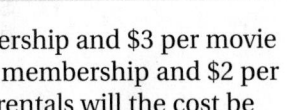

MATHEMATICAL PRACTICES

THINK AND DISCUSS

1. Explain how to use a graph to solve a system of linear equations.

2. Explain how to check a solution of a system of linear equations.

3. **GET ORGANIZED** Copy and complete the graphic organizer. In each box, write a step for solving a linear system by graphing. More boxes may be added.

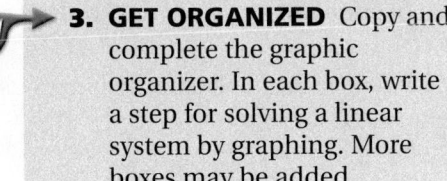

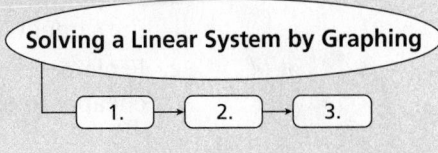

Solving a Linear System by Graphing

1. → 2. → 3.

Exercises

GUIDED PRACTICE

1. **Vocabulary** Describe a *solution of a system of linear equations*.

SEE EXAMPLE 1   Tell whether the ordered pair is a solution of the given system.

2. $(2, -2)$; $\begin{cases} 3x + y = 4 \\ x - 3y = -4 \end{cases}$ 3. $(3, -1)$; $\begin{cases} x - 2y = 5 \\ 2x - y = 7 \end{cases}$ 4. $(-1, 5)$; $\begin{cases} -x + y = 6 \\ 2x + 3y = 13 \end{cases}$

SEE EXAMPLE 2   Solve each system by graphing. Check your answer.

5. $\begin{cases} y = \dfrac{1}{2}x \\ y = -x + 3 \end{cases}$ 6. $\begin{cases} y = x - 2 \\ 2x + y = 1 \end{cases}$ 7. $\begin{cases} -2x - 1 = y \\ x + y = 3 \end{cases}$

SEE EXAMPLE 3   8. To deliver mulch, Lawn and Garden charges $30 per cubic yard of mulch plus a $30 delivery fee. Yard Depot charges $25 per cubic yard of mulch plus a $55 delivery fee. For how many cubic yards will the cost be the same? What will that cost be?

PRACTICE AND PROBLEM SOLVING

Independent Practice

For Exercises	See Example
9–11	1
12–15	2
16	3

Tell whether the ordered pair is a solution of the given system.

9. $(1, -4)$; $\begin{cases} x - 2y = 8 \\ 4x - y = 8 \end{cases}$ 10. $(-2, 1)$; $\begin{cases} 2x - 3y = -7 \\ 3x + y = -5 \end{cases}$ 11. $(5, 2)$; $\begin{cases} 2x + y = 12 \\ -3y - x = -11 \end{cases}$

Solve each system by graphing. Check your answer.

Extra Practice

See Extra Practice for more Skills Practice and Applications Practice exercises.

12. $\begin{cases} y = \dfrac{1}{2}x + 2 \\ y = -x - 1 \end{cases}$ 13. $\begin{cases} y = x \\ y = -x + 6 \end{cases}$ 14. $\begin{cases} -2x - 1 = y \\ x = -y + 3 \end{cases}$ 15. $\begin{cases} x + y = 2 \\ y = x - 4 \end{cases}$

16. **Multi-Step** Angelo runs 7 miles per week and increases his distance by 1 mile each week. Marc runs 4 miles per week and increases his distance by 2 miles each week. In how many weeks will Angelo and Marc be running the same distance? What will that distance be?

17. **School** The school band sells carnations on Valentine's Day for $2 each. They buy the carnations from a florist for $0.50 each, plus a $16 delivery charge.

   a. Write a system of equations to describe the situation.

   b. Graph the system. What does the solution represent?

   c. Explain whether the solution shown on the graph makes sense in this situation. If not, give a reasonable solution.

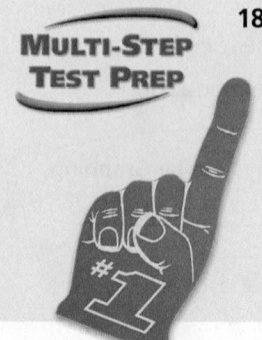

MULTI-STEP TEST PREP

18. a. The Warrior baseball team is selling hats as a fund-raiser. They contacted two companies. Hats Off charges a $50 design fee and $5 per hat. Top Stuff charges a $25 design fee and $6 per hat. Write an equation for each company's pricing.

   b. Graph the system of equations from part **a**. For how many hats will the cost be the same? What is that cost?

   c. Explain when it is cheaper for the baseball team to use Top Stuff and when it is cheaper to use Hats Off.

Graphing Calculator Use a graphing calculator to graph and solve the systems of equations in Exercises 19–22. Round your answer to the nearest tenth.

19. $\begin{cases} y = 4.7x + 2.1 \\ y = 1.6x - 5.4 \end{cases}$

20. $\begin{cases} 4.8x + 0.6y = 4 \\ y = -3.2x + 2.7 \end{cases}$

21. $\begin{cases} y = \dfrac{5}{4}x - \dfrac{2}{3} \\ \dfrac{8}{3}x + y = \dfrac{5}{9} \end{cases}$

22. $\begin{cases} y = 6.9x + 12.4 \\ y = -4.1x - 5.3 \end{cases}$

Landscaping

Middleton Place Gardens, South Carolina, are the United States' oldest landscaped gardens. The gardens were established in 1741 and opened to the public in the 1920s.

23. **Landscaping** The gardeners at Middleton Place Gardens want to plant a total of 45 white and pink hydrangeas in one flower bed. In another flower bed, they want to plant 120 hydrangeas. In this bed, they want 2 times the number of white hydrangeas and 3 times the number of pink hydrangeas as in the first bed. Use a system of equations to find how many white and how many pink hydrangeas the gardeners should buy altogether.

24. **Fitness** Rusty burns 5 Calories per minute swimming and 11 Calories per minute jogging. In the morning, Rusty burns 200 Calories walking and swims for x minutes. In the afternoon, Rusty will jog for x minutes. How many minutes must he jog to burn at least as many Calories y in the afternoon as he did in the morning? Round your answer up to the next whole number of minutes.

25. A tree that is 2 feet tall is growing at a rate of 1 foot per year. A 6-foot tall tree is growing at a rate of 0.5 foot per year. In how many years will the trees be the same height?

26. **Critical Thinking** Write a real-world situation that could be represented by the system $\begin{cases} y = 3x + 10 \\ y = 5x + 20 \end{cases}$.

27. **Write About It** When you graph a system of linear equations, why does the intersection of the two lines represent the solution of the system?

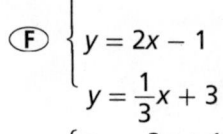

28. Taxi company A charges $4 plus $0.50 per mile. Taxi company B charges $5 plus $0.25 per mile. Which system best represents this problem?

(A) $\begin{cases} y = 4x + 0.5 \\ y = 5x + 0.25 \end{cases}$

(C) $\begin{cases} y = -4x + 0.5 \\ y = -5x + 0.25 \end{cases}$

(B) $\begin{cases} y = 0.5x + 4 \\ y = 0.25x + 5 \end{cases}$

(D) $\begin{cases} y = -0.5x + 4 \\ y = -0.25x + 5 \end{cases}$

29. Which system of equations represents the given graph?

(F) $\begin{cases} y = 2x - 1 \\ y = \dfrac{1}{3}x + 3 \end{cases}$

(H) $\begin{cases} y = 2x + 1 \\ y = \dfrac{1}{3}x - 3 \end{cases}$

(G) $\begin{cases} y = -2x + 1 \\ y = 2x - 3 \end{cases}$

(J) $\begin{cases} y = -2x - 1 \\ y = 3x - 3 \end{cases}$

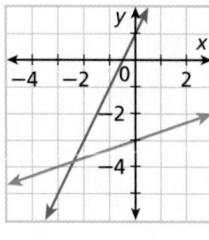

30. **Gridded Response** Which value of b will make the system $y = 2x + 2$ and $y = 2.5x + b$ intersect at the point $(2, 6)$?

CHALLENGE AND EXTEND

31. Entertainment If the pattern in the table continues, in what month will the number of sales of VCRs and DVD players be the same? What will that number be?

Total Number Sold				
Month	1	2	3	4
VCRs	500	490	480	470
DVD Players	250	265	280	295

32. Long Distance Inc. charges a $1.45 connection charge and $0.03 per minute. Far Away Calls charges a $1.52 connection charge and $0.02 per minute.

    a. For how many minutes will a call cost the same from both companies? What is that cost?

    b. When is it better to call using Long Distance Inc.? Far Away Calls? Explain.

    c. What if...? Long Distance Inc. raised its connection charge to $1.50 and Far Away Calls decreased its connection charge by 2 cents. How will this affect the graphs? Now which company is better to use for calling long distance? Why?

Career Path

Learn It Online
Career Resources Online

Ethan Reynolds
Applied Sciences major

Q: What math classes did you take in high school?
A: Career Math, Algebra, and Geometry

Q: What are you studying and what math classes have you taken?
A: I am really interested in aviation. I am taking Statistics and Trigonometry. Next year I will take Calculus.

Q: How is math used in aviation?
A: I use math to interpret aeronautical charts. I also perform calculations involving wind movements, aircraft weight and balance, and fuel consumption. These skills are necessary for planning and executing safe air flights.

Q: What are your future plans?
A: I could work as a commercial or corporate pilot or even as a flight instructor. I could also work toward a bachelor's degree in aviation management, air traffic control, aviation electronics, aviation maintenance, or aviation computer science.

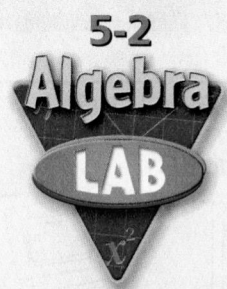

Model Systems of Linear Equations

You can use algebra tiles to model and solve some systems of linear equations.

Use with Solving Systems by Substitution

KEY

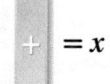 = 1

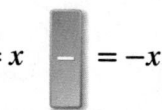

$\boxed{-}$ = -1

= x   = -x

REMEMBER

When two expressions are equal, you can substitute one for the other in any expression or equation.

Learn It Online
Lab Resources Online

MATHEMATICAL
PRACTICES
Use appropriate tools strategically.

CC.9-12.A.REI.6 Solve systems of linear equations exactly and approximately (e.g., with graphs), focusing on pairs of linear equations in two variables.

Activity

Use algebra tiles to model and solve $\begin{cases} y = 2x - 3 \\ x + y = 9 \end{cases}$.

MODEL		ALGEBRA
[tiles diagram: x, y, 9]	The first equation is solved for y. Model the second equation, $x + y = 9$, by substituting $2x - 3$ for y.	$x + y = 9$ $x + (2x - 3) = 9$ $3x - 3 = 9$
[tiles diagram]	Add 3 yellow tiles on both sides of the mat. This represents adding 3 to both sides of the equation. Remove zero pairs.	$3x - 3 = \quad 9$ $\underline{+3 \qquad +3}$ $3x = 12$
[tiles diagram]	Divide each side into 3 equal groups. Align one x-tile with each group on the right side. One x-tile is equivalent to 4 yellow tiles. $x = 4$	$\dfrac{3x}{3} = \dfrac{12}{3}$ $x = 4$

To solve for *y*, substitute 4 for *x* in one of the equations:
$$y = 2x - 3$$
$$= 2(4) - 3$$
$$= 5$$

The solution is (4, 5).

Try This

Model and solve each system of equations.

1. $\begin{cases} y = x + 3 \\ 2x + y = 6 \end{cases}$

2. $\begin{cases} 2x + 3 = y \\ x + y = 6 \end{cases}$

3. $\begin{cases} 2x + 3y = 1 \\ x = -1 - y \end{cases}$

4. $\begin{cases} y = x + 1 \\ 2x - y = -5 \end{cases}$

COMMON CORE

5-2 Solving Systems by Substitution

CC.9-12.A.REI.6 Solve systems of linear equations exactly and approximately (e.g., with graphs), focusing on pairs of linear equations in two variables. *Also* **CC.9-12.A.CED.3***

CAMPING OUT FOR THE BEST TICKETS ISN'T WHAT IT USED TO BE...

Off the Mark by Mark Parisi. Cartoon copyrighted by Mark Parisi, printed with permission.

Objective
Solve systems of linear equations in two variables by substitution.

Why learn this?

You can solve systems of equations to help select the best value among high-speed Internet providers. (See Example 3.)

Sometimes it is difficult to identify the exact solution to a system by graphing. In this case, you can use a method called *substitution*.

The goal when using substitution is to reduce the system to one equation that has only one variable. Then you can solve this equation, and substitute into an original equation to find the value of the other variable.

Know it!
.Note

Solving Systems of Equations by Substitution
Step 1 Solve for one variable in at least one equation, if necessary.
Step 2 Substitute the resulting expression into the other equation.
Step 3 Solve that equation to get the value of the first variable.
Step 4 Substitute that value into one of the original equations and solve.
Step 5 Write the values from Steps 3 and 4 as an ordered pair, (x, y), and check.

EXAMPLE 1   Solving a System of Linear Equations by Substitution

Solve each system by substitution.

A $\begin{cases} y = 2x \\ y = x + 5 \end{cases}$

Step 1 $y = 2x$ *Both equations are solved for y.*
       $y = x + 5$

Step 2 $y = x + 5$ *Substitute 2x for y in the second equation.*
      $2x = x + 5$

Step 3 $\underline{-x -x}$ *Solve for x.*
       $x = 5$

Step 4 $y = 2x$ *Write one of the original equations.*
       $y = 2(5)$ *Substitute 5 for x.*
       $y = 10$

Step 5 $(5, 10)$ *Write the solution as an ordered pair.*

Check   Substitute $(5, 10)$ into both equations in the system.

$y = 2x$	
10	$2(5)$
10	$10 \checkmark$

$y = x + 5$	
10	$5 + 5$
10	$10 \checkmark$

Helpful Hint

You can substitute the value of one variable into *either* of the original equations to find the value of the other variable.

336   *Chapter 5 Systems of Equations and Inequalities*

Solve each system by substitution.

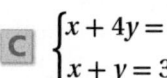 $\begin{cases} 2x + y = 5 \\ y = x - 4 \end{cases}$

Step 1 $y = x - 4$ *The second equation is solved for y.*

Step 2 $2x + y = 5$

$2x + (x - 4) = 5$ *Substitute x − 4 for y in the first equation.*

Step 3 $3x - 4 = 5$ *Simplify. Then solve for x.*

$\underline{\quad\ +4 \quad +4\quad}$ *Add 4 to both sides.*

$3x \quad = \quad 9$

$\dfrac{3x}{3} = \dfrac{9}{3}$ *Divide both sides by 3.*

$x = 3$

Step 4 $y = x - 4$ *Write one of the original equations.*

$y = 3 - 4$ *Substitute 3 for x.*

$y = -1$

Step 5 $(3, -1)$ *Write the solution as an ordered pair.*

C $\begin{cases} x + 4y = 6 \\ x + y = 3 \end{cases}$

Step 1 $x + 4y = 6$ *Solve the first equation for x by subtracting 4y from both sides.*

$\underline{\quad\ -4y \quad -4y\quad}$

$x \quad = \quad 6 - 4y$

Step 2 $x + y = 3$

$(6 - 4y) + y = 3$ *Substitute 6 − 4y for x in the second equation.*

Step 3 $6 - 3y = 3$ *Simplify. Then solve for y.*

$\underline{\ -6 \qquad\quad -6\ }$ *Subtract 6 from both sides.*

$-3y = -3$

$\dfrac{-3y}{-3} = \dfrac{-3}{-3}$ *Divide both sides by −3.*

$y = 1$

Step 4 $x + y = 3$ *Write one of the original equations.*

$x + 1 = 3$ *Substitute 1 for y.*

$\underline{\quad\ -1 \quad -1\quad}$ *Subtract 1 from both sides.*

$x \quad = 2$

Step 5 $(2, 1)$ *Write the solution as an ordered pair.*

Helpful Hint

Sometimes neither equation is solved for a variable. You can begin by solving either equation for either *x* or *y*.

 Solve each system by substitution.

1a. $\begin{cases} y = x + 3 \\ y = 2x + 5 \end{cases}$ **1b.** $\begin{cases} x = 2y - 4 \\ x + 8y = 16 \end{cases}$ **1c.** $\begin{cases} 2x + y = -4 \\ x + y = -7 \end{cases}$

Sometimes you substitute an expression for a variable that has a coefficient. When solving for the second variable in this situation, you can use the Distributive Property.

EXAMPLE 2 **Using the Distributive Property**

Solve $\begin{cases} 4y - 5x = 9 \\ x - 4y = 11 \end{cases}$ by substitution.

Step 1 $\quad x - 4y = \quad 11$

$$\underline{\quad + 4y \quad + 4y}$$

$$x \quad = \quad 4y + 11$$

Solve the second equation for x by adding 4y to each side.

Caution!

When you solve one equation for a variable, you must substitute the value or expression into the *other* original equation, not the one that has just been solved.

Step 2 $\qquad\qquad 4y - 5x = 9$

$$4y - 5(4y + 11) = 9$$

Substitute 4y + 11 for x in the first equation.

Step 3 $\quad 4y - 5(4y) - 5(11) = 9$

Distribute −5 to the expression in parentheses. Simplify. Solve for y.

$$4y - 20y - 55 = 9$$

$$-16y - 55 = \quad 9$$

$$\underline{\quad + 55 \quad + 55}$$

Add 55 to both sides.

$$-16y \quad = \quad 64$$

$$\frac{-16y}{-16} = \frac{64}{-16}$$

Divide both sides by −16.

$$y = -4$$

Step 4 $\qquad x - 4y = 11$

Write one of the original equations.

$$x - 4(-4) = 11$$

Substitute −4 for y.

$$x + 16 = \quad 11$$

Simplify.

$$\underline{\quad - 16 \quad - 16}$$

Subtract 16 from both sides.

$$x \quad = -5$$

Step 5 $(-5, -4)$

Write the solution as an ordered pair.

 **2.** Solve $\begin{cases} -2x + y = 8 \\ 3x + 2y = 9 \end{cases}$ by substitution.

Student to Student

Solving Systems by Substitution

Erika Chu
Terrell High School

I always look for a variable with a coefficient of 1 or −1 when deciding which equation to solve for x or y.

For the system

$$\begin{cases} 2x + y = 14 \\ -3x + 4y = -10 \end{cases}$$

I would solve the first equation for y because it has a coefficient of 1.

$$2x + y = 14$$

$$y = -2x + 14$$

Then I use substitution to find the values of x and y.

$$-3x + 4y = -10$$

$$-3x + 4(-2x + 14) = -10$$

$$-3x + (-8x) + 56 = -10$$

$$-11x + 56 = -10$$

$$-11x = -66$$

$$x = 6$$

$$y = -2x + 14$$

$$y = -2(6) + 14 = 2$$

The solution is (6, 2).

EXAMPLE 3 *Consumer Economics Application*

One high-speed Internet provider has a $50 setup fee and costs $30 per month. Another provider has no setup fee and costs $40 per month.

a. In how many months will both providers cost the same? What will that cost be?

Write an equation for each option. Let t represent the total amount paid and m represent the number of months.

	Total paid	is	setup fee	plus	cost per month	times	months.
Option 1	t	$=$	50	$+$	30	$\cdot$	m
Option 2	t	$=$	0	$+$	40	$\cdot$	m

Step 1 $t = 50 + 30m$ *Both equations are solved for t.*
$t = 40m$

Step 2 $50 + 30m = 40m$ *Substitute 50 + 30m for t in the second equation.*

Step 3 $\dfrac{-30m \qquad -30m}{50 \quad = \quad 10m}$ *Solve for m. Subtract 30m from both sides.*

$\dfrac{50}{10} = \dfrac{10m}{10}$ *Divide both sides by 10.*

$5 = m$

Step 4 $t = 40m$ *Write one of the original equations.*
$= 40(5)$ *Substitute 5 for m.*
$= 200$

Step 5 $(5, 200)$ *Write the solution as an ordered pair.*

In 5 months, the total cost for each option will be the same—$200.

b. If you plan to cancel in 1 year, which is the cheaper provider? Explain.

Option 1: $t = 50 + 30(12) = 410$ Option 2: $t = 40(12) = 480$
Option 1 is cheaper.

3. One cable television provider has a $60 setup fee and charges $80 per month, and another provider has a $160 equipment fee and charges $70 per month.

    a. In how many months will the cost be the same? What will that cost be?

    b. If you plan to move in 6 months, which is the cheaper option? Explain.

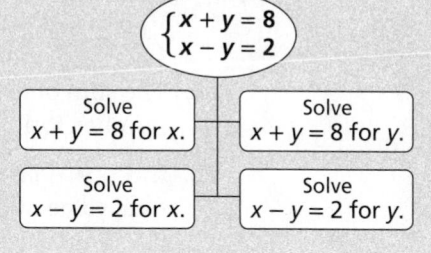

THINK AND DISCUSS

1. If you graphed the equations in Example 1A, where would the lines intersect?

2. GET ORGANIZED Copy and complete the graphic organizer. In each box, solve the system by substitution using the first step given. Show that each method gives the same solution.

$$\begin{cases} x + y = 8 \\ x - y = 2 \end{cases}$$

Solve $x + y = 8$ for x.	Solve $x + y = 8$ for y.
Solve $x - y = 2$ for x.	Solve $x - y = 2$ for y.

GUIDED PRACTICE

Solve each system by substitution.

SEE EXAMPLE 1

1. $\begin{cases} y = 5x - 10 \\ y = 3x + 8 \end{cases}$

2. $\begin{cases} 3x + y = 2 \\ 4x + y = 20 \end{cases}$

3. $\begin{cases} y = x + 5 \\ 4x + y = 20 \end{cases}$

SEE EXAMPLE 2

4. $\begin{cases} x - 2y = 10 \\ \frac{1}{2}x - 2y = 4 \end{cases}$

5. $\begin{cases} y - 4x = 3 \\ 2x - 3y = 21 \end{cases}$

6. $\begin{cases} x = y - 8 \\ -x - y = 0 \end{cases}$

SEE EXAMPLE 3

7. **Consumer Economics** The Strauss family is deciding between two lawn-care services. Green Lawn charges a $49 startup fee, plus $29 per month. Grass Team charges a $25 startup fee, plus $37 per month.

   a. In how many months will both lawn-care services cost the same? What will that cost be?

   b. If the family will use the service for only 6 months, which is the better option? Explain.

PRACTICE AND PROBLEM SOLVING

Independent Practice

For Exercises	See Example
8–10	1
11–16	2
17	3

Extra Practice
See Extra Practice for more Skills Practice and Applications Practice exercises.

Solve each system by substitution.

8. $\begin{cases} y = x + 3 \\ y = 2x + 4 \end{cases}$

9. $\begin{cases} y = 2x + 10 \\ y = -2x - 6 \end{cases}$

10. $\begin{cases} x + 2y = 8 \\ x + 3y = 12 \end{cases}$

11. $\begin{cases} 2x + 2y = 2 \\ -4x + 4y = 12 \end{cases}$

12. $\begin{cases} y = 0.5x + 2 \\ -y = -2x + 4 \end{cases}$

13. $\begin{cases} -x + y = 4 \\ 3x - 2y = -7 \end{cases}$

14. $\begin{cases} 3x + y = -8 \\ -2x - y = 6 \end{cases}$

15. $\begin{cases} x + 2y = -1 \\ 4x - 4y = 20 \end{cases}$

16. $\begin{cases} 4x = y - 1 \\ 6x - 2y = -3 \end{cases}$

17. **Recreation** Casey wants to buy a gym membership. One gym has a $150 joining fee and costs $35 per month. Another gym has no joining fee and costs $60 per month.

   a. In how many months will both gym memberships cost the same? What will that cost be?

   b. If Casey plans to cancel in 5 months, which is the better option for him? Explain.

Solve each system by substitution. Check your answer.

18. $\begin{cases} x = 5 \\ x + y = 8 \end{cases}$

19. $\begin{cases} y = -3x + 4 \\ x = 2y + 6 \end{cases}$

20. $\begin{cases} 3x - y = 11 \\ 5y - 7x = 1 \end{cases}$

21. $\begin{cases} \frac{1}{2}x + \frac{1}{3}y = 6 \\ x - y = 2 \end{cases}$

22. $\begin{cases} x = 7 - 2y \\ 2x + y = 5 \end{cases}$

23. $\begin{cases} y = 1.2x - 4 \\ 2.2x + 5 = y \end{cases}$

24. The sum of two numbers is 50. The first number is 43 less than twice the second number. Write and solve a system of equations to find the two numbers.

25. **Money** A jar contains n nickels and d dimes. There are 20 coins in the jar, and the total value of the coins is $1.40. How many nickels and how many dimes are in the jar? (*Hint:* Nickels are worth $0.05 and dimes are worth $0.10.)

26. **Multi-Step** Use the receipts below to write and solve a system of equations to find the cost of a large popcorn and the cost of a small drink.

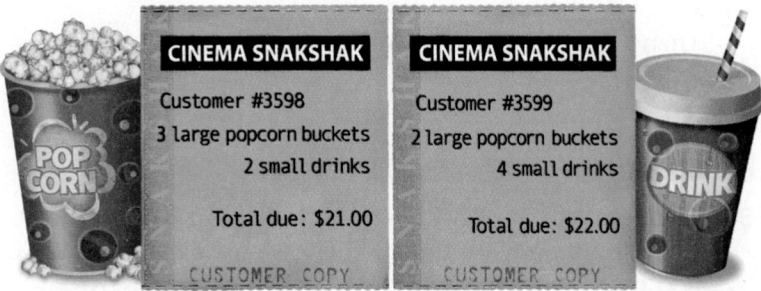

CINEMA SNAKSHAK

Customer #3598

3 large popcorn buckets
2 small drinks

Total due: $21.00

CUSTOMER COPY

CINEMA SNAKSHAK

Customer #3599

2 large popcorn buckets
4 small drinks

Total due: $22.00

CUSTOMER COPY

27. **Finance** Helene invested a total of $1000 in two simple-interest bank accounts. One account paid 5% annual interest; the other paid 6% annual interest. The total amount of interest she earned after one year was $58. Write and solve a system of equations to find the amount invested in each account. (*Hint:* Change the interest rates into decimals first.)

 Geometry Two angles whose measures have a sum of 90° are called complementary angles. For Exercises 28–30, *x* and *y* represent the measures of complementary angles. Use this information and the equation given in each exercise to find the measure of each angle.

28. $y = 4x - 10$ 29. $x = 2y$ 30. $y = 2(x - 15)$

31. **Aviation** With a headwind, a small plane can fly 240 miles in 3 hours. With a tailwind, the plane can fly the same distance in 2 hours. Follow the steps below to find the rates of the plane and wind.

a. Copy and complete the table. Let *p* be the rate of the plane and *w* be the rate of the wind.

	Rate	•	Time	=	Distance
With Headwind	$p - w$	•		=	240
With Tailwind		•	2	=	

b. Use the information in each row to write a system of equations.

c. Solve the system of equations to find the rates of the plane and wind.

32. **Write About It** Explain how to solve a system of equations by substitution.

33. **Critical Thinking** Explain the connection between the solution of a system solved by graphing and the solution of the same system solved by substitution.

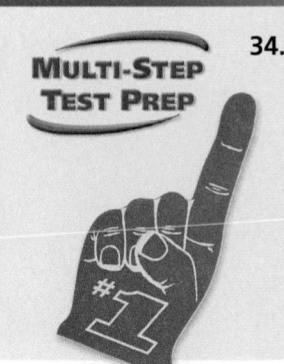
34. At the school store, Juanita bought 2 books and a backpack for a total of $26 before tax. Each book cost $8 less than the backpack.

a. Write a system of equations that can be used to find the price of each book and the price of the backpack.

b. Solve this system by substitution.

c. Solve this system by graphing. Discuss advantages and disadvantages of solving by substitution and solving by graphing.

35. Estimation Use the graph to estimate the solution to

$\begin{cases} 2x - y = 6 \\ x + y = -0.6 \end{cases}$. Round your answer to the nearest tenth.

Then solve the system by substitution.

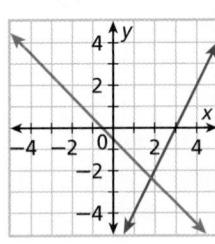

36. Elizabeth met 24 of her cousins at a family reunion. The number of male cousins m was 6 less than twice the number of female cousins f. Which system can be used to find the number of male cousins and female cousins?

Ⓐ $\begin{cases} m + f = 24 \\ f = 2m - 6 \end{cases}$ Ⓑ $\begin{cases} m + f = 24 \\ f = 2m \end{cases}$ Ⓒ $\begin{cases} m = 24 + f \\ m = f - 6 \end{cases}$ Ⓓ $\begin{cases} f = 24 - m \\ m = 2f - 6 \end{cases}$

37. Which problem is best represented by the system $\begin{cases} d = n + 5 \\ d + n = 12 \end{cases}$?

Ⓕ Roger has 12 coins in dimes and nickels. There are 5 more dimes than nickels.

Ⓖ Roger has 5 coins in dimes and nickels. There are 12 more dimes than nickels.

Ⓗ Roger has 12 coins in dimes and nickels. There are 5 more nickels than dimes.

Ⓙ Roger has 5 coins in dimes and nickels. There are 12 more nickels than dimes.

CHALLENGE AND EXTEND

38. A car dealership has 378 cars on its lot. The ratio of new cars to used cars is 5:4. Write and solve a system of equations to find the number of new and used cars on the lot.

Solve each system by substitution.

39. $\begin{cases} 2r - 3s - t = 12 \\ s + 3t = 10 \\ t = 4 \end{cases}$

40. $\begin{cases} x + y + z = 7 \\ y + z = 5 \\ 2y - 4z = -14 \end{cases}$

41. $\begin{cases} a + 2b + c = 19 \\ -b + c = -5 \\ 3b + 2c = 15 \end{cases}$

5-3 Solving Systems by Elimination

CC.9-12.A.REI.5 Prove that, given a system of two equations in two variables, replacing one equation by the sum of that equation and a multiple of the other produces a system with the same solutions. *Also* **CC.9-12.A.REI.6, CC.9-12.A.CED.3***

Objectives
Solve systems of linear equations in two variables by elimination.

Compare and choose an appropriate method for solving systems of linear equations.

Why learn this?

You can solve a system of linear equations to determine how many flowers of each type you can buy to make a bouquet. (See Example 4.)

Another method for solving systems of equations is *elimination*. Like substitution, the goal of elimination is to get one equation that has only one variable.

Remember that an equation stays balanced if you add equal amounts to both sides. Consider the system $\begin{cases} x - 2y = -19 \\ 5x + 2y = 1 \end{cases}$. Since $5x + 2y = 1$, you can add $5x + 2y$ to one side of the first equation and 1 to the other side and the balance is maintained.

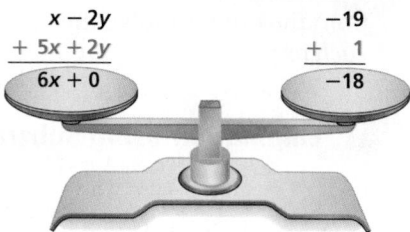

$x - 2y$		-19
$+\ 5x + 2y$		$+\ \ \ 1$
$6x + 0$		-18

Since $-2y$ and $2y$ have **opposite coefficients**, you can eliminate the y by adding the two equations. The result is one equation that has only one variable: $6x = -18$.

When you use the elimination method to solve a system of linear equations, align all like terms in the equations. Then determine whether any like terms can be eliminated because they have opposite coefficients.

Solving Systems of Equations by Elimination
Step 1 Write the system so that like terms are aligned.
Step 2 Eliminate one of the variables and solve for the other variable.
Step 3 Substitute the value of the variable into one of the original equations and solve for the other variable.
Step 4 Write the answers from Steps 2 and 3 as an ordered pair, (x, y), and check.

Later in this lesson you will learn how to multiply one or more equations by a number in order to produce opposites that can be eliminated.

EXAMPLE 1 **Elimination Using Addition**

Solve $\begin{cases} x - 2y = -19 \\ 5x + 2y = 1 \end{cases}$ by elimination.

Step 1 $\quad x - 2y = -19$ *Write the system so that like terms are aligned.*

$\quad\quad\quad\quad \underline{+\ 5x + 2y = \quad 1}$ *Notice that $-2y$ and $2y$ are opposites.*

Step 2 $\quad 6x\ + 0 = -18$ *Add the equations to eliminate y.*

$\quad\quad\quad\quad\quad 6x = -18$ *Simplify and solve for x.*

$\quad\quad\quad\quad\quad \dfrac{6x}{6} = \dfrac{-18}{6}$ *Divide both sides by 6.*

$\quad\quad\quad\quad\quad\quad x = -3$

Step 3 $\ x - 2y = -19$ *Write one of the original equations.*

$\quad\quad\quad -3 - 2y = -19$ *Substitute -3 for x.*

$\quad\quad\quad \underline{+3 \quad\quad\quad +3}$ *Add 3 to both sides.*

$\quad\quad\quad\quad\ -2y = -16$

$\quad\quad\quad\quad\ \dfrac{-2y}{-2} = \dfrac{-16}{-2}$ *Divide both sides by -2.*

$\quad\quad\quad\quad\quad\ y = 8$

Step 4 $(-3, 8)$ *Write the solution as an ordered pair.*

> **Helpful Hint**
>
> Check your answer.
>
> | $x - 2y = -19$ | |
> |---|---|
> | $-3 - 2(8)$ | -19 |
> | $-3 - 16$ | -19 |
> | -19 | $-19\ ✓$ |
>
> | $5x + 2y = 1$ | |
> |---|---|
> | $5(-3) + 2(8)$ | 1 |
> | $-15 + 16$ | 1 |
> | 1 | $1\ ✓$ |

 **1.** Solve $\begin{cases} y + 3x = -2 \\ 2y - 3x = 14 \end{cases}$ by elimination. Check your answer.

When two equations each contain the same term, you can subtract one equation from the other to solve the system. To subtract an equation, add the opposite of *each* term.

EXAMPLE 2 **Elimination Using Subtraction**

Solve $\begin{cases} 3x + 4y = 18 \\ -2x + 4y = 8 \end{cases}$ by elimination.

Step 1 $\quad\quad 3x + 4y = 18$

$\quad\quad\quad -(-2x + 4y = \ 8)$ *Notice that both equations contain 4y.*

$\quad\quad\quad\quad 3x + 4y = \ 18$ *Add the opposite of each term*

$\quad\quad\quad\quad \underline{+\ 2x - 4y = -8}$ *in the second equation.*

Step 2 $\quad\quad 5x +\ \ 0 = 10$ *Eliminate y.*

$\quad\quad\quad\quad\quad\quad 5x = 10$ *Simplify and solve for x.*

$\quad\quad\quad\quad\quad\quad\quad x = 2$

Step 3 $\ -2x + 4y = \ 8$ *Write one of the original equations.*

$\quad\quad\ -2(2) + 4y = \ 8$ *Substitute 2 for x.*

$\quad\quad\quad\ -4 + 4y = \ 8$

$\quad\quad\quad \underline{+4 \quad\quad\quad +4}$ *Add 4 to both sides.*

$\quad\quad\quad\quad\quad\ 4y = 12$ *Simplify and solve for y.*

$\quad\quad\quad\quad\quad\ \ y = 3$

Step 4 $\quad\quad (2, 3)$ *Write the solution as an ordered pair.*

> **Remember!**
>
> Remember to check by substituting your answer into both original equations.

 **2.** Solve $\begin{cases} 3x + 3y = 15 \\ -2x + 3y = -5 \end{cases}$ by elimination. Check your answer.

In some cases, you will first need to multiply one or both of the equations by a number so that one variable has opposite coefficients.

EXAMPLE 3 **Elimination Using Multiplication First**

Solve each system by elimination.

A $\begin{cases} 2x + y = 3 \\ -x + 3y = -12 \end{cases}$

Helpful Hint

In Example 3A, you could have also multiplied the first equation by −3 to eliminate y.

Step 1
$$2x + y = 3$$
$$+\ 2(-x + 3y = -12)$$
$$2x + y = 3$$

Multiply each term in the second equation by 2 to get opposite x-coefficients.

$$+(-2x + 6y = -24)$$

Add the new equation to the first equation to eliminate x.

Step 2
$$7y = -21$$
$$y = -3$$

Solve for y.

Step 3
$$2x + y = 3$$ Write one of the original equations.
$$2x + (-3) = 3$$ Substitute −3 for y.
$$\underline{+\ \ 3 \quad +3}$$ Add 3 to both sides.
$$2x = 6$$ Solve for x.
$$x = 3$$

Step 4 $(3, -3)$ Write the solution as an ordered pair.

B $\begin{cases} 7x - 12y = -22 \\ 5x - 8y = -14 \end{cases}$

Step 1
$$2(7x - 12y = -22)$$
$$+\ (-3)(5x - 8y = -14)$$
$$14x - 24y = -44$$

Multiply the first equation by 2 and the second equation by −3 to get opposite y-coefficients.

$$+(-15x + 24y = 42)$$

Add the new equations to eliminate y.

Step 2
$$-x = -2$$
$$x = 2$$ Solve for x.

Step 3
$$7x - 12y = -22$$ Write one of the original equations.
$$7(2) - 12y = -22$$ Substitute 2 for x.
$$14 - 12y = -22$$
$$\underline{-14 \qquad\ -14}$$ Subtract 14 from both sides.
$$-12y = -36$$ Solve for y.
$$y = 3$$

Step 4 $(2, 3)$ Write the solution as an ordered pair.

 Solve each system by elimination. Check your answer.

3a. $\begin{cases} 3x + 2y = 6 \\ -x + y = -2 \end{cases}$ **3b.** $\begin{cases} 2x + 5y = 26 \\ -3x - 4y = -25 \end{cases}$

EXAMPLE 4

Consumer Economics Application

Sam spent $24.75 to buy 12 flowers for his mother. The bouquet contained roses and daisies. How many of each type of flower did Sam buy?

Write a system. Use r for the number of roses and d for the number of daisies.

$$2.50r + 1.75d = 24.75 \qquad \text{\textit{The cost of roses and daisies totals \$24.75.}}$$

$$r + d = 12 \qquad \text{\textit{The total number of roses and daisies is 12.}}$$

ROSES
$2.50 each

DAISIES
$1.75 each

Step 1
$$2.50r + 1.75d = 24.75$$
$$+ (-2.50)(r + d = 12)$$

Multiply the second equation by −2.50 to get opposite r-coefficients.

$$2.50r + 1.75d = 24.75$$
$$+ (-2.50r - 2.50d = -30.00)$$

Add this equation to the first equation to eliminate r.

Step 2
$$-0.75d = -5.25$$
$$d = 7 \qquad \text{\textit{Solve for d.}}$$

Step 3
$$r + d = 12 \qquad \text{\textit{Write one of the original equations.}}$$
$$r + 7 = 12 \qquad \text{\textit{Substitute 7 for d.}}$$
$$\underline{-7 \quad -7} \qquad \text{\textit{Subtract 7 from both sides.}}$$
$$r = 5$$

Step 4
$$(5, 7) \qquad \text{\textit{Write the solution as an ordered pair.}}$$

Sam can buy 5 roses and 7 daisies.

4. What if...? Sally spent $14.85 to buy 13 flowers. She bought lilies, which cost $1.25 each, and tulips, which cost $0.90 each. How many of each flower did Sally buy?

All systems can be solved in more than one way. For some systems, some methods may be better than others.

Systems of Linear Equations

METHOD	USE WHEN...	EXAMPLE
Graphing	• Both equations are solved for y. • You want to estimate a solution.	$\begin{cases} y = 3x + 2 \\ y = -2x + 6 \end{cases}$
Substitution	• A variable in either equation has a coefficient of 1 or −1. • Both equations are solved for the same variable. • Either equation is solved for a variable.	$\begin{cases} x + 2y = 7 \\ x = 10 - 5y \end{cases}$ or $\begin{cases} x = 2y + 10 \\ x = 3y + 5 \end{cases}$
Elimination	• Both equations have the same variable with the same or opposite coefficients. • A variable term in one equation is a multiple of the corresponding variable term in the other equation.	$\begin{cases} 3x + 2y = 8 \\ 5x + 2y = 12 \end{cases}$ or $\begin{cases} 6x + 5y = 10 \\ 3x + 2y = 15 \end{cases}$

THINK AND DISCUSS

1. Explain how multiplying the second equation in a system by -1 and eliminating by adding is the same as elimination by subtraction. Give an example of a system for which this applies.

2. Explain why it does not matter which variable you solve for first when solving a system by elimination.

Know it!
Note

3. **GET ORGANIZED** Copy and complete the graphic organizer. In each box, write an example of a system of equations that you could solve using the given method.

Solving Systems of Linear Equations
- Substitution
- Elimination using addition or subtraction
- Elimination using multiplication

5-3 Exercises

Learn It Online
Homework Help Online
Parent Resources Online

GUIDED PRACTICE

Solve each system by elimination. Check your answer.

SEE EXAMPLE 1

1. $\begin{cases} -x + y = 5 \\ x - 5y = -9 \end{cases}$

2. $\begin{cases} x + y = 12 \\ x - y = 2 \end{cases}$

3. $\begin{cases} 2x + 5y = -24 \\ 3x - 5y = 14 \end{cases}$

SEE EXAMPLE 2

4. $\begin{cases} x - 10y = 60 \\ x + 14y = 12 \end{cases}$

5. $\begin{cases} 5x + y = 0 \\ 5x + 2y = 30 \end{cases}$

6. $\begin{cases} -5x + 7y = 11 \\ -5x + 3y = 19 \end{cases}$

SEE EXAMPLE 3

7. $\begin{cases} 2x + 3y = 12 \\ 5x - y = 13 \end{cases}$

8. $\begin{cases} -3x + 4y = 12 \\ 2x + y = -8 \end{cases}$

9. $\begin{cases} 2x + 4y = -4 \\ 3x + 5y = -3 \end{cases}$

SEE EXAMPLE 4

10. **Consumer Economics** Each family in a neighborhood is contributing $20 worth of food to the neighborhood picnic. The Harlin family is bringing 12 packages of buns. The hamburger buns cost $2.00 per package. The hot-dog buns cost $1.50 per package. How many packages of each type of bun did they buy?

PRACTICE AND PROBLEM SOLVING

Independent Practice

For Exercises	See Example
11–13	1
14–16	2
17–19	3
20	4

Extra Practice

See Extra Practice for more Skills Practice and Applications Practice exercises.

Solve each system by elimination. Check your answer.

11. $\begin{cases} -x + y = -1 \\ 2x - y = 0 \end{cases}$

12. $\begin{cases} -2x + y = -20 \\ 2x + y = 48 \end{cases}$

13. $\begin{cases} 3x - y = -2 \\ -2x + y = 3 \end{cases}$

14. $\begin{cases} x - y = 4 \\ x - 2y = 10 \end{cases}$

15. $\begin{cases} x + 2y = 5 \\ 3x + 2y = 17 \end{cases}$

16. $\begin{cases} 3x - 2y = -1 \\ 3x - 4y = 9 \end{cases}$

17. $\begin{cases} x - y = -3 \\ 5x + 3y = 1 \end{cases}$

18. $\begin{cases} 9x - 3y = 3 \\ 3x + 8y = -17 \end{cases}$

19. $\begin{cases} 5x + 2y = -1 \\ 3x + 7y = 11 \end{cases}$

20. **Multi-Step** Mrs. Gonzalez bought centerpieces to put on each table at a graduation party. She spent $31.50. There are 8 tables each requiring either a candle or vase. Candles cost $3 and vases cost $4.25. How many of each type did she buy?

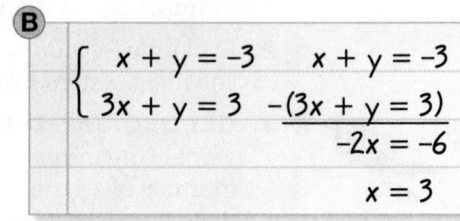

21. Geometry The difference between the length and width of a rectangle is 2 units. The perimeter is 40 units. Write and solve a system of equations to determine the length and width of the rectangle. (*Hint:* The perimeter of a rectangle is $2\ell + 2w$.)

22. /// ERROR ANALYSIS /// Which is incorrect? Explain the error.

A

$$\begin{cases} x + y = -3 & x + y = -3 \\ 3x + y = 3 & -(3x + y = 3) \end{cases}$$
$$\overline{ -2x = 0}$$
$$x = 0$$

B

$$\begin{cases} x + y = -3 & x + y = -3 \\ 3x + y = 3 & -(3x + y = 3) \end{cases}$$
$$\overline{ -2x = -6}$$
$$x = 3$$

Math History

In 1247, Qin Jiushao wrote *Mathematical Treatise in Nine Sections*. Its contents included solving systems of equations and the Chinese Remainder Theorem.

23. Chemistry A chemist has a bottle of a 1% acid solution and a bottle of a 5% acid solution. She wants to mix the two solutions to get 100 mL of a 4% acid solution. Follow the steps below to find how much of each solution she should use.

	1% Solution	+	5% Solution	=	4% Solution
Amount of Solution (mL)	x	+	y	=	▨
Amount of Acid (mL)	$0.01x$	+	▨	=	$0.04(100)$

a. Copy and complete the table.

b. Use the information in the table to write a system of equations.

c. Solve the system of equations to find how much she will use from each bottle to get 100 mL of a 4% acid solution.

Critical Thinking Which method would you use to solve each system? Explain.

24. $\begin{cases} \dfrac{1}{2}x - 5y = 30 \\ \dfrac{1}{2}x + 7y = 6 \end{cases}$

25. $\begin{cases} -x + 2y = 3 \\ 4x - 5y = -3 \end{cases}$

26. $\begin{cases} 3x - y = 10 \\ 2x - y = 7 \end{cases}$

27. $\begin{cases} 3y + x = 10 \\ x = 4y + 2 \end{cases}$

28. $\begin{cases} y = -4x \\ y = 2x + 3 \end{cases}$

29. $\begin{cases} 2x + 6y = 12 \\ 4x + 5y = 15 \end{cases}$

30. Business A local boys club sold 176 bags of mulch and made a total of $520. They did not sell any of the expensive cocoa mulch. Use the table to determine how many bags of each type of mulch they sold.

Mulch Prices ($)	
Cocoa	4.75
Hardwood	3.50
Pine Bark	2.75

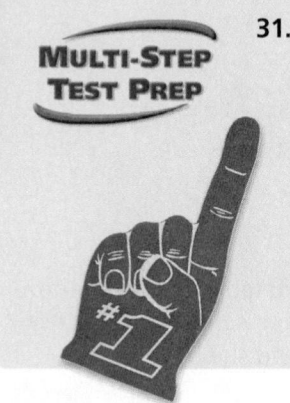

MULTI-STEP TEST PREP

31. a. The school store is running a promotion on school supplies. Different supplies are placed on two shelves. You can purchase 3 items from shelf A and 2 from shelf B for $16. Or you can purchase 2 items from shelf A and 3 from shelf B for $14. Write a system of equations that can be used to find the individual prices for the supplies on shelf A and on shelf B.

b. Solve the system of equations by elimination.

c. If the supplies on shelf A are normally $6 each and the supplies on shelf B are normally $3 each, how much will you save on each package plan from part **a**?

32. Write About It Solve the system $\begin{cases} 3x + y = 1 \\ 2x + 4y = -6 \end{cases}$. Explain how you can check your solution algebraically and graphically.

33. A math test has 25 problems. Some are worth 2 points, and some are worth 3 points. The test is worth 60 points total. Which system can be used to determine the number of 2-point problems and the number of 3-point problems on the test?

Ⓐ $\begin{cases} x + y = 25 \\ 2x + 3y = 60 \end{cases}$ Ⓑ $\begin{cases} x + y = 60 \\ 2x + 3y = 25 \end{cases}$ Ⓒ $\begin{cases} x - y = 25 \\ 2x + 3y = 60 \end{cases}$ Ⓓ $\begin{cases} x - y = 60 \\ 2x - 3y = 25 \end{cases}$

34. An electrician charges $15 plus $11 per hour. Another electrician charges $10 plus $15 per hour. For what amount of time will the cost be the same? What is that cost?

    Ⓕ 1 hour; $25   Ⓗ $1\frac{1}{2}$ hours; $30

    Ⓖ $1\frac{1}{4}$ hours; $28.75   Ⓙ $1\frac{3}{4}$ hours; $32.50

35. Short Response Three hundred fifty-eight tickets to the school basketball game on Friday were sold. Student tickets were $1.50, and nonstudent tickets were $3.25. The school made $752.25.

  a. Write a system of linear equations that could be used to determine how many student and how many nonstudent tickets were sold. Define the variables you use.

  b. Solve the system you wrote in part **a.** How many student and how many nonstudent tickets were sold?

CHALLENGE AND EXTEND

Solve each system by any method.

36. $\begin{cases} x + 16\frac{1}{2} = -\frac{3}{4}y \\ y = \frac{1}{2}x \end{cases}$ **37.** $\begin{cases} 2x + y + z = 17 \\ \frac{1}{2}z = 5 \\ x - y = 5 \end{cases}$ **38.** $\begin{cases} x - 2y - z = -1 \\ -x + 2y + 4z = -11 \\ 2x + y + z = 1 \end{cases}$

39. The sum of the digits of a two-digit number is 5. If the number is multiplied by 3, the result is 42. Write and solve a system of equations to find the number. (*Hint:* One equation involves the digits in the number. The other equation involves the values of the digits.)

Connecting Algebra to

Number Theory

Solving Classic Problems

You can use systems of linear equations to solve some "classic" math problems that are common in textbooks and puzzle books.

Example 1

Yuri is twice as old as Zack. Four years from now, the sum of their ages will be 23. How old is Yuri?

Step 1 Write a system. Let y represent Yuri's age. Let z represent Zack's age.

Yuri is twice as old as Zack.   In 4 years, the sum of their ages will be 23.

$$y = 2z$$

$$(y + 4) + (z + 4) = 23$$
$$y + z + 8 = 23$$
$$y + z = 15$$

Step 2 Solve the equations for y.

$$\begin{cases} y = 2z \\ y + z = 15 \end{cases} \rightarrow \begin{cases} y = 2z \\ y = -z + 15 \end{cases}$$

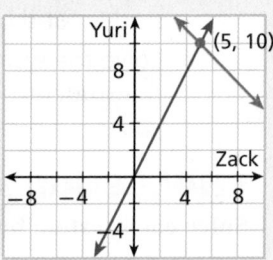

Step 3 Graph $y = 2z$ and $y = -z + 15$.

The lines appear to intersect at $(5, 10)$.

The solution $(5, 10)$ means that Yuri is 10 years old.

Example 2

Mandy has 11 coins in dimes and quarters. The value of her coins is $2.15. How many dimes does she have?

Step 1 Write a system. Let d be the number of dimes. Let q be the number of quarters.

The total number of coins is 11.   The value of the coins is $2.15.

$$q + d = 11$$

$$0.25q + 0.10d = 2.15$$
$$100(0.25q + 0.10d = 2.15)$$
$$25q + 10d = 215$$
$$5q + 2d = 43$$

Step 2 Solve the first equation for d.

$$d = 11 - q$$

Step 3 Substitute $11 - q$ for d in the second equation.

$$5q + 2(11 - q) = 43$$
$$3q + 22 = 43 \qquad \textit{Distribute 2 and then combine like terms.}$$
$$3q = 21$$
$$q = 7 \qquad \textit{Solve for q.}$$

Step 4 Substitute 7 for q in one of the original equations.

$$q + d = 11$$
$$7 + d = 11$$
$$d = 4$$

The solution $(4, 7)$ means that there are 4 dimes and 7 quarters. Mandy has 4 dimes.

Example 3

When the digits of a two-digit number are reversed, the new number is 45 less than the original number. The sum of the digits is 7. What is the original number?

Step 1 Write expressions for the original number and the new number. Let a represent the tens digit. Let b represent the ones digit.

The original number: The new number:
$$10a + b$$ $$10b + a$$

Step 2 Write a system.

The new number is 45 less
than the original number.   The sum of the digits is 7.
$$10b + a = (10a + b) - 45$$ $$a + b = 7$$
$$9b - 9a = -45$$
$$b - a = -5 \longrightarrow a - b = 5$$

Step 3 Add the equations to eliminate b. Solve for a.

$$
\begin{array}{r}
a - b = 5 \\
+ (a + b = 7) \\
\hline
2a = 12 \\
a = 6
\end{array}
$$

Step 4 Substitute 6 for a in one of the original equations.

$$a + b = 7$$
$$6 + b = 7$$
$$b = 1$$

The solution is $(6, 1)$. This means that 6 is the tens digit and 1 is the ones digit. The original number is 61.

Check Check your solution using the original problem.
The sum of the digits is 7: $6 + 1 = 7$ ✓
When the digits are reversed, the new number is 45 less than the original number: $16 = 61 - 45$ ✓

Try This

1. The sum of the digits of a two-digit number is 17. When the digits are reversed, the new number is 9 more than the original number. What is the original number?

2. Vic has 14 coins in nickels and quarters. The value of his coins is $1.70. How many quarters does he have?

3. Grace is 8 years older than her brother Sam. The sum of their ages is 24. How old is Grace?

5-4 Solving Special Systems

CC.9-12.A.REI.6 Solve systems of linear equations exactly and approximately (e.g., with graphs), focusing on pairs of linear equations in two variables. *Also* **CC.9-12.A.CED.2*, CC.9-12.A.CED.3***

Objectives
Solve special systems of linear equations in two variables.

Classify systems of linear equations and determine the number of solutions.

Vocabulary
consistent system
inconsistent system
independent system
dependent system

Why learn this?

Linear systems can be used to analyze business growth, such as comic book sales. (See Example 4.)

When two lines intersect at a point, there is exactly one solution to the system. A system with at least one solution is a **consistent system**.

When the two lines in a system do not intersect, they are parallel lines. There are no ordered pairs that satisfy both equations, so there is no solution. A system that has no solution is an **inconsistent system**.

EXAMPLE **1** **Systems with No Solution**

Show that $\begin{cases} y = x - 1 \\ -x + y = 2 \end{cases}$ has no solution.

Method 1 Compare slopes and y-intercepts.

$\quad y = x - 1 \rightarrow y = 1x - 1$ *Write both equations in slope-intercept form.*
$\quad -x + y = 2 \rightarrow y = 1x + 2$ *The lines are parallel because they have the same slope and different y-intercepts.*

This system has no solution.

Method 2 Graph the system.
     The lines are parallel.

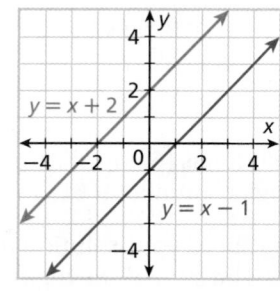

This system has no solution.

Method 3 Solve the system algebraically. Use the substitution method.

$\quad -x + (x - 1) = 2$ *Substitute x − 1 for y in the second equation, and solve.*
$\quad\quad\quad\quad -1 = 2$ ✗   *False*

This system has no solution.

1. Show that $\begin{cases} y = -2x + 5 \\ 2x + y = 1 \end{cases}$ has no solution.

If two linear equations in a system have the same graph, the graphs are coincident lines, or the same line. There are infinitely many solutions of the system because every point on the line represents a solution of both equations.

EXAMPLE 2 **Systems with Infinitely Many Solutions**

Show that $\begin{cases} y = 2x + 1 \\ 2x - y + 1 = 0 \end{cases}$ has infinitely many solutions.

Method 1 Compare slopes and y-intercepts.

$$y = 2x + 1 \rightarrow y = 2x + 1$$
$$2x - y + 1 = 0 \rightarrow y = 2x + 1$$

Write both equations in slope-intercept form. The lines have the same slope and the same y-intercept.

If this system were graphed, the graphs would be the same line. There are infinitely many solutions.

Method 2 Solve the system algebraically. Use the elimination method.

$$y = 2x + 1 \rightarrow -2x + y = 1 \qquad \textit{Write equations to line up like terms.}$$
$$2x - y + 1 = 0 \rightarrow \underline{+2x - y = -1} \qquad \textit{Add the equations.}$$
$$0 = 0 \checkmark \quad \textit{True. The equation is an identity.}$$

There are infinitely many solutions.

Caution!

$0 = 0$ is a true statement. It does not mean the system has zero solutions or no solution.

CHECK IT OUT! **2.** Show that $\begin{cases} y = x - 3 \\ x - y - 3 = 0 \end{cases}$ has infinitely many solutions.

Consistent systems can either be independent or dependent.
- An **independent system** has exactly one solution. The graph of an independent system consists of two intersecting lines.
- A **dependent system** has infinitely many solutions. The graph of a dependent system consists of two coincident lines.

Know it! Note

Classification of Systems of Linear Equations

CLASSIFICATION	CONSISTENT AND INDEPENDENT	CONSISTENT AND DEPENDENT	INCONSISTENT
Number of Solutions	Exactly one	Infinitely many	None
Description	Different slopes	Same slope, same y-intercept	Same slope, different y-intercepts
Graph	Intersecting lines	Coincident lines	Parallel lines

EXAMPLE 3 **Classifying Systems of Linear Equations**

Classify each system. Give the number of solutions.

A $\begin{cases} 2y = x + 2 \\ -\dfrac{1}{2}x + y = 1 \end{cases}$

$2y = x + 2 \rightarrow y = \dfrac{1}{2}x + 1$ *Write both equations in slope-intercept form.*

$-\dfrac{1}{2}x + y = 1 \rightarrow y = \dfrac{1}{2}x + 1$ *The lines have the same slope and the same y-intercepts. They are the same.*

The system is consistent and dependent. It has infinitely many solutions.

B $\begin{cases} y = 2(x - 1) \\ y = x + 1 \end{cases}$

$y = 2(x - 1) \rightarrow y = 2x - 2$ *Write both equations in slope-intercept form.*

$y = x + 1 \rightarrow y = 1x + 1$ *The lines have different slopes. They intersect.*

The system is consistent and independent. It has one solution.

 **CHECK IT OUT!** Classify each system. Give the number of solutions.

3a. $\begin{cases} x + 2y = -4 \\ -2(y + 2) = x \end{cases}$ **3b.** $\begin{cases} y = -2(x - 1) \\ y = -x + 3 \end{cases}$ **3c.** $\begin{cases} 2x - 3y = 6 \\ y = \dfrac{2}{3}x \end{cases}$

EXAMPLE 4 *Business Application*

The sales manager at Comics Now is comparing its sales with the sales of its competitor, Dynamo Comics. If the sales patterns continue, will the sales for Comics Now ever equal the sales for Dynamo Comics? Explain.

Comic Books Sold per Year (thousands)	2005	2006	2007	2008
Comics Now	130	170	210	250
Dynamo Comics	180	220	260	300

Use the table to write a system of linear equations. Let y represent the sales total and x represent the number of years since 2005.

	Sales total	equals	increase in sales per year	times	years	plus	beginning sales.
Comics Now	y	=	40	•	x	+	130
Dynamo Comics	y	=	40	•	x	+	180

Helpful Hint

The increase in sales is the difference between sales each year.

$\begin{cases} y = 40x + 130 \\ y = 40x + 180 \end{cases}$

$y = 40x + 130$ *Both equations are in slope-intercept form.*

$y = 40x + 180$ *The lines have the same slope, but different y-intercepts.*

The graphs of the two equations are parallel lines, so there is no solution. If the patterns continue, sales for the two companies will never be equal.

 **CHECK IT OUT!** **4.** Matt has $100 in a checking account and deposits $20 per month. Ben has $80 in a checking account and deposits $30 per month. Will the accounts ever have the same balance? Explain.

THINK AND DISCUSS

1. What methods can be used to determine the number of solutions of a system of linear equations?

Know it!
·Note

2. **GET ORGANIZED** Copy and complete the graphic organizer. In each box, write the word or words that describes a system with that number of solutions and sketch a graph.

Linear System of Equations

No solution

Exactly one

Infinitely many

5-4 Exercises

Learn It Online
Homework Help Online
Parent Resources Online

GUIDED PRACTICE

1. Vocabulary A _____?_____ system can be independent or dependent. (*consistent* or *inconsistent*)

SEE EXAMPLE 1 Show that each system has no solution.

2. $\begin{cases} y = x + 1 \\ -x + y = 3 \end{cases}$

3. $\begin{cases} 3x + y = 6 \\ y = -3x + 2 \end{cases}$

4. $\begin{cases} -y = 4x + 1 \\ 4x + y = 2 \end{cases}$

SEE EXAMPLE 2 Show that each system has infinitely many solutions.

5. $\begin{cases} y = -x + 3 \\ x + y - 3 = 0 \end{cases}$

6. $\begin{cases} y = 2x - 4 \\ 2x - y - 4 = 0 \end{cases}$

7. $\begin{cases} -7x + y = -2 \\ 7x - y = 2 \end{cases}$

SEE EXAMPLE 3 Classify each system. Give the number of solutions.

8. $\begin{cases} y = 2x + 3 \\ -2y = 2x + 6 \end{cases}$

9. $\begin{cases} y = -3x - 1 \\ 3x + y = 1 \end{cases}$

10. $\begin{cases} 9y = 3x + 18 \\ \frac{1}{3}x - y = -2 \end{cases}$

SEE EXAMPLE 4 **11. Athletics** Micah walks on a treadmill at 4 miles per hour. He has walked 2 miles when Luke starts running at 6 miles per hour on the treadmill next to him. If their rates continue, will Luke's distance ever equal Micah's distance? Explain.

PRACTICE AND PROBLEM SOLVING

Show that each system has no solution.

12. $\begin{cases} y = 2x - 2 \\ -2x + y = 1 \end{cases}$

13. $\begin{cases} x + y = 3 \\ y = -x - 1 \end{cases}$

14. $\begin{cases} x + 2y = -4 \\ y = -\frac{1}{2}x - 4 \end{cases}$

15. $\begin{cases} -6 + y = 2x \\ y = 2x - 36 \end{cases}$

Show that each system has infinitely many solutions.

16. $\begin{cases} y = -2x + 3 \\ 2x + y - 3 = 0 \end{cases}$

17. $\begin{cases} y = x - 2 \\ x - y - 2 = 0 \end{cases}$

18. $\begin{cases} x + y = -4 \\ y = -x - 4 \end{cases}$

19. $\begin{cases} -9x - 3y = -18 \\ 3x + y = 6 \end{cases}$

Independent Practice

For Exercises	See Example
12–15	1
16–19	2
20–22	3
23	4

Extra Practice

See Extra Practice for more Skills Practice and Applications Practice exercises.

Classify each system. Give the number of solutions.

20. $\begin{cases} y = -x + 5 \\ x + y = 5 \end{cases}$

21. $\begin{cases} y = -3x + 2 \\ y = 3x \end{cases}$

22. $\begin{cases} y - 1 = 2x \\ y = 2x - 1 \end{cases}$

23. **Sports** Mandy is skating at 5 miles per hour. Nikki is skating at 6 miles per hour and started 1 mile behind Mandy. If their rates stay the same, will Mandy catch up with Nikki? Explain.

24. **Multi-Step** Photocopier A can print 35 copies per minute. Photocopier B can print 35 copies per minute. Copier B is started and makes 10 copies. Copier A is then started. If the copiers continue, will the number of copies from machine A ever equal the number of copies from machine B? Explain.

25. **Entertainment** One week Trey rented 4 DVDs and 2 video games for $18. The next week he rented 2 DVDs and 1 video game for $9. Find the rental costs for each video game and DVD. Explain your answer.

26. Rosa bought 1 pound of cashews and 2 pounds of peanuts for $10. At the same store, Sabrina bought 2 pounds of cashews and 1 pound of peanuts for $11. Find the cost per pound for cashews and peanuts.

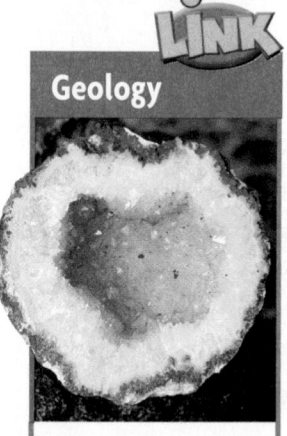

Geology

27. **Geology** Pam and Tommy collect geodes. Pam's parents gave her 2 geodes to start her collection, and she buys 4 every year. Tommy has 2 geodes that were given to him for his birthday. He buys 4 every year. If Pam and Tommy continue to buy the same amount of geodes per year, when will Tommy have as many geodes as Pam? Explain your answer.

Geodes are rounded, hollow rock formations. Most are partially or completely filled with layers of colored quartz crystals. The world's largest geode was discovered in Spain in 2000. It is 26 feet long and 5.6 feet high.

28. Use the data given in the tables.

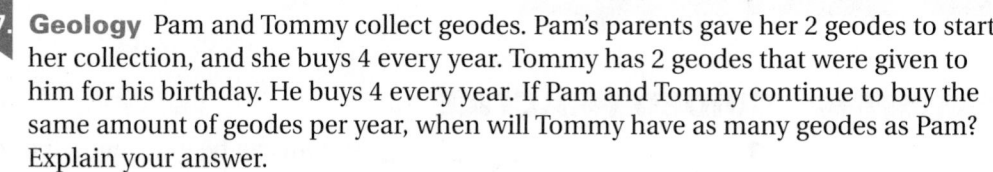

x	3	4	5	6
y	6	8	10	12

x	12	13	14	15
y	24	26	28	30

a. Write an equation to describe the data in each table.

b. Graph the system of equations from part **a.** Describe the graph.

c. How could you have predicted the graph by looking at the equations?

d. **What if...?** Each y-value in the second table increases by 1. How does this affect the graphs of the two equations? How can you tell how the graphs would be affected without actually graphing?

29. **Critical Thinking** Describe the graphs of two equations if the result of solving the system by substitution or elimination is the statement $1 = 3$.

MULTI-STEP TEST PREP

30. The Crusader pep club is selling team buttons that support the sports teams. They contacted Buttons, Etc. which charges $50 plus $1.10 per button, and Logos, which charges $40 plus $1.10 per button.

a. Write an equation for each company's cost.

b. Use the system from part **a** to find when the price for both companies is the same. Explain.

c. What part of the equation should the pep club negotiate to change so that the cost of Buttons, Etc. is the same as Logos? What part of the equation should change in order to get a better price?

31. **///ERROR ANALYSIS///** Student A says there is no solution to the graphed system of equations. Student B says there is one solution. Which student is incorrect? Explain the error.

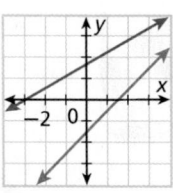

32. **Write About It** Compare the graph of a system that is consistent and independent with the graph of a system that is consistent and dependent.

33. Which of the following classifications fit the following system?

$$\begin{cases} 2x - y = 3 \\ 6x - 3y = 9 \end{cases}$$

    Ⓐ Inconsistent and independent   Ⓒ Inconsistent and dependent

    Ⓑ Consistent and independent   Ⓓ Consistent and dependent

34. Which of the following would be enough information to classify a system of two linear equations?

    Ⓕ The graphs have the same slope.

    Ⓖ The y-intercepts are the same.

    Ⓗ The graphs have different slopes.

    Ⓙ The y-intercepts are different.

CHALLENGE AND EXTEND

35. What conditions are necessary for the system $\begin{cases} y = 2x + p \\ y = 2x + q \end{cases}$ to have infinitely many solutions? no solution?

36. Solve the systems in parts **a** and **b.** Use this information to make a conjecture about all solutions that exist for the system in part **c.**

    a. $\begin{cases} 3x + 4y = 0 \\ 4x + 3y = 0 \end{cases}$ **b.** $\begin{cases} 2x + 5y = 0 \\ 5x + 2y = 0 \end{cases}$ **c.** $\begin{cases} ax + by = 0 \\ bx + ay = 0 \end{cases}$, for $a > 0, b > 0, a \neq b$

MULTI-STEP TEST PREP

MATHEMATICAL
PRACTICES

Make sense of problems and
persevere in solving them.

Systems of Equations

We've Got Spirit Some cheerleaders are going to sell spirit bracelets
and foam fingers to raise money for traveling to away games.

1. Two companies, Spirit for You
and Go Team, are interested
in providing the foam fingers.
The cheerleaders plan to sell
100 foam fingers. Based on this
information, which company
should they choose? Explain your
reasoning.

Company	Design fee	Cost per item
Spirit for You	$35	$2.50
Go Team	$20	$3.00

2. The cheerleaders sold foam fingers for
$5 and spirit bracelets for $4. They sold
40 more foam fingers than bracelets,
and they earned $965. Write a system of
equations to describe this situation.

3. Solve this system using at least two
different methods. Explain each
method.

4. Using the company you chose in
Problem 1, how much profit did the
cheerleaders make from the foam
fingers alone? (*Hint:* profit =
amount earned − expenses)

5. What is the maximum price the
cheerleaders could pay for each spirit
bracelet in order to make a total profit
of $500?

READY TO GO ON?

Quiz for Lessons 5-1 Through 5-4

✓ 5-1 Solving Systems by Graphing

Tell whether the ordered pair is a solution of the given system.

1. $(-2, 1)$; $\begin{cases} y = -2x - 3 \\ y = x + 3 \end{cases}$

2. $(9, 2)$; $\begin{cases} x - 4y = 1 \\ 2x - 3y = 3 \end{cases}$

3. $(3, -1)$; $\begin{cases} y = -\frac{1}{3}x \\ y + 2x = 5 \end{cases}$

Solve each system by graphing.

4. $\begin{cases} y = x + 5 \\ y = \frac{1}{2}x + 4 \end{cases}$

5. $\begin{cases} y = -x - 2 \\ 2x - y = 2 \end{cases}$

6. $\begin{cases} \frac{2}{3}x + y = -3 \\ 4x + y = 7 \end{cases}$

7. **Banking** Christiana and Marlena opened their first savings accounts on the same day. Christiana opened her account with $50 and plans to deposit $10 every month. Marlena opened her account with $30 and plans to deposit $15 every month. After how many months will their two accounts have the same amount of money? What will that amount be?

✓ 5-2 Solving Systems by Substitution

Solve each system by substitution.

8. $\begin{cases} y = -x + 5 \\ 2x + y = 11 \end{cases}$

9. $\begin{cases} 4x - 3y = -1 \\ 3x - y = -2 \end{cases}$

10. $\begin{cases} y = -x \\ y = -2x - 5 \end{cases}$

✓ 5-3 Solving Systems by Elimination

Solve each system by elimination.

11. $\begin{cases} x + 3y = 15 \\ 2x - 3y = -6 \end{cases}$

12. $\begin{cases} x + y = 2 \\ 2x + y = -1 \end{cases}$

13. $\begin{cases} -2x + 5y = -1 \\ 3x + 2y = 11 \end{cases}$

14. It takes Akira 10 minutes to make a black and white drawing and 25 minutes for a color drawing. On Saturday he made a total of 9 drawings in 2 hours. Write and solve a system of equations to determine how many drawings of each type Akira made.

✓ 5-4 Solving Special Systems

Solve each system of linear equations.

15. $\begin{cases} y = -2x - 6 \\ 2x + y = 5 \end{cases}$

16. $\begin{cases} x + y = 2 \\ 2x + 2y = -6 \end{cases}$

17. $\begin{cases} y = -2x + 4 \\ 2x + y = 4 \end{cases}$

Classify each system. Give the number of solutions.

18. $\begin{cases} 3x = -6y + 3 \\ 2y = -x + 1 \end{cases}$

19. $\begin{cases} y = -4x + 2 \\ 4x + y = -2 \end{cases}$

20. $\begin{cases} 4x - 3y = 8 \\ y = 4(x + 2) \end{cases}$

COMMON CORE

5-5 Solving Linear Inequalities

CC.9-12.A.REI.12 Graph the solutions to a linear inequality in two variables as a halfplane (excluding the boundary in the case of a strict inequality), …. *Also* **CC.9-12.A.CED.3***

Objective
Graph and solve linear inequalities in two variables.

Vocabulary
linear inequality
solution of a linear
  inequality

Who uses this?

Consumers can use linear inequalities to determine how much food they can buy for an event. (See Example 3.)

A **linear inequality** is similar to a linear equation, but the equal sign is replaced with an inequality symbol. A **solution of a linear inequality** is any ordered pair that makes the inequality true.

EXAMPLE **1** **Identifying Solutions of Inequalities**

Tell whether the ordered pair is a solution of the inequality.

A $(7, 3); y < x - 1$

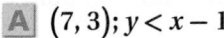

y	<	$x - 1$
3		$7 - 1$
3	<	6 ✓

Substitute (7, 3) for (x, y).

$(7, 3)$ is a solution.

B $(4, 5); y > 3x + 2$

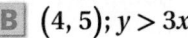

y	>	$3x + 2$
5		$3(4) + 2$
5		$12 + 2$
5	>	14 ✗

Substitute (4, 5) for (x, y).

$(4, 5)$ is not a solution.

 Tell whether the ordered pair is a solution of the inequality.

1a. $(4, 5); y < x + 1$ **1b.** $(1, 1); y > x - 7$

A linear inequality describes a region of a coordinate plane called a *half-plane*. All points in the region are solutions of the linear inequality. The boundary line of the region is the graph of the related equation.

When the inequality is written as $y \le$ or $y \ge$, the points on the boundary line are solutions of the inequality, and the line is solid.

When the inequality is written as $y <$ or $y >$, the points on the boundary line are not solutions of the inequality, and the line is dashed.

When the inequality is written as $y >$ or $y \ge$, the points above the boundary line are solutions of the inequality.

When the inequality is written as $y <$ or $y \le$, the points below the boundary line are solutions of the inequality.

	Graphing Linear Inequalities	
Step 1	Solve the inequality for *y*.	
Step 2	Graph the boundary line. Use a solid line for ≤ or ≥. Use a dashed line for < or >.	
Step 3	Shade the half-plane above the line for *y* > or *y* ≥. Shade the half-plane below the line for *y* < or *y* ≤. Check your answer.	

E X A M P L E 2 **Graphing Linear Inequalities in Two Variables**

Graph the solutions of each linear inequality.

A $y < 3x + 4$

Step 1 The inequality is already solved for *y*.

Step 2 Graph the boundary line $y = 3x + 4$. Use a dashed line for <.

Step 3 The inequality is <, so shade below the line.

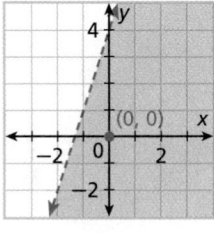

Check

y	$<$	$3x + 4$
0		$3(0) + 4$
0		$0 + 4$
0	$<$	4 ✓

Substitute (0, 0) for (x, y) because it is not on the boundary line.

The point (0, 0) satisfies the inequality, so the graph is shaded correctly.

B $3x + 2y \geq 6$

Step 1 Solve the inequality for *y*.

$$3x + 2y \geq \quad 6$$
$$\underline{-3x \qquad\quad -3x}$$
$$2y \geq -3x + 6$$
$$y \geq -\frac{3}{2}x + 3$$

Step 2 Graph the boundary line $y = -\frac{3}{2}x + 3$. Use a solid line for ≥.

Step 3 The inequality is ≥, so shade above the line.

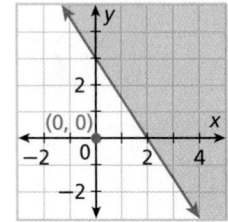

Check

y	$\geq$	$\frac{3}{2}x + 3$
0		$\frac{3}{2}(0) + 3$
0		$0 + 3$
0	$\geq$	3 ✗

A false statement means that the half-plane containing (0, 0) should NOT be shaded. (0, 0) is not one of the solutions, so the graph is shaded correctly.

Graph the solutions of each linear inequality.

2a. $4x - 3y > 12$ **2b.** $2x - y - 4 > 0$ **2c.** $y \geq -\frac{2}{3}x + 1$

EXAMPLE 3 *Consumer Economics Application*

Sarah can spend at most $7.50 on vegetables for a party. Broccoli costs $1.25 per bunch and carrots cost $0.75 per package.

a. Write a linear inequality to describe the situation.

Let x represent the number of bunches of broccoli and let y represent the number of packages of carrots.

Write an inequality. Use $\leq$ for "at most."

Cost of broccoli	plus	cost of carrots	is at most	$7.50.
$1.25x$	$+$	$0.75y$	$\leq$	7.50

Solve the inequality for y.

$$1.25x + 0.75y \leq 7.50$$

$$100(1.25x + 0.75y) \leq 100(7.50)$$ *You can multiply both sides of the inequality by 100 to eliminate the decimals.*

$$125x + 75y \leq 750$$
$$\underline{-125x \qquad\qquad -125x}$$ *Subtraction Property of Inequality*

$$75y \leq 750 - 125x$$

$$\frac{75y}{75} \leq \frac{750 - 125x}{75}$$ *Division Property of Inequality*

$$y \leq 10 - \frac{5}{3}x$$

b. Graph the solutions.

Step 1 Since Sarah cannot buy a negative amount of vegetables, the system is graphed only in Quadrant I. Graph the boundary line $y = -\frac{5}{3}x + 10$. Use a solid line for $\leq$.

Step 2 Shade below the line. Sarah must buy whole numbers of bunches or packages. All points on or below the line with whole-number coordinates represent combinations of broccoli and carrots that Sarah can buy.

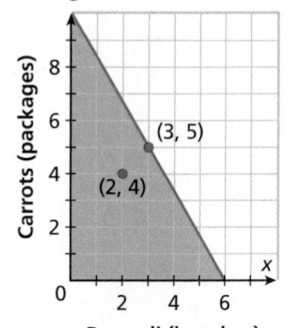

Vegetable Combinations

c. Give two combinations of vegetables that Sarah can buy.

Two different combinations that Sarah could buy for $7.50 or less are 2 bunches of broccoli and 4 packages of carrots, or 3 bunches of broccoli and 5 packages of carrots.

3. Dirk is going to bring two types of olives to the Honor Society induction and can spend no more than $6. Green olives cost $2 per pound and black olives cost $2.50 per pound.

    a. Write a linear inequality to describe the situation.

    b. Graph the solutions.

    c. Give two combinations of olives that Dirk could buy.

EXAMPLE 4 **Writing an Inequality from a Graph**

Write an inequality to represent each graph.

A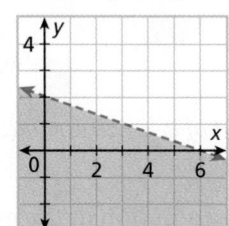

y-intercept: 2; slope: $-\frac{1}{3}$

Write an equation in slope-intercept form.

$$y = mx + b \longrightarrow y = -\frac{1}{3}x + 2$$

The graph is shaded *below* a *dashed* boundary line.

Replace $=$ with $<$ to write the inequality $y < -\frac{1}{3}x + 2$.

B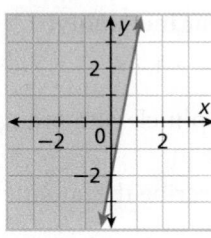

y-intercept: -2; slope: 5

Write an equation in slope-intercept form.

$$y = mx + b \longrightarrow y = 5x + (-2)$$

The graph is shaded *above* a *solid* boundary line.

Replace $=$ with $\geq$ to write the inequality $y \geq 5x - 2$.

C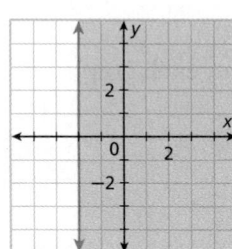

y-intercept: none; slope: undefined

The graph is a vertical line at $x = -2$.

The graph is shaded on the *right* side of a *solid* boundary line.

Replace $=$ with $\geq$ to write the inequality $x \geq -2$.

 Write an inequality to represent each graph.

4a.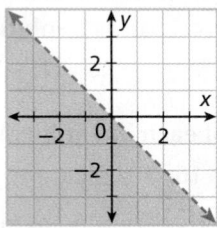

4b.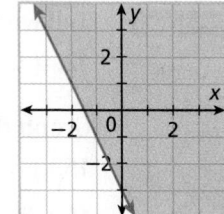

MATHEMATICAL PRACTICES

THINK AND DISCUSS

1. Tell how graphing a linear inequality is the same as graphing a linear equation. Tell how it is different.

2. Explain how you would write a linear inequality from a graph.

 **3. GET ORGANIZED** Copy and complete the graphic organizer.

Inequality	$y < 5x + 2$	$y > 7x - 3$	$y \leq 9x + 1$	$y \geq -3x - 2$
Symbol	$<$			
Boundary Line	Dashed			
Shading	Below			

GUIDED PRACTICE

1. **Vocabulary** Can a *solution of a linear inequality* lie on a dashed boundary line? Explain.

SEE EXAMPLE 1 **Tell whether the ordered pair is a solution of the given inequality.**

2. $(0, 3)$; $y \leq -x + 3$ 3. $(2, 0)$; $y > -2x - 2$ 4. $(-2, 1)$; $y < 2x + 4$

SEE EXAMPLE 2 **Graph the solutions of each linear inequality.**

5. $y \leq -x$ 6. $y > 3x + 1$ 7. $-y < -x + 4$ 8. $-y \geq x + 1$

SEE EXAMPLE 3 9. **Multi-Step** Jack is making punch with orange juice and pineapple juice. He can make at most 16 cups of punch.

   a. Write an inequality to describe the situation.

   b. Graph the solutions.

   c. Give two combinations of cups of orange juice and pineapple juice that Jack can use in his punch.

SEE EXAMPLE 4 **Write an inequality to represent each graph.**

10.
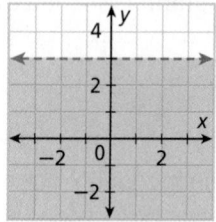

11.
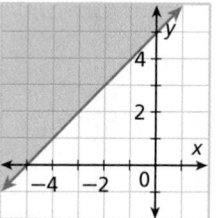

PRACTICE AND PROBLEM SOLVING

Independent Practice	
For Exercises	See Example
12–14	1
15–18	2
19	3
20–21	4

Extra Practice

See Extra Practice for more Skills Practice and Applications Practice exercises.

Tell whether the ordered pair is a solution of the given inequality.

12. $(2, 3)$; $y \geq 2x + 3$ 13. $(1, -1)$; $y < 3x - 3$ 14. $(0, 7)$; $y > 4x + 7$

Graph the solutions of each linear inequality.

15. $y > -2x + 6$ 16. $-y \geq 2x$ 17. $x + y \leq 2$ 18. $x - y \geq 0$

19. **Multi-Step** Beverly is serving hamburgers and hot dogs at her cookout. Hamburger meat costs $3 per pound, and hot dogs cost $2 per pound. She wants to spend no more than $30.

   a. Write an inequality to describe the situation.

   b. Graph the solutions.

   c. Give two combinations of pounds of hamburger and hot dogs that Beverly can buy.

Write an inequality to represent each graph.

20.
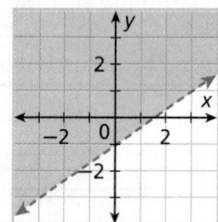

21.
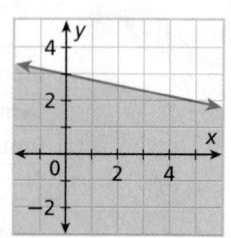

22. **Business** An electronics store makes $125 profit on every DVD player it sells and $100 on every CD player it sells. The store owner wants to make a profit of at least $500 a day selling DVD players and CD players.

   a. Write a linear inequality to determine the number of DVD players x and the number of CD players y that the owner needs to sell to meet his goal.

   b. Graph the linear inequality.

   c. Describe the possible values of x. Describe the possible values of y.

   d. List three combinations of DVD players and CD players that the owner could sell to meet his goal.

Graph the solutions of each linear inequality.

23. $y \leq 2 - 3x$ **24.** $-y < 7 + x$ **25.** $2x - y \leq 4$ **26.** $3x - 2y > 6$

 27. **Geometry** Marvin has 18 yards of fencing that he can use to put around a rectangular garden.

   a. Write an inequality to describe the possible lengths and widths of the garden.

   b. Graph the inequality and list three possible solutions to the problem.

   c. What are the dimensions of the largest *square* garden that can be fenced in with whole-number dimensions?

28. **Hobbies** Stephen wants to buy yellow tangs and clown fish for his saltwater aquarium. He wants to spend no more than $77 on fish. At the store, yellow tangs cost $15 each and clown fish cost $11 each. Write and graph a linear inequality to find the number of yellow tangs x and the number of clown fish y that Stephen could purchase. Name a solution of your inequality that is not reasonable for the situation. Explain.

Graph each inequality on a coordinate plane.

29. $y > 1$ **30.** $-2 < x$ **31.** $x \geq -3$ **32.** $y \leq 0$

33. $0 \geq x$ **34.** $-12 + y > 0$ **35.** $x + 7 < 7$ **36.** $-4 \geq x - y$

37. **School** At a high school football game, tickets at the gate cost $7 per adult and $4 per student. Write a linear inequality to determine the number of adult and student tickets that need to be sold so that the amount of money taken in at the gate is at least $280. Graph the inequality and list three possible solutions.

38. **Critical Thinking** Why must a region of a coordinate plane be shaded to show all solutions of a linear inequality?

39. **Write About It** Give a real-world situation that can be described by a linear inequality. Then graph the inequality and give two solutions.

MULTI-STEP TEST PREP

40. Gloria is making teddy bears. She is making boy and girl bears. She has enough stuffing to create 50 bears. Let x represent the number of girl bears and y represent the number of boy bears.

   a. Write an inequality that shows the possible number of boy and girl bears Gloria can make.

   b. Graph the inequality.

   c. Give three possible solutions for the numbers of boy and girl bears that can be made.

41. **///ERROR ANALYSIS///** Student A wrote $y < 2x - 1$ as the inequality represented by the graph. Student B wrote $y \leq 2x - 1$ as the inequality represented by the graph. Which student is incorrect? Explain the error.

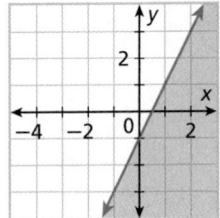

42. **Write About It** How do you decide to shade above or below a boundary line? What does this shading represent?

43. Which point is a solution of the inequality $y > -x + 3$?

 Ⓐ $(0, 3)$ Ⓑ $(1, 4)$ Ⓒ $(-1, 4)$ Ⓓ $(0, -3)$

44. Which inequality is represented by the graph at right?

 Ⓕ $2x + y \geq 3$ Ⓗ $2x + y \leq 3$

 Ⓖ $2x + y > 3$ Ⓙ $2x + y < 3$

45. Which of the following describes the graph of $3 \leq x$?

 Ⓐ The boundary line is dashed, and the shading is to the right.

 Ⓑ The boundary line is dashed, and the shading is to the left.

 Ⓒ The boundary line is solid, and the shading is to the right.

 Ⓓ The boundary line is solid, and the shading is to the left.

CHALLENGE AND EXTEND

Graph each inequality.

46. $0 \geq -6 - 2x - 5y$ 47. $y > |x|$ 48. $y \geq |x - 3|$

49. A linear inequality has the points $(0, 3)$ and $(-3, 1.5)$ as solutions on the boundary line. Also, the point $(1, 1)$ is not a solution. Write the linear inequality.

50. Two linear inequalities are graphed on the same coordinate plane. The point $(0, 0)$ is a solution of both inequalities. The entire coordinate plane is shaded except for Quadrant I. What are the two inequalities?

5-6 Solving Systems of Linear Inequalities

CC.9-12.A.REI.12 Graph the … solution set to a system of linear inequalities in two variables as the intersection of the corresponding half- planes. *Also* **CC.9-12.A.CED.3***

Objective
Graph and solve systems of linear inequalities in two variables.

Vocabulary
system of linear inequalities
solutions of a system of linear inequalities

Who uses this?

The owner of a surf shop can use systems of linear inequalities to determine how many surfboards and wakeboards need to be sold to make a certain profit. (See Example 4.)

A **system of linear inequalities** is a set of two or more linear inequalities containing two or more variables. The **solutions of a system of linear inequalities** are all of the ordered pairs that satisfy all the linear inequalities in the system.

EXAMPLE 1 Identifying Solutions of Systems of Linear Inequalities

Tell whether the ordered pair is a solution of the given system.

Remember!

An ordered pair must be a solution of all inequalities to be a solution of the system.

A $(2, 1)$; $\begin{cases} y < -x + 4 \\ y \le x + 1 \end{cases}$

$(2, 1)$

$y < -x + 4$
1 | $-2 + 4$
$1 < 2$ ✓

$(2, 1)$

$y \le x + 1$
1 | $2 + 1$
$1 \le 3$ ✓

$(2, 1)$ is a solution to the system because it satisfies both inequalities.

B $(2, 0)$; $\begin{cases} y \ge 2x \\ y < x + 1 \end{cases}$

$(2, 0)$

$y \ge 2x$
0 | $2(2)$
$0 \ge 4$ ✗

$(2, 0)$

$y < x + 1$
0 | $2 + 1$
$0 < 3$ ✓

$(2, 0)$ is not a solution to the system because it does not satisfy both inequalities.

 Tell whether the ordered pair is a solution of the given system.

1a. $(0, 1)$; $\begin{cases} y < -3x + 2 \\ y \ge x - 1 \end{cases}$

1b. $(0, 0)$; $\begin{cases} y > -x + 1 \\ y > x - 1 \end{cases}$

To show all the solutions of a system of linear inequalities, graph the solutions of each inequality. The solutions of the system are represented by the overlapping shaded regions. Below are graphs of Examples 1A and 1B.

Example 1A

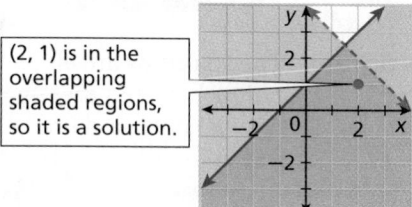

(2, 1) is in the overlapping shaded regions, so it is a solution.

Example 1B

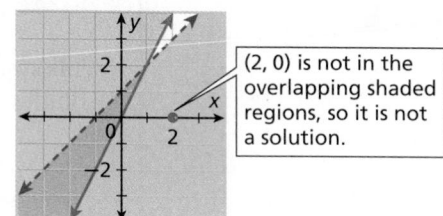

(2, 0) is not in the overlapping shaded regions, so it is not a solution.

EXAMPLE 2 **Solving a System of Linear Inequalities by Graphing**

Graph the system of linear inequalities. Give two ordered pairs that are solutions and two that are not solutions.

$$\begin{cases} 8x + 4y \le 12 \\ y > \dfrac{1}{2}x - 2 \end{cases}$$

$8x + 4y \le 12$ *Solve the first inequality for y.*
    $4y \le -8x + 12$
      $y \le -2x + 3$

Graph the system.

$$\begin{cases} y \le -2x + 3 \\ y > \dfrac{1}{2}x - 2 \end{cases}$$

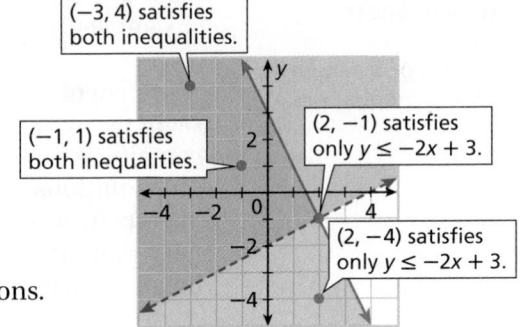

(−3, 4) satisfies both inequalities.

(−1, 1) satisfies both inequalities.

(2, −1) satisfies only $y \le -2x + 3$.

(2, −4) satisfies only $y \le -2x + 3$.

$(-1, 1)$ and $(-3, 4)$ are solutions.
$(2, -1)$ and $(2, -4)$ are not solutions.

CHECK IT OUT! Graph each system of linear inequalities. Give two ordered pairs that are solutions and two that are not solutions.

2a.  $\begin{cases} y \le x + 1 \\ y > 2 \end{cases}$ **2b.** $\begin{cases} y > x - 7 \\ 3x + 6y \le 12 \end{cases}$

Previously, you saw that in systems of linear equations, if the lines are parallel, there are no solutions. With systems of linear inequalities, that is not always true.

EXAMPLE 3 **Graphing Systems with Parallel Boundary Lines**

Graph each system of linear inequalities. Describe the solutions.

A $\begin{cases} y < 2x - 3 \\ y > 2x + 2 \end{cases}$ **B** $\begin{cases} y > x - 3 \\ y \le x + 1 \end{cases}$ **C** $\begin{cases} y \le -3x - 2 \\ y \le -3x + 4 \end{cases}$

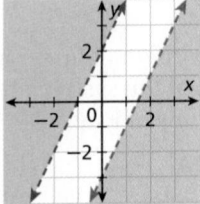   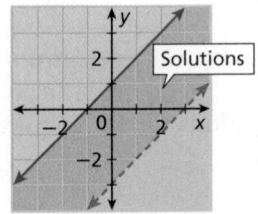   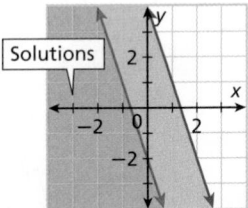

This system has no solution. | The solutions are all points between the parallel lines and on the solid line. | The solutions are the same as the solutions of $y \le -3x - 2$.

 Graph each system of linear inequalities. Describe the solutions.

3a. $\begin{cases} y > x + 1 \\ y \leq x - 3 \end{cases}$ **3b.** $\begin{cases} y \geq 4x - 2 \\ y \leq 4x + 2 \end{cases}$ **3c.** $\begin{cases} y > -2x + 3 \\ y > -2x \end{cases}$

EXAMPLE **4**   *Business Application*

A surf shop makes the profits given in the table. The shop owner sells at least 10 surfboards and at least 20 wakeboards per month. He wants to earn at least $2000 a month. Show and describe all possible combinations of surfboards and wakeboards that the store owner needs to sell to meet his goals. List two possible combinations.

Profit per Board Sold ($)	
Surfboard	150
Wakeboard	100

Step 1 Write a system of inequalities.
Let *x* represent the number of surfboards and *y* represent the number of wakeboards.

$x \geq 10$	*He sells at least 10 surfboards.*
$y \geq 20$	*He sells at least 20 wakeboards.*
$150x + 100y \geq 2000$	*He wants to earn a total of at least $2000.*

Step 2 Graph the system.
The graph should be in only the first quadrant because sales are not negative.

Step 3 Describe all possible combinations.
To meet the sales goals, the shop could sell any combination represented by an ordered pair of whole numbers in the solution region. Answers must be whole numbers because the shop cannot sell part of a surfboard or wakeboard.

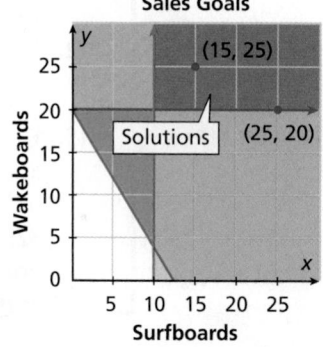
Sales Goals

Step 4 List two possible combinations.
Two possible combinations are:
15 surfboards and 25 wakeboards
25 surfboards and 20 wakeboards

> **Caution!**
>
> An ordered pair solution of the system need not have whole numbers, but answers to many application problems may be restricted to whole numbers.

 **4.** At her party, Alice is serving pepper jack cheese and cheddar cheese. She wants to have at least 2 pounds of each. Alice wants to spend at most $20 on cheese. Show and describe all possible combinations of the two cheeses Alice could buy. List two possible combinations.

Price per Pound ($)	
Pepper Jack	4
Cheddar	2

MATHEMATICAL PRACTICES

THINK AND DISCUSS

1. How would you write a system of linear inequalities from a graph?

2. GET ORGANIZED Copy and complete each part of the graphic organizer. In each box, draw a graph and list one solution.

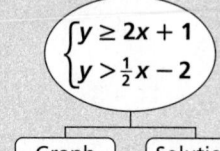
$\begin{cases} y \geq 2x + 1 \\ y > \frac{1}{2}x - 2 \end{cases}$

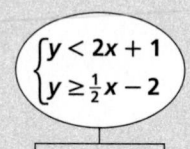
$\begin{cases} y < 2x + 1 \\ y \geq \frac{1}{2}x - 2 \end{cases}$

Graph   Solution   Graph   Solution

GUIDED PRACTICE

1. **Vocabulary** A solution of a system of inequalities is a solution of _____?_____ of the inequalities in the system. (*at least one* or *all*)

SEE EXAMPLE 1 Tell whether the ordered pair is a solution of the given system.

2. $(0, 0); \begin{cases} y < -x + 3 \\ y < x + 2 \end{cases}$
3. $(0, 0); \begin{cases} y < 3 \\ y > x - 2 \end{cases}$
4. $(1, 0); \begin{cases} y > 3x \\ y \le x + 1 \end{cases}$

SEE EXAMPLE 2 Graph each system of linear inequalities. Give two ordered pairs that are solutions and two that are not solutions.

5. $\begin{cases} y < 2x - 1 \\ y > 2 \end{cases}$
6. $\begin{cases} x < 3 \\ y > x - 2 \end{cases}$
7. $\begin{cases} y \ge 3x \\ 3x + y \ge 3 \end{cases}$
8. $\begin{cases} 2x - 4y \le 8 \\ y > x - 2 \end{cases}$

SEE EXAMPLE 3 Graph each system of linear inequalities. Describe the solutions.

9. $\begin{cases} y > 2x + 3 \\ y < 2x \end{cases}$
10. $\begin{cases} y \le -3x - 1 \\ y \ge -3x + 1 \end{cases}$
11. $\begin{cases} y > 4x - 1 \\ y \le 4x + 1 \end{cases}$

12. $\begin{cases} y < -x + 3 \\ y > -x + 2 \end{cases}$
13. $\begin{cases} y > 2x - 1 \\ y > 2x - 4 \end{cases}$
14. $\begin{cases} y \le -3x + 4 \\ y \le -3x - 3 \end{cases}$

SEE EXAMPLE 4 15. **Business** Sandy makes $2 profit on every cup of lemonade that she sells and $1 on every cupcake that she sells. Sandy wants to sell at least 5 cups of lemonade and at least 5 cupcakes per day. She wants to earn at least $25 per day. Show and describe all the possible combinations of lemonade and cupcakes that Sandy needs to sell to meet her goals. List two possible combinations.

PRACTICE AND PROBLEM SOLVING

Independent Practice

For Exercises	See Example
16–18	1
19–22	2
23–28	3
29	4

Tell whether the ordered pair is a solution of the given system.

16. $(0, 0); \begin{cases} y > -x - 1 \\ y < 2x + 4 \end{cases}$
17. $(0, 0); \begin{cases} x + y < 3 \\ y > 3x - 4 \end{cases}$
18. $(1, 0); \begin{cases} y > 3x \\ y > 3x + 1 \end{cases}$

Extra Practice

See Extra Practice for more Skills Practice and Applications Practice exercises.

Graph each system of linear inequalities. Give two ordered pairs that are solutions and two that are not solutions.

19. $\begin{cases} y < -3x - 3 \\ y \ge 0 \end{cases}$
20. $\begin{cases} y < -1 \\ y > 2x - 1 \end{cases}$
21. $\begin{cases} y > 2x + 4 \\ 6x + 2y \ge -2 \end{cases}$
22. $\begin{cases} 9x + 3y \le 6 \\ y > x \end{cases}$

Graph each system of linear inequalities. Describe the solutions.

23. $\begin{cases} y < 3 \\ y > 5 \end{cases}$
24. $\begin{cases} y < x - 1 \\ y > x - 2 \end{cases}$
25. $\begin{cases} x \ge 2 \\ x \le 2 \end{cases}$

26. $\begin{cases} y > -4x - 3 \\ y < -4x + 2 \end{cases}$
27. $\begin{cases} y > -1 \\ y > 2 \end{cases}$
28. $\begin{cases} y \le 2x + 1 \\ y \le 2x - 4 \end{cases}$

29. **Multi-Step** Linda works at a pharmacy for $15 an hour. She also baby-sits for $10 an hour. Linda needs to earn at least $90 per week, but she does not want to work more than 20 hours per week. Show and describe the number of hours Linda could work at each job to meet her goals. List two possible solutions.

30. **Farming** Tony wants to plant at least 40 acres of corn and at least 50 acres of soybeans. He wants no more than 200 acres of corn and soybeans. Show and describe all the possible combinations of the number of acres of corn and of soybeans Tony could plant. List two possible combinations.

Graph each system of linear inequalities.

31. $\begin{cases} y \geq -3 \\ y \geq 2 \end{cases}$
32. $\begin{cases} y > -2x - 1 \\ y > -2x - 3 \end{cases}$
33. $\begin{cases} x \leq -3 \\ x \geq 1 \end{cases}$
34. $\begin{cases} y < 4 \\ y > 0 \end{cases}$

Write a system of linear inequalities to represent each graph.

35.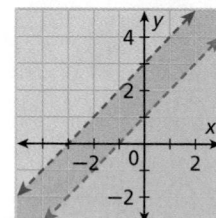

36.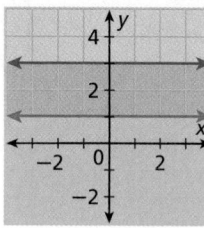

37.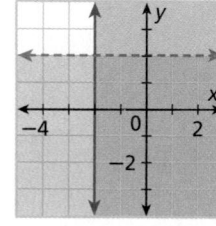

38. **Military** For males to enter the United States Air Force Academy, located in Colorado Springs, CO, they must be at least 17 but less than 23 years of age. Their standing height must be not less than 60 inches and not greater than 80 inches. Graph all possible heights and ages for eligible male candidates. Give three possible combinations.

39. **/// ERROR ANALYSIS ///** Two students wrote a system of linear inequalities to describe the graph. Which student is incorrect? Explain the error.

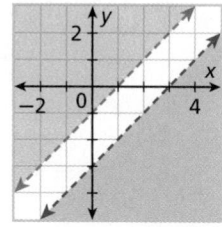

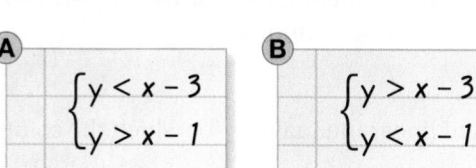

Ⓐ $\begin{cases} y < x - 3 \\ y > x - 1 \end{cases}$

Ⓑ $\begin{cases} y > x - 3 \\ y < x - 1 \end{cases}$

40. **Recreation** Vance wants to fence in a rectangular area for his dog. He wants the length of the rectangle to be at least 30 feet and the perimeter to be no more than 150 feet. Graph all possible dimensions of the rectangle.

41. **Critical Thinking** Can the solutions of a system of linear inequalities be the points on a line? Explain.

MULTI-STEP TEST PREP

42. Gloria is starting her own company making teddy bears. She has enough bear bodies to create 40 bears. She will make girl bears and boy bears.

   a. Write an inequality to show this situation.

   b. Gloria will charge $15 for girl bears and $12 for boy bears. She wants to earn at least $540 a week. Write an inequality to describe this situation.

   c. Graph this situation and locate the solution region.

43. **Write About It** What must be true of the boundary lines in a system of two linear inequalities if there is no solution of the system? Explain.

44. Which point is a solution of $\begin{cases} 2x + y \geq 3 \\ y \geq -2x + 1 \end{cases}$?

Ⓐ $(0, 0)$ Ⓑ $(0, 1)$ Ⓒ $(1, 0)$ Ⓓ $(1, 1)$

45. Which system of inequalities best describes the graph?

Ⓕ $\begin{cases} y < 2x - 3 \\ y > 2x + 1 \end{cases}$ Ⓗ $\begin{cases} y < 2x - 3 \\ y < 2x + 1 \end{cases}$

Ⓖ $\begin{cases} y > 2x - 3 \\ y < 2x + 1 \end{cases}$ Ⓙ $\begin{cases} y > 2x - 3 \\ y > 2x + 1 \end{cases}$

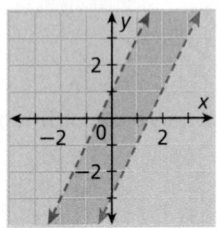

46. **Short Response** Graph and describe $\begin{cases} y + x > 2 \\ y \leq -3x + 4 \end{cases}$. Give two possible solutions of the system.

CHALLENGE AND EXTEND

47. **Estimation** Graph the given system of inequalities. Estimate the area of the overlapping solution regions.
$$\begin{cases} y \geq 0 \\ y \leq x + 3.5 \\ y \leq -x + 3.5 \end{cases}$$

48. Write a system of linear inequalities for which $(-1, 1)$ and $(1, 4)$ are solutions and $(0, 0)$ and $(2, -1)$ are not solutions.

49. Graph $|y| < 1$.

50. Write a system of linear inequalities for which the solutions are all the points in the third quadrant.

5-6 Technology LAB

Solve Systems of Linear Inequalities

A graphing calculator gives a visual solution to a system of linear inequalities.

Use with Solving Systems of Linear Inequalities

MATHEMATICAL PRACTICES
Use appropriate tools strategically.

CC.9-12.A.REI.12 Graph the ... solution set to a system of linear inequalities in two variables as the intersection of the corresponding half-planes.

Activity

Graph the system $\begin{cases} y > 2x - 4 \\ 2.75y - x < 6 \end{cases}$. **Give two ordered pairs that are solutions.**

1 The first inequality is solved for y.

2 Graph the first inequality. First graph the boundary line $y = 2x - 4$. Press **Y=** and enter $2x - 4$ for **Y1**.

The inequality contains the symbol $>$. The solution region is above the boundary line. Press ◄ to move the cursor to the left of **Y1**. Press **ENTER** until the icon that looks like a region above a line appears. Press **GRAPH**.

3 Solve the second inequality for y.

$$2.75y - x < 6$$
$$2.75y < x + 6$$
$$y < \frac{x + 6}{2.75}$$

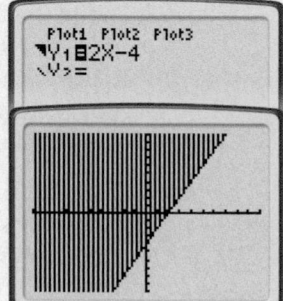

4 Graph the second inequality. First graph the boundary line $y = \frac{x + 6}{2.75}$. Press **Y=** and enter $(x + 6)/2.75$ for **Y2**.

The inequality contains the symbol $<$. The solution region is below the boundary line. Press ◄ to move the cursor to the left of **Y2**. Press **ENTER** until the icon that looks like a region below a line appears. Press **GRAPH**.

5 The solutions of the system are represented by the overlapping shaded regions. The points $(0, 0)$ and $(-1, 0)$ are in the shaded region.

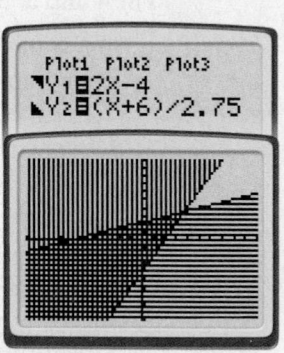

Check Test $(0, 0)$ in both inequalities.   Test $(-1, 0)$ in both inequalities.

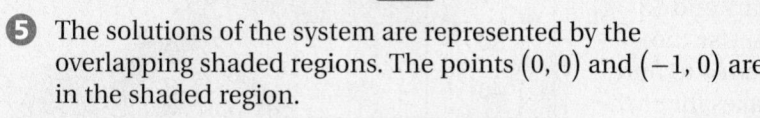

Try This

Graph each system. Give two ordered pairs that are solutions.

1. $\begin{cases} x + 5y > -10 \\ x - y < 4 \end{cases}$

2. $\begin{cases} y > x - 2 \\ y \le x + 2 \end{cases}$

3. $\begin{cases} y > x - 2 \\ y \le 3 \end{cases}$

4. $\begin{cases} y < x - 3 \\ y - 3 > x \end{cases}$

MULTI-STEP TEST PREP

Make sense of problems and persevere in solving them.

Equations and Formulas

Bearable Sales Gloria makes teddy bears. She dresses some as girl bears with dresses and bows and some as boy bears with bow ties. She is running low on supplies. She has only 100 eyes, 30 dresses, and 60 ties that can be used as bows on the girls and bow ties on the boys.

1. Write the inequalities that describe this situation. Let x represent the number of boy bears and y represent the number of girl bears.

2. Graph the inequalities and locate the region showing the number of boy and girl bears Gloria can make.

3. List at least three combinations of girl and boy bears that Gloria can make.

For 4 and 5, use the table.

4. Using the boundary line in your graph from Problem 2, copy and complete the table with the corresponding number of girl bears.

5. Gloria sells the bears for profit. She makes a profit of $8 for the girl bears and $5 for the boy bears. Use the table from Problem 4 to find the profit she makes for each given combination.

6. Which combination is the most profitable? Explain. Where does it lie on the graph?

Bear Combinations	
Boy	Girl
0	
10	
20	
30	
40	
50	

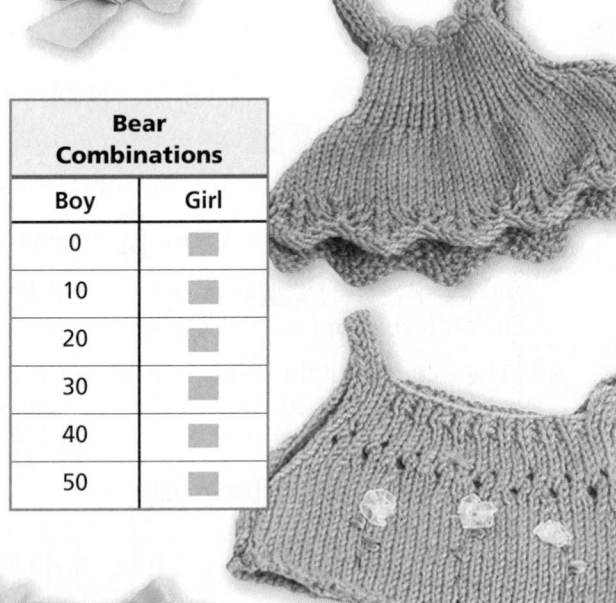

READY TO GO ON?

Quiz for Lessons 5-5 Through 5-6

✅ 5-5 Solving Linear Inequalities

Tell whether the ordered pair is a solution of the inequality.

1. $(3, -2)$; $y < -2x + 1$ **2.** $(2, 1)$; $y \geq 3x - 5$ **3.** $(1, -6)$; $y \leq 4x - 10$

Graph the solutions of each linear inequality.

4. $y \geq 4x - 3$ **5.** $3x - y < 5$ **6.** $2x + 3y < 9$ **7.** $y \leq -\dfrac{1}{2}x$

8. Theo's mother has given him at most $150 to buy clothes for school. The pants cost $30 each and the shirts cost $15 each. Write a linear inequality to describe the situation. Graph the solutions and give three combinations of pants and shirts that Theo could buy.

Write an inequality to represent each graph.

9.
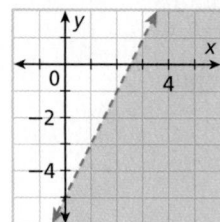

10.
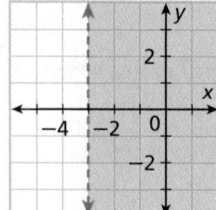

11.
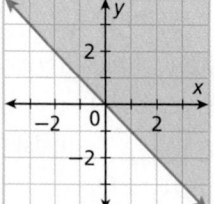

✅ 5-6 Solving Systems of Linear Inequalities

Tell whether the ordered pair is a solution of the given system.

12. $(-3, -1)$; $\begin{cases} y > -2 \\ y < x + 4 \end{cases}$ **13.** $(-3, 0)$; $\begin{cases} y \leq x + 4 \\ y \geq -2x - 6 \end{cases}$ **14.** $(0, 0)$; $\begin{cases} y \geq 3x \\ 2x + y < -1 \end{cases}$

Graph each system of linear inequalities. Give two ordered pairs that are solutions and two that are not solutions.

15. $\begin{cases} y > -2 \\ y < x + 3 \end{cases}$ **16.** $\begin{cases} x + y \leq 2 \\ 2x + y \geq -1 \end{cases}$ **17.** $\begin{cases} 2x - 5y \leq -5 \\ 3x + 2y < 10 \end{cases}$

Graph each system of linear inequalities. Describe the solutions.

18. $\begin{cases} y \geq x + 1 \\ y \geq x - 4 \end{cases}$ **19.** $\begin{cases} y \geq 2x - 1 \\ y < 2x - 3 \end{cases}$ **20.** $\begin{cases} y < -3x + 5 \\ y > -3x - 2 \end{cases}$

21. A grocer sells mangos for $4/lb and apples for $3/lb. The grocer starts with 45 lb of mangos and 50 lb of apples each day. The grocer's goal is to make at least $300 by selling mangos and apples each day. Show and describe all possible combinations of mangos and apples that could be sold to meet the goal. List two possible combinations.

Study Guide: Review

Vocabulary

consistent system

dependent system

inconsistent system

independent system

linear inequality

solution of a linear inequality

solution of a system of linear equations

solutions of a system of linear inequalities

system of linear equations

system of linear inequalities

Complete the sentences below with vocabulary words from the list above.

1. A(n) ___?___ is a system that has exactly one solution.

2. A set of two or more linear equations that contain the same variable(s) is a(n) ___?___ .

3. The ___?___ consists of all the ordered pairs that satisfy all the inequalities in the system.

4. A system consisting of equations of parallel lines with different y-intercepts is a(n) ___?___ .

5. A(n) ___?___ consists of two intersecting lines.

5-1 Solving Systems by Graphing

EXAMPLE

■ Solve $\begin{cases} y = 2x - 2 \\ x + 2y = 16 \end{cases}$ by graphing.

Check your answer.

$\begin{cases} y = 2x - 2 \\ y = -\dfrac{1}{2}x + 8 \end{cases}$ *Write the second equation in slope-intercept form.*

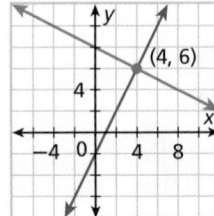

(4, 6)

The solution appears to be at $(4, 6)$.

$y = 2x - 2$		$x + 2y = 16$	
6	$2(4) - 2$	$4 + 2(6)$	16
6	$6\checkmark$		$16 \mid 16\checkmark$

The ordered pair $(4, 6)$ makes both equations true, so it is a solution of the system.

EXERCISES

Tell whether the ordered pair is a solution of the given system.

6. $(0, -5)$; $\begin{cases} y = -6x + 5 \\ x - y = 5 \end{cases}$

7. $(4, 3)$; $\begin{cases} x - 2y = -2 \\ y = \dfrac{1}{2}x + 1 \end{cases}$

8. $\left(1\dfrac{3}{4}, 7\dfrac{1}{4}\right)$; $\begin{cases} x + y = 9 \\ 2y = 6x + 4 \end{cases}$

9. $(-1, -1)$; $\begin{cases} y = -2x + 5 \\ 3y = 6x + 3 \end{cases}$

Solve each system by graphing. Check your answer.

10. $\begin{cases} y = 3x + 2 \\ y = -2x - 3 \end{cases}$

11. $\begin{cases} y = -\dfrac{1}{3}x + 5 \\ 2x - 2y = -2 \end{cases}$

12. Raheel is comparing the cost of two parking garages. Garage A charges a flat fee of $6 per car plus $0.50 per hour. Garage B charges a flat fee of $2 per car plus $1 per hour. After how many hours will the cost at garage A be the same as the cost at garage B? What will that cost be?

5-2 Solving Systems by Substitution

EXAMPLE

■ Solve $\begin{cases} 2x - 3y = -2 \\ y - 3x = 10 \end{cases}$ by substitution.

Step 1 $\quad y - 3x = 10$ *Solve the second*
$\qquad\qquad y = 3x + 10$ *equation for y.*

Step 2 $\qquad\quad 2x - 3y = -2$ *Substitute 3x + 10*
$\qquad 2x - 3(3x + 10) = -2$ *for y in the first*
$\qquad\qquad\qquad\qquad\qquad\qquad$ *equation.*

Step 3 $\quad 2x - 9x - 30 = -2$ *Solve for x.*
$\qquad\qquad -7x - 30 = -2$
$\qquad\qquad\qquad -7x = 28$
$\qquad\qquad\qquad\quad x = -4$

Step 4 $\qquad\quad y - 3x = 10$ *Substitute −4 for x.*
$\qquad\qquad y - 3(-4) = 10$
$\qquad\qquad\quad y + 12 = 10$ *Find the value of y.*
$\qquad\qquad\qquad\quad y = -2$

Step 5 $(-4, -2)$ *Write the solution as an*
$\qquad\qquad\qquad\qquad\qquad$ *ordered pair.*

To check the solution, substitute $(-4, -2)$ into both equations in the system.

EXERCISES

Solve each system by substitution.

13. $\begin{cases} y = x + 3 \\ y = 2x + 12 \end{cases}$ **14.** $\begin{cases} y = -4x \\ y = 2x - 3 \end{cases}$

15. $\begin{cases} 2x + y = 4 \\ 3x + y = 3 \end{cases}$ **16.** $\begin{cases} x + y = -1 \\ y = -2x + 3 \end{cases}$

17. $\begin{cases} x = y - 7 \\ -y - 2x = 8 \end{cases}$ **18.** $\begin{cases} \frac{1}{2}x + y = 9 \\ 3x - 4y = -6 \end{cases}$

19. The Nash family's car needs repairs. Estimates for parts and labor from two garages are shown below.

Garage	Parts ($)	Labor ($ per hour)
Motor Works	650	70
Jim's Car Care	800	55

For how many hours of labor will the total cost of fixing the car be the same at both garages? What will that cost be? Which garage will be cheaper if the repairs require 8 hours of labor? Explain.

5-3 Solving Systems by Elimination

EXAMPLE

■ Solve $\begin{cases} 2x - 3y = -8 \\ x + 4y = 7 \end{cases}$ by elimination.

Step 1
$\qquad\quad 2x - 3y = -8$ *Multiply the*
$+(-2)(x + 4y = 7)$ *second*
$\qquad\qquad\qquad\qquad\qquad$ *equation by −2.*
$\qquad\quad 2x - 3y = -8$ *Eliminate x.*
$+(-2x - 8y = -14)$

Step 2 $\qquad\quad -11y = -22$ *Solve for y.*
$\qquad\qquad\qquad\quad y = 2$

Step 3 $\quad 2x - 3y = -8$
$\qquad 2x - 3(2) = -8$ *Substitute 2 for y.*
$\qquad\quad 2x - 6 = -8$ *Simplify and solve*
$\qquad\qquad\quad 2x = -2$ *for x.*
$\qquad\qquad\qquad x = -1$

Step 4 $(-1, 2)$ *Write the solution as*
$\qquad\qquad\qquad\qquad\qquad$ *an ordered pair.*

To check the solution, substitute $(-1, 2)$ into both equations in the system.

EXERCISES

Solve each system by elimination.

20. $\begin{cases} 4x + y = -1 \\ 2x - y = -5 \end{cases}$ **21.** $\begin{cases} x + 2y = -1 \\ x + y = 2 \end{cases}$

22. $\begin{cases} x + y = 12 \\ 2x + 5y = 27 \end{cases}$ **23.** $\begin{cases} 3x - 2y = -6 \\ \frac{1}{3}x + 3y = 9 \end{cases}$

Solve each system by any method. Explain why you chose each method. Check your answer.

24. $\begin{cases} 3x + y = 2 \\ y = -4x \end{cases}$ **25.** $\begin{cases} y = \frac{1}{3}x - 6 \\ y = -2x + 1 \end{cases}$

26. $\begin{cases} 2y = -3x \\ y = -2x + 2 \end{cases}$ **27.** $\begin{cases} x - y = 0 \\ 3x + y = 8 \end{cases}$

EXAMPLES

Classify each system. Give the number of solutions.

■ $\begin{cases} y = 3x + 4 \\ 6x - 2y = -8 \end{cases}$

Use the substitution method because the first equation is solved for y.

$6x - 2(3x + 4) = -8$ *Substitute $3x + 4$ for y in*
$6x - 6x - 8 = -8$ *the second equation.*
$-8 = -8$ ✓   *True*

The equation is an identity. There are infinitely many solutions.

This system is **consistent** and **dependent**. When graphed, the two lines are coincident (the same line)—they have identical slopes and y-intercepts.

■ $\begin{cases} y = 2x - 1 \\ 2x - y = -2 \end{cases}$

Compare slopes and y-intercepts. Write both equations in slope-intercept form.

$\begin{cases} y = 2x - 1 & \Rightarrow y = 2x - 1 \\ 2x - y = -2 & \Rightarrow y = 2x + 2 \end{cases}$

The lines have the same slope and different y-intercepts. The lines are parallel.

The lines never intersect, so this system is **inconsistent**. It has **no solution.**

■ $\begin{cases} 2x - y = 6 \\ y = x - 1 \end{cases}$

Write both equations in slope-intercept form.

$\begin{cases} 2x - y = 6 & \Rightarrow y = 2x - 6 \\ y = x - 1 & \Rightarrow y = 1x - 1 \end{cases}$

The lines intersect because they have different slopes.

The system is **consistent** and **independent**. There is **one solution**: $(5, 4)$.

EXERCISES

Solve each system of linear equations.

28. $\begin{cases} y = \dfrac{1}{4}x - 3 \\ y = \dfrac{1}{4}x + 5 \end{cases}$ 29. $\begin{cases} y = -x + 4 \\ x + y = 4 \end{cases}$

30. $\begin{cases} y = 3x + 2 \\ y = 2x \end{cases}$ 31. $\begin{cases} -4x - y = 6 \\ \dfrac{1}{2}y = -2x - 3 \end{cases}$

32. $\begin{cases} x + 2y = 8 \\ y = -\dfrac{1}{2}x + 4 \end{cases}$ 33. $\begin{cases} y - 2x = -1 \\ y + 2x = -5 \end{cases}$

34. Tristan and his friend Marco just started DVD collections. They continue to get DVDs at the rate shown in the table below. Will Tristan ever have the same number of DVDs as Marco? Explain.

DVD Collections			
	Month 1	Month 2	Month 3
Tristan	2	7	12
Marco	8	12	16

Classify each system. Give the number of solutions.

35. $\begin{cases} y = \dfrac{1}{2}x + 2 \\ y = \dfrac{1}{4}x - 8 \end{cases}$ 36. $\begin{cases} y = 3x - 7 \\ y = 3x + 2 \end{cases}$

37. $\begin{cases} 2x + y = 2 \\ y - 2 = -2x \end{cases}$ 38. $\begin{cases} -3x - y = -5 \\ y = -3x - 5 \end{cases}$

39. $\begin{cases} 2x + 3y = 1 \\ 3x + 2y = 1 \end{cases}$ 40. $\begin{cases} x + \dfrac{1}{2}y = 3 \\ 2x = 6 - y \end{cases}$

41. The two parallel lines graphed below represent a system of equations. Classify the system and give the number of solutions.

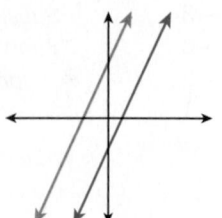

5-5 Solving Linear Inequalities

EXAMPLE

■ Graph the solutions of $x - 2y < 6$.

Step 1 Solve the inequality for y.
$$x - 2y < 6$$
$$-2y < -x + 6$$
$$y > \frac{1}{2}x - 3$$

Step 2 Graph $y = \frac{1}{2}x - 3$.
Use a dashed line for $>$.

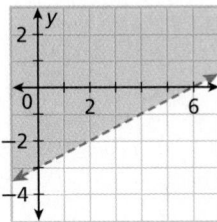

Step 3 The inequality is $>$, so shade above the boundary line.

Check Substitute $(0, 0)$ for (x, y).
$$\begin{array}{c|c} x - 2y & < 6 \\ \hline 0 - 2(0) & 6 \\ 0 & \overset{?}{<} 6 \checkmark \end{array}$$

$(0, 0)$ satisfies the inequality, so the graph is shaded correctly.

EXERCISES

Tell whether the ordered pair is a solution of the inequality.

42. $(0, -3); y < 2x - 3$

43. $(2, -1); y \geq x - 3$

44. $(6, 0); y > -3x + 4$

45. $(10, 10); y \leq x - 3$

Graph the solutions of each linear inequality.

46. $y < -2x + 5$ **47.** $x - y \geq 2$

48. $-x + 2y \geq 6$ **49.** $y > -4x$

50. $x + y + 4 > 0$ **51.** $5 - y \geq 2x$

52. The Mathematics Club is selling pizza and lemonade to raise money for a trip. They estimate that the trip will cost at least $450. They earn $2 on each slice of pizza and $1 on each bottle of lemonade. Write an inequality to describe the situation. Graph the solutions and then give two combinations of the number of pizza slices and number of lemonade bottles they could sell to meet their goal.

5-6 Solving Systems of Linear Inequalities

EXAMPLES

■ Graph $\begin{cases} y < -x + 5 \\ y \geq 2x - 3 \end{cases}$. Give two ordered pairs that are solutions and two that are not solutions.

Graph both inequalities.

The solutions of the system are represented by the overlapping shaded regions.

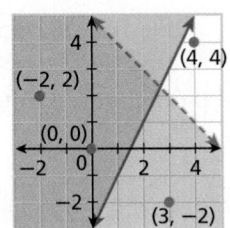

The points $(0, 0)$ and $(-2, 2)$ are solutions of the system.

The points $(3, -2)$ and $(4, 4)$ are not solutions.

EXERCISES

Tell whether the ordered pair is a solution of the given system.

53. $(3, 3); \begin{cases} y > -2x + 9 \\ y \geq x \end{cases}$ **54.** $(-1, 0); \begin{cases} 2x - y > -5 \\ y \leq -3x - 3 \end{cases}$

Graph each system of linear inequalities. Give two ordered pairs that are solutions and two that are not solutions.

55. $\begin{cases} y \geq x + 4 \\ y > 6x - 3 \end{cases}$ **56.** $\begin{cases} y \leq -2x + 8 \\ y > 3x - 5 \end{cases}$

57. $\begin{cases} -x + 2y > 6 \\ x + y < 4 \end{cases}$ **58.** $\begin{cases} x - y > 7 \\ x + 3y \leq 15 \end{cases}$

Graph each system of linear inequalities.

59. $\begin{cases} y > -x - 6 \\ y < -x + 5 \end{cases}$ **60.** $\begin{cases} 4x + 2y \geq 10 \\ 6x + 3y < -9 \end{cases}$

CHAPTER TEST

Tell whether the ordered pair is a solution of the given system.

1. $(1, -4);$ $\begin{cases} y = -4x \\ y = 2x - 2 \end{cases}$

2. $(0, -1);$ $\begin{cases} 3x - y = 1 \\ x + 5y = -5 \end{cases}$

3. $(3, 2);$ $\begin{cases} x - 2y = -1 \\ -3x + 2y = 5 \end{cases}$

Solve each system by graphing.

4. $\begin{cases} y = x - 3 \\ y = -2x - 3 \end{cases}$

5. $\begin{cases} 2x + y = -8 \\ y = \frac{1}{3}x - 1 \end{cases}$

6. $\begin{cases} y = -x + 4 \\ x = y + 2 \end{cases}$

Solve each system by substitution.

7. $\begin{cases} y = -6 \\ y = -2x - 2 \end{cases}$

8. $\begin{cases} -x + y = -4 \\ y = 2x - 11 \end{cases}$

9. $\begin{cases} x - 3y = 3 \\ 2x = 3y \end{cases}$

10. The costs for services at two kennels are shown in the table. Joslyn plans to board her dog and have him bathed once during his stay. For what number of days will the cost for boarding and bathing her dog at each kennel be the same? What will that cost be? If Joslyn plans a week-long vacation, which is the cheaper service? Explain.

Kennel Costs		
	Boarding ($ per day)	Bathing ($)
Pet Care	30	15
Fido's	28	27

Solve each system by elimination.

11. $\begin{cases} 3x - y = 7 \\ 2x + y = 3 \end{cases}$

12. $\begin{cases} 4x + y = 0 \\ x + y = -3 \end{cases}$

13. $\begin{cases} 2x + y = 3 \\ x - 2y = -1 \end{cases}$

Classify each system. Give the number of solutions.

14. $\begin{cases} y = 6x - 1 \\ 6x - y = 1 \end{cases}$

15. $\begin{cases} y = -3x - 3 \\ 3x + y = 3 \end{cases}$

16. $\begin{cases} 2x - y = 1 \\ -4x + y = 1 \end{cases}$

Graph the solutions of each linear inequality.

17. $y < 2x - 5$

18. $-y \geq 8$

19. $y > \frac{1}{3}x$

Graph each system of linear inequalities. Give two ordered pairs that are solutions and two that are not solutions.

20. $\begin{cases} y > \frac{1}{2}x - 5 \\ y \leq 4x - 1 \end{cases}$

21. $\begin{cases} y > -x + 4 \\ 3x - y > 3 \end{cases}$

22. $\begin{cases} y \geq 2x \\ y - 2x < 6 \end{cases}$

23. Ezra and Tava sold at least 150 coupon books. Ezra sold at most 30 books more than twice the number Tava sold. Show and describe all possible combinations of the numbers of coupon books Ezra and Tava sold. List two possible combinations.

COLLEGE ENTRANCE EXAM PRACTICE

FOCUS ON ACT

Four scores are reported for the ACT Mathematics Test: one score based on all 60 problems and one for each content area. The three content areas are: Pre-Algebra/Elementary Algebra, Intermediate Algebra/Coordinate Geometry, and Plane Geometry/Trigonometry.

Taking classes that cover the content areas on the ACT is a good idea. This way you will have skills from each area of the test. Preparation over a long term is better than cramming at the last minute.

You may want to time yourself as you take this practice test. It should take you about 5 minutes to complete.

1. Which system of inequalities is represented by the graph?

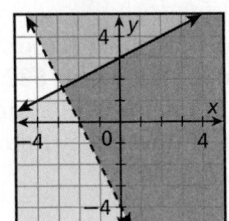

(A) $\begin{cases} -x + 2y < 6 \\ 2x + y > -4 \end{cases}$

(B) $\begin{cases} x - 2y \le 6 \\ 2x - y \ge 4 \end{cases}$

(C) $\begin{cases} -x + 2y \le 6 \\ 2x + y \ge 4 \end{cases}$

(D) $\begin{cases} -x + 2y \le 6 \\ 2x + y > -4 \end{cases}$

(E) $\begin{cases} x - 2y \le 6 \\ 2x - y > 4 \end{cases}$

2. What is the y-value of the solution of the given system?

$\begin{cases} 4x + 3y = 1 \\ -4x + 3y = -7 \end{cases}$

(F) -1

(G) 0

(H) 1

(J) 2

(K) 6

3. Wireless phone company A charges $20 per month plus $0.12 per minute. Wireless phone company B charges $50 per month plus $0.06 per minute. For how many minutes of calls will the monthly bills be the same?

(A) 80 minutes

(B) 100 minutes

(C) 160 minutes

(D) 250 minutes

(E) 500 minutes

4. Which of the following systems of equations does NOT have a solution?

(F) $\begin{cases} x + 5y = 30 \\ -4x + 5y = 10 \end{cases}$

(G) $\begin{cases} x + 5y = -30 \\ -4x + 5y = 10 \end{cases}$

(H) $\begin{cases} x + 5y = -30 \\ -4x + 5y = -10 \end{cases}$

(J) $\begin{cases} -4x + 5y = -10 \\ -8x + 10y = -20 \end{cases}$

(K) $\begin{cases} -4x + 5y = -10 \\ -4x + 5y = -30 \end{cases}$

CHAPTER 5

TEST TACKLER

Standardized Test Strategies

Any Question Type: Read the Problem for Understanding

Standardized test questions may vary in format including multiple choice, gridded response, and short or extended response. No matter what format the test uses, read each question carefully and critically. Do not rush. Be sure you completely understand what you are asked to do and what your response should include.

EXAMPLE

Extended Response

An interior decorator charges a consultation fee of \$50 plus \$12 per hour. Another interior decorator charges a consultation fee of \$5 plus \$22 per hour. Write a system of equations to find the amount of time for which the cost of both decorators will be the same. Graph the system. After how many hours will the cost be the same for both decorators? What will the cost be?

Read the problem again.

What information are you given?

the consultation fees and hourly rates of two decorators

What are you asked to do?

1. Write a system of equations.
2. Graph the system.
3. Interpret the solution to the system.

What should your response include?

1. a system of equations with variables defined
2. a graph of the system
3. the time when the cost is the same for both decorators
4. the cost at that time

Read each test item and answer the questions that follow.

After you answer each item, read the item again to be sure your response includes everything that is asked for.

Item A

Short Response Which value of b will make the lines intersect at the point $(-2, 14)$?

$$\begin{cases} y = -6x + 2 \\ y = 4x + b \end{cases}$$

1. What information are you given?

2. What are you asked to do?

3. Ming's answer to this test problem was $y = 4x + 22$. Did Ming answer correctly? Explain.

Item B

Extended Response Solve the system by using elimination. Explain how you can check your solution algebraically and graphically.

$$\begin{cases} 4x + 10y = -48 \\ 6x - 10y = 28 \end{cases}$$

4. What method does the problem ask you to use to solve the system of equations?

5. What methods does the problem ask you to use to check your solution?

6. How many parts are there to this problem? List what needs to be included in your response.

Item C

Gridded Response What is the x-coordinate of the solution to this system? $\begin{cases} y = 6x + 9 \\ y = 12x - 15 \end{cases}$

7. What question is being asked?

8. A student correctly found the solution of the system to be $(4, 33)$. What should the student mark on the grid so that the answer is correct?

Item D

Short Response Write an inequality to represent the graph below. Give a real-world situation that this inequality could describe.

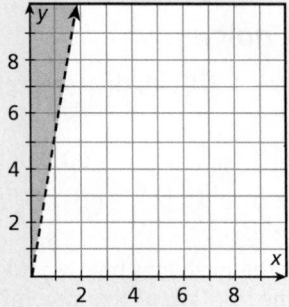

9. As part of his answer, a student wrote the following response:

The point $(1, 5)$ is not a solution to the inequality because it lies on the line, but $(2, 12)$ is a solution because it lies above the line.

Is his response appropriate? Explain.

10. What should the response include so that it answers all parts of the problem?

Item E

Multiple Choice Taylor bikes 50 miles per week and increases her distance by 2 miles each week. Josie bikes 30 miles per week and increases her distance by 10 miles each week. In how many weeks will Taylor and Josie be biking the same distance?

(A) 2.5 weeks   (C) 55 weeks

(B) 7.5 weeks   (D) 110 weeks

11. What question is being asked?

12. Carson incorrectly selected option C as his answer. What question did he most likely answer?

CUMULATIVE ASSESSMENT

Multiple Choice

1. If $a > 0$ and $b < 0$, which of the following must be true?

(A) $ab > 0$ (C) $a + b > 0$

(B) $ab < 0$ (D) $a + b < 0$

2. Which of the problems below could be solved by finding the solution of this system?

$$\begin{cases} 2x + 2y = 56 \\ y = \frac{1}{3}x \end{cases}$$

(F) The area of a rectangle is 56 square units. The width is one-third the length. Find the length of the rectangle.

(G) The area of a rectangle is 56 square units. The length is one-third the perimeter. Find the length of the rectangle.

(H) The perimeter of a rectangle is 56 units. The length is one-third more than the width. Find the length of the rectangle.

(J) The perimeter of a rectangle is 56 units. The width is one-third the length. Find the length of the rectangle.

3. What is the slope of a line perpendicular to a line that passes through $(3, 8)$ and $(1, -4)$?

(A) $-\frac{1}{6}$ (C) 2

(B) $-\frac{1}{2}$ (D) 6

4. Which inequality is graphed below?

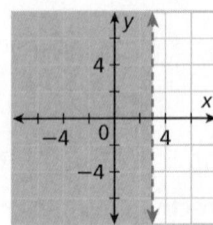

(F) $-x > -3$ (H) $2x < -6$

(G) $-y > -3$ (J) $3y < 9$

5. A chemist has a bottle of a 10% acid solution and a bottle of a 30% acid solution. He mixes the solutions together to get 500 mL of a 25% acid solution. How much of the 30% solution did he use?

(A) 125 mL   (C) 375 mL

(B) 150 mL   (D) 450 mL

6. Which ordered pair is NOT a solution of the system graphed below?

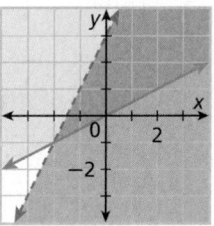

(F) $(0, 0)$ (H) $(1, 1)$

(G) $(0, 3)$ (J) $(2, 1)$

7. Which of the following best classifies a system of linear equations whose graph is two intersecting lines?

(A) inconsistent and dependent

(B) inconsistent and independent

(C) consistent and dependent

(D) consistent and independent

8. Which ordered pair is a solution of this system?

$$\begin{cases} 2x - y = -2 \\ \frac{1}{3}y = x \end{cases}$$

(F) $(0, 2)$ (H) $(2, 6)$

(G) $(1, 3)$ (J) $(3, 8)$

9. Where does the graph of $5x - 10y = 30$ cross the y-axis?

(A) $(0, -3)$ (C) $(6, 0)$

(B) $\left(0, \frac{1}{2}\right)$ (D) $(0, -6)$

 **HOT TIP!** Most standardized tests allow you to write in your test booklet. Cross out each answer choice you eliminate. This may keep you from accidentally marking an answer other than the one you think is right. However, don't draw in your math book!

10. Hillary needs markers and poster board for a project. The markers are $0.79 each and the poster board is $1.89 per sheet. She needs at least 4 sheets of poster board. Hillary has $15 to spend on project materials. Which system models this information?

(F) $\begin{cases} p \geq 4 \\ 0.79m + 1.89p \leq 15 \end{cases}$

(G) $\begin{cases} 0.79m \geq 1.89p \\ 4p \leq 15 \end{cases}$

(H) $\begin{cases} 4p \geq 1.89 \\ m + 4p \leq 15 \end{cases}$

(J) $\begin{cases} p + m \leq 15 \\ 0.79m + 1.89p \geq 4 \end{cases}$

11. Find the slope of the line described by $4x - 2y = -8$.

(A) -2 (C) 2

(B) $-\frac{1}{2}$ (D) 4

Gridded Response

12. The floor in the entranceway of Kendra's house is square and measures 6.5 feet on each side. Colored tiles have been set in the center of the floor in a square measuring 4 feet on each side. The remaining floor consists of white tiles.

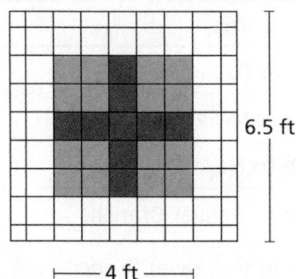

6.5 ft

4 ft

How many square feet of the entranceway floor consists of white tiles?

13. What value of y will make the line passing through $(4, -4)$ and $(-8, y)$ have a slope of $-\frac{1}{2}$?

14. What value of k will make the system $y - 5x = -1$ and $y = kx + 3$ inconsistent?

Short Response

15. The data in the table represents a linear relationship between x and y. Find the missing y-value. Explain your answer.

x	y
-3	-15
-1	-7
0	-3
2	
5	17

16. Graph $y > \frac{-x}{3} - 1$ on a coordinate plane. Name one point that is a solution of the inequality.

17. Marc and his brother Ty start saving money at the same time. Marc has $145 and will add $10 to his savings every week. Ty has $20 and will add $15 to his savings every week. After how many weeks will Marc and Ty have the same amount saved? What is that amount? Show your work.

18. A movie producer is looking for extras to act as office employees in his next movie. The producer needs extras that are at least 40 years old but less than 70 years old. They should be at least 60 inches tall but less than 75 inches tall. Graph all the possible combinations of ages and heights for extras that match the producer's needs. Let x represent age and y represent height. Show your work.

19. Graph the system $\begin{cases} y < -2x + 3 \\ y \geq 6x + 6. \end{cases}$

a. Is $(0, 0)$ a solution of the system you graphed? Explain why or why not.

b. Is $(-4, 5)$ a solution of the system you graphed? Explain why or why not.

Extended Response

20. Every year, Erin knits scarves and sells them at the craft fair. This year she used $6 worth of yarn for each scarf. She also paid $50 to rent a table at the fair. She sold every scarf for $10.

a. Write a system of linear equations to represent the amount Erin spent and the amount she collected. Tell what your variables represent. Tell what each equation in the system represents.

b. Use any method to solve the system you wrote in part a. Show your work. How many scarves did Erin need to sell to make a profit? Explain.

c. Describe two ways you could check your solution to part b. Check your solution by using one of those ways. Show your work.

Real-World CONNECTIONS

New Jersey

Pine Barrens

⭐ Kayaking and Canoeing in the Pine Barrens

The Pine Barrens, or Pinelands, of New Jersey cover over 1 million acres in southern and central New Jersey. Kayaking on the Wading and Oswego Rivers is a popular summertime activity. There are several campgrounds and canoe and kayak rentals located along the rivers.

Choose one or more strategies to solve each problem.

1. A group of kayakers starts at Evans Bridge and kayaks to Beaver Branch. Two other groups of kayakers start at Oswego Lake. One of these groups heads toward Harrisville, and the other heads toward Bodine Field. A fourth group starts at Speedwell and kayaks to Chips Folly. Draw a mapping diagram to represent the starting and ending points of the trips. Tell whether the relation is a function. Explain.

For 2 and 3, use the table.

2. If the average speed of canoes on the river is $1\frac{1}{2}$ miles per hour, about how far is it from Oswego Lake to Beaver Branch?

3. All river trips must be completed by 4:30 P.M. What is the latest time a canoetrip can start in order to make it from Speedwell to Evans Bridge?

| Approximate Canoe Trip Times on the Wading and Oswego Rivers ||
Trip	Time (h)
Evans Bridge to Beaver Branch	2
Hawkins Bridge to Evans Bridge	3
Oswego Lake to Harrisville	4
Oswego Lake to Beaver Branch	$4\frac{1}{2}$
Hawkins Bridge to Beaver Branch	5
Speedwell to Evans Bridge	6
Speedwell to Beaver Branch	8

American Black Bear

American black bears are the most common bears in the United States. They can be found in 11 of the 21 counties in New Jersey. Most wild male black bears weigh between 125 and 600 pounds, while females generally weigh between 90 and 300 pounds. Their weight depends upon their age, the season of the year, and how much food is available.

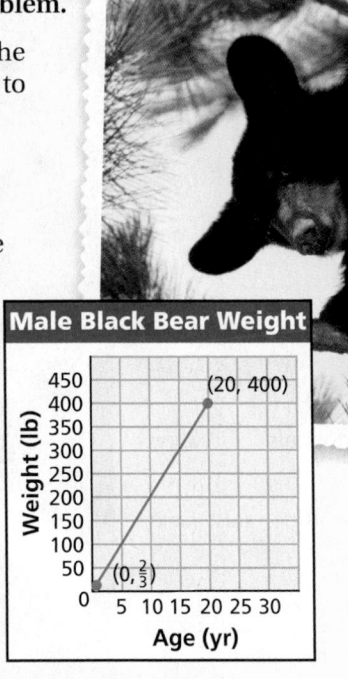

Choose one or more strategies to solve each problem.

1. Black bears hibernate for about 5 months in the winter. They must store 50 to 60 pounds of fat to survive hibernation. During the month before hibernation, a black bear may consume up to 20,000 Calories per day. If a bear consumes an average of 18,500 Calories per day in the month of August, about how many total Calories will he consume that month?

For 2, use the graph.

2. A male bear weighed $\frac{2}{3}$ pound at birth. When he died at 20 years of age, he weighed 400 pounds. Use the graph to estimate how much the bear weighed when he was 7 years old.

Male Black Bear Weight

Weight (lb): 450, 400, 350, 300, 250, 200, 150, 100, 50, 0
(20, 400)
$(0, \frac{2}{3})$
Age (yr): 0 5 10 15 20 25 30

3. A white-tailed deer is running from a black bear at 20 miles per hour. It is $\frac{1}{3}$ mile in front of the bear. The bear is running at 30 miles per hour. How long will it take the bear to catch the deer? Assume both continue running at that same pace.

4. During the hibernation months, the bear's heart rate slows to about 10 beats per minute. If the bear hibernates for 155 days, how many times will his heart beat?

CHAPTER

6

Exponents and Polynomials

COMMON CORE

6A Exponents

6-1	Integer Exponents	N.RN.1
6-2	Rational Exponents	N.RN.1

6B Polynomials

6-3	Polynomials	A.SSE.1a
Lab	Model Polynomial Addition and Subtraction	A.APR.1
6-4	Adding and Subtracting Polynomials	A.APR.1
Lab	Model Polynomial Multiplication	A.APR.1
6-5	Multiplying Polynomials	A.APR.1
Ext	Closure	A.APR.1
6-6	Special Products of Binomials	A.APR.1

Chapter Focus

- Use exponents to describe numbers.
- Perform operations with polynomials.

Every Second *Counts*

How many seconds until you graduate? The concepts in this chapter will help you find and use large numbers such as this one.

Learn It Online
Chapter Project Online

© Charles Gupton Photography

ARE YOU READY?

☑ Vocabulary

Match each term on the left with a definition on the right.

1. Associative Property

2. coefficient

3. Commutative Property

4. exponent

5. like terms

A. a number that is raised to a power

B. a number that is multiplied by a variable

C. a property of addition and multiplication that states you can add or multiply numbers in any order

D. the number of times a base is used as a factor

E. terms that contain the same variables raised to the same powers

F. a property of addition and multiplication that states you can group the numbers in any order

☑ Exponents

Write each expression using a base and an exponent.

6. $4 \cdot 4 \cdot 4 \cdot 4 \cdot 4 \cdot 4 \cdot 4$

7. $5 \cdot 5$

8. $(-10)(-10)(-10)(-10)$

9. $x \cdot x \cdot x$

10. $k \cdot k \cdot k \cdot k \cdot k$

11. 9

☑ Evaluate Powers

Evaluate each expression.

12. 3^4

13. -12^2

14. 5^3

15. 2^5

16. 4^3

17. $(-1)^6$

☑ Multiply Decimals

Multiply.

18. 0.006×10

19. 25.25×100

20. 2.4×6.5

☑ Combine Like Terms

Simplify each expression.

21. $6 + 3p + 14 + 9p$

22. $8y - 4x + 2y + 7x - x$

23. $(12 + 3w - 5) + 6w - 3 - 5w$

24. $6n - 14 + 5n$

☑ Squares and Square Roots

Tell whether each number is a perfect square. If so, identify its positive square root.

25. 42

26. 81

27. 36

28. 50

29. 100

30. 4

31. 1

32. 12

Study Guide: Preview

Where You've Been

Previously, you

- wrote and evaluated exponential expressions.
- simplified algebraic expressions by combining like terms.

In This Chapter

You will study

- how to evaluate and simplify expressions containing exponents.
- how to add, subtract, and multiply polynomials by using properties of exponents and combining like terms.

Where You're Going

You can use the skills in this chapter

- to model area, perimeter, and volume in geometry.
- to express very small or very large quantities in science classes such as Chemistry, Physics, and Biology.
- in the real world to model business profits and population growth or decline.

Key Vocabulary/Vocabulario

binomial	binomio
closure	cerradura
degree of a monomial	grado de un monomio
degree of a polynomial	grado de un polinomio
element	elemento
leading coefficient	coeficiente principal
monomial	monomio
perfect-square trinomial	trinomio cuadrado perfecto
polynomial	polinomio
set	conjunto
standard form of a polynomial	forma estándar de un polinomio
subset	subconjunto
trinomial	trinomio

Vocabulary Connections

To become familiar with some of the vocabulary terms in the chapter, consider the following. You may refer to the chapter, the glossary, or a dictionary if you like.

1. A **polynomial** written in standard form may have more than one algebraic term. What do you think the **leading coefficient** of a polynomial is?

2. A simple definition of **monomial** is "an expression with exactly one term." If the prefix *mono-* means "one" and the prefix *bi-* means "two," define the word **binomial** .

3. What words do you know that begin with the prefix *tri-*? What do they all have in common? Define the word **trinomial** based on the prefix *tri-* and the information given in Problem 2.

Reading *and* Writing Math

Reading Strategy: Read and Understand the Problem

Follow this strategy when solving word problems.

• Read the problem through once.

• Identify exactly what the problem asks you to do.

• Read the problem again, slowly and carefully, to break it into parts.

• Highlight or underline the key information.

• Make a plan to solve the problem.

---

29. Multi-Step Linda works at a pharmacy for $15 an hour. She also baby-sits for $10 an hour. Linda needs to earn at least $90 per week, but she does not want to work more than 20 hours per week. Show and describe the number of hours Linda could work at each job to meet her goals. List two possible solutions.

Step 1	Identify exactly what the problem asks you to do.	• Show and describe the number of hours Linda can work at each job and earn at least $90 per week, without working more than 20 hours per week. • List two possible solutions of the system.
Step 2	Break the problem into parts. Highlight or underline the key information.	• Linda has two jobs. She makes **$15 per hour** at one job and **$10 per hour** at the other job. • She wants to earn **at least $90 per week.** • She does **not** want to work **more than 20 hours per week.**
Step 3	Make a plan to solve the problem.	• Write a system of inequalities. • Solve the system. • Identify two possible solutions of the system.

For the problem below,

    a. identify exactly what the problem asks you to do.

    b. break the problem into parts. Highlight or underline the key information.

    c. make a plan to solve the problem.

1. The difference between the length and the width of a rectangle is 14 units. The area is 120 square units. Write and solve a system of equations to determine the length and the width of the rectangle. (*Hint:* The formula for the area of a rectangle is $A = \ell w$.)

Integer Exponents

CC.9-12.N.RN.1 Explain how the definition of the meaning of rational exponents follows from extending the properties of integer exponents to those values, allowing for a notation for radicals in terms of rational exponents.

Objectives
Evaluate expressions containing zero and integer exponents.

Simplify expressions containing zero and integer exponents.

Who uses this?

Manufacturers can use negative exponents to express very small measurements.

In 1930, the Model A Ford was one of the first cars to boast precise craftsmanship in mass production. The car's pistons had a diameter of $3\frac{7}{8}$ inches; this measurement could vary by at most 10^{-3} inch.

You have seen positive exponents. Recall that to simplify 3^2, use 3 as a factor 2 times: $3^2 = 3 \cdot 3 = 9$.

Remember!

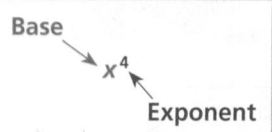

Base
x^4
Exponent

But what does it mean for an exponent to be negative or 0? You can use a table and look for a pattern to figure it out.

Power	5^5	5^4	5^3	5^2	5^1	5^0	5^{-1}	5^{-2}
Value	3125	625	125	25	5	▇	▇	▇

$\div 5 \quad \div 5 \quad \div 5 \quad \div 5$

When the exponent decreases by one, the value of the power is divided by 5. Continue the pattern of dividing by 5:

$$5^0 = \frac{5}{5} = 1 \qquad 5^{-1} = \frac{1}{5} = \frac{1}{5^1} \qquad 5^{-2} = \frac{1}{5} \div 5 = \frac{1}{25} = \frac{1}{5^2}$$

Know it!
Note

Integer Exponents

	WORDS	NUMBERS	ALGEBRA
	Zero exponent—Any nonzero number raised to the zero power is 1.	$3^0 = 1 \quad 123^0 = 1$ $(-16)^0 = 1 \quad \left(\frac{3}{7}\right)^0 = 1$	If $x \neq 0$, then $x^0 = 1$.
	Negative exponent—A nonzero number raised to a negative exponent is equal to 1 divided by that number raised to the opposite (positive) exponent.	$3^{-2} = \frac{1}{3^2} = \frac{1}{9}$ $2^{-4} = \frac{1}{2^4} = \frac{1}{16}$	If $x \neq 0$ and n is an integer, then $x^{-n} = \frac{1}{x^n}$.

Reading Math

2^{-4} is read "2 to the negative fourth power."

Notice the phrase "nonzero number" in the table above. This is because 0^0 and 0 raised to a negative power are both undefined. For example, if you use the pattern given above the table with a base of 0 instead of 5, you would get $0^0 = \frac{0}{0}$. Also, 0^{-6} would be $\frac{1}{0^6} = \frac{1}{0}$. Since division by 0 is undefined, neither value exists.

EXAMPLE  **Manufacturing Application**

The diameter for the Model A Ford piston could vary by at most 10^{-3} inch. Simplify this expression.

$$10^{-3} = \frac{1}{10^3} = \frac{1}{10 \cdot 10 \cdot 10} = \frac{1}{1000}$$

10^{-3} inch is equal to $\frac{1}{1000}$ inch, or 0.001 inch.

CHECK IT OUT!

1. A sand fly may have a wingspan up to 5^{-3} m. Simplify this expression.

EXAMPLE 2 **Zero and Negative Exponents**

Simplify.

A 2^{-3}

$$2^{-3} = \frac{1}{2^3} = \frac{1}{2 \cdot 2 \cdot 2} = \frac{1}{8}$$

B 5^0

$5^0 = 1$ *Any nonzero number raised to the zero power is 1.*

Caution!

In $(-3)^{-4}$, the base is negative because the negative sign is inside the parentheses.

In -3^{-4} the base (3) is positive.

C $(-3)^{-4}$

$$(-3)^{-4} = \frac{1}{(-3)^4} = \frac{1}{(-3)(-3)(-3)(-3)} = \frac{1}{81}$$

D -3^{-4}

$$-3^{-4} = -\frac{1}{3^4} = -\frac{1}{3 \cdot 3 \cdot 3 \cdot 3} = -\frac{1}{81}$$

CHECK IT OUT! Simplify.

2a. 10^{-4}　　　**2b.** $(-2)^{-4}$　　　**2c.** $(-2)^{-5}$　　　**2d.** -2^{-5}

EXAMPLE 3 **Evaluating Expressions with Zero and Negative Exponents**

Evaluate each expression for the given value(s) of the variable(s).

A x^{-1} for $x = 2$

2^{-1}　　　　　　　　　　*Substitute 2 for x.*

$2^{-1} = \frac{1}{2^1} = \frac{1}{2}$　　　*Use the definition $x^{-n} = \frac{1}{x^n}$.*

B $a^0 b^{-3}$ for $a = 8$ and $b = -2$

$8^0 \cdot (-2)^{-3}$　　　　　　*Substitute 8 for a and −2 for b.*

$1 \cdot \dfrac{1}{(-2)^3}$　　　　　　*Simplify expressions with exponents.*

$1 \cdot \dfrac{1}{(-2)(-2)(-2)}$　　*Write the power in the denominator as a product.*

$1 \cdot \dfrac{1}{-8}$　　　　　　　*Simplify the power in the denominator.*

$-\dfrac{1}{8}$　　　　　　　　　*Simplify.*

CHECK IT OUT! Evaluate each expression for the given value(s) of the variable(s).

3a. p^{-3} for $p = 4$　　　　　　**3b.** $8a^{-2}b^0$ for $a = -2$ and $b = 6$

What if you have an expression with a negative exponent in a denominator, such as $\frac{1}{x^{-8}}$?

$$x^{-n} = \frac{1}{x^n}, \text{ or } \frac{1}{x^n} = x^{-n} \qquad \textit{Definition of negative exponent}$$

$$\frac{1}{x^{-8}} = x^{-(-8)} \qquad \textit{Substitute } -8 \textit{ for } n.$$

$$= x^8 \qquad \textit{Simplify the exponent on the right side.}$$

So if a base with a negative exponent is in a denominator, it is equivalent to the same base with the opposite (positive) exponent in the numerator.

An expression that contains negative or zero exponents is not considered to be simplified. Expressions should be rewritten with only positive exponents.

EXAMPLE 4 **Simplifying Expressions with Zero and Negative Exponents**

Simplify.

A $3y^{-2}$

$3y^{-2} = 3 \cdot y^{-2}$

$\qquad = 3 \cdot \dfrac{1}{y^2}$

$\qquad = \dfrac{3}{y^2}$

B $\dfrac{-4}{k^{-4}}$

$\dfrac{-4}{k^{-4}} = -4 \cdot \dfrac{1}{k^{-4}}$

$\qquad = -4 \cdot k^4$

$\qquad = -4k^4$

C $\dfrac{x^{-3}}{a^0 y^5}$

$\dfrac{x^{-3}}{a^0 y^5} = \dfrac{1}{x^3 \cdot 1 \cdot y^5} \qquad a^0 = 1 \text{ and } x^{-3} = \dfrac{1}{x^3}.$

$\qquad = \dfrac{1}{x^3 y^5}$

CHECK IT OUT! Simplify.

4a. $2r^0 m^{-3}$ **4b.** $\dfrac{r^{-3}}{7}$ **4c.** $\dfrac{g^4}{h^{-6}}$

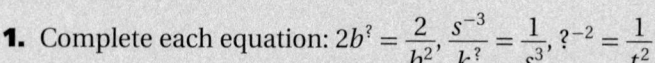

MATHEMATICAL PRACTICES

THINK AND DISCUSS

1. Complete each equation: $2b^? = \dfrac{2}{b^2}, \dfrac{s^{-3}}{k^?} = \dfrac{1}{s^3}, ?^{-2} = \dfrac{1}{t^2}$

2. GET ORGANIZED Copy and complete the graphic organizer. In each box, describe how to simplify, and give an example.

> **Simplifying Expressions with Negative Exponents**
>
> | For a negative exponent in the numerator . . . | For a negative exponent in the denominator . . . |

GUIDED PRACTICE

SEE EXAMPLE 1

1. **Medicine** A typical virus is about 10^{-7} m in size. Simplify this expression.

SEE EXAMPLE 2

Simplify.

2. 6^{-2} 3. 3^0 4. -5^{-2} 5. 3^{-3} 6. 1^{-8}

7. -8^{-3} 8. 10^{-2} 9. $(4.2)^0$ 10. $(-3)^{-3}$ 11. 4^{-2}

SEE EXAMPLE 3

Evaluate each expression for the given value(s) of the variable(s).

12. b^{-2} for $b = -3$ 13. $(2t)^{-4}$ for $t = 2$

14. $(m-4)^{-5}$ for $m = 6$ 15. $2x^0 y^{-3}$ for $x = 7$ and $y = -4$

SEE EXAMPLE 4

Simplify.

16. $4m^0$ 17. $3k^{-4}$ 18. $\dfrac{7}{r^{-7}}$ 19. $\dfrac{x^{10}}{d^{-3}}$

20. $2x^0 y^{-4}$ 21. $\dfrac{f^{-4}}{g^{-6}}$ 22. $\dfrac{c^4}{d^{-3}}$ 23. $p^7 q^{-1}$

PRACTICE AND PROBLEM SOLVING

Independent Practice	
For Exercises	See Example
24	1
25–36	2
37–42	3
43–57	4

Extra Practice

See Extra Practice for more Skills Practice and Applications Practice exercises.

24. **Biology** One of the smallest bats is the northern blossom bat, which is found from Southeast Asia to Australia. This bat weighs about 2^{-1} ounce. Simplify this expression.

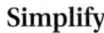

Simplify.

25. 8^0 26. 5^{-4} 27. 3^{-4} 28. -9^{-2}

29. -6^{-2} 30. 7^{-2} 31. $\left(\dfrac{2}{5}\right)^0$ 32. 13^{-2}

33. $(-3)^{-1}$ 34. $(-4)^2$ 35. $\left(\dfrac{1}{2}\right)^{-2}$ 36. -7^{-1}

Evaluate each expression for the given value(s) of the variable(s).

37. x^{-4} for $x = 4$ 38. $\left(\dfrac{2}{3}v\right)^{-3}$ for $v = 9$

39. $(10 - d)^0$ for $d = 11$ 40. $10m^{-1}n^{-5}$ for $m = 10$ and $n = -2$

41. $(3ab)^{-2}$ for $a = \dfrac{1}{2}$ and $b = 8$ 42. $4w^v x^v$ for $w = 3$, $v = 0$, and $x = -5$

Simplify.

43. k^{-4} 44. $2z^{-8}$ 45. $\dfrac{1}{2b^{-3}}$ 46. $c^{-2}d$ 47. $-5x^{-3}$

48. $4x^{-6}y^{-2}$ 49. $\dfrac{2f^0}{7g^{-10}}$ 50. $\dfrac{r^{-5}}{s^{-1}}$ 51. $\dfrac{s^5}{t^{-12}}$ 52. $\dfrac{3w^{-5}}{x^{-6}}$

53. $b^0 c^0$ 54. $\dfrac{2}{3}m^{-1}n^5$ 55. $\dfrac{q^{-2}r^0}{s^0}$ 56. $\dfrac{a^{-7}b^2}{c^3 d^{-4}}$ 57. $\dfrac{h^3 k^{-1}}{6m^2}$

Evaluate each expression for $x = 3$, $y = -1$, and $z = 2$.

58. z^{-5} **59.** $(x + y)^{-4}$ **60.** $(yz)^0$ **61.** $(xyz)^{-1}$

62. $(xy - 3)^{-2}$ **63.** x^{-y} **64.** $(yz)^{-x}$ **65.** xy^{-4}

66. **///ERROR ANALYSIS///** Look at the two equations below. Which is incorrect? Explain the error.

Ⓐ
$$5x^{-3} = \frac{1}{5x^3}$$

Ⓑ
$$5x^{-3} = \frac{5}{x^3}$$

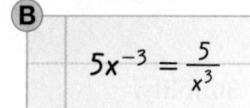

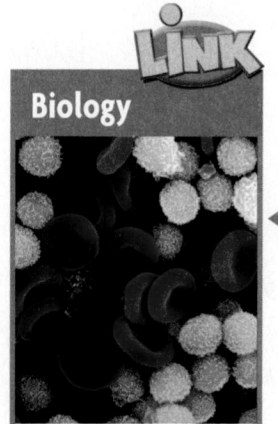

Simplify.

67. $a^3 b^{-2}$ **68.** $c^{-4} d^3$ **69.** $v^0 w^2 y^{-1}$ **70.** $(a^2 b^{-7})^0$ **71.** $-5y^{-6}$

72. $\dfrac{2a^{-5}}{b^{-6}}$ **73.** $\dfrac{2a^3}{b^{-1}}$ **74.** $\dfrac{m^2}{n^{-3}}$ **75.** $\dfrac{x^{-8}}{3y^{12}}$ **76.** $-\dfrac{20p^{-1}}{5q^{-3}}$

 77. **Biology** Human blood contains red blood cells, white blood cells, and platelets. The table shows the sizes of these components. Simplify each expression.

Blood Components	
Part	**Size (m)**
Red blood cell	$125{,}000^{-1}$
White blood cell	$3(500)^{-2}$
Platelet	$3(1000)^{-2}$

Tell whether each statement is sometimes, always, or never true.

78. If n is a positive integer, then $x^{-n} = \frac{1}{x^n}$.

79. If x is positive, then x^{-n} is negative.

80. If n is zero, then x^{-n} is 1.

81. If n is a negative integer, then $x^{-n} = 1$.

82. If x is zero, then x^{-n} is 1.

83. If n is an integer, then $x^{-n} > 1$.

84. **Critical Thinking** Find the value of $2^3 \cdot 2^{-3}$. Then find the value of $3^2 \cdot 3^{-2}$. Make a conjecture about the value of $a^n \cdot a^{-n}$.

 **85.** **Write About It** Explain in your own words why 2^{-3} is the same as $\frac{1}{2^3}$.

Find the missing value.

86. $\dfrac{1}{4} = 2^{\blacksquare}$ **87.** $9^{-2} = \dfrac{1}{\blacksquare}$ **88.** $\dfrac{1}{64} = \blacksquare^{-2}$ **89.** $\dfrac{\blacksquare}{3} = 3^{-1}$

90. $7^{-2} = \dfrac{1}{\blacksquare}$ **91.** $10^{\blacksquare} = \dfrac{1}{1000}$ **92.** $3 \cdot 4^{-2} = \dfrac{3}{\blacksquare}$ **93.** $2 \cdot \dfrac{1}{5} = 2 \cdot 5^{\blacksquare}$

 MULTI-STEP TEST PREP

94. a. The product of the frequency f and the wavelength w of light in air is a constant v. Write an equation for this relationship.

 b. Solve this equation for wavelength. Then write this equation as an equation with f raised to a negative exponent.

 c. The units for frequency are hertz (Hz). One hertz is one cycle per second, which is often written as $\frac{1}{s}$. Rewrite this expression using a negative exponent.

95. Which is NOT equivalent to the other three?

(A) $\dfrac{1}{25}$ (B) 5^{-2} (C) 0.04   (D) -25

96. Which is equal to 6^{-2}?

(F) $6(-2)$ (G) $(-6)(-6)$ (H) $-\dfrac{1}{6 \cdot 6}$ (J) $\dfrac{1}{6 \cdot 6}$

97. Simplify $\dfrac{a^3 b^{-2}}{c^{-1}}$.

(A) $\dfrac{a^3 c}{b^2}$ (B) $\dfrac{a^3 b^2}{-c}$ (C) $\dfrac{a^3}{-b^2 c}$ (D) $\dfrac{c}{a^3 b^2}$

98. Gridded Response Simplify $\left[2^{-2} + (6 + 2)^0\right]$.

99. Short Response If a and b are real numbers and n is a positive integer, write a simplified expression for the product $a^{-n} \cdot b^0$ that contains only positive exponents. Explain your answer.

CHALLENGE AND EXTEND

100. Multi-Step Copy and complete the table of values below. Then graph the ordered pairs and describe the shape of the graph.

x	-4	-3	-2	-1	0	1	2	3	4
$y = 2^x$									

101. Multi-Step Copy and complete the table. Then write a rule for the values of 1^n and $(-1)^n$ when n is any negative integer.

n	-1	-2	-3	-4	-5
1^n					
$(-1)^n$					

6-2 Rational Exponents

CC.9-12.N.RN.1 Explain how the definition of the meaning of rational exponents follows from extending the properties of integer exponents to those values, allowing for a notation for radicals in terms of rational exponents. *Also* **CC.9-12.N.RN.2**

Objective
Evaluate and simplify expressions containing rational exponents.

Why learn this?
You can use rational exponents to find the number of Calories animals need to consume each day to maintain health. (See Example 3.)

Vocabulary
index

Recall that the radical symbol $\sqrt{}$ is used to indicate roots. The **index** is the small number to the left of the radical symbol that tells which root to take. For example, $\sqrt[3]{}$ represents a cube root. Since $2^3 = 2 \cdot 2 \cdot 2 = 8$, $\sqrt[3]{8} = 2$.

Another way to write nth roots is by using exponents that are fractions. For example, for $b > 1$, suppose $\sqrt{b} = b^k$.

$$\sqrt{b} = b^k$$
$$\left(\sqrt{b}\right)^2 = \left(b^k\right)^2 \quad \textit{Square both sides.}$$
$$b^1 = b^{2k} \quad \textit{Power of a Power Property}$$
$$1 = 2k \quad \textit{If } b^m = b^n, \textit{ then } m = n.$$
$$\frac{1}{2} = k \quad \textit{Divide both sides by 2.}$$

Helpful Hint

When $b = 0$, $\sqrt[n]{b} = 0$.
When $b = 1$, $\sqrt[n]{b} = 1$.

So for all $b > 1$, $\sqrt{b} = b^{\frac{1}{2}}$.

Definition of $b^{\frac{1}{n}}$

WORDS	NUMBERS	ALGEBRA
A number raised to the power of $\frac{1}{n}$ is equal to the nth root of that number.	$3^{\frac{1}{2}} = \sqrt{3}$ $5^{\frac{1}{4}} = \sqrt[4]{5}$ $2^{\frac{1}{7}} = \sqrt[7]{2}$	If $b > 1$ and n is an integer, where $n \geq 2$, then $b^{\frac{1}{n}} = \sqrt[n]{b}$. $b^{\frac{1}{2}} = \sqrt{b}$, $b^{\frac{1}{3}} = \sqrt[3]{b}$, $b^{\frac{1}{4}} = \sqrt[4]{b}$, and so on.

EXAMPLE 1 Simplifying $b^{\frac{1}{n}}$

Simplify each expression.

A $125^{\frac{1}{3}}$

$$125^{\frac{1}{3}} = \sqrt[3]{125} = \sqrt[3]{5^3} \qquad \textit{Use the definition of } b^{\frac{1}{n}}.$$
$$= 5$$

Remember!

$\sqrt{}$ is equivalent to $\sqrt[2]{}$.

B $64^{\frac{1}{6}} + 25^{\frac{1}{2}}$

$$64^{\frac{1}{6}} + 25^{\frac{1}{2}} = \sqrt[6]{64} + \sqrt{25} \qquad \textit{Use the definition of } b^{\frac{1}{n}}.$$
$$= \sqrt[6]{2^6} + \sqrt{5^2}$$
$$= 2 + 5 = 7$$

 **Simplify each expression.**

1a. $81^{\frac{1}{4}}$

1b. $121^{\frac{1}{2}} + 256^{\frac{1}{4}}$

A fractional exponent can have a numerator other than 1, as in the expression $b^{\frac{2}{3}}$. You can write the exponent as a product in two different ways.

$$b^{\frac{2}{3}} = b^{\frac{1}{3} \cdot 2}$$
$$= \left(b^{\frac{1}{3}}\right)^2 \qquad \text{Power of a Power Property}$$
$$= \left(\sqrt[3]{b}\right)^2 \qquad \text{Definition of } b^{\frac{1}{n}}$$

$$b^{\frac{2}{3}} = b^{2 \cdot \frac{1}{3}}$$
$$= \left(b^2\right)^{\frac{1}{3}}$$
$$= \sqrt[3]{b^2}$$

 **Definition of $b^{\frac{m}{n}}$**

WORDS	NUMBERS	ALGEBRA
A number raised to the power of $\frac{m}{n}$ is equal to the nth root of the number raised to the mth power.	$8^{\frac{2}{3}} = \left(\sqrt[3]{8}\right)^2 = 2^2 = 4$ $8^{\frac{2}{3}} = \sqrt[3]{8^2} = \sqrt[3]{64} = 4$	If $b > 1$ and m and n are integers, where $m \geq 1$ and $n \geq 2$, then $b^{\frac{m}{n}} = \left(\sqrt[n]{b}\right)^m = \sqrt[n]{b^m}$.

EXAMPLE  **Simplifying Expressions with Fractional Exponents**

Simplify each expression.

A $216^{\frac{2}{3}}$

$$216^{\frac{2}{3}} = \left(\sqrt[3]{216}\right)^2 \qquad \text{Definition of } b^{\frac{m}{n}}$$
$$= \left(\sqrt[3]{6^3}\right)^2$$
$$= (6)^2 = 36$$

B $32^{\frac{4}{5}}$

$$32^{\frac{4}{5}} = \left(\sqrt[5]{32}\right)^4$$
$$= \left(\sqrt[5]{2^5}\right)^4$$
$$= (2)^4 = 16$$

 Simplify each expression.

2a. $16^{\frac{3}{4}}$

2b. $1^{\frac{2}{5}}$

2c. $27^{\frac{4}{3}}$

EXAMPLE  **Biology Application**

The approximate number of Calories C that an animal needs each day is given by $C = 72m^{\frac{3}{4}}$, where m is the animal's mass in kilograms. Find the number of Calories that a 16 kg dog needs each day.

$$C = 72m^{\frac{3}{4}}$$
$$= 72(16)^{\frac{3}{4}} \qquad \text{Substitute 16 for } m.$$
$$= 72 \cdot \left(\sqrt[4]{16}\right)^3 \qquad \text{Definition of } b^{\frac{m}{n}}$$
$$= 72 \cdot \left(\sqrt[4]{2^4}\right)^3$$
$$= 72 \cdot (2)^3$$
$$= 72 \cdot 8 = 576$$

The dog needs 576 Calories per day to maintain health.

 **3.** Find the number of Calories that an 81 kg panda needs each day.

Remember that $\sqrt{\ }$ always indicates a nonnegative square root. When you simplify variable expressions that contain $\sqrt{\ }$, such as $\sqrt{x^2}$, the answer cannot be negative. But x may be negative. Therefore you simplify $\sqrt{x^2}$ as $|x|$ to ensure the answer is nonnegative.

When x is...	and n is...	x^n is...	and $\sqrt[n]{x^n}$ is...
Positive	Even	Positive	Positive
Negative	Even	Positive	Positive
Positive	Odd	Positive	Positive
Negative	Odd	Negative	Negative

When n is even, you must simplify $\sqrt[n]{x^n}$ to $|x|$, because you do not know whether x is positive or negative. When n is odd, simplify $\sqrt[n]{x^n}$ to x.

EXAMPLE **4** **Using Properties of Exponents to Simplify Expressions**

Simplify. All variables represent nonnegative numbers.

A $\sqrt[3]{x^9 y^3}$

$$\sqrt[3]{x^9 y^3} = \left(x^9 y^3\right)^{\frac{1}{3}} \qquad \textit{Definition of } b^{\frac{1}{n}}$$

$$= \left(x^9\right)^{\frac{1}{3}} \cdot \left(y^3\right)^{\frac{1}{3}} \qquad \textit{Power of a Product Property}$$

$$= \left(x^{9 \cdot \frac{1}{3}}\right) \cdot \left(y^{3 \cdot \frac{1}{3}}\right) \qquad \textit{Power of a Power Property}$$

$$= \left(x^3\right) \cdot \left(y^1\right) = x^3 y \qquad \textit{Simplify exponents.}$$

B $\left(x^2 y^{\frac{1}{2}}\right)^4 \sqrt[3]{y^3}$

$$\left(x^2 y^{\frac{1}{2}}\right)^4 \sqrt[3]{y^3} = \left(x^2 y^{\frac{1}{2}}\right)^4 \cdot y \qquad \sqrt[3]{y^3} = y$$

$$= \left(x^{2 \cdot 4}\right) \cdot \left(y^{\frac{1}{2} \cdot 4}\right) \cdot y \qquad \textit{Power of a Product Property}$$

$$= \left(x^8\right) \cdot \left(y^2\right) \cdot y \qquad \textit{Simplify exponents.}$$

$$= x^8 \cdot y^{2+1} = x^8 y^3 \qquad \textit{Product of Powers Property}$$

 Simplify. All variables represent nonnegative numbers.

4a. $\sqrt[4]{x^4 y^{12}}$

4b. $\dfrac{\left(xy^{\frac{1}{2}}\right)^2}{\sqrt[5]{x^5}}$

THINK AND DISCUSS

1. Explain how to find the value of $\left(\sqrt[10]{25}\right)^5$.

2. GET ORGANIZED Copy and complete the graphic organizer. In each cell, provide the definition and a numerical example of each type of exponent.

Exponent	Definition	Numerical Example
$b^{\frac{1}{n}}$		
$b^{\frac{m}{n}}$		

Exercises

GUIDED PRACTICE

1. **Vocabulary** In the expression $\sqrt[5]{3x}$, what is the *index*?

Simplify each expression.

SEE EXAMPLE **1**

2. $8^{\frac{1}{3}}$

3. $16^{\frac{1}{2}}$

4. $0^{\frac{1}{6}}$

5. $27^{\frac{1}{3}}$

6. $81^{\frac{1}{2}}$

7. $216^{\frac{1}{3}}$

8. $1^{\frac{1}{9}}$

9. $625^{\frac{1}{4}}$

10. $36^{\frac{1}{2}} + 1^{\frac{1}{3}}$

11. $8^{\frac{1}{3}} + 64^{\frac{1}{2}}$

12. $81^{\frac{1}{4}} + 8^{\frac{1}{3}}$

13. $25^{\frac{1}{2}} - 1^{\frac{1}{4}}$

SEE EXAMPLE **2**

14. $81^{\frac{3}{4}}$

15. $8^{\frac{5}{3}}$

16. $125^{\frac{2}{3}}$

17. $25^{\frac{3}{2}}$

18. $36^{\frac{3}{2}}$

19. $64^{\frac{4}{3}}$

20. $1^{\frac{3}{4}}$

21. $0^{\frac{2}{3}}$

SEE EXAMPLE **3**

22. **Geometry** Given a square with area a, you can use the formula $P = 4a^{\frac{1}{2}}$ to find the perimeter P of the square. Find the perimeter of a square that has an area of 64 m^2.

SEE EXAMPLE **4**

Simplify. All variables represent nonnegative numbers.

23. $\sqrt{x^4y^2}$

24. $\sqrt[4]{z^4}$

25. $\sqrt{x^6y^6}$

26. $\sqrt[3]{a^{12}b^6}$

27. $\left(a^{\frac{1}{2}}\right)^2 \sqrt{a^2}$

28. $\left(x^{\frac{1}{3}}\right)^6 \sqrt[4]{y^4}$

29. $\dfrac{\left(z^{\frac{1}{3}}\right)^3}{\sqrt{z^2}}$

30. $\dfrac{\sqrt[3]{x^6y^9}}{x^2}$

PRACTICE AND PROBLEM SOLVING

Extra Practice
See Extra Practice for more Skills Practice and Applications Practice exercises.

Simplify each expression.

31. $100^{\frac{1}{2}}$

32. $1^{\frac{1}{5}}$

33. $512^{\frac{1}{3}}$

34. $729^{\frac{1}{2}}$

35. $32^{\frac{1}{5}}$

36. $196^{\frac{1}{2}}$

37. $256^{\frac{1}{8}}$

38. $400^{\frac{1}{2}}$

39. $125^{\frac{1}{3}} + 81^{\frac{1}{2}}$

40. $25^{\frac{1}{2}} - 81^{\frac{1}{4}}$

41. $121^{\frac{1}{2}} - 243^{\frac{1}{5}}$

42. $256^{\frac{1}{4}} + 0^{\frac{1}{3}}$

43. $4^{\frac{3}{2}}$

44. $27^{\frac{2}{3}}$

45. $256^{\frac{3}{4}}$

46. $64^{\frac{5}{6}}$

47. $100^{\frac{3}{2}}$

48. $1^{\frac{5}{3}}$

49. $9^{\frac{5}{2}}$

50. $243^{\frac{2}{5}}$

51. **Biology** Biologists use a formula to estimate the mass of a mammal's brain. For a mammal with a mass of m grams, the approximate mass B of the brain, also in grams, is given by $B = \frac{1}{8}m^{\frac{2}{3}}$. Find the approximate mass of the brain of a mouse that has a mass of 64 grams.

Simplify. All variables represent nonnegative numbers.

52. $\sqrt[3]{a^6c^9}$

53. $\sqrt[3]{8m^3}$

54. $\sqrt[4]{x^{16}y^4}$

55. $\sqrt[3]{27x^6}$

56. $\left(x^{\frac{1}{2}}y^3\right)^2 \sqrt{x^2}$

57. $\left(a^2b^4\right)^{\frac{1}{2}} \sqrt[3]{b^6}$

58. $\dfrac{\sqrt[3]{x^6y^6}}{yx^2}$

59. $\dfrac{\left(a^2b^{\frac{1}{2}}\right)^4}{\sqrt{b^2}}$

Fill in the boxes to make each statement true.

60. $256^{\frac{\blacksquare}{4}} = 4$

61. $\blacksquare^{\frac{1}{5}} = 1$

62. $225^{\frac{1}{\blacksquare}} = 15$

63. $\blacksquare^{\frac{1}{6}} = 0$

64. $64^{\frac{\blacksquare}{3}} = 16$

65. $\blacksquare^{\frac{3}{4}} = 125$

66. $27^{\frac{4}{\blacksquare}} = 81$

67. $36^{\frac{\blacksquare}{2}} = 216$

Simplify each expression.

68. $\left(\dfrac{81}{169}\right)^{\frac{1}{2}}$

69. $\left(\dfrac{8}{27}\right)^{\frac{1}{3}}$

70. $\left(\dfrac{256}{81}\right)^{\frac{1}{4}}$

71. $\left(\dfrac{1}{16}\right)^{\frac{1}{2}}$

72. $\left(\dfrac{9}{16}\right)^{\frac{3}{2}}$

73. $\left(\dfrac{8}{27}\right)^{\frac{2}{3}}$

74. $\left(\dfrac{16}{81}\right)^{\frac{3}{4}}$

75. $\left(\dfrac{4}{49}\right)^{\frac{3}{2}}$

76. $\left(\dfrac{4}{25}\right)^{\frac{3}{2}}$

77. $\left(\dfrac{1}{81}\right)^{\frac{3}{4}}$

78. $\left(\dfrac{27}{64}\right)^{\frac{2}{3}}$

79. $\left(\dfrac{8}{125}\right)^{\frac{4}{3}}$

80. **Multi-Step** Scientists have found that the life span of a mammal living in captivity is related to the mammal's mass. The life span in years L can be approximated by the formula $L = 12m^{\frac{1}{5}}$, where m is the mammal's mass in kilograms. How much longer is the life span of a lion compared with that of a wolf?

Typical Mass of Mammals	
Mammal	**Mass (kg)**
Koala	8
Wolf	32
Lion	243
Giraffe	1024

81. **Geometry** Given a sphere with volume V, the formula $r = 0.62V^{\frac{1}{3}}$ may be used to approximate the sphere's radius r. Find the approximate radius of a sphere that has a volume of 27 in^3.

82. **Critical Thinking** Show that a number raised to the power $\frac{1}{3}$ is the same as the cube root of that number. (*Hint:* Use properties of exponents to find the cube of $b^{\frac{1}{3}}$. Then compare this with the cube of $\sqrt[3]{b}$. Use the fact that if two numbers have the same cube, then they are equal.)

83. **Critical Thinking** Compare $n^{\frac{2}{3}}$ and $n^{\frac{3}{2}}$ for values of n greater than 1. When simplifying each of these expressions, will the result be greater than n or less than n? Explain.

84. **///ERROR ANALYSIS///** Two students simplified $64^{\frac{3}{2}}$. Which solution is incorrect? Explain the error.

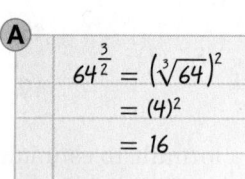

A

$$64^{\frac{3}{2}} = \left(\sqrt[3]{64}\right)^2$$
$$= (4)^2$$
$$= 16$$

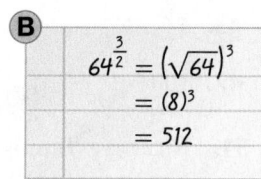

B

$$64^{\frac{3}{2}} = \left(\sqrt{64}\right)^3$$
$$= (8)^3$$
$$= 512$$

MULTI-STEP TEST PREP

85. You can estimate an object's distance in inches from a light source by using the formula $d = \left(0.8\dfrac{L}{B}\right)^{\frac{1}{2}}$, where L is the light's luminosity in lumens and B is the light's brightness in lumens per square inch.

a. Find an object's distance to a light source with a luminosity of 4000 lumens and a brightness of 32 lumens per square inch.

b. Suppose the brightness of this light source decreases to 8 lumens per square inch. How does the object's distance from the source change?

86. **Write About It** You can write $4^{\frac{3}{2}}$ as $4^{3 \cdot \frac{1}{2}}$ or as $4^{\frac{1}{2} \cdot 3}$. Use the Power of a Power Property to show that both expressions are equal. Is one method easier than the other? Explain.

87. What is $9^{\frac{1}{2}} + 8^{\frac{1}{3}}$?

　Ⓐ 4　　　　　Ⓑ 5　　　　　Ⓒ 6　　　　　Ⓓ 10

88. Which expression is equal to 8?

　Ⓕ $4^{\frac{3}{2}}$　　　　Ⓖ $16^{\frac{1}{2}}$　　　　Ⓗ $32^{\frac{4}{5}}$　　　　Ⓙ $64^{\frac{3}{2}}$

89. Which expression is equivalent to $\sqrt[3]{a^9 b^3}$?

　Ⓐ $a^2 b$　　　　Ⓑ a^3　　　　Ⓒ $a^3 b$　　　　Ⓓ $a^3 b^3$

90. Which of the following is NOT equal to $16^{\frac{3}{2}}$?

　Ⓕ $\left(\sqrt{16}\right)^3$　　Ⓖ 4^3　　Ⓗ $\left(\sqrt[3]{16}\right)^2$　　Ⓙ $\sqrt{16^3}$

CHALLENGE AND EXTEND

Use properties of exponents to simplify each expression.

91. $\left(a^{\frac{1}{3}}\right)\left(a^{\frac{1}{3}}\right)\left(a^{\frac{1}{3}}\right)$

92. $\left(x^{\frac{1}{2}}\right)^5 \left(x^{\frac{3}{2}}\right)$

93. $\left(x^{\frac{1}{3}}\right)^4 \left(x^5\right)^{\frac{1}{3}}$

You can use properties of exponents to help you solve equations. For example, to solve $x^3 = 64$, raise both sides to the $\frac{1}{3}$ power to get $\left(x^3\right)^{\frac{1}{3}} = 64^{\frac{1}{3}}$. Simplifying both sides gives $x = 4$. Use this method to solve each equation. Check your answer.

94. $y^5 = 32$

95. $27x^3 = 729$

96. $1 = \frac{1}{8}x^3$

97. **Geometry** The formula for the surface area of a sphere S in terms of its volume V is $S = (4\pi)^{\frac{1}{3}}(3V)^{\frac{2}{3}}$. What is the surface area of a sphere that has a volume of 36π cm^3? Leave the symbol π in your answer. What do you notice?

MULTI-STEP TEST PREP

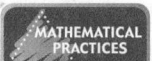

Make sense of problems and persevere in solving them.

Exponents

I See the Light! The speed of light is the product of its frequency f and its wavelength w. In air, the speed of light is 3×10^8 m/s.

1. Write an equation for the relationship described above, and then solve this equation for frequency. Write this equation as an equation with w raised to a negative exponent.

2. Wavelengths of visible light range from 400 to 700 nanometers (10^{-9} meters). Use a graphing calculator and the relationship you found in Problem 1 to graph frequency as a function of wavelength. Sketch the graph with the axes clearly labeled. Describe your graph.

3. The speed of light in water is $\frac{3}{4}$ of its speed in air. Find the speed of light in water.

4. When light enters water, some colors bend more than others. How much the light bends depends on its wavelength. This is what creates a rainbow. The frequency of green light is about 5.9×10^{14} cycles per second. Find the wavelength of green light in water.

5. When light enters water, colors with shorter wavelengths bend more than colors with longer wavelengths. Violet light has a frequency of 7.5×10^{14} cycles per second, and red light has a frequency of 4.6×10^{14} cycles per second. Which of these colors of light will bend more when it enters water? Justify your answer.

READY TO GO ON?

Quiz for Lessons 6-1 Through 6-2

6-1 Integer Exponents

Evaluate each expression for the given value(s) of the variable(s).

1. t^{-6} for $t = 2$

2. n^{-3} for $n = -5$

3. $r^0 s^{-2}$ for $r = 8$ and $s = 10$

Simplify.

4. $5k^{-3}$

5. $\dfrac{x^4}{y^{-6}}$

6. $8f^{-4}\,g^0$

7. $\dfrac{a^{-3}}{b^{-2}}$

8. Measurement Metric units can be written in terms of a base unit. The table shows some of these equivalencies. Simplify each expression.

Selected Metric Prefixes					
Milli-	Centi-	Deci-	Deka-	Hecto-	Kilo-
10^{-3}	10^{-2}	10^{-1}	10^1	10^2	10^3

6-2 Rational Exponents

Simplify each expression. All variables represent nonnegative numbers.

9. $81^{\frac{1}{2}}$

10. $125^{\frac{1}{3}}$

11. $4^{\frac{3}{2}}$

12. $0^{\frac{2}{9}}$

13. $\sqrt{x^8 y^4}$

14. $\sqrt[3]{r^9}$

15. $\sqrt[6]{z^{12}}$

16. $\sqrt[3]{p^3 q^{12}}$

6-3 Polynomials

CC.9-12.A.SSE.1a Interpret parts of an expression, such as terms, factors, and coefficients.

Objectives
Classify polynomials and write polynomials in standard form.

Evaluate polynomial expressions.

Vocabulary
monomial
degree of a monomial
polynomial
degree of a polynomial
standard form of a
   polynomial
leading coefficient
quadratic
cubic
binomial
trinomial

Who uses this?

Pyrotechnicians can use polynomials to plan complex fireworks displays. (See Example 5.)

A **monomial** is a number, a variable, or a product of numbers and variables with whole-number exponents.

Monomials	Not Monomials
$5 \quad x \quad -7xy \quad 0.5x^4$	$-0.3x^{-2} \quad 4x - y \quad \dfrac{2}{x^3}$

The **degree of a monomial** is the sum of the exponents of the variables. A constant has degree 0.

EXAMPLE 1 **Finding the Degree of a Monomial**

Find the degree of each monomial.

A $-2a^2b^4$
The degree is 6.   *Add the exponents of the variables: 2 + 4 = 6*

B 4
$4x^0$ *There is no variable, but you can write 4 as $4x^0$.*
The degree is 0.

C $8y$
$8y^1$ *A variable written without an exponent has exponent 1.*
The degree is 1.

Remember!

The *terms* of an expression are the parts being added or subtracted.

CHECK IT OUT! Find the degree of each monomial.
   1a. $1.5k^2m$ **1b.** $4x$ **1c.** $2c^3$

A **polynomial** is a monomial or a sum or difference of monomials. The **degree of a polynomial** is the degree of the term with the greatest degree.

EXAMPLE 2 **Finding the Degree of a Polynomial**

Find the degree of each polynomial.

A $4x - 18x^5$
$4x$: degree 1 $-18x^5$: degree 5   *Find the degree of each term.*

The degree of the polynomial is the greatest degree, 5.

Find the degree of each polynomial.

B $0.5x^2y + 0.25xy + 0.75$
$0.5x^2y$: degree 3 $0.25xy$: degree 2 0.75: degree 0
The degree of the polynomial is the greatest degree, 3.

C $6x^4 + 9x^2 - x + 3$
$6x^4$: degree 4 $9x^2$: degree 2 $-x$: degree 1 3: degree 0
The degree of the polynomial is the greatest degree, 4.

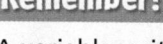
CHECK IT OUT! **Find the degree of each polynomial.**
2a. $5x - 6$ **2b.** $x^3y^2 + x^2y^3 - x^4 + 2$

The terms of a polynomial may be written in any order. However, polynomials that contain only one variable are usually written in *standard form*.

The **standard form of a polynomial** that contains one variable is written with the terms in order from greatest degree to least degree. When written in standard form, the coefficient of the first term is called the **leading coefficient**.

EXAMPLE 3 **Writing Polynomials in Standard Form**

Write each polynomial in standard form. Then give the leading coefficient.

A $20x - 4x^3 + 2 - x^2$

Find the degree of each term. Then arrange them in descending order.

$$\underbrace{20x}\ \underbrace{-4x^3}\ \underbrace{+2}\ \underbrace{-x^2} \rightarrow \underbrace{-4x^3}\ \underbrace{-x^2}\ \underbrace{+20x}\ \underbrace{+2}$$
Degree: 1   3   0   2   3   2   1   0

The standard form is $-4x^3 - x^2 + 20x + 2$. The leading coefficient is -4.

B $y^3 + y^5 + 4y$

Find the degree of each term. Then arrange them in descending order.

$$\underbrace{y^3}\ \underbrace{+y^5}\ \underbrace{+4y} \rightarrow \underbrace{y^5}\ \underbrace{+y^3}\ \underbrace{+4y}$$
Degree: 3   5   1   5   3   1

The standard form is $y^5 + y^3 + 4y$. The leading coefficient is 1.

Remember!

A variable written without a coefficient has a coefficient of 1.

$y^5 = 1y^5$

CHECK IT OUT! **Write each polynomial in standard form. Then give the leading coefficient.**
3a. $16 - 4x^2 + x^5 + 9x^3$ **3b.** $18y^5 - 3y^8 + 14y$

Some polynomials have special names based on their degree and the number of terms they have.

Degree	Name
0	Constant
1	Linear
2	**Quadratic**
3	**Cubic**
4	Quartic
5	Quintic
6 or more	6th degree, 7th degree, and so on

Terms	Name
1	Monomial
2	**Binomial**
3	**Trinomial**
4 or more	Polynomial

EXAMPLE 4 **Classifying Polynomials**

Classify each polynomial according to its degree and number of terms.

A $5x - 6$

Degree: 1   Terms: 2 $5x - 6$ is a linear binomial.

B $y^2 + y + 4$

Degree: 2   Terms: 3 $y^2 + y + 4$ is a quadratic trinomial.

C $6x^7 + 9x^2 - x + 3$

Degree: 7   Terms: 4 $6x^7 + 9x^2 - x + 3$ is a 7th-degree polynomial.

 Classify each polynomial according to its degree and number of terms.

4a. $x^3 + x^2 - x + 2$ **4b.** 6 **4c.** $-3y^8 + 18y^5 + 14y$

EXAMPLE 5 *Physics Application*

A firework is launched from a platform 6 feet above the ground at a speed of 200 feet per second. The firework has a 5-second fuse. The height of the firework in feet is given by the polynomial $-16t^2 + 200t + 6$, where t is the time in seconds. How high will the firework be when it explodes?

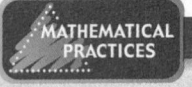

Substitute the time for t to find the firework's height.

$$-16t^2 + 200t + 6$$
$$-16(5)^2 + 200(5) + 6 \quad \text{\textit{The time is}}$$
$$-16(25) + 200(5) + 6 \quad \text{\textit{5 seconds.}}$$
$$-400 + 1000 + 6 \quad \text{\textit{Evaluate the polynomial by using the}}$$
$$606 \quad \quad \text{\textit{order of operations.}}$$

When the firework explodes, it will be 606 feet above the ground.

 **5. What if...?** Another firework with a 5-second fuse is launched from the same platform at a speed of 400 feet per second. Its height is given by $-16t^2 + 400t + 6$. How high will this firework be when it explodes?

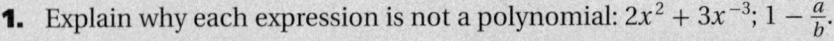

THINK AND DISCUSS

1. Explain why each expression is not a polynomial: $2x^2 + 3x^{-3}$; $1 - \dfrac{a}{b}$.

2. **GET ORGANIZED** Copy and complete the graphic organizer. In each oval, write an example of the given type of polynomial.

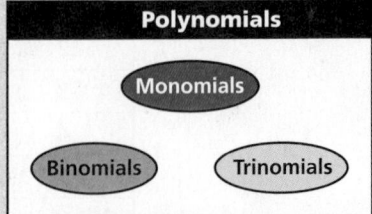

Exercises

GUIDED PRACTICE

Vocabulary Match each polynomial on the left with its classification on the right.

1. $2x^3 + 6$
2. $3x^3 + 4x^2 - 7$
3. $5x^2 - 2x + 3x^4 - 6$

   a. quartic polynomial
   b. quadratic polynomial
   c. cubic trinomial
   d. cubic binomial

SEE EXAMPLE 1   Find the degree of each monomial.

4. 10^6 5. $-7xy^2$ 6. $0.4n^8$ 7. 2

SEE EXAMPLE 2   Find the degree of each polynomial.

8. $x^2 - 2x + 1$ 9. $0.75a^2b - 2a^3b^5$ 10. $15y - 84y^3 + 100 - 3y^2$

11. $r^3 + r^2 - 5$ 12. $a^3 + a^2 - 2a$ 13. $3k^4 + k^3 - 2k^2 + k$

SEE EXAMPLE 3   Write each polynomial in standard form. Then give the leading coefficient.

14. $-2b + 5 + b^2$ 15. $9a^8 - 8a^9$ 16. $5s^2 - 3s + 3 - s^7$

17. $2x + 3x^2 - 1$ 18. $5g - 7 + g^2$ 19. $3c^2 + 5c^4 + 5c^3 - 4$

SEE EXAMPLE 4   Classify each polynomial according to its degree and number of terms.

20. $x^2 + 2x + 3$ 21. $x - 7$ 22. $8 + k + 5k^4$

23. $q^2 + 6 - q^3 + 3q^4$ 24. $5k^2 + 7k^3$ 25. $2a^3 + 4a^2 - a^4$

SEE EXAMPLE 5   26. **Geometry** The surface area of a cone
is approximated by the polynomial
$3.14r^2 + 3.14r\ell$, where r is the radius
and ℓ is the slant height. Find the
approximate surface area of
this cone.

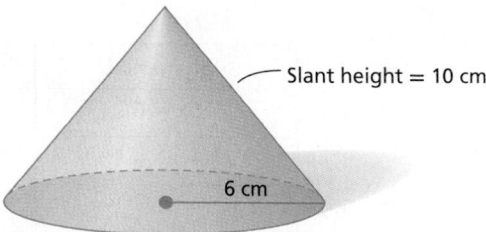

Slant height = 10 cm

6 cm

PRACTICE AND PROBLEM SOLVING

Independent Practice

For Exercises	See Example
27–34	1
35–40	2
41–49	3
50–57	4
58	5

Find the degree of each monomial.

27. $3y^4$ 28. $6k$ 29. $2a^3b^2c$ 30. 325

31. $2y^4z^3$ 32. $9m^5$ 33. p 34. 5

Find the degree of each polynomial.

35. $a^2 + a^4 - 6a$ 36. $3^2b - 5$ 37. $3.5y^2 - 4.1y - 6$

38. $-5f^4 + 2f^6 + 10f^8$ 39. $4n^3 - 2n$ 40. $4r^3 + 4r^6$

Extra Practice

See Extra Practice for
more Skills Practice and
Applications Practice
exercises.

Write each polynomial in standard form. Then give the leading coefficient.

41. $2.5 + 4.9t^3 - 4t^2 + t$ 42. $8a - 10a^2 + 2$ 43. $x^7 - x + x^3 - x^5 + x^{10}$

44. $-m + 7 - 3m^2$ 45. $3x^2 + 5x - 4 + 5x^3$ 46. $-2n + 1 - n^2$

47. $4d + 3d^2 - d^3 + 5$ 48. $3s^2 + 12s^3 + 6$ 49. $4x^2 - x^5 - x^3 + 1$

Classify each polynomial according to its degree and number of terms.

50. 12

51. $6k$

52. $3.5x^3 - 4.1x - 6$

53. $4g + 2g^2 - 3$

54. $2x^2 - 6x$

55. $6 - s^3 - 3s^4$

56. $c^2 + 7 - 2c^3$

57. $-y^2$

58. Transportation The polynomial $3.675v + 0.096v^2$ is used by transportation officials to estimate the stopping distance in feet for a car whose speed is v miles per hour on flat, dry pavement. What is the stopping distance for a car traveling at 30 miles per hour?

Tell whether each statement is sometimes, always, or never true.

59. A monomial is a polynomial.

60. A trinomial is a 3rd-degree polynomial.

61. A binomial is a trinomial.

62. A polynomial has two or more terms.

63. Geometry A piece of 8.5-by-11-inch cardboard has identical squares cut from its corners. It is then folded into a box with no lid. The volume of the box in cubic inches is $4c^3 - 39c^2 + 93.5c$, where c is the side length of the missing squares in inches.

    a. What is the volume of the box if $c = 1$ in.?

    b. What is the volume of the box if $c = 1.5$ in.?

    c. What is the volume of the box if $c = 4.25$ in.?

    d. Critical Thinking Does your answer to part **c** make sense? Explain why or why not.

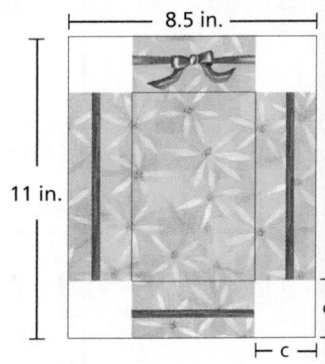

Copy and complete the table by evaluating each polynomial for the given values of x.

	Polynomial	$x = -2$	$x = 0$	$x = 5$
64.	$5x - 6$	$5(-2) - 6 = -16$	$5(0) - 6 = -6$	▪
65.	$x^5 + x^3 + 4x$	▪	▪	▪
66.	$-10x^2$	▪	▪	▪

Give one example of each type of polynomial.

67. quadratic trinomial

68. linear binomial

69. constant monomial

70. cubic monomial

71. quintic binomial

72. 12th-degree trinomial

73. Write About It Explain the steps you would follow to write the polynomial $4x^3 - 3 + 5x^2 - 2x^4 - x$ in standard form.

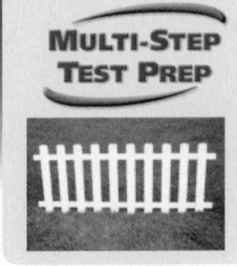
MULTI-STEP TEST PREP

74. a. The perimeter of the rectangle shown is $12x + 6$. What is the degree of this polynomial?

    b. The area of the rectangle is $8x^2 + 12x$. What is the degree of this polynomial?

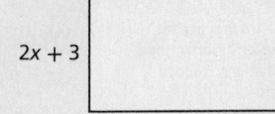

$2x + 3$

$4x$

75. 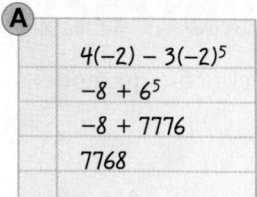**ERROR ANALYSIS**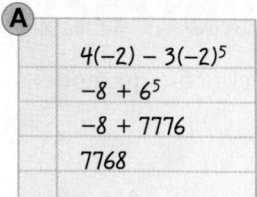 Two students evaluated $4x - 3x^5$ for $x = -2$. Which is incorrect? Explain the error.

A
$4(-2) - 3(-2)^5$
$-8 + 6^5$
$-8 + 7776$
7768

B
$4(-2) - 3(-2)^5$
$-8 - 3(-32)$
$-8 + 96$
88

76. Which polynomial has the highest degree?

(A) $3x^8 - 2x^7 + x^6$ (B) $5x - 100$ (C) $25x^{10} + 3x^5 - 15$ (D) $134x^2$

77. What is the value of $-3x^3 + 4x^2 - 5x + 7$ when $x = -1$?

(F) 3   (G) 13   (H) 9   (J) 19

78. Short Response A toy rocket is launched from the ground at 75 feet per second. The polynomial $-16t^2 + 75t$ gives the rocket's height in feet after t seconds. Make a table showing the rocket's height after 1 second, 2 seconds, 3 seconds, and 4 seconds. At which of these times will the rocket be the highest?

CHALLENGE AND EXTEND

79. Medicine Doctors and nurses use growth charts and formulas to tell whether a baby is developing normally. The polynomial $0.016m^3 - 0.390m^2 + 4.562m + 50.310$ gives the average length in centimeters of a baby boy between 0 and 10 months of age, where m is the baby's age in months.

   a. What is the average length of a 2-month-old baby boy? a 5-month-old baby boy? Round your answers to the nearest centimeter.

   b. What is the average length of a newborn (0-month-old) baby boy?

   c. How could you find the answer to part **b** without doing any calculations?

80. Consider the binomials $4x^5 + x$, $4x^4 + x$, and $4x^3 + x$.

   a. Without calculating, which binomial has the greatest value for $x = 5$?

   b. Are there any values of x for $4x^3 + x$ which will have the greatest value? Explain.

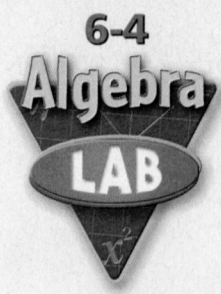

6-4 Algebra LAB

Model Polynomial Addition and Subtraction

You can use algebra tiles to model polynomial addition and subtraction.

Use with Adding and Subtracting Polynomials

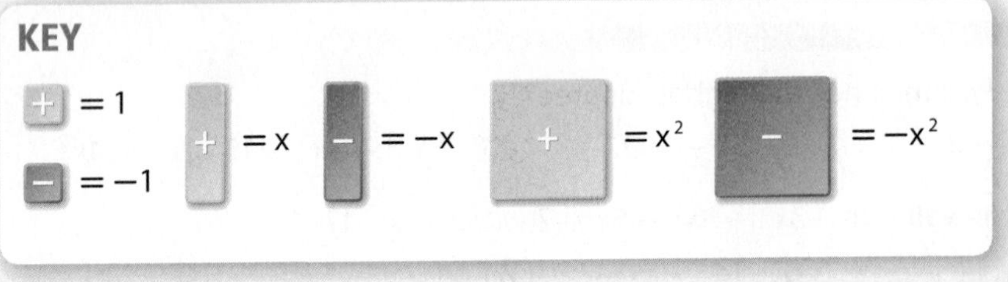

Learn It Online
Lab Resources Online

MATHEMATICAL PRACTICES **Use appropriate tools strategically.**

CC.9-12.A.APR.1 Understand that polynomials form a system analogous to the integers, namely, they are closed under the operations of addition, subtraction, and multiplication; add, subtract, and multiply polynomials.

Activity 1

Use algebra tiles to find $(2x^2 - x) + (x^2 + 3x - 1)$.

MODEL		ALGEBRA
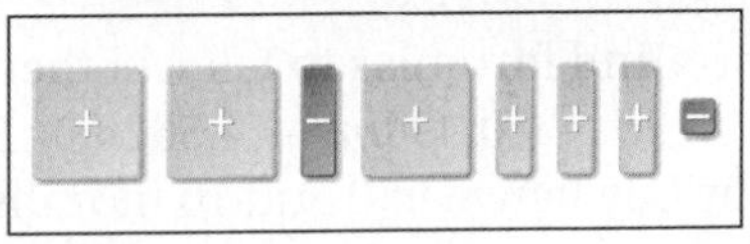	*Use tiles to represent all terms from both expressions.*	$(2x^2 - x) + (x^2 + 3x - 1)$
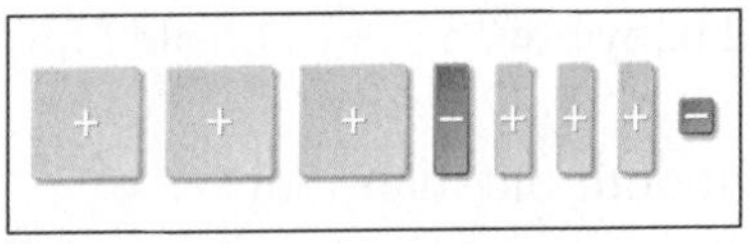	*Rearrange tiles so that like tiles are together. Like tiles are the same size and shape.*	$(2x^2 + x^2) + (-x + 3x) - 1$
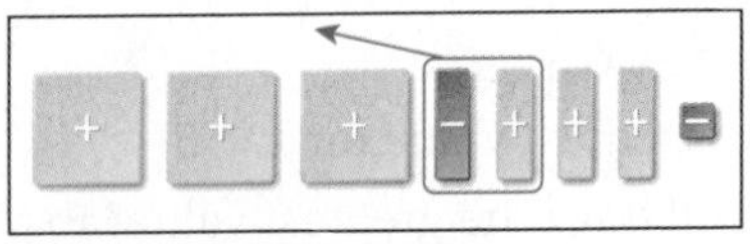	*Remove any zero pairs.*	$3x^2 - x + x + 2x - 1$
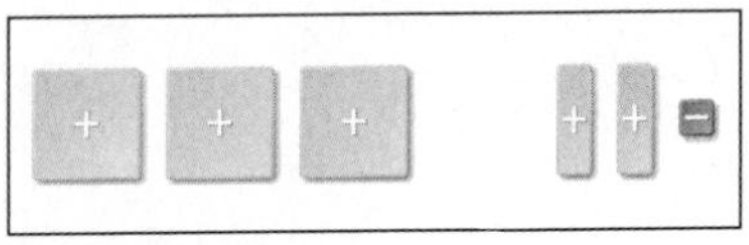	*The remaining tiles represent the sum.*	$3x^2 + 2x - 1$

Try This

Use algebra tiles to find each sum.

1. $(-2x^2 + 1) + (-x^2)$

2. $(3x^2 + 2x + 5) + (x^2 - x - 4)$

3. $(x - 3) + (2x - 2)$

4. $(5x^2 - 3x - 6) + (x^2 + 3x + 6)$

5. $-5x^2 + (2x^2 + 5x)$

6. $(x^2 - x - 1) + (6x - 3)$

Activity 2

Use algebra tiles to find $(2x^2 + 6) - 4x^2$.

MODEL		ALGEBRA
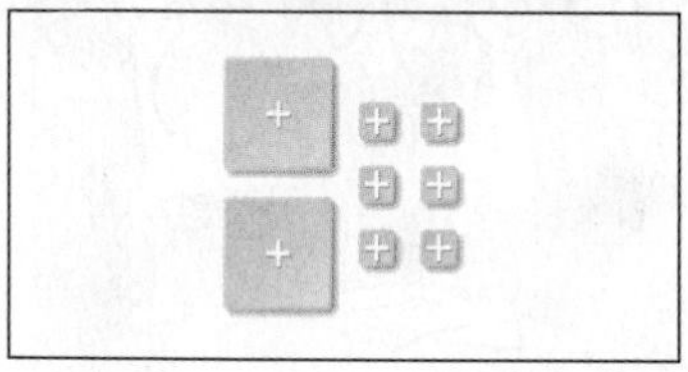	Use tiles to represent the terms in the first expression.	$2x^2 + 6$

To subtract $4x^2$, you would remove 4 yellow x^2-tiles, but there are not enough to do this. Remember that subtraction is the same as adding the opposite, so rewrite $(2x^2 + 6) - 4x^2$ as $(2x^2 + 6) + (-4x^2)$.

MODEL		ALGEBRA
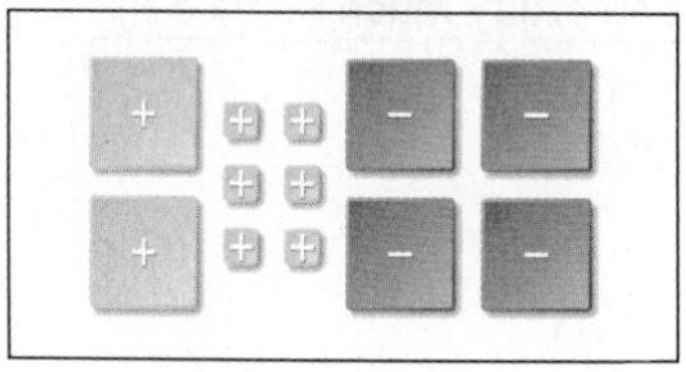	Add 4 red x^2-tiles.	$2x^2 + 6 + (-4x^2)$
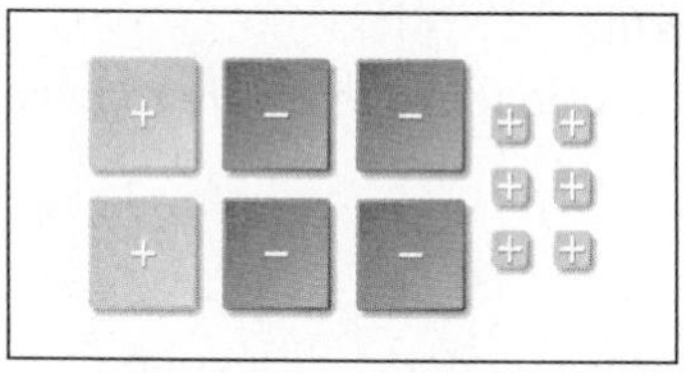	Rearrange tiles so that like tiles are together.	$2x^2 + (-4x^2) + 6$
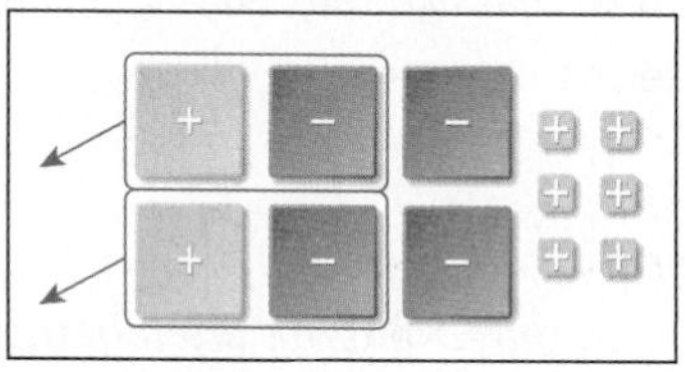	Remove zero pairs.	$2x^2 + (-2x^2) + (-2x^2) + 6$
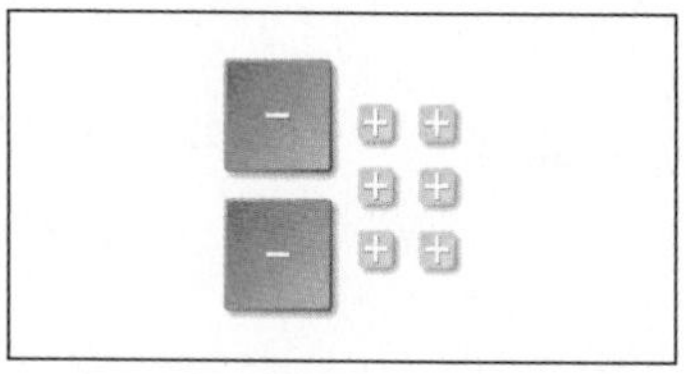	The remaining tiles represent the difference.	$-2x^2 + 6$

Try This

Use algebra tiles to find each difference.

7. $(6x^2 + 4x) - 3x^2$

8. $(2x^2 + x - 7) - 5x$

9. $(3x + 6) - 6$

10. $(8x + 5) - (-2x)$

11. $(x^2 + 2x) - (-4x^2 + x)$

12. $(3x^2 - 4) - (x^2 + 6x)$

13.  [+] [−] represents a zero pair. Use algebra tiles to model two other zero pairs.

14. When is it not necessary to "add the opposite" for polynomial subtraction using algebra tiles?

6-4 Adding and Subtracting Polynomials

CC.9-12.A.APR.1 Understand that polynomials … are closed under the operations of addition, subtraction, and multiplication; add, subtract, and multiply polynomials.

Objective
Add and subtract polynomials.

Who uses this?
Business owners can add and subtract polynomials that model profit. (See Example 4.)

Just as you can perform operations on numbers, you can perform operations on polynomials. To add or subtract polynomials, combine like terms.

"This one pretty much sums it up."

EXAMPLE 1 **Adding and Subtracting Monomials**

Add or subtract.

 A $15m^3 + 6m^2 + 2m^3$

$15m^3 + 6m^2 + 2m^3$ *Identify like terms.*
$15m^3 + 2m^3 + 6m^2$ *Rearrange terms so that like terms are together.*
$17m^3 + 6m^2$ *Combine like terms.*

B $3x^2 + 5 - 7x^2 + 12$

$3x^2 + 5 - 7x^2 + 12$ *Identify like terms.*
$3x^2 - 7x^2 + 5 + 12$ *Rearrange terms so that like terms are together.*
$-4x^2 + 17$ *Combine like terms.*

C $0.9y^5 - 0.4y^5 + 0.5x^5 + y^5$

$0.9y^5 - 0.4y^5 + 0.5x^5 + y^5$ *Identify like terms.*
$0.9y^5 - 0.4y^5 + y^5 + 0.5x^5$ *Rearrange terms so that like terms are together.*
$1.5y^5 + 0.5x^5$ *Combine like terms.*

D $2x^2y - x^2y - x^2y$

$2x^2y - x^2y - x^2y$ *All terms are like terms.*
0 *Combine.*

> **Remember!**
> Like terms are constants or terms with the same variable(s) raised to the same power(s).

 **CHECK IT OUT!** **Add or subtract.**

1a. $2s^2 + 3s^2 + s$ **1b.** $4z^4 - 8 + 16z^4 + 2$
1c. $2x^8 + 7y^8 - x^8 - y^8$ **1d.** $9b^3c^2 + 5b^3c^2 - 13b^3c^2$

Polynomials can be added in either vertical or horizontal form.

In vertical form, align the like terms and add:

$$
\begin{array}{r}
5x^2 + 4x + 1 \\
+\ 2x^2 + 5x + 2 \\
\hline
7x^2 + 9x + 3
\end{array}
$$

In horizontal form, use the Associative and Commutative Properties to regroup and combine like terms:

$$(5x^2 + 4x + 1) + (2x^2 + 5x + 2)$$
$$= (5x^2 + 2x^2) + (4x + 5x) + (1 + 2)$$
$$= 7x^2 + 9x + 3$$

EXAMPLE 2 **Adding Polynomials**

Add.

A $(2x^2 - x) + (x^2 + 3x - 1)$

$(2x^2 - x) + (x^2 + 3x - 1)$ *Identify like terms.*

$(2x^2 + x^2) + (-x + 3x) + (-1)$ *Group like terms together.*
                                         Combine like terms.

$3x^2 + 2x - 1$

B $(-2ab + b) + (2ab + a)$

$(-2ab + b) + (2ab + a)$ *Identify like terms.*

$(-2ab + 2ab) + b + a$ *Group like terms together.*

$0 + b + a$ *Combine like terms.*

$b + a$ *Simplify.*

C $(4b^5 + 8b) + (3b^5 + 6b - 7b^5 + b)$

$(4b^5 + 8b) + (3b^5 + 6b - 7b^5 + b)$ *Identify like terms.*

$(4b^5 + 8b) + (-4b^5 + 7b)$ *Combine like terms in the second polynomial.*

$$\begin{array}{r} 4b^5 + 8b \\ + \, {-4b^5} + 7b \\ \hline 0 \quad + 15b \end{array}$$ *Use the vertical method.*

                     Combine like terms.

$15b$ *Simplify.*

D $(20.2y^2 + 6y + 5) + (1.7y^2 - 8)$

$(20.2y^2 + 6y + 5) + (1.7y^2 - 8)$ *Identify like terms.*

$$\begin{array}{r} 20.2y^2 + 6y + 5 \\ + \; 1.7y^2 + 0y - 8 \\ \hline 21.9y^2 + 6y - 3 \end{array}$$

Use the vertical method.

Write 0y as a placeholder in the second polynomial.

Combine like terms.

> **Writing Math**
>
> When you use the Associative and Commutative Properties to rearrange the terms, the sign in front of each term must stay with that term.

2. Add $(5a^3 + 3a^2 - 6a + 12a^2) + (7a^3 - 10a)$.

To subtract polynomials, remember that subtracting is the same as adding the opposite. To find the opposite of a polynomial, you must write the opposite of *each* term in the polynomial:

$$-(2x^3 - 3x + 7) = -2x^3 + 3x - 7$$

EXAMPLE 3 **Subtracting Polynomials**

Subtract.

A $(2x^2 + 6) - (4x^2)$

$(2x^2 + 6) + (-4x^2)$ *Rewrite subtraction as addition of the opposite.*

$(2x^2 + 6) + (-4x^2)$ *Identify like terms.*

$(2x^2 - 4x^2) + 6$ *Group like terms together.*

$-2x^2 + 6$ *Combine like terms.*

B $(a^4 - 2a) - (3a^4 - 3a + 1)$

$(a^4 - 2a) + (-3a^4 + 3a - 1)$ *Rewrite subtraction as addition of the opposite.*

$(a^4 - 2a) + (-3a^4 + 3a - 1)$ *Identify like terms.*

$(a^4 - 3a^4) + (-2a + 3a) - 1$ *Group like terms together.*

$-2a^4 + a - 1$ *Combine like terms.*

Subtract.

C $\left(3x^2 - 2x + 8\right) - \left(x^2 - 4\right)$

$\left(3x^2 - 2x + 8\right) + \left(-x^2 + 4\right)$ *Rewrite subtraction as addition of the opposite.*

$\left(3x^2 - 2x + 8\right) + \left(-x^2 + 4\right)$ *Identify like terms.*

$$
\begin{array}{r}
3x^2 - 2x\ + 8 \\
+\ -x^2 + 0x\ + 4 \\
\hline
2x^2 - 2x + 12
\end{array}
$$

    Use the vertical method.
    Write 0x as a placeholder.
    Combine like terms.

D $\left(11z^3 - 2z\right) - \left(z^3 - 5\right)$

$\left(11z^3 - 2z\right) + \left(-z^3 + 5\right)$ *Rewrite subtraction as addition of the opposite.*

$\left(11z^3 - 2z\right) + \left(-z^3 + 5\right)$ *Identify like terms.*

$$
\begin{array}{r}
11z^3 - 2z + 0 \\
+\ -z^3 + 0z + 5 \\
\hline
10z^3 - 2z + 5
\end{array}
$$

    Use the vertical method.
    Write 0 and 0z as placeholders.
    Combine like terms.

 **3.** Subtract $\left(2x^2 - 3x^2 + 1\right) - \left(x^2 + x + 1\right)$.

EXAMPLE 4   *Business Application*

The profits of two different manufacturing plants can be modeled as shown, where x is the number of units produced at each plant.

Eastern:
$-0.03x^2 + 25x - 1500$

Southern:
$-0.02x^2 + 21x - 1700$

Write a polynomial that represents the difference of the profits at the eastern plant and the profits at the southern plant.

$$
\begin{array}{l}
\left(-0.03x^2 + 25x - 1500\right) \\
-\left(-0.02x^2 + 21x - 1700\right)
\end{array}
$$
    Eastern plant profits
    Southern plant profits

$$
\begin{array}{r}
-0.03x^2 + 25x - 1500 \\
+\left(+0.02x^2 - 21x + 1700\right) \\
\hline
-0.01x^2 +\ \ 4x +\ \ 200
\end{array}
$$
    Write subtraction as addition of the opposite.
    Combine like terms.

 **4.** Use the information above to write a polynomial that represents the total profits from both plants.

MATHEMATICAL PRACTICES

THINK AND DISCUSS

1. Identify the like terms in the following list: $-12x^2$, $-4.7y$, $\frac{1}{5}x^2y$, y, $3xy^2$, $-9x^2$, $5x^2y$, $-12x$

2. Describe how to find the opposite of $9t^2 - 5t + 8$.

3. GET ORGANIZED Copy and complete the graphic organizer. In each box, write an example that shows how to perform the given operation.

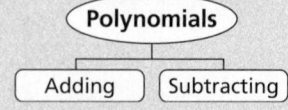

Know it!
Note

GUIDED PRACTICE

SEE EXAMPLE 1

Add or subtract.

1. $7a^2 - 10a^2 + 9a$

2. $13x^2 + 9y^2 - 6x^2$

3. $0.07r^4 + 0.32r^3 + 0.19r^4$

4. $\frac{1}{4}p^3 + \frac{2}{3}p^3$

5. $5b^3c + b^3c - 3b^3c$

6. $-8m + 5 - 16 + 11m$

SEE EXAMPLE 2

Add.

7. $(5n^3 + 3n + 6) + (18n^3 + 9)$

8. $(3.7q^2 - 8q + 3.7) + (4.3q^2 - 2.9q + 1.6)$

9. $(-3x + 12) + (9x^2 + 2x - 18)$

10. $(9x^4 + x^3) + (2x^4 + 6x^3 - 8x^4 + x^3)$

SEE EXAMPLE 3

Subtract.

11. $(6c^4 + 8c + 6) - (2c^4)$

12. $(16y^2 - 8y + 9) - (6y^2 - 2y + 7y)$

13. $(2r + 5) - (5r - 6)$

14. $(-7k^2 + 3) - (2k^2 + 5k - 1)$

SEE EXAMPLE 4

15. Geometry Write a polynomial that represents the measure of angle ABD.

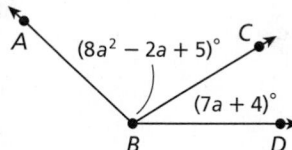

PRACTICE AND PROBLEM SOLVING

Independent Practice	
For Exercises	See Example
16–24	1
25–28	2
29–32	3
33–34	4

Extra Practice

See Extra Practice for more Skills Practice and Applications Practice exercises.

Add or subtract.

16. $4k^3 + 6k^2 + 9k^3$

17. $5m + 12n^2 + 6n - 8m$

18. $2.5a^4 - 8.1b^4 - 3.6b^4$

19. $2d^5 + 1 - d^5$

20. $7xy - 4x^2y - 2xy$

21. $-6x^3 + 5x + 2x^3 + 4x^3$

22. $x^2 + x + 3x + 2x^2$

23. $3x^3 - 4 - x^3 - 1$

24. $3b^3 - 2b - 1 - b^3 - b$

Add.

25. $(2t^2 - 8t) + (8t^2 + 9t)$

26. $(-7x^2 - 2x + 3) + (4x^2 - 9x)$

27. $(x^5 - x) + (x^4 + x)$

28. $(-2z^3 + z + 2z^3 + z) + (3z^3 - 5z^2)$

Subtract.

29. $(t^3 + 8t^2) - (3t^3)$

30. $(3x^2 - x) - (x^2 + 3x - x)$

31. $(5m + 3) - (6m^3 - 2m^2)$

32. $(3s^2 + 4s) - (-10s^2 + 6s)$

33. Photography The measurements of a photo and its frame are shown in the diagram. Write a polynomial that represents the width of the photo.

34. Geometry The length of a rectangle is represented by $4a + 3b$, and its width is represented by $7a - 2b$. Write a polynomial for the perimeter of the rectangle.

$6w^2 + 8$

?

$w^2 - 3w + 2$

Add or subtract.

35. $(2t - 7) + (-t + 2)$

36. $(4m^2 + 3m) + (-2m^2)$

37. $(4n - 2) - 2n$

38. $(-v - 7) - (-2v)$

39. $(4x^2 + 3x - 6) + (2x^2 - 4x + 5)$

40. $(2z^2 - 3z - 3) + (2z^2 - 7z - 1)$

41. $(5u^2 + 3u + 7) - (u^3 + 2u^2 + 1)$

42. $(-7h^2 - 4h + 7) - (7h^2 - 4h + 11)$

43. Geometry The length of a rectangle is represented by $2x + 3$, and its width is represented by $3x + 7$. The perimeter of the rectangle is 35 units. Find the value of x.

44. Write About It If the parentheses are removed from $(3m^2 - 5m) + (12m^2 + 7m - 10)$, is the new expression equivalent to the original? If the parentheses are removed from $(3m^2 - 5m) - (12m^2 + 7m - 10)$, is the new expression equivalent to the original? Explain.

45. /// **ERROR ANALYSIS** /// Two students found the sum of the polynomials $(-3n^4 + 6n^3 + 4n^2)$ and $(8n^4 - 3n^2 + 9n)$. Which is incorrect? Explain the error.

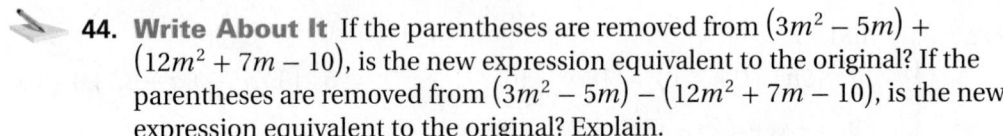

A	B
$-3n^4 + 6n^3 + 4n^2 + 0n$ $+8n^4 + 0n^3 - 3n^2 + 9n$ $\overline{5n^4 + 6n^3 + n^2 + 9n}$	$-3n^4 + 6n^3 + 4n^2$ $+8n^4 - 3n^2 + 9n$ $\overline{5n^4 + 3n^3 + 13n^2}$

Copy and complete the table by finding the missing polynomials.

	Polynomial 1	Polynomial 2	Sum
46.	$x^2 - 6$	$3x^2 - 10x + 2$	▓
47.	$12x + 5$	▓	$15x + 11$
48.	▓	$5x^4 + 8$	$6x^4 - 3x^2 - 1$
49.	$7x^3 - 6x - 3$	▓	$7x^3 + 11$
50.	$2x^3 + 5x^2$	$7x^3 - 5x^2 + 1$	▓
51.	▓	$x + x^2 + 6$	$3x^2 + 2x + 1$

52. Critical Thinking Does the order in which you add polynomials affect the sum? Does the order in which you subtract polynomials affect the difference? Explain.

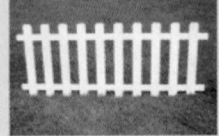

53. a. Ian plans to build a fenced dog pen. At first, he planned for the pen to be a square of length x feet on each side, but then he decided that a square may not be best. He added 4 feet to the length and subtracted 3 feet from the width. Draw a diagram to show the dimensions of the new pen.

b. Write a polynomial that represents the amount of fencing that Ian will need for the new dog pen.

c. How much fencing will Ian need if $x = 15$?

54. What is the missing term?

$$\left(-14y^2 + 9y^2 - 12y + 3\right) + \left(2y^2 + \blacksquare - 6y - 2\right) = \left(-3y^2 - 15y + 1\right)$$

Ⓐ $-6y$ Ⓑ $-3y$ Ⓒ $3y$ Ⓓ $6y$

55. Which is NOT equivalent to $-5t^3 - t$?

Ⓕ $-\left(5t^3 + t\right)$ Ⓗ $\left(t^3 + 6t\right) - \left(6t^3 + 7t\right)$

Ⓖ $\left(2t^3 - 4t\right) - \left(-7t - 3t\right)$ Ⓙ $\left(2t^3 - 3t^2 + t\right) - \left(7t^3 - 3t^2 + 2t\right)$

56. Extended Response Tammy plans to put a wallpaper border around the perimeter of her room. She will not put the border across the doorway, which is 3 feet wide.

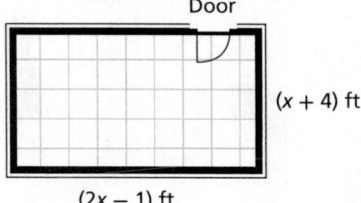

Door

$(x + 4)$ ft

$(2x - 1)$ ft

    a. Write a polynomial that represents the number of feet of wallpaper border that Tammy will need.

    b. A local store has 50 feet of the border that Tammy has chosen. What is the greatest whole-number value of x for which this amount would be enough for Tammy's room? Justify your answer.

    c. Determine the dimensions of Tammy's room for the value of x that you found in part **b.**

CHALLENGE AND EXTEND

 57. Geometry The legs of the isosceles triangle at right measure $\left(x^3 + 5\right)$ units. The perimeter of the triangle is $\left(2x^3 + 3x^2 + 8\right)$ units. Write a polynomial that represents the measure of the base of the triangle.

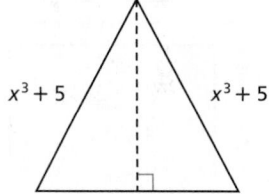

$x^3 + 5$ $x^3 + 5$

58. Write two polynomials whose sum is $4m^3 + 3m$.

59. Write two polynomials whose difference is $4m^3 + 3m$.

60. Write three polynomials whose sum is $4m^3 + 3m$.

61. Write two monomials whose sum is $4m^3 + 3m$.

62. Write three trinomials whose sum is $4m^3 + 3m$.

6-5

Algebra LAB

Model Polynomial Multiplication

Use with Multiplying Polynomials

You can use algebra tiles to multiply polynomials. Use the length and width of a rectangle to represent the factors. The area of the rectangle represents the product.

KEY

 = 1
= −1
 = x   = −x   = x^2

REMEMBER
- The product of two values with the same sign is positive.
- The product of two values with different signs is negative.

Activity 1

MATHEMATICAL PRACTICES Use appropriate tools strategically.

CC.9-12.A.APR.1 Understand that polynomials form a system analogous to the integers, namely, they are closed under the operations of addition, subtraction, and multiplication; add, subtract, and multiply polynomials.

Use algebra tiles to find $2(x + 1)$.

MODEL		ALGEBRA
	Place the first factor in a column along the left side of the grid. This will be the width of the rectangle.	$2(x + 1)$
	Place the second factor across the top of the grid. This will be the length of the rectangle.	
	Fill in the grid with tiles that have the same width as the tiles in the left column and the same length as the tiles in the top row.	
	The area of the rectangle inside the grid represents the product.	$x + x + 1 + 1$ $2x + 2$

The rectangle has an area of $2x + 2$, so $2(x + 1) = 2x + 2$. Notice that this is the same product you would get by using the Distributive Property to multiply $2(x + 1)$.

Try This

Use algebra tiles to find each product.

1. $3(x + 2)$ **2.** $2(2x + 1)$ **3.** $3(x + 1)$ **4.** $3(2x + 2)$

Activity 2

Use algebra tiles to find $2x(x - 3)$.

MODEL		ALGEBRA
	Place tiles to form the length and width of a rectangle and fill in the rectangle. The product of two values with the same sign (same color) is positive (yellow). The product of two values with different signs (different colors) is negative (red).	$2x(x - 3)$
	The area of the rectangle inside the grid represents the product. The rectangle has an area of $2x^2 - 6x$, so $2x(x - 3) = 2x^2 - 6x$.	$x^2 + x^2 - x - x - x - x - x - x$ $2x^2 - 6x$

Try This

Use algebra tiles to find each product.

5. $3x(x - 2)$ **6.** $x(2x - 1)$ **7.** $x(x + 1)$ **8.** $(8x + 5)(-2x)$

Activity 3

Use algebra tiles to find $(x + 1)(x - 2)$.

MODEL		ALGEBRA
	Place tiles for each factor to form the length and width of a rectangle. Fill in the grid and remove any zero pairs.	$(x + 1)(x - 2)$ $x^2 - x - x + x - 1 - 1$
	The area inside the grid represents the product. The remaining area is $x^2 - x - 2$, so $(x + 1)(x - 2) = x^2 - x - 2$.	$x^2 - x - 1 - 1$ $x^2 - x - 2$

Try This

Use algebra tiles to find each product.

9. $(x + 2)(x - 3)$ **10.** $(x - 1)(x + 3)$ **11.** $(x - 2)(x - 3)$ **12.** $(x + 1)(x + 2)$

6-5 Multiplying Polynomials

CC.9-12.A.APR.1 Understand that polynomials … are closed under the operations of addition, subtraction, and multiplication; add, subtract, and multiply polynomials.

Objective
Multiply polynomials.

Why learn this?
You can multiply polynomials to write expressions for areas, such as the area of a dulcimer. (See Example 5.)

To multiply monomials and polynomials, you will use some of the properties of exponents that you learned earlier in this chapter.

EXAMPLE 1 **Multiplying Monomials**

Multiply.

A $(5x^2)(4x^3)$

$(5x^2)(4x^3)$

$(5 \cdot 4)(x^2 \cdot x^3)$ *Group factors with like bases together.*

$20x^5$ *Multiply.*

B $(-3x^3y^2)(4xy^5)$

$(-3x^3y^2)(4xy^5)$

$(-3 \cdot 4)(x^3 \cdot x)(y^2 \cdot y^5)$ *Group factors with like bases together.*

$-12x^4y^7$ *Multiply.*

> **Remember!**
>
> When multiplying powers with the same base, keep the base and add the exponents.
>
> $x^2 \cdot x^3 = x^{2+3} = x^5$

C $\left(\frac{1}{2}a^3b\right)(a^2c^2)(6b^2)$

$\left(\frac{1}{2}a^3b\right)(a^2c^2)(6b^2)$

$\left(\frac{1}{2} \cdot 6\right)(a^3 \cdot a^2)(b \cdot b^2)(c^2)$ *Group factors with like bases together.*

$3a^5b^3c^2$ *Multiply.*

CHECK IT OUT! Multiply.

1a. $(3x^3)(6x^2)$ **1b.** $(2r^2t)(5t^3)$ **1c.** $\left(\frac{1}{3}x^2y\right)(12x^3z^2)(y^4z^5)$

To multiply a polynomial by a monomial, use the Distributive Property.

EXAMPLE 2 **Multiplying a Polynomial by a Monomial**

Multiply.

A $5(2x^2 + x + 4)$

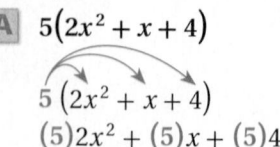

$(5)2x^2 + (5)x + (5)4$ *Distribute 5.*

$10x^2 + 5x + 20$ *Multiply.*

© Pat and Chuck Blackley

Multiply.

B $2x^2y(3x - y)$

$$\overparen{(2x^2y)(3x - y)}$$

$(2x^2y)3x + (2x^2y)(-y)$ *Distribute $2x^2y$.*

$(2 \cdot 3)(x^2 \cdot x)y + 2(-1)(x^2)(y \cdot y)$ *Group like bases together.*

$6x^3y - 2x^2y^2$ *Multiply.*

C $4a(a^2b + 2b^2)$

$$\overparen{4a(a^2b + 2b^2)}$$

$(4a)a^2b + (4a)2b^2$ *Distribute $4a$.*

$(4)(a \cdot a^2)(b) + (4 \cdot 2)(a)(b^2)$ *Group like bases together.*

$4a^3b + 8ab^2$ *Multiply.*

 CHECK IT OUT!

Multiply.

2a. $2(4x^2 + x + 3)$ **2b.** $3ab(5a^2 + b)$ **2c.** $5r^2s^2(r - 3s)$

To multiply a binomial by a binomial, you can apply the Distributive Property more than once:

$$\overparen{(x + 3)}(x + 2) = x(x + 2) + 3(x + 2)$$ *Distribute.*

$$= \overparen{x(x + 2)} + \overparen{3(x + 2)}$$

$$= x(x) + x(2) + 3(x) + 3(2)$$ *Distribute again.*

$$= x^2 + 2x + 3x + 6$$ *Multiply.*

$$= x^2 + 5x + 6$$ *Combine like terms.*

Another method for multiplying binomials is called the FOIL method.

1. Multiply the **F**irst terms. $\overset{F}{\overparen{(x+3)(x+2)}} \rightarrow x \cdot x = x^2$

2. Multiply the **O**uter terms. $\overset{O}{\overparen{(x+3)(x+2)}} \rightarrow x \cdot 2 = 2x$

3. Multiply the **I**nner terms. $(x+3)\overset{I}{\overparen{(x+3)(x+2)}} \rightarrow 3 \cdot x = 3x$

4. Multiply the **L**ast terms. $\underset{L}{\overparen{(x+3)(x+2)}} \rightarrow 3 \cdot 2 = 6$

$$(x+3)(x+2) = x^2 + 2x + 3x + 6 = x^2 + 5x + 6$$

     F   O   I   L

EXAMPLE 3 **Multiplying Binomials**

Multiply.

A $(x + 2)(x - 5)$

$(x + 2)(x - 5)$

$x(x - 5) + 2(x - 5)$ *Distribute.*

$x(x) + x(-5) + 2(x) + 2(-5)$ *Distribute again.*

$x^2 - 5x + 2x - 10$ *Multiply.*

$x^2 - 3x - 10$ *Combine like terms.*

B $(x + 5)^2$

$(x + 5)(x + 5)$ *Write as a product of two binomials.*

$(x \cdot x) + (x \cdot 5) + (5 \cdot x) + (5 \cdot 5)$ *Use the FOIL method.*

$x^2 + 5x + 5x + 25$ *Multiply.*

$x^2 + 10x + 25$ *Combine like terms.*

C $(3a^2 - b)(a^2 - 2b)$

$3a^2(a^2) + 3a^2(-2b) - b(a^2) - b(-2b)$ *Use the FOIL method.*

$3a^4 - 6a^2b - a^2b + 2b^2$ *Multiply.*

$3a^4 - 7a^2b + 2b^2$ *Combine like terms.*

> **Helpful Hint**
>
> In the expression $(x + 5)^2$, the base is $(x + 5)$.
> $(x + 5)^2 =$
> $(x + 5)(x + 5)$

 **CHECK IT OUT!**   **3a.** $(a + 3)(a - 4)$ **3b.** $(x - 3)^2$ **3c.** $(2a - b^2)(a + 4b^2)$

To multiply polynomials with more than two terms, you can use the Distributive Property several times. Multiply $(5x + 3)$ by $(2x^2 + 10x - 6)$:

$$(5x + 3)(2x^2 + 10x - 6) = 5x(2x^2 + 10x - 6) + 3(2x^2 + 10x - 6)$$

$$= 5x(2x^2 + 10x - 6) + 3(2x^2 + 10x - 6)$$

$$= 5x(2x^2) + 5x(10x) + 5x(-6) + 3(2x^2) + 3(10x) + 3(-6)$$

$$= 10x^3 + 50x^2 - 30x + 6x^2 + 30x - 18$$

$$= 10x^3 + 56x^2 - 18$$

You can also use a rectangle model to multiply polynomials with more than two terms. This is similar to finding the area of a rectangle with length $(2x^2 + 10x - 6)$ and width $(5x + 3)$:

	$2x^2$	$+ 10x$	$- 6$
$5x$	$10x^3$	$50x^2$	$-30x$
$+ 3$	$6x^2$	$30x$	-18

Write the product of the monomials in each row and column.

To find the product, add all of the terms inside the rectangle by combining like terms and simplifying if necessary.

$$10x^3 + 6x^2 + 50x^2 + 30x - 30x - 18$$

$$10x^3 + 56x^2 - 18$$

Another method that can be used to multiply polynomials with more than two terms is the vertical method. This is similar to methods used to multiply whole numbers.

$$2x^2 + 10x - 6$$

$$\underline{\times \qquad\qquad 5x + 3}$$

$$6x^2 + 30x - 18 \qquad \text{\textit{Multiply each term in the top polynomial by 3.}}$$

$$\underline{+\ 10x^3 + 50x^2 - 30x} \qquad \text{\textit{Multiply each term in the top polynomial by 5x,}}$$
$$\qquad\qquad\qquad\qquad\qquad\qquad \text{\textit{and align like terms.}}$$

$$10x^3 + 56x^2 \ \ + 0x - 18 \qquad \text{\textit{Combine like terms by adding vertically.}}$$
$$10x^3 + 56x^2 \qquad\quad - 18 \qquad \text{\textit{Simplify.}}$$

EXAMPLE **4** **Multiplying Polynomials**

Multiply.

Helpful Hint

A polynomial with *m* terms multiplied by a polynomial with *n* terms has a product that, before simplifying, has *mn* terms. In Example 4A, there are 2 · 3, or 6, terms before simplifying.

A $(x + 2)(x^2 - 5x + 4)$

$(x + 2)(x^2 - 5x + 4)$

$x(x^2 - 5x + 4) + 2(x^2 - 5x + 4)$ *Distribute.*

$x(x^2) + x(-5x) + x(4) + 2(x^2) + 2(-5x) + 2(4)$ *Distribute again.*

$x^3 + 2x^2 - 5x^2 - 10x + 4x + 8$ *Simplify.*

$x^3 - 3x^2 - 6x + 8$ *Combine like terms.*

B $(3x - 4)(-2x^3 + 5x - 6)$

$(3x - 4)(-2x^3 + 5x - 6)$

$$-2x^3 + \ 0x^2 + \ 5x - \ 6 \qquad \text{\textit{Add 0x}}^2 \text{ \textit{as a placeholder.}}$$

$$\underline{\times \qquad\qquad\qquad\qquad 3x - \ 4}$$

$$8x^3 + \ 0x^2 - 20x + 24 \qquad \text{\textit{Multiply each term in the top}}$$
$$\qquad\qquad\qquad\qquad\qquad\qquad\qquad \text{\textit{polynomial by −4.}}$$

$$\underline{+\ -6x^4 + 0x^3 + 15x^2 - 18x} \qquad \text{\textit{Multiply each term in the top polynomial}}$$
$$\qquad\qquad\qquad\qquad\qquad\qquad\qquad\qquad \text{\textit{by 3x, and align like terms.}}$$

$$-6x^4 + 8x^3 + 15x^2 - 38x + 24 \qquad \text{\textit{Combine like terms by adding vertically.}}$$

C $(x - 2)^3$

$[(x - 2)(x - 2)](x - 2)$ *Write as the product of three binomials.*

$[x \cdot x + x(-2) + (-2)\,x + (-2)(-2)](x - 2)$ *Use the FOIL method on the first two factors.*

$(x^2 - 2x - 2x + 4)(x - 2)$ *Multiply.*

$(x^2 - 4x + 4)(x - 2)$ *Combine like terms.*

$(x - 2)(x^2 - 4x + 4)$ *Use the Commutative Property of Multiplication.*

$x(x^2 - 4x + 4) + (-2)(x^2 - 4x + 4)$ *Distribute.*

$x(x^2) + x(-4x) + x(4) + (-2)(x^2) + (-2)(-4x) + (-2)(4)$ *Distribute again.*

$x^3 - 4x^2 + 4x - 2x^2 + 8x - 8$ *Simplify.*

$x^3 - 6x^2 + 12x - 8$ *Combine like terms.*

Multiply.

D $(2x + 3)(x^2 - 6x + 5)$

	x^2	$-6x$	$+5$
$2x$	$2x^3$	$-12x^2$	$10x$
$+3$	$3x^2$	$-18x$	15

Write the product of the monomials in each row and column.

$2x^3 + 3x^2 - 12x^2 - 18x + 10x + 15$ *Add all terms inside the rectangle.*

$2x^3 - 9x^2 - 8x + 15$ *Combine like terms.*

 **Multiply.**

4a. $(x + 3)(x^2 - 4x + 6)$

4b. $(3x + 2)(x^2 - 2x + 5)$

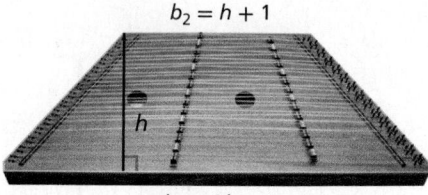

$b_2 = h + 1$

h

$b_1 = 2h - 1$

EXAMPLE 5   *Music Application*

A dulcimer is a musical instrument that is sometimes shaped like a trapezoid.

A   Write a polynomial that represents the area of the dulcimer shown.

$A = \dfrac{1}{2}h(b_1 + b_2)$ *Write the formula for area of a trapezoid.*

$= \dfrac{1}{2}h[(2h - 1) + (h + 1)]$ *Substitute $2h - 1$ for b_1 and $h + 1$ for b_2.*

$= \dfrac{1}{2}h(3h)$ *Combine like terms.*

$= \dfrac{3}{2}h^2$ *Simplify.*

The area is represented by $\dfrac{3}{2}h^2$.

B   Find the area of the dulcimer when the height is 22 inches.

$A = \dfrac{3}{2}h^2$ *Use the polynomial from part a.*

$= \dfrac{3}{2}(22)^2$ *Substitute 22 for h.*

$= \dfrac{3}{2}(484) = 726$

The area is 726 square inches.

 **5.** The length of a rectangle is 4 meters shorter than its width.

   a. Write a polynomial that represents the area of the rectangle.

   b. Find the area of the rectangle when the width is 6 meters.

THINK AND DISCUSS

1. Compare the vertical method for multiplying polynomials with the vertical method for multiplying whole numbers.

2. GET ORGANIZED Copy and complete the graphic organizer. In each box, multiply two polynomials using the given method.

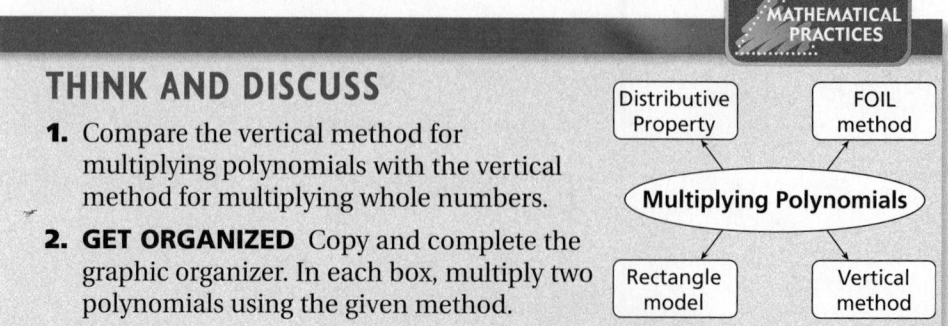

MATHEMATICAL PRACTICES

Exercises

Learn It Online
Homework Help Online
Parent Resources Online

GUIDED PRACTICE

Multiply.

SEE EXAMPLE 1

1. $(2x^2)(7x^4)$

2. $(-5mn^3)(4m^2n^2)$

3. $(6rs^2)(s^3t^2)\left(\frac{1}{2}r^4t^3\right)$

4. $\left(\frac{1}{3}a^5\right)(12a)$

5. $(-3x^4y^2)(-7x^3y)$

6. $(-2pq^3)(5p^2q^2)(-3q^4)$

SEE EXAMPLE 2

7. $4(x^2 + 2x + 1)$

8. $3ab(2a^2 + 3b^3)$

9. $2a^3b(3a^2b + ab^2)$

10. $-3x(x^2 - 4x + 6)$

11. $5x^2y(2xy^3 - y)$

12. $5m^2n^3 \cdot mn^2(4m - n)$

SEE EXAMPLE 3

13. $(x + 1)(x - 2)$

14. $(x + 1)^2$

15. $(x - 2)^2$

16. $(y - 3)(y - 5)$

17. $(4a^3 - 2b)(a - 3b^2)$

18. $(m^2 - 2mn)(3mn + n^2)$

SEE EXAMPLE 4

19. $(x + 5)(x^2 - 2x + 3)$

20. $(3x + 4)(x^2 - 5x + 2)$

21. $(2x - 4)(-3x^3 + 2x - 5)$

22. $(-4x + 6)(2x^3 - x^2 + 1)$ **23.** $(x - 5)(x^2 + x + 1)$

24. $(a + b)(a - b)(b - a)$

SEE EXAMPLE 5

25. Photography The length of a rectangular photograph is 3 inches less than twice the width.

  a. Write a polynomial that represents the area of the photograph.

  b. Find the area of the photograph when the width is 4 inches.

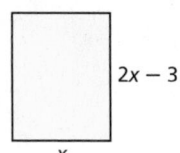
$2x - 3$
x

PRACTICE AND PROBLEM SOLVING

Multiply.

Independent Practice	
For Exercises	See Example
26–34	1
35–43	2
44–52	3
53–61	4
62	5

Extra Practice

See Extra Practice for more Skills Practice and Applications Practice exercises.

26. $(3x^2)(8x^5)$

27. $(-2r^3s^4)(6r^2s)$

28. $(15xy^2)\left(\frac{1}{3}x^2z^3\right)(y^3z^4)$

29. $(-2a^3)(-5a)$

30. $(6x^3y^2)(-2x^2y)$

31. $(-3a^2b)(-2b^3)(-a^3b^2)$

32. $(7x^2)(xy^5)(2x^3y^2)$

33. $(-4a^3bc^2)(a^3b^2c)(3ab^4c^5)$ **34.** $(12mn^2)(2m^2n)(mn)$

35. $9s(s + 6)$

36. $9(2x^2 - 5x)$

37. $3x(9x^2 - 4x)$

38. $3(2x^2 + 5x + 4)$

39. $5s^2t^3(2s - 3t^2)$

40. $x^2y^3 \cdot 5x^2y(6x + y^2)$

41. $-5x(2x^2 - 3x - 1)$

42. $-2a^2b^3(3ab^2 - a^2b)$

43. $-7x^3y \cdot x^2y^2(2x - y)$

44. $(x + 5)(x - 3)$

45. $(x + 4)^2$

46. $(m - 5)^2$

47. $(5x - 2)(x + 3)$

48. $(3x - 4)^2$

49. $(5x + 2)(2x - 1)$

50. $(x - 1)(x - 2)$

51. $(x - 8)(7x + 4)$

52. $(2x + 7)(3x + 7)$

53. $(x + 2)(x^2 - 3x + 5)$

54. $(2x + 5)(x^2 - 4x + 3)$

55. $(5x - 1)(-2x^3 + 4x - 3)$

56. $(x - 3)(x^2 - 5x + 6)$

57. $(2x^2 - 3)(4x^3 - x^2 + 7)$

58. $(x - 4)^3$

59. $(x - 2)(x^2 + 2x + 1)$

60. $(2x + 10)(4 - x + 6x^3)$

61. $(1 - x)^3$

62. Geometry The length of the rectangle at right is 3 feet longer than its width.

  a. Write a polynomial that represents the area of the rectangle.

  b. Find the area of the rectangle when the width is 5 feet.

$x + 3$
x

63. A square tabletop has side lengths of $(4x - 6)$ units. Write a polynomial that represents the area of the tabletop.

64. a. Marie is creating a garden. She designs a rectangular garden with a length of $(x + 4)$ feet and a width of $(x + 1)$ feet. Draw a diagram of Marie's garden with the length and width labeled.

b. Write a polynomial that represents the area of Marie's garden.

c. What is the area when $x = 4$?

65. Copy and complete the table below.

	A	Degree of A	B	Degree of B	A · B	Degree of A · B
	$2x^2$	2	$3x^5$	5	$6x^7$	7
a.	$5x^3$	▨	$2x^2 + 1$	▨	▨	▨
b.	$x^2 + 2$	▨	$x^2 - x$	▨	▨	▨
c.	$x - 3$	▨	$x^3 - 2x^2 + 1$	▨	▨	▨

d. Use the results from the table to complete the following: The product of a polynomial of degree m and a polynomial of degree n has a degree of ▨.

 Geometry Write a polynomial that represents the area of each rectangle.

66.
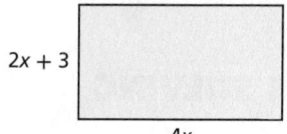
$2x + 3$

$4x$

67.
$3(2x + 1)$
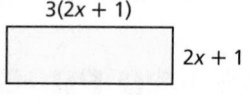
$2x + 1$

68.
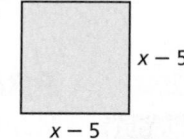
$x - 5$

$x - 5$

69. Sports The length of a regulation team handball court is twice its width.

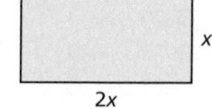
x

$2x$

a. Write a polynomial that represents the area of the court.

b. The width of a team handball court is 20 meters. Find the area of the court.

Multiply.

70. $(1.5a^3)(4a^6)$

71. $(2x + 5)(x - 6)$

72. $(3g - 1)(g + 5)$

73. $(4x - 2y)(2x - 3y)$

74. $(x + 3)(x - 3)$

75. $(1.5x - 3)(4x + 2)$

76. $(x - 10)(x + 4)$

77. $x^2(x + 3)$

78. $(x + 1)(x^2 + 2x)$

79. $(x - 4)(2x^2 + x - 6)$

80. $(a + b)(a - b)^2$

81. $(2p - 3q)^3$

82. Multi-Step A rectangular swimming pool is 25 feet long and 10 feet wide. It is surrounded by a fence that is x feet from each side of the pool.

a. Draw a diagram of this situation.

b. Write expressions for the length and width of the fenced region. (*Hint:* How much longer is one side of the fenced region than the corresponding side of the pool?)

c. Write an expression for the area of the fenced region.

 83. Write About It Explain why the FOIL method can be used to multiply only two binomials at a time.

 **84. Geometry** Write a polynomial that represents the volume of the rectangular prism.

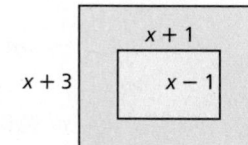

$x + 2$

$x + 5$

x

85. Critical Thinking Is there any value for x that would make the statement $(x + 3)^3 = x^3 + 3^3$ true? Give an example to justify your answer.

86. Estimation The length of a rectangle is 1 foot more than its width. Write a polynomial that represents the area of the rectangle. Estimate the width of the rectangle if its area is 25 square feet.

TEST PREP

87. Which of the following products is equal to $a^2 - 5a - 6$?

Ⓐ $(a - 1)(a - 5)$ Ⓑ $(a - 2)(a - 3)$ Ⓒ $(a + 1)(a - 6)$ Ⓓ $(a + 2)(a - 3)$

88. Which of the following is equal to $2a(a^2 - 1)$?

Ⓕ $2a^2 - 2a$ Ⓖ $2a^3 - 1$ Ⓗ $2a^3 - 2a$ Ⓙ $2a^2 - 1$

89. What is the degree of the product of $3x^3y^2z$ and x^2yz?

Ⓐ 5 Ⓑ 6 Ⓒ 7 Ⓓ 10

CHALLENGE AND EXTEND

Simplify.

90. $6x^2 - 2(3x^2 - 2x + 4)$ **91.** $x^2 - 2x(x + 3)$ **92.** $x(4x - 2) + 3x(x + 1)$

93. The diagram shows a sandbox and the frame that surrounds it.

  a. Write a polynomial that represents the area of the sandbox.

  b. Write a polynomial that represents the area of the frame that surrounds the sandbox.

$x + 5$

$x + 1$

$x + 3$

$x - 1$

94. Geometry The side length of a square is $(8 + 2x)$ units. The area of this square is the same as the perimeter of another square with a side length of $(x^2 + 48)$ units. Find the value of x.

95. Write a polynomial that represents the product of three consecutive integers. Let x represent the first integer.

96. Find m and n so that $x^m(x^n + x^{n-2}) = x^5 + x^3$.

97. Find a so that $2x^a(5x^{2a-3} + 2x^{2a+2}) = 10x^3 + 4x^8$

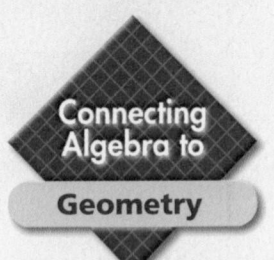

Volume and Surface Area

The volume V of a three-dimensional figure is the amount of space it occupies. The surface area S is the total area of the two-dimensional surfaces that make up the figure.

Rectangular Prism

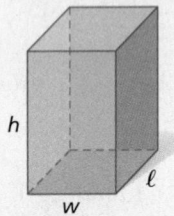

$V = \ell wh$
$S = 2(\ell w + \ell h + wh)$

Cylinder

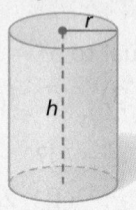

$V = \pi r^2 h$
$S = 2\pi r^2 + 2\pi rh$

Cone

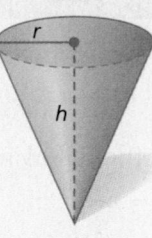

$V = \frac{1}{3}\pi r^2 h$

Pyramid

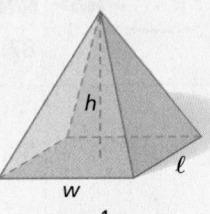

$V = \frac{1}{3}\ell wh$

Example

Write and simplify a polynomial expression for the volume of the cone. Leave the symbol π in your answer.

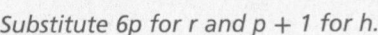

$V = \frac{1}{3}\pi r^2 h$ — *Choose the correct formula.*

$= \frac{1}{3}\pi(6p)^2(p+1)$ — *Substitute 6p for r and p + 1 for h.*

$= \frac{1}{3}\pi(36p^2)(p+1)$ — *Use the Power of a Product Property.*

$= \frac{1}{3}(36)\pi[p^2(p+1)]$ — *Use the Associative and Commutative Properties of Multiplication.*

$= 12\pi p^2(p+1)$ — *Distribute 12πp².*

$= 12\pi p^3 + 12\pi p^2$

Try This

Write and simplify a polynomial expression for the volume of each figure.

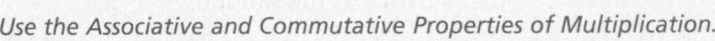

1.

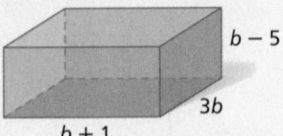

2.

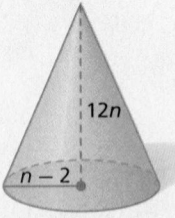

3.

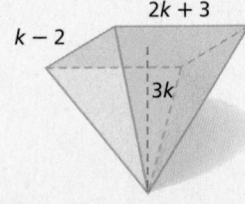

Write and simplify a polynomial expression for the surface area of each figure.

4.

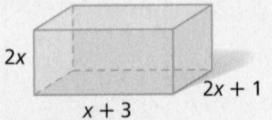

5.

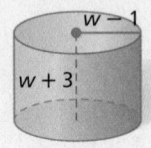

6.

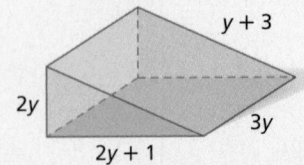

Closure

CC.9-12.A.APR.1 Understand that polynomials form a system analogous to the integers, namely, they are closed under the operations of addition, subtraction, and multiplication; add, subtract, and multiply polynomials. *Also* CC.9-12.N.RN.3

Objective
Identify sets and the operations under which they are closed.

Vocabulary
set
element
subset
closure

A **set** is a collection of objects. Each object in a set is called an **element** of the set. A set may have no elements, a finite number of elements, or an infinite number of elements. For example, $N = \{1, 2, 3, \ldots\}$ describes the set of natural numbers.

A **subset** is a set contained entirely within another set. For example, $A = \{2, 6, 11, 50\}$ is a subset of set N above. Also, N is a subset of the set of real numbers. The diagram below shows other subsets of the real numbers.

Real Numbers

Rational Numbers (Q)   Irrational Numbers

$\frac{27}{4}$ $0.\overline{3}$ $-\frac{10}{11}$

Integers (Z) $\sqrt{17}$

-3 -2

-1 Whole Numbers (W) $-\sqrt{11}$

0 $\sqrt{2}$

Natural Numbers (N)

1 3

4.5 2 $\frac{5}{9}$ π

A set of numbers is *closed*, or has **closure**, under a given operation if the result of the operation on any two numbers in the set is also in the set. For example, the set of even numbers is closed under addition, since the sum of two even numbers is also an even number.

Closure Properties of the Real Numbers

WORDS	NUMBERS	ALGEBRA
The real numbers are closed under addition, subtraction, and multiplication.	$6.1 + \sqrt{2}$, $6.1 - \sqrt{2}$, and $6.1 \times \sqrt{2}$ are all real numbers.	For real numbers a and b, $a + b$, $a - b$, and ab are real numbers.

EXAMPLE 1 **Determining Closure of Sets of Numbers**

A Is the set $\{-1, 0, 1\}$ closed under multiplication?

Multiply each pair of elements in the set. Check whether each product is in the set.

$-1 \times (-1) = 1$ ✓ $-1 \times 1 = -1$ ✓ $0 \times 1 = 0$ ✓
$-1 \times 0 = 0$ ✓ $0 \times 0 = 0$ ✓ $1 \times 1 = 1$ ✓

The set $\{-1, 0, 1\}$ is closed under multiplication.

Helpful Hint

Remember the Commutative Property of Multiplication.

If $1 \times (-1) = -1$, then $-1 \times 1 = -1$. Only one instance needs to be tested.

B Show that the set of irrational numbers is not closed under multiplication.

Find two irrational numbers whose product is not an irrational number.

$$\sqrt{2} \times \sqrt{2} = \sqrt{4} = 2 \qquad \textit{2 is not irrational.}$$

The set of irrational numbers is not closed under multiplication.

 **1.** Show that the set of whole numbers is not closed under subtraction.

The set of polynomials also has closure under certain operations. The closure properties of polynomials are similar to the closure properties of real numbers.

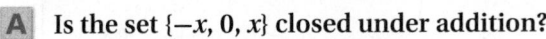

Closure Properties of Polynomials		
WORDS	**EXAMPLES**	**ALGEBRA**
The set of all polynomials is closed under addition, subtraction, and multiplication.	$x^2 + (x + 1)$, $x^2 - (x + 1)$ and $x^2(x + 1)$ are all polynomials.	For polynomials p and q, $p + q$, $p - q$, and pq are all polynomials.

EXAMPLE 2 **Determining Closure of Sets of Polynomials**

A Is the set $\{-x, 0, x\}$ closed under addition?

Add each pair of elements in the set. Check whether each sum is in the set.

$-x + 0 = -x$ ✓ $-x + (-x) = -2x$ ✗ $0 + 0 = 0$ ✓
$-x + x = 0$ ✓ $0 + x = x$ ✓ $x + x = 2x$ ✗

The set $\{-x, 0, x\}$ is not closed under addition.

B Show that the set of polynomials is not closed under division.

Find two polynomials, a and b, such that their quotient, $\frac{a}{b}$, is not a polynomial. Try $a = x + 1$ and $b = 0$.

$\dfrac{x + 1}{0}$ = undefined   *The result is not a polynomial.*

The set of polynomials is not closed under division.

 **2.** Is the set $\{x, x + 1, x^2 - 1\}$ closed under division?

EXTENSION
Exercises

Determine whether the following sets are closed under addition, subtraction, multiplication, and division.

1. $\{-1, 0, 1\}$ **2.** $\{0, 8\}$ **3.** $\{x^2, 1\}$

4. $\{0, x\}$ **5.** $\{-x^3, 1, x^3\}$ **6.** $\{-x, 1, x + 1\}$

7. $\{-1, 1\}$ **8.** $\{-1, 0, x\}$ **9.** $\{-1, x + 3, 1\}$

10. The set of whole numbers   **11.** The set of natural numbers   **12.** The set of integers

13. Polynomials without a constant term   **14.** The set of rational numbers   **15.** The set of real numbers

 16. **Write About It** Compare closure properties under the four operations for the set of rational numbers and the set of irrational numbers.

6-6

Special Products of Binomials

CC.9-12.A.APR.1 Understand that polynomials form a system analogous to the integers, namely, they are closed under the operations of addition, subtraction, and multiplication; add, subtract, and multiply polynomials.

Objective
Find special products of binomials.

Vocabulary
perfect-square trinomial
difference of two squares

Why learn this?

You can use special products to find areas, such as the area of a deck around a pond. (See Example 4.)

Imagine a square with sides of length $(a + b)$:

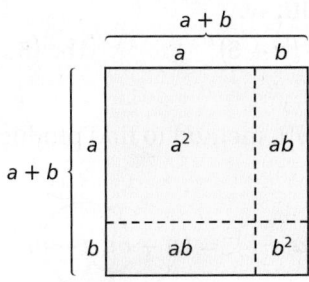

The area of this square is $(a + b)(a + b)$, or $(a + b)^2$. The area of this square can also be found by adding the areas of the smaller squares and rectangles inside. The sum of the areas inside is $a^2 + ab + ab + b^2$.

This means that $(a + b)^2 = a^2 + 2ab + b^2$.

You can use the FOIL method to verify this:

$$(a + b)^2 = (a + b)(a + b) = a^2 + ab + ab + b^2$$
$$= a^2 + 2ab + b^2$$

A trinomial of the form $a^2 + 2ab + b^2$ is called a *perfect-square trinomial*. A **perfect-square trinomial** is a trinomial that is the result of squaring a binomial.

EXAMPLE 1   **Finding Products in the Form $(a + b)^2$**

Multiply.

A $(x + 4)^2$

$(a + b)^2 = a^2 + 2ab + b^2$ *Use the rule for $(a + b)^2$.*

$(x + 4)^2 = x^2 + 2(x)(4) + 4^2$ *Identify a and b: a = x and b = 4.*

$\qquad = x^2 + 8x + 16$ *Simplify.*

B $(3x + 2y)^2$

$(a + b)^2 = a^2 + 2ab + b^2$ *Use the rule for $(a + b)^2$.*

$(3x + 2y)^2 = (3x)^2 + 2(3x)(2y) + (2y)^2$ *Identify a and b: a = 3x and b = 2y.*

$\qquad = 9x^2 + 12xy + 4y^2$ *Simplify.*

Multiply.

 $\left(4 + s^2\right)^2$

$\left(a + b\right)^2 = a^2 + 2ab + b^2$ *Use the rule for $(a + b)^2$.*

$\left(4 + s^2\right)^2 = (4)^2 + 2(4)\left(s^2\right) + \left(s^2\right)^2$ *Identify a and b: a = 4 and b = s^2.*

$= 16 + 8s^2 + s^4$ *Simplify.*

D $\left(-m + 3\right)^2$

$\left(a + b\right)^2 = a^2 + 2ab + b^2$ *Use the rule for $(a + b)^2$.*

$\left(-m + 3\right)^2 = (-m)^2 + 2(-m)(3) + 3^2$ *Identify a and b: a = −m and b = 3.*

$= m^2 - 6m + 9$ *Simplify.*

CHECK IT OUT! **Multiply.**

1a. $\left(x + 6\right)^2$ **1b.** $\left(5a + b\right)^2$ **1c.** $\left(1 + c^3\right)^2$

You can use the FOIL method to find products in the form $\left(a - b\right)^2$:

$$\left(a - b\right)^2 = (a - b)(a - b) = a^2 - ab - ab + b^2$$

$$= a^2 - 2ab + b^2$$

A trinomial of the form $a^2 - 2ab + b^2$ is also a perfect-square trinomial because it is the result of squaring the binomial $\left(a - b\right)$.

EXAMPLE 2 **Finding Products in the Form $\left(a - b\right)^2$**

Multiply.

A $\left(x - 5\right)^2$

$\left(a - b\right)^2 = a^2 - 2ab + b^2$ *Use the rule for $(a - b)^2$.*

$\left(x - 5\right)^2 = x^2 - 2(x)(5) + 5^2$ *Identify a and b: a = x and b = 5.*

$= x^2 - 10x + 25$ *Simplify.*

B $\left(6a - 1\right)^2$

$\left(a - b\right)^2 = a^2 - 2ab + b^2$ *Use the rule for $(a - b)^2$.*

$\left(6a - 1\right)^2 = (6a)^2 - 2(6a)(1) + (1)^2$ *Identify a and b: a = 6a and b = 1.*

$= 36a^2 - 12a + 1$ *Simplify.*

C $\left(4c - 3d\right)^2$

$\left(a - b\right)^2 = a^2 - 2ab + b^2$ *Use the rule for $(a - b)^2$.*

$\left(4c - 3d\right)^2 = (4c)^2 - 2(4c)(3d) + (3d)^2$ *Identify a and b: a = 4c and b = 3d.*

$= 16c^2 - 24cd + 9d^2$ *Simplify.*

D $\left(3 - x^2\right)^2$

$\left(a - b\right)^2 = (a)^2 - 2ab + b^2$ *Use the rule for $(a - b)^2$.*

$\left(3 - x^2\right)^2 = (3)^2 - 2(3)\left(x^2\right) + \left(x^2\right)^2$ *Identify a and b: a = 3 and b = x^2.*

$= 9 - 6x^2 + x^4$ *Simplify.*

CHECK IT OUT! **Multiply.**

2a. $\left(x - 7\right)^2$ **2b.** $\left(3b - 2c\right)^2$ **2c.** $\left(a^2 - 4\right)^2$

You can use an area model to see that $(a + b)(a - b) = a^2 - b^2$.

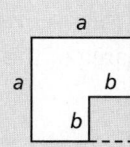

Begin with a square with area a^2. Remove a square with area b^2. The area of the new figure is $a^2 - b^2$.

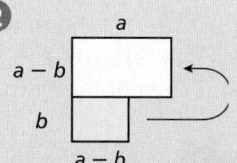

Then remove the smaller rectangle on the bottom. Turn it and slide it up next to the top rectangle.

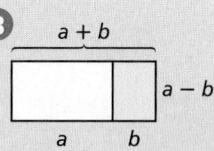

The new arrangement is a rectangle with length $a + b$ and width $a - b$. Its area is $(a + b)(a - b)$.

So $(a + b)(a - b) = a^2 - b^2$. A binomial of the form $a^2 - b^2$ is called a **difference of two squares**.

EXAMPLE 3 **Finding Products in the Form $(a + b)(a - b)$**

Multiply.

A $(x + 6)(x - 6)$

$(a + b)(a - b) = a^2 - b^2$ *Use the rule for $(a + b)(a - b)$.*

$(x + 6)(x - 6) = x^2 - 6^2$ *Identify a and b: a = x and b = 6.*

$= x^2 - 36$ *Simplify.*

B $(x^2 + 2y)(x^2 - 2y)$

$(a + b)(a - b) = a^2 - b^2$ *Use the rule for $(a + b)(a - b)$.*

$(x^2 + 2y)(x^2 - 2y) = (x^2)^2 - (2y)^2$ *Identify a and b: $a = x^2$ and b = 2y.*

$= x^4 - 4y^2$ *Simplify.*

C $(7 + n)(7 - n)$

$(a + b)(a - b) = a^2 - b^2$ *Use the rule for $(a + b)(a - b)$.*

$(7 + n)(7 - n) = 7^2 - n^2$ *Identify a and b: a = 7 and b = n.*

$= 49 - n^2$ *Simplify.*

 **Multiply.**

3a. $(x + 8)(x - 8)$ **3b.** $(3 + 2y^2)(3 - 2y^2)$ **3c.** $(9 + r)(9 - r)$

EXAMPLE 4 *Problem-Solving Application*

A square koi pond is surrounded by a gravel path. Write an expression that represents the area of the path.

MATHEMATICAL PRACTICES

Make sense of problems and persevere in solving them.

1. **Understand the Problem**

The **answer** will be an expression that represents the area of the path.

List the important information:

• The pond is a square with a side length of $x - 2$.

• The path has a side length of $x + 2$.

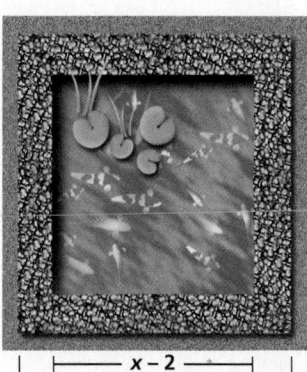

2 Make a Plan

The area of the pond is $(x - 2)^2$. The total area of the path plus the pond is $(x + 2)^2$. You can subtract the area of the pond from the total area to find the area of the path.

3 Solve

Step 1 Find the total area.

$$(x + 2)^2 = x^2 + 2(x)(2) + 2^2 \qquad \textit{Use the rule for } (a + b)^2\text{: } a = x \text{ and } b = 2.$$

$$= \boxed{x^2 + 4x + 4}$$

Step 2 Find the area of the pond.

$$(x - 2)^2 = x^2 - 2(x)(2) + 2^2 \qquad \textit{Use the rule for } (a - b)^2\text{: } a = x \text{ and } b = 2.$$

$$= \boxed{x^2 - 4x + 4}$$

Remember!

To subtract a polynomial, add the opposite of *each* term.

Step 3 Find the area of the path.

area of path	=	total area	−	area of pond

$$a = \boxed{x^2 + 4x + 4} - \left(\boxed{x^2 - 4x + 4} \right)$$

$$= x^2 + 4x + 4 - x^2 + 4x - 4 \qquad \textit{Identify like terms.}$$

$$= (x^2 - x^2) + (4x + 4x) + (4 - 4) \quad \textit{Group like terms together.}$$

$$= 8x$$

The area of the path is $8x$. *Combine like terms.*

4 Look Back

Suppose that $x = 10$. Then one side of the path is 12, and the total area is 12^2, or 144. Also, if $x = 10$, one side of the pond is 8, and the area of the pond is 8^2, or 64. This means the area of the path is $144 - 64 = 80$.

According to the solution above, the area of the path is $8x$. If $x = 10$, then $8x = 8(10) = 80$. ✓

 **4.** Write an expression that represents the area of the swimming pool at right.

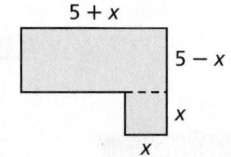

Special Products of Binomials

Perfect-Square Trinomials

$$(a + b)^2 = (a + b)(a + b) = a^2 + 2ab + b^2$$
$$(a - b)^2 = (a - b)(a - b) = a^2 - 2ab + b^2$$

Difference of Two Squares

$$(a + b)(a - b) = a^2 - b^2$$

THINK AND DISCUSS

1. Use the FOIL method to verify that $(a + b)(a - b) = a^2 - b^2$.

2. When a binomial is squared, the middle term of the resulting trinomial is twice the _____?_____ of the first and last terms.

3. GET ORGANIZED Copy and complete the graphic organizer. Complete the special product rules and give an example of each.

Special Products of Binomials		
Perfect-Square Trinomials		Difference of Two Squares
$(a + b)^2 = ?$	$(a - b)^2 = ?$	$(a + b)(a - b) = ?$

6-6 Exercises

Learn It Online
Homework Help Online
Parent Resources Online

GUIDED PRACTICE

1. Vocabulary In your own words, describe a *perfect-square trinomial*.

Multiply.

SEE EXAMPLE **1**

2. $(x + 7)^2$ **3.** $(2 + x)^2$ **4.** $(x + 1)^2$

5. $(2x + 6)^2$ **6.** $(5x + 9)^2$ **7.** $(2a + 7b)^2$

SEE EXAMPLE **2**

8. $(x - 6)^2$ **9.** $(x - 2)^2$ **10.** $(2x - 1)^2$

11. $(8 - x)^2$ **12.** $(6p - q)^2$ **13.** $(7a - 2b)^2$

SEE EXAMPLE **3**

14. $(x + 5)(x - 5)$ **15.** $(x + 6)(x - 6)$ **16.** $(5x + 1)(5x - 1)$

17. $(2x^2 + 3)(2x^2 - 3)$ **18.** $(9 - x^3)(9 + x^3)$ **19.** $(2x - 5y)(2x + 5y)$

SEE EXAMPLE **4**

20. Geometry Write a polynomial that represents the area of the figure.

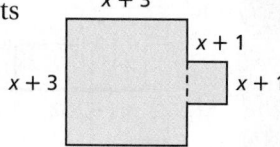

PRACTICE AND PROBLEM SOLVING

Independent Practice	
For Exercises	See Example
21–26	1
27–32	2
33–38	3
39	4

Extra Practice

See Extra Practice for more Skills Practice and Applications Practice exercises.

Multiply.

21. $(x + 3)^2$ **22.** $(4 + z)^2$ **23.** $(x^2 + y^2)^2$

24. $(p + 2q^3)^2$ **25.** $(2 + 3x)^2$ **26.** $(r^2 + 5t)^2$

27. $(s^2 - 7)^2$ **28.** $(2c - d^3)^2$ **29.** $(a - 8)^2$

30. $(5 - w)^2$ **31.** $(3x - 4)^2$ **32.** $(1 - x^2)^2$

33. $(a - 10)(a + 10)$ **34.** $(y + 4)(y - 4)$ **35.** $(7x + 3)(7x - 3)$

36. $(x^2 - 2)(x^2 + 2)$ **37.** $(5a^2 + 9)(5a^2 - 9)$ **38.** $(x^3 + y^2)(x^3 - y^2)$

39. Entertainment Write a polynomial that represents the area of the circular puzzle. Remember that the formula for area of a circle is $A = \pi r^2$, where r is the radius of the circle. Leave the symbol π in your answer.

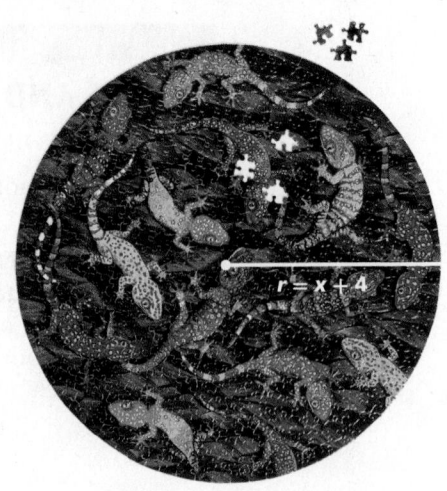

r = x + 4

40. Multi-Step A square has sides that are $(x - 1)$ units long and a rectangle has a length of x units and a width of $(x - 2)$ units.

   a. What are the possible values of x? Explain.

   b. Which has the greater area, the square or the rectangle?

   c. What is the difference in the areas?

Multiply.

41. $(x + y)^2$ **42.** $(x - y)^2$ **43.** $(x^2 + 4)(x^2 - 4)$

44. $(x^2 + 4)^2$ **45.** $(x^2 - 4)^2$ **46.** $(1 - x)^2$

47. $(1 + x)^2$ **48.** $(1 - x)(1 + x)$ **49.** $(x^3 - a^3)(x^3 - a^3)$

50. $(5 + n)(5 + n)$ **51.** $(6a - 5b)(6a + 5b)$ **52.** $(r - 4t^4)(r - 4t^4)$

Copy and complete the tables to verify the special products of binomials.

	a	b	$(a - b)^2$	$a^2 - 2ab + b^2$
	1	4	$(1 - 4)^2 = 9$	$1^2 - 2(1)(4) + 4^2 = 9$
53.	2	4	▨	▨
54.	3	2	▨	▨

	a	b	$(a + b)^2$	$a^2 + 2ab + b^2$
55.	1	4	▨	▨
56.	2	5	▨	▨
57.	3	0	▨	▨

	a	b	$(a + b)(a - b)$	$a^2 - b^2$
58.	1	4	▨	▨
59.	2	3	▨	▨
60.	3	2	▨	▨

61. Math History The Babylonians used tables of squares and the formula $ab = \dfrac{(a + b)^2 - (a - b)^2}{4}$ to multiply two numbers. Use this formula to find the product $35 \cdot 24$.

62. Critical Thinking Find a value of c that makes $16x^2 - 24x + c$ a perfect-square trinomial.

63. /// ERROR ANALYSIS /// Explain the error below. What is the correct product?

$$(a - b)^2 = a^2 - b^2$$

MULTI-STEP TEST PREP

64. a. Michael is fencing part of his yard. He started with a square of length x on each side. He then added 3 feet to the length and subtracted 3 feet from the width. Make a sketch to show the fenced area with the length and width labeled.

b. Write a polynomial that represents the area of the fenced region.

c. Michael bought a total of 48 feet of fencing. What is the area of his fenced region?

65. Critical Thinking The polynomial $ax^2 - 49$ is a difference of two squares. Find all possible values of a between 1 and 100 inclusive.

 66. Write About It When is the product of two binomials also a binomial? Explain and give an example.

TEST PREP

67. What is $(5x - 6y)(5x - 6y)$?

    Ⓐ $25x^2 - 22xy + 36y^2$ Ⓒ $25x^2 + 22xy + 36y^2$

    Ⓑ $25x^2 - 60xy + 36y^2$ Ⓓ $25x^2 + 60xy + 36y^2$

68. Which product is represented by the model?

    Ⓕ $(2x + 5)(2x + 5)$ Ⓗ $(5x + 2)(5x - 2)$

    Ⓖ $(5x - 2)(5x - 2)$ Ⓙ $(5x + 2)(5x + 2)$

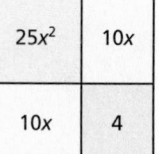

69. If $a + b = 12$ and $a^2 - b^2 = 96$ what is the value of a?

    Ⓐ 2   Ⓑ 4   Ⓒ 8   Ⓓ 10

70. If $rs = 15$ and $(r + s)^2 = 64$, what is the value of $r^2 + s^2$?

    Ⓕ 25   Ⓖ 30   Ⓗ 34   Ⓙ 49

CHALLENGE AND EXTEND

71. Multiply $(x + 4)(x + 4)(x - 4)$.   **72.** Multiply $(x + 4)(x - 4)(x - 4)$.

73. If $x^2 + bx + c$ is a perfect-square trinomial, what is the relationship between b and c?

74. You can multiply two numbers by rewriting the numbers as the difference of two squares. For example:

$$36 \cdot 24 = (30 + 6)(30 - 6) = 30^2 - 6^2 = 900 - 36 = 864$$

Use this method to multiply $27 \cdot 19$. Explain how you rewrote the numbers.

MULTI-STEP TEST PREP

MATHEMATICAL PRACTICES

Make sense of problems and persevere in solving them.

Polynomials

Don't Fence Me In James has 500 feet of fencing to enclose a rectangular region on his farm for some sheep.

1. Make a sketch of three possible regions that James could enclose and give the corresponding areas.

2. If the length of the region is x, find an expression for the width.

3. Use your answer to Problem 2 to write an equation for the area of the region.

4. Graph your equation from Problem 3 on your calculator. Sketch the graph.

5. James wants his fenced region to have the largest area possible using 500 feet of fencing. Find this area using the graph or a table of values.

6. What are the length and width of the region with the area from Problem 5? Describe this region.

READY TO GO ON?

Quiz for Lessons 6-3 Through 6-6

✓ 6-3 Polynomials

Write each polynomial in standard form and give the leading coefficient.

1. $4r^2 + 2r^6 - 3r$ **2.** $y^2 + 7 - 8y^3 + 2y$ **3.** $-12t^3 - 4t + t^4$

4. $n + 3 + 3n^2$ **5.** $2 + 3x^3$ **6.** $-3a^2 + 16 + a^7 + a$

Classify each polynomial according to its degree and number of terms.

7. $2x^3 + 5x - 4$ **8.** $5b^2$ **9.** $6p^2 + 3p - p^4 + 2p^3$

10. $x^2 + 12 - x$ **11.** $-2x^3 - 5 + x - 2x^7$ **12.** $5 - 6b^2 + b - 4b^4$

13. Business The function $C(x) = x^3 - 15x + 14$ gives the cost to manufacture x units of a product. What is the cost to manufacture 900 units?

✓ 6-4 Adding and Subtracting Polynomials

Add or subtract.

14. $(10m^3 + 4m^2) + (7m^2 + 3m)$ **15.** $(3t^2 - 2t) + (9t^2 + 4t - 6)$

16. $(12d^6 - 3d^2) + (2d^4 + 1)$ **17.** $(6y^3 + 4y^2) - (2y^2 + 3y)$

18. $(7n^2 - 3n) - (5n^2 + 5n)$ **19.** $(b^2 - 10) - (-5b^3 + 4b)$

20. Geometry The measures of the sides of a triangle are shown as polynomials. Write a simplified polynomial to represent the perimeter of the triangle.

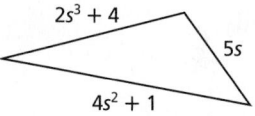

✓ 6-5 Multiplying Polynomials

Multiply.

21. $2h^3 \cdot 5h^5$ **22.** $(s^8 t^4)(-6st^3)$ **23.** $2ab(5a^3 + 3a^2 b)$

24. $(3k + 5)^2$ **25.** $(2x^3 + 3y)(4x^2 + y)$ **26.** $(p^2 + 3p)(9p^2 - 6p - 5)$

27. Geometry Write a simplified polynomial expression for the area of a parallelogram whose base is $(x + 7)$ units and whose height is $(x - 3)$ units.

✓ 6-6 Special Products of Binomials

Multiply.

28. $(d + 9)^2$ **29.** $(3 + 2t)^2$ **30.** $(2x + 5y)^2$ **31.** $(m - 4)^2$

32. $(a - b)^2$ **33.** $(3w - 1)^2$ **34.** $(c + 2)(c - 2)$ **35.** $(5r + 6)(5r - 6)$

36. Sports A child's basketball has a radius of $(x - 5)$ inches. Write a polynomial that represents the surface area of the basketball. (The formula for the surface area of a sphere is $S = 4\pi r^2$, where r represents the radius of the sphere.) Leave the symbol π in your answer.

Study Guide: Review

Vocabulary

binomial	index	quadratic
cubic	leading coefficient	standard form of a
degree of a monomial	monomial	polynomial
degree of a polynomial	perfect-square trinomial	trinomial
difference of two squares	polynomial	

Complete the sentences below with vocabulary words from the list above.

1. A(n) ___?___ polynomial is a polynomial of degree 3.

2. When a polynomial is written with the terms in order from highest to lowest degree, it is in ___?___ .

3. A(n) ___?___ is a number, a variable, or a product of numbers and variables with whole-number exponents.

4. A(n) ___?___ is a polynomial with three terms.

6-1 Integer Exponents

EXAMPLES

Simplify.

■ -2^{-4}

$$-2^{-4} = -\frac{1}{2^4} = -\frac{1}{2 \cdot 2 \cdot 2 \cdot 2} = -\frac{1}{16}$$

■ 3^0

$3^0 = 1$ *Any nonzero number raised to the zero power is 1.*

■ **Evaluate** $r^3 s^{-4}$ **for** $r = -3$ **and** $s = 2$.

$r^3 s^{-4}$

$$(-3)^3 (2)^{-4} = \frac{(-3)(-3)(-3)}{2 \cdot 2 \cdot 2 \cdot 2} = -\frac{27}{16}$$

■ **Simplify** $\dfrac{a^{-3} b^4}{c^{-2}}$.

$$\frac{a^{-3} b^4}{c^{-2}} = \frac{b^4 c^2}{a^3}$$

EXERCISES

5. The diameter of a certain bearing is 2^{-5} in. Simplify this expression.

Simplify.

6. $(3.6)^0$ **7.** $(-1)^{-4}$

8. 5^{-3} **9.** 10^{-4}

Evaluate each expression for the given value(s) of the variable(s).

10. b^{-4} for $b = 2$ **11.** $\left(\dfrac{2}{5} b\right)^{-4}$ for $b = 10$

12. $-2p^3 q^{-3}$ for $p = 3$ and $q = -2$

Simplify.

13. m^{-2} **14.** bc^0

15. $-\dfrac{1}{2} x^{-2} y^{-4}$ **16.** $\dfrac{2b^6}{c^{-4}}$

17. $\dfrac{3a^2 c^{-2}}{4b^0}$ **18.** $\dfrac{q^{-1} r^{-2}}{s^{-3}}$

6-2 Rational Exponents

EXAMPLES

■ Simplify $\sqrt[3]{r^6 s^{12}}$.

$\sqrt[3]{r^6 s^{12}} = \left(r^6 s^{12}\right)^{\frac{1}{3}}$ *Definition of $b^{\frac{1}{n}}$*

$= \left(r^6\right)^{\frac{1}{3}} \cdot \left(s^{12}\right)^{\frac{1}{3}}$ *Power of a Product Property*

$= \left(r^{6 \cdot \frac{1}{3}}\right) \cdot \left(s^{12 \cdot \frac{1}{3}}\right)$ *Power of a Power Property*

$= \left(r^2\right) \cdot \left(s^4\right)$ *Simplify exponents.*

$= r^2 s^4$

EXERCISES

Simplify each expression.

19. $81^{\frac{1}{2}}$

20. $343^{\frac{1}{3}}$

21. $64^{\frac{2}{3}}$

22. $\left(2^6\right)^{\frac{1}{2}}$

Simplify each expression. All variables represent nonnegative numbers.

23. $\sqrt[5]{z^{10}}$

24. $\sqrt[3]{125x^6}$

25. $\sqrt{x^8 y^6}$

26. $\sqrt[3]{m^6 n^{12}}$

6-3 Polynomials

EXAMPLES

■ Find the degree of the polynomial $3x^2 + 8x^5$.

$3x^2 + 8x^5$ *$8x^5$ has the highest degree.*

The degree is 5.

■ Classify the polynomial $y^3 - 2y$ according to its degree and number of terms.

Degree: 3
Terms: 2

The polynomial $y^3 - 2y$ is a **cubic binomial**.

EXERCISES

Find the degree of each polynomial.

27. 5

28. $8st^3$

29. $3z^6$

30. $6h$

Write each polynomial in standard form. Then give the leading coefficient.

31. $2n - 4 + 3n^2$

32. $2a - a^4 - a^6 + 3a^3$

Classify each polynomial according to its degree and number of terms.

33. $2s - 6$

34. $-8p^5$

35. $-m^4 - m^2 - 1$

36. 2

6-4 Adding and Subtracting Polynomials

Add.

- $(h^3 - 2h) + (3h^2 + 4h) - 2h^3$

  $(h^3 - 2h) + (3h^2 + 4h) - 2h^3$

  $(h^3 - 2h^3) + (3h^2) + (4h - 2h)$

  $-h^3 + 3h^2 + 2h$

Subtract.

- $(n^3 + 5 - 6n^2) - (3n^2 - 7)$

  $(n^3 + 5 - 6n^2) + (-3n^2 + 7)$

  $(n^3 + 5 - 6n^2) + (-3n^2 + 7)$

  $n^3 + (-6n^2 - 3n^2) + (5 + 7)$

  $n^3 - 9n^2 + 12$

Add or subtract.

37. $3t + 5 - 7t - 2$

38. $4x^5 - 6x^6 + 2x^5 - 7x^5$

39. $-h^3 - 2h^2 + 4h^3 - h^2 + 5$

40. $(3m - 7) + (2m^2 - 8m + 6)$

41. $(12 + 6p) - (p - p^2 + 4)$

42. $(3z - 9z^2 + 2) + (2z^2 - 4z + 8)$

43. $(10g - g^2 + 3) - (-4g^2 + 8g - 1)$

44. $(-5x^3 + 2x^2 - x + 5) - (-5x^3 + 3x^2 - 5x - 3)$

6-5 Multiplying Polynomials

Multiply.

- $(2x - 4)(3x + 5)$

  $2x(3x) + 2x(5) - 4(3x) - 4(5)$

  $6x^2 + 10x - 12x - 20$

  $6x^2 - 2x - 20$

- $(b - 2)(b^2 + 4b - 5)$

  $b(b^2) + b(4b) - b(5) - 2(b^2) - 2(4b) - 2(-5)$

  $b^3 + 4b^2 - 5b - 2b^2 - 8b + 10$

  $b^3 + 2b^2 - 13b + 10$

Multiply.

45. $(2r)(4r)$

46. $(3a^5)(2ab)$

47. $(-3xy)(-6x^2y)$

48. $(3s^3t^2)(2st^4)\left(\dfrac{1}{2} s^2 t^8\right)$

49. $2(x^2 - 4x + 6)$

50. $-3ab(ab - 2a^2b + 5a)$

51. $(a + 3)(a - 6)$

52. $(b - 9)(b + 3)$

53. $(x - 10)(x - 2)$

54. $(t - 1)(t + 1)$

55. $(2q + 6)(4q + 5)$

56. $(5g - 8)(4g - 1)$

6-6 Special Products of Binomials

EXAMPLES

Multiply.

- $(2h - 6)^2$
  $(2h - 6)^2 = (2h)^2 + 2(2h)(-6) + (-6)^2$
  $4h^2 - 24h + 36$

- $(4x - 3)(4x + 3)$
  $(4x - 3)(4x + 3) = (4x)^2 - 3^2$
  $16x^2 - 9$

EXERCISES

Multiply.

57. $(p - 4)^2$

58. $(x + 12)^2$

59. $(m + 6)^2$

60. $(3c + 7)^2$

61. $(2r - 1)^2$

62. $(3a - b)^2$

63. $(2n - 5)^2$

64. $(h - 13)^2$

65. $(x - 1)(x + 1)$

66. $(z + 15)(z - 15)$

67. $(c^2 - d)(c^2 + d)$

68. $(3k^2 + 7)(3k^2 - 7)$

CHAPTER TEST

Evaluate each expression for the given value(s) of the variable(s).

1. $\left(\frac{1}{3}b\right)^{-2}$ for $b = 12$

2. $\left(14 - a^0 b^2\right)^{-3}$ for $a = -2$ and $b = 4$

Simplify.

3. $2r^{-3}$

4. $-3f^0 g^{-1}$

5. $m^2 n^{-3}$

6. $\frac{1}{2} s^{-5} t^3$

7. Geometry The surface area of a cone is approximated by the polynomial $3.14r^2 + 3.14r\ell$, where r is the radius and ℓ is the slant height. Find the approximate surface area of a cone when $\ell = 5$ cm and $r = 3$ cm.

Simplify each expression. All variables represent nonnegative numbers.

8. $\left(\frac{27}{125}\right)^{\frac{1}{3}}$

9. $\sqrt[3]{43^3}$

10. $\sqrt{25y^8}$

11. $\sqrt[5]{3^5 t^{10}}$

Add or subtract.

12. $3a - 4b + 2a$

13. $\left(2b^2 - 4b^3\right) - \left(6b^3 + 8b^2\right)$

14. $-9g^2 + 3g - 4g^3 - 2g + 3g^2 - 4$

Multiply.

15. $-5\left(r^2 s - 6\right)$

16. $(2t - 7)(t + 4)$

17. $\left(4g - 1\right)\left(4g^2 - 5g - 3\right)$

18. $(m + 6)^2$

19. $(3t - 7)(3t + 7)$

20. $\left(3x^2 - 7\right)^2$

21. Carpentry Carpenters use a tool called a *speed square* to help them mark right angles. A speed square is a right triangle.

    a. Write a polynomial that represents the area of the speed square shown.

    b. Find the area when $x = 4.5$ in.

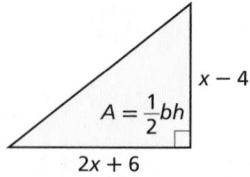

$x - 4$

$A = \frac{1}{2}bh$

$2x + 6$

COLLEGE ENTRANCE EXAM PRACTICE

FOCUS ON SAT

When you receive your SAT scores, you will find a percentile for each score. The percentile tells you what percent of students scored lower than you on the same test. Your percentile at the national and state levels may differ because of the different groups being compared.

You may use some types of calculators on the math section of the SAT. For about 40% of the test items, a graphing calculator is recommended. Bring a calculator that you are comfortable using. You won't have time to figure out how a new calculator works.

You may want to time yourself as you take this practice test. It should take you about 7 minutes to complete.

---

1. If $(x + 1)(x + 4) - (x - 1)(x - 2) = 0$, what is the value of x?

(A) -1

(B) $-\dfrac{1}{4}$

(C) 0

(D) $\dfrac{1}{4}$

(E) 1

---

2. Which of the following is equal to 4^5?

    I. $3^5 \times 1^5$

    II. 2^{10}

    III. $4^0 \times 4^5$

(A) I only

(B) II only

(C) I and II only

(D) II and III only

(E) I, II, and III

---

3. If $x^{-4} = 81$, then $x =$

(A) -3

(B) $\dfrac{1}{4}$

(C) $\dfrac{1}{3}$

(D) 3

(E) 9

---

4. What is the value of $2x^3 - 4x^2 + 3x + 1$ when $x = -2$?

(A) -37

(B) -25

(C) -5

(D) 7

(E) 27

---

5. What is the area of a rectangle with a length of $x - a$ and a width of $x + b$?

(A) $x^2 - a^2$

(B) $x^2 + b^2$

(C) $x^2 - abx + ab$

(D) $x^2 - ax - bx - ab$

(E) $x^2 + bx - ax - ab$

---

6. For integers greater than 0, define the following operations.

$$a\,\square\,b = 2a^2 + 3b$$

$$a\,\triangle\,b = 5a^2 - 2b$$

What is $(a\,\square\,b) + (a\,\triangle\,b)$?

(A) $7a^2 + b$

(B) $-3a^2 + 5b$

(C) $7a^2 - b$

(D) $3a^2 - 5b$

(E) $-3a^2 - b$

Any Question Type: Use a Diagram

When a test item includes a diagram, use it to help solve the problem. Gather as much information from the drawing as possible. However, keep in mind that diagrams are not always drawn to scale and can be misleading.

EXAMPLE 1

Multiple Choice What is the height of the triangle when $x = 4$ and $y = 1$?

- Ⓐ 2
- Ⓒ 8
- Ⓑ 4
- Ⓓ 16

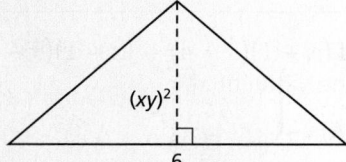

In the diagram, the height appears to be less than 6, so you might eliminate choices C and D. However, doing the math shows that the height is actually greater than 6. Do not rely solely on visual information. Always use the numbers given in the problem.

The height of the triangle is $(xy)^2$.

When $x = 4$ and $y = 1$, $(xy)^2 = (4 \cdot 1)^2 = (4)^2 = 16$.

Choice D is the correct answer.

If a test item does not have a diagram, draw a quick sketch of the problem situation. Label your diagram with the data given in the problem.

EXAMPLE 2

Short Response A square placemat is lying in the middle of a rectangular table. The side length of the placemat is $\left(\frac{x}{2}\right)$. The length of the table is $12x$, and the width is $8x$. Write a polynomial to represent the area of the placemat. Then write a polynomial to represent the area of the table that surrounds the placemat.

Use the information in the problem to draw and label a diagram. Then write the polynomials.

area of placemat $= s^2 = \left(\frac{x}{2}\right)^2 = \left(\frac{x}{2}\right)\left(\frac{x}{2}\right) = \frac{x^2}{4}$

area of table $= \ell w = (12x)(8x) = 96x^2$

area of table − area of placemat $= 96x^2 - \frac{x^2}{4} = \frac{384x^2 - x^2}{4} = \frac{383x^2}{4}$

The area of the placemat is $\frac{x^2}{4}$.

The area of the table that surrounds the placemat is $\frac{383x^2}{4}$.

Read each test item and answer the questions that follow.

Item A

Short Response The width of a rectangle is 1.5 feet more than 4 times its length. Write a polynomial expression for the area of the rectangle. What is the area when the length is 16.75 feet?

1. What is the unknown measure in this problem?

2. How will drawing a diagram help you solve the problem?

3. Draw and label a sketch of the situation.

Item B

Multiple Choice Rectangle *ABDC* is similar to rectangle *MNPO*. If the width of rectangle *ABDC* is 8, what is its length?

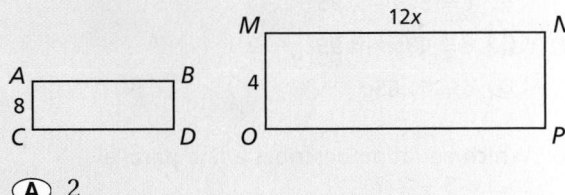

Ⓐ 2

Ⓑ 2*x*

Ⓒ 24*x*

Ⓓ 24

4. Look at the dimensions in the diagram. Do you think that the length of rectangle *ABDC* is greater or less than the length of rectangle *MNPO*?

5. Do you think the drawings reflect the information in the problem accurately? Why or why not?

6. Draw your own sketch to match the information in the problem.

Item C

Short Response Write a polynomial expression for the area of triangle *QRP*. Write a polynomial expression for the area of triangle *MNP*. Then use these expressions to write a polynomial expression for the area of *QRNM*.

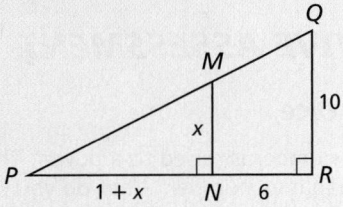

7. Describe how redrawing the figure can help you better understand the information in the problem.

8. After reading this test item, a student redrew the figure as shown below. Is this a correct interpretation of the original figure? Explain.

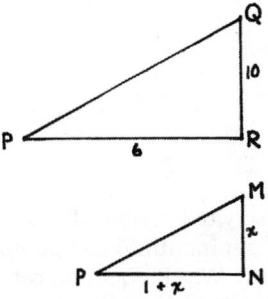

Item D

Multiple Choice The measure of angle *XYZ* is $(x^2 + 10x + 15)°$. What is the measure of angle *XYW*?

Ⓕ $(6x + 15)°$

Ⓖ $(2x^2 + 14x + 15)°$

Ⓗ $(14x + 15)°$

Ⓙ $(6x^2 + 15)°$

9. What information does the diagram provide that the problem does not?

10. Will the measure of angle *XYW* be less than or greater than the measure of angle *XYZ*? Explain.

STANDARDIZED TEST PREP

CUMULATIVE ASSESSMENT

Multiple Choice

1. A negative number is raised to a power. The result is a negative number. What do you know about the power?

Ⓐ It is an even number.

Ⓑ It is an odd number.

Ⓒ It is zero.

Ⓓ It is a whole number.

2. Which expression represents the phrase *eight less than the product of a number and two*?

Ⓕ $2 - 8x$

Ⓖ $8 - 2x$

Ⓗ $2x - 8$

Ⓙ $\frac{x}{2} - 8$

3. An Internet service provider charges a $20 set-up fee plus $12 per month. A competitor charges $15 per month. Which equation can you use to find x, the number of months when the total charge will be the same for both companies?

Ⓐ $15 = 20 + 12x$

Ⓑ $20 + 12x = 15x$

Ⓒ $20x + 12 = 15x$

Ⓓ $20 = 15x + 12x$

4. Which is a solution of the inequality $7 - 3(x - 3) > 2(x + 3)$?

Ⓕ 0

Ⓖ 2

Ⓗ 5

Ⓙ 12

5. One dose of Ted's medication contains 0.625 milligram, or $\frac{5}{8}$ milligram, of a drug. Which expression is equivalent to 0.625?

Ⓐ $5(4)^{-2}$

Ⓑ $5(2)^{-4}$

Ⓒ $5(-2)^3$

Ⓓ $5(2)^{-3}$

6. Find the product $(b - 8)^2$.

Ⓕ $b^2 + 64$

Ⓖ $b^2 - 64$

Ⓗ $b^2 - 16b - 64$

Ⓙ $b^2 - 16b + 64$

7. Janet is ordering game cartridges from an online retailer. The retailer's prices, including shipping and handling, are given in the table below.

Game Cartridges	Total Cost ($)
1	54.95
2	104.95
3	154.95
4	204.95

Which equation best describes the relationship between the total cost c and the number of game cartridges g?

Ⓐ $c = 54.95g$

Ⓑ $c = 51g + 0.95$

Ⓒ $c = 50g + 4.95$

Ⓓ $c = 51.65g$

8. Which equation describes a line parallel to $y = 5 - 2x$?

Ⓕ $y = -2x + 8$

Ⓗ $y = 5 + \frac{1}{2}x$

Ⓖ $y = 2x - 5$

Ⓙ $y = 5 - \frac{1}{2}x$

9. A square has sides of length $x - 4$. A rectangle has a length of $x + 2$ and a width of $2x - 1$. What is the total combined area of the square and the rectangle?

Ⓐ $10x - 14$

Ⓑ $4x - 3$

Ⓒ $3x^2 - 5x + 14$

Ⓓ $3x^2 + 3x - 18$

10. Jennifer has a pocketful of change, all in nickels and quarters. There are 11 coins with a total value of $1.15. Which system of equations can you use to find the number of each type of coin?

Ⓕ $\begin{cases} n + q = 11 \\ n + q = 1.15 \end{cases}$

Ⓖ $\begin{cases} n + q = 11 \\ 5n + 25q = 1.15 \end{cases}$

Ⓗ $\begin{cases} 5n + 25q = 11 \\ n + q = 1.15 \end{cases}$

Ⓙ $\begin{cases} n + q = 11 \\ 0.05n + 0.25q = 1.15 \end{cases}$

11. Which of the following is a true statement?

Ⓐ $\left[(a^m)^n\right]^p = a^{m+n+p}$

Ⓑ $\left[(a^m)^n\right]^p = a^{mn+p}$

Ⓒ $\left[(a^m)^n\right]^p = a^{mnp}$

Ⓓ $\left[(a^m)^n\right]^p = (a^{m+n})^p$

12. The drama club needs to raise at least $1400 for a field trip. The club was given $150 by the school administration. Club members are selling key chains for $5 each. Which inequality represents the number of key chains k that the drama club needs to sell to go on its field trip?

Ⓕ $150 + 5k \geq 1400$

Ⓖ $5k - 150 \geq 1400$

Ⓗ $5k + 150 \leq 1400$

Ⓙ $150 \leq 5k + 1400$

Gridded Response

13. Evaluate the expression $3b^{-2}c^0$ for $b = 2$ and $c = -3$.

14. What is the slope of the line described by $-3y = -6x - 12$?

15. The volume of a plastic cylinder is 64 cubic centimeters. A glass cylinder has the same height and a radius that is half that of the plastic cylinder. What is the volume in cubic centimeters of the glass cylinder?

Short Response

16. A sweater that normally sells for $35 was marked down 20% and placed on the sale rack. Later, the sweater was marked down an additional 30% and placed on the clearance rack.

   a. Find the price of the sweater while on the sale rack. Show your work.

   b. Find the price of the sweater while on the clearance rack. Show your work.

17. A set of positive integers (a, b, c) is called a *Pythagorean triple* if $a^2 + b^2 = c^2$.

   a. Find a^2, b^2, and c^2 when $a = 2x$, $b = x^2 - 1$, and $c = x^2 + 1$. Show your work.

   b. Is $(2x, x^2 - 1, x^2 + 1)$ a Pythagorean triple? Explain your reasoning.

18. Ron is making an ice sculpture. The block of ice is in the shape of a rectangular prism with a length of $(x + 2)$ inches, a width of $(x - 2)$ inches, and a height of $2x$ inches.

   a. Write and simplify a polynomial expression for the volume of the block of ice. Show your work.

   b. The final volume of the ice sculpture is $(x^3 + 4x^2 - 10x + 1)$ cubic inches. Write an expression for the volume of ice that Ron carved away. Show your work.

19. Simplify the expression $(3 \cdot a^2 \cdot b^{-4} \cdot a \cdot b^{-3})^{-3}$ using two different methods. Show that the results are the same.

Extended Response

20. Look at the pentagon below.

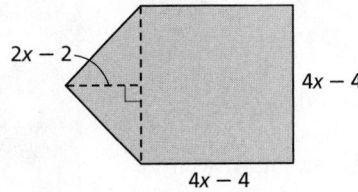

   a. Write and simplify an expression that represents the area of the pentagon. Show your work or explain your answer.

   b. Show one method of checking that your expression in part **a** is correct.

   c. The triangular part of the pentagon can be rearranged to form a square. Write the area of this square as the square of a binomial.

   d. Expand the product that you wrote in part **c**. What type of polynomial is this?

   e. Is the square of a binomial ever a binomial? Explain your reasoning.

Factoring Polynomials

COMMON CORE

Chapter Focus

• Factor polynomials.
• Apply factoring techniques to solve problems involving area and volume.

High Fliers

You can use polynomials to model area. When given the area of a kite as a polynomial, you can factor to find the kite's dimensions.

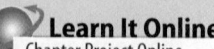
Learn It Online
Chapter Project Online

ARE YOU READY?

✓ Vocabulary

Match each term on the left with a definition on the right.

1. binomial
2. composite number
3. factor
4. multiple
5. prime number

A. a whole number greater than 1 that has more than two positive factors

B. a polynomial with two terms

C. the product of any number and a whole number

D. a number that is written as the product of its prime factors

E. a whole number greater than 1 that has exactly two positive factors, itself and 1

F. a number that is multiplied by another number to get a product

✓ Multiples

Write the first four multiples of each number.

6. 3
7. 4
8. 8
9. 15

✓ Factors

Tell whether the second number is a factor of the first number.

10. 20, 5
11. 50, 6
12. 120, 8
13. 245, 7

✓ Prime and Composite Numbers

Tell whether each number is prime or composite. If the number is composite, write it as the product of two numbers.

14. 2
15. 7
16. 10
17. 38
18. 115
19. 147
20. 151
21. 93

✓ Multiply Monomials and Polynomials

Multiply.

22. $2(x + 5)$
23. $3h(h + 1)$
24. $xy(x^2 - xy^3)$
25. $6m(m^2 - 4m - 1)$

✓ Multiply Binomials

Find each product.

26. $(x + 3)(x + 8)$
27. $(b - 7)(b + 1)$
28. $(2p - 5)(p - 1)$
29. $(3n + 4)(2n + 3)$

Study Guide: Preview

Where You've Been

Previously, you

- used properties of exponents to evaluate and simplify expressions.
- added and subtracted polynomials by combining like terms.
- multiplied polynomials.

In This Chapter

You will study

- greatest common factors.
- how to factor polynomials.
- how to factor special products.
- how to choose a factoring method.

Where You're Going

You can use the skills in this chapter

- in Geometry to solve area problems.
- in Physics to solve quadratic equations.
- in the real world to calculate dimensions in landscaping, construction, or design work.

Key Vocabulary/Vocabulario

greatest common factor	máximo común divisor
prime factorization	factorización prima

Vocabulary Connections

To become familiar with the vocabulary terms in the chapter, consider the following. You may refer to the chapter, the glossary, or a dictionary if you like.

1. The word *factor* refers to a number or polynomial that is multiplied by another number or polynomial to form a product. What do you think the word *factor* means when it is used as a verb (action word)?

2. List some words that end with the suffixes *-ize* or *-ization*. What does the ending *-ization* seem to mean? What do you think *factorization* means?

3. The words *prime, primer, primary*, and *primitive* all come from the same root word. What are the meanings of these words? How can their meanings help you understand what a *prime factor* is?

4. What is a prime number? How might the **prime factorization** of a number differ from another factorization?

5. What does the word *common* mean? How can you use this meaning to understand the term **greatest common factor** ?

Reading and Writing Math

Reading Strategy: Read a Lesson for Understanding

To help you learn new concepts, you should read each lesson with a purpose. As you read a lesson, make notes. Include the main ideas of the lesson and any questions you have. In class, listen for explanations of the vocabulary, clarification of the examples, and answers to your questions.

Reading Tips

Objectives
Evaluate and multiply by powers of 10.

Convert between standard notation and scientific notation.

> The objectives tell you the main idea of the lesson.

If a power of 10 has a negative integer exponent, does that make the number negative?
How do I enter numbers written in scientific notation into my calculator?

> Write down questions you have as you read the lesson.

EXAMPLE 1 Evaluating Powers of 10

Find the value of each power of 10.

A 10^{-3}

Start with 1 and move the decimal point three places to the left.

0. 0 0 1

0.001

> Work through the examples and write down any questions you have.

CHECK IT OUT!

> Practice what you've learned in the Check It Out sections.

Try This

Read the lesson for your next class. Then answer the questions below.

1. What are the lesson objectives?

2. What vocabulary, formulas, and symbols are new?

3. Which examples, if any, are unclear?

4. What questions do you have about the lesson?

7-1 Factors and Greatest Common Factors

Objectives
Write the prime factorization of numbers.

Find the GCF of monomials.

Vocabulary
prime factorization
greatest common factor

Who uses this?
Web site designers who sell electronic greeting cards can use the greatest common factor of numbers to design their Web sites. (See Example 4.)

The numbers that are multiplied to find a product are called *factors* of that product. A number is divisible by its factors.

You can use the factors of a number to write the number as a product. The number 12 can be factored several ways.

> **Remember!**
>
> A prime number is a whole number that has exactly two positive factors, itself and 1. The number 1 is not prime because it only has one positive factor.

Factorizations of 12

$1 \cdot 12 \qquad 2 \cdot 6 \qquad 3 \cdot 4 \qquad 1 \cdot 4 \cdot 3 \qquad \boxed{2 \cdot 2 \cdot 3}$

The order of the factors does not change the product, but there is only one example above that cannot be factored further. The circled factorization is the **prime factorization** because all the factors are prime numbers. The prime factors can be written in any order, and, except for changes in the order, there is only one way to write the prime factorization of a number.

EXAMPLE 1 **Writing Prime Factorizations**

Write the prime factorization of 60.

Method 1 Factor tree
Choose any two factors of 60 to begin. Keep finding factors until each branch ends in a prime factor.

```
        60
       /  \
     ②  •  30
           /  \
         10  •  ③
         /  \
       ②  •  ⑤
```

$60 = 2 \cdot 2 \cdot 5 \cdot 3$

Method 2 Ladder diagram
Choose a prime factor of 60 to begin. Keep dividing by prime factors until the quotient is 1.

```
2 | 60
3 | 30
2 | 10
5 | 5
    1
```

$60 = 2 \cdot 3 \cdot 2 \cdot 5$

The prime factorization of 60 is $2 \cdot 2 \cdot 3 \cdot 5$ or $2^2 \cdot 3 \cdot 5$.

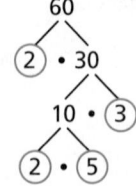
CHECK IT OUT! Write the prime factorization of each number.
1a. 40 **1b.** 33 **1c.** 49 **1d.** 19

Factors that are shared by two or more whole numbers are called *common factors*. The greatest of these common factors is called the **greatest common factor** , or GCF.

> Factors of 12: 1, 2, 3, 4, 6, 12
>
> Factors of 32: 1, 2, 4, 8, 16, 32
>
> Common factors: 1, 2, ④
>
> The greatest of the common factors is 4.

EXAMPLE 2 **Finding the GCF of Numbers**

Find the GCF of each pair of numbers.

A **24 and 60**

Method 1 List the factors.

factors of 24: 1, 2, 3, 4, 6, 8, ⑫, 24 *List all the factors.*
factors of 60: 1, 2, 3, 4, 5, 6, 10, ⑫, 15, 20, 30, 60 *Circle the GCF.*

The GCF of 24 and 60 is 12.

B **18 and 27**

Method 2 Use prime factorization.

$18 = 2 \cdot \boxed{3} \cdot \boxed{3}$ *Write the prime factorization of each number.*
$27 = \boxed{3} \cdot \boxed{3} \cdot 3$ *Align the common factors.*

$3 \cdot 3 = 9$

The GCF of 18 and 27 is 9.

 **Find the GCF of each pair of numbers.**
2a. 12 and 16 **2b.** 15 and 25

You can also find the GCF of monomials that include variables. To find the GCF of monomials, write the prime factorization of each coefficient and write all powers of variables as products. Then find the product of the common factors.

EXAMPLE 3 **Finding the GCF of Monomials**

Find the GCF of each pair of monomials.

A $3x^3$ **and** $6x^2$

$3x^3 = \boxed{3} \cdot \boxed{x} \cdot \boxed{x} \cdot x$ *Write the prime factorization of each*
$6x^2 = 2 \cdot \boxed{3} \cdot \boxed{x} \cdot \boxed{x}$ *coefficient and write powers as products.*
 Align the common factors.

$3 \cdot x \cdot x = 3x^2$ *Find the product of the common factors.*

The GCF of $3x^3$ and $6x^2$ is $3x^2$.

Helpful Hint

If two terms contain the same variable raised to different powers, the GCF will contain that variable raised to the lower power.

B $4x^2$ **and** $5y^3$

$4x^2 = 2 \cdot 2 \cdot \quad x \cdot x$ *Write the prime factorization of each*
$5y^3 = \quad 5 \cdot \quad y \cdot y \cdot y$ *coefficient and write powers as products.*
 Align the common factors.
 There are no common factors other than 1.

The GCF of $4x^2$ and $5y^3$ is 1.

 **Find the GCF of each pair of monomials.**
3a. $18g^2$ and $27g^3$ **3b.** $16a^6$ and $9b$ **3c.** $8x$ and $7v^2$

EXAMPLE **4** *Technology Application*

Garrison is creating a Web page that offers electronic greeting cards. He has 24 special occasion designs and 42 birthday designs. The cards will be displayed with the same number of designs in each row. Special occasion and birthday designs will not appear in the same row. How many rows will there be if Garrison puts the greatest possible number of designs in each row?

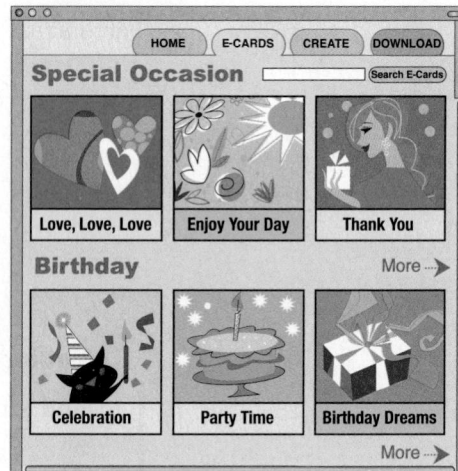

The 24 special occasion designs and 42 birthday designs must be divided into groups of equal size. The number of designs in each row must be a common factor of 24 and 42.

factors of 24: 1, 2, 3, 4, ⑥ 8, 12, 24
factors of 42: 1, 2, 3, ⑥ 7, 14, 21, 42

Find the common factors of 24 and 42.

The GCF of 24 and 42 is 6.

The greatest possible number of designs in each row is 6. Find the number of rows of each group of designs when there are 6 designs in each row.

$$\frac{24 \text{ special occasion designs}}{6 \text{ designs per row}} = 4 \text{ rows}$$

$$\frac{42 \text{ birthday designs}}{6 \text{ designs per row}} = 7 \text{ rows}$$

When the greatest possible number of designs is in each row, there are 11 rows in total.

 **4.** Adrianne is shopping for a CD storage unit. She has 36 CDs by pop music artists and 48 CDs by country music artists. She wants to put the same number of CDs on each shelf without putting pop music and country music CDs on the same shelf. If Adrianne puts the greatest possible number of CDs on each shelf, how many shelves does her storage unit need?

THINK AND DISCUSS

1. Describe two ways you can find the prime factorization of a number.

2. GET ORGANIZED Copy and complete the graphic organizer. Show how to write the prime factorization of $100x^2$ by filling in each box.

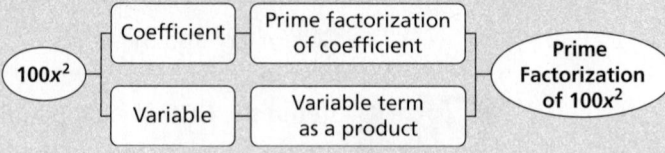

GUIDED PRACTICE

1. **Vocabulary** Define the term *greatest common factor* in your own words.

SEE EXAMPLE **1** **Write the prime factorization of each number.**

2. 20   **3.** 36   **4.** 27   **5.** 54

6. 96   **7.** 7   **8.** 100   **9.** 75

SEE EXAMPLE **2** **Find the GCF of each pair of numbers.**

10. 12 and 60   **11.** 14 and 49   **12.** 55 and 121

SEE EXAMPLE **3** **Find the GCF of each pair of monomials.**

13. $6x^2$ and $5x^2$ **14.** $15y^3$ and $-20y$ **15.** $13q^4$ and $2p^2$

SEE EXAMPLE **4**

16. Samantha is making beaded necklaces using 54 glass beads and 18 clay beads. She wants each necklace to have the same number of beads, but each necklace will have only one type of bead. If she puts the greatest possible number of beads on each necklace, how many necklaces can she make?

PRACTICE AND PROBLEM SOLVING

Independent Practice

For Exercises	See Example
17–24	1
25–27	2
28–30	3
31	4

Extra Practice

See Extra Practice for more Skills Practice and Applications Practice exercises.

Write the prime factorization of each number.

17. 18   **18.** 64   **19.** 12   **20.** 150

21. 17   **22.** 226   **23.** 49   **24.** 63

Find the GCF of each pair of numbers.

25. 36 and 63   **26.** 14 and 15   **27.** 30 and 40

Find the GCF of each pair of monomials.

28. $8a^2$ and 11   **29.** $9s$ and $63s^3$ **30.** $-64n^4$ and $24n^2$

31. José is making fruit-filled tart shells for a party. He has 72 raspberries and 108 blueberries. The tarts will each have the same number of berries. Raspberries and blueberries will not be in the same tart. If he puts the greatest possible number of fruits in each tart, how many tarts can he make?

Find the GCF of each pair of products.

32. $3 \cdot 5 \cdot t$ and $2 \cdot 2 \cdot 5 \cdot t \cdot t$

33. $-1 \cdot 2 \cdot 2 \cdot x \cdot x$ and $2 \cdot 2 \cdot 7 \cdot x \cdot x \cdot x$

34. $2 \cdot 2 \cdot 2 \cdot 11 \cdot x \cdot x \cdot x$ and $3 \cdot 11$

35. $2 \cdot 5 \cdot n \cdot n \cdot n$ and $-1 \cdot 2 \cdot 3 \cdot n$

36. **Write About It** The number 2 is even and is prime. Explain why all other prime numbers are odd numbers.

37. Critical Thinking The GCF of two numbers is 1. Explain whether this means the two numbers must be prime.

38. Multi-Step Angelo is making a rectangular floor for a clubhouse with an area of 84 square feet. The length of each side of the floor is a whole number of feet.

   a. What are the possible lengths and widths for Angelo's clubhouse floor?

   b. What is the minimum perimeter for the clubhouse floor?

   c. What is the maximum perimeter for the clubhouse floor?

39. Music The Cavaliers and the Blue Devils are two of the marching bands that are members of Drum Corps International (DCI). DCI bands are made up of percussionists, brass players, and color guard members who use flags and other props.

In 2004, there were 35 color guard members in the Cavaliers and 40 in the Blue Devils. The two color guards will march in rows with the same number of people in each row without mixing the guards together. If the greatest possible number of people are in each row, how many rows will there be?

For each set of numbers, determine which two numbers have a GCF greater than 1, and find that GCF.

40. 11, 12, 14   **41.** 8, 20, 63   **42.** 16, 21, 27

43. 32, 63, 105   **44.** 25, 35, 54   **45.** 35, 54, 72

46. Number Sense The prime factorization of 24 is $2^3 \cdot 3$. Without using a diagram, write the prime factorization of 48. Explain your reasoning.

Fill in each diagram. Then write the prime factorization of the number.

47.

48.

49.

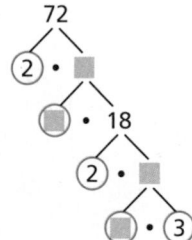
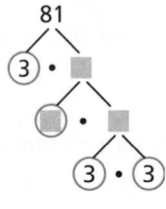
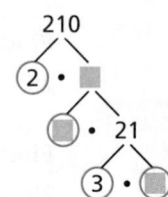

50.

```
  | 56
2 | 28
2 | ▩
▩ | 7
    1
```

51.

```
  | 108
  | 54
3 | ▩
▩ | 9
3 | 3
    1
```

52.

```
2 | 136
  | 68
2 | ▩
▩ | 17
    1
```

53.

```
2 | 48
2 | ▩
  | 12
2 | ▩
  | 3
    1
```

54.

```
  | 140
2 | ▩
  | 35
7 | 7
    1
```

55.

```
2 | 40
  | 20
  | ▩
5 | ▩
    1
```

56. The equation for the motion of an object with constant acceleration is $d = vt + \frac{1}{2}at^2$ where d is distance traveled in feet, v is starting velocity in ft/s, a is acceleration in ft/s^2, and t is time in seconds.

    a. A toy car begins with a velocity of 2 ft/s and accelerates at 2 ft/s^2. Write an expression for the distance the toy car travels after t seconds.

    b. What is the GCF of the terms in your expression from part **a**?

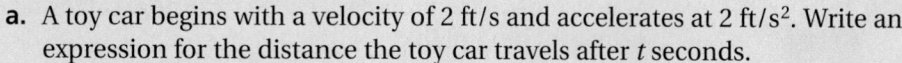

57. Which set of numbers has a GCF greater than 6?

    Ⓐ 18, 24, 36   Ⓑ 30, 35, 40   Ⓒ 11, 29, 37   Ⓓ 16, 24, 48

58. The slope of a line is the GCF of 48 and 12. The y-intercept is the GCF of the slope and 8. Which equation describes the line?

    Ⓕ $y = 12x + 4$ Ⓖ $y = 6x + 2$ Ⓗ $y = 4x + 4$ Ⓙ $y = 3x + 1$

59. Extended Response Patricia is making a dog pen in her back yard. The pen will be rectangular and have an area of 24 square feet. Draw and label a diagram that shows all possible whole-number dimensions for the pen. Find the perimeter of each rectangle you drew. Which dimensions should Patricia use in order to spend the least amount of money on fencing materials? Explain your reasoning.

CHALLENGE AND EXTEND

Find the GCF of each set.

60. $4n^3, 16n^2, 8n$

61. $27y^3, 18y^2, 81y$

62. $100, 25s^5, 50s$

63. $2p^4r, 8p^3r^2, 16p^2r^3$

64. $2x^3y, 8x^2y^2, 17xy^3$

65. $8a^4b^3, 4a^3b^3, 12a^2b^3$

66. Geometry The area of a triangle is 10 in^2. What are the possible whole-number dimensions for the base and height of the triangle?

67. Number Sense The GCF of three different numbers is 7. The sum of the three numbers is 105. What are the three numbers?

68. Critical Thinking Find three different *composite* numbers whose GCF is 1. (*Hint:* A composite number has factors other than 1 and itself.)

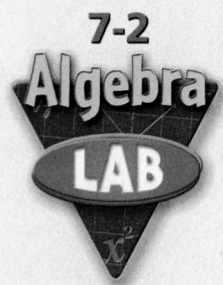

7-2
Algebra
LAB

Model Factoring

You can use algebra tiles to write a polynomial as the product of its factors. This process is called *factoring*. Factoring is the reverse of multiplying.

Use with Factoring by GCF

Use appropriate tools strategically.

CC.9-12.A.SSE.2 Use the structure of an expression to identify ways to rewrite it.

KEY

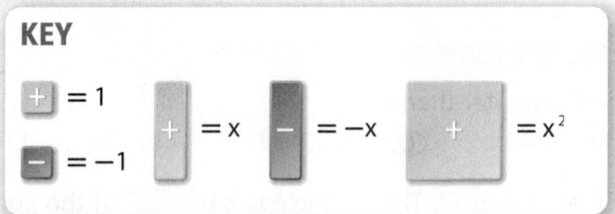

$+$ = 1

$-$ = −1

$+$ = x $-$ = −x $+$ = x^2

Activity

Use algebra tiles to factor $4x + 8$.

MODEL		ALGEBRA
	Model $4x + 8$.	$4x + 8$
	Arrange the tiles into a rectangle. The total area represents $4x + 8$. The length and width represent the factors. The rectangle has a width of $x + 2$ and a length of 4.	$4x + 8 = 4(x + 2)$

Use algebra tiles to factor $x^2 - 2x$.

MODEL		ALGEBRA
	Model $x^2 - 2x$.	$x^2 - 2x$
	Arrange the tiles into a rectangle. The total area represents $x^2 - 2x$. The length and width represent the factors. The rectangle has a width of $x - 2$ and a length of x.	$x^2 - 2x = x(x - 2)$

Try This

Use algebra tiles to factor each polynomial.

1. $3x + 9$ **2.** $2x + 8$ **3.** $4x - 12$ **4.** $3x - 12$

5. $2x^2 + 2x$ **6.** $x^2 + 4x$ **7.** $x^2 - 3x$ **8.** $2x^2 - 4x$

7-2 Factoring by GCF

CC.9-12.A.SSE.2 Use the structure of an expression to identify ways to rewrite it.

Objective
Factor polynomials by using the greatest common factor.

Why learn this?
You can determine the dimensions of a solar panel by factoring an expression representing the panel's area. (See Example 2.)

Recall that the Distributive Property states that $ab + ac = a(b + c)$. The Distributive Property allows you to factor out the GCF of the terms in a polynomial to write a factored form of the polynomial.

A polynomial is in its factored form when it is written as a product of monomials and polynomials that cannot be factored further. The expression $2(3x - 4x)$ is not fully factored because the terms in the parentheses have a common factor of x.

EXAMPLE 1 Factoring by Using the GCF

Factor each polynomial. Check your answer.

Writing Math

Aligning common factors can help you find the greatest common factor of two or more terms.

A $4x^2 - 3x$

$$4x^2 = 2 \cdot 2 \cdot \boxed{x} \cdot x$$
$$3x = \qquad 3 \cdot \boxed{x}$$
$$\qquad\qquad\qquad\quad \downarrow$$
$$\qquad\qquad\qquad\quad x$$

Find the GCF.

The GCF of $4x^2$ and $3x$ is x.

$$4x(x) - 3(x)$$

Write terms as products using the GCF as a factor.

$$x(4x - 3)$$

Use the Distributive Property to factor out the GCF.

Check $x(4x - 3)$
$4x^2 - 3x \checkmark$

Multiply to check your answer.
The product is the original polynomial.

B $10y^3 + 20y^2 - 5y$

$$10y^3 = \quad 2 \cdot \boxed{5} \cdot \boxed{y} \cdot y \cdot y$$
$$20y^2 = 2 \cdot 2 \cdot 5 \cdot \boxed{y} \cdot y$$
$$5y = \qquad\qquad \boxed{5} \cdot \boxed{y}$$
$$\qquad\qquad\qquad\qquad \downarrow \quad \downarrow$$
$$\qquad\qquad\qquad\quad 5 \cdot y = 5y$$

Find the GCF.

The GCF of $10y^3$, $20y^2$, and $5y$ is $5y$.

$$2y^2(5y) + 4y(5y) - 1(5y)$$

Write terms as products using the GCF as a factor.

$$5y(2y^2 + 4y - 1)$$

Use the Distributive Property to factor out the GCF.

Check $5y(2y^2 + 4y - 1)$
$10y^3 + 20y^2 - 5y \checkmark$

Multiply to check your answer.
The product is the original polynomial.

Factor each polynomial. Check your answer.

C $-12x - 8x^2$

$\quad -1(12x + 8x^2)$ *Both coefficients are negative. Factor out -1.*

$\quad\quad 12x = \boxed{2} \cdot \boxed{2} \cdot 3 \cdot \boxed{x}$ *Find the GCF.*
$\quad\quad 8x^2 = \boxed{2} \cdot \boxed{2} \cdot 2 \cdot \boxed{x} \cdot x$

$\quad\quad\quad\quad 2 \cdot 2 \cdot \quad x = 4x$ *The GCF of $12x$ and $8x^2$ is $4x$.*

$\quad -1[3(4x) + 2x(4x)]$ *Write each term as a product using the GCF.*
$\quad -1[4x(3 + 2x)]$ *Use the Distributive Property to factor out*
$\quad -1(4x)(3 + 2x)$ *the GCF.*
$\quad -4x(3 + 2x)$

Check

$\quad -4x(3 + 2x) = -12x - 8x^2$ ✓ *Multiply to check your answer.*

D $5x^2 + 7$

$\quad\quad 5x^2 = 5 \quad \cdot x \cdot x$ *Find the GCF.*
$\quad\quad\quad 7 = \quad 7$

$\quad\quad 5x^2 + 7$ *There are no common factors other than 1.*

The polynomial cannot be factored.

 **Factor each polynomial. Check your answer.**
1a. $5b + 9b^3$ **1b.** $9d^2 - 8^2$
1c. $-18y^3 - 7y^2$ **1d.** $8x^4 + 4x^3 - 2x^2$

To write expressions for the length and width of a rectangle whose area is expressed as a polynomial, you need to write the polynomial as a product. You can write a polynomial as a product by factoring it.

EXAMPLE 2 *Science Application*

Mandy's calculator is powered by solar energy. The area of the solar panel is $(7x^2 + x)$ cm². Factor this polynomial to find possible expressions for the dimensions of the solar panel.

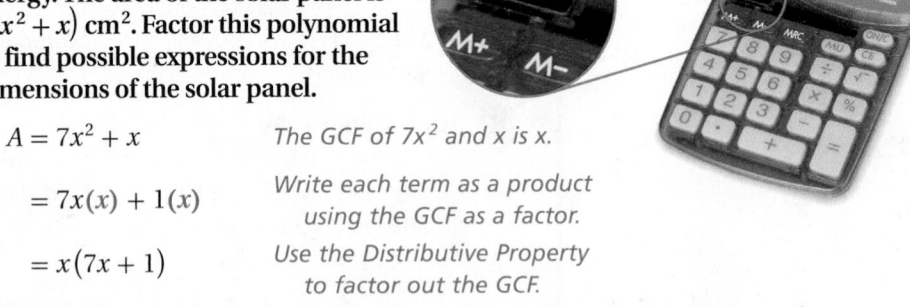

$\quad A = 7x^2 + x$ *The GCF of $7x^2$ and x is x.*

$\quad\quad = 7x(x) + 1(x)$ *Write each term as a product using the GCF as a factor.*

$\quad\quad = x(7x + 1)$ *Use the Distributive Property to factor out the GCF.*

Possible expressions for the dimensions of the solar panel are x cm and $(7x + 1)$ cm.

 **2. What if...?** The area of the solar panel on another calculator is $(2x^2 + 4x)$ cm². Factor this polynomial to find possible expressions for the dimensions of the solar panel.

Sometimes the GCF of terms is a binomial. This GCF is called a *common binomial factor*. You factor out a common binomial factor the same way you factor out a monomial factor.

EXAMPLE 3 **Factoring Out a Common Binomial Factor**

Factor each expression.

A $7(x-3) - 2x(x-3)$

$7(x-3) - 2x(x-3)$ *(x − 3) is a common binomial factor.*

$(x-3)(7 - 2x)$ *Factor out (x − 3).*

B $-t(t^2 + 4) + (t^2 + 4)$

$-t(t^2 + 4) + (t^2 + 4)$ *(t² + 4) is a common binomial factor.*

$-t(t^2 + 4) + 1(t^2 + 4)$ *(t² + 4) = 1(t² + 4)*

$(t^2 + 4)(-t + 1)$ *Factor out (t² + 4).*

C $9x(x+4) - 5(4+x)$

$9x(x+4) - 5(4+x)$ *(x + 4) = (4 + x), so (x + 4) is a common binomial factor.*

$9x(x+4) - 5(x+4)$

$(x+4)(9x - 5)$ *Factor out (x + 4).*

D $-3x^2(x+2) + 4(x-7)$

$-3x^2(x+2) + 4(x-7)$ *There are no common factors.*

The expression cannot be factored.

CHECK IT OUT! Factor each expression.

3a. $4s(s+6) - 5(s+6)$ **3b.** $7x(2x+3) + (2x+3)$

3c. $3x(y+4) - 2y(x+4)$ **3d.** $5x(5x-2) - 2(5x-2)$

You may be able to factor a polynomial by grouping. When a polynomial has four terms, you can make two groups and factor out the GCF from each group.

EXAMPLE 4 **Factoring by Grouping**

Factor each polynomial by grouping. Check your answer.

A $12a^3 - 9a^2 + 20a - 15$

$(12a^3 - 9a^2) + (20a - 15)$ *Group terms that have a common number or variable as a factor.*

$3a^2(4a - 3) + 5(4a - 3)$ *Factor out the GCF of each group.*

$3a^2(4a - 3) + 5(4a - 3)$ *(4a − 3) is a common factor.*

$(4a - 3)(3a^2 + 5)$ *Factor out (4a − 3).*

Check $(4a - 3)(3a^2 + 5)$ *Multiply to check your solution.*

$4a(3a^2) + 4a(5) - 3(3a^2) - 3(5)$

$12a^3 + 20a - 9a^2 - 15$

$12a^3 - 9a^2 + 20a - 15 ✓$ *The product is the original polynomial.*

Factor each polynomial by grouping. Check your answer.

$\boxed{B}$ $9x^3 + 18x^2 + x + 2$

$\quad\quad (9x^3 + 18x^2) + (x + 2)$ *Group terms.*

$\quad\quad 9x^2(x + 2) + 1(x + 2)$ *Factor out the GCF of each group.*

$\quad\quad 9x^2(x + 2) + 1(x + 2)$ *(x + 2) is a common factor.*

$\quad\quad (x + 2)(9x^2 + 1)$ *Factor out (x + 2).*

Check $(x + 2)(9x^2 + 1)$ *Multiply to check your solution.*

$\quad\quad x(9x^2) + x(1) + 2(9x^2) + 2(1)$

$\quad\quad 9x^3 + x + 18x^2 + 2$

$\quad\quad 9x^3 + 18x^2 + x + 2 \checkmark$ *The product is the original polynomial.*

 Factor each polynomial by grouping. Check your answer.

4a. $6b^3 + 8b^2 + 9b + 12$ **4b.** $4r^3 + 24r + r^2 + 6$

Helpful Hint

If two quantities are opposites, their sum is 0.

$(5 - x) + (x - 5)$
$5 - x + x - 5$
$(-x + x) + (5 - 5)$
$0 + 0$
0

Recognizing opposite binomials can help you factor polynomials. The binomials $(5 - x)$ and $(x - 5)$ are opposites. Notice $(5 - x)$ can be written as $-1(x - 5)$.

$\quad -1(x - 5) = (-1)(x) + (-1)(-5)$ *Distributive Property*

$\quad\quad\quad\quad\quad\quad = -x + 5$ *Simplify.*

$\quad\quad\quad\quad\quad\quad = 5 - x$ *Commutative Property of*

$\quad$ So, $(5 - x) = -1(x - 5).$ *Addition*

EXAMPLE 5   **Factoring with Opposites**

Factor $3x^3 - 15x^2 + 10 - 2x$ by grouping.

$\quad 3x^3 - 15x^2 + 10 - 2x$

$\quad (3x^3 - 15x^2) + (10 - 2x)$ *Group terms.*

$\quad 3x^2(x - 5) + 2(5 - x)$ *Factor out the GCF of each group.*

$\quad 3x^2(x - 5) + 2(-1)(x - 5)$ *Write (5 − x) as −1(x − 5).*

$\quad 3x^2(x - 5) - 2(x - 5)$ *Simplify. (x − 5) is a common factor.*

$\quad (x - 5)(3x^2 - 2)$ *Factor out (x − 5).*

 Factor each polynomial by grouping. Check your answer.

5a. $15x^2 - 10x^3 + 8x - 12$ **5b.** $8y - 8 - x + xy$

MATHEMATICAL PRACTICES

THINK AND DISCUSS

1. Explain how finding the GCF of monomials helps you factor a polynomial.

2. GET ORGANIZED Copy and complete the graphic organizer.

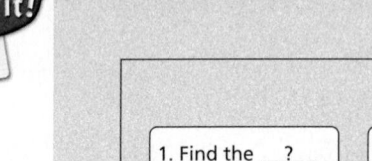

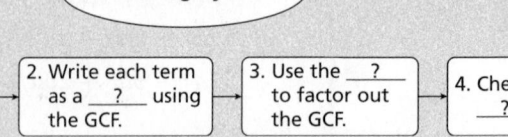

Factoring by GCF

1. Find the __?__ common factor.

2. Write each term as a __?__ using the GCF.

3. Use the __?__ to factor out the GCF.

4. Check by __?__.

GUIDED PRACTICE

SEE EXAMPLE 1

Factor each polynomial. Check your answer.

1. $15a - 5a^2$

2. $10g^3 - 3g$

3. $-35x + 42$

4. $-4x^2 - 6x$

5. $12h^4 + 8h^2 - 6h$

6. $3x^2 - 9x + 3$

7. $9m^2 + m$

8. $14n^3 + 7n + 7n^2$

9. $36f + 18f^2 + 3$

10. $-15b^2 + 7b$

SEE EXAMPLE 2

11. Physics A model rocket is fired vertically into the air at 320 ft/s. The expression $-16t^2 + 320t$ gives the rocket's height after t seconds. Factor this expression.

SEE EXAMPLE 3

Factor each expression.

12. $5(m - 2) - m(m - 2)$

13. $2b(b + 3) + 5(b + 3)$

14. $4(x - 3) - x(y + 2)$

Factor each polynomial by grouping. Check your answer.

SEE EXAMPLE 4

15. $x^3 + 4x^2 + 2x + 8$

16. $6x^3 + 4x^2 + 3x + 2$

17. $4b^3 - 6b^2 + 10b - 15$

18. $2m^3 + 4m^2 + 6m + 12$

19. $7r^3 - 35r^2 + 6r - 30$

20. $10a^3 + 4a^2 + 5a + 2$

SEE EXAMPLE 5

21. $2r^2 - 6r + 12 - 4r$

22. $6b^2 - 3b + 4 - 8b$

23. $14q^2 - 21q + 6 - 4q$

24. $3r - r^2 + 2r - 6$

25. $2m^3 - 6m^2 + 9 - 3m$

26. $6a^3 - 9a^2 - 12 + 8a$

PRACTICE AND PROBLEM SOLVING

Independent Practice	
For Exercises	See Example
27–35	1
36	2
37–42	3
43–48	4
49–54	5

Extra Practice

See Extra Practice for more Skills Practice and Applications Practice exercises.

Factor each polynomial. Check your answer.

27. $9y^2 + 45y$

28. $36d^3 + 24$

29. $-14x^4 + 5x^2$

30. $-15f - 10f^2$

31. $-4d^4 + d^3 - 3d^2$

32. $14x^3 + 63x^2 - 7x$

33. $21c^2 + 14c$

34. $33d^3 + 22d + 11$

35. $-5g^3 - 15g^2$

36. Finance After t years, the amount of money in a savings account that earns simple interest is $P + Prt$, where P is the starting amount and r is the yearly interest rate. Factor this expression.

Factor each expression.

37. $6a(a - 2) - 5b(b + 4)$

38. $-4x(x + 2) + 9(x + 2)$

39. $6y(y - 7) + (y - 7)$

40. $a(x - 3) + 2b(x - 3)$

41. $-3(2 + b) + 4b(b + 2)$

42. $5(3x - 2) + x(3x - 2)$

Factor each polynomial by grouping. Check your answer.

43. $2a^3 - 8a^2 + 3a - 12$

44. $x^3 + 3x^2 + 5x + 15$

45. $6x^3 + 18x^2 + x + 3$

46. $7x^3 + 2x^2 + 28x + 8$

47. $n^3 - 2n^2 + 5n - 10$

48. $10b^3 - 16b^2 + 25b - 40$

49. $2m^3 - 2m^2 + 3 - 3m$

50. $2d^3 - d^2 - 3 + 6d$

51. $6f^3 - 8f^2 + 20 - 15f$

52. $5k^2 - k^3 + 3k - 15$

53. $b^3 - 2b - 8 + 4b^2$

54. $20 - 15x - 6x^2 + 8x$

Fill in the missing part of each factorization.

55. $16v + 12v^2 = 4v\left(4 + \blacksquare\right)$

56. $15x - 25x^2 = 5x\left(3 - \blacksquare\right)$

57. $-16k^3 - 24k^2 = -8k^2\left(\blacksquare + 3\right)$

58. $-x - 10 = -1\left(\blacksquare + 10\right)$

Copy and complete the table.

	Polynomial	Number of Terms	Name	Completely Factored Form
	$3y + 3x + 9$	3	trinomial	$3(y + x + 3)$
59.	$x^2 + 5x$	$\blacksquare$	$\blacksquare$	$\blacksquare$
60.	$28c^2 - 49c$	$\blacksquare$	$\blacksquare$	$\blacksquare$
61.	$a^4 + a^3 + a^2$	$\blacksquare$	$\blacksquare$	$\blacksquare$
62.	$36 + 99r - 40r^2 - 110r^3$	$\blacksquare$	$\blacksquare$	$\blacksquare$

63. Personal Finance The final amount of money earned by a certificate of deposit (CD) after n years is $P(1 + r)^n$, where P is the original amount contributed and r is the interest rate as a decimal.

Year	Amount of CD
2004	$100.00
2005	$200.00
2006	$400.00

Justin's aunt purchased three CDs with the same interest rate to help him pay for college. The table shows the amount of the CD she purchased each year. In 2007, she paid $800.00 directly to the college.

a. Let $x = 1 + r$. Write expressions in terms of x for the value of the CDs purchased in 2004, 2005, and 2006 when Justin started college in 2007.

b. Write a polynomial in terms of x to represent the total value of the CDs purchased in 2004, 2005, and 2006 plus the amount paid to the college in 2007.

c. Factor the polynomial in part **b** by grouping. Evaluate the factored form of the polynomial when the interest rate is 9%. (*Hint*: Remember that $x = 1 +$ the interest rate expressed as a decimal.)

64. Write About It Describe how to find the area of the figure shown. Show each step and write your answer in factored form.

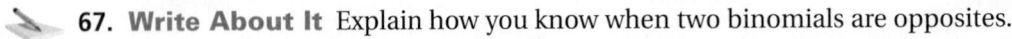

65. Critical Thinking Show two methods of factoring the expression $3a - 3b - 4a + 4b$.

66. Geometry The area of a triangle is $\frac{1}{2}\left(x^3 - 2x + 2x^2 - 4\right)$. The height h is $x + 2$. Write an expression for the base b of the triangle. $\left(Hint:$ Area of a triangle $= \frac{1}{2}bh\right)$

67. Write About It Explain how you know when two binomials are opposites.

68. a. The Multiplication Property of Zero states that the product of any number and 0 is 0. What must be true about either a or b to make $ab = 0$?

b. A toy car's distance in feet from the starting point is given by the equation $d = t(3 - t)$. Explain why $t(3 - t) = 0$ means that either $t = 0$ or $3 - t = 0$.

c. When $d = 0$, the car is at the starting point. Use the fact that $t = 0$ or $3 - t = 0$ when $d = 0$ to find the two times when the car is at the starting point.

Fill in each blank with a property or definition that justifies the step.

69. $7x^3 + 2x + 21x^2 + 6 = 7x^3 + 21x^2 + 2x + 6$ **a.** _____?_____

$= (7x^3 + 21x^2) + (2x + 6)$ **b.** _____?_____

$= 7x^2(x + 3) + 2(x + 3)$ **c.** _____?_____

$= (x + 3)(7x^2 + 2)$ **d.** _____?_____

70. ///**ERROR ANALYSIS**/// Which factorization of $3n^3 - n^2$ is incorrect? Explain.

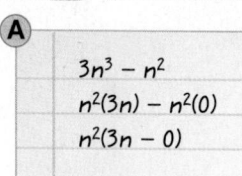

A
$3n^3 - n^2$
$n^2(3n) - n^2(0)$
$n^2(3n - 0)$

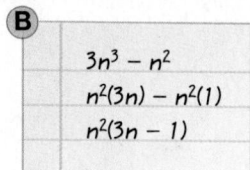

B
$3n^3 - n^2$
$n^2(3n) - n^2(1)$
$n^2(3n - 1)$

TEST PREP

71. Which is the complete factorization of $24x^3 - 12x^2$?

Ⓐ $6(4x^3 - 2x^2)$ Ⓑ $12(2x^3 - x^2)$ Ⓒ $12x(2x^2 - x)$ Ⓓ $12x^2(2x - 1)$

72. Which is NOT a factor of $18x^2 + 36x$?

Ⓕ 1   Ⓖ $4x$ Ⓗ $x + 2$ Ⓙ $18x$

73. The area of a rectangle is represented by the polynomial $x^2 + 3x - 6x - 18$. Which of the following could represent the length and width of the rectangle?

Ⓐ Length: $x + 3$; width: $x + 6$ Ⓒ Length: $x + 3$; width: $x - 6$

Ⓑ Length: $x - 3$; width: $x - 6$ Ⓓ Length: $x - 3$; width: $x + 6$

CHALLENGE AND EXTEND

Factor each polynomial.

74. $6ab^2 - 24a^2$

75. $-72a^2b^2 - 45ab$

76. $-18a^2b^2 + 21ab$

77. $ab + bc + ad + cd$

78. $4y^2 + 8ay - y - 2a$

79. $x^3 - 4x^2 + 3x - 12$

 80. Geometry The area between two concentric circles is called an *annulus*. The formula for area of an annulus is $A = \pi R^2 - \pi r^2$, where R is the radius of the larger circle and r is the radius of the smaller circle.

a. Factor the GCF from the formula for area of an annulus.

b. Use your answer from part **a** to find the area of an annulus with $R = 12$ cm and $r = 5$ cm

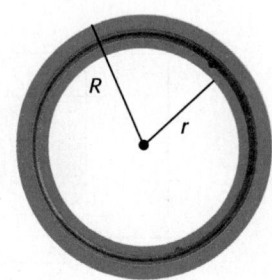

7-3 Algebra LAB

Model Factorization of Trinomials

You can use algebra tiles to write a trinomial as a product of two binomials. This is called *factoring a trinomial*.

Use with Factoring
$x^2 + bx + c$

KEY

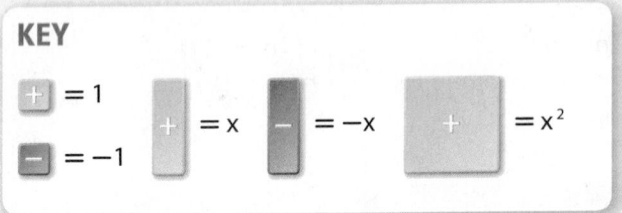

$\boxed{+} = 1$

$\boxed{-} = -1$

$= x$ $= -x$ $= x^2$

MATHEMATICAL PRACTICES

Use appropriate tools strategically.

CC.9-12.A.SSE.2 Use the structure of an expression to identify ways to rewrite it.

Activity 1

Use algebra tiles to factor $x^2 + 7x + 6$.

MODEL		ALGEBRA
	Model $x^2 + 7x + 6$.	$x^2 + 7x + 6$
	Try to arrange all of the tiles in a rectangle. Start by placing the x^2-tile in the upper left corner.	
	Arrange the unit tiles in a rectangle so that the top left corner of this rectangle touches the bottom right corner of the x^2-tile.	$x^2 + 7x + 6 \neq (x + 2)(x + 3)$
	Arrange the x-tiles so that all the tiles together make one large rectangle.	
	This arrangement does not work because two x-tiles are left over.	
	Rearrange the unit tiles to form another rectangle.	
	Fill in the empty spaces with x-tiles. All 7 x-tiles fit. This is the correct arrangement.	$x^2 + 7x + 6 = (x + 1)(x + 6)$
	The total area represents the trinomial. The length and width represent the factors.	

The rectangle has width $x + 1$ and length $x + 6$. So $x^2 + 7x + 6 = (x + 1)(x + 6)$.

Use algebra tiles to factor each trinomial.

1. $x^2 + 2x + 1$ **2.** $x^2 + 3x + 2$ **3.** $x^2 + 6x + 5$ **4.** $x^2 + 6x + 9$

5. $x^2 + 5x + 4$ **6.** $x^2 + 6x + 8$ **7.** $x^2 + 5x + 6$ **8.** $x^2 + 8x + 12$

Activity 2

Use algebra tiles to factor $x^2 + x - 2$.

MODEL		ALGEBRA
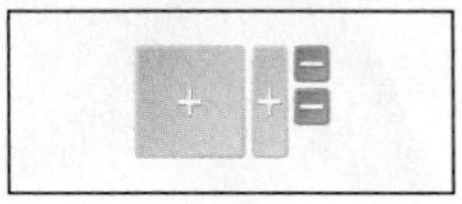	Model $x^2 + x - 2$.	$x^2 + x - 2$
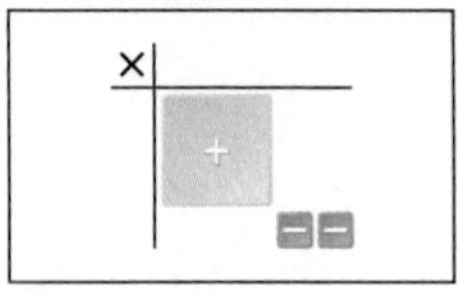 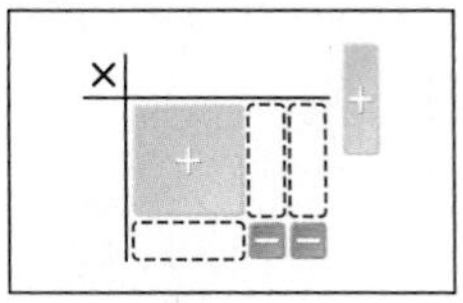	Start by placing the x^2-tile in the upper left corner. Arrange the unit tiles in a rectangle so that the top left corner of this rectangle touches the bottom right corner of the x^2-tile. To make a rectangle, you need to fill in the empty spaces, but there aren't enough x-tiles to fill in the empty spaces.	
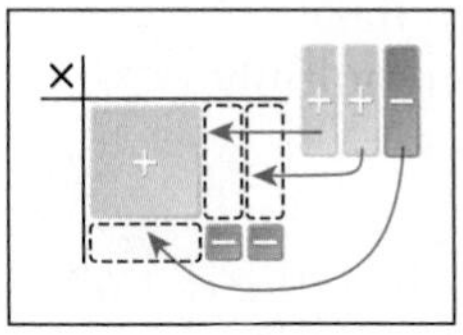	Add a zero pair. Arrange the x-tiles to complete the rectangle. Remember that the product of two positive values is positive and the product of a positive and a negative value is negative.	
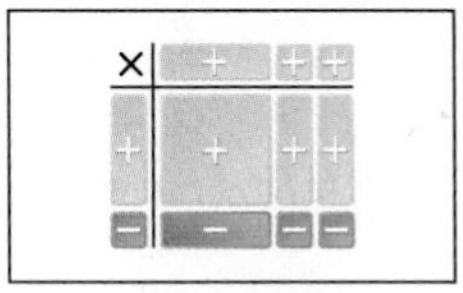	The total area represents the trinomial. The length and width represent the factors.	$x^2 + x - 2 = (x - 1)(x + 2)$

The rectangle has width $x - 1$ and length $x + 2$. So, $x^2 + x - 2 = (x - 1)(x + 2)$.

Try This

9. Why can you add one red $-x$-tile and one yellow x-tile?

Use algebra tiles to factor each trinomial.

10. $x^2 - x - 2$ **11.** $x^2 - 2x - 3$ **12.** $x^2 - 5x + 4$ **13.** $x^2 - 7x + 10$

14. $x^2 - 2x + 1$ **15.** $x^2 - 6x + 5$ **16.** $x^2 + 5x - 6$ **17.** $x^2 + 3x - 4$

18. $x^2 - x - 6$ **19.** $x^2 + 3x - 10$ **20.** $x^2 - 2x - 8$ **21.** $x^2 + x - 12$

COMMON CORE

7-3 Factoring $x^2 + bx + c$

CC.9-12.A.SSE.2 Use the structure of an expression to identify ways to rewrite it.

Objective
Factor quadratic trinomials of the form $x^2 + bx + c$.

Why learn this?
Factoring polynomials will help you find the dimensions of rectangular shapes, such as a fountain. (See Exercise 71.)

Previously, you learned how to multiply two binomials using the Distributive Property or the FOIL method. In this lesson, you will learn how to factor a trinomial into two binomials.

Notice that when you multiply $(x + 2)(x + 5)$, the constant term in the trinomial is the product of the constants in the binomials.

$$(x + 2)(x + 5) = x^2 + 7x + 10$$

You can use this fact to factor a trinomial into its binomial factors. Look for two numbers that are factors of the constant term in the trinomial. Write two binomials with those numbers, and then multiply to see if you are correct.

EXAMPLE 1 **Factoring Trinomials by Guess and Check**

Factor $x^2 + 19x + 60$ by guess and check.

$(\blacksquare + \blacksquare)(\blacksquare + \blacksquare)$ *Write two sets of parentheses.*

$(x + \blacksquare)(x + \blacksquare)$ *The first term is x^2, so the variable terms have a coefficient of 1.*

Remember!

When you multiply two binomials, multiply:

First terms
Outer terms
Inner terms
Last terms

The constant term in the trinomial is 60.

$(x + 1)(x + 60) = x^2 + 61x + 60$ ✗   *Try factors of 60 for the constant*
$(x + 2)(x + 30) = x^2 + 32x + 60$ ✗   *terms in the binomials.*
$(x + 3)(x + 20) = x^2 + 23x + 60$ ✗
$(x + 4)(x + 15) = x^2 + 19x + 60$ ✓

The factors of $x^2 + 19x + 60$ are $(x + 4)$ and $(x + 15)$.

$x^2 + 19x + 60 = (x + 4)(x + 15)$

Factor each trinomial by guess and check.
1a. $x^2 + 10x + 24$ **1b.** $x^2 + 7x + 12$

The guess and check method is usually not the most efficient method of factoring a trinomial. Look at the product of $(x + 3)$ and $(x + 4)$.

$$(x+3)(x+4) = x^2 + 7x + 12$$

The coefficient of the middle term is the sum of 3 and 4. The third term is the product of 3 and 4.

Factoring $x^2 + bx + c$

WORDS	EXAMPLE		
To factor a quadratic trinomial of the form $x^2 + bx + c$, find two factors of c whose sum is b.	To factor $x^2 + 9x + 18$, look for factors of 18 whose sum is 9.		
	Factors of 18	**Sum**	
	1 and 18	19 ✗	
If no such integers exist, the trinomial is not factorable.	2 and 9	11 ✗	
	3 and 6	9 ✓	$x^2 + 9x + 18 = (x + 3)(x + 6)$

When c is positive, its factors have the same sign. The sign of b tells you whether the factors are positive or negative. When b is positive, the factors are positive, and when b is negative, the factors are negative.

EXAMPLE 2 **Factoring $x^2 + bx + c$ When c Is Positive**

Factor each trinomial. Check your answer.

A $x^2 + 6x + 8$

$(x + \blacksquare)(x + \blacksquare)$ $b = 6$ and $c = 8$; look for factors of 8 whose sum is 6.

Factors of 8	Sum	
1 and 8	9	✗
2 and 4	6	✓

The factors needed are 2 and 4.

$(x + 2)(x + 4)$

Check $(x + 2)(x + 4) = x^2 + 4x + 2x + 8$ Use the FOIL method.

$= x^2 + 6x + 8$ ✓   The product is the original polynomial.

B $x^2 + 5x + 6$

$(x + \blacksquare)(x + \blacksquare)$ $b = 5$ and $c = 6$; look for factors of 6 whose sum is 5.

Factors of 6	Sum	
1 and 6	7	✗
2 and 3	5	✓

The factors needed are 2 and 3.

$(x + 2)(x + 3)$

Check $(x + 2)(x + 3) = x^2 + 3x + 2x + 6$ Use the FOIL method.

$= x^2 + 5x + 6$ ✓

The product is the original polynomial.

Factor each trinomial. Check your answer.

 $x^2 - 10x + 16$
$$\left(x + \blacksquare\right)\left(x + \blacksquare\right)$$

b = −10 and c = 16; look for factors of 16 whose sum is −10.

Factors of 16	Sum	
−1 and −16	−17	✗
−2 and −8	−10	✓

The factors needed are −2 and −8.

$$(x - 2)(x - 8)$$

Check $(x - 2)(x - 8) = x^2 - 8x - 2x + 16$ *Use the FOIL method.*
$$= x^2 - 10x + 16 \checkmark$$ *The product is the original polynomial.*

CHECK IT OUT!

Factor each trinomial. Check your answer.

2a. $x^2 + 8x + 12$ **2b.** $x^2 - 5x + 6$

2c. $x^2 + 13x + 42$ **2d.** $x^2 - 13x + 40$

When *c* is negative, its factors have opposite signs. The sign of *b* tells you which factor is positive and which is negative. The factor with the greater absolute value has the same sign as *b*.

E X A M P L E 3 Factoring $x^2 + bx + c$ When *c* Is Negative

Factor each trinomial.

A $x^2 + 7x - 18$
$$\left(x + \blacksquare\right)\left(x + \blacksquare\right)$$

b = 7 and c = −18; look for factors of −18 whose sum is 7. The factor with the greater absolute value is positive.

Factors of −18	Sum	
−1 and 18	17	✗
−2 and 9	7	✓

The factors needed are −2 and 9.

$$(x - 2)(x + 9)$$

B $x^2 - 5x - 24$
$$\left(x + \blacksquare\right)\left(x + \blacksquare\right)$$

b = −5 and c = −24; look for factors of −24 whose sum is −5. The factor with the greater absolute value is negative.

Factors of −24	Sum	
1 and −24	−23	✗
2 and −12	−10	✗
3 and −8	−5	✓

The factors needed are 3 and −8.

$$(x + 3)(x - 8)$$

Helpful Hint

If you have trouble remembering the rules for which factor is positive and which is negative, you can try all the factor pairs and check their sums.

CHECK IT OUT!

Factor each trinomial. Check your answer.

3a. $x^2 + 2x - 15$ **3b.** $x^2 - 6x + 8$ **3c.** $x^2 - 8x - 20$

A polynomial and the factored form of the polynomial are equivalent expressions. When you evaluate these two expressions for the same value of the variable, the results are the same.

EXAMPLE 4 **Evaluating Polynomials**

Factor $n^2 + 11n + 24$. Show that the original polynomial and the factored form have the same value for $n = 0, 1, 2, 3,$ and 4.

$n^2 + 11n + 24$

$(n + \blacksquare)(n + \blacksquare)$ *b = 11 and c = 24; look for factors of 24 whose sum is 11.*

Factors of 24	Sum	
1 and 24	25	✗
2 and 12	14	✗
3 and 8	11	✓

The factors needed are 3 and 8.

$(n + 3)(n + 8)$

Evaluate the original polynomial and the factored form for $n = 0, 1, 2, 3,$ and 4.

n	$n^2 + 11n + 24$
0	$0^2 + 11(0) + 24 = 24$
1	$1^2 + 11(1) + 24 = 36$
2	$2^2 + 11(2) + 24 = 50$
3	$3^2 + 11(3) + 24 = 66$
4	$4^2 + 11(4) + 24 = 84$

n	$(n + 3)(n + 8)$
0	$(0 + 3)(0 + 8) = 24$
1	$(1 + 3)(1 + 8) = 36$
2	$(2 + 3)(2 + 8) = 50$
3	$(3 + 3)(3 + 8) = 66$
4	$(4 + 3)(4 + 8) = 84$

The original polynomial and the factored form have the same value for the given values of n.

 CHECK IT OUT! 4. Factor $n^2 - 7n + 10$. Show that the original polynomial and the factored form have the same value for $n = 0, 1, 2, 3,$ and 4.

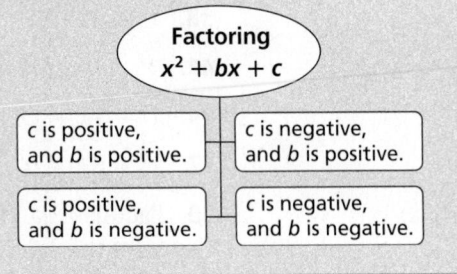 MATHEMATICAL PRACTICES

THINK AND DISCUSS

1. Explain in your own words how to factor $x^2 + 9x + 14$. Show how to check your answer.

2. Explain how you can determine the signs of the factors of c when factoring a trinomial of the form $x^2 + bx + c$.

 Know it! Note

3. GET ORGANIZED Copy and complete the graphic organizer. In each box, write an example of a trinomial with the given properties and factor it.

Factoring $x^2 + bx + c$

c is positive, and b is positive.	c is negative, and b is positive.
c is positive, and b is negative.	c is negative, and b is negative.

GUIDED PRACTICE

SEE EXAMPLE 1

Factor each trinomial by guess and check.

1. $x^2 + 13x + 36$

2. $x^2 + 11x + 24$

3. $x^2 + 14x + 40$

Factor each trinomial. Check your answer.

SEE EXAMPLE 2

4. $x^2 + 4x + 3$

5. $x^2 + 10x + 16$

6. $x^2 + 15x + 44$

7. $x^2 - 7x + 6$

8. $x^2 - 9x + 14$

9. $x^2 - 11x + 24$

SEE EXAMPLE 3

10. $x^2 - 6x - 7$

11. $x^2 + 6x - 27$

12. $x^2 + x - 30$

13. $x^2 - x - 2$

14. $x^2 - 3x - 18$

15. $x^2 - 4x - 45$

SEE EXAMPLE 4

16. Factor $n^2 + 6n - 7$. Show that the original polynomial and the factored form have the same value for $n = 0, 1, 2, 3,$ and 4.

PRACTICE AND PROBLEM SOLVING

Independent Practice	
For Exercises	See Example
17–19	1
20–25	2
26–31	3
32	4

Extra Practice
See Extra Practice for more Skills Practice and Applications Practice exercises.

Factor each trinomial by guess and check.

17. $x^2 + 13x + 30$

18. $x^2 + 11x + 28$

19. $x^2 + 16x + 48$

Factor each trinomial. Check your answer.

20. $x^2 + 12x + 11$

21. $x^2 + 16x + 28$

22. $x^2 + 15x + 36$

23. $x^2 - 6x + 5$

24. $x^2 - 9x + 18$

25. $x^2 - 12x + 32$

26. $x^2 + x - 12$

27. $x^2 + 4x - 21$

28. $x^2 + 9x - 36$

29. $x^2 - 12x - 13$

30. $x^2 - 10x - 24$

31. $x^2 - 2x - 35$

32. Factor $n^2 - 12n - 45$. Show that the original polynomial and the factored form have the same value for $n = 0, 1, 2, 3,$ and 4.

Match each trinomial with its correct factorization.

33. $x^2 + 3x - 10$

A. $(x - 2)(x - 5)$

34. $x^2 - 7x + 10$

B. $(x + 1)(x + 10)$

35. $x^2 - 9x - 10$

C. $(x - 2)(x + 5)$

36. $x^2 + 11x + 10$

D. $(x + 1)(x - 10)$

 37. Write About It Compare multiplying binomials with factoring polynomials into binomial factors.

Factor each trinomial. Check your answer.

38. $x^2 + x - 20$

39. $x^2 - 11x + 18$

40. $x^2 - 4x - 21$

41. $x^2 + 10x + 9$

42. $x^2 - 12x + 32$

43. $x^2 + 13x + 42$

44. $x^2 - 7x + 12$

45. $x^2 + 11x + 18$

46. $x^2 - 6x - 27$

47. $x^2 + 5x - 24$

48. $x^2 - 10x + 21$

49. $x^2 + 4x - 45$

50. Factor $n^2 + 11n + 28$. Show that the original polynomial and the factored form have the same value for $n = 0, 1, 2, 3,$ and 4.

51. Estimation The graph shows the areas of rectangles with dimensions $(x + 1)$ yards and $(x + 2)$ yards. Estimate the value of x for a rectangle with area 9 square yards.

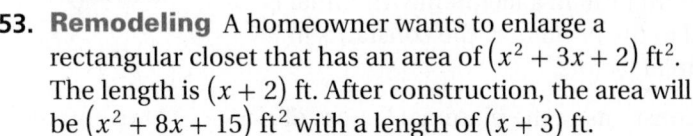

52. Geometry The area of a rectangle in square feet can be represented by $x^2 + 8x + 12$. The length is $(x + 6)$ ft. What is the width of the rectangle?

53. Remodeling A homeowner wants to enlarge a rectangular closet that has an area of $(x^2 + 3x + 2)$ ft². The length is $(x + 2)$ ft. After construction, the area will be $(x^2 + 8x + 15)$ ft² with a length of $(x + 3)$ ft.

  a. Find the dimensions of the closet before construction.

  b. Find the dimensions of the closet after construction.

  c. By how many feet will the length and width increase after construction?

Art Write the polynomial modeled and then factor.

54.

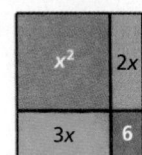

55.

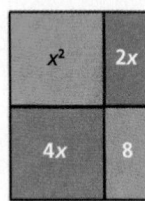

56.

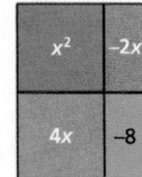

Copy and complete the table.

	$x^2 + bx + c$	Sign of c	Binomial Factors	Signs of Numbers in Binomials
	$x^2 + 4x + 3$	Positive	$(x + 1)(x + 3)$	Both positive
57.	$x^2 - 4x + 3$	▨	$(x\ \blacksquare\ 1)(x\ \blacksquare\ 3)$	▨
58.	$x^2 + 2x - 3$	▨	$(x\ \blacksquare\ 1)(x\ \blacksquare\ 3)$	▨
59.	$x^2 - 2x - 3$	▨	$(x\ \blacksquare\ 1)(x\ \blacksquare\ 3)$	▨

60. Geometry A rectangle has area $x^2 + 6x + 8$. The length is $x + 4$. Find the width of the rectangle. Could the rectangle be a square? Explain why or why not.

MULTI-STEP TEST PREP

61. The equation for the motion of an object with constant acceleration is $d = vt + \frac{1}{2}at^2$ where d is distance traveled in feet, v is starting velocity in feet per second, a is acceleration in feet per second squared, and t is time in seconds.

  a. Janna has two toy race cars on a track. One starts with a velocity of 0 ft/s and accelerates at 2 ft/s². Write an equation for the distance the car travels in time t.

  b. The second car travels at a constant speed of 4 ft/s. Write an equation for the distance the second car travels in time t. (*Hint:* When speed is constant, the acceleration is 0 ft/s².)

  c. By setting the equations equal to each other you can determine when the cars have traveled the same distance: $t^2 = 4t$. This can be written as $t^2 - 4t = 0$. Factor the left side of the equation.

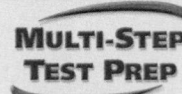

62. Construction The length of a rectangular porch is $(x + 7)$ ft. The area of the porch is $(x^2 + 9x + 14)$ ft². Find the width of the porch.

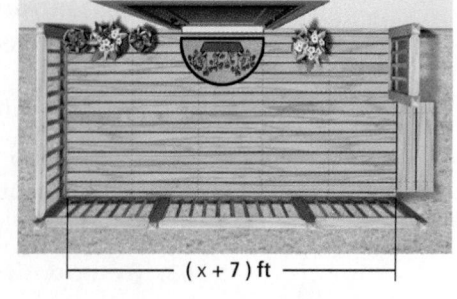

$(x + 7)$ ft

Tell whether each statement is true or false. If false, explain.

63. The third term in a factorable trinomial is equal to the product of the constants in its binomial factors.

64. The constants in the binomial factors of $x^2 + x - 2$ are both negative.

65. The correct factorization of $x^2 - 3x - 4$ is $(x + 4)(x - 1)$.

66. All trinomials of the form $x^2 + bx + c$ can be factored.

Fill in the missing part of each factorization.

67. $x^2 - 6x + 8 = (x - 2)(x - \blacksquare)$

68. $x^2 - 2x - 8 = (x + 2)(x - \blacksquare)$

69. $x^2 + 2x - 8 = (x - 2)(x + \blacksquare)$

70. $x^2 + 6x + 8 = (x + 2)(x + \blacksquare)$

71. Construction The area of a rectangular fountain is $(x^2 + 12x + 20)$ ft². The width is $(x + 2)$ ft.

   a. Find the length of the fountain.

   b. A 2-foot walkway is built around the fountain. Find the dimensions of the outside border of the walkway.

   c. Find the total area covered by the fountain and walkway.

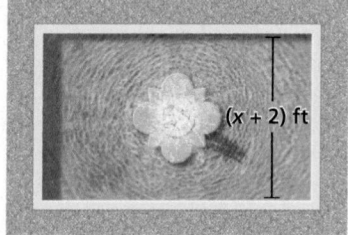

$(x + 2)$ ft

72. Critical Thinking Find all possible values of b so that $x^2 + bx + 6$ can be factored into binomial factors.

TEST PREP

73. Which is the correct factorization of $x^2 - 10x - 24$?

   Ⓐ $(x - 4)(x - 6)$ Ⓒ $(x - 2)(x + 12)$

   Ⓑ $(x + 4)(x - 6)$ Ⓓ $(x + 2)(x - 12)$

74. Which value of b would make $x^2 + bx - 20$ factorable?

   Ⓕ 9   Ⓖ 12   Ⓗ 19   Ⓙ 21

75. Which value of b would NOT make $x^2 + bx - 36$ factorable?

   Ⓐ 5   Ⓑ 9   Ⓒ 15   Ⓓ 16

76. Short Response What are the factors of $x^2 + 2x - 24$? Show and explain each step of factoring the polynomial.

CHALLENGE AND EXTEND

Factor each expression.

77. $x^4 + 18x^2 + 81$ **78.** $y^4 - 5y^2 - 24$ **79.** $d^4 + 22d^2 + 21$

80. $(u + v)^2 + 2(u + v) - 3$ **81.** $(de)^2 - (de) - 20$ **82.** $(m - n)^2 - 4(m - n) - 45$

83. Find all possible values of b such that, when $x^2 + bx + 28$ is factored, both constants in the binomials are positive.

84. Find all possible values of b such that, when $x^2 + bx + 32$ is factored, both constants in the binomials are negative.

85. The area of Beth's rectangular garden is $(x^2 + 13x + 42)$ ft². The width is $(x + 6)$ ft.

Item	Cost
Fertilizer	0.28 ($/ft²)
Fencing	2.00 ($/ft)

   a. What is the length of the garden?

   b. Find the perimeter in terms of x.

   c. Find the cost to fence the garden when x is 5.

   d. Find the cost of fertilizer when x is 5.

   e. Find the total cost to fence and fertilize Beth's garden when x is 5.

Career Path

Learn It Online
Career Resources Online

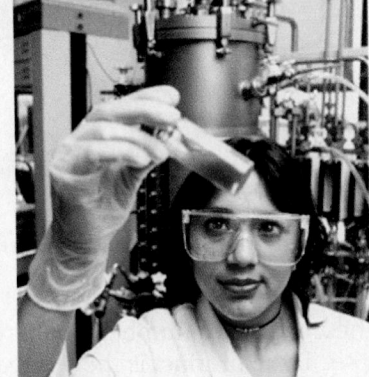

Jessica Rubino
Environmental Sciences major

Q: What math classes did you take in high school?

A: Algebra 1, Algebra 2, and Geometry

Q: What college math classes have you taken?

A: I took several computer modeling and programming classes as well as Statistics and Probability.

Q: How is math used in some of your projects?

A: Computer applications help me analyze data collected from a local waste disposal site. I used my mathematical knowledge to make recommendations on how to preserve surrounding water supplies.

Q: What plans do you have for the future?

A: I enjoy my studies in the area of water pollution. I would also like to research more efficient uses of natural energy resources.

Janine Wiedel Photolibrary/Alamy

7-4 Factoring $ax^2 + bx + c$

CC.9-12.A.SSE.2 Use the structure of an expression to identify ways to rewrite it.

Objective
Factor quadratic trinomials of the form $ax^2 + bx + c$.

Why learn this?
The height of a football that has been kicked can be modeled by a factored polynomial. (See Exercise 69.)

You have already factored trinomials of the form $x^2 + bx + c$. Now you will factor trinomials of the form $ax^2 + bx + c$, where $a \neq 0$ or 1.

When you multiply $(3x + 2)(2x + 5)$, the coefficient of the x^2-term is the product of the coefficients of the x-terms. Also, the constant term in the trinomial is the product of the constants in the binomials.

$$(3x+2)(2x+5) = 6x^2 + 19x + 10$$

To factor a trinomial like $ax^2 + bx + c$ into its binomial factors, write two sets of parentheses: $(\blacksquare x + \blacksquare)(\blacksquare x + \blacksquare)$.

Write two numbers that are factors of a next to the x's and two numbers that are factors of c in the other blanks. Then multiply to see if the product is the original trinomial. If there are not two such integers, the trinomial is unfactorable.

EXAMPLE 1 **Factoring $ax^2 + bx + c$ by Guess and Check**

Factor $4x^2 + 16x + 15$ by guess and check.

$(\blacksquare + \blacksquare)(\blacksquare + \blacksquare)$ *Write two sets of parentheses.*

$(\blacksquare x + \blacksquare)(\blacksquare x + \blacksquare)$ *The first term is $4x^2$, so at least one variable term has a coefficient other than 1.*

The coefficient of the x^2-term is 4. The constant term in the trinomial is 15.

$(1x + 15)(4x + 1) = 4x^2 + 61x + 15$ ✗   *Try factors of 4 for the coefficients and factors of 15 for the constant terms.*

$(1x + 5)(4x + 3) = 4x^2 + 23x + 15$ ✗

$(1x + 3)(4x + 5) = 4x^2 + 17x + 15$ ✗

$(1x + 1)(4x + 15) = 4x^2 + 19x + 15$ ✗

$(2x + 15)(2x + 1) = 4x^2 + 32x + 15$ ✗

$(2x + 5)(2x + 3) = 4x^2 + 16x + 15$ ✓

The factors of $4x^2 + 16x + 15$ are $(2x + 5)$ and $(2x + 3)$.

$4x^2 + 16x + 15 = (2x + 5)(2x + 3)$

 Factor each trinomial by guess and check.

1a. $6x^2 + 11x + 3$ **1b.** $3x^2 - 2x - 8$

AP Photo/Peter Cosgrove

So, to factor $ax^2 + bx + c$, check the factors of a and the factors of c in the binomials. The sum of the products of the outer and inner terms should be b.

Product = a — 　　　　　　 — Product = c

$$(\boxed{}x + \boxed{})(\boxed{}x + \boxed{}) = ax^2 + bx + c$$

Sum of outer and inner products = b

Since you need to check all the factors of a and all the factors of c, it may be helpful to make a table. Then check the products of the outer and inner terms to see if the sum is b. You can multiply the binomials to check your answer.

EXAMPLE 2 **Factoring $ax^2 + bx + c$ When c Is Positive**

Factor each trinomial. Check your answer.

A $2x^2 + 11x + 12$

$(\boxed{}x + \boxed{})(\boxed{}x + \boxed{})$　　　$a = 2$ and $c = 12$; Outer + Inner = 11

Factors of 2	Factors of 12	Outer + Inner	
1 and 2	1 and 12	$1(12) + 2(1) = 14$	✗
1 and 2	12 and 1	$1(1) + 2(12) = 25$	✗
1 and 2	2 and 6	$1(6) + 2(2) = 10$	✗
1 and 2	6 and 2	$1(2) + 2(6) = 14$	✗
1 and 2	3 and 4	$1(4) + 2(3) = 10$	✗
1 and 2	4 and 3	$1(3) + 2(4) = 11$	✓

$(x + 4)(2x + 3)$

Check　$(x + 4)(2x + 3) = 2x^2 + 3x + 8x + 12$　　*Use the FOIL method.*
$$= 2x^2 + 11x + 12 \checkmark$$

B $5x^2 - 14x + 8$

$(\boxed{}x + \boxed{})(\boxed{}x + \boxed{})$　　　$a = 5$ and $c = 8$; Outer + Inner = -14

Factors of 5	Factors of 8	Outer + Inner	
1 and 5	-1 and -8	$1(-8) + 5(-1) = -13$	✗
1 and 5	-8 and -1	$1(-1) + 5(-8) = -41$	✗
1 and 5	-2 and -4	$1(-4) + 5(-2) = -14$	✓

$(x - 2)(5x - 4)$

Check　$(x - 2)(5x - 4) = 5x^2 - 4x - 10x + 8$　　*Use the FOIL method.*
$$= 5x^2 - 14x + 8 \checkmark$$

Remember!

When b is negative and c is positive, the factors of c are both negative.

Factor each trinomial. Check your answer.

2a. $6x^2 + 17x + 5$　　**2b.** $9x^2 - 15x + 4$　　**2c.** $3x^2 + 13x + 12$

When c is negative, one factor of c will be positive and the other factor will be negative. Only some of the factors are shown in the examples, but you may need to check all of the possibilities.

EXAMPLE 3 **Factoring $ax^2 + bx + c$ When c Is Negative**

Factor each trinomial. Check your answer.

A $4y^2 + 7y - 2$

$(\boxed{}y + \boxed{})(\boxed{}y + \boxed{})$ *a = 4 and c = −2; Outer + Inner = 7*

Factors of 4	Factors of −2	Outer + Inner	
1 and 4	1 and −2	$1(-2) + 4(1) = 2$	✗
1 and 4	−1 and 2	$1(2) + 4(-1) = -2$	✗
1 and 4	2 and −1	$1(-1) + 4(2) = 7$	✓

$(y + 2)(4y - 1)$

Check $(y + 2)(4y - 1) = 4y^2 - y + 8y - 2$ *Use the FOIL method.*

$= 4y^2 + 7y - 2$ ✓

B $4x^2 + 19x - 5$

$(\boxed{}x + \boxed{})(\boxed{}x + \boxed{})$ *a = 4 and c = −5; Outer + Inner = 19*

Factors of 4	Factors of −5	Outer + Inner	
1 and 4	1 and −5	$1(-5) + 4(1) = -1$	✗
1 and 4	−1 and 5	$1(5) + 4(-1) = 1$	✗
1 and 4	5 and −1	$1(-1) + 4(5) = 19$	✓

$(x + 5)(4x - 1)$

Check $(x + 5)(4x - 1) = 4x^2 - x + 20x - 5$ *Use the FOIL method.*

$= 4x^2 + 19x - 5$ ✓

C $2x^2 - 7x - 15$

$(\boxed{}x + \boxed{})(\boxed{}x + \boxed{})$ *a = 2 and c = −15; Outer + Inner = −7*

Factors of 2	Factors of −15	Outer + Inner	
1 and 2	1 and −15	$1(-15) + 2(1) = -13$	✗
1 and 2	−1 and 15	$1(15) + 2(-1) = 13$	✗
1 and 2	3 and −5	$1(-5) + 2(3) = 1$	✗
1 and 2	−3 and 5	$1(5) + 2(-3) = -1$	✗
1 and 2	5 and −3	$1(-3) + 2(5) = 7$	✗
1 and 2	−5 and 3	$1(3) + 2(-5) = -7$	✓

$(x - 5)(2x + 3)$

Check $(x - 5)(2x + 3) = 2x^2 + 3x - 10x - 15$ *Use the FOIL method.*

$= 2x^2 - 7x - 15$ ✓

Factor each trinomial. Check your answer.

3a. $6x^2 + 7x - 3$ **3b.** $4n^2 - n - 3$

Student to Student

Factoring $ax^2 + bx + c$

Reggie Wilson
Franklin High School

When a, b, and c are positive, I like to use a box to help me factor. I look for factors of ac that add to b. Then I arrange the terms in a box and factor.

To factor $6x^2 + 7x + 2$, first I find the factors I need.

$ac = 2(6) = 12$ $b = 7$

Factors of 12	Sum
1 and 12	13
2 and 6	8
3 and 4	7

Then I rewrite the trinomial as $6x^2 + 3x + 4x + 2$.

Now I arrange $6x^2 + 3x + 4x + 2$ in a box and factor out the common factors from each row and column.

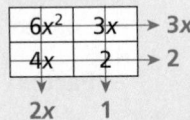

The factors are $(2x + 1)$ and $(3x + 2)$.

When the leading coefficient is negative, factor out -1 from each term before using other factoring methods.

EXAMPLE **4**   **Factoring $ax^2 + bx + c$ When a Is Negative**

Factor $-2x^2 - 15x - 7$.

$-1(2x^2 + 15x + 7)$ *Factor out -1.*

$-1(\boxed{}x + \boxed{})(\boxed{}x + \boxed{})$ *a = 2 and c = 7; Outer + Inner = 15*

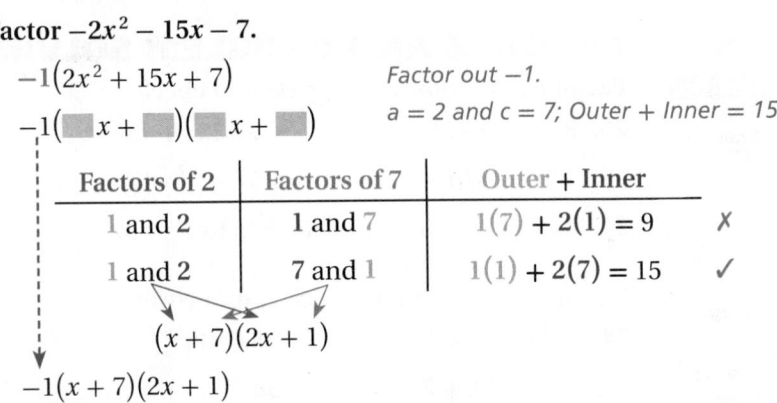

Factors of 2	Factors of 7	Outer + Inner	
1 and 2	1 and 7	$1(7) + 2(1) = 9$	✗
1 and 2	7 and 1	$1(1) + 2(7) = 15$	✓

$(x + 7)(2x + 1)$

$-1(x + 7)(2x + 1)$

> **Caution!**
>
> When you factor out -1 in an early step, you must carry it through the rest of the steps.

 **CHECK IT OUT!**   Factor each trinomial. Check your answer.

4a. $-6x^2 - 17x - 12$ **4b.** $-3x^2 - 17x - 10$

 MATHEMATICAL PRACTICES

THINK AND DISCUSS

1. Let a, b, and c be positive. If $ax^2 + bx + c$ is the product of two binomials, what do you know about the signs of the numbers in the binomials?

2. GET ORGANIZED Copy and complete the graphic organizer. Write each of the following trinomials in the appropriate box and factor each one.

$3x^2 + 10x - 8$ $3x^2 + 10x + 8$
$3x^2 - 10x + 8$ $3x^2 - 10x - 8$

Factoring $ax^2 + bx + c$	
$c > 0$	
$b > 0$	$b < 0$
$c < 0$	
$b < 0$	$b > 0$

© Stockbyte

7-4 Exercises

GUIDED PRACTICE

SEE EXAMPLE 1

Factor each trinomial by guess and check.

1. $2x^2 + 9x + 10$

2. $5x^2 + 31x + 6$

3. $5x^2 + 7x - 6$

4. $6x^2 + 37x + 6$

5. $3x^2 - 14x - 24$

6. $6x^2 + x - 2$

Factor each trinomial. Check your answer.

SEE EXAMPLE 2

7. $5x^2 + 11x + 2$

8. $2x^2 + 11x + 5$

9. $4x^2 - 9x + 5$

10. $2y^2 - 11y + 14$

11. $5x^2 + 9x + 4$

12. $3x^2 + 7x + 2$

SEE EXAMPLE 3

13. $4a^2 + 8a - 5$

14. $15x^2 + 4x - 3$

15. $2x^2 + x - 6$

16. $6n^2 - 11n - 10$

17. $10x^2 - 9x - 1$

18. $7x^2 - 3x - 10$

SEE EXAMPLE 4

19. $-2x^2 + 5x + 12$

20. $-4n^2 - 16n + 9$

21. $-5x^2 + 7x + 6$

22. $-6x^2 + 13x - 2$

23. $-4x^2 - 8x + 5$

24. $-5x^2 + x + 18$

PRACTICE AND PROBLEM SOLVING

Independent Practice

For Exercises	See Example
25–33	1
34–42	2
43–48	3
49–51	4

Factor each trinomial by guess and check.

25. $9x^2 + 9x + 2$

26. $2x^2 + 7x + 5$

27. $3n^2 + 8n + 4$

28. $10d^2 + 17d + 7$

29. $4c^2 - 17c + 15$

30. $6x^2 + 14x + 4$

31. $8x^2 + 22x + 5$

32. $6x^2 - 13x + 6$

33. $5x^2 + 9x - 18$

Factor each trinomial. Check your answer.

Extra Practice

See Extra Practice for more Skills Practice and Applications Practice exercises.

34. $6x^2 + 23x + 7$

35. $10n^2 - 17n + 7$

36. $3x^2 + 11x + 6$

37. $7x^2 + 15x + 2$

38. $3n^2 + 4n + 1$

39. $3x^2 - 19x + 20$

40. $6x^2 + 11x + 4$

41. $4x^2 - 31x + 21$

42. $10x^2 + 31x + 15$

43. $12y^2 + 17y - 5$

44. $3x^2 + 10x - 8$

45. $4x^2 + 4x - 3$

46. $2n^2 - 7n - 4$

47. $3x^2 - 4x - 15$

48. $3n^2 - n - 4$

49. $-4x^2 - 4x + 15$

50. $-3x^2 + 16x - 16$

51. $-3x^2 - x + 2$

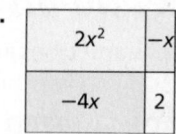 **Geometry** For Exercises 52–54, write the polynomial modeled and then factor.

52.

$12x^2$	$24x$
$3x$	6

53.

$2x^2$	$-x$
$-4x$	2

54.

$5x^2$	$-4x$
$35x$	-28

Factor each trinomial, if possible.

55. $9n^2 + 17n + 8$

56. $2x^2 - 7x - 4$

57. $4x^2 - 12x + 5$

58. $5x^2 - 4x + 12$

59. $3x^2 + 14x + 16$

60. $-3x^2 - 11x + 4$

61. $6x^2 - x - 12$

62. $10a^2 + 11a + 3$

63. $4x^2 - 12x + 9$

64. Geometry The area of a rectangle is $(6x^2 + 11x + 5)$ cm². The width is $(x + 1)$ cm. What is the length of the rectangle?

$(x + 1)$ cm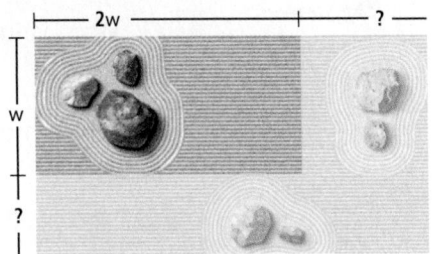

65. Write About It Write a paragraph describing how to factor $6x^2 + 13x + 6$. Show each step you would take and explain your steps.

Complete each factorization.

66.
$8x^2 + 18x - 5$
$8x^2 + 20x - 2x - 5$
$(8x^2 + 20x) - (2x + 5)$
$\blacksquare(\blacksquare + \blacksquare) - \blacksquare(2x + 5)$
$(\blacksquare - \blacksquare)(2x + 5)$

67.
$4x^2 + 9x + 2$
$4x^2 + 8x + x + 2$
$(4x^2 + 8x) + (x + 2)$
$\blacksquare(\blacksquare + \blacksquare) + \blacksquare(x + 2)$
$(\blacksquare + \blacksquare)(x + 2)$

68. Gardening The length of Rebecca's rectangular garden was two times the width w. Rebecca increased the length and width of the garden so that the area of the new garden is $(2w^2 + 7w + 6)$ square yards. By how much did Rebecca increase the length and the width?

69. Physics The height of a football that has been thrown or kicked can be described by the expression $-16t^2 + vt + h$ where t is the time in seconds, v is the initial upward velocity, and h is the initial height in feet.

a. Write an expression for the height of a football at time t when the initial upward velocity is 20 feet per second and the initial height is 6 feet.

b. Factor your expression from part **a**.

c. Find the height of the football after 1 second.

70. /// ERROR ANALYSIS /// A student attempted to factor $2x^2 + 11x + 12$ as shown. Find and explain the error.

$2x^2 + 11x + 12$		
Factors of 12	Sum	
1 and 12	13	✓
2 and 6	8	✗
3 and 4	7	✗
$(2x + 1)(x + 12)$		

MULTI-STEP TEST PREP

71. The equation $d = 2t^2$ gives the distance from the start point of a toy boat that starts at rest and accelerates at 4 cm/s². The equation $d = 10t - 8$ gives the distance from the start point of a second boat that starts at rest 8 cm behind the first boat and travels at a constant rate of 10 cm/s.

a. By setting the equations equal to each other, you can determine when the cars are the same distance from the start point: $2t^2 = 10t - 8$. Use properties of algebra to collect all terms on the left side of the equation, leaving 0 on the right side.

b. Factor the expression on the left side of the equation.

c. The boats are the same distance from the start point at $t = 1$ and $t = 4$. Explain how the factors you found in part **b** were used to find these two times.

HMH

Match each trinomial with its correct factorization.

72. $6x^2 - 29x - 5$ **A.** $(x + 5)(6x + 1)$

73. $6x^2 - 31x + 5$ **B.** $(x - 5)(6x - 1)$

74. $6x^2 + 31x + 5$ **C.** $(x + 5)(6x - 1)$

75. $6x^2 + 29x - 5$ **D.** $(x - 5)(6x + 1)$

76. Critical Thinking The quadratic trinomial $ax^2 + bx + c$ has $a > 0$ and can be factored into the product of two binomials.

    a. Explain what you know about the signs of the constants in the factors if $c > 0$.

    b. Explain what you know about the signs of the constants in the factors if $c < 0$.

77. What value of b would make $3x^2 + bx - 8$ factorable?

    Ⓐ 3   Ⓑ 10   Ⓒ 11   Ⓓ 25

78. Which product of binomials is represented by the model?

    Ⓕ $(x + 4)(3x + 5)$ Ⓗ $(x + 3)(5x + 4)$

    Ⓖ $(x + 4)(5x + 3)$ Ⓙ $(x + 5)(3x + 4)$

$5x^2$	$4x$
$15x$	12

79. Which binomial is a factor of $24x^2 - 49x + 2$?

    Ⓐ $x - 2$ Ⓑ $x - 1$ Ⓒ $x + 1$ Ⓓ $x + 2$

80. Which value of c would make $2x^2 + x + c$ NOT factorable?

    Ⓕ -15 Ⓖ -9 Ⓗ -6 Ⓙ -1

CHALLENGE AND EXTEND

Factor each trinomial. Check your answer.

81. $1 + 4x + 4x^2$ **82.** $1 - 14x + 49x^2$ **83.** $1 + 18x + 81x^2$

84. $25 + 30x + 9x^2$ **85.** $4 + 20x + 25x^2$ **86.** $4 - 12x + 9x^2$

87. Find all possible values of b such that $3x^2 + bx + 2$ can be factored.

88. Find all possible values of b such that $3x^2 + bx - 2$ can be factored.

89. Find all possible values of b such that $5x^2 + bx + 1$ can be factored.

Technology LAB

Use a Graph to Factor Polynomials

You can use a graphing calculator to help factor polynomials.

Use with Factoring
$ax^2 + bx + c$

Use appropriate tools strategically.

CC.9-12.A.SSE.3a Factor a quadratic expression to reveal the zeros of the function it defines. *Also* **CC.9-12.A.SSE.2**

🪐 **Learn It Online**
Lab Resources Online

Activity

Factor $x^2 - 3x - 4$ using algebra and check your factorization using a graphing calculator.

1 $x^2 - 3x - 4$

$(x + \blacksquare)(x + \blacksquare)$ *$b = -3$ and $c = -4$; look for factors of -4 whose sum is -3.*

$(x - 4)(x + 1)$ *$-4(1) = -4$; $-4 + 1 = -3$*

2 Press [Y=] and enter $x^2 - 3x - 4$ for **Y1**.

3 Press [GRAPH] to view the graph of the equation.

4 Press [TRACE] and use the left and right buttons to move the cursor along the graph. The graph appears to cross the x-axis at $x = -1$ and $x = 4$.

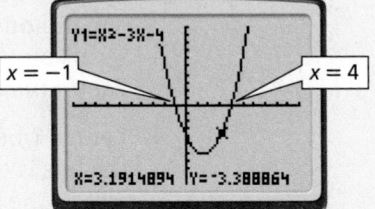

5 To find the value of y at $x = -1$, enter -1 and press [ENTER] while in *Trace* mode. The calculator gives you a value for y. Then enter 4 to find the value of y at $x = 4$.

The calculator tells you that $y = 0$ at $x = -1$ and at $x = 4$.

Notice that for a function with a binomial factor of the form $(x - a)$, it appears that a is an x-intercept.

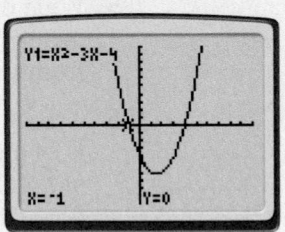

Try This

Graph each trinomial and use the graph to predict the factors. Then factor each trinomial using algebra.

1. $x^2 - x - 2$ **2.** $x^2 + 5x + 6$ **3.** $x^2 + x - 12$

4. $x^2 + 12x - 64$ **5.** $x^2 - 4x - 5$ **6.** $3x^2 + 16x - 12$

MULTI-STEP TEST PREP

Make sense of problems and persevere in solving them.

Factoring

Red Light, Green Light The equation for the motion of an object with constant acceleration is $d = vt + \frac{1}{2}at^2$ where d is distance traveled in meters, v is starting velocity in m/s, a is acceleration in m/s², and t is time in seconds.

1. A car is stopped at a traffic light. The light changes to green and the driver starts to drive, accelerating at a rate of 4 m/s². Write an equation for the distance the car travels in time t.

Speed = 15 m/s

Acceleration = 4 m/s²

2. A bus is traveling at a speed of 15 m/s. The driver approaches the same traffic light in another traffic lane. He does not brake, and continues at the same speed. Write an equation for the distance the bus travels in time t. (*Hint:* At a constant speed, the acceleration is 0 m/s².)

3. Set the equations equal to each other so you can determine when the car and bus are the same distance from the intersection. Collect all the terms on the left side of this new equation, leaving 0 on the right side. Factor the expression on the left side of the equation.

4. Let $t = 0$ be the point at which the car is just starting to drive and the bus is even with the car. Find the other time when the vehicles will be the same distance from the intersection.

5. What distance will the two vehicles have traveled when they are again at the same distance from the intersection?

6. A truck traveling at 16 m/s is 24 meters behind the bus at $t = 0$. The equation $d = -24 + 16t$ gives the position of the truck. At what time will the truck be the same distance from the intersection as the bus? What will that distance be?

READY TO GO ON?

Quiz for Lessons 7-1 Through 7-4

7-1 Factors and Greatest Common Factors

Write the prime factorization of each number.

1. 54 **2.** 42 **3.** 50 **4.** 120 **5.** 44 **6.** 78

Find the GCF of each pair of monomials.

7. $6p^3$ and $2p$ **8.** $12x^3$ and $18x^4$

9. -15 and $20s^4$ **10.** $3a$ and $4b^2$

11. Brent is making a wooden display case for his baseball collection. He has 24 balls from American League games and 30 balls from National League games. He wants to display the same number of baseballs in each row and does not want to put American League baseballs in the same row as National League baseballs. How many rows will Brent need in the display case to put the greatest number of baseballs possible in each row?

7-2 Factoring by GCF

Factor each polynomial. Check your answer.

12. $2d^3 + 4d$ **13.** $m^2 - 8m^5$

14. $12x^4 - 8x^3 - 4x^2$ **15.** $3k^2 + 6k - 3$

16. The surface area of a cone can be found using the expression $s\pi r + \pi r^2$, where s represents the slant height and r represents the radius of the base. Factor this expression.

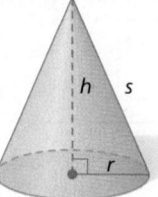

Factor each polynomial by grouping. Check your answer.

17. $w^3 - 4w^2 + w - 4$ **18.** $3x^3 + 6x^2 - 4x - 8$

19. $2p^3 - 6p^2 + 15 - 5p$ **20.** $n^3 - 6n^2 + 5n - 30$

7-3 Factoring $x^2 + bx + c$

Factor each trinomial. Check your answer.

21. $n^2 + 9n + 20$ **22.** $d^2 - 6d - 7$ **23.** $x^2 - 6x + 8$

24. $y^2 + 7y - 30$ **25.** $k^2 - 6k + 5$ **26.** $c^2 - 10c + 24$

27. Simplify and factor the expression $n(n + 3) - 4$. Show that the original expression and the factored form have the same value for $n = 0, 1, 2, 3$, and 4.

7-4 Factoring $ax^2 + bx + c$

Factor each trinomial. Check your answer.

28. $2x^2 + 11x + 5$ **29.** $3n^2 + 16n + 21$ **30.** $5y^2 - 7y - 6$

31. $4g^2 - 10g + 6$ **32.** $6p^2 - 18p - 24$ **33.** $12d^2 + 7d - 12$

34. The area of a rectangle is $(8x^2 + 8x + 2)$ cm^2. The width is $(2x + 1)$ cm. What is the length of the rectangle?

7-5 Factoring Special Products

CC.9-12.A.SSE.2 Use the structure of an expression to identify ways to rewrite it.

Objectives
Factor perfect-square trinomials.

Factor the difference of two squares.

Who uses this?
Urban planners can use the area of a square park to find its length and width. (See Example 2.)

Previously, you studied the patterns of some special products of binomials. You can use those patterns to factor certain polynomials.

A trinomial is a perfect square if:
- The **first** and **last** terms are perfect squares.
- The **middle** term is two times one factor from the first term and one factor from the last term.

$$9x^2 + 12x + 4$$
$$3x \cdot 3x \quad 2(3x \cdot 2) \quad 2 \cdot 2$$

Know it!
·*Note*

Perfect-Square Trinomials

PERFECT-SQUARE TRINOMIAL	EXAMPLES
$a^2 + 2ab + b^2 = (a + b)(a + b) = (a + b)^2$	$x^2 + 6x + 9 = (x + 3)(x + 3) = (x + 3)^2$
$a^2 - 2ab + b^2 = (a - b)(a - b) = (a - b)^2$	$x^2 - 2x + 1 = (x - 1)(x - 1) = (x - 1)^2$

EXAMPLE **1** **Recognizing and Factoring Perfect-Square Trinomials**

Determine whether each trinomial is a perfect square. If so, factor. If not, explain.

A $x^2 + 12x + 36$

$$x^2 + 12x + 36$$
$$x \cdot x \quad 2(x \cdot 6) \quad 6 \cdot 6$$

The trinomial is a perfect square. Factor.

Method 1 Factor.
$$x^2 + 12x + 36$$

Factors of 36	Sum	
1 and 36	37	✗
2 and 18	20	✗
3 and 12	15	✗
4 and 9	13	✗
6 and 6	12	✓

$$(x + 6)(x + 6)$$

Method 2 Use the rule.
$$x^2 + 12x + 36 \quad a = x, b = 6$$
$$x^2 + 2(x)(6) + 6^2 \quad \textit{Write the trinomial as } a^2 + 2ab + b^2.$$
$$(x + 6)^2 \quad \textit{Write the trinomial as } (a + b)^2.$$

Determine whether each trinomial is a perfect square. If so, factor. If not, explain.

B $4x^2 - 12x + 9$

$$4x^2 - 12x + 9$$

$2x \cdot 2x \qquad 2(2x \cdot 3) \qquad 3 \cdot 3$ *The trinomial is a perfect square. Factor.*

$$\begin{array}{ll} 4x^2 - 12x + 9 & a = 2x,\ b = 3 \\ (2x)^2 - 2(2x)(3) + 3^2 & a^2 - 2ab + b^2 \\ (2x - 3)^2 & (a - b)^2 \end{array}$$

C $x^2 + 9x + 16$

$$x^2 + 9x + 16$$

$x \cdot x \qquad 2(x \cdot 4) \qquad 4 \cdot 4 \qquad\qquad 2(x \cdot 4) \neq 9x$

$x^2 + 9x + 16$ is not a perfect-square trinomial because $9x \neq 2(x \cdot 4)$.

CHECK IT OUT! Determine whether each trinomial is a perfect square. If so, factor. If not, explain.

1a. $x^2 + 4x + 4$ **1b.** $x^2 - 14x + 49$ **1c.** $9x^2 - 6x + 4$

Helpful Hint

You can check your answer by using the FOIL method.

For Example 1B,
$(2x - 3)^2 =$
$(2x - 3)(2x - 3) =$
$4x^2 - 6x - 6x + 9 =$
$4x^2 - 12x + 9$

EXAMPLE 2

Problem-Solving Application

The park in the center of the Place des Vosges in Paris, France, is in the shape of a square. The area of the park is $(25x^2 + 70x + 49)$ ft². The side length of the park is in the form $cx + d$, where c and d are whole numbers. Find an expression in terms of x for the perimeter of the park. Find the perimeter when $x = 8$ ft.

MATHEMATICAL PRACTICES

Make sense of problems and persevere in solving them.

1 Understand the Problem

The **answer** will be an expression for the perimeter of the park and the value of the expression when $x = 8$.

List the **important information:**
- The park is a square with area $(25x^2 + 70x + 49)$ ft².
- The side length of the park is in the form $cx + d$, where c and d are whole numbers.

2 Make a Plan

The formula for the area of a square is area $= (\text{side})^2$.

Factor $25x^2 + 70x + 49$ to find the side length of the park. Write a formula for the perimeter of the park, and evaluate the expression for $x = 8$.

Solve

$$25x^2 + 70x + 49 \qquad a = 5x,\ b = 7$$
$$(5x)^2 + 2(5x)(7) + 7^2 \quad \textit{Write the trinomial as } a^2 + 2ab + b^2.$$
$$(5x + 7)^2 \qquad \textit{Write the trinomial as } (a + b)^2.$$

$$25x^2 + 70x + 49 = (5x + 7)(5x + 7)$$

The side length of the park is $(5x + 7)$ ft.

Write a formula for the perimeter of the park.

$$P = 4s \qquad\qquad \textit{Write the formula for the perimeter of a square.}$$
$$= 4(5x + 7) \qquad \textit{Substitute the side length for s.}$$
$$= 20x + 28 \qquad \textit{Distribute 4.}$$

An expression for the perimeter of the park in feet is $20x + 28$.

Evaluate the expression when $x = 8$.

$$P = 20x + 28$$
$$= 20(8) + 28 \qquad \textit{Substitute 8 for x.}$$
$$= 188$$

When $x = 8$ ft, the perimeter of the park is 188 ft.

 **Look Back**

For a square with a perimeter of 188 ft, the side length is $\frac{188}{4} = 47$ ft and the area is $47^2 = 2209$ ft^2.

Evaluate $25x^2 + 70x + 49$ for $x = 8$:
$$25(8)^2 + 70(8) + 49$$
$$1600 + 560 + 49$$
$$2209 \checkmark$$

CHECK IT OUT!

2. What if...? A company produces square sheets of aluminum, each of which has an area of $(9x^2 + 6x + 1)$ m^2. The side length of each sheet is in the form $cx + d$, where c and d are whole numbers. Find an expression in terms of x for the perimeter of a sheet. Find the perimeter when $x = 3$ m.

Previously, you learned that the difference of two squares has the form $a^2 - b^2$. The difference of two squares can be written as the product $(a + b)(a - b)$. You can use this pattern to factor some polynomials.

A polynomial is a difference of two squares if:
- There are two terms, one subtracted from the other.
- Both terms are perfect squares.

$$4x^2 - 9$$
$$2x \cdot 2x \quad 3 \cdot 3$$

 **Know it! Note**

Difference of Two Squares	
DIFFERENCE OF TWO SQUARES	**EXAMPLE**
$a^2 - b^2 = (a + b)(a - b)$	$x^2 - 9 = (x + 3)(x - 3)$

EXAMPLE 3 **Recognizing and Factoring the Difference of Two Squares**

Determine whether each binomial is a difference of two squares. If so, factor. If not, explain.

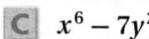

Reading Math

Recognize a difference of two squares: the coefficients of variable terms are perfect squares, powers on variable terms are even, and constants are perfect squares.

A $x^2 - 81$

$$x^2 - 81$$
$$\overset{\diagup\ \diagdown}{x \cdot x \quad 9 \cdot 9}$$

The polynomial is a difference of two squares.

$$x^2 - 9^2 \qquad a = x,\ b = 9$$
$$(x + 9)(x - 9) \qquad \text{Write the polynomial as } (a + b)(a - b).$$
$$x^2 - 81 = (x + 9)(x - 9)$$

B $9p^4 - 16q^2$

$$9p^4 - 16q^2$$
$$\overset{\diagup\ \diagdown}{3p^2 \cdot 3p^2 \quad 4q \cdot 4q}$$

The polynomial is a difference of two squares.

$$(3p^2)^2 - (4q)^2 \qquad a = 3p^2,\ b = 4q$$
$$(3p^2 + 4q)(3p^2 - 4q) \qquad \text{Write the polynomial as } (a + b)(a - b).$$
$$9p^4 - 16q^2 = (3p^2 + 4q)(3p^2 - 4q)$$

C $x^6 - 7y^2$

$$x^6 - 7y^2$$
$$\overset{\diagup\ \diagdown}{x^3 \cdot x^3}$$

$7y^2$ is not a perfect square.

$x^6 - 7y^2$ is not the difference of two squares because $7y^2$ is not a perfect square.

CHECK IT OUT! Determine whether the binomial is a difference of two squares. If so, factor. If not, explain.

3a. $1 - 4x^2$ **3b.** $p^8 - 49q^6$ **3c.** $16x^2 - 4y^5$

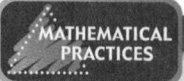

THINK AND DISCUSS

1. The binomial $1 - x^4$ is a difference of two squares. Use the rule to identify a and b in $1 - x^4$.

2. The polynomial $x^2 + 8x + 16$ is a perfect-square trinomial. Use the rule to identify a and b in $x^2 + 8x + 16$.

3. GET ORGANIZED Copy and complete the graphic organizer. Write an example of each type of special product and factor it.

Special Product	Factored Form
Perfect-square trinomial with positive coefficient of middle term	
Perfect-square trinomial with negative coefficient of middle term	
Difference of two squares	

GUIDED PRACTICE

SEE EXAMPLE 1 Determine whether each trinomial is a perfect square. If so, factor. If not, explain.

1. $x^2 - 4x + 4$ **2.** $x^2 - 4x - 4$ **3.** $9x^2 - 12x + 4$

4. $x^2 + 2x + 1$ **5.** $x^2 - 6x + 9$ **6.** $x^2 - 6x - 9$

SEE EXAMPLE 2 **7. City Planning** A city purchases a square plot of land with an area of $(x^2 + 24x + 144)$ yd^2 for a park. The dimensions of the plot are of the form $ax + b$, where a and b are whole numbers. Find an expression for the perimeter of the park. Find the perimeter when $x = 10$ yd.

SEE EXAMPLE 3 Determine whether each binomial is a difference of two squares. If so, factor. If not, explain.

8. $1 - 4x^2$ **9.** $s^2 - 4^2$ **10.** $81x^2 - 1$

11. $4x^4 - 9y^2$ **12.** $x^8 - 50$ **13.** $x^6 - 9$

PRACTICE AND PROBLEM SOLVING

Independent Practice	
For Exercises	See Example
14–19	1
20	2
21–26	3

Extra Practice

See Extra Practice for more Skills Practice and Applications Practice exercises.

Determine whether the trinomial is a perfect square. If so, factor. If not, explain.

14. $4x^2 - 4x + 1$ **15.** $4x^2 - 4x - 1$ **16.** $36x^2 - 12x + 1$

17. $25x^2 + 10x + 4$ **18.** $9x^2 + 18x + 9$ **19.** $16x^2 - 40x + 25$

20. Measurement You are given a sheet of paper and told to cut out a square piece with an area of $(4x^2 - 44x + 121)$ mm^2. The dimensions of the square have the form $ax - b$, where a and b are whole numbers. Find an expression for the perimeter of the square you cut out. Find the perimeter when $x = 41$ mm.

Determine whether each binomial is a difference of two squares. If so, factor. If not, explain.

21. $1^2 - 4x^2$ **22.** $25m^2 - 16n^2$ **23.** $4x - 9y$

24. $49p^{12} - 9q^6$ **25.** $9^2 - 100x^4$ **26.** $x^3 - y^3$

Find the missing term in each perfect-square trinomial.

27. $x^2 + 14x + \blacksquare$ **28.** $9x^2 + \blacksquare + 25$ **29.** $\blacksquare - 36y + 81$

Factor each polynomial using the rule for perfect-square trinomials or the rule for a difference of two squares. Tell which rule you used.

30. $x^2 - 8x + 16$ **31.** $100x^2 - 81y^2$ **32.** $36x^2 + 24x + 4$

33. $4r^6 - 25s^6$ **34.** $49x^2 - 70x + 25$ **35.** $x^{14} - 144$

36. Write About It What is similar about a perfect-square trinomial and a difference of two squares? What is different?

37. Critical Thinking Describe two ways to create a perfect-square trinomial.

38. For what value of b would $(x + b)(x + b)$ be the factored form of $x^2 - 22x + 121$?

39. For what value of c are the factors of $x^2 + cx + 256$ the same?

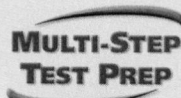

40. Juanita designed a vegetable garden in the shape of a square and purchased fencing for that design. Then she decided to change the design to a rectangle.

   a. The square garden had an area of x^2 ft². The area of the rectangular garden is $(x^2 - 25)$ ft². Factor this expression.

   b. The rectangular garden must have the same perimeter as the square garden, so Juanita added a number of feet to the length and subtracted the same number of feet from the width. Use your factors from part **a** to determine how many feet were added to the length and subtracted from the width.

   c. If the original length of the square garden was 8 feet, what are the length and width of the new garden?

41. Multi-Step The area of a square is represented by $25z^2 - 40z + 16$.

   a. What expression represents the length of a side of the square?

   b. What expression represents the perimeter of the square?

   c. What are the length of a side, the perimeter, and the area of the square when $z = 3$?

42. Multi-Step A small rectangle is drawn inside a larger rectangle as shown.

   a. What is the area of each rectangle?

   b. What is the area of the green region?

   c. Factor the expression for the area of the green region. (*Hint:* First factor out the common factor of 3 and then factor the binomial.)

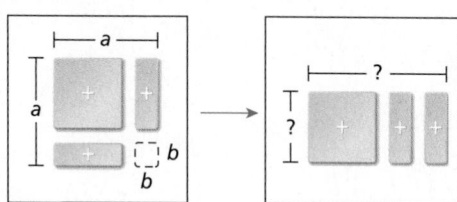

43. Evaluate each expression for the values of x.

	x	$x^2 + 10x + 25$	$(x + 5)^2$	$(x - 5)^2$	$x^2 - 10x + 25$	$x^2 - 25$
a.	−5					
b.	−1					
c.	0					
d.	1					
e.	5					

44. In the table above, which columns have equivalent values? Explain why.

45. Geometry A model for the difference of two squares is shown below. Copy and complete the second figure by writing the missing labels.

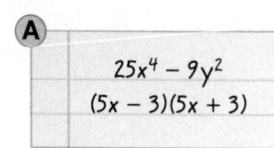

46. /// ERROR ANALYSIS /// Two students factored $25x^4 - 9y^2$. Which is incorrect? Explain the error.

Ⓐ
$25x^4 - 9y^2$
$(5x - 3)(5x + 3)$

Ⓑ
$25x^4 - 9y^2$
$(5x^2 - 3y)(5x^2 + 3y)$

47. A polynomial expression is evaluated for the x- and y-values shown in the table. Which expression could have been evaluated to give the values shown in the third column?

x	y	Value of Expression
0	0	0
−1	−1	0
1	1	0
1	−1	4

Ⓐ $x^2 - y^2$

Ⓑ $x^2 + 2xy + y^2$

Ⓒ $x^2 - 2xy + y^2$

Ⓓ None of the above

48. The area of a square is $4x^2 + 20x + 25$. Which expression can also be used to model the area of the square?

Ⓕ $(2x - 5)(5 - 2x)$ Ⓗ $(2x - 5)^2$

Ⓖ $(2x + 5)(2x - 5)$ Ⓙ $(2x + 5)^2$

49. Gridded Response Evaluate the polynomial expression $x^2 - 18x + 81$ for $x = 10$.

CHALLENGE AND EXTEND

50. The binomial $81x^4 - 16$ can be factored using the rule for a difference of two squares.

  a. Fill in the factorization: $81x^4 - 16$
  $$\left(9x^2 + \blacksquare\right)\left(\blacksquare - \blacksquare\right)$$

  b. One binomial from part **a** can be further factored. Identify the binomial and factor it.

  c. Write your own binomial that can be factored twice as the difference of two squares.

51. The expression $4 - (v + 2)^2$ is the difference of two squares, because it fits the rule $a^2 - b^2$.

  a. Identify a and b in the expression.

  b. Factor and simplify $4 - (v + 2)^2$.

The *difference of cubes* is an expression of the form $a^3 - b^3$. It can be factored according to the rule $a^3 - b^3 = (a - b)(a^2 + ab + b^2)$. For each binomial, identify a and b, and factor using the rule.

52. $x^3 - 1$ **53.** $27y^3 - 64$ **54.** $n^6 - 8$

Mental Math

Recognizing patterns of special products can help you perform multiplication mentally.

Remember these special products.

Patterns of Special Products	
Difference of Two Squares	$(a + b)(a - b) = a^2 - b^2$
Perfect-Square Trinomial	$(a + b)^2 = a^2 + 2ab + b^2$ $(a - b)^2 = a^2 - 2ab + b^2$

Example 1

Simplify $17^2 - 7^2$.

This expression is a difference of two squares with $a = 17$ and $b = 7$.

$$a^2 - b^2 = (a + b)(a - b)$$ *Write the rule for a difference of two squares.*

$$17^2 - 7^2 = (17 + 7)(17 - 7)$$ *Substitute 17 for a and 7 for b.*

$$= (24)(10)$$ *Simplify.*

$$= 240$$

Example 2

Simplify $14^2 + 2(14)(6) + 6^2$.

This expression is a perfect-square trinomial with $a = 14$ and $b = 6$.

$$a^2 + 2ab + b^2 = (a + b)^2$$ *Write the rule for a perfect-square trinomial.*

$$14^2 + 2(14)(6) + 6^2 = (14 + 6)^2$$ *Substitute 14 for a and 6 for b.*

$$= (20)^2$$ *Simplify.*

$$= 400$$

Try This

Simplify each expression using the rules for special products.

1. $18^2 - 12^2$
2. $11^2 + 2(11)(14) + 14^2$
3. $22^2 - 18^2$
4. $38^2 - 2(38)(27) + 27^2$
5. $29^2 - 2(29)(17) + 17^2$
6. $55^2 + 2(55)(45) + 45^2$
7. $14^2 - 9^2$
8. $13^2 - 12^2$
9. $14^2 + 2(14)(16) + 16^2$

7-6 Choosing a Factoring Method

CC.9-12.A.SSE.2 Use the structure of an expression to identify ways to rewrite it.

Objectives
Choose an appropriate method for factoring a polynomial.

Combine methods for factoring a polynomial.

Why learn this?
You will need to factor polynomials to solve quadratic equations, which have many applications in physics. (See Exercise 42.)

The height of a leaping ballet dancer can be modeled by a quadratic polynomial. Solving an equation that contains that polynomial may require factoring the polynomial.

Recall that a polynomial is in its fully factored form when it is written as a product that cannot be factored further.

EXAMPLE 1 Determining Whether an Expression Is Completely Factored

Tell whether each expression is completely factored. If not, factor it.

A $2x(x^2 + 4)$

$2x(x^2 + 4)$ *Neither 2x nor x^2 + 4 can be factored further.*

$2x(x^2 + 4)$ is completely factored.

B $(2x + 6)(x + 5)$

$(2x + 6)(x + 5)$ *2x + 6 can be further factored.*

$2(x + 3)(x + 5)$ *Factor out 2, the GCF of 2x and 6.*

$2(x + 3)(x + 5)$ is completely factored.

> **Caution!** //////
> $x^2 + 4$ is a *sum* of squares, and cannot be factored.

CHECK IT OUT! Tell whether each expression is completely factored. If not, factor it.

1a. $5x^2(x - 1)$ **1b.** $(4x + 4)(x + 1)$

To factor a polynomial completely, you may need to use more than one factoring method. Use the steps below to factor a polynomial completely.

Factoring Polynomials
Step 1 Check for a greatest common factor.
Step 2 Check for a pattern that fits the difference of two squares or a perfect-square trinomial.
Step 3 To factor $x^2 + bx + c$, look for two numbers whose sum is b and whose product is c. To factor $ax^2 + bx + c$, check factors of a and factors of c in the binomial factors. The sum of the products of the outer and inner terms should be b.
Step 4 Check for common factors.

EXAMPLE 2 **Factoring by GCF and Recognizing Patterns**

Factor $-2xy^2 + 16xy - 32x$ completely. Check your answer.

$$-2xy^2 + 16xy - 32x$$
$$-2x(y^2 - 8y + 16)$$ *Factor out the GCF. $y^2 - 8y + 16$ is a perfect-square trinomial of the form $a^2 - 2ab + b^2$.*
$$-2x(y - 4)^2$$ *$a = y, b = 4$*

Check $-2x(y - 4)^2 = -2x(y^2 - 8y + 16)$
$$= -2xy^2 + 16xy - 32x \checkmark$$

 **CHECK IT OUT!** Factor each polynomial completely. Check your answer.

2a. $4x^3 + 16x^2 + 16x$　　　　**2b.** $2x^2y - 2y^3$

If none of the factoring methods work, the polynomial is unfactorable.

EXAMPLE 3 **Factoring by Multiple Methods**

Factor each polynomial completely.

A $2x^2 + 5x + 4$

$$2x^2 + 5x + 4$$ *The GCF is 1 and there is no pattern.*
$$(\boxed{}x + \boxed{})(\boxed{}x + \boxed{})$$ *$a = 2$ and $c = 4$; Outer + Inner = 5*

Remember!

For a polynomial of the form $ax^2 + bx + c$, if there are no integers whose sum is b and whose product is ac, then the polynomial is unfactorable.

Factors of 2	Factors of 4	Outer + Inner	
1 and 2	1 and 4	$1(4) + 2(1) = 6$	✗
1 and 2	4 and 1	$1(1) + 2(4) = 9$	✗
1 and 2	2 and 2	$1(2) + 2(2) = 6$	✗

$2x^2 + 5x + 4$ is unfactorable.

B $3n^4 - 15n^3 + 12n^2$

$$3n^2(n^2 - 5n + 4)$$ *Factor out the GCF. There is no pattern.*
$$(n + \boxed{})(n + \boxed{})$$ *$b = -5$ and $c = 4$; look for factors of 4 whose sum is -5.*

Factors of 4	Sum	
-1 and -4	-5	✓

The factors needed are -1 and -4.

$$3n^2(n - 1)(n - 4)$$

C $4x^3 + 18x^2 + 20x$

$$2x(2x^2 + 9x + 10)$$ *Factor out the GCF. There is no pattern.*
$$(\boxed{}x + \boxed{})(\boxed{}x + \boxed{})$$ *$a = 2$ and $c = 10$; Outer + Inner = 9*

Factors of 2	Factors of 10	Outer + Inner	
1 and 2	1 and 10	$1(10) + 2(1) = 12$	✗
1 and 2	10 and 1	$1(11) + 2(10) = 21$	✗
1 and 2	2 and 5	$1(5) + 2(2) = 9$	✓

$$(x + 2)(2x + 5)$$

$$2x(x + 2)(2x + 5)$$

 $p^5 - p$

$\quad p(p^4 - 1)$ *Factor out the GCF.*

$\quad p(p^2 + 1)(p^2 - 1)$ *$p^4 - 1$ is a difference of two squares.*

$\quad p(p^2 + 1)(p + 1)(p - 1)$ *$p^2 - 1$ is a difference of two squares.*

CHECK IT OUT! **Factor each polynomial completely. Check your answer.**

3a. $3x^2 + 7x + 4$ **3b.** $2p^5 + 10p^4 - 12p^3$

3c. $9q^6 + 30q^5 + 24q^4$ **3d.** $2x^4 + 18$

Know it! Note

Methods to Factor Polynomials

Any Polynomial—Look for the greatest common factor.

$ab - ac = a(b - c)$	$6x^2y + 10xy^2 = 2xy(3x + 5y)$

Binomials—Look for a difference of two squares.

$a^2 - b^2 = (a + b)(a - b)$	$x^2 - 9y^2 = (x + 3y)(x - 3y)$

Trinomials—Look for perfect-square trinomials and other factorable trinomials.

$a^2 + 2ab + b^2 = (a + b)^2$ $a^2 - 2ab + b^2 = (a - b)^2$	$x^2 + 4x + 4 = (x + 2)^2$ $x^2 - 2x + 1 = (x - 1)^2$
$x^2 + bx + c = (x + \blacksquare)(x + \blacksquare)$ $ax^2 + bx + c = (\blacksquare x + \blacksquare)(\blacksquare x + \blacksquare)$	$x^2 + 3x + 2 = (x + 1)(x + 2)$ $6x^2 + 7x + 2 = (2x + 1)(3x + 2)$

Polynomials of Four or More Terms—Factor by grouping.

$ax + bx + ay + by = x(a + b) + y(a + b)$ $= (x + y)(a + b)$	$2x^3 + 4x^2 + x + 2 = (2x^3 + 4x^2) + (x + 2)$ $= 2x^2(x + 2) + 1(x + 2)$ $= (x + 2)(2x^2 + 1)$

MATHEMATICAL PRACTICES

THINK AND DISCUSS

1. Give an expression that includes a polynomial that is not completely factored.

2. Give an example of an unfactorable binomial and an unfactorable trinomial.

 **Know it! Note**

3. GET ORGANIZED Copy the graphic organizer. Draw an arrow from each expression to the method you would use to factor it.

Factoring Methods	
Polynomial	**Method**
1. $16x^4 - 25y^8$	**A.** Factoring out the GCF
2. $x^2 + 10x + 25$	**B.** Factoring by grouping
3. $9t^2 + 27t + 18t^4$	**C.** Unfactorable
4. $a^2 + 3a - 7a - 21$	**D.** Difference of two squares
5. $100b^2 + 81$	**E.** Perfect-square trinomial

Exercises

GUIDED PRACTICE

SEE EXAMPLE **1**

Tell whether each expression is completely factored. If not, factor it.

1. $3x(9x^2 + 1)$

2. $2(4x^3 - 3x^2 - 8x)$

3. $2k^2(4 - k^3)$

4. $(2x + 3)(3x - 5)$

5. $4(4p^4 - 1)$

6. $a(a^3 + 2ab + b^2)$

Factor each polynomial completely. Check your answer.

SEE EXAMPLE **2**

7. $3x^5 - 12x^3$

8. $4x^3 + 8x^2 + 4x$

9. $8pq^2 + 8pq + 2p$

10. $18rs^2 - 2r$

11. $mn^5 - m^3n$

12. $2x^2y - 20xy + 50y$

SEE EXAMPLE **3**

13. $6x^4 - 3x^3 - 9x^2$

14. $3y^2 + 14y + 4$

15. $p^5 + 3p^3 + p^2 + 3$

16. $7x^5 + 21x^4 - 28x^3$

17. $2z^2 + 11z + 6$

18. $9p^2 - q^2 + 3p$

PRACTICE AND PROBLEM SOLVING

Independent Practice	
For Exercises	See Example
19–24	1
25–30	2
31–36	3

Extra Practice

See Extra Practice for more Skills Practice and Applications Practice exercises.

Tell whether each expression is completely factored. If not, factor it.

19. $2x(y^3 - 4y^2 + 5y)$

20. $2r(25r^6 - 36)$

21. $3n^2(n^2 - 25)$

22. $2m(m + 1)(m + 4)$

23. $2y^2(4x^2 + 9)$

24. $4(7g + 9h^2)$

Factor each polynomial completely. Check your answer.

25. $-4x^3 + 24x^2 - 36x$

26. $24r^2 - 6r^4$

27. $5d^2 - 60d + 135$

28. $4y^8 + 36y^7 + 81y^6$

29. $98x^3 - 50xy^2$

30. $4x^3y - 4x^2y - 8xy$

31. $5x^2 - 10x + 14$

32. $121x^2 + 36y^2$

33. $p^4 - 16$

34. $4m^6 - 30m^5 + 36m^4$

35. $2k^3 + 3k^2 + 6k + 9$

36. $ab^4 - 16a$

Write an expression for each situation. Factor your expression.

37. the square of Ella's age plus 12 times Ella's age plus 36

38. the square of the distance from point A to point B minus 81

39. the square of the number of seconds Bob can hold his breath minus 16 times the number of seconds plus 28

40. three times the square of the number of apples on a tree minus 22 times the number of apples plus 35

41. the square of Beth's score minus 49

42. Physics The height in meters of a ballet dancer's center of mass when she leaps can be modeled by the polynomial $-5t^2 + 30t + 1$, where t is time in seconds after the jump. Tell whether the polynomial is fully factored when written as $-1(5t^2 - 30t - 1)$. Explain.

 43. Write About It When asked to factor a polynomial completely, you first determine that the terms in the polynomial do not share any common factors. What would be your next step?

Factor and simplify each expression.

44. $12(x + 1)^2 + 60(x + 1) + 75$

45. $(2x + 3)^2 - (x - 4)^2$

46. $45x(x - 2)^2 + 60x(x - 2) + 20x$

47. $(3x - 5)^2 - (y + 2)^2$

MULTI-STEP TEST PREP

48. a. The area of a Marci's rectangular flower garden is $(x^2 + 2x - 15)$ ft². Factor this expression.

b. Draw a diagram of the garden and label the length and width with your factors from part **a.**

c. Find the length and width of the flower garden if $x = 7$ ft.

49. Critical Thinking Show two methods of factoring $4x^2 - 100$.

50. Estimation Estimate the value of $2x^2 + 5xy + 3y^2$ when $x = -10.1$ and $y = 10.05$. (*Hint:* Factor the expression first.)

51. ///ERROR ANALYSIS/// Examine the factorization shown. Explain why the factorization is incorrect.

$12x^2 - 12x - 3$
$3(4x^2 - 4x - 1)$
$3(2x - 1)(2x - 1)$

Math History

Blaise Pascal was a French mathematician who lived in the 1600s.

Math History Use the following information for Exercises 52–54.

The triangle at right is called *Pascal's Triangle*. The triangle starts with 1 and each of the other numbers in the triangle is the sum of the two numbers in the row above it.

0						1				
1					1		1			
2				1		2		1		
3			1		3		3		1	
4		1		4		6		4		1
5	1		5		10		10		5	1

Pascal's Triangle can be used to write the product of a binomial raised to an integer power. The numbers in each row give you the coefficients of each term in the product.

$$(a + b)^3 = a^3 + 3a^2b + 3ab^2 + b^3$$

The numbers in row 3 are 1, 3, 3, 1. These are the coefficients of the terms in the product $(a + b)^3$. The power of a decreases in each term and the power of b increases in each term.

Use the patterns you see in Pascal's Triangle to write the power of the binomial $a + b$ given by each polynomial.

52. $a^6 + 6a^5b + 15a^4b^2 + 20a^3b^3 + 15a^2b^4 + 6ab^5 + b^6 = (a + b)^\blacksquare$

53. $a^8 + 8a^7b + 28a^6b^2 + 56a^5b^3 + 70a^4b^4 + 56a^3b^5 + 28a^2b^6 + 8ab^7 + b^8 = (a + b)^\blacksquare$

54. $a^7 + 7a^6b + 21a^5b^2 + 35a^4b^3 + 35a^3b^4 + 21a^2b^5 + 7ab^6 + b^7 = (a + b)^\blacksquare$

TEST PREP

55. Which expression equals $6x^2 + 7x - 10$?

Ⓐ $(6x + 2)(x - 5)$
Ⓑ $(2x + 5)(3x - 2)$
Ⓒ $(x + 2)(6x - 5)$
Ⓓ $(3x + 2)(2x - 5)$

56. What is the complete factorization of $16x^{12} - 256$?

Ⓕ $16(x^6 + 4)(x^6 - 4)$
Ⓖ $(4x^6 + 16)(4x^6 - 16)$
Ⓗ $16(x^6 + 4)(x^3 + 2)(x^3 - 2)$
Ⓙ $(4x^6 + 16)(2x^3 + 4)(2x^3 - 4)$

57. Which of the expressions below represents the fifth step of the factorization?

Step 1: $40a^3 - 60a^2 - 10a + 15$

Step 2: $5(8a^3 - 12a^2 - 2a + 3)$

Step 3: $5[(8a^3 - 12a^2) - (2a - 3)]$

Step 4: $5[4a^2(2a - 3) - 1(2a - 3)]$

Step 5: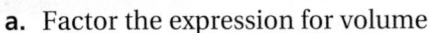

Step 6: $5(2a - 3)(2a + 1)(2a - 1)$

(A) $5(2a - 3)(2a + 3)(4a^2 - 1)$

(B) $5(2a - 3)(4a^2 + 1)$

(C) $5(2a - 3)(4a^2 - 1)$

(D) $5(2a - 3)(2a - 3)(4a^2 - 1)$

58. Short Response Use the polynomial $8x^3 + 24x^2 + 18x$ for the following.

  a. Factor the polynomial. Explain each step and tell whether you used any rules for special products.

  b. Explain another set of steps that could be used to factor the polynomial.

CHALLENGE AND EXTEND

59. Geometry The volume of the cylinder shown is represented by the expression $72\pi p^3 + 48\pi p^2 + 8\pi p$. The height of the cylinder is $8p$.

$V = \pi r^2 h$

  a. Factor the expression for volume.

  b. What expression represents the radius of the cylinder?

  c. If the radius is 4 cm, what are the height and volume of the cylinder?

Factor.

60. $g^7 + g^3 + g^5 + g^4$

61. $h^2 + h^8 + h^6 + h^4$

62. $x^{n+2} + x^{n+1} + x^n$

63. $x^{n+5} + x^{n+4} + x^{n+3}$

64. Geometry The rectangular prism has the dimensions shown.

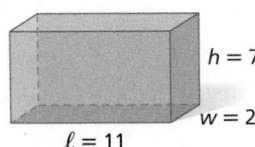

$h = 7$

$w = 2$

$\ell = 11$

  a. Write expressions for the height and length of the prism using w.

  b. Write a polynomial that represents the volume of the prism using w.

MULTI-STEP TEST PREP

MATHEMATICAL PRACTICES

Make sense of problems and persevere in solving them.

Factoring

Shaping the Environment The Environmental Awareness Club is going to plant a garden on the front lawn of the school. Henry suggests a garden in the shape of a square. Theona suggests a rectangular shape.

Width = ?

1. Henry's plans include a square garden with an area of $(x^2 + 12x + 36)$ m². Write expressions for the length and width of the square garden.

2. A drawing of the square garden shows a length of 12 m. What is the width of the square garden? What is the value of x? What is the total area of the square garden?

Length = 12 m

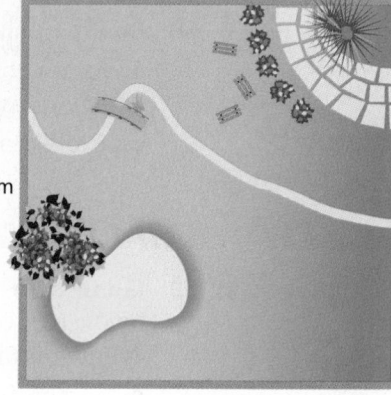

3. Theona's plans include a rectangular garden with an area of $(x^2 + 14x + 24)$ m². Write expressions for the length and width of the rectangular garden.

Width = ?

4. A drawing of the rectangular garden shows that the length is 6 m longer than the length of the square garden. What is the width of the rectangular garden? How much shorter is the width of the rectangular garden than the square garden?

Length = (12 + 6) m

5. Find the perimeter of each garden in terms of x.

6. Which plan should the club choose if they want the garden that covers the most area? Which plan should the club choose if they want the garden that requires the least fencing around it? Explain your reasoning.

READY TO GO ON?

Quiz for Lessons 7-5 Through 7-6

7-5 Factoring Special Products

Determine whether each trinomial is a perfect square. If so, factor. If not, explain.

1. $x^2 + 8x + 16$

2. $4x^2 - 20x + 25$

3. $x^2 + 3x + 9$

4. $2x^2 - 4x + 4$

5. $9x^2 - 12x + 4$

6. $x^2 - 12x - 36$

7. An architect is designing square windows with an area of $(x^2 + 20x + 100)$ ft^2. The dimensions of the windows are of the form $ax + b$, where a and b are whole numbers. Find an expression for the perimeter of the windows. Find the perimeter of a window when $x = 4$ ft.

Determine whether each trinomial is a difference of two squares. If so, factor. If not, explain.

8. $x^2 - 121$

9. $4t^2 - 20$

10. $1 - 9y^4$

11. $25m^2 - 4m^6$

12. $16x^2 + 49$

13. $r^4 - t^2$

14. The area of a square is $(36d^2 - 36d + 9)$ in^2.

    a. What expression represents the length of a side of the square?

    b. What expression represents the perimeter of the square?

    c. What are the length of a side, the perimeter, and the area of the square when $d = 2$ in.?

7-6 Choosing a Factoring Method

Tell whether each expression is completely factored. If not, factor it.

15. $5(x^2 + 3x + 1)$

16. $6x(5x^2 - x)$

17. $3t(t^4 - 9)$

18. $2(m^2 - 10m + 25)$

19. $3(2y^2 - 5)(y + 1)$

20. $(2n + 6)(n - 4)$

Factor each polynomial completely. Check your answer.

21. $3x^3 - 12x^2 + 12x$

22. $16m^3 - 4m$

23. $5x^3y - 45xy$

24. $3t^2 + 5t - 1$

25. $3c^2 + 12c - 63$

26. $x^5 - 81x$

Write an expression for each situation. Then factor your expression.

27. the difference of the square of a board's length and 36

28. the square of Michael's age minus 8 times Michael's age plus 16

29. two times the square of a car's speed plus 2 times the car's speed minus 12

30. three times the cube of Jessie's height plus 3 times the square of Jessie's height minus 6 times Jessie's height

31. Write an expression for the area of the shaded region. Then factor the expression.

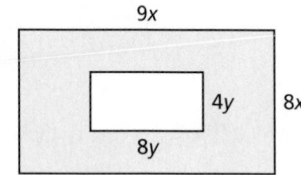

Vocabulary

greatest common factor   prime factorization

Complete the sentences below with vocabulary words from the list above.

1. A number written as a product so that each of its factors has no factors other than 1 and itself is the ___?___ .

2. The ___?___ of two monomials is the greatest of the factors that the monomials share.

7-1 Factors and Greatest Common Factors

EXAMPLES

■ **Write the prime factorization of 84.**

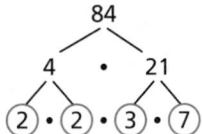

Write as a product.
Continue until all factors are prime.

■ **Write the prime factorization of 75.**

$$\begin{array}{r|r} 3 & 75 \\ 5 & 25 \\ 5 & 5 \\ \hline & 1 \end{array}$$

Keep dividing by prime factors until the quotient is 1.

$75 = 3 \cdot 5 \cdot 5 = 3 \cdot 5^2$

■ **Find the GCF of 36 and 90.**

$36 = 2 \cdot \boxed{2} \cdot \boxed{3} \cdot \boxed{3}$
$90 = \quad\; \boxed{2} \cdot \boxed{3} \cdot \boxed{3} \cdot 5$

Write the prime factorization of each number.

$2 \cdot 3 \cdot 3 = 18$

Find the product of the common factors.

The GCF of 36 and 90 is 18.

■ **Find the GCF of $10x^5$ and $4x^2$.**

$10x^5 = \boxed{2} \cdot 5 \cdot \boxed{x} \cdot \boxed{x} \cdot x \cdot x \cdot x$
$4x^2 \;= \boxed{2} \cdot 2 \cdot \boxed{x} \cdot \boxed{x}$

Write the prime factorization of each coefficient.
Write powers as products.

$2 \cdot \quad x \cdot x = 2x^2$

Find the product of the common factors.

The GCF of $10x^5$ and $4x^2$ is $2x^2$.

EXERCISES

Write the prime factorization of each number.

3. 12   **4.** 20

5. 32   **6.** 23

7. 40   **8.** 64

9. 66   **10.** 114

Find the GCF of each pair of numbers.

11. 15 and 50

12. 36 and 132

13. 29 and 30

14. 54 and 81

15. 20 and 48

Find the GCF of each pair of monomials.

16. $9m$ and 3

17. $4x$ and $2x^2$

18. $-18b^4$ and $27b^2$

19. $100r$ and $25r^5$

20. A hardware store carries 42 types of boxed nails and 36 types of boxed screws. The store manager wants to build a rack so that he can display the hardware in rows. He wants to put the same number of boxes in each row, but he wants no row to contain both nails and screws. What is the greatest number of boxes that he can display in one row? How many rows will there be if the manager puts the greatest number of boxes in each row?

7-2 Factoring by GCF

EXAMPLES

■ **Factor $3t^3 - 9t^2$. Check your answer.**

$3t^3 = 3 \cdot t \cdot t \cdot t$
$9t^2 = 3 \cdot 3 \cdot t \cdot t$ *Find the GCF.*

GCF: $3 \cdot t \cdot t = 3t^2$

$3t^3 - 9t^2 = 3t^2(t) - 3t^2(3)$
$\qquad\qquad = 3t^2(t - 3)$ *Factor out the GCF.*

Check $3t^2(t - 3) = 3t^3 - 9t^2$ ✓

■ **Factor $-12s - 6s^3$. Check your answer.**

$-1(12s + 6s^3)$ *Factor out -1.*

$12s = 2 \cdot 2 \cdot 3 \cdot s$
$6s^3 = 2 \cdot 3 \cdot s \cdot s \cdot s$ *Find the GCF.*

GCF: $2 \cdot 3 \cdot s = 6s$

$-1(12s + 6s^3)$
$-1[(6s)(2) + (6s)(s^2)]$
$-1[(6s)(2 + s^2)]$
$-6s(2 + s^2)$ *Factor out the GCF.*

Check $-6s(2 + s^2) = -12s - 6s^3$ ✓

■ **Factor $5(x - 7) + 3x(x - 7)$ by grouping.**

$5(x - 7) + 3x(x - 7)$ *$(x - 7)$ is a common factor.*

$(x - 7)(5 + 3x)$ *Factor out $(x - 7)$.*

■ **Factor $6b^3 + 8b + 15b^2 + 20$ by grouping.**

$(6b^3 + 8b) + (15b^2 + 20)$ *Group terms that have a common factor.*

$2b(3b^2 + 4) + 5(3b^2 + 4)$ *Factor each group.*

$(3b^2 + 4)(2b + 5)$ *Factor out $(3b^2 + 4)$.*

■ **Factor $2m^3 - 6m^2 + 15 - 5m$. Check your answer.**

$(2m^3 - 6m^2) + (15 - 5m)$ *Group terms.*
$2m^2(m - 3) + 5(3 - m)$ *Factor each group.*

$2m^2(m - 3) + 5(-1)(m - 3)$ *Rewrite $(3 - m)$ as $(-1)(m - 3)$.*

$2m^2(m - 3) - 5(m - 3)$ *Simplify.*
$(m - 3)(2m^2 - 5)$ *Factor out $(m - 3)$.*

Check $(m - 3)(2m^2 - 5)$

$\qquad\qquad 2m^3 - 5m - 6m^2 + 15$
$\qquad\qquad 2m^3 - 6m^2 + 15 - 5m$ ✓

EXERCISES

Factor each polynomial. Check your answer.

21. $5x - 15x^3$ **22.** $-16b + 32$

23. $-14v - 21$ **24.** $4a^2 - 12a - 8$

25. $5g^5 - 10g^3 - 15g$ **26.** $40p^2 - 10p + 30$

27. A civil engineer needs the area of a rectangular lot to be $(6x^2 + 5x)$ ft². Factor this polynomial to find possible expressions for the dimensions of the lot.

Factor each expression.

28. $2x(x - 4) + 9(x - 4)$

29. $t(3t + 5) - 6(3t + 5)$

30. $5(6 - n) - 3n(6 - n)$

31. $b(b + 4) + 2(b + 4)$

32. $x^2(x - 3) + 7(x - 3)$

Factor each polynomial. Check your answer.

33. $n^3 + n - 4n^2 - 4$

34. $6b^2 - 8b + 15b - 20$

35. $2h^3 - 7h + 14h^2 - 49$

36. $3t^2 + 18t + t + 6$

37. $10m^3 + 15m^2 - 2m - 3$

38. $8p^3 + 4p - 6p^2 - 3$

39. $5r - 10 + 2r - r^2$

40. $b^3 - 5b + 15 - 3b^2$

41. $6t - t^3 - 4t^2 + 24$

42. $12h - 3h^2 + h - 4$

43. $d - d^2 + d - 1$

44. $6b - 5b^2 + 10b - 12$

45. $5t - t^2 - t + 5$

46. $8b^2 - 2b^3 - 5b + 20$

47. $3r - 3r^2 - 1 + r$

48. Write an expression for the area of each of the two rectangles shown. Then write and factor an expression for the combined area.

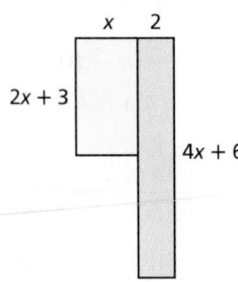

7-3 Factoring $x^2 + bx + c$

EXAMPLES

Factor each trinomial. Check your answer.

- $x^2 + 14x + 45$

  $(x + \blacksquare)(x + \blacksquare)$ *Look for factors of 45*

  $(x + 9)(x + 5)$ *whose sum is 14.*

  Check $(x + 9)(x + 5) = x^2 + 5x + 9x + 45$

  $= x^2 + 14x + 45 ✓$

- $x^2 + 6x - 27$

  $(x + \blacksquare)(x - \blacksquare)$ *Look for factors of −27*

  $(x + 9)(x - 3)$ *whose sum is 6.*

  Check $(x + 9)(x - 3) = x^2 - 3x + 9x - 27$

  $= x^2 + 6x - 27 ✓$

EXERCISES

Factor each trinomial. Check your answer.

49. $x^2 + 6x + 5$ **50.** $x^2 + 6x + 8$

51. $x^2 + 8x + 15$ **52.** $x^2 - 8x + 12$

53. $x^2 + 10x + 25$ **54.** $x^2 - 13x + 22$

55. $x^2 + 24x + 80$ **56.** $x^2 - 26x + 120$

57. $x^2 + 5x - 84$ **58.** $x^2 - 5x - 24$

59. $x^2 - 3x - 28$ **60.** $x^2 + 4x - 5$

61. $x^2 + x - 6$ **62.** $x^2 + x - 20$

63. $x^2 - 2x - 48$ **64.** $x^2 - 5x - 36$

65. $x^2 - 6x - 72$ **66.** $x^2 - 3x - 70$

67. $x^2 + 14x - 120$ **68.** $x^2 + 6x - 7$

69. The rectangle shown has an area of $\left(y^2 + 8y + 15\right)$ m². What is the width of the rectangle?

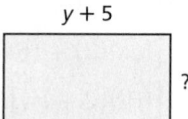

7-4 Factoring $ax^2 + bx + c$

EXAMPLES

Factor each trinomial.

- $6x^2 + 17x + 5$

  $(\blacksquare x + \blacksquare)(\blacksquare x + \blacksquare)$ *a = 6 and c = 5;*

  Outer + Inner = 17

Factors of 6	Factors of 5	Outer + Inner
1 and 6	5 and 1	$1(1) + 6(5) = 31$ ✗
2 and 3	1 and 5	$2(5) + 3(1) = 13$ ✗
2 and 3	5 and 1	$1(1) + 3(5) = 17$ ✓

  $(2x + 5)(3x + 1)$

- $2n^2 - n - 10$

  $(\blacksquare n + \blacksquare)(\blacksquare n + \blacksquare)$ *a = 2 and c = −10;*

  Outer + Inner = −1

Factors of 2	Factors of −10	Outer + Inner
1 and 2	1 and −10	$1(-10) + 2(1) = -8$ ✗
1 and 2	−1 and 10	$1(10) + 2(-1) = 8$ ✗
1 and 2	2 and −5	$1(-5) + 2(2) = -1$ ✓

  $(1n + 2)(2n - 5) = (n + 2)(2n - 5)$

EXERCISES

Factor each trinomial. Check your answer.

70. $2x^2 + 11x + 5$ **71.** $3x^2 + 10x + 7$

72. $2x^2 - 3x + 1$ **73.** $3x^2 + 8x + 4$

74. $5x^2 + 28x + 15$ **75.** $6x^2 - 19x + 15$

76. $4x^2 + 13x + 10$ **77.** $3x^2 + 10x + 8$

78. $7x^2 - 37x + 10$ **79.** $9x^2 + 18x + 8$

80. $2x^2 - x - 1$ **81.** $3x^2 - 11x - 4$

82. $2x^2 - 11x + 5$ **83.** $7x^2 - 19x - 6$

84. $5x^2 - 9x - 2$ **85.** $-6x^2 - x + 2$

86. $6x^2 - x - 5$ **87.** $6x^2 + 17x - 14$

88. $-4x^2 + 8x + 5$ **89.** $-10x^2 + 11x + 6$

90. Write the polynomial modeled and then factor.

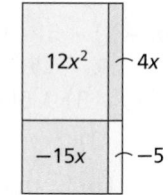

7-5 Factoring Special Products

- Determine whether $x^2 + 18x + 81$ is a perfect square. If so, factor. If not, explain.

$$x^2 + 18x + 81$$

$$x \cdot x \quad 2(x \cdot 9) \quad 9 \cdot 9$$

The trinomial is of the form $a^2 + 2ab + b^2$, so it is a perfect-square trinomial.

$$x^2 + 18x + 81 = (x + 9)^2$$

- Determine whether $49x^4 - 25y^6$ is a difference of two squares. If so, factor. If not, explain.

$$49x^4 - 25y^6$$

$$7x^2 \cdot 7x^2 \quad 5y^3 \cdot 5y^3$$

The binomial is a difference of two squares.

$$(7x^2)^2 - (5y^3)^2$$

$a = 7x^2, b = 5x^3$

$$(7x^2 + 5y^3)(7x^2 - 5y^3)$$

Write the binomial as $(a + b)(a - b)$.

$$49x^4 - 25y^6 = (7x^2 + 5y^3)(7x^2 - 5y^3)$$

Determine whether each trinomial is a perfect square. If so, factor. If not, explain.

91. $x^2 + 12x + 36$

92. $x^2 + 5x + 25$

93. $4x^2 - 2x + 1$

94. $9x^2 + 12x + 4$

95. $16x^2 + 8x + 4$

96. $x^2 + 14x + 49$

Determine whether each binomial is a difference of two squares. If so, factor. If not, explain.

97. $100x^2 - 81$

98. $x^2 - 2$

99. $5x^4 - 10y^6$

100. $(-12)^2 - (x^3)^2$

101. $121b^2 + 9c^8$

102. $100p^2 - 25q^2$

Factor each polynomial using the rule for perfect-square trinomials or the rule for a difference of two squares. Tell which rule you used.

103. $x^2 - 25$

104. $x^2 + 20x + 100$

105. $j^2 - k^4$

106. $9x^2 - 42x + 49$

107. $81x^2 + 144x + 64$

108. $16b^4 - 121c^6$

7-6 Choosing a Factoring Method

- Tell whether $(3x - 9)(x + 4)$ is completely factored. If not, factor it.

$(3x - 9)(x + 4)$ *$3x - 9$ can be factored.*

$3(x - 3)(x + 4)$ *Factor out 3, the GCF of $3x$ and 9.*

- $3ab^2 - 48a$

$3a(b^2 - 16)$ *Factor out the GCF.*

$3a(b + 4)(b - 4)$ *Factor the difference of two squares.*

Check $3a(b + 4)(b - 4) = 3a(b^2 - 16)$

$= 3ab^2 - 48a$ ✓

- $2m^3 + 4m^2 - 48m$

$2m(m^2 + 2m - 24)$ *Factor out the GCF.*

$2m(m - 4)(m + 6)$ *Factor the trinomial.*

Check $2m(m - 4)(m + 6)$

$2m(m^2 + 2m - 24)$

$2m^3 + 4m^2 - 48m$ ✓

Tell whether each polynomial is completely factored. If not, factor it.

109. $4x^2 + 10x + 6 = (4x + 6)(x + 1)$

110. $3y^2 + 75 = 3(y^2 + 25)$

111. $b^4 - 81 = (b^2 + 9)(b^2 - 9)$

112. $x^2 - 6x + 9 = (x - 3)^2$

Factor each polynomial completely. Check your answer.

113. $4x^2 - 64$

114. $3b^5 - 6b^4 - 24b^3$

115. $a^4b^3 - a^2b^5$

116. $t^{20} - t^4$

117. $5x^2 + 20x + 15$

118. $2x^4 - 50x^2$

119. $8t + 32 + 2st + 8s$

120. $25m^3 - 90m^2 - 40m$

121. $32x^4 - 48x^3 + 8x^2 - 12x$

122. $6s^4t + 12s^3t^2 + 6s^2t^3$

123. $10m^3 + 4m^2 - 90m - 36$

Find the GCF of each pair of monomials.

1. $3t^4$ and $8t^2$ **2.** $2y^3$ and $-12y$ **3.** $15n^5$ and $9n^4$

4. Write the prime factorization of 360.

5. A coin collector is arranging a display of three types of nickels. The types of nickels and number of each type are shown in the table. The collector wants to arrange them in rows with the same number in each row without having different types in the same row. How many rows will she need if she puts the greatest possible number of nickels in each row?

Type of Nickel	Number of Nickels
Liberty	16
Buffalo	24
Jefferson	40

Factor each expression.

6. $24m^2 + 4m^3$ **7.** $9x^5 - 12x$ **8.** $-2r^4 - 6$

9. $3(c - 5) + 4c(c - 5)$ **10.** $10x^3 + 4x - 25x^2 - 10$ **11.** $4y^3 - 4y^2 - 3 + 3y$

12. A model rocket is shot vertically from a deck into the air at a speed of 50 m/s. The expression $-5t^2 + 50t + 5$ gives the approximate height of the rocket after t seconds. Factor this expression.

Factor each trinomial.

13. $x^2 + 6x + 5$ **14.** $x^2 - 4x - 21$ **15.** $x^2 - 8x + 15$

16. $2x^2 + 9x + 7$ **17.** $2x^2 + 9x - 18$ **18.** $-3x^2 - 2x + 8$

Determine whether each trinomial is a perfect square. If so, factor. If not, explain.

19. $a^2 + 14a + 49$ **20.** $2x^2 + 10x + 25$ **21.** $9t^2 - 6t + 1$

Determine whether each binomial is a difference of two squares. If so, factor. If not, explain.

22. $b^2 - 16$ **23.** $25y^2 - 10$ **24.** $9a^2 - b^{10}$

25. A company is producing square sheets of plastic. Each has an area of $\left(9x^2 + 30x + 25\right)$ ft². The dimensions of each sheet are of the form $ax + b$, where a and b are whole numbers. Find an expression for the perimeter of a sheet. Find the perimeter when $x = 4$ ft.

Tell whether each expression is completely factored. If not, factor it.

26. $(6x - 3)(x + 5)$ **27.** $\left(v^5 + 10\right)\left(v^5 - 10\right)$ **28.** $(2b + 3)(3b - 2)$

Factor each polynomial completely.

29. $8x^3 + 72x^2 + 160x$ **30.** $3x^5 - 27x^3$ **31.** $8x^3 + 64x^2 - 20x - 160$

32. $cd^4 - c^7d^6$ **33.** $100x^2 - 80x + 16$ **34.** $7m^8 - 7$

COLLEGE ENTRANCE EXAM PRACTICE

FOCUS ON ACT

The ACT Mathematics test booklet usually has writing space for scratch work. You may not bring your own scratch paper to the testing center. Remember that any scratch work done in the test booklet is for your use only and will not be scored. Be sure to transfer your final answer to the answer sheet.

If you are unsure how to solve a problem, look through the answer choices. They may provide you with a clue to the solution method. It may take longer to work backward from the answer choices, so make sure you monitor your time.

You may want to time yourself as you take this practice test. It should take you about 6 minutes to complete.

---

1. What is the value of $c^2 - d^2$ if $c + d = 7$ and $c - d = -2$?

   (A) -14

   (B) -5

   (C) 5

   (D) 14

   (E) 45

---

2. Which of the following is the complete factorization of $6a^3b + 3a^2b^3$?

   (F) $6a^3b^3$

   (G) $9a^5b^4$

   (H) $3ab(2a^2 + ab^2)$

   (J) $3a^2b(2a + b^2)$

   (K) $(6a^3b)(3a^2b^3)$

---

3. Which of the following is a factor of $x^2 + 3x - 18$?

   (A) $x + 2$

   (B) $x + 3$

   (C) $x + 6$

   (D) $x + 9$

   (E) $x + 18$

---

4. The binomial $x - 3$ is NOT a factor of which of the following trinomials?

   (F) $2x^2 - x - 3$

   (G) $2x^2 - 5x - 3$

   (H) $2x^2 - 8x + 6$

   (J) $3x^2 - 6x - 9$

   (K) $3x^2 - 10x + 3$

---

5. For what value of n is $4x^2 + 20x + n^2 = (2x + n)^2$ true for any real number x?

   (A) 4

   (B) 5

   (C) 8

   (D) 10

   (E) 25

---

6. What is the factored form of $x^2 + \dfrac{2x}{3} + \dfrac{x}{2} + \dfrac{2}{6}$?

   (F) $\left(x + \dfrac{1}{3}\right)\left(x + \dfrac{1}{2}\right)$

   (G) $\left(x + \dfrac{1}{2}\right)\left(x + \dfrac{2}{3}\right)$

   (H) $\left(x + \dfrac{2}{3}\right)\left(x + \dfrac{1}{6}\right)$

   (J) $(x + 2)\left(x + \dfrac{1}{3}\right)$

   (K) $\left(x + \dfrac{1}{3}\right)\left(x + \dfrac{2}{3}\right)$

TEST TACKLER

Standardized Test Strategies

Any Question Type: Translate Words to Math

When reading a word problem, look for key words and context clues to help you translate the words into a mathematical equation or expression.

Some key words, such as those shown in this table, represent certain mathematical operations.

Action	Math Operation
Combining, increasing	Addition
Decreasing, reducing	Subtraction
Increasing or decreasing by a factor	Multiplication
Separating	Division

EXAMPLE

Short Response The polynomial $x^2 + 7x + 12$ represents the area of a rectangle in square meters. The width is $(x + 3)$ meters. Find the combined measure of the length and the width.

Use action words and context clues to translate the words into equations.

$x^2 + 7x + 12$ **represents** the **area of a rectangle** in square meters.
$x^2 + 7x + 12 \quad = \quad A$
The **width** is $(x + 3)$ meters.
$w = (x + 3)$
Find the **combined measure** of the **length** and the **width**.
$m \quad = \quad \ell \quad + \quad w$

Now use the equations to solve the problem.

$A = \ell w$	*Write the formula for area of a rectangle.*
$x^2 + 7x + 12 = \ell(x + 3)$	*Substitute $x^2 + 7x + 12$ for A and $(x + 3)$ for w.*
$(x + \boxed{?})(x + 3)$	*Factor $x^2 + 7x + 12$ to find an expression for the length.*
$(x + 4)(x + 3)$	*$3(4) = 12$; $3 + 4 = 7$*

The length is $(x + 4)$.

$m = \ell + w$	*Write the equation for the combined measure of the length and width.*
$m = (x + 4) + (x + 3)$	*Substitute $(x + 4)$ for ℓ and $(x + 3)$ for w.*
$m = 2x + 7$	*Combine like terms.*

The combined measure of the length and width is $(2x + 7)$ meters.

Sometimes you cannot write an expression or equation in the order that the key words appear. For example, the expression "4 years younger than Maria" is written mathematically as $m - 4$.

Read each test item and answer the questions that follow.

Item A
Short Response The width of Alvin's rectangular mural is 6 times the length x. Alvin plans to make a new mural with an area of $(6x^2 - 24x + 24)$ square meters. By how much did Alvin decrease the area of the mural? Show your work.

---

1. What key words or context clues are in the first sentence of the test item? Use these clues to write an expression that represents the width of the rectangle.

2. Write an equation to represent the area of Alvin's first mural.

3. What math operation does the key word *decrease* represent?

Item B
Multiple Choice Which factored expression represents the phrase shown below?

the square of the number of hours it takes to empty a cistern minus 20 times the number of hours plus 64

Ⓐ $(h - 16)(h - 4)$ Ⓒ $(h - 8)(h - 8)$

Ⓑ $(h^2 - 20)(h - 64)$ Ⓓ $(h - 16)(h + 4)$

---

4. Which word in the phrase tells you to use an exponent in your expression?

5. What is the unknown value in the expression? Define a variable to represent this value.

6. Identify other key words and the mathematical operation phrase each one represents.

Item C
Multiple Choice A company owns two packaging plants. The polynomial $0.05x^2 + 16x - 9400$ models one plant's profit, where x is the number of units packaged. The polynomial $-0.01x^2 + 17x - 5400$ models the other plant's profit. If x is 25,000, what is the total profit of both plants?

Ⓐ $-\$5,830,300$

Ⓑ $\$25,810,200$

Ⓒ $\$31,640,500$

Ⓓ $\$37,471,000$

---

7. What mathematical symbol does the word *models* represent?

8. Write an equation for each plant that can be used to determine its profit P.

9. What mathematical operation does the term "total profit" represent?

Item D
Gridded Response One of the bases of a trapezoid is 12 meters greater than its height. The other base is 4 meters less than its height. Find the area of the trapezoid when the height is 6 meters.

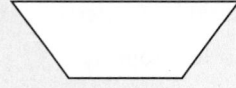

---

10. Identify the unknown dimension, and assign it a variable.

11. A student is unsure how many bases a trapezoid has. Identify the context clues that can help this student.

12. Make a list of the key words in the problem, and link each word to its mathematical meaning.

13. Write an expression for each base of the trapezoid.

STANDARDIZED TEST PREP

CUMULATIVE ASSESSMENT

Multiple Choice

1. A rectangle has an area of $(x^2 + 5x - 24)$ square units. Which of the following are possible expressions for the length and the width of the rectangle?

 (A) Length: $(x - 24)$ units; width: $(x + 1)$ units

 (B) Length: $(x - 4)$ units; width: $(x + 6)$ units

 (C) Length: $(x - 3)$ units; width: $(x + 8)$ units

 (D) Length: $(x + 12)$ units; width: $(x - 2)$ units

2. Which property of real numbers is used to transform the equation in Step 1 into the equation in Step 2?

 Step 1: $4(x - 5) + 8 = 88$
 Step 2: $4x - 20 + 8 = 88$
 Step 3: $4x - 12 = 88$
 Step 4: $4x = 100$
 Step 5: $4x = 25$

 (F) Commutative Property of Multiplication

 (G) Associative Property of Multiplication

 (H) Multiplication Property

 (J) Distributive Property

3. If $\frac{2}{3}x - 9 = 3$, what is the value of the expression $8x - 3$?

 (A) -75 (C) 61

 (B) -35 (D) 141

4. Carlos and Bonita were just hired at a manufacturing plant. Carlos will earn $12.50 per hour. He will receive a hiring bonus of $300. Bonita will not get a hiring bonus, but she will earn $14.50 per hour. Which equation can you use to determine the number of hours h when both employees will have earned the same total amount?

 (F) $300 + 14.50h = 12.50h$

 (G) $14.50h + 300 = 12.50h$

 (H) $14.50h + 12.50h = 300$

 (J) $300 + 12.50h = 14.50h$

5. Which of the following expressions is equivalent to $x^2 - 8x + 16$?

 (A) $(x + 4)^2$ (C) $(x + 8)(x + 2)$

 (B) $(x + 4)(x - 4)$ (D) $(x - 4)^2$

6. An amusement park has two jumping attractions called moonbounces in the shape of similar cubes. The larger moonbounce has a volume of 4800 cubic feet. The smaller moonbounce is half the length of the larger one. What is the volume of the smaller moonbounce?

 (F) 300 cubic feet

 (G) 600 cubic feet

 (H) 1200 cubic feet

 (J) 2400 cubic feet

7. What is the value of y if the line through $(1, -1)$ and $(2, 2)$ is parallel to the line through $(-2, 1)$ and $(-1, y)$?

 (A) -8 (C) 3

 (B) -2 (D) 4

8. Which of the following shows the complete factorization of $2x^3 + 4x^2 - 6x$?

 (F) $(2x^2 - 2x)(x + 3)$

 (G) $2x(x^2 + 2x - 3)$

 (H) $2x(x - 1)(x + 3)$

 (J) $2(x^3 + 2x^2 - 3x)$

9. Which graph shows the solution set of the compound inequality $-9 \le 5 - 2x \le 13$?

 (A)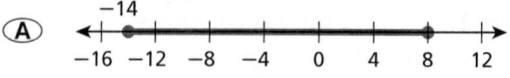

 (B)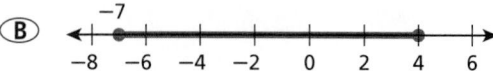

 (C)

 (D)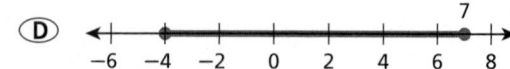

10. Which point lies on the graph of both functions?

$f(x) = 2x - 10$
$g(x) = 10 - 2x$

(F) $(5, 0)$ (H) $(0, 0)$

(G) $(1, -8)$ (J) $(2, 6)$

11. Hayley plans to solve the system of equations below.

$$\begin{cases} x + 3y = 8 \\ 5x - y = 8 \end{cases}$$

Which of the following does NOT show an equation Hayley can use to solve the system of equations?

(A) $x + 3(5x - 8) = 8$

(B) $5(8 - 3y) - y = 8$

(C) $x = 8 - 3y$

(D) $5x - (-x + 8) = 8$

12. Which value of b would make $x^2 + bx - 2$ factorable?

(F) -2 (H) 0

(G) -1 (J) 3

13. Which expression is equivalent to $5(x - 2) + 4x$?

(A) $5x - 10$ (C) $9x - 10$

(B) $9x - 2$ (D) $20x - 2$

Gridded Response

14. The complete factorization of $-12x^3 + 14x^2 + 6x$ is $-2x(ax + 1)(2x - 3)$. What is the value of a?

15. The expression $x^2 + x + b$ is a perfect-square trinomial. What is the value of b?

16. Margaret is buying a $35 sweater that is on sale for 20% off. What is the total price of the sweater, in dollars, when 5% sales tax is added?

17. A car is traveling at a constant speed. In 4 hours, the car travels 220 miles. How many hours will it take the car to travel 550 miles?

Short Response

18. The area of a certain circle is $\pi(9x^2 + 6x + 1)$ square centimeters. Find an expression for the length of the circle's radius. Explain how you found your answer.

19. A rectangle has an area of $(x^2 - 25)$ square feet.

a. Use factoring to write possible expressions for the length and width of the rectangle.

b. Use your expressions from part **a** to write an expression for the perimeter of the rectangle. Simplify the expression.

c. Use your expressions from parts **a** and **b** to find the perimeter and the area of the rectangle when $x = 10$ feet. Show your work.

20. What are 2 values of b that will make $2x^2 - bx - 20$ factorable? Explain your answer.

21. Show that you can factor the expression $x^2y - 12 + 3y - 4x^2$ by grouping in two different ways.

Extended Response

22. The diagram below can be used to show that the expression $(a + b)^2$ is equivalent to the expression $a^2 + 2ab + b^2$.

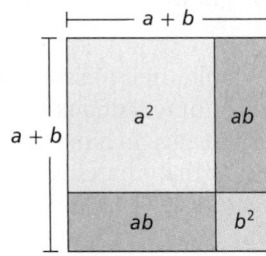

a. Make a diagram similar to the one above to model the expression $(a + b + c)^2$. Label each distinct area.

b. Use the labels from your diagram to write an expression equivalent to $(a + b + c)^2$.

c. Show that your expression in part **b** is equivalent to $(a + b + c)^2$ by evaluating each expression for $a = 4$, $b = 2$, and $c = 1$.

d. Factor $x^2 + y^2 + 9 + 2xy + 6x + 6y$. Show or explain how you found your answer.

Real-World CONNECTIONS

South Carolina

Columbia

Myrtle Beach

⭐ Alligator Adventure

Alligator Adventure is a tourist attraction in North Myrtle Beach, South Carolina. Its exhibits feature alligators, snakes, Galapagos tortoises, bears, frogs, lizards, tropical birds, and crocodiles.

Choose one or more strategies to solve each problem.

1. At birth, alligators are about 8 inches long. Adult male alligators can grow up to 18 feet long. How many times as long as a newborn alligator is an alligator that measures 18 feet?

2. Alligators build their nests out of dirt, grass, and leaves. The female alligator will deposit 40 to 50 eggs in her nest. Suppose there were 40 eggs in a nest and 80 percent of them hatched. The baby alligators each weigh 3 ounces. What is the total weight of the hatched alligators?

3. Most alligators have U-shaped snouts while most crocodiles have V-shaped snouts. Which of the equations below has a graph that could model the shape of an alligator's snout? Explain.

$$y = 3x - 4$$
$$y = x^2 - 12$$
$$y = |x^2 - 4|$$

Melton Memorial Observatory

Melton Memorial Observatory is run by the University of South Carolina in Columbia, South Carolina. The table lists some of the stars that can be seen from the observatory.

A light-year is the distance light can travel in one year, which is 9,500,000,000,000 kilometers.

Eight of the Brightest Stars as Seen from Earth				
Name	Rank	Apparent Magnitude	Distance from Earth (light-years)	Temperature (kelvins)
Sirius	1	−1.46	8.6	9,400
Arcturus	4	−0.04	34	4,290
Vega	5	0.03	25	9,600
Procyon	8	0.38	11.4	6,500
Altair	12	0.77	16	7,550
Spica	14	0.98	220	22,400
Deneb	20	1.25	1500	8,400
Regulus	25	1.35	69	12,000

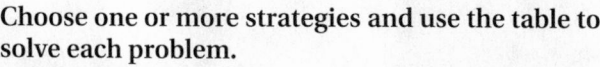

Deneb · Vega

Choose one or more strategies and use the table to solve each problem.

1. Order the stars from closest to Earth to farthest from Earth.

2. Identify which star is farthest from and which is closest to Earth. Approximate how many times as far as the closest star the farthest star is.

Apparent magnitude is a measure of how bright a star (or other object) appears from Earth. The lower the apparent magnitude of a star, the brighter the star appears.

3. Describe the correlation between apparent magnitude and distance from Earth in light-years. Make a scatter plot to support your answer.

COMMON CORE

Chapter Focus

- Graph quadratic functions.
- Solve quadratic equations.
- Use quadratic functions and equations to solve real-world problems.

FREE *Falling*

Physicists use quadratic equations to describe the motion of falling objects, such as water over a waterfall.

Learn It Online
Chapter Project Online

ARE YOU READY?

✓ Vocabulary

Match each term on the left with a definition on the right.

1. factoring

2. quadratic

3. trinomial

4. x-intercept

A. the process of writing a number or an algebraic expression as a product

B. the x-coordinate(s) of the point(s) where a graph intersects the x-axis

C. a polynomial with three terms

D. a polynomial with degree 2

E. the first number of an ordered pair of numbers that describes the location of a point on the coordinate plane

✓ Graph Functions

Graph each function for the given domain.

5. $y = -2x + 8$; D: $\{-4, -2, 0, 2, 4\}$

6. $y = (x + 1)^2$; D: $\{-3, -2, -1, 0, 1\}$

7. $y = x^2 + 3$; D: $\{-2, -1, 0, 1, 2\}$

8. $y = 2x^2$; D: all real numbers

✓ Multiply Binomials

Find each product.

9. $(m + 2)(m + 5)$

10. $(y - 7)(y + 2)$

11. $(2a + 4)(5a + 6)$

12. $(x + 1)(x + 1)$

13. $(t + 5)(t + 5)$

14. $(3n - 8)(3n - 8)$

✓ Factor Trinomials

Factor each polynomial completely.

15. $x^2 - 2x + 1$

16. $x^2 - x - 2$

17. $x^2 - 6x + 5$

18. $x^2 - x - 12$

19. $x^2 - 9x + 18$

20. $x^2 - 7x - 18$

✓ Squares and Square Roots

Find each square root.

21. $\sqrt{36}$

22. $\sqrt{121}$

23. $-\sqrt{64}$

24. $\sqrt{16}\ \sqrt{81}$

25. $\sqrt{\dfrac{9}{25}}$

26. $-\sqrt{6(24)}$

✓ Solve Multi-Step Equations

Solve each equation.

27. $3m + 5 = 11$

28. $3t + 4 = 10$

29. $5n + 13 = 28$

30. $2(k - 4) + k = 7$

31. $10 = \dfrac{r}{3} + 8$

32. $2(y - 6) = 8.6$

Study Guide: Preview

Where You've Been

Previously, you

- identified and graphed linear functions.
- transformed linear functions.
- solved linear equations.
- factored quadratic polynomials, including perfect-square trinomials.

In This Chapter

You will study

- identifying and graphing quadratic functions.
- transforming quadratic equations.
- solving quadratic equations.
- using factoring to graph quadratic functions and solve quadratic equations.

Where You're Going

You can use the skills in this chapter

- to determine the maximum height of a ball thrown into the air.
- to graph higher-degree polynomials in future math classes, including Algebra 2.
- to solve problems about the height of launched or thrown objects in Physics.

Key Vocabulary/Vocabulario

axis of symmetry	eje de simetría
completing the square	completar el cuadrado
maximum	máximo
minimum	mínimo
parabola	parábola
quadratic equation	ecuación cuadrática
quadratic function	función cuadrática
vertex	vértice
zero of a function	cero de una función

Vocabulary Connections

To become familiar with some of the vocabulary terms in the chapter, consider the following. You may refer to the chapter, the glossary, or a dictionary if you like.

1. The value of a function is determined by its rule. The rule is an algebraic expression. What is true about the algebraic expression that determines a **quadratic function** ?

2. The shape of a **parabola** is similar to the shape of an open parachute. Predict the shape of a *parabola*.

3. A **minimum** is a point on the graph of a curve with the least *y*-coordinate. How might a **maximum** be described?

4. An axis is an imaginary line. Use this information and your understanding of symmetry to define the term **axis of symmetry** .

Study Strategy: Learn Vocabulary

Mathematics has a vocabulary all its own. Many new terms appear on the pages of your textbook. Learn these new terms as they are introduced. They will give you the necessary tools to understand new concepts.

Some tips to learning new vocabulary include:

• Look at the **context** in which a new word appears.

• Use **prefixes** or **suffixes** to figure out the word's meaning.

• Relate the new term to familiar **everyday words.** Keep in mind that a word's mathematical meaning may not exactly match its everyday meaning.

polynomial = many
intersection = overlap
conversion = change

Vocabulary Word	Study Tip	Definition
Polynomial	*The prefix "poly-" means many.*	*One monomial or the sum or the difference of monomials*
Intersection	*Relate it to the meaning of the "intersection of two roads".*	*The overlapping region that shows the solution to a system of inequalities*
Conversion Factor	*Relate it to the word "convert", which means change or alter.*	*Used to convert a measurement to different units*

Complete the chart.

	Vocabulary Word	Study Tips	Definition
1.	Trinomial	▪	▪
2.	Independent system	▪	▪
3.	Variable	▪	▪

Use the context of each sentence to define the underlined word. Then relate the word to everyday words.

4. If two linear equations in a system have the same graph, the graphs are called <u>coincident</u> lines, or simply the same line.

5. In the formula $d = rt$, d is <u>isolated</u>.

8-1 Identifying Quadratic Functions

CC.9-12.F.IF.7 Graph functions expressed symbolically and show key features of the graph, ... *
a. Graph … quadratic functions and show intercepts, maxima, and minima. *Also* CC.9-12.A.REI.10

Objectives
Identify quadratic functions and determine whether they have a minimum or maximum.

Graph a quadratic function and give its domain and range.

Vocabulary
quadratic function
parabola
vertex
minimum
maximum

Why learn this?
The height of a soccer ball after it is kicked into the air can be described by a quadratic function. (See Exercise 51.)

The function $y = x^2$ is shown in the graph. Notice that the graph is not linear. This function is a *quadratic function*. A **quadratic function** is any function that can be written in the standard form $y = ax^2 + bx + c$, where a, b, and c are real numbers and $a \neq 0$. The function $y = x^2$ can be written as $y = 1x^2 + 0x + 0$, where $a = 1$, $b = 0$, and $c = 0$.

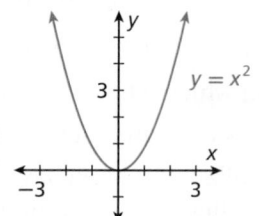

Previously, you identified linear functions by finding that a constant change in x corresponded to a constant change in y. The differences between y-values for a constant change in x-values are called *first differences*.

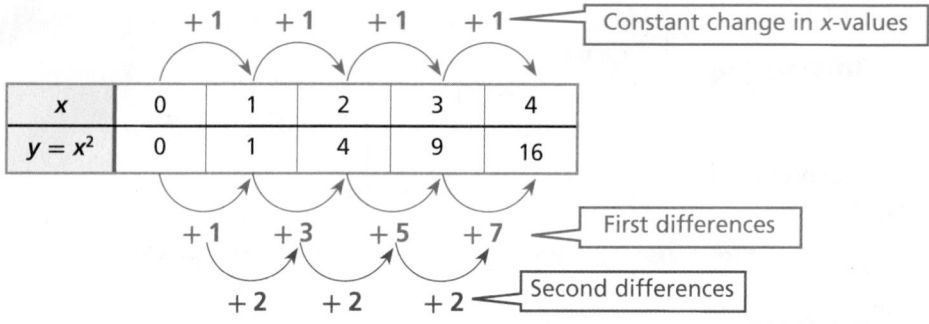

x	0	1	2	3	4
y = x²	0	1	4	9	16

Constant change in *x*-values
First differences
Second differences

Notice that the quadratic function $y = x^2$ does not have constant first differences. It has constant *second differences*. This is true for all quadratic functions.

EXAMPLE 1 Identifying Quadratic Functions

Tell whether each function is quadratic. Explain.

A

x	y
−4	8
−2	2
0	0
2	2
4	8

+2, +2, +2, +2

−6, −2, +2, +6

+4, +4, +4

Since you are given a table of ordered pairs with a constant change in x-values, see if the second differences are constant.

Find the first differences, then find the second differences.

The function is quadratic. The second differences are constant.

B $y = -3x + 20$ *Since you are given an equation, use $y = ax^2 + bx + c$.*

This is not a quadratic function because the value of a is 0.

Caution!
Be sure there is a constant change in *x*-values before you try to find first or second differences.

Aflo Foto Agency

Helpful Hint

In a quadratic function, only a cannot equal 0. It is okay for the values of b and c to be 0.

Tell whether each function is quadratic. Explain.

 C $y + 3x^2 = -4$

$$\underline{-3x^2 \quad -3x^2}$$
$$y = -3x^2 - 4$$

Try to write the function in the form $y = ax^2 + bx + c$ by solving for y. Subtract $3x^2$ from both sides.

This is a quadratic function because it can be written in the form $y = ax^2 + bx + c$ where $a = -3$, $b = 0$, and $c = -4$.

CHECK IT OUT! **Tell whether each function is quadratic. Explain.**

1a. $\{(-2, 4), (-1, 1), (0, 0), (1, 1), (2, 4)\}$ **1b.** $y + x = 2x^2$

The graph of a quadratic function is a curve called a **parabola**. To graph a quadratic function, generate enough ordered pairs to see the shape of the parabola. Then connect the points with a smooth curve.

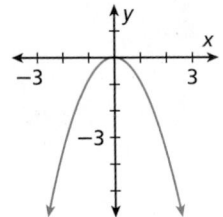

EXAMPLE 2 **Graphing Quadratic Functions by Using a Table of Values**

Use a table of values to graph each quadratic function.

 A $y = 2x^2$

x	$y = 2x^2$
-2	8
-1	2
0	0
1	2
2	8

Make a table of values. Choose values of x and use them to find values of y.

Graph the points. Then connect the points with a smooth curve.

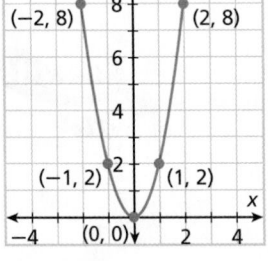

B $y = -2x^2$

x	$y = -2x^2$
-2	-8
-1	-2
0	0
1	-2
2	-8

Make a table of values. Choose values of x and use them to find values of y.

Graph the points. Then connect the points with a smooth curve.

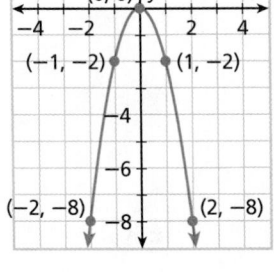

CHECK IT OUT! Use a table of values to graph each quadratic function.

2a. $y = x^2 + 2$ **2b.** $y = -3x^2 + 1$

As shown in the graphs in Examples 2A and 2B, some parabolas open upward and some open downward. Notice that the only difference between the two equations is the value of a. When a quadratic function is written in the form $y = ax^2 + bx + c$, the value of a determines the direction a parabola opens.

- A parabola opens **upward** when $a > 0$.
- A parabola opens **downward** when $a < 0$.

 **EXAMPLE 3** **Identifying the Direction of a Parabola**

Tell whether the graph of each quadratic function opens upward or downward. Explain.

 A $y = 4x^2$

$y = 4x^2$

$a = 4$ *Identify the value of a.*

Since $a > 0$, the parabola opens upward.

B $2x^2 + y = 5$

     $2x^2 + y = 5$

  $\underline{-2x^2 \qquad -2x^2}$ *Write the function in the form $y = ax^2 + bx + c$*

      $y = -2x^2 + 5$ *by solving for y. Subtract $2x^2$ from both sides.*

       $a = -2$ *Identify the value of a.*

Since $a < 0$, the parabola opens downward.

 Tell whether the graph of each quadratic function opens upward or downward. Explain.

3a. $f(x) = -4x^2 - x + 1$ **3b.** $y - 5x^2 = 2x - 6$

The highest or lowest point on a parabola is the **vertex**. If a parabola opens upward, the vertex is the lowest point. If a parabola opens downward, the vertex is the highest point.

Minimum and Maximum Values		
WORDS	If $a > 0$, the parabola opens upward, and the y-value of the vertex is the **minimum** value of the function.	If $a < 0$, the parabola opens downward, and the y-value of the vertex is the **maximum** value of the function.
GRAPHS	$y = x^2 + 6x + 9$ 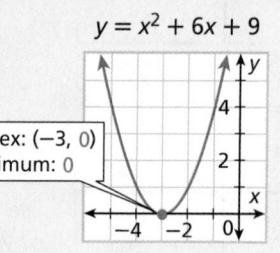 Vertex: $(-3, 0)$ Minimum: 0	$y = -x^2 + 6x - 4$ 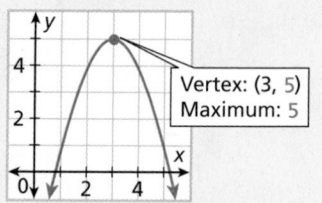 Vertex: $(3, 5)$ Maximum: 5

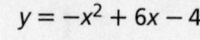

EXAMPLE 4 **Identifying the Vertex and the Minimum or Maximum**

Identify the vertex of each parabola. Then give the minimum or maximum value of the function.

A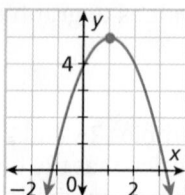

The vertex is $(1, 5)$, and the maximum is 5.

B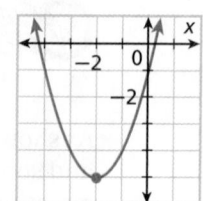

The vertex is $(-2, -5)$, and the minimum is -5.

 **CHECK IT OUT!** Identify the vertex of each parabola. Then give the minimum or maximum value of the function.

4a.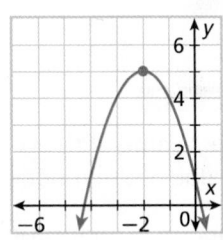

4b.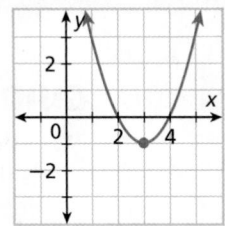

You may not be able to see the entire graph, but that does not mean the graph stops. Remember that the arrows indicate that the graph continues.

Unless a specific domain is given, you may assume that the domain of a quadratic function is all real numbers. You can find the range of a quadratic function by looking at its graph.

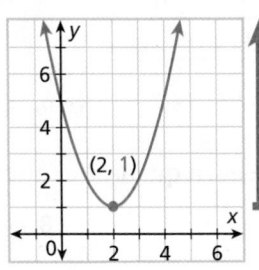

For the graph of $y = x^2 - 4x + 5$, the **range** begins at the minimum value of the function, where $y = 1$. All the y-values of the function are greater than or equal to 1. So the range is $y \geq 1$.

EXAMPLE 5 **Finding Domain and Range**

Find the domain and range.

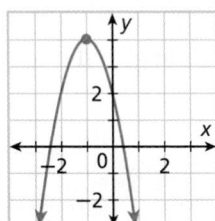

Step 1 The graph opens downward, so identify the maximum.
The vertex is $(-1, 4)$, so the maximum is 4.

Step 2 Find the domain and range.
D: all real numbers
R: $y \leq 4$

 **CHECK IT OUT!** Find the domain and range.

5a.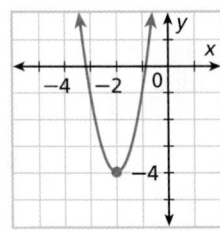

5b.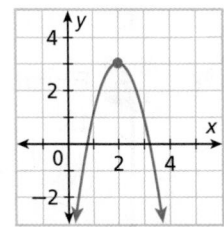

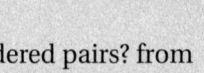 MATHEMATICAL PRACTICES

THINK AND DISCUSS

1. How can you identify a quadratic function from ordered pairs? from looking at the function rule?

2. **GET ORGANIZED** Copy and complete the graphic organizer below. In each box, describe a way of identifying quadratic functions.

> Identifying Quadratic Functions
>
> Forms a parabola

GUIDED PRACTICE

1. **Vocabulary** The y-value of the vertex of a parabola that opens upward is the _____?_____ value of the function. (*maximum* or *minimum*)

SEE EXAMPLE 1 | Tell whether each function is quadratic. Explain.

2. $y + 6x = -14$

3. $2x^2 + y = 3x - 1$

4.

x	-4	-3	-2	-1	0
y	39	18	3	-6	-9

5. $\{(-10, 15), (-9, 17), (-8, 19), (-7, 21), (-6, 23)\}$

SEE EXAMPLE 2 | Use a table of values to graph each quadratic function.

6. $y = 4x^2$ 7. $y = \dfrac{1}{2}x^2$ 8. $y = -x^2 + 1$ 9. $y = -5x^2$

SEE EXAMPLE 3 | Tell whether the graph of each quadratic function opens upward or downward. Explain.

10. $y = -3x^2 + 4x$ 11. $y = 1 - 2x + 6x^2$ 12. $y + x^2 = -x - 2$

13. $y + 2 = x^2$ 14. $y - 2x^2 = -3$ 15. $y + 2 + 3x^2 = 1$

SEE EXAMPLE 4 | Identify the vertex of each parabola. Then give the minimum or maximum value of the function.

16.
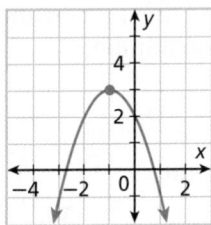

17.
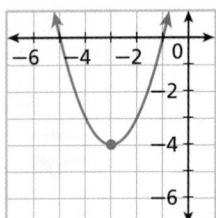

SEE EXAMPLE 5 | Find the domain and range.

18.
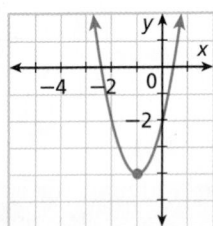

19.
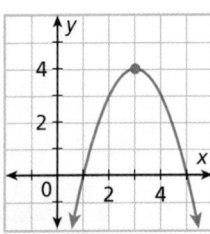

20.
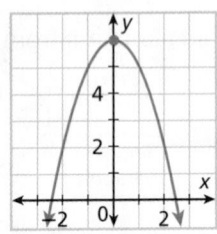

21.
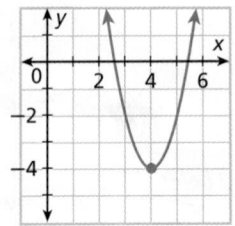

PRACTICE AND PROBLEM SOLVING

Independent Practice

For Exercises	See Example
22–25	1
26–29	2
30–32	3
33–34	4
35–38	5

Extra Practice

See Extra Practice for more Skills Practice and Applications Practice exercises.

Tell whether each function is quadratic. Explain.

22.

x	−2	−1	0	1	2
y	−1	0	4	9	15

23. $-3x^2 + x = y - 11$

24. $\{(0, -3), (1, -2), (2, 1), (3, 6), (4, 13)\}$ **25.** $y = \dfrac{2}{3}x - \dfrac{4}{9} + \dfrac{1}{6}x^2$

Use a table of values to graph each quadratic function.

26. $y = x^2 - 5$ **27.** $y = -\dfrac{1}{2}x^2$ **28.** $y = -2x^2 + 2$ **29.** $y = 3x^2 - 2$

Tell whether the graph of each quadratic function opens upward or downward. Explain.

30. $y = 7x^2 - 4x$ **31.** $x - 3x^2 + y = 5$ **32.** $y = -\dfrac{2}{3}x^2$

Identify the vertex of each parabola. Then give the minimum or maximum value of the function.

33.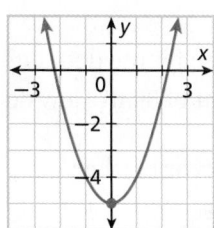

34.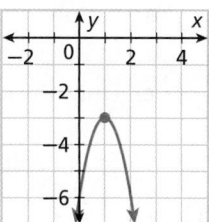

Find the domain and range.

35.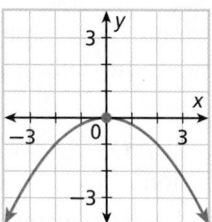

36.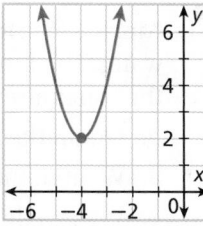

37.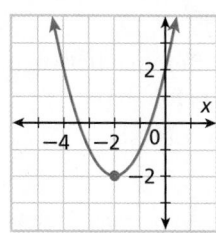

38.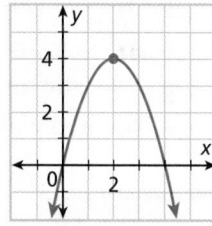

Tell whether each statement is sometimes, always, or never true.

39. The graph of a quadratic function is a straight line.

40. The range of a quadratic function is the set of all real numbers.

41. The highest power of the independent variable in a quadratic function is 2.

42. The graph of a quadratic function contains the point $(0, 0)$.

43. The vertex of a parabola occurs at the minimum value of the function.

44. The graph of a quadratic function that has a minimum opens upward.

Tell whether each function is quadratic. If it is, write the function in standard form. If not, explain why not.

45. $y = 3x - 1$

46. $y = 2x^2 - 5 + 3x$

47. $y = (x + 1)^2$

48. $y = 5 - (x - 1)^2$

49. $y = 3x^2 - 9$

50. $y = (x + 1)^3 - x^2$

51. Estimation The graph shows the approximate height y in meters of a volleyball x seconds after it is served.

   a. Estimate the time it takes for the volleyball to reach its greatest height.

   b. Estimate the greatest height that the volleyball reaches.

   c. Critical Thinking If the domain of a quadratic function is all real numbers, why is the domain of this function limited to nonnegative numbers?

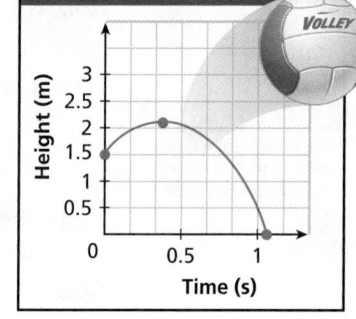

Volleyball's Height

52. Sports The height in feet of a soccer ball x seconds after it is kicked into the air is modeled by the function $y = 48x - 16x^2$.

   a. Graph the function.

   b. In this situation, what values make sense for the domain?

   c. Does the soccer ball ever reach a height of 50 ft? How do you know?

Tell whether each function is linear, quadratic, or neither.

53. $y = \frac{1}{2}x - x^2$

54. $y = \frac{1}{2}x - 3$

55. $y + 3 = -x^2$

56. $y - 2x^2 = 0$

57. $y = \frac{1}{2}x(x^2)$

58. $y = \frac{3}{x^2}$

59. $y = \frac{3}{2}x$

60. $x^2 + 2x + 1 = y$

61. Marine Biology A scientist records the motion of a dolphin as it jumps from the water. The function $h(t) = -16t^2 + 32t$ models the dolphin's height in feet above the water after t seconds.

   a. Graph the function.

   b. What domain makes sense for this situation?

   c. What is the dolphin's maximum height above the water?

   d. How long is the dolphin out of the water?

62. Write About It Explain how to tell the difference between a linear function and a quadratic function when given each of the following:

   a. ordered pairs   **b.** the function rule   **c.** the graph

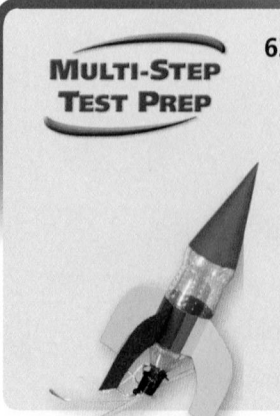

MULTI-STEP TEST PREP

63. A rocket team is using simulation software to create and study water bottle rockets. The team begins by simulating the launch of a rocket without a parachute. The table gives data for one rocket design.

   a. Show that the data represent a quadratic function.

   b. Graph the function.

   c. The acceleration due to gravity is 9.8 m/s^2. How is this number related to the data for this water bottle rocket?

Time (s)	Height (m)
0	0
1	34.3
2	58.8
3	73.5
4	78.4
5	73.5
6	58.8
7	34.3
8	0

64. Critical Thinking Given the function $-3 - y = x^2 + x$, why is it incorrect to state that the parabola opens upward and has a minimum?

65. Which of the following is the graph of a quadratic function?

Ⓐ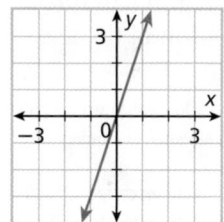

Ⓒ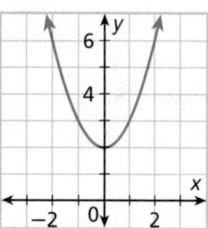

Ⓑ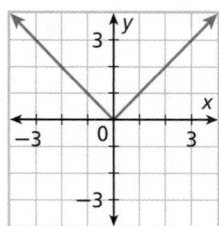

Ⓓ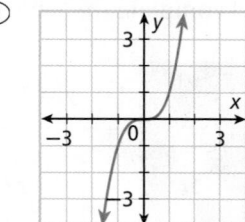

66. Which of the following quadratic functions has a maximum?

Ⓕ $2x^2 - y = 3x - 2$

Ⓖ $y = x^2 + 4x + 16$

Ⓗ $y - x^2 + 6 = 9x$

Ⓙ $y + 3x^2 = 9$

67. Short Response Is the function $f(x) = 5 - 2x^2 + 3x$ quadratic? Explain your answer by using two different methods of identification.

CHALLENGE AND EXTEND

68. Multi-Step A rectangular picture measuring 6 in. by 10 in. is surrounded by a frame with uniform width x. Write a quadratic function to show the combined area of the picture and frame.

 69. Graphing Calculator Use a graphing calculator to find the domain and range of the quadratic functions $y = x^2 - 4$ and $y = -(x + 2)^2$.

8-2 Algebra LAB

Use with Characteristics of Quadratic Functions

Explore the Axis of Symmetry

Every graph of a quadratic function is a parabola that is symmetric about a vertical line through its vertex called the *axis of symmetry*.

There is a relationship between a and b in the quadratic function and the equation of the axis of symmetry.

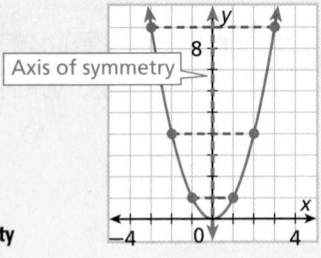

MATHEMATICAL PRACTICES Look for and express regularity in repeated reasoning.

CC.9-12.F.IF.7 Graph functions expressed symbolically and show key features of the graph, …. *
a. Graph … quadratic functions and show intercepts, maxima, and minima.

Activity

1 Copy and complete the table.

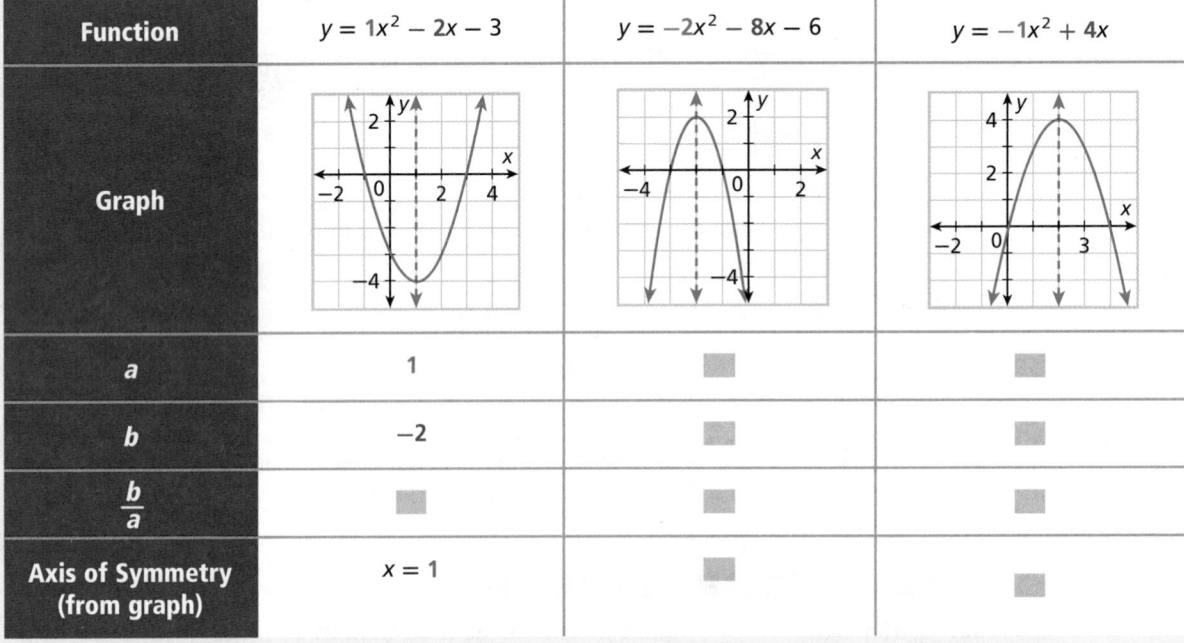

Function	$y = 1x^2 - 2x - 3$	$y = -2x^2 - 8x - 6$	$y = -1x^2 + 4x$
Graph			
a	1	▦	▦
b	-2	▦	▦
$\dfrac{b}{a}$	▦	▦	▦
Axis of Symmetry (from graph)	$x = 1$	▦	▦

2 Compare the axis of symmetry with $\frac{b}{a}$ in your chart. What can you multiply $\frac{b}{a}$ by to get the number in the equation of the axis of symmetry? (*Hint:* Write and solve an equation to find the value.) Check your answer for each function.

3 Use your answer from Problem 2 to complete the equation of the axis of symmetry of a quadratic function. $x = $ _____?_____

Try This

For the graph of each quadratic function, find the equation of the axis of symmetry.

1. $y = 2x^2 + 12x - 7$ **2.** $y = 4x^2 + 8x - 12$ **3.** $y = 5x^2 - 20x + 10$

4. $y = -3x^2 + 9x + 1$ **5.** $y = x^2 - 7$ **6.** $y = 3x^2 + x + 4$

8-2 Characteristics of Quadratic Functions

CC.9-12.F.IF.7 Graph functions expressed symbolically and show key features of the graph, ...*
a. Graph ... quadratic functions and show intercepts, maxima, and minima. *Also* **CC.9-12.F.IF.8,**
CC.9-12.F.IF.4*

Objectives
Find the zeros of a quadratic function from its graph.

Find the axis of symmetry and the vertex of a parabola.

Vocabulary
zero of a function
axis of symmetry

Who uses this?
Engineers can use characteristics of quadratic functions to find the height of the arch supports of bridges. (See Example 5.)

Recall that an x-intercept of a function is a value of x when $y = 0$. A **zero of a function** is an x-value that makes the function equal to 0. So a zero of a function is the same as an x-intercept of a function. Since a graph intersects the x-axis at the point or points containing an x-intercept these intersections are also at the zeros of the function. A quadratic function may have one, two, or no zeros.

EXAMPLE **Finding Zeros of Quadratic Functions From Graphs**

Find the zeros of each quadratic function from its graph. Check your answer.

A $y = x^2 - x - 2$

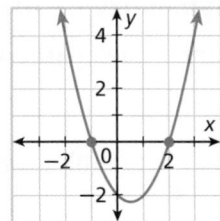

The zeros appear to be -1 and 2.
Check
$$y = x^2 - x - 2$$
$$y = (-1)^2 - (-1) - 2$$
$$= 1 + 1 - 2 = 0 \checkmark$$
$$y = 2^2 - 2 - 2$$
$$= 4 - 2 - 2 = 0 \checkmark$$

B $y = -2x^2 + 4x - 2$

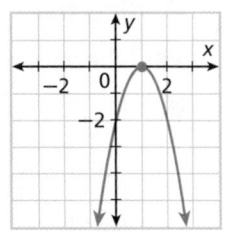

The only zero appears to be 1.
Check
$$y = -2x^2 + 4x - 2$$
$$y = -2(1)^2 + 4(1) - 2$$
$$= -2(1) + 4 - 2$$
$$= -2 + 4 - 2$$
$$= 0 \checkmark$$

C $y = \frac{1}{4}x^2 + 1$

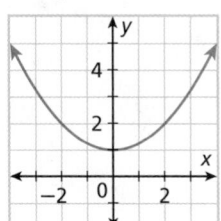

The graph does not cross the x-axis, so there are no zeros of this function.

Helpful Hint
Notice that if a parabola has only one zero, the zero is the x-coordinate of the vertex.

 Find the zeros of each quadratic function from its graph. Check your answer.

1a. $y = -4x^2 - 2$

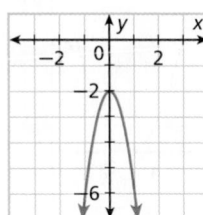

1b. $y = x^2 - 6x + 9$

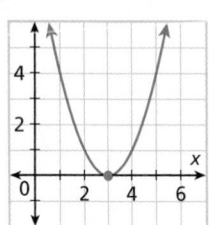

A vertical line that divides a parabola into two symmetrical halves is the **axis of symmetry**. The axis of symmetry always passes through the vertex of the parabola. You can use the zeros to find the axis of symmetry.

Finding the Axis of Symmetry by Using Zeros

WORDS	NUMBERS	GRAPH
One Zero If a function has one zero, use the x-coordinate of the vertex to find the axis of symmetry.	Vertex: $(3, 0)$ Axis of symmetry: $x = 3$	
Two Zeros If a function has two zeros, use the average of the two zeros to find the axis of symmetry.	$\dfrac{-4 + 0}{2} = \dfrac{-4}{2} = -2$ Axis of symmetry: $x = -2$	

EXAMPLE 2 **Finding the Axis of Symmetry by Using Zeros**

Find the axis of symmetry of each parabola.

A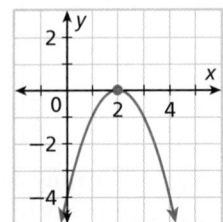

$(2, 0)$ *Identify the x-coordinate of the vertex.*

The axis of symmetry is $x = 2$.

B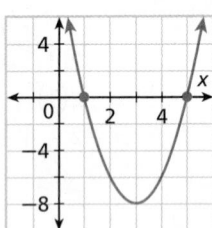

$\dfrac{1 + 5}{2} = \dfrac{6}{2} = 3$ *Find the average of the zeros.*

The axis of symmetry is $x = 3$.

 Find the axis of symmetry of each parabola.

2a. 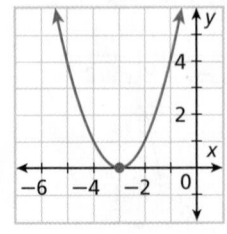   **2b.**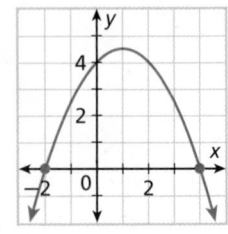

If a function has no zeros or they are difficult to identify from a graph, you can use a formula to find the axis of symmetry. The formula works for all quadratic functions.

Finding the Axis of Symmetry by Using the Formula	
FORMULA	**EXAMPLE**
For a quadratic function $y = ax^2 + bx + c$, the axis of symmetry is the vertical line $$x = -\frac{b}{2a}.$$	$y = 2x^2 + 4x + 5$ $$x = -\frac{b}{2a}$$ $$= -\frac{4}{2(2)} = -1$$ The axis of symmetry is $x = -1$.

E X A M P L E 3 **Finding the Axis of Symmetry by Using the Formula**

Find the axis of symmetry of the graph of $y = x^2 + 3x + 4$.

Step 1 Find the values of a and b.
$y = 1x^2 + 3x + 4$
$a = 1, b = 3$

Step 2 Use the formula $x = -\frac{b}{2a}$.
$$x = -\frac{3}{2(1)} = -\frac{3}{2} = -1.5$$

The axis of symmetry is $x = -1.5$.

 **3.** Find the axis of symmetry of the graph of $y = 2x^2 + x + 3$.

Once you have found the axis of symmetry, you can use it to identify the vertex.

Finding the Vertex of a Parabola
Step 1 To find the x-coordinate of the vertex, find the axis of symmetry by using zeros or the formula.
Step 2 To find the corresponding y-coordinate, substitute the x-coordinate of the vertex into the function.
Step 3 Write the vertex as an ordered pair.

E X A M P L E 4 **Finding the Vertex of a Parabola**

Find the vertex.

A $y = -x^2 - 2x$

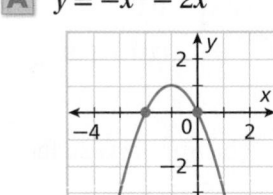

Step 1 Find the x-coordinate.
The zeros are -2 and 0.
$$x = \frac{-2 + 0}{2} = \frac{-2}{2} = -1$$

Step 2 Find the corresponding y-coordinate.
$y = -x^2 - 2x$ *Use the function rule.*
$= -(-1)^2 - 2(-1) = 1$ *Substitute −1 for x.*

Step 3 Write the ordered pair.
$(-1, 1)$

The vertex is $(-1, 1)$.

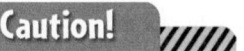

Caution!

In Example 4A Step 2, use the order of operations to simplify.
$-(-1)^2 = -(1) = -1$

Find the vertex.

B $y = 5x^2 - 10x + 3$

Step 1 Find the x-coordinate.

$a = 5, b = -10$ *Identify a and b.*

$x = -\dfrac{b}{2a}$

$= -\dfrac{-10}{2(5)} = -\dfrac{-10}{10} = 1$ *Substitute 5 for a and −10 for b.*

The x-coordinate of the vertex is 1.

Step 2 Find the corresponding y-coordinate.

$y = 5x^2 - 10x + 3$ *Use the function rule.*

$= 5(1)^2 - 10(1) + 3$ *Substitute 1 for x.*

$= 5 - 10 + 3$

$= -2$

Step 3 Write the ordered pair.

The vertex is $(1, -2)$.

 **4.** Find the vertex of the graph of $y = x^2 - 4x - 10$.

EXAMPLE 5   *Architecture Application*

The height above water level of a curved arch support for a bridge can be modeled by $f(x) = -0.007x^2 + 0.84x + 0.8$, where x is the distance in feet from where the arch support enters the water. Can a sailboat that is 24 feet tall pass under the bridge? Explain.

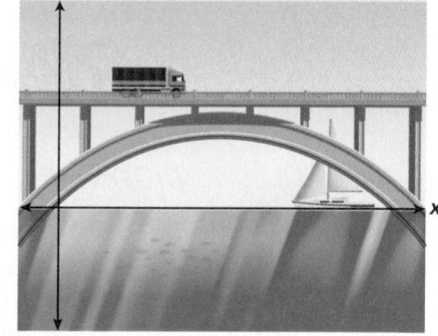

The vertex represents the highest point of the arch support.

Step 1 Find the x-coordinate.

$a = -0.007, b = 0.84$ *Identify a and b.*

$x = -\dfrac{b}{2a}$

$= -\dfrac{0.84}{2(-0.007)} = 60$ *Substitute −0.007 for a and 0.84 for b.*

Step 2 Find the corresponding y-coordinate.

$f(x) = -0.007x^2 + 0.84x + 0.8$ *Use the function rule.*

$= -0.007(60)^2 + 0.84(60) + 0.8$ *Substitute 60 for x.*

$= 26$

Since the height of the arch support is 26 feet, the sailboat can pass under the bridge.

 **5.** The height of a small rise in a roller coaster track is modeled by $f(x) = -0.07x^2 + 0.42x + 6.37$, where x is the horizontal distance in feet from a support pole at ground level. Find the greatest height of the rise.

THINK AND DISCUSS

1. How do you find the zeros of a function from its graph?

2. Describe how to find the axis of symmetry of a quadratic function if its graph does not cross the x-axis

3. **GET ORGANIZED** Copy and complete the graphic organizer. In each box, sketch a graph that fits the given description.

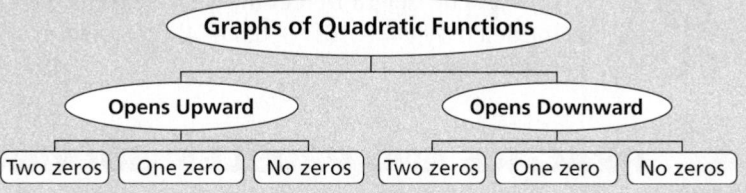

8-2 Exercises

Learn It Online
Homework Help Online
Parent Resources Online

GUIDED PRACTICE

Vocabulary Apply the vocabulary from this lesson to answer each question.

1. Why is the *zero of a function* the same as an x-intercept of a function?

2. Where is the *axis of symmetry* of a parabola located?

SEE EXAMPLE **1**

Find the zeros of each quadratic function from its graph. Check your answer.

3. $y = x^2 + 2x + 1$

4. $y = 9 - x^2$

5. $y = -x^2 - x - 4$

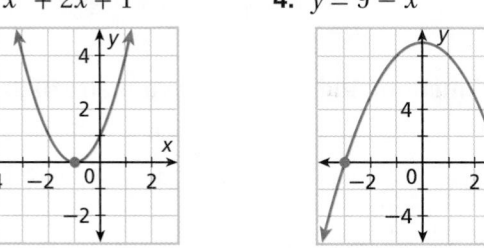

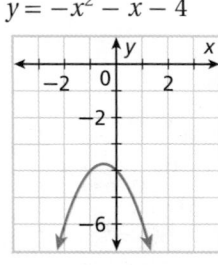

SEE EXAMPLE **2**

Find the axis of symmetry of each parabola.

6.

7.

8.

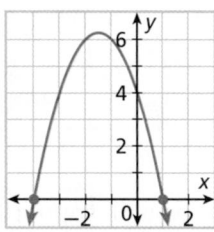

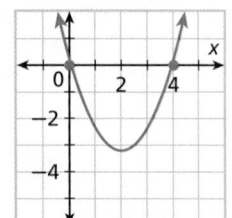

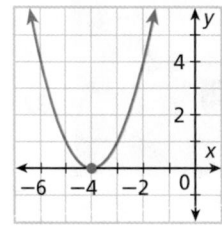

SEE EXAMPLE **3**

For each quadratic function, find the axis of symmetry of its graph.

9. $y = x^2 + 4x - 7$

10. $y = 3x^2 - 18x + 1$

11. $y = 2x^2 + 3x - 4$

12. $y = -3x^2 + x + 5$

SEE EXAMPLE 4 Find the vertex.

13. $y = -5x^2 + 10x + 3$

14. $y = x^2 + 4x - 7$

15. $y = \frac{1}{2}x^2 + 2x$

16. $y = -x^2 + 6x + 1$

17.

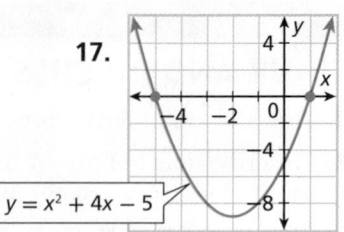

$y = x^2 + 4x - 5$

SEE EXAMPLE 5 **18. Archery** The height in feet above the ground of an arrow after it is shot can be modeled by $y = -16t^2 + 63t + 4$. Can the arrow pass over a tree that is 68 feet tall? Explain.

PRACTICE AND PROBLEM SOLVING

Independent Practice	
For Exercises	**See Example**
19–21	1
22–24	2
25–28	3
29–33	4
34	5

Extra Practice

See Extra Practice for more Skills Practice and Applications Practice exercises.

Find the zeros of each quadratic function from its graph. Check your answer.

19. $y = \frac{1}{4}x^2 - x + 3$

20. $y = -\frac{1}{3}x^2$

21. $y = x^2 + 10x + 16$

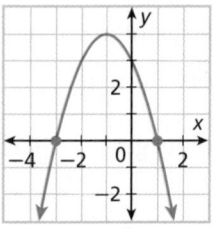
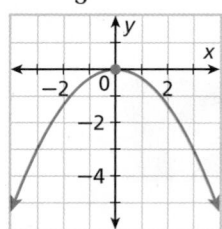
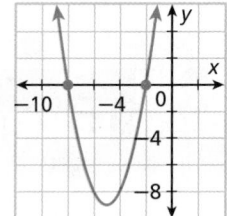

Find the axis of symmetry of each parabola.

22.

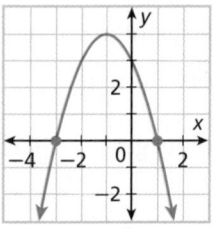

23.

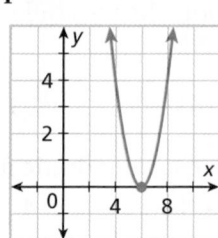

24.

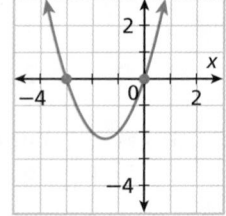

For each quadratic function, find the axis of symmetry of its graph.

25. $y = x^2 + x + 2$

26. $y = 3x^2 - 2x - 6$

27. $y = \frac{1}{2}x^2 - 5x + 4$

28. $y = -2x^2 + \frac{1}{3}x - \frac{3}{4}$

Find the vertex.

29. $y = x^2 + 7x$

30. $y = -x^2 + 8x + 16$

31. $y = -2x^2 - 8x - 3$

32. $y = -x^2 + \frac{1}{2}x + 2$

33.

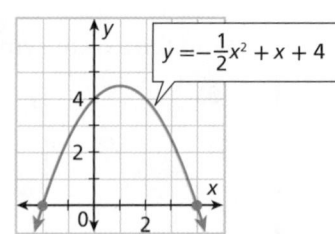

$y = -\frac{1}{2}x^2 + x + 4$

Engineering

This arched bridge spans a river near the city of Yokote in northwestern Japan.

34. Engineering The height in feet of the curved arch support for a bridge over a creek can be modeled by $f(x) = -0.628x^2 + 4.5x$, where x is the horizontal distance in feet from where the arch support enters the water. If there is a flood that raises the level of the creek by 5.5 feet, will the top of the arch support be above the water? Explain.

35. Critical Thinking What conclusion can be drawn about the axis of symmetry of any quadratic function for which $b = 0$?

36. a. Use the graph of the height of a water bottle rocket to estimate the coordinates of the parabola's vertex.

b. What does the vertex represent?

c. Find the zeros of the function. What do they represent?

d. Find the axis of symmetry. How is it related to the vertex and the zeros?

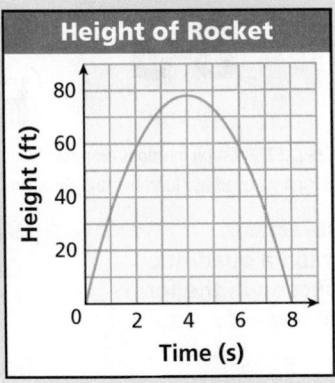

 Graphing Calculator Tell how many zeros each quadratic function has.

37. $y = 8x^2 - 4x + 2$ **38.** $0 = y + 16x^2$ **39.** $\frac{1}{4}x^2 - 7x - 12 = y - 4$

 40. Write About It If you are given the axis of symmetry of a quadratic function and know that the function has two zeros, how would you describe the location of the two zeros?

 **TEST PREP**

41. Which function has the zeros shown in the graph?

   Ⓐ $y = x^2 + 2x + 8$ Ⓒ $y = x^2 + 2x - 8$

   Ⓑ $y = x^2 - 2x - 8$ Ⓓ $y = 2x^2 - 2x + 8$

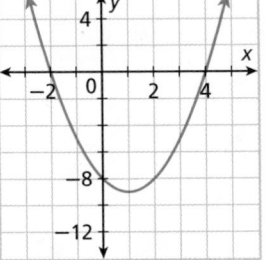

42. Which of the following functions has a graph with an axis of symmetry of $x = -\frac{1}{2}$?

   Ⓕ $y = 2x^2 - 2x + 5$ Ⓗ $2x^2 + y = 2x + 5$

   Ⓖ $2x + 5 = 2x^2 - y$ Ⓙ $2x - y = 5 - 2x^2$

43. Gridded Response For the graph of $f(x) = -3 + 20x - 5x^2$, what is the x-coordinate of its vertex?

CHALLENGE AND EXTEND

44. Describe the domain and range of a quadratic function that has exactly one zero and whose graph opens downward.

 45. Graphing Calculator The height in feet of a parabolic bridge support is modeled by $f(x) = -0.01x^2 + 20$, where $y = -5$ represents ground level and the x-axis represents the middle of the bridge. Find the height and the width of the bridge support.

8-3 Graphing Quadratic Functions

CC.9-12.F.IF7 Graph functions expressed symbolically and show key features of the graph, …. *
a. Graph … quadratic functions and show intercepts, maxima, and minima. *Also* **CC.9-12.F.IF.4***, **CC.9-12.F.IF.8**

Objective
Graph a quadratic function in the form $y = ax^2 + bx + c$.

Why use this?

Graphs of quadratic functions can help you determine how high an object is tossed or kicked. (See Exercise 14.)

Recall that a *y*-intercept is the *y*-coordinate of the point where a graph intersects the *y*-axis. The *x*-coordinate of this point is always 0. For a quadratic function written in the form $y = ax^2 + bx + c$, when $x = 0$, $y = c$. So the *y*-intercept of a quadratic function is *c*.

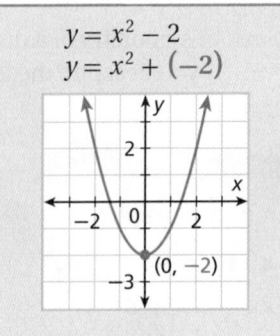

$$y = x^2 - 2$$
$$y = x^2 + (-2)$$

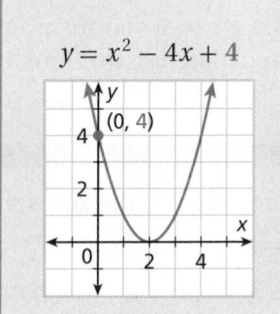

$$y = x^2 - 4x + 4$$

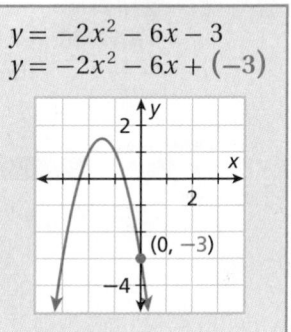

$$y = -2x^2 - 6x - 3$$
$$y = -2x^2 - 6x + (-3)$$

Previously, you found the axis of symmetry and vertex of a parabola. You can use these characteristics, the *y*-intercept, and symmetry to graph a quadratic function.

EXAMPLE 1 **Graphing a Quadratic Function**

Graph $y = x^2 - 4x - 5$.

Step 1 Find the axis of symmetry.

$$x = -\frac{-4}{2(1)}$$ *Use $x = -\dfrac{b}{2a}$. Substitute 1 for a and −4 for b.*

$$= 2$$ *Simplify.*

The axis of symmetry is $x = 2$.

Step 2 Find the vertex.

$$y = x^2 - 4x - 5$$

$$= 2^2 - 4(2) - 5$$ *The x-coordinate of the vertex is 2. Substitute 2 for x.*

$$= 4 - 8 - 5$$ *Simplify.*

$$= -9$$ *The y-coordinate is −9.*

The vertex is $(2, -9)$.

Step 3 Find the *y*-intercept.

$$y = x^2 - 4x - 5$$

$$y = x^2 - 4x + (-5)$$ *Identify c.*

The *y*-intercept is -5; the graph passes through $(0, -5)$.

Step 4 Find two more points on the same side of the axis of symmetry as the point containing the y-intercept.

Since the axis of symmetry is $x = 2$, choose x-values less than 2.

Let $x = 1$.

$y = 1^2 - 4(1) - 5$ *Substitute x-coordinates.*

$= 1 - 4 - 5$ *Simplify.*

$= -8$

Let $x = -1$.

$y = (-1)^2 - 4(-1) - 5$

$= 1 + 4 - 5$

$= 0$

Two other points are $(1, -8)$ and $(-1, 0)$.

Helpful Hint

Because a parabola is symmetrical, each point is the same number of units away from the axis of symmetry as its reflected point.

Step 5 Graph the **axis of symmetry**, the **vertex**, the point containing the **y-intercept**, and **two other points**.

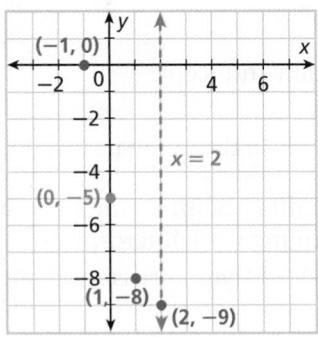

Step 6 **Reflect** the points across the axis of symmetry. Connect the points with a smooth curve.

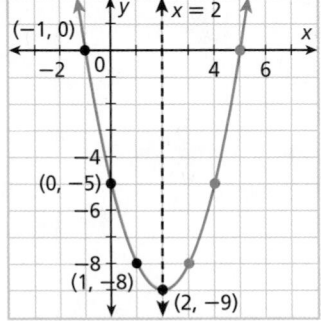

CHECK IT OUT!

Graph each quadratic function.

1a. $y = 2x^2 + 6x + 2$

1b. $y + 6x = x^2 + 9$

EXAMPLE 2

Problem-Solving Application

The height in feet of a football that is kicked can be modeled by the function $f(x) = -16x^2 + 64x$, where x is the time in seconds after it is kicked. Find the football's maximum height and the time it takes the football to reach this height. Then find how long the football is in the air.

MATHEMATICAL PRACTICES

Make sense of problems and persevere in solving them.

1 **Understand the Problem**

The **answer** includes three parts: the maximum height, the time to reach the maximum height, and the time to reach the ground.

List the important information:
- The function $f(x) = -16x^2 + 64x$ models the approximate height of the football after x seconds.

Remember!

The vertex is the highest or lowest point on a parabola. Therefore, in the example, it gives the maximum height of the football.

2 **Make a Plan**

Find the vertex of the graph because the maximum height of the football and the time it takes to reach it are the coordinates of the vertex. The football will hit the ground when its height is 0, so find the zeros of the function. You can do this by graphing.

Solve

Step 1 Find the axis of symmetry.

$$x = -\frac{64}{2(-16)}$$ *Use $x = -\frac{b}{2a}$. Substitute −16 for a and 64 for b.*

$$= -\frac{64}{-32} = 2$$ *Simplify.*

The axis of symmetry is $x = 2$.

Step 2 Find the vertex.

$$y = -16x^2 + 64x$$
$$= -16(2)^2 + 64(2)$$ *The x-coordinate of the vertex is 2. Substitute 2 for x.*
$$= -16(4) + 128$$ *Simplify.*
$$= -64 + 128$$
$$= 64$$ *The y-coordinate is 64.*

The vertex is $(2, 64)$.

Step 3 Find the y-intercept.

$$y = -16x^2 + 64x + 0$$ *Identify c.*

The y-intercept is 0; the graph passes through $(0, 0)$.

Step 4 Find another point on the same side of the axis of symmetry as the point containing the y-intercept.

Since the axis of symmetry is $x = 2$, choose an x-value that is less than 2. Let $x = 1$.

$$y = -16(1)^2 + 64(1)$$ *Substitute 1 for x.*
$$= -16 + 64$$ *Simplify.*
$$= 48$$

Another point is $(1, 48)$.

Step 5 Graph the **axis of symmetry**, the **vertex**, the point containing the **y-intercept**, and the **other point**. Then **reflect** the points across the axis of symmetry. Connect the points with a smooth curve.

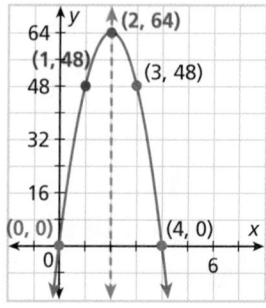

The vertex is $(2, 64)$. So at 2 seconds, the football has reached its maximum height of 64 feet. The graph shows the zeros of the function are 0 and 4. At 0 seconds the football has not yet been kicked, and at 4 seconds it reaches the ground. The football is in the air for 4 seconds.

4 **Look Back**

Check by substituting $(2, 64)$ and $(4, 0)$ into the function.

$$64 = -16(2)^2 + 64(2) \qquad 0 = -16(4)^2 + 64(4)$$
$$64 = -64 + 128 \qquad\qquad 0 = -256 + 256$$
$$64 = 64 \checkmark \qquad\qquad\quad 0 = 0 \checkmark$$

 **2.** As Molly dives into her pool, her height in feet above the water can be modeled by the function $f(x) = -16x^2 + 16x + 12$ where x is the time in seconds after she begins diving. Find the maximum height of her dive and the time it takes Molly to reach this height. Then find how long it takes her to reach the pool.

THINK AND DISCUSS

1. Explain how to find the y-intercept of a quadratic function that is written in the form $ax^2 - y = bx + c$.

2. Explain how to graph a quadratic function.

3. What do the vertex and zeros of the function represent in the situation in the Check It Out for Example 2?

4. **GET ORGANIZED** Copy and complete the graphic organizer using your own quadratic function.

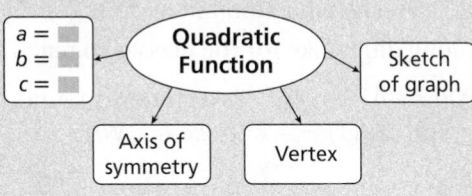

8-3 Exercises

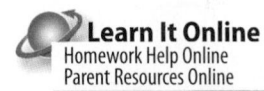
Learn It Online
Homework Help Online
Parent Resources Online

GUIDED PRACTICE

SEE EXAMPLE 1

Graph each quadratic function.

1. $y = x^2 - 2x - 3$
2. $-y - 3x^2 = -3$
3. $y = 2x^2 + 2x - 4$
4. $y = x^2 + 4x - 8$
5. $y + x^2 + 5x + 2 = 0$
6. $y = 4x^2 + 2$

SEE EXAMPLE 2

7. **Multi-Step** The height in feet of a golf ball that is hit from the ground can be modeled by the function $f(x) = -16x^2 + 96x$, where x is the time in seconds after the ball is hit. Find the ball's maximum height and the time it takes the ball to reach this height. Then find how long the ball is in the air.

PRACTICE AND PROBLEM SOLVING

Independent Practice

For Exercises	See Example
8–13	1
14	2

Extra Practice

See Extra Practice for more Skills Practice and Applications Practice exercises.

Graph each quadratic function.

8. $y = -4x^2 + 12x - 5$
9. $y = 3x^2 + 12x + 9$
10. $y - 7x^2 - 14x = 3$
11. $y = -x^2 + 2x$
12. $y - 1 = 4x^2 + 8x$
13. $y = -2x^2 - 3x + 4$

14. **Multi-Step** A juggler tosses a ring into the air. The height of the ring in feet above the juggler's hands can be modeled by the function $f(x) = -16x^2 + 16x$, where x is the time in seconds after the ring is tossed. Find the ring's maximum height above the juggler's hands and the time it takes the ring to reach this height. Then find how long the ring is in the air.

For each quadratic function, find the axis of symmetry and the vertex of its graph.

15. $y = x^2 - 8x$
16. $y = -x^2 + 6x - 4$
17. $y = 4 - 3x^2$
18. $y = -2x^2 - 4$
19. $y = -x^2 - x - 4$
20. $y = x^2 + 8x + 16$

Graph each quadratic function. On your graph, label the coordinates of the vertex. Draw and label the axis of symmetry.

21. $y = -x^2$

22. $y = -x^2 + 4x$

23. $y = x^2 - 6x + 4$

24. $y = x^2 - x$

25. $y = 3x^2 - 4$

26. $y = -2x^2 - 16x - 25$

27. **Travel** While on a vacation in Italy, Rudy visited the Leaning Tower of Pisa. When he leaned over the railing to look down from the tower, his sunglasses fell off. The height in meters of the sunglasses as they fell can be approximated by the function $y = -5x^2 + 50$, where x is the time in seconds.

  a. Graph the function. (*Hint:* Use a graphing calculator.)

  b. What is a reasonable domain and range?

  c. How long did it take for the glasses to reach the ground?

28. ///**ERROR ANALYSIS**/// Two students found the equation of the axis of symmetry for the graph of $f(x) = -x^2 - 2x + 1$. Who is incorrect? Explain the error.

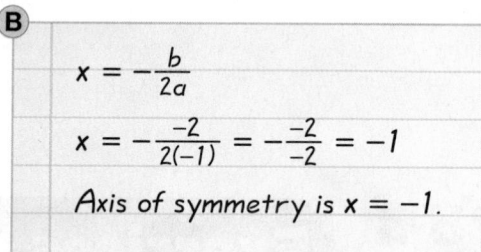

29. **Critical Thinking** The point $(5, 4)$ lies on the graph of a quadratic function whose axis of symmetry is $x = 2$. Find another point on the graph. Explain how you found the point.

Engineering Use the graph for Exercises 30–32. The velocity v in centimeters per second of a fluid flowing in a pipe varies according to the radius r of the pipe.

30. Find the radius of the pipe when the velocity is 7 cm/s.

31. Find the velocity of the fluid when the radius is 2 cm.

32. What is a reasonable domain for this function? Explain.

33. **Critical Thinking** The graph of a quadratic function has the vertex $(0, 5)$. One point on the graph is $(1, 6)$. Find another point on the graph. Explain how you found the point.

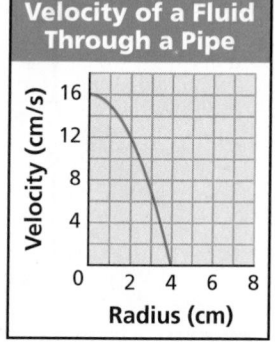

34. **Write About It** Explain how the vertex and the range can help you graph a quadratic function.

35. A water bottle rocket is shot upward with an initial velocity of $v_i = 45$ ft/s from the roof of a school, which is at h_i, 50 ft above the ground. The equation $h = -\frac{1}{2}at^2 + v_i t + h_i$ models the rocket's height as a function of time. The acceleration due to gravity a is 32 ft/s^2.

  a. Write the equation for height as a function of time for this situation.

  b. Find the vertex of this parabola.

  c. Sketch the graph of this parabola and label the vertex.

  d. What do the coordinates of the vertex represent in terms of time and height?

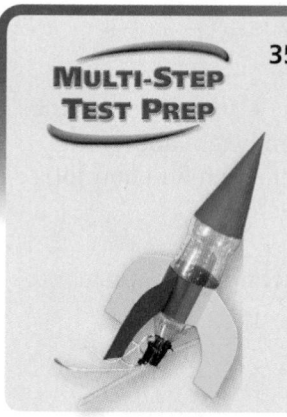

36. Copy and complete the table for each function.

Function	Graph Opens	Axis of Symmetry	Vertex	Zeros	Domain and Range
$y = x^2 + 4$	■	$x = $ ■	(■ , ■)	■	D: ■ R: ■
$y = -x^2 + 4$	■	$x = $ ■	(■ , ■)	■	D: ■ R: ■
$y + 8 - x^2 = -2x$	■	$x = $ ■	(■ , ■)	■	D: ■ R: ■

TEST PREP

37. Which is the axis of symmetry for the graph of $f(x) = 6 - 5x + \frac{1}{2}x^2$?

   Ⓐ $x = 5$ Ⓑ $x = \dfrac{1}{20}$ Ⓒ $x = -5$ Ⓓ $x = -\dfrac{1}{20}$

38. What are the coordinates of the vertex for the graph of $f(x) = x^2 - 5x + 6$?

   Ⓕ $\left(-\dfrac{5}{2}, -\dfrac{1}{4}\right)$ Ⓖ $\left(-\dfrac{5}{2}, \dfrac{1}{4}\right)$ Ⓗ $\left(\dfrac{5}{2}, \dfrac{1}{4}\right)$ Ⓙ $\left(\dfrac{5}{2}, -\dfrac{1}{4}\right)$

39. Which function's graph has an axis of symmetry of $x = 1$ and a vertex of $(1, 8)$?

   Ⓐ $y = -x^2 + x + 8$ Ⓒ $y = 2x^2 - 4x - 8$
   Ⓑ $y = x^2 + 8x + 1$ Ⓓ $y = -3x^2 + 6x + 5$

40. Short Response Graph $y = x^2 + 3x + 2$. What are the zeros, the axis of symmetry, and the coordinates of the vertex? Show your work.

CHALLENGE AND EXTEND

41. The graph of a quadratic function has its vertex at $(1, -4)$ and one zero of the function is 3. Find the other zero. Explain how you found the other zero.

42. The x-intercepts of a quadratic function are 3 and -3. The y-intercept is 6. What are the coordinates of the vertex? Does the function have a maximum or a minimum? Explain.

8-4
Technology LAB

Use with Transforming Quadratic Functions

The Family of Quadratic Functions

Functions whose graphs share the same basic characteristics form a *family of functions*. All quadratic functions form a family because their graphs are all parabolas. You can use a graphing calculator to explore the family of quadratic functions.

Learn It Online
Lab Resources Online

Activity

Describe how the value of a affects the graph of $y = ax^2$.

1 Press **Y=**. Enter Y_1 through Y_4 as shown.

Notice that Y_2 represents the parent function $y = x^2$. To make it stand out from the other functions, change its line style. When you enter Y_2, move the cursor to the line style indicator by pressing **◄**. Then press **ENTER** to cycle through the choices until a thicker line appears.

Line style indicator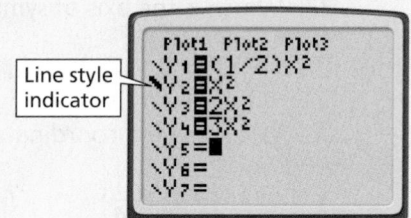

2 Press **GRAPH**.

Keep in mind the values of a as the functions are graphed. The graphing calculator will graph the functions in order.

Notice that the graph of $y = \frac{1}{2}x^2$ is wider than the graph of the parent function. The graphs of $y = 2x^2$ and $y = 3x^2$ are narrower than the graph of the parent function.

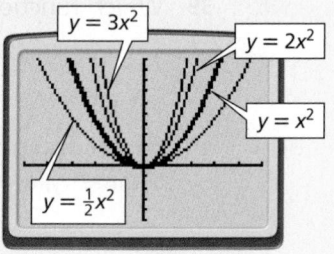
$y = 3x^2$
$y = 2x^2$
$y = x^2$
$y = \frac{1}{2}x^2$

MATHEMATICAL PRACTICES **Use appropriate tools strategically.**

CC.9-12.F.BF.3 Identify the effect on the graph of replacing $f(x)$ by $f(x) + k$, $kf(x)$, $f(kx)$, and $f(x + k)$ for specific values of k … and illustrate an explanation of the effects on the graph using technology.
CC.9-12.F.IF.7*

Try This

1. How would the graph of $y = 6x^2$ compare with the graph of the parent function?

2. How would the graph of $y = \frac{1}{5}x^2$ compare with the graph of the parent function?

3. **Make a Conjecture** Make a conjecture about the effect of a on the graph of $y = ax^2$.

Consider the graphs of $y = -\frac{1}{2}x^2$, $y = -x^2$, $y = -2x^2$, and $y = -3x^2$.

4. Describe the differences in the graphs.

5. How would the graph of $y = -8x^2$ compare with the graph of $y = -x^2$?

6. How do these results affect your conjecture from Problem 3?

Consider the graphs of $y = x^2 - 1$, $y = x^2$, $y = x^2 + 2$, and $y = x^2 + 4$.

7. Describe the differences in the graphs.

8. How would the graph of $y = x^2 - 7$ compare with the graph of the parent function?

9. **Make a Conjecture** Make a conjecture about the effect of c on the graph of $y = x^2 + c$.

8-4 Transforming Quadratic Functions

CC.9-12.F.BF.3 Identify the effect on the graph of replacing $f(x)$ by $f(x) + k$, $kf(x)$, $f(kx)$, and $f(x + k)$ for specific values of k (both positive and negative); .... Also **CC.9-12.F.IF.7***, **CC.9-12.F.IF.5***

Objective
Graph and transform quadratic functions.

Remember!

Recall that the graphs of all linear functions are transformations of the linear parent function, $f(x) = x$.

Why learn this?
You can compare how long it takes raindrops to reach the ground from different heights. (See Exercise 18.)

The quadratic parent function is $f(x) = x^2$. The graph of all other quadratic functions are transformations of the graph of $f(x) = x^2$.

For the parent function $f(x) = x^2$:
- The axis of symmetry is $x = 0$, or the y-axis.
- The vertex is $(0, 0)$.
- The function has only one zero, 0.

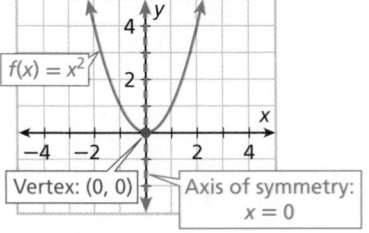

$f(x) = x^2$

Vertex: $(0, 0)$ Axis of symmetry: $x = 0$

Compare the coefficients in the following functions.	Compare the graphs of the same functions.

$$f(x) = x^2 \qquad g(x) = \frac{1}{2}x^2$$

$$h(x) = -3x^2$$

$$f(x) = 1x^2 + 0x + 0$$
$$g(x) = \frac{1}{2}x^2 + 0x + 0$$
$$h(x) = -3x^2 + 0x + 0$$

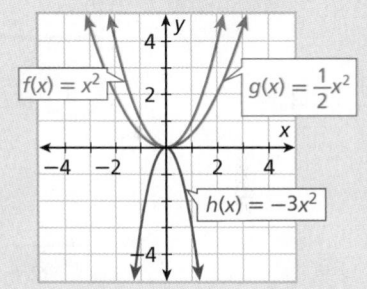

$f(x) = x^2$ $g(x) = \frac{1}{2}x^2$

$h(x) = -3x^2$

Same	Different
• $b = 0$ • $c = 0$	• Value of a

Same	Different
• Axis of symmetry is $x = 0$. • Vertex is $(0, 0)$.	• Widths of parabolas

The value of a in a quadratic function determines not only the direction a parabola opens, but also the width of the parabola.

Know it! Note

Width of a Parabola

WORDS	EXAMPLES	
The graph of $f(x) = ax^2$ is **narrower** than the graph of $f(x) = x^2$ if $\lvert a \rvert > 1$ and **wider** if $\lvert a \rvert < 1$.	Compare the graphs of $g(x)$ and $h(x)$ with the graph of $f(x)$. $\lvert -2 \rvert$? 1 $\qquad$ $\left\lvert \frac{1}{4} \right\rvert$? 1 $2 > 1$ $\qquad$ $\frac{1}{4} < 1$ narrower $\qquad$ wider	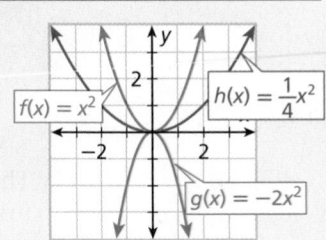 $f(x) = x^2$ $\quad$ $h(x) = \frac{1}{4}x^2$ $g(x) = -2x^2$

EXAMPLE 1 **Comparing Widths of Parabolas**

Order the functions from narrowest graph to widest.

A $f(x) = -2x^2, g(x) = \frac{1}{3}x^2, h(x) = 4x^2$

Step 1 Find $|a|$ for each function.

$$|-2| = 2 \qquad \left|\frac{1}{3}\right| = \frac{1}{3} \qquad |4| = 4$$

Step 2 Order the functions.

$h(x) = 4x^2$

$f(x) = -2x^2$ *The function with the narrowest graph has the greatest value for |a|.*

$g(x) = \frac{1}{3}x^2$

Check Use a graphing calculator to compare the graphs.

$h(x) = 4x^2$ has the narrowest graph, and $g(x) = \frac{1}{3}x^2$ has the widest graph. ✓

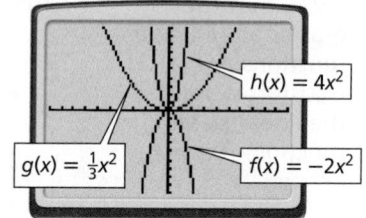

B $f(x) = 2x^2, g(x) = -2x^2$

Step 1 Find $|a|$ for each function.
$$|2| = 2 \qquad |-2| = 2$$

Step 2 Order the functions from narrowest graph to widest. Since the absolute values are equal, the graphs are the same width.

 Order the functions from narrowest graph to widest.

1a. $f(x) = -x^2, g(x) = \frac{2}{3}x^2$

1b. $f(x) = -4x^2, g(x) = 6x^2, h(x) = 0.2x^2$

Compare the coefficients in the following functions.	Compare the graphs of the same functions.
$f(x) = x^2 \qquad g(x) = x^2 - 4$ $h(x) = x^2 + 3$ $f(x) = 1x^2 + 0x + 0$ $g(x) = 1x^2 + 0x + (-4)$ $h(x) = 1x^2 + 0x + 3$	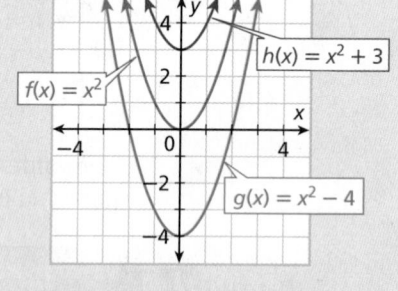

Same	Different	Same	Different
• $a = 1$ • $b = 0$	• Value of c	• Axis of symmetry is $x = 0$. • Width of parabola	• Vertex of parabola

The value of c makes these graphs look different. The value of c in a quadratic function determines not only the value of the y-intercept but also a vertical translation of the graph of $f(x) = ax^2$ up or down the y-axis.

Vertical Translations of a Parabola

The graph of the function $f(x) = x^2 + c$ is the graph of $f(x) = x^2$ translated vertically.

- If $c > 0$, the graph of $f(x) = x^2$ is translated c units **up**.
- If $c < 0$, the graph of $f(x) = x^2$ is translated c units **down**.

EXAMPLE **2** **Comparing Graphs of Quadratic Functions**

Compare the graph of each function with the graph of $f(x) = x^2$.

A $g(x) = -\frac{1}{3}x^2 + 2$

When comparing graphs, it is helpful to draw them on the same coordinate plane.

Method 1 Compare the graphs.

- The graph of $g(x) = -\frac{1}{3}x^2 + 2$ is wider than the graph of $f(x) = x^2$.
- The graph of $g(x) = -\frac{1}{3}x^2 + 2$ opens **downward**, and the graph of $f(x) = x^2$ opens **upward**.
- The axis of symmetry is the same.
- The vertex of $f(x) = x^2$ is $(0, 0)$. The vertex of $g(x) = -\frac{1}{3}x^2 + 2$ is translated **2 units up** to $(0, 2)$.

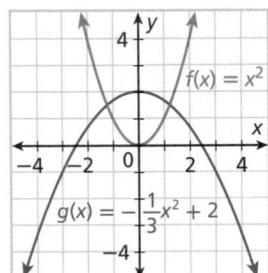

B $g(x) = 2x^2 - 3$

Method 2 Use the functions.

- Since $|2| > |1|$, the graph of $g(x) = 2x^2 - 3$ is **narrower** than the graph of $f(x) = x^2$.
- Since $-\frac{b}{2a} = 0$ for both functions, the axis of symmetry is the same.
- The vertex of $f(x) = x^2$ is $(0, 0)$. The vertex of $g(x) = 2x^2 - 3$ is translated **3 units down** to $(0, -3)$.

Check Use a graph to verify all comparisons.

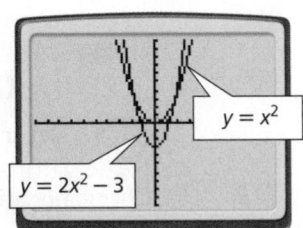

$y = x^2$

$y = 2x^2 - 3$

CHECK IT OUT! Compare the graph of each function with the graph of $f(x) = x^2$.

2a. $g(x) = -x^2 - 4$ **2b.** $g(x) = 3x^2 + 9$ **2c.** $g(x) = \frac{1}{2}x^2 + 2$

The quadratic function $h(t) = -16t^2 + c$ can be used to approximate the height h in feet above the ground of a falling object t seconds after it is dropped from a height of c feet. This model is used only to approximate the height of falling objects because it does not account for air resistance, wind, and other real-world factors.

8-4 Transforming Quadratic Functions **547**

EXAMPLE **3** *Physics Application*

Two identical water balloons are dropped from different heights as shown in the diagram.

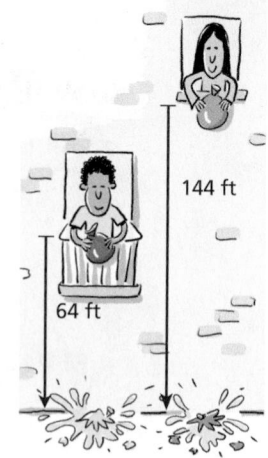

a. Write the two height functions and compare their graphs.

Step 1 Write the height functions. The *y*-intercept *c* represents the original height.

$h_1(t) = -16t^2 + 64$ *Dropped from 64 feet*
$h_2(t) = -16t^2 + 144$ *Dropped from 144 feet*

144 ft

64 ft

Step 2 Use a graphing calculator. Since time and height cannot be negative, set the window for nonnegative values.

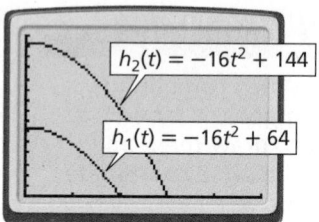
$h_2(t) = -16t^2 + 144$
$h_1(t) = -16t^2 + 64$

The graph of h_2 is a vertical translation of the graph of h_1. Since the balloon in h_2 is dropped from 80 feet higher than the one in h_1, the *y*-intercept of h_2 is 80 units higher.

b. Use the graphs to tell when each water balloon reaches the ground.

The zeros of each function are when the water balloons reach the ground.

The water balloon dropped from 64 feet reaches the ground in 2 seconds. The water balloon dropped from 144 feet reaches the ground in 3 seconds.

Check These answers seem reasonable because the water balloon dropped from a greater height should take longer to reach the ground.

3. Two tennis balls are dropped, one from a height of 16 feet and the other from a height of 100 feet.

    a. Write the two height functions and compare their graphs.

    b. Use the graphs to tell when each tennis ball reaches the ground.

THINK AND DISCUSS

1. Describe how the graph of $f(x) = x^2 + c$ differs from the graph of $f(x) = x^2$ when the value of *c* is positive and when the value of *c* is negative.

2. Tell how to determine whether a graph of a function is wider or narrower than the graph of $f(x) = x^2$.

3. GET ORGANIZED Copy and complete the graphic organizer by explaining how each change affects the graph $f(x) = ax^2 + c$.

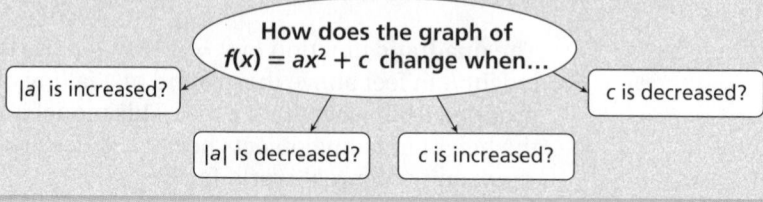

How does the graph of
$f(x) = ax^2 + c$ change when...

|a| is increased?

c is decreased?

|a| is decreased?

c is increased?

GUIDED PRACTICE

SEE EXAMPLE 1

Order the functions from narrowest graph to widest.

1. $f(x) = 3x^2$, $g(x) = 2x^2$

2. $f(x) = 5x^2$, $g(x) = -5x^2$

3. $f(x) = \frac{3}{4}x^2$, $g(x) = -2x^2$, $h(x) = -8x^2$

4. $f(x) = x^2$, $g(x) = -\frac{4}{5}x^2$, $h(x) = 3x^2$

SEE EXAMPLE 2

Compare the graph of each function with the graph of $f(x) = x^2$.

5. $g(x) = x^2 + 6$

6. $g(x) = -2x^2 + 5$

7. $g(x) = \frac{1}{3}x^2$

8. $g(x) = -\frac{1}{4}x^2 - 2$

SEE EXAMPLE 3

9. Multi-Step Two baseballs are dropped, one from a height of 16 feet and the other from a height of 256 feet.

    a. Write the two height functions and compare their graphs.

    b. Use the graphs to tell when each baseball reaches the ground.

PRACTICE AND PROBLEM SOLVING

Independent Practice

For Exercises	See Example
10–13	1
14–17	2
18	3

Order the functions from narrowest graph to widest.

10. $f(x) = x^2$, $g(x) = 4x^2$

11. $f(x) = -2x^2$, $g(x) = \frac{1}{2}x^2$

12. $f(x) = -x^2$, $g(x) = -\frac{5}{8}x^2$, $h(x) = \frac{1}{2}x^2$

13. $f(x) = -5x^2$, $g(x) = -\frac{3}{8}x^2$, $h(x) = 3x^2$

Extra Practice

See Extra Practice for more Skills Practice and Applications Practice exercises.

Compare the graph of each function with the graph of $f(x) = x^2$.

14. $g(x) = \frac{1}{2}x^2 - 10$

15. $g(x) = -4x^2 - 2$

16. $g(x) = \frac{2}{3}x^2 - 9$

17. $g(x) = -\frac{1}{5}x^2 + 1$

18. Multi-Step A raindrop falls from a cloud at an altitude of 10,000 ft. Another raindrop falls from a cloud at an altitude of 14,400 ft.

    a. Write the two height functions and compare their graphs.

    b. Use the graphs to tell when each raindrop reaches the ground.

Tell whether each statement is sometimes, always, or never true.

19. The graphs of $f(x) = ax^2$ and $g(x) = -ax^2$ have the same width.

20. The function $f(x) = ax^2 + c$ has three zeros.

21. The graph of $y = ax^2 + 1$ has its vertex at the origin.

22. The graph of $y = -x^2 + c$ intersects the x-axis.

23. Data Collection Use a graphing calculator and a motion detector to graph the height of a falling object over time.

    a. Find a function to model the height of the object while it is in motion.

    b. Critical Thinking Explain why the value of a in your function is not -16.

Write a function to describe each of the following.

24. The graph of $f(x) = x^2 + 10$ is translated 10 units down.

25. The graph of $f(x) = 3x^2 - 2$ is translated 4 units down.

26. The graph of $f(x) = 0.5x^2$ is narrowed.

27. The graph of $f(x) = -5x^2$ is narrowed and translated 2 units up.

28. The graph of $f(x) = x^2 - 7$ is widened and has no x-intercept.

Match each function to its graph.

29. $f(x) = 4x^2 - 3$ **30.** $f(x) = \frac{1}{4}x^2 - 3$ **31.** $f(x) = 4x^2 + 3$ **32.** $f(x) = -\frac{1}{4}x^2 - 3$

A. 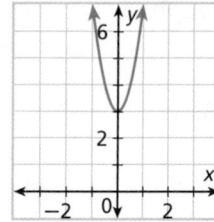   **B.** 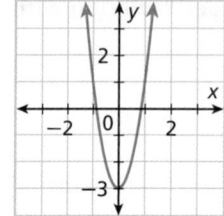   **C.** 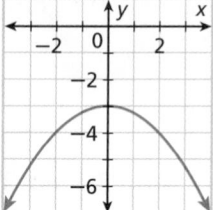   **D.**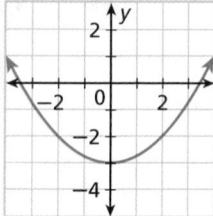

33. Critical Thinking For what values of a and c will $f(x) = ax^2 + c$ have one zero?

34. Physics The graph compares the heights of two identical coconuts that fell from different trees.

   a. What are the starting heights of each coconut?

   b. What is a possible function for the blue graph?

   c. Estimate the time for each coconut to reach the ground.

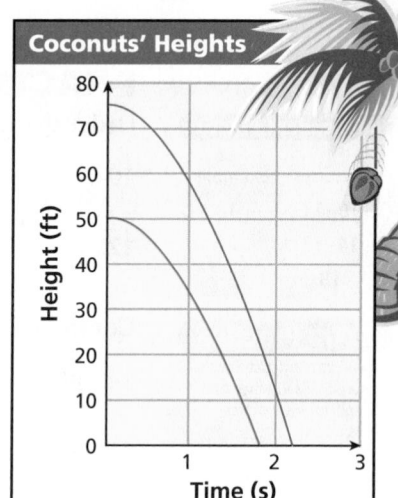

35. Give an example of a quadratic function for each description.

   a. Its graph opens upward.

   b. Its graph has the same width as in part **a**, but the graph opens downward.

   c. Its graph is narrower than the graph in part **a**.

36. Critical Thinking Describe how the effect that the value of c has on the graph of $y = x^2 + c$ is similar to the effect that the value of b has on the graph of $y = x + b$.

 37. Write About It Explain how you know, without graphing, what the graph of $f(x) = \frac{1}{10}x^2 - 5$ looks like.

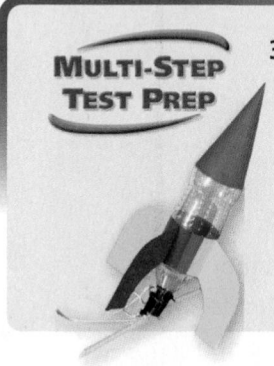

MULTI-STEP TEST PREP

38. a. Use a graphing calculator to graph $y = (x - 3)^2$. Compare this graph to the graph of $y = x^2$. How does this differ from $y = x^2 - 3$?

   b. The equation $h = -16(x - 2)^2 + 64$ describes the height in feet of a water bottle rocket as a function of time. What is the highest point that the rocket will reach? When will it return to the ground?

   c. How can the vertex be located from the equation? from the graph?

39. Which function's graph is the result of shifting the graph of $f(x) = -x^2 - 4$ 3 units down?

  Ⓐ $g(x) = -x^2 - 1$ Ⓒ $g(x) = -4x^2 - 4$

  Ⓑ $g(x) = -\dfrac{1}{3}x^2 - 4$ Ⓓ $g(x) = -x^2 - 7$

40. Which of the following is true when the graph of $f(x) = x^2 + 4$ is transformed into the graph of $g(x) = 2x^2 + 4$?

  Ⓕ The new function has more zeroes than the old function.

  Ⓖ Both functions have the same vertex.

  Ⓗ The function is translated up.

  Ⓙ The axis of symmetry changes.

41. **Gridded Response** For what value of c will $f(x) = x^2 + c$ have one zero?

CHALLENGE AND EXTEND

 42. **Graphing Calculator** Graph the functions $f(x) = (x + 1)^2$, $g(x) = (x + 4)^2$, $h(x) = (x - 2)^2$, and $k(x) = (x - 5)^2$. Make a conjecture about the result of transforming the graph of $f(x) = x^2$ into the graph of $f(x) = (x - h)^2$.

43. Using the function $f(x) = x^2$, write each new function:

  a. The graph is translated 7 units down.

  b. The graph is reflected across the x-axis and translated 2 units up.

  c. Each y-value is halved, and then the graph is translated 1 unit up.

MULTI-STEP TEST PREP

MATHEMATICAL
PRACTICES

Make sense of
problems and
persevere in
solving them.

Quadratic Functions

The Sky's the Limit The
Physics Club is using computer
simulation software to design a
water bottle rocket that doesn't
have a parachute. The data for
their current design are shown
in the table.

1. Tell whether the data
satisfy a quadratic
function.

2. Graph the function from
Problem 1.

3. Find and label the zeros,
axis of symmetry, and
vertex.

Time (s)	Height (ft)
0	0
1	80
2	128
3	144
4	128
5	80

4. Explain what the x- and
y-coordinates of the vertex represent in the context of the problem.

5. Estimate how many seconds it will take the rocket to reach 110 feet.
Explain.

READY TO GO ON?

CHAPTER

8

SECTION 8A

Quiz for Lessons 8-1 Through 8-4

8-1 Identifying Quadratic Functions

Tell whether each function is quadratic. Explain.

1. $y + 2x^2 = 3x$

2. $x^2 + y = 4 + x^2$

3. $\{(2, 12), (-1, 3), (0, 0), (1, 3)\}$

Tell whether the graph of each quadratic function opens upward or downward and whether the parabola has a maximum or a minimum.

4. $y = -x^2 - 7x + 18$

5. $y - 2x^2 = 4x + 3$

6. $y = 5x - 0.5x^2$

7. Graph the function $y = \frac{1}{2}x^2 - 2$ and give the domain and range.

8-2 Characteristics of Quadratic Functions

Find the zeros of each quadratic function from its graph. Then find the axis of symmetry.

8.
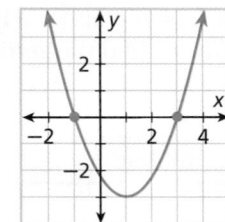

9.
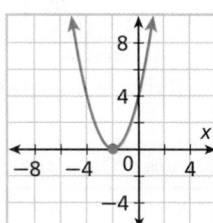

10.
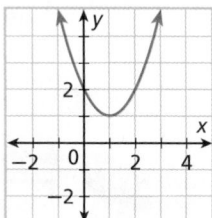

Fnd the vertex.

11. $y = x^2 + 6x + 2$

12. $y = 3 + 4x - 2x^2$

13. $y = 3x^2 + 12x - 12$

14. The height in feet of the curved roof of an aircraft hangar can be modeled by $y = -0.02x^2 + 1.6x$, where x is the horizontal distance in feet from one wall at ground level. What is the greatest height of the hangar?

8-3 Graphing Quadratic Functions

Graph each quadratic function.

15. $y = x^2 + 3x + 9$

16. $y = x^2 - 2x - 15$

17. $y = x^2 - 2x - 8$

18. $y = 2x^2 - 6$

19. $y = 4x^2 + 8x - 2$

20. $y = 2x^2 + 10x + 1$

8-4 Transforming Quadratic Functions

Compare the graph of each function with the graph of $f(x) = x^2$.

21. $g(x) = x^2 - 2$

22. $g(x) = \frac{2}{3}x^2$

23. $g(x) = 5x^2 + 3$

24. $g(x) = -x^2 + 4$

25. The pilot of a hot-air balloon drops a sandbag onto a target from a height of 196 feet. Later, he drops an identical sandbag from a height of 676 feet.

a. Write the two height functions and compare their graphs. Use $h(t) = -16t^2 + c$, where c is the height of the balloon.

b. Use the graphs to tell when each sandbag will reach the ground.

8-5 Solving Quadratic Equations by Graphing

CC.9-12.A.REI.11 Explain why the *x*- coordinates of the points where the graphs of the equations $y = f(x)$ and $y = g(x)$ intersect are the solutions of the equation $f(x) = g(x)$; find the solutions approximately, ...* Also **CC.9-12.A.REI.4, CC.9-12.F.IF.7*, CC.9-12.F.IF.4***

Objective
Solve quadratic equations by graphing.

Vocabulary
quadratic equation

Who uses this?
Dolphin trainers can use solutions of quadratic equations to plan the choreography for their shows. (See Example 2.)

Every quadratic function has a related *quadratic equation*. A **quadratic equation** is an equation that can be written in the standard form $ax^2 + bx + c = 0$, where *a*, *b*, and *c* are real numbers and $a \neq 0$.

When writing a quadratic function as its related quadratic equation, you replace *y* with 0.

$$y = ax^2 + bx + c$$
$$0 = ax^2 + bx + c$$
$$ax^2 + bx + c = 0$$

One way to solve a quadratic equation in standard form is to graph the related function and find the *x*-values where $y = 0$. In other words, find the zeros of the related function. Recall that a quadratic function may have two, one, or no zeros.

Solving Quadratic Equations by Graphing
Step 1 Write the related function.
Step 2 Graph the related function.
Step 3 Find the zeros of the related function.

EXAMPLE 1 Solving Quadratic Equations by Graphing

Solve each equation by graphing the related function.

A $2x^2 - 2 = 0$

Step 1 Write the related function.

$2x^2 - 2 = y$, or $y = 2x^2 + 0x - 2$

Step 2 Graph the function.
- The axis of symmetry is $x = 0$.
- The vertex is $(0, -2)$.
- Two other points are $(1, 0)$ and $(2, 6)$.
- Graph the points and **reflect** them across the axis of symmetry.

Step 3 Find the zeros.

The zeros appear to be -1 and 1.

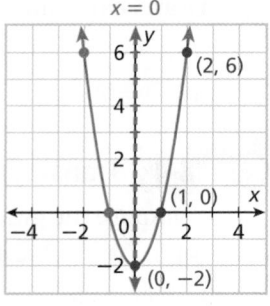

Check

$2x^2 - 2 = 0$	
$2(-1)^2 - 2$	0
$2(1) - 2$	0
$2 - 2$	0
0	0 ✓

Substitute -1 and 1 for x in the quadratic equation.

$2x^2 - 2 = 0$	
$2(1)^2 - 2$	0
$2(1) - 2$	0
$2 - 2$	0
0	0 ✓

Solve each equation by graphing the related function.

B $-x^2 - 4x - 4 = 0$

Step 1 Write the related function.

$y = -x^2 - 4x - 4$

Step 2 Graph the function.

- The axis of symmetry is $x = -2$.
- The vertex is $(-2, 0)$.
- The y-intercept is -4.
- Another point is $(-1, -1)$.
- Graph the points and **reflect** them across the axis of symmetry.

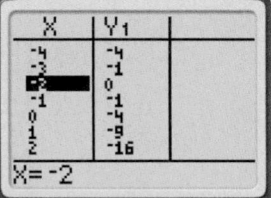

Step 3 Find the zeros.

The only zero appears to be -2.

Check

$$-x^2 - 4x - 4 = 0$$

$-(-2)^2 - 4(-2) - 4$	0
$-(4) + 8 - 4$	0
$4 - 4$	0
0	0 ✓

You can also confirm the solution by using the **Table** function. Enter the equation and press **2nd** **GRAPH** (TABLE). When $y = 0$, $x = -2$. The x-intercept is -2.

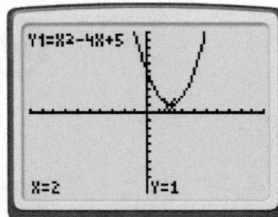

C $x^2 + 5 = 4x$

Step 1 Write the related function.

$x^2 - 4x + 5 = 0$

$y = x^2 - 4x + 5$

Step 2 Graph the function.
Use a graphing calculator.

Step 3 Find the zeros.
The function appears to have no zeros.

The equation has no real-number solutions.

Check reasonableness   Use the table function.

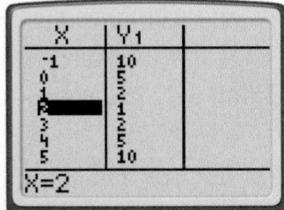

There are no zeros in the Y1 column. Also, the signs of the values in this column do not change. The function appears to have no zeros.

Solve each equation by graphing the related function.

1a. $x^2 - 8x - 16 = 2x^2$

1b. $6x + 10 = -x^2$

1c. $-x^2 + 4 = 0$

EXAMPLE 2 Aquatics Application

A dolphin jumps out of the water. The quadratic function $y = -16x^2 + 20x$ models the dolphin's height above the water after x seconds. How long is the dolphin out of the water?

When the dolphin leaves the water, its height is 0, and when the dolphin reenters the water, its height is 0. So solve $0 = -16x^2 + 20x$ to find the times when the dolphin leaves and reenters the water.

Step 1 Write the related function.

$0 = -16x^2 + 20x$

$y = -16x^2 + 20x$

Step 2 Graph the function.

Use a graphing calculator.

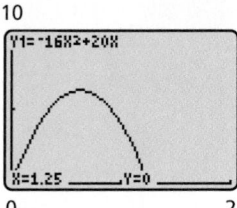

Step 3 Use TRACE to estimate the zeros.

The zeros appear to be 0 and 1.25.

The dolphin leaves the water at 0 seconds and reenters the water at 1.25 seconds.

The dolphin is out of the water for 1.25 seconds.

Check $0 = -16x^2 + 20x$

0	$-16(1.25)^2 + 20(1.25)$	*Substitute 1.25 for x in the quadratic equation.*
0	$-16(1.5625) + 25$	
0	$-25 + 25$	
0	$0 \checkmark$	

 **CHECK IT OUT!** **2. What if...?** Another dolphin jumps out of the water. The quadratic function $y = -16x^2 + 32x$ models the dolphin's height above the water after x seconds. How long is the dolphin out of the water?

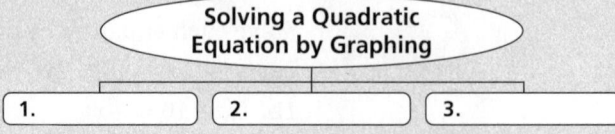 MATHEMATICAL PRACTICES

THINK AND DISCUSS

1. Describe the graph of a quadratic function whose related quadratic equation has only one solution.

2. Describe the graph of a quadratic function whose related quadratic equation has no real solutions.

3. Describe the graph of a quadratic function whose related quadratic equation has two solutions.

4. GET ORGANIZED Copy and complete the graphic organizer. In each of the boxes, write the steps for solving quadratic equations by graphing.

Solving a Quadratic Equation by Graphing

| 1. | 2. | 3. |

GUIDED PRACTICE

1. **Vocabulary** Write two words related to the graph of a quadratic function that can be used to find the solution of the related *quadratic equation*.

SEE EXAMPLE 1   Solve each equation by graphing the related function.

2. $x^2 - 4 = 0$
3. $x^2 = 16$
4. $-2x^2 - 6 = 0$
5. $-x^2 + 12x - 36 = 0$
6. $-x^2 = -9$
7. $2x^2 = 3x^2 - 2x - 8$
8. $x^2 - 6x + 9 = 0$
9. $8x = -4x^2 - 4$
10. $x^2 + 5x + 4 = 0$
11. $x^2 + 2 = 0$
12. $x^2 - 6x = 7$
13. $x^2 + 5x = -8$

SEE EXAMPLE 2   14. **Sports** A baseball coach uses a pitching machine to simulate pop flies during practice. The quadratic function $y = -16x^2 + 80x$ models the height of the baseball after x seconds. How long is the baseball in the air?

PRACTICE AND PROBLEM SOLVING

Independent Practice

For Exercises	See Example
15–23	1
24	2

Solve each equation by graphing the related function.

15. $-x^2 + 16 = 0$
16. $3x^2 = -7$
17. $5x^2 - 12x + 10 = x^2 + 10x$
18. $x^2 + 10x + 25 = 0$
19. $-4x^2 - 24x = 36$
20. $-9x^2 + 10x - 9 = -8x$
21. $-x^2 - 1 = 0$
22. $3x^2 - 27 = 0$
23. $4x^2 - 4x + 5 = 2x^2$

Extra Practice

See Extra Practice for more Skills Practice and Applications Practice exercises.

24. **Geography** Yosemite Falls in California is made of three smaller falls. The upper fall drops 1450 feet. The height h in feet of a water droplet falling from the upper fall to the next fall is modeled by $h(t) = -16t^2 + 1450$, where t is the time in seconds after the initial fall. Estimate the time it takes for the droplet to reach the next cascade.

Tell whether each statement is always, sometimes, or never true.

25. If the graph of a quadratic function has its vertex at the origin, then the related quadratic equation has exactly one solution.

26. If the graph of a quadratic function opens upward, then the related quadratic equation has two solutions.

27. If the graph of a quadratic function has its vertex on the x-axis, then the related quadratic equation has exactly one solution.

28. If the graph of a quadratic function has its vertex in the first quadrant, then the related quadratic equation has two solutions.

29. A quadratic equation in the form $ax^2 - c = 0$, where $a < 0$ and $c > 0$, has two solutions.

30. **Graphing Calculator** A fireworks shell is fired from a mortar. Its height is modeled by the function $h(t) = -16(t - 7)^2 + 784$, where t is the time in seconds and h is the height in feet.

   a. Graph the function.

   b. If the shell is supposed to explode at its maximum height, at what height should it explode?

   c. If the shell does not explode, how long will it take to return to the ground?

31. Athletics The graph shows the height y in feet of a gymnast jumping off a vault after x seconds.

   a. How long does the gymnast stay in the air?

   b. What is the maximum height that the gymnast reaches?

   c. Explain why the function $y = -5x^2 + 10x$ cannot accurately model the gymnast's motion.

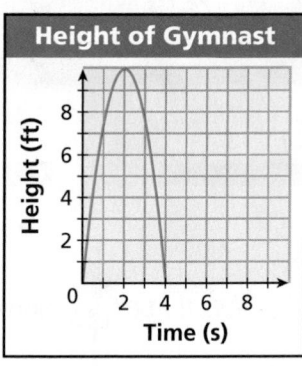

Height of Gymnast

32. Graphing Calculator Use a graphing calculator to solve the equation $x^2 = x + 12$ by graphing $y_1 = x^2$ and $y_2 = x + 12$ and finding the x-coordinates of the points of intersection. (*Hint:* Find the points of intersection by using the [2nd] [TRACE] function after graphing.)

Biology

33. Biology The quadratic function $y = -5x^2 + 7x$ approximates the height y in meters of a kangaroo x seconds after it has jumped. How long does it take the kangaroo to return to the ground?

For Exercises 34–36, use the table to determine the solutions of the related quadratic equation.

Some species of kangaroos are able to jump 30 feet in distance and 6 feet in height.

34.

x	y
-2	-1
-1	0
0	-1
1	-4
2	-9

35.

x	y
-2	-6
-1	0
0	2
1	0
2	-6

36.

x	y
-2	6
-1	3
0	2
1	3
2	6

37. Geometry The hypotenuse of a right triangle is 4 cm longer than one leg and 8 cm longer than the other leg. Let x represent the length of the hypotenuse.

   a. Write an expression for the length of each leg in terms of x.

   b. Use the Pythagorean Theorem to write an equation that can be solved for x.

   c. Find the solutions of your equation from part **b.**

   d. Critical Thinking What do the solutions of your equation represent? Are both solutions reasonable? Explain.

38. Write About It Explain how to find solutions of a quadratic equation by analyzing a table of values.

39. Critical Thinking Explain why a quadratic equation in the form $ax^2 - c = 0$, where $a > 0$ and $c > 0$, will always have two solutions. Explain why a quadratic equation in the form $ax^2 + c = 0$, where $a > 0$ and $c > 0$, will never have any real-number solutions.

MULTI-STEP TEST PREP

40. The quadratic equation $0 = -16t^2 + 80t$ gives the time t in seconds when a golf ball is at height 0 feet.

   a. How long is the golf ball in the air?

   b. What is the maximum height of the golf ball?

   c. After how many seconds is the ball at its maximum height?

   d. What is the height of the ball after 3.5 seconds? Is there another time when the ball reaches that height? Explain.

41. Use the graph to find the number of solutions of $-2x^2 + 2 = 0$.

Ⓐ 0   Ⓒ 2

Ⓑ 1   Ⓓ 3

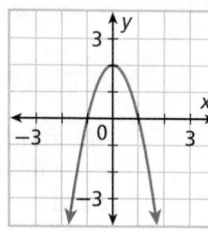

42. Which graph could be used to find the solutions of $x^2 = -4x + 12$?

Ⓕ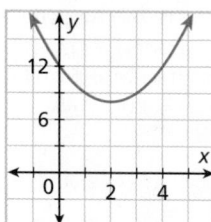

Ⓗ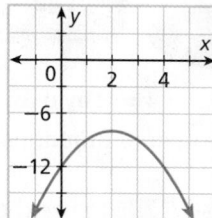

Ⓖ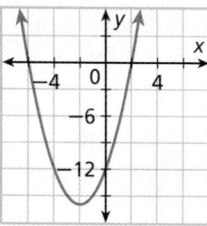

Ⓙ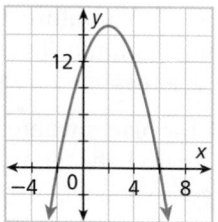

43. Short Response Find the solutions of $2x^2 + x - 1 = 0$ by graphing. Explain how the graph of the related function shows the solutions of the equation.

CHALLENGE AND EXTEND

Graphing Calculator Use a graphing calculator to approximate the solutions of each quadratic equation.

44. $\dfrac{5}{16}x + \dfrac{1}{4}x^2 = \dfrac{3}{5}$

45. $1200x^2 - 650x - 100 = -200x - 175$

46. $\dfrac{1}{5}x + \dfrac{3}{4}x^2 = \dfrac{7}{12}$

47. $400x^2 - 100 = -300x + 456$

8-5

Technology LAB

Use with Solving Quadratic Equations by Graphing

Activity 1

Explore Roots, Zeros, and x-Intercepts

The solutions, or *roots*, of a quadratic equation are the x-intercepts, or zeros, of the related quadratic function. You can use tables or graphs on a graphing calculator to understand the connections between zeros, roots, and x-intercepts.

MATHEMATICAL PRACTICES Use appropriate tools strategically.

CC.9-12.A.REI.11 Explain why the x- coordinates of the points where the graphs of the equations $y = f(x)$ and $y = g(x)$ intersect are the solutions of the equation $f(x) = g(x)$; ....* *Also* **CC.9-12.A.REI.4**

Learn It Online
Lab Resources Online

Solve $5x^2 + 8x - 4 = 0$ by using a table.

1 Enter the related function in **Y₁**.

2 Press **2nd** **GRAPH** to use the **TABLE** function.

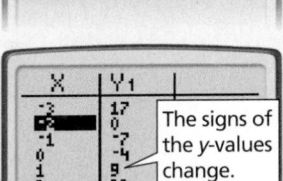

3 Scroll through the values by using ▲ and ▼ . Look for values of 0 in the **Y₁** column. The corresponding x-value is a zero of the function. There is one zero at −2.

Also look for places where the signs of nonzero y-values change. There is a zero between the corresponding x-values. So there is another zero somewhere between 0 and 1.

The signs of the y-values change.

4 To get a better estimate of the zero, change the table settings. Press **2nd** **WINDOW** to view the **TABLE SETUP** screen. Set **TblStart = 0** and the step value △**Tbl = .1**. Press **2nd** **GRAPH** to see the table again. The table will show you more x-values between 0 and 1.

5 Scroll through the values by using ▲ and ▼ . The second zero is at 0.4.

The zeros of the function, −2 and 0.4, are the solutions, or roots, of the equation $5x^2 + 8x - 4 = 0$. Check the solutions algebraically.

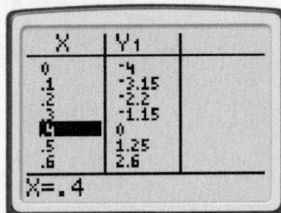

Check

$5x^2 + 8x - 4 = 0$		$5x^2 + 8x - 4 = 0$	
$5(-2)^2 + 8(-2) - 4$	0	$5(0.4)^2 + 8(0.4) - 4$	0
$5(4) - 16 - 4$	0	$5(0.16) + 3.2 - 4$	0
$20 - 16 - 4$	0	$0.8 + 3.2 - 4$	0
0	0 ✓	0	0 ✓

Try This

Solve each equation by using a table.

1. $x^2 - 4x - 5 = 0$ 2. $x^2 - x - 6 = 0$ 3. $2x^2 + x - 1 = 0$ 4. $5x^2 - 6x - 8 = 0$

5. **Critical Thinking** How would you find the zero of a function that showed a sign change in the y-values between the x-values 1.2 and 1.3?

6. **Make a Conjecture** If you scrolled up and down the list and found only positive y-values, what might you conclude?

Activity 2

Solve $5x^2 + x - 8.4 = 0$ by using a table and a graph.

1 Enter the related function in Y_1.

2 To view both the table and the graph at the same time, set your calculator to the Graph-Table mode. Press **MODE** and select **G-T**.

3 Press **GRAPH**. You should see the graph and the table. Notice that the function appears to have one negative zero and one positive zero near the y-axis.

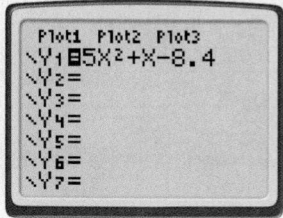

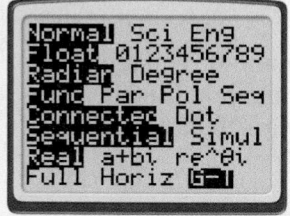

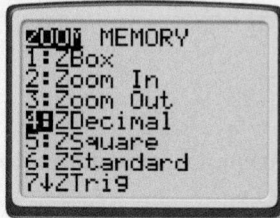

4 To get a closer view of the graph, press **ZOOM** and select **4:ZDecimal**.

5 Press **TRACE**. Use ◄ to scroll to find the negative zero. The graph and the table show that the zero is -1.4.

6 Use ► to scroll and find the positive zero. The graph and the table show that the zero is 1.2.

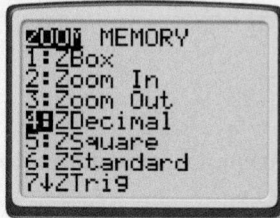

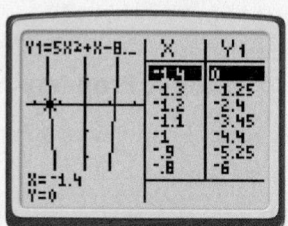

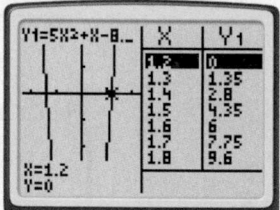

The solutions are -1.4 and 1.2. Check the solutions algebraically.

$5x^2 + x - 8.4 = 0$	
$5(-1.4)^2 + (-1.4) - 8.4$	0
$5(1.96) - 1.4 - 8.4$	0
$9.8 - 1.4 - 8.4$	0
0	$0 \checkmark$

$5x^2 + x - 8.4 = 0$	
$5(1.2)^2 + (1.2) - 8.4$	0
$5(1.44) + 1.2 - 8.4$	0
$7.2 + 1.2 - 8.4$	0
0	$0 \checkmark$

Try This

Solve each equation by using a table and a graph.

7. $2x^2 - x - 3 = 0$ **8.** $5x^2 + 13x + 6 = 0$ **9.** $10x^2 - 3x - 4 = 0$ **10.** $x^2 - 2x - 0.96 = 0$

11. Critical Thinking Suppose that when you graphed a quadratic function, you could see only one side of the graph and one zero. What methods would you use to try to find the other zero?

8-6 Solving Quadratic Equations by Factoring

CC.9-12.A.REI.4b Solve quadratic equations by … factoring…. *Also* CC.9-12.A.SSE.3

Objective
Solve quadratic equations by factoring.

Who uses this?
In order to determine how many seconds she will be in the air, a high diver can use a quadratic equation. (See Example 3.)

You have solved quadratic equations by graphing. Another method used to solve quadratic equations is to factor and use the Zero Product Property.

Zero Product Property

For all real numbers *a* and *b*,

WORDS	NUMBERS	ALGEBRA
If the product of two quantities equals zero, at least one of the quantities equals zero.	$3(0) = 0$ $0(4) = 0$	If $ab = 0$, then $a = 0$ or $b = 0$.

EXAMPLE 1 **Using the Zero Product Property**

Use the Zero Product Property to solve each equation. Check your answer.

A $(x - 3)(x + 7) = 0$

$x - 3 = 0$ or $x + 7 = 0$ *Use the Zero Product Property.*

$x = 3$ or $x = -7$ *Solve each equation.*

The solutions are 3 and −7.

Check

$(x - 3)(x + 7) = 0$	
$(3 - 3)(3 + 7)$	0
$(0)(10)$	0
0	0 ✓

Substitute each solution for x into the original equation.

$(x - 3)(x + 7) = 0$	
$(-7 - 3)(-7 + 7)$	0
$(-10)(0)$	0
0	0 ✓

B $(x)(x - 5) = 0$

$x = 0$ or $x - 5 = 0$ *Use the Zero Product Property.*

$x = 5$ *Solve the second equation.*

The solutions are 0 and 5.

Check

$(x)(x - 5) = 0$	
$(0)(0 - 5)$	0
$(0)(-5)$	0
0	0 ✓

Substitute each solution for x into the original equation.

$(x)(x - 5) = 0$	
$(5)(5 - 5)$	0
$(5)(0)$	0
0	0 ✓

Use the Zero Product Property to solve each equation. Check your answer.

1a. $(x)(x + 4) = 0$ **1b.** $(x + 4)(x - 3) = 0$

If a quadratic equation is written in standard form, $ax^2 + bx + c = 0$, you may need to factor before using the Zero Product Property to solve the equation.

EXAMPLE 2 **Solving Quadratic Equations by Factoring**

Solve each quadratic equation by factoring. Check your answer.

A $x^2 + 7x + 10 = 0$

$(x + 5)(x + 2) = 0$ *Factor the trinomial.*

$x + 5 = 0$ or $x + 2 = 0$ *Use the Zero Product Property.*

$x = -5$ or $x = -2$ *Solve each equation.*

The solutions are -5 and -2.

Helpful Hint

You may want to review factoring techniques before solving quadratic equations.

Check

$x^2 + 7x + 10 = 0$		$x^2 + 7x + 10 = 0$	
$(-5)^2 + 7(-5) + 10$	0	$(-2)^2 + 7(-2) + 10$	0
$25 - 35 + 10$	0	$4 - 14 + 10$	0
	$0 \mid 0 ✓$		$0 \mid 0 ✓$

B $x^2 + 2x = 8$

$$
\begin{aligned}
x^2 + 2x &= 8 \\
-8 \quad &-8 \\
\hline
x^2 + 2x - 8 &= 0
\end{aligned}
$$
The equation must be written in standard form. So subtract 8 from both sides.

$(x + 4)(x - 2) = 0$ *Factor the trinomial.*

$x + 4 = 0$ or $x - 2 = 0$ *Use the Zero Product Property.*

$x = -4$ or $x = 2$ *Solve each equation.*

The solutions are -4 and 2.

Check Graph the related quadratic function. The zeros of the related function should be the same as the solutions from factoring.

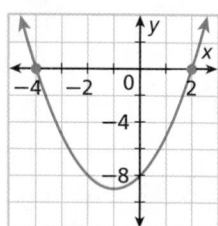

The graph of $y = x^2 + 2x - 8$ shows two zeros that appear to be -4 and 2, the same as the solutions from factoring. ✓

C $x^2 + 2x + 1 = 0$

$(x + 1)(x + 1) = 0$ *Factor the trinomial.*

$x + 1 = 0$ or $x + 1 = 0$ *Use the Zero Product property.*

$x = -1$ or $x = -1$ *Solve each equation.*

Both factors result in the same solution, so there is one solution, -1.

Check Use a graphing calculator to graph the related function.

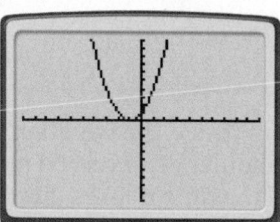

The graph of $y = x^2 + 2x + 1$ shows one zero that appears to be -1, the same as the solution from factoring. ✓

Solve each quadratic equation by factoring. Check your answer.

D $-2x^2 = 18 - 12x$

$$-2x^2 + 12x - 18 = 0 \qquad \text{\textit{Write the equation in standard form.}}$$
$$-2(x^2 - 6x + 9) = 0 \qquad \text{\textit{Factor out the GCF, } -2.}$$
$$-2(x - 3)(x - 3) = 0 \qquad \text{\textit{Factor the trinomial.}}$$
$$-2 \neq 0 \quad \text{or} \quad x - 3 = 0 \qquad \text{\textit{Use the Zero Product Property. } -2 \textit{ cannot equal 0.}}$$
$$x = 3 \qquad \text{\textit{Solve the remaining equation.}}$$

The only solution is 3.

Check $\quad -2x^2 = 18 - 12x$

$-2(3)^2$	$18 - 12(3)$	*Substitute 3 into the original equation.*
-18	$18 - 36$	
-18	-18 ✓	

CHECK IT OUT! Solve each quadratic equation by factoring. Check your answer.

2a. $x^2 - 6x + 9 = 0$ **2b.** $x^2 + 4x = 5$

2c. $30x = -9x^2 - 25$ **2d.** $3x^2 - 4x + 1 = 0$

EXAMPLE 3   *Sports Application*

The height of a diver above the water during a dive can be modeled by $h = -16t^2 + 8t + 48$, where h is height in feet and t is time in seconds. Find the time it takes for the diver to reach the water.

48 ft

$$h = -16t^2 + 8t + 48$$

$$0 = -16t^2 + 8t + 48 \qquad \text{\textit{The diver reaches the water when $h = 0$.}}$$

$$0 = -8(2t^2 - t - 6) \qquad \text{\textit{Factor out the GCF, -8.}}$$

$$0 = -8(2t + 3)(t - 2) \qquad \text{\textit{Factor the trinomial.}}$$

$$-8 \neq 0, \, 2t + 3 = 0 \quad \text{or} \; t - 2 = 0 \qquad \text{\textit{Use the Zero Product Property.}}$$

$$2t = -3 \; \text{or} \qquad t = 2 \qquad \text{\textit{Solve each equation.}}$$

$$t = -\frac{3}{2} \; \text{✗} \qquad \text{\textit{Since time cannot be negative, $-\frac{3}{2}$ does not make sense in this situation.}}$$

It takes the diver 2 seconds to reach the water.

Check $\quad 0 = -16t^2 + 8t + 48$

0	$-16(2)^2 + 8(2) + 48$	*Substitute 2 into the original equation.*
0	$-64 + 16 + 48$	
0	0 ✓	

CHECK IT OUT! **3. What if...?** The equation for the height above the water for another diver can be modeled by $h = -16t^2 + 8t + 24$. Find the time it takes this diver to reach the water.

THINK AND DISCUSS

1. Explain two ways to solve $x^2 + x - 6 = 0$. How are these two methods similar?

2. Describe the relationships among the solutions of $x^2 - 4x - 12 = 0$, the zeros and x-intercepts of $y = x^2 - 4x - 12$, and the factors of $x^2 - 4x - 12$.

3. GET ORGANIZED Copy and complete the graphic organizer. In each box, write a step used to solve a quadratic equation by factoring.

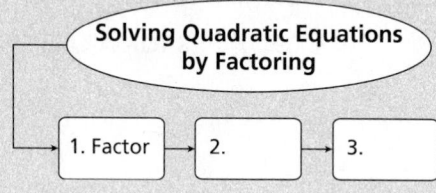

Solving Quadratic Equations by Factoring

1. Factor → 2. → 3.

8-6 Exercises

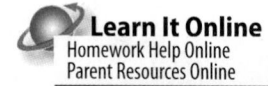
Learn It Online
Homework Help Online
Parent Resources Online

GUIDED PRACTICE

SEE EXAMPLE 1

Use the Zero Product Property to solve each equation. Check your answer.

1. $(x + 2)(x - 8) = 0$ **2.** $(x - 6)(x - 5) = 0$ **3.** $(x + 7)(x + 9) = 0$

4. $(x)(x - 1) = 0$ **5.** $(x)(x + 11) = 0$ **6.** $(3x + 2)(4x - 1) = 0$

SEE EXAMPLE 2

Solve each quadratic equation by factoring. Check your answer.

7. $x^2 + 4x - 12 = 0$ **8.** $x^2 - 8x - 9 = 0$ **9.** $x^2 - 5x + 6 = 0$

10. $x^2 - 3x = 10$ **11.** $x^2 + 10x = -16$ **12.** $x^2 + 2x = 15$

13. $x^2 - 8x + 16 = 0$ **14.** $-3x^2 = 18x + 27$ **15.** $x^2 + 36 = 12x$

16. $2x^2 + 5x - 3 = 0$ **17.** $2x^2 + 7x + 6 = 0$ **18.** $2x^2 + 6x = -18$

SEE EXAMPLE 3

19. Games A group of friends tries to keep a beanbag from touching the ground. On one kick, the beanbag's height can be modeled by $h = -16t^2 + 14t + 2$, where h is the height in feet above the ground and t is the time in seconds. Find the time it takes the beanbag to reach the ground.

PRACTICE AND PROBLEM SOLVING

Independent Practice

For Exercises	See Example
20–25	1
26–31	2
32	3

Use the Zero Product Property to solve each equation. Check your answer.

20. $(x - 8)(x + 6) = 0$ **21.** $(x + 4)(x + 7) = 0$ **22.** $(x - 2)(x - 5) = 0$

23. $(x - 9)(x) = 0$ **24.** $(x)(x + 25) = 0$ **25.** $(2x + 1)(3x - 1) = 0$

Extra Practice

See Extra Practice for more Skills Practice and Applications Practice exercises.

Solve each quadratic equation by factoring. Check your answer.

26. $x^2 + 8x + 15 = 0$ **27.** $x^2 - 2x - 8 = 0$ **28.** $x^2 - 4x + 3 = 0$

29. $3x^2 - 2x - 1 = 0$ **30.** $4x^2 - 9x + 2 = 0$ **31.** $-x^2 = 4x + 4$

32. **Multi-Step** The height of a flare can be approximated by the function $h = -16t^2 + 95t + 6$, where h is the height in feet and t is the time in seconds. Find the time it takes the flare to hit the ground.

Determine the number of solutions of each equation.

33. $(x + 8)(x + 8) = 0$

34. $(x - 3)(x + 3) = 0$

35. $(x + 7)^2 = 0$

36. $3x^2 + 12x + 9 = 0$

37. $x^2 + 12x + 40 = 4$

38. $(x - 2)^2 = 9$

39. **///ERROR ANALYSIS///** Which solution is incorrect? Explain the error.

A

| $x^2 + x - 2 = 0$ |
| $(x - 1)(x + 2) = 0$ |
| $x = 1$ or $x = -2$ |

B

| $x^2 + x - 2 = 0$ |
| $(x - 1)(x + 2) = 0$ |
| $x = -1$ or $x = 2$ |

40. **Number Theory** Write an equation that could be used to find two consecutive even integers whose product is 24. Let x represent the first integer. Solve the equation and give the two integers.

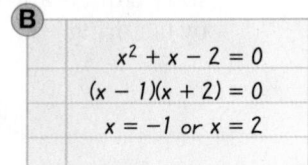

41. **Geometry** The photo shows a traditional thatched house as found in Santana, Madeira, in Portugal. The front of the house is in the shape of a triangle. Suppose the base of the triangle is 1 m less than its height and the area of the triangle is 15 m². Find the height of the triangle. $\left(Hint:\ Use\ A = \frac{1}{2}bh.\right)$

42. **Multi-Step** The length of a rectangle is 1 ft less than 3 times the width. The area is 310 ft². Find the dimensions of the rectangle.

43. **Physics** The height of a fireworks rocket in meters can be approximated by $h = -5t^2 + 30t$, where h is the height in meters and t is time in seconds. Find the time it takes the rocket to reach the ground after it has been launched.

44. **Geometry** One base of a trapezoid is the same length as the height of the trapezoid. The other base is 4 cm more than the height. The area of the trapezoid is 48 cm². Find the length of the shorter base. $\left(Hint:\ Use\ A = \frac{1}{2}h(b_1 + b_2)\right)$.

45. **Critical Thinking** Can you solve $(x - 2)(x + 3) = 5$ by solving $x - 2 = 5$ and $x + 3 = 5$? Why or why not?

46. **Write About It** Explain why you set each factor equal to zero when solving a quadratic equation by factoring.

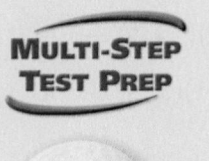

MULTI-STEP TEST PREP

47. A tee box is 48 feet above its fairway. When a golf ball is hit from the tee box with an initial vertical velocity of 32 ft/s, the quadratic equation $0 = -16t^2 + 32t + 48$ gives the time t in seconds when a golf ball is at height 0 feet on the fairway.

   a. Solve the quadratic equation by factoring to see how long the ball is in the air.

   b. What is the height of the ball at 1 second?

   c. Is the ball at its maximum height at 1 second? Explain.

48. What are the solutions to $(x - 1)(2x + 5) = 0$?

    Ⓐ -1 and $\dfrac{5}{2}$ Ⓒ 1 and $-\dfrac{5}{2}$

    Ⓑ -1 and $\dfrac{2}{5}$ Ⓓ 1 and $-\dfrac{2}{5}$

49. Which graph could be used to solve the equation $(x - 3)(x - 2) = 0$?

Ⓕ 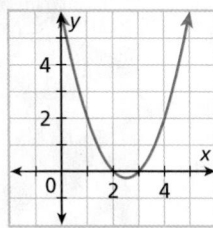   Ⓗ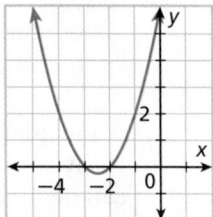

Ⓖ 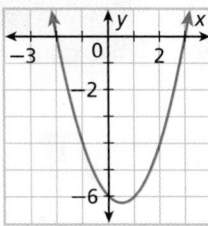   Ⓙ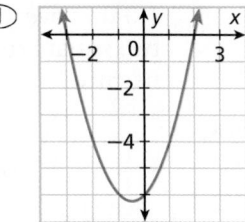

CHALLENGE AND EXTEND

Solve each equation by factoring.

50. $6x^2 + 11x = 10$ **51.** $0.2x^2 + 1 = -1.2x$ **52.** $\dfrac{1}{3}x^2 = 2x - 3$

53. $75x - 45 = -30x^2$ **54.** $x^2 = -4(2x + 3)$ **55.** $\dfrac{x(x - 3)}{2} = 5$

56. $x(x - 10)(x - 3) = 0$ **57.** $x^3 + 2x^2 + x = 0$ **58.** $x^3 + 4x^2 = 0$

Geometry Use the diagram for Exercises 59–61.

59. Write a polynomial to represent the area of the larger rectangle.

60. Write a polynomial to represent the area of the smaller rectangle.

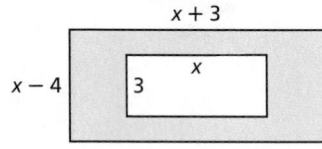

61. Write a polynomial to represent the area of the shaded region. Then solve for x given that the area of the shaded region is 48 square units.

8-7 Solving Quadratic Equations by Using Square Roots

CC.9-12.A.REI.4b Solve quadratic equations by inspection (e.g., for $x^2 = 49$), taking square roots, … *Also* **CC.9-12.A.CED.3*, CC.9-12.A.CED.1*, CC.9-12.F.BF.1***

Objective
Solve quadratic equations by using square roots.

Why learn this?
Square roots can be used to find how much fencing is needed for a pen at a zoo. (See Example 4.)

Some quadratic equations cannot be easily solved by factoring. Square roots can be used to solve some of these quadratic equations. Recall from Lesson 1-5 that every positive real number has two square roots, one positive and one negative.

$$3(3) = 3^2 = 9 \longrightarrow \sqrt{9} = 3 \longleftarrow \text{Positive square root of 9}$$

$$(-3)(-3) = (-3)^2 = 9 \longrightarrow -\sqrt{9} = -3 \longleftarrow \text{Negative square root of 9}$$

When you take the square root of a positive real number and the sign of the square root is not indicated, you must find both the positive and negative square root. This is indicated by $\pm\sqrt{}$.

Reading Math

The expression ± 3 is read "plus or minus three."

$$\pm\sqrt{9} = \pm 3 \longleftarrow \text{Positive and negative square roots of 9}$$

Know it!
Note

Square-Root Property

WORDS	NUMBERS	ALGEBRA
To solve a quadratic equation in the form $x^2 = a$, take the square root of both sides.	$x^2 = 15$ $x = \pm\sqrt{15}$	If $x^2 = a$ and a is a positive real number, then $x = \pm\sqrt{a}$.

EXAMPLE 1 **Using Square Roots to Solve $x^2 = a$**

Solve using square roots.

A $x^2 = 16$

$x = \pm\sqrt{16}$ *Solve for x by taking the square root of both*
$x = \pm 4$ *sides. Use ± to show both square roots.*

The solutions are 4 and −4.

Check

$x^2 = 16$		
$(4)^2$	16	
	16	$16 ✓$

Substitute 4 and −4 into the original equation.

$x^2 = 16$	
$(-4)^2$	16
	$16 \quad 16 ✓$

Solve using square roots.

 B $x^2 = -4$

$x = \pm\sqrt{-4}$ *There is no real number whose square is negative.*

There is no real solution.

 **Solve using square roots. Check your answer.**

1a. $x^2 = 121$ **1b.** $x^2 = 0$ **1c.** $x^2 = -16$

If necessary, use inverse operations to isolate the squared part of a quadratic equation before taking the square root of both sides.

EXAMPLE **2** |  **Using Square Roots to Solve Quadratic Equations**

Solve using square roots.

A $x^2 + 5 = 5$

$$x^2 + 5 = 5$$

$$\underline{-5 \quad -5}$$ *Subtract 5 from both sides.*

$$x^2 = 0$$

$$x = \pm\sqrt{0} = 0$$ *Take the square root of both sides.*

The solution is 0.

> **Helpful Hint**
>
> 0 is neither positive nor negative.

B $4x^2 - 25 = 0$

$$4x^2 - 25 = 0$$

$$\underline{+25 \quad +25}$$ *Add 25 to both sides.*

$$\frac{4x^2}{4} = \frac{25}{4}$$ *Divide both sides by 4.*

$$x^2 = \frac{25}{4}$$

$$x = \pm\sqrt{\frac{25}{4}} = \pm\frac{5}{2}$$ *Take the square root of both sides. Use ± to show both square roots.*

The solutions are $\frac{5}{2}$ and $-\frac{5}{2}$.

C $(x + 2)^2 = 9$

$$(x + 2)^2 = 9$$

$$x + 2 = \pm\sqrt{9}$$ *Take the square root of both sides. Use ± to show both square roots.*

$$x + 2 = \pm 3$$

$$x + 2 = 3 \text{ or } x + 2 = -3$$ *Write two equations, using both the positive and negative square roots, and solve each equation.*

$$\underline{-2 \quad -2 \qquad\qquad -2 \quad -2}$$

$$x = 1 \text{ or } x = -5$$

The solutions are 1 and −5.

Check

$(x + 2)^2 = 9$	
$(1 + 2)^2$	9
3^2	9
9	9 ✓

$(x + 2)^2 = 9$	
$(-5 + 2)^2$	9
$(-3)^2$	9
9	9 ✓

 **Solve by using square roots. Check your answer.**

2a. $100x^2 + 49 = 0$ **2b.** $(x - 5)^2 = 16$

When solving quadratic equations by using square roots, you may need to find the square root of a number that is not a perfect square. In this case, the answer is an irrational number. You can approximate the solutions.

EXAMPLE 3 Solve the equation $0 = -2x^2 + 80$. Round to the nearest hundredth.

$$0 = -2x^2 + 80$$

$$\underline{-80 \qquad\qquad -80}$$ *Subtract 80 from both sides.*

$$\frac{-80}{-2} = \frac{-2x^2}{-2}$$ *Divide both sides by −2.*

$$40 = x^2$$

$$\pm\sqrt{40} = x$$ *Take the square root of both sides.*

$$x \approx \pm 6.32$$ *Find $\sqrt{40}$ on a calculator.*

The approximate solutions are 6.32 and −6.32.

Check Use a graphing calculator to support your answer.

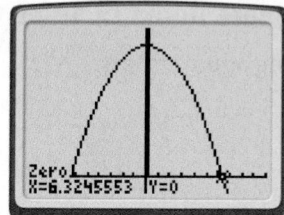

Use the zero function.
The approximate solutions
are 6.32 and −6.32. ✓

 Solve. Round to the nearest hundredth.

3a. $0 = 90 - x^2$ **3b.** $2x^2 - 64 = 0$ **3c.** $x^2 + 45 = 0$

EXAMPLE 4 *Career Application*

A zookeeper is buying fencing to enclose a pen at the zoo. The pen is an isosceles right triangle. There is already a fence on the side that borders a path. The area of the pen will be 4500 square feet. The zookeeper can buy the fencing in whole feet only. How many feet of fencing should he buy?

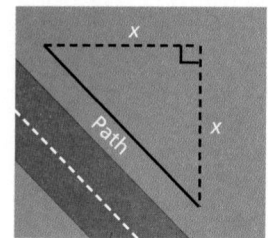

Let x represent the length of one of the sides.

$$\frac{1}{2}bh = A$$ *Use the formula for area of a triangle.*

$$\frac{1}{2}x(x) = 4500$$ *Substitute x for both b and h and 4500 for A.*

$$(2)\frac{1}{2}x^2 = 4500(2)$$ *Simplify. Multiply both sides by 2.*

$$x^2 = 9000$$

$$x = \pm\sqrt{9000}$$ *Take the square root of both sides.*

$$x \approx \pm 94.9$$ *Find $\sqrt{9000}$ on a calculator.*

Negative numbers are not reasonable for length, so $x \approx 94.9$ is the only solution that makes sense. Therefore, the zookeeper needs $95 + 95$, or 190, feet of fencing.

Remember!

An isosceles triangle has at least two sides of the same length.

 **4.** A house is on a lot that is shaped like a trapezoid. The solid lines show the boundaries, where x represents the width of the front yard. Find the width of the front yard, given that the area is 6000 square feet. Round to the nearest foot. $\left(\text{Hint: Use } A = \frac{1}{2}h(b_1 + b_2).\right)$

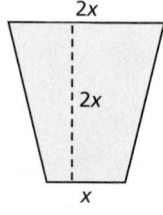

THINK AND DISCUSS

1. Explain why there are no solutions to the quadratic equation $x^2 = -9$.

2. Describe how to estimate the solutions of $4 = x^2 - 16$. What are the approximate solutions?

3. **GET ORGANIZED** Copy and complete the graphic organizer. In each box, write an example of a quadratic equation with the given number of solutions. Solve each equation.

Solving Quadratic Equations by Using Square Roots When the Equation Has...

| No real solutions | One solution | Two solutions |

8-7 Exercises

Learn It Online
Homework Help Online
Parent Resources Online

GUIDED PRACTICE

Solve using square roots. Check your answer.

SEE EXAMPLE 1

1. $x^2 = 225$
2. $x^2 = 49$
3. $x^2 = -100$
4. $x^2 = 400$
5. $-25 = x^2$
6. $36 = x^2$

SEE EXAMPLE 2

7. $3x^2 - 75 = 0$
8. $0 = 81x^2 - 25$
9. $49x^2 + 64 = 0$
10. $16x^2 + 10 = 131$
11. $(x - 3)^2 = 64$
12. $(x - 9)^2 = 25$

SEE EXAMPLE 3

Solve. Round to the nearest hundredth.

13. $3x^2 = 81$
14. $0 = x^2 - 60$
15. $100 - 5x^2 = 0$

SEE EXAMPLE 4

16. **Geometry** The length of a rectangle is 3 times its width. The area of the rectangle is 170 square meters. Find the width. Round to the nearest tenth of a meter. (*Hint:* Use $A = \ell w$.)

PRACTICE AND PROBLEM SOLVING

Solve using square roots. Check your answer.

For Exercises	See Example
17–22	1
23–28	2
29–34	3
35	4

17. $x^2 = 169$
18. $x^2 = 25$
19. $x^2 = -36$
20. $x^2 = 10,000$
21. $-121 = x^2$
22. $625 = x^2$
23. $4 - 81x^2 = 0$
24. $(2x + 1)^2 = 25$
25. $64x^2 - 5 = 20$
26. $(x - 7)^2 = 1$
27. $49x^2 + 1 = 170$
28. $81x^2 + 17 = 81$

Extra Practice

See Extra Practice for more Skills Practice and Applications Practice exercises.

Solve. Round to the nearest hundredth.

29. $4x^2 = 88$
30. $x^2 - 29 = 0$
31. $x^2 + 40 = 144$
32. $3x^2 - 84 = 0$
33. $50 - x^2 = 0$
34. $2x^2 - 10 = 64$

35. **Entertainment** For a scene in a movie, a sack of money is dropped from the roof of a 600 ft skyscraper. The height of the sack above the ground is given by $h = -16t^2 + 600$, where t is the time in seconds. How long will it take the sack to reach the ground? Round to the nearest tenth of a second.

Solve for the indicated variable. Assume all values are positive.

36. $A = \pi r^2$ for r

37. $d = \frac{1}{2} at^2$ for t

38. $F = \frac{mv^2}{r}$ for v

39. **Number Theory** If $a = 2b$ and $2ab = 36$, find all possible solutions for a and b.

40. **Geometry** The geometric mean of two positive numbers a and b is the positive number x such that $\frac{a}{x} = \frac{x}{b}$. Find the geometric mean of 2 and 18.

41. **Estimation** The area y of any rectangle with side length x and one side twice as long as the other is represented by $y = 2x^2$. Use the graph to estimate the dimensions of such a rectangle whose area is 35 square feet.

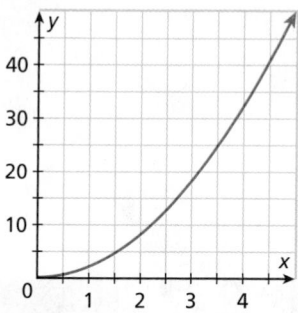

42. **Physics** The period of a pendulum is the amount of time it takes to swing back and forth one time. The relationship between the length of the pendulum L in inches and the length of the period t in seconds can be approximated by $L = 9.78t^2$. Find the period of a pendulum whose length is 60 inches. Round to the nearest tenth of a second.

43. **///ERROR ANALYSIS///** Which solution is incorrect? Explain the error.

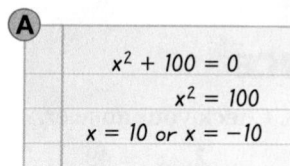

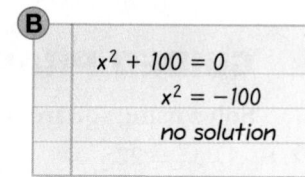

Determine whether each statement is always, sometimes, or never true.

44. There are two solutions to $x^2 = n$ when n is positive.

45. If n is a rational number, then the solutions to $x^2 = n$ are rational numbers.

46. **Multi-Step** The height in feet of a soccer ball kicked upward from the ground with initial velocity 60 feet per second is modeled by $h = -16t^2 + 60t$, where t is the time in seconds. Find the time it takes for the ball to return to the ground.

47. **Critical Thinking** For the equation $x^2 = a$, describe the values of a that will result in each of the following.

   a. two solutions

   b. one solution

   c. no solution

MULTI-STEP TEST PREP

48. The equation $d = 16t^2$ describes the distance d in feet that a golf ball falls in relation to the number of seconds t that it falls.

   a. How many seconds will it take a golf ball to drop to the ground from a height of 4 feet?

   b. Make a table and graph the function.

   c. How far will the golf ball drop in 1 second?

   d. How many seconds will it take the golf ball to drop 64 feet?

For the quadratic equation $x^2 + a = 0$, determine whether each value of a will result in two rational solutions. Explain.

49. $-\dfrac{1}{2}$ **50.** $\dfrac{1}{2}$ **51.** $-\dfrac{1}{4}$ **52.** $\dfrac{1}{4}$

53. Write About It Explain why the quadratic equation $x^2 + 4 = 0$ has no real solutions but the quadratic equation $x^2 - 4 = 0$ has two solutions.

 **TEST PREP**

54. The formula for finding the approximate volume of a cylinder is $V = 3.14r^2h$, where r is the radius and h is the height. The height of a cylinder is 100 cm, and the approximate volume is 1256 cm³. Find the radius of the cylinder.

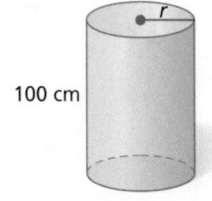
100 cm

    (A) 400 cm   (C) 4 cm

    (B) 20 cm   (D) 2 cm

55. Which best describes the positive solution of $\frac{1}{2}x^2 = 20$?

    (F) Between 4 and 5   (H) Between 6 and 7

    (G) Between 5 and 6   (J) Between 7 and 8

56. Which best describes the solutions of $81x^2 - 169 = 0$?

    (A) Two rational solutions   (C) No solution

    (B) Two irrational solutions   (D) One solution

CHALLENGE AND EXTEND

Find the solutions of each equation without using a calculator.

57. $288x^2 - 19 = -1$ **58.** $-75x^2 = -48$ **59.** $x^2 = \dfrac{128}{242}$

 60. Geometry The Pythagorean Theorem states that $a^2 + b^2 = c^2$ if a and b represent the lengths of the legs of a right triangle and c represents the length of the hypotenuse.

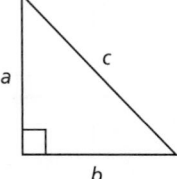

    a. Find the length of the hypotenuse if the lengths of the legs are 9 cm and 12 cm.

    b. Find the length of each leg of an isosceles right triangle whose hypotenuse is 10 cm. Round to the nearest tenth of a centimeter.

Algebra LAB

Use with Completing the Square

Model Completing the Square

One way to solve a quadratic equation is by using a procedure called *completing the square*. In this procedure, you add something to a quadratic expression to make it a perfect-square trinomial. This procedure can be modeled with algebra tiles.

KEY

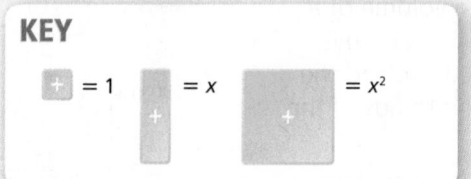

$\boxed{+} = 1$ $= x$ $= x^2$

MATHEMATICAL PRACTICES

Use appropriate tools strategically.

CC.9-12.A.REI. 4a Use the method of completing the square to transform any quadratic equation in *x* into an equation of the form $(x - p)^2 = q$ that has the same solutions....

Activity

Use algebra tiles to model $x^2 + 6x$. Add unit tiles to complete a perfect-square trinomial. Then write the new expression in factored form.

MODEL		ALGEBRA
	Arrange the tiles to form part of a large square. Part of the square is missing. How many one-tiles do you need to complete it?	$x^2 + 6x$
	Complete the square by placing 9 one-tiles on the mat. $x^2 + 6x + 9$ is a perfect-square trinomial.	$x^2 + 6x + 9$
	Use the length and the width of the square to rewrite the area expression in factored form.	$(x + 3)^2$

Try This

Use algebra tiles to model each expression. Add unit tiles to complete a perfect-square trinomial. Then write the new expression in factored form.

1. $x^2 + 4x$ **2.** $x^2 + 2x$ **3.** $x^2 + 10x$ **4.** $x^2 + 8x$

5. Make a Conjecture Examine the pattern in Problems 1–4. How many unit tiles would you have to add to make $x^2 + 12x$ a perfect-square trinomial?

8-8 Completing the Square

CC.9-12.A.REI. 4a Use the method of completing the square to transform any quadratic equation in *x* into an equation of the form $(x - p)^2 = q$ that has the same solutions…. *Also* **CC.9-12.A.CED.1***

Objective
Solve quadratic equations by completing the square.

Vocabulary
completing the square

Who uses this?
Landscapers can solve quadratic equations to find dimensions of patios. (See Example 4.)

Previously, you solved quadratic equations by isolating x^2 and then using square roots. This method works if the quadratic equation, when written in standard form, is a perfect square.

When a trinomial is a perfect square, there is a relationship between the coefficient of the *x*-term and the constant term.

$$x^2 + 6x + 9 \qquad x^2 - 8x + 16$$

$$\left(\frac{6}{2}\right)^2 = 9 \qquad \left(\frac{-8}{2}\right)^2 = 16$$

Divide the coefficient of the x-term by 2, then square the result to get the constant term.

An expression in the form $x^2 + bx$ is not a perfect square. However, you can use the relationship shown above to add a term to $x^2 + bx$ to form a trinomial that is a perfect square. This is called **completing the square**.

Completing the Square

WORDS	NUMBERS	ALGEBRA
To complete the square of $x^2 + bx$, add $\left(\frac{b}{2}\right)^2$ to the expression. This will form a perfect-square trinomial.	$x^2 + 6x + \blacksquare$ $x^2 + 6x + \left(\frac{6}{2}\right)^2$ $x^2 + 6x + 9$ $(x + 3)^2$	$x^2 + bx + \blacksquare$ $x^2 + bx + \left(\frac{b}{2}\right)^2$ $\left(x + \frac{b}{2}\right)^2$

EXAMPLE 1 **Completing the Square**

Complete the square to form a perfect-square trinomial.

A $x^2 + 10x + \blacksquare$
$x^2 + 10x$ *Identify b.*
$\left(\frac{10}{2}\right)^2 = 5^2 = 25$ *Find $\left(\frac{b}{2}\right)^2$.*
$x^2 + 10x + 25$ *Add $\left(\frac{b}{2}\right)^2$ to the expression.*

B $x^2 - 9x + \blacksquare$
$x^2 + -9x$
$\left(\frac{-9}{2}\right)^2 = \frac{81}{4}$
$x^2 - 9x + \frac{81}{4}$

Complete the square to form a perfect-square trinomial.

1a. $x^2 + 12x + \blacksquare$ **1b.** $x^2 - 5x + \blacksquare$ **1c.** $8x + x^2 + \blacksquare$

To solve a quadratic equation in the form $x^2 + bx = c$, first complete the square of $x^2 + bx$. Then you can solve using square roots.

Solving a Quadratic Equation by Completing the Square
Step 1 Write the equation in the form $x^2 + bx = c$.
Step 2 Find $\left(\frac{b}{2}\right)^2$.
Step 3 Complete the square by adding $\left(\frac{b}{2}\right)^2$ to both sides of the equation.
Step 4 Factor the perfect-square trinomial.
Step 5 Take the square root of both sides.
Step 6 Write two equations, using both the positive and negative square root, and solve each equation.

EXAMPLE 2 **Solving $x^2 + bx = c$ by Completing the Square**

Solve by completing the square. Check your answer.

A $x^2 + 14x = 15$

Step 1	$x^2 + 14x = 15$	*The equation is in the form $x^2 + bx = c$.*
Step 2	$\left(\frac{14}{2}\right)^2 = 7^2 = 49$	*Find $\left(\frac{b}{2}\right)^2$.*
Step 3	$x^2 + 14x + 49 = 15 + 49$	*Complete the square.*
Step 4	$(x + 7)^2 = 64$	*Factor and simplify.*
Step 5	$x + 7 = \pm 8$	*Take the square root of both sides.*
Step 6	$x + 7 = 8$ or $x + 7 = -8$	*Write and solve two equations.*
	$x = 1$ or $x = -15$	

Helpful Hint

$(x + 7)(x + 7) = (x + 7)^2$. So the square root of $(x + 7)^2$ is $x + 7$.

The solutions are 1 and -15.

Check

$x^2 + 14x = 15$	
$(1)^2 + 14(1)$	15
$1 + 14$	15
15	15 ✓

$x^2 + 14x = 15$	
$(-15)^2 + 14(-15)$	15
$225 - 210$	15
15	15 ✓

B $x^2 - 2x - 2 = 0$

Step 1	$x^2 + (-2)x = 2$	*Write in the form $x^2 + bx = c$.*
Step 2	$\left(\frac{-2}{2}\right)^2 = (-1)^2 = 1$	*Find $\left(\frac{b}{2}\right)^2$.*
Step 3	$x^2 - 2x + 1 = 2 + 1$	*Complete the square.*
Step 4	$(x - 1)^2 = 3$	*Factor and simplify.*
Step 5	$x - 1 = \pm\sqrt{3}$	*Take the square root of both sides.*
Step 6	$x - 1 = \sqrt{3}$ or $x - 1 = -\sqrt{3}$	*Write and solve*
	$x = 1 + \sqrt{3}$ or $x = 1 - \sqrt{3}$	*two equations.*

Writing Math

The expressions $1 + \sqrt{3}$ and $1 - \sqrt{3}$ can be written as one expression: $1 \pm \sqrt{3}$, which is read as "1 plus or minus the square root of 3."

The solutions are $1 + \sqrt{3}$ and $1 - \sqrt{3}$.

Check Use a graphing calculator to check your answer.

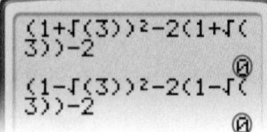

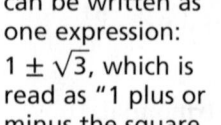 Solve by completing the square. Check your answer.

2a. $x^2 + 10x = -9$ **2b.** $t^2 - 8t - 5 = 0$

EXAMPLE 3

Solving $ax^2 + bx = c$ by Completing the Square

Solve by completing the square.

A $-2x^2 + 12x - 20 = 0$

Step 1 $\dfrac{-2x^2}{-2} + \dfrac{12x}{-2} - \dfrac{20}{-2} = \dfrac{0}{-2}$ *Divide by −2 to make a = 1.*

$x^2 - 6x + 10 = 0$ *Write in the form $x^2 + bx = c$.*

$x^2 - 6x = -10$

$x^2 + (-6)x = -10$

Step 2 $\left(\dfrac{-6}{2}\right)^2 = (-3)^2 = 9$ *Find $\left(\dfrac{b}{2}\right)^2$.*

Step 3 $x^2 - 6x + 9 = -10 + 9$ *Complete the square.*

Step 4 $(x - 3)^2 = -1$ *Factor and simplify.*

There is no real number whose square is negative, so there are no real solutions.

B $3x^2 - 10x = -3$

Step 1 $\dfrac{3x^2}{3} - \dfrac{10}{3}x = \dfrac{-3}{3}$ *Divide by 3 to make a = 1.*

$x^2 - \dfrac{10}{3}x = -1$

$x^2 + \left(-\dfrac{10}{3}\right)x = -1$ *Write in the form $x^2 + bx = c$.*

Step 2 $\left(-\dfrac{10}{3} \cdot \dfrac{1}{2}\right)^2 = \left(-\dfrac{10}{6}\right)^2 = \dfrac{100}{36} = \dfrac{25}{9}$ *Find $\left(\dfrac{b}{2}\right)^2$.*

Step 3 $x^2 - \dfrac{10}{3}x + \dfrac{25}{9} = -1 + \dfrac{25}{9}$ *Complete the square.*

$x^2 - \dfrac{10}{3}x + \dfrac{25}{9} = -\dfrac{9}{9} + \dfrac{25}{9}$ *Rewrite using like denominators.*

Step 4 $\left(x - \dfrac{5}{3}\right)^2 = \dfrac{16}{9}$ *Factor and simplify.*

Step 5 $x - \dfrac{5}{3} = \pm\dfrac{4}{3}$ *Take the square root of both sides.*

Step 6 $x - \dfrac{5}{3} = \dfrac{4}{3}$ or $x - \dfrac{5}{3} = -\dfrac{4}{3}$ *Write and solve two equations.*

$x = 3$ or $x = \dfrac{1}{3}$

The solutions are 3 and $\dfrac{1}{3}$.

Remember!

Dividing by 2 is the same as multiplying by $\dfrac{1}{2}$.

Solve by completing the square.

3a. $3x^2 - 5x - 2 = 0$ **3b.** $4t^2 - 4t + 9 = 0$

EXAMPLE 4

Problem-Solving Application

A landscaper is designing a rectangular brick patio. She has enough bricks to cover 144 square feet. She wants the length of the patio to be 10 feet greater than the width. What dimensions should she use for the patio?

1 **Understand the Problem**

The **answer** will be the length and width of the patio.

 **Geometry**

List the important information:
- There are enough bricks to cover 144 square feet.
- One edge of the patio is to be 10 feet longer than the other edge.

 Make a Plan

Set the formula for the area of a rectangle equal to 144, the area of the patio. Solve the equation.

 Solve

Let x be the width.

Then $x + 10$ is the length.

Use the formula for area of a rectangle.

ℓ	$\cdot$	w	$=$	A
length	**times**	**width**	**=**	**area of patio**
$(x + 10)$	$\cdot$	x	$=$	144

Step 1 $x^2 + 10x = 144$ *Simplify.*

Step 2 $\left(\dfrac{10}{2}\right)^2 = 5^2 = 25$ *Find $\left(\dfrac{b}{2}\right)^2$.*

Step 3 $x^2 + 10x + 25 = 144 + 25$ *Complete the square by adding 25 to both sides.*

Step 4 $(x + 5)^2 = 169$ *Factor the perfect-square trinomial.*

Step 5 $x + 5 = \pm 13$ *Take the square root of both sides.*

Step 6 $x + 5 = 13$ or $x + 5 = -13$ *Write and solve two equations.*

$x = 8$ or $x = -18$

Negative numbers are not reasonable for length, so $x = 8$ is the only solution that makes sense.

The width is 8 feet, and the length is $8 + 10$, or 18, feet.

 Look Back

The length of the patio is 10 feet greater than the width. Also, $8(18) = 144$.

 **4.** An architect designs a rectangular room with an area of 400 ft^2. The length is to be 8 ft longer than the width. Find the dimensions of the room. Round your answers to the nearest tenth of a foot.

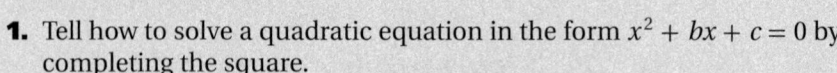

THINK AND DISCUSS

1. Tell how to solve a quadratic equation in the form $x^2 + bx + c = 0$ by completing the square.

2. GET ORGANIZED Copy and complete the graphic organizer. In each box, write and solve an example of the given type of quadratic equation.

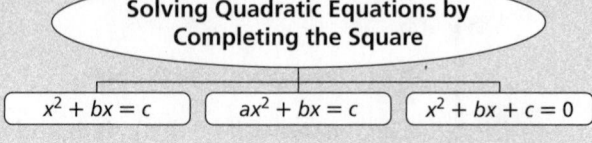

Solving Quadratic Equations by Completing the Square

| $x^2 + bx = c$ | $ax^2 + bx = c$ | $x^2 + bx + c = 0$ |

Exercises

Learn It Online
Homework Help Online
Parent Resources Online

GUIDED PRACTICE

1. **Vocabulary** Describe in your own words how to *complete the square* for the equation $1 = x^2 + 4x$.

SEE EXAMPLE 1 Complete the square to form a perfect-square trinomial.

2. $x^2 + 14x + \blacksquare$

3. $x^2 - 4x + \blacksquare$

4. $x^2 - 3x + \blacksquare$

Solve by completing the square.

SEE EXAMPLE 2

5. $x^2 + 6x = -5$

6. $x^2 - 8x = 9$

7. $x^2 + x = 30$

8. $x^2 + 2x = 21$

9. $x^2 - 10x = -9$

10. $x^2 + 16x = 91$

SEE EXAMPLE 3

11. $-x^2 - 5x = -5$

12. $-x^2 - 3x + 2 = 0$

13. $-6x = 3x^2 + 9$

14. $2x^2 - 6x = -10$

15. $-x^2 + 8x - 6 = 0$

16. $4x^2 + 16 = -24x$

SEE EXAMPLE 4

17. **Multi-Step** The length of a rectangle is 4 meters longer than the width. The area of the rectangle is 80 square meters. Find the length and width. Round your answers to the nearest tenth of a meter.

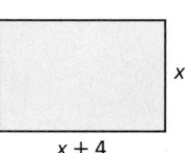

x

$x + 4$

PRACTICE AND PROBLEM SOLVING

For Exercises	See Example
18–20	1
21–26	2
27–32	3
33	4

Independent Practice

Complete the square to form a perfect-square trinomial.

18. $x^2 - 16x + \blacksquare$

19. $x^2 - 2x + \blacksquare$

20. $x^2 + 11x + \blacksquare$

Solve by completing the square.

21. $x^2 - 10x = 24$

22. $x^2 - 6x = -9$

23. $x^2 + 15x = -26$

24. $x^2 + 6x = 16$

25. $x^2 - 2x = 48$

26. $x^2 + 12x = -36$

27. $-x^2 + x + 6 = 0$

28. $2x^2 = -7x - 29$

29. $-x^2 - x + 1 = 0$

30. $3x^2 - 6x - 9 = 0$

31. $-x^2 = 15x + 30$

32. $2x^2 + 20x - 10 = 0$

33. **Geometry** The base of a parallelogram is 8 inches longer than twice the height. The area of the parallelogram is 64 square inches. What is the height?

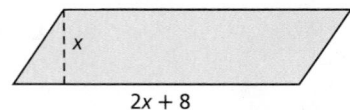

x

$2x + 8$

Extra Practice
See Extra Practice for more Skills Practice and Applications Practice exercises.

Solve each equation by completing the square.

34. $3x^2 + x = 10$

35. $x^2 = 2x + 6$

36. $2a^2 = 5a + 12$

37. $2x^2 + 5x = 3$

38. $4x = 7 - x^2$

39. $8x = -x^2 + 20$

40. **Hobbies** The height in feet h of a water bottle rocket launched from a rooftop is given by the equation $h = -16t^2 + 320t + 32$, where t is the time in seconds. After the rocket is fired, how long will it take to return to the ground? Solve by completing the square. Round your answer to the nearest tenth of a second.

Complete each trinomial so that it is a perfect square.

41. $x^2 + 18x + \blacksquare$

42. $x^2 - 100x + \blacksquare$

43. $x^2 - 7x + \blacksquare$

44. $x^2 + \blacksquare x + 4$

45. $x^2 - \blacksquare x + \dfrac{81}{4}$

46. $x^2 + \blacksquare x + \dfrac{1}{36}$

47. Multi-Step A roped-off area of width x is created around a 34-by-10-foot rectangular museum display of Egyptian artifacts, as shown. The combined area of the display and the roped-off area is 640 square feet.

  a. Write an equation for the combined area.

  b. Find the width of the roped-off area.

48. Graphing Calculator Compare solving a quadratic equation by completing the square with finding the solutions on a graphing calculator.

  a. Complete the square to solve $2x^2 - 3x - 2 = 0$.

  b. Use your graphing calculator to graph $y = 2x^2 - 3x - 2$.

  c. Explain how to use this graph to find the solutions of $2x^2 - 3x - 2 = 0$.

  d. Compare the two methods of solving the equation. What are the advantages and disadvantages of each?

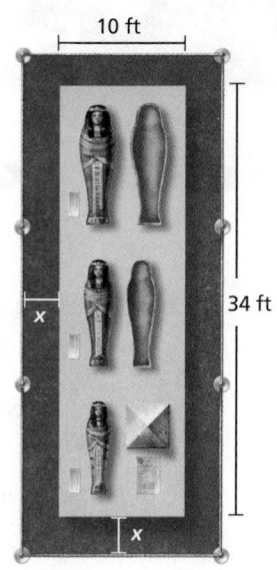

49. ///**ERROR ANALYSIS**/// Explain the error below. What is the correct answer?

$$x^2 + 4x = 77$$
$$x^2 + 4x + 4 = 77 + 4$$
$$(x + 2)^2 = 81$$
$$x + 2 = 9$$
$$x = 7$$

Solve each equation by completing the square.

50. $5x^2 - 50x = 55$ **51.** $3x^2 + 36x = -30$ **52.** $28x - 2x^2 = 26$

53. $-36x = 3x^2 + 108$ **54.** $0 = 4x^2 + 32x + 44$ **55.** $16x + 40 = -2x^2$

56. $x^2 + 5x + 6 = 10x$ **57.** $x^2 + 3x + 18 = -3x$ **58.** $4x^2 + x + 1 = 3x^2$

 59. Write About It Jamal prefers to solve $x^2 + 20x - 21 = 0$ by completing the square. Heather prefers to solve $x^2 + 11x + 18 = 0$ by factoring. Explain their reasoning.

60. Critical Thinking What should be done to the binomial $x^2 + y^2$ to make it a perfect-square trinomial? Explain.

MULTI-STEP TEST PREP

61. The function $h(t) = -16t^2 + vt + c$ models the height in feet of a golf ball after t seconds when it is hit with initial vertical velocity v from initial height c feet. A golfer stands on a tee box that is 32 feet above the fairway. He hits the golf ball from the tee at an initial vertical velocity of 64 feet per second.

  a. Write an equation that gives the time t when the golf ball lands on the fairway at height 0.

  b. What number would be added to both sides of the equation in part **a** to complete the square while solving for t?

  c. Solve the equation from part **a** by completing the square to find the time it takes the ball to reach the fairway. Round to the nearest tenth of a second.

62. **Write About It** Compare solving an equation of the form $x^2 + bx + c = 0$ by completing the square and solving an equation of the form $ax^2 + bx + c = 0$ by completing the square.

63. What value of c will make $x^2 + 16x + c$ a perfect-square trinomial?

    (A) 32   (B) 64   (C) 128   (D) 256

64. What value of b will make $x^2 + b + 25$ a perfect-square trinomial?

    (F) 5   (G) $5x$ (H) 10   (J) $10x$

65. Which of the following is closest to a solution of $3x^2 + 2x - 4 = 0$?

    (A) 0   (B) 1   (C) 2   (D) 3

66. **Short Response** Solve $x^2 - 8x - 20 = 0$ by completing the square. Explain each step in your solution.

CHALLENGE AND EXTEND

Solve each equation by completing the square.

67. $6x^2 + 5x = 6$ 68. $7x + 3 = 6x^2$ 69. $4x = 1 - 3x^2$

70. What should be done to the binomial $ax^2 + bx$ to obtain a perfect-square trinomial?

71. Solve $ax^2 + bx = 0$ for x.

72. **Geometry** The hypotenuse of a right triangle is 20 cm. One of the legs is 4 cm longer than the other leg. Find the area of the triangle. (*Hint:* Use the Pythagorean Theorem.)

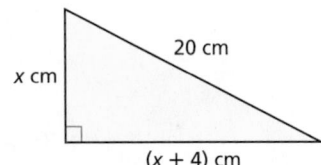

20 cm

x cm

(x + 4) cm

8-9 The Quadratic Formula and the Discriminant

CC.9-12.A.REI.4b Solve quadratic equations by … the quadratic formula.… *Also* **CC.9-12.A.REI.4a, CC.9-12.A.REI.1**

Objectives
Solve quadratic equations by using the Quadratic Formula.

Determine the number of solutions of a quadratic equation by using the discriminant.

Vocabulary
discriminant

Why learn this?
You can use the discriminant to determine whether the weight in a carnival strength test will reach a certain height. (See Exercise 4.)

Previously, you completed the square to solve quadratic equations. If you complete the square of $ax^2 + bx + c = 0$, you can derive the *Quadratic Formula*. The Quadratic Formula can be used to solve *any* quadratic equation.

Numbers		**Algebra**
$2x^2 + 6x + 1 = 0$		$ax^2 + bx + c = 0,\ a \neq 0$
$\frac{2}{2}x^2 + \frac{6}{2}x + \frac{1}{2} = \frac{0}{2}$	Divide both sides by a.	$\frac{a}{a}x^2 + \frac{b}{a}x + \frac{c}{a} = \frac{0}{a}$
$x^2 + 3x + \frac{1}{2} = 0$		$x^2 + \frac{b}{a}x + \frac{c}{a} = 0$
$x^2 + 3x = -\frac{1}{2}$	Subtract $\frac{c}{a}$ from both sides.	$x^2 + \frac{b}{a}x = -\frac{c}{a}$
$x^2 + 3x + \left(\frac{3}{2}\right)^2 = -\frac{1}{2} + \left(\frac{3}{2}\right)^2$	Complete the square.	$x^2 + \frac{b}{a}x + \left(\frac{b}{2a}\right)^2 = -\frac{c}{a} + \left(\frac{b}{2a}\right)^2$
$\left(x + \frac{3}{2}\right)^2 = \frac{9}{4} - \frac{1}{2}$	Factor and simplify.	$\left(x + \frac{b}{2a}\right)^2 = \frac{b^2}{4a^2} - \frac{c}{a}$
$\left(x + \frac{3}{2}\right)^2 = \frac{9}{4} - \frac{2}{4}$	Use common denominators.	$\left(x + \frac{b}{2a}\right)^2 = \frac{b^2}{4a^2} - \frac{4ac}{4a^2}$
$\left(x + \frac{3}{2}\right)^2 = \frac{7}{4}$	Simplify.	$\left(x + \frac{b}{2a}\right)^2 = \frac{b^2 - 4ac}{4a^2}$
$x + \frac{3}{2} = \pm\frac{\sqrt{7}}{2}$	Take square roots.	$x + \frac{b}{2a} = \pm\frac{\sqrt{b^2 - 4ac}}{2a}$
$x = -\frac{3}{2} \pm \frac{\sqrt{7}}{2}$	Subtract $\frac{b}{2a}$ from both sides.	$x = -\frac{b}{2a} \pm \frac{\sqrt{b^2 - 4ac}}{2a}$
$x = \frac{-3 \pm \sqrt{7}}{2}$	Simplify.	$x = \frac{-b \pm \sqrt{b^2 - 4ac}}{2a}$

Remember!
To add fractions, you need a common denominator.
$$\frac{b^2}{4a^2} - \frac{c}{a} = \frac{b^2}{4a^2} - \frac{c}{a}\left(\frac{4a}{4a}\right)$$
$$= \frac{b^2}{4a^2} - \frac{4ac}{4a^2}$$
$$= \frac{b^2 - 4ac}{4a^2}$$

Know it!
Note

The Quadratic Formula

The solutions of $ax^2 + bx + c = 0$, where $a \neq 0$, are $x = \dfrac{-b \pm \sqrt{b^2 - 4ac}}{2a}$.

©Powerstock/SuperStock

EXAMPLE 1 **Using the Quadratic Formula**

Solve using the Quadratic Formula.

A $2x^2 + 3x - 5 = 0$

$2x^2 + 3x + (-5) = 0$ *Identify a, b, and c.*

$x = \dfrac{-b \pm \sqrt{b^2 - 4ac}}{2a}$ *Use the Quadratic Formula.*

$x = \dfrac{-3 \pm \sqrt{3^2 - 4(2)(-5)}}{2(2)}$ *Substitute 2 for a, 3 for b, and −5 for c.*

$x = \dfrac{-3 \pm \sqrt{9 - (-40)}}{4}$ *Simplify.*

$x = \dfrac{-3 \pm \sqrt{49}}{4} = \dfrac{-3 \pm 7}{4}$ *Simplify.*

$x = \dfrac{-3 + 7}{4}$ or $x = \dfrac{-3 - 7}{4}$ *Write as two equations.*

$x = 1$ or $x = -\dfrac{5}{2}$ *Simplify.*

B $2x = x^2 - 3$

$1x^2 + (-2)x + (-3) = 0$ *Write in standard form. Identify a, b, and c.*

$x = \dfrac{-(-2) \pm \sqrt{(-2)^2 - 4(1)(-3)}}{2(1)}$ *Substitute 1 for a, −2 for b, and −3 for c.*

$x = \dfrac{2 \pm \sqrt{4 - (-12)}}{2}$ *Simplify.*

$x = \dfrac{2 \pm \sqrt{16}}{2} = \dfrac{2 \pm 4}{2}$ *Simplify.*

$x = \dfrac{2 + 4}{2}$ or $x = \dfrac{2 - 4}{2}$ *Write as two equations.*

$x = 3$ or $x = -1$ *Simplify.*

> **Helpful Hint**
>
> You can graph the related quadratic function to see if your solutions are reasonable.

 Solve using the Quadratic Formula.

1a. $-3x^2 + 5x + 2 = 0$ **1b.** $2 - 5x^2 = -9x$

Many quadratic equations can be solved by graphing, factoring, taking the square root, or completing the square. Some cannot be easily solved by any of these methods, but you can use the Quadratic Formula to solve any quadratic equation.

EXAMPLE 2 **Using the Quadratic Formula to Estimate Solutions**

Solve $x^2 - 2x - 4 = 0$ using the Quadratic Formula.

$x = \dfrac{-(-2) \pm \sqrt{(-2)^2 - 4(1)(-4)}}{2(1)}$

$x = \dfrac{2 \pm \sqrt{4 - (-16)}}{2} = \dfrac{2 \pm \sqrt{20}}{2}$

$x = \dfrac{2 + \sqrt{20}}{2}$ or $x = \dfrac{2 - \sqrt{20}}{2}$

Use a calculator: $x \approx 3.24$ or $x \approx -1.24$.

Check reasonableness

 **2.** Solve $2x^2 - 8x + 1 = 0$ using the Quadratic Formula.

If the quadratic equation is in standard form, the **discriminant** of a quadratic equation is $b^2 - 4ac$, the part of the equation under the radical sign. Recall that quadratic equations can have two, one, or no real solutions. You can determine the number of solutions of a quadratic equation by evaluating its discriminant.

Equation	$x^2 - 4x + 3 = 0$	$x^2 + 2x + 1 = 0$	$x^2 - 2x + 2 = 0$
Discriminant	$a = 1, b = -4, c = 3$	$a = 1, b = 2, c = 1$	$a = 1, b = -2, c = 2$
	$b^2 - 4ac$	$b^2 - 4ac$	$b^2 - 4ac$
	$(-4)^2 - 4(1)(3)$	$2^2 - 4(1)(1)$	$(-2)^2 - 4(1)(2)$
	$16 - 12$	$4 - 4$	$4 - 8$
	4	0	-4
	The discriminant is positive.	The discriminant is zero.	The discriminant is negative.
Graph of Related Function	Notice that the related function has two x-intercepts.	Notice that the related function has one x-intercept.	Notice that the related function has no x-intercepts.
	![graph with points (1, 0) and (3, 0)]	![graph with point (-1, 0)]	![graph with no x-intercepts]
Number of Solutions	two real solutions	one real solution	no real solutions

The Discriminant of Quadratic Equation $ax^2 + bx + c = 0$

If $b^2 - 4ac > 0$, the equation has two real solutions.

If $b^2 - 4ac = 0$, the equation has one real solution.

If $b^2 - 4ac < 0$, the equation has no real solutions.

EXAMPLE 3   **Using the Discriminant**

Find the number of real solutions of each equation using the discriminant.

A $3x^2 + 10x + 2 = 0$
$a = 3, b = 10, c = 2$
$b^2 - 4ac$
$10^2 - 4(3)(2)$
$100 - 24$
76
$b^2 - 4ac$ is positive.
There are two real solutions.

B $9x^2 - 6x + 1 = 0$
$a = 9, b = -6, c = 1$
$b^2 - 4ac$
$(-6)^2 - 4(9)(1)$
$36 - 36$
0
$b^2 - 4ac$ is zero.
There is one real solution.

C $x^2 + x + 1 = 0$
$a = 1, b = 1, c = 1$
$b^2 - 4ac$
$1^2 - 4(1)(1)$
$1 - 4$
-3
$b^2 - 4ac$ is negative.
There are no real solutions.

Find the number of real solutions of each equation using the discriminant.

3a. $2x^2 - 2x + 3 = 0$ **3b.** $x^2 + 4x + 4 = 0$ **3c.** $x^2 - 9x + 4 = 0$

The height h in feet of an object shot straight up with initial velocity v in feet per second is given by $h = -16t^2 + vt + c$, where c is the beginning height of the object above the ground.

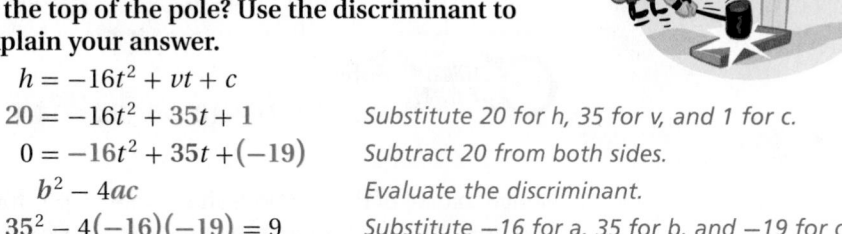

EXAMPLE 4 *Physics Application*

Helpful Hint

If the object is shot straight up from the ground, the initial height of the object above the ground equals 0.

A weight 1 foot above the ground on a carnival strength test is shot straight up with an initial velocity of 35 feet per second. Will it ring the bell at the top of the pole? Use the discriminant to explain your answer.

$h = -16t^2 + vt + c$	
$20 = -16t^2 + 35t + 1$	*Substitute 20 for h, 35 for v, and 1 for c.*
$0 = -16t^2 + 35t + (-19)$	*Subtract 20 from both sides.*
$b^2 - 4ac$	*Evaluate the discriminant.*
$35^2 - 4(-16)(-19) = 9$	*Substitute −16 for a, 35 for b, and −19 for c.*

The discriminant is positive, so the equation has two solutions. The weight will reach a height of 20 feet so it will ring the bell.

 **4. What if...?** Suppose the weight is shot straight up with an initial velocity of 20 feet per second. Will it ring the bell? Use the discriminant to explain your answer.

There is no one correct way to solve a quadratic equation. Many quadratic equations can be solved using several different methods.

EXAMPLE 5 **Solving Using Different Methods**

Solve $x^2 + 7x + 6 = 0$.

Method 1 Solve by graphing.

$y = x^2 + 7x + 6$ *Write the related quadratic function and graph it.*

The solutions are the x-intercepts, -6 and -1.

Method 2 Solve by factoring.

$x^2 + 7x + 6 = 0$	
$(x + 6)(x + 1) = 0$	*Factor.*
$x + 6 = 0$ or $x - 1 = 0$	*Use the Zero Product Property.*
$x = -6$ or $x = -1$	*Solve each equation.*

Method 3 Solve by completing the square.

$x^2 + 7x + 6 = 0$	
$x^2 + 7x = -6$	
$x^2 + 7x + \dfrac{49}{4} = -6 + \dfrac{49}{4}$	*Add $\left(\dfrac{b}{2}\right)^2$ to both sides.*
$\left(x + \dfrac{7}{2}\right)^2 = \dfrac{25}{4}$	*Factor and simplify.*
$x + \dfrac{7}{2} = \pm\dfrac{5}{2}$	*Take the square root of both sides.*
$x + \dfrac{7}{2} = \dfrac{5}{2}$ or $x + \dfrac{7}{2} = -\dfrac{5}{2}$	*Solve each equation.*
$x = -1$ or $x = -6$	

Method 4 Solve using the Quadratic Formula.

$$1x^2 + 7x + 6 = 0 \qquad \textit{Identify a, b, and c.}$$

$$x = \frac{-7 \pm \sqrt{7^2 - 4(1)(6)}}{2(1)} \qquad \textit{Substitute 1 for a, 7 for b, and 6 for c.}$$

$$x = \frac{-7 \pm \sqrt{49 - 24}}{2} = \frac{-7 \pm \sqrt{25}}{2} = \frac{-7 \pm 5}{2} \qquad \textit{Simplify.}$$

$$x = \frac{-7 + 5}{2} \ \text{ or } \ x = \frac{-7 - 5}{2} \qquad \textit{Write as two equations.}$$

$$x = -1 \quad \text{ or } \quad x = -6 \qquad \textit{Solve each equation.}$$

 Solve.

5a. $x^2 + 7x + 10 = 0$ **5b.** $-14 + x^2 = 5x$ **5c.** $2x^2 + 4x - 21 = 0$

Notice that all of the methods in Example 5 produce the same solutions, -1 and -6. The only method you cannot use to solve $x^2 + 7x + 6 = 0$ is using square roots. Sometimes one method is better for solving certain types of equations. The table below gives some advantages and disadvantages of the different methods.

Methods of Solving Quadratic Equations

METHOD	ADVANTAGES	DISADVANTAGES
Graphing	• Always works to give approximate solutions • Can quickly see the number of solutions	• Cannot always get an exact solution
Factoring	• Good method to try first • Straightforward if the equation is factorable	• Complicated if the equation is not easily factorable • Not all quadratic equations are factorable.
Using square roots	• Quick when the equation has no x-term	• Cannot easily use when there is an x-term
Completing the square	• Always works	• Sometimes involves difficult calculations
Using the Quadratic Formula	• Always works • Can always find exact solutions	• Other methods may be easier or less time consuming.

Student to Student *Solving Quadratic Equations*

Binh Pham
Johnson High School

No matter what method I use, I like to check my answers for reasonableness by graphing.

I used the Quadratic Formula to solve $2x^2 - 7x - 10 = 0$. I found that $x \approx -1.09$ and $x \approx 4.59$. Then I graphed $y = 2x^2 - 7x - 10$. The x-intercepts appeared to be close to -1 and 4.5, so I knew my solutions were reasonable.

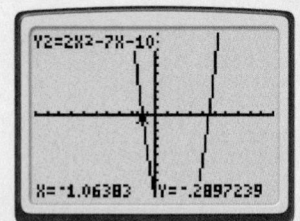

Comstock Images/Getty Images

THINK AND DISCUSS

1. Describe how to use the discriminant to find the number of real solutions to a quadratic equation.

2. Choose a method to solve $x^2 + 5x + 4 = 0$ and explain why you chose that method.

3. Describe how the discriminant can be used to determine if an object will reach a given height.

4. GET ORGANIZED Copy and complete the graphic organizer. In each box, write the number of real solutions.

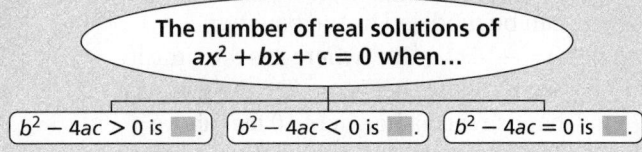

The number of real solutions of
$ax^2 + bx + c = 0$ when...

$b^2 - 4ac > 0$ is ▢. | $b^2 - 4ac < 0$ is ▢. | $b^2 - 4ac = 0$ is ▢.

8-9 Exercises

Learn It Online
Homework Help Online
Parent Resources Online

GUIDED PRACTICE

1. Vocabulary If the *discriminant* is negative, the quadratic equation has _____?_____ real solution(s). (*no, one,* or *two*)

Solve using the Quadratic Formula.

SEE EXAMPLE **1**

2. $x^2 - 5x + 4 = 0$ **3.** $2x^2 = 7x - 3$ **4.** $x^2 - 6x - 7 = 0$

5. $x^2 = -14x - 40$ **6.** $3x^2 - 2x = 8$ **7.** $4x^2 - 4x - 3 = 0$

SEE EXAMPLE **2**

8. $2x^2 - 6 = 0$ **9.** $x^2 + 6x + 3 = 0$ **10.** $x^2 - 7x + 2 = 0$

11. $3x^2 = -x + 5$ **12.** $x^2 - 4x - 7 = 0$ **13.** $2x^2 + x - 5 = 0$

SEE EXAMPLE **3**

Find the number of real solutions of each equation using the discriminant.

14. $2x^2 + 4x + 3 = 0$ **15.** $x^2 + 4x + 4 = 0$ **16.** $2x^2 - 11x + 6 = 0$

17. $x^2 + x + 1 = 0$ **18.** $3x^2 = 5x - 1$ **19.** $-2x + 3 = 2x^2$

20. $2x^2 + 12x = -18$ **21.** $5x^2 + 3x = -4$ **22.** $8x = 1 - x^2$

SEE EXAMPLE **4**

23. Hobbies The height above the ground in meters of a model rocket on a particular launch can be modeled by the equation $h = -4.9t^2 + 102t + 100$, where t is the time in seconds after its engine burns out 100 m above the ground. Will the rocket reach a height of 600 m? Use the discriminant to explain your answer.

SEE EXAMPLE **5**

Solve.

24. $x^2 + x - 12 = 0$ **25.** $x^2 + 6x + 9 = 0$ **26.** $2x^2 - x - 1 = 0$

27. $4x^2 + 4x + 1 = 0$ **28.** $2x^2 + x - 7 = 0$ **29.** $9 = 2x^2 + 3x$

PRACTICE AND PROBLEM SOLVING

Independent Practice

For Exercises	See Example
30–32	1
33–35	2
36–38	3
39	4
40–42	5

Extra Practice

See Extra Practice for more Skills Practice and Applications Practice exercises.

Solve using the Quadratic Formula.

30. $3x^2 = 13x - 4$

31. $x^2 - 10x + 9 = 0$

32. $1 = 3x^2 + 2x$

33. $x^2 - 4x + 1 = 0$

34. $3x^2 - 5 = 0$

35. $2x^2 + 7x = -4$

Find the number of real solutions of each equation using the discriminant.

36. $3x^2 - 6x + 3 = 0$

37. $x^2 - 3x - 8 = 0$

38. $7x^2 + 6x + 2 = 0$

39. Multi-Step A gymnast who can stretch her arms up to reach 6 feet jumps straight up on a trampoline. The height of her feet above the trampoline can be modeled by the equation $h = -16x^2 + 12x$, where x is the time in seconds after her jump. Do the gymnast's hands reach a height of 10 feet above the trampoline? Use the discriminant to explain. (*Hint:* Let $h = 10 - 6$, or 4.)

10 ft

Solve.

40. $x^2 + 4x + 3 = 0$

41. $x^2 + 2x = 15$

42. $x^2 - 12 = -x$

Write each equation in standard form. Use the discriminant to determine the number of solutions. Then find any real solutions.

43. $2x = 3 + 2x^2$

44. $x^2 = 2x + 9$

45. $2 = 7x + 4x^2$

46. $-7 = x^2$

47. $-12x = -9x^2 - 4$

48. $x^2 - 14 = 0$

Multi-Step Use the discriminant to determine the number of x-intercepts. Then find them.

49. $y = 2x^2 - x - 21$

50. $y = 5x^2 + 12x + 8$

51. $y = x^2 - 10x + 25$

52. Copy and complete the table.

Quadratic Equation	Discriminant	Number of Real Solutions
$x^2 + 12x - 20 = 0$	▨	▨
$8x + x^2 = -16$	▨	▨
$0.5x^2 + x - 3 = 0$	▨	▨
$-3x^2 - 2x = 1$	▨	▨

53. Sports A diver begins on a platform 10 meters above the surface of the water. The diver's height is given by the equation $h(t) = -4.9t^2 + 3.5t + 10$, where t is the time in seconds after the diver jumps.

   a. How long does it take the diver to reach a point 1 meter above the water?

   b. How many solutions does the equation you used in part **a** have?

   c. Do all of the solutions to the equation make sense in the situation? Explain.

54. Critical Thinking How many real solutions does the equation $x^2 = k$ have when $k > 0$, when $k < 0$, and when $k = 0$? Use the discriminant to explain.

55. Write About It How can you use the discriminant to save time?

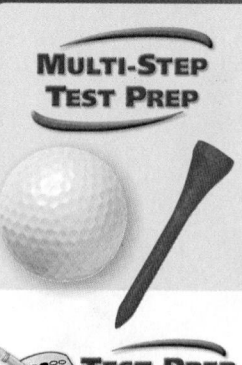

56. The equation $0 = -16t^2 + 80t + 20$ gives the time t in seconds when a golf ball is at height 0 feet.

    a. Will the height of the ball reach 130 feet? Explain.

    b. Will the golf ball reach a height of 116 feet? If so, when?

    c. Solve the given quadratic equation using the Quadratic Formula.

TEST PREP

57. How many real solutions does $4x^2 - 3x + 1 = 0$ have?

    Ⓐ 0   Ⓑ 1   Ⓒ 2   Ⓓ 4

58. For which of the following conditions does $ax^2 + bx + c = 0$ have two real solutions?

    I. $b^2 = 4ac$

    II. $b^2 > 4ac$

    III. $a = b, c = b$

    Ⓕ I only   Ⓖ II only   Ⓗ III only   Ⓙ II and III

59. Extended Response Use the equation $0 = x^2 + 2x + 1$ to answer the following.

    a. How many solutions does the equation have?

    b. Solve the equation by graphing.

    c. Solve the equation by factoring.

    d. Solve the equation by using the Quadratic Formula.

    e. Explain which method was easiest for you. Why?

CHALLENGE AND EXTEND

60. Agriculture A rancher has 80 yards of fencing to build a rectangular pen. Let w be the width of the pen. Write an equation giving the area of the pen. Find the dimensions of the pen when the area is 400 square yards.

61. Agriculture A farmer wants to fence a four-sided field using an existing fence along the south side of the field. He has 1000 feet of fencing. He makes the northern boundary perpendicular to and twice as long as the western boundary. The eastern and western boundaries have to be parallel, but the northern and southern ones do not.

    a. Can the farmer enclose an area of 125,000 square feet? Explain why or why not. $\left(\text{Hint: Use the formula for the area of a trapezoid, } A = \frac{1}{2} h(b_1 + b_2).\right)$

    b. What geometric shape will the field be?

8-10 Nonlinear Systems

CC.9-12.A.REI.7 Solve a simple system consisting of a linear equation and a quadratic equation in two variables algebraically and graphically.

Objective
Solve systems of equations in two variables in which one equation is linear and the other is quadratic.

Vocabulary
nonlinear system of equations

Why learn this?

You can solve a nonlinear system to find how long it takes for two objects to reach the same height. (See Example 4.)

Recall that a system of linear equations is a set of two or more linear equations. A solution of a system is an ordered pair that satisfies each equation in the system. Points where the graphs of the equations intersect represent solutions of the system.

A **nonlinear system of equations** is a system in which at least one of the equations is nonlinear. For example, a system that contains one quadratic equation and one linear equation is a nonlinear system.

A system made up of a linear equation and a quadratic equation can have no solution, one solution, or two solutions, as shown below.

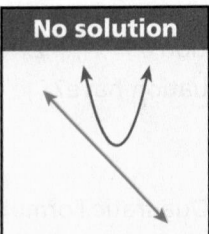

No solution

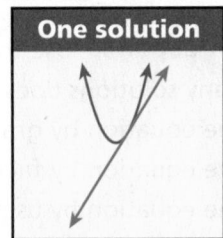

One solution

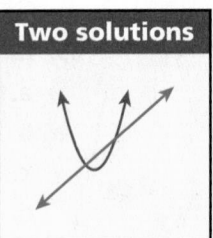

Two solutions

EXAMPLE 1 Solving a Nonlinear System by Graphing

Solve the system by graphing. Check your answer.

$$\begin{cases} y = x^2 - 2x - 3 \\ y = -x - 1 \end{cases}$$

Step 1 Graph $y = x^2 - 2x - 3$.

The axis of symmetry is $x = 1$.

The vertex is $(1, -4)$.

The y-intercept is -3.

Another point is $(-1, 0)$.

Graph the points and reflect them across the axis of symmetry.

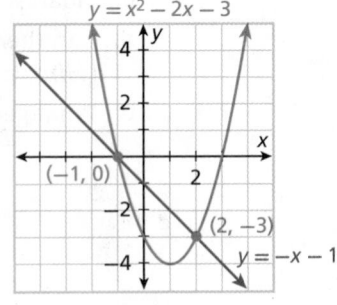

Step 2 Graph $y = -x - 1$.

The slope is -1.

The y-intercept is -1.

Step 3 Find the points where the two graphs intersect.

The solutions appear to be $(-1, 0)$ and $(2, -3)$.

Remember!

A quadratic function has the form
$y = ax^2 + bx + c$.
To graph a quadratic function, start by using $x = -\frac{b}{2a}$
to find the axis of symmetry and the vertex.

Check

Substitute $(-1, 0)$ into the system.   Substitute $(2, -3)$ into the system.

$y = x^2 - 2x - 3$		$y = -x - 1$		$y = x^2 - 2x - 3$		$y = -x - 1$	
0	$(-1)^2 - 2(-1) - 3$	0	$-(-1) - 1$	-3	$2^2 - 2(2) - 3$	-3	$-2 - 1$
0	$1 + 2 - 3$	0	$1 - 1$	-3	$4 - 4 - 3$	-3	$-3\ \checkmark$
0	$0\ \checkmark$	0	$0\ \checkmark$	-3	$-3\ \checkmark$		

The solutions are $(-1, 0)$ and $(2, -3)$.

 1. Solve the system by graphing. Check your answer.
$$\begin{cases} y = x^2 - 4x + 5 \\ y = x + 1 \end{cases}$$

EXAMPLE 2

Solving a Nonlinear System by Substitution

Solve the system by substitution.
$$\begin{cases} y = 2x^2 - 3x + 4 \\ y = x + 2 \end{cases}$$

$y = 2x^2 - 3x + 4$ *Both equations are solved for y.*

$y = x + 2$

$\quad\quad y = 2x^2 - 3x + 4$

$\quad x + 2 = 2x^2 - 3x + 4$ *Substitute x + 2 for y in the first equation.*

$\underline{-(x + 2) \quad\quad -(x + 2)}$ *Subtract x + 2 from both sides.*

$\quad\quad 0 = 2x^2 - 4x + 2$

$\quad\quad 0 = 2(x^2 - 2x + 1)$ *Factor out the GCF, 2.*

$\quad\quad 0 = 2(x - 1)(x - 1)$ *Factor the trinomial.*

$\quad\quad 2 \neq 0; \quad x - 1 = 0$ *Use the Zero Product Property; 2 cannot equal 0.*

$\quad\quad\quad\quad\quad\quad x = 1$ *Solve the remaining equation.*

$y = x + 2$ *Write one of the original equations.*

$y = 1 + 2$ *Substitute 1 for x.*

$y = 3$

The solution is $(1, 3)$.

Check
Use a graphing calculator.

The graph supports the result found above. This system has exactly one real solution. The graph of the system consists of a line and a parabola that meet in exactly one point.

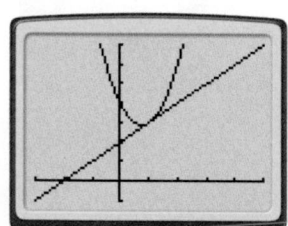

 2. Solve the system by substitution. Check your answer.
$$\begin{cases} y = 3x^2 - 3x + 1 \\ y = -3x + 4 \end{cases}$$

EXAMPLE 3 Solving a Nonlinear System by Elimination

Solve each system by elimination.

A $\begin{cases} 4x - y = 2 \\ y = x^2 + 1 \end{cases}$

$$4x - y = 2$$ *Write the system to align the y-terms.*

$$\underline{+ \quad\quad y = x^2 + 1}$$ *Add the equations to eliminate y.*

$$4x = x^2 + 3$$

$$\underline{- 4x \quad\quad - 4x}$$ *Subtract 4x from both sides.*

$$0 = x^2 - 4x + 3$$

$$0 = (x - 1)(x - 3)$$ *Factor the trinomial.*

$x - 1 = 0$ or $x - 3 = 0$ *Use the Zero Product Property.*

$x = 1$ or $x = 3$ *Solve the equations.*

$y = x^2 + 1$ $y = x^2 + 1$ *Write one of the original equations.*

$y = 1^2 + 1$ $y = 3^2 + 1$ *Substitute each x-value and solve for y.*

$y = 2$ $y = 10$

The solutions are $(1, 2)$ and $(3, 10)$.

B $\begin{cases} y = x^2 + x - 1 \\ 2x - 3y = 6 \end{cases}$

$$y = x^2 + x - 1$$ *Write the system to align the y-terms.*

$$2x - 3y = 6$$

$$3(y) = 3(x^2 + x - 1)$$ *Multiply each term in the first equation by 3.*

$$2x - 3y = 6$$

$$3y = 3x^2 + 3x - 3$$

$$\underline{+ \, 2x - 3y = 6}$$ *Add the second equation to the new first equation to eliminate y.*

$$2x = 3x^2 + 3x + 3$$

$$0 = 3x^2 + x + 3$$ *Subtract 2x from both sides.*

$$x = \frac{-1 \pm \sqrt{(1)^2 - 4(3)(3)}}{2(3)}$$ *Use the Quadratic Formula,*

$$x = \frac{-1 \pm \sqrt{1 - 36}}{6}$$ $x = \frac{-b \pm \sqrt{b^2 - 4ac}}{2a}.$

$$x = \frac{-1 \pm \sqrt{-35}}{6}$$ *Note the discriminant: $b^2 - 4ac = -35$. Its value is negative, so there are no real solutions.*

There are no real solutions.

Check Use a graphing calculator.
      To graph $2x - 3y = 6$, first solve for y.

$$2x - 3y = 6$$

$$-3y = -2x + 6$$

$$y = \frac{2}{3}x - 2$$

The graph supports that there are no real solutions.

Remember!

The elimination method is a good choice when both equations have the same variable term with the same or opposite coefficients or when a variable term in one equation is a multiple of the corresponding variable term in the other equation.

3a. $\begin{cases} 2x - y = 2 \\ y = x^2 - 5 \end{cases}$ **3b.** $\begin{cases} y = x^2 - 2x - 5 \\ 5x - 2y = 5 \end{cases}$

EXAMPLE 4 *Physics Application*

An elevator is rising at a constant rate of 20 feet per second. Its height in feet after t seconds is given by $h = 20t$. At the instant the elevator is at ground level, a ball is thrown upward with an initial velocity of 80 feet per second from ground level. The height in feet of the ball after t seconds is given by $h = -16t^2 + 80t$. Find the time it takes for the ball and the elevator to reach the same height.

Solve the system $\begin{cases} h = -16t^2 + 80t \\ h = 20t \end{cases}$ by substitution.

> **Helpful Hint**
>
> When $t = 0$, the ball and elevator are at the same height because they are both at ground level.

$$-16t^2 + 80t = 20t \qquad \text{Substitute } -16t^2 + 80t \text{ for } h \text{ in the second equation.}$$

$$\underline{ -20t \quad -20t} \qquad \text{Subtract } 20t \text{ from both sides.}$$

$$-16t^2 + 60t = 0$$

$$-4t(4t - 15) = 0 \qquad \text{Factor out the GCF, } -4t.$$

$$-4t = 0 \quad \text{or} \quad 4t - 15 = 0 \quad \text{Use the Zero Product Property.}$$

$$t = 0 \qquad\qquad 4t = 15 \quad \text{Solve the remaining equations.}$$

$$t = 3.75$$

It takes 3.75 seconds for the ball and the elevator to reach the same height.

 **4.** An elevator is rising at a constant rate of 8 feet per second. Its height in feet after t seconds is given by $h = 8t$. At the instant the elevator is at ground level, a ball is dropped from a height of 120 feet. The height in feet of the ball after t seconds is given by $h = -16t^2 + 120$. Find the time it takes for the ball and the elevator to reach the same height.

THINK AND DISCUSS

1. How is solving the systems in this lesson similar to solving systems of linear equations? How is it different?

2. When using elimination to solve a linear/quadratic system, which variable will be eliminated? Why?

3. A system of linear equations can have infinitely many solutions. Why can't a linear/quadratic system have infinitely many solutions?

4. **GET ORGANIZED** Copy and complete the graphic organizer by sketching diagrams to show examples. Write *not possible* for any cases that are not possible.

System of Equations	Number of Solutions			
	0	1	2	infinite
Linear				
Linear/Quadratic				

GUIDED PRACTICE

Vocabulary Apply the vocabulary from this lesson to answer each question.

1. A system of equations that includes a linear equation and a quadratic equation is _____?_____. (*linear*, *nonlinear*, or *quadratic*)

2. Sketch a nonlinear system of equations that has two solutions. The system should include one quadratic equation and one linear equation.

SEE EXAMPLE **1** Solve each system by graphing. Check your answers.

3. $\begin{cases} y = 2x^2 - 7x + 6 \\ y = x \end{cases}$

4. $\begin{cases} y = x^2 - 2x - 5 \\ y = 2x - 8 \end{cases}$

SEE EXAMPLE **2** Solve each system by substitution. Check your answers.

5. $\begin{cases} y = x^2 - 4x + 3 \\ y = x - 3 \end{cases}$

6. $\begin{cases} y = 2x^2 - 5x + 3 \\ y = -3x + 15 \end{cases}$

SEE EXAMPLE **3** Solve each system by elimination. Check your answers.

7. $\begin{cases} y = x^2 - 3 \\ 4x - y = 6 \end{cases}$

8. $\begin{cases} y = x^2 + 7x + 12 \\ 3x - y = 5 \end{cases}$

SEE EXAMPLE **4** 9. **Physics** A bird is flying upwards such that its height in feet after t seconds is given by $h = 4t$. At the instant the bird passes the height of a ball being held out of a window, the ball is thrown upward with an initial velocity of 80 feet per second. The height in feet of the ball after t seconds is given by $h = -16t^2 + 80t$. Find the time it takes for the ball and the bird to reach the same height.

PRACTICE AND PROBLEM SOLVING

Solve each system by graphing. Check your answers.

Independent Practice

For Exercises	See Example
10–13	1
14–17	2
18–21	3
22–25	4

10. $\begin{cases} y = x^2 - 4 \\ y = 5x - 10 \end{cases}$

11. $\begin{cases} y = x^2 - 3 \\ x - 6y = 18 \end{cases}$

12. $\begin{cases} y = x^2 + 4x + 7 \\ y = x + 5 \end{cases}$

13. $\begin{cases} y = 2x^2 - 8x + 3 \\ y = 6x - 21 \end{cases}$

Extra Practice

See Extra Practice for more Skills Practice and Applications Practice exercises.

Solve each system by substitution. Check your answers.

14. $\begin{cases} y = x^2 + 7x + 2 \\ y = 5x + 5 \end{cases}$

15. $\begin{cases} y = 2x^2 - 3 \\ y = 2x + 9 \end{cases}$

16. $\begin{cases} y = x^2 - 5 \\ y = -2x + 3 \end{cases}$

17. $\begin{cases} y = 5x^2 - 2x \\ y = 10x + 9 \end{cases}$

Solve each system by elimination. Check your answers.

18. $\begin{cases} y = 2x^2 - 3x + 1 \\ 5x - y = -1 \end{cases}$

19. $\begin{cases} y = x^2 - 5 \\ x - 3y = 15 \end{cases}$

20. $\begin{cases} y = 2x^2 - x + 7 \\ 2x + 3y = 6 \end{cases}$

21. $\begin{cases} y = x^2 + 5x \\ 9x - y = 3 \end{cases}$

22. **Demographics** The growing population of town A can be modeled by the equation $P(t) = 8t^2 + 2000$, where t represents number of years after 2010. The growing population of town B can be modeled by the equation $P(t) = 100t + 3000$. In which year will the populations of the towns be approximately equal?

23. **Finance** The value of Danielle's investments is modeled by the equation $V(t) = 3t^2 + 70t + 100$, where t represents the number of months after she made her initial investment. Jeffrey has no money invested in stocks, but he deposits the same amount every month into a savings account that he opened at the same time as Danielle began investing. His savings account balance can be modeled by the equation $V(t) = 50t + 275$. After how many months will the value of Danielle's investments be equal to the balance of Jeffrey's savings account?

24. **Amusement Parks** A ride at an amusement park consists of an observation deck that travels directly up into the air at a constant rate of 40 feet per second. Its height in feet after t seconds is given by $h = 40t$. At the instant the deck is at ground level, a ball is thrown up with initial velocity 60 feet per second from ground level. The height in feet of the ball after t seconds is given by $h = -16t^2 + 60t$. Find the time it takes for the ball and the deck to reach the same height. Round your answer to the nearest hundredth.

25. **Business** A company's weekly revenue can be modeled by the equation $C(p) = 0.75p^2 + 10p + 200$, where p represents the number of products sold. The weekly cost of running the business is modeled by the equation $C(p) = 80p + 700$. How many products must the company sell in a week to break even (when revenue equal the costs of running the business)?

Determine whether the point is a solution of the system of equations.

26. $\begin{cases} y = x^2 - 9x + 2 \\ 2x + y = -16 \end{cases}$; $(-2, -12)$

27. $\begin{cases} y = x^2 + 2x - 9 \\ y = 8x \end{cases}$; $(3, 24)$

28. $\begin{cases} y = x^2 - 6x - 1 \\ 3x - 4y = -3 \end{cases}$; $(7, 6)$

29. $\begin{cases} y = 3x^2 - 7x + 6 \\ y = x + 1 \end{cases}$; $(1, 2)$

30. $\begin{cases} y = 2x^2 - 5x + 5 \\ y = x + 5 \end{cases}$; $(3, 8)$

31. $\begin{cases} y = 3x^2 + 4x - 1 \\ 9x - 2y = -5 \end{cases}$; $(-1, -2)$

32. $\begin{cases} y = 2x^2 - 25 \\ 4x - y = 5 \end{cases}$; $(5, 25)$

33. $\begin{cases} y = x^2 + 3x + 8 \\ 5x - y = 28 \end{cases}$; $(2, -18)$

34. **Write About It** Explain in your own words when you should use the substitution method to solve a nonlinear system, and when you should use the elimination method.

35. **Critical Thinking** Describe a scenario in which you might use the graphing method to solve a system of nonlinear equations, even if you didn't expect the solution(s) to consist of integer coordinates.

36. **Estimation** Estimate the solution(s) to the system by graphing.

$\begin{cases} y = x^2 + 6x - 2 \\ y = 0.5x + 7 \end{cases}$

37. **/// ERROR ANALYSIS ///** Below are two solutions to the system of equations $\begin{cases} y = x^2 - 4x + 5 \\ 4x + 3y = 11 \end{cases}$. Which is incorrect? Explain the error.

A

$y = x^2 - 4x + 5 \rightarrow \quad -3y = -3x^2 + 12x - 15$

$4x + 3y = 11 \quad \rightarrow \underline{\quad 4x + 3y = 11 \quad}$

$\qquad\qquad\qquad 4x + 0 = -3x^2 + 12x - 4$

$\qquad\qquad\qquad\quad 0 = -3x^2 + 8x - 4$

$\qquad\qquad\qquad\quad 0 = (-3x + 2)(x - 2)$

$\qquad -3x + 2 = 0 \quad \text{or} \quad x - 2 = 0$

$\qquad\qquad -3x = -2 \qquad\qquad x = 2$

$\qquad\qquad\quad x = \dfrac{2}{3}$

$\quad 4x + 3y = 11 \qquad\qquad 4x + 3y = 11$

$\quad 4\left(\dfrac{2}{3}\right) + 3y = 11 \qquad 4(2) + 3y = 11$

$\quad \dfrac{8}{3} + 3y = 11 \qquad\qquad 8 + 3y = 11$

$\quad 3y = \dfrac{25}{3} \qquad\qquad\qquad 3y = 3$

$\quad y = \dfrac{25}{9} \qquad\qquad\qquad y = 1$

The solutions are $\left(\dfrac{2}{3}, \dfrac{25}{9}\right)$ and $(2, 1)$.

B

$y = x^2 - 4x + 5 \rightarrow \quad -3y = x^2 - 4x + 5$

$4x + 3y = 11 \quad \rightarrow \underline{\quad 4x + 3y = 11 \quad}$

$\qquad\qquad\qquad 4x + 0 = x^2 - 4x + 5$

$\qquad\qquad\qquad\quad 0 = x^2 - 8x + 5$

$\qquad x = \dfrac{-b \pm \sqrt{b^2 - 4ac}}{2a}$

$\qquad x = \dfrac{-(-8) \pm \sqrt{(-8)^2 - 4(1)(5)}}{2(1)}$

$\qquad x = \dfrac{8 \pm \sqrt{44}}{2}$

$\qquad x = \dfrac{8 \pm 2\sqrt{11}}{2}$

$\qquad x = 4 \pm \sqrt{11} \approx 7.32 \quad \text{or} \quad 0.68$

$\quad 4x + 3y \approx 11 \qquad\qquad 4x + 3y \approx 11$

$\quad 4(7.32) + 3y \approx 11 \qquad 4(0.68) + 3y \approx 11$

$\quad 29.28 + 3y \approx 11 \qquad\quad 2.72 + 3y \approx 11$

$\qquad\quad 3y \approx -18.28 \qquad\qquad 3y \approx 8.28$

$\qquad\quad y \approx -6.09 \qquad\qquad\quad y \approx 2.76$

The solutions are approximately $(7.32, -6.09)$ and $(0.68, 2.76)$.

TEST PREP

38. Which are the solutions to the system of equations below?

$\begin{cases} y = x^2 - 5x - 2 \\ y = -7x + 1 \end{cases}$

   Ⓐ $(-3, 22)$ and $(1, -6)$ Ⓒ $(-1, 8)$ and $(2, -10)$

   Ⓑ $(-3, 22)$ and $(-1, 8)$ Ⓓ $(1, -6)$ and $(2, -10)$

39. For which system of equations is $(2, 6)$ a solution?

   Ⓕ $\begin{cases} y = x^2 + 4x - 2 \\ y = -3x - 2 \end{cases}$ Ⓗ $\begin{cases} y = 3x^2 - x - 4 \\ y = -5x + 16 \end{cases}$

   Ⓖ $\begin{cases} y = x^2 - 4x + 14 \\ x - y = 4 \end{cases}$ Ⓙ $\begin{cases} y = 2x^2 + 9 \\ y = 5x - 4 \end{cases}$

40. Which system below has no real solutions?

   Ⓐ $\begin{cases} 3y + x = 9 \\ y = (x - 3)^2 \end{cases}$ Ⓒ $\begin{cases} y = x - 4x^2 \\ x = -2 - y \end{cases}$

   Ⓑ $\begin{cases} y = 2x^2 - 2 \\ x - y = 5 \end{cases}$ Ⓓ $\begin{cases} y = 2x - 7 \\ y = x^2 - 7 \end{cases}$

41. Which is the graph of $\begin{cases} y = 2x - 1 \\ y = 2x^2 + 4x - 5 \end{cases}$?

 F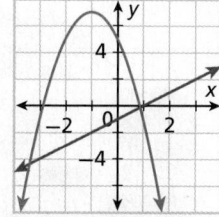

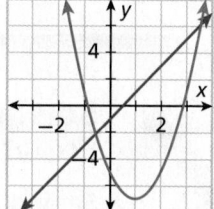 **H**

 G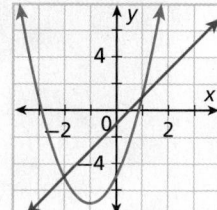

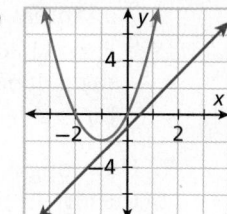 **J**

CHALLENGE AND EXTEND

Find the *x*-coordinate(s) of the solution(s) of each system.

42. $\begin{cases} y = 3x^2 + 4x - 7 \\ 3x + 5y = 8 \end{cases}$ **43.** $\begin{cases} y = x^2 - 3x - 5 \\ 3x + 2y = 8 \end{cases}$ **44.** $\begin{cases} y = x^2 + x - 2 \\ 3x + 2y = 3 \end{cases}$ **45.** $\begin{cases} y = 4x^2 - 9 \\ y = 7x - 2 \end{cases}$

46. A system of two equations contains one quadratic equation and one linear equation. The quadratic equation in the system is $y = x^2 + 5x - 9$. The solutions of the system are $(3, 15)$ and $(-1, -13)$. What is the linear equation in the system?

47. Physics The formula for the height of an object in free fall (neglecting air resistance) is $h(t) = -16t^2 + v_0 t + h_0$, where v_0 is the object's initial velocity in feet per second and h_0 is the object's initial height above the ground in feet. One ball is thrown with an initial velocity of 90 ft/s from a height of 20 ft. A second ball is thrown at the exact same instant with an initial velocity of 80 ft/s and a height of 30 ft. After how many seconds will the balls reach the same height?

MULTI-STEP TEST PREP

Make sense of problems and persevere in solving them.

Solving Quadratic Equations

Seeing Green A golf player hits a golf ball from a tee with an initial vertical velocity of 80 feet per second. The height of the golf ball t seconds after it is hit is given by $h = -16t^2 + 80t$.

1. How long is the golf ball in the air?

2. What is the maximum height of the golf ball?

3. How long after the golf ball is hit does it reach its maximum height?

4. What is the height of the golf ball after 3.5 seconds?

5. At what times is the golf ball 64 feet in the air? Explain.

READY TO GO ON?

Quiz for Lessons 8-5 Through 8-10

8-5 **Solving Quadratic Equations by Graphing**

Solve each equation by graphing the related function.

1. $x^2 - 9 = 0$ **2.** $x^2 + 3x - 4 = 0$ **3.** $4x^2 + 8x = 32$

4. The height of a fireworks rocket launched from a platform 35 meters above the ground can be approximated by $h = -5t^2 + 30t + 35$, where h is the height in meters and t is the time in seconds. Find the time it takes the rocket to reach the ground after it is launched.

8-6 **Solving Quadratic Equations by Factoring**

Use the Zero Product Property to solve each equation.

5. $(x + 1)(x + 3) = 0$ **6.** $(x - 6)(x - 3) = 0$ **7.** $(x + 6)(x - 3) = 0$ **8.** $(x + 7)(x - 10) = 0$

Solve each quadratic equation by factoring.

9. $x^2 - 4x - 32 = 0$ **10.** $x^2 - 8x + 15 = 0$ **11.** $x^2 + x = 6$ **12.** $-8x - 33 = -x^2$

8-7 **Solving Quadratic Equations by Using Square Roots**

Solve using square roots.

13. $3x^2 = 48$ **14.** $36x^2 - 49 = 0$ **15.** $-12 = x^2 - 21$

8-8 **Completing the Square**

Solve by completing the square.

16. $x^2 + 2x = 3$ **17.** $x^2 - 5 = 2x$ **18.** $x^2 + 7x = 8$

19. The width of a rectangle is 4 feet shorter than its length. The area of the rectangle is 42 square feet. Find the length and width. Round your answer to the nearest tenth of a foot.

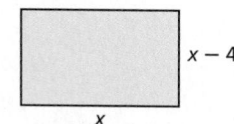

8-9 **Using the Quadratic Formula and the Discriminant**

Solve using the Quadratic Formula. Round your answer to the nearest hundredth.

20. $x^2 + 5x + 1 = 0$ **21.** $3x^2 + 1 = 2x$ **22.** $5x + 8 = 3x^2$

Find the number of real solutions of each equation using the discriminant.

23. $2x^2 - 3x + 4 = 0$ **24.** $x^2 + 1 + 2x = 0$ **25.** $x^2 - 5 + 4x = 0$

8-10 **Nonlinear Systems**

26. Solve the system by graphing. Check your answer. $\begin{cases} y = x^2 - 7 \\ y = x - 7 \end{cases}$

27. Solve the system by substitution. Check your answer. $\begin{cases} y = 2x^2 + x + 7 \\ y = 4x + 5 \end{cases}$

EXTENSION Cubic Functions and Equations

CC.9-12.F.IF.7c Graph polynomial functions, identifying zeros when suitable factorizations are available, and showing end behavior. *Also* **CC.9-12.A.REI.10, CC.9-12.A.REI.11*, CC.9-12.A.APR.3**

Objectives
Recognize and graph cubic functions.

Solve cubic equations.

Vocabulary
cubic function
cubic equation

A **cubic function** is a function that can be written in the form $f(x) = ax^3 + bx^2 + cx + d$, where $a \neq 0$. The parent cubic function is $f(x) = x^3$. To graph this function, choose several values of x and find ordered pairs.

x	f(x)
2	8
1	1
0	0
−1	−1
−2	−8

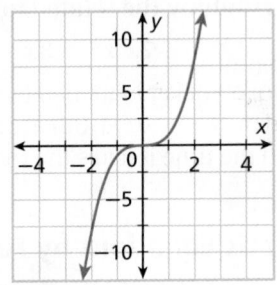

From the graph of $f(x) = x^3$, you can see
- the general shape of a cubic function.
- that the domain and the range are all real numbers.
- that the x-intercept and the y-intercept are both 0.

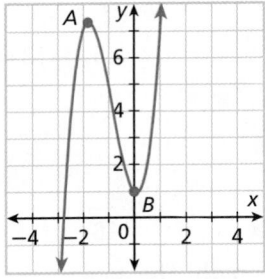

The graph of $f(x) = 2x^3 + 5x^2 - x + 1$ illustrates another characteristic of the graphs of cubic functions. Points A and B are called *turning points*. In general, the graph of a cubic function will have two turning points.

EXAMPLE **1** **Graphing Cubic Functions**

Graph $f(x) = -2x^3 + 3x^2 + x - 4$. **Identify the intercepts and give the domain and range.**

x	$f(x) = -2x^3 + 3x^2 + x - 4$	f(x)
−1	$-2(-1)^3 + 3(-1)^2 - 1 - 4$	0
0	$-2(0)^3 + 3(0)^2 + 0 - 4$	−4
1	$-2(1)^3 + 3(1)^2 + 1 - 4$	−2
2	$-2(2)^3 + 3(2)^2 + 2 - 4$	−6

Choose positive, negative, and zero values for x, and find ordered pairs.

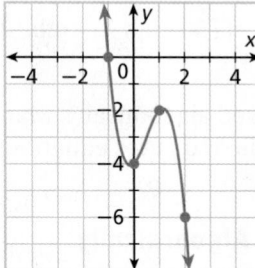

Plot the ordered pairs and connect them with a smooth curve.

Notice that, in general, this graph falls from left to right. This is because the value of a is negative.

The x-intercept is -1. The y-intercept is -4. The domain and range are all real numbers.

 **CHECK IT OUT!** Graph each cubic function. Identify the intercepts and give the domain and range.

1a. $f(x) = (x - 1)^3$ **1b.** $f(x) = 2x^3 - 12x^2 + 18x$

Previously, you saw that every quadratic function has a related quadratic equation. Cubic functions also have related *cubic equations*. A **cubic equation** is an equation that can be written in the form $ax^3 + bx^2 + cx + d = 0$, where $a \neq 0$.

One way to solve a cubic equation is by graphing the related function and finding its zeros.

EXAMPLE 2 **Solving Cubic Equations by Graphing**

Solve $x^3 - 2x^2 - x = -2$ by graphing. Check your answer.

Step 1 Rewrite the equation in the form $ax^3 + bx^2 + cx + d = 0$.

$x^3 - 2x^2 - x = -2$

$x^3 - 2x^2 - x + 2 = 0$ *Add 2 to both sides of the equation.*

Step 2 Write and graph the related function: $f(x) = x^3 - 2x^2 - x + 2$

x	$f(x) = x^3 - 2x^2 - x + 2$	$f(x)$
-1	$(-1)^3 - 2(-1)^2 - (-1) + 2$	0
0	$(0)^3 - 2(0)^2 - 0 + 2$	2
1	$(1)^3 - 2(1)^2 - 1 + 2$	0
2	$(2)^3 - 2(2)^2 - 2 + 2$	0
3	$(3)^3 - 2(3)^2 - 3 + 2$	8

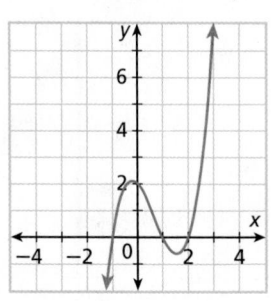

Step 3 Find the zeros.

The zeros appear to be -1, 1, and 2. Check these values in the original equation.

$x^3 - 2x^2 - x = -2$		$x^3 - 2x^2 - x = -2$		$x^3 - 2x^2 - x = -2$	
$(-1)^3 - 2(-1)^2 - (-1)$	-2	$1^3 - 2(1)^2 - 1$	-2	$2^3 - 2(2)^2 - 2$	-2
$(-1) - 2 + 1$	-2	$1 - 2 - 1$	-2	$x - 8 - 2$	-2
-2	$-2 \checkmark$	-2	$-2 \checkmark$	-2	$-2 \checkmark$

CHECK IT OUT! Solve each equation by graphing. Check your answer.

2a. $x^3 - 2x^2 - 25x = -50$ **2b.** $2x^3 + 12x^2 = 30x + 200$

Cubic equations can also be solved algebraically. Many of the methods used to solve quadratic equations can be applied to cubic equations as well.

EXAMPLE 3

Solving Cubic Equations Algebraically

Solve each equation. Check your answer.

A $(x + 5)^3 = 27$

$$\sqrt[3]{(x + 5)^3} = \sqrt[3]{27}$$ *Take the cube root of both sides.*

$$x + 5 = 3$$

$$x = -2$$ *Subtract 5 from both sides.*

Check

$$(x + 5)^3 = 27$$

$(-2 + 5)^3$	27
3^3	27
27	27 ✓

Substitute –2 for x in the original equation.

B $x^3 + 3x^2 = -2x$

$$x^3 + 3x^2 + 2x = 0$$ *Add 2x to both sides.*

$$x(x^2 + 3x + 2) = 0$$ *Factor out x on the left side.*

$$x(x + 1)(x + 2) = 0$$ *Factor the quadratic trinomial.*

$$x = 0 \text{ or } x + 1 = 0 \text{ or } x + 2 = 0$$ *Zero Product Property*

$$x = -1 \text{ or } \quad x = -2$$ *Solve each equation.*

The solutions are 0, –1, and –2.

Remember!

The factored expression must equal zero to use the Zero Product Property.

Check

$x^3 + 3x^2 = -2x$		$x^3 + 3x^2 = -2x$		$x^3 + 3x^2 = -2x$	
$0^3 + 3(0)^2$	$-2(0)$	$(-1)^3 + 3(-1)^2$	$-2(-1)$	$(-2)^3 + 3(-2)^2$	$-2(-2)$
$0 + 0$	0	$-1 + 3(1)$	2	$-8 + 3(4)$	4
0	0 ✓	$-1 + 3$	2	$-8 + 12$	4
			2 2 ✓		4 4 ✓

C $x^3 - 3.125x = -1.25x^2$

$$x^3 + 1.25x^2 - 3.125x = 0$$ *Add 1.25x² to both sides.*

$$x(x^2 + 1.25x - 3.125) = 0$$ *Factor out x on the left side.*

$$x = 0 \text{ or } x^2 + 1.25x - 3.125 = 0$$ *Zero Product Property*

$$x = \frac{-1.25 \pm \sqrt{(1.25)^2 - 4(1)(-3.125)}}{2(1)}$$ *Quadratic Formula*

$$x = \frac{-1.25 \pm 3.75}{2}$$ *Simplify.*

$$x = -2.5 \text{ or } x = 1.25$$

The solutions are –2.5, 0, and 1.25.

Check   Use a graphing calculator.

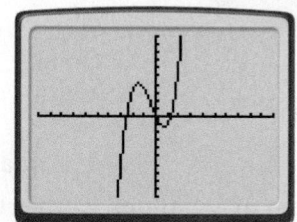

Graph the related function and look for the zeros.

The solutions look reasonable.

 **Solve each equation. Check your answer.**

3a. $(x + 2)^3 = 64$ **3b.** $4x^3 - 12x^2 + 4x = 0$ **3c.** $x^3 + 3x^2 = 10x$

EXTENSION

Exercises

Graph each cubic function. Identify the intercepts and give the domain and range.

1. $f(x) = x^3 - 2x^2 + 3x + 6$

2. $g(x) = -4x^3 + 2x - 2$

Solve each equation by graphing. Check your answer.

3. $2x^3 - 6x = -4x^2$

4. $-3x^3 + 12x^2 + 12x = 48$

Solve each equation. Check your answer.

5. $(x - 9)^3 = 64$ **6.** $8x + 4x^2 = 4x^3$ **7.** $5x^3 + 3x^2 = 4x$

8. The Send-It Store uses shipping labels that are x in. tall and $2x$ in. wide. Six labels fit on the front of the store's standard shipping box with an area of $3x$ in^2 left over. Three labels fit on the side of the box. The volume of the box is $108x$ in^3. What is the area of one label?

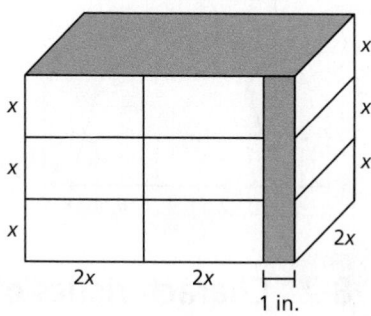

9. a. Graph the functions $f(x) = x^3$, $f(x) = x^3 + 1$, and $f(x) = x^3 + 2$ on the same coordinate plane. Describe any patterns you observe. Predict the shape of the graph of $f(x) = x^3 + c$.

b. Graph the functions $g(x) = x^3$, $g(x) = (x - 1)^3$, and $g(x) = (x - 2)^3$ on the same coordinate plane. Describe any patterns you observe. Predict the shape of the graph of $g(x) = (x - c)^3$.

Use a graphing calculator to find the approximate solution(s) of each cubic equation. Round to the nearest hundredth.

10. $100x^3 - 40x^2 = 6x$

11. $2x^3 - 5x^2 + 4x = -3$

12. $-1.32x^3 - 3.65x^2 = -0.43x$

13. $\frac{3}{5}x^3 + x^2 - \frac{1}{2}x = 9$

14. Critical Thinking How many zeros can a cubic function have? What does this tell you about the number of real solutions possible for a cubic equation?

Study Guide: Review

Vocabulary

axis of symmetry   minimum   quadratic function

completing the square   nonlinear system of equations   vertex

discriminant   parabola   zero of a function

maximum   quadratic equation

Complete the sentences below with vocabulary words from the list above.

1. The ___?___ is the highest or lowest point on a parabola.

2. A ___?___ can also be called an *x*-intercept of the function.

8-1 Identifying Quadratic Functions

EXAMPLE

■ Use a table of values to graph $y = -5x^2 + 40x$.

Step 1 Make a table of values. Choose values of *x* and use them to find values of *y*.

x	0	1	3	4	6	7	8
y	0	35	75	80	60	35	0

Step 2 Plot the points and connect them.

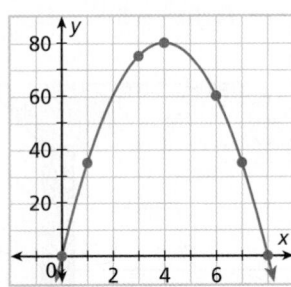

EXERCISES

Tell whether each function is quadratic. Explain.

3. $y = 2x^2 + 9x - 5$ **4.** $y = -4x + 3$

5. $y = -\dfrac{1}{2}x^2$ **6.** $y = 5x^3 + 8$

Use a table of values to graph each quadratic function.

7. $y = 6x^2$ **8.** $y = -4x^2$

9. $y = \dfrac{1}{4}x^2$ **10.** $y = -3x^2$

Tell whether the graph of each function opens upward or downward. Explain.

11. $y = 5x^2 - 12$ **12.** $y = -x^2 + 3x - 7$

8-2 Characteristics of Quadratic Functions

EXAMPLE

■ Find the zeros of $y = 2x^2 - 4x - 6$ from its graph.

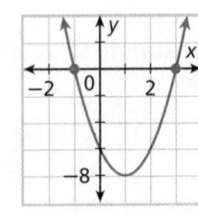

Use the graph to find the zeros.
The zeros are −1 and 3.

EXERCISES

Find the zeros of each quadratic function from its graph. Check your answer.

13. $y = x^2 + 3x - 10$ **14.** $y = x^2 - x - 2$

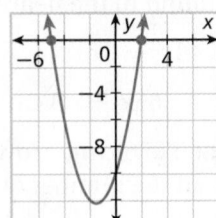 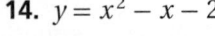 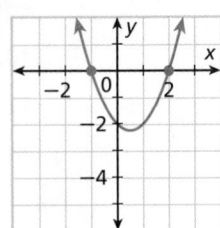

8-3 Graphing Quadratic Functions

EXAMPLE

■ Graph $y = 2x^2 - 8x - 10$.

Step 1 Find the axis of symmetry.

$$x = \frac{-b}{2a} = \frac{-(-8)}{2(2)} = \frac{8}{4} = 2$$

The axis of symmetry is $x = 2$.

Step 2 Find the vertex.

$$y = 2x^2 - 8x - 10$$
$$y = 2(2)^2 - 8(2) - 10$$
$$y = -18$$

The vertex is $(2, -18)$.

Step 3 Find the y-intercept.
$c = -10$

Step 4 Find one more point on the graph.

$$y = 2(-1)^2 - 8(-1) - 10 = 0 \qquad \textit{Let } x = -1.$$
Use $(-1, 0)$.

Step 5 Graph the axis of symmetry and the points. **Reflect** the points and connect with a smooth curve.

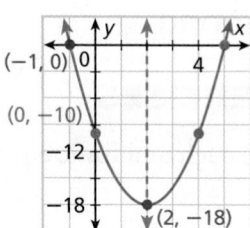

EXERCISES

Graph each quadratic function.

15. $y = x^2 + 6x + 6$

16. $y = x^2 - 4x - 12$

17. $y = x^2 - 8x + 7$

18. $y = 2x^2 - 6x - 8$

19. $3x^2 + 6x = y - 3$

20. $2 - 4x^2 + y = 8x - 10$

21. Water that is sprayed upward from a sprinkler with an initial velocity of 20 m/s can be approximated by the function $y = -5x^2 + 20x$, where y is the height of a drop of water x seconds after it is released. Graph this function. Find the time it takes a drop of water to reach its maximum height, the water's maximum height, and the time it takes the water to reach the ground.

8-4 Transforming Quadratic Functions

EXAMPLE

■ Compare the graph of $g(x) = 3x^2 - 4$ with the graph of $f(x) = x^2$. Use the functions.

- Both graphs open upward because $a > 0$.

- The axis of symmetry is the same, $x = 0$, because $b = 0$ in both functions.

- The graph of $g(x)$ is narrower than the graph of $f(x)$ because $|3| > |1|$.

- The vertex of $f(x)$ is $(0, 0)$. The vertex of $g(x)$ is translated 4 units down to $(0, -4)$.

- $f(x)$ has one zero at the origin. $g(x)$ has two zeros because the vertex is below the origin and the parabola opens upward.

EXERCISES

Compare the widths of the graphs of the given quadratic functions. Order functions with different widths from narrowest graph to widest.

22. $f(x) = 2x^2$, $g(x) = 4x^2$

23. $f(x) = 6x^2$, $g(x) = -6x^2$

24. $f(x) = x^2$, $g(x) = \frac{1}{3}x^2$, $h(x) = 3x^2$

Compare the graph of each function with the graph of $f(x) = x^2$.

25. $g(x) = x^2 + 5$

26. $g(x) = 3x^2 - 1$

27. $g(x) = 2x^2 + 3$

8-5 Solving Quadratic Equations by Graphing

EXAMPLE

■ Solve $-4 = 4x^2 - 8x$ by graphing the related function.

Step 1 Write the equation in standard form.

$$0 = 4x^2 - 8x + 4$$

Step 2 Graph the related function.

$$y = 4x^2 - 8x + 4$$

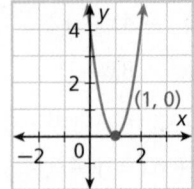

Step 3 Find the zeros.
The only zero is 1. The solution is $x = 1$.

EXERCISES

Solve each equation by graphing the related function.

28. $0 = x^2 + 4x + 3$

29. $0 = x^2 + 6x + 9$

30. $-4x^2 = 3$

31. $x^2 + 5 = 6x$

32. $-4x^2 = 64 - 32x$

33. $9 = 9x^2$

34. $-3x^2 + 2x = 5$

8-6 Solving Quadratic Equations by Factoring

EXAMPLE

■ Solve $3x^2 - 6x = 24$ by factoring.

$3x^2 - 6x = 24$	*Write the equation in*
$3x^2 - 6x - 24 = 0$	*standard form.*
$3(x^2 - 2x - 8) = 0$	*Factor out 3.*
$3(x + 2)(x - 4) = 0$	*Factor the trinomial.*
	Zero Product
$3 \neq 0, x + 2 = 0$ or $x - 4 = 0$	*Property*
$x = -2$ or $x = 4$	*Solve each equation.*

EXERCISES

Solve each quadratic equation by factoring.

35. $x^2 + 6x + 5 = 0$ 36. $x^2 + 9x + 14 = 0$

37. $x^2 - 2x - 15 = 0$ 38. $2x^2 - 2x - 4 = 0$

39. $x^2 + 10x + 25 = 0$ 40. $4x^2 - 36x = -81$

41. A rectangle is 2 feet longer than it is wide. The area of the rectangle is 48 square feet. Write and solve an equation that can be used to find the width of the rectangle.

8-7 Solving Quadratic Equations by Using Square Roots

EXAMPLE

■ Solve $2x^2 = 98$ using square roots.

$\dfrac{2x^2}{2} = \dfrac{98}{2}$	*Divide both sides of the equation by 2 to isolate x^2.*
$x^2 = 49$	
$x = \pm\sqrt{49}$	*Take the square root of both sides.*
$x = \pm 7$	*Use $\pm$ to show both roots.*

The solutions are -7 and 7.

EXERCISES

Solve using square roots.

42. $5x^2 = 320$ 43. $-x^2 + 144 = 0$

44. $x^2 = -16$ 45. $x^2 + 7 = 7$

46. $2x^2 = 50$ 47. $4x^2 = 25$

48. A rectangle is twice as long as it is wide. The area of the rectangle is 32 square feet. Find the rectangle's width.

8-8 Completing the Square

EXAMPLE

EXAMPLE

■ Solve $x^2 - 6x = -5$ by completing the square.

$$\left(\frac{-6}{2}\right)^2 = 9 \qquad \textit{Find } \left(\frac{b}{2}\right)^2.$$

$$x^2 - 6x + 9 = -5 + 9$$
$$x^2 - 6x + 9 = 4 \qquad \textit{Complete the square.}$$
$$(x-3)^2 = 4 \qquad \textit{Factor the trinomial.}$$
$$x - 3 = \pm\sqrt{4} \qquad \begin{array}{l}\textit{Take the square root of}\\ \textit{both sides.}\end{array}$$
$$x - 3 = \pm 2 \qquad \textit{Use the } \pm \textit{ symbol.}$$
$$x - 3 = 2 \text{ or } x - 3 = -2 \quad \textit{Solve each}$$
$$x = 5 \quad \text{ or } \quad x = 1 \qquad \textit{equation.}$$

The solutions are 5 and 1.

EXERCISES

Solve by completing the square.

49. $x^2 + 2x = 48$

50. $x^2 + 4x = 21$

51. $2x^2 - 12x + 10 = 0$

52. $x^2 - 10x = -20$

53. A homeowner is planning an addition to her house. She wants the new family room to be a rectangle with an area of 192 square feet. The contractor says that the length needs to be 4 more feet than the width. What will the dimensions of the new room be?

8-9 The Quadratic Formula and the Discriminant

EXAMPLE

■ Solve $x^2 + 4x + 4 = 0$ using the Quadratic Formula.

$$x = \frac{-b \pm \sqrt{b^2 - 4ac}}{2a} \qquad \begin{array}{l}\textit{Write the Quadratic}\\ \textit{Formula.}\end{array}$$

$$= \frac{-4 \pm \sqrt{4^2 - 4(1)(4)}}{2(1)} \qquad \begin{array}{l}\textit{Substitute for a, b,}\\ \textit{and c.}\end{array}$$

$$= \frac{-4 \pm \sqrt{16 - 16}}{2} \qquad \textit{Simplify.}$$

$$= \frac{-4 \pm \sqrt{0}}{2} = \frac{-4}{2} = -2$$

The solution is $x = -2$.

EXERCISES

Solve using the Quadratic Formula.

54. $x^2 - 5x - 6 = 0$　　**55.** $2x^2 - 9x - 5 = 0$

56. $4x^2 - 8x + 4 = 0$　　**57.** $x^2 - 6x = -7$

Find the number of real solutions of each equation using the discriminant.

58. $x^2 - 12x + 36 = 0$

59. $3x^2 + 5 = 0$

60. $2x^2 - 13x = -20$

61. $6x^2 - 20 = 15x + 1$

8-10 Nonlinear Systems

EXAMPLE

■ Solve $\begin{cases} y = x^2 \\ y = x + 2 \end{cases}$ by substitution.

$$x + 2 = x^2. \qquad \begin{array}{l}\textit{Substitute x + 2 for y in}\\ \textit{the first equation.}\end{array}$$
$$0 = x^2 - x - 2$$
$$0 = (x - 2)(x + 1) \qquad \textit{Factor the trinomial.}$$
$$x - 2 = 0 \text{ or } x + 1 = 0 \quad \textit{Solve the equations.}$$
$$x = 2 \qquad \text{ or } x = -1 \qquad \textit{Write one of the}$$
$$y = x + 2 \qquad y = x + 2 \qquad \textit{original equations.}$$
$$y = 2 + 2 \qquad y = -1 + 2 \quad \textit{Substitute each x-value}$$
$$y = 4 \qquad y = 1 \qquad \textit{and solve for y.}$$

The solutions are (2, 4) and (−1, 1).

EXERCISES

Solve each system.

62. $\begin{cases} y = x^2 - 4 \\ y = -2x - 1 \end{cases}$

63. $\begin{cases} y = x^2 - 3x - 1 \\ y = 2x - 5 \end{cases}$

64. $\begin{cases} y = x^2 + 5x + 4 \\ y = -2x - 6 \end{cases}$

CHAPTER TEST

Tell whether each function is quadratic. Explain.

1. $\{(10, 50), (11, 71), (12, 94), (13, 119), (14, 146)\}$ 2. $3x^2 + y = 4 + 3x^2$

3. Tell whether the graph of $y = -2x^2 + 7x - 5$ opens upward or downward and whether the parabola has a maximum or a minimum.

4. Estimate the zeros of the quadratic function.

5. Find the axis of symmetry of the parabola.

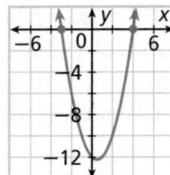

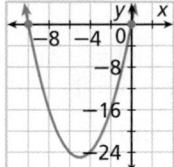

6. Find the vertex of the graph of $y = x^2 + 6x + 8$.

7. Graph the quadratic function $y = x^2 - 4x + 2$.

Compare the graph of each function with the graph of $f(x) = x^2$.

8. $g(x) = -x^2 - 2$ 9. $h(x) = \frac{1}{3}x^2 + 1$ 10. $g(x) = 3x^2 - 4$

11. A hammer is dropped from a 40-foot scaffold. Another one is dropped from a 60-foot scaffold.

   a. Write the two height functions and compare their graphs. Use $h(t) = -16t^2 + c$, where c is the height of the scaffold.

   b. Use the graphs to estimate when each hammer will reach the ground.

12. A rocket is launched with an initial vertical velocity of 110 m/s. The height of the rocket in meters is approximated by the quadratic equation $h = -5t^2 + 110t$ where t is the time after launch in seconds. About how long does it take for the rocket to return to the ground?

Solve each quadratic equation by factoring.

13. $x^2 + 6x + 5 = 0$ 14. $x^2 - 12x = -36$ 15. $x^2 - 81 = 0$

Solve by using square roots.

16. $-2x^2 = -72$ 17. $9x^2 - 49 = 0$ 18. $3x^2 + 12 = 0$

Solve by completing the square.

19. $x^2 + 10x = -21$ 20. $x^2 - 6x + 4 = 0$ 21. $2x^2 + 16x = 0$

Solve each quadratic equation. Round to the nearest hundredth if necessary.

22. $x^2 + 3x - 40 = 0$ 23. $2x^2 + 7x = -5$ 24. $8x^2 + 3x - 1 = 0$

Find the number of real solutions of each equation using the discriminant.

25. $4x^2 - 4x + 1 = 0$ 26. $2x^2 + 5x - 25 = 0$ 27. $\frac{1}{2}x^2 + 8 = 0$

28. Solve the system. $\begin{cases} y = x^2 + 7x + 6 \\ y = x + 1 \end{cases}$

COLLEGE ENTRANCE EXAM PRACTICE

FOCUS ON SAT SUBJECT TESTS

In addition to the SAT, some colleges require the SAT Subject Tests for admission. Colleges that don't require the SAT Subject Tests may still use the scores to learn about your academic background and to place you in the appropriate college math class.

Take the SAT Subject Test in mathematics while the material is still fresh in your mind. You are not expected to be familiar with all of the test content, but you should have completed at least three years of college-prep math.

You may want to time yourself as you take this practice test. It should take you about 6 minutes to complete.

---

1. The graph below corresponds to which of the following quadratic functions?

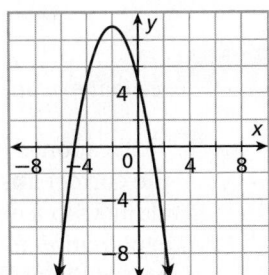

(A) $f(x) = x^2 + 4x - 5$

(B) $f(x) = -x^2 - 4x + 3$

(C) $f(x) = -x^2 + 5x - 4$

(D) $f(x) = -x^2 - 4x + 5$

(E) $f(x) = -x^2 - 3x + 5$

---

2. What is the sum of the solutions to the equation $9x^2 - 6x = 8$?

(A) $\dfrac{4}{3}$

(B) $\dfrac{2}{3}$

(C) $\dfrac{1}{3}$

(D) $-\dfrac{2}{3}$

(E) $-\dfrac{8}{3}$

---

3. If $h(x) = ax^2 + bx + c$, where $b^2 - 4ac < 0$ and $a < 0$, which of the following statements must be true?

I. The graph of $h(x)$ has no points in the first or second quadrants.

II. The graph of $h(x)$ has no points in the third or fourth quadrants.

III. The graph of $h(x)$ has points in all quadrants.

(A) I only

(B) II only

(C) III only

(D) I and II only

(E) None of the statements are true.

---

4. What is the axis of symmetry for the graph of a quadratic function whose zeros are -2 and 4?

(A) $x = -2$

(B) $x = 0$

(C) $x = 1$

(D) $x = 2$

(E) $x = 6$

---

5. How many real-number solutions does $0 = x^2 - 7x + 1$ have?

(A) None

(B) One

(C) Two

(D) All real numbers

(E) It is impossible to determine.

TEST TACKLER

Standardized Test Strategies

Extended Response: Explain Your Reasoning

Extended response test items often include multipart questions that evaluate your understanding of a math concept. To receive full credit, you must answer the problem correctly, show all of your work, and explain your reasoning. Use complete sentences and show your problem-solving method clearly.

EXAMPLE 1

Extended Response Given $\frac{1}{2}x^2 + y = 4x - 3$ and $y = 2x - 12x$, identify which is a quadratic function. Provide an explanation for your decision. For the quadratic function, tell whether the graph of the function opens upward or downward and whether the parabola has a maximum or a minimum. Explain your reasoning.

Read the solutions provided by two different students.

Student A   *Excellent explanation*

> The quadratic function is $\frac{1}{2}x^2 + y = 4X - 3$ because it can be written in standard form,
> $Y = -\frac{1}{2}x^2 + 4X - 3$, where a, b, and c are real numbers and $a \neq 0$. The other function, $Y = 2X - 12X$, is not quadratic because there is no x^2-term.
>
> The graph of this function will open downward because a, which is equal to $-\frac{1}{2}$, is less than 0. Because the parabola opens downward, the graph will have a maximum.

The response includes the correct answers along with a detailed explanation for each part of the problem. The explanation is written using complete sentences and is presented in an order that is easy to follow and to understand. It is obvious that this student knows how to determine and interpret a quadratic function.

Student B   *Poor explanation*

> $\frac{1}{2}x^2 + y = 4x - 3$ There is an x^2.
>
> When I graphed the function on my calculator, I saw a parabola that opened downward.
>
> It had a maximum.

The response includes the correct answers, but the explanation does not include details. The reason for defining the function as quadratic does not show knowledge of the concept. The student shows a lack of understanding of how to write and interpret a quadratic function in standard form.

Include as many details as possible to support your reasoning. This increases the chance of getting full credit for your response.

Read each test item and answer the questions that follow.

1. What should a student include in the explanation to receive full credit?

2. Read the two explanations below. Which explanation is better? Why?

Student A

Range: $0 \le y \le 10$ Domain: $0 \le x \le 2$
Second differences are -1: quadratic

Student B

The function is quadratic because the second differences are constant: -1. The domain and range are determined by the points $(0, 10)$ and $(2, 0)$. The range is $0 \le y \le 10$, and the domain is $0 \le x \le 2$.

3. A student correctly found the following answers. Use this information to write a clear and concise explanation.

Axis of symmetry is the vertical line at $x = 2$.
Vertex is at $(2, 28)$.
28 meters; 2 seconds

4. Read the two responses below.

   a. Which student provided the better explanation? Why?

   b. What advice would you give the other student to improve his or her explanation?

Student C

Graph the function $h = -16t^2 + 96t$, and then find the zeros. The first zero is when $t = 0$, when the rocket is launched. The second zero is when the rocket hits the ground: $t = 6$. The difference between 6 and 0 is the time that the rocket is in the air: 6 seconds.

Student D

6 seconds.
Graph the function to find how long the rocket is in the air, and find the values where it crosses the x-axis.

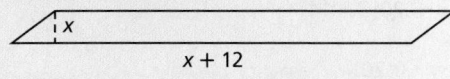
5. Read the following response. Identify any areas that need improvement. Rewrite the response so that it will receive full credit.

$x^2 + 12x + 36 = 49$ Complete the square.
$(x + 6)^2 = 49$
$x + 6 = \sqrt{49}$
$x + 6 = \pm 7; \; x = 1 \text{ or } -13$

base $= 13$, height $= 1$

CUMULATIVE ASSESSMENT

Multiple Choice

1. Which expression is NOT equal to the other three?

  Ⓐ 0^1 Ⓒ 1^0

  Ⓑ 1^1 Ⓓ $(-1)^0$

2. Which function's graph is a translation of the graph of $f(x) = 3x^2 + 4$ seven units down?

  Ⓕ $f(x) = -4x^2 + 4$

  Ⓖ $f(x) = 10x^2 + 4$

  Ⓗ $f(x) = 3x^2 - 3$

  Ⓙ $f(x) = 3x^2 + 11$

3. The area of a circle in square units is $\pi\left(9x^2 + 42x + 49\right)$. Which expression represents the circumference of the circle in units?

  Ⓐ $\pi(3x + 7)$

  Ⓑ $2\pi(3x + 7)$

  Ⓒ $2\pi(3x + 7)^2$

  Ⓓ $6x + 14$

4. CyberCafe charges a computer station rental fee of $5, plus $0.20 for each quarter-hour spent surfing. Which expression represents the total amount Carl will pay to use a computer station for three and a half hours?

  Ⓕ $5 + 0.20(3.5)$

  Ⓖ $5 + 0.20(3.5)(4)$

  Ⓗ $5 + \dfrac{0.20}{3.5 \div 4}$

  Ⓙ $5 + \dfrac{1}{4} \cdot \dfrac{0.20}{3.5}$

5. What is the numerical solution to the equation *five less than three times a number equals four more than eight times the number?*

  Ⓐ $-\dfrac{9}{5}$ Ⓒ $\dfrac{1}{11}$

  Ⓑ $-\dfrac{1}{5}$ Ⓓ $\dfrac{1}{5}$

6. Which is a possible situation for the graph?

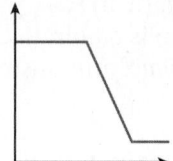

  Ⓕ A car travels at a steady speed, slows down in a school zone, and then resumes its previous speed.

  Ⓖ A child climbs the ladder of a slide and then slides down.

  Ⓗ A person flies in an airplane for a while, parachutes out, and gets stuck in a tree.

  Ⓙ The number of visitors increases in the summer, declines in the fall, and levels off in the winter.

7. Which of the following is the graph of $f(x) = -x^2 + 2$?

  Ⓐ 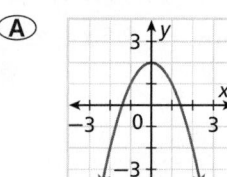   Ⓒ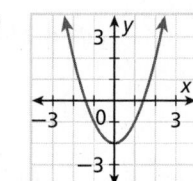

  Ⓑ 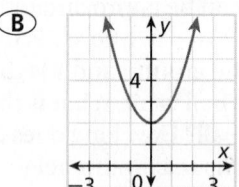   Ⓓ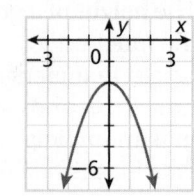

8. The value of y varies directly with x, and $y = 40$ when $x = -5$. Find y when $x = 8$.

  Ⓕ 25   Ⓗ -8

  Ⓖ -1 Ⓙ -64

9. What is the slope of the line that passes through the points $(4, 7)$ and $(5, 3)$?

  Ⓐ 4   Ⓒ $-\dfrac{1}{4}$

  Ⓑ $\dfrac{1}{4}$ Ⓓ -4

10. Putting Green Mini Golf charges a $4 golf club rental fee plus $1.25 per game. Good Times Golf charges a $1.25 golf club rental fee plus $3.75 per game. Which system of equations could be solved to determine for how many games the cost is the same at both places?

(F) $\begin{cases} y = 4x + 1.25 \\ y = 3.75 + 1.25x \end{cases}$

(G) $\begin{cases} y = 4 - 1.25x \\ y = -3.75 + 1.25x \end{cases}$

(H) $\begin{cases} y = 1.25x + 4 \\ y = 3.75x + 1.25 \end{cases}$

(J) $\begin{cases} y = 1.25x - 4 \\ y = 1.25x + 3.75 \end{cases}$

11. The graph of which quadratic function has an axis of symmetry of $x = -2$?

(A) $y = 2x^2 - x + 3$

(B) $y = 4x^2 + 2x + 3$

(C) $y = x^2 - 2x + 3$

(D) $y = x^2 + 4x + 3$

12. Which polynomial is the product of $x - 4$ and $x^2 - 4x + 1$?

(F) $-4x^2 + 17x - 4$

(G) $x^3 - 8x^2 + 17x - 4$

(H) $x^3 + 17x - 4$

(J) $x^3 - 15x + 4$

Gridded Response

13. The length of a rectangle is 2 units greater than the width. The area of the rectangle is 24 square units. What is its width in units?

14. Find the value of the discriminant of the equation $0 = -2x^2 + 3x + 4$.

15. What is the positive solution of $4x^2 = 10x + 2$? Round your answer to the nearest hundredth if necessary.

Short Response

16. The data in the table shows ordered pair solutions to a linear function. Find the missing y-value. Show your work.

x	y
-2	-7
-1	-3
0	▆
1	5
2	9

17. Answer the following questions using the function $f(x) = 2x^2 + 4x - 1$.

a. Make a table of values and give five points on the graph.

b. Find the axis of symmetry and vertex. Show all calculations.

18. a. Show how to solve $x^2 - 2x - 8 = 0$ by graphing the related function. Show all your work.

b. Show another way to solve the equation in part **a**. Show all your work.

19. What can you say about the value of a if the graph of $y = ax^2 - 8$ has no x-intercepts? Explain.

Extended Response

20. The graph shows the quadratic function $f(x) = ax^2 + bx + c$.

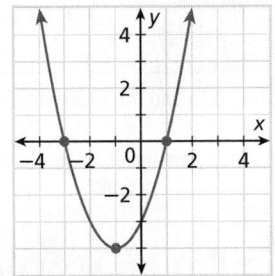

a. What are the solutions of the equation $0 = ax^2 + bx + c$? Explain how you know.

b. If the point $(-5, 12)$ lies on the graph of $f(x)$, the point $(a, 12)$ also lies on the graph. Find the value of a.

c. What do you know about the relationship between the values of a and b? Use the coordinates of the vertex in your explanation.

d. Use what you know about solving quadratic equations by factoring to make a conjecture about the values of a, b, and c in the function $f(x) = ax^2 + bx + c$.

CHAPTER 9

Exponential Functions

COMMON CORE

Chapter Focus

- Graph and use exponential functions to model real-world problems.
- Compare linear, quadratic, and exponential functions.

Population Explosion

The concepts in this chapter are used to model many real-world phenomena, such as changes in wildlife populations.

Learn It Online
Chapter Project Online

ARE YOU READY?

✓ Vocabulary

Match each term on the left with a definition on the right.

1. like terms   **A.** the set of second elements of a relation

2. square root   **B.** terms that contain the same variables raised to the same powers

3. domain   **C.** the set of first elements of a relation

4. perfect square   **D.** a number that tells how many times a base is used as a factor

5. exponent   **E.** a number whose positive square root is a whole number

     F. one of two equal factors of a number

✓ Evaluate Powers

Find the value of each expression.

6. 2^4 **7.** 5^0 **8.** $7 \cdot 3^2$ **9.** $3 \cdot 5^3$

10. 3^5 **11.** $-6^2 + 8^1$ **12.** $40 \cdot 2^3$ **13.** $7^2 \cdot 3^1$

✓ Graph Functions

Graph each function.

14. $y = 8$ **15.** $y = x + 3$ **16.** $y = x^2 - 4$ **17.** $y = x^2 + 2$

✓ Fractions, Decimals, and Percents

Write each percent as a decimal.

18. 50%   **19.** 25%   **20.** 15.2%   **21.** 200%

22. 1.9%   **23.** 0.3%   **24.** 0.1%   **25.** 1.04%

✓ Squares and Square Roots

Find each square root.

26. $\sqrt{36}$ **27.** $\sqrt{81}$ **28.** $\sqrt{25}$ **29.** $\sqrt{64}$

✓ Pythagorean Theorem

Find the length of the hypotenuse in each right triangle.

30.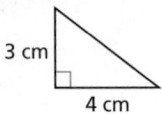

31.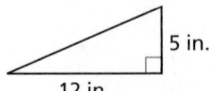

32.

✓ Multiply Monomials and Polynomials

Multiply.

33. $5(2m - 3)$ **34.** $3x(8x + 9)$ **35.** $2t(3t - 1)$ **36.** $4r(4r - 5)$

Study Guide: Preview

Where You've Been

Previously, you
- identified and extended arithmetic sequences.
- identified and graphed linear functions and quadratic functions.
- solved linear and quadratic equations.

In This Chapter

You will study
- another type of sequence—geometric sequences.
- compare linear, quadratic, and linear functions
- compare several types of exponential functions

Where You're Going

You can use the skills in this chapter
- to analyze more complicated functions in later math courses, such as Calculus.
- to explore exponential growth and decay models that are used in science.
- to make informed decisions about finances.

Key Vocabulary/Vocabulario

common ratio	razón común
compound interest	interés compuesto
exponential decay	decrecimiento exponencial
exponential function	función exponencial
exponential growth	crecimiento exponencial
geometric sequence	sucesión geométrica

Vocabulary Connections

To become familiar with some of the vocabulary terms in the chapter, consider the following. You may refer to the chapter, the glossary, or a dictionary if you like.

1. What does it mean when several items have something "in common"? What is a ratio? What do you think **common ratio** means?

2. What is an *exponent*? What do you think an **exponential function** might involve?

3. Two types of functions that you will study in this chapter are **exponential growth** and **exponential decay**. What is the difference in the way these two types of functions behave?

4. You have calculated *simple interest*. What is the difference between *simple interest* and **compound interest**?

Study Strategy: Remember Properties

In math, there are many formulas, properties, and rules that you should commit to memory.

To memorize a property, create flash cards. Write the name of the property on one side of a card. Write the property on the other side of the card. You might also include a diagram or an example if helpful. Study your flash cards on a regular basis.

Sample Flash Card

Back

Front

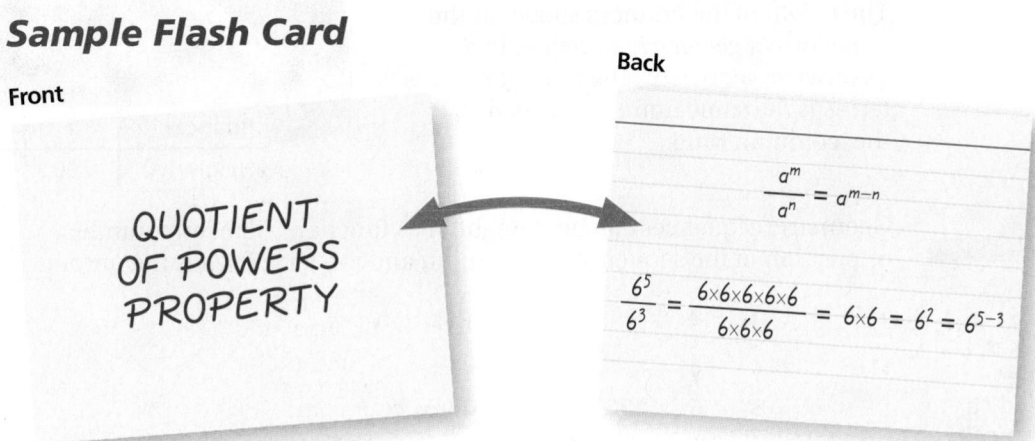

QUOTIENT OF POWERS PROPERTY

$$\frac{a^m}{a^n} = a^{m-n}$$

$$\frac{6^5}{6^3} = \frac{6 \times 6 \times 6 \times 6 \times 6}{6 \times 6 \times 6} = 6 \times 6 = 6^2 = 6^{5-3}$$

Knowing when and how to apply a mathematical property is as important as memorizing the property itself.

To know what property to apply, read the problem carefully and look for key words.

> A professional baseball player earns an annual salary of **$5.7 x 10^6**. There are **162 games** in a baseball season. How much does the player earn **per game**?

The key words have been highlighted. You are asked for an amount *per game* so you need to find a quotient. The annual salary is given in *exponential form* so you will need to use the *quotient of powers property*.

Try This

Read each problem. Then write the property needed to solve it. What key words helped you identify the property?

1. Light travels at about 1.86×10^5 miles per second. Find the approximate distance that light travels in one year if there are about 3.15×10^7 seconds in a year.

2. The area of a rectangular pool is 120 square feet. The length is 1 foot less than twice the width. What is the perimeter of the pool?

COMMON CORE

9-1 Geometric Sequences

CC.9-12.F.IF.3 Recognize that sequences are functions, sometimes defined recursively, whose domain is a subset of the integers. *Also* **CC.9-12.F.LE.2***, **CC.9-12.F.BF.2***

Objectives
Recognize and extend geometric sequences.

Find the *n*th term of a geometric sequence.

Vocabulary
geometric sequence
common ratio

Who uses this?

Bungee jumpers can use geometric sequences to calculate how high they will bounce.

The table shows the heights of a bungee jumper's bounces.

The height of the bounces shown in the table form a *geometric sequence*. In a **geometric sequence** , the ratio of successive terms is the same number *r*, called the **common ratio** .

Bounce	1	2	3
Height (ft)	200	80	32

Writing Math

The variable *a* is often used to represent terms in a sequence. The variable a_4 (read "*a* sub 4") is the fourth term in a sequence.

Geometric sequences can be thought of as functions. The term number, or position in the sequence, is the input, and the term itself is the output.

$$
\begin{array}{cccc}
1 & 2 & 3 & 4 \quad \longleftarrow \text{ Position} \\
\downarrow & \downarrow & \downarrow & \downarrow \\
3 & 6 & 12 & 24 \quad \longleftarrow \text{ Term} \\
a_1 & a_2 & a_3 & a_4
\end{array}
$$

To find a term in a geometric sequence, multiply the previous term by *r*.

Finding a Term of a Geometric Sequence

The *n*th term of a geometric sequence with **common ratio** *r* is

$$a_n = a_{n-1}r$$

EXAMPLE 1 **Extending Geometric Sequences**

Find the next three terms in each geometric sequence.

A 1, 3, 9, 27, ...

Step 1 Find the value of *r* by dividing each term by the one before it.

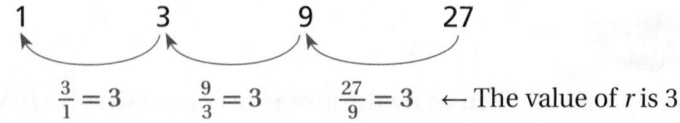

$$\frac{3}{1} = 3 \qquad \frac{9}{3} = 3 \qquad \frac{27}{9} = 3 \quad \longleftarrow \text{ The value of } r \text{ is 3.}$$

Step 2 Multiply each term by 3 to find the next three terms.

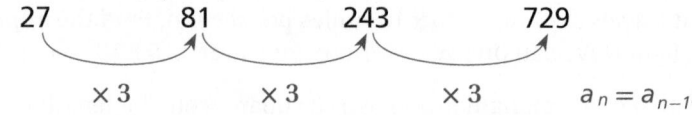

$$\times 3 \qquad \times 3 \qquad \times 3 \qquad a_n = a_{n-1}r$$

The next three terms are 81, 243, and 729.

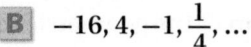

Helpful Hint

When the terms in a geometric sequence alternate between positive and negative, the value of r is negative.

B $-16, 4, -1, \frac{1}{4}, ...$

Step 1 Find the value of r by dividing each term by the one before it.

$$-16 \qquad 4 \qquad -1 \qquad \frac{1}{4}$$

$$\frac{4}{-16} = -\frac{1}{4} \qquad \frac{-1}{4} = -\frac{1}{4} \qquad \frac{\frac{1}{4}}{-1} = -\frac{1}{4} \qquad \leftarrow \text{The value of } r \text{ is } -\frac{1}{4}.$$

Step 2 Multiply each term by $-\frac{1}{4}$ to find the next three terms.

$$\frac{1}{4} \qquad -\frac{1}{16} \qquad \frac{1}{64} \qquad -\frac{1}{256}$$

$$\times \left(-\frac{1}{4}\right) \quad \times \left(-\frac{1}{4}\right) \quad \times \left(-\frac{1}{4}\right) \qquad a_n = a_{n-1} r$$

The next three terms are $-\frac{1}{16}, \frac{1}{64}$, and $-\frac{1}{256}$.

CHECK IT OUT! Find the next three terms in each geometric sequence.

1a. $5, -10, 20, -40, ...$ **1b.** $512, 384, 288, ...$

To find the output a_n of a geometric sequence when n is a large number, you need an equation, or function rule.

The pattern in the table shows that to get the nth term, multiply the first term by the common ratio raised to the power $n - 1$.

Words	Numbers	Algebra
1st term	3	a_1
2nd term	$3 \cdot 2^1 = 6$	$a_1 \cdot r^1$
3rd term	$3 \cdot 2^2 = 12$	$a_1 \cdot r^2$
4th term	$3 \cdot 2^3 = 24$	$a_1 \cdot r^3$
nth term	$3 \cdot 2^{n-1}$	$a_1 \cdot r^{n-1}$

If the first term of a geometric sequence is a_1, the nth term is a_n, and the common ratio is r, then

$$a_n = a_1 r^{n-1}$$

nth term   1st term   Common ratio

EXAMPLE 2 **Finding the nth Term of a Geometric Sequence**

A The first term of a geometric sequence is 128, and the common ratio is 0.5. What is the 10th term of the sequence?

$a_n = a_1 r^{n-1}$ — *Write the formula.*

$a_{10} = 128(0.5)^{10-1}$ — *Substitute 128 for a_1, 10 for n, and 0.5 for r.*

$= 128(0.5)^9$ — *Simplify the exponent.*

$= 0.25$ — *Use a calculator.*

B For a geometric sequence, $a_1 = 8$ and $r = 3$. Find the 5th term of this sequence.

$a_n = a_1 r^{n-1}$ — *Write the formula.*

$a_5 = 8(3)^{5-1}$ — *Substitute 8 for a_1, 5 for n, and 3 for r.*

$= 8(3)^4$ — *Simplify the exponent.*

$= 648$ — *Use a calculator.*

When writing a function rule for a sequence with a negative common ratio, remember to enclose r in parentheses.

$-2^{12} \neq (-2)^{12}$

C What is the 13th term of the geometric sequence 8, −16, 32, −64, … ?

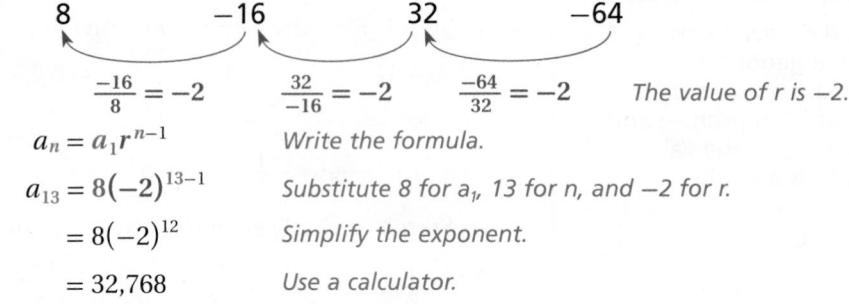

8   −16   32   −64

$\frac{-16}{8} = -2$ $\frac{32}{-16} = -2$ $\frac{-64}{32} = -2$ *The value of r is −2.*

$a_n = a_1 r^{n-1}$ *Write the formula.*

$a_{13} = 8(-2)^{13-1}$ *Substitute 8 for a_1, 13 for n, and −2 for r.*

$= 8(-2)^{12}$ *Simplify the exponent.*

$= 32{,}768$ *Use a calculator.*

 **2.** What is the 8th term of the sequence 1000, 500, 250, 125, … ?

EXAMPLE **3** **Sports Application**

A bungee jumper jumps from a bridge. The diagram shows the bungee jumper's height above the ground at the top of each bounce. The heights form a geometric sequence. What is the bungee jumper's height at the top of the 5th bounce?

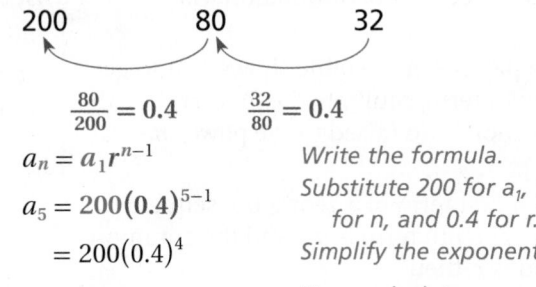

200   80   32

$\frac{80}{200} = 0.4$ $\frac{32}{80} = 0.4$

$a_n = a_1 r^{n-1}$ *Write the formula.*

$a_5 = 200(0.4)^{5-1}$ *Substitute 200 for a_1, 5 for n, and 0.4 for r.*

$= 200(0.4)^4$ *Simplify the exponent.*

$= 5.12$ *Use a calculator.*

First bounce 200 ft

Second bounce 80 ft

Third bounce 32 ft

The height of the 5th bounce is 5.12 feet.

 **3.** The table shows a car's value for 3 years after it is purchased. The values form a geometric sequence. How much will the car be worth in the 10th year?

Year	Value ($)
1	10,000
2	8,000
3	6,400

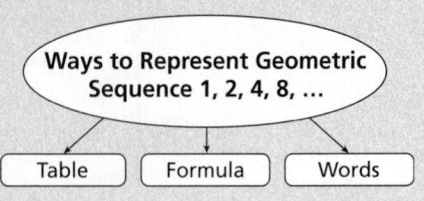

MATHEMATICAL PRACTICES

THINK AND DISCUSS

1. How do you determine whether a sequence is geometric?

2. GET ORGANIZED Copy and complete the graphic organizer. In each box, write a way to represent the geometric sequence.

Ways to Represent Geometric Sequence 1, 2, 4, 8, …

Table   Formula   Words

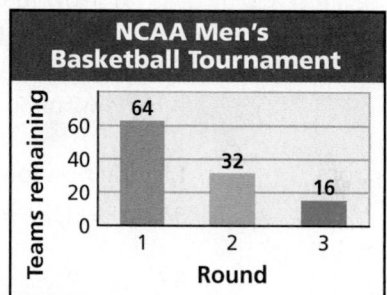
GUIDED PRACTICE

1. **Vocabulary** What is the *common ratio* of a geometric sequence?

SEE EXAMPLE 1   **Find the next three terms in each geometric sequence.**

2. 2, 4, 8, 16, …

3. 400, 200, 100, 50, …

4. 4, −12, 36, −108, …

SEE EXAMPLE 2   5. The first term of a geometric sequence is 1, and the common ratio is 10. What is the 10th term of the sequence?

6. What is the 11th term of the geometric sequence 3, 6, 12, 24, … ?

SEE EXAMPLE 3   7. **Sports** In the NCAA men's basketball tournament, 64 teams compete in round 1. Fewer teams remain in each following round, as shown in the graph, until all but one team have been eliminated. The numbers of teams in each round form a geometric sequence. How many teams compete in round 5?

NCAA Men's Basketball Tournament

(Bar graph: Teams remaining vs. Round. Round 1: 64, Round 2: 32, Round 3: 16)

PRACTICE AND PROBLEM SOLVING

Independent Practice

For Exercises	See Example
8–13	1
14–15	2
16	3

Find the next three terms in each geometric sequence.

8. −2, 10, −50, 250, …

9. 32, 48, 72, 108, …

10. 625, 500, 400, 320, …

11. 6, 42, 294, …

12. 6, −12, 24, −48, …

13. $40, 10, \frac{5}{2}, \frac{5}{8}, …$

Extra Practice

See Extra Practice for more Skills Practice and Applications Practice exercises.

14. The first term of a geometric sequence is 18 and the common ratio is 3.5. What is the 5th term of the sequence?

15. What is the 14th term of the geometric sequence 1000, 100, 10, 1, … ?

16. **Physical Science** A ball is dropped from a height of 500 meters. The table shows the height of each bounce, and the heights form a geometric sequence. How high does the ball bounce on the 8th bounce? Round your answer to the nearest tenth of a meter.

Bounce	Height (m)
1	400
2	320
3	256

Find the missing term(s) in each geometric sequence.

17. 20, 40, ▧, ▧, …

18. ▧, 6, 18, ▧, …

19. 9, 3, 1, ▧, …

20. 3, 12, ▧, 192, ▧, …

21. $7, 1, ▧, ▧, \frac{1}{343}, …$

22. $▧, 100, 25, ▧, \frac{25}{16}, …$

23. −3, ▧, −12, 24, ▧, …

24. ▧, ▧, 1, −3, 9, …

25. 1, 17, 289, ▧, …

Determine whether each sequence could be geometric. If so, give the common ratio.

26. 2, 10, 50, 250, …

27. $15, 5, \frac{5}{3}, \frac{5}{9}, …$

28. 6, 18, 24, 38, …

29. 9, 3, −1, −5, …

30. 7, 21, 63, 189, …

31. 4, 1, −2, −4, …

32. Multi-Step Billy earns money by mowing lawns for the summer. He offers two payment plans, as shown at right.

   a. Do the payments for plan 2 form a geometric sequence? Explain.

   b. If you were one of Billy's customers, which plan would you choose? (Assume that the summer is 10 weeks long.) Explain your choice.

33. Measurement When you fold a piece of paper in half, the thickness of the folded piece is twice the thickness of the original piece. A piece of copy paper is about 0.1 mm thick.

   a. How thick is a piece of copy paper that has been folded in half 7 times?

   b. Suppose that you could fold a piece of copy paper in half 12 times. How thick would it be? Write your answer in centimeters.

List the first four terms of each geometric sequence.

34. $a_1 = 3$, $a_n = 3(2)^{n-1}$ **35.** $a_1 = -2$, $a_n = -2(4)^{n-1}$ **36.** $a_1 = 5$, $a_n = 5(-2)^{n-1}$

37. $a_1 = 2$, $a_n = 2(2)^{n-1}$ **38.** $a_1 = 2$, $a_n = 2(5)^{n-1}$ **39.** $a_1 = 12$, $a_n = 12\left(\frac{1}{4}\right)^{n-1}$

40. Critical Thinking What happens to the terms of a geometric sequence when r is doubled? Use an example to support your answer.

41. Geometry The steps below describe how to make a geometric figure by repeating the same process over and over on a smaller and smaller scale.

   Step 1 (stage 0) Draw a large square.

   Step 2 (stage 1) Divide the square into four equal squares.

   Step 3 (stage 2) Divide each small square into four equal squares.

   Step 4 Repeat Step 3 indefinitely.

   a. Draw stages 0, 1, 2, and 3.

   b. How many small squares are in each stage? Organize your data relating stage and number of small squares in a table.

   c. Does the data in part **b** form a geometric sequence? Explain.

   d. Write a rule to find the number of small squares in stage n.

 42. Write About It Write a series of steps for finding the nth term of a geometric sequence when you are given the first several terms.

MULTI-STEP TEST PREP

43. a. Three years ago, the annual tuition at a university was $3000. The following year, the tuition was $3300, and last year, the tuition was $3630. If the tuition has continued to grow in the same manner, what is the tuition this year? What do you expect it to be next year?

   b. What is the common ratio?

   c. What would you predict the tuition was 4 years ago? How did you find that value?

44. Which of the following is a geometric sequence?

    Ⓐ $\frac{1}{2}$, 1, $\frac{3}{2}$, 2, …   Ⓒ 3, 8, 13, 18, …

    Ⓑ −2, −6, −10, −14, …   Ⓓ 5, 10, 20, 40, …

45. Which equation represents the nth term in the geometric sequence
2, −8, 32, −128, …?

    Ⓕ $a_n = (-4)^n$ Ⓖ $a_n = (-4)^{n-1}$ Ⓗ $a_n = 2(-4)^n$ Ⓙ $a_n = 2(-4)^{n-1}$

46. The frequency of a musical note, measured in hertz (Hz), is called its pitch. The
pitches of the A keys on a piano form a geometric sequence, as shown.

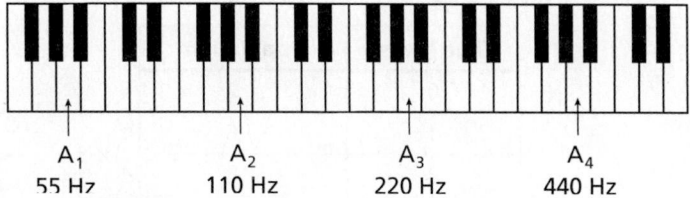

    A₁   A₂   A₃   A₄

    55 H₂   110 Hz   220 Hz   440 Hz

What is the frequency of A_7?

    Ⓐ 880 Hz   Ⓑ 1760 Hz   Ⓒ 3520 Hz   Ⓓ 7040 Hz

CHALLENGE AND EXTEND

Find the next three terms in each geometric sequence.

47. $x, x^2, x^3, …$ **48.** $2x^2, 6x^3, 18x^4, …$ **49.** $\frac{1}{y^3}, \frac{1}{y^2}, \frac{1}{y}, …$ **50.** $\frac{1}{(x+1)^2}, \frac{1}{x+1}, 1, …$

51. The 10th term of a geometric sequence is 0.78125. The common ratio is −0.5. Find
the first term of the sequence.

52. The first term of a geometric sequence is 12 and the common ratio is $\frac{1}{2}$. Is 0 a term in
this sequence? Explain.

53. A geometric sequence starts with 14 and has a common ration of 0.4. Colin finds
that another number in the sequence is 0.057344. Which term in the sequence did
Colin find?

54. The first three terms of a sequence are 1, 2, and 4. Susanna said the 8th term of this
sequence is 128. Paul said the 8th term is 29. Explain how the students found their
answers. Why could these both be considered correct answers?

9-2 Exponential Functions

CC.9-12.F.IF.7e Graph exponential ... functions, showing intercepts and end behavior, ... *Also* CC.9-12.F.LE.1*,
CC.9-12.F.IF.4*, CC.9-12.F.IF.8, CC.9-12.A.REI.10

Objectives
Evaluate exponential functions.

Identify and graph exponential functions.

Vocabulary
exponential function

Who uses this?
Scientists model populations with exponential functions.

The table and the graph show an insect population that increases over time.

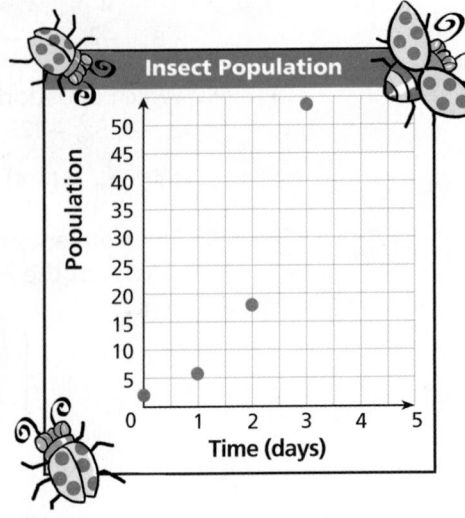

Insect Population

Time (days)	Population
0	2
1	6
2	18
3	54

× 3
× 3
× 3

A function rule that describes the pattern above is $f(x) = 2(3)^x$. This type of function, in which the independent variable appears in an exponent, is an **exponential function**. Notice that 2 is the starting population and 3 is the amount by which the population is multiplied each day.

Know it!
.Note

> ## Exponential Functions
> An exponential function has the form $f(x) = ab^x$, where $a \neq 0$, $b \neq 1$, and $b > 0$.

EXAMPLE 1 Evaluating an Exponential Function

A The function $f(x) = 2(3)^x$ models an insect population after x days. What will the population be on the 5th day?

$f(x) = 2(3)^x$ *Write the function.*

$f(5) = 2(3)^5$ *Substitute 5 for x.*

$= 2(243)$ *Evaluate 3^5.*

$= 486$ *Multiply.*

There will be 486 insects on the 5th day.

Helpful Hint

In Example 1B, round your answer to the nearest whole number because there can only be a whole number of prairie dogs.

B The function $f(x) = 1500(0.995)^x$, where x is the time in years, models a prairie dog population. How many prairie dogs will there be in 8 years?

$f(x) = 1500(0.995)^x$

$f(8) = 1500(0.995)^8$ *Substitute 8 for x.*

≈ 1441 *Use a calculator. Round to the nearest whole number.*

There will be about 1441 prairie dogs in 8 years.

CHECK IT OUT!

1. The function $f(x) = 8(0.75)^x$ models the width of a photograph in inches after it has been reduced by 25% x times. What is the width of the photograph after it has been reduced 3 times?

Remember that linear functions have constant first differences and quadratic functions have constant second differences. Exponential functions do not have constant differences, but they do have *constant ratios*.

As the *x*-values increase by a constant amount, the *y*-values are multiplied by a constant amount. This amount is the constant ratio and is the value of *b* in $f(x) = ab^x$.

x	$f(x) = 2(3)^x$
1	6
2	18
3	54
4	162

+1 ×3
+1 ×3
+1 ×3

EXAMPLE 2 **Identifying an Exponential Function**

Tell whether each set of ordered pairs satisfies an exponential function. Explain your answer.

A $\{(-1, 1.5), (0, 3), (1, 6), (2, 12)\}$

x	y
−1	1.5
0	3
1	6
2	12

+1 ×2
+1 ×2
+1 ×2

This is an exponential function. As the *x*-values increase by a constant amount, the *y*-values are multiplied by a constant amount.

B $\{(-1, -9), (1, 9), (3, 27), (5, 45)\}$

x	y
−1	−9
1	9
3	27
5	45

+2 ×(−1)
+2 ×3
+2 ×$\frac{5}{3}$

This is *not* an exponential function. As the *x*-values increase by a constant amount, the *y*-values are *not* multiplied by a constant amount.

CHECK IT OUT!  Tell whether each set of ordered pairs satisfies an exponential function. Explain your answer.

2a. $\{(-1, 1), (0, 0), (1, 1), (2, 4)\}$ **2b.** $\{(-2, 4), (-1, 2), (0, 1), (1, 0.5)\}$

To graph an exponential function, choose several values of *x* (positive, negative, and 0) and generate ordered pairs. Plot the points and connect them with a smooth curve.

EXAMPLE 3 **Graphing $y = ab^x$ with $a > 0$ and $b > 1$**

Graph $y = 3(4)^x$.

Choose several values of x and generate ordered pairs.

x	$y = 3(4)^x$
−1	0.75
0	3
1	12
2	48

Graph the ordered pairs and connect with a smooth curve.

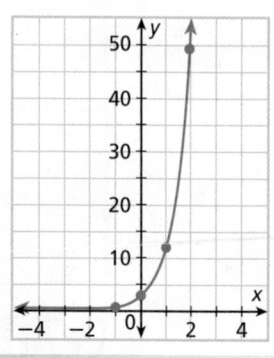

CHECK IT OUT!  **3a.** Graph $y = 2^x$. **3b.** Graph $y = 0.2(5)^x$.

EXAMPLE 4 Graphing $y = ab^x$ with $a < 0$ and $b > 1$

Graph $y = -5(2)^x$.

Choose several values of x and generate ordered pairs.

x	$y = -5(2)^x$
−1	−2.5
0	−5
1	−10
2	−20

Graph the ordered pairs and connect with a smooth curve.

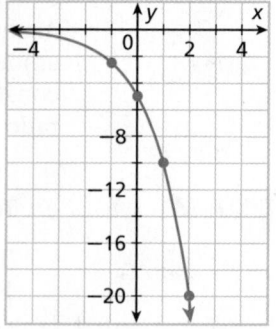

CHECK IT OUT! **4a.** Graph $y = -6^x$. **4b.** Graph $y = -3(3)^x$.

EXAMPLE 5 Graphing $y = ab^x$ with $0 < b < 1$

Graph each exponential function.

A $y = 3\left(\frac{1}{2}\right)^x$

Choose several values of x and generate ordered pairs.

x	$y = 3\left(\frac{1}{2}\right)^x$
−1	6
0	3
1	1.5
2	0.75

Graph the ordered pairs and connect with a smooth curve.

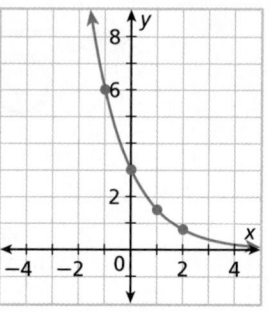

B $y = -2(0.4)^x$

Choose several values of x and generate ordered pairs.

x	$y = -2(0.4)^x$
−2	−12.5
−1	−5
0	−2
1	−0.8

Graph the ordered pairs and connect with a smooth curve.

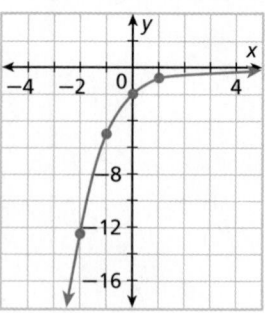

CHECK IT OUT! Graph each exponential function.
5a. $y = 4\left(\frac{1}{4}\right)^x$ **5b.** $y = -2(0.1)^x$

The box summarizes the general shapes of exponential function graphs.

Graphs of Exponential Functions	
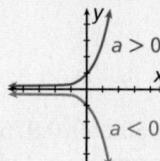	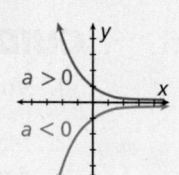
For $y = ab^x$, if $b > 1$, then the graph will have one of these shapes.	For $y = ab^x$, if $0 < b < 1$, then the graph will have one of these shapes.

E X A M P L E 6 *Statistics Application*

In the year 2000, the world population was about 6 billion, and it was growing by 1.21% each year. At this growth rate, the function $f(x) = 6(1.0121)^x$ gives the population, in billions, x years after 2000. Using this model, in about what year does the population reach 7 billion?

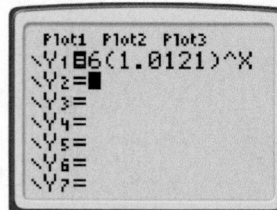

Enter the function into the Y= editor of a graphing calculator.

Caution! /////

The function values give the population *in billions*, so a y-value of 7 means 7 billion.

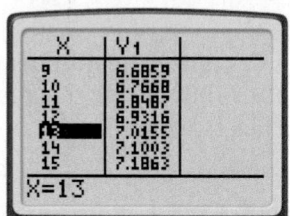

TABLE

Press 2nd GRAPH. *Use the arrow keys to find a y-value as close to 7 as possible. The corresponding x-value is 13.*

The world population reaches 7 billion in about 2013.

6. An accountant uses $f(x) = 12{,}330(0.869)^x$, where x is the time in years since the purchase, to model the value of a car. When will the car be worth $2000?

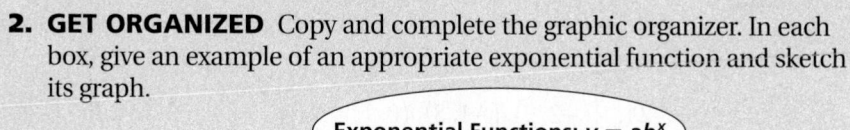
MATHEMATICAL PRACTICES

THINK AND DISCUSS

1. How can you find the constant ratio of a set of exponential data?

2. GET ORGANIZED Copy and complete the graphic organizer. In each box, give an example of an appropriate exponential function and sketch its graph.

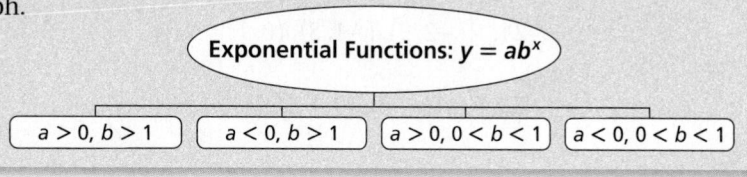

Exponential Functions: $y = ab^x$

| $a > 0, b > 1$ | $a < 0, b > 1$ | $a > 0, 0 < b < 1$ | $a < 0, 0 < b < 1$ |

GUIDED PRACTICE

1. **Vocabulary** Tell whether $y = 3x^4$ is an *exponential function*. Explain your answer.

SEE EXAMPLE 1

2. **Physics** The function $f(x) = 50{,}000(0.975)^x$, where x represents the underwater depth in meters, models the intensity of light below the water's surface in lumens per square meter. What is the intensity of light 200 meters below the surface? Round your answer to the nearest whole number.

SEE EXAMPLE 2

Tell whether each set of ordered pairs satisfies an exponential function. Explain your answer.

3. $\{(-1, -1), (0, 0), (1, -1), (2, -4)\}$ 4. $\{(0, 1), (1, 4), (2, 16), (3, 64)\}$

Graph each exponential function.

SEE EXAMPLE 3

5. $y = 3^x$ 6. $y = 5^x$

7. $y = 10(3)^x$ 8. $y = 5(2)^x$

SEE EXAMPLE 4

9. $y = -2(3)^x$ 10. $y = -4(2)^x$

11. $y = -3(2)^x$ 12. $y = 2(3)^x$

SEE EXAMPLE 5

13. $y = -\left(\frac{1}{4}\right)^x$ 14. $y = \left(\frac{1}{3}\right)^x$

15. $y = 2\left(\frac{1}{4}\right)^x$ 16. $y = -2(0.25)^x$

SEE EXAMPLE 6

17. The function $f(x) = 57.8(1.02)^x$ gives the number of passenger cars, in millions, in the United States x years after 1960. Using this model, in about what year does the number of passenger cars reach 200 million?

PRACTICE AND PROBLEM SOLVING

Independent Practice

For Exercises	See Example
18–20	1
21–24	2
25–27	3
28–30	4
31–33	5
34	6

Extra Practice

See Extra Practice for more Skills Practice and Applications Practice exercises.

18. **Sports** If a golf ball is dropped from a height of 27 feet, the function $f(x) = 27\left(\frac{2}{3}\right)^x$ gives the height in feet of each bounce, where x is the bounce number. What will be the height of the 4th bounce?

19. Suppose the depth of a lake can be described by the function $y = 334(0.976)^x$, where x represents the number of weeks from today. Today, the depth of the lake is 334 ft. What will the depth be in 6 weeks? Round your answer to the nearest whole number.

20. **Physics** A ball rolling down a slope travels continuously faster. Suppose the function $y = 1.3(1.41)^x$ describes the speed of the ball in inches per minute. How fast will the ball be rolling in 15 minutes? Round your answer to the nearest hundredth.

Tell whether each set of ordered pairs satisfies an exponential function. Explain your answer.

21. $\left\{(-2, 9), (-1, 3), (0, 1), \left(1, \frac{1}{3}\right)\right\}$ 22. $\{(-1, 0), (0, 1), (1, 4), (2, 9)\}$

23. $\{(-1, -5), (0, -3), (1, -1), (2, 1)\}$ 24. $\{(-3, 6.25), (-2, 12.5), (-1, 25), (0, 50)\}$

Graph each exponential function.

25. $y = 1.5^x$

26. $y = \frac{1}{3}(3)^x$

27. $y = 100(0.7)^x$

28. $y = -2(4)^x$

29. $y = -1(5)^x$

30. $y = -\frac{1}{2}(4)^x$

31. $y = 4\left(\frac{1}{2}\right)^x$

32. $y = -2\left(\frac{1}{3}\right)^x$

33. $y = 0.5(0.25)^x$

34. Technology Moore's law states that the maximum number of transistors that can fit on a silicon chip doubles every two years. The function $f(x) = 42(1.41)^x$ models the number of transistors, in millions, that can fit on a chip, where x is the number of years since 2000. Using this model, in what year can a chip hold 1 billion transistors?

35. Multi-Step A computer randomly creates three different functions. The functions are $y = (3.1x + 7)^2$, $y = 4.8(2)^x$, and $y = \frac{1}{5}(6)^x$. The computer then generates the y value 38.4. Given the three different functions, determine which one is exponential *and* produces the generated number.

36. Contests As a promotion, a clothing store draws the name of one of its customers each week. The prize is a coupon for the store. If the winner is not present at the drawing, he or she cannot claim the prize, and the amount of the coupon increases for the following week's drawing. The function $f(x) = 20(1.2)^x$ gives the amount of the coupon in dollars after x weeks of the prize going unclaimed.

Clothes for everyone!
Math Apparel
Win Valuable Store Coupon

Must be present to win!

a. What is the amount of the coupon after 2 weeks of the prize going unclaimed?

b. After how many weeks of the prize going unclaimed will the amount of the coupon be greater than $100?

c. What is the original amount of the coupon?

d. Find the percent increase each week.

37. Critical Thinking In the definition of exponential function, the value of b cannot be 1, and the value of a cannot be 0. Why?

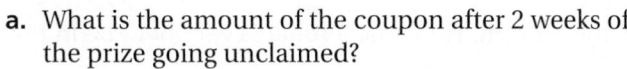

Graphing Calculator Graph each group of functions on the same screen. How are their graphs alike? How are they different?

38. $y = 2^x$, $y = 3^x$, $y = 4^x$

39. $y = \left(\frac{1}{2}\right)^x$, $y = \left(\frac{1}{3}\right)^x$, $y = \left(\frac{1}{4}\right)^x$

Evaluate each of the following for the given value of x.

40. $f(x) = 4^x$; $x = 3$

41. $f(x) = -(0.25)^x$; $x = 1.5$

42. $f(x) = 0.4(10)^x$; $x = -3$

MULTI-STEP TEST PREP

43. a. The annual tuition at a community college since 2001 is modeled by the equation $C = 2000(1.08)^n$, where C is the tuition cost and n is the number of years since 2001. What was the tuition cost in 2001?

b. What is the annual percentage of tuition increase?

c. Find the tuition cost in 2006.

44. Write About It Your employer offers two salary plans. With plan A, your salary is $f(x) = 10{,}000(2x)$, where x is the number of years you have worked for the company. With plan B, your salary is $g(x) = 10{,}000(2)^x$. Which plan would you choose? Why?

45. Which graph shows an exponential function?

Ⓐ
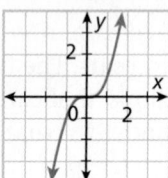

Ⓒ
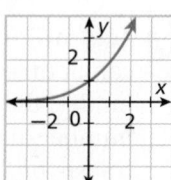

Ⓑ
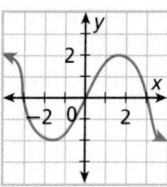

Ⓓ
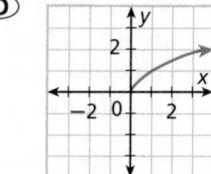

46. The function $f(x) = 15(1.4)^x$ represents the area in square inches of a photograph after it has been enlarged x times by a factor of 140%. What is the area of the photograph after it has been enlarged 4 times?

Ⓕ 5.6 square inches

Ⓖ 57.624 square inches

Ⓗ 41.16 square inches

Ⓙ 560 square inches

47. Look at the pattern. How many squares will there be in the nth stage?

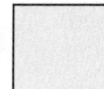
Stage 0

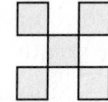
Stage 1

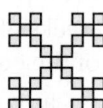
Stage 2

Ⓐ $5n$ Ⓑ $2.5 \cdot 2^n$ Ⓒ 25^{n-1} Ⓓ 5^n

CHALLENGE AND EXTEND

Solve each equation.

48. $4^x = 64$

49. $\left(\dfrac{1}{3}\right)^x = \dfrac{1}{27}$

50. $2^x = \dfrac{1}{16}$

51. Graph the following functions: $y = 2(2)^x$, $y = 3(2)^x$, $y = -2(2)^x$. Then make a conjecture about the relationship between the value of a and the y-intercept of $y = ab^x$.

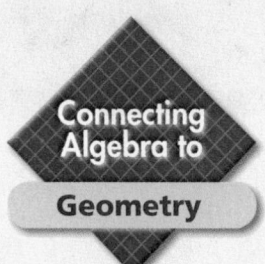

Changing Dimensions

What happens to the volume of a three-dimensional figure when you repeatedly double the dimensions?

Recall these formulas for the volumes of common three-dimensional figures.

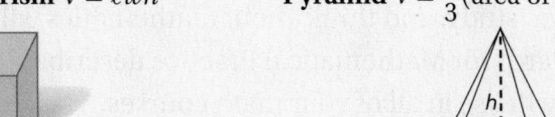

Cube $V = s^3$ **Rectangular Prism** $V = \ell w h$ **Pyramid** $V = \frac{1}{3}(\text{area of base}) \cdot h$

Base

Changing the dimensions of three-dimensional figures results in geometric sequences.

Example

Find the volume of a cube with a side length of 3 cm. Double the side length and find the new volume. Repeat two more times. Show the patterns for the side lengths and volumes as geometric sequences. Identify the common ratios.

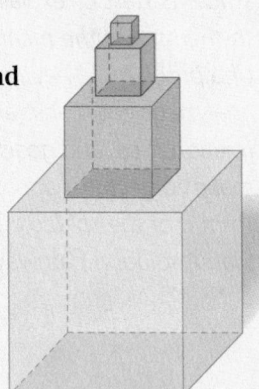

Cube	Side Length (cm)	Volume (cm³)
1	3	27
2	6	216
3	12	1,728
4	24	13,824

×2 (between side lengths)   ×8 (between volumes)

The side lengths and the volumes form geometric sequences. The sequence of the side lengths has a common ratio of 2. The sequence of the volumes has a common ratio of 2^3, or 8.

The patterns in the example above are a specific instance of a general rule.

> When the dimensions of a solid figure are multiplied by x, the volume of the figure is multiplied by x^3.

Try This

1. The large rectangular prism at right is 8 in. wide, 16 in. long, and 32 in. tall. The dimensions are multiplied by $\frac{1}{2}$ to create each next smaller prism. Show the patterns for the dimensions and the volumes as geometric sequences. Identify the common ratios.

2. A pyramid has a height of 8 cm and a square base of 3 cm on each edge. Triple the dimensions two times. Show the patterns for the dimensions and the volumes as geometric sequences. Identify the common ratios.

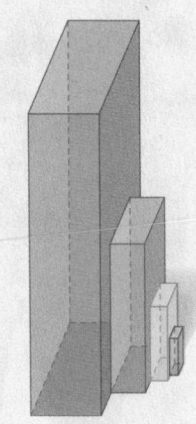

Mastering *the* Standards

for Mathematical Practice

The topics described in the Standards for Mathematical Content will vary from year to year. However, the *way* in which you learn, study, and think about mathematics will not. The Standards for Mathematical Practice describe skills that you will use in all of your math courses.

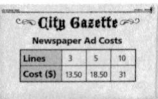

Mathematical Practices

1. *Make sense of problems and persevere in solving them.*
2. *Reason abstractly and quantitatively.*
3. *Construct viable arguments and critique the reasoning of others.*
4. *Model with mathematics.*
5. *Use appropriate tools strategically.*
6. *Attend to precision.*
7. *Look for and make use of structure.*
8. *Look for and express regularity in repeated reasoning.*

① Make sense of problems and persevere in solving them.

Mathematically proficient students start by explaining to themselves the meaning of a problem... They analyze givens, constraints, relationships, and goals. They make conjectures about the form... of the solution and plan a solution pathway...

In your book

Focus on Problem Solving describes a four-step plan for problem solving. The plan is introduced at the beginning of your book, and practice with the plan appears throughout the book.

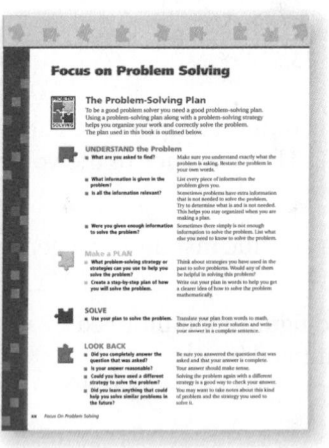

EXAMPLE 5   **Problem-Solving Application**

The cost to place an ad in a newspaper for one week is a linear function of the number of lines in the ad. The costs for 3, 5, and 10 lines are shown. Write an equation in slope-intercept form that represents the function. Then find the cost of an ad that is 18 lines long.

City Gazette
Newspaper Ad Costs

Lines	3	5	10
Cost ($)	13.50	18.50	31

Understand the Problem

• The **answer** will have two parts—an equation in slope-intercept form and the cost of an ad that is 18 lines long.
• The ordered pairs given in the table satisfy the equation.

Make a Plan

First, find the slope. Then use point-slope form to write the equation. Finally, write the equation in slope-intercept form.

Solve

Step 1 Choose any two ordered pairs from the table to find the slope.

$m = \dfrac{y_2 - y_1}{x_2 - x_1} = \dfrac{18.50 - 13.50}{5 - 3} = \dfrac{5}{2} = 2.5$ Use (3, 13.50) and (5, 18.50).

Step 2 Substitute the slope and any ordered pair from the table into the point-slope form.

$y - y_1 = m(x - x_1)$
$y - 31 = 2.5(x - 10)$ Use (10, 31).

Step 3 Write the equation in slope-intercept form by solving for y.

$y - 31 = 2.5(x - 10)$
$y - 31 = 2.5x - 25$ Distribute 2.5.
$y = 2.5x + 6$ Add 31 to both sides.

Step 4 Find the cost of an ad containing 18 lines by substituting 18 for x.

$y = 2.5x + 6$
$y = 2.5(18) + 6 = 51$
The cost of an ad containing 18 lines is $51.

Look Back

Check the equation by substituting the ordered pairs (3, 13.50) and (5, 18.50).

$y = 2.5x + 6$		$y = 2.5x + 6$	
13.50	2.5(3) + 6	18.50	2.5(5) + 6
13.5	7.5 + 6	18.5	12.5 + 6
13.5	13.5 ✓	18.5	18.5 ✓

Quiz for Lessons 9-1 and 9-2

9-1 Geometric Sequences

Find the next three terms in each geometric sequence.

1. 3, 6, 12, 24, …

2. $-1, 2, -4, 8, …$

3. $-2400, -1200, -600, -300, …$

4. The first term of a geometric sequence is 2 and the common ratio is 3. What is the 8th term of the sequence?

9-2 Exponential Functions

5. The function $f(x) = 3(1.1)^x$ gives the length (in inches) of an image after being enlarged by 10% x times. What is the length of the image after it has been enlarged 4 times? Round your answer to the nearest hundredth.

Graph each exponential function.

6. $y = 3^x$

7. $y = 2(2)^x$

8. $y = -2(4)^x$

9. $y = -(0.5)^x$

10. The function $f(x) = 40(0.8)^x$ gives the amount of a medication in milligrams present in a patient's system x hours after taking a 40-mg dose. In how many hours will there be less than 2 mg of the drug in a patient's system?

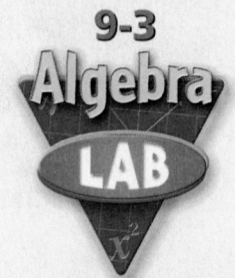

9-3

Algebra LAB

Model Growth and Decay

You can fold and cut paper to model quantities that increase or decrease exponentially.

Look for and express regularity in repeated reasoning.

Use with Exponential Growth and Decay

CC.9-12.F.LE.2 Construct linear and exponential functions, including arithmetic and geometric sequences, given a graph, a description of a relationship, or two input-output pairs (include reading these from a table).* Also **CC.9-12.F.LE.1***

Activity 1

1 Copy the table at right.

2 Fold a piece of notebook paper in half. Then open it back up. Count the number of regions created by the fold. Record your answer in the table.

3 Now fold the paper in half twice. Record the number of regions created by the folds in the table.

4 Repeat this process for 3, 4, and 5 folds.

Folds	Regions
0	1
1	
2	
3	
4	
5	

Try This

1. When the number of folds increases by 1, the number of regions ____?____ .

2. For each row of the table, write the number of regions as a power of 2.

3. Write an exponential expression for the number of regions formed by n folds.

4. If you could fold the paper 8 times, how many regions would be formed?

5. How many times would you have to fold the paper to make 512 regions?

Activity 2

1 Copy the table at right.

2 Begin with a square piece of paper. The area of the paper is 1 square unit. Cut the paper in half. Each piece has an area of $\frac{1}{2}$ square unit. Record the result in the table.

3 Cut one of those pieces in half again, and record the area of one of the new, smaller pieces in the table.

4 Repeat this process for 3, 4, and 5 cuts.

Cuts	Area
0	1
1	
2	
3	
4	
5	

Try This

6. When the number of cuts increases by 1, the area ____?____ .

7. For each row of the table, write the area as a power of 2.

8. Write an exponential expression for the area after n cuts.

9. What would be the area after 7 cuts?

10. How many cuts would you have to make to get an area of $\frac{1}{256}$ square unit?

9-3 Exponential Growth and Decay

CC.9-12.F.LE.2 Construct linear and exponential functions … given a graph, a description of a relationship, or two input-output pairs …* *Also* **CC.9-12.F.LE.5*, CC.9-12.F.LE.1*, CC.9-12.F.BF.1***

Objective
Solve problems involving exponential growth and decay.

Vocabulary
exponential growth
compound interest
exponential decay
half-life

Why learn this?

Exponential growth and decay describe many real-world situations, such as the value of artwork. (See Example 1.)

Exponential growth occurs when a quantity increases by the same rate r in each time period t. When this happens, the value of the quantity at any given time can be calculated as a function of the rate and the original amount.

Know it!
Note

Exponential Growth

An exponential growth function has the form $y = a(1 + r)^t$, where $a > 0$.

y represents the final amount.

a represents the original amount.

r represents the rate of growth expressed as a decimal.

t represents time.

EXAMPLE 1 **Exponential Growth**

Helpful Hint

In Example 1, round to the nearest hundredth because the problem deals with money. This means you are rounding to the nearest cent.

The original value of a painting is $1400, and the value increases by 9% each year. Write an exponential growth function to model this situation. Then find the value of the painting in 25 years.

Step 1 Write the exponential growth function for this situation.

$y = a(1 + r)^t$ *Write the formula.*

$= 1400(1 + 0.09)^t$ *Substitute 1400 for a and 0.09 for r.*

$= 1400(1.09)^t$ *Simplify.*

Step 2 Find the value in 25 years.

$y = 1400(1.09)^t$

$= 1400(1.09)^{25}$ *Substitute 25 for t.*

$\approx 12{,}072.31$ *Use a calculator and round to the nearest hundredth.*

The value of the painting in 25 years is $12,072.31.

CHECK IT OUT!

1. A sculpture is increasing in value at a rate of 8% per year, and its value in 2000 was $1200. Write an exponential growth function to model this situation. Then find the sculpture's value in 2006.

© Wendy Stone/CORBIS

A common application of exponential growth is *compound interest*. Recall that simple interest is earned or paid only on the principal. **Compound interest** is interest earned or paid on *both* the principal and previously earned interest.

Compound Interest

$$A = P\left(1 + \frac{r}{n}\right)^{nt}$$

A represents the balance after *t* years.

P represents the principal, or original amount.

r represents the annual interest rate expressed as a decimal.

n represents the number of times interest is compounded per year.

t represents time in years.

EXAMPLE *Finance Application*

Write a compound interest function to model each situation. Then find the balance after the given number of years.

A **$1000 invested at a rate of 3% compounded quarterly; 5 years**

  Step 1 Write the compound interest function for this situation.

$$A = P\left(1 + \frac{r}{n}\right)^{nt}$$ *Write the formula.*

$$= 1000\left(1 + \frac{0.03}{4}\right)^{4t}$$ *Substitute 1000 for P, 0.03 for r, and 4 for n.*

$$= 1000(1.0075)^{4t}$$ *Simplify.*

  Step 2 Find the balance after 5 years.

$$A = 1000(1.0075)^{4(5)}$$ *Substitute 5 for t.*

$$= 1000(1.0075)^{20}$$

$$\approx 1161.18$$ *Use a calculator and round to the nearest hundredth.*

  The balance after 5 years is $1161.18.

B **$18,000 invested at a rate of 4.5% compounded annually; 6 years**

  Step 1 Write the compound interest function for this situation.

$$A = P\left(1 + \frac{r}{n}\right)^{nt}$$ *Write the formula.*

$$= 18{,}000\left(1 + \frac{0.045}{1}\right)^{t}$$ *Substitute 18,000 for P, 0.045 for r, and 1 for n.*

$$= 18{,}000(1.045)^{t}$$ *Simplify.*

  Step 2 Find the balance after 6 years.

$$A = 18{,}000(1.045)^{6}$$ *Substitute 6 for t.*

$$\approx 23{,}440.68$$ *Use a calculator and round to the nearest hundredth.*

  The balance after 6 years is $23,440.68.

Write a compound interest function to model each situation. Then find the balance after the given number of years.

2a. $1200 invested at a rate of 3.5% compounded quarterly; 4 years

2b. $4000 invested at a rate of 3% compounded monthly; 8 years

Exponential decay occurs when a quantity decreases by the same rate r in each time period t. Just like exponential growth, the value of the quantity at any given time can be calculated by using the rate and the original amount.

Exponential Decay

An exponential decay function has the form $y = a(1 - r)^t$, where $a > 0$.

  y represents the final amount.

  a represents the original amount.

  r represents the rate of decay as a decimal.

  t represents time.

Notice an important difference between exponential growth functions and exponential decay functions. For exponential growth, the value inside the parentheses will be greater than 1 because r is added to 1. For exponential decay, the value inside the parentheses will be less than 1 because r is subtracted from 1.

EXAMPLE 3 **Exponential Decay**

The population of a town is decreasing at a rate of 1% per year. In 2000 there were 1300 people. Write an exponential decay function to model this situation. Then find the population in 2008.

Step 1 Write the exponential decay function for this situation.

$y = a(1 - r)^t$ *Write the formula.*

$ = 1300(1 - 0.01)^t$ *Substitute 1300 for a and 0.01 for r.*

$ = 1300(0.99)^t$ *Simplify.*

Step 2 Find the population in 2008.

$y = 1300(0.99)^8$ *Substitute 8 for t.*

$ \approx 1200$ *Use a calculator and round to the nearest whole number.*

The population in 2008 is approximately 1200 people.

Helpful Hint

In Example 3, round your answer to the nearest whole number because there can only be a whole number of people.

3. The fish population in a local stream is decreasing at a rate of 3% per year. The original population was 48,000. Write an exponential decay function to model this situation. Then find the population after 7 years.

A common application of exponential decay is *half-life*. The **half-life** of a substance is the time it takes for one-half of the substance to decay into another substance.

Half-life

$A = P(0.5)^t$

  A represents the final amount.

  P represents the original amount.

  t represents the number of half-lives in a given time period.

EXAMPLE 4   *Science Application*

Fluorine-20 has a half-life of 11 seconds.

A Find the amount of fluorine-20 left from a 40-gram sample after 44 seconds.

Step 1 Find *t*, the number of half-lives in the given time period.

$$\frac{44 \text{ s}}{11 \text{ s}} = 4$$ *Divide the time period by the half-life.*
                               The value of t is 4.

Step 2 $A = P(0.5)^t$ *Write the formula.*

        $= 40(0.5)^4$ *Substitute 40 for P and 4 for t.*

        $= 2.5$ *Use a calculator.*

There are 2.5 grams of fluorine-20 remaining after 44 seconds.

B Find the amount of fluorine-20 left from a 40-gram sample after 2.2 minutes. Round your answer to the nearest hundredth.

Step 1 Find *t*, the number of half-lives in the given time period.

$$2.2(60) = 132$$ *Find the number of seconds in 2.2 minutes.*

$$\frac{132 \text{ s}}{11 \text{ s}} = 12$$ *Divide the time period by the half-life.*
                       The value of t is $\frac{132}{11} = 12$.

Step 2 $A = P(0.5)^t$ *Write the formula.*

        $= 40(0.5)^{12}$ *Substitute 40 for P and 12 for t.*

        ≈ 0.01 *Use a calculator. Round to the nearest hundredth.*

There is about 0.01 gram of fluorine-20 remaining after 2.2 minutes.

CHECK IT OUT!

4a. Cesium-137 has a half-life of 30 years. Find the amount of cesium-137 left from a 100-milligram sample after 180 years.

4b. Bismuth-210 has a half-life of 5 days. Find the amount of bismuth-210 left from a 100-gram sample after 5 weeks. (*Hint:* Change 5 weeks to days.)

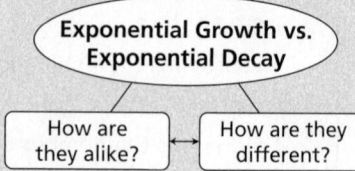

MATHEMATICAL
PRACTICES

THINK AND DISCUSS

1. Describe three real-world situations that can be described by exponential growth or exponential decay functions.

2. The population of a town after *t* years can be modeled by $P = 1000(1.02)^t$. Is the population increasing or decreasing? By what percentage rate?

3. An exponential function is a function of the form $y = ab^x$. Explain why both exponential growth functions and exponential decay functions are exponential functions.

4. GET ORGANIZED Copy and complete the graphic organizer.

Exponential Growth vs. Exponential Decay

How are they alike?   How are they different?

Exercises

GUIDED PRACTICE

1. **Vocabulary** The function $y = 0.68(2)^x$ is an example of _____?_____.
   (*exponential growth* or *exponential decay*)

SEE EXAMPLE 1 Write an exponential growth function to model each situation. Then find the value of the function after the given amount of time.

2. The cost of tuition at a college is $12,000 and is increasing at a rate of 6% per year; 4 years.

3. The number of student-athletes at a local high school is 300 and is increasing at a rate of 8% per year; 5 years.

SEE EXAMPLE 2 Write a compound interest function to model each situation. Then find the balance after the given number of years.

4. $1500 invested at a rate of 3.5% compounded annually; 4 years

5. $4200 invested at a rate of 2.8% compounded quarterly; 6 years

SEE EXAMPLE 3 Write an exponential decay function to model each situation. Then find the value of the function after the given amount of time.

6. The value of a car is $18,000 and is depreciating at a rate of 12% per year; 10 years.

7. The amount (to the nearest hundredth) of a 10-mg dose of a certain antibiotic decreases in your bloodstream at a rate of 16% per hour; 4 hours.

SEE EXAMPLE 4

8. Bismuth-214 has a half-life of approximately 20 minutes. Find the amount of bismuth-214 left from a 30-gram sample after 1 hour.

9. Mendelevium-258 has a half-life of approximately 52 days. Find the amount of mendelevium-258 left from a 44-gram sample after 156 days.

PRACTICE AND PROBLEM SOLVING

Independent Practice

For Exercises	See Example
10–13	1
14–17	2
18–19	3
20	4

Extra Practice

See Extra Practice for more Skills Practice and Applications Practice exercises.

Write an exponential growth function to model each situation. Then find the value of the function after the given amount of time.

10. Annual sales for a company are $149,000 and are increasing at a rate of 6% per year; 7 years.

11. The population of a small town is 1600 and is increasing at a rate of 3% per year; 10 years.

12. A new savings account starts at $700 and increases at 1.2% yearly; 8 years.

13. Membership of a local club grows at a rate of 7.8% yearly and currently has 30 members; 6 years.

Write a compound interest function to model each situation. Then find the balance after the given number of years.

14. $28,000 invested at a rate of 4% compounded annually; 5 years

15. $7000 invested at a rate of 3% compounded quarterly; 10 years

16. $3500 invested at a rate of 1.8% compounded monthly; 4 years

17. $12,000 invested at a rate of 2.6% compounded annually; 15 years

Write an exponential decay function to model each situation. Then find the value of the function after the given amount of time.

18. The population of a town is 18,000 and is decreasing at a rate of 2% per year; 6 years.

19. The value of a book is $58 and decreases at a rate of 10% per year; 8 years.

20. The half-life of bromine-82 is approximately 36 hours. Find the amount of bromine-82 left from an 80-gram sample after 6 days.

Identify each of the following functions as exponential growth or decay. Then give the rate of growth or decay as a percent.

21. $y = 3(1.61)^t$ 22. $y = 39(0.098)^t$ 23. $y = a\left(\dfrac{2}{3}\right)^t$ 24. $y = a\left(\dfrac{3}{2}\right)^t$

25. $y = a(1.1)^t$ 26. $y = a(0.8)^t$ 27. $y = a\left(\dfrac{5}{4}\right)^t$ 28. $y = a\left(\dfrac{1}{2}\right)^t$

Write an exponential growth or decay function to model each situation. Then find the value of the function after the given amount of time.

29. The population of a country is 58,000,000 and grows by 0.1% per year; 3 years.

30. An antique car is worth $32,000, and its value grows by 7% per year; 5 years.

31. An investment of $8200 loses value at a rate of 2% per year; 7 years.

32. A new car is worth $25,000, and its value decreases by 15% each year; 6 years.

33. The student enrollment in a local high school is 970 students and increases by 1.2% per year; 5 years.

Atlantic Ocean
North Sea
England
Testwood

34. **Archaeology** Carbon-14 dating is a way to determine the age of very old organic objects. Carbon-14 has a half-life of about 5700 years. An organic object with $\frac{1}{2}$ as much carbon-14 as its living counterpart died 5700 years ago. In 1999, archaeologists discovered the oldest bridge in England near Testwood, Hampshire. Carbon dating of the wood revealed that the bridge was 3500 years old. Suppose that when the bridge was built, the wood contained 15 grams of carbon-14. How much carbon-14 would it have contained when it was found by the archaeologists? Round to the nearest hundredth.

A computer-generated image of what the bridge at Testwood might have looked like

35. **///ERROR ANALYSIS///** Two students were asked to find the value of a $1000-item after 3 years. The item was depreciating (losing value) at a rate of 40% per year. Which is incorrect? Explain the error.

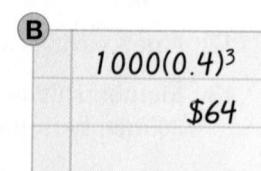

A
$1000(0.6)^3$
$216

B
$1000(0.4)^3$
$64

36. **Critical Thinking** The value of a certain car can be modeled by the function $y = 20,000(0.84)^t$, where t is time in years. Will the value ever be zero? Explain.

37. The value of a rare baseball card increases every year at a rate of 4%. Today, the card is worth $300. The owner expects to sell the card as soon as the value is over $600. How many years will the owner wait before selling the card? Round your answer to the nearest whole number.

MULTI-STEP
TEST PREP

38. a. The annual tuition at a prestigious university was $20,000 in 2002. It generally increases at a rate of 9% each year. Write a function to describe the cost as a function of the number of years since 2002. Use 2002 as year zero when writing the function rule.

b. What do you predict the cost of tuition will be in 2008?

c. Use a table of values to find the first year that the cost of the tuition is more than twice the cost in 2002.

39. Multi-Step At bank A, $600 is invested with an interest rate of 5% compounded annually. At bank B, $500 is invested with an interest rate of 6% compounded quarterly. Which account will have a larger balance after 10 years? 20 years?

40. Estimation The graph shows the decay of 100 grams of sodium-24. Use the graph to estimate the number of hours it will take the sample to decay to 10 grams. Then estimate the half-life of sodium-24.

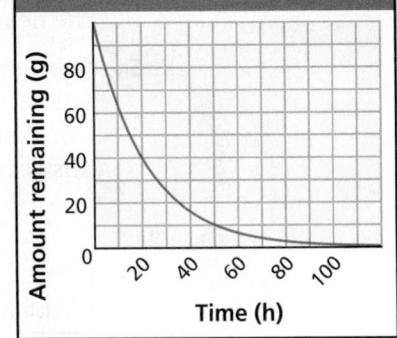

41. Graphing Calculator Use a graphing calculator to graph $y = 10(1 + r)^x$ for $r = 10\%$ and $r = 20\%$. Compare the two graphs. How does the value of r affect the graphs?

42. Write About It Write a real-world situation that could be modeled by $y = 400(1.08)^t$.

43. Write About It Write a real-world situation that could be modeled by $y = 800(0.96)^t$.

44. Critical Thinking The amount of water in a container doubles every minute. After 6 minutes, the container is full. Your friend says it was half full after 3 minutes. Do you agree? Why or why not?

TEST PREP

45. A population of 500 is decreasing by 1% per year. Which function models this situation?

Ⓐ $y = 500(0.01)^t$ Ⓑ $y = 500(0.1)^t$ Ⓒ $y = 500(0.9)^t$ Ⓓ $y = 500(0.99)^t$

46. Which function is NOT an exponential decay model?

Ⓕ $y = 5\left(\dfrac{1}{3}\right)^x$ Ⓖ $y = -5\left(\dfrac{1}{3}\right)^x$ Ⓗ $y = 5(3)^{-x}$ Ⓙ $y = 5(3^{-1})^x$

47. Stephanie wants to save $1000 for a down payment on a car that she wants to buy in 3 years. She opens a savings account that pays 5% interest compounded annually. About how much should Stephanie deposit now to have enough money for the down payment in 3 years?

Ⓐ $295   Ⓑ $333   Ⓒ $500   Ⓓ $865

48. Short Response In 2000, the population of a town was 1000 and was growing at a rate of 5% per year.

a. Write an exponential growth function to model this situation.

b. In what year is the population 1300? Show how you found your answer.

CHALLENGE AND EXTEND

49. You invest $700 at a rate of 6% compounded quarterly. Use a graph to estimate the number of years it will take for your investment to increase to $2300.

50. Omar invested $500 at a rate of 4% compounded annually. How long will it take for Omar's money to double? How long would it take if the interest were 8% compounded annually?

51. An 80-gram sample of a radioactive substance decayed to 10 grams after 300 minutes. Find the half-life of the substance.

52. Praseodymium-143 has a half-life of 2 weeks. The original measurement for the mass of a sample was lost. After 6 weeks, 15 grams of praseodymium-143 remain. How many grams was the original sample?

53. Phillip invested some money in a business 8 years ago. Since then, his investment has grown at an average rate of 1.3% compounded quarterly. Phillip's investment is now worth $250,000. How much was his original investment? Round your answer to the nearest dollar.

54. Personal Finance Anna has a balance of $200 that she owes on her credit card. She plans to make a $30 payment each month. There is also a 1.5% finance charge (interest) on the remaining balance each month. Copy and complete the table to answer the questions below. You may add more rows to the table as necessary.

Month	Balance ($)	Monthly Payment ($)	Remaining Balance ($)	1.5% Finance Charge ($)	New Balance ($)
1	200	30	170	2.55	172.55
2	172.55	30			
3		30			
4		30			

a. How many months will it take Anna to pay the entire balance?

b. By the time Anna pays the entire balance, how much total interest will she have paid?

COMMON CORE

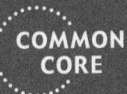

Mastering the *Standards*

for Mathematical Practice

The topics described in the Standards for Mathematical Content will vary from year to year. However, the *way* in which you learn, study, and think about mathematics will not. The Standards for Mathematical Practice describe skills that you will use in all of your math courses.

Mathematical Practices

1. *Make sense of problems and persevere in solving them.*
2. *Reason abstractly and quantitatively.*
3. *Construct viable arguments and critique the reasoning of others.*
4. *Model with mathematics.*
5. *Use appropriate tools strategically.*
6. *Attend to precision.*
7. *Look for and make use of structure.*
8. *Look for and express regularity in repeated reasoning.*

4 Model with mathematics.

Mathematically proficient students can apply... mathematics... to... problems... in everyday life, society, and the workplace...

In your book

Multi-Step Test Prep and **Real-World Connections** apply mathematics to other disciplines and in real-world scenarios.

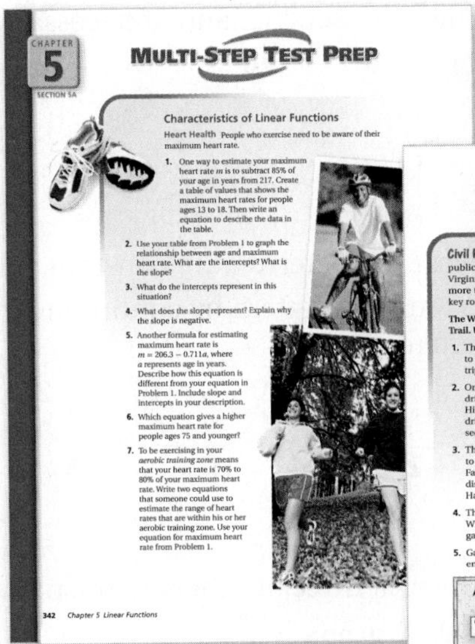
CHAPTER 5
SECTION 5A

MULTI-STEP TEST PREP

Characteristics of Linear Functions

Heart Health People who exercise need to be aware of their maximum heart rate.

1. One way to estimate your maximum heart rate m is to subtract 85% of your age in years from 217. Create a table of values that shows the maximum heart rates for people ages 13 to 18. Then write an equation to describe the data in the table.
2. Use your table from Problem 1 to graph the relationship between age and maximum heart rate. What are the intercepts? What is the slope?
3. What do the intercepts represent in this situation?
4. What does the slope represent? Explain why the slope is negative.
5. Another formula for estimating maximum heart rate is $m = 206.3 - 0.711a$, where a represents age in years. Describe how this equation is different from your equation in Problem 1. Include slope and intercepts in your description.
6. Which equation gives a higher maximum heart rate for people ages 75 and younger?
7. To be exercising in your *aerobic training zone* means that your heart rate is 70% to 80% of your maximum heart rate. Write two equations that someone could use to estimate the range of heart rates that are within his or her aerobic training zone. Use your equation for maximum heart rate from Problem 1.

342 *Chapter 5 Linear Functions*

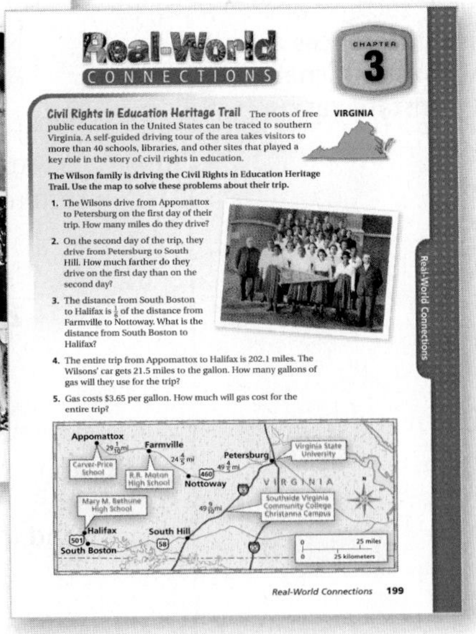
Real-World CONNECTIONS

CHAPTER 3

Civil Rights in Education Heritage Trail The roots of free public education in the United States can be traced to southern Virginia. A self-guided driving tour of the area takes visitors to more than 40 schools, libraries, and other sites that played a key role in the story of civil rights in education.

VIRGINIA

The Wilson family is driving the Civil Rights in Education Heritage Trail. Use the map to solve these problems about their trip.

1. The Wilsons drive from Appomattox to Petersburg on the first day of their trip. How many miles do they drive?
2. On the second day of the trip, they drive from Petersburg to South Hill. How much farther do they drive on the first day than on the second day?
3. The distance from South Boston to Halifax is $\frac{1}{6}$ of the distance from Farmville to Nottoway. What is the distance from South Boston to Halifax?
4. The entire trip from Appomattox to Halifax is 202.1 miles. The Wilsons' car gets 21.5 miles to the gallon. How many gallons of gas will they use for the trip?
5. Gas costs $3.65 per gallon. How much will gas cost for the entire trip?

Real-World Connections 199

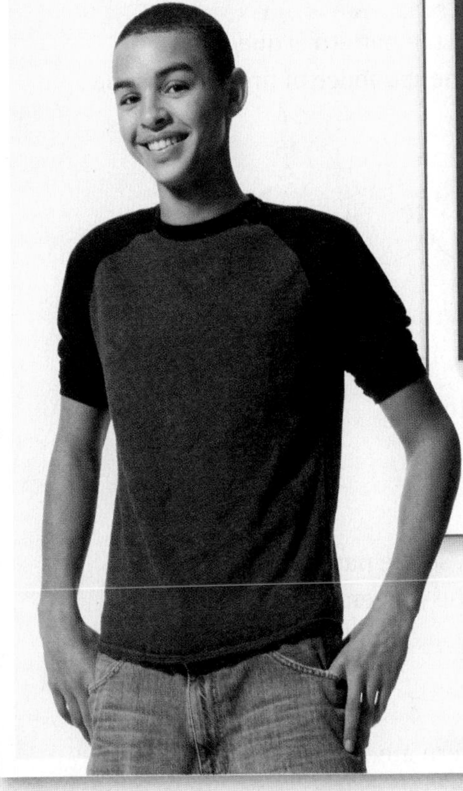

PhotoDisc/Getty Images

EXTENSION Patterns and Recursion

CC.9-12.F.IF.3 Recognize that sequences are functions, sometimes defined recursively, whose domain is a subset of the integers. *Also* **CC.9-12.F.BF.2*, CC.9-12.F.LE.2***

Objective
Identify and extend patterns using recursion.

Vocabulary
recursive pattern

In a **recursive pattern** or *recursive sequence*, each term is defined using one or more previous terms. For example, the sequence 1, 4, 7, 10, 13, ... can be defined recursively as follows: The first term is 1 and each term after the first is equal to the preceding term plus 3.

You can use recursive techniques to identify patterns. The table summarizes the characteristics of four types of patterns.

Using Recursive Techniques to Identify Patterns	
Type of Pattern	**Characteristics**
Linear	First differences are constant.
Quadratic	Second differences are constant.
Cubic	Third differences are constant.
Exponential	Ratios between successive terms are constant.

EXAMPLE 1

Identifying and Extending a Pattern

Identify the type of pattern. Then find the next three numbers in the pattern.

Helpful Hint

You may need to use trial and error when identifying a pattern. If first, second, and third differences are not constant, check for constant ratios.

A 4, 6, 10, 16, 24, ...

Find first, second, and, if necessary, third differences.

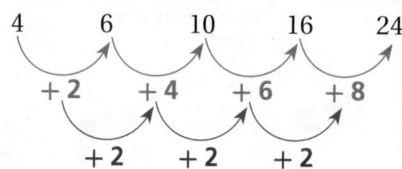

Second differences are constant, so the pattern is quadratic.

Extend the pattern by continuing the sequence of first and second differences.

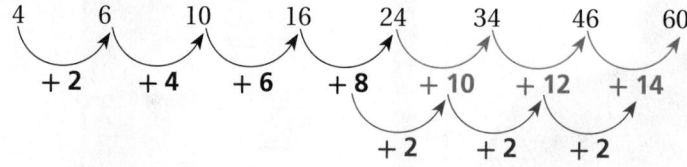

The next three numbers in the pattern are 34, 46, and 60.

B $\frac{1}{8}, \frac{1}{2}, 2, 8, 32$

Find the ratio between successive terms.

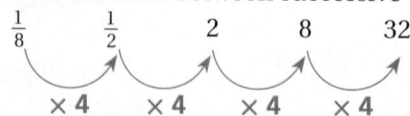

Ratios between terms are constant, so the pattern is exponential.

Extend the pattern by continuing the sequence of ratios.

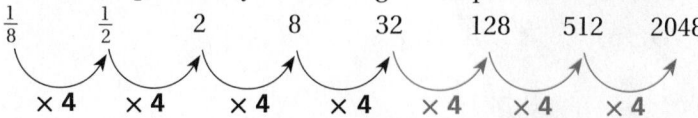

The next three numbers in the pattern are 128, 512, and 2048.

 Identify the type of pattern. Then find the next three numbers in the pattern.

1a. 56, 47, 38, 29, 20, ...   **1b.** 1, 8, 27, 64, 125, ...

You can use a similar process to determine whether a function is linear, quadratic, cubic, or exponential. Note that before comparing *y*-values, you must first make sure there is a constant change in the corresponding *x*-values.

Using Recursive Techniques to Identify Functions	
Type of Function	**Characteristics** **(Given a Constant Change in *x*-values)**
Linear	First differences of *y*-values are constant.
Quadratic	Second differences of *y*-values are constant.
Cubic	Third differences of *y*-values are constant.
Exponential	Ratios between successive *y*-values are constant.

EXAMPLE 2 **Identifying a Function**

The ordered pairs {(−4, −4), (0, 0), (4, 4), (8, 32), (12, 108)} satisfy a function. Determine whether the function is linear, quadratic, cubic, or exponential. Then find three additional ordered pairs that satisfy the function.

Make a table. Check for a constant change in the *x*-values. Then find first, second, and third differences of *y*-values.

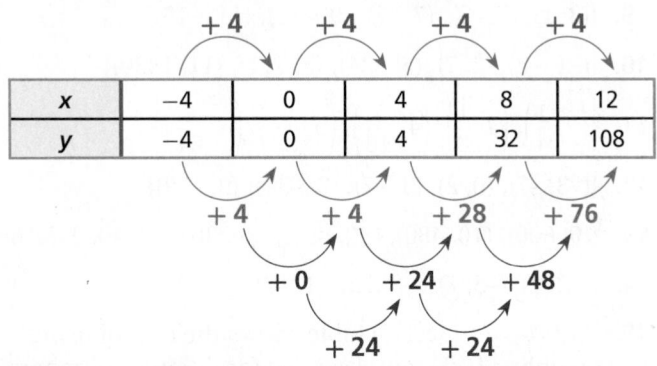

There is a constant change in the *x*-values. Third differences are constant. The function is a cubic function.

To find additional ordered pairs, extend the pattern by working backward from the constant third differences.

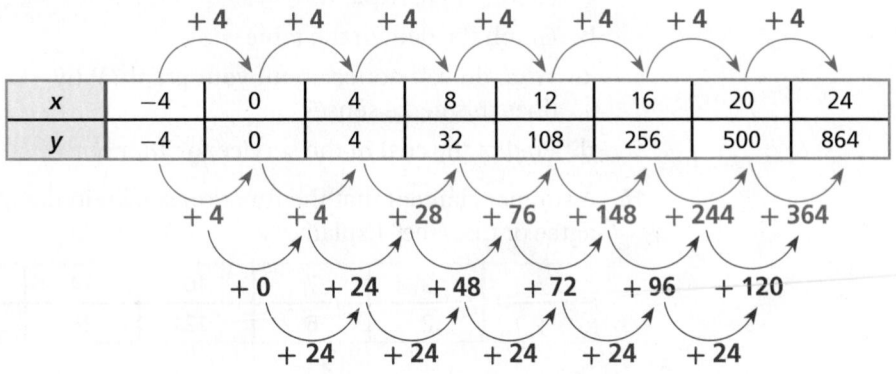

Helpful Hint

In Example 2, the constant third differences are 24. To extend the pattern, first find each second difference by adding 24 to the previous second difference. Then find each first difference by adding the second difference below to the previous first difference.

Three additional ordered pairs that satisfy this function are (16, 256), (20, 500), and (24, 864).

 **CHECK IT OUT!** Several ordered pairs that satisfy a function are given. Determine whether the function is linear, quadratic, cubic, or exponential. Then find three additional ordered pairs that satisfy the function.

2a. {(0, 1), (1, 3), (2, 9), (3, 19), (4, 33)}

2b. $\left\{\left(1, \frac{1}{2}\right), \left(3, \frac{1}{6}\right), \left(5, \frac{1}{18}\right), \left(7, \frac{1}{54}\right), \left(9, \frac{1}{162}\right)\right\}$

EXTENSION Exercises

Identify the type of pattern. Then find the next three numbers in the pattern.

1. 25, 28, 31, 34, 37, ...

2. 20, 45, 80, 125, 180, ...

3. 128, 64, 32, 16, 8, ...

4. 4, 32, 108, 256, 500, ...

5. $\frac{1}{2}, \frac{3}{4}, 1, 1\frac{1}{4}, 1\frac{1}{2}$, ...

6. 0.3, 0.03, 0.003, 0.0003, 0.00003, ...

7. 127, 66, 29, 10, 3, ...

8. 2, 8, 18, 32, 50, ...

Several ordered pairs that satisfy a function are given. Determine whether the function is linear, quadratic, cubic, or exponential. Then find three additional ordered pairs that satisfy the function.

9. {(3, 1), (5, –3), (7, –7), (9, –11), (11, –15)}

10. {(–1, –2), (2, 7), (5, 124), (8, 511), (11, 1330)}

11. $\left\{\left(2, \frac{1}{4}\right), \left(3, \frac{1}{8}\right), \left(4, \frac{1}{16}\right), \left(5, \frac{1}{32}\right), \left(6, \frac{1}{64}\right)\right\}$

12. {(–3, –7), (0, 2), (3, –7), (6, –34), (9, –79)}

13. {(0, 600), (10, 480), (20, 384), (30, 307.2), (40, 245.76)}

14. {(–8, 2), (–5, 7), (–2, 12), (1, 17), (4, 22)}

15. Entertainment The table shows the cost of using an online DVD rental service for different numbers of months.

a. Determine whether the function that models the data is linear, quadratic, cubic, or exponential. Explain.

b. Graph the data in the table.

c. What do you notice about your graph? Why does this make sense?

d. Predict the cost of the service for 18 months.

Online DVD Rentals	
Months	**Cost ($)**
3	50
6	92
9	134
12	176
15	218

16. A student claimed that the function shown in the table is a quadratic function. Do you agree or disagree? Explain.

x	3	7	10	14	17
y	2	6	12	20	30

+4   +6   +8   +10

+2   +2   +2

17. Business The table shows the annual sales for a small company.

Annual Sales	
Year	Sales ($)
2006	513,000
2007	516,000
2008	521,000
2009	528,000
2010	537,000

   a. Determine whether the function that models the data is linear, quadratic, cubic, or exponential. Explain.

   b. Suppose sales continue to grow according to the pattern in the table. Predict the annual sales for 2011, 2012, and 2013.

   c. If the pattern continues, in what year will annual sales be $17,000 greater than the previous year's sales?

18. Critical Thinking Use the table for the following problems.

x	0	1	2	3	4
y	3	6	■	■	■

   a. Copy and complete the table so that the function is a linear function.

   b. Copy and complete the table so that the function is a quadratic function.

   c. Copy and complete the table so that the function is an exponential function.

   d. For which of these three types of functions is there more than one correct way to complete the table? Explain.

Use the description to write the first five terms in each numerical pattern.

19. The first term is 8. Each following term is 11 less than the term before it.

20. The first term is 1000. Each following term is 40% of the term before it.

21. The first two terms are 1 and 2. Each following term is the sum of the two terms before it.

Make a table for a function that has the given characteristics. Include at least five ordered pairs.

22. The function is linear. The first differences are -3.

23. The function is quadratic. The second differences are 6.

24. The function is cubic. The third differences are 1.

A *recursive formula* for a sequence shows how to find the value of a term from one or more terms that come before it. For example, the recursive formula $a_n = a_{n-1} + 3$ tells you that each term is equal to the preceding term plus 3. Given that $a_1 = 5$, you can use the formula to generate the sequence 5, 8, 11, 14, ...

Write the first four terms of each sequence.

25. $a_n = a_{n-1} + 2;\ a_1 = 12$

26. $a_n = a_{n-1} - 7;\ a_1 = 16$

27. $a_n = 2a_{n-1};\ a_1 = 4$

28. $a_n = 0.6a_{n-1};\ a_1 = 100$

29. $a_n = 5a_{n-1} - 2;\ a_1 = 0$

30. $a_n = (a_{n-1})^2;\ a_1 = -2$

31. A *recursive function* defines a function for whole numbers by referring to the value of the function at previous whole numbers. Consider the recursive function $f(n) = f(n-1) + 5$ with $f(0) = 1$.

   a. According to the formula, $f(1) = f(0) + 5$. What is the value of $f(1)$?

   b. Use the formula to find $f(2)$, $f(3)$, $f(4)$, and $f(5)$.

   c. Graph $f(n)$ by plotting points at $x = 0$, $x = 1$, $x = 2$, $x = 3$, $x = 4$, and $x = 5$.

   d. What do you notice about your graph? What does this tell you about $f(n)$?

Mastering *the* Standards

for Mathematical Practice

The topics described in the Standards for Mathematical Content will vary from year to year. However, the *way* in which you learn, study, and think about mathematics will not. The Standards for Mathematical Practice describe skills that you will use in all of your math courses.

Mathematical Practices

1. Make sense of problems and persevere in solving them.
2. Reason abstractly and quantitatively.
3. Construct viable arguments and critique the reasoning of others.
4. Model with mathematics.
5. Use appropriate tools strategically.
6. Attend to precision.
7. Look for and make use of structure.
8. Look for and express regularity in repeated reasoning.

⑤ Use appropriate tools strategically.

Mathematically proficient students consider the available tools when solving a... problem... [and] are... able to use technological tools to explore and deepen their understanding...

In your book

Algebra Labs and **Technology Labs** use concrete and technological tools to explore mathematical concepts.

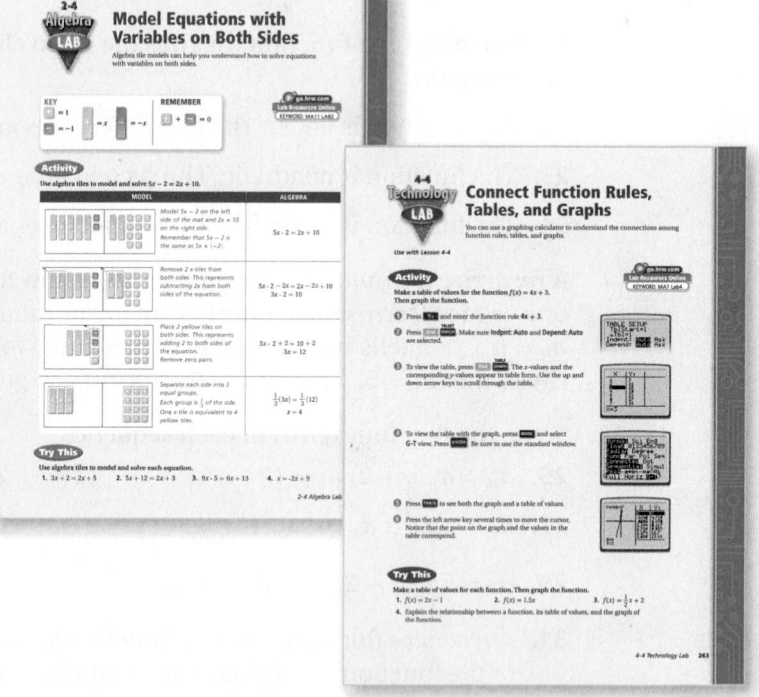

Getty Images/Image Source

CC.9-12.F.LE.1 Distinguish between situations that can be modeled with linear functions and with exponential functions.* *Also* CC.9-12.F.LE.2*, CC.9-12.A.CED.2*, CC.9-12.F.IF.4*, CC.9-12.F.IF.7*, CC.9-12.F.BF.1*

9-4 Linear, Quadratic, and Exponential Models

Objectives
Compare linear, quadratic, and exponential models.

Given a set of data, decide which type of function models the data and write an equation to describe the function.

Why learn this?
Different situations in sports can be described by linear, quadratic, or exponential models.

Look at the tables and graphs below. The data show three ways you have learned that variable quantities can be related. The relationships shown are linear, quadratic, and exponential.

Linear		Quadratic		Exponential	
Training Heart Rate		**Volleyball Height**		**Volleyball Tournament**	
Age (yr)	Beats/min	Time (s)	Height (ft)	Round	Teams Left
20	170	0.4	10.44	1	16
30	161.5	0.8	12.76	2	8
40	153	1	12	3	4
50	144.5	1.2	9.96	4	2

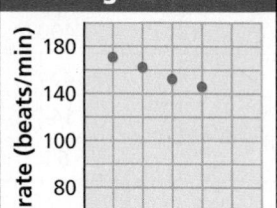

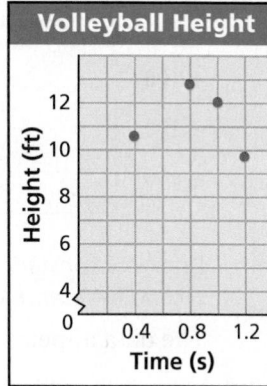

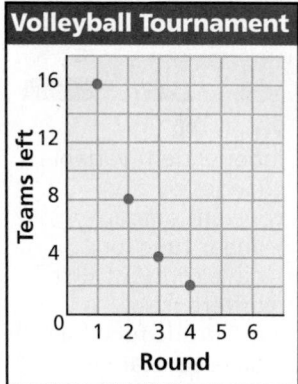

In the real world, people often gather data and then must decide what kind of relationship (if any) they think best describes their data.

EXAMPLE 1 Graphing Data to Choose a Model

Graph each data set. Which kind of model best describes the data?

Time (h)	0	1	2	3
Bacteria	10	20	40	80

Plot the data points and connect them.
The data appear to be exponential.

Bacteria Population

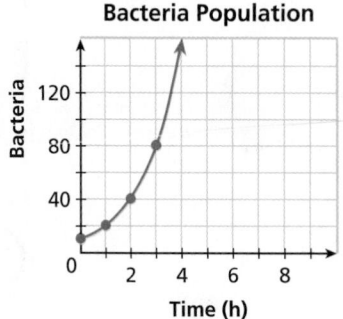

Graph each data set. Which kind of model best describes the data?

B

°C	0	5	10	15	20
°F	32	41	50	59	68

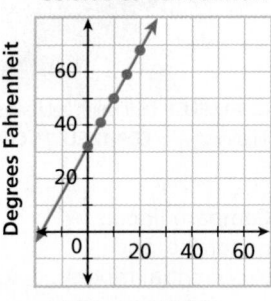

Celsius to Fahrenheit

Plot the data points and connect them.

The data appear to be linear.

 CHECK IT OUT! **Graph each data set. Which kind of model best describes the data?**

1a. $\{(-3, 0.30), (-2, 0.44), (0, 1), (1, 1.5), (2, 2.25), (3, 3.38)\}$

1b. $\{(-3, -14), (-2, -9), (-1, -6), (0, -5), (1, -6), (2, -9), (3, -14)\}$

Another way to decide which kind of relationship (if any) best describes a data set is to use patterns.

EXAMPLE 2   **Using Patterns to Choose a Model**

Look for a pattern in each data set to determine which kind of model best describes the data.

A

Height of Bridge Suspension Cables

Cable's Distance from Tower (ft)	Cable's Height (ft)
0	400
100	256
200	144
300	64

+100 between distances; −144, −112, −80 between heights; +32, +32 second differences.

For every constant change in distance of +100 feet, there is a constant second difference of +32.

The data appear to be quadratic.

B

Value of a Car

Car's Age (yr)	Value ($)
0	20,000
1	17,000
2	14,450
3	12,282.50

+1 between ages; ×0.85, ×0.85, ×0.85 ratios.

For every constant change in age of +1 year, there is a constant ratio of 0.85.

The data appear to be exponential.

> **Remember!**
>
> When the independent variable changes by a constant amount,
> • linear functions have constant first differences.
> • quadratic functions have constant second differences.
> • exponential functions have a constant ratio.

 **CHECK IT OUT!** **2.** Look for a pattern in the data set $\{(-2, 10), (-1, 1), (0, -2), (1, 1), (2, 10)\}$ to determine which kind of model best describes the data.

After deciding which model best fits the data, you can write a function. Recall the general forms of linear, quadratic, and exponential functions.

General Forms of Functions

LINEAR	QUADRATIC	EXPONENTIAL
$y = mx + b$	$y = ax^2 + bx + c$	$y = ab^x$

EXAMPLE **3** *Problem-Solving Application*

Make sense of problems and persevere in solving them.

Use the data in the table to describe how the ladybug population is changing. Then write a function that models the data. Use your function to predict the ladybug population after one year.

Ladybug Population	
Time (mo)	Ladybugs
0	10
1	30
2	90
3	270

1 **Understand the Problem**

The **answer** will have three parts—a description, a function, and a prediction.

2 **Make a Plan**

Determine whether the data is linear, quadratic, or exponential. Use the general form to write a function. Then use the function to find the population after one year.

3 **Solve**

Step 1 Describe the situation in words.

Ladybug Population	
Time (mo)	Ladybugs
0	10
1	30
2	90
3	270

+1 × 3

Each month, the ladybug population is multiplied by 3. In other words, the population triples each month.

Step 2 Write the function.

There is a constant ratio of 3. The data appear to be exponential.

$y = ab^x$ *Write the general form of an exponential function.*
$y = a(3)^x$ *Substitute the constant ratio, 3, for b.*
$10 = a(3)^0$ *Choose an ordered pair from the table, such as (0, 10). Substitute for x and y.*
$10 = a(1)$ *Simplify. $3^0 = 1$*
$10 = a$ *The value of a is 10.*
$y = 10(3)^x$ *Substitute 10 for a in $y = a(3)^x$.*

Helpful Hint

You can choose any given ordered pair to substitute for *x* and *y*. However, it is often easiest to choose an ordered pair that contains 0.

Step 3 Predict the ladybug population after one year.

$$y = 10(3)^x \quad \text{\textit{Write the function.}}$$
$$= 10(3)^{12} \quad \text{\textit{Substitute 12 for x (1 year = 12 mo).}}$$
$$= 5{,}314{,}410 \quad \text{\textit{Use a calculator.}}$$

There will be 5,314,410 ladybugs after one year.

 Look Back

You chose the ordered pair $(0, 10)$ to write the function. Check that every other ordered pair in the table satisfies your function.

$y = 10(3)^x$	
30	$10(3)^1$
30	$10(3)$
30	30 ✓

$y = 10(3)^x$	
90	$10(3)^2$
90	$10(9)$
90	90 ✓

$y = 10(3)^x$	
270	$10(3)^3$
270	$10(27)$
270	270 ✓

 **3.** Use the data in the table to describe how the oven temperature is changing. Then write a function that models the data. Use your function to predict the temperature after 1 hour.

Oven Temperature				
Time (min)	0	10	20	30
Temperature (°F)	375	325	275	225

Student to Student

Checking Units

Michael Gambhir
Warren High School

I used to get a lot of answers wrong because of the units. If a question asked for the value of something after 1 year, I would always just substitute 1 into the function.

I finally figured out that you have to check what x is. If x represents months and you're trying to find the value after 1 year, then you have to substitute 12, not 1, because there are 12 months in a year.

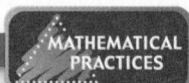

THINK AND DISCUSS

1. Do you think that every data set will be able to be modeled by a linear, quadratic, or exponential function? Why or why not?

2. In Example 3, is it certain that there will be 5,314,410 ladybugs after one year? Explain.

 **3. GET ORGANIZED** Copy and complete the graphic organizer. In each box, list some characteristics and sketch a graph of each type of model.

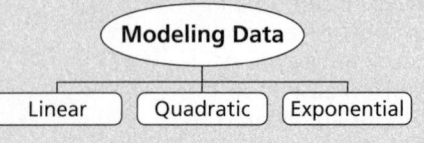

age fotostock

GUIDED PRACTICE

SEE EXAMPLE **1**   Graph each data set. Which kind of model best describes the data?

1. $\{(-1, 4), (-2, 0.8), (0, 20), (1, 100), (-3, 0.16)\}$

2. $\{(0, 3), (1, 9), (2, 11), (3, 9), (4, 3)\}$

3. $\{(2, -7), (-2, -9), (0, -8), (4, -6), (6, -5)\}$

SEE EXAMPLE **2**   Look for a pattern in each data set to determine which kind of model best describes the data.

4. $\{(-2, 1), (-1, 2.5), (0, 3), (1, 2.5), (2, 1)\}$

5. $\{(-2, 0.75), (-1, 1.5), (0, 3), (1, 6), (2, 12)\}$

6. $\{(-2, 2), (-1, 4), (0, 6), (1, 8), (2, 10)\}$

SEE EXAMPLE **3**   7. **Consumer Economics** Use the data in the table to describe the cost of grapes. Then write a function that models the data. Use your function to predict the cost of 6 pounds of grapes.

Total Cost of Grapes				
Amount (lb)	1	2	3	4
Cost ($)	1.79	3.58	5.37	7.16

PRACTICE AND PROBLEM SOLVING

Independent Practice

For Exercises	See Example
8–10	1
11–13	2
14	3

Graph each data set. Which kind of model best describes the data?

8. $\{(-3, -5), (-2, -8), (-1, -9), (0, -8), (1, -5), (2, 0), (3, 7)\}$

9. $\{(-3, -1), (-2, 0), (-1, 1), (0, 2), (1, 3), (2, 4), (3, 5)\}$

10. $\{(0, 0.1), (2, 0.9), (3, 2.7), (4, 8.1)\}$

Extra Practice

See Extra Practice for more Skills Practice and Applications Practice exercises.

Look for a pattern in each data set to determine which kind of model best describes the data.

11. $\{(-2, 5), (-1, 4), (0, 3), (1, 2), (2, 1)\}$

12. $\{(-2, 12), (-1, 15), (0, 16), (1, 15), (2, 12)\}$

13. $\{(-2, 8), (-1, 4), (0, 2), (1, 1), (2, 0.5)\}$

14. **Business** Use the data in the table to describe how the company's sales are changing. Then write a function that models the data. Use your function to predict the amount of sales after 10 years.

Company Sales				
Year	0	1	2	3
Sales ($)	25,000	30,000	36,000	43,200

15. **Multi-Step** Jay's hair grows about 6 inches each year. Write a function that describes the length ℓ in inches that Jay's hair will grow for each year k. Which kind of model best describes the function?

Tell which kind of model best describes each situation.

16. The height of a plant at weekly intervals over the last 6 weeks was 1 inches, 1.5 inches, 2 inches, 2.5 inches, 3 inches., and 3.5 inches.

17. The number of games a baseball player played in the last four years was 162, 162, 162, and 162.

18. The height of a ball in a certain time interval was recorded as 30.64 feet, 30.96 feet, 31 feet, 30.96 feet, and 30.64 feet.

Write a function to model each set of data.

19.

x	−1	0	1	2	4
y	0.05	0.2	0.8	3.2	51.2

20.

x	−2	0	2	4	8
y	5	4	3	2	0

Tell which kind of model best describes each graph.

21.
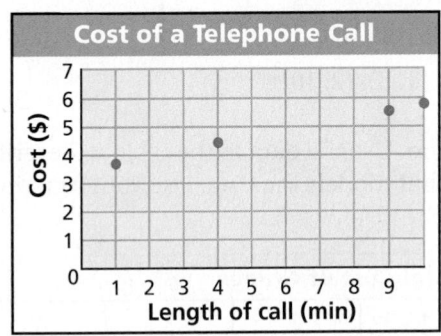

22.
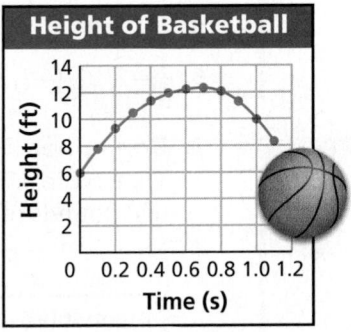

23. **Write About It** Write a set of data that you could model with an exponential function. Explain why the exponential model would work.

24. **///ERROR ANALYSIS///** A student concluded that the data set would best be modeled by a quadratic function. Explain the student's error.

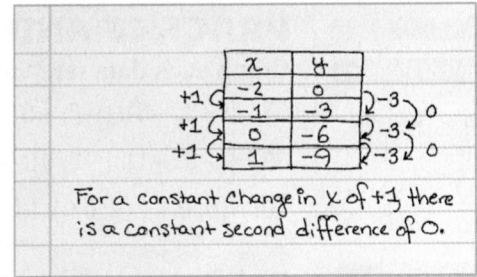

25. **Critical Thinking** Sometimes the graphs of quadratic data and exponential data can look very similar. Describe how you can tell them apart.

MULTI-STEP TEST PREP

26. **a.** Examine the two models that represent annual tuition for two colleges. Describe each model as linear, quadratic, or exponential.
   b. Write a function rule for each model.
   c. Both models have the same values for 2004. What does this mean?
   d. Why do both models have the same value for year 1?

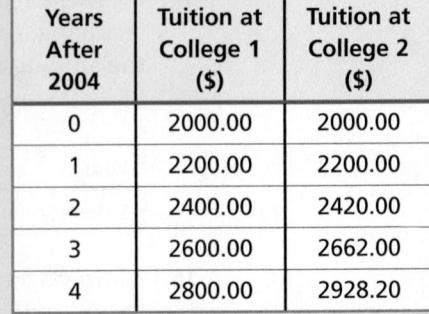

Years After 2004	Tuition at College 1 ($)	Tuition at College 2 ($)
0	2000.00	2000.00
1	2200.00	2200.00
2	2400.00	2420.00
3	2600.00	2662.00
4	2800.00	2928.20

Chapter 9 Exponential Functions

27. Which function best models the data: $\{(-4, -2), (-2, -1), (0, 0), (2, 1), (4, 2)\}$?

(A) $y = \left(\dfrac{1}{2}\right)^{x}$ (B) $y = \dfrac{1}{2}x^{2}$ (C) $y = \dfrac{1}{2}x$ (D) $y = \left(\dfrac{1}{2}x\right)^{2}$

28. A city's population is increasing at a rate of 2% per year. Which type of model describes this situation?

(F) Exponential (G) Quadratic (H) Linear (J) None of these

29. Which data set is best modeled by a linear function?

(A) $\{(-2, 0), (-1, 2), (0, -4), (1, -1), (2, 2)\}$

(B) $\{(-2, 2), (-1, 4), (0, 6), (1, 16), (2, 32)\}$

(C) $\{(-2, 2), (-1, 4), (0, 6), (1, 8), (2, 10)\}$

(D) $\{(-2, 0), (-1, 5), (0, 7), (1, 5), (2, 0)\}$

CHALLENGE AND EXTEND

30. Finance An accountant estimates that a certain new automobile worth $18,000 will lose value at a rate of 16% per year.

a. Make a table that shows the worth of the car for years 0, 1, 2, 3, and 4. What is the real-world meaning of year 0?

b. Which type of model best represents the data in your table? Explain.

c. Write a function for your data.

d. What is the value of the car after $5\frac{1}{2}$ years?

e. What is the value of the car after 8 years?

31. Pet Care The table shows general guidelines for the weight of a Great Dane at various ages.

a. None of the three models in this lesson—linear, quadratic, or exponential—fits this data exactly. Which of these is the *best* model for the data? Explain your choice.

b. What would you predict for the weight of a Great Dane who is 1 year old?

c. Do you think you could use your model to find the weight of a Great Dane at any age? Why or why not?

Great Dane	
Age (mo)	Weight (kg)
2	12
4	23
6	33
8	40
10	45

EXTENSION Linear and Nonlinear Rates of Change

CC.9-12.F.IF.6 Calculate and interpret the average rate of change of a function (presented symbolically or as a table) over a specified interval. Estimate the rate of change from a graph.*

Objectives
Identify linear and nonlinear rates of change.

Compare rates of change.

Recall that a *rate of change* is a ratio that compares the amount of change in a dependent variable to the amount of change in an independent variable.

$$\text{rate of change} = \frac{\text{change in dependent variable}}{\text{change in independent variable}}$$

The table shows the price of one ounce of gold in 2005 and 2008. The year is the independent variable and the price is the dependent variable. The rate of change is $\frac{870-513}{2008-2005} = \frac{357}{3} = 119$, or \$119 per year.

Price of Gold	
Year	Price ($/oz)
2005	513
2008	870

EXAMPLE 1 **Identifying Constant and Variable Rates of Change**

Determine whether each function has a constant or variable rate of change.

A {(0, 0), (1, 4), (3, 8), (6, 8), (8, 6)}

Find the ratio of the amount of change in the dependent variable *y* to the corresponding amount of change in the independent variable *x*.

x	y
0	0
1	4
3	8
6	8
8	6

+1 → +4
+2 → +4
+3 → +0
+2 → −2

The rates of change are
$\frac{4}{1} = 4$, $\frac{4}{2} = 2$, $\frac{0}{3} = 0$, and $\frac{-2}{2} = -1$.
The function has a variable rate of change.

B {(0, 1), (1, 2), (4, 5), (6, 7), (7, 8)}

Find the ratio of the amount of change in the dependent variable *y* to the corresponding amount of change in the independent variable *x*.

x	y
0	1
1	2
4	5
6	7
7	8

+1 → +1
+3 → +3
+2 → +2
+1 → +1

The rates of change are
$\frac{1}{1} = 1$, $\frac{3}{3} = 1$, $\frac{2}{2} = 1$, and $\frac{1}{1} = 1$.
The function has a constant rate of change.

 **CHECK IT OUT!** Determine whether each function has a constant or variable rate of change.

1a. {(−3, 10), (0, 7), (1, 6), (4, 3), (7, 0)}

1b. {(−2, −3), (2, 5), (3, 7), (5, 9), (8, 12)}

The functions in Examples 1A and 1B are graphed below.

Example 1A (variable rate of change)

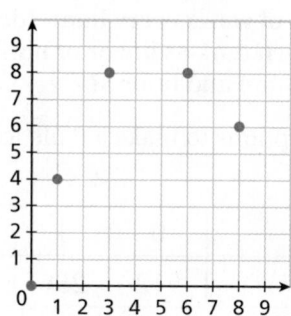

Example 1B (constant rate of change)

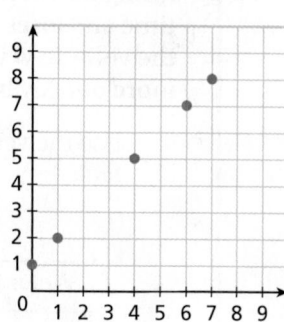

A function is a *linear function* if and only if the function has a constant rate of change. The graph of such a function is a straight line and the rate of change is the slope of the line, as in Example 1B.

A function with a variable rate of change, as in Example 1A, is a *nonlinear function*. Examples of nonlinear functions include quadratic functions and exponential functions.

EXAMPLE 2   **Identifying Linear and Nonlinear Functions**

Use rates of change to determine whether each function is linear or nonlinear.

A

x	y
−2	0
0	1
1	1.5
4	3
10	6

+2, +1, +3, +6 (x changes); +1, +0.5, +1.5, +3 (y changes)

Find the rates of change.

$$\frac{1}{2} \quad \frac{0.5}{1} = \frac{1}{2} \quad \frac{1.5}{3} = \frac{1}{2} \quad \frac{3}{6} = \frac{1}{2}$$

There is a constant rate of change, $\frac{1}{2}$, so this function is linear.

B

x	y
−6	18
−2	2
2	2
0	0
4	8

+4, +4, −2, +4 (x changes); −16, +0, −2, +8 (y changes)

Find the rates of change.

$$\frac{-16}{4} = -4 \quad \frac{0}{4} = 0 \quad \frac{-2}{-2} = 1 \quad \frac{8}{4} = \frac{1}{2}$$

The rates of change are not constant, so this function is nonlinear.

 **CHECK IT OUT!**   Use rates of change to determine whether each function is linear or nonlinear.

2a.

x	y
−2	$\frac{1}{4}$
−1	$\frac{1}{2}$
0	1
3	8
4	16

2b.

x	y
−5	3
−1	3
1	3
3	3
7	3

When you are given a verbal description of a function, you can determine whether the function is linear or nonlinear by making a table of values and examining the rates of change. You can compare two functions by comparing their rates of change.

EXAMPLE 3 | *Physical Science Application*

Two water tanks contain 512 gallons of water each. Tank A begins to drain, losing half of its volume of water every hour. Tank B begins to drain at the same time and loses 40 gallons of water every hour. Identify the function that gives the volume of water in each tank as linear or nonlinear. Which tank loses water more quickly between hour 4 and hour 5?

Use the verbal descriptions to make a table for the volume of water in each tank.

Time (h)	0	1	2	3	4	5
Water in Tank A (gal)	512	256	128	64	32	16

Time (h)	0	1	2	3	4	5
Water in Tank B (gal)	512	472	432	392	352	312

For tank A, the rates of change are –256, –128, –64, –32, and –16, so the rate of change is variable and the function is nonlinear.

For tank B, the rates of change are all –40, so the rate of change is constant and the function is linear.

Between hours 4 and 5, the volume of water in tank A decreases at a rate of 16 gallons per hour. The volume of water in tank B decreases at a rate of 40 gallons per hour. Tank B loses water more quickly.

3. Reka and Charlotte each invest $500. Each month, Charlotte's investment grows by $25, while Reka's investment grows by 5% of the previous month's amount. Identify the function that gives the value of each investment as linear or nonlinear. Who is earning money more quickly between month 3 and month 4?

EXTENSION

Exercises

Use rates of change to determine whether each function is linear or nonlinear.

1.

x	4	5	7	10	12
y	–2	–1	1	4	6

2.

x	–2	3	4	6	8
y	–4	6	8	14	20

3.

x	0	3	9	12	18
y	14	12	8	6	2

4.

x	–8	–6	–4	–2	0
y	–3	1	3	5	9

5. Hobbies Caitlin and Greg collect stamps. Each starts with a collection of 50 stamps. Caitlin adds 15 stamps to her collection each week. Greg adds 1 stamp to his collection the first week, 3 stamps the second week, 5 stamps the third week, and so on. Identify the function that gives the number of stamps in each collection as linear or nonlinear. Which collection is growing more quickly between week 5 and week 6?

Determine whether each function has a constant or variable rate of change.

6.
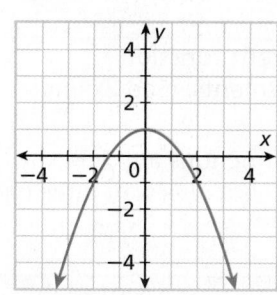

7.
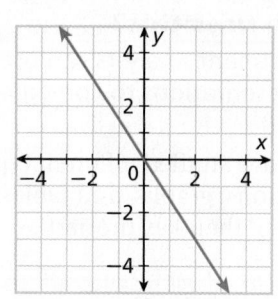

8.
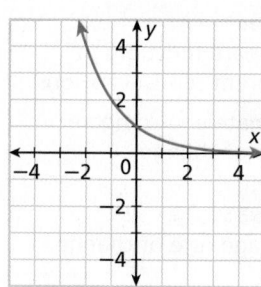

9. $y = 2x^2$

10. $y + 1 = 3x$

11. $y = -7$

12. $y = \frac{1}{5}x$

13. $y = 5^x$

14. $y = x^2 + 1$

15. $y = 3\sqrt{x}$

16. $y = \frac{x - 3}{2x}$

17. $x + y = 6.25$

Determine whether each statement is sometimes, always, or never true.

18. A function whose graph is a straight line has a variable rate of change.

19. A quadratic function has a constant rate of change.

20. The rate of change of a linear function is negative.

21. The rate of change between two points on the graph of a nonlinear function is 0.

22. Critical Thinking The figure shows the graph of the exponential function $y = \left(\frac{1}{2}\right)^x$.

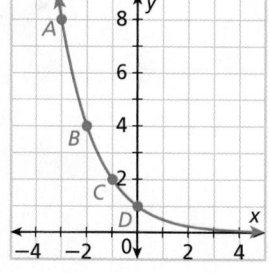

  a. Find the rates of change between points A and B, between points B and C, and between points A and D.

  b. What do you notice about the rates of change you found in part **a**? Do you think this would be true for the rate of change between any two points on the graph?

  c. How do your findings about the rates of change relate to the shape of the graph?

23. A model rocket is launched from the ground. The graph shows the height of the rocket at various times.

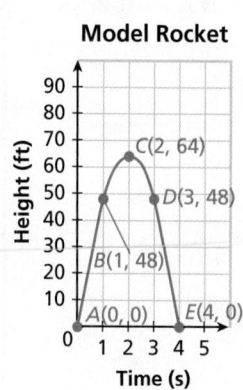

Model Rocket

  a. Find the rates of change between points A and B and between points B and C.

  b. Which rate of change is greater? What does this tell you about the motion of the rocket?

  c. Find the rates of change between points C and D and between points D and E.

  d. What does the sign of the rates of change you found in part **c** tell you about the motion of the rocket? Explain.

9-5 Comparing Functions

CC.9-12.F.IF.9 Compare properties of two functions each represented in a different way (algebraically, graphically, numerically in tables, or by verbal descriptions). *Also* **CC.9-12.F.IF.6***, **CC.9-12.F.LE.3***

Objectives
Compare functions in different representations.

Estimate and compare rates of change.

Vocabulary
average rate of change

Who uses this?
Investment analysts can use different function representations to compare investments. (See Example 2.)

You have studied different types of functions and how they can be represented as equations, graphs, and tables. Below is a review of three types of functions and some of their key properties.

	Linear	Quadratic	Exponential
Equation	$y = mx + b$ Example: $y = 2x + 1$	$y = ax^2 + bx + c,$ $a \neq 0$ Example: $y = x^2 - 2x + 3$	$y = ab^x, a \neq 0, b \neq 1,$ $b > 0$ Example: $y = 0.5(2)^x$
Graph			
Table	<table><tr><td>x</td><td>y</td></tr><tr><td>0</td><td>1</td></tr><tr><td>1</td><td>3</td></tr><tr><td>2</td><td>5</td></tr><tr><td>3</td><td>7</td></tr><tr><td>4</td><td>9</td></tr></table> +2, +2, +2, +2	<table><tr><td>x</td><td>y</td></tr><tr><td>0</td><td>3</td></tr><tr><td>1</td><td>2</td></tr><tr><td>2</td><td>3</td></tr><tr><td>3</td><td>6</td></tr><tr><td>4</td><td>11</td></tr></table> −1, +1, +3, +5 and +2, +2, +2	<table><tr><td>x</td><td>y</td></tr><tr><td>0</td><td>0.5</td></tr><tr><td>1</td><td>1</td></tr><tr><td>2</td><td>2</td></tr><tr><td>3</td><td>4</td></tr><tr><td>4</td><td>8</td></tr></table> ×2, ×2, ×2, ×2
	Constant first differences	Constant second differences	Constant ratios

---

EXAMPLE 1 Comparing Linear Functions

Deirdre and Beth each deposit money into their checking accounts weekly. Their account information for the past several weeks is shown below.

Deirdre's Account

Weeks	Account Balance ($)
0	60
1	75
2	90
3	105
4	120

Beth's Account

Compare the accounts by finding slopes and *y*-intercepts and interpreting those values in the context of the situation.

	Deirdre	Beth	Interpret and Compare.
Slope	**Slope** Use (1, 75) and (2, 90). $\frac{90-75}{2-1} = 15$	**Slope** Use (1, 60) and (2, 80). $\frac{80-60}{2-1} = 20$	The slope is the rate of change. Beth is saving at a higher rate.
y-intercept	(0, 60) *y*-intercept = 60	(0, 40) *y*-intercept = 40	The *y*-intercept is the beginning account balance. Deirdre started with more money.

1. Dave and Arturo each deposit money into their checking accounts weekly. Their account information for the past several weeks is shown. Compare the accounts by finding and interpreting slopes and *y*-intercepts.

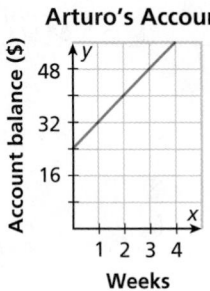

Arturo's Account

Dave's Account

Weeks	0	1	2	3
Account Balance ($)	30	42	54	66

Remember that nonlinear functions do not have a constant rate of change. One way to compare two nonlinear functions is to calculate their *average rates of change* over a certain interval. For a function $f(x)$ whose graph contains the points (x_1, y_1) and (x_2, y_2), the **average rate of change** over the interval $[x_1, x_2]$ is the slope of the line through (x_1, y_1) and (x_2, y_2).

Reading Math

The notation [0, 20] means all *x*-values from 0 to 20, including 0 and 20.

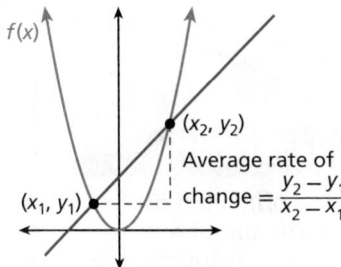

$f(x)$

(x_2, y_2)

Average rate of change $= \frac{y_2 - y_1}{x_2 - x_1}$

(x_1, y_1)

EXAMPLE 2

Comparing Exponential Functions

An investment analyst offers two different investment options for her customers. Compare the investments by finding and interpreting the average rates of change from year 0 to year 20.

Investment A

Years	Value ($)
0	10.00
5	13.38
10	17.91
15	23.97
20	32.07
25	42.92

Investment B

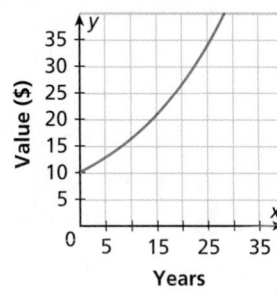

Calculate the average rates of change over [0, 20] by using the points whose x-coordinates are 0 and 20.

Investment A

$$\frac{32.07 - 10.00}{20 - 0} = \frac{22.07}{20} \approx 1.10 \quad \textit{Use (0, 10.00) and (20, 32.07).}$$

Investment B

$$\frac{27 - 10}{20 - 0} = \frac{17}{20} = 0.85 \qquad \textit{Use the graph to estimate. When x = 20,}$$
$$\textit{y} \approx \textit{27. Use (0, 10) and (20, 27).}$$

From year 0 to year 20, investment A increased at an average rate of $1.10 per year, while investment B increased at an average rate of $0.85 per year.

 **2.** Compare the same investments' average rates of change from year 10 to year 25.

EXAMPLE 3 Comparing Quadratic Functions

Students in an engineering class were given an assignment to design a parabola-shaped bridge. Two students' models are shown at right. Compare the models by finding and interpreting maximums, x-intercepts, and average rates of change over the x-interval [0, 20].

Rosetta's Plan

$$y = -0.01x^2 + 1.2x$$

Marco's Plan

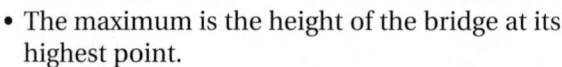

- The maximum is the height of the bridge at its highest point.
- The difference of the x-intercepts is the length of the bridge.
- The average rate of change over [0, 20] indicates the steepness of the bridge over the first 20 horizontal feet.

For Rosetta's plan, use the function.

Remember!

The minimum or maximum of a quadratic function is the y-value of the vertex.

Step 1 Find the maximum.

$$x = -\frac{b}{2a} = -\frac{1.2}{2(-0.01)} = \frac{1.2}{0.02} = 60 \quad \textit{Find the x-value of the vertex.}$$

$$y = -0.01(60)^2 + 1.2(60) \qquad \textit{Substitute 60 into the function}$$
$$= -36 + 72 = 36 \qquad \textit{to find the y-value of the vertex.}$$

The vertex is (60, 36) and the maximum is 36.

Step 2 Find the x-intercepts.

$$-0.01x^2 + 1.2x = 0 \qquad \textit{Write the related equation.}$$
$$-x(0.01x - 1.2) = 0 \qquad \textit{Solve for x.}$$
$$x = 0 \text{ or } 0.01x - 1.2 = 0$$
$$0.01x = 1.2$$
$$x = 120$$

The x-intercepts are 0 and 120.

Step 3 Find the average rate of change over [0, 20].

At $x = 0$, $y = -0.01(0)^2 + 1.2(0) = 0$ *Find the points whose x-coordinates*

At $x = 20$, $y = -0.01(20)^2 + 1.2(20)$ *are 0 and 20.*

$$= -4 + 24 = 20$$

Use (0, 0) and (20, 20): $\dfrac{20 - 0}{20 - 0} = 1$

For Marco's plan, use the graph.

Step 1 Find the maximum.

The maximum is slightly greater than 24, between 24 and 32.

Step 2 Find the *x*-intercepts.

The *x*-intercepts are 0 and 100.

Step 3 Find the average rate of change over [0, 20].

Use (0, 0) and (20, 16): $\dfrac{16 - 0}{20 - 0} = \dfrac{16}{20} = 0.8$

	Rosetta's Bridge	Marco's Bridge	Interpret and Compare.
Maximum Height	36 ft	just over 24 ft	Rosetta's bridge is taller.
Length	120 – 0 = 120 ft	100 – 0 = 100 ft	Rosetta's bridge is longer.
Average Steepness Over [0, 20]	1	0.8	Rosetta's bridge is steeper over [0, 20].

3. What if...? Suppose Rosetta uses $y = -0.01x^2 + 1.1x$ and Marco uses the same plan as above. Compare Marco's model with Rosetta's new model.

EXAMPLE **4** **Comparing Different Types of Functions**

A town has approximately 1000 homes. The town council is considering plans for future development. Plan A calls for an increase of 200 homes per year. Plan B calls for a 10% increase each year. Compare the plans.

Let *x* be the number of years. Let *y* be the number of homes. Write functions to model each plan.

Plan A: $y = 200x + 1000$

Plan B: $y = 1000(1.10)^x$

Use your calculator to graph both functions.

The graphs show that under plan A, there will be more homes built than under plan B in early years.

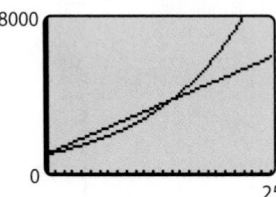

But by the end of the 15th year, the number of homes built under plan B exceeds the number of homes built under plan A. From that point on, plan B results in more homes than plan A by ever-increasing amounts every year.

4. Two neighboring schools use different models for anticipated growth in enrollment: School A has 850 students and predicts an increase of 100 students per year. School B also has 850 students, but predicts an increase of 8% per year. Compare the models.

THINK AND DISCUSS

1. Explain why you need to use the word *average* when comparing rates of change for quadratic or exponential functions, but not for linear functions.

2. A function can be represented by an equation or a graph. Describe a possible advantage of each representation.

3. GET ORGANIZED Copy and complete the graphic organizer. Complete the sentence in each column by writing important values to compare.

Comparing Functions			
Linear to Linear	**Exponential to Exponential**	**Quadratic to Quadratic**	**Linear to Quadratic**
Compare...	Compare...	Compare...	Compare...

9-5 Exercises

GUIDED PRACTICE

SEE EXAMPLE 1

1. Personal Finance Fay and Kara each withdraw money from their savings accounts weekly, as shown. Compare the accounts by finding and interpreting slopes and *y*-intercepts.

Fay's Account

Weeks	0	1	2	3
Account Balance ($)	425	375	325	255

Kara's Account

SEE EXAMPLE 2

2. Biology A biologist tracked the hourly growth of two different strains of bacteria in the lab. Her data are shown below. Compare the number of bacteria by finding and interpreting the average rates of change from hour 0 to hour 4.

Bacteria A

Hours	Number of Bacteria
0	5
1	15
2	45
3	135
4	405

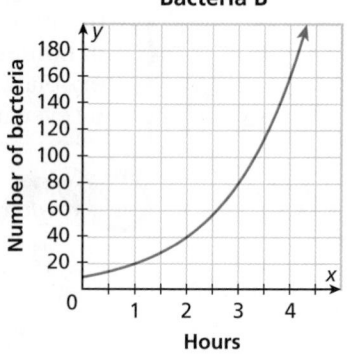

Bacteria B

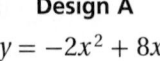

SEE EXAMPLE 3

3. **Architecture** An architect designs arch-shaped passageways in the form of a parabola. Models for two of his designs are shown at right. Compare the designs by finding and interpreting maximums, x-intercepts, and average rates of change over the interval [0, 2].

SEE EXAMPLE 4

4. **Business** A bicycle store has approximately 200 bicycles in stock. The store owner is considering plans for expanding his inventory. Plan A calls for an increase of 30 bicycles per year. Plan B calls for a 10% increase each year. Compare the plans.

Design A
$$y = -2x^2 + 8x$$

Design B

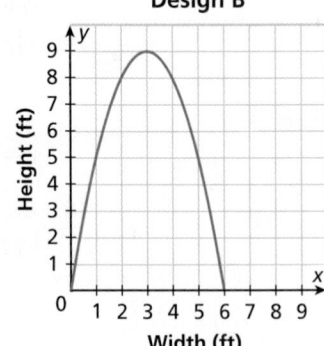

PRACTICE AND PROBLEM SOLVING

5. **Recreation** Kevin and Darius each hiked a mountain trail at different rates, as shown below. Compare the hikes by finding and interpreting slopes and y-intercepts.

Kevin's Hike

Time (h)	0	1	2	3
Distance from Camp (mi)	1.5	3.5	5.5	7.5

Darius's Hike
$$y = 2.2x + 1$$

6. **Anthropology** An archeologist used these functions to model the changing populations of two ancient cities as they grew in size. Compare the populations by finding and interpreting the average rates of change over the interval [0, 40].

City A

Area (mi²)	Population
0	0
10	31
20	89
30	164
40	252
50	353

City B

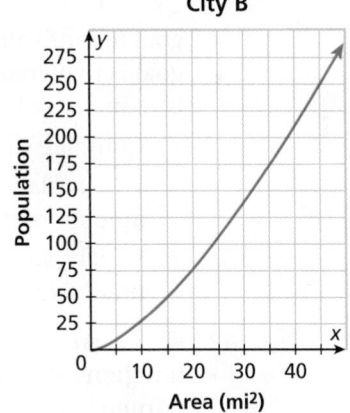

7. **Physics** Rhea's science teacher launched two model rockets straight up into the air. The functions that model the heights of the rockets are shown below. Compare the functions by finding and interpreting maximums, x-intercepts, and average rates of change over the x-interval [0, 2].

Rocket A
$$y = -16x^2 + 80x$$

Rocket B

Time (s)	0	1	2	3	4
Height (ft)	0	48	64	48	0

8. **Recreation** A summer boating camp has 75 boats. The camp director is considering two proposals for increasing the number of boats to match the increase in the number of campers. Proposal A recommends increasing the number of boats by 5 boats per year. Proposal B recommends a 5% increase each year. Compare the proposals.

9. Three functions are given below. Make a table of values for each function using nonnegative coordinates. Then graph all 3 functions on the same coordinate plane. Compare and interpret the tables, graphs, and rates of change over [0, 4].

   $y = 5x + 30$ $\qquad\qquad$ $y = 3 + 5^x$ $\qquad\qquad$ $y = 3x^2 + 5x$

10. **Business** The revenue of a company based on the price of its product is modeled by the function below.

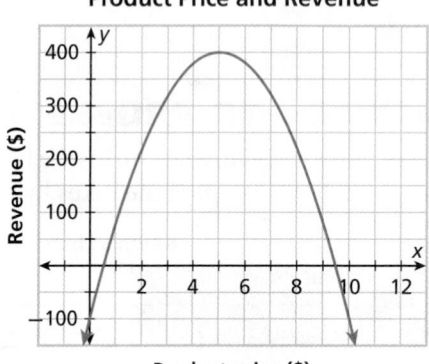

Product Price and Revenue

   a. Estimate the average rate of change over [0, 4].

   b. What price that will yield the maximum revenue?

11. **Critical Thinking** A karate center has 120 students. The director wants to set a goal to motivate her instructors to increase student enrollment. Under plan A, the goal is to increase the number of students by 12% each year. Under plan B, the goal is to increase the number of students by 20 each year.

   a. Compare the plans.

   b. Which plan should the director choose to double the enrollment in the shortest amount of time? Explain.

   c. Which plan should she use to triple the enrollment in the shortest amount of time? Explain.

12. **Write About It** Compare the characteristics of linear, quadratic, and exponential functions, including any of the following that are applicable: rate of change, x-intercept, and maximum/minimum. Explain how to decide which type of function is being shown on a graph and in a table.

13. Tanya has $2000 in her savings account. She wants to save more money. She is considering two savings plans. Under plan A, she will increase her account balance by $1000 per year. Under plan B, she will increase her account balance by 20% each year. How much more will she save with plan B after 10 years? Round your answer to the nearest dollar.

   Ⓐ $383 $\qquad\qquad\qquad\qquad$ Ⓒ $12,000

   Ⓑ $9,562 $\qquad\qquad\qquad\qquad$ Ⓓ $12,383

14. The equation for the motion of a model rocket fired straight up with an initial velocity of 64 feet per second is $h = 64t - 16t^2$. Which could be the graph of this function?

F
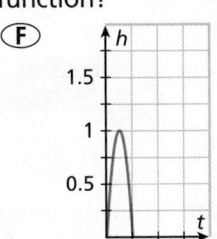

G
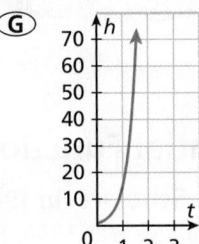

H
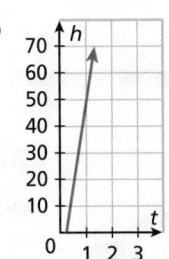

J
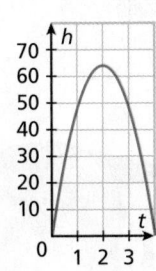

CHALLENGE AND EXTEND

15. Two functions are shown below.

Function A

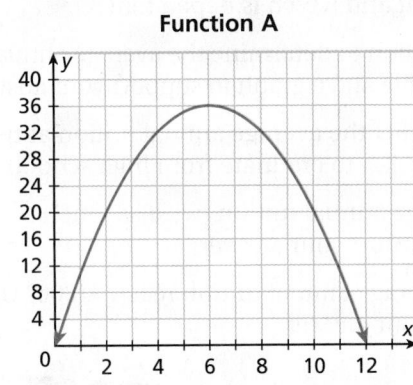

Function B

$$y = 12 - 2^x$$

a. Estimate the average rate of change over the intervals [0, 4], [0, 6], [4, 6], [7, 10], and [8, 12] for both functions.

b. Explain how the average rate of change varies for each function.

c. **What if...?** For function B, if y is doubled while x remains the same, what is the effect on the rate of change over [0, 4]?

MULTI-STEP TEST PREP

Make sense of problems and persevere in solving them.

Exponential Functions

Dollars for Scholars In 1980, the average annual tuition at two-year colleges was $350. Since then, the cost of tuition has increased by an average of 9% each year.

1. What type of function should you use to model this situation?

2. Write a function rule that models the annual growth in tuition at two-year colleges since 1980. Let 1980 be year zero in your function. Identify the variables, and tell which is independent and which is dependent.

3. Use your function to determine the average annual tuition in 2006. Use a table and a graph to support your answer.

4. Use your function to predict the average annual tuition at two-year colleges for the year you plan to graduate from high school.

5. In what year is the average annual tuition twice as much as in 1980? Use a table and a graph to support your answer.

6. In what year does the average annual tuition reach $1000? Use a table and a graph to support your answer.

Quiz for Lessons 9-3 Through 9-5

☑ **9-3** Exponential Growth and Decay

Write a function to model each situation. Then find the value of the function after the given amount of time.

1. Fiona's salary is $30,000, and she expects to receive a 3% raise each year; 10 years.

2. $2000 is invested at a rate of 4.5% compounded monthly; 3 years.

3. A $1200 computer is losing value at a rate of 20% per year; 4 years.

4. Strontium-90 has a half-life of 29 years. About how much strontium-90 will be left from a 100-mg sample after 290 years? Round your answer to the nearest thousandth.

☑ **9-4** Linear, Quadratic, and Exponential Models

Graph each data set. Which kind of model best describes the data?

5. $\{(-2, 5), (3, 10), (0, 1), (1, 2), (0.5, 1.25)\}$ **6.** $\{(0, 3), (2, 12), (-1, 1.5), (-3, 0.375), (4, 48)\}$

Look for a pattern in each data set to determine which kind of model best describes the data.

7. $\{(-2, -6), (-1, -5), (0, -4), (1, -3), (2, -2)\}$ **8.** $\{(-2, -24), (-1, -12), (0, -6), (1, -3)\}$

☑ **9-5** Comparing Functions

9. The rocket club launched two model rockets straight up into the air. The height of Rocket A can be modeled by the function $y = -16x^2 + 88x$. The function that models the height of the Rocket B is shown in the table below. Compare the functions by finding and interpreting maximums, x-intercepts, and average rates of change over the x-interval [0, 2].

Time (seconds) x	0	1	2	3	4
Height (feet) y	0	80	128	144	128

Vocabulary

common ratio

compound interest

exponential decay

exponential function

exponential growth

geometric sequence

half-life

Complete the sentences below with vocabulary words from the list above.

1. 3, 6, 12, 24, ... is an example of a(n) ___?___ .

2. A(n) ___?___ function has the form $y = a(1 - r)^t$, where $a > 0$.

3. In the formula $a_n = a_1 r^{n-1}$, the variable r represents the ___?___ .

4. $f(x) = 2^x$ is an example of a(n) ___?___ .

9-1 Geometric Sequences

EXAMPLE

■ What is the 10th term of the geometric sequence −6400, 3200, −1600, 800, ...?

Find the common ratio by dividing consecutive terms.

$\dfrac{3200}{-6400} = -0.5 \qquad \dfrac{-1600}{3200} = -0.5$

$a_n = a_1 r^{n-1}$ *Write the formula.*

$a_{10} = -6400(-0.5)^{10-1}$ *Substitute.*

$\phantom{a_{10}} = -6400(-0.5)^9$ *Simplify.*

$\phantom{a_{10}} = 12.5$

EXERCISES

Find the next three terms in each geometric sequence.

5. 1, 3, 9, 27, ...

6. 3, −6, 12, −24, ...

7. 80, 40, 20, 10, ...

8. −1, −4, −16, −64, ...

9. The first term of a geometric sequence is 4 and the common ratio is 5. What is the 10th term?

10. What is the 15th term of the geometric sequence 4, 12, 36, 108, ...?

9-2 Exponential Functions

- Tell whether the ordered pairs $\{(1, 4), (2, 16), (3, 36), (4, 64)\}$ satisfy an exponential function. Explain.

x	y
1	4
2	16
3	36
4	64

As the x-values increase by a constant amount, the y-values are not multiplied by a constant amount. This function is not exponential.

EXERCISES

Tell whether each set of ordered pairs satisfies an exponential function. Explain.

11. $\{(0, 1), (2, 9), (4, 81), (6, 729)\}$

12. $\{(-2, -8), (-1, -4), (0, 0), (1, 4)\}$

Graph each exponential function.

13. $y = 4^x$ **14.** $y = \left(\dfrac{1}{4}\right)^x$

9-3 Exponential Growth and Decay

EXAMPLE

- The value of a piece of antique furniture has been increasing at a rate of 2% per year. In 1990, its value was $800. Write an exponential growth function to model the situation. Then find the value of the furniture in the year 2010.

Step 1 $y = a(1 + r)^t$ *Write the formula.*

$y = 800(1 + 0.02)^t$ *Substitute.*

$y = 800(1.02)^t$ *Simplify.*

Step 2 $y = 800(1.02)^{20}$ *Substitute 20 for t.*

≈ 1188.76 *Simplify and round.*

The furniture's value will be $1188.76.

EXERCISES

15. The number of students in the book club is increasing at a rate of 15% per year. In 2001, there were 9 students in the book club. Write an exponential growth function to model the situation. Then find the number of students in the book club in the year 2008.

16. The population of a small town is decreasing at a rate of 4% per year. In 1970, the population was 24,500. Write an exponential decay function to model the situation. Then find the population in the year 2020.

EXAMPLE

■ Use the data in the table to describe how Jasmin's debt is changing. Then write a function that models the data. Use your function to predict Jasmin's debt after 8 years.

Jasmin's Debt	
Years	Debt ($)
1	130
2	260
3	520
4	1040

+1 ⟶ ×2 (between rows)

Jasmin's debt doubles every year.

For a constant change in time $(+1)$, there is a constant ratio of 2, so the data is exponential.

$y = ab^x$	*Write the general form.*
$y = a(2)^x$	*Substitute 2 for b.*
$130 = a(2)^1$	*Substitute (1, 130) for x and y.*
$a = 65$	*Solve for a.*
$y = 65(2)^x$	*Replace a and b in $y = ab^x$.*
$y = 65(2)^8$	*Substitute 8 for x.*
$y = 16,640$	*Simplify with a calculator.*

Jasmin's debt in 8 years will be $16,640.

EXERCISES

Graph each data set. Which kind of model best describes the data?

17. $\{(-2, -12), (-1, -3), (0, 0), (1, -3), (2, -12)\}$

18. $\{(-2, -2), (-1, 2), (0, 6), (1, 10), (2, 14)\}$

19. $\left\{\left(-2, -\frac{1}{4}\right), \left(-1, -\frac{1}{2}\right), (0, -1), (1, -2), (2, -4)\right\}$

Look for a pattern in each data set to determine which kind of model best describes the data.

20. $\{(0, 2), (1, 6), (2, 18), (3, 54), (4, 162)\}$

21. $\{(0, 0), (2, -20), (4, -80), (6, -180), (8, -320)\}$

22. $\{(-8, 5), (-4, 3), (0, 1), (4, -1), (8, -3)\}$

23. Write a function that models the data. Then use your function to predict how long the humidifier will produce steam with 10 quarts of water.

Input and Output of a Humidifier	
Water Volume (qt)	Steam Time (h)
3	4.5
4	6
5	7.5
6	9

9-5 Comparing Functions

EXAMPLE

Decide which linear function is increasing at a greater rate.

- Function 1 has x-intercept 4 and y-intercept –2.

- Function 2 includes the points in the table below.

x	−2	−1	0	1
y	−11	−6	−1	4

The points (4, 0) and (0, –2) are on the graph of Function 1. Its slope of is $\frac{0-(-2)}{4-0} = \frac{1}{2}$. The table for Function 2 shows that for each increase of 1 in the value of x there is an increase of 5 in the value of y. Its slope is 5. So, Function 2 is increasing more rapidly.

EXAMPLE

Use the given information to decide which quadratic function has the lesser minimum value.

- Function 1: The function whose equation is $y = 3x^2 - 12x + 1$.

- Function 2: The function whose graph is shown.

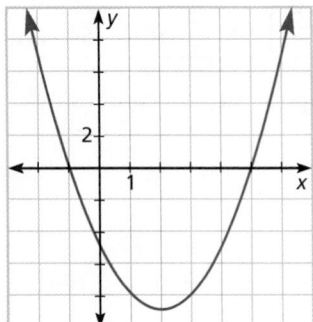

The minimum value of Function 1 is –11. It can be found by identifying the y-value of the vertex of its parabola. The minimum value of Function 2 can be seen on the graph of the function; it is –9. So, Function 1 has the lesser minimum value.

EXERCISES

24. Decide which linear function is increasing at a greater rate.

- Function 1 has x-intercept –7 and y-intercept 4.

- Function 2 includes the points in the table.

x	0	2	4	6
y	−8	−3	2	7

25. Use the given information to decide which quadratic function has the greater maximum value.

- Function 1: The function whose equation is $y = -x^2 + 4x + 2$.

- Function 2: The function whose graph is shown.

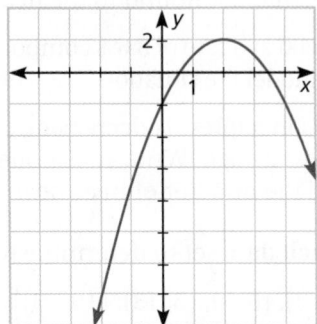

26. Michael is studying population changes in two types of birds living on an island. Compare the populations by finding and interpreting the average rates of change over the interval [0, 18]

Bird A

Time (months)	0	6	12	18
Population (thousands)	8.3	8.6	8.8	9.1

Bird B

$y = 3.6(1.06)^x$

CHAPTER TEST

Find the next three terms in each geometric sequence.

1. 2, 6, 18, 54, …

2. 4800, 2400, 1200, 600, …

3. −4, 20, −100, 500, …

4. Communication If school is cancelled, the school secretary calls 2 families. Each of those families calls 2 other families. In the third round of calls, each of the 4 families calls 2 more families. If this pattern continues, how many families are called in the seventh round of calls?

Graph each exponential function.

5. $y = -2(4)^x$

6. $y = 3(2)^x$

7. $y = 4\left(\dfrac{1}{2}\right)^x$

8. $-\left(\dfrac{1}{3}\right)^x$

9. A teacher is repeatedly enlarging a diagram on a photocopier. The function $f(x) = 3(1.25)^x$ represents the length of the diagram, in centimeters, after x enlargements. What is the length after 5 enlargements? Round to the nearest centimeter.

10. Chelsea invested $5600 at a rate of 3.6% compounded quarterly. Write a compound interest function to model the situation. Then find the balance after 6 years.

11. The number of trees in a forest is decreasing at a rate of 5% per year. The forest had 24,000 trees 15 years ago. Write an exponential decay function to model the situation. Then find the number of trees now.

Look for a pattern in each data set to determine which kind of model best describes the data.

12. $\{(-10, -17), (-5, -7), (0, 3), (5, 13), (10, 23)\}$

13. $\{(1, 3), (2, 9), (3, 27), (4, 81), (5, 243)\}$

14. Use the data in the table to describe how the bacteria population is changing. Then write a function that models the data. Use your function to predict the bacteria population after 10 hours.

Bacteria Population				
Time (h)	0	1	2	3
Bacteria	6	18	54	162

15. Greta is measuring how much two different candles burn over time. Compare the two candles by finding and interpreting slopes and y-intercepts.

- Candle 1 was 6 inches tall and burned for 1.5 hours.

- Candle 2 reached the heights at certain times shown in the table.

Time (hours)	0	0.5	1	1.5	2
Height (inches)	9	7.5	6	4.5	3

16. The information below models the population of fish living in two different lakes. Compare the populations by finding and interpreting the average rates of change over the interval [0, 50].

Fish in Lake A

Time (years)	0	10	30	50
Population (thousands)	32	33.3	36.1	39.1

Fish in Lake B

$y = 45(1.007)^x$

COLLEGE ENTRANCE EXAM PRACTICE

FOCUS ON SAT MATHEMATICS SUBJECT TESTS

Colleges use standardized test scores to confirm what your academic record indicates. Because courses and instruction differ from school to school, standardized tests are one way in which colleges try to compare students fairly when making admissions decisions.

You will need to use a calculator on the SAT Mathematics Subject Tests. If you do not already have a graphing calculator, consider getting one because it may give you an advantage when solving some problems. Spend time getting used to your calculator before the test.

You may want to time yourself as you take this practice test. It should take you about 6 minutes to complete.

---

1. Which function models a population of 450 that is increasing by 2% per year?

   (A) $y = 450(0.02)^t$

   (B) $y = 450(0.2)^t$

   (C) $y = 450(1.2)^t$

   (D) $y = 450(1.02)^t$

   (E) $y = 450(0.98)^t$

---

2. Which data set is best modeled by an exponential growth function?

   (A) {(2, 12), (4, 23), (6, 33), (8, 40)}

   (B) {(3, 0.1), (6, 0.2), (9, 0.3), (12, 0.4)}

   (C) {(−1, 2), (0, 8), (1, 32), (2, 128)}

   (D) {(−2, 12), (−1, 6), (0, 3), (1, 1.5)}

   (E) {(0, 0), (1, 3), (2, 12), (3, 27)}

---

3. Brandon has $1500 in his savings account. Under plan A, he will increase his balance by $800 per year. Under plan B, he will increase his balance by 25% each year. To the nearest dollar, how much more will he save with plan B after 10 years?

   (A) $383

   (B) $2,476

   (C) $4,470

   (D) $6,392

   (E) $7,162

---

4. The third term of a geometric sequence is 32 and the fifth term is 512. What is the eighth term of the sequence?

   (A) 544

   (B) 1232

   (C) 8192

   (D) 32,768

   (E) 2,097,152

---

5. A band releases a new CD and tracks its sales. The table shows the number of copies sold each week (in thousands). Which type of function best models this data?

CD Sales	
Week	Copies Sold (thousands)
1	129.5
2	155
3	179.5
4	203
5	225.5
6	247

   (A) Linear function

   (B) Quadratic function

   (C) Exponential function

   (D) Square-root function

   (E) Absolute-value function

Any Question Type: Spatial Reasoning

Some test questions include a three-dimensional figure. You must use spatial reasoning to correctly interpret the figure.

EXAMPLE 1

Which of the following shows the top view of the solid figure?

Ⓐ   Ⓑ   Ⓒ   Ⓓ

Notice that the isometric drawing shows three sides of the figure: the top, front, and right side. Use the isometric drawing to make a foundation plan of the figure.

Count the number of cubes at the widest part of the figure and at the longest part of the figure.

*The widest part is 3 cubes across.
The longest part is 4 cubes deep.*

Draw a 3-by-4 grid.

Each cube on the bottom level of the figure corresponds to a square on the grid.

Start at the front of the figure. Shade in each square of the grid that corresponds to a cube on the bottom level of the figure.

Using the foundation plan, you can see that choice B shows the top view of the solid.

Imagine that you are stacking blocks to help you to visualize the solid figure. Each square shown in the drawing represents a face of one block.

Read each test item and answer the questions that follow.

Item A

Multiple Choice Which solid is represented by these top, side, and front views?

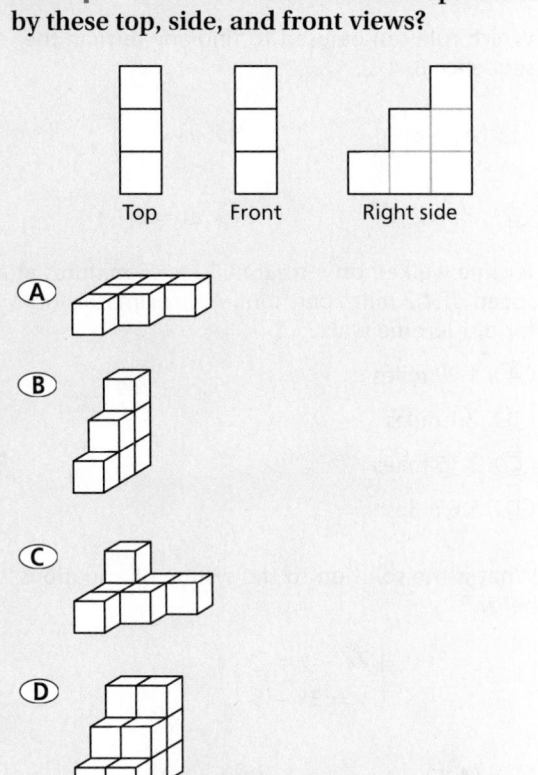

Top   Front   Right side

(A)

(B)

(C)

(D)

1. How many cubes can you see if you are looking down on the figure? How do you know?

2. How many cubes can you see if you are looking at the front of the figure? How do you know?

3. How many cubes high is the highest stack of the figure? Explain how you know.

4. Using your answers from Problems 1–3, what is the correct answer choice?

Item B

Short Response The drawing shows a foundation plan of a solid figure made of stacked cubes. The numbers in the squares identify the number of cubes in each stack. Draw a three-dimensional view of this solid figure.

2	4	6
2	2	3
2	1	1

5. Draw the top view of the figure.

6. If you were to look at the figure from the right or from the front, how many cubes high is the highest stack? Explain how you know.

7. A student drew this figure as his response. Do you agree that this is the correct drawing? If so, explain how you know. If not, what did the student do wrong?

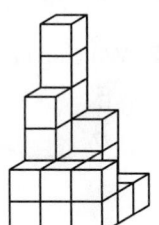

Item C

Short Response Draw the top view and front view of the solid figure.

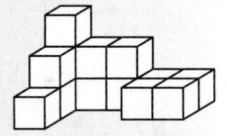

8. If you look down on the figure, how many cubes do you see?

9. Create a base plan or foundation plan for the figure.

10. Nolan drew his version of the top view of the figure. Is he correct? If not, show how you would change his drawing so that it is correct.

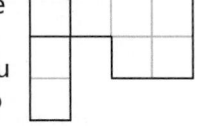

11. If you look at the figure from the front, how tall is the highest stack of cubes and how short is the shortest stack of cubes?

12. Draw the front view of the figure.

STANDARDIZED TEST PREP

Learn It Online
State Test Practice

CUMULATIVE ASSESSMENT

Multiple Choice

1. A sequence is defined by the rule $a_n = -3(2)^{n-1}$. What is the 5th term of the sequence?

(A) 5

(B) -30

(C) -48

(D) -216

2. Which could be the graph of $y = -2^x$?

(F)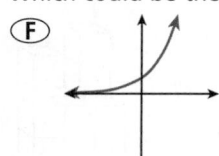

(G)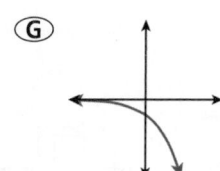

(H)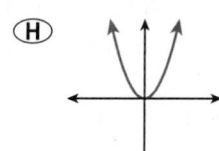

(J)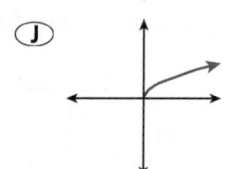

3. What is the slope of the line described by $4x - 3y = 12$?

(A) 4

(B) 3

(C) $\frac{4}{3}$

(D) $-\frac{3}{4}$

4. Which rule can be used to find any term in the sequence 8, 4, 2, 1, ...?

(F) $a_n = 8\left(\frac{1}{2}\right)^n$

(H) $a_n = \left(\frac{1}{2}\right)^{n-1}$

(G) $a_n = 2(1)^n$

(J) $a_n = 8\left(\frac{1}{2}\right)^{n-1}$

5. Jerome walked on a treadmill for 45 minutes at a speed of 4.2 miles per hour. Approximately how far did Jerome walk?

(A) 1.89 miles

(B) 2.1 miles

(C) 3.15 miles

(D) 5.6 miles

6. What is the solution to the system of equations below?

$$\begin{cases} 2x - y = 2 \\ y = 3x - 5 \end{cases}$$

(F) $(4, 6)$

(H) $(2, 1)$

(G) $(3, 4)$

(J) $(0, 2)$

7. What is the complete factorization of $2x^3 + 18x$?

(A) $2x(x^2 + 9)$

(B) $2x(x + 3)^2$

(C) $2x(x + 3)(x - 3)$

(D) $2(x^3 + 18)$

8. Which ordered pair lies on the graph of $y = 3(2)^{x+1}$?

(F) $(-1, 0)$

(H) $(1, 12)$

(G) $(0, 9)$

(J) $(3, 24)$

When a test item gives an equation to be solved, it may be quicker to work backward from the answer choices by substituting them into the equation. If time remains, check your answer by solving the equation.

9. Simplify the expression $4(2d - 1) - 6d$.

   Ⓐ $2d$

   Ⓑ $2d - 4$

   Ⓒ $-4d + 3$

   Ⓓ $2d - 1$

10. Which is an arithmetic sequence?

   I   3, 6, 9, 12, 15, …

   II 1, 10, 100, 1000, …

   III 4000, −2000, 1000, −500, …

   Ⓕ I only

   Ⓖ II and III

   Ⓗ I and III

   Ⓙ III only

Gridded Response

11. The function $f(x) = 30,000(0.8)^x$ gives the value of a vehicle, where x is the number of years after purchase. According to the function, what will be the value of the car in dollars 8 years after purchase? Round your answer to the nearest whole dollar.

12. The graph of $f(x)$ is shown below. How many zeros does $f(x)$ have?

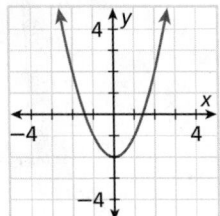

13. Rosalind purchased a sewing machine at a 20%-off sale. The original selling price of the machine was $340. What was the sale price in dollars?

14. Two planes leave an airport, one heading due north and the other heading due west. After several minutes, the first plane is 12 miles north of the airport, and the second plane is 15 miles west of the airport. Estimate the distance between the two planes to the nearest hundredth of a mile.

Short Response

15. The table shows the number of people newly infected by a certain virus with one person as the original source.

Week	1	2	3	4	5	6	7
Newly Infected People	1	3	9	27	81	243	729

   a. Is the data set best described by a linear function, a quadratic function, or an exponential function? Write a function to model the data.

   b. Use the function to predict the number of people that will become infected in the 10th week. Show your work.

16. Ella and Mia went on a camping trip. The total cost for their trip was $124, which the girls divided evenly. Ella paid for 4 nights at the campsite and $30 for supplies. Mia paid for 2 nights at the campsite and $46 for supplies.

   a. Write an equation that could be used to find the cost of one night's stay at the campsite. Explain what each variable in your equation represents.

   b. Solve your equation from part a to find the cost of one night's stay at the campsite. Show your work.

Extended Response

17. Regina is beginning a training program to prepare for a race. In week 1, she will run 3 miles during each workout. Each week thereafter, she plans to increase the distance of her runs by 20%.

   a. Write an equation to show the number of miles Regina plans to run during her workouts each week. Use the variable n to represent the week number.

   b. Make a table of values to show the distances of the runs in Regina's workouts for the first 6 weeks. Round each distance to the nearest hundredth of a mile. Then graph the points.

   c. Explain how to use your equation from part a to determine how many miles Regina will run during each workout in week 8. Then find this number.

   d. Explain how to the use your graph from part b to determine how many miles Regina will run during each workout in week 8. How does the graph verify the answer you found in part c?

CHAPTER 10 Data Analysis and Probability

COMMON CORE

Chapter Focus

• Organize and display data to answer questions.
• Use descriptive statistics to summarize data sets.
• Understand experimental probability and theoretical probability.
• Use probability to make appropriate predictions.

You're *the Designer*

Research studies are designed to gather and analyze data in order to answer questions. The results are displayed in tables and graphs.

Learn It Online
Chapter Project Online

ARE YOU READY?

✓ Vocabulary

Match each term on the left with a definition on the right.

1. difference

2. factor

3. natural numbers

4. ratio

5. sum

   A. the result of an addition

   B. a whole number that is multiplied by another whole number to get a product

   C. numbers that can be expressed in the form $\frac{a}{b}$, where a and b are both integers and $b \neq 0$

   D. the result of a subtraction

   E. a comparison of two quantities by division

   F. the counting numbers: 1, 2, 3, …

✓ Solve Proportions

Solve each proportion.

6. $\frac{3}{4} = \frac{x}{12}$

7. $\frac{15}{9} = \frac{3}{x}$

8. $\frac{10}{20} = \frac{x}{100}$

9. $\frac{250}{1500} = \frac{x}{100}$

✓ Compare and Order Real Numbers

Compare. Write <, >, or =.

10. 20 ▨ 13

11. $\frac{2}{3}$ ▨ $\frac{1}{2}$

12. $\frac{3}{4}$ ▨ $\frac{7}{9}$

13. 0.75 ▨ $\frac{9}{12}$

Order the numbers from least to greatest.

14. $\frac{1}{2}, \frac{4}{5}, \frac{1}{8}, \frac{3}{4}, \frac{2}{3}$

15. $0.12, \frac{2}{5}, \frac{3}{4}, 0.3, \frac{1}{3}$

✓ Multiply Decimals

Multiply.

16. 0.25×300

17. 0.5×4000

18. 0.05×200

19. 0.125×9600

✓ Divide Decimals

Divide.

20. $435 \div 10$

21. $32 \div 100$

22. $777 \div 1000$

23. $295 \div 10{,}000$

✓ Fractions, Decimals, and Percents

Write the equivalent decimal.

24. $\frac{3}{5}$

25. 45%

26. $\frac{3}{4}$

27. 8%

Write the equivalent percent.

28. $\frac{1}{4}$

29. 0.2

30. 0.36

31. $\frac{1}{10}$

Study Guide: Preview

Where You've Been

Previously, you
- read information from tables and graphs.
- added, subtracted, multiplied, and divided real numbers.
- worked with ratios and percents.

In This Chapter

You will study
- how to organize data in tables, graphs, and plots.
- how to find the central tendency of a data set by calculating mean, median, and mode.
- writing experimental and theoretical probability as ratios, percents, and decimals.

Where You're Going

You can use the skills in this chapter
- to present your findings from science laboratory experiments in an appropriate and accurate graphical form.
- to be more informed about statistical information in the news and not to be misled by how it is presented.

Key Vocabulary/Vocabulario

dependent events	sucesos dependientes
experimental probability	probabilidad experimental
frequency	frecuencia
independent events	sucesos independientes
median	mediana
outlier	valor extremo
probability	probabilidad
quartile	cuartil
theoretical probability	probabilidad teórica

Vocabulary Connections

To become familiar with some of the vocabulary terms in the chapter, consider the following. You may refer to the chapter, the glossary, or a dictionary if you like.

1. The *median strip* is the middle region that divides a highway in half. Use this knowledge to define **median** as it relates to a set of data.

2. The word **quartile** starts with the prefix *quart-*. What are some other words that start with the prefix *quart-*? What do they all have in common?

3. **Probability** is the chance something will happen. Based on your understanding of the words *experiment* and *theory*, compare and contrast the terms **experimental probability** and **theoretical probability**.

Study Strategy: Prepare for Your Final Exam

Math is a cumulative subject, so your final exam will probably cover all of the material you have learned since the beginning of the course. Preparation is essential for you to be successful on your final exam. It may help you to make a study timeline like the one below.

2 weeks before the final:

- Look at previous exams and homework to determine areas I need to focus on; rework problems that were incorrect or incomplete.

- Make a list of all formulas, definitions, and properties I need to know for the final.

- Create a practice exam using problems from the book that are similar to problems from each exam.

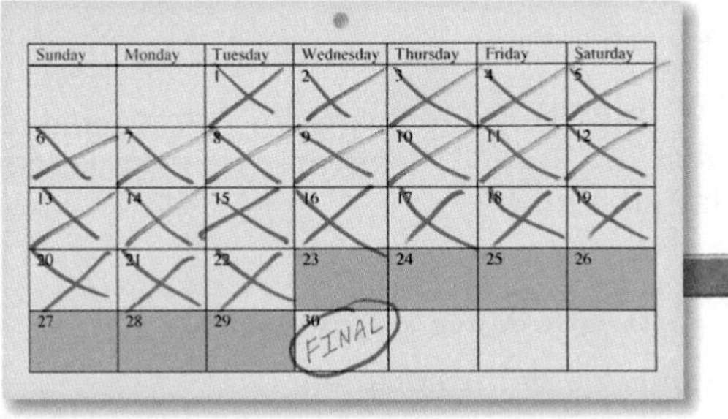

1 week before the final:

- Take the practice exam and check it. For each problem I miss, find 2 or 3 similar ones and work those.

- Work with a friend in the class to quiz each other on formulas, definitions, and properties from my list.

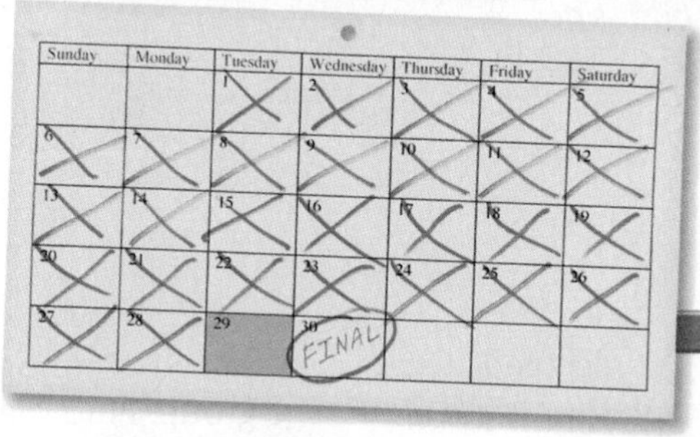

1 day before the final:

- Make sure I have pencils, calculator (check batteries!), and ruler.

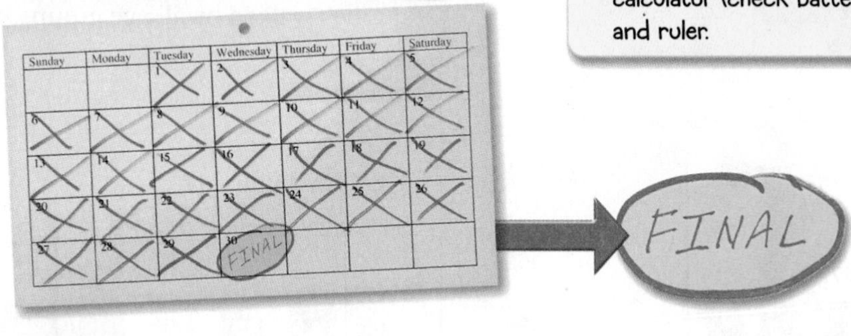

FINAL

Try This

1. Create a timeline that you will use to study for your final exam.

Bar and Circle Graphs

Data displayed in bar graphs and circle graphs can be used to solve equations. In these problems, parts of the graphs are missing.

Example 1

The top part of this graph was torn off. If Warren received 15% of the votes, how many votes did Adams receive?

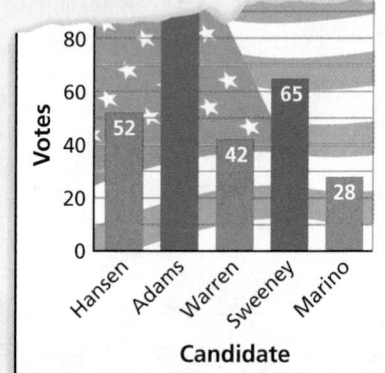

Step 1 Find the total number of votes. Let t represent the total.

15%	of	the total votes	is	42 votes.
0.15	•	t	=	42

$$0.15t = 42$$

$$t = 280 \text{ votes}$$

Step 2 Find the number of votes Adams received.

Let a represent the number of votes received by Adams. Let h, w, s, and m represent the number of votes received by Hansen, Warren, Sweeney, and Marino.

$$t = a + h + w + s + m$$
$$280 = a + 52 + 42 + 65 + 28 \quad \textit{Substitute the numbers shown on the graph.}$$
$$280 = a + 187 \quad \textit{Simplify the right side of the equation.}$$
$$\underline{-187 \qquad -187} \quad \textit{Subtract 187 from both sides.}$$
$$93 = a$$

Adams received 93 votes.

Try This

1. The missing bar is twice as tall as the bar for week 2. How many total miles did Kim bike in these five weeks?

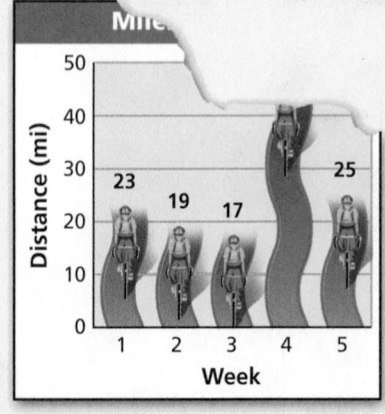

2. People aged 20–29 years walked 275 more miles than the oldest age group. Find the total miles walked by all age groups.

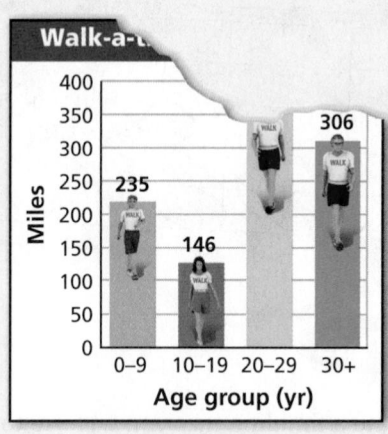

Remember that a circle graph represents all the data in a data set. The percent represented by each section is a part of the whole data set, so the sum of all the percents must be 100%.

Example 2

A survey asked people in a neighborhood to agree or disagree with the following statement:

"We need a traffic light at Jefferson Avenue and Third Street."

If 35% of the people disagreed with the statement, how many people had no opinion?

The number of people who answered "no opinion" is missing from the graph.

Opinion Survey

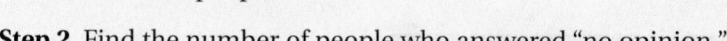

Step 1 Find the total number of people who answered the survey. Let t represent the total number of people.

35%	of	the total number of people	is	63 people.
0.35	•	t	=	63

$$0.35t = 63$$
$$t = 180 \text{ people}$$

Step 2 Find the number of people who answered "no opinion."

Let n represent the number of "no opinion" answers. Let d, s, g, and a represent the number of "disagree," "strongly disagree," "strongly agree," and "agree" answers.

$$t = n + d + s + g + a$$
$$180 = n + 63 + 45 + 36 + 27 \qquad \textit{Substitute the numbers shown on the graph.}$$
$$180 = n + 171 \qquad \textit{Simplify the right side of the equation.}$$
$$\underline{-171 \qquad -171} \qquad \textit{Subtract 171 from both sides.}$$
$$9 = n$$

There were 9 people who had no opinion.

Try This

3. The students in a junior high school voted on their choice for a field trip. Sixteen students voted for the natural history museum. How many students voted for the winning choice?

Field Trip Vote

Aquarium 25% Zoo 20%

Planetarium ? Museum 20%

4. At the fall dance recital, 40% of the tickets were sold to adults. What percent of the sales were to seniors?

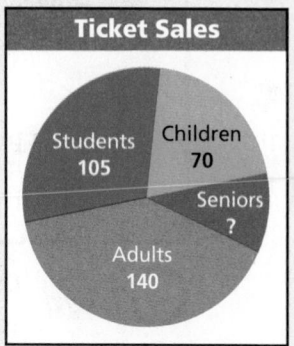

Ticket Sales

Students 105 Children 70

Seniors ?

Adults 140

10-1 Organizing and Displaying Data

COMMON CORE

CC.9-12.S.ID.1 Represent data with plots on the real number line (dot plots, histograms, and box plots).

Objectives
Organize data in tables and graphs.

Choose a table or graph to display data.

Vocabulary
bar graph
line graph
circle graph

Who uses this?
Nutritionists can display health information about food in bar graphs.

Bar graphs, line graphs, and *circle graphs* can be used to present data in a visual way.

A **bar graph** displays data with vertical or horizontal bars. Bar graphs are a good way to display data that can be organized into categories. Using a bar graph, you can quickly compare the categories.

EXAMPLE 1 Reading and Interpreting Bar Graphs

Use the graph to answer each question.

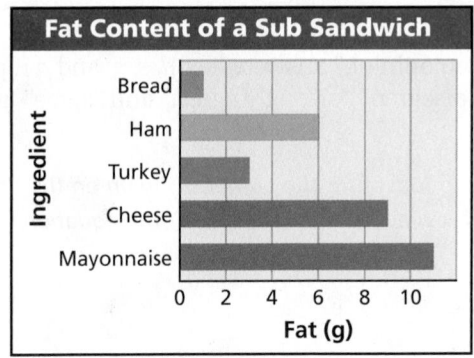

Fat Content of a Sub Sandwich

A Which ingredient contains the most fat?
mayonnaise   *The bar for mayonnaise is the longest.*

B How many more grams of fat are in ham than in turkey?
$6 - 3 = 3$ *There are 6 grams of fat in ham and 3 grams of fat in turkey.*

C How many total fat grams are in this sandwich?
$1 + 6 + 3 + 9 + 11 = 30$ *Add the number of fat grams for each ingredient.*

D What percent of the total fat grams in this sandwich are from turkey?
$\frac{3}{30} = \frac{1}{10} = 10\%$ *Out of 30 total fat grams, 3 fat grams are from turkey.*

Use the graph to answer each question.
1a. Which ingredient contains the least amount of fat?
1b. Which ingredients contain at least 8 grams of fat?

Victoria Smith/HMH

A double-bar graph can be used to compare two data sets. A double-bar graph has a key to distinguish between the two sets of data.

EXAMPLE 2 **Reading and Interpreting Double Bar Graphs**

Use the graph to answer each question.

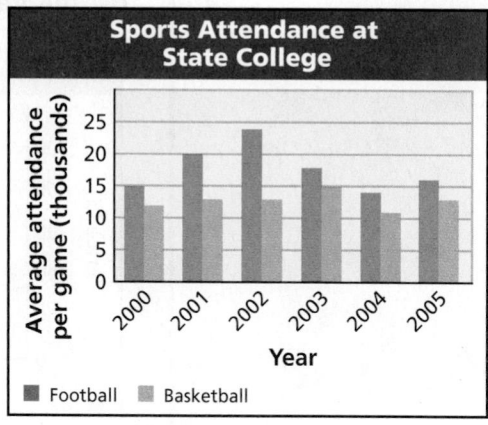

A In which year did State College have the greatest average attendance for basketball?

2003

Find the tallest orange bar.

B On average, how many more people attended a football game than a basketball game in 2001?

$20,000 - 13,000 = 7000$

Find the height of each bar for 2001 and subtract.

2. Use the graph to determine which years had the same average basketball attendance. What was the average attendance for those years?

A **line graph** displays data using line segments. Line graphs are a good way to display data that changes over a period of time.

EXAMPLE 3 **Reading and Interpreting Line Graphs**

Use the graph to answer each question.

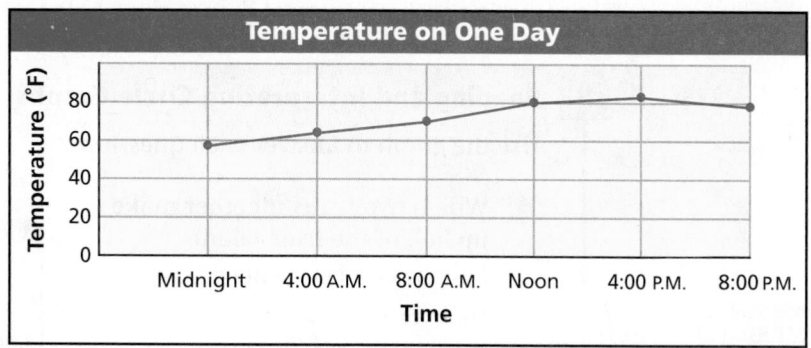

A At what time was the temperature the warmest?

4:00 P.M.   *Identify the highest point.*

B During which 4-hour time period did the temperature increase the most?

From 8:00 A.M. to noon   *Look for the segment with the greatest positive slope.*

3. Use the graph to estimate the difference in temperature between 4:00 A.M. and noon.

A double-line graph can be used to compare how two related data sets change over time. A double-line graph has a key to distinguish between the two sets of data.

EXAMPLE 4 **Reading and Interpreting Double-Line Graphs**

Use the graph to answer each question.

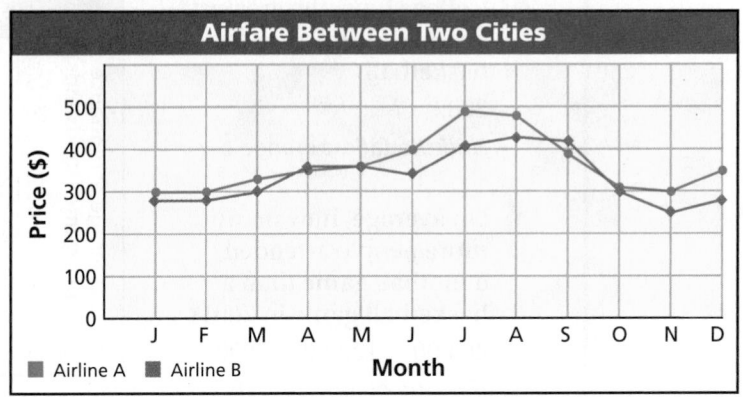

A In which month(s) did airline B charge more than airline A?

April and September   *Identify the points when the purple line is higher than the blue line.*

B During which month(s) did the airlines charge the same airfare?

May   *Look for the point where the data points overlap.*

 **4.** Use the graph to describe the general trend of the data.

A **circle graph** shows parts of a whole. The entire circle represents 100% of the data and each sector represents a percent of the total. Circle graphs are good for comparing each category of data to the whole set.

EXAMPLE 5 **Reading and Interpreting Circle Graphs**

Use the graph to answer each question.

A Which two fruits together make up half of the fruit salad?

bananas and strawberries

Look for two fruits that together make up half of the circle.

Reading Math

The sections of a circle graph are called *sectors*.

B Which fruit is used more than any other?

cantaloupe

Look for the largest sector of the graph.

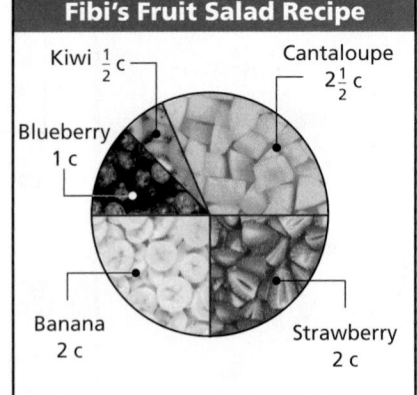

 **5.** Use the graph to determine what percent of the fruit salad is cantaloupe.

Sam Dudgeon/HMH

EXAMPLE **6** **Choosing and Creating an Appropriate Display**

Use the given data to make a graph. Explain why you chose that type of graph.

A

Livestock Show Entries	
Animal	**Number**
Chicken	38
Goat	10
Horse	32
Pig	12
Sheep	25

A bar graph is appropriate for this data because it will be a good way to compare categories.

Step 1 Determine an appropriate scale and interval. The scale must include all of the data values. The scale is separated into equal parts, called intervals.

Step 2 Use the data to determine the lengths of the bars. Draw bars of equal width. The bars should not touch.

Step 3 Title the graph and label the horizontal and vertical scales.

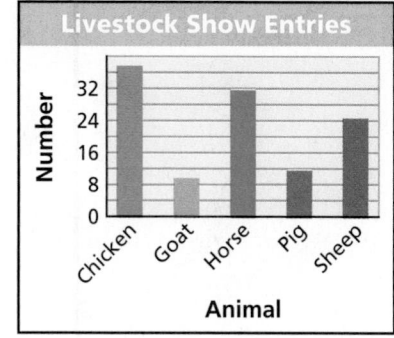

B

Division of Crops	
Crop	**Area (acres)**
Corn	70
Fallow	50
Mixed vegetables	10
Soybeans	40
Wheat	30

A circle graph is appropriate for this data because it shows categories as parts of a whole.

Step 1 Calculate the percent of the total represented by each category.

Corn: $\frac{70}{200} = 0.35 = 35\%$

Soybeans: $\frac{40}{200} = 0.2 = 20\%$

Fallow: $\frac{50}{200} = 0.25 = 25\%$

Wheat: $\frac{30}{200} = 0.15 = 15\%$

Mixed vegetables: $\frac{10}{200} = 0.05 = 5\%$

Step 2 Find the angle measure for each sector of the graph. Since there are 360° in a circle, multiply each percent by 360°.

Corn: $0.35 \times 360° = 126°$
Fallow: $0.25 \times 360° = 90°$
Mixed vegetables: $0.05 \times 360° = 18°$
Soybeans: $0.2 \times 360° = 72°$
Wheat: $0.15 \times 360° = 54°$

Step 3 Use a compass to draw a circle. Mark the center and use a straightedge to draw one radius. Then use a protractor to draw each central angle.

Step 4 Title the graph and label each sector.

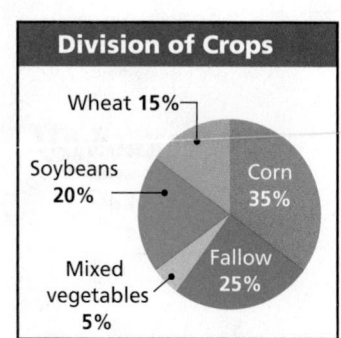

Use the given data to make a graph. Explain why you chose that type of graph.

  C

Chinnick College Enrollment	
Year	Students
1930	586
1955	2,361
1980	15,897
2005	21,650

A line graph is appropriate for this data because it will show the change in enrollment over a period of time.

Step 1 Determine the scale and interval for each set of data. Time should be plotted on the horizontal axis because it is independent.

Step 2 Plot a point for each pair of values. Connect the points using line segments.

Step 3 Title the graph and label the horizontal and vertical scales.

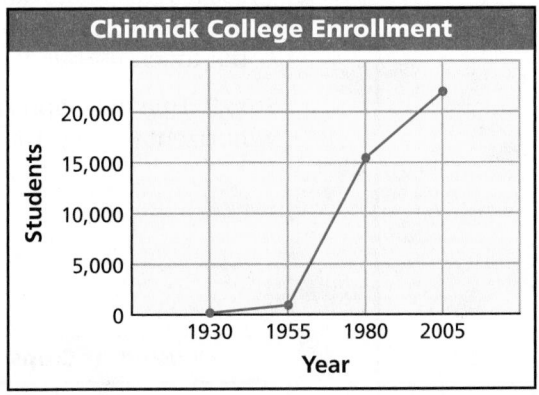

6. Use the given data to make a graph. Explain why you chose that type of graph.

The data below shows how Vera spends her time during a typical 5-day week during the school year.

Vera's Schedule					
Activity	Sleeping	Eating	School	Sports	Homework	Other
Time (h)	45	8	30	10	10	17

MATHEMATICAL PRACTICES

THINK AND DISCUSS

1. What are some comparisons you can make by looking at a bar graph?

2. Name some key components of a good line graph.

3. **GET ORGANIZED** Copy and complete the graphic organizer. In each box, tell which kind of graph is described.

Know it!
Note

Graph Type
- Compares categories
- Shows change over time
- Shows how a whole is divided in parts

Exercises

GUIDED PRACTICE

Vocabulary Use the vocabulary from this lesson to answer the following questions.

1. In a *circle graph*, what does each sector represent?

2. In a *line graph*, how does the slope of a line segment relate to the rate of change?

SEE EXAMPLE 1 Use the bar graph for Exercises 3 and 4.

3. Estimate the total number of animals at the shelter.

4. There are 3 times as many ___?___ as ___?___ at the animal shelter.

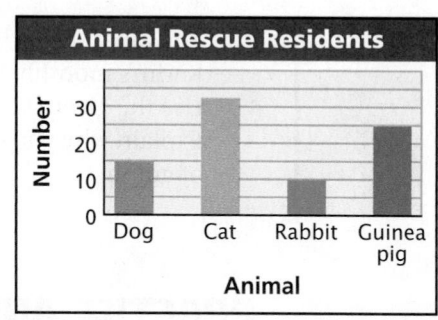

SEE EXAMPLE 2 Use the double-bar graph for Exercises 5–7.

5. About how much more is a club level seat at stadium A than at stadium B?

6. Which type of seat is the closest in price at the two stadiums?

7. Describe one relationship between the ticket prices at stadium A and stadium B.

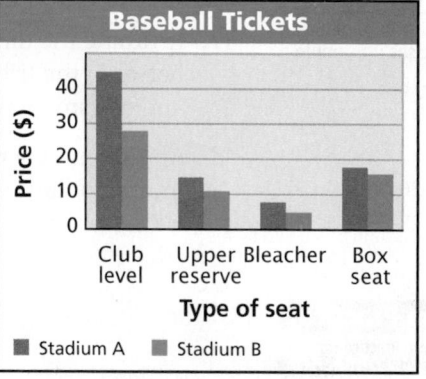

SEE EXAMPLE 3 Use the line graph for Exercises 8 and 9.

8. Estimate the number of tickets sold during the week of the greatest sales.

9. Which one-week period of time saw the greatest change in sales?

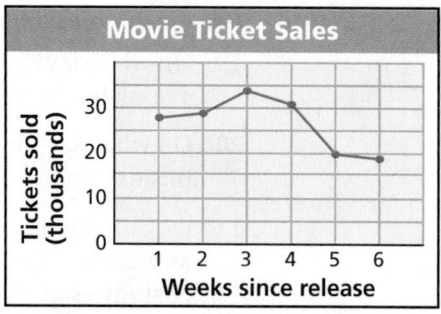

SEE EXAMPLE 4 Use the double-line graph for Exercises 10–12.

10. When was the support for the two candidates closest?

11. Estimate the difference in voter support for the two candidates five weeks before the election.

12. Describe the general trend(s) of voter support for the two candidates.

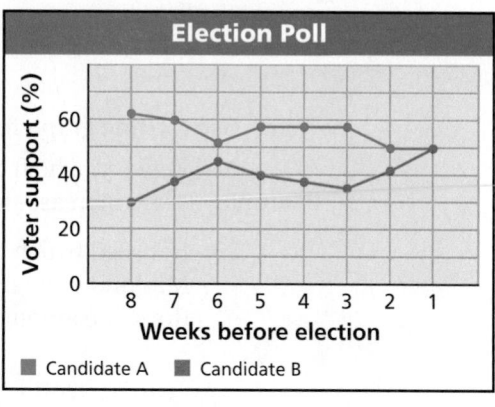

Use the circle graph for Exercises 13–15.

13. Which color is least represented in the ball playpen?

14. There are 500 balls in the playpen. How many are yellow?

15. Which two colors are approximately equally represented in the ball playpen?

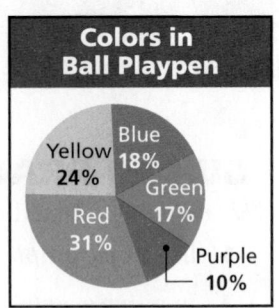

Colors in Ball Playpen

Yellow 24%
Blue 18%
Green 17%
Red 31%
Purple 10%

16. The table shows the breakdown of Karim's monthly budget of $100. Use the given data to make a graph. Explain why you chose that type of graph.

Item/Activity	Spending ($)
Clothing	35
Food	25
Entertainment	25
Other	15

PRACTICE AND PROBLEM SOLVING

Independent Practice

For Exercises	See Example
17–18	1
19–21	2
22–23	3
24–26	4
27–28	5
29	6

Extra Practice

See Extra Practice for more Skills Practice and Applications Practice exercises.

Use the bar graph for Exercises 17 and 18.

17. Estimate the difference in population between the tribes with the largest and the smallest population.

18. Approximately what percent of the total population shown in the table is Cherokee?

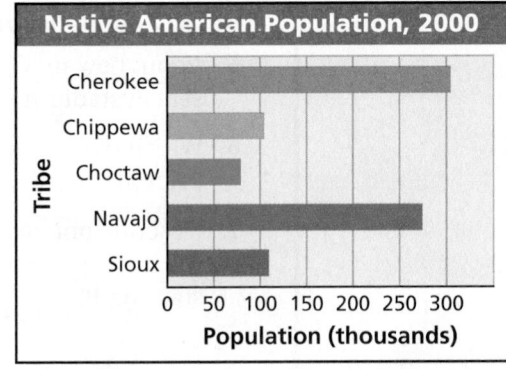

Native American Population, 2000

Source: U.S. Census Bureau

Use the double bar graph for Exercises 19–21.

19. On what day did Ray do the most overall business?

20. On what day did Ray have the busiest lunch?

21. On Sunday, about how many times as great was the number of dinner customers as the number of lunch customers?

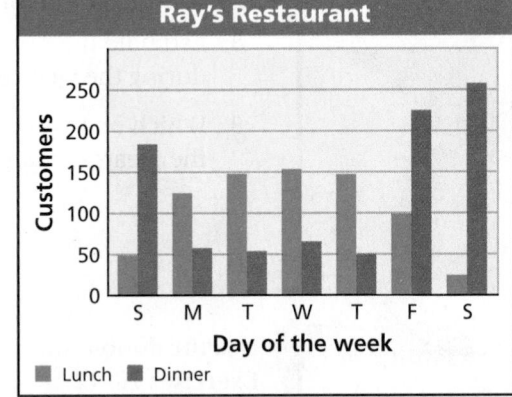

Ray's Restaurant

■ Lunch ■ Dinner

Use the line graph for Exercises 22 and 23.

22. Between which two games did Marlon's score increase the most?

23. Between which three games did Marlon's score increase by about the same amount?

Marlon's Video Game Scores

Use the double-line graph for Exercises 24–26.

24. What was the average value per share of Juan's two stocks in July 2004?

25. Which stock's value changed the most over any time period?

26. Describe the trend of the values of both stocks.

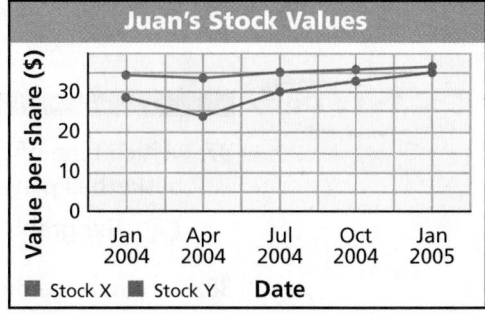

Use the circle graph for Exercises 27 and 28.

27. About what percent of the total number of cars are hopper cars?

28. About what percent of the total number of cars are gondola or tank cars?

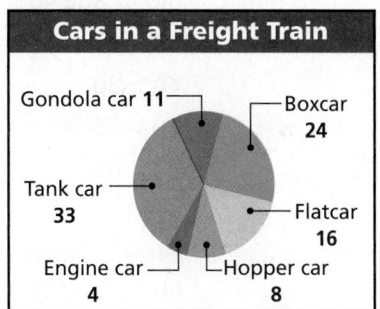

29. The table shows the weight of twin babies at various times from birth to four weeks old. Use the given data to make a graph. Explain why you chose that type of graph.

Age (days)	Boy's Weight (lb)	Girl's Weight (lb)
1	5.3	5.7
3	5.0	5.2
7	5.5	5.9
14	6.2	6.8
28	7.9	7.5

Write *bar, double-bar, line, double-line*, or *circle* to indicate the type of graph that would best display the data described.

30. attendance at a carnival each year over a ten-year period

31. attendance at two different carnivals each year over a ten-year period

32. attendance at five different carnivals during the same year

33. attendance at a carnival by age group as it relates to total attendance

34. **Critical Thinking** Give an example of real-world data that would best be displayed by each type of graph: line graph, circle graph, double-bar graph.

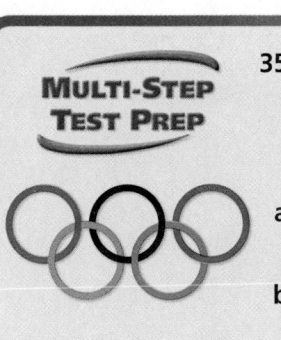

MULTI-STEP TEST PREP

35. The first modern Olympic Games took place in 1896 in Athens, Greece. The circle graph shows the total number of medals won by several countries at the Olympic Games of 1896.

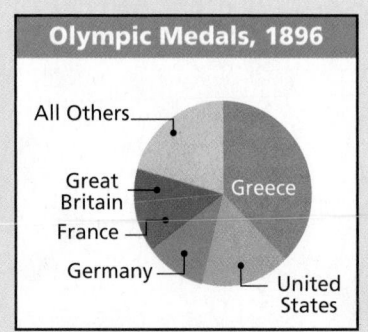

a. Which country won the most medals? Estimate the percent of the medals won by this country.

b. Which country won the second most medals? Estimate the percent of the medals won by this country.

36. Write About It Explain how you could use a line graph to make predictions.

37. Which type of graph would best display the contribution of each high school basketball player to the team, in terms of points scored?

(A) Bar graph   (B) Line graph   (C) Double-line graph   (D) Circle graph

38. At what age did Marianna have 75% more magazine subscriptions than she did at age 40?

(F) 25

(G) 30

(H) 35

(J) 45

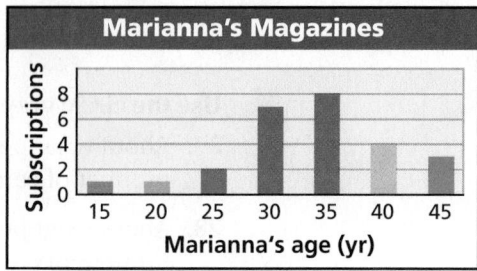

39. Short Response The table shows the number of students in each algebra class. Make a graph to display the data. Explain why you chose that type of graph.

Teacher	Students
Mr. Abrams	34
Ms. Belle	29
Mr. Marvin	25
Ms. Swanson	27

CHALLENGE AND EXTEND

Students and teachers at Lauren's school went on one of three field trips.

40. On which trip were there more boys than girls?

41. A total of 60 people went to the museum. Estimate the number of girls who went to the museum.

42. Explain why it is not possible to determine whether fewer teachers went to the museum than to the zoo or the opera.

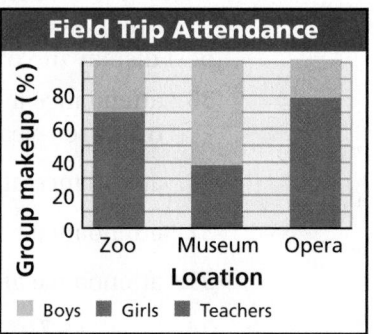

COMMON CORE

10-2 Frequency and Histograms

CC.9-12.S.ID.1 Represent data with plots on the real number line (dot plots, histograms, and box plots).

Objectives
Create stem-and-leaf plots.

Create frequency tables and histograms.

Vocabulary
stem-and-leaf plot
frequency
frequency table
histogram
cumulative frequency

Why learn this?
Stem-and-leaf plots can be used to organize data, like the number of students in elective classes. (See Example 1.)

A **stem-and-leaf plot** arranges data by dividing each data value into two parts. This allows you to see each data value.

The digits other than the last digit of each value are called a stem. ⟶ $2 | 3$ ⟵ The last digit of a value is called a leaf.

Key: 2|3 means 23 ⟵ The key tells you how to read each value.

EXAMPLE **1** Making a Stem-and-Leaf Plot

A The numbers of students in each of the elective classes at a school are given below. Use the data to make a stem-and-leaf plot.

24, 14, 12, 25, 32, 18, 23, 24, 9, 18, 34, 28, 24, 27

Number of Students in Elective Classes

Stem	Leaves
0	9
1	2 4 8 8
2	3 4 4 4 5 7 8
3	2 4

Key: 2|3 means 23

The *tens digits* are the stems.

The *ones digits* are the leaves. List the leaves from least to greatest within each row.

Title the graph and add a key.

Writing Math

Stems are always consecutive numbers. In Example 1B, neither player has scores that start with 15, so there are no leaves in that row.

B Marty's and Bill's scores for ten games of bowling are given below. Use the data to make a back-to-back stem-and-leaf plot.

Marty: 137, 149, 167, 134, 121, 127, 143, 123, 168, 162
Bill: 129, 138, 141, 124, 139, 160, 149, 145, 128, 130

Bowling Scores

Marty		Bill
7 3 1	12	4 8 9
7 4	13	0 8 9
9 3	14	1 5 9
	15	
8 7 2	16	0

Key: |14|1 means 141
3|14| means 143

The *first two digits* are the stems.

The *ones digits* are the leaves.

Put Marty's scores on the left side and Bill's scores on the right.

Title the graph and add a key.

The graph shows that three of Marty's scores were higher than Bill's highest score.

1. The temperatures in degrees Celsius for two weeks are given below. Use the data to make a stem-and-leaf plot.

7, 32, 34, 31, 26, 27, 23, 19, 22, 29, 30, 36, 35, 31

Tom Stewart/CORBIS

The **frequency** of a data value is the number of times it occurs. A **frequency table** shows the frequency of each data value. If the data is divided into intervals, the table shows the frequency of each interval.

EXAMPLE 2 Making a Frequency Table

The final scores for each golfer in a tournament are given below. Use the data to make a frequency table with intervals.

77, 71, 70, 82, 75, 76, 72, 70, 77, 74, 71, 75, 68, 72, 75, 74

Step 1 Identify the least and greatest values.

The least value is 68. The greatest value is 82.

Step 2 Divide the data into equal intervals.

For this data set, use an interval of 3.

Step 3 List the intervals in the first column of the table. Count the number of data values in each interval and list the count in the last column. Give the table a title.

Golf Tournament Scores	
Scores	**Frequency**
68–70	3
71–73	4
74–76	6
77–79	2
80–82	1

 **2.** The numbers of days of Maria's last 15 vacations are listed below. Use the data to make a frequency table with intervals.

4, 8, 6, 7, 5, 4, 10, 6, 7, 14, 12, 8, 10, 15, 12

A **histogram** is a bar graph used to display the frequency of data divided into equal intervals. The bars must be of equal width and should touch, but not overlap.

EXAMPLE 3 Making a Histogram

Use the frequency table in Example 2 to make a histogram.

Step 1 Use the scale and interval from the frequency table.

Step 2 Draw a bar for the number of scores in each interval.

All bars should be the same width. The bars should touch, but not overlap.

Step 3 Title the graph and label the horizontal and vertical scales.

Helpful Hint

The intervals in a histogram must be of equal size.

 **3.** Make a histogram for the number of days of Maria's last 15 vacations.

4, 8, 6, 7, 5, 4, 10, 6, 7, 14, 12, 8, 10, 15, 12

Cumulative frequency shows the frequency of all data values less than or equal to a given value. You could just count the number of values, but if the data set has many values, you might lose track. Recording the data in a cumulative frequency table can help you keep track of the data values as you count.

EXAMPLE 4 **Making a Cumulative Frequency Table**

The heights in inches of the players on a school basketball team are given below.

72, 68, 71, 70, 73, 69, 79, 76, 72, 75, 72, 74, 68, 70, 69, 75, 72, 71, 73, 76

a. Use the data to make a cumulative frequency table.

Step 1 Choose intervals for the first column of the table.

Step 2 Record the frequency of values in each interval for the second column.

Step 3 Add the frequency of each interval to the frequencies of all the intervals before it. Put that number in the third column of the table.

Step 4 Title the table.

Basketball Players' Heights		
Height (in.)	Frequency	Cumulative Frequency
68–70	6	6
71–73	8	14
74–76	5	19
77–79	1	20

b. How many players have heights under 74 in?

All heights under 74 in. are displayed in the first two rows of the table, so look at the cumulative frequency shown in the second row.
There are 14 players with heights under 74 in.

4. The numbers of vowels in each sentence of a short essay are listed below.

33, 36, 39, 37, 34, 35, 43, 35, 28, 32, 36, 35, 29, 40, 33, 41, 37

a. Use the data to make a cumulative frequency table.

b. How many sentences contain 35 vowels or fewer?

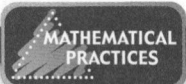

THINK AND DISCUSS

1. In a stem-and-leaf plot, the number of _____?_____ is always the same as the number of data values. (*stems* or *leaves*)

2. Explain how to make a histogram from a stem-and-leaf plot.

3. GET ORGANIZED Copy and complete the graphic organizer.

Bar Graphs vs Histograms

How are they alike? | How are they different?

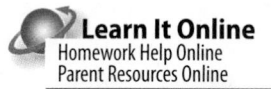

GUIDED PRACTICE

1. **Vocabulary** A(n) ____?____ is a data display that shows individual data values. (*stem-and-leaf plot* or *histogram*)

SEE EXAMPLE **1**

2. **Sports** The ages of professional basketball players at the time the players were recruited are given. Use the data to make a stem-and-leaf plot.

Ages When Recruited
21   23   21   18   22   19   24   22   21   22   20   21

3. **Weather** The average monthly rainfall for two cities (in inches) is given below. Use the data to make a back-to-back stem-and-leaf plot.

Average Monthly Rainfall (in.)											
Austin, TX	1.9	2.4	1.9	3.0	3.6	3.3	1.9	2.1	3.2	3.5	2.2	2.3
New York, NY	3.3	3.1	3.9	3.7	4.2	3.3	4.1	4.1	3.6	3.3	4.2	3.6

SEE EXAMPLE **2**

4. **Sports** The finishing times of runners in a 5K race, to the nearest minute, are given. Use the data to make a frequency table with intervals.

Finishing Times in 5K Race (to the nearest minute)
19   25   23   29   32   30   21   22   24
19   28   26   31   34   30   28   25   24

SEE EXAMPLE **3**

5. **Biology** The breathing intervals of gray whales are given. Use the frequency table to make a histogram for the data.

Breathing Intervals (min)	
Interval	**Frequency**
5–7	4
8–10	7
11–13	7
14–16	8

SEE EXAMPLE **4**

6. The scores made by a group of eleventh-grade students on the mathematics portion of the SAT are given.

Scores on Mathematics Portion of SAT
520   560   720   690   540   630   790   540
600   580   710   500   540   660   630

   a. Use the data to make a cumulative frequency table.

   b. How many students scored 650 or higher on the mathematics portion of the SAT?

PRACTICE AND PROBLEM SOLVING

7. The numbers of people who visited a park each day over two weeks during different seasons are given below. Use the data to make a back-to-back stem-and-leaf plot.

Visitors to a Park													
Summer	25	25	26	27	27	57	59	22	23	29	22	23	54	53
Winter	11	12	13	9	30	27	4	19	14	19	21	33	35	9

Independent Practice

For Exercises	See Example
7–8	1
9	2
10	3
11	4

Extra Practice

See Extra Practice for more Skills Practice and Applications Practice exercises.

8. **Weather** The daily high temperatures in degrees Fahrenheit in a town during one month are given. Use the data to make a stem-and-leaf plot.

Daily High Temperatures (°F)									
68	72	79	77	70	72	75	71	64	64
68	62	70	71	78	83	83	87	91	89
87	75	73	70	69	69	62	58	71	76

9. The overall GPAs of several high school seniors are given. Use the data to make a frequency table with intervals.

Overall GPAs								
3.6	2.9	3.1	3.0	2.5	2.6	3.8	2.9	
2.2	2.9	3.1	3.3	3.6	3.0	2.3	2.8	2.9

10. **Chemistry** The atomic masses of the nonmetal elements are given in the table. Use the frequency table to make a histogram for the data.

Atomic Masses of Nonmetal Elements					
Interval	0–49.9	50–99.9	100–149.9	150–199.9	200–249.9
Frequency	11	3	2	0	2

11. The numbers of pretzels found in several samples of snack mix are given in the table.

   a. Use the data to make a cumulative frequency table.

   b. How many samples of snack mix had fewer than 42 pretzels?

Numbers of Pretzels				
42	39	39	38	40
41	44	42	38	44
47	36	40	40	43	38

Automobiles

Solar cars usually weigh between 330 and 880 pounds. A conventional car weighs over 4000 pounds.

12. **Automobiles** The table shows gas mileage for the most economical cars in July 2004, including three hybrids.

Gas Mileage of Economical Cars									
Mileage in City (mi/gal)	32	60	48	38	36	60	35	38	32
Mileage on Highway (mi/gal)	38	51	47	46	47	66	43	46	40

Make a back-to-back stem-and-leaf plot for the data.

13. Damien's math test scores are given in the table:

   a. Make a stem-and-leaf plot of Damien's test scores.

   b. Make a histogram of the test scores using intervals of 5.

   c. Make a histogram of the test scores using intervals of 10.

   d. Make a histogram of the test scores using intervals of 20.

   e. How does the size of the interval affect the appearance of the histogram?

   f. **Write About It** Which histogram makes Damien's grades look highest? Explain.

Damien's Math Test Scores		
75	84	68
72	59	88
72	77	81
84	60	70

14. ///ERROR ANALYSIS/// Two students made stem-and-leaf plots for the following data: 530, 545, 550, 555, 570. Which is incorrect? Explain the error.

A

Stem	Leaves
53	0
54	5
55	0 5
57	0

Key: 52|5 means 525

B

Stem	Leaves
53	0
54	5
55	0 5
56	
57	0

Key: 52|5 means 525

15. The 2004 Olympic results for women's weightlifting in the 48 kg weight class are 210, 205, 200, 190, 187.5, 182.5, 180, 177.5, 175, 172.5, 170, 167.5, and 165, measured in kilograms. Medals are awarded to the athletes who can lift the most weight.

   a. Create a frequency table beginning at 160 and using intervals of 10 kg.
   b. Create a histogram of the data.
   c. Tara Cunningham from the United States lifted 172.5 kg. Did she win a medal? How do you know?

16. **Entertainment** The top ten movies in United States theaters for the weekend of June 25–27, 2004, grossed the following amounts (in millions of dollars). Create a histogram for the data. Make the first interval 5–9.9.

Ticket Sales (million $)				
23.9	19.7	18.8	13.5	13.1
11.2	10.2	7.5	6.1	5.1

17. **Critical Thinking** Margo's homework assignment is to make a data display of some data she finds in a newspaper. She found a frequency table with the given intervals.

Explain why Margo must be careful when drawing the bars of the histogram.

Age
Under 18
18–30
31–54
55 and older

TEST PREP

18. What data value occurs most often in the stem-and-leaf plot?

   Ⓐ 7
   Ⓒ 47
   Ⓑ 4.7
   Ⓓ 777

Stem	Leaves
3	2 3 4 4 7 9
4	0 1 5 7 7 7 8
5	1 2 2 3

Key: 3|2 means 3.2

19. The table shows the results of a survey about time spent on the Internet each month. Which statement is NOT supported by the data in the table?

Time Spent on the Internet per Month		
Time (h)	Frequency	Cumulative Frequency
0–4	4	4
5–9	6	10
10–14	3	13
15–19	16	29
20–24	12	41
25–29	7	48
30–34	2	50

   Ⓕ The interval of 30 to 34 h/mo has the lowest frequency.
   Ⓖ More than half of those who responded spend more than 20 h/mo on the Internet.
   Ⓗ Only four people responded that they spend less than 5 h/mo on the Internet.
   Ⓙ Sixteen people responded that they spend less than 20 h/mo on the Internet.

20. The frequencies of starting salary ranges for college graduates are noted in the table. Which histogram best reflects the data?

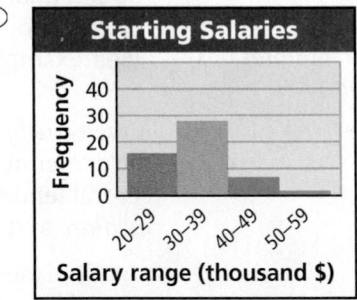

Starting Salaries

Salary Range ($)	Frequency
20,000–29,000	~~||||~~ ~~||||~~ ~~||||~~ ~~||||~~ ~~||||~~ ||
30,000–39,000	~~||||~~ ~~||||~~ ~~||||~~ ~~||||~~ ~~||||~~ ~~||||~~ ~~||||~~
40,000–49,000	~~||||~~ ~~||||~~ ~~||||~~	
50,000–59,000		

(A)

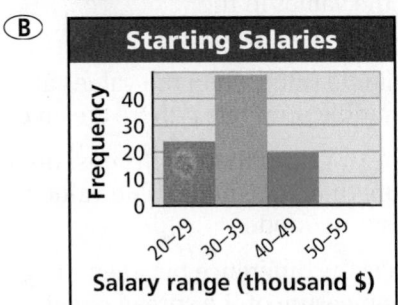

(B)

(C)

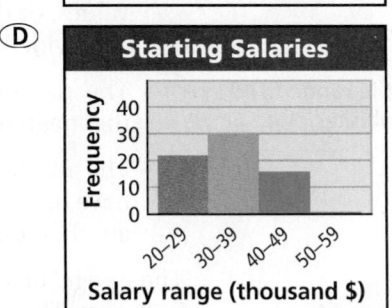

(D)

CHALLENGE AND EXTEND

21. The cumulative frequencies of each interval have been given. Use this information to complete the frequency column.

Interval	Frequency	Cumulative Frequency
13–16		8
17–20		16
21–24		57
25–28		123

10-3 Data Distributions

CC.9-12.S.ID.2 Use statistics appropriate to the shape of the data distribution to compare center (median, mean) and spread (interquartile range, standard deviation) of two or more different data sets. *Also* **CC.9-12.S.ID.3, CC.9-12.S.ID.1**

Objectives
Describe the central tendency of a data set.

Create and interpret box-and-whisker plots.

Vocabulary
mean
median
mode
range
outlier
first quartile
third quartile
interquartile range (IQR)
box-and-whisker plot

Who uses this?

Sports analysts examine data distributions to make predictions. (See Example 4.)

A *measure of central tendency* describes the center of a set of data. Measures of central tendency include the *mean, median,* and *mode.*

- The **mean** is the average of the data values, or the sum of the values in the set divided by the number of values in the set.

- The **median** is the middle value when the values are in numerical order, or the mean of the two middle numbers if there are an even number of values.

- The **mode** is the value or values that occur most often. A data set may have one mode or more than one mode. If no value occurs more often than another, the data set has no mode.

The **range** of a set of data is the difference between the greatest and least values in the set. The range is one measure of the spread of a data set.

E X A M P L E **1** **Finding Mean, Median, Mode, and Range of a Data Set**

The numbers of hours Isaac did homework on six days are 3, 8, 4, 6, 5, and 4. Find the mean, median, mode, and range of the data set.

3, 4, 4, 5, 6, 8   *Write the data in numerical order.*

mean: $\dfrac{3 + 4 + 4 + 5 + 6 + 8}{6} = \dfrac{30}{6} = 5$ *Add all the values and divide by the number of values.*

median: 3, 4, 4, 5, 6, 8   *There is an even number of values. Find the*
       The median is 4.5.   *mean of the two middle values.*

mode: 4   *4 occurs more than any other value.*

range: $8 - 3 = 5$ *Subtract the least value from the greatest value.*

1. The weights in pounds of five cats are 12, 14, 12, 16, and 16. Find the mean, median, mode, and range of the data set.

A value that is very different from the other values in a data set is called an **outlier**. In the data set below, one value is much greater than the other values.

EXAMPLE 2 **Determining the Effects of Outliers**

Identify the outlier in the data set $\{7, 10, 54, 9, 12, 8, 5\}$, and determine how the outlier affects the mean, median, mode, and range of the data.

5, 7, 8, 9, 10, 12, 54   *Write the data in numerical order.*

The outlier is 54.   *Look for a value much greater or less than the rest.*

With the Outlier:

mean: $\dfrac{5 + 7 + 8 + 9 + 10 + 12 + 54}{7}$

$= 15$

median: 5, 7, 8, ⑨ 10, 12, 54
The median is 9.

mode: Each value occurs once.
There is no mode.

range: $54 - 5 = 49$

Without the Outlier:

mean: $\dfrac{5 + 7 + 8 + 9 + 10 + 12}{6}$

$= 8.5$

median: 5, 7, ⑧|⑨ 10, 12
The median is 8.5.

mode: Each value occurs once.
There is no mode.

range: $12 - 5 = 7$

The outlier increases the mean by 6.5, the median by 0.5, and the range by 42. It has no effect on the mode.

2. Identify the outlier in the data set $\{21, 24, 3, 27, 30, 24\}$, and determine how the outlier affects the mean, median, mode, and range of the data.

As you can see in Example 2, an outlier can strongly affect the mean of a data set, while having little or no impact on the median and mode. Therefore, the mean may not be the best measure to describe a data set that contains an outlier. In such cases, the median or mode may better describe the center of the data set.

EXAMPLE 3 **Choosing a Measure of Central Tendency**

Niles scored 70, 74, 72, 71, 73, and 96 on his six geography tests. For each question, choose the mean, median, or mode, and give its value.

A Which measure gives Niles's test average?
The average of Niles's scores is the mean.

mean: $\dfrac{70 + 74 + 72 + 71 + 73 + 96}{6} = 76$

B Which measure best describes Niles's typical score? Explain.
The outlier of 96 causes the mean to be greater than all but one of the test scores, so it is not the best measure in this situation.

The data set has no mode.

The median best describes the typical score.

median: 70, 71, ⑦②|⑦③ 74, 96   *Find the mean of the two middle values.*
The median is 72.5.

Josh scored 75, 75, 81, 84, and 85 on five tests. For each question, choose the mean, median, or mode, and give its value.

3a. Which measure describes the score Josh received most often?

3b. Which measure should Josh use to convince his parents that he is doing well in school? Explain.

Measures of central tendency describe how data cluster around one value. Another way to describe a data set is by its spread—how the data values are spread out from the center.

Quartiles divide a data set into four equal parts. Each quartile contains one-fourth of the values in the set. The **first quartile** is the median of the lower half of the data set. The second quartile is the median of the data set, and the **third quartile** is the median of the upper half of the data set.

The **interquartile range (IQR)** of a data set is the difference between the third and first quartiles. It represents the range of the middle half of the data.

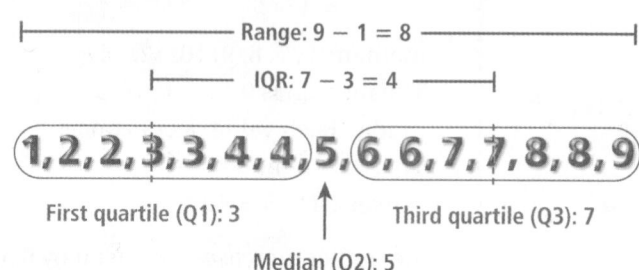

A **box-and-whisker plot** can be used to show how the values in a data set are distributed. You need five values to make a box-and-whisker plot: the minimum (or least value), first quartile, median, third quartile, and maximum (or greatest value).

EXAMPLE 4   *Sports Application*

The numbers of runs scored by a softball team in 20 games are given. Use the data to make a box-and-whisker plot.

3, 4, 8, 12, 7, 5, 4, 12, 3, 9, 11, 4, 14, 8, 2, 10, 3, 10, 9, 7

Step 1 Order the data from least to greatest.

2, 3, 3, 3, 4, 4, 4, 5, 7, 7, 8, 8, 9, 9, 10, 10, 11, 12, 12, 14

Step 2 Identify the five needed values.

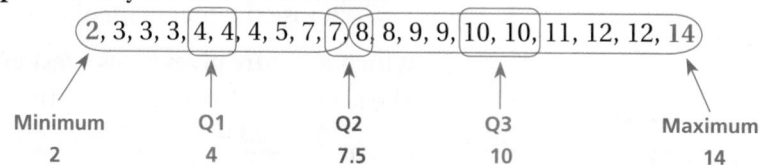

Step 3 Draw a number line and plot a point above each of the five needed values. Draw a box through the first and third quartiles and a vertical line through the median. Draw lines from the box to the minimum and maximum.

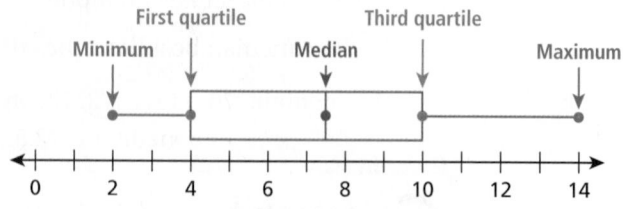

4. Use the data to make a box-and-whisker plot.

13, 14, 18, 13, 12, 17, 15, 12, 13, 19, 11, 14, 14, 18, 22, 23

EXAMPLE 5 **Reading and Interpreting Box-and-Whisker Plots**

The box-and-whisker plots show the ticket sales, in millions of dollars, of the top 25 movies in 2000 and 2007 (for the United States only).

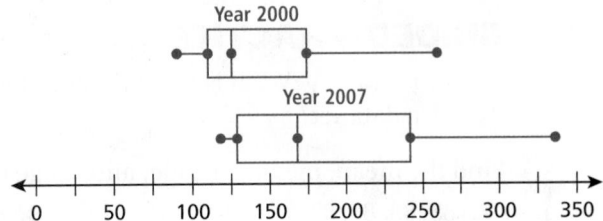

Year 2000

Year 2007

A Which data set has a greater median? Explain.

The vertical line in the box for 2007 is farther to the right than the vertical line in the box for 2000.

The data set for 2007 has a greater median.

B Which data set has a greater interquartile range? Explain.

The length of the box for 2007 is greater than the length of the box for 2000.

The data set for 2007 has a greater interquartile range.

C About how much more were the ticket sales for the top movie in 2007 than for the top movie in 2000?

2007 maximum: **about $335 million**   *Read the maximum values from*
2000 maximum: **about $260 million**   *the box-and-whisker plots.*
$335 - 260 = 75$ *Subtract the maximum values.*

The ticket sales for the top movie in 2007 were about $75 million more than for the top movie in 2000.

 Use the box-and-whisker plots above to answer each question.

5a. Which data set has a smaller range? Explain.

5b. About how much more was the median ticket sales for the top 25 movies in 2007 than in 2000?

THINK AND DISCUSS

1. Explain when the median is a value in the data set.

2. Give an example of a data set for which the mean is twice the median. Explain how you determined your answer.

3. Suppose the minimum in a data set is the same as the first quartile. How would this affect a box-and-whisker plot of the data?

 **4. GET ORGANIZED** Copy and complete the graphic organizer. Tell which measure of central tendency answers each question.

Measures of Central Tendency	
Measure	**Used to Answer**
	What is the average?
	What is the halfway point of the data?
	What is the most common value?

GUIDED PRACTICE

1. **Vocabulary** What is the difference between the *range* and the *interquartile range* of a data set?

SEE EXAMPLE 1 Find the mean, median, mode, and range of each data set.

2. 85, 83, 85, 82

3. 12, 22, 33, 34, 44, 44

4. 10, 26, 25, 10, 20, 22, 25, 20

5. 71, 73, 75, 78, 78, 80, 85, 86

SEE EXAMPLE 2 Identify the outlier in each data set, and determine how the outlier affects the mean, median, mode, and range of the data.

6. 10, 96, 12, 17, 15

7. 64, 75, 72, 13, 64

SEE EXAMPLE 3 Adrienne scored 82, 54, 85, 91, and 83 on her last five science tests. For each question, choose the mean, median, or mode, and give its value.

8. Which measure best describes Adrienne's typical score? Explain.

9. Which measure should Adrienne use to convince her soccer coach she is doing well in science? Explain.

SEE EXAMPLE 4 Use the data to make a box-and-whisker plot.

10. 21, 31, 26, 24, 28, 26

11. 12, 13, 42, 62, 62, 82

SEE EXAMPLE 5 The box-and-whisker plots show the scores, in thousands of points, of two players on a video game. Use the box-and-whisker plots to answer each question.

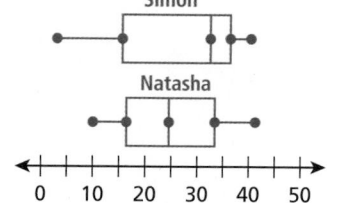

12. Which player has a higher median score? Explain.

13. Which player had the lowest score? Estimate this score.

PRACTICE AND PROBLEM SOLVING

Find the mean, median, mode, and range of each data set.

Independent Practice	
For Exercises	See Example
14–17	1
18–19	2
20–21	3
22–23	4
24-26	5

14. 75, 63, 89, 91

15. 1, 2, 2, 2, 3, 3, 3, 4

16. 19, 25, 31, 19, 34, 22, 31, 34

17. 58, 58, 60, 60, 60, 61, 63

Identify the outlier in each data set, and determine how the outlier affects the mean, median, mode, and range of the data.

18. 42, 8, 54, 37, 29

19. 3, 8, 3, 3, 23, 8

Extra Practice
See Extra Practice for more Skills Practice and Applications Practice exercises.

Lamont bowled 153, 145, 148, and 166 in four games. For each question, choose the mean, median, or mode, and give its value.

20. Which measure gives Lamont's average score?

21. Which measure should Lamont use to convince his parents to let him join a bowling league? Explain.

Use the data to make a box-and-whisker plot.

22. 62, 63, 62, 64, 68, 62, 62

23. 85, 90, 81, 100, 92, 85

The box-and-whisker plots show the prices, in dollars, of athletic shoes at two sports apparel stores. Use the box-and-whisker plots to answer each question.

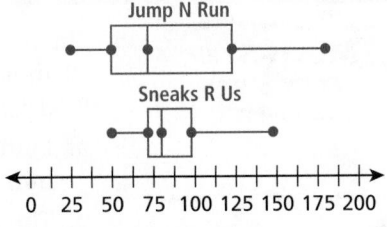

24. Which store has the greater median price? About how much greater?

25. Which store has the smaller interquartile range? What does this tell you about the data sets?

26. Estimate the difference in price between the most expensive shoe type at Jump N Run and the most expensive shoe at Sneaks R Us.

Find the mean, median, mode, and range of each data set.

27. 1, 2, 3, 4, 5, 6, 7, 8, 9, 10

28. 5, 6, 6, 5, 5

29. 2.1, 4.3, 6.5, 1.2, 3.4

30. $0, \frac{1}{4}, \frac{1}{2}, \frac{3}{4}, 1$

31. 23, 25, 26, 25, 23

32. −3, −3, −3, −2, −2, −1

33. 1, 4, 9, 16, 25, 36

34. 1, 0, 0, 1, 1, 4

35. Estimation Estimate the mean of $16\frac{7}{8}$, $12\frac{1}{4}$, $22\frac{1}{10}$, $18\frac{5}{7}$, $19\frac{1}{3}$, $13\frac{8}{11}$, and $13\frac{8}{11}$.

Tell whether each statement is sometimes, always, or never true.

36. The mean is a value in the data set.

37. The median is a value in the data set.

38. If a data set has one mode, the mode is a value in the data set.

39. The mean is affected by including an outlier.

40. The mode is affected by including an outlier.

41. Sports The table shows the attendance at six football games at Jefferson High School. Which measure of central tendency best indicates the typical attendance at a football game? Why?

Attendance at Football Games	
Eagles vs. Bulldogs	743
Eagles vs. Panthers	768
Eagles vs. Coyotes	835
Eagles vs. Bears*	1218
Eagles vs. Colts	797
Eagles vs. Mustangs	854

*Homecoming Game

42. Weather The high temperatures in degrees Fahrenheit on 11 consecutive days were 68, 71, 75, 74, 75, 71, 73, 71, 72, 74, and 79. Find the mean, median, mode, and range of the temperatures. Describe the effect on the mean, median, mode, and range if the next day's temperature was 70 °F.

43. Advertising A home-decorating store sells five types of candles, which are priced at $3, $2, $2, $2, and $15. If the store puts an ad in the paper titled "Best Local Candle Prices," which measure of central tendency should it advertise? Justify your answer.

Use the data to make a box-and-whisker plot.

44. 25, 28, 26, 16, 18, 15, 25, 28, 26, 16

45. 2, 3, 5, 7, 11, 13, 17, 19, 23, 29, 31

46. 1, 1, 1, 1, 2, 2, 2, 2, 3, 3, 4, 4, 4, 4, 4

47. 50, 52, 45, 62, 36, 55, 40, 50, 65, 33

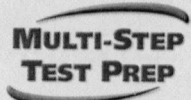

48. The results in Olympic pole-vaulting are given as heights in meters. In the 2008 Olympic Games in Beijing, the following results occurred for the men's pole-vault finals: 5.96, 5.85, 5.70, 5.70, 5.70, 5.70, 5.60, 5.60, 5.60, 5.45, 5.45.

a. Find the mean, median, mode, and range of this data set. Round to the nearest hundredth if needed.

b. The gold medal was won by Steve Hooker of Australia. What was his height in the pole-vault finals?

49. Business The salaries for the eight employees at a small company are shown in the stem-and-leaf plot. Find the mean and median of the salaries. Which measure better describes the typical salary of an employee at this company? Explain.

50. Critical Thinking Use the data set {1, 2, 3, 5, 8, 13, 21, 34} to complete the following.

a. Find the mean of the data set.

b. What happens to the mean of the data set if every number is increased by 2?

c. What happens to the mean of the data set if every number is multiplied by 2?

Salaries ($1000)

Stem	Leaves
2	0 0 3 5 5
3	0 5
4	
5	
6	
7	8

Key: 2|0 means $20,000

51. Allison has taken 5 tests worth 100 points each. Her scores are shown in the grade book below. What score does she need on her next test to have a mean of 90%?

Student	Test 1	Test 2	Test 3	Test 4	Test 5	Test 6	Average
Allison	88	85	89	92	90		

52. Astronomy The table shows the number of moons of the planets in our solar system. What is the mean number of moons per planet? Is Earth's value of one moon typical for the solar system? Explain.

Planet	Mercury	Venus	Earth	Mars	Jupiter	Saturn	Uranus	Neptune
Moons	0	0	1	2	63	60	27	13

53. Write About It Explain how an outlier with a large value will affect the mean. Explain how an outlier with a small value will affect the mean.

54. Which value is always represented on a box-and-whisker plot?

Ⓐ Mean   Ⓑ Median   Ⓒ Mode   Ⓓ Range

55. The lengths in feet of the alligators at a zoo are 9, 7, 12, 6, and 10. The lengths in feet of the crocodiles at the zoo are 13, 10, 8, 19, 18, and 16. What is the difference between the mean length of the crocodiles and the mean length of the alligators?

Ⓕ 0.5 foot   Ⓖ 5.2 feet   Ⓗ 8 feet   Ⓙ 11.4 feet

56. The mean score on a test is 50. Which CANNOT be true?

    (A) Half the scores are 0, and half the scores are 100.

    (B) The range is 50.

    (C) Half the scores are 25, and half the scores are 50.

    (D) Every score is 50.

57. Short Response The table shows the weights in pounds of six dogs. How does the mean weight of the dogs change if Rex's weight is not included in the data set?

Weights of Dogs (lb)			
Duffy	23	Rex	62
Rocky	15	Skipper	34
Pepper	21	Sunny	19

CHALLENGE AND EXTEND

58. List a set of data values with the following measures of central tendency:

    mean: 8   median: 7   mode: 6

59. Collect a set of data about your classmates or your school. For example, you might collect data about the number of points per game scored by your school's basketball team. Use the data you collect to make a box-and-whisker plot.

60. A *weighted average* is an average in which each data value has an importance, or weight, assigned to it. A teacher uses the following weights when determining course grades: homework 25%, tests 30%, and final exam 45%. The table shows Nathalie's scores in the class.

Homework	78, 83, 95, 82, 79, 93
Tests	88, 92, 81
Final exam	90

    a. Find the mean of Nathalie's homework scores and the mean of her test scores.

    b. Find Nathalie's weighted average for the class. To do so, multiply the homework mean, the test mean, and the final exam score by their corresponding weights. Then add the products.

    c. What if...? What would Nathalie's mean score for the class be if her teacher did not use a weighted average?

EXTENSION Dot Plots and Distributions

CC.9-12.S.ID.3 Interpret differences in shape, center, and spread in the context of the data sets, accounting for possible
effects of extreme data points (outliers). *Also* CC.9-12.S.ID.1

A **dot plot** is a data representation that uses a number line and x's, dots, or other symbols to show frequency. Dot plots are sometimes called line plots.

EXAMPLE 1 Making a Dot Plot

Objectives
Create dot plots.

Use a dot plot to describe the shape of a data distribution.

Vocabulary
dot plot
uniform distribution
symmetric distribution
skewed distribution

Mrs. Montoya asked her junior and senior students how many minutes each of them spent studying math in one day, rounded to the nearest five minutes. The results are shown below. Make a dot plot showing the data for juniors and a dot plot showing the data for seniors.

Time Spent Studying Math (min)	Frequency (Juniors)	Frequency (Seniors)
5	2	0
10	1	1
15	3	2
20	4	3
25	5	4
30	5	4
35	4	6
40	3	5
45	2	4

Find the least and greatest values in each data set. Then use these values to draw a number line for each graph. For each student, place a dot above the number line for the number of minutes he or she spent studying.

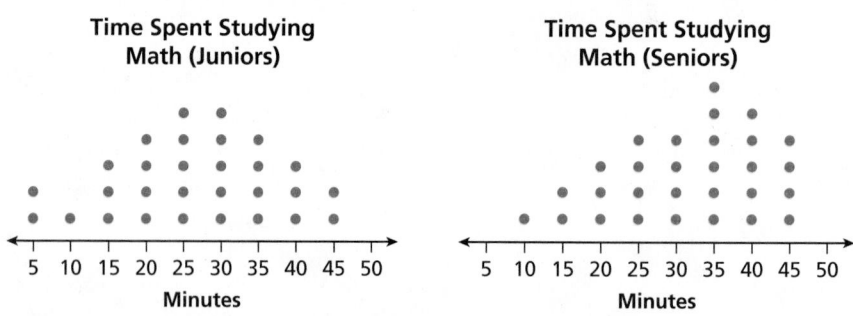

1. The cafeteria offers items at six different prices. John counted how many items were sold at each price for one week. Make a dot plot of the data.

Price ($)	1.50	2.00	2.50	3.00	3.50	4.00	4.50
Items	3	3	5	8	6	5	3

A dot plot gives a visual representation of the distribution, or "shape", of the data. The dot plots in Example 1 have different shapes because the data sets are distributed differently.

Types of Distributions

UNIFORM DISTRIBUTION	SYMMETRIC DISTRIBUTION	SKEWED DISTRIBUTION
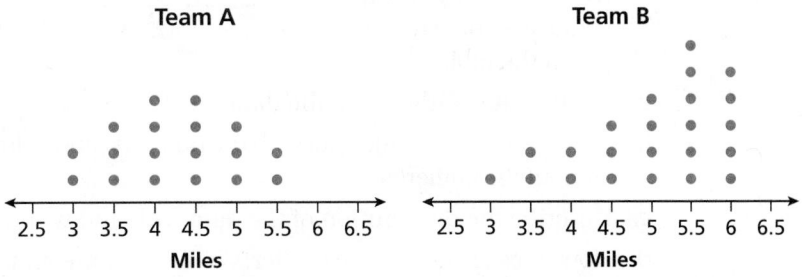		
In a **uniform distribution**, all data points have an approximately equal frequency.	In a **symmetric distribution**, a vertical line can be drawn and the result is a graph divided in two parts that are approximate mirror images of each other.	In a **skewed distribution**, the data is not uniform or symmetric. The data may be skewed to the right or skewed to the left.

EXAMPLE 2 **Shapes of Data Distributions**

The data table shows the number of miles run by members of two track teams during one day. Make a dot plot and determine the type of distribution for each team. Explain what the distribution means for each.

Miles	3	3.5	4	4.5	5	5.5	6
Team A	2	3	4	4	3	2	0
Team B	1	2	2	3	4	6	5

Make dot plots of the data.

Team A

Team B

The data for team A show a symmetric distribution. The distances run are evenly distributed about the mean.

The data for team B show a skewed left distribution. Most team members ran a distance greater than the mean.

2. Data for team C members are shown below. Make a dot plot and determine the type of distribution. Explain what the distribution means.

Miles	3	3.5	4	4.5	5	5.5	6
Team C	3	2	2	2	3	2	2

1. **Biology** Michael is collecting data for the growth of plants after one week. He planted nine seeds for each of three different types of plants and recorded his data in the table below.

Growth of Plants (in.)		
Type A	Type B	Type C
0.9	2.1	1.9
0.9	2.2	2.0
1.0	2.2	2.0
1.0	2.2	2.1
1.1	2.3	2.1
1.2	2.3	2.1
1.2	2.4	2.2
1.3	2.5	2.2
1.4	2.6	2.3

a. Create a dot plot for each type of plant.

b. Describe the distributions.

c. Which data value(s) occur(s) the most often in each dot plot? the least often?

d. For each dot plot, list the heights in order from least frequent to most frequent.

2. **Nutrition** Julia researched grape juice brands to determine how many grams of sugar each brand contained per serving (8 fluid ounces = 1 serving). The data she collected is shown in the table.

Grams of Sugar in Grape Juice (per serving)					
15	0	36	18	30	10
30	15	35	30	36	30
36	30	38	16	35	16

a. Identify any outlier(s) in the data set.

b. Make a dot plot for the data with the outlier(s) and a dot plot for the data without the outlier(s).

c. Describe the distribution of the data with and without the outlier(s).

d. How does excluding the outlier(s) affect the mean, median, and mode of the data set?

3. The frequency table shows the number of siblings of each student in a class. Use the table to make a dot plot of the data, and describe the distribution.

Number of Siblings	Frequency
0	7
1	9
2	5
3	1
4	1

4. School The list below shows which grade each member of a high school marching band belongs to.

9, 12, 9, 10, 9, 12, 9, 9, 11, 12, 12, 10, 10, 9, 9, 11, 9, 10,
10, 12, 9, 12, 11, 9, 12, 11, 10, 9, 12, 12, 9, 9, 11, 12

a. Make a dot plot of the data.

b. Explain how you can use the dot plot to find the mean, median, and mode of the data set. Then find each of these values.

Use the dot plot for Exercises 5 and 6.

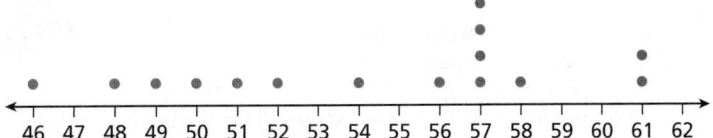

5. Write About It Compare stem-and-leaf plots and dot plots.

a. How are they similar and how are they different?

b. What information can you get from each graph?

c. Can you make a dot plot given a stem-and-leaf plot? Explain.

d. Can you make a stem-and-leaf plot given a dot plot? If so, make a stem-and-leaf plot of the data in the dot plot at right. If not, explain why not.

6. Write About It Compare histograms and dot plots.

a. How are they similar and how are they different?

b. What information can you get from each graph?

c. Can you make a dot plot given a histogram? Explain.

d. Can you make a histogram given a dot plot? If so, make a histogram of the data in the dot plot at right. If not, explain why not.

7. Multi-Step Gather data on the heights of people in your classroom. Separate the data for males from the data for females. Make two dot plots representing the data collected for each group. Compare the dot plots and the distributions of the data.

8. The dot plot at right shows an example of a *bimodal distribution.* Why is this an appropriate name for this type of distribution?

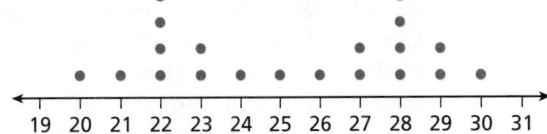

9. Critical Thinking Magdalene and Peter conducted the same experiment. Both of their data sets had the same mean. Both made dot plots of their data that showed symmetric distributions, but Peter's dot plot shows a greater range than Magdalene's dot plot. Identify which plot below belongs to Peter and which belongs to Magdalene.

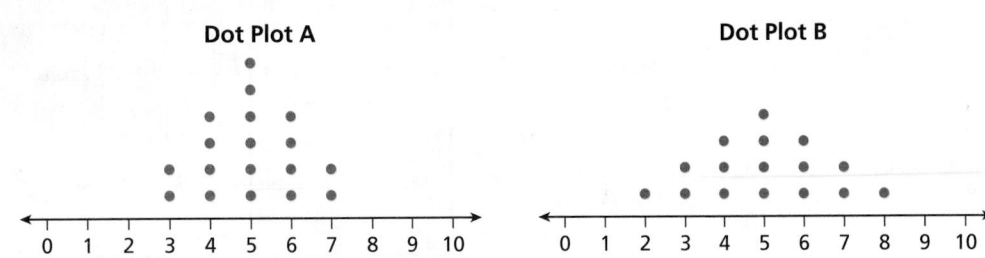

Biology

Even though identical twins share the same DNA, they are often of different heights. According to one study, the average height difference between identical twins is 1.7 cm.

10-3
Technology LAB

Use Technology to Make Graphs

You can use a spreadsheet program to create bar graphs, line graphs, and circle graphs. You can also use a graphing calculator to make a box-and-whisker plot.

Use with Data Distributions

 **Use appropriate tools strategically.**

Activity 1

CC.9-12.S.ID.1 Represent data with plots on the real number line (dot plots, histograms, and box plots).

Many colors are used on the flags of the 50 United States. The table shows the number of flags that use each color. Use a spreadsheet program to make a bar graph to display the data.

Color	Black	Blue	Brown	Gold	Green	Purple	Red	White
Number	27	46	20	36	24	4	34	42

1. Enter the data from the table in the first two columns of the spreadsheet.

2. Select the cells containing the titles and the data.
   Then click the Chart Wizard icon, 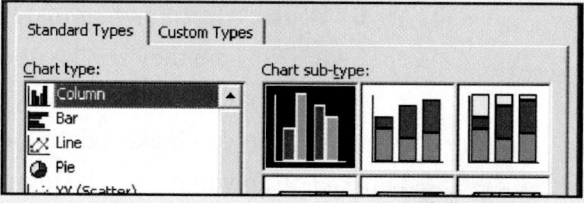.
   Click Column from the list on the left, and then choose the small picture of a vertical bar graph. Click Next.

3. The next screen shows the range of cells used to make the graph. Click Next.

4. Give the chart a title and enter titles for the *x*-axis and *y*-axis. Click the Legend tab, and then click the box next to Show Legend to turn off the key. (A key is needed when making a double-bar graph.) Click Next.

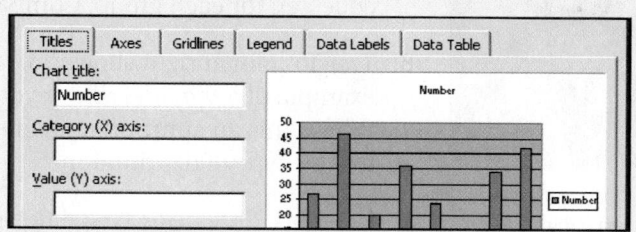

5. Click Finish to place the chart in the spreadsheet.

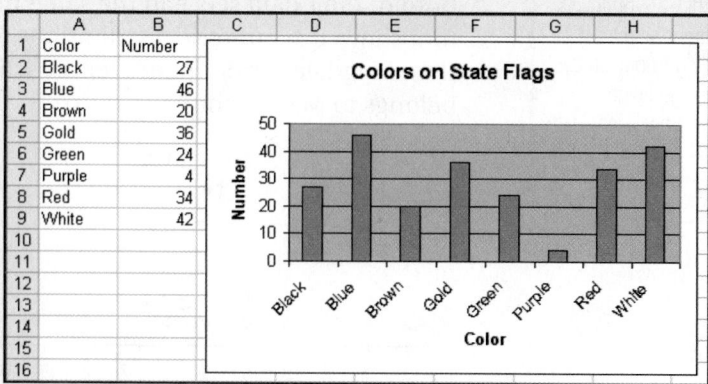

1. The table shows the average number of hours of sleep people at different ages get each night. Use a spreadsheet program to make a bar graph to display the data.

Age (yr)	3–9	10–13	14–18	19–30	31–45	46–50	51+
Sleep (h)	11	10	9	8	7.5	6	5.5

Activity 2

Adrianne is a waitress at a restaurant. The amounts Adrianne made in tips during her last 15 shifts are listed below. Use a graphing calculator to make a box-and-whisker plot to display the data. Give the minimum, first quartile, median, third quartile, and maximum values.

$58, $63, $40, $44, $57, $59, $61, $53, $54, $58, $57, $57, $58, $58, $56

1 To make a list of the data, press **STAT**, select **Edit**, and enter the values in List 1 **(L1)**. Press **ENTER** after each value.

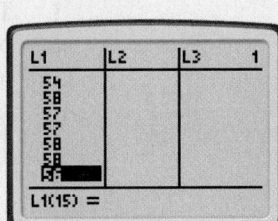

2 To use the **STAT PLOT** editor to set up the box-and-whisker plot, press **2nd** **Y=**, and then **ENTER**.

Press **ENTER** to select **Plot 1**.

3 Select **On**. Then use the arrow keys to choose the fifth type of graph, a box-and-whisker plot.

Xlist should be **L1** and **Freq:** should be 1.

4 Press **ZOOM** and select **9: ZoomStat** to see the graph in the statistics window.

5 Use **TRACE** and the arrow keys to move the cursor along the graph to the five important values: minimum **(MinX)**, first quartile **(Q1)**, median **(MED)**, third quartile **(Q3)**, and maximum **(MaxX)**.

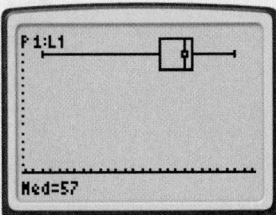

minimum: 40

first quartile: 54

median: 57

third quartile: 58

maximum: 63

Try This

2. The average length in inches of the ten longest bones in the human body are listed. Use a graphing calculator to make a box-and-whisker plot to display the data. What are the minimum, first quartile, median, third quartile, and maximum values of the data set?

19.88, 16.94, 15.94, 14.35, 11.10, 10.40, 9.45, 9.06, 7.28, 6.69

10-4 Misleading Graphs and Statistics

CC.9-12.S.IC.6 Evaluate reports based on data.

GUARANTEED NOT TO BREAK DOWN (while parked)

Objectives
Recognize misleading graphs.

Recognize misleading statistics.

Vocabulary
random sample

Why learn this?
A misleading graph can be used to distort the results of a student council election. (See Example 3.)

Graphs can be used to influence what people believe. The way a data set is displayed can influence how the data are interpreted.

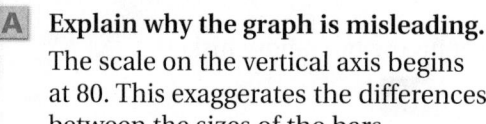

EXAMPLE 1 Misleading Bar Graphs

The graph shows the size of tomatoes on plants that were treated with different fertilizers.

Effect of Fertilizer

82.8 g   81.9 g   83.4 g   85.2 g

A   B   C   D

Fertilizer

A Explain why the graph is misleading.

The scale on the vertical axis begins at 80. This exaggerates the differences between the sizes of the bars.

B What might someone believe because of the graph?

Someone might believe that the tomato treated with fertilizer D is much larger than the other tomatoes. It is only 3.3 grams larger than the tomato treated with fertilizer B.

CHECK IT OUT!

1. Who might want to use the graph above? Explain.

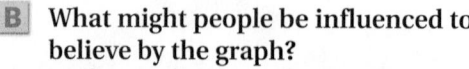

EXAMPLE 2 Misleading Line Graphs

The graph shows the average price of gasoline in the U.S. in September.

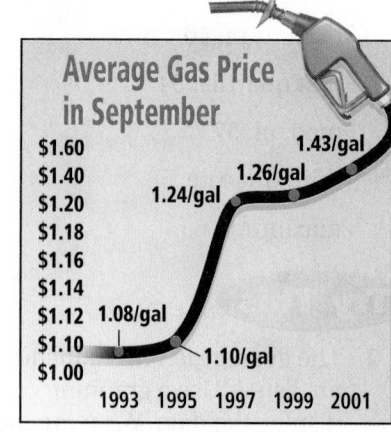

Average Gas Price in September

$1.60 $1.40 $1.20 $1.18 $1.16 $1.14 $1.12 $1.10 $1.00

1.08/gal   1.24/gal   1.26/gal   1.43/gal   1.10/gal

1993   1995   1997   1999   2001

A Explain why the graph is misleading.

The intervals on the vertical axis are not equal.

B What might people be influenced to believe by the graph?

Someone might believe that the price of gasoline increased the most between 1995 and 1997. However, the change between 1995 and 1997 was only $0.14/gal while the change between 1999 and 2001 was $0.17/gal.

CHECK IT OUT!

2. Who might want to use the graph above? Explain.

A circle graph compares each category of a data set to the whole. When any category is not represented in the graph, it may appear that another category represents a greater percentage of the total than it should.

 EXAMPLE 3 **Misleading Circle Graphs**

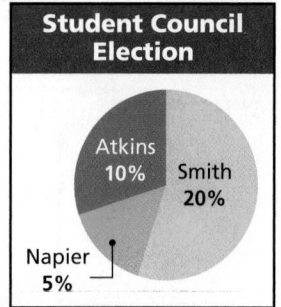

The graph shows what percent of the total votes were received by three candidates for student council president.

A Explain why the graph is misleading.

The sections of the graph do not add to 100%, so the votes for at least one of the candidates is not represented.

B What might people be influenced to believe by the graph?

Someone might believe that Smith won the election.

 3. Who might want to use the graph above? Explain.

Statistics can be misleading because of the way the data is collected or the way the results are reported. A sufficiently large *random sample* is a good way to collect unbiased data. In a **random sample**, all members of the group being surveyed have an equal chance of being selected.

 EXAMPLE 4 **Misleading Statistics**

A researcher surveys people leaving a basketball game about what they like to watch on TV. Explain why the following statement is misleading: "80% of people like to watch sports on TV."

The sample is biased because people who attend sporting events are more likely to watch sports on TV than people who watch TV but do not attend sporting events.

 **4.** A researcher asks 4 people if they have seasonal allergies. Three people respond yes. Explain why the following statement is misleading: "75% of people have seasonal allergies."

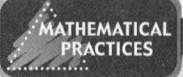

THINK AND DISCUSS

1. Give an example of a situation in which someone might intentionally try to make a graph misleading.

 **2. GET ORGANIZED** Copy and complete the graphic organizer. Add more boxes if needed.

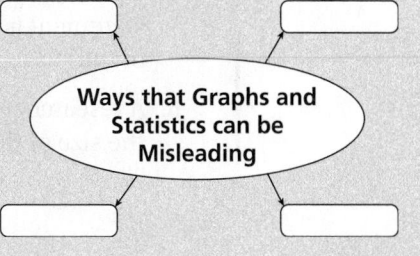

GUIDED PRACTICE

1. **Vocabulary** Explain in your own words what the term *random sample* means.

SEE EXAMPLE 1

2. The graph shows the average salaries of employees at three companies.

   a. Explain why the graph is misleading.

   b. What might someone believe because of the graph?

   c. Who might want to use this graph? Explain.

$ Average Salaries $

$42,800 — 42,700
$42,400
$42,000
$41,600   41,550   41,800
$41,200
$40,800   Company   Company   Company
              X   Y   Z

SEE EXAMPLE 2

3. The graph shows hotel occupancy in San Francisco over four years.

   a. Explain why the graph is misleading.

   b. What might someone believe because of the graph?

   c. Who might want to use this graph? Explain.

San Francisco Tourism

100
95
90   92%   Hotel
85   87%   occupancy
80
75   80%
70   79%   78%
65
      Jun   Oct   Jun   Jun   Oct
      2000   2000   2001   2002   2002

SEE EXAMPLE 3

4. The graph shows the nutritional information for a granola bar.

   a. Explain why the graph is misleading.

   b. What might someone believe because of the graph?

   c. Who might want to use this graph? Explain.

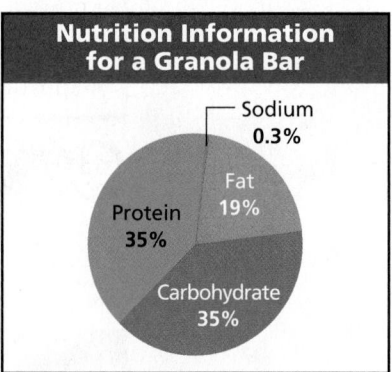

Nutrition Information for a Granola Bar

Sodium 0.3%
Fat 19%
Protein 35%
Carbohydrate 35%

SEE EXAMPLE 4

5. Three students were surveyed about their favorite teacher. Two students answer Mr. Gregory, and one answers Mr. Blaine. Explain why the following statement is misleading: "Mr. Gregory is the favorite teacher of a majority of the students."

6. A researcher surveys people at a shopping mall about whether they favor enlarging the size of the mall parking lot. Explain why the following statement is misleading: "85% of the community is in favor of enlarging the parking lot."

PRACTICE AND PROBLEM SOLVING

Independent Practice

For Exercises	See Example
7	1
8	2
9	3
10	4

Extra Practice

See Extra Practice for more Skills Practice and Applications Practice exercises.

7. The graph shows the median rent for men and women in a metropolitan area.

   a. Explain why the graph is misleading.

   b. What might someone believe because of the graph?

   c. Who might want to use this graph? Explain.

Metropolitan Area Median Rent 2000

8. The graph shows the export prices of Colombian arabica coffee over nine years.

   a. Explain why the graph is misleading.

   b. What might someone believe because of the graph?

   c. Who might want to use this graph? Explain.

Colombian Arabica Coffee
Export Price/lb

9. The graph shows how the state spent tax dollars during 1999 and 2000.

   a. Explain why the graph is misleading.

   b. What might someone believe because of the graph?

   c. Who might want to use this graph? Explain.

10. A college math course has one section with 240 students and 8 sections with 30 students. Explain why the following statement is misleading: "The average class size for the course is 53 students."

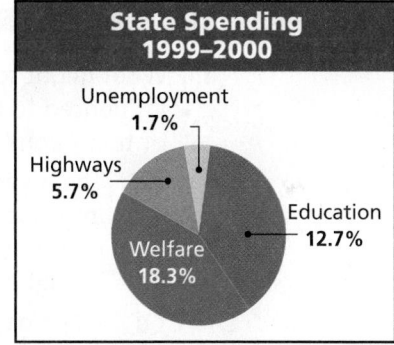

State Spending 1999–2000

Unemployment 1.7%
Highways 5.7%
Education 12.7%
Welfare 18.3%

MULTI-STEP TEST PREP

11. The table shows scores from the women's gymnastics finals in the floor exercise at the 2004 Summer Olympic Games.

   a. Find the average score for the women in the finals.

   b. Would it be misleading to describe the data using the average score? Explain.

   c. Make a graph for this data that could convince someone that the difference between the first place score and the eighth place score was very small.

Rank	Name	Score
1	Catalina Ponor	9.750
2	Nicoleta Sofronie	9.562
3	Patricia Moreno	9.487
4	Fei Cheng	9.412
5	Daiane dos Santos	9.375
6	Mohini Bhardwaj	9.312
7	Kate Richardson	9.312
8	Alina Kozich	8.500

12. **///ERROR ANALYSIS///** The graph shows the population of a city over time. Which conclusion is incorrect? Explain why the conclusion is incorrect and how the graph was misleading.

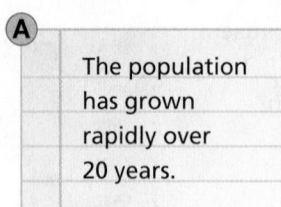

A
| The population |
| has grown |
| rapidly over |
| 20 years. |

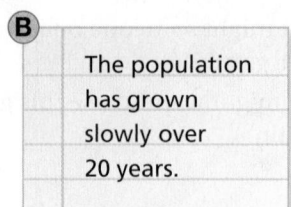

B
| The population |
| has grown |
| slowly over |
| 20 years. |

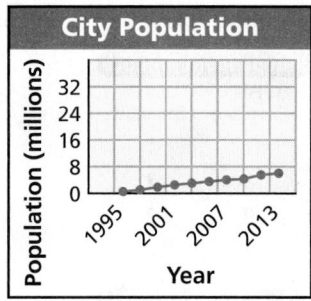

City Population

13. The table shows the average connection speeds of some broadband Internet service providers.

Provider	Connection Speed (Kbps)
Speedy Online	954
TelQuick	914
Alacrity	858

   a. Construct a display that suggests that Speedy Online is much faster than the other services.

   b. Construct a display that suggests that all of the services offer about the same connection speeds.

    **c. Write About It** Where might you expect to see your graph from part **b**? Explain.

14. **Critical Thinking** Explain how a graph can show truthful data but still be misleading.

TEST PREP

15. What might someone be influenced to believe because of the graph?

   Ⓐ The measles vaccine was introduced when the mortality rate was at its highest.

   Ⓑ The measles vaccine was unnecessary.

   Ⓒ The measles vaccine dramatically decreased the mortality rate.

   Ⓓ The measles vaccine increased the mortality rate.

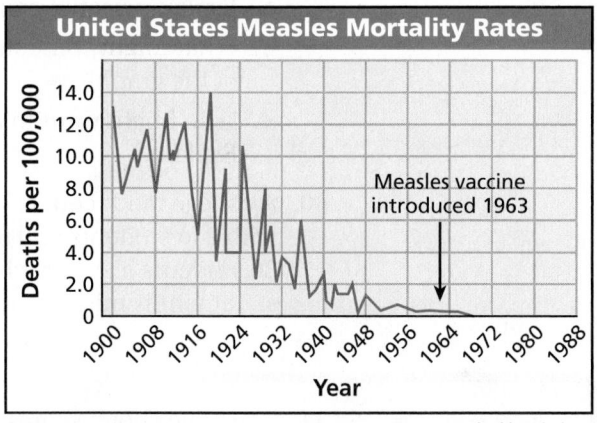

United States Measles Mortality Rates

Source: www.healthsentinel.com

16. The table shows the number of votes cast in the 2000 U.S. presidential election and in the 2002 French presidential election. What additional information is needed to determine whether the following statement is misleading?

Country	Votes Cast
United States	105,405,100
France	29,497,272

   "American voters are more likely to vote than French voters."

   Ⓕ The number of candidates in each election

   Ⓖ The legal voting age in France

   Ⓗ The number of registered voters in the United States in 2000 and France in 2002

   Ⓙ The number of polling locations in the United States in 2000 and France in 2002

17. Logic A fingerprint analyst is studying a fingerprint that was found in the chemistry lab. He reports that the fingerprint belongs to Dr. Arenson. Below are two questions the analyst was asked and the answers he gave.

Question 1: What are the chances that the fingerprint belongs to someone else who has the same fingerprint as Dr. Arenson?

Answer: One in several billion.

Question 2: What are the chances that the fingerprint was wrongly identified?

Answer: About 1 in 100.

a. What is the difference between the two questions?

b. What does the answer to question 1 lead you to believe?

c. Who do you think might have asked question 1?

d. What does the answer to question 2 lead you to believe?

e. Who do you think might have asked question 2?

History

Florence Nightingale (1820–1910) served as a nurse in the Crimean War. In 1854, she brought the first female nurses to military hospitals.

18. History Graphs like the one at right were created by Florence Nightingale. Nightingale served as a nurse during the Crimean War and was concerned with the unsanitary conditions the soldiers lived in. Each "wedge" of the circle represents a month between April 1854 and March 1855.

a. What do you think Florence Nightingale wanted to show with this graph?

b. Who do you think Nightingale showed the graph to?

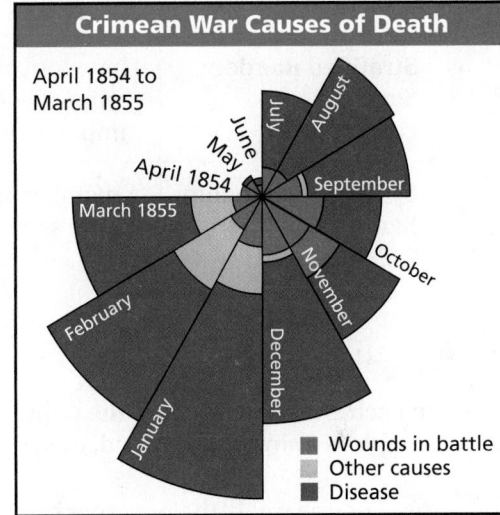

Crimean War Causes of Death

April 1854 to March 1855

■ Wounds in battle
■ Other causes
■ Disease

Source: The Florence Nightingale Museum

Sampling and Bias

If you wanted to collect data about a very large group of people, you would most likely need to survey a smaller group. The large group that contains all the people you could survey is called a *population*. The smaller group is called a *sample*.

You have learned that a random sample is a good way of collecting data that is unbiased. There are different ways of selecting a random sample.

Random Samples		
Type	**Definition**	**Example**
Simple Random Sample	Every member of the population has an equal chance of being chosen for the sample.	The names of all students in your class are placed in a hat and three names are chosen at random.
Stratified Random Sample	The population is divided into similar groups. Then a simple random sample is chosen from each group.	Your class is divided into boys and girls and two students are chosen at random from each group.
Systematic Random Sample	A member of the population is chosen for the sample at a regular interval.	Every third student who comes into the classroom is chosen.

Example 1

In each situation, identify the population and the sample. Tell whether each sample is a simple, stratified, or systematic random sample.

A **For one week, the manager of a pet supplies store asks every tenth customer what brand of pet food they buy.**

population: all customers at the pet supplies store during one week

sample: every tenth customer during that same week

The sample is systematic because one member of the population is chosen for the sample at a regular interval.

B **Every person who enters a theater one evening places their ticket stub in a bowl. The theater owner chooses five ticket stubs to award prizes.**

population: all people who put their ticket stub in the bowl

sample: five ticket stubs chosen from the bowl

The sample is simple because every member of the population has the same chance of being chosen.

C **One student from each classroom at a school is chosen at random for a committee.**

population: all students at a school

sample: one student from each classroom

The sample is stratified because the population is divided into similar groups and one member is chosen at random from each group.

1. Choose a topic to research. Describe the population, why you need to choose a sample, and the sample.
2. Choose whether to use a simple, stratified, or systematic random sample. Explain your choice and the process you would use to choose your sample.

A random sample is not biased because no part of the population is favored over another. In a biased sample, one or more parts of the population have an advantage for being chosen for the sample.

There are two main types of biased samples.

Biased Samples		
Type	**Definition**	**Example**
Convenience Sample	Those members of the population that are easily accessed are chosen for the sample.	A reporter questions people he personally knows.
Voluntary Response Sample	Members of the population who want to participate make up the sample.	A reporter questions people who fill out comment cards and indicate that they would like to be contacted.

Example 2

In each situation, identify the population and the sample. Tell whether each sample is a convenience or voluntary response sample. Explain why the sample is biased.

A A website asks visitors to complete a survey about Internet usage.

population: all visitors to the website

sample: those visitors who choose to complete the survey

The sample is a voluntary response sample because visitors to the website chose whether to complete the survey. The sample is biased because those visitors who choose to complete the survey may not be representative of all visitors to the website.

B A reporter asks people leaving a shopping center through one door about their shopping habits.

population: all people at the shopping center

sample: people who leave from one door at the shopping center

The sample is a convenience sample because the people leaving through the chosen door are easily accessed. The sample is biased because people leaving through another door do not have an opportunity to be chosen.

Try This

3. Choose a topic to research. Describe the population, why you need to choose a sample, and the sample.
4. Assume that you want an unbiased sample. Choose whether to use a simple, stratified, or systematic random sample. Explain your choice and the process you would use to choose your sample.
5. Describe how a biased sample could be chosen for this same situation.

MULTI-STEP TEST PREP

MATHEMATICAL PRACTICES

Make sense of problems and persevere in solving them.

Data Analysis

USA! USA! USA! In 708 B.C.E., the Olympic Games included the pentathlon. This event included the discus, javelin, long jump, running, and wrestling. The winner of the pentathlon was considered a "super athlete." The modern pentathlon of the Olympic Games includes five disciplines: target shooting, fencing, swimming, horseback riding, and cross-country running.

1. The pentathlon includes five events. What type of graph should be used to show what percent of this event is made up of each discipline?

2. Do you think the winner of the modern pentathlon must win each of the five events? Explain.

3. Thirty-two men competed in the modern pentathlon in the 2004 Olympic Games. The chart shows the total points for the competitors.

Pentathlon Scores
5480 5428 5392 5356 5340
5332 5320 5295 5276 5252 5200 5196
5192 5184 5180 5172 5144 5132 5084
5084 5068 5016 4976 4936 4932 4916
4904 4848 4732 4676 4420 4388

Find the mean, median, and mode of this data set. Which value best describes the data? Explain.

4. Find the minimum, first quartile, third quartile, and maximum values of the data set above. Use these values and the median to make a box-and-whisker plot of the data.

READY TO GO ON?

Quiz for Lessons 10-1 Through 10-4

✓ 10-1 Organizing and Displaying Data

Use the circle graph for 1–3.

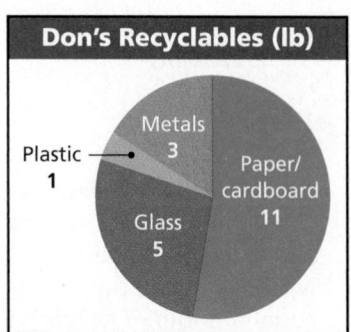

Don's Recyclables (lb)

Metals 3
Plastic 1
Paper/cardboard 11
Glass 5

1. Which material represents over 50% of Don's recyclables?

2. How many pounds of materials does Don recycle?

3. What percent of Don's recyclables are glass?

4. The table shows the total proceeds for a fund-raiser at various times during the day. Choose a type of graph to display the given data. Make the graph, and explain why you chose that type of graph.

Time	Total Proceeds (thousand $)	Time	Total Proceeds (thousand $)
3:00 P.M.	1.5	6:00 P.M.	6.5
4:00 P.M.	2	7:00 P.M.	8
5:00 P.M.	4	8:00 P.M.	9.5

✓ 10-2 Frequency and Histograms

5. The Miller family is going to buy a new car. The approximate prices of the cars they are considering are given. Use the data to make a stem-and-leaf plot.

$24,000, $28,000, $26,000, $32,000, $30,000, $41,000, $27,000, $22,000, $26,000, $33,000

6. The number of people at a caterer's last 12 parties are given below.

16, 18, 17, 19, 15, 25, 18, 17, 18, 16, 17, 19

a. Use the data to make a frequency table with intervals.

b. Use your frequency table from part **a** to make a histogram.

✓ 10-3 Data Distributions

7. The daily high temperatures on 14 consecutive days in one city were 59 °F, 49 °F, 48 °F, 46 °F, 47 °F, 51 °F, 49 °F, 43 °F, 45 °F, 52 °F, 51 °F, 51 °F, 51 °F, and 38 °F.

a. Find the mean, median, and mode of the temperatures.

b. Which value describes the average high temperature for the 14 days?

c. Which value best describes the high temperatures? Explain.

8. Use the temperature data above to make a box-and-whisker plot.

✓ 10-4 Misleading Graphs and Statistics

9. The graph shows the value of a company's stock over time. Explain why the graph is misleading. What might people be influenced to believe because of the graph? Who might want to use this graph?

10. The results of an online survey of 230 people showed that 92% of the population felt very comfortable using technology. Explain why this statistic is misleading.

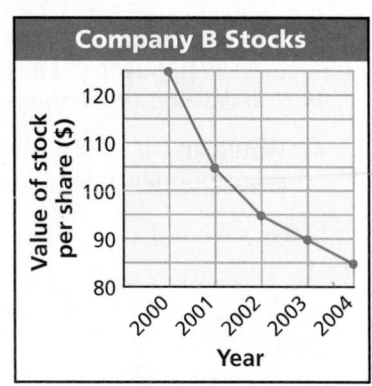

Company B Stocks

Value of stock per share ($)

120
110
100
90
80

2000 2001 2002 2003 2004

Year

10-5
Algebra LAB

Simulations

A simulation can be used to model an experiment that would be difficult or inconvenient to actually perform. In this lab, you will conduct simulations.

Use with Experimental Probability

 **Use appropriate tools strategically.**

Activity

The local movie theater is offering an opportunity for customers to win a free night at the movies. To win, you must collect six different letters to spell CINEMA. Each movie ticket sold during this promotion will have one of the six letters stamped on the back of the ticket. An equal number of tickets will be stamped with each of the letters.

1 Since there are six different letters that appear on the tickets an equal number of times, you can use a number cube to simulate collecting the six letters.

Each of the numbers on the number cube will represent a letter. Each roll of the number cube will represent purchasing one movie ticket, and the number rolled will represent the letter stamped on the ticket.

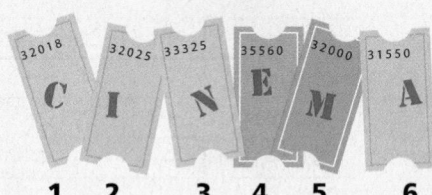

2 The table shows the results of rolling the number cube until each number has been rolled once.

a. Based on the results shown in the table, how many rolls did it take to get all six numbers?

b. Based on the results in the table, how many movie tickets would you expect to have to buy to get all six letters? If you purchased this number of tickets, would you be sure to win? Explain.

Number on Cube	Letter on Ticket	Frequency
1	C	I
2	I	JHT I
3	N	IIII
4	E	II
5	M	II
6	A	III

Try This

1. Repeat the simulation four more times and record the results.

2. Find the average number of rolls from all five simulations
$\left(\dfrac{\text{total number of rolls from 5 simulations}}{5}\right)$.

3. Based on your answer to Problem 2, how many movie tickets would you expect to have to buy to get all six letters? Is this number different from the answer you gave based on the results in the table above?

4. Would any of your answers have been different if you had used a different correspondence between the numbers and letters? Explain.

10-5 Experimental Probability

CC.9-12.S.CP.1 Describe events as subsets of a sample space (the set of outcomes) using characteristics (or categories) of the outcomes, or as unions, intersections, or complements of other events ("or," "and," "not").

Objectives
Determine the experimental probability of an event.

Use experimental probability to make predictions.

Vocabulary
experiment
trial
outcome
sample space
event
probability
experimental probability
prediction

Why learn this?
Experimental probability can be used by manufacturers for quality control. (See Example 4.)

An **experiment** is an activity involving chance. Each repetition or observation of an experiment is a **trial**, and each possible result is an **outcome**. The **sample space** of an experiment is the set of all possible outcomes.

Experiment	Rolling a number cube	Tossing a coin	Spinning a game spinner
Sample Space	{1, 2, 3, 4, 5, 6}	{heads, tails}	{red, blue, green, yellow}

EXAMPLE **1** **Identifying Sample Spaces and Outcomes**

Identify the sample space and the outcome shown for each experiment.

A **tossing two coins**
Sample space: {HH, HT, TH, TT}
Outcome shown: heads, tails (H, T)

B **spinning a game spinner**
Sample space: {yellow, red, blue, green}
Outcome shown: green

 **1.** Identify the sample space and the outcome shown for the experiment: rolling a number cube.

An **event** is an outcome or set of outcomes in an experiment. **Probability** is the measure of how likely an event is to occur. Probabilities are written as fractions or decimals from 0 to 1, or as percents from 0% to 100%.

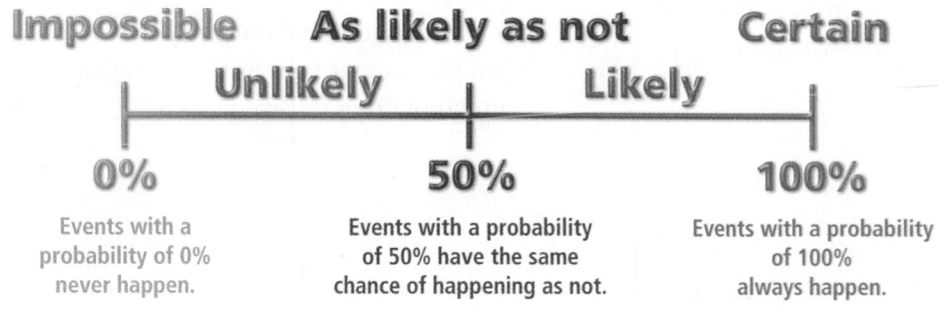

EXAMPLE 2   **Estimating the Likelihood of an Event**

Write *impossible, unlikely, as likely as not, likely,* or *certain* to describe each event.

A   **There are 31 days in August.**

August always has 31 days. This event is *certain*.

B   **Carlos correctly guesses a number between 1 and 1000.**

Carlos must pick one outcome out of 1000 possible outcomes. This event is *unlikely*.

C   **A coin lands heads up.**

Heads is one of two possible outcomes. This event is *as likely as not*.

D   **Cecilia rolls a 10 on a standard number cube.**

A standard number cube is numbered 1 through 6. This event is *impossible*.

 **2.** Write *impossible, unlikely, as likely as not, likely,* or *certain* to describe the event: Anthony rolls a number less than 7 on a standard number cube.

You can estimate the probability of an event by performing an experiment. The **experimental probability** of an event is the ratio of the number of times the event occurs to the number of trials. The more trials performed, the more accurate the estimate is likely to be.

Experimental Probability

$$\text{experimental probability} = \frac{\text{number of times the event occurs}}{\text{number of trials}}$$

EXAMPLE 3   **Finding Experimental Probability**

An experiment consists of spinning a spinner. Use the results in the table to find the experimental probability of each event.

Outcome	Frequency
Red	7
Blue	8
Green	5

Helpful Hint

Probabilities can be expressed as fractions, decimals, or percents. For Example 3, the probabilities are:

3A: $\frac{2}{5} = 0.4 = 40\%$

3B: $\frac{3}{4} = 0.75 = 75\%$

A   **spinner lands on blue**

$$\frac{\text{number of times the event occurs}}{\text{number of trials}} = \frac{8}{7 + 8 + 5}$$

$$= \frac{8}{20}$$

$$= \frac{2}{5}$$

B   **spinner does not land on green**

When the spinner does not land on green, it must land on red or blue.

$$\frac{\text{number of times the event occurs}}{\text{number of trials}} = \frac{7 + 8}{7 + 8 + 5}$$

$$= \frac{15}{20}$$

$$= \frac{3}{4}$$

 **Use the information in Example 3 to find the experimental probability of each event.**

3a. spinner lands on red

3b. spinner does not land on red

You can use experimental probability to make *predictions*. A **prediction** is an estimate or guess about something that has not yet happened.

 EXAMPLE 4 *Quality Control Application*

A manufacturer inspects 800 light bulbs and finds that 796 of them have no defects.

A **What is the experimental probability that a light bulb chosen at random has no defects?**

Find the experimental probability that a light bulb has no defects.

$$\frac{\text{number of times the event occurs}}{\text{number of trials}} = \frac{796}{800}$$

$$= 99.5\%$$

The experimental probability that a light bulb has no defects is 99.5%.

B **The manufacturer sent a shipment of 2400 light bulbs to a retail store. Predict the number of light bulbs in the shipment that are likely to have no defects.**

Find 99.5% of 2400.

$$0.995(2400) = 2388$$

The manufacturer predicts that 2388 light bulbs have no defects.

 **4.** A manufacturer inspects 1500 electric toothbrush motors and finds that 1497 of them have no defects.

a. What is the experimental probability that a motor chosen at random will have no defects?

b. There are 35,000 motors in a warehouse. Predict the number of motors that are likely to have no defects.

THINK AND DISCUSS

1. Explain the difference between an outcome and an event.

2. Is the experimental probability of an event always the same? Explain why or why not.

 **3. GET ORGANIZED** Copy and complete the graphic organizer. In each box, write an example of an event that has the given likelihood.

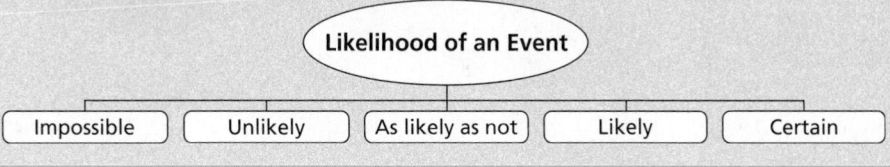

Learn It Online
Homework Help Online
Parent Resources Online

GUIDED PRACTICE

1. Vocabulary Give an example of an *event* that has two possible *outcomes*.

SEE EXAMPLE 1 Identify the sample space and the outcome shown for each experiment.

2. rolling a number cube   **3.** spinning a spinner   **4.** tossing 3 coins

 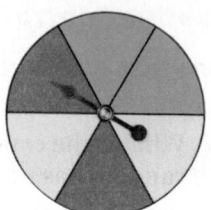 

SEE EXAMPLE 2 Write *impossible, unlikely, as likely as not, likely,* or *certain* to describe each event.

5. Peter was born in January. Thomas was born in June. Peter and Thomas have the same birthday.

6. The football team won 9 of its last 10 games. The team will win the next game.

7. A board game has a rule that if you roll the game cube and get a 6, you get an extra turn. You get an extra turn on your first roll.

SEE EXAMPLE 3 An experiment consists of rolling a number cube. Use the results in the table to find the experimental probability of each event.

Outcome	1	2	3	4	5	6
Frequency	5	6	2	2	3	7

8. rolling a 6

9. rolling an even number

10. not rolling a 6

SEE EXAMPLE 4 **11. Sports** One game of bowling consists of ten frames. Elyse usually rolls 3 strikes in each game.

a. What is the experimental probability that Elyse will roll a strike on any frame?

b. Predict the number of strikes Elyse will roll in 18 games.

PRACTICE AND PROBLEM SOLVING

Identify the sample space and the outcome shown for each experiment.

12. tossing two coins   **13.** spinning a spinner   **14.** selecting a marble

Independent Practice	
For Exercises	See Example
12–14	1
15–17	2
18–20	3
21	4

Extra Practice
See Extra Practice for more Skills Practice and Applications Practice exercises.

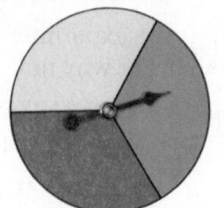 

Write *impossible, unlikely, as likely as not, likely,* or *certain* to describe each event.

15. Marlo purchased a new pair of shoes. She takes one shoe out of the box. The shoe is for the left foot.

16. Sam takes the bus to school. The bus came late twice in the last two weeks. The bus will be late today.

17. Tammy dropped two quarters on the floor. At least one of them lands heads up.

An experiment consists of randomly choosing a marble from a bag. Use the results in the table to find the experimental probability of each event.

Outcome	Frequency
Red	4
Blue	6
Green	6
Yellow	9

18. choosing a yellow marble

19. choosing a blue marble

20. not choosing a green marble

21. Sports A ski lodge inspects 80 skis and finds 4 to be defective.

    a. What is the experimental probability that a ski chosen at random will be defective?

    b. The lodge has 420 skis. Predict the number of skis that are likely to be defective.

22. The table shows the results of a survey asking students the season of their birthday. What is the experimental probability that a student has a birthday during the summer?

Season	Birthdays
Fall	39
Winter	27
Spring	33
Summer	51

23. You and your friend can either go swimming or to a movie on Thursday. The weather forecast says there is a 70% chance of rain on Thursday. Should you plan on going swimming or to a movie? Explain.

24. Critical Thinking Tell why it is important to repeat an experiment many times.

25. Write About It Explain what it means for an event to have a 50-50 chance of happening.

26. How many outcomes are in the sample space for an experiment consisting of rolling two standard number cubes?

27. Estimation A manufacturing company produced 986 units in one day. Of those, 9 units were found to be defective. Estimate the experimental probability that a unit produced that day was defective. Then predict approximately how many units will be defective when 5680 units are produced in one week.

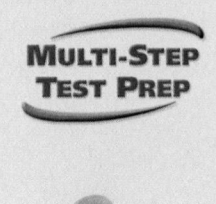

MULTI-STEP TEST PREP

28. In a standard deck of cards, there are 13 cards in each of four suits: hearts, diamonds, clubs, and spades. The hearts and diamonds are red and the clubs and spades are black. Ricardo randomly drew cards from a standard deck of 52 cards. The table shows the results.

Outcome	Frequency
Hearts	7
Diamonds	7
Clubs	8
Spades	6

    a. Find the experimental probability of drawing a club.

    b. Find the experimental probability of drawing a black suit.

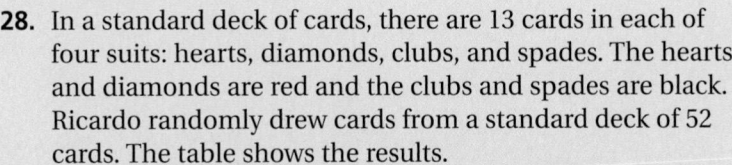

Sam Dudgeon/HMH

29. Alex rolls two standard number cubes. What is the likelihood that the sum of the numbers is less than 4?

(A) Impossible (B) Unlikely (C) As likely as not (D) Likely

30. A community reported that $\frac{2}{3}$ of the residents had a pet and $\frac{1}{2}$ of the pet owners had a dog. If there are 84 residents in the community, how many residents are likely to have a dog?

(F) 14 (G) 28 (H) 42 (J) 56

31. What is the probability that a number chosen at random from the list below will be a solution of the inequality $3x + 2 \leq 23$?

−8, −7, −6, −5, −4, −3, −2, −1, 0, 1, 2, 3, 4, 5, 6, 7, 8, 9

(A) $\frac{17}{18}$ (B) $\frac{8}{9}$ (C) $\frac{1}{9}$ (D) $\frac{1}{18}$

32. **Short Response** A coin was tossed 50 times. It landed showing heads 6 more times than it landed showing tails. What is the experimental probability of the coin landing on heads? Show your work.

CHALLENGE AND EXTEND

A coin is tossed 3 times. Use the sample space for this experiment to describe each event below as *impossible, unlikely, as likely as not, likely,* or *certain.* Justify each answer.

33. At least 2 heads

34. 2 heads and 1 tail

35. 2 tails and 1 head

36. 3 tails

37. One coin is tossed 20 times.

    a. The experimental probability of the coin showing heads is 65%. How many times did the coin show tails?

    b. If the coin is tossed ten more times, how many more times must the coin land showing tails for the experimental probability of tails to be 50%?

10-5
Technology LAB

Use with Experimental Probability

Use Random Numbers

A calculator can be used to model an experiment that would be difficult or inconvenient to perform. To do this, you will use random numbers.

MATHEMATICAL PRACTICES **Use appropriate tools strategically.**

CC.9-12.S.IC.1 Decide if a specified model is consistent with results from a given data-generating process, e.g., using simulation.

Activity

You can use a calculator to explore the experimental probability that at least 2 people in a group of 6 people were born in the same month. Assume that all months are equally likely to be a person's birth month.

❶ Represent each month with an integer. Since there are 12 months, use the numbers 1–12.

To set your calculator up to generate random numbers, press . Then use the arrow keys to highlight **PRB**. Select **5: randInt(**.

```
MATH NUM CPX PRB
1:rand
2:nPr
3:nCr
4:!
5:randInt(
6:randNorm(
7:randBin(
```

❷ Now give the start number, 1, press ⟨ , ⟩, and give the end number, 12.

Each time you press ENTER the calculator will return an integer from 1 to 12.

❸ You are considering a group of 6 people. This means you need 6 random numbers.

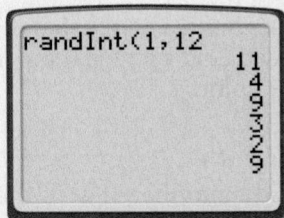

```
randInt(1,12
            11
             4
             9
             3
             2
             9
```

	Person					
	1	2	3	4	5	6
Trial 1	11	4	9	3	2	9
Trial 2	3	8	10	12	6	2

In the first trial, the number 9 appears twice. This means that two people have a birth day in the ninth month, September.

In the second trial, no number appears more than once. This means that none of the people were born in the same month.

Try This

1. Repeat the experiment until you have 10 trials of the experiment. Count the number of trials in which a number appears more than once. Divide this number by the number of trials, 10, to find the experimental probability that at least 2 people in a group of 6 people will have the same birth month.

2. Gather the results from at least 100 trials of the experiment. (Either perform all of the trials yourself or combine data with your classmates.) Using your results, what is the experimental probability that at least 2 people in a group of 6 people will have the same birth month? Compare the results from 100 trials to the results of 10 trials.

3. How could you set up the experiment to find the experimental probability that at least 2 people in a group of 6 people will have the same birthday (same month and same date)?

10-6 Theoretical Probability

CC.9-12.S.CP.1 Describe events as subsets of a sample space … using characteristics (or categories) of the outcomes, or as unions, intersections, or complements of other events ….

Objectives
Determine the theoretical probability of an event.

Convert between probabilities and odds.

Vocabulary
equally likely
theoretical probability
fair
complement
odds

Why learn this?
Theoretical probability can be used to determine the likelihood of different weather conditions. (See Example 2.)

A developing tornado near Amarillo, Texas.

When the outcomes in the sample space of an experiment have the same chance of occurring, the outcomes are said to be **equally likely**.

Equally likely outcomes

There is the same chance that the spinner will land on any of the colors.

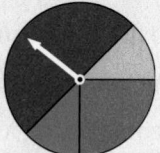

Not equally likely outcomes

There is a greater chance that the spinner will land on blue than on any other color.

The **theoretical probability** of an event is the ratio of the number of ways the event can occur to the total number of equally likely outcomes.

> ### Theoretical Probability
> $$\text{theoretical probability} = \frac{\text{number of ways the event can occur}}{\text{total number of equally likely outcomes}}$$

An experiment in which all outcomes are equally likely is said to be **fair**. You can usually assume that experiments involving coins and number cubes are fair.

EXAMPLE 1 Finding Theoretical Probability

An experiment consists of rolling a number cube. Find the theoretical probability of each outcome.

Caution!
The use of the word *experiment* does not necessarily mean you are looking for experimental probability.

A rolling a 3

$$\frac{\text{number of ways the event can occur}}{\text{total number of equally likely outcomes}} = \frac{1}{6}$$

There is one 3 on a number cube.

$$= 0.1\overline{6}$$

$$= 16\frac{2}{3}\%$$

Digital Vision/Getty Images

An experiment consists of rolling a number cube. Find the theoretical probability of each outcome.

B rolling a number greater than 3

$$\frac{\text{number of ways the event can occur}}{\text{total number of equally likely outcomes}} = \frac{3}{6} = \frac{1}{2} \qquad \text{\textit{There are 3 numbers greater than 3.}}$$

$$= 0.5 = 50\%$$

 **CHECK IT OUT!** An experiment consists of rolling a number cube. Find the theoretical probability of each outcome.

1a. rolling an even number   **1b.** rolling a multiple of 3

When you toss a coin, there are two possible outcomes, heads or tails. The table below shows the theoretical probabilities and experimental results of tossing a coin 10 times.

Reading Math

The probability of an event can be written as *P*(event). *P*(heads) means "the probability that heads will be the outcome."

	P(heads)	P(tails)	P(heads) + P(tails)
Experimental Probability	$\frac{3}{10}$	$\frac{7}{10}$	$\frac{3}{10} + \frac{7}{10} = \frac{10}{10} = 1$
Theoretical Probability	$\frac{1}{2}$	$\frac{1}{2}$	$\frac{1}{2} + \frac{1}{2} = \frac{2}{2} = 1$

The sum of the probability of heads and the probability of tails is 1, or 100%. This is because it is certain that one of the two outcomes will always occur.

$$P(\text{event happening}) + P(\text{event not happening}) = 1$$

The **complement** of an event is all the outcomes in the sample space that are not included in the event. The sum of the probabilities of an event and its complement is 1, or 100%, because the event will either happen or not happen. Two events are *complementary events* if the sum of their probabilities equals 1 and if one event occurs if and only if the other does not.

$$P(\text{event}) + P(\text{complement of event}) = 1$$

EXAMPLE 2 Finding Probability by Using the Complement

The weather forecaster predicts a 20% chance of snow. What is the probability that it will not snow?

$$P(\text{snow}) + P(\text{not snow}) = \quad 100\% \qquad \text{\textit{Either it will snow or it will}}$$
$$20\% + P(\text{not snow}) = \quad 100\% \qquad \text{\textit{not snow.}}$$
$$\underline{-20\% \qquad\qquad\qquad -20\%} \qquad \text{\textit{Subtract 20\% from both sides.}}$$
$$P(\text{not snow}) = \quad 80\%$$

 **CHECK IT OUT!** **2.** A jar has green, blue, purple, and white marbles. The probability of choosing a green marble is 0.2, the probability of choosing blue is 0.3, and the probability of choosing purple is 0.1. What is the probability of choosing white?

Atlo Foto Agency/Alamy

Odds are another way to indicate the likelihood of an event. **Odds** express likelihood by comparing the number of ways an event can happen to the number of ways an event can fail to happen. The *odds in favor of an event* describe the likelihood that the event will occur. The *odds against an event* describe the likelihood that the event will not occur.

Odds are usually written with a colon in the form $a:b$, but can also be written as a to b or $\frac{a}{b}$.

Odds

ODDS IN FAVOR OF AN EVENT WITH EQUALLY LIKELY OUTCOMES

$$\text{odds in favor} = \frac{\text{number of ways an event can happen}}{\text{number of ways an event can fail to happen}}$$

$$= a:b$$

ODDS AGAINST AN EVENT WITH EQUALLY LIKELY OUTCOMES

$$\text{odds against} = \frac{\text{number of ways an event can fail to happen}}{\text{number of ways an event can happen}}$$

$$= b:a$$

a represents the number of ways an event can occur.

b represents the number of ways an event can fail to occur.

The two numbers given as the odds will add up to the total number of possible outcomes. You can use this relationship to convert between odds and probabilities.

EXAMPLE **3** **Converting Between Odds and Probabilities**

A **The probability of choosing a red card from a standard deck of playing cards is 50%. What are the odds of choosing a red card?**

The probability of choosing a red card is 50%, so the probability of not drawing a red card is 100% − 50% = 50%.

Odds in favor = 50 : 50, or 1 : 1

The odds in favor of choosing a red card are 1 : 1.

Reading Math

You may see an outcome called "favorable." This does not mean that the outcome is good or bad. A favorable outcome is the outcome you are looking for in a probability experiment.

B **The odds against choosing a green marble from a bag are 5 : 3. What is the probability of choosing a green marble?**

The odds against green are 5 : 3, so the odds in favor of green are 3 : 5. This means there are 3 favorable outcomes and 5 unfavorable outcomes for a total of 8 possible outcomes.

$$\frac{\text{number of ways event can happen}}{\text{total possible outcomes}} = \frac{3}{8}$$

The probability of choosing a green marble is $\frac{3}{8}$.

CHECK IT OUT!

3. The odds in favor of winning a free drink are 1 : 24. What is the probability of winning a free drink?

Victoria Smith/HMH

THINK AND DISCUSS

1. Tell how to find the probability of the complement of an event.

2. GET ORGANIZED Copy and complete the graphic organizer using the spinner.

Probabilities on Spinner	
P(gray)	
P(not gray)	
Odds in favor of gray	
Odds against gray	

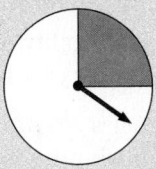

10-6 Exercises

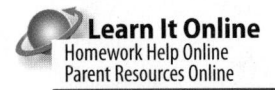
Learn It Online
Homework Help Online
Parent Resources Online

GUIDED PRACTICE

1. Vocabulary All of the outcomes in the sample space that are not included in the event are called the ___?___. (*theoretical probability*, *complement*, or *odds*)

SEE EXAMPLE **1** **Find the theoretical probability of each outcome.**

2. rolling a number divisible by 3 on a number cube

3. tossing 2 coins and both landing with tails showing

4. randomly choosing the letter S from the letters in STARS

5. rolling a prime number on a number cube

SEE EXAMPLE **2** **6.** A spinner is green, red, and blue. The probability that the spinner will land on green is 15% and red is 35%. What is the probability the spinner will land on blue?

7. The probability of choosing a red marble from a bag is $\frac{1}{3}$. What is the probability of not choosing a red marble?

8. You have a $\frac{1}{50}$ chance of winning. What is the probability you will not win?

9. There is a $\frac{1}{10}$ chance that you will be chosen as class representative. What is the probability that you will not be chosen?

SEE EXAMPLE **3** **10.** The odds against a spinner landing on blue are 3 : 1. What is the probability of the spinner landing on blue?

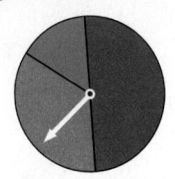

11. The probability of choosing an ace from a deck of cards is $\frac{1}{13}$. What are the odds of choosing an ace?

12. The probability of not winning a game is 80%. What are the odds of winning?

13. The odds in favor of a spinner landing on blue are 1 : 3. What is the probability of landing on blue?

PRACTICE AND PROBLEM SOLVING

Find the theoretical probability of each outcome.

Independent Practice

For Exercises	See Example
14–16	1
17–19	2
20–22	3

Extra Practice

See Extra Practice for more Skills Practice and Applications Practice exercises.

14. rolling a 5 on a number cube

15. tossing 2 coins and 1 landing with heads showing, the other with tails showing

16. randomly choosing a blue marble from a bag of 5 blue marbles, 8 red marbles, and 7 yellow marbles

17. The probability of a spinner landing on yellow is $\frac{4}{9}$. What is the probability of it not landing on yellow?

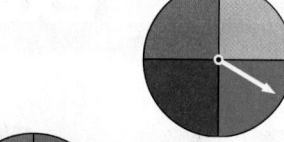

18. There is a 3% probability of winning a game. Find the probability of not winning the game.

19. There is a 15% chance it will snow and a 15% chance it will rain. What is the probability that it will neither snow nor rain?

20. The odds against winning a contest are 99:1. What is the probability of not winning the contest?

21. The odds of choosing a white marble from a bag are 1:9. Find the probability of not choosing a white marble.

22. The probability of a spinner landing on green is 25%. What are the odds of the spinner not landing on green?

Use the spinner for Exercises 23–28.

23. $P(\text{red})$

24. $P(\text{green})$

25. $P(\text{not blue})$

26. odds in favor of yellow

27. odds against red

28. odds against green

29. **Write About It** A number cube is rolled. Which event has a greater theoretical probability: rolling a number less than 3 or rolling a number greater than three? Explain.

30. **///ERROR ANALYSIS///** The odds in favor of an event are 1:4. Two students converted these odds into the probability of the event NOT happening. Which is incorrect? Explain the error.

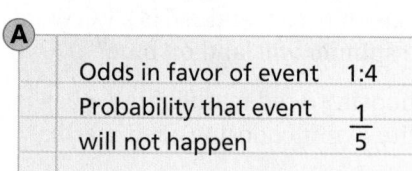

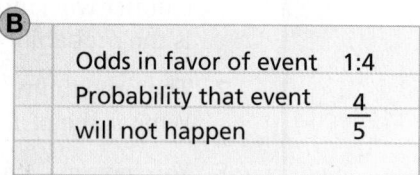

31. **Critical Thinking** The odds in favor of a certain event are the same as the odds against that event. What is the probability of the event occurring?

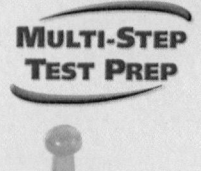

MULTI-STEP TEST PREP

32. Chutes and Ladders is a children's game that uses a spinner with the numbers 1 through 6.

   a. What is the probability of spinning a 3?

   b. What is the probability of spinning an odd number?

   c. What is the probability of spinning a number that is less than or equal to 4?

Sam Dudgeon/HMH

33. **Write About It** Explain how to convert odds to probability.

34. **Geometry** The radius of each circle in the diagram is given. Find the probability that a point chosen at random will lie in the red area of the diagram. (*Hint:* Find the ratio of the red area to the total area of the diagram.)

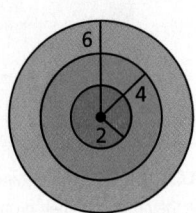

35. Two coins are tossed. What is the probability that at least one of the coins lands with heads showing?

    (A) 25%   (B) $33\frac{1}{3}\%$ (C) 50%   (D) 75%

36. A standard number cube is rolled. Which has the greatest probability?

    (F) P(even)   (G) P(less than 5)   (H) P(not 2)   (J) P(greater than 3)

37. Find the probability that a point chosen at random would fall in the yellow area.

    (A) $\frac{1}{6}$ (C) $\frac{4}{9}$

    (B) $\frac{2}{9}$ (D) $\frac{2}{3}$

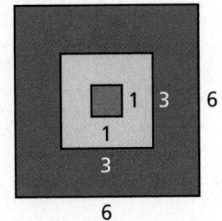

CHALLENGE AND EXTEND

Use the results of 3 coin-tossing experiments in the table for Exercise 38.

38. Find the experimental probability of the coin showing heads for

    a. experiment 1.

    b. experiment 2.

    c. experiment 3.

    d. Find the theoretical probability of the coin showing heads.

     e. **Write About It** How do the experimental probabilities of each experiment compare to the theoretical probability?

	Experiment		
	1	**2**	**3**
Number of Tosses	10	100	1000
Heads	4	48	502

10-7 Independent and Dependent Events

CC.9-12.S.CP.2 Understand that two events *A* and *B* are independent if the probability of *A* and *B* occurring together is the product of their probabilities … *Also* **CC.9-12.S.CP.6, CC.9-12.S.CP.3, CC.9-12.S.CP.5, CC.9-12.S.CP.1**

Objectives
Find the probability of independent events.

Find the probability of dependent events.

Vocabulary
independent events
dependent events

Why learn this?

You may need to understand independent and dependent events to determine the number of reading selections available.

Adam's teacher gives the class two lists of titles and asks each student to choose two of them to read. Adam can choose one title from each list or two titles from the same list.

One title from each list		Two titles from the same list	
(Animal Farm)	*Never Cry Wolf*	*(Animal Farm)*	*~~Animal Farm~~*
Ethan Frome	*Night*	*Ethan Frome*	*Ethan Frome*
Frankenstein	*Things Fall Apart*	*Frankenstein*	*(Frankenstein)*
Great Expectations	*Wish You Well*	*Great Expectations*	*Great Expectations*
Jane Eyre	*(Wuthering Heights)*	*Jane Eyre*	*Jane Eyre*

Choosing a title from one list does not affect the number of titles to choose from on the other list. The events are *independent*.

Choosing a title from one of the lists changes the number of titles that can be chosen from the same list. The events are *dependent*.

Events are **independent events** if the occurrence of one event does not affect the probability of the other. Events are **dependent events** if the occurrence of one event does affect the probability of the other.

EXAMPLE 1 **Classifying Events as Independent or Dependent**

Tell whether each set of events is independent or dependent. Explain your answer.

A A dime lands heads up and a nickel lands heads up.

The result of tossing a dime does not affect the result of tossing a nickel, so the events are independent.

B You choose a colored game piece in a board game, and then your sister picks another color.

Your sister cannot pick the same color you picked, and there are fewer game pieces for your sister to choose from after you choose, so the events are dependent.

CHECK IT OUT! Tell whether each set of events is independent or dependent. Explain your answer.

1a. A number cube lands showing an odd number. It is rolled a second time and lands showing 6.

1b. One student in your class is chosen for a project. Then another student in the class is chosen.

Independent and Dependent Events

I use the everyday meanings of independent and dependent to remember their mathematical meanings.

The math class I take next year depends on which math classes I have already taken.

For dependent events, the occurrence of one affects the probability of the other.

The history class I take next year is independent from (does not depend on) which math classes I have taken.

For independent events, the occurrence of one does not affect the occurrence of the other.

Lydia Delgado
Northridge High
School

Suppose an experiment involves tossing two fair coins. The sample space of outcomes is shown by the tree diagram. Determine the theoretical probability of both coins landing heads up.

1st Coin

2nd Coin

H

H
T

T

H
T

There are four possible outcomes in the sample space: $\{(H, H), (H, T), (T, H), (T, T)\}$

Only one outcome includes both coins landing heads up.

The theoretical probability of both coins landing heads up is $\frac{1}{4}$.

Now look back at the separate theoretical probabilities of each coin landing heads up. The theoretical probability in each case is $\frac{1}{2}$. The product of these two probabilities is $\frac{1}{4}$, the same probability shown by the tree diagram.

To determine the probability of two independent events, multiply the probabilities of the two events.

Probability of Independent Events

If A and B are independent events, then $P(A \text{ and } B) = P(A) \cdot P(B)$.

EXAMPLE 2 **Finding the Probability of Independent Events**

A An experiment consists of randomly selecting a marble from a bag, replacing it, and then selecting another marble. The bag contains 7 blue marbles and 3 yellow marbles. What is the probability of selecting a yellow marble and then a blue marble?

Because the first marble is replaced after it is selected, the sample space for each selection is the same. The events are independent.

$P(\text{yellow, blue}) = P(\text{yellow}) \cdot P(\text{blue})$

$= \frac{3}{10} \cdot \frac{7}{10}$

$= \frac{21}{100}$

The probability of selecting yellow is $\frac{3}{10}$, and the probability of selecting blue is $\frac{7}{10}$.

B When a person rolls 2 number cubes and they land showing the same number, we say the person rolled doubles. What is the probability of rolling doubles 3 times in a row?

The result of one roll does not affect any following rolls. The events are independent.

When you roll 2 number cubes, there are 36 possible outcomes, six of which are doubles:

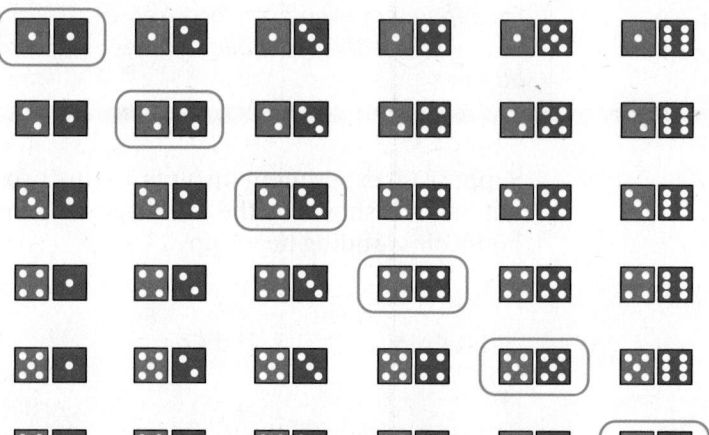

So, the probability of rolling doubles once is $P(\text{double}) = \dfrac{6}{36} = \dfrac{1}{6}$.

$P(\text{double, double, double}) = P(\text{double}) \cdot P(\text{double}) \cdot P(\text{double})$

$$= \frac{1}{6} \cdot \frac{1}{6} \cdot \frac{1}{6}$$

$$= \frac{1}{216}$$

 **2.** An experiment consists of spinning the spinner twice. What is the probability of spinning two odd numbers?

Suppose an experiment involves drawing marbles from a bag. Determine the theoretical probability of drawing a red marble and then drawing a second red marble *without replacing the first one.*

1st Draw   **2nd Draw**

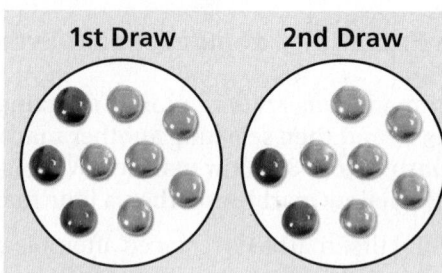

The sample space for the second draw is not the same as the sample space for the first draw. There are fewer marbles in the bag for the second draw.

This means the events are dependent.

Probability of drawing a red marble on the first draw $= \dfrac{3}{9} = \dfrac{1}{3}$

Probability of drawing a red marble on the second draw $= \dfrac{2}{8} = \dfrac{1}{4}$

To determine the probability of two dependent events, multiply the probability of the first event times the probability of the second event after the first event has occurred.

Probability of Dependent Events

If A and B are dependent events, then $P(A \text{ and } B) = P(A) \cdot P(B \text{ after } A)$.

EXAMPLE **3**

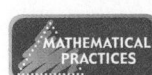

MATHEMATICAL PRACTICES

Make sense of problems and persevere in solving them.

Problem-Solving Application

There are 7 pink flowers and 5 yellow flowers in a bunch. Jane selects a flower at random, and then Leah selects a flower at random from the remaining flowers. What is the probability that Jane selects a pink flower and Leah selects a yellow flower?

1 **Understand the Problem**

The **answer** will be the probability that a yellow flower is chosen after a pink flower is chosen.

List the **important information:**

• Jane chooses a pink flower from 7 pink flowers and 5 yellow flowers.
• Leah chooses a yellow flower from 6 pink flowers and 5 yellow flowers.

2 **Make a Plan**

Draw a diagram.

Flowers Jane can choose from: Flowers Leah can choose from:

⬤⬤⬤⬤⬤⬤⬤ 7 pink   ⬤⬤⬤⬤⬤⬤ 6 pink
⬤⬤⬤⬤⬤ 5 yellow   ⬤⬤⬤⬤⬤ 5 yellow
12 total   11 total

After Jane selects a flower, the sample space changes. So the events are dependent.

3 **Solve**

$$P(\text{pink and yellow}) = P(\text{pink}) \cdot P(\text{yellow after pink})$$

$$= \frac{7}{12} \cdot \frac{5}{11} \qquad \textit{Jane selects one of 7 pink flowers from 12 total flowers. Then Leah selects one of 5 yellow flowers from the 11 flowers left.}$$

$$= \frac{35}{132}$$

The probability that Jane selects a pink flower and Leah selects a yellow flower is $\frac{35}{132}$.

4 **Look Back**

Drawing a diagram helps you see how the sample space changes. This means the events are dependent, so you can use the formula for probability of dependent events.

3. A bag has 10 red marbles, 12 white marbles, and 8 blue marbles. Two marbles are randomly drawn from the bag. What is the probability of drawing a blue marble and then a red marble?

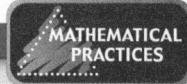
THINK AND DISCUSS

1. Give an example of two events that are dependent. Explain why the events are dependent.

2. GET ORGANIZED Copy and complete the graphic organizer.

	Example	Probability
Dependent Events	$A =$ $B =$	$P(A \text{ and } B) =$
Independent Events	$A =$ $B =$	$P(A \text{ and } B) =$

10-7 Exercises

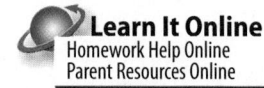
Learn It Online
Homework Help Online
Parent Resources Online

GUIDED PRACTICE

1. Vocabulary Two events are _____?_____ if the occurrence of one event affects the probability of the other event. (*independent* or *dependent*)

SEE EXAMPLE 1 **Tell whether each set of events is independent or dependent. Explain your answers.**

2. You draw a heart from a deck of cards and set it aside. Then you draw a club from the deck of cards.

3. You guess "true" on two true-false questions.

4. You select a kitten to adopt from an animal shelter. Then your friend selects a kitten to adopt.

5. You order from a menu, and then your friend orders.

6. A doctors' office schedules several patients. Then you make an appointment.

SEE EXAMPLE 2 **7.** A coin is tossed three times. What is the probability of the coin landing heads up three times?

8. Seven cards are numbered from 1 to 7 and placed in a box. One card is selected at random and replaced. Another card is randomly selected. What is the probability of selecting two odd numbers?

9. Stacey rolls two number cubes. What is the probability that the sum of the numbers on the two number cubes is 7?

10. A number cube is rolled twice and a coin is tossed once. What is the probability of the coin landing heads up and the number cube landing with 2 showing both times?

11. A spinner with four equal sections of red, yellow, green, and blue is spun twice. What is the probability that it lands on yellow and then on green?

Sam Dudgeon/HMH

12. A bag contains 4 red marbles, 3 white marbles, and 6 blue marbles. What is the probability of randomly selecting a red marble, setting it aside, and then randomly selecting a white marble from the bag?

13. Seven cards are numbered from 1 to 7 and placed in a box. One card is selected at random and not replaced. Another card is randomly selected. What is the probability of selecting two odd numbers?

14. There are 15 boys and 14 girls in a room. Two of them are selected at random to take a survey. What is the probability that the two people selected will be girls?

PRACTICE AND PROBLEM SOLVING

Independent Practice

For Exercises	See Example
15–16	1
17–19	2
20–22	3

Extra Practice

See Extra Practice for more Skills Practice and Applications Practice exercises.

Tell whether each set of events is independent or dependent. Explain your answer.

15. The teacher randomly selects two students from the class.

16. You roll a 3 on a number cube and choose a 3 from a deck of cards.

17. A number cube is rolled three times. What is the probability of rolling three even numbers?

18. Ten cards are numbered from 1 to 10 and placed in a box. One card is selected at random and replaced. Another card is randomly selected. What is the probability of selecting two even numbers?

19. Stacey rolls a number cube and tosses a coin. What is the probability that she rolls a 5 and the coin lands heads up?

20. A bag contains 5 red marbles, 3 white marbles, and 4 blue marbles. What is the probability of randomly selecting a red marble, setting it aside, and then randomly selecting another red marble from the bag?

21. Ten cards are numbered from 1 to 10 and placed in a box. One card is selected at random and not replaced. Another card is randomly selected. What is the probability of selecting two even numbers?

22. A game has 6 colored playing pieces. They are red, yellow, green, blue, purple, and white. You and a friend each pick a game piece without looking. What is the probability that your friend picks the blue piece and then you pick the yellow piece?

School

23. **School** On a multiple-choice test, each question has 4 possible answers. A student does not know the answers to three questions, so the student guesses.

 a. What is the probability that the student gets all three questions wrong?

 b. What is the probability that the student gets all three questions right?

Tell whether each set of events is independent or dependent. Explain your answer.

24. Pick "Joe" from a box of names, replace it, and then pick "Craig."

25. Pick "Joe" from a box of names, set it aside, and then pick "Craig."

26. Roll a prime number on a number cube and get tails when tossing a coin.

27. Roll an even number, then an odd number, and then a 1 on a number cube.

 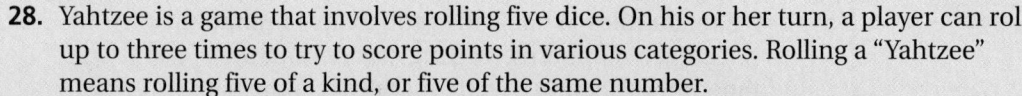

MULTI-STEP TEST PREP

28. Yahtzee is a game that involves rolling five dice. On his or her turn, a player can roll up to three times to try to score points in various categories. Rolling a "Yahtzee" means rolling five of a kind, or five of the same number.

  a. Juan has rolled twice and has three 5's showing. He rolls the remaining two dice. What is the probability that both dice will land showing 5?

  b. Shauna has two 3's showing. She has one more roll with the remaining three dice. What is the probability that all three dice will land showing 3?

  c. Mike rolls all five number cubes and all of them land showing 6. What is the probability of getting five 6's in one roll?

29. A bag contains 3 red, 5 blue, and 2 white marbles.

  a. Find the probability of randomly picking a red marble, replacing it, and then picking a blue marble.

  b. Find the probability of randomly picking a red marble, setting it aside, and then picking a blue marble.

  c. Find the probability of randomly picking a red marble, replacing it, and then picking another red marble.

  d. Find the probability of randomly picking a red marble, setting it aside, and then picking another red marble.

30. Entertainment Joe and Maria are playing a board game. On each turn, the player rolls two number cubes. Both players have two turns remaining.

  a. Joe will win if he rolls double 6's on both turns. What is the probability that Joe will roll double 6's on both turns?

  b. Maria will win if she rolls 2 on the first turn and 12 on the second turn. What is the probability that Maria will roll 2 on the first turn and 12 on the second turn?

   c. Write About It Who has the better probability of winning? Explain.

31. Tamika has $2.50 in quarters in her pocket, including four state quarters. She reaches into her pocket and takes out two quarters, one at a time. What is the probability that they are both state quarters?

32. Ten cards are numbered 1 through 10 and placed in a bag. You draw a card, set it aside, and draw another card. What is the probability that you will draw two numbers that are divisible by 3?

33. Critical Thinking What is the probability of a coin landing heads up on two tosses if it lands tails up on the first toss? Explain.

 34. Write About It Explain what it means for two events to be independent.

TEST PREP

35. A number cube is rolled twice. What is the probability of getting a 2 on both rolls?

  Ⓐ $\frac{1}{3}$ Ⓑ $\frac{1}{4}$ Ⓒ $\frac{1}{9}$ Ⓓ $\frac{1}{36}$

36. In baseball, Julio averages 3 hits in every 10 at bats. What is the probability that he will get hits in both of his next two at bats?

  Ⓕ 0.03   Ⓖ 0.09   Ⓗ 0.3   Ⓙ 0.9

Sam Dudgeon/HMH

37. Two people from a group of 30 will be selected at random for a prize. Twenty people in the group are women. What is the probability that both people selected will be men?

  Ⓐ $\dfrac{3}{29}$ Ⓑ $\dfrac{38}{87}$ Ⓒ $\dfrac{56}{87}$ Ⓓ $\dfrac{1}{10}$

38. Ravi has 10 pairs of socks in a drawer, but none of the pairs are matched up. Each pair is a different color, and one pair is blue. Ravi has to pick his socks in the dark so he does not wake his brother. Which expression can be used to find the probability that Ravi will choose a blue sock and then the matching sock?

  Ⓕ $\dfrac{1}{20}+\dfrac{1}{20}$ Ⓖ $\dfrac{1}{10}\cdot\dfrac{1}{20}$ Ⓗ $\dfrac{1}{20}+\dfrac{1}{19}$ Ⓙ $\dfrac{1}{10}\cdot\dfrac{1}{19}$

CHALLENGE AND EXTEND

39. Basketball Terrance has made 90% of the free throws he has attempted at basketball practice. What is the probability that he will make the next three free throws he attempts?

40. A number cube is rolled three times. What is the probability of rolling a 5 at least once?

Geometry Use the grid for Exercises 41–44.

On the grid at right, one small square represents 1% probability.

The shaded rows represent the probability that event *A* occurs.

The shaded columns represent the probability that event *B* occurs.

The area where the shaded rows and columns overlap represents the probability that both events occur.

Use the grid to find each probability.

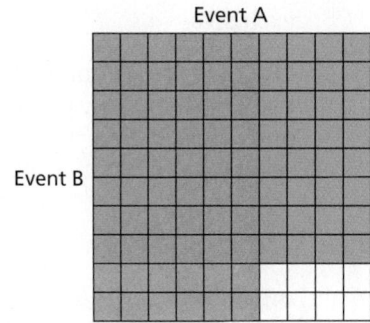

41. Event *A* occurs.

42. Event *B* occurs.

43. Event *A* occurs AND event *B* occurs.

44. Neither event *A* nor event *B* occurs.

10-7
Algebra
LAB

Use with Independent and Dependent Events

Compound Events

When two events cannot happen at the same time, they are called *mutually exclusive* events. When two events can happen at the same time, they are called *inclusive* events. You can use sample spaces to determine the probabilities of mutually exclusive events and inclusive events.

When finding the probablity of a compound event, you should first determine whether the simple events involved are dependent or independent.

Activity 1

 **Look for and express regularity in repeated reasoning.**

CC.9-12.S.CP.7 Apply the Addition Rule, $P(A \text{ or } B) = P(A) + P(B) - P(A \text{ and } B)$, and interpret the answer in terms of the model.

Suppose you are playing Monopoly and are "just visiting" the Jail. If you roll 7 on your next turn, you will land on Community Chest. If you roll 12, you will land on Chance. What is the probability that on your next roll you land on either Community Chest or Chance?

You cannot land on Community Chest and Chance at the same time, so the events are mutually exclusive. You cannot roll 7 and 12 at the same time, so those events are also mutually exclusive.

The table shows some of the totals when rolling two fair dice. Copy and complete the table. Use one color to circle all rolls with a total of 7. Use a second color to circle all rolls with a total of 12.

+	1	2	3	4	5	6
1	2	3	4	5	▢	▢
2	3	4	▢	▢	▢	▢
3	4	5	▢	▢	▢	▢
4	5	▢	▢	▢	▢	▢
5	6	▢	▢	▢	▢	▢
6	7	▢	▢	▢	▢	▢

Try This

1. What is the total number of possible rolls?

2. What is the probability that the total will be 7?

3. What is the probability that the total will be 12?

4. What is the probability that the total will be 7 or 12?

5. What do you notice about the probabilities in Problems 2, 3, and 4?

Suppose you are three spaces away from Community Chest and eight spaces away from Chance.

6. What is the probability that on your next roll the total will be 3?

7. What is the probability that on your next roll the total will be 8?

8. What is the probability that on your next roll the total will be 3 or 8?

9. Complete the following statement:

   The probability that one of two mutually exclusive events will occur is the
   ___?___ of the probabilities of the individual events.

In this lab, you discovered this rule: If A and B are mutually exclusive events, then $P(A \text{ or } B) = P(A) + P(B)$.

Activity 2

Suppose you are playing Yahtzee and on the last roll of your turn, you roll two of the five dice. You need to roll either a 1 or a 5 to make what is called a "small straight" (four consecutive numbers).

What is the probability that you will make a small straight?

You can roll a 1 and a 5 at the same time on different dice. These events are inclusive.

(If you roll a 1 and a 5, you will need to look at only four of the dice to make a small straight.)

There are three outcomes that involve rolling a 1 or rolling a 5.

Case 1	Case 2	Case 3
At least one 1	At least one 5	Both a 1 and a 5

Try This

10. Find the probability of Case 1, rolling at least one 1.

   a. What is the probability of rolling ⚀ on the first die and any number on the second die?

   b. What is the probability of rolling any number on the first die and ⚀ on the second die?

   c. What is the probability of rolling ⚀ on the first die and ⚀ on the second die?

   d. Parts **a** and **b** both include rolling ⚀ on the first die and ⚀ on the second die. You need to count this outcome only once, so subtract the probability from part **c** from the sum of parts **a** and **b**.

11. Find the probability of Case 2, rolling at least one 5. (*Hint:* Repeat the steps in Problem 10.)

12. Find the probability of Case 3, rolling a 1 and a 5.

13. The probability of rolling a small straight, is the probability of rolling ⚀ *or* ⚄.

   Subtract the probability of rolling both ⚀ *and* ⚄ from the sum of the probabilities of rolling ⚀ on one of the dice (Problem 10) and rolling ⚄ on one of the dice (Problem 11).

14. Complete the following statement:

   The probability that one of two inclusive events will occur is the ___?___ of the probabilities of the individual events ___?___ the probability of the intersection of the two events.

In this lab, you discovered this rule:

If A and B are inclusive events, then $P(A \text{ or } B) = P(A) + P(B) - P(A \text{ and } B)$.

Sam Dudgeon/HMH

MULTI-STEP TEST PREP

MATHEMATICAL
PRACTICES

Make sense of
problems and
persevere in
solving them.

Probability

The Games People Play Probability is involved in most board
and card games.

1. There are 108 cards in a deck for
   the game Uno. The table shows
   the number of each type of card
   found in an Uno deck. What is the
   probability of randomly selecting
   a red card from a complete deck of
   Uno cards?

Type of Card	Number in Deck
Blue cards, 0–9	19
Green cards, 0–9	19
Red cards, 0–9	19
Yellow cards, 0–9	19
Draw Two	8 (2 in each color)
Reverse	8 (2 in each color)
Skip	8 (2 in each color)
Wild	4
Wild Draw Four	4

2. Robert is playing Monopoly. He
   starts the game on the GO space.
   He wants to avoid the Income Tax
   space, which he will land on if he
   rolls a 4 with the two dice. What is
   the probability that he will land on
   the Income Tax space?

3. In the game Battleship, each player chooses locations for small ships
   on a 10-by-10 grid. Each player guesses grid spaces to try to locate
   the other player's ships. A correct guess equals a hit, and by hitting
   each space occupied by a ship, the ship is sunk. The battleship
   piece occupies four grid spaces. What is the probability that a player
   randomly guesses a correct grid space and hits the other player's
   battleship?

(t).Sam Dudgeon/HMH; (b),© Handout/ Hasbro/ Ray Stubblebine/Reuters/CORBIS

Quiz for Lessons 10-5 Through 10-7

✅ 10-5 Experimental Probability

An experiment consists of pushing the random select button on a CD player for a disc with five tracks. Use the results in the table to find the experimental probability of each event.

Outcome	Frequency
Track 1	4
Track 2	6
Track 3	2
Track 4	5
Track 5	3

1. Selecting track 4
2. Selecting track 3
3. Not selecting track 2
4. Selecting an odd numbered track
5. Selecting one of the first 3 tracks
6. Ms. Bleakman checks 32 papers and finds 2 with no name. What is the experimental probability that a paper chosen at random will have no name? Ms. Bleakman has the papers of 176 students. Predict the number of papers she will find with no name.

✅ 10-6 Theoretical Probability

Find the theoretical probability of each outcome.

7. Landing on an odd number when spinning a spinner with 4 equal spaces marked 1, 4, 6, 8
8. Randomly selecting a vowel from all the letters in the word VOWELS
9. Picking a red marble out of a bag with 3 green, 5 blue, 2 red, and 6 yellow marbles
10. The probability of winning a certain prize is 5%. What are the odds of winning the prize?
11. The odds of choosing a winning ticket are 2:8. What is the probability of choosing a winning ticket?
12. The probability of snow is 70%. What are the odds of it not snowing?

✅ 10-7 Independent and Dependent Events

13. A physical education class has 12 boys and 18 girls. Each day, the teacher randomly selects a team captain. Assume that no student is absent. What is the probability that the team captain is a girl two days in a row?
14. After reading to a kindergarten class at the library, Tobey gives out stickers. He has 9 zoo animal stickers and 16 scratch-n-sniff stickers. If Tobey gives the stickers out at random, what is the probability that the first child gets a scratch-n-sniff sticker and the second child gets a zoo animal sticker?

Vocabulary

bar graph	first quartile	outcome
box-and-whisker plot	frequency	outlier
circle graph	frequency table	prediction
complement	histogram	probability
cumulative frequency	independent events	random sample
dependent events	interquartile range (IQR)	range
equally likely	line graph	sample space
event	mean	stem-and-leaf plot
experiment	median	theoretical probability
experimental probability	mode	third quartile
fair	odds	trial

Complete the sentences below with vocabulary words from the list above.

1. A(n) ____?____ is one possible result of an experiment.

2. The ____?____ is the difference between the third and first quartiles.

3. Two events are ____?____ if the occurrence of one event does not affect the probability of the other.

10-1 Organizing and Displaying Data

EXAMPLE

The circle graph shows the post-graduation plans for a high school's 500 graduating seniors.

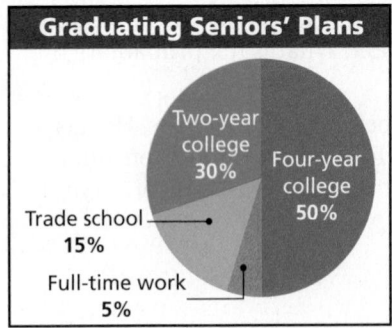

■ How many seniors plan to attend a four-year college?

50% of 500   *Find the percentage.*

$0.50 \times 500 = 250$

250 students plan to attend a four-year college.

EXERCISES

Use the double-bar graph for Exercises 4 and 5.

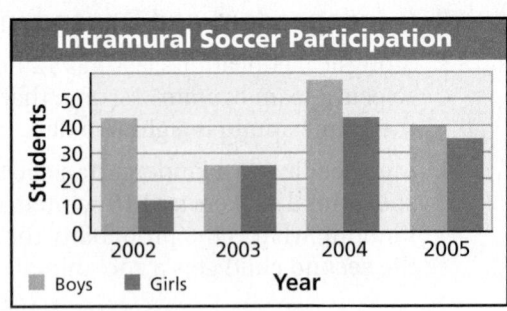

4. In which year did the same number of boys and girls participate?

5. How many more boys than girls participated during 2004?

10-2 Frequency and Histograms

EXAMPLE

- The lives (in hours) of each light bulb in a test are given below. Use the data to make a frequency table and a histogram.

  22, 28, 25, 21, 19, 21, 25,
  21, 22, 18, 20, 29, 25, 26

  Identify the least and greatest values. Divide the data into equal intervals.

Light Bulb Life (h)	
Life	Frequency
18–20	3
21–23	5
24–26	4
27–29	2

  Draw a bar for the number of hours in each interval. The bars touch, but do not overlap.

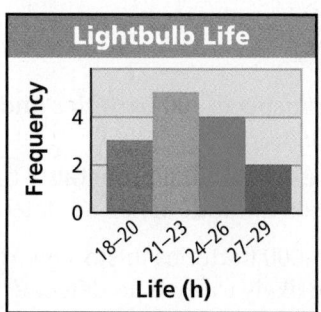

EXERCISES

6. The weights of packages shipped by an online retailer are given below. Use the data to make a stem-and-leaf plot.

Package Weight (lb)										
14	9	22	24	7	1	19	22	28	18	12

7. The numbers of people who attended two different plays are shown in the table below. Make a back-to-back stem-and-leaf plot.

Play Attendance	
Comedy Camp	Days and Days
104 62 83 102	103 105 80 135
104 120 81	109 128 82
126 122	132 139

8. The capacities of the gas tanks on several new vehicles are shown below. Use the data to make a frequency table with intervals.

Gas Tank Capacity (gal)										
15	12	12	15	18	26	25	12	15	18	11
10	12	16	15	16	18	25	21	18	20	21

9. Use your frequency table from Exercise 9 to make a histogram.

10-3 Data Distributions

EXAMPLE

- Consider the following ages of the winners of an art contest: 13, 15, 14, 18, 12, 10, 11, 13. Find the mean and mode of the data.

  mean:

  $$\frac{10 + 11 + 12 + 13 + 13 + 14 + 15 + 18}{8}$$

  $$= \frac{106}{8}$$

  $$= 13.25$$

  mode: 13   *13 occurs most often.*

EXERCISES

Find the mean, median, mode, and range of each data set.

10. Years of playing experience of the members of a musical ensemble:

    5, 14, 25, 7, 8, 10, 12, 33, 12

Herman has five pairs of cowboy boots. The prices were $120, $137, $120, $145, and $482.
mean: $200.80   median: $137   mode: $120

11. Which value best describes the price Herman paid? Explain.

Use the data to make a box-and-whisker plot.

12. 25, 28, 2, 24, 28, 21, 18, 29, 31, 12, 6, 19, 27, 3

10-4 Misleading Graphs and Statistics

EXAMPLE

■ Explain why the graph is misleading.

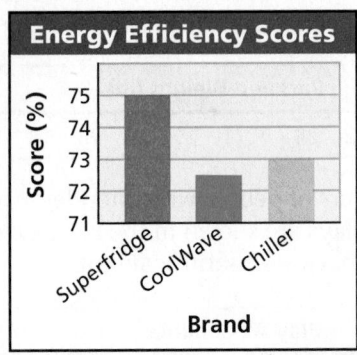

The vertical axis begins at 71. This exaggerates the difference in the heights of the bars.

EXERCISES

The graph shows the cost of admission to an amusement park over 20 years.

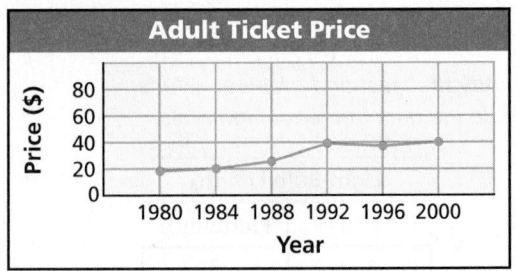

13. Explain why the graph is misleading.

14. What might someone believe because of the graph?

10-5 Experimental Probability

EXAMPLES

The manager of a photo processing lab inspects 500 photos and finds that 4 have flaws.

■ What is the experimental probability that a photo is flawed?

$$\frac{\text{number of times the event occurs}}{\text{number of trials}} = \frac{4}{500} = 0.8\%$$

■ In one month, the lab processes 13,000 photos. Predict the number that are likely to be flawed.

$0.008 \cdot 13,000 = 104$ *Find 0.8% of 13,000.*
104 photos are likely to be flawed.

EXERCISES

A manufacturer inspects 800 batteries and finds that 796 have no defects.

15. What is the experimental probability that a battery chosen at random has no defects?

16. There are 25,000 batteries in storage. How many batteries are likely to have no defects?

17. Another storage area holds 50,000 batteries. How many batteries are likely to have a defect?

10-6 Theoretical Probability

EXAMPLE

■ A jar contains red, green, brown, and blue marbles. The probability of choosing red is 0.30, of choosing green is 0.20, and of choosing brown is 0.25. Find the probability of choosing blue.

$$P(\text{blue}) + P(\text{not blue}) = 1$$
$$P(\text{blue}) + P(\text{red, green, or brown}) = 1$$
$$P(\text{blue}) + (0.30 + 0.20 + 0.25) = 1$$
$$P(\text{blue}) + 0.75 = 1$$
$$P(\text{blue}) = 0.25$$

EXERCISES

Find the theoretical probability of each outcome.

18. Rolling a number less than 4 on a standard number cube

19. Randomly selecting a month that starts with "J" from all month names

20. Randomly selecting a vowel from the letters in EQUATION

10-7 Independent and Dependent Events

A hardware store shelf holds 12 cans of red paint, 4 cans of yellow paint, and 6 cans of black paint.

- Syd selects one can at random and replaces it. Then she selects another can at random. What is the probability that Syd selects a red can and then a yellow can?

  $P(\text{red, yellow}) = P(\text{red}) \cdot P(\text{yellow})$

  $\qquad = \dfrac{12}{22} \cdot \dfrac{4}{22}$ *Independent events*

  $\qquad = \dfrac{48}{484} = \dfrac{12}{121}$

- Gene selects one can at random and then selects another can at random from the remaining cans. What is the probability that Gene selects two cans of black paint?

  $P(\text{black, black}) = P(\text{black}) \cdot P(\text{black after black})$

  $\qquad = \dfrac{6}{22} \cdot \dfrac{5}{21}$ *Dependent events*

  $\qquad = \dfrac{30}{462} = \dfrac{5}{77}$

EXERCISES

Tell whether each set of events is independent or dependent. Explain your answers.

21. A computer generates a random number and then generates another random number.

22. You roll two number cubes. One is a 6 and the other is a 1.

23. Two audience members are called to the stage.

A lottery machine contains different-colored balls. There are 64 green, 128 yellow, 1 golden, and 3 silver balls. Find the probability of each event.

24. A yellow ball is drawn and set aside. Then a green ball is drawn.

25. A golden ball is drawn and set aside. Then another golden ball is drawn.

26. A green ball is drawn and replaced. Then another green ball is drawn.

CHAPTER TEST

1. The table shows the population of Oakville. Use the data to make a graph. Explain why you chose that type of graph.

2. Which ten-year period saw the greatest change in population?

3. Describe the trend in Oakville's population.

Population of Oakville	
Year	Population
1970	20,851
1980	14,229
1990	11,198
2000	9,579

The high temperatures in degrees Fahrenheit for two weeks are given:
64, 66, 63, 58, 59, 55, 51, 54, 61, 62, 68, 70, 63, 63.

4. Use the data to make a stem-and-leaf plot.

5. Use the data to make a frequency table with intervals.

6. Use your frequency table from Problem 5 to make a histogram.

The lengths of statements during a town council meeting are given.

7. Find the mean, median, mode, and range of the data.

8. Use the data to make a box-and-whisker plot.

Length of Statement (min)						
6	25	12	14	2	13	38
22	21	14	3	8	5	17

A manufacturer inspects 500 watches and finds that 498 have no defects.

9. What is the experimental probability that a watch chosen at random has no defects?

10. There are 30,000 watches in a warehouse. Predict the number of watches that are likely to have no defects.

The graph shows how the money raised by a charity is spent.

11. Explain why the graph is misleading.

12. What might someone believe because of the graph?

13. Who might want to use this graph?

14. A bag contains 12 cards, each with a different month of the year printed on it. A card is selected at random. What is the probability that the month begins with *A*?

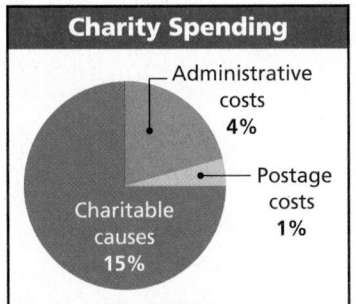

Charity Spending

Administrative costs **4%**

Postage costs **1%**

Charitable causes **15%**

15. The odds of spinning red on a spinner are 2 : 7. What is the probability of not spinning red?

16. A bag has 14 red marbles and 10 white marbles. Rosa randomly picks two marbles from the bag, one at a time. What is the probability that Rosa picks two white marbles?

COLLEGE ENTRANCE EXAM PRACTICE

FOCUS ON SAT MATHEMATICS SUBJECT TEST

There are two levels of SAT Subject Tests: Mathematics Level 1 and Mathematics Level 2. Each test has 50 multiple-choice questions. The content of each test is very different. Getting a high score on one test does not mean you will get a high score on the other test.

You can write all over the test book to sketch figures, do scratch work, or cross out incorrect answers to help you eliminate choices. Remember to mark your final answer on the answer sheet because the test book is not used for scoring.

You may want to time yourself as you take this practice test. It should take you about 6 minutes to complete.

---

1. At a certain high school, the ratio of left-handed to right-handed basketball players is 1:4. If there are a total of 20 players on the team, how many players are right-handed?

   (A) 1

   (B) 4

   (C) 5

   (D) 12

   (E) 16

---

2. Your friend randomly selects 2 movies from your collection to borrow. Your collection includes 9 comedies, 5 dramas, 3 mysteries, 1 musical, and 2 horror movies. What is the probability that both movies are comedies?

   (A) $\dfrac{1}{36}$

   (B) $\dfrac{18}{95}$

   (C) $\dfrac{81}{400}$

   (D) $\dfrac{2}{9}$

   (E) $\dfrac{331}{380}$

---

3. A student's test scores are 88, 87, 82, 95, and 89. If the student needs an average test score of at least 90 to obtain a grade of A, what must the minimum score be on the last test of the semester?

   (A) 88

   (B) 88.2

   (C) 91

   (D) 99

   (E) 100

---

4. What is the probability of not getting a 2 on the spinner?

   (A) 0.10

   (B) 0.25

   (C) 0.50

   (D) 0.75

   (E) 1

---

5. If $x - 3 = 4 - 2(x + 5)$, then $x = ?$

   (A) -3

   (B) -1

   (C) 1

   (D) $\dfrac{3}{2}$

   (E) $\dfrac{11}{3}$

TEST TACKLER

Standardized Test Strategies

Multiple Choice: *None of the Above* or *All of the Above*

In some multiple-choice test items, one of the options is *None of the above* or *All of the above*. To answer these types of items, first determine whether each of the other options is true or false. If you find that more than one option is true, then the correct choice is likely to be *All of the above*. If none of the options are true, the correct choice is *None of the above*.

If you do not know how to solve the problem and have to guess, *All of the above* is most often correct, and *None of the above* is usually incorrect.

EXAMPLE

There are 8 players on the chess team. Which of the following expressions gives the number of ways in which the coach can choose 2 players to start the game?

(A) $_8C_2$

(C) 28

(B) $\dfrac{8!}{2!(6!)}$

(D) All of the above

Notice that choice D is All of the above. *This means that you must look at each option. As you consider each option, mark it true or false in your test booklet.*

A Because order does not matter, this is a combination problem. The number of combinations of 8 players, taken 2 at a time, is given by $_nC_r$, where $n = 8$ and $r = 2$, so $_8C_2$ is a correct model of the combination. Choice A is true.

B The number of combinations of 8 players, taken 2 at a time, is given by $_nC_r = \dfrac{n!}{r!(n - r)!}$, where $n = 8$ and $r = 2$.

$$_nC_r = \frac{n!}{r!(n - r)!} = \frac{8!}{2!(8 - 2)!} = \frac{8!}{2!(6)!}$$

Choice B is a correct model of the combination. Choice B is also true. The answer is likely to be choice D, *All of the above*, but you should also check whether choice C is true.

C The number of combinations of 8 players, taken 2 at a time, is given by $_nC_r = \dfrac{n!}{r!(n - r)!}$, where $n = 8$ and $r = 2$.

$$_nC_r = \frac{n!}{r!(n - r)!} = \frac{8!}{2!(8 - 2)!} = \frac{8!}{2!(6)!} = 28$$

Choice C is a correct model of the combination. Choice C is true as well.

Because A, B, and C are all true, the correct response is D, *All of the above*.

Be careful of problems that contain more than one negative word, such as *no*, *not*, or *never*. Read the problem and each option twice before selecting an answer.

Read each test item and answer the questions that follow.

Item A
The mean score on a test is 68. Which CANNOT be true?

(A) Every score is 68.

(B) Half of the scores are 68, and half of the scores are 0.

(C) Half of the scores are 94, and half of the scores are 42.

(D) None of the above

1. What is the definition of *mean*?

2. If you find that an option is true, is that the correct response? Explain.

3. Willie determined that A and C could both be true, so he chose D as his response. Do you agree? Why or why not?

Item B
What is the probability of rolling a 2 on a number cube?

(F) $16.\overline{6}\%$

(G) $1 - P(\text{rolling } 1, 3, 4, 5, \text{ or } 6)$

(H) $\frac{1}{6}$

(J) All of the above

4. What is the complement of rolling a 2? Is choice G correct? Explain.

5. If you roll a number cube, how many possible outcomes are there? How does this information help you solve this problem?

6. Is the value given in choice H equivalent to any other choice? If so, which one(s)?

7. How many choices are true? What is the correct response to the test item?

Item C
Suppose that a dart lands at a random point on the circular dartboard. Find the probability that the dart does NOT land inside the center circle.

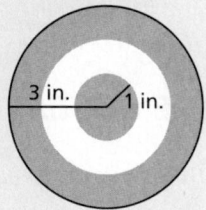

(A) $\frac{1}{9}$

(B) 8π

(C) $\frac{8}{9}$

(D) None of the above

8. Kyle finds that choices A and B are both false. To save time, he selects choice D as his answer because he figures it is likely that choice C will also be false. Do you think Kyle made a wise decision? Why or why not?

9. What is the formula for the area of a circle? What is the total area of this dartboard? How can you determine the area of the dartboard outside the center circle?

10. Determine whether choices A, B, and C are true, and then give the correct response to this test item.

Item D
Each gym member receives a 3-digit locker combination. Digits are from 0–9 and may repeat. What is the probability that you will receive a code consisting of three identical numbers?

(F) $\frac{1}{100}$

(G) $\frac{10}{_{10}C_3}$

(H) $_{10}P_3 = \frac{10!}{7!}$

(J) All of the above

11. How can you determine whether choice J is the correct response to the test item?

12. Are the values given in choices F, G, and H equivalent? What does this tell you about choice J?

CUMULATIVE ASSESSMENT

Multiple Choice

1. Josephine has 9 cousins. Her friend Summer has *s* more cousins. Which expression can be used to show the number of cousins Summer has?

  (A) $9 \div s$ (C) $9 + s$

  (B) $9s$ (D) $9 - s$

2. A negative number raised to an exponent is positive. Which of the following is NOT true?

  (F) The number could be even.

  (G) The number could be odd.

  (H) The exponent could be even.

  (J) The exponent could be odd.

3. A computer game normally sells for $40. Niko bought it when it went on sale for 25% off. The sales tax was 6%. How much did Niko pay for the game?

  (A) $10.60   (C) $31.80

  (B) $12.40   (D) $32.40

4. The graph shows the profit made at a family yard sale that lasted 8 hours. Between which hours did the profit increase at the slowest rate?

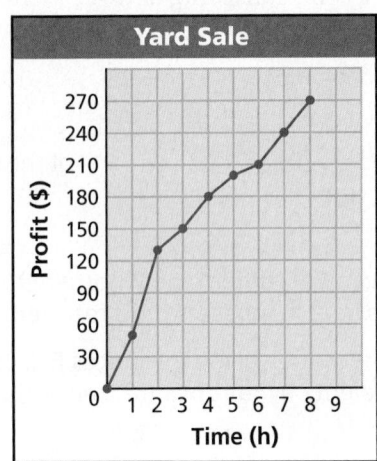

  (F) 0–1   (H) 5–6

  (G) 1–2   (J) 7–8

5. Which of the following is one of the five values needed to make a box-and-whisker plot?

  (A) Mean   (C) Mode

  (B) Median   (D) Average

6. Which value is a solution of $2(1 - x) < 12$?

  (F) -7 (H) -5

  (G) -6 (J) -4

7. What is the median of the data presented in this stem-and-leaf plot?

Stem	Leaves
6	0 2 2 2 5 8
7	3 4 4 6 7
8	2 5 8 9

Key: 8 | 2 means 0.82

  (A) 0.62

  (B) 0.74

  (C) 6.2

  (D) 7.4

8. Which of the following does NOT represent a function?

  (F) $\{(-4, 3), (-2, 1), (-2, -1), (-4, -3)\}$

  (G)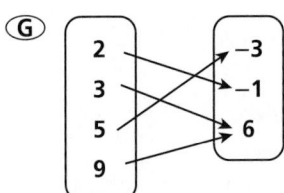

  (H)

x	−4	−3	−2	−1	0	1
y	4	3	2	1	0	−1

  (J)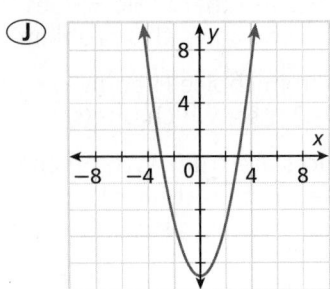

 **If you are allowed to write in your test booklet, you may want to add additional information to a given diagram. Be sure to mark your answer on the answer sheet since your marks on the test booklet will not be graded.**

9. Which of these equations describes a line parallel to $x + 2y = 6$?

(A) $y = \frac{1}{2}x$

(B) $y = -\frac{1}{2}x + 4$

(C) $y = -2x + 6$

(D) $y = 2x + 3$

10. What is the probability that the spinner will NOT land on white?

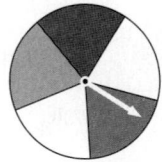

(F) 20%

(G) 40%

(H) 50%

(J) 60%

11. Which equation is NOT true?

(A) $55 + 27 + 45 = 100 + 27$

(B) $5 \cdot 7 \cdot \frac{2}{5} = 2 \cdot 7$

(C) $14(126) = 14(100) + 14(26)$

(D) $31(152) = 30(150) + 1(2)$

12. Which is a factor of $4x^2 + 24x + 36$?

(F) $x + 12$

(G) $2x + 6$

(H) $2x + 18$

(J) $4x + 18$

Gridded Response

13. Yvette is choosing between two stores to get her family pictures taken. Say Cheese charges a $20 sitting fee and $14 per sheet of pictures. Picture Me charges a $12 sitting fee and $18 per sheet of pictures. For how many sheets will the total cost be the same at both stores?

14. Brian plays basketball. In the past, he has made 4 out of every 5 free throws. What is the probability, as a decimal, that Brian will make the next two free throws?

15. What is the next term in the geometric sequence 2000, 1600, 1280, 1024,...?

Short Response

16. An experiment consists of tossing 3 coins at the same time.

a. Identify the sample space.

b. What is the probability of tossing 2 tails and 1 head?

c. Which is more likely to occur: tossing exactly 1 tail or tossing at least 2 heads? Explain.

17. If 8% of a number is 4, what is 12% of the number? Explain your reasoning.

18. Nat surveyed 30 twelfth-grade students and found that 27 of them were in favor of allowing seniors to leave campus for lunch. As a result, Nat reported that "90% of the student body supports off-campus lunch privileges for seniors." Was Nat's statistic misleading? Explain.

19. As part of a challenge problem, a math teacher writes the following expression on the board:

$$-(-x).$$

a. If x is 12, what is the value of the expression?

b. If x is a negative number, is the value of the expression positive or negative? Explain how you found your answer.

c. Simplify the expression.

Extended Response

20. The ages of the first 15 people to enter a community center for bingo one evening are 77, 85, 76, 73, 69, 70, 84, 82, 76, 74, 89, 83, 68, 91, and 88.

a. Find the mean, median, mode, and range of the data.

b. Create a box-and-whisker plot of the data.

c. The sixteenth person to enter the center is 39 years old. Calculate the mean, median, mode, and range of the data with the 16 people.

d. Create a box-and-whisker plot with the 16 people.

e. When the sixteenth person was added, which measure of central tendency changed the most? Which measure changed the least? Explain.

f. How did the addition of the sixteenth person affect the box-and-whisker plot?

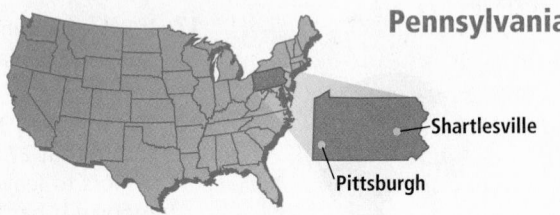

Pennsylvania

Shartlesville

Pittsburgh

⭐ Roadside America Indoor Miniature Village

The Roadside America Indoor Miniature Village in Shartlesville, Pennsylvania, is sometimes referred to as the World's Greatest Indoor Miniature Village. The exhibit uses miniature buildings and realistic landscaping to show what life was like in the 1700s, 1800s, and 1900s. Laurence Gieringer built the village using a $\frac{3}{8}$-inch-to-1-foot scale.

Choose one or more strategies to solve each problem.

1. Suppose a model of a building is made of 180 one-inch cubes. The area of the base of the model is 15 in². How tall is the miniature building? Using a scale of $\frac{3}{8}$ inch to 1 foot, how tall is the actual building?

2. There are about 4000 miniature people in the village. This number is about 100 more than thirteen times the number of buildings in the village. Estimate the number of miniature buildings in the village.

For 3, use the map.

3. It might be helpful to use a coordinate grid when designing a miniature village. Suppose you decide to arrange it as shown. About how far is it from the school to the post office along a straight line?

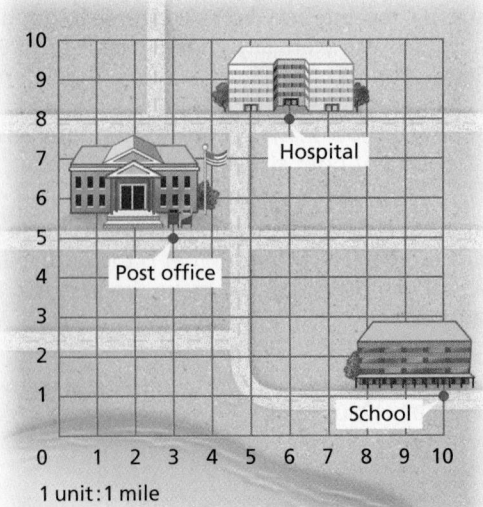

1 unit : 1 mile

⭐ The National Aviary

The National Aviary is located on the north side of Pittsburgh. It is America's only independent indoor nonprofit bird zoo. The aviary is home to more than 600 birds of over 200 species, many of which are threatened or endangered in the wild. Visitors can see birds from almost every continent. Visitors can even feed the birds flying around in a 200,000-cubic-foot indoor rainforest where it actually rains every 15 minutes.

Choose one or more strategies to solve each problem.

For 1 and 2, use the circle graph.

1. The red-crowned crane is the second rarest crane species. The total population of red-crowned cranes in the wild is about 2000 birds. The circle graph shows the approximate percent of this population in four countries where they are found. About how many red-crowned cranes live in Japan?

2. About how many of the total population of red-crowned cranes living in the wild do not live in North Korea or South Korea?

3. One exhibit at the aviary contains bald eagles. An eagle can see a rabbit from about one mile away. The average person must be 1650 feet away to see the same rabbit. Do humans or eagles see farther? How many times as far?

4. It is estimated that only one of every 18 attempts by an eagle to hunt for food is successful. Because of this, eagles use a great deal of energy hunting and have to spend a lot of time resting quietly. According to this information, if you observe an eagle diving for a fish, what is the probability that he is not going to catch the fish on the first try?

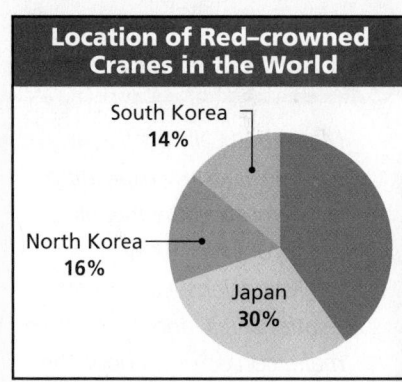

Location of Red–crowned Cranes in the World

South Korea 14%
North Korea 16%
Japan 30%

Mastering *the* Standards

for Mathematical Practice

The topics described in the Standards for Mathematical Content will vary from year to year. However, the *way* in which you learn, study, and think about mathematics will not. The Standards for Mathematical Practice describe skills that you will use in all of your math courses.

Mathematical Practices

1. *Make sense of problems and persevere in solving them.*
2. *Reason abstractly and quantitatively.*
3. *Construct viable arguments and critique the reasoning of others.*
4. *Model with mathematics.*
5. *Use appropriate tools strategically.*
6. *Attend to precision.*
7. *Look for and make use of structure.*
8. *Look for and express regularity in repeated reasoning.*

1 Make sense of problems and persevere in solving them.

Mathematically proficient students start by explaining to themselves the meaning of a problem... They analyze givens, constraints, relationships, and goals. They make conjectures about the form... of the solution and plan a solution pathway...

In your book

Focus on Problem Solving describes a four-step plan for problem solving. The plan is introduced at the beginning of your book, and practice with the plan appears throughout the book.

EXAMPLE 5 *Problem-Solving Application*

The cost to place an ad in a newspaper for one week is a linear function of the number of lines in the ad. The costs for 3, 5, and 10 lines are shown. Write an equation in slope-intercept form that represents the function. Then find the cost of an ad that is 18 lines long.

City Gazette

Newspaper Ad Costs

Lines	3	5	10
Cost ($)	13.50	18.50	31

1 Understand the Problem

• The **answer** will have two parts—an equation in slope-intercept form and the cost of an ad that is 18 lines long.
• The ordered pairs given in the table satisfy the equation.

2 Make a Plan

First, find the slope. Then use point-slope form to write the equation. Finally, write the equation in slope-intercept form.

3 Solve

Step 1 Choose any two ordered pairs from the table to find the slope.

$$m = \frac{y_2 - y_1}{x_2 - x_1} = \frac{18.50 - 13.50}{5 - 3} = \frac{5}{2} = 2.5 \quad \textit{Use (3, 13.50) and (5, 18.50).}$$

Step 2 Substitute the slope and any ordered pair from the table into the point-slope form.

$$y - y_1 = m(x - x_1)$$
$$y - 31 = 2.5(x - 10) \qquad \textit{Use (10, 31).}$$

Step 3 Write the equation in slope-intercept form by solving for y.

$$y - 31 = 2.5(x - 10)$$
$$y - 31 = 2.5x - 25 \qquad \textit{Distribute 2.5.}$$
$$y = 2.5x + 6 \qquad \textit{Add 31 to both sides.}$$

Step 4 Find the cost of an ad containing 18 lines by substituting 18 for x.

$$y = 2.5x + 6$$
$$y = 2.5(18) + 6 = 51$$

The cost of an ad containing 18 lines is $51.

4 Look Back

Check the equation by substituting the ordered pairs (3, 13.50) and (5, 18.50).

$y = 2.5x + 6$		$y = 2.5x + 6$	
13.50	2.5(3) + 6	18.50	2.5(5) + 6
13.5	7.5 + 6	18.5	12.5 + 6
13.5	13.5 ✓	18.5	18.5 ✓

Focus on Problem Solving

The Problem-Solving Plan

To be a good problem solver you need a good problem-solving plan. Using a problem-solving plan along with a problem-solving strategy helps you organize your work and correctly solve the problem. The plan used in this book is outlined below.

UNDERSTAND the Problem

- **What are you asked to find?** Make sure you understand exactly what the problem is asking. Restate the problem in your own words.
- **What information is given in the problem?** List every piece of information the problem gives you.
- **Is all the information relevant?** Sometimes problems have extra information that is not needed to solve the problem. Try to determine what is and is not needed. This helps you stay organized when you are making a plan.
- **Were you given enough information to solve the problem?** Sometimes there simply is not enough information to solve the problem. List what else you need to know to solve the problem.

Make a PLAN

- **What problem-solving strategy or strategies can you use to help you solve the problem?** Think about strategies you have used in the past to solve problems. Would any of them be helpful in solving this problem?
- **Create a step-by-step plan of how you will solve the problem.** Write out your plan in words to help you get a clearer idea of how to solve the problem mathematically.

SOLVE

- **Use your plan to solve the problem.** Translate your plan from words to math. Show each step in your solution and write your answer in a complete sentence.

LOOK BACK

- **Did you completely answer the question that was asked?** Be sure you answered the question that was asked and that your answer is complete.
- **Is your answer reasonable?** Your answer should make sense.
- **Could you have used a different strategy to solve the problem?** Solving the problem again with a different strategy is a good way to check your answer.
- **Did you learn anything that could help you solve similar problems in the future?** You may want to take notes about this kind of problem and the strategy you used to solve it.

Student Handbook

19.95

3²

63.40

Lesson 1-1

Give two ways to write each algebraic expression in words.

1. $x + 8$ **2.** $6(y)$ **3.** $g - 4$ **4.** $\dfrac{12}{h}$

Evaluate each expression for $a = 4$, $b = 2$, and $c = 5$.

5. $b + c$ **6.** $\dfrac{a}{b}$ **7.** $c - a$ **8.** ab

Write an algebraic expression for each verbal expression. Then evaluate the algebraic expression for the given values of y.

	Verbal	Algebraic	$y = 9$	$y = 6$
9.	y reduced by 4	▨	▨	▨
10.	the quotient of y and 3	▨	▨	▨
11.	5 more than y	▨	▨	▨
12.	the sum of y and 2	▨	▨	▨

Lesson 1-2

Solve each equation. Check your answer.

13. $x - 9 = 5$ **14.** $4 = y - 12$ **15.** $a + \dfrac{3}{5} = 7$

16. $7.3 = b + 3.4$ **17.** $-6 + j = 5$ **18.** $-1.7 = -6.1 + k$

Write an equation to represent each relationship. Then solve the equation.

19. A number decreased by 7 is equal to 10.   **20.** The sum of 6 and a number is -3.

Lesson 1-3

Solve each equation. Check your answer.

21. $\dfrac{n}{5} = 15$ **22.** $-6 = \dfrac{k}{4}$ **23.** $\dfrac{r}{2.6} = 5$

24. $3b = 27$ **25.** $56 = -7d$ **26.** $-3.6 = -2f$

27. $\dfrac{1}{4}z = 3$ **28.** $12 = \dfrac{4}{5}g$ **29.** $\dfrac{1}{3}a = -5$

Write an equation to represent each relationship. Then solve the equation.

30. A number multiplied by 4 is -20.   **31.** The quotient of a number and 5 is 7.

Lesson 1-4

Solve each equation. Check your answer.

32. $2k + 7 = 15$ **33.** $11 - 5m = -4$ **34.** $23 = 9 - 2d$

35. $\dfrac{2}{5}b + 6 = 10$ **36.** $\dfrac{f}{3} - 4 = 2$ **37.** $6n + 4 = 22$

Write an equation to represent each relationship. Solve each equation.

38. The difference of 11 and 4 times a number equals 3.

39. Thirteen less than 5 times a number is equal to 7.

Lesson 1-5

Solve each equation. Check your answer.

40. $5b - 3 = 4b + 1$

41. $3g + 7 = 11g - 17$

42. $-8 + 4y = y - 6 + 3y - 2$

43. $7 + 3d - 5 = -1 + 2d - 12 + d$

Write an equation to represent each relationship. Then solve the equation.

44. Three more than one-half a number is the same as 17 minus three times the number.

45. Two times the difference of a number and 4 is the same as 5 less than the number.

Lesson 1-6

Solve each equation for the indicated variable.

46. $q - 3r = 2$ for r

47. $\dfrac{5 - c}{6} = d - 7$ for c

48. $2x + 3\dfrac{y}{4} = 5$ for y

49. $2fgh - 3g = 10$ for h

Lesson 1-7

Solve each equation. Check your answer.

50. $|a| = 13$

51. $|x| - 16 = 3$

52. $|g + 5| = 11$

53. $|7s| - 6 = 8$

54. $\left|\dfrac{f}{2} + 1\right| = 15$

55. $|p - 5| - 12 = -9$

56. $500 = 25|z| + 200$

57. $|7j + 14| - 5 = 16$

58. $\dfrac{|p - 2| - 15}{5} = -1$

Lesson 1-8

59. A car traveled 210 miles in 3 hours. Find the unit rate in miles per hour.

60. A printer printed 60 pages in 5 minutes. Find the unit rate in pages per minute.

Solve each proportion.

61. $\dfrac{h}{4} = \dfrac{5}{6}$

62. $\dfrac{5}{m} = \dfrac{2}{5}$

63. $\dfrac{r}{3} = \dfrac{10}{7}$

64. $\dfrac{2}{3} = \dfrac{2x}{8}$

65. $\dfrac{5}{x - 3} = \dfrac{3}{10}$

66. $\dfrac{b - 2}{4} = \dfrac{7}{12}$

Lesson 1-9

67. In the diagram, $ABCD \sim EFGH$. Find (a) the value of x and (b) the value of y.

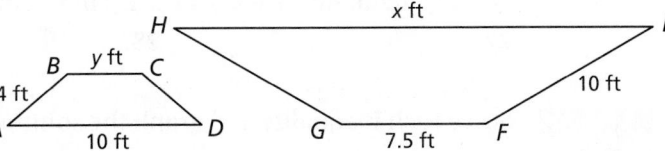

Lesson 1-10

Choose the more precise measurement in each pair.

68. 7.25 lb; 7 lb

69. 11 in.; 11.6 inches

70. 3.3 cm; 3.28 cm

71. 5.6 cm; 55.8 mm

72. 1372 mg; 1.4 g

73. 1100 m; 1 km

74. Scale A measures a mass of exactly 12.000 ounces to be 12.015 ounces. Scale B measures the mass to be 12.02 ounces. Which scale is more precise? Which is more accurate?

Write the possible range of each measurement. Round to the nearest hundredth if necessary.

75. 10 mg ± 0.5%

76. 15 cm ± 1%

77. 80 lb ± 0.2%

Lesson 2-1

Describe the solutions of each inequality in words.

1. $3 + v < -2$ **2.** $15 \le k + 4$ **3.** $-3 + n > 6$ **4.** $1 - 4x \ge -2$

Graph each inequality.

5. $f \ge 2$ **6.** $m < -1$ **7.** $\sqrt{4^2 + 3^2} > c$ **8.** $(-1 - 1)^2 \le p$

Write the inequality shown by each graph.

9.

10.

11.

12.

13.

14.

Write each inequality with the variable on the left. Graph the solutions.

15. $14 > b$ **16.** $9 \le g$ **17.** $-2 < x$ **18.** $-4 \ge k$

Lesson 2-2

Solve each inequality and graph the solutions.

19. $8 \ge d - 4$ **20.** $-5 < 10 + w$ **21.** $a + 4 \le 7$ **22.** $9 + j > 2$

Write an inequality to represent each statement. Solve the inequality and graph the solutions.

23. Five more than a number v is less than or equal to 9.

24. A number t decreased by 2 is at least 7.

25. Three less than a number r is less than -1.

26. A number k increased by 1 is at most -2.

Use the inequality $4 + z \le 11$ to fill in the missing numbers.

27. $z \le \blacksquare$ **28.** $z - \blacksquare \le 4$ **29.** $z - 3 \le \blacksquare$

Lesson 2-3

Solve each inequality and graph the solutions.

30. $24 > 4b$ **31.** $27g \le 81$ **32.** $\frac{x}{5} < 3$ **33.** $10y \ge 2$

34. $4p < -2$ **35.** $\frac{3s}{8} > 3$ **36.** $0 \ge \frac{3}{7}d$ **37.** $\frac{a}{8} \ge \frac{3}{4}$

38. $-3k \le -12$ **39.** $\frac{-2e}{5} \ge 4$ **40.** $8 < -12y$ **41.** $-3.5 > 14c$

42. $9 > \frac{h}{-2}$ **43.** $49 > -7m$ **44.** $60 \le -12c$ **45.** $-\frac{1}{3}q < -6$

Write an inequality for each statement. Solve the inequality and graph the solutions.

46. The product of $\frac{1}{2}$ and a number is not more than 6.

47. The quotient of r and -5 is greater than 3.

48. The product of -11 and a number is greater than -33.

49. The quotient of w and -4 is less than or equal to -6.

Lesson 2-4

Solve each inequality and graph the solutions.

50. $3t - 2 < 5$

51. $-6 < 5b - 4$

52. $4 < \dfrac{2f + 3}{2}$

53. $10 \le 3(4 - r)$

54. $\dfrac{2}{3} + \dfrac{3}{4}h < \dfrac{4}{3}$

55. $\dfrac{1}{5}(10k - 2) > 1$

56. $-n - 3 < -2^3$

57. $37 - 4d \le \sqrt{3^2 + 4^2}$

58. $-\dfrac{3}{4}\left(8q - 2^2\right) < -3$

Use the inequality $-6 - 2w \ge 10$ to fill in the missing numbers.

59. $w \le \blacksquare$

60. $w - 3 \le \blacksquare$

61. $\blacksquare + w \le 1$

Write an inequality for each statement. Solve the inequality and graph the solutions.

62. Twelve is less than or equal to the product of 6 and the difference of 5 and a number.

63. The difference of one-third a number and 8 is more than -4.

64. One-fourth of the sum of $2x$ and 4 is more than 5.

Lesson 2-5

Solve each inequality and graph the solutions.

65. $4v - 2 \le 3v$

66. $2(7 - s) > 4(s + 2)$

67. $\dfrac{1}{3}u - \dfrac{5}{2} \ge \dfrac{1}{6}u$

Solve each inequality.

68. $3 + 3c < 6 + 3c$

69. $4(k + 2) \ge 4k + 5$

70. $2(5 - b) \le 3 - 2b$

Write an inequality to represent each relationship. Solve your inequality.

71. The difference of three times a number and 5 is more than the number times 4.

72. One less than a number is greater than the product of 3 and the difference of 5 and the number.

Lesson 2-6

Solve each compound inequality and graph the solutions.

73. $6 < 3 + x < 8$

74. $-1 \le b + 4 \le 3$

75. $k + 5 \le -3$ OR $k + 5 \ge 1$

76. $r - 3 > 2$ OR $r + 1 < 4$

Write the compound inequality shown by each graph.

77.

-3 -2 -1 0 1 2 3

78.

-6 -4 -2 0 2 4 6

Write and graph a compound inequality for the numbers described.

79. all real numbers less than 2 and greater than or equal to -1

80. all real numbers between -3 and 1

Lesson 2-7

Solve each inequality and graph the solutions.

81. $|n + 5| \le 26$

82. $|x| + 6 < 13$

83. $4|k| \le 12$

84. $|c - 8| > 18$

85. $6|p| \ge 48$

86. $|3 + t| - 1 \ge 5$

Solve each inequality.

87. $|a| - 2 \le -5$

88. $2|w| + 5 < 3$

89. $|s| + 12 > 8$

Write and solve an absolute-value inequality for each expression. Graph the solutions on a number line.

90. All numbers whose absolute value is greater than 14.

91. All numbers whose absolute value multiplied by 3 is less than 27.

Lesson 3-1

Choose the graph that best represents each situation.

1. A person blows up a balloon with a steady airstream.

2. A person blows up a balloon and then lets it deflate.

3. A person blows up a balloon slowly at first and then uses more and more air.

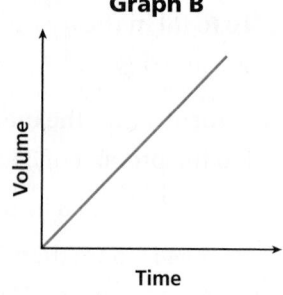

Lesson 3-2

Express each relation as a table, as a graph, and as a mapping diagram.

4. $\{(0, 2), (-1, 3), (-2, 5)\}$

5. $\{(2, 8), (4, 6), (6, 4), (8, 2)\}$

Give the domain and range of each relation. Tell whether the relation is a function. Explain.

6. $\{(3, 4), (-1, 2), (2, -3), (5, 0)\}$

7. $\{(5, 4), (0, 2), (5, -3), (0, 1)\}$

8.

x	2	0	1	2	−1
y	1	0	−1	−2	−3

9.

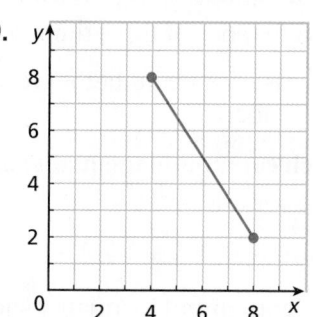

Lesson 3-3

Determine a relationship between the x- and y-variables. Write an equation.

10. $\{(1, 3), (2, 6), (3, 9), (4, 12)\}$

11.

x	1	2	3	4
y	1	4	9	16

Identify the independent and dependent variables. Write an equation in function notation for each situation.

12. A science tutor charges students $15 per hour.

13. A circus charges a $10 entry fee and $1.50 for each pony ride.

14. For $f(a) = 6 - 4a$, find $f(a)$ when $a = 2$ and when $a = -3$.

15. For $g(d) = \frac{2}{5}d + 3$, find $g(d)$ when $d = 10$ and when $d = -5$.

16. For $h(w) = 2 - w^2$, find $h(w)$ when $w = -1$ and when $w = -2$.

17. Complete the table for $f(t) = 7 + 3t$.

t	0	1	2	3
f(t)				

18. Complete the table for $h(s) = 2s + s^3 - 6$.

s	−1	0	1	2
h(s)				

Lesson 3-4

Graph each function for the given domain.

19. $2x - y = 2$; D: $\{-2, -1, 0, 1\}$

20. $f(x) = x^2 - 1$; D: $\{-3, -1, 0, 2\}$

Graph each function.

21. $f(x) = 4 - 2x$

22. $y + 3 = 2x$

23. $y = -5 + x^2$

24. Use a graph of the function $y = \frac{5}{2} - 2x$ to find the value of y when $x = \frac{1}{2}$. Check your answer.

25. Find the value of x so that $(x, 4)$ satisfies $y = -x + 8$.

26. Find the value of y so that $(-3, y)$ satisfies $y = 15 - 2x^2$.

For each function, determine whether the given points are on the graph.

27. $y = \frac{x}{3} + 4$; $(-3, 3)$ and $(3, 5)$

28. $y = x^2 - 1$; $(-2, 3)$ and $(2, 5)$

Lesson 3-5

Describe the correlation illustrated by each scatter plot.

29.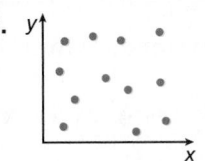

30.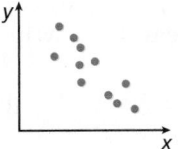

31.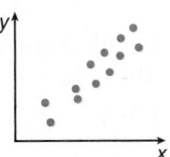

Identify the correlation you would expect to see between each pair of data sets. Explain.

32. the number of chess pieces captured and the number of pieces still on the board

33. a person's height and the color of the person's eyes

Choose the scatter plot that best represents the described relationship. Explain.

34. the number of students in a class and the grades on a test

35. the number of students in a class and the number of empty desks

Graph A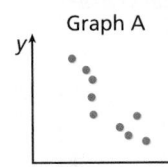

Graph B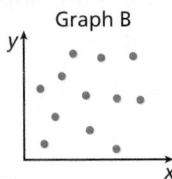

Lesson 3-6

Determine whether each sequence appears to be an arithmetic sequence. If so, find the common difference and the next three terms.

36. $-10, -7, -4, -1, \ldots$

37. $8, 5, 1, -4, \ldots$

38. $1, -2, 3, -4, \ldots$

39. $-19, -9, 1, 11, \ldots$

Find the indicated term of each arithmetic sequence.

40. 15th term: $-5, -1, 3, 7, \ldots$

41. 20th term: $a_1 = 2$; $d = -5$

42. 12th term: $8, 16, 24, 32, \ldots$

43. 21st term: $5.2, 5.17, 5.14, 5.11, \ldots$

Find the common difference for each arithmetic sequence.

44. $0, 7, 14, 21, \ldots$

45. $132, 121, 110, 99, \ldots$

46. $\frac{1}{4}, 1, \frac{7}{4}, \frac{10}{4}, \ldots$

47. $1.4, 2.2, 3, 3.8, \ldots$

48. $-7, -2, 3, 8, \ldots$

49. $7.28, 7.21, 7.14, 7.07, \ldots$

Find the next four terms in each arithmetic sequence.

50. $-3, -6, -9, -12, \ldots$

51. $2, 9, 16, 23, \ldots$

52. $-\frac{1}{3}, \frac{1}{3}, 1, \frac{5}{3}, \ldots$

53. $-4.3, -3.2, -2.1, -1, \ldots$

Lesson 4-1

Identify whether each graph represents a function. Explain. If the graph does represent a function, is the function linear?

1.
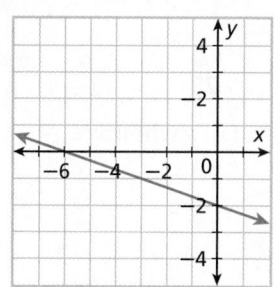

2.
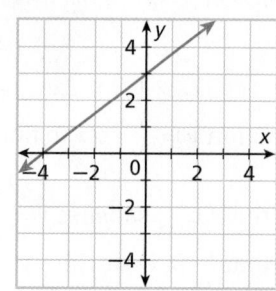

3.
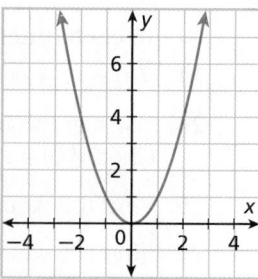

Tell whether the given ordered pairs satisfy a linear function. Explain.

4.

x	−4	−2	0	2	4
y	7	6	5	4	3

5.

x	2	5	8	11	14
y	12	8	7	3	3

Tell whether each equation is linear. If so, write the equation in standard form and give the values of A, B, and C.

6. $y = 8 - 3x$
7. $\frac{x}{3} = 4 - 2y$
8. $-3 + xy = 2$
9. $4x = -3 - 3y$

Lesson 4-2

Find the x- and y-intercepts.

10. $-4x = 2y - 1$
11. $x - y = 3$
12. $2x - 3y = 12$
13. $2.5x + 2.5y = 5$

Use intercepts to graph the line described by each equation.

14. $15 = -3x - 5y$
15. $4y = 2x + 8$
16. $y = 6 - 3x$
17. $-2y = x + 2$

Lesson 4-3

Find the slope of each line.

18.
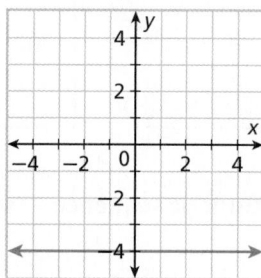

19.
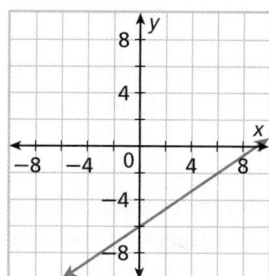

Lesson 4-4

Find the slope of the line that contains each pair of points.

20. $(-1, 2)$ and $(-4, 8)$
21. $(2, 6)$ and $(0, 1)$
22. $(-2, 3)$ and $(4, 0)$

Find the slope of the line described by each equation.

23. $2y = 42 - 6x$
24. $3x + 4y = 12$
25. $3x = 15 + 5y$

Lesson 4-5

Tell whether each equation represents a direct variation. If so, identify the constant of variation.

26. $x - 2y = 0$
27. $x - y = 3$
28. $3y = 2x$

29. The value of y varies directly with x, and $y = 2$ when $x = -3$. Find y when $x = 6$.

30. The value of y varies directly with x, and $y = -3$ when $x = 9$. Find y when $x = 12$.

Lesson 4-6

Write the equation that describes each line in slope-intercept form.

31. slope = 2, y-intercept = -2

32. slope = 0.25, y-intercept = 4

33. slope = -2, (5, 4) is on the line.

34. slope = $\frac{1}{3}$, $(-8, 0)$ is on the line.

35.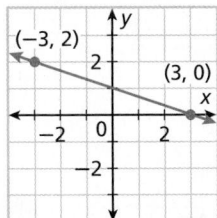

36.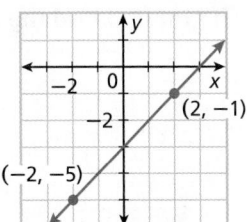

Write each equation in slope-intercept form. Then graph the line described by the equation.

37. $2y = x - 3$

38. $-3x - 2y = 1$

39. $2y - \frac{1}{2}x = 2$

Lesson 4-7

Write an equation in point-slope form for the line with the given slope that contains the given point.

40. slope = 2; (0, 3)

41. slope = -1; (1, -1)

42. slope = $\frac{1}{2}$; (2, 4)

Write the equation that describes each line in slope-intercept form.

43. slope = 3, $(-2, -5)$ is on the line.

44. $(-1, 1)$ and $(1, -2)$ are on the line.

45. (3, 1) and (2, -3) are on the line.

46. x-intercept = 4, y-intercept = -5

Your wingspan is the distance between the tips of your middle fingers when your arms are stretched out at your sides. The table shows the wingspans and heights in centimeters of several people.

Wingspan (cm)	158	175	166	171	189
Height (cm)	157	166	169	162	180

47. Find an equation for a line of best. How well does the line fit the data?

48. Use your equation to predict the height of a person with a wingspan of 184 cm.

Lesson 4-8

Write an equation in slope-intercept form for the line that is parallel to the given line and that passes through the given point.

49. $y = -2x + 3$; (1, 4)

50. $y = x - 5$; (2, -4)

51. $y = 3x$; $(-1, 5)$

Write an equation in slope-intercept form for the line that is perpendicular to the given line and that passes through the given point.

52. $y = x + 1$; (3, -2)

53. $y = -4x - 1$; $(-1, 0)$

54. $y = 4x + 5$; (2, -1)

Lesson 4-9

Graph $f(x)$ and $g(x)$. Then describe the transformation(s) from the graph of $f(x)$ to the graph of $g(x)$.

55. $f(x) = x$, $g(x) = x + 2$

56. $f(x) = x$, $g(x) = x - \frac{1}{2}$

57. $f(x) = 6x + 1$, $g(x) = 2x + 1$

58. $f(x) = 3x - 1$, $g(x) = 9x - 1$

59. $f(x) = x$, $g(x) = 2x - 1$

60. $f(x) = x + 1$, $g(x) = -\frac{1}{2}x$

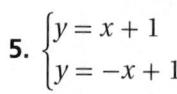

Lesson 5-1

Tell whether the ordered pair is a solution of the given system.

1. $(1, 3)$; $\begin{cases} 2x - 3y = -7 \\ -5x + 3y = 4 \end{cases}$

2. $(-2, 2)$; $\begin{cases} 4x + 3y = -2 \\ -2x - 2y = 2 \end{cases}$

3. $(4, -3)$; $\begin{cases} -2x - 3y = 1 \\ x + 2y = -2 \end{cases}$

Use the given graph to find the solution of each system.

4. $\begin{cases} y = \dfrac{1}{2}x - 1 \\ y = -\dfrac{1}{2}x + 3 \end{cases}$

5. $\begin{cases} y = x + 1 \\ y = -x + 1 \end{cases}$

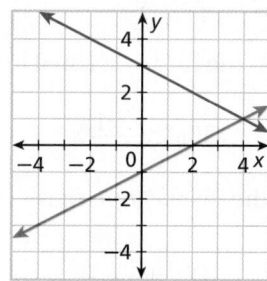

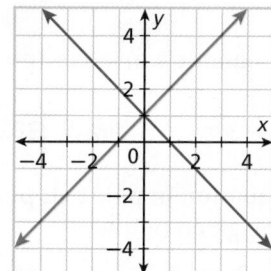

Solve each system by graphing. Check your answer.

6. $\begin{cases} y = x + 1 \\ y = -2x - 2 \end{cases}$

7. $\begin{cases} 3x + y = -8 \\ 3y = \dfrac{1}{2}x - 5 \end{cases}$

8. $\begin{cases} x = 2 - 2y \\ -1 = -2x - 3y \end{cases}$

Lesson 5-2

Solve each system by substitution.

9. $\begin{cases} y = 12 - 3x \\ y = 2x - 3 \end{cases}$

10. $\begin{cases} 2x + y = -6 \\ -5x + y = 1 \end{cases}$

11. $\begin{cases} y = 11 - 3x \\ -2x + y = 1 \end{cases}$

12. $\begin{cases} 2x + 3y = 2 \\ -\dfrac{1}{2}x + 2y = -6 \end{cases}$

13. $\begin{cases} 3x - 2y = -3 \\ y = 7 - 4x \end{cases}$

14. $\begin{cases} 4y - 2x = -2 \\ x + 3y = -4 \end{cases}$

Two angles whose measures have a sum of 90° are called complementary angles. For Exercises 15–17, x and y represent the measures of complementary angles. Use this information and the equation given in each exercise to find the measure of each angle.

15. $y = 9x - 10$

16. $y - 4x = 15$

17. $y = 2x + 15$

Lesson 5-3

Solve each system by elimination.

18. $\begin{cases} x - 3y = -1 \\ -x + 2y = -2 \end{cases}$

19. $\begin{cases} -3x - y = 1 \\ 5x + y = -5 \end{cases}$

20. $\begin{cases} -x - 3y = -1 \\ 3x + 3y = 9 \end{cases}$

21. $\begin{cases} 3x - 2y = 2 \\ 3x + y = 8 \end{cases}$

22. $\begin{cases} 5x - 2y = -15 \\ 2x - 2y = -12 \end{cases}$

23. $\begin{cases} -4x - 2y = -4 \\ -4x + 3y = -24 \end{cases}$

24. $\begin{cases} -3x - 3y = 3 \\ 2x + y = -4 \end{cases}$

25. $\begin{cases} 4x - 3y = -1 \\ 2x - 2y = -4 \end{cases}$

26. $\begin{cases} 3x + 6y = 0 \\ 7x + 4y = 20 \end{cases}$

Lesson 5-4

Solve each system of linear equations.

27. $\begin{cases} y = 2x + 4 \\ -2x + y = 6 \end{cases}$

28. $\begin{cases} -y = 3 - 5x \\ y - 5x = 6 \end{cases}$

29. $\begin{cases} y + 2 = 3x \\ 3x - y = -1 \end{cases}$

30. $\begin{cases} 2y = 6 - 6x \\ 3y + 9x = 9 \end{cases}$

31. $\begin{cases} y - 1 = -3x \\ 12x + 4y = 4 \end{cases}$

32. $\begin{cases} 4x - 2y = 4 \\ 3y = 6(x - 1) \end{cases}$

Classify each system. Give the number of solutions.

33. $\begin{cases} 2y = 2(4x - 3) \\ y - 1 = 4x \end{cases}$

34. $\begin{cases} 3y + 6x = 9 \\ 2(y - 3) = -4x \end{cases}$

35. $\begin{cases} 3x - 13 = 2y \\ -3y = 2x \end{cases}$

Lesson 5-5

Tell whether the ordered pair is a solution of the given inequality.

36. $(3, 6); y > 2x + 4$

37. $(-2, -8); y \le 3x - 2$

38. $(-3, 3); y \ge -2x + 5$

Graph the solutions of each linear inequality.

39. $y > 2x$

40. $y \le -3x + 2$

41. $y \ge 2x - 1$

42. $-y < -x + 4$

43. $y \ge -2x + 4$

44. $y > -x - 3$

45. $y < \frac{1}{2}x + 1\frac{1}{2}$

46. $y \le 4x - (-1)$

Write an inequality to represent each graph.

47.

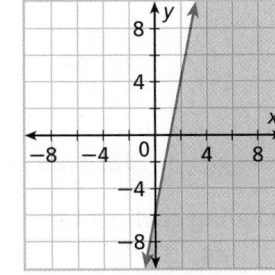

48.

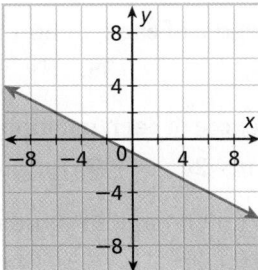

Lesson 5-6

Tell whether the ordered pair is a solution of the given system.

49. $(2, 5); \begin{cases} y > 3x - 3 \\ y \ge x + 1 \end{cases}$

50. $(3, 9); \begin{cases} y > -3x - 2 \\ y < 2x + 3 \end{cases}$

51. $(2, 3); \begin{cases} y > 2x \\ y \le x - 3 \end{cases}$

Graph each system of linear inequalities. Give two ordered pairs that are solutions and two that are not solutions.

52. $\begin{cases} x + 4y < 2 \\ 2y > 3x + 8 \end{cases}$

53. $\begin{cases} y \le 6 - 2x \\ x - 2y < -2 \end{cases}$

54. $\begin{cases} 2x - 2 > -3y \\ -x + 3y \ge -10 \end{cases}$

Graph each system of linear inequalities. Describe the solutions.

55. $\begin{cases} y > 2x + 1 \\ y < 2x - 2 \end{cases}$

56. $\begin{cases} y < 3x - 1 \\ y > 3x - 4 \end{cases}$

57. $\begin{cases} y \ge -x + 2 \\ y \ge -x + 5 \end{cases}$

58. $\begin{cases} y \ge 2x - 3 \\ y \ge 2x + 3 \end{cases}$

59. $\begin{cases} y > -4x - 2 \\ y \le -4x - 5 \end{cases}$

60. $\begin{cases} y \ge -2x + 1 \\ y < -2x + 6 \end{cases}$

Lesson 6-1

Simplify.

1. 3^{-4} **2.** 5^{-3} **3.** -4^0 **4.** -2^{-5} **5.** 6^{-3}

6. $(-2)^{-4}$ **7.** 1^{-7} **8.** $(-4)^{-3}$ **9.** $(-5)^0$ **10.** $(-1)^{-5}$

Evaluate each expression for the given value(s) of the variable(s).

11. x^{-4} for $x = 2$ **12.** $(c+3)^{-3}$ for $c = -6$

13. $3j^{-7}k^{-1}$ for $j = -2$ and $k = 3$ **14.** $(2n-2)^{-4}$ for $n = 3$

Simplify.

15. $b^4 g^{-5}$ **16.** $\dfrac{k^{-3}}{r^5}$ **17.** $5s^{-3}c^0$ **18.** $\dfrac{z^{-4}}{5t^{-2}}$

19. $\dfrac{f^2}{3a^{-4}}$ **20.** $\dfrac{-3t^4}{q^{-5}}$ **21.** $\dfrac{a^0 k^{-4}}{p^2}$ **22.** $3f^{-1}y^{-5}$

Lesson 6-2

Simplify each expression.

23. $27^{\frac{1}{3}}$ **24.** $256^{\frac{1}{4}}$ **25.** $169^{\frac{1}{2}}$ **26.** $0^{\frac{1}{5}}$

27. $4^{\frac{3}{2}}$ **28.** $49^{\frac{3}{2}}$ **29.** $36^{\frac{3}{2}}$ **30.** $16^{\frac{5}{4}}$

Simplify. All variables represent nonnegative numbers.

31. $\sqrt{x^2 y^6}$ **32.** $\sqrt[3]{a^9 b^{15}}$ **33.** $\dfrac{(m^8)^{\frac{1}{2}}}{\sqrt{m^4}}$ **34.** $\left(\sqrt[5]{g^{60}}\right)^{\frac{1}{3}} \sqrt[7]{t^{14}}$

Lesson 6-3

Find the degree of each monomial.

35. 4^7 **36.** $x^3 y$ **37.** $\dfrac{r^6 st^2}{2}$ **38.** 9^0

Find the degree of each polynomial.

39. $a^2 b + b - 2^2$ **40.** $5x^4 y^2 - y^5 z^2$ **41.** $3g^4 h + h^2 + 4j^6$ **42.** $4nm^7 - m^6 p^3 + p$

Write each polynomial in standard form. Then give the leading coefficient.

43. $4r - 5r^3 + 2r^2$ **44.** $-3b^2 + 7b^6 + 4 - b$ **45.** $\dfrac{1}{2}t^3 + t - \dfrac{1}{3}t^5 + 4$

Classify each polynomial according to its degree and number of terms.

46. $3x^2 + 4x - 5$ **47.** $-4x^2 + x^6 - 4 + x^3$ **48.** $x^3 - 7^2$

Lesson 6-4

Add or subtract.

49. $4y^3 - 2y + 3y^3$ **50.** $9k^2 + 5 - 10k^2 - 6$

51. $7 - 3n^2 + 4 + 2n^2$ **52.** $(9x^6 - 5x^2 + 3) + (6x^2 - 5)$

53. $(2y^5 - 5y^2) + (3y^5 - y^3 + 2y^2)$ **54.** $(r^3 + 2r + 1) - (2r^3 - 4)$

55. $(10s^2 + 5) - (5s^2 + 3s - 2)$ **56.** $(2s^7 - 6s^3 + 2) - (3s^7 + 2)$

Lesson 6-5

Multiply.

57. $(3a^7)(2a^4)$

58. $(-3xy^3)(2x^2z)(yz^4)$

59. $(4k\ell^3m)(-2k^2m^2)$

60. $3jk^2(2j^2 + k)$

61. $4q^3r^2(2qr^2 + 3q)$

62. $3xy^2(2x^2y - 3y)$

63. $(x - 3)(x + 1)$

64. $(x - 2)(x - 3)$

65. $(x^2 + 2xy)(3x^2y - 2)$

66. $(x^2 - 3x)(2xy - 3y)$

67. $(x - 2)(x^2 + 3x - 4)$

68. $(2x - 1)(-2x^2 - 3x + 4)$

69. $(x + 3)(2x^4 - 3x^2 - 5)$

70. $(3a + b)(2a^2 + ab - 2b^2)$

71. $(a^2 - b)(3a^2 - 2ab + 3b^2)$

Lesson 6-6

Multiply.

72. $(x + 3)^2$

73. $(3 + 2x)^2$

74. $(4x + 2y)^2$

75. $(3x - 2)^2$

76. $(5 - 2x)^2$

77. $(3x - 5y)^2$

78. $(3 + x)(3 - x)$

79. $(x - 5)(x + 5)$

80. $(2x + 1)(2x - 1)$

81. $(x^2 + 4)(x^2 - 4)$

82. $(2 + 3x^3)(2 - 3x^3)$

83. $(4x^3 - 3y)(4x^3 + 3y)$

Lesson 7-1

Write the prime factorization of each number.

1. 24   **2.** 78   **3.** 88   **4.** 63

5. 128   **6.** 102   **7.** 71   **8.** 125

Find the GCF of each pair of numbers.

9. 18 and 66   **10.** 24 and 104   **11.** 30 and 75

12. 24 and 120   **13.** 36 and 99   **14.** 42 and 72

Find the GCF of each pair of monomials.

15. $4a^3$ and $9a^4$ **16.** $6q^2$ and $15q^5$ **17.** $6x^2$ and $14y^3$

18. $4z^2$ and $10z^5$ **19.** $5g^3$ and $9g$ **20.** $12x^2$ and $21y^2$

Lesson 7-2

Factor each polynomial. Check your answer.

21. $6b^2 - 15b^3$ **22.** $11t^4 - 9t^3$ **23.** $10v^3 - 25v$

24. $12r + 16r^3$ **25.** $17a^4 - 35a^2$ **26.** $9f + 18f^5 + 12f^2$

Factor each expression.

27. $3(a + 3) + 4a(a + 3)$ **28.** $5(k - 4) - 2k(k - 4)$ **29.** $5(c - 3) + 4c^2(c - 3)$

30. $3(t - 4) + t(t - 4)$ **31.** $5(2r - 1) - s(2r - 1)$ **32.** $7(3d + 4) - 2e(3d + 4)$

Factor each polynomial by grouping. Check your answer.

33. $x^3 + 3x^2 - 2x - 6$ **34.** $2m^3 - 3m^2 + 8m - 12$ **35.** $3k^3 - k^2 + 15k - 5$

36. $15r^3 + 25r^2 - 6r - 10$ **37.** $12n^3 - 6n^2 - 10n + 5$ **38.** $4z^3 - 3z^2 + 4z - 3$

39. $2k^2 - 3k + 12 - 8k$ **40.** $3p^2 - 2p + 8 - 12p$ **41.** $10d^2 - 6d + 9 - 15d$

42. $6a^3 - 4a^2 + 10 - 15a$ **43.** $12s^3 - 2s^2 + 3 - 18s$ **44.** $4c^3 - 3c^2 + 15 - 20c$

Lesson 7-3

Factor each trinomial. Check your answer.

45. $x^2 + 15x + 36$ **46.** $x^2 + 13x + 40$ **47.** $x^2 + 10x + 16$

48. $x^2 - 9x + 18$ **49.** $x^2 - 11x + 28$ **50.** $x^2 - 13x + 42$

51. $x^2 + 4x - 21$ **52.** $x^2 - 5x - 36$ **53.** $x^2 - 7x - 30$

54. Factor $c^2 - 2c - 48$. Show that the original polynomial and the factored form describe the same sequence of values for $c = 0, 1, 2, 3,$ and 4.

Copy and complete the table.

	$x^2 + bx + c$	Sign of c	Binomial factors	Sign of Numbers in Binomials
	$x^2 + 9x + 20$	Positive	$(x + 4)(x + 5)$	Both positive
55.	$x^2 - x - 20$	?	?	?
56.	$x^2 - 2x - 8$	?	?	?
57.	$x^2 - 6x + 8$	?	?	?

Lesson 7-4

Factor each trinomial. Check your answer.

58. $2x^2 + 13x + 15$ **59.** $3x^2 + 14x + 16$ **60.** $8x^2 - 16x + 6$

61. $6x^2 + 11x + 4$ **62.** $3x^2 - 11x + 6$ **63.** $10x^2 - 31x + 15$

64. $6x^2 - 5x - 4$ **65.** $8x^2 - 14x - 15$ **66.** $4x^2 - 11x + 6$

67. $12x^2 - 13x + 3$ **68.** $6x^2 - 7x - 10$ **69.** $6x^2 + 7x - 3$

70. $2x^2 + 5x - 12$ **71.** $6x^2 - 5x - 6$ **72.** $8x^2 + 10x - 3$

73. $10x^2 - 11x - 6$ **74.** $4x^2 - x - 5$ **75.** $6x^2 - 7x - 20$

76. $-2x^2 + 11x - 5$ **77.** $-6x^2 - x + 12$ **78.** $-8x^2 - 10x - 3$

79. $-4x^2 + 16x - 15$ **80.** $-10x^2 + 21x + 10$ **81.** $-3x^2 + 13x - 14$

Lesson 7-5

Determine whether each trinomial is a perfect square. If so, factor. If not, explain why.

82. $x^2 - 8x + 16$ **83.** $4x^2 - 4x + 1$ **84.** $x^2 - 8x + 9$

85. $9x^2 - 14x + 4$ **86.** $4x^2 + 12x + 9$ **87.** $x^2 + 8x - 16$

88. $9x^2 - 42x + 49$ **89.** $4x^2 + 18x + 25$ **90.** $16x^2 - 24x + 9$

Determine whether each trinomial is the difference of two squares. If so, factor. If not, explain why.

91. $4 - 16x^4$ **92.** $-t^2 - 35$ **93.** $c^2 - 25$

94. $g^5 - 9$ **95.** $v^4 - 64$ **96.** $x^2 - 120$

97. $x^2 - 36$ **98.** $9m^2 - 15$ **99.** $25c^2 - 16$

Find the missing term in each perfect-square trinomial.

100. $4x^2 - 20x +$ ▨   **101.** $9x^2 +$ ▨ $+ 1$ **102.** ▨ $- 56x + 49$

103. $9b^2 -$ ▨ $+ 25$ **104.** ▨ $+ 28a + 49$ **105.** $4a^2 + 4a +$ ▨

Lesson 7-6

Tell whether each expression is completely factored. If not, factor.

106. $5(16x^2 + 4)$ **107.** $3r(4x - 9)$ **108.** $(9d - 6)(2d - 7)$

109. $(5 - h)(6 - 5h)$ **110.** $12y^2 - 2y - 24$ **111.** $3f(2f^2 + 5fg + 2g^2)$

Factor each polynomial completely. Check your answer.

112. $12b^3 - 48b$ **113.** $24w^4 - 20w^3 - 16w^2$ **114.** $18k^3 - 32k$

115. $4a^3 + 12a^2 - a^2b - 3ab$ **116.** $3x^3y - 6x^2y^2 + 3xy^3$ **117.** $36p^2q - 64q^3$

118. $32a^4 - 8a^2$ **119.** $m^3 + 5m^2n + 6mn^2$ **120.** $4x^2 - 3x^2 - 16x + 48x$

121. $18d^2 + 3d - 6$ **122.** $2r^2 - 9r - 18$ **123.** $8y^2 + 4y - 4$

124. $81 - 36u^2$ **125.** $8x^4 + 12x^2 - 20$ **126.** $10j^3 + 15j^2 - 70j$

127. $27z^3 - 18z^2 + 3z$ **128.** $4b^2 + 2b - 72$ **129.** $3f^2 - 3g^2$

Lesson 8-1

Tell whether each function is quadratic. Explain.

1. $y + 4x^2 = 2x - 3$ **2.** $4x - y = 3$ **3.** $3x^2 - 4 = y + x$

4.

x	−6	−4	−2	0	2
y	−5	−6	−4	2	11

5.

x	0	1	2	3	4
y	−5	−5	−3	1	7

Tell whether the graph of each quadratic function opens upward or downward. Then use a table of values to graph each function.

6. $y = -3x^2$ **7.** $y = \frac{2}{3}x^2$ **8.** $y = x^2 + 2$ **9.** $y = -4x^2 + 2x$

Identify the vertex of each parabola. Then find the domain and range.

10. 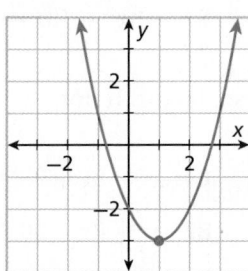 **11.** 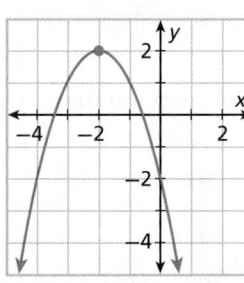 **12.**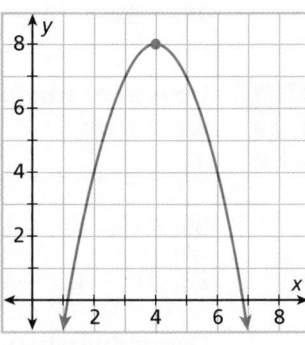

Lesson 8-2

Find the zeros of each quadratic function and the axis of symmetry of each parabola from the graph.

13. 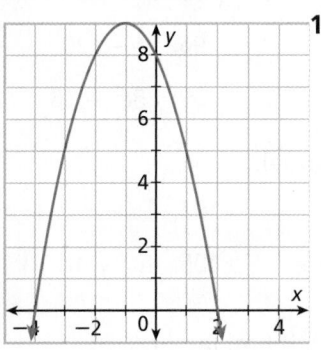 **14.** 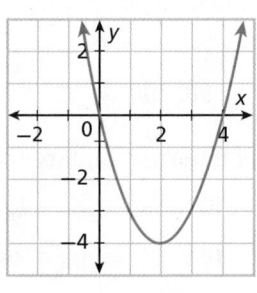 **15.**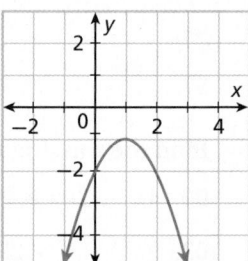

Find the vertex.

16. $y = 3x^2 - 6x + 2$ **17.** $y = -2x^2 + 8x - 3$ **18.** $y = x^2 + 2x - 4$

Lesson 8-3

Graph each quadratic function.

19. $y = x^2 - 4x + 1$ **20.** $y = -x^2 - x + 4$ **21.** $y = 3x^2 - 3x + 1$

22. $y - 2 = 2x^2$ **23.** $y + 3x^2 = 3x - 1$ **24.** $y - 4 = x^2 + 2x$

Lesson 8-4

Order the functions from narrowest to widest.

25. $f(x) = 2x^2$, $g(x) = -4x^2$, $h(x) = -x^2$ **26.** $f(x) = 3x^2$, $g(x) = \frac{1}{2}x^2$, $h(x) = -2x^2$

27. $f(x) = 4x^2$, $g(x) = x^2$, $h(x) = -\frac{1}{4}x^2$ **28.** $f(x) = 2x^2$, $g(x) = 5x^2$, $h(x) = -3x^2$

Compare the graph of each function with the graph of $f(x) = x^2$.

29. $g(x) = 2x^2 - 2$ **30.** $g(x) = -\frac{1}{2}x^2$ **31.** $g(x) = -3x^2 + 1$

Lesson 8-5

Solve each quadratic equation by graphing the related function.

32. $x^2 - x - 2 = 0$ **33.** $x^2 - 2x + 8 = 0$ **34.** $2x^2 + 4x - 6 = 0$

35. $2x^2 + 9x = -4$ **36.** $2x^2 + 3 = 0$ **37.** $2x^2 - 2x - 12 = 0$

38. $3x^2 = -3x + 6$ **39.** $x^2 = 4$ **40.** $2x^2 + 6x - 20 = 0$

Lesson 8-6

Use the Zero Product Property to solve each equation. Check your answer.

41. $(x + 3)(x - 2) = 0$ **42.** $(x - 4)(x + 2) = 0$ **43.** $(x)(x - 4) = 0$

44. $(2x + 6)(x - 2) = 0$ **45.** $(3x - 1)(x + 3) = 0$ **46.** $(x)(2x - 4) = 0$

Solve each quadratic equation by factoring. Check your answer.

47. $x^2 + 5x + 6 = 0$ **48.** $x^2 - 3x - 4 = 0$ **49.** $x^2 + x - 12 = 0$

50. $x^2 + x - 6 = 0$ **51.** $x^2 - 6x + 5 = 0$ **52.** $x^2 + 4x - 12 = 0$

Lesson 8-7

Solve using square roots. Check your answer.

53. $x^2 = 169$ **54.** $x^2 = 121$ **55.** $x^2 = 289$

56. $x^2 = -64$ **57.** $x^2 = 81$ **58.** $x^2 = -441$

59. $4x^2 - 196 = 0$ **60.** $0 = 3x^2 - 48$ **61.** $24x^2 + 96 = 0$

Solve. Round to the nearest hundredth.

62. $4x^2 = 160$ **63.** $0 = 3x^2 - 66$ **64.** $250 - 5x^2 = 0$

65. $0 = 9x^2 - 72$ **66.** $48 - 2x^2 = 42$ **67.** $6x^2 = 78$

Lesson 8-8

Complete the square to form a perfect-square trinomial.

68. $x^2 - 8x + \blacksquare$ **69.** $x^2 + x + \blacksquare$ **70.** $x^2 + 10x + \blacksquare$

71. $x^2 - 5x + \blacksquare$ **72.** $x^2 + 6x + \blacksquare$ **73.** $x^2 - 7x + \blacksquare$

Solve by completing the square.

74. $x^2 + 6x = 91$ **75.** $x^2 + 10x = -16$ **76.** $x^2 - 4x = 12$

77. $x^2 - 8x = -12$ **78.** $x^2 - 12x = -35$ **79.** $-x^2 - 6x = 5$

80. $-x^2 - 4x + 77 = 0$ **81.** $-x^2 = 10x + 9$ **82.** $-x^2 + 63 = -2x$

Lesson 8-9

Solve using the quadratic formula.

83. $x^2 + 3x - 4 = 0$ **84.** $x^2 - 2x - 8 = 0$ **85.** $x^2 + 2x - 3 = 0$

86. $x^2 - x - 10 = 0$ **87.** $2x^2 - x - 4 = 0$ **88.** $2x^2 + 3x - 3 = 0$

Find the number of real solutions of each equation using the discriminant.

89. $x^2 + 4x + 1 = 0$ **90.** $2x^2 - 3x + 2 = 0$ **91.** $x^2 - 5x + 2 = 0$

92. $2x^2 - 4x + 2 = 0$ **93.** $x^2 + 2x - 5 = 0$ **94.** $2x^2 - 2x - 3 = 0$

Lesson 8-10

Solve each system of equations.

95. $\begin{cases} y = -x - 1 \\ y = x^2 - 3 \end{cases}$ **96.** $\begin{cases} y = -3x \\ y = x^2 + 2 \end{cases}$ **97.** $\begin{cases} y = 3x - 2 \\ y = -3x^2 + 4 \end{cases}$

98. $\begin{cases} y = -x + 6 \\ y = x^2 - x + 2 \end{cases}$ **99.** $\begin{cases} y = x - 1 \\ y = x^2 - 5x + 3 \end{cases}$ **100.** $\begin{cases} y = 2x - 7 \\ y = x^2 - 2x - 4 \end{cases}$

Extra Practice Chapter 9 ▪ Skills Practice

Lesson 9-1

Find the next three terms in each geometric sequence.

1. 1, 5, 25, 125 ...
2. 736, 368, 184, 92, ...
3. −2, 6, −18, 54, ...

4. 8, 2, $\frac{1}{2}$, $\frac{1}{8}$, ...
5. 7, −14, 28, −56, ...
6. $\frac{1}{9}$, $\frac{1}{3}$, 1, 3, ...

7. The first term of a geometric sequence is 2, and the common ratio is 3. What is the 8th term of the sequence?

8. What is the 8th term of the geometric sequence 600, 300, 150, 75, ...?

Lesson 9-2

Tell whether each set of ordered pairs satisfies an exponential function. Explain your answer.

9. $\left\{\left(-1, \frac{1}{2}\right), (0, 2), (1, 8), (2, 32)\right\}$
10. $\left\{\left(-1, -\frac{1}{2}\right), (0, 0), \left(1, \frac{1}{2}\right), (2, 4)\right\}$

11. $\left\{(-1, 4), (0, 1), \left(1, \frac{1}{4}\right), \left(2, \frac{1}{16}\right)\right\}$
12. $\left\{(0, 0), (1, 3), (2, 12), (3, 27)\right\}$

Graph each exponential function.

13. $y = 3(2)^x$
14. $y = \frac{1}{2}(4)^x$
15. $y = -3^x$

16. $y = -\frac{1}{2}(2)^x$
17. $y = 5\left(\frac{1}{2}\right)^x$
18. $y = -2(0.25)^x$

Lesson 9-3

Write an exponential growth function to model each situation. Then find the value of the function after the given amount of time.

19. The rent for an apartment is $6600 per year and increasing at a rate of 4% per year; 5 years.

20. A museum has 1200 members and the number of members is increasing at a rate of 2% per year; 8 years.

Write a compound interest function to model each situation. Then find the balance after the given number of years.

21. $4000 invested at a rate of 4% compounded quarterly; 3 years

22. $5200 invested at a rate of 2.5% compounded annually; 6 years

Write an exponential decay function to model each situation. Then find the value of the function after the given amount of time.

23. The cost of a stereo system is $800 and is decreasing at a rate of 6% per year; 5 years.

24. The population of a town is 14,000 and is decreasing at a rate of 2% per year; 10 years.

Lesson 9-4

Graph each data set. Which kind of model best describes the data?

25. $\{(0, 3), (1, 0), (2, -1), (3, 0), (4, 3)\}$

26. $\{(-4, -4), (-3, -3.5), (-2, -3), (-1, -2.5), (0, -2), (1, -1.5)\}$

27. $\{(0, 4), (1, 2), (2, 1), (3, 0.5), (4, 0.25)\}$

Look for a pattern in each data set to determine which kind of model best describes the data.

28. $\{(-1, -5), (0, -5), (1, -3), (2, 1), (3, 7)\}$

29. $\{(0, 0.25), (1, 0.5), (2, 1), (3, 2), (4, 4)\}$

30. $\{(-2, 11), (-1, 8), (0, 5), (1, 2), (2, -1)\}$

Lesson 9-5

31. Identify the type of functions shown. Compare the functions by finding and interpreting slopes and y-intercepts.

Function A

x	0	1	2	3	4
y	2	5	8	11	14

Function B

$y = 3x - 4$

32. Identify the type of functions shown. Compare the functions by finding and interpreting maximums, minimums, x-intercepts, and average rates of change over the x-interval $[0, 10]$.

Function A

$y = 0.5x^2 + 3x - 3$

Function B

x	0	2	4	6	8	10
y	-3	1	1	-3	-11	-23

33. Identify the type of functions shown. Compare the functions by finding the average rates of change over the interval $[0, 4]$.

Function A

x	0	1	2	3	4
y	3	4.5	6.8	10.1	15.2

Function B

$y = 3(0.5)^x$

Lesson 10-1

Use the line graph for Exercises 1–4.

1. In what year was the population the greatest?

2. Estimate the population in 2005.

3. During which one-year period did the population increase by the greatest amount?

4. Estimate the amount by which the population decreased from 2005 to 2006.

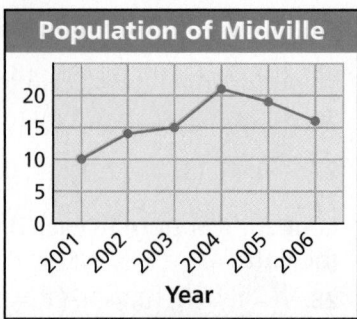

Use the circle graph for Exercises 5–7.

5. Which candidate received the fewest votes?

6. Which two candidates received approximately the same number of votes?

7. A total of 400 students voted in the election. How many votes did Velez receive?

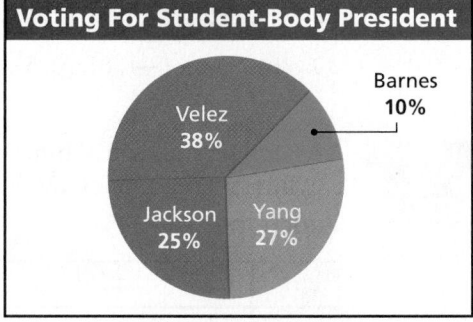

Lesson 10-2

The daily high temperatures in degrees Celsius during a two-week period in Madison, Wisconsin, are given at right.

8. Use the data to make a stem-and-leaf plot.

9. Use the data to make a frequency table with intervals.

10. Use the frequency table from Exercise 9 to make a histogram for the data.

11. Use the data to make a cumulative frequency table.

High Temperatures (°C)						
22	25	28	33	29	24	19
19	18	25	32	30	32	25

Lesson 10-3

Find the mean, median, mode, and range of each data set.

12. 42, 45, 48, 45

13. 66, 68, 68, 62, 61, 68, 65, 60

Identify the outlier in each data set, and determine how the outlier affects the mean, median, mode, and range of the data.

14. 4, 8, 15, 8, 71, 7, 6

15. 36, 7, 50, 40, 38, 48, 40

Use the data to make a box-and-whisker plot.

16. 7, 8, 10, 2, 5, 1, 10, 8, 5, 5

17. 54, 64, 50, 48, 53, 55, 57

Lesson 10-4

18. The graph shows the ages of people who listen to a radio program.

    a. Explain why the graph is misleading.

    b. What might someone believe because of the graph?

    c. Who might want to use this graph? Explain.

19. A researcher surveys people at the Elmwood library about the number of hours they spend reading each day. Explain why the following statement is misleading: "People in Elmwood read for an average of 1.5 hours per day."

Ages of Radio Program Listeners

25 to 36
30%

Under 18
15%

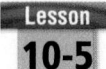

Lesson 10-5

20. Identify the sample space and the outcome shown for the spinner at right.

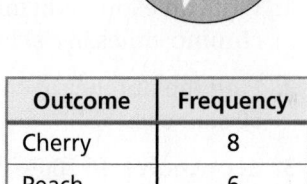

Write *impossible, unlikely, as likely as not, likely,* or *certain* to describe each event.

21. Two people sitting next to each other on a bus have the same birthday.

22. Dylan rolls a number greater than 1 on a standard number cube.

An experiment consists of randomly choosing a fruit snack from a box. Use the results in the table to find the experimental probability of each event.

Outcome	Frequency
Cherry	8
Peach	6
Blueberry	6

23. choosing a blueberry fruit snack

24. choosing a cherry fruit snack

25. not choosing a cherry fruit snack

Lesson 10-6

Find the theoretical probability of each outcome.

26. rolling an even number on a number cube

27. tossing two coins and both landing tails up

28. randomly choosing a prime number from a bag that contains ten slips of paper numbered 1 through 10

29. The probability of choosing a green marble from a bag is $\frac{3}{7}$. What is the probability of not choosing a green marble?

30. The odds against winning a game are 8:3. What is the probability of winning the game?

Lesson 10-7

Tell whether each set of events is independent or dependent. Explain your answer.

31. You pick a bottle from a basket containing chilled drinks, and then your friend chooses a bottle.

32. You roll a 6 on a number cube and you toss a coin that lands heads up.

33. A number cube is rolled three times. What is the probability of rolling three numbers greater than 4?

34. An experiment consists of randomly selecting a marble from a bag, replacing it, and then selecting another marble. The bag contains 3 blue marbles, 2 orange marbles, and 5 yellow marbles. What is the probability of selecting a blue marble and then a yellow marble?

35. Madeleine has 3 nickels and 5 quarters in her pocket. She randomly chooses one coin and does not replace it. Then she randomly chooses another coin. What is the probability that she chooses two quarters?

Biology Use the following information for Exercises 1 and 2.

In general, skin cells in the human body contain 46 chromosomes. *(Lesson 1-1)*

1. Write an expression for the number of chromosomes in c skin cells.

2. Find the number of chromosomes in 8, 15, and 50 skin cells.

3. **Economics** In 2004, the average price of an ounce of gold was $47 more than the average price in 2003. The 2004 price was $410. Write and solve an equation to find the average price of an ounce of gold in 2003. *(Lesson 1-2)*

4. During a renovation, 36 seats were removed from a theater. The theater now seats 580 people. Write and solve an equation to find the number of seats in the theater before the renovation. *(Lesson 1-2)*

5. A case of juice drinks contains 12 bottles and costs $18. Write and solve an equation to find the cost of each drink. *(Lesson 1-2)*

6. **Astronomy** Objects weigh about 3 times as much on Earth as they do on Mars. A rock weighs 42 lb on Mars. Write and solve an equation to find the rock's weight on Earth. *(Lesson 1-2)*

7. The county fair's admission fee is $8 and each ride costs $2.50. Sonia spent a total of $25.50. How many rides did she go on? *(Lesson 1-4)*

8. At the beginning of a block party, the temperature was 84°. During the party, the temperature dropped 3° every hour. At the end of the party, the temperature was 66°. How long was the party? *(Lesson 1-4)*

9. **Consumer Economics** A health insurance policy costs $700 per year, plus $15 for each visit to the doctor's office. A different plan costs $560 per year, but each office visit is $50. Find the number of office visits for which the two plans have the same total cost. *(Lesson 1-5)*

10. **Geometry** The formula $A = \frac{1}{2}bh$ gives the area A of a triangle with base b and height h. *(Lesson 1-6)*

    a. Solve $A = \frac{1}{2}bh$ for h.

    b. Find the height of a triangle with an area of 30 square feet and a base of 6 feet.

11. Charles is hanging a poster on his wall. He wants the top of the poster to be 84 inches from the floor but would be happy for it to be 3 inches higher or lower. Write and solve an absolute-value equation to find the maximum and minimum acceptable heights. *(Lesson 1-7)*

12. The ratio of students to adults on a school trip is 9:2. There are 6 adults on the trip. How many students are there? *(Lesson 1-8)*

13. A cheetah can reach speeds of up to 103 feet per second. Use dimensional analysis to convert the cheetah's speed to miles per hour. Round to the nearest tenth. *(Lesson 1-8)*

14. Write and solve a proportion to find the height of the flagpole. *(Lesson 1-9)*

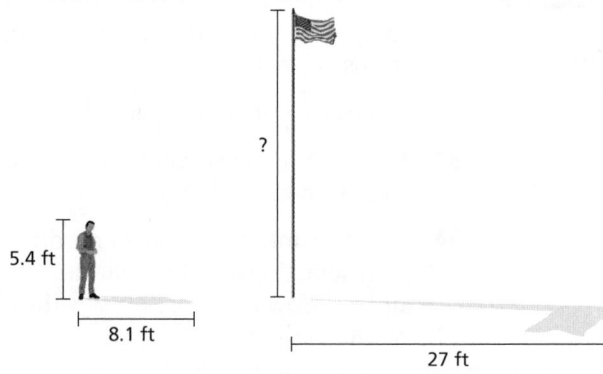

15. **Coins** Alex and Aretha found the mass of a half dollar coin with an exact mass of 11.340 g. Alex's measure was 11.3 g. Aretha's was 11.338 g. Whose measure was more precise? Whose is more accurate? *(Lesson 1-10)*

16. **Manufacturing** The weight of a box of Wheat Treats cereal is 16 oz with a tolerance of 0.2 oz. Is a box with a weight of 15.85 oz acceptable? Explain. *(Lesson 1-10)*

Extra Practice Chapter 2 ▪ Applications Practice

1. At a food-processing factory, each box of cereal must weigh at least 15 ounces. Define a variable and write an inequality for the acceptable weights of the cereal boxes. Graph the solutions. *(Lesson 2-1)*

2. In order to qualify for a discounted entry fee at a museum, a visitor must be less than 13 years old. Define a variable and write an inequality for the ages that qualify for the discounted entry fee. Graph the solutions. *(Lesson 2-1)*

3. A restaurant can seat no more than 102 customers at one time. There are already 96 customers in the restaurant. Write and solve an inequality to find out how many additional customers could be seated in the restaurant. *(Lesson 2-2)*

4. **Meteorology** A hurricane is a tropical storm with a wind speed of at least 74 mi/h. A meteorologist is tracking a storm whose current wind speed is 63 mi/h. Write and solve an inequality to find out how much greater the wind speed must be in order for this storm to be considered a hurricane. *(Lesson 2-2)*

Hobbies Use the following information for Exercises 5–7.

When setting up an aquarium, it is recommended that you have no more than one inch of fish per gallon of water. For example, in a 30-gallon tank, the total length of the fish should be at most 30 inches. *(Lesson 2-3)*

Freshwater Fish	
Name	Length (in.)
Red tail catfish	3.5
Blue gourami	1.5

5. Write an inequality to show the possible numbers of blue gourami you can put in a 10-gallon aquarium.

6. Find the possible numbers of blue gourami you can put in a 10-gallon aquarium.

7. Find the possible numbers of red tail catfish you can put in a 20-gallon aquarium.

8. The admission fee at an amusement park is $12, and each ride costs $3.50. The park also offers an all-day pass with unlimited rides for $33. For what numbers of rides is it cheaper to buy the all-day pass? *(Lesson 2-4)*

9. The table shows the cost of Internet access at two different cafes. For how many hours of access is the cost at Cyber Station less than the cost at Web World? *(Lesson 2-5)*

Internet Access	
Cafe	Cost
Cyber Station	$12 one-time membership fee $1.50 per hour
Web World	No membership fee $2.25 per hour

10. Larissa is considering two summer jobs. A job at the mall pays $400 per week plus $15 for every hour of overtime. A job at the movie theater pays $360 per week plus $20 for every hour of overtime. How many hours of overtime would Larissa have to work in order for the job at the movie theater to pay a higher salary than the job at the mall? *(Lesson 2-5)*

11. **Health** For maximum safety, it is recommended that food be stored at a temperature between 34 °F and 40 °F inclusive. Write a compound inequality to show the temperatures that are within the recommended range. Graph the solutions. *(Lesson 2-6)*

12. **Physics** Color is determined by the wavelength of light. Wavelengths are measured in nanometers (nm). Our eyes see the color green when light has a wavelength between 492 nm and 577 nm inclusive. Write a compound inequality to show the wavelengths that produce green light. Graph the solutions. *(Lesson 2-6)*

13. Allison ran a mile in 8 minutes. She wants to run a second mile within 0.75 minute of her time for the first mile. Write and solve an absolute-value inequality to find the range of acceptable times for the second mile. *(Lesson 2-7)*

1. Donnell drove on the highway at a constant speed and then slowed down as she approached her exit. Sketch a graph to show the speed of Donnell's car over time. Tell whether the graph is continuous or discrete. *(Lesson 3-1)*

2. Lori is buying mineral water for a party. The bottles are available in six-packs. Sketch a graph showing the number of bottles Lori will have if she buys 1, 2, 3, 4, or 5 six-packs. Tell whether the graph is continuous or discrete. *(Lesson 3-1)*

3. **Health** To exercise effectively, it is important to know your maximum heart rate. You can calculate your maximum heart rate in beats per minute by subtracting your age from 220. *(Lesson 3-2)*

   a. Express the age x and the maximum heart rate y as a relation in table form by showing the maximum heart rate for people who are 20, 30, 35, and 40 years old.

   b. Is this relation a function? Explain.

4. **Sports** The table shows the number of games won by four baseball teams and the number of home runs each team hit. Is this relation a function? Explain. *(Lesson 3-2)*

Season Statistics	
Wins	Home Runs
95	185
93	133
80	140
93	167

5. Michael uses 5.5 cups of flour for each loaf of bread that he bakes. He plans to bake a maximum of 4 loaves. Write a function to describe the number of cups of flour used. Find a reasonable domain and range for the function. *(Lesson 3-3)*

6. A gym offers the following special rate. New members pay a $425 initiation fee and then pay $90 per year for 1, 2, or 3 years. Write a function to describe the situation. Find a reasonable domain and range for the function. *(Lesson 3-3)*

7. The function $y = 3.5x$ describes the number of miles y that the average turtle can walk in x hours. Graph the function. Use the graph to estimate how many miles a turtle can walk in 4.5 hours. *(Lesson 3-4)*

8. **Earth Science** The Kangerdlugssuaq glacier in Greenland is flowing into the sea at the rate of 1.6 meters per hour. The function $y = 1.6x$ describes the number of meters y that flow into the sea in x hours. Graph the function. Use the graph to estimate the number of meters that flow into the sea in 8 hours. *(Lesson 3-4)*

9. The scatter plot shows a relationship between the number of lemonades sold in a day and the day's high temperature. Based on this relationship, predict the number of lemonades that will be sold on a day when the high temperature is 96 °F. *(Lesson 3-5)*

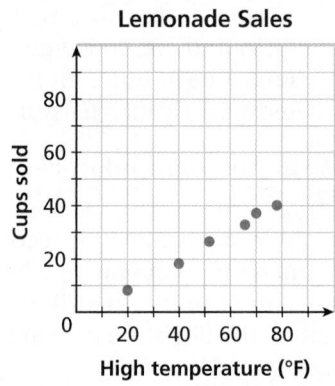

Lemonade Sales

10. In month 1 the Elmwood Public Library had 85 Spanish books in its collection. Each month, the librarian plans to order 8 new Spanish books. How many Spanish books will the library have in month 15? *(Lesson 3-6)*

11. Nikki purchases a card that she can use to ride the bus in her town. Each time she rides the bus $1.50 is deducted from the value of the card. After her first ride, there is $43.50 left on the card. How much money will be left on the card after Nikki has taken 12 bus rides? *(Lesson 3-6)*

1. Jennifer is having prints made of her photographs. Each print costs $1.50. The function $f(x) = 1.50x$ gives the total cost of the x prints. Graph this function and give its domain and range. *(Lesson 4-1)*

2. The Chang family lives 400 miles from Denver. They drive to Denver at a constant speed of 50 mi/h. The function $f(x) = 400 - 50x$ gives their distance in miles from Denver after x hours. *(Lesson 4-2)*

   a. Graph this function and find the intercepts.

   b. What does each intercept represent?

3. **History** The table shows the number of nations in the United Nations in different years. Find the rate of change for each time interval. During which time interval did the U.N. grow at the greatest rate? *(Lesson 4-3)*

Year	1945	1950	1960	1975
Number of Nations	51	60	99	144

4. The graph shows the temperature of an oven at different times. Find the slope of the line. Then tell what the slope represents. *(Lesson 4-4)*

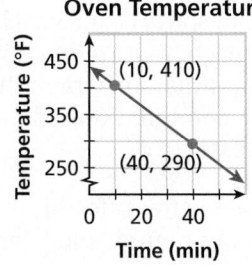

Oven Temperature

(10, 410)
(40, 290)

5. **Sports** Competitive race-walkers move at a speed of about 9 miles per hour. Write a direct variation equation for the distance y that a race-walker will cover in x hours. Then graph. *(Lesson 4-5)*

6. A bicycle rental costs $10 plus $1.50 per hour. *(Lesson 4-6)*

   a. Write an equation that represents the cost as a function of the number of hours.

   b. Identify the slope and y-intercept and describe their meaning.

   c. Find the cost of renting a bike for 6 hours.

7. A hot-air balloon is moving at a constant rate. Its altitude is a linear function of time, as shown in the table. Write an equation in slope-intercept form that represents this function. Then find the balloon's altitude after 25 minutes. *(Lesson 4-7)*

Balloon's Altitude	
Time (min)	Altitude (m)
0	250
7	215
12	190

8. The table shows weights and fuel efficiencies of five cars. *(Lesson 4-8)*

Weight (thousands of pounds)	Fuel efficiency (mi/gal)
3.5	18
2.8	22
2.1	24
4.1	17
2.2	36

   a. Find an equation for a line of best. How well does the line fit the data?

   b. Predict the fuel efficiency of a car that weighs 3000 pounds.

9. **Geometry** Show that the points $A(2, 3)$, $B(3, 1)$, $C(-1, -1)$, and $D(-2, 1)$ are the vertices of a rectangle. *(Lesson 4-9)*

10. A phone plan for international calls costs $12.50 per month plus $0.04 per minute. The monthly cost for x minutes of calls is given by the function $f(x) = 0.04x + 12.50$. How will the graph change if the phone company raises the monthly fee to $14.50? if the cost per minute is raised to $0.05? *(Lesson 4-10)*

1. Net Sounds, an online music store, charges $12 per CD plus $3 for shipping and handling. Web Discs charges $10 per CD plus $9 for shipping and handling. For how many CDs will the cost be the same? What will that cost be? *(Lesson 5-1)*

2. At Rocco's Restaurant, a large pizza costs $12 plus $1.25 for each additional topping. At Pizza Palace, a large pizza costs $15 plus $0.75 for each additional topping. For how many toppings will the cost be the same? What will that cost be? *(Lesson 5-1)*

Use the following information for Exercises 3 and 4.

The coach of a baseball team is deciding between two companies that manufacture team jerseys. One company charges a $60 setup fee and $25 per jersey. The other company charges a $200 setup fee and $15 per jersey. *(Lesson 5-2)*

3. For how many jerseys will the cost at the two companies be the same? What will that cost be?

4. The coach is planning to purchase 20 jerseys. Which company is the better option? Why?

5. **Geometry** The length of a rectangle is 5 inches greater than the width. The sum of the length and width is 41 inches. Find the length and width of the rectangle. *(Lesson 5-2)*

6. At a movie theater, tickets cost $9.50 for adults and $6.50 for children. A group of 7 moviegoers pays a total of $54.50. How many adults and how many children are in the group? *(Lesson 5-3)*

7. **Business** A grocer is buying large quantities of fruit to resell at his store. He purchases apples at $0.50 per pound and pears at $0.75 per pound. The grocer spends a total of $17.25 for 27 pounds of fruit. How many pounds of each fruit does he buy? *(Lesson 5-3)*

8. Bricks are available in two sizes. Large bricks weigh 9 pounds, and small bricks weigh 4.5 pounds. A bricklayer has 14 bricks that weigh a total of 90 pounds. How many of each type of brick are there? *(Lesson 5-3)*

9. **Sports** The table shows the time it took two runners to complete the Boston Marathon in several different years. If the patterns continue, will Shanna ever complete the marathon in the same number of minutes as Maria? Explain. *(Lesson 5-4)*

Marathon Times (min)				
	2003	2004	2005	2006
Shanna	190	182	174	166
Maria	175	167	159	151

10. Jordan leaves his house and rides his bike at 10 mi/h. After he goes 4 miles, his brother Tim leaves the house and rides in the same direction at 12 mi/h. If their rates stay the same, will Tim ever catch up to Jordan? Explain. *(Lesson 5-4)*

11. Charmaine is buying almonds and cashews for a reception. She wants to spend no more than $18. Almonds cost $4 per pound, and cashews cost $5 per pound. Write a linear inequality to describe the situation. Graph the solutions. Then give two combinations of nuts that Charmaine could buy. *(Lesson 5-5)*

12. Luis is buying T-shirts to give out at a school fund-raiser. He must spend less than $100 for the shirts. Child shirts cost $5 each, and adult shirts cost $8 each. Write a linear inequality to describe the situation. Graph the solutions. Then give two combinations of shirts that Luis could buy. *(Lesson 5-5)*

13. Nicholas is buying treats for his dog. Beef cubes cost $3 per pound, and liver cubes cost $2 per pound. He wants to buy at least 2 pounds of each type of treat, and he wants to spend no more than $14. Graph all possible combinations of the treats that Nicholas could buy. List two possible combinations. *(Lesson 5-6)*

14. **Geometry** The perimeter of a rectangle is at most 20 inches. The length and the width are each at least 3 inches. Graph all possible combinations of lengths and widths that result in such a rectangle. List two possible combinations. *(Lesson 5-6)*

1. The eye of a bee is about 10^{-3} m in diameter. Simplify this expression. *(Lesson 6-1)*

2. A typical stroboscopic camera has a shutter speed of 10^{-6} seconds. Simplify this expression. *(Lesson 6-1)*

3. Carl has 4 identical cubes lined up in a row and wants to find the total length of the cubes. He knows that the volume of one cube is 343 in³. Use the formula $s = V^{\frac{1}{3}}$ to find the length of one cube. What is the length of the row of cubes? *(Lesson 6-2)*

4. A rock is thrown off a 220-foot cliff with an initial velocity of 50 feet per second. The height of the rock above the ground is given by the polynomial $-16t^2 - 50t + 220$, where t is the time in seconds after the rock has been thrown. What is the height of the rock above the ground after 2 seconds? *(Lesson 6-3)*

5. The sum of the first n natural numbers is given by the polynomial $\frac{1}{2}n^2 + \frac{1}{2}n$. Use this polynomial to find the sum of the first 9 natural numbers. *(Lesson 6-3)*

6. **Biology** The population of insects in a meadow depends on the temperature. A biologist models the population of insect A with the polynomial $0.02x^2 + 0.5x + 8$ and the population of insect B with the polynomial $0.04x^2 - 0.2x + 12$, where x represents the temperature in degrees Fahrenheit. *(Lesson 6-4)*

   a. Write a polynomial that represents the total population of both insects.

   b. Write a polynomial that represents the difference of the populations of insect B and insect A.

7. **Geometry** The length of the rectangle shown is 1 inch longer than 3 times the width.

   a. Write a polynomial that represents the area of the rectangle.

   b. Find the area of the rectangle when the width is 4 inches. *(Lesson 6-5)*

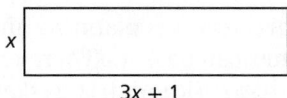

x

$3x + 1$

8. A cabinet maker starts with a square piece of wood and then cuts a square hole from its center as shown. Write a polynomial that represents the area of the remaining piece of wood. *(Lesson 6-6)*

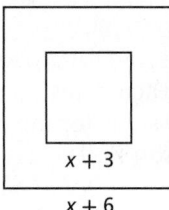

$x + 3$

$x + 6$

1. Ms. Andrews's class has 12 boys and 18 girls. For a class picture, the students will stand in rows on a set of steps. Each row must have the same number of students, and each row will contain only boys or girls. How many rows will there be if Ms. Andrews puts the maximum number of students in each row? *(Lesson 7-1)*

2. A museum director is planning an exhibit of Native American baskets. There are 40 baskets from North America and 32 baskets from South America. The baskets will be displayed on shelves so that each shelf has the same number of baskets. Baskets from North and South America will not be placed together on the same shelf. How many shelves will be needed if each shelf holds the maximum number of baskets? *(Lesson 7-1)*

3. The area of a rectangular painting is $(3x^2 + 5x)$ ft^2. Factor this polynomial to find possible expressions for the dimensions of the painting. *(Lesson 7-2)*

4. **Geometry** The surface area of a cylinder with radius r and height h is given by the expression $2\pi r^2 + 2\pi rh$. Factor this expression. *(Lesson 7-2)*

5. The area of a rectangular classroom in square feet is given by $x^2 + 9x + 18$. The width of the classroom is $(x + 3)$ ft. What is the length of the classroom? *(Lesson 7-3)*

Gardening Use the following information for Exercises 6 and 7.

A rectangular flower bed has a width of $(x + 4)$ ft. The bed will be enlarged by increasing the length, as shown. *(Lesson 7-3)*

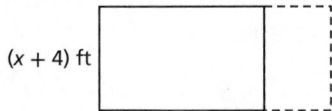

(x + 4) ft

6. The original flower bed has an area of $(x^2 + 9x + 20)$ ft^2. What is its length?

7. The enlarged flower bed will have an area of $(x^2 + 12x + 32)$ ft^2. What will be the new length of the flower bed?

8. A rectangular poster has an area of $(6x^2 + 19x + 15)$ in^2. The width of the poster is $(2x + 3)$ in. What is the length of the poster? *(Lesson 7-4)*

9. **Physics** The height of an object thrown upward with a velocity of 38 feet per second from an initial height of 5 feet can be modeled by the polynomial $-16t^2 + 38t + 5$, where t is the time in seconds. Factor this expression. Then use the factored expression to find the object's height after $\frac{1}{2}$ second. *(Lesson 7-4)*

10. A rectangular pool has an area of $(9x^2 + 30x + 25)$ ft^2. The dimensions of the pool are of the form $ax + b$, where a and b are whole numbers. Find an expression for the perimeter of the pool. Then find the perimeter when $x = 5$. *(Lesson 7-5)*

11. **Geometry** The area of a square is $9x^2 - 24x + 16$. Find the length of each side of the square. Is it possible for x to equal 1 in this situation? Why or why not? *(Lesson 7-5)*

Architecture Use the following information for Exercises 12–14.

An architect is designing a rectangular hotel room. A balcony that is 5 feet wide runs along the length of the room, as shown in the figure. *(Lesson 7-6)*

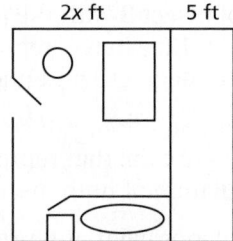

2x ft   5 ft

12. The area of the room, including the balcony, is $(4x^2 + 12x + 5)$ ft^2. Tell whether the polynomial is fully factored. Explain.

13. Find the length and width of the room (including the balcony).

14. How long is the balcony when $x = 9$?

1. The table shows the height of a ball at various times after being thrown into the air. Tell whether the function is quadratic. Explain. *(Lesson 8-1)*

Time (s)	0	0.5	1	1.5	2
Height (ft)	4	20	28	28	20

2. The height of the curved roof of a camping tent can be modeled by $f(x) = -0.5x^2 + 3x$, where x is the width in feet. Find the height of the tent at its tallest point. *(Lesson 8-2)*

3. **Engineering** A small bridge passes over a stream. The height in feet of the bridge's curved arch support can be modeled by $f(x) = -0.25x^2 + 2x + 1.5$, where the x-axis represents the level of the water. Find the greatest height of the arch support. *(Lesson 8-2)*

4. **Sports** The height in meters of a football that is kicked from the ground is approximated by $f(x) = -5x^2 + 20x$, where x is the time in seconds after the ball is kicked. Find the ball's maximum height and the time it takes the ball to reach this height. Then find how long the ball is in the air. *(Lesson 8-3)*

5. **Physics** Two golf balls are dropped, one from a height of 400 feet and the other from a height of 576 feet. *(Lesson 8-4)*

   a. Compare the graphs that show the time it takes each golf ball to reach the ground.

   b. Use the graphs to tell when each golf ball reaches the ground.

6. A model rocket is launched into the air with an initial velocity of 144 feet per second. The quadratic function $y = -16x^2 + 144x$ models the height of the rocket after x seconds. How long is the rocket in the air? *(Lesson 8-5)*

7. A gymnast jumps on a trampoline. The quadratic function $y = -16x^2 + 24x$ models her height in feet above the trampoline after x seconds. How long is the gymnast in the air? *(Lesson 8-5)*

8. A child standing on a rock tosses a ball into the air. The height of the ball above the ground is modeled by $h = -16t^2 + 28t + 8$, where h is the height in feet and t is the time in seconds. Find the time it takes the ball to reach the ground. *(Lesson 8-6)*

9. **Geometry** The base of the triangle in the figure is five times the height. The area of the triangle is 400 in². Find the height of the triangle to the nearest tenth. *(Lesson 8-7)*

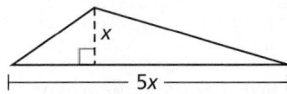

10. The length of a rectangular swimming pool is 8 feet greater than the width. The pool has an area of 240 ft². Find the length and width of the pool. *(Lesson 8-8)*

11. **Geometry** One base of a trapezoid is 4 ft longer than the other base. The height of the trapezoid is equal to the shorter base. The trapezoid's area is 80 ft². Find the height. $\left(Hint: A = \frac{1}{2}h(b_1 + b_2) \right)$ *(Lesson 8-8)*

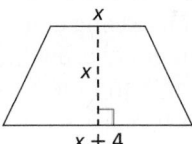

12. A referee tosses a coin into the air at the start of a football game to decide which team will get the ball. The height of the coin above the ground is modeled by $h = -16t^2 + 12t + 4$, where h is the height in feet and t is the time in seconds after the coin is tossed. Will the coin reach a height of 8 feet? Use the discriminant to explain your answer. *(Lesson 8-9)*

13. The population in thousands of Millville can be modeled by the equation $P(t) = t^2 + 2t$. The population in thousands of Barton can be modeled by the equation $y = 8t + 15$. In both cases, t is the number of years since 2010. In what year will the populations of the two towns be approximately equal? *(Lesson 8-10)*

1. Scientists who are developing a vaccine track the number of new infections of a disease each year. The values in the table form a geometric sequence. To the nearest whole number, how many new infections will there be in the 6th year? *(Lesson 9-1)*

Year	Number of New Infections
1	12,000
2	9000
3	6750

2. **Finance** For a savings account that earns 5% interest each year, the function $f(x) = 2000(1.05)^x$ gives the value of a $2000 investment after x years. *(Lesson 9-2)*

   a. Find the investment's value after 5 years.

   b. Approximately how many years will it take for the investment to be worth $3100?

3. **Chemistry** Cesium-137 has a half-life of 30 years. Find the amount left from a 200-gram sample after 150 years. *(Lesson 9-3)*

4. The cost of tuition at a dance school is $300 a year and is increasing at a rate of 3% a year. Write an exponential growth function to model the situation and find the cost of tuition after 4 years. *(Lesson 9-3)*

5. Use the data in the table to describe how the price of the company's stock is changing. Then write a function that models the data. Use your function to predict the price of the company's stock after 7 years. *(Lesson 9-4)*

Stock Prices				
Year	0	1	2	3
Price ($)	10.00	11.00	12.20	13.31

6. Use the data in the table to describe the rate at which Susan reads. Then write a function that models the data. Use your function to predict the number of pages Susan will read in 6 hours. *(Lesson 9-4)*

Total Number of Pages Read				
Time (h)	1	2	3	4
Pages	48	96	144	192

7. **Savings** Mary has $50 in her savings account. She is considering two options for increasing her savings. Option A recommends increasing the amount in her savings by $5 per month. Option B recommends a 5% increase each month. Compare the options. *(Lesson 9-5)*

8. **Critical Thinking** A tutoring center has 100 students. The director wants to set a goal to motivate her instructors to increase student enrollment. Under plan A, the goal is to increase the number of students by 15% each year. Under plan B, the goal is to increase the number of students by 25 each year.

   a. Compare the plans.

   b. Which plan should the director choose to double the enrollment in the shortest amount of time? Explain.

   c. When will the center have about the same number of students enrolled under both plans? Will this happen more than once? Explain. *(Lesson 9-5)*

Geography Use the following information for Exercises 1–3.

The bar graph shows the areas of the Great Lakes. *(Lesson 10-1)*

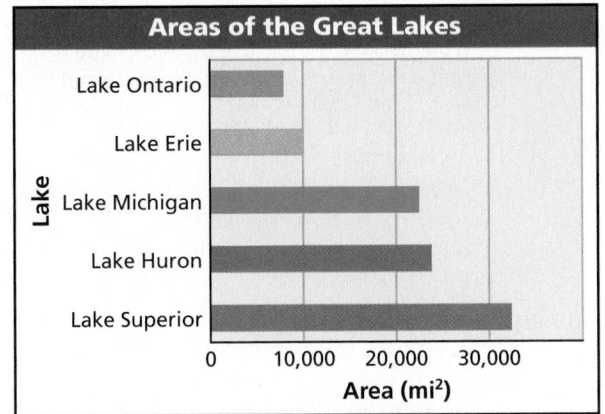

1. Estimate the difference in the areas between the lake with the greatest area and the lake with the least area.

2. Estimate the total area of the five lakes.

3. Approximately what percent of the total area is Lake Superior?

4. The scores of 18 students on a Spanish exam are given below. Use the data to make a stem-and-leaf plot. *(Lesson 10-2)*

Exam Scores								
65	94	92	75	71	83	77	73	91
82	63	79	80	77	99	76	80	88

5. The numbers of customers who visited a hair salon each day are given below. Use the data to make a frequency table with intervals. *(Lesson 10-2)*

Number of Customers Per Day						
32	35	29	44	41	25	35
40	41	32	33	28	33	34

Sports Use the following information for Exercises 6 and 7.

The numbers of points scored by a college football team in 11 games are given below. *(Lesson 10-3)*

10 17 17 14 21 7 10 14 17 17 21

6. Find the mean, median, mode, and range of the data set.

7. Use the data to make a box-and-whisker plot.

8. The weekly salaries of five employees at a restaurant are $450, $500, $460, $980, and $520. Explain why the following statement is misleading: "The average salary is $582." *(Lesson 10-4)*

9. The graph shows the sales figures for three sales representatives. Explain why the graph is misleading. What might someone believe because of the graph? *(Lesson 10-4)*

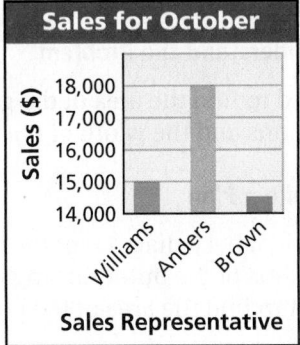

10. A manager inspects 120 stereos that were built at a factory. She finds that 6 are defective. What is the experimental probability that a stereo chosen at random will be defective? *(Lesson 10-5)*

Travel Use the following information for Exercises 11–13.

A row of an airplane has 2 window seats, 3 middle seats, and 4 aisle seats. You are randomly assigned a seat in the row. *(Lesson 10-6)*

11. Find the probability that you are assigned a window seat.

12. Find the odds in favor of being assigned a window seat.

13. Find the probability that you are not assigned a middle seat.

14. A class consists of 19 boys and 16 girls. The teacher selects one student at random to be the class president and then selects a different student to be vice president. What is the probability that both students are girls? *(Lesson 10-7)*

Problem Solving Handbook

Draw a Diagram

You can draw a diagram to help you visualize what the words of a problem are describing.

Problem Solving Strategies

Draw a Diagram   Make a Table
Make a Model   Solve a Simpler Problem
Guess and Test   Use Logical Reasoning
Work Backward   Use a Venn Diagram
Find a Pattern   Make an Organized List

EXAMPLE

A gardener wants to plant a 2.5-foot-wide border of flowers around a rectangular herb garden. The herb garden is 12 feet long and 7.5 feet wide. What is the area of the border?

 Understand the Problem

You need to find the area of the garden's border. You are given the garden's dimensions and the width of the border.

 Make a Plan

Draw and label a diagram of the herb garden with the surrounding border. Find the dimensions of the outer rectangle. Then find the area of the inner rectangle and subtract to find the area of the border.

 Solve

length of outer rectangle: 2.5 ft + 12 ft + 2.5 ft = 17 ft
width of outer rectangle: 2.5 ft + 7.5 ft + 2.5 ft = 12.5 ft

Find the area of each rectangle:

area of outer rectangle: 17 ft × 12.5 ft = 212.5 ft²
area of inner rectangle: 12 ft × 7.5 ft = 90 ft²

Subtract:

area of border: 212.5 ft² − 90 ft² = 122.5 ft²

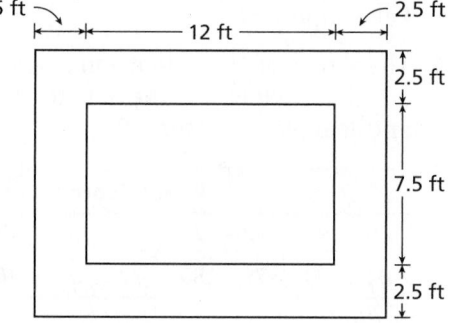

 Look Back

To check your answer, solve the problem in a different way.

Divide the border into four parts and find the area of each part. Then add the areas.

17 ft × 2.5 ft = 42.5 ft²	7.5 ft × 2.5 ft = 18.75 ft² ft²
17 ft × 2.5 ft = 42.5 ft²	7.5 ft × 2.5 ft = 18.75 ft²

42.5 ft² + 42.5 ft² + 18.75 ft² + 18.75 ft² + = 122.5 ft²

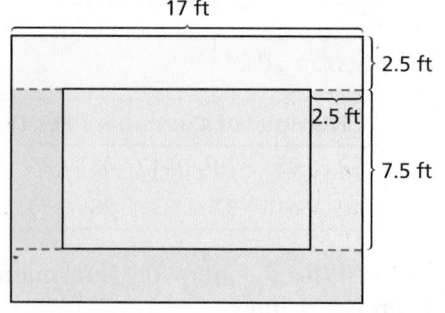

PRACTICE

1. A circular fish pond is surrounded by a circular border of stones that is 18 inches wide. The fish pond is 4 feet in diameter. What is the area of the border? (Use 3.14 for π.)

2. Thirty-two teams are in the first round of a softball tournament. A team is eliminated as soon as it loses a game. How many games need to be played to determine the winner? (*Hint:* Use a tree diagram.)

Make a Model

You can **make a model,** or representation of the objects in a problem, to help you solve it.

 Problem Solving Strategies

Draw a Diagram	Make a Table
Make a Model	Solve a Simpler Problem
Guess and Test	Use Logical Reasoning
Work Backward	Use a Venn Diagram
Find a Pattern	Make an Organized List

EXAMPLE

Mr. Duncan is using blue and white square tiles to create a pattern on his kitchen wall. The entire design will have 8 rows with 15 tiles in each row. The bottom row alternates colors starting with blue, and the row above that alternates colors starting with white. He will continue this alternating pattern so that the same two colors are never next to each other. How many of each color tile does Mr. Duncan need to complete the entire design?

1. Understand the Problem

You need to find how many of each color tile are needed. You know the number of rows and the number of tiles in each row. The colors alternate so that the same two colors are never next to each other.

2. Make a Plan

Use blocks (preferably blue and white, but any two colors would work) to make a model of the first two rows. Count how many of each color you use. Then multiply to find how many of each color would be used in the entire design.

3. Solve

Create the bottom row. Start with a blue block and alternate colors across the row until you have used 15 blocks.

Create the row above the bottom row. Start with a white block.

You could build all 8 rows and just count the number of each color, but each group of two rows will be the same, so this way is quicker.

There will be a total of 8 rows: 4 that start with blue and 4 that start with white. Count how many of each color are used above and multiply each number by 4.

$$\text{blue: } 15 \times 4 = 60$$
$$\text{white: } 15 \times 4 = 60$$

Mr. Duncan needs 60 blue tiles and 60 white tiles.

4. Look Back

The grid is 15 units by 8 units, so there are $15 \times 8 = 120$ squares in the grid. Add the number of blue and white tiles to see if the sum is 120: $60 + 60 = 120$.

PRACTICE

1. Mr. Duncan decides to tile another area of his kitchen wall. This design will have 12 rows with 10 tiles in each row. The bottom row will repeat this pattern: blue, white, blue, blue, white. The row above the bottom row will repeat this pattern: white, green, white, white, green. He will use these two patterns for each of the remaining rows so that the first colors of each row always alternate. How many of each color tile will Mr. Duncan need?

Problem-Solving Handbook

Guess and Test

The **guess and test** strategy can be used when you cannot think of another way to solve the problem. Begin by making a reasonable guess, and then test it to see whether your guess is correct. If not, adjust the guess accordingly and test again. Keep guessing and testing until you correctly solve the problem.

Problem Solving Strategies

Draw a Diagram	Make a Table
Make a Model	Solve a Simpler Problem
Guess and Test	Use Logical Reasoning
Work Backward	Use a Venn Diagram
Find a Pattern	Make an Organized List

EXAMPLE

The manager of a college computer lab purchased 24 printers at a total cost of $3120. Some of the printers were laser, and some were ink jet. The laser printers cost $250 each, and the ink jet printers cost $70 each. How many of each type of printer did the manager purchase?

1. Understand the Problem

You know the cost of each type of printer and the total number of printers. You need to find the number of each type of printer purchased.

2. Make a Plan

Make reasonable first guesses for each type of printer. The sum must be 24. Then multiply each guess by the cost of each printer. Find the total and compare it to $3120. Adjust the guess as needed and continue until you find the solution.

3. Solve

Use a table to organize your guesses.

	Laser Printers	Ink Jet Printers	Total Priners	Total Cost	
1st guess	12	12	24	$12(\$250) + 12(\$70)$ $\$3000 + \$840 = \$3840$	*Too high—try fewer laser printers.*
2nd guess	6	18	24	$6(\$250) + 18(\$70)$ $\$1500 + \$1260 = \$2760$	*Too low—try more laser printers.*
3rd guess	8	16	24	$8(\$250) + 16(\$70)$ $\$2000 + \$1120 = \$3120$	*Correct!*

The manager purchased 8 laser printers and 16 ink jet printers.

4. Look Back

The total spent is $3120, and the total number of printers is 24. The solution is correct.

PRACTICE

1. All 350 seats were sold for a concert in the park. Adult tickets cost $15, and child tickets cost $5. Ticket sales totaled $4350. How many of each type of ticket were sold?

2. Jane is 3 times as old as Theo. Luke is 5 years older than Theo. Zoe is 8 years younger than twice Theo's age, and Cassie is 6 years younger than Theo. The sum of their ages is 71. How old is each person?

Problem-Solving Handbook

Work Backward

You can **work backward** to solve a problem when you know the ending value and are asked to find the initial value.

Draw a Diagram	Make a Table
Make a Model	Solve a Simpler Problem
Guess and Test	Use Logical Reasoning
Work Backward	Use a Venn Diagram
Find a Pattern	Make an Organized List

EXAMPLE

Lee Ann is taking a vacation in Paris, France. Her flight arrived in Paris at 9:35 A.M. on Tuesday. The plane left New York City and flew for 7 hours and 55 minutes to Nice, France, where there was a layover of 1 hour 12 minutes. From Nice the plane flew 1 hour and 25 minutes to Paris. Paris time is 6 hours ahead of New York City time. What time did the plane leave New York City?

1 Understand the Problem

You are asked to find the time that the plane left New York City. You know when the flight arrived in Paris, the length of the stops that were made along the way, and the time difference between New York City and Paris.

2 Make a Plan

Work backward from the time the plane arrived in Paris, using inverse operations. Then apply the time difference between the two cities.

3 Solve

Subtract the length of time it took to fly from Nice to Paris from the time Lee Ann arrived in Paris.

9:35 A.M. − 1 hour 25 minutes = 8:10 A.M.

Subtract the length of the layover in Nice.

8:10 A.M. − 1 hour 12 minutes = 6:58 A.M.

Subtract the length of the flight from New York to Nice.

6:58 A.M. − 7 hours 55 minutes = 11:03 P.M. Monday

Since Paris time is ahead of New York time, subtract the time difference.

11:03 P.M., Monday − 6 hours = 5:03 P.M. Monday

Lee Ann's flight left New York City on Monday at 5:03 P.M.

4 Look Back

Work forward to check your answer.

5:03 P.M. Monday + 6 h + 7 h 55 min + 1 h 12 min + 1 h 25 min
= 5:03 P.M. Monday + 16 h 32 min
= 9:35 A.M. Tuesday

This matches the information given in the problem.

PRACTICE

1. A bus arrives in Dallas, Texas, at 10:59 A.M. on Friday. The bus left Atlanta, Georgia, and took 12 hours and 15 minutes to arrive in Shreveport, Louisiana, where there was a 45-minute layover. From Shreveport it took 4 hours and 29 minutes to get to Dallas. Dallas time is 1 hour behind Atlanta time. What time did the bus leave Atlanta?

2. Carolina bought a DVD player that was on sale for 90% of the original price. The total amount she paid was $135.72, which included a sales tax of $5.22. What was the original price of the DVD player?

Find a Pattern

If a problem involves a sequence of numbers or figures, it is often necessary to **find a pattern** to solve the problem.

 Problem Solving Strategies

Draw a Diagram	Make a Table
Make a Model	Solve a Simpler Problem
Guess and Test	Use Logical Reasoning
Work Backward	Use a Venn Diagram
Find a Pattern	Make an Organized List

EXAMPLE

Darian created the following sequence of stars:

How many stars will be in the 6th figure?

 Understand the Problem

You need to find the number of stars in the 6th figure. You can find the number in the first four figures by counting.

 Make a Plan

Count the number of stars in each of the first four figures. Use the information to find a pattern and determine a general rule.

 Solve

Look for a pattern between the position of each figure in the sequence and the number of stars in that figure.

Position	1	2	3	4
Stars	2	6	12	20

The number of stars is the square of the position number plus the position number. This rule written algebraically is $n^2 + n$.

Evaluate the expression for $n = 6$: $n^2 + n$

$$6^2 + 6 = 36 + 6 = 42$$

There will be 42 stars in the 6th figure.

 Look Back

Look for another pattern. The number of stars in each position increases by 4, then by 6, then by 8. That is, the amount of increase always increases by 2. So the number of stars in the 5th position will be 20 + 10, or 30, and the number of stars in the 6th position will be 30 + 12, or 42.

PRACTICE

1. The first three figures of a pattern are shown. How many circles will be in the 10th figure?

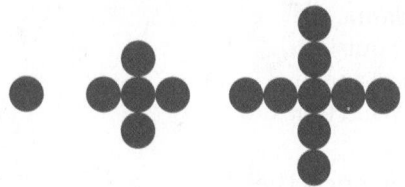

2. Lily drew the first four figures of a pattern. How many squares will be in the 7th figure?

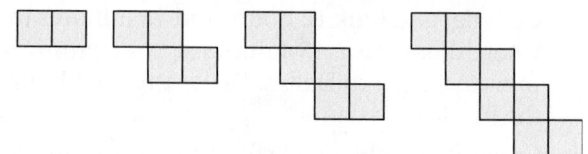

Problem-Solving Handbook

Make a Table

You can **make a table** to solve problems because
the rows and columns can help you arrange
information. Sometimes this also allows you to discover
relationships that might otherwise be hard to notice.

Problem Solving Strategies

Draw a Diagram	Make a Table
Make a Model	Solve a Simpler Problem
Guess and Test	Use Logical Reasoning
Work Backward	Use a Venn Diagram
Find a Pattern	Make an Organized List

EXAMPLE

A scientist begins a culture with 500 bacteria. The number of bacteria triples every
30 minutes. How many bacteria are in the culture after $2\frac{1}{2}$ hours?

 Understand the Problem

You are asked to find the number of bacteria in the culture after $2\frac{1}{2}$ hours.
You know the initial number of bacteria, and you know that the population
triples every half hour.

 Make a Plan

Make a table with rows for time and number of bacteria. Start with the initial
number in the culture. Increase the time in 30-minute increments and triple the
number of bacteria with each increase. Keep extending the table until the time is
$2\frac{1}{2}$ hours (150 minutes).

 Solve

Time (min)	0	30	60	90	120	150
Bacteria	500	1500	4500	13,500	40,500	121,500

There are 121,500 bacteria in the culture after $2\frac{1}{2}$ hours.

Look Back

Check your answer by solving a simpler problem. The number of bacteria in the
culture triples five times (150 min ÷ 30 min = 5). Start with 5 instead of 500 and triple
the number five times.

$5 \times 3 = 15$

$15 \times 3 = 45$

$45 \times 3 = 135$

$135 \times 3 = 405$

$405 \times 3 = 1215$

Multiply by 100 to find the total if you had started with 500; $1215 \times 100 = 121,500$

PRACTICE

1. A dietician's report states that a 125-pound woman needs to eat about 1750
   Calories a day to maintain her weight. It also states that a 132-pound woman
   needs 1848 Calories and a 139-pound woman needs 1946 Calories a day. Based
   on these values, how many Calories does a 160-pound woman need to eat each
   day to maintain her weight?

2. Simon opened a savings account with an initial deposit of $200. At the end of
   each year, the account earns 4% interest. If he does not deposit or withdraw any
   additional money, what would his balance be at the end of 6 years?

Problem-Solving Handbook

Solve a Simpler Problem

Sometimes a problem contains numbers that make it seem difficult to solve. You can **solve a simpler problem** by rewriting the numbers so they are easier to compute.

Problem Solving Strategies

Draw a Diagram	Make a Table
Make a Model	**Solve a Simpler Problem**
Guess and Test	Use Logical Reasoning
Work Backward	Use a Venn Diagram
Find a Pattern	Make an Organized List

EXAMPLE

During a skating competition, Jules skated around the track 35 times. One lap is 0.9 mile. If Jules finished in 1 hour 30 minutes, what was his average speed?

 Understand the Problem

You are asked to find Jules's average speed for 35 laps. You know the distance of each lap and the amount of time it took him to finish the competition.

 Make a Plan

Solve a simpler problem by using easier numbers to do the computations.

 Solve

Find the total distance skated.

$35(0.9)$	*There were 35 laps that measured 0.9 mile.*
$35(1 - 0.1)$	*Write 0.9 as 1 − 0.1*
$35(1) - 3.5(0.1)$	*Use the Distributive Property.*
$35 - 3.5$	
31.5	

Use the distance formula to find the average speed.

$d = rt$	
$31.5 = r \times 1.5$	*1 hour 30 minutes = 1.5 hours*
$\dfrac{31.5}{1.5} = r$	*Solve for r.*
$\dfrac{315}{15} = r$	*Multiply the numerator and denominator by 10 to eliminate the decimals.*
$\dfrac{1}{15}(315) = r$	
$\dfrac{1}{15}(300 + 15) = r$	*Write 315 as 300 + 15.*
$\dfrac{1}{15}(300) + \dfrac{1}{15}(15) = r$	*Use the Distributive Property.*
$20 + 1 = r$	
$21 = r$	

Jules skated at an average speed of 21 miles per hour.

 Look Back

Each lap is a little less than 1 mile, so 35 laps is a little less than 35 miles. Round this distance to 30 miles and use $d = rt$ to find the rate when the time is 1.5 hours: $30 \text{ mi} = (1.5 \text{ h})r \longrightarrow r = 20 \text{ mi/h}$. This is close to 21 mi/h.

PRACTICE

1. Diana swam 24 laps in the pool today. One lap is 200 feet. She swam at an average rate of 4 feet per second. How many minutes did Diana swim?

Use Logical Reasoning

Use logical reasoning to solve problems when you are given several facts and can use common sense to find a missing fact.

 Problem Solving Strategies

Draw a Diagram	Make a Table
Make a Model	Solve a Simpler Problem
Guess and Test	**Use Logical Reasoning**
Work Backward	Use a Venn Diagram
Find a Pattern	Make an Organized List

EXAMPLE 1

Five players on a baseball team wear the numbers 2, 12, 15, 34, and 42. Their positions are pitcher, catcher, first base, left field, and center field. The pitcher's number is less than the left fielder's number. The center fielder's number is greater than 25, and the left fielder wears an even number. The catcher wears number 34. What is the pitcher's number?

1. Understand the Problem

You want to find the jersey number of the pitcher. You know there are five positions and five jersey numbers. Some information about who wears which number is given.

2. Make a Plan

Organize the information in a table. Start with the fact that the catcher wears number 34 and use logical reasoning to determine the numbers of the other positions.

3. Solve

The catcher wears number 34. No other player wears 34, and the catcher wears no other number. Enter *Y's* and *N's* in the chart as shown.

The center fielder's number is greater than 25, so he must wear number 42. The left fielder cannot wear number 15 (because it is odd), and he cannot have the least number (the pitcher's number is less than his). The left fielder must wear 12.

The pitcher's number is less than 12 (the left fielder's), so he must wear number 2.

	2	12	15	34	42
Pitcher	Y	N	N	N	N
Catcher	N	N	N	Y	N
First Base	N	N	Y	N	N
Left Fielder	N	Y	N	N	N
Center Fielder	N	N	N	N	Y

Y = yes; N = no

Once you enter Y in a cell, enter N in the remaining cells for the row and the column that include it.

The pitcher wears number 2.

4. Look Back

Complete the chart if needed. Read the problem while looking at the chart to make sure there are no contradictions.

PRACTICE

1. Rose, Jill, Gaby, and Chloe bowled the scores 110, 125, 144, and 150. Jill did not bowl the 110. The person who bowled the 150 is Rose's sister and Jill's aunt. Chloe bowled the 125. What score did Jill bowl?

Use a Venn Diagram

You can **use a Venn diagram** to display relationships among sets of numbers. Circles are used to represent the individual sets.

Problem Solving Strategies

Draw a Diagram
Make a Model
Guess and Test
Work Backward
Find a Pattern

Make a Table
Solve a Simpler Problem
Use Logical Reasoning
Use a Venn Diagram
Make an Organized List

EXAMPLE

At a local supermarket, 194 people were given samples of two brands of orange juice. Their opinions were as follows: 120 people liked brand A, 101 people liked brand B, and 15 people did not like either brand. How many people liked only brand A?

 Understand the Problem

The total number of people was 194, and 15 of them did not like either brand. The statement "120 people liked brand A" means some of the 120 people liked *only* brand A and some liked brand A *and* brand B. The statement "101 people liked brand B" means some of the 101 people liked *only* brand B and some liked brand A *and* brand B.

2 Make a Plan

Use a Venn diagram to show the relationship among the groups of people.

3 Solve

Draw and label two intersecting circles to show the sets of people who liked brand A and brand B. Write 15 in the area labeled "Neither."

Out of 194 people, 15 liked neither brand. Subtract 15 from 194 to find how many people liked at least one brand: $194 - 15 = 179$.

Add the number of people who liked brand A to the number of people who liked brand B: $120 + 101 = 221$. You know there are only 179 people who liked at least one brand, so subtract 179 from 221: $221 - 179 = 42$. This means 42 people were counted twice, and that 42 people liked both brands. Write 42 in the area labeled both.

Out of 120 people who liked brand A, 42 also liked brand B. Subtract 42 from 120 to find the number of people who liked only brand A: $120 - 42 = 78$.

So 78 people liked only brand A.

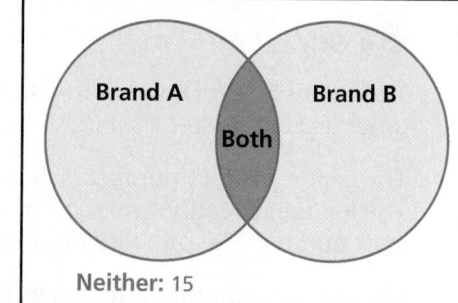

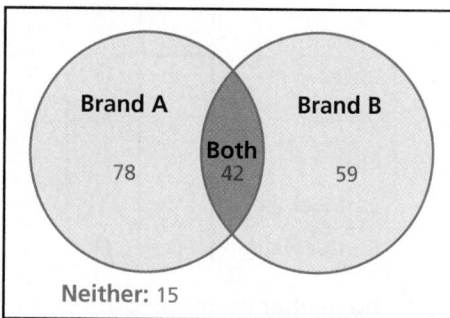

4 Look Back

Find the number of people who liked brand B only: $101 - 42 = 59$. Add all the numbers in the Venn diagram. The sum of the number who liked only brand A, the number who liked only brand B, the number who liked both brands, and the number who liked neither brand should be the total number of people surveyed: $78 + 59 + 42 + 15 = 194$.

PRACTICE

In a group of 138 people, 55 own a cat, 27 own a cat and a dog, and 42 own neither pet.

1. How many people own only a cat?

2. How many people own a dog?

Problem-Solving Handbook

Make an Organized List

If a problem asks you to find all the possible ways in which something can happen, you can **make an organized list** to keep track of the outcomes.

Problem Solving Strategies

Draw a Diagram   Make a Table
Make a Model   Solve a Simpler Problem
Guess and Test   Use Logical Reasoning
Work Backward   Use a Venn Diagram
Find a Pattern   **Make an Organized List**

EXAMPLE

A fair coin is tossed 4 times. What is the probability that it lands heads up at least 3 times?

1. Understand the Problem

You need to find the probability that a coin tossed 4 times lands heads up 3 or 4 times.

2. Make a Plan

The formula for probability is:

$$\text{probability} = \frac{\text{number of favorable outcomes}}{\text{total number of outcomes}}$$

The total number of outcomes is the number of items in the list. The number of favorable outcomes is the number of times the coin lands heads up 3 or 4 times.

Make an organized list of the coin tosses to find the total number of outcomes.

3. Solve

Start with heads for all 4 tosses, then heads for the first 3 tosses, then heads for the first 2 tosses, and then heads for the first toss. Repeat the pattern for tails.

HHHH	HTHH	TTTT	THTT	*There are 16 total*
HHHT	HTHT	TTTH	THTH	*outcomes.*
HHTH	HTTH	TTHT	THHT	*There are 5 favorable*
HHTT	HTTT	TTHH	THHH	*outcomes.*

The probability that the coin lands heads up 3 or 4 times is $\frac{5}{16}$.

4. Look Back

Double-check that each combination is listed and that no combination is written more than once. You can also use the Fundamental Counting Principle to check the total number of outcomes. For each of the 4 coin tosses, there are 2 possible outcomes, so the total number of outcomes is $2 \times 2 \times 2 \times 2 = 16$.

PRACTICE

1. A beagle, a fox terrier, an Afghan hound, and a golden retriever are competing in the finals of a dog show. How many ways can the dogs finish in first, second, and third place?

2. Two number cubes are rolled. What is the probability that the sum of the numbers rolled is an odd number?

Problem-Solving Handbook

1-1

Check It Out! **1a.** 4 decreased by n; n less than 4 **1b.** the quotient of t and 5; t divided by 5 **1c.** the sum of 9 and q; q added to 9 **1d.** the product of 3 and h; 3 times h **2a.** $65t$ **2b.** $m + 5$ **2c.** $32d$ **3a.** 6 **3b.** 7 **3c.** 3 **4. a.** $63s$, **b.** 756 bottles; 1575 bottles; 3150 bottles

Exercises **1.** variable **3.** the quotient of f and 3; f divided by 3 **5.** 9 decreased by y; y less than 9 **7.** the sum of t and 12; t increased by 12 **9.** x decreased by 3; the difference of x and 3 **11.** $w + 4$ **13.** 12 **15.** 6 **17.** the product of 5 and p; 5 groups of p **19.** the sum of 3 and x; 3 increased by x **21.** negative 3 times s; the product of negative 3 and s **23.** 14 decreased by t; the difference of 14 and t **25.** $t + 20$ **27.** 1 **29.** 2 **31a.** $h - 40$, **b.** 0; 4; 8; 12 **33.** $2x$ **35.** $y + 10$ **37.** $9w$; 9 in^2; 72 in^2; 81 in^2; 99 in^2 **39.** 13; 14; 15; 16 **41.** 6; 10; 13; 15 **43a.** $47.84 + m$; **b.** $58.53 - s$ **45.** $x + 7$; 19; 21 **47.** $x + 3$; 15; 17 **49.** F **51.** 36 **53.** 1. **55.** 45° **57.** 90° **59.** $\frac{1}{2}$ **61.** 1 **63.** Multiply the previous term by 3; 729, 2187, 6561.

1-2

Check It Out! **1a.** 8.8 **1b.** 0 **1c.** 25 **2a.** $\frac{1}{2}$ **2b.** -10 **2c.** 8 **3a.** 9.3 **3b.** 2 **3c.** 44 **4.** 35 years old

Exercises **3.** 21 **5.** 16.3 **7.** $\frac{1}{2}$ **9.** 0 **11.** 2.3 **13.** 1.2 **15.** 32 **17.** 3.7 **19.** $\frac{17}{6}$ **21.** 9 **23.** 17 **25.** $\frac{4}{7}$ **27.** 10.5 **29.** 9 **31.** 0 **33.** -17 **35.** -3100 **37.** -0.5 **39.** 0.05 **41.** 15 **43.** 1545 **45.** 30 **47.** $\frac{1}{3}$ **49.** $a + 500 = 4732$; $4232 **51.** $x - 10 = 12$; $x = 22$ **53.** $x + 8 = 16$; $x = 8$ **55.** $5 + x = 6$; $x = 1$ **57.** $x - 4 = 9$; $x = 13$ **59.** $m + 560 = 1680$; $1120 **61.** $63 + x = 90$; $x = 27$ **63.** $x + 15 = 90$; $x = 75$ **65.** $h - 47 = 28$; 75 **69.** J **71.** $-\frac{12}{5}$ **73.** $-\frac{13}{12}$ **75.** 10 **77.** 90

1-3

Check It Out! **1a.** 50 **1b.** -39 **1c.** 56 **2a.** 4 **2b.** -20 **2c.** 5 **3a.** $-\frac{5}{4}$ **3b.** 1 **3c.** 612 **4.** 15,000 ft

Exercises **1.** 32 **3.** 14 **5.** 19 **7.** 7 **9.** 5 **11.** 2.5 **13.** 14 **15.** -9 **17.** $\frac{1}{8}$ **19.** $16c = 192$; $12 **21.** 24 **23.** -36 **25.** -150 **27.** 55 **29.** -3 **31.** 1 **33.** 13 **35.** 0.3 **37.** 2 **39.** -16 **41.** -3.5 **43.** -2 **45.** $\frac{7}{10}s = 392$; $560 **49.** $4s = 84$; 21 in. **51.** $4s = 16.4$; 4.1 cm **53.** $-3x = 12$; $x = -4$ **55.** $\frac{x}{3} = -8$; $x = -24$ **57.** $6.25h = 50$; 8 h **59.** $0.05m = 13.80$; 276 min **61.** -2 **63.** 0; $8y = 0$; 0 **65a.** number of data values **c.** 185,300 acres **67.** 7 **69.** 605 **71.** $\frac{3}{16}$ **73.** 5.7 **75.** $\frac{2}{3}g = 2$; 3 g **77.** D **79.** B **81a.** $6c = 4.80$ **b.** $c = $0.80 **83.** 2 **85.** 9 **87.** 2 **89.** -20 **91.** -132 **93.** Multiply both sides by a.

1-4

Check It Out! **1a.** 1 **1b.** 6 **1c.** 0 **2a.** $\frac{55}{4}$ **2b.** $\frac{1}{2}$ **2c.** 15 **3a.** $-\frac{5}{6}$ **3b.** 5 **3c.** 8 **4.** $60 **5.** -42

Exercises **1.** 2 **3.** -18 **5.** 2 **7.** 66 **9.** $\frac{5}{4}$ **11.** -12 **13.** 16 **15.** -3.2 **17.** 4 **19.** 15 passes **21.** 4 **23.** -4 **25.** 4 **27.** 5 **29.** -9 **31.** $\frac{1}{4}$ **33.** 1 **35.** 3 **37.** $\frac{28}{5}$ **39.** 3 **41.** 8 **43.** 7 **45.** $-\frac{1}{2}$ **47.** $x = 40$ **49.** $x = 35$ **51.** $8 - 3n = 2$; $n = 2$ **53a.** $1963 - 5s = 1863$; $s = 20$ **53b.** 3 **55.** 8 **57.** 4.5 **59.** -10 **61.** 10 **63.** $5k - 70 = 60$; 26 in. **65.** Stan: 36; Mark: 37; Wayne: 38 **67a.** 45,000; 112,500; 225,000; 337,500; $225n$ **67b.** $c = 225n$ **71.** H **73.** 27 **75.** $6\frac{1}{5}$ **77.** 14.5 **79.** -6

1-5

Check It Out! **1a.** -2 **1b.** 2 **2a.** 4 **2b.** -2 **3a.** no solution **3b.** all real numbers **4.** 10 years old

Exercises **3.** 1 **5.** 40 **7.** $-\frac{2}{3}$ **9.** 3 **11.** no solution **13.** all real numbers **15.** 6 **17.** 6 **19.** 2.85

21. 10 **23.** 6 **25.** 14 **27.** $\frac{3}{4}$ **29.** -4 **31.** no solution **33a.** 15 weeks **33b.** 180 lb **35.** $x - 30 = 14 - 3x$; $x = 11$ **37.** -4 **39.** 7 **41.** -3 **43.** 2 **45.** 1 **47.** $-\frac{7}{5}$ **49.** 4 **51.** no solution **53.** 9 **59.** F **61.** H **63.** 2 **65.** no solution **67.** -20 **69.** 6, 7, 8 **71.** $1.68

1-6

Check It Out! **1.** about 1.46 h **2.** $i = f + gt$ **3a.** $t = \frac{5 - b}{2}$ **3b.** $V = \frac{m}{D}$

Exercises **3.** $w = \frac{V}{\ell h}$ **5.** $m = 4n + 8$ **7.** $a = \frac{10}{b + c}$ **9.** $I = A - P$ **11.** $x = \frac{k + 5}{y}$ **13.** $\frac{x - 2}{z} = y$ **15.** $x = 5(a + g)$ **17.** $x = \frac{y - b}{m}$ **19.** $T = \frac{PV}{nR}$ **21.** $T = M + R$ **23.** $b = \frac{c - 2a}{2}$ **25.** $r = 7 - ax$ **27.** $x = \frac{5 - 4y}{3}$ **31.** $a = \frac{t - g}{-0.0035}$ **35.** C **37.** D **39.** $a = \frac{5}{2}\left(c + \frac{3}{4}b\right)$ **41.** $d = 500\left(t - \frac{1}{2}\right)$ **43.** $s = \frac{v^2 - u^2}{2a}$ **45.** 120 s

1-7

Check It Out! **1a.** -7, 7 **1b.** -5.5, 10.5 **2a.** no solutions **2b.** 4 **3.** $|x - 134| = 0.18$; minimum height: 133.82 m; maximum height: 134.18 m

Exercises **1.** -6, 6 **3.** -2, 2 **5.** $-\frac{3}{2}, \frac{1}{2}$ **7.** no solutions **9.** no solutions **11.** 2.8 **13.** $|x - 207| = 2$; mile markers 205 and 209 **15.** -9, 13 ft **17.** -2, 2 **19.** 18.8, 65.28 **21.** $-\frac{14}{3}$, 4 **23.** 0 **25.** 0 **27.** $\frac{2}{3}$ **29.** $|x - 5| = 0.001$; 4.999 mm; 5.001 mm **31.** $|x - 7| = 2$; 5, 9 **33.** $|x - 1500| = 75$; 1575 bricks; 1425 bricks **35.** $|x| = 3$ **37.** $|x - 2| = 3$ **39.** sometimes **41.** always **43a.** $|t - 24| = 5$ **43b.** 19; 29 **43c.** yes **43d.** The measurements are correct to within 5 mi/h. **47.** C **49.** B **51.** Division Property of Equality; Subtraction Property of Equality; Division Property of Equality

1-8

Check It Out! 1. 12 **2.** $7.50/h
3. 20.5 ft/s **4a.** −20 **4b.** 5.75
5. 6 in.

Exercises 1. The ratios are
equivalent. **3.** 682 trillion **5.** 18,749
lb/cow **7.** 0.075 page/min
9. 18 mi/gal **11.** $\frac{3}{5}$ **13.** 39 **15.** 6.5
17. 23 **19.** $\frac{3}{5} = \frac{h}{4.9}$; 2.94 m **21.** 72
23. $403.90/oz **25.** 2498.4 km/h
27. 10 **29.** −1 **31.** 13 **33.** 1.2 **35.** $\frac{1}{9}$
37. 45 **39.** $84 **43.** 1.625 **45.** 3
47. $-\frac{2}{7}$ **49.** $\frac{11}{3}$ **51.** 3 **53.** 24
55. −120 **59.** A **61.** D **63.** 40°; 50°
65. 0.0006722 people/m²

1-9

Check It Out! 1. 2.8 in.
2a. $\frac{150}{x} = \frac{45}{195}$; 650 cm **2b.** $\frac{5.5}{x} = \frac{3.5}{28}$;
44 ft **3.** The ratio of the perimeters
is equal to the ratio of the
corresponding sides.

Exercises 3. 10 ft **7.** 7 in. **11.** 480 ft²
13. 4 **15.** 2.8 ft **17.** 4 cm
21. $\frac{1.5}{x} = \frac{4.5}{36}$; 12 m **23.** k^2 **25.** G
27. $w = 4$; $x = 7.5$; $y = 8$
29. 16.6 cm

1-10

Check It Out! 1a. 17 oz **1b.** 7.85
m **1c.** 6000 g **2a.** C **2b.** C **3.** no;
C **4a.** 3.89 cm–4.31 cm **4b.** 463.12
m–486.88 m **4c.** 84.57 mg–85.43 mg

Exercises 1. precise **3.** 4.3 mL **5.**
2.37 mg **7.** 47.3 ft **9a.** 1 **9b.** 1 **11.**
no; ball 4 **13.** 49 lb–51 lb **15.**
24 cm–26 cm **17.** 240 mm–260
mm **19.** 4337 mg **21.** 11,000
lb **23.** 6.83 cm **25.** 0.0127 m **27a.**
Chandra **27b.** Lucy **29.** 44.1
lb–45.9 lb **31.** 36.44°C–37.56°C **33.**
28.8 ft–31.2 ft **35.** 0.19 cm–0.21
cm **37.** 5456 mi **39.** 120 ft **41.**
6 kg **43.** 16,453.2 mL **45.** 0.265
cm **47.** 165 ft **49.** neither **51.** 475.0
mL **53.** 50 kg ± 4% **55.** 750 kg ±
2% **57.** 425 lb ± 2% **59.** 175 km ±
3% **61.** ball 4 **65.** J **67.** 0.04% **69.**
384,326 km–384,480 km

Study Guide: Review

1. literal equation **2.** ratio **3.**
constant **4.** 1.99g **5.** $t + 3$ **6.** 5
7. 5 **8.** 6 **9.** 150 ÷ m; 30; 25; 15
10. 36 **11.** −2 **12.** −21 **13.** 18

14. $\frac{9}{8}$ **15.** $\frac{7}{3}$ **16.** $27 + s = 108$; 81
17. 7 **18.** $-\frac{10}{3}$ **19.** −90 **20.** 13
21. 0 **22.** −2 **23.** 17.5 **24.** −5
25. 40 **26.** −3 **27.** $-\frac{1}{2}$ **28.** 15
29. 18 **30.** 1 **31.** 41; 123°; 57°
32. −2 **33.** −2 **34.** 1 **35.** $-\frac{2}{3}$ **36.** no
solution **37.** all real numbers
38. 9 **39.** $n = \frac{360}{c}$ **40.** $a = \frac{2S}{n} - \ell$
41. 3.7 gal **42.** $x = 15, -27$ **43.** y
$= 7, 3$ **44.** $y = 9, -9$ **45.** $x = 17.4,$
-6.6 **46.** $g = -4, -8$ **47.** $x = \frac{5}{7}, -\frac{5}{7}$
48. $|x - 55| = 5$; minimum speed:
50 mi/h; maximum speed: 60 mi/h
49. $3\frac{1}{3}$c **50.** 1080 m/h **51.** 0.85 mi/
min **52.** 1.6 **53.** 54 **54.** 5 **55.** −3
56. 2.5 cm **57.** 16 ft **58.** The ratio
of the areas is the square of the ratio
of the radii. **59.** 12 in. **60.** 37.0 g **61.**
550 cm **62.** 1.5 L **63.** 480 lb–520
lb **64.** 19.9 oz–20.1 oz **65.** 72.75
kg–77.25 kg **66.** 931.5 mm–1138.5
mm

2-1

Check It Out! **1.** all real numbers greater than 4

2a.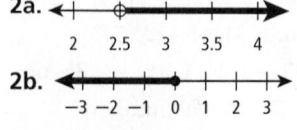
2 2.5 3 3.5 4

2b.
−3 −2 −1 0 1 2 3

2c.
−6 −5 −4 −3 −2 −1 0

3. $x < 2.5$ **4.** d = amount employee can earn per hour; $d \geq 8.25$

8.25
0 2 4 6 8 10 12

Exercises 1. A solution of an inequality makes the inequality true when substituted for the variable. **3.** all real numbers greater than −3 **5.** all real numbers greater than or equal to 3 **11.** $b > -8\frac{1}{2}$ **13.** $d < -7$ **15.** $f \leq 14$ **17.** $r < 140$ where r is positive **19.** all real numbers less than 2 **21.** all real numbers less than or equal to 12 **27.** $v < -11$ **29.** $x > -3.3$ **31.** $z \geq 9$ **33.** y = years of experience; $y \geq 5$ **35.** h is less than −5. **37.** r is greater than or equal to −2. **39.** $p \leq 17$ **41.** $f > 0$ **43.** p = profits; $p < 10{,}000$ **45.** e = elevation; $e \leq 5000$ **51.** D **53.** C **59.** D **61.** C **65.** <

2-2

Check It Out! **1a.** $s \leq 9$
0 3 6 9 12

1b. $t < 5\frac{1}{2}$
4 $4\frac{1}{2}$ 5 $5\frac{1}{2}$ 6

1c. $q < 11$
9 10 11 12 13

2. $11 + m \leq 15$; $m \leq 4$ where m is nonnegative; Sarah can consume 4 mg or less without exceeding the RDA. **3.** $250 + p > 282$; $p > 32$; Josh needs to bench press more than 32 additional pounds to break the school record.

Exercises 1. $p > 6$ **3.** $x \leq -15$ **5.** $102 + t \leq 104$; $t \leq 2$ where t is

nonnegative **7.** $a \geq 5$ **9.** $x < 15$ **11.** $1400 + 243 + w \leq 2000$; $w \leq 357$ where w is nonnegative **13.** $x - 10 > 32$; $x > 42$ **15.** $r - 13 \leq 15$; $r \leq 28$ **17.** $q > 51$ **19.** $p \leq 0.8$ **21.** $c > -202$ **23.** $x \geq 0$ **25.** $21 + d \leq 30$; $d \leq 9$ where d is nonnegative **27.** $x < 3$; B **29.** $x \leq 3$; D **31.** $p \leq 40{,}421$ where p is nonnegative **35. a.** $411 + 411 = 882$ miles **b.** $822 + m \leq 1000$ **c.** $m \leq 178$, but m cannot be negative. **37.** F **39.** J **41.** $r \leq 5\frac{1}{10}$ **43.** sometimes **45.** always

2-3

Check It Out! **1a.** $k > 6$
0 2 4 6 8 10 12

1b. $q \leq -10$
−18 −16 −14 −12 −10

1c. $g > 36$
34 35 36 37 38

2a. $x \geq -10$
−10 −8 −6 −4 −2

2b. $h > -17$
−19 −18 −17 −16 −15

3. 0, 1, 2, 3, 4, 5, 6, 7, 8, 9, 10, 11, or 12 servings

Exercises 1. $b > 9$ **3.** $d > 18$ **5.** $m \leq 1.1$ **7.** $s > -2$ **9.** $x > 5$ **11.** $n > -0.4$ **13.** $d > -3$ **15.** $t > -72$ **17.** 0, 1, 2, 3, 4, 5, or 6 nights **19.** $j \leq 12$ **21.** $d < 7$ **23.** $h \leq \frac{8}{7}$ **25.** $c \leq -12$ **27.** $b \geq \frac{1}{10}$ **29.** $b \leq -16$ **31.** $r < -\frac{3}{2}$ **33.** $y < 2$ **35.** $t > 4$ **37.** $z < -11$ **39.** $k \leq -7$ **41.** $p \geq -12$ **43.** $x > -3$ **45.** $x < 20$ **47.** $p \leq -6$ **49.** $b < 2$ **51.** $7x \geq 21$; $x \geq 3$ **53.** $-\frac{4}{5}b \leq -16$; $b \geq 20$ **57.** C **59.** A **67.** B **71.** $g \leq -\frac{14}{5}$ **73.** $m > \frac{4}{15}$ **75.** $x = 5$

2-4

Check It Out! **1a.** $x \leq -6$
−8 −6 −4 −2 0

1b. $x < -11$
−13 −12 −11 −10 −9

1c. $n \leq -10$
−12 −11 −10 −9 −8

2a. $m > 10$
8 9 10 11 12

2b. $x > -4$
−6 −5 −4 −3 −2 −1 0

2c. $x > 2\frac{1}{3}$
$2\frac{1}{3}$
0 1 2 3 4

3. $\frac{95 + x}{2} \geq 90$; $95 + x \geq 180$; $x \geq 85$; Jim's score must be at least 85.

Exercises 1. $m > 6$ **3.** $x \leq -2$ **5.** $x > -16$ **7.** $x \geq -9$ **9.** $x > -\frac{1}{2}$ **11.** $x \leq 19$ **13.** $x > 1$ **15.** sales of more than $9000 **17.** $x \leq 1$ **19.** $w < -2$ **21.** $x < -6$ **23.** $f < -4.5$ **25.** $w > 0$ **27.** $v > \frac{2}{3}$ **29.** $x > -5$ **31.** $x < -2$ **33.** $a \geq 11$ **35.** $x > 3$ **37.** starting at 29 min **39.** $x \leq 2$ **41.** $x < 4$ **43.** $x < -6$ **45.** $r < 8$ **47.** $x < 7$ **49.** $p \geq 18$ **51.** $\frac{1}{2}x + 9 < 33$; $x < 48$ **53.** $4(x + 12) \leq 16$; $x \leq -8$ **55.** B **57.** A **59.** 24 months or more **61a.**

Number	Process	Cost
1	350 + 3	353
2	350 + 3(2)	356
3	350 + 3(3)	359
10	350 + 3(10)	380
n	350 + 3n	350 + 3n

b. $c = 350 + 3n$ **c.** $350 + 3n \leq 500$; $n \leq 50$; 50 CDs or fewer **65.** G **67.** 59 **69.** $x > 5$ **71.** $x > 0$ **73.** $x \geq 0$ **75.** $-3x > 0$

2-5

Check It Out! **1a.** $x \leq -2$
−3 −2 −1 0 1 2 3

1b. $t < -1$
−3 −2 −1 0 1 2 3

2. more than 160 flyers

3a. $r \leq 2$
−3 −2 −1 0 1 2 3

 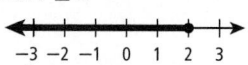

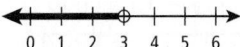

3b. $x < 3$

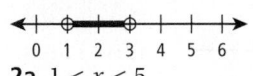

4a. no solutions **4b.** all real numbers

Exercises 1. $x < 3$ **3.** $x < 2$
5. $c < -2$ **7.** at least 34 pizzas
9. $p < -17$ **11.** $x > 3$ **13.** $t < 6.8$
15. no solutions **17.** all real
numbers **19.** no solutions
21. $y > -2$ **23.** $b \geq -7$ **25.** $m > 5$
27. $x \geq 2$ **29.** $w \geq 6$ **31.** $r \geq -4$
33. no solutions **35.** all real numbers
37. all real numbers **39.** $t < -7$
41. $x > 3$ **43.** $x < 2$ **45.** $x > -2$
47. $x \leq -6$ **49.** 27 s
51a. $400 + 4.50n$ **b.** $12n$ **c.** $400 +$
$4.50n < 12n$; $n > 53\frac{1}{3}$; 54 CDs or
more **53.** $5x - 10 < 6x - 8$; $x > -2$
55. $\frac{3}{4}x \geq x - 5$; $x \leq 20$
59. x can never be greater than
itself plus 1. **61.** D **63.** A
67. $x < -3$ **69.** $w \geq -1\frac{6}{7}$

2-6

Check It Out! 1. $1.0 < c < 3.0$

2a. $1 < x < 5$

2b. $-3 \leq n < 2$

3a. $r < 10$ OR $r > 14$

3b. $x \geq 3$ OR $x < -1$

4a. $-9 < y < -2$

4b. $x \leq -13$ OR $x \geq 2$

Exercises 1. intersection
3. $-5 < x < 5$ **5.** $0 < x < 3$
7. $x < -8$ OR $x > 4$ **9.** $n < 1$ OR $n > 4$
11. $-5 \leq a \leq -3$ **13.** $c < 1$ OR $c \geq 9$
15. $16 \leq k \leq 50$ **17.** $3 \leq n \leq 6$
19. $2 < x < 6$ **21.** $x < 0$ OR $x > 3$
23. $x < -3$ OR $x > 2$
25. $q < 0$ OR $q \geq 2$ **27.** $-2 < s < 1$
29a. $225 + 80n$ gives the cost of the
studio and technicians; the band
will spend between $200 and $550.

b. $-0.3125 \leq n \leq 4.0625$; n cannot
be a negative number **c.** $155
31. $1 \leq x \leq 2$ **33.** $-10 \leq x \leq 10$
35. $t < 0$ OR $t > 100$ **37.** $-2 < x < 5$
39. $a < 0$ OR $a > 1$ **41.** $n < 2$ OR $n > 5$
43. $7 \leq m \leq 60$ **47.** D **49.** B
51. $0.5 < c < 3$ **53.** $s \leq 6$ OR $s \geq 9$
55. $-1 \leq x \leq 3$

2-7

Check It Out! 1a. $-3 \leq x \leq 3$

1b. $-15 \leq x \leq 9$

2a. $x \leq -2$ OR $x \geq 2$

2b. $x \leq -6$ OR $x \geq 1$

3. $|p - 125| \leq 75$; $50 \leq p \leq 200$

4a. all real numbers **4b.** no
solutions

Exercises 1. $-3 \leq x \leq 3$
3. $-2 < x < 2$ **5.** $4 < x < 6$
7. $x < -22$ OR $x > 22$ **9.** $x \leq -4$
OR $x \geq 4$ **11.** $x \leq 1$ OR $x \geq 5$
13. $|x - 55| \leq 25$; $30 \leq x \leq 80$
15. no solutions **17.** all real
numbers **19.** no solutions
21. $2 < x < 4$ **23.** $-3 < x < 3$
25. $-6 < x < 0$ **27.** $x \leq -10$ OR
$x \geq 10$ **29.** $x \leq -10$ OR $x \geq 6$
31. $x < -1$ OR $x > 2$ **33.** no
solutions **35.** all real numbers
37. no solutions **39.** always
41. sometimes **43.** $|x - 2| \leq 3$;
$-1 \leq x \leq 5$ **45.** $|a| \leq 2$ **47.** $|c| \geq 6\frac{1}{2}$
49a. 10,010 Hz **49b.** $|x - 10,010| \leq$
9990 **51.** $|n - 23| > 12$ **53.** $k \leq 1$;
the inequality is equivalent to
$|x| < k - 1$, and this has no solutions
when the expression on the right side
is less than or equal to 0 (i.e., when
$k - 1 \leq 0$ or $k \leq 1$). **55.** B **57.** B

Study Guide: Review

1. inequality **2.** union **3.** compound
inequality **4.** intersection
5. solution of an inequality

6.

7.

8.

9.

10.

11.

12. $a < 2$ **13.** $k \geq -3.5$
14. $q < -10$ **15.** $t =$ temperature;
$t \geq 72$ **16.** $s =$ students; $s \leq 12$
where s is a natural number
17. $m =$ minutes; $m < 30$ where m
is nonnegative **18.** $t < 7$ **19.** $k \leq 2$
20. $m > -5$ **21.** $x \geq 4.5$ **22.** $w < 9.5$
23. $a < 5$ **24.** $h < 1$ **25.** $v < -2$
26. 5.5 mi or more **27.** $18 or
less **28.** $a \leq 5$ **29.** $t > -3$ **30.** $p > 8$
31. $x \leq -25$ **32.** $n > 6$ **33.** $g < -12$
34. $k > -7$ **35.** $r < -9$ **36.** $h < -3$
37. $g < 2.5$ **38.** 0, 1, 2, 3, 4, 5,
6, 7 **39.** at least 334 lanyards
40. $x < 5$ **41.** $t \geq 6$ **42.** $m > -11$
43. $x < -1$ **44.** $h > -3$
45. $x > 1\frac{1}{2}$ **46.** $b \leq 10$ **47.** $y >$
$3\frac{1}{2}$ **48.** $n > -15$ **49.** 0, 1, 2, 3, 4, 5,
6, 7, 8, 9, 10, 11, 12, or 13 **50.** $m <$
-1 **51.** $y \geq -2$ **52.** $c < -3$
53. $q \leq -4$ **54.** $x > 2$ **55.** $t < 3$
56. no solutions **57.** all real numbers
58. $p > -\frac{1}{2}$ **59.** all real numbers
60. $k > 2$ **61.** no solutions
62. $8.75 > m$ **63.** $-10 < t < 4$
64. $-6 < k \leq 7$ **65.** $r > 7$ OR $r < -2$
66. no solutions **67.** $-2 < p \leq 5$
68. all real numbers **69.** $68 \leq t \leq 84$
70. $102 \leq n \leq 183.6$ **71.** $-22 \leq x \leq$
22 **72.** $x < -12$ OR $x > 4$ **73.** $-4 \leq$
$x \leq 4$ **74.** $-18 < x < 0$ **75.** $x \leq -3$
OR $x \geq 3$ **76.** $-3 < x < 3$ **77.** $x < -13.9$
OR $x > 13.9$ **78.** $-12.5 < x < 2.1$
79. $x \leq 5$ OR $x \geq 9$ **80.** $x \leq -4$
OR $x \geq 4$ **81.** no solutions
82. $-16.8 \leq x \leq 5.8$ **83.** $|d - 72| \leq 4$;
$68 \leq d \leq 76$

3-1

Check It Out! 1. C
2a. discrete;

Keyboarding

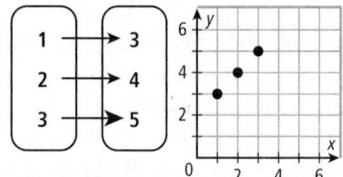

2b. continuous;

Water Tank

3. Possible answer: When the number of students reaches a certain point, the number of pizzas bought increases.

Exercises 1. continuous 3. B
5. C 11. A 13. continuous 19. The point of intersection represents the time of day when you will be the same distance from the base of the mountain on both the hike up and the hike down. 23. C

3-2

Check It Out! 1.

x	y
1	3
2	4
3	5

2a. D: {6, 5, 2, 1}; R: {−4, −1, 0}
2b. D: {1, 4, 8}; R: {1, 4}
3a. D: {−6, −4, 1, 8}; R: {1, 2, 9}; yes; each domain value is paired with exactly one range value. 3b. D: {2, 3, 4}; R: {−5, −4, −3}; no; the domain value 2 is paired with both −5 and −4.

Exercises

3.
x	y
1	1
1	2

5.
x	y
−7	7
−3	3
−1	1
5	−5

7. D: {−5, 0, 2, 5}; R: {−20, −8, 0, 7} 9. D: {2, 3, 5, 6, 8}; R: {4, 9, 25, 36, 81} 11. D: {1}; R: {−2, 0, 3, 8}; no 13. D: {−2, −1, 0, 1, 2}; R: {1}; yes

15.
x	y
−2	−4
−1	−1
0	0
1	−1
2	−4

17. D: {3}; R: $1 \leq y \leq 5$
19. D: $−2 \leq x \leq 2$; R: $0 \leq y \leq 2$; yes 21. yes 23. yes 25. yes
27. no 29a. D: $0 \leq t \leq 5$; R: $0 \leq v \leq 750$ b. yes c. (2, 300); (3.5, 525)
33. G 35a. {(−3, 5), (−1, 7), (0, 9), (1, 11), (3, 13)} b. D: {−3, −1, 0, 1, 3}; R: {5, 7, 9, 11, 13} c. yes
37. all real numbers

3-3

Check It Out! 1. $y = 3x$
2a. independent: time; dependent: cost 2b. independent: pounds; dependent: cost 3a. independent: pounds; dependent: cost; $f(x) = 1.69x$ 3b. independent: people; dependent: cost; $f(x) = 6 + 29.99x$
4a. 1; −7 4b. −5; 101 5. $f(x) = 500x$; D: {0, 1, 2, 3}; R: {0, 500, 1000, 1500}

Exercises 1. dependent

3. $y = x − 2$ 5. independent: size of bottle; dependent: cost of water
7. independent: hours; dependent: cost; $f(h) = 75h$ 9. 2; 9 11. −1; −15
13. $y = −2x$ 15. independent: size of lawn; dependent: cost
17. independent: days late; dependent: total cost; $f(x) = 3.99 + 0.99x$ 19. independent: gallons of gas; dependent: miles; $f(x) =$

28x 21. 7; 10 23. $f(n) = 2n + 5$; D: {1, 2, 3, 4}; R: {$7, $9, $11, $13}
25.
z	1	2	3	4
g(z)	−3	−1	1	3

27. $f(−6.89) \approx −16$; $f(1.01) \approx 8$; $f(4.67) \approx 20$ 33. D 35. 3.5
37. 44.1 m

3-4

Check It Out! 1a.

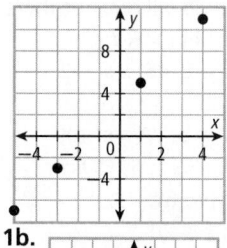

1b.

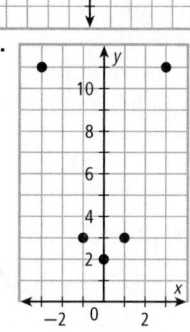

2a.

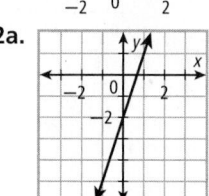

2b.

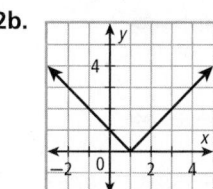

3. $x = 3$ 4. Possible answer: about 32.5 mi

Average Speed of Lava Flow

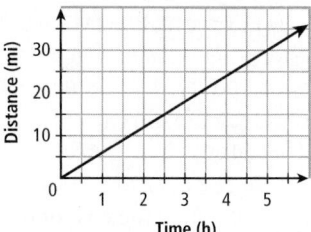

Exercises

1.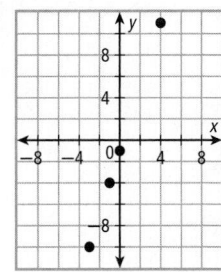

3.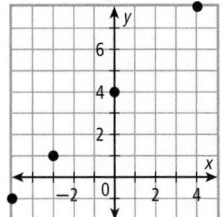

5.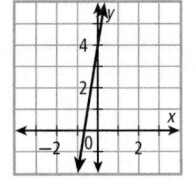

7.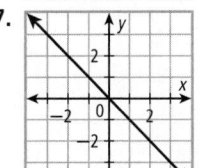

9.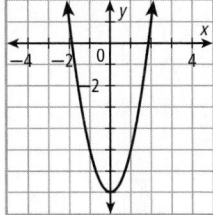

11. $y = -1$

13.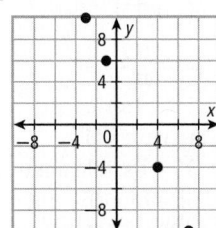

15.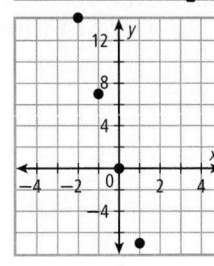

17.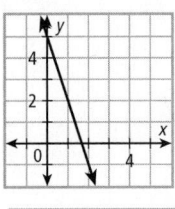

19.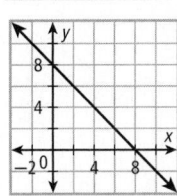

21.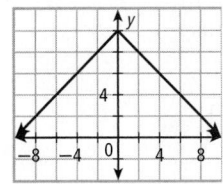

23.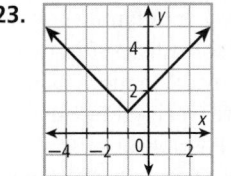

25. $y = 5$

29.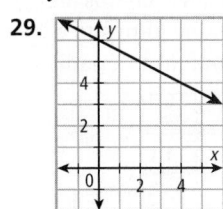

31.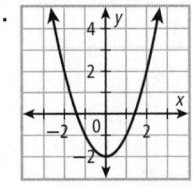

33.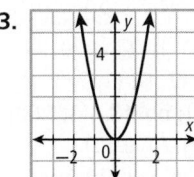

35.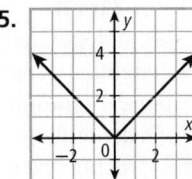

37. $x = 1$ **39.** $y = -8$ **41.** yes;

yes **43.** no; yes **45.** no; yes; yes
47. yes; no; yes **55a.** $v = 10,000 - 1500h$ **b.** 8500 gal

c.

Time (h)	Volume (gal)
0	10,000
1	8,500
2	7,000
3	5,500
4	4,000

59. J **61.** J **63.** $y = 4x + 64$

3-5

Check It Out!

1. Football Team Score

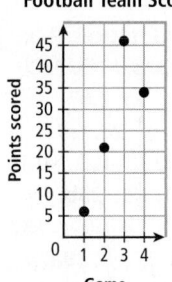

2. positive **3a.** No correlation; the temperature in Houston has nothing to do with the number of cars sold in Boston. **3b.** Positive; as the number of family members increases, more food is needed, so the grocery bill increases too. **3c.** Negative; as the number of times you sharpen your pencil increases, the length of the pencil decreases. **4.** Graph A; it cannot be graph B because graph B shows negative minutes; it cannot be graph C because graph C shows the temperature of the pie increasing, a positive correlation. **5.** about 75 rolls

Exercises 3. no **5.** positive
7. negative **9.** positive **11.** A
15. positive **17.** positive **19.** A
23. positive **25.** B

27a.

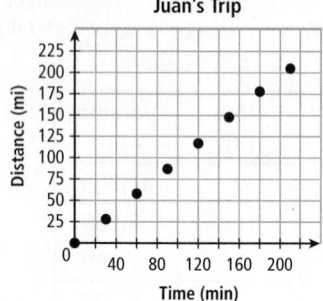

Juan's Trip

b. positive **29.** C

3-6

Check It Out! 1a. yes; $\frac{1}{2}$; $\frac{5}{4}$, $\frac{7}{4}$, $\frac{9}{4}$
1b. no **2a.** −343 **2b.** 19.6 **3.** 750 lb

Exercises 1. common difference
3. yes; −0.7; −0.7, −1.4, −2.1
5. no **7.** −53 **9.** no **11.** yes; −9;
−58, −67, −76 **13.** 5.9 **15.** 9500
mi **17.** $\frac{1}{4}$ **19.** −2.2 **21.** 0.07
23. $-\frac{3}{8}$, $-\frac{1}{2}$, $-\frac{5}{8}$, $-\frac{3}{4}$ **25.** −0.2,
−0.7, −1.2, −1.7 **27.** −0.3, −0.1,
0.1, 0.3 **29.** 22 **31.** 122 **33b.** $9,
$11, $13, $15; $a_n = 2n + 7$ **c.** $37
d. no **35.** −104.5 **37.** $\frac{20}{3}$ **39a.** $a_n =$
$6 + 3(n − 1)$ **b.** 48 **c.** $7800 **d.** $a_n =$
$7 + 3(n − 1)$; $8200
41a.

Time Interval	Mile Marker
1	520
2	509
3	498
4	487
5	476
6	465

b. $a_n = 520 + (n − 1)(−11)$
c. number of miles per interval
d. 421 **43.** F **45.** 173 and 182; 20th
and 21st terms **47a.** session 16; yes
b. Thursday

Study Guide: Review

1. domain **2.** negative
correlation **3.** term

4. continuous

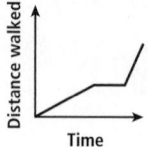

5. continuous

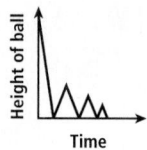

6. continuous

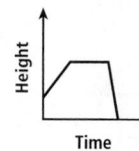

7. Possible answer: A family buys a
fish tank and some fish. After two
weeks, they buy some more fish.
After two more weeks, they buy
more fish. **8.** Possible answer: A
monkey swings from a high branch
to a lower branch. He climbs along
the branch. Then he jumps to a
higher branch and takes a nap.

9.

x	−1	0	2
y	0	1	1

10.

x	−2	−1	2	3
y	−1	1	3	4

11. D: {−4, −2, 0, 2}; R: { −1, 1, 3, 5}
12. D: {−2, −1, 0, 1, 2}; R: {−1, 0}
13. D: {0, 1, 4}; R: {−2, −1, 0, 1, 2}
14. D: $-4 \leq x \leq 3$; R: $-3 \leq y \leq 5$
15. D: {−5, −3, −1, 1}; R: {−3, −2,
−1, 0}; yes **16.** D: {−4, −2, 0, 2};
R: {−2, 1}; yes **17.** D: {1, 2, 3 ,4};
R: {−1, 0, 1, 2, 3}; no **18.** {(1, 5.00),
(2, 6.50), (3, 8.00), (4, 9.50),
(5, 11.00)}; yes **19.** yes **20.** y is 7
less than x; $y = x − 7$. **21.** y is
9 times x; $y = 9x$. **22.** independent:
number of cakes; dependent: cost;
$f(c) = 6c$ **23.** independent: number
of CDs Raul will buy; dependent:
number of CDs Tim will buy; $g(n)$
$= 2n$ **24.** 14 **25.** −11 **26.** 6; −1

27.

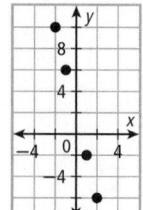

28.

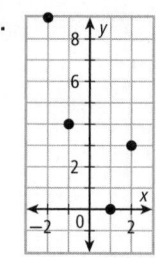

29.

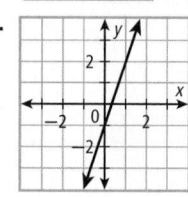

30.

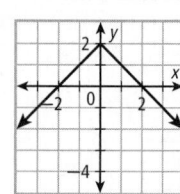

31.

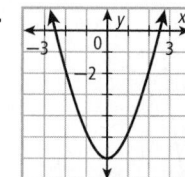

32.

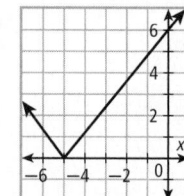

33. Possible answer: $44
34. negative **35.** Possible answer:
33 **36.** yes; −6; −4, −10, −16
37. no **38.** no **39.** yes; 2.5; 2, 4.5, 7
40. 105 **41.** −62 **42.** 20 **43.** $408
44. −15.5 °C

Mastering the Standards

for Mathematical Practice

The topics described in the Standards for Mathematical Content will vary from year to year. However, the *way* in which you learn, study, and think about mathematics will not. The Standards for Mathematical Practice describe skills that you will use in all of your math courses.

Mathematical Practices

1. *Make sense of problems and persevere in solving them.*
2. *Reason abstractly and quantitatively.*
3. *Construct viable arguments and critique the reasoning of others.*
4. *Model with mathematics.*
5. *Use appropriate tools strategically.*
6. *Attend to precision.*
7. *Look for and make use of structure.*
8. *Look for and express regularity in repeated reasoning.*

④ Model with mathematics.

Mathematically proficient students can apply... mathematics... to... problems... in everyday life, society, and the workplace...

In your book

Multi-Step Test Prep and **Real-World Connections** apply mathematics to other disciplines and in real-world scenarios.

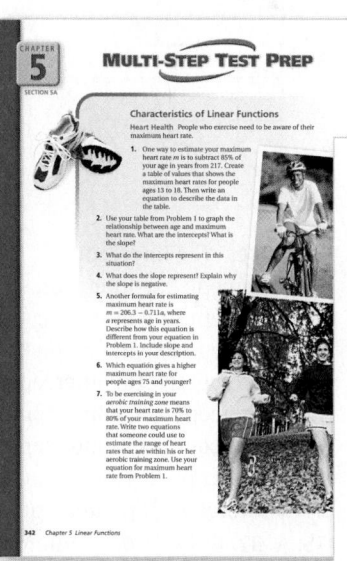

PhotoDisc/Getty Images

4-1

Check It Out! 1a. Yes; each domain value is paired with exactly one range value; yes **1b.** Yes; each domain value is paired with exactly one range value; yes **1c.** No; each domain value is not paired with exactly one range value.
2. Yes; a constant change of +2 in x corresponds to a constant change of −1 in y.
3a. yes

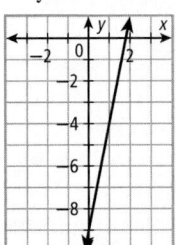

3b. yes

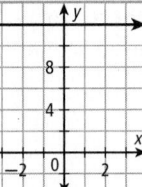

3c. no
4.

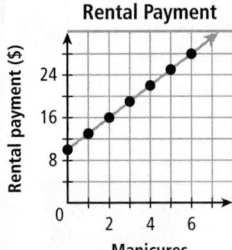

D: {0, 1, 2, 3, …}
R: {$10, $13, $16, $19, …}

Exercises 1. No; it is not in the form $Ax + By = C$. **3.** yes; yes
5. yes **7.** yes **9.** yes **11.** no **15.** yes; no **17.** yes; no **19.** yes **23.** no
27. yes; yes **29.** yes; yes
31. yes; $-4x + y = 2$; $A = -4$; $B = 1$; $C = 2$ **33.** no **35.** yes; $x = 7$; $A = 1$; $B = 0$; $C = 7$ **37.** yes; $3x - y = 1$; $A = 3$; $B = -1$; $C = 1$ **39.** yes; $5x - 2y = -3$; $A = 5$, $B = -2$, $C = -3$ **41.** no **55.** no **57.** C
63. not linear

4-2

Check It Out! 1a. x-intercept: −2; y-intercept: 3 **1b.** x-intercept: −10; y-intercept: 6 **1c.** x-intercept: 4; y-intercept: 8
2a.

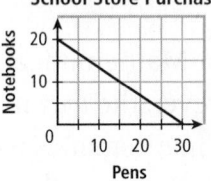

School Store Purchases

x-intercept: 30; y-intercept: 20
2b. x-intercept: number of pens that can be purchased if no notebooks are purchased; y-intercept: number of notebooks that can be purchased if no pens are purchased

3a.

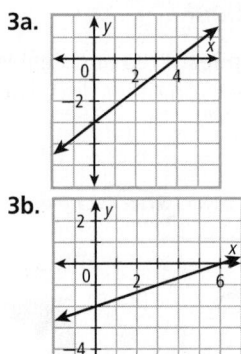

3b.

Exercises 1. y-intercept
3. x-intercept: 2; y-intercept: −4
5. x-intercept: 2; y-intercept: −1
7. x-intercept: 2; y-intercept: 8
13. x-intercept: −1; y-intercept: 3
15. x-intercept: −4; y-intercept: 2
17. x-intercept: −4; y-intercept: 2
19. x-intercept: 2; y-intercept: 8
21. x-intercept: $\frac{1}{8}$; y-intercept: −1
35. A **37.** B **41.** F **47.** x-intercept: 950; y-intercept: −55

4-3

Check It Out! 1. day 1 to day 6: −53; day 6 to day 16: −7.5; day 16 to day 22: 0; day 22 to day 30: −4.375; from day 1 to day 6

2.

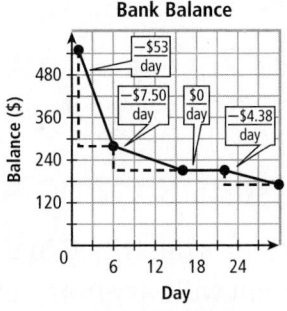

Bank Balance

3. $-\frac{2}{5}$ **4a.** undefined **4b.** 0
5a. undefined **5b.** positive

Exercises 1. constant **5.** $-\frac{3}{4}$
7. undefined **9.** undefined
11. positive **15.** 1 **17.** 0
19. positive **23.** $\frac{17}{18}$ **29.** C **31.** G

4-4

Check It Out! 1a. $m = 0$ **1b.** $m = 3$
1c. $m = 2$ **2a.** $m = \frac{1}{2}$ **2b.** $m = -3$
2c. $m = 2$ **2d.** $m = -\frac{3}{2}$ **3.** $m = \frac{1}{2}$; the height of the plant is increasing at a rate of 1 cm every 2 days.
4. $m = -\frac{2}{3}$

Exercises 1. 1 **3.** $-\frac{1}{2}$ **5.** 10 **7.** $\frac{1}{540}$
9. $-\frac{5}{9}$ **11.** −4 **13.** undefined
15. $-\frac{3}{4}$ **17.** $-\frac{9}{5000}$ **19.** $-\frac{13}{5}$
23a. Car 1; 20 mi/h **b.** The speed and the slope are both equal to the distance divided by time. **c.** 20 mi/h
25a. $y = 220 - x$ **27.** G **29.** $-\frac{b}{a}$
31. $\frac{3}{2} - y$ **33.** $x = \frac{1}{2}$ **35.** $x = -3$
37. $x = 0$

4-5

Check It Out! 1a. no **1b.** yes; $-\frac{3}{4}$
1c. yes; −3 **2a.** No; possible answer: the value of $\frac{y}{x}$ is not the same for each ordered pair. **2b.** Yes; possible answer: the value of $\frac{y}{x}$ is the same for each ordered pair.
2c. No; possible answer: the value of $\frac{y}{x}$ is not the same for each ordered pair. **3.** 90

4. $y = 4x$

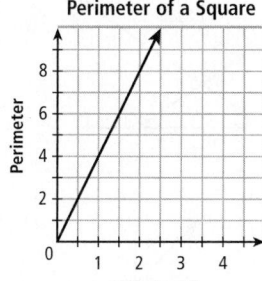

Perimeter of a Square

Exercises 1. direct variation
3. yes; -4 **5.** no **7.** 18 **9.** $y = 7x$
11. yes; $\frac{1}{4}$ **13.** yes **15.** -16
17. $y = 2.50x$ **19.** no **21.** $y = -3x$

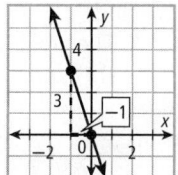

The value of k is -3, and the graph shows that the slope of the line is -3.
25. $y = 2x$

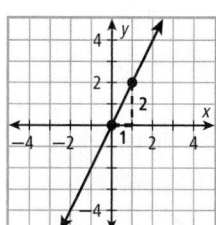

The value of k is 2, and the graph shows that the slope of the line is 2.
29. $k = -\frac{2}{9}x$

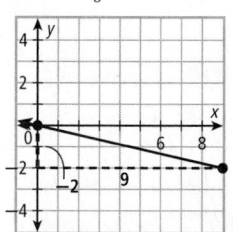

The value of k is $-\frac{2}{9}$, and the graph shows that the slope of the line is $-\frac{2}{9}$.
33. $y = -6x$

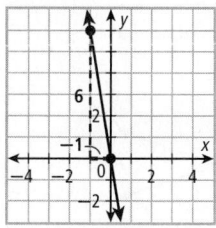

The value of k is -6, and the graph shows that the slope of the line is -6. **41.** C **43.** B

4-6

Check It Out!
1a.

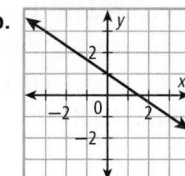

1b.

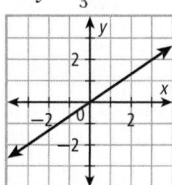

2a. $y = -12x - \frac{1}{2}$ **2b.** $y = x$
2c. $y = 8x - 25$
3a. $y = \frac{2}{3}x$

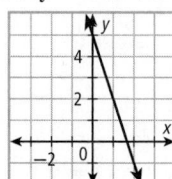

3b. $y = -3x + 5$

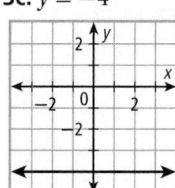

3c. $y = -4$

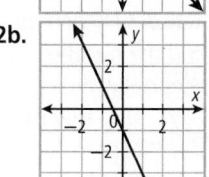

4a. $y = 18x + 200$ **4b.** slope: 18; cost per person; y-intercept: 200; fee **4c.** $3800

Exercises
1.

5. $y = x - 2$ **7.** $y = -3$

9. $y = -2x - 1$ **11.** $y = 3x - 1$
13a. $y = 18x + 10$ **b.** slope: 18; Helen's speed; y-intercept: 10; distance she has already biked
c. 46 mi

15.

17.

19. $y = 5x - 9$ **21.** $y = -\frac{1}{2}x + 7$
23. $y = \frac{1}{2}x + 4$ **25.** $y = -2x + 8$
29. possible **31.** impossible
33. C **37.** B **39.** B **41.** $y = \frac{1}{3}x - 3$
43. -6

4-7

Check It Out!
1a. $y - 1 = 2\left(x - \frac{1}{2}\right)$
1b. $y + 4 = 0(x - 3)$

2a.

2b.

3a. $y = \frac{1}{3}x + 2$ **3b.** $y = 6x - 8$
4. x-intercept: -3; y-intercept: 9
5. $y = 2.25x + 6$; $53.25

Exercises 1. $y + 6 = \frac{1}{5}(x - 2)$
3. $y + 7 = 0(x - 3)$ **7.** $y = -\frac{1}{3}x + 7$
9. $y = -x$ **11.** $y = -\frac{1}{2}x + 4$
13. x-intercept: 3; y-intercept: -3
15. x-intercept: -1; y-intercept: 3

17. $y - 5 = \frac{2}{9}(x + 1)$ **19.** $y - 8 = 8(x - 1)$ **23.** $y = -\frac{2}{7}x + 1$ **25.** $y = -6x + 57$ **27.** $y = -\frac{11}{2}x + 18$ **29.** $y = 2x - 6$ **31.** x-intercept: 1; y-intercept: -2 **33.** x-intercept: -6; y-intercept: 9 **35.** $y = -\frac{1}{500}x + 212$; 200 °F **41.** never **43a.** $y - 11 = 2.5(x - 2)$ **b.** 6 in. **c.** $16\frac{5}{8}$ in. **47.** $y = -8$; $x = 4$ **49.** A **53a.** $(0, 12)$ and $(6, 8)$ **b.** $y = -\frac{2}{3}x + 12$ **c.** 18 min **55.** H **57.** $y = -3x + \frac{11}{4}$

4-8

Check It Out! 1. $y = -\frac{1}{2}x + 6$: 16; $y = -x + 8$: 30; $y = -\frac{1}{2}x + 6$ is better. **2a.** $y \approx 0.04x + 6.38$ **2b.** slope: cost is \$0.04/yd; y-int.: \$6.38 is added to the cost of every ball of yarn. **2c.** \$46.38 **3.** $y \approx -2.74x + 84.32$; very well $(r \approx -0.88)$ **4.** strong positive correlation; likely cause-and-effect (more education often contributes to higher earnings)

Exercises 1. residual **3.** $y = x + 1$: 19; $y = x - 1$: 23; $y = x + 1$ is better. **5.** $y \approx -0.53x + 8.8$; very well $(y \approx -0.91)$ **7.** $y = -x + 8$: 7; $y = -\frac{1}{2}x + 6$: 9; $y = -x + 8$ is better. **9.** $y \approx 0.2x + 2$; very well $(r \approx 0.94)$ **13a.** $y \approx 0.48x + 12.03$ **13b.** A player will score 0.48 run for every hit. **13c.** A player with no hits will score 12.03 runs. **13d.** There is a strong correlation between the number of hits and the number of runs, since the correlation cofficient is $r \approx 0.84$. **13e.** ≈ 60 runs **15a.** $y \approx 115.36x + 1065$; $r \approx 0.96$ **15b.** Slope: each year there will be 115.36 more visitors than the previous year; y-intercept: there were 1065 visitors in year 0. **15c.** yes; $r \approx 0.96$, which is very close to 1. **15d.** No; the passage of time likely does not cause changes in the number of visitors. **17.** B **19a.** 1000

4-9

Check It Out! 1a. $y = 2x + 2$ and $y = 2x + 1$ **1b.** $y = 3x$ and $y - 1 = 3(x + 2)$

2. slope of $\overline{AB} = 0$; slope of $\overline{BC} = \frac{5}{3}$; slope of $\overline{CD} = 0$; slope of $\overline{AD} = \frac{5}{3}$; $\overline{AB}$ is parallel to $\overline{CD}$ because they have the same slope. $\overline{AD}$ is parallel to $\overline{BC}$ because they have the same slope. Since opposite sides are parallel, $ABCD$ is a parallelogram. **3.** $y = -4$ and $x = 3$; $y - 6 = 5(x + 4)$ and $y = -\frac{1}{5}x + 2$ **4.** slope of $\overline{PQ} = 2$; slope of $\overline{QR} = -1$; slope of $\overline{PR} = -\frac{1}{2}$; $\overline{PQ}$ is perpendicular to $\overline{PR}$ because the product of their slopes is -1. Since PQR contains a right angle, PQR is a right triangle. **5a.** $y = \frac{4}{5}x + 3$ **5b.** $y = -\frac{1}{5}x + 2$

Exercises 1. parallel **3.** $y = \frac{3}{4}x - 1$ and $y - 3 = \frac{3}{4}(x - 5)$ **5.** $y = \frac{2}{3}x - 4$ and $y = -\frac{3}{2}x + 2$; $y = -1$ and $x = 3$ **9.** $x = 7$ and $x = -9$; $y = -\frac{5}{6}x + 8$ and $y = -\frac{5}{6}x - 4$ **11.** $y = -3x + 2$ and $3x + y = 27$; $y = \frac{1}{2}x - 1$ and $-x + 2y = 17$ **13.** $y = 6x$ and $y = -\frac{1}{6}x$; $y = \frac{1}{6}x$ and $y = -6x$ **15.** $x - 6y = 15$ and $y = -6x - 8$; $y = 3x - 2$ and $3y = -x - 11$ **17.** $y = -\frac{6}{7}x$ **19.** neither **21.** parallel **23.** $y = \frac{1}{2}x - 5$ **25.** $y = 2x + 5$ **27.** $y = 3x + 13$ **29.** $y = -x + 5$ **31.** $y = 4x - 23$ **33.** $y = -\frac{3}{4}x$ **35.** $y = -x + 1$ **37.** $y = \frac{2}{5}x - \frac{31}{5}$ **39.** $y = -\frac{1}{5}x - \frac{11}{5}$ **41.** $y = -\frac{1}{2}x - \frac{1}{2}$ **43.** $y = \frac{1}{2}x + 6$ **45.** $y = x - 3$ **47.** $y = -4$ **51a.** $y = 50x$ **b.** $y = 50x + 30$ **53.** H **57.** $-\frac{1}{5}$

4-10

Check It Out!

1.

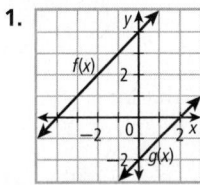

translation 6 units down

2.

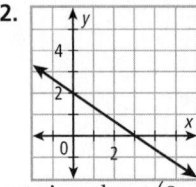

rotation about $(0, -1)$ (less steep)

3.

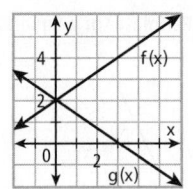

$g(x) = -\frac{2}{3}x + 2$

4.

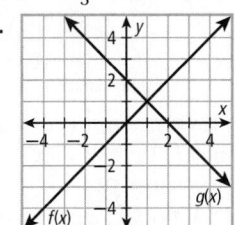

reflection across y-axis and translation 2 units up **5.** The graph will be rotated about $(0, 175)$ and become less steep; the graph will be translated 5 units up.

Exercises 1. translation
3.

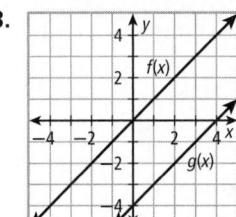

translation 4 units down

7.

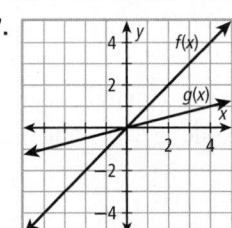

rotation about $(0, 0)$ (less steep)

9.

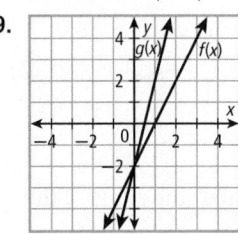

rotation about $(0, -2)$ (steeper)

13.

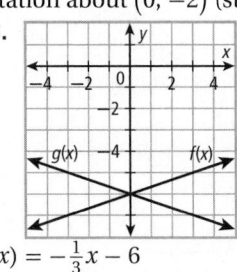

$g(x) = -\frac{1}{3}x - 6$

17.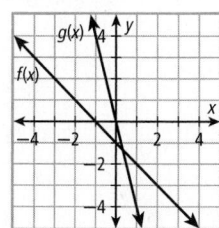

rotation about $(0, 0)$ (steeper) and translation 1 unit up

23.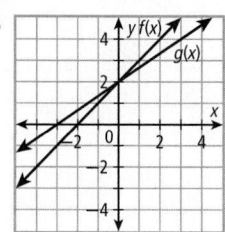

rotation about $(0, 2)$ (less steep)

27.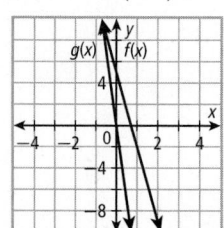

rotation about $(0, 0)$ (steeper) and translation 5 units down

31. rotation about $(0, 0)$ (steeper)

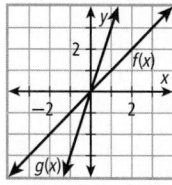

They have different slopes and the same y-intercept.

37.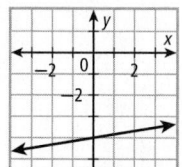

$g(x) = \frac{1}{6}x - 4$ **39.** translation 9 units down **41.** rotation about $(0, 0)$ (steeper) **43.** rotation about $(0, 0)$ (steeper) **45a.** \$300 **b.** 20%
c. Commission changes to 25%. Base pay changes to \$400. **49.** D

Study Guide: Review

1. translation; rotation; reflection
2. y-intercept **3.** slope; y-intercept
4. No; a constant change of $+2$ in x corresponds to different changes in y. **5.** Yes; a constant change of $+1$ in x corresponds to a constant change of $+2$ in y.
6. Yes; a constant change of $+1$ in x corresponds to a constant change of -2 in y. **7.** No; a constant change of -1 in y corresponds to different changes in x. **8.** $5x + y = 1$; $A = 5$; $B = 1$; $C = 1$
9. $x + 6y = -2$; $A = 1$; $B = 6$; $C = -2$ **10.** $7x - 4y = 0$; $A = 7$; $B = -4$; $C = 0$ **11.** $y = 9$; $A = 0$; $B = 1$; $C = 9$
12.

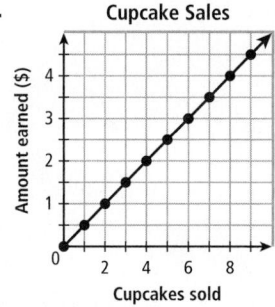

Cupcake Sales

D: whole numbers;
R: nonnegative multiples of 0.5
13. x-intercept: 2; y-intercept: -4
14. x-intercept: 5; y-intercept: 6
15. x-intercept: 3; y-intercept: -9
16. x-intercept: $-\frac{1}{2}$; y-intercept: 1
17. x-intercept: -18; y-intercept: 3
18. x-intercept: $\frac{1}{3}$; y-intercept: $-\frac{1}{4}$
19.

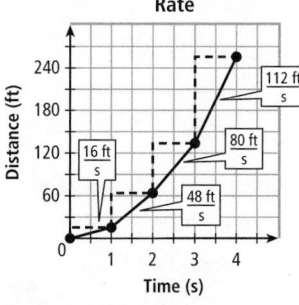

Rate

20. 5 **21.** $-\frac{4}{3}$ **22.** -3 **23.** $-\frac{1}{2}$
24. 3 **25.** 7 **26.** 4 **27.** -5 **28.** -1
29. 1 **30.** 2 **31.** undefined **32.** 0
33. yes; -6 **34.** yes; 1 **35.** no
36. yes; $-\frac{1}{2}$ **37.** -12

38. $y = 8x$

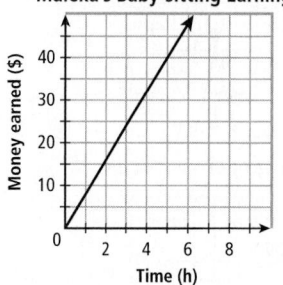

Maleka's Baby-sitting Earnings

39.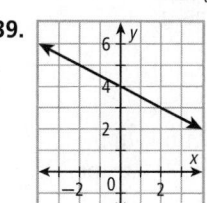

40.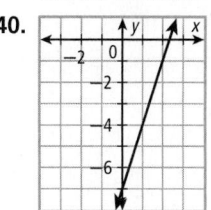

41. $y = \frac{1}{3}x + 5$ **42.** $y = 4x - 9$

43.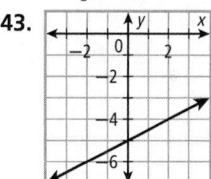

44.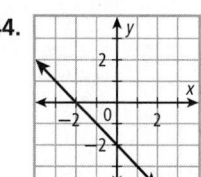

45. $y = 2x + 1$ **46.** $y = -5x - 26$
47. $y = 2x + 2$ **48.** $y = 2x + 8$
49. $y = 0.5x$: 4.5; $y = x - 1$: 6.25;
$y = 0.5x$ is the better fit. **50.** $y \approx 2.3x - 16$; extremely well ($r \approx 0.99$)
51. $y = -\frac{1}{3}x$ and $y = -\frac{1}{3}x - 6$
52. $y - 2 = -4(x - 1)$ and $y = -4x - 2$ **53.** $y - 1 = -5(x - 6)$ and $y = \frac{1}{5}x + 2$ **54.** $y - 2 = 3(x + 1)$ and $y = -\frac{1}{3}x$ **55.** $y = 2x - 3$
56.

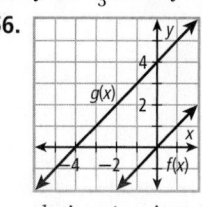

translation 4 units up

57.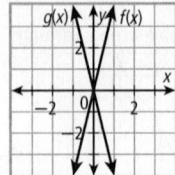

reflection across *y*-axis

58.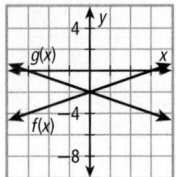

reflection across *y*-axis

59. translation 2 units up;
rotation about $(0, 3)$ (steeper)

Mastering the Standards

for Mathematical Practice

The topics described in the Standards for Mathematical Content will vary from year to year. However, the *way* in which you learn, study, and think about mathematics will not. The Standards for Mathematical Practice describe skills that you will use in all of your math courses.

Mathematical Practices

1. *Make sense of problems and persevere in solving them.*
2. *Reason abstractly and quantitatively.*
3. *Construct viable arguments and critique the reasoning of others.*
4. *Model with mathematics.*
5. *Use appropriate tools strategically.*
6. *Attend to precision.*
7. *Look for and make use of structure.*
8. *Look for and express regularity in repeated reasoning.*

---

⑤ Use appropriate tools strategically.

Mathematically proficient students consider the available tools when solving a... problem... [and] are... able to use technological tools to explore and deepen their understanding...

In your book

Algebra Labs and **Technology Labs** use concrete and technological tools to explore mathematical concepts.

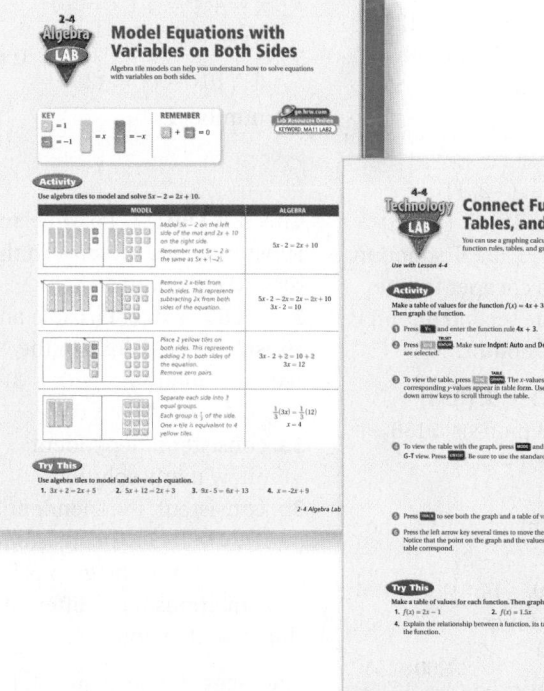

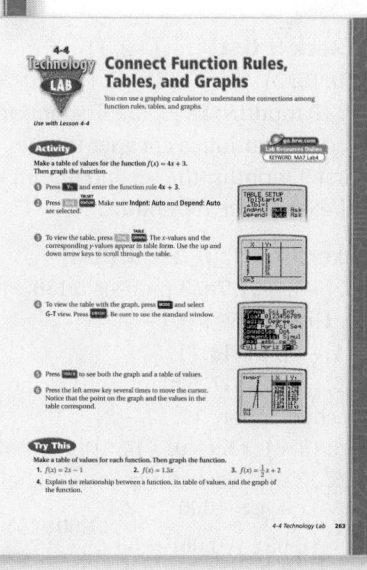

5-1

Check It Out! 1a. yes 1b. no
2a. $(-2, 3)$ 2b. $(3, -2)$ 3. 5 movies; $25

Exercises 1. an ordered pair that satisfies both equations 3. yes
5. $(2, 1)$ 7. $(-4, 7)$ 9. no 11. yes
13. $(3, 3)$ 15. $(3, -1)$

17a. $\begin{cases} y = 2x \\ y = 16 + 0.50x \end{cases}$

b.

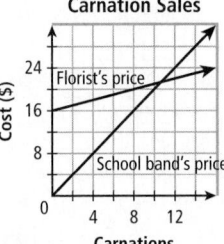

Carnation Sales

It represents how many carnations need to be sold to break even.
c. No, because the solution is not a whole number of carnations; 11 carnations. 19. $(-2.4, -9.3)$
21. $(0.3, -0.3)$ 23. 45 white; 120 pink 25. 8 yr 29. C 31. month 11; 400

5-2

Check It Out! 1a. $(-2, 1)$
1b. $(0, 2)$ 1c. $(3, -10)$ 2. $(-1, 6)$
3. 10 months; $860; the first option; the first option is cheaper for the first 9 months; the second option is cheaper after 10 months.

Exercises 1. $(9, 35)$ 3. $(3, 8)$
5. $(-3, -9)$ 7a. 3 months; $136
b. Green Lawn 9. $(-4, 2)$
11. $(-1, 2)$ 13. $(1, 5)$
15. $(3, -2)$ 17. 6 months; $360; the second option 19. $(2, -2)$
21. $(8, 6)$ 23. $(-9, -14.8)$
25. 12 nickels; 8 dimes
27. $\begin{cases} x + y = 1000 \\ 0.05x + 0.06y = 58 \end{cases}$; $200 at 5%; $800 at 6%

29. $x = 60°$; $y = 30°$
35. Possible estimate: $(1.75, -2.5)$; $(1.8, -2.4)$ 37. F 39. $r = 5$; $s = -2$; $t = 4$ 41. $a = 9$; $b = 5$; $c = 0$

5-3

Check It Out! 1. $(-2, 4)$ 2. $(4, 1)$
3a. $(2, 0)$ 3b. $(3, 4)$ 4. 9 lilies; 4 tulips

Exercises 1. $(-4, 1)$ 3. $(-2, -4)$
5. $(-6, 30)$ 7. $(3, 2)$ 9. $(4, -3)$
11. $(-1, -2)$ 13. $(1, 5)$ 15. $\left(6, -\frac{1}{2}\right)$
17. $(-1, 2)$ 19. $(-1, 2)$

21. $\begin{cases} \ell - w = 2 \\ 2\ell + 2w = 40 \end{cases}$; length: 11 units; width: 9 units

25. $(3, 3)$ 27. $\left(\frac{46}{7}, \frac{8}{7}\right)$ 29. $\left(\frac{15}{7}, \frac{9}{7}\right)$

31a. $\begin{cases} 3A + 2B = 16 \\ 2A + 3B = 14 \end{cases}$ b. $A = 4$; $B = 2$
c. Buying the first package will save $8; buying the second package will save $7. 33. A 35a. s = number of student tickets; n = number of nonstudent tickets;

$\begin{cases} s + n = 358 \\ 1.50s + 3.25n = 752.25 \end{cases}$

b. $s = 235$; $n = 123$; 235 student tickets, 123 nonstudent tickets
37. $x = 4$; $y = -1$; $z = 10$

39. $\begin{cases} x + y = 5 \\ 3(10x + y) = 42 \end{cases}$; $x = 1$; $y = 4$;
the number is 14.

5-4

Check It Out! 1. Possible answer: Substitute $-2x + 5$ for y in the second equation: $2x + (-2x + 5) = 1$; $5 = 1$ ✗ 2. Possible answer: Substitute $x - 3$ for y in the second equation: $x - (x - 3) - 3 = 0$; $3 - 3 = 0$; $0 = 0$ ✔
3a. consistent, dependent; infinitely many solutions
3b. consistent, independent; one solution 3c. inconsistent; no solution 4. Yes; the graphs of the two equations have different slopes so they intersect.

Exercises 1. consistent 3. Possible answer: Substitute $-3x + 2$ for y in the first equation: $3x + (-3x + 2) = 6$; $2 = 6$ ✗ 5. Possible answer: Substitute $-x + 3$ for y in the second equation: $x + (-x + 3) - 3 = 0$; $0 = 0$ ✔ 7. Possible answer: Add the two equations:

$\begin{array}{r} -7x + y = -2 \\ +7x - y = 2 \\ \hline 0 + 0 = 0 \\ 0 = 0 \checkmark \end{array}$

9. inconsistent; no solutions
11. yes 13. Possible answer: Substitute $-x - 1$ for y in the first equation: $x + (-x - 1) = 3$; $-1 = 3$ ✗ 15. Possible answer: Compare slopes and intercepts. $-6 + y = 2x \to y = 2x - 6$; $y = 2x - 36$; the lines have the same slope and different y-intercepts. Therefore the lines are parallel. 17. Possible answer: Substitute $x - 2$ for y in the second equation: $x - (x - 2) - 2 = 0$; $2 - 2 = 0$; $0 = 0$ ✔
19. Possible answer: Compare slopes and intercepts. $-9x - 3y = -18 \to y = -3x + 6$; $3x + y = 6 \to y = -3x + 6$; the lines have the same slope and the same y-intercepts. Therefore the graphs are one line. 21. consistent, independent; one solution 23. Yes; the graphs of the two equations have different slopes, so they intersect. 27. They will always have the same number; both started with 2 and add 4 every year. 29. The graph will be 2 parallel lines. 31. A 33. D
35. $p = q$; $p \neq q$

5-5

Check It Out! 1a. no 1b. yes
2a.

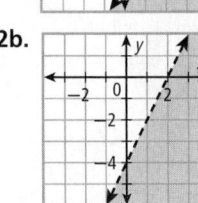

2b.

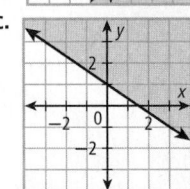

2c.

3a. $2.5b + 2g \le 6$

3b.

Olive Combinations

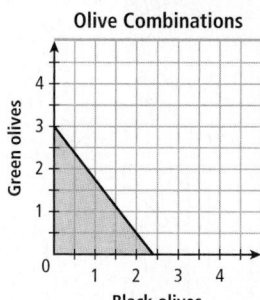

3c. Possible answer: (1 lb black, 1 lb green), (0.5 lb black, 2 lb green)

4a. $y < -x$ **4b.** $y \ge -2x - 3$

Exercises **3.** yes

5.

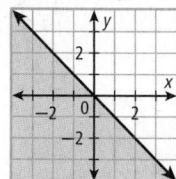

7.

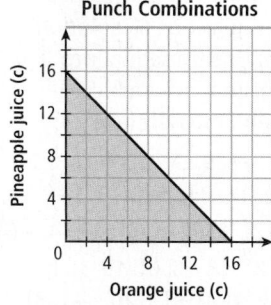

9a. $r + p \le 16$

b.

Punch Combinations

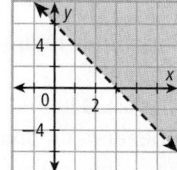

c. Possible answer: (2 c orange, 2 c pineapple), (4 c orange, 10 c pineapple) **11.** $y \ge x + 5$ **13.** yes

15.

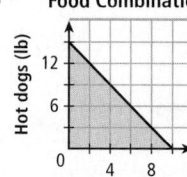

19a. $3x + 2y \le 30$

b.

Food Combinations

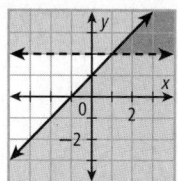

c. Possible answer: (3 lb hamburger, 2 lb hot dogs), (5 lb hamburger, 6 lb hot dogs) **21.** $y \le -\frac{1}{5}x + 3$

23.

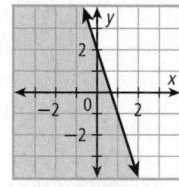

25.

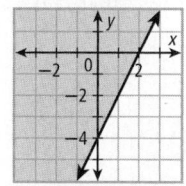

29.

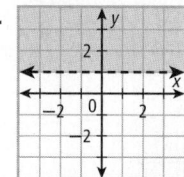

31.

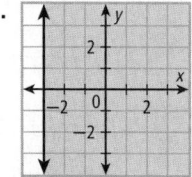

33.

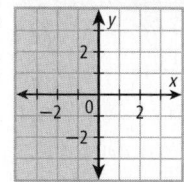

35.

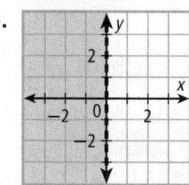

37. $7a + 4s \ge 280$ **41.** A **43.** B **45.** C

47.

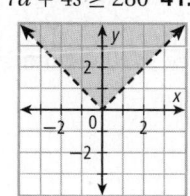

49. $y \ge \frac{1}{2}x + 3$

5-6

Check It Out! **1a.** yes **1b.** no

2a.

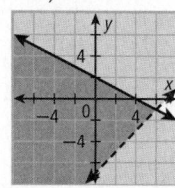

Possible answer: solutions: $(3, 3)$, $(4, 4)$; not solutions: $(-3, 1)$, $(-1, -4)$

2b.

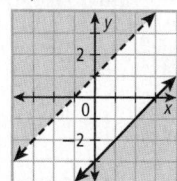

Possible answer: solutions: $(0, 0)$, $(3, -2)$; not solutions: $(4, 4)$, $(1, -6)$

3a.

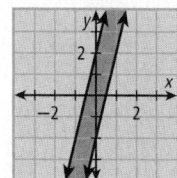

no solutions

3b.

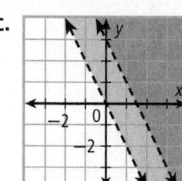

all points between and on the parallel lines

3c.

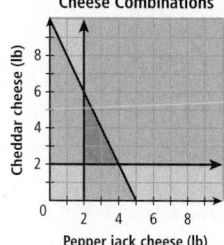

same as solutions of $y > -2x + 3$

4.

Cheese Combinations

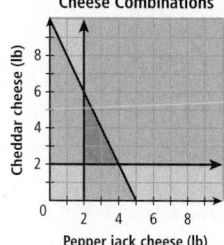

Possible answer: (3 lb pepper jack, 2 lb cheddar), (2.5 lb pepper jack, 4 lb cheddar)

Exercises 1. all **3.** yes

5.

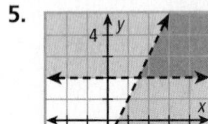

Possible answer: solutions: $(3, 3)$, $(4, 3)$; not solutions: $(0, 0)$, $(2, 1)$

7.

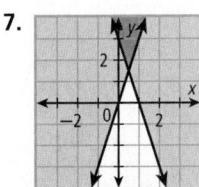

Possible answer: solutions: $(0, 4)$, $(1, 4)$; not solutions: $(2, -1)$, $(3, 1)$

9.

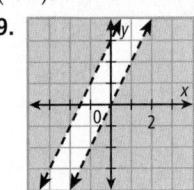

no solutions

11.

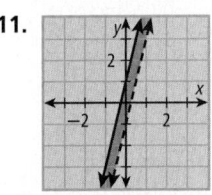

all points between the parallel lines and on the solid line

13.

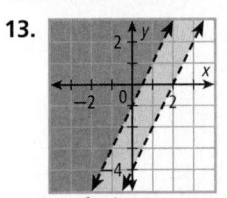

same solutions as $y > 2x - 1$

15. Sales Goals

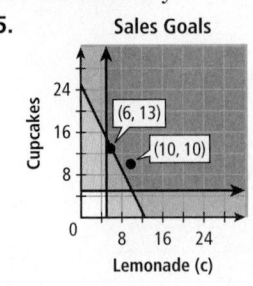

Possible answer: (6 lemonade, 13 cupcakes), (10 lemonade, 10

cupcakes) **17.** yes

19.

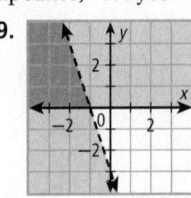

Possible answer: solutions: $(-2, 0)$, $(-3, 1)$; not solutions: $(0, 0)$, $(1, 4)$

21.

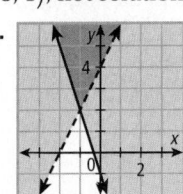

Possible answer: solutions: $(-1, 3)$, $(0, 5)$; not solutions: $(0, 0)$, $(1, 4)$

23.

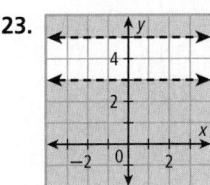

no solutions

25.

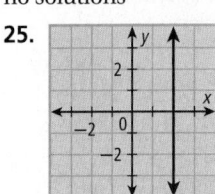

All points are solutions.

27.

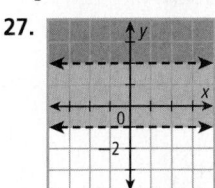

same solutions as $y > 2$

29. Linda's Work Hours

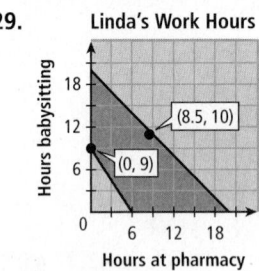

Possible answer:
$\left(0 \text{ h at pharmacy, } 9 \text{ h babysitting}\right)$,
$\left(8.5 \text{ h at pharmacy, } 10 \text{ h babysitting}\right)$

31.

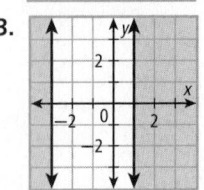

33.

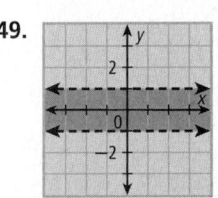

35. $\begin{cases} y > x + 1 \\ y < x + 3 \end{cases}$

37. $\begin{cases} y < 2 \\ x \geq -2 \end{cases}$

39. Student B **45.** G
47. about 12 square units

49.

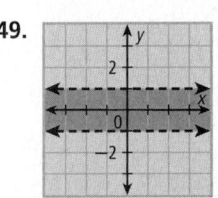

Study Guide: Review

1. independent system **2.** system of linear equations **3.** solution of a system of linear inequalities **4.** inconsistent system **5.** independent system **6.** no

7. yes **8.** yes **9.** no **10.** $(-1, -1)$ **11.** $(3, 4)$ **12.** 8 h; $10 **13.** $(-9, -6)$ **14.** $\left(\frac{1}{2}, -2\right)$ **15.** $(-1, 6)$ **16.** $(4, -5)$ **17.** $(-5, 2)$ **18.** $(6, 6)$ **19.** 10 h; $1350; Motor Works **20.** $(-1, 3)$ **21.** $(5, -3)$ **22.** $(11, 1)$ **23.** $(0, 3)$ **24.** $(-2, 8)$ **25.** $(3, -5)$ **26.** $(4, -6)$ **27.** $(2, 2)$ **28.** no solution **29.** infinitely many solutions **30.** $(-2, -4)$ **31.** infinitely many solutions **32.** infinitely many solutions **33.** $(-1, -3)$ **34.** no **35.** consistent, independent; one solution **36.** inconsistent; no solution **37.** consistent, dependent; infinitely many solutions **38.** inconsistent; no solution **39.** consistent, independent; one solution **40.** consistent, dependent; infinitely many solutions

41. inconsistent; no solution **42.** no **43.** yes **44.** yes

45. no

46.

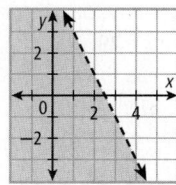

47.

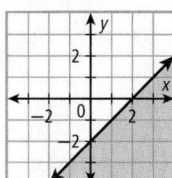

48.

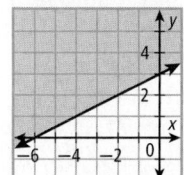

49.

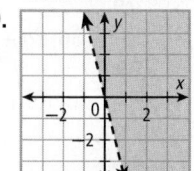

50.

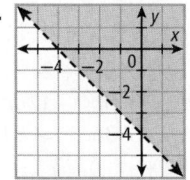

51.

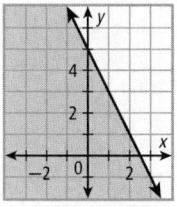

52. x = slices of pizza; y = bottles of soda; $2x + y \geq 450$

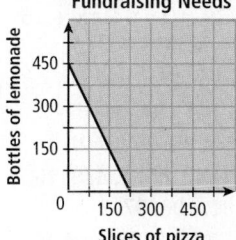

Possible answer: $(200, 50)$, $(150, 150)$ **53.** no **54.** yes

55.

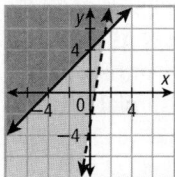

Possible answer: solutions: $(-6, 6)$, $(-10, 0)$; not solutions: $(0, 0)$, $(4, -4)$

56.

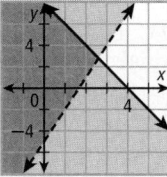

Possible answer: solutions: $(0, 0)$, $(-5, 0)$; not solutions: $(8, 0)$, $(3, -3)$

57.

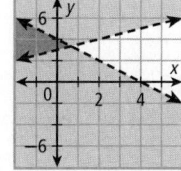

Possible answer: solutions: $(-6, 2)$, $(-8, 1)$; not solutions: $(0, 0)$, $(4, 1)$

58.

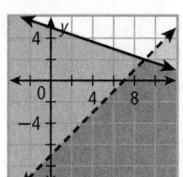

Possible answer: solutions: $(8, -8)$, $(9, 0)$; not solutions: $(0, 0)$, $(0, -4)$

59.

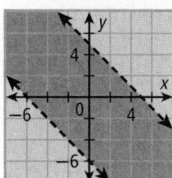

60.

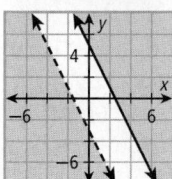

Selected Answers ▪ Chapter 6

6-1

Check It Out! 1. $\frac{1}{125}$ m 2a. $\frac{1}{10,000}$
2b. $\frac{1}{16}$ 2c. $-\frac{1}{32}$ 2d. $-\frac{1}{32}$ 3a. $\frac{1}{64}$
3b. 2 4a. $\frac{2}{m^3}$ 4b. $\frac{1}{7r^3}$ 4c. g^4h^6

Exercises 1. $\frac{1}{10,000,000}$ m 3. 1 5. $\frac{1}{27}$
7. $-\frac{1}{512}$ 9. 1 11. $\frac{1}{16}$ 13. $\frac{1}{256}$
15. $-\frac{1}{32}$ 17. $\frac{3}{k^4}$ 19. $x^{10}d^3$ 21. $\frac{g^6}{f^4}$
23. $\frac{p^7}{q}$ 25. 1 27. $\frac{1}{81}$ 29. $-\frac{1}{36}$ 31. 1
33. $-\frac{1}{3}$ 35. 4 37. $\frac{1}{256}$ 39. 1 41. $\frac{1}{144}$
43. $\frac{1}{k^4}$ 45. $\frac{b^3}{2}$ 47. $-\frac{5}{x^3}$ 49. $\frac{2g^{10}}{7}$
51. s^5t^{12} 53. 1 55. $\frac{1}{q^2}$ 57. $\frac{h^3}{6m^2k}$
59. $\frac{1}{16}$ 61. $-\frac{1}{6}$ 63. 3 65. 3 67. $\frac{a^3}{b^2}$
69. $\frac{w^2}{y}$ 71. $-\frac{5}{y^6}$ 73. $2a^3b$ 75. $\frac{1}{3x^8y^{12}}$
79. never 81. sometimes
83. sometimes 87. 81 89. 1 91. -3
93. -1 95. D 97. A

6-2

Check It Out! 1a. 3 1b. 15
2a. 8 2b. 1 2c. 81 3. 1944
4a. xy^3 4b. xy

Exercises 1. 5 3. 4 5. 3 7. 6 9. 5
11. 10 13. 4 15. 32 17. 125 19. 256
21. 0 23. x^2y 25. x^3y^3 27. a^2 29. 1
31. 10 33. 8 35. 2 37. 2 39. 14
41. 8 43. 8 45. 64 47. 1000
49. 243 51. $2g$ 53. $2m$ 55. $3x^2$
57. ab^4 59. a^8b 61. 1 63. 0 65. 625
67. 3 69. $\frac{2}{3}$ 71. $\frac{1}{4}$ 73. $\frac{4}{9}$ 75. $\frac{8}{343}$
77. $\frac{1}{27}$ 79. $\frac{16}{625}$ 81. 1.86 in. 83. $n^{\frac{2}{3}}$
will be less than n because $\frac{2}{3} < 1$.
$n^{\frac{3}{2}}$ will be greater than n because
$\frac{3}{2} > 1$. 85a. 10 in. 85b. The distance
doubles (20 in.). 87. B 89. C 91. a
93. x^3 95. 3 97. 36π cm^2; both
volume and surface area are
described by 36π (although the units
are different).

6-3

Check It Out! 1a. 3 1b. 1 1c. 3
2a. 1 2b. 5 3a. $x^5 + 9x^3 - 4x^2 +$
16; 1 3b. $-3y^8 + 18y^5 + 14y$; -3
4a. cubic polynomial 4b. constant
monomial 4c. 8th degree trinomial
5. 1606 ft

Exercises 1. d 3. a 5. 3 7. 0 9. 8

11. 3 13. 4 15. $-8a^9 + 9a^8$; -8
17. $3x^2 + 2x - 1$; 3 19. $5c^4 + 5c^3 +$
$3c^2 - 4$; 5 21. linear binomial
23. quartic polynomial 25. quartic
trinomial 27. 4 29. 6 31. 7 33. 1
35. 4 37. 2 39. 3 41. $4.9t^3 - 4t^2 +$
$t + 2.5$; 4.9 43. $x^{10} + x^7 - x^5 +$
$x^3 - x$; 1 45. $5x^3 + 3x^2 + 5x - 4$; 5
47. $-d^3 + 3d^2 + 4d + 5$; -1
49. $-x^5 - x^3 + 4x^2 + 1$; -1
51. linear monomial 53. quadratic
trinomial 55. quartic trinomial
57. quadratic monomial 59. always
61. never 63a. 58.5 in^3 b. 66 in^3
c. 0 d. yes 65. -48; 0; 3270 75. A is
incorrect 77. J 79a. 58 cm; 65 cm
b. 50.310 cm

6-4

Check It Out! 1a. $5s^2 + s$
1b. $20z^4 - 6$ 1c. $x^8 + 6y^8$ 1d. b^3c^2
2. $12a^3 + 15a^2 - 16a$ 3. $-2x^2 - x$
4. $-0.05x^2 + 46x - 3200$

Exercises 1. $-3a^2 + 9a$ 3. $0.26r^4 +$
$0.32r^3$ 5. $3b^3c$ 7. $23n^3 + 3n + 15$
9. $9x^2 - x - 6$ 11. $4c^4 + 8c + 6$
13. $-3r + 11$ 15. $8a^2 + 5a + 9$
17. $12n^2 + 6n - 3m$ 19. $d^5 + 1$
21. $5x$ 23. $2x^3 - 5$ 25. $10t^2 + t$
27. $x^5 + x^4$ 29. $-2t^3 + 8t^2$
31. $-6m^3 + 2m^2 + 5m + 3$
33. $4w^2 + 6w + 4$ 35. $t - 5$
37. $2n - 2$ 39. $6x^2 - x - 1$
41. $-u^3 + 3u^2 + 3u + 6$ 43. $x = \frac{3}{2}$,
or 1.5 45. B is incorrect. 47. $3x + 6$
49. $6x + 14$ 51. $2x^2 + x - 5$ 55. G
57. $3x^2 - 2$

6-5

Check It Out! 1a. $18x^5$ 1b. $10r^2t^4$
1c. $4x^5y^5z^7$ 2a. $8x^2 + 2x + 6$
2b. $15a^3b + 3ab^2$ 2c. $5r^3s^2 - 15r^2s^3$
3a. $a^2 - a - 12$ 3b. $x^2 - 6x + 9$
3c. $2a^2 + 7ab^2 - 4b^4$ 4a. $x^3 - x^2 -$
$6x + 18$ 4b. $3x^3 - 4x^2 + 11x + 10$
5a. $x^2 - 4x$ 5b. 12 m^2

Exercises 1. $14x^6$ 3. $3r^5s^5t^5$
5. $21x^7y^3$ 7. $4x^2 + 8x + 4$
9. $6a^5b^2 + 2a^4b^3$
11. $10x^3y^4 - 5x^2y^2$ 13. $x^2 - x - 2$
15. $x^2 - 4x + 4$

17. $4a^4 - 2ab - 12a^3b^2 + 6b^3$
19. $x^3 + 3x^2 - 7x + 15$
21. $-6x^4 + 12x^3 + 4x^2 - 18x + 20$
23. $x^3 - 4x^2 - 4x - 5$ 25a. $2x^2 - 3x$
b. 20 in^2 27. $-12r^5s^5$ 29. $10a^4$
31. $-6a^5b^6$ 33. $-12a^7b^7c^8$
35. $9s^2 + 54s$ 37. $27x^3 - 12x^2$
39. $10s^3t^3 - 15s^2t^5$ 41. $-10x^3 +$
$15x^2 + 5x$ 43. $-14x^6y^3 + 7x^5y^4$
45. $x^2 + 8x + 16$ 47. $5x^2 + 13x - 6$
49. $10x^2 - x - 2$ 51. $7x^2 - 52x - 32$
53. $x^3 - x^2 - x + 10$
55. $-10x^4 + 2x^3 + 20x^2 - 19x + 3$
57. $8x^5 - 12x^3 - 2x^4 + 17x^2 - 21$
59. $x^3 - 3x - 2$ 61. $-x^3 + 3x^2 - 3x$
$+ 1$ 63. $16x^2 - 48x + 36$ 65a. 3; 2;
$10x^5 + 5x^3$; 5 b. 2; 2; $x^4 - x^3 + 2x^2$
$- 2x$; 4 c. 1; 3; $x^4 - 5x^3 + 6x^2 + x -$
3; 4 d. $m + n$ 67. $12x^2 + 12x + 3$
69a. $2x^2$ b. 800 m^2 71. $2x^2 - 7x -$
30 73. $8x^2 - 16xy + 6y^2$ 75. $6x^2 -$
$9x - 6$ 77. $x^3 + 3x^2$ 79. $2x^3 -$
$7x^2 - 10x + 24$ 81. $8p^3 - 36p^2q +$
$54pq^2 - 27q^3$ 87. C 89. D
91. $-x^2 - 6$ 93. a. $x^2 - 1$ b. $8x +$
16 95. $x^3 + 3x^2 + 2x$ 97. $a = 2$

6-6

Check It Out! 1a. $x^2 + 12x + 36$
1b. $25a^2 + 10ab + b^2$ 1c. $1 + 2c^3 + c^6$
2a. $x^2 - 14x + 49$ 2b. $9b^2 - 12bc +$
$4c^2$ 2c. $a^4 - 8a^2 + 16$ 3a. $x^2 - 64$
3b. $9 - 4y^4$ 3c. $81 - r^2$ 4. 25

Exercises 3. $4 + 4x + x^2$ 5. $4x^2 +$
$24x + 36$ 7. $4a^2 + 28ab + 49b^2$
9. $x^2 - 4x + 4$ 11. $64 - 16x + x^2$
13. $49a^2 - 28ab + 4b^2$ 15. $x^2 - 36$
17. $4x^4 - 9$ 19. $4x^2 - 25y^2$
21. $x^2 + 6x + 9$ 23. $x^4 + 2x^2y^2 + y^4$
25. $4 + 12x + 9x^2$ 27. $s^4 - 14s^2 + 49$
29. $a^2 - 16a + 64$ 31. $9x^2 - 24x +$
16 33. $a^2 - 100$ 35. $49x^2 - 9$
37. $25a^4 - 81$ 39. $\pi x^2 + 8\pi x + 16\pi$
41. $x^2 + 2xy + y^2$ 43. $x^4 - 16$
45. $x^4 - 8x^2 + 16$ 47. $1 + 2x + x^2$
49. $x^6 - 2a^3x^3 + a^6$ 51. $36a^2 -$
$25b^2$ 53. 4; 4 55. 25; 25 57. 9; 9
59. -5; -5 61. 840 65. 1, 4, 9, 16,
25, 36, 49, 64, 81, 100 67. B
69. D 71. $x^3 + 4x^2 - 16x - 64$
73. $b = \pm 2\sqrt{c}$

Selected Answers ▪ Chapter 6

1. cubic **2.** standard form of a polynomial **3.** monomial
4. trinomial **5.** $\frac{1}{32}$ in. **6.** 1 **7.** 1
8. $\frac{1}{125}$ **9.** $\frac{1}{10,000}$, or 0.0001 **10.** $\frac{1}{16}$
11. $\frac{1}{256}$ **12.** $\frac{27}{4}$ **13.** $\frac{1}{m^2}$ **14.** b
15. $-\frac{1}{2x^2y^4}$ **16.** $2b^6c^4$ **17.** $\frac{3a^2}{4c^2}$ **18.** $\frac{s^3}{qr^2}$
19. 9 **20.** 7 **21.** 16 **22.** 8 **23.** z^2
24. $5x^2$ **25.** x^4y^3 **26.** m^2n^4 **27.** 0

28. 3 **29.** 6 **30.** 1 **31.** $3n^2 + 2n - 4$; 3 **32.** $-a^6 - a^4 + 3a^3 + 2a$; -1
33. linear binomial **34.** quintic monomial **35.** quartic trinomial
36. constant monomial **37.** $-4t + 3$
38. $-6x^6 - x^5$ **39.** $3h^3 - 3h^2 + 5$
40. $2m^2 - 5m - 1$ **41.** $p^2 + 5p + 8$
42. $-7z^2 - z + 10$ **43.** $3g^2 + 2g + 4$
44. $-x^2 + 4x + 8$ **45.** $8r^2$ **46.** $6a^6b$
47. $18x^3y^2$ **48.** $3s^6t^{14}$ **49.** $2x^2 - 8x + 12$ **50.** $-3a^2b^2 + 6a^3b^2 - 15a^2b$

51. $a^2 - 3a - 18$ **52.** $b^2 - 6b - 27$
53. $x^2 - 12x + 20$ **54.** $t^2 - 1$ **55.** $8q^2 + 34q + 30$ **56.** $20g^2 - 37g + 8$
57. $p^2 - 8p + 16$ **58.** $x^2 + 24x + 144$ **59.** $m^2 + 12m + 36$ **60.** $9c^2 + 42c + 49$ **61.** $4r^2 - 4r + 1$ **62.** $9a^2 - 6ab + b^2$ **63.** $4n^2 - 20n + 25$ **64.** $h^2 - 26h + 169$ **65.** $x^2 - 1$ **66.** $z^2 - 225$
67. $c^4 - d^2$ **68.** $9k^4 - 49$

Selected Answers ▪ Chapter 7

7-1

Check It Out! 1a. $2^3 \cdot 5$ **1b.** $3 \cdot 11$
1c. 7^2 **1d.** 19 **2a.** 4 **2b.** 5 **3a.** $9g^2$
3b. 1 **3c.** 1 **4.** 7

Exercises 3. $3^2 \cdot 2^2$ **5.** $3^3 \cdot 2$ **7.** 7
(prime) **9.** $3 \cdot 5^2$ **11.** 7 **13.** x^2
15. 1 **17.** $2 \cdot 3^2$ **19.** $2^2 \cdot 3$
21. 17 **23.** 7^2 **25.** 9 **27.** 10 **29.** $9s$
31. 5 **33.** $4x^2$ **35.** $2n$ **39.** 15
rows **41.** 8 and 20; 4 **43.** 63 and
105; 21 **45.** 54 and 72; 18 **47.** 36; 2;
9; 3 **49.** 105; 5; 7 **51.** 2; 2; 27; 3
53. 24; 2; 6; 3 **55.** 2; 2; 10, 5 **57.** D
61. $9y$ **63.** $2p^2r$ **65.** $4a^2b^3$

7-2

Check It Out! 1a. $b(5 + 9b^2)$
1b. cannot be factored
1c. $-y^2(18y + 7)$
1d. $2x^2(4x^2 + 2x - 1)$
2. $2x$ cm; $(x + 2)$ cm
3a. $(4s - 5)(s + 6)$ **3b.** $(7x + 1)$
$(2x + 3)$
3c. cannot be factored **3d.** $(5x - 2)^2$
4a. $(2b^2 + 3)(3b + 4)$
4b. $(4r + 1)(r^2 + 6)$
5a. $(5x^2 - 4)(3 - 2x)$
5b. $(8 + x)(y - 1)$

Exercises 1. $5a(3 - a)$ **3.** $7(-5x + 6)$
5. $2h(6h^3 + 4h - 3)$ **7.** $m(9m + 1)$
9. $3(12f + 6f^2 + 1)$ **11.** $16t(-t + 20)$
13. $(2b + 5)(b + 3)$
15. $(x^2 + 2)(x + 4)$
17. $(2b^2 + 5)(2b - 3)$
19. $(7r^2 + 6)(r - 5)$
21. $2(r - 2)(r - 3)$
23. $(7q - 2)(2q - 3)$
25. $(2m^2 - 3)(m - 3)$ **27.** $9y(y + 5)$
29. $x^2(-14x^2 + 5)$
31. $-d^2(4d^2 - d + 3)$
33. $7c(3c + 2)$ **35.** $-5g^2(g + 3)$
37. cannot be factored
39. $(6y + 1)(y - 7)$
41. $(-3 + 4b)(b + 2)$
43. $(2a^2 + 3)(a - 4)$
45. $(6x^2 + 1)(x + 3)$
47. $(n^2 + 5)(n - 2)$
49. $(2m^2 - 3)(m - 1)$
51. $(2f^2 - 5)(3f - 4)$
53. $(b^2 - 2)(b + 4)$ **55.** $3v$
57. $2k$ **59.** 2; binomial; $x(x + 5)$
61. 3; trinomial; $a^2(a^2 + a + 1)$

63a. $100x^3$; $200x^2$; $400x$
b. $100x^3 + 200x^2 + 400x + 800$
c. $100(x^2 + 4)(x + 2)$; 1603.12
67. The sum of opposite binomials
is 0. **69a.** Commutative Property
of Addition **b.** Associative Property
of Addition **c.** Distributive
Property **d.** Distributive Property
71. D **73.** C **75.** $-9ab(8ab + 5)$
77. $(a + c)(b + d)$
79. $(x^2 + 3)(x - 4)$

7-3

Check It Out! 1a. $(x + 4)(x + 6)$
1b. $(x + 4)(x + 3)$ **2a.** $(x + 6)(x + 2)$
2b. $(x - 6)(x + 1)$ **2c.** $(x + 6)(x + 7)$
2d. $(x - 8)(x - 5)$ **3a.** $(x + 5)(x - 3)$
3b. $(x - 4)(x - 2)$ **3c.** $(x - 10)$
$(x + 2)$

4.

n	$n^2 - 7n + 10$
0	$0^2 - 7(0) + 10 = 10$
1	$1^2 - 7(1) + 10 = 4$
2	$2^2 - 7(2) + 10 = 0$
3	$3^2 - 7(3) + 10 = -2$
4	$4^2 - 7(4) + 10 = -2$

n	$(n - 5)(n - 2)$
0	$(0 - 5)(0 - 2) = 10$
1	$(1 - 5)(1 - 2) = 4$
2	$(2 - 5)(2 - 2) = 0$
3	$(3 - 5)(3 - 2) = -2$
4	$(4 - 5)(4 - 2) = -2$

Exercises 1. $(x + 4)(x + 9)$
3. $(x + 4)(x + 10)$ **5.** $(x + 2)(x + 8)$
7. $(x - 1)(x - 6)$ **9.** $(x - 3)(x - 8)$
11. $(x + 9)(x - 3)$ **13.** $(x - 2)(x + 1)$
15. $(x - 9)(x + 5)$ **17.** $(x + 3)(x + 10)$
19. $(x + 4)(x + 12)$ **21.** $(x + 2)$
$(x + 14)$ **23.** $(x - 1)(x - 5)$
25. $(x - 4)(x - 8)$ **27.** $(x + 7)(x - 3)$
29. $(x - 13)(x + 1)$ **31.** $(x - 7)(x + 5)$
33. C **35.** D **37.** They are inverse
operations. **39.** $(x - 2)(x - 9)$
41. $(x + 1)(x + 9)$ **43.** $(x + 6)(x + 7)$
45. $(x + 2)(x + 9)$ **47.** $(x - 3)(x + 8)$
49. $(x - 5)(x + 9)$ **51.** approximately
1.5 **55.** $x^2 + 6x + 8$; $(x + 4)(x + 2)$
57. Positive; $-$, $-$; Both negative
59. Negative; $+$, $-$; Positive;
Negative **61a.** $d = t^2$ **b.** $d = 4t$

c. $t(t - 4)$ **63.** true **65.** false **67.** 4
69. 4 **71a.** $(x + 10)$ ft **b.** $\ell = (x + 14)$ ft;
$w = (x + 6)$ ft **c.** $A = (x^2 + 20x + 84)$
ft^2
73. D **75.** C **77.** $(x^2 + 9)(x^2 + 9)$
79. $(d^2 + 21)(d^2 + 1)$
81. $(de - 5)(de + 4)$ **83.** 16; 11; 29
85a. $(x + 7)$ ft **b.** $(4x + 26)$ ft
c. $92.00 **d.** $36.96 **e.** $128.96

7-4

Check It Out! 1a. $(3x + 1)(2x + 3)$
1b. $(3x + 4)(x - 2)$
2a. $(2x + 5)(3x + 1)$
2b. $(3x - 4)(3x - 1)$
2c. $(3x + 4)(x + 3)$
3a. $(3x - 1)(2x + 3)$
3b. $(4n + 3)(n - 1)$
4a. $-1(2x + 3)(3x + 4)$
4b. $-1(3x + 2)(x + 5)$

Exercises 1. $(2x + 5)(x + 2)$
3. $(5x - 3)(x + 2)$ **5.** $(3x + 4)(x - 6)$
7. $(x + 2)(5x + 1)$
9. $(4x - 5)(x - 1)$
11. $(5x + 4)(x + 1)$
13. $(2a - 1)(2a + 5)$
15. $(2x - 3)(x + 2)$
17. $(10x + 1)(x - 1)$
19. $(2x + 3)(4 - x)$
21. $-1(5x + 3)(x - 2)$
23. $-1(2x - 1)(2x + 5)$
25. $(3x + 2)(3x + 1)$
27. $(n + 2)(3n + 2)$
29. $(4c - 5)(c - 3)$
31. $(2x + 5)(4x + 1)$
33. $(5x - 6)(x + 3)$
35. $(10n - 7)(n - 1)$
37. $(7x + 1)(x + 2)$
39. $(3x - 4)(x - 5)$
41. $(x - 7)(4x - 3)$
43. $(4y - 1)(3y + 5)$
45. $(2x - 1)(2x + 3)$
47. $(3x + 5)(x - 3)$
49. $-1(2x - 3)(2x + 5)$
51. $-1(3x - 2)(x + 1)$
53. $2x^2 - 5x + 2$; $(x - 2)(2x - 1)$
55. $(9n + 8)(n + 1)$
57. $(2x - 1)(2x - 5)$
59. $(3x + 8)(x + 2)$
61. $(3x + 4)(2x - 3)$
63. $(2x - 3)(2x - 3)$
65. $(2x + 3)(3x + 2)$
69a. $-16t^2 + 20t + 6$

b. $-2(4t+1)(2t-3)$ **c.** 10 ft **71.** D
73. B **77.** B **79.** A
81. $(2x+1)(2x+1)$
83. $(9x+1)(9x+1)$
85. $(5x+2)(5x+2)$ **87.** $-7; -5; 5; 7$
89. $-6; 6$

7-5

Check It Out! 1a. yes; $(x+2)^2$
1b. yes; $(x-7)^2$ **1c.** no; $-6x \neq$
$2(3x)(2)$ **2.** $4(3x+1)$ m; 40 m
3a. yes; $(1-2x)(1+2x)$
3b. yes; $(p^4+7q^3)(p^4-7q^3)$
3c. No; $4y^5$ is not a perfect square.

Exercises 1. yes; $(x-2)^2$ **3.** yes;
$(3x-2)^2$ **5.** yes; $(x-3)^2$
7. $4(x+12)$; 88 yd **9.** yes; $(s+4)$
$(s-4)$ **11.** yes; $(2x^2+3y)(2x^2-3y)$
13. yes; x^3+3x^3-3 **15.** No; the
last term must be positive. **17.** no;
$10x \neq 2(5x)(2)$ **19.** yes; $(4x-5)^2$
21. yes; $(1+2x)(1-2x)$ **23.** No;
$4x$ and $9y$ are not perfect squares.
25. yes; $(9-10x^2)(9+10x^2)$
27. 49 **29.** $4y^2$
31. $(10x+9y)(10x-9y)$; difference
of 2 squares
33. $(2r^3+5s^3)(2r^3-5s^3)$;
difference of 2 squares
35. $(x^7+12)(x^7-12)$; difference of
2 squares **39.** $c=32$ **41a.** $5z-4$
b. $20z-16$ **c.** 11; 44; 121
43a. 0; 0; 100; 100; 0 **b.** 16; 16; 36;
36; -24 **c.** 25; 25; 25; 25; -25
d. 36; 36; 16; 16; -24 **e.** 100; 100; 0;
0; 0 **45.** $a-b; a+b$ **47.** C **49.** 1
51a. $a=2; b=v+2$
b. $[2+(v+2)][2-(v+2)] =$
$(v+4)(-v) = -v^2-4v$ **53.** $a=3y$;
$b=y$; $(3y-4)(9y^2+12y+16)$

7-6

Check It Out! 1a. yes **1b.** no;
$4(x+1)^2$ **2a.** $4x(x+2)^2$
2b. $2y(x-y)(x+y)$
3a. $(3x+4)(x+1)$
3b. $2p^3(p+6)(p-1)$
3c. $3q^4(3q+4)(q+2)$ **3d.** $2(x^4+9)$

Exercises 1. yes **3.** yes **5.** no;
$4(2p^2+1)(2p^2-1)$
7. $3x^3(x+2)(x-2)$ **9.** $2p(2q+1)^2$
11. $mn(n^2+m)(n^2-m)$

13. $3x^2(2x-3)(x+1)$
15. $(p^3+1)(p^2+3)$
17. unfactorable **19.** no;
$2xy(y^2-4y+5)$
21. no; $3n^2(n+5)(n-5)$ **23.** yes
25. $-4x(x-3)^2$ **27.** $5(d-3)(d-9)$
29. $2x(7x+5y)(7x-5y)$
31. unfactorable
33. $(p^2+4)(p+2)(p-2)$
35. $(k^2+3)(2k+3)$ **37.** x^2+12x+
$36 = (x+6)^2$ **39.** $s^2-16s+28 =$
$(s-2)(s-14)$ **41.** $b^2-49 =$
$(b+7)(b-7)$ **45.** $(3x-1)(x+7)$
47. $(3x+y-3)(3x-y-7)$
53. 8 **55.** C **57.** C **59a.** $V =$
$8p[\pi(3p+1)^2]$ **b.** $r = (3p+1)$ cm
c. $h = 8$ cm; $V = 128\pi$ cm^3
61. $h^2(h^4+1)(h^2+1)$
63. $x^{n+3}(x^2+x+1)$

Study Guide: Review

1. prime factorization **2.** greatest
common factor **3.** $2^2 \cdot 3$ **4.** $2^2 \cdot 5$
5. 2^5 **6.** prime **7.** $2^3 \cdot 5$ **8.** 2^6
9. $2 \cdot 3 \cdot 11$ **10.** $2 \cdot 3 \cdot 19$ **11.** 5
12. 12 **13.** 1 **14.** 27 **15.** 4 **16.** 3
17. $2x$ **18.** $9b^2$ **19.** $25r$ **20.** 6 boxes;
13 rows **21.** $5x(1-3x^2)$
22. $16(-b+2)$ **23.** $-7(2v+3)$
24. $4(a^2-3a-2)$
25. $5g(g^2-3)(g^2+1)$
26. $10(4p^2-p+3)$
27. $(6x+5)$ ft by x ft
28. $(2x+9)(x-4)$
29. $(t-6)(3t+5)$
30. $(5-3n)(6-n)$
31. $(b+2)(b+4)$
32. $(x^2+7)(x-3)$
33. $(n^2+1)(n-4)$
34. $(2b+5)(3b-4)$
35. $(2h^2-7)(h+7)$
36. $(3t+1)(t+6)$
37. $(5m^2-1)(2m+3)$
38. $(4p-3)(2p^2+1)$
39. $-1(r-5)(r-2)$
40. $(b^2-5)(b-3)$
41. $(t+4)(-t^2+6)$
42. $-1(3h-1)(h-4)$
43. $-1(d-1)^2$ **44.** $(2-b)(5b-4)$
45. $(t+1)(5-t)$
46. $(2b^2+5)(4-b)$
47. $-1(3r-1)(r-1)$

48. left rectangle: $2x^2+3x$; right
rectangle: $8x+12$; combined:
$2x^2+8x+3x+12$; $(2x+3)(x+4)$
49. $(x+1)(x+5)$ **50.** $(x+2)(x+4)$
51. $(x+3)(x+5)$ **52.** $(x-6)(x-2)$
53. $(x+5)^2$ **54.** $(x-2)(x-11)$
55. $(x+4)(x+20)$
56. $(x-6)(x-20)$
57. $(x+12)(x-7)$
58. $(x+3)(x-8)$
59. $(x+4)(x-7)$ **60.** $(x-1)(x+5)$
61. $(x+3)(x-2)$ **62.** $(x+5)(x-4)$
63. $(x-8)(x+6)$ **64.** $(x-9)(x+4)$
65. $(x-12)(x+6)$
66. $(x-10)(x+7)$
67. $(x+20)(x-6)$
68. $(x+7)(x-1)$ **69.** $(y+3)$ m
70. $(2x+1)(x+5)$
71. $(3x+7)(x+1)$
72. $(2x-1)(x-1)$
73. $(3x+2)(x+2)$
74. $(5x+3)(x+5)$
75. $(2x-3)(3x-5)$
76. $(4x+5)(x+2)$
77. $(3x+4)(x+2)$
78. $(7x-2)(x-5)$
79. $(3x+2)(3x+4)$
80. $(2x+1)(x-1)$
81. $(3x+1)(x-4)$
82. $(2x-1)(x-5)$
83. $(7x+2)(x-3)$
84. $(5x+1)(x-2)$
85. $-1(2x-1)(3x+2)$
86. $(6x+5)(x-1)$
87. $(3x-2)(2x+7)$
88. $-1(2x+1)(2x-5)$
89. $-1(2x-3)(5x+2)$
90. $12x^2-11x-5$; $(4x-5)(3x+1)$
91. yes; $(x+6)^2$ **92.** no; $5x \neq 2(x)(5)$
93. no; $-2x \neq 2(2x)(1)$
94. yes; $(3x+2)^2$ **95.** no; $8x \neq$
$2(4x)(2)$ **96.** yes; $(x+7)^2$ **97.** yes;
$(10x-9)(10x+9)$ **98.** No; 2 is
not a perfect square. **99.** No; 5
and 10 are not perfect squares.
100. yes; $(-12+x^3)(-12-x^3)$
101. no; terms must be subtracted
102. yes; $(10p-5q)(10p+5q)$
103. $(x-5)(x+5)$; difference of 2
squares **104.** $(x+10)^2$; perfect-
square trinomial **105.** $(j-k^2)(j+k^2)$;
difference of 2 squares
106. $(3x-7)^2$; perfect-square
trinomial

107. $(9x + 8)^2$; perfect-square
trinomial **108.** $(4b^2 - 11c^3)$
$(4b^2 + 11c^3)$; difference of 2 squares
109. no; $2(2x + 3)(x + 1)$
110. yes **111.** no; $(b^2 + 9)(b - 3)$
$(b + 3)$ **112.** yes **113.** $4(x - 4)$

$(x + 4)$ **114.** $3b^3(b - 4)(b + 2)$
115. $a^2b^3(a - b)(a + b)$
116. $t^4 (t^8 + 1)(t^4 + 1)(t^2 + 1)$
$(t + 1)(t - 1)$ **117.** $5(x + 3)(x + 1)$
118. $2x^2(x - 5)(x + 5)$
119. $2(s + 4)(t + 4)$

120. $5m(5m + 2)(m - 4)$
121. $4x(4x^2 + 1)(2x - 3)$
122. $6s^2t (s + t^2)$
123. $2(m + 3)(m - 3)(5m + 2)$

Mastering the Standards

for Mathematical Practice

The topics described in the Standards for Mathematical Content will vary from year to year. However, the *way* in which you learn, study, and think about mathematics will not. The Standards for Mathematical Practice describe skills that you will use in all of your math courses.

Mathematical Practices

1. *Make sense of problems and persevere in solving them.*
2. *Reason abstractly and quantitatively.*
3. *Construct viable arguments and critique the reasoning of others.*
4. *Model with mathematics.*
5. *Use appropriate tools strategically.*
6. *Attend to precision.*
7. *Look for and make use of structure.*
8. *Look for and express regularity in repeated reasoning.*

① Make sense of problems and persevere in solving them.

Mathematically proficient students start by explaining to themselves the meaning of a problem... They analyze givens, constraints, relationships, and goals. They make conjectures about the form... of the solution and plan a solution pathway...

In your book

Focus on Problem Solving describes a four-step plan for problem solving. The plan is introduced at the beginning of your book, and practice with the plan appears throughout the book.

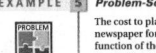

EXAMPLE 5 **Problem-Solving Application**

The cost to place an ad in a newspaper for one week is a linear function of the number of lines in the ad. The costs for 3, 5, and 10 lines are shown. Write an equation in slope-intercept form that represents the function. Then find the cost of an ad that is 18 lines long.

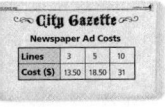

City Gazette

Newspaper Ad Costs

Lines	3	5	10
Cost ($)	13.50	18.50	31

Understand the Problem

- The **answer** will have two parts—an equation in slope-intercept form and the cost of an ad that is 18 lines long.
- The ordered pairs given in the table satisfy the equation.

Make a Plan

First, find the slope. Then use point-slope form to write the equation. Finally, write the equation in slope-intercept form.

Solve

Step 1 Choose any two ordered pairs from the table to find the slope.

$m = \dfrac{y_2 - y_1}{x_2 - x_1} = \dfrac{18.50 - 13.50}{5 - 3} = \dfrac{5}{2} = 2.5$ *Use (3, 13.50) and (5, 18.50).*

Step 2 Substitute the slope and any ordered pair from the table into the point-slope form.

$y - y_1 = m(x - x_1)$

$y - 31 = 2.5(x - 10)$ *Use (10, 31).*

Step 3 Write the equation in slope-intercept form by solving for y.

$y - 31 = 2.5(x - 10)$

$y - 31 = 2.5x - 25$ *Distribute 2.5.*

$y = 2.5x + 6$ *Add 31 to both sides.*

Step 4 Find the cost of an ad containing 18 lines by substituting 18 for x.

$y = 2.5x + 6$

$y = 2.5(18) + 6 = 51$

The cost of an ad containing 18 lines is $51.

Look Back

Check the equation by substituting the ordered pairs (3, 13.50) and (5, 18.50).

$y = 2.5x + 6$		$y = 2.5x + 6$	
13.50	2.5(3) + 6	18.50	2.5(5) + 6
13.5	7.5 + 6	18.5	12.5 + 6
13.5	13.5 ✓	18.5	18.5 ✓

8-1

Check It Out! **1a.** Yes; the second differences are constant. **1b.** Yes; the function can be written in the form $y = ax^2 + bx + c$.

2a.

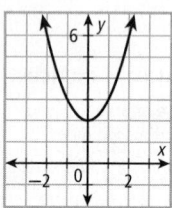

2b.

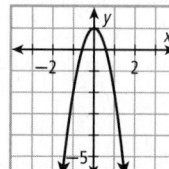

3a. Because $a < 0$, the parabola opens downward. **3b.** Because $a > 0$, the parabola opens upward. **4a.** vertex: $(-2, 5)$; maximum: 5 **4b.** vertex: $(3, -1)$; minimum: -1 **5a.** D: all real numbers; R: $y \geq 4$ **5b.** D: all real numbers; R: $y \leq 3$

Exercises **1.** minimum **3.** yes **5.** no

7.

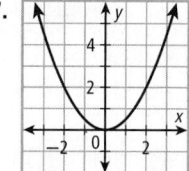

9.

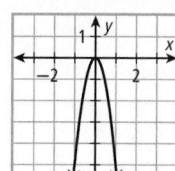

11. upward; $a > 0$ **13.** upward; $a > 0$ **15.** downward; $a < 0$ **17.** $(-3, -4)$; minimum: -4 **19.** D: all real numbers; R: $y \leq 4$ **21.** D: all real numbers; R: $y \geq -4$ **23.** yes **25.** yes **31.** upward; $a > 0$ **33.** vertex: $(0, -5)$; minimum: -5 **35.** D: all real numbers; R: $y \leq 0$ **37.** D: all real numbers; R: $y \geq -2$ **39.** never **41.** always **43.** sometimes **45.** no **47.** yes **9.** yes **53.** quadratic **55.** quadratic

57. neither **59.** linear **61b.** $t \geq 0$ **c.** 16 ft **d.** 2 s **65.** C **67.** yes

8-2

Check It Out! **1a.** no zeros **1b.** 3 **2a.** $x = -3$ **2b.** $x = 1$ **3.** $x = -\frac{1}{4}$ **4.** $(2, -14)$ **5.** 7 ft

Exercises **3.** -1 **5.** no zeros **7.** $x = 2$ **9.** $x = -2$ **11.** $x = -\frac{3}{4}$ **13.** $(1, 8)$ **15.** $(-2, -2)$ **17.** $(-2, -9)$ **19.** no zeros **21.** $-8, -2$ **23.** $x = 6$ **25.** $x = -\frac{1}{2}$ **27.** $x = 5$ **29.** $(-3.5, -12.25)$ **31.** $(-2, 5)$ **33.** $(1, 4.5)$ **35.** $x = 0$. **37.** 0 **39.** 2 **41.** B **43.** 2 **45.** 25 ft; 100 ft

8-3

Check It Out!

1a.

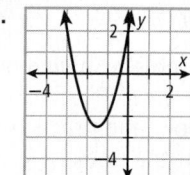

1b.

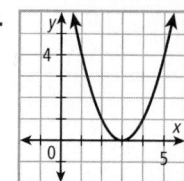

2. maximum height: 16 ft at 0.5 s; time it takes to reach the pool: 1.5 s

Exercises **1.**

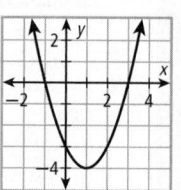

3.

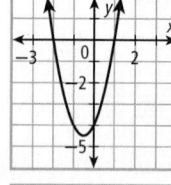

5.

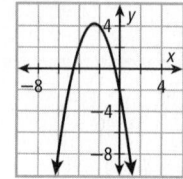

7. maximum height: 144 ft at 3 s; time in the air: 6 s

9.

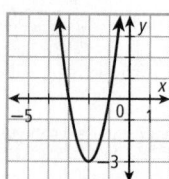

11.

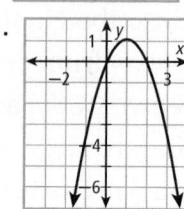

13.

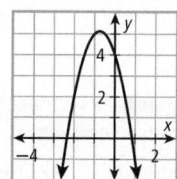

15. $x = 4$; $(4, -16)$ **17.** $x = 0$; $(0, 4)$ **19.** $x = -\frac{1}{2}$; $\left(-\frac{1}{2}, -\frac{15}{4}\right)$ **21.** vertex: $(0, 0)$; axis of symmetry: $x = 0$ **23.** vertex: $(3, -5)$; axis of symmetry: $x = 3$ **25.** vertex: $(0, -4)$; axis of symmetry: $x = 0$ **27b.** D: $0 \leq x \leq 3.16$; R: $0 \leq y \leq 50$ **c.** about 3.16 s **31.** 12 cm/s **35a.** $h(t) = -16t^2 + 45t + 50$ **b.** approximately $(1.4, 81.6)$ **37.** A **39.** D **41.** -1

8-4

Check It Out! **1a.** $f(x), g(x)$ **1b.** $g(x), f(x), h(x)$ **2a.** same width, same axis of symmetry, opens upward, translated 4 units down **2b.** narrower, same axis of symmetry, opens upward, translated 9 units up **2c.** wider, same axis of symmetry, opens upward, translated 2 units up **3a.** The graph of the ball that is dropped from a height of 100 ft is a vertical translation of the graph of the ball that is dropped from a height of 16 ft. The y-intercept of the graph of the ball that is dropped from 100 ft is 84 units higher. **3b.** The ball that is dropped from 16 ft reaches the ground in 1 s. The ball that is dropped from 100 ft reaches the ground in 2.5 s.

Exercises 1. $f(x), g(x)$ **3.** $h(x)$, $g(x), f(x)$ **5.** same width, same axis of symmetry, opens upward, translated 6 units up **7.** wider, same axis of symmetry, opens upward, same vertex **9a.** $h_1(t) = -16t^2 + 16$, $h_2(t) = -16t^2 + 256$; the graph of h_2 is a vertical translation of the graph of h_1. The y-intercept of h_2 is 240 units higher. **b.** The baseball that is dropped from 256 ft reaches the ground in 4 s. The baseball that is dropped from 16 ft reaches the ground in 1 s. **11.** $f(x), g(x)$ **13.** $f(x)$, $h(x), g(x)$ **19.** always **21.** never **25.** $f(x) = 3x^2 - 6$ **29.** B **31.** A **39.** D **41.** 0 **43a.** $f(x) = x^2 - 7$ **b.** $f(x) = -x^2 + 2$ **c.** $f(x) = \frac{1}{2}x^2 + 1$

8-5

Check It Out! 1a. $x = -4$ **1b.** no real solutions **1c.** $x = -2$ or $x = 2$ **2.** 2 s

Exercises 1. zeros, x-intercepts **3.** $-4, 4$ **5.** 6 **7.** $-2, 4$ **9.** -1 **11.** no real solutions **13.** no real solutions **15.** $x = -4$ or $x = 4$ **17.** $x = \frac{1}{2}$ or $x = 5$ **19.** $x = -3$ **21.** no real solutions **23.** no real solutions **25.** always **27.** always **29.** never **31a.** 4 s **b.** 10 ft **33.** 1.4 s **35.** $-1, 1$ **41.** C **45.** no real solutions **47.** $x \approx -1.6$ or $x \approx 0.86$

8-6

Check It Out! 1a. $0, -4$ **1b.** $-4, 3$ **2a.** 3 **2b.** $1, -5$ **2c.** $-\frac{5}{3}$ **2d.** $\frac{1}{3}, 1$ **3.** 1.5 s

Exercises 1. $-2, 8$ **3.** $-7, -9$ **5.** $-11, 0$ **7.** $-6, 2$ **9.** $2, 3$ **11.** $-8, -2$ **13.** 4 **15.** 6 **17.** $-2, -\frac{3}{2}$ **19.** 1 s **21.** $-4, -7$ **23.** $0, 9$ **25.** $-\frac{1}{2}, \frac{1}{3}$ **27.** $-2, 4$ **29.** $-\frac{1}{3}, 1$ **31.** -2 **33.** 1 **35.** 1 **37.** 1 **39.** B **41.** 6 m **43.** 6 s **45.** no **47a.** 3 s **b.** 64 ft **c.** yes **49.** F **51.** $-5, -1$ **53.** $\frac{1}{2}, -3$ **55.** $-2, 5$ **57.** $-1, 0$ **59.** $x^2 - x - 12$ **61.** $x^2 - 4x - 12 = 48; x = 10$

8-7

Check It Out! 1a. ± 11 **1b.** 0 **1c.** no real solutions **2a.** no real solutions **2b.** 9, 1 **3a.** ± 9.49 **3b.** ± 5.66 **3c.** no real solutions **4.** 45 ft

Exercises 1. ± 15 **3.** no real solutions **5.** no real solutions **7.** ± 5 **9.** no real solutions **11.** $11, -5$ **13.** ± 5.20 **15.** ± 4.47 **17.** ± 13 **19.** no real solutions **21.** no real solutions **23.** $\pm \frac{2}{9}$ **25.** $\pm \frac{5}{8}$ **27.** $\pm \frac{13}{7}$ **29.** ± 4.69 **31.** ± 10.20 **33.** ± 7.07 **35.** 6.1 s **37.** $t = \sqrt{\frac{2d}{a}}$ **39.** $a = -6$ and $b = -3$ or $a = 6$ and $b = 3$ **41.** about 4.2 ft by 8.4 ft **43.** A **45.** sometimes **47a.** $a > 0$ **b.** $a = 0$ **c.** $a < 0$ **49.** no; $x = \pm\sqrt{\frac{1}{2}}$, irrational **51.** yes; $x = \pm\frac{1}{2}$, rational **55.** H **57.** $\pm\frac{1}{4}$ **59.** $\pm\frac{8}{11}$

8-8

Check It Out! 1a. 36 **1b.** $\frac{25}{4}$ **1c.** 16 **2a.** $-9, -1$ **2b.** $4 \pm \sqrt{21}$ **3a.** $-\frac{1}{3}, 2$ **3b.** no real solutions **4.** 16.4 ft by 24.4 ft

Exercises 3. 4 **5.** $-5, -1$ **7.** $-6, 5$ **9.** $1, 9$ **11.** $\frac{-5 \pm 3\sqrt{5}}{2}$ **13.** no real solutions **15.** $4 \pm \sqrt{10}$ **17.** 7.2 m; 11.2 m **19.** 1 **21.** $-2, 12$ **23.** $-13, -2$ **25.** $-6, 8$ **27.** $-2, 3$ **29.** $\frac{-1 \pm \sqrt{5}}{2}$ **31.** $\frac{-15 \pm \sqrt{105}}{2}$ **33.** 4 in. **35.** $1 \pm \sqrt{7}$ **37.** $-3, \frac{1}{2}$ **39.** $-10, 2$ **41.** 81 **43.** $\frac{49}{4}$ **45.** 9 **47a.** $(10 + 2x)(24 + 2x) = 640$ **b.** 3 ft **51.** $-6 \pm \sqrt{26}$ **53.** -6 **55.** no real solutions **57.** no real solutions **61a.** $-16t^2 + 64t + 32 = 0$ **b.** 4 **c.** 4.4 s **63.** B **65.** B **67.** $-\frac{3}{2}, \frac{2}{3}$ **69.** $-\frac{2}{3} - \frac{\sqrt{7}}{3}, -\frac{2}{3} + \frac{\sqrt{7}}{3}$ **71.** $0, -\frac{b}{a}$

8-9

Check It Out! 1a. $2, -\frac{1}{3}$ **1b.** $2, -\frac{1}{5}$ **2.** $\frac{8 - \sqrt{56}}{4} \approx 0.13$, $\frac{8 + \sqrt{56}}{4} \approx 3.87$ **3a.** 0 **3b.** 1 **3c.** 2 **4.** No; for the equation $45 = -16t^2 + 20t + 0$, the discriminant is negative, so the weight will not ring the bell. **5a.** $-2, -5$ **5b.** $-2, 7$

5c. $\frac{-4 - \sqrt{184}}{4} \approx -4.39$, $\frac{-4 + \sqrt{184}}{4} \approx 2.39$

Exercises 1. no **3.** $\frac{1}{2}, 3$ **5.** $-4, -10$ **7.** $-\frac{1}{2}, \frac{3}{2}$ **9.** $\frac{-6 - \sqrt{24}}{2} \approx -5.45, \frac{-6 - \sqrt{24}}{2}$ ≈ -0.55 **11.** $\frac{-1 - \sqrt{61}}{6} \approx 1.14, \frac{-1 + \sqrt{61}}{6} \approx$ -1.47 **13.** $\frac{-1 - \sqrt{41}}{4} \approx -1.85$, $\frac{-1 + \sqrt{41}}{4} \approx 1.35$ **15.** 1 **17.** 0 **19.** 2 **21.** 0 **23.** yes **25.** -3 **27.** $-\frac{1}{2}$ **29.** $-3, \frac{3}{2}$ **31.** $1, 9$ **33.** $\frac{4 - \sqrt{12}}{2} \approx 0.27$, $\frac{4 + \sqrt{12}}{2} \approx 3.73$ **35.** $\frac{-7 - \sqrt{17}}{4} \approx 2.78$, $\frac{-7 + \sqrt{17}}{4} \approx -0.72$ **37.** 2 **39.** no **41.** $-5, 3$ **43.** no real solutions **45.** 2 solutions; $-2, \frac{1}{4}$ **47.** 1 solution; $\frac{2}{3}$ **49.** 2 x-intercepts; $\frac{7}{2}, -3$ **51.** 1 x-intercept; 5 **57.** A **59a.** 1 **b.** -1 **c.** -1 **d.** -1

8-10

Check It Out! 1. $(1, 2), (4, 5)$ **2.** $(-1, 7), (1, 1)$ **3a.** $(3, 4), (-1, -4)$ **3b.** $(5, 10), (-0.5, -3.75)$ **4.** 2.5 s

Exercises 1. nonlinear **3.** $(1, 1)$, $(3, 3)$ **5.** $(3, 0), (2, -1)$ **7.** $(1, -2), (3, 6)$ **9.** 4.75 s **11.** $(0, -3)$ **13.** $(3, -3)$, $(4, 3)$ **15.** $(3, 15), (-2, 5)$ **17.** $(3, 39)$, $\left(-\frac{3}{5}, 3\right)$ **19.** $(0, -5), \left(\frac{1}{3}, -\frac{44}{9}\right)$ **21.** $(1, 6), (3, 24)$ **23.** 5 mo **25.** 100 **27.** no **29.** yes **31.** yes **33.** no **37.** B; the left side of the equation was multiplied by -3, but the right side was not. **39.** H **41.** G **43.** $\frac{-3 \pm \sqrt{153}}{-4}$ **45.** $\frac{7 \pm \sqrt{161}}{8}$ **47.** 1 s

Study Guide: Review

1. vertex **2.** zero of a function **3.** Yes; it is in standard form. **4.** No; $a = 0$ **5.** Yes; it is in standard form. **6.** No; a quadratic function does not have a power of x greater than 2.

7.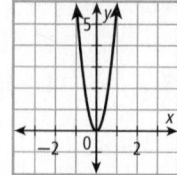

8.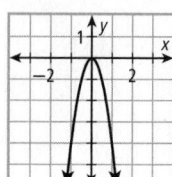

9.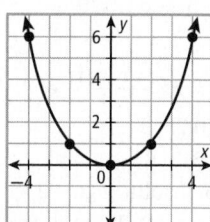

10.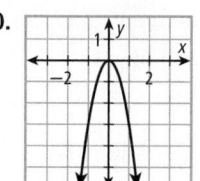

11. upward **12.** downward
13. −5 and 2 **14.** −1 and 2

15.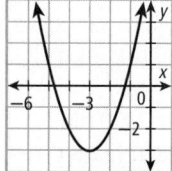

16.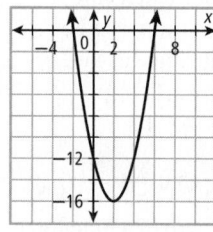

17.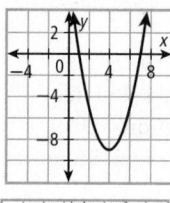

18.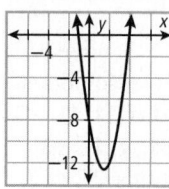

19.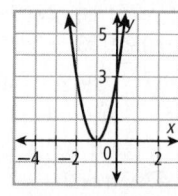

20.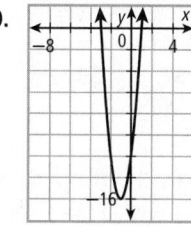

21.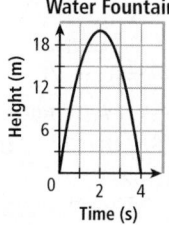

In 2 seconds, the water reaches its maximum height of 20 meters. It takes a total of 4 seconds for the water to reach the ground. **22.** $g(x)$, $f(x)$ **23.** The graphs have the same width. **24.** $h(x)$, $f(x)$, $g(x)$ **25.** same width, same axis of symmetry, opens upward, vertex translated 5 units up **26.** narrower, same axis of symmetry, opens upward, vertex translated 1 unit down **27.** narrower, same axis of symmetry, opens upward, vertex translated 3 units up **28.** $x = -3$ or $x = -1$ **29.** $x = -3$ **30.** no real solutions **31.** $x = 1$ or $x = 5$ **32.** $x = 4$ **33.** $x = 1$ or $x = -1$ **34.** no real solutions **35.** $x = -5$ or $x = -1$ **36.** $x = -7$ or $x = -2$ **37.** $x = -3$ or $x = 5$ **38.** $x = -1$ or $x = 2$ **39.** $x = -5$ **40.** $x = 4.5$ **41.** $x^2 + 2x = 48$; 6 ft **42.** $x = -8$ or $x = 8$ **43.** $x = -12$ or $x = 12$ **44.** no real solutions **45.** $x = 0$ **46.** $x = -5$ or $x = 5$ **47.** $x = -\frac{5}{2}$ or $x = \frac{5}{2}$ **48.** 4 ft **49.** $x = -8$ or $x = 6$ **50.** $x = -7$ or $x = 3$ **51.** $x = 1$ or $x = 5$ **52.** $x = 5 \pm \sqrt{5}$ **53.** 16 ft by 12 ft **54.** $x = -1$ or $x = 6$ **55.** $x = -\frac{1}{2}$ or $x = 5$ **56.** $x = 1$ **57.** $x = \frac{6 \pm \sqrt{8}}{2}$ **58.** 1 **59.** 0 **60.** 2 **61.** 2 **62.** $(-3, 5)$, $(1, -3)$ **63.** $(1, -3)$, $(4, 3)$ **64.** $(-2, -2)$, $(-5, 4)$

Mastering the Standards

for Mathematical Practice

The topics described in the Standards for Mathematical Content will vary from year to year. However, the *way* in which you learn, study, and think about mathematics will not. The Standards for Mathematical Practice describe skills that you will use in all of your math courses.

> **Mathematical Practices**
>
> 1. *Make sense of problems and persevere in solving them.*
> 2. *Reason abstractly and quantitatively.*
> 3. *Construct viable arguments and critique the reasoning of others.*
> 4. *Model with mathematics.*
> 5. *Use appropriate tools strategically.*
> 6. *Attend to precision.*
> 7. *Look for and make use of structure.*
> 8. *Look for and express regularity in repeated reasoning.*

④ Model with mathematics.

Mathematically proficient students can apply... mathematics... to... problems... in everyday life, society, and the workplace...

In your book

Multi-Step Test Prep and **Real-World Connections** apply mathematics to other disciplines and in real-world scenarios.

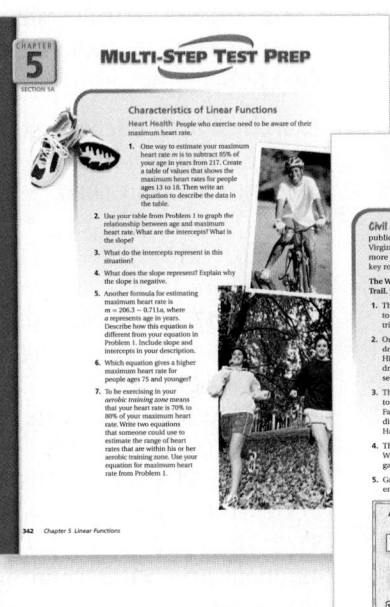

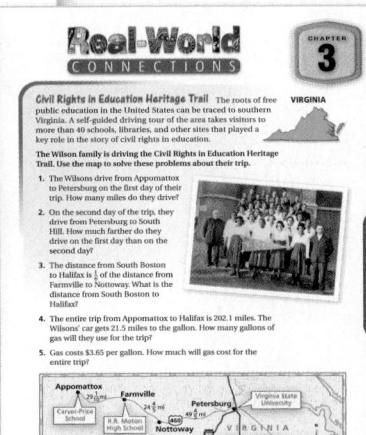

9-1

Check It Out! **1a.** 80, −160, 320
1b. 216, 162, 121.5 **2.** 7.8125
3. $1342.18

Exercises 3. 25, 12.5, 6.25
5. 1,000,000,000 **7.** 4 **9.** 162, 243,
364.5 **11.** 2058; 14,406; 100,842
13. $\frac{5}{32}, \frac{5}{128}, \frac{5}{512}$ **15.** 0.0000000001, or
1×10^{-10} **17.** 80; 160 **19.** $\frac{1}{3}$ **21.** $\frac{1}{7}; \frac{1}{49}$
23. 6; −48 **25.** 4913 **27.** yes; $\frac{1}{3}$ **29.** no
31. no **33a.** 1.28 cm **b.** 40.96 cm
35. −2, −8, −32, −128
37. 2, 4, 8, 16 **39.** 12, 3, $\frac{3}{4}, \frac{3}{16}$
43a. $3993; $4392.30 **b.** 1.1
c. $2727.27 **45.** J **47.** x^4, x^5, x^6
49. 1, y, y^2 **51.** −400 **53.** the 7th
term

9-2

Check It Out! **1.** 3.375 in. **2a.** no
2b. yes

3a.

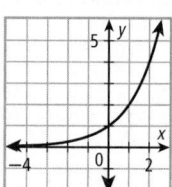

3b.

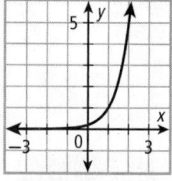

4a.

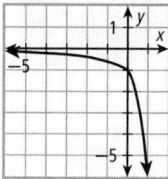

4b.

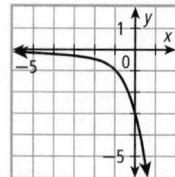

5a.

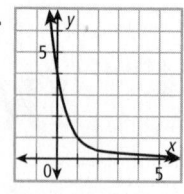

5b.

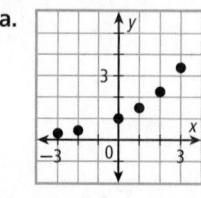

6. after about 13 yr

Exercises 1. no **3.** no **17.** about
2023 **19.** 289 ft **21.** yes **23.** no
35. $y = 4.8(2)^x$ **41.** −0.125
43a. $2000 **b.** 8% **c.** $2938.66
45. C **45.** C **47.** D **49.** 3 **51.** The
value of a is the y-intercept.

9-3

Check It Out! **1.** $y = 1200(1.08)^t$;
$1904.25 **2a.** $A = 1200(1.00875)^{4t}$;
$1379.49 **2b.** $A = 4000(1.0025)^{12t}$;
$5083.47 **3.** $y = 48,000(0.97)^t$; 38,783
4a. 1.5625 mg **4b.** 0.78125 g

Exercises 1. exponential growth
3. $y = 300(1.08)^t$; 441 **5.** $A =$
$4200(1.007)^{4t}$; $4965.43 **7.** $y =$
$10(0.84)^t$; 4.98 mg **9.** 5.5 g **11.** $y =$
$1600(1.03)^t$; 2150 **13.** $A = 30(1.078)^t$;
47 members **15.** $A = 7000(1.0075)^{4t}$;
$9438.44 **17.** $A = 12,000(1.026)^t$;
$17,635.66 **19.** $y = 58(0.9)^t$; $24.97
21. growth; 61% **23.** decay; $33\frac{1}{3}$%
25. growth; 10% **27.** growth; 25%
29. $y = 58,000,000(1.001)^t$;
58,174,174 **31.** $y = 8200(0.98)^t$;
$7118.63 **33.** $y = 970(1.012)^t$; 1030
35. B **37.** 18 yr **39.** A; B **45.** D **47.** D
49. about 20 yr **51.** 100 min, or 1 h
40 min **53.** $225,344

9-4

Check It Out!

1a.

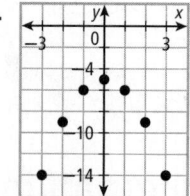

exponential

1b.

quadratic
2. quadratic **3.** The oven
temperature decreases by 50 °F
every 10 min; $y = -5x + 375$; 75 °F

Exercises 1. exponential
3. linear **5.** exponential **7.** Grapes
cost $1.79/lb; $y = 1.79x$; $10.74
11. linear **13.** exponential
15. $\ell = 6k$; linear **17.** linear
19. $y = 0.2(4)^x$ **21.** linear **27.** C
29. C

9-5

Check It Out! **1.** Slope: Dave is
saving at a higher rate ($12/wk)
than Arturo ($8/wk); y-int.: Dave
started with more money ($30)
than Arturo ($24). **2.** A increased
about $1.67/yr; B increased about
$1.13/yr. **3.** Rosetta's new model:
max ht. = 30.25 ft; length = 110 ft;
avg. steepness over [0, 20] = 0.9;
new bridge is taller, longer, and
steeper over [0, 20] than Marco's.
4. A: $y = 100x + 850$; B: $y =$
$850(1.08)^x$; school A's enrollment
will exceed school B's enrollment
at first, but school B will have
more students by the end of the
11th year. After that, school B's
enrollment exceeds school A's
enrollment by ever-increasing
amounts each year.

Exercises 1. Slope: Kara is
withdrawing at a higher rate ($75/
wk) than Fay ($50/wk); y-int.: Kara
started with more money ($500)
than Fay ($425). **3.** A: x-int. = 0, 4;
max. = 8; avg. rate of chg. over
[0, 2] = 4; B: x-int. = 0, 6; max. = 9;
avg. rate of chg. over [0, 2] = 4; B is
taller and wider. Both are equally
steep over [0, 2].

5. Slope: Darius is hiking faster (2.2 mi/h) than Kevin (2 mi/h); *y*-int.: Kevin started farther from camp (1.5 mi) than Darius (1 mi). **7.** A: *x*-int. = 0, 5; max = 100; avg. rate of chg. over [0, 2] = 48; B: *x*-int. = 0, 4; max = 64; avg. rate of chg. over [0, 2] = 32. A is faster, will go higher, and covers more horizontal distance than B.
13. A

15a.

	A	B
[0, 4]	8	−3.75
[0, 6]	6	−10.5
[4, 6]	2	−24
[7, 10]	−5	−298.7
[8, 12]	−8	−960

15b. A: rate of chg. is pos. and decreasing until (6, 36), when it becomes neg. and decreasing. B has ever-decreasing neg. rate of chg. **15c.** It is halved.

Study Guide: Review

1. geometric sequences
2. exponential decay **3.** common ratio **4.** exponential function
5. 81, 243, 729 **6.** 48, −96, 192
7. 5, 2.5, 1.25 **8.** −256, −1024, −4096
9. 7,812,500 **10.** 19,131,876 **11.** yes
12. no

13.

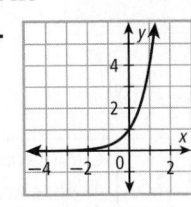

14.

15. $y = 9(1.15)^t$; 24
16. $y = 24,500(0.96)^t$; 3182
17. quadratic **18.** linear
19. exponential **20.** exponential
21. quadratic **22.** linear
23. $y = 1.5x$; 15 h **24.** The slope of Function 1 is $\frac{4}{7}$. The slope of Function 2 is $\frac{2}{5}$. Function 1 is increasing at a greater rate.
25. Function 1 has a maximum value of 6. Function 2 has a maximum value of 2. So Function 1 has the greater maximum value.
26. The population of Bird B is increasing more rapidly, but starts at a smaller population; Bird A: 44 birds per month; Bird B: 372 birds per month.

10-1

Check It Out! 1a. bread
1b. cheese and mayonnaise
2. 2001, 2002, and 2005; about
13,000 **3.** about 18 °F **4.** Prices
increased from January through
July or August, and then prices
decreased through November.
5. 31.25%
6.

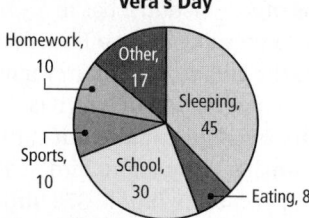

Vera's Day

Homework, 10; Other, 17; Sleeping, 45; Sports, 10; School, 30; Eating, 8

A circle graph shows parts of a
whole.

Exercises 1. one part of a whole
3. 82 animals **5.** $15 **7.** Prices at
stadium A are greater than prices at
stadium B. **9.** between weeks 4 and
5 **11.** 18% **13.** purple **15.** blue and
green **17.** 225,000 **19.** Friday
21. 3.5 times **23.** games 3, 4, and 5
25. Stock Y changed the most
between April and July of 2004.
27. $8\frac{1}{3}$% **31.** double line **33.** circle
35a. Greece; about 40% **b.** United
States; about 15% **37.** D **41.** 19
girls

10-2

Check It Out!

1.

Temperature (°C)

Stem	Leaves
0	7
1	9
2	2 3 6 7 9
3	0 1 1 2 4 5 6 6

Key: 1|9 means 19

2.

Interval	Frequency
4–6	5
7–9	4
10–12	4
13–15	2

3.

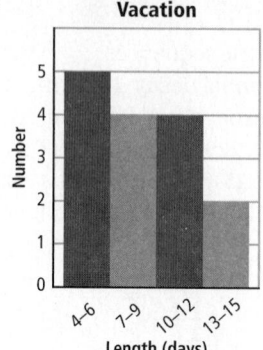

Vacation

Number vs. Length (days): 4–6, 7–9, 10–12, 13–15

4a.

Interval	Frequency	Cumulative Frequency
28–31	2	2
32–35	7	9
36–39	5	14
40–43	3	17

4b. 9

Exercises 1. stem-and-leaf plot
3.

Austin	Stem	New York
9 9 9	1	
4 3 2 1	2	
6 5 3 2 0	3	1 3 3 3 6 6 7 9
	4	1 1 2 2

5.

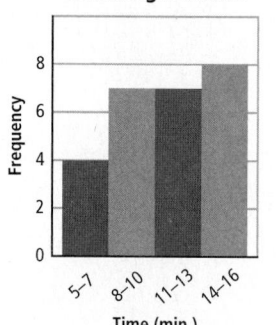

Breathing Intervals

Frequency vs. Time (min.): 5–7, 8–10, 11–13, 14–16

7.

Summer	Stem	Winter
	0	4 9 9
	1	1 2 3 4 9 9
9 7 7 6 5 5 3 3 2 2	2	1 7
	3	0 3 5
	4	
9 7 4 3	5	

Key: |2|1 means 21
7|2| means 27

9.

Interval	Frequency
2.0–2.4	2
2.5–2.9	7
3.0–3.4	5
3.5–3.9	3

11a.

Interval	Frequency	Cumulative Frequency
36–38	4	4
39–41	6	10
42–44	5	15
45–47	1	16

b. 10

15a.

Interval	Frequency
160–169.9	2
170–179.9	4
180–189.9	3
190–199.9	1
200–209.9	2
210–219.9	1

19. G **21.** 8; 8; 41; 66

10-3

Check It Out! 1. mean: 14 lb;
median: 14 lb; modes: 12 lb and
16 lb; range: 4 lb **2.** 3; the outlier
decreases the mean by 3.7 and
increases the range by 18. It has no
effect on the median and mode.
3a. mode: 7 **3b.** Median: 81; the
median is greater than either the
mean or the mode.

4.

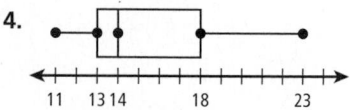

11 13 14   18   23

5a. The data set for 2000; the
distance between the points for the
least and greatest values is less for
2000 than for 2007. **5b.** about $40
million

Exercises **3.** mean: 31.5; median: 33.5; mode: 44; range: 32 **5.** mean: 78.25; median: 78; mode: 78; range: 15 **7.** 13; the outlier decreases the mean by 11.15 and the median by 4. It increases the range by 51 and has no effect on the mode.
9. Median: 83; the median is greater than the mean, and there is no mode. **13.** Simon; about 3000 points **15.** mean: 2.5; median: 2.5; modes: 2 and 3; range: 3 **17.** mean: 60; median: 60; mode: 60; range: 5
19. 23; the outlier increases the mean by 3, the median by 2.5, and the range by 15. It has no effect on the mode. **21.** Mean: 153; the mean is greater than the median, and there is no mode. **25.** Sneaks R Us; the middle half of the data doesn't vary as much at Sneaks R Us as at Jump N Run. **27.** mean: 5.5; median: 5.5; mode: none; range: 9 **29.** mean: 3.5; median: 3.4; mode: none; range: 5.3
31. mean: 24.4; median: 25; modes: 23 and 25; range: 3 **33.** mean: $15\frac{1}{6}$; median: $12\frac{1}{2}$; mode: none; range: 35 **37.** sometimes **39.** always
41. Median; the mean is affected by the outlier of 1218, and there is no mode. **43.** Median or mode; the store wants their prices to seem low, and the median and mode are both $2.80 less than the mean. **49.** Mean: $32,000; median: $25,000; median; the outlier of $78,000 increases the mean significantly. **51.** 96 **53.** increase the mean; decrease the mean **55.** G **57.** The mean decreases by 6.6 lb.

10-4

Check It Out! **1.** Possible answer: company D; the fertilizer from company D appears to be more effective than the other fertilizers. **2.** Possible answer: taxi drivers; the drivers could justify charging higher rates by using this graph, which seems to show that gas prices have increased

dramatically. **3.** Possible answer: Smith; Smith might want to show that he or she got many more votes than Atkins or Napier. **4.** The sample size is much too small.

Exercises **3a.** The vertical scale does not start at 0, and the categories on the horizontal scale are not at equal time intervals.
b. Possible answer: Tourism is decreasing rapidly. **5.** The sample size is too small. **7a.** The vertical scale does not start at 0.
b. Possible answer: Single men pay significantly more than single women.
9a. The sectors of the graph do not add to 100%.
b. Possible answer: Nearly half of the state's spending was for welfare. **15.** B

10-5

Check It Out! **1.** sample space: {1, 2, 3, 4, 5, 6}; outcome shown: 3 **2.** certain **3a.** $\frac{7}{20}$ **3b.** $\frac{13}{20}$ **4a.** 99.8% **4b.** 34,930

Exercises **3.** sample space: {blue, red, yellow, green}; outcome shown:red **5.** impossible **7.** unlikely
9. $\frac{3}{5}$ **11a.** 30% **b.** 54 **13.** sample space: {blue, red, yellow}; outcome shown: blue **15.** as likely as not **17.** likely **19.** $\frac{6}{25}$ **21a.** 5% **b.** 21 **27.** about 1%; about 57 **29.** B **31.** B **33.** as likely as not **35.** unlikely **37a.** 7 **b.** 8

10-6

Check It Out! **1a.** 50% **1b.** $33\frac{1}{3}$% **2.** 0.4 **3.** $\frac{1}{25}$

Exercises **1.** complement **3.** 25% **5.** $\frac{1}{2}$ **7.** $\frac{2}{3}$ **9.** $\frac{9}{10}$ **11.** 1:12 **13.** $\frac{1}{4}$ **15.** 50% **17.** $\frac{5}{9}$ **19.** 70% **21.** $\frac{9}{10}$ **23.** $\frac{1}{5}$ **25.** $\frac{4}{5}$ **27.** 4:1 **31.** $\frac{1}{2}$ **35.** D **37.** B

10-7

Check It Out! **1a.** Independent; the result of rolling the number cube the first time does not affect the result of the second roll.
1b. Dependent; choosing the first student leaves fewer students to choose from the second time. **2.** $\frac{1}{4}$
3. $\frac{8}{87}$

Exercises **1.** dependent
3. independent **5.** independent
7. $\frac{1}{8}$ **9.** $\frac{1}{6}$ **11.** $\frac{1}{16}$ **13.** $\frac{2}{7}$
15. dependent **17.** $\frac{1}{8}$ **19.** $\frac{1}{12}$
21. $\frac{2}{9}$ **23a.** $\frac{27}{64}$ **b.** $\frac{1}{64}$ **25.** dependent
27. independent **29a.** $\frac{3}{20}$ **b.** $\frac{1}{6}$
c. $\frac{9}{100}$ **d.** $\frac{1}{15}$ **31.** $\frac{2}{15}$ **35.** D **37.** A
39. 72.9% **41.** 80% **43.** 48%

Study Guide: Review

1. outcome **2.** interquartile range
3. independent events **4.** 2003
5. 14 more boys

6.

Stem	Leaves
0	1 7 9
1	2 4 8 9
2	2 2 4 8

Key: 1|2 means 12

7.

Comedy Camp		Days and Days
2	6	
	7	
3 1	8	0 2
	9	
4 4 2	10	3 5 9
	11	
6 2 0	12	8
	13	2 5 9

Key: |12|8 means 128
4|10| means 104

8.

Gas Tank Capacities		
Capacity	Tally	Frequency
10–14	‖‖ ‖	6
15–19	‖‖ ‖‖	10
20–24	‖‖	3
25–29	‖‖	3

9.

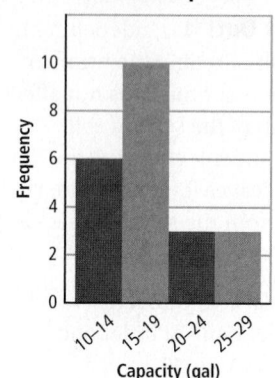

Gas Tank Capacities

10. mean: 14; median: 12; mode: 12; range: 28 **11.** Median; the mean is higher than 4 of the 5 prices; the mode is the lowest price.

12.

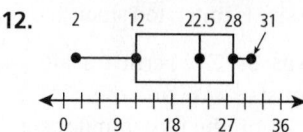

13. The scale on the vertical axis is too large. This makes the slopes of the segments less steep.

14. Someone might believe that the price has been relatively stable when in fact it has doubled.

15. 99.5% **16.** 24,875 **17.** 250 **18.** $\frac{1}{2}$

19. $\frac{1}{4}$ **20.** $\frac{5}{8}$ **21.** independent

22. independent **23.** dependent

24. $\frac{2048}{9555}$ **25.** 0 **26.** $\frac{256}{2401}$

Glossary/Glosario

Learn It Online
Multilingual Glossary

ENGLISH	SPANISH	EXAMPLES
absolute value The absolute value of x is the distance from zero to x on a number line, denoted $|x|$. $$|x| = \begin{cases} x & \text{if } x \geq 0 \\ -x & \text{if } x < 0 \end{cases}$$	**valor absoluto** El valor absoluto de x es la distancia de cero a x en una recta numérica, y se expresa $|x|$. $$|x| = \begin{cases} x & \text{si } x \geq 0 \\ -x & \text{si } x < 0 \end{cases}$$	$|3| = 3$ $|-3| = 3$
absolute-value equation An equation that contains absolute-value expressions.	**ecuación de valor absoluto** Ecuación que contiene expresiones de valor absoluto.	$|x + 4| = 7$
absolute-value function A function whose rule contains absolute-value expressions.	**función de valor absoluto** Función cuya regla contiene expresiones de valor absoluto.	$y = |x + 4|$
absolute-value inequality An inequality that contains absolute-value expressions.	**desigualdad de valor absoluto** Desigualdad que contiene expresiones de valor absoluto.	$|x + 4| > 7$
accuracy The closeness of a given measurement or value to the actual measurement or value.	**exactitud** Cercanía de una medida o un valor a la medida o el valor real.	
acute angle An angle that measures greater than 0° and less than 90°.	**ángulo agudo** Ángulo que mide más de 0° y menos de 90°.	
acute triangle A triangle with three acute angles.	**triángulo acutángulo** Triángulo con tres ángulos agudos.	
Addition Property of Equality For real numbers a, b, and c, if $a = b$, then $a + c = b + c$.	**Propiedad de igualdad de la suma** Dados los números reales a, b y c, si $a = b$, entonces $a + c = b + c$.	$\begin{aligned} x - 6 &= 8 \\ +6 & +6 \\ \hline x &= 14 \end{aligned}$
Addition Property of Inequality For real numbers a, b, and c, if $a < b$, then $a + c < b + c$. Also holds true for $>$, $\leq$, $\geq$, and $\neq$.	**Propiedad de desigualdad de la suma** Dados los números reales a, b y c, si $a < b$, entonces $a + c < b + c$. Es válido también para $>$, $\leq$, $\geq$ y $\neq$.	$\begin{aligned} x - 6 &< 8 \\ +6 & +6 \\ \hline x &< 14 \end{aligned}$
additive inverse The opposite of a number. Two numbers are additive inverses if their sum is zero.	**inverso aditivo** El opuesto de un número. Dos números son inversos aditivos si su suma es cero.	The additive inverse of 5 is −5. The additive inverse of −5 is 5.

ENGLISH	SPANISH	EXAMPLES

AND A logical operator representing the intersection of two sets.

Y Operador lógico que representa la intersección de dos conjuntos.

$A = \{2, 3, 4, 5\}$ $B = \{1, 3, 5, 7\}$
The set of values that are in A AND B is $A \cap B = \{3, 5\}$.

---

angle A figure formed by two rays with a common endpoint.

ángulo Figura formada por dos rayos con un extremo común.

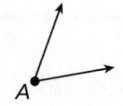

---

area The number of nonoverlapping unit squares of a given size that will exactly cover the interior of a plane figure.

área Cantidad de cuadrados unitarios de un determinado tamaño no superpuestos que cubren exactamente el interior de una figura plana.

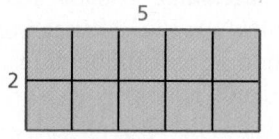

The area is 10 square units.

---

arithmetic sequence A sequence whose successive terms differ by the same nonzero number d, called the *common difference*.

sucesión aritmética Sucesión cuyos términos sucesivos difieren en el mismo número distinto de cero d, denominado *diferencia común*.

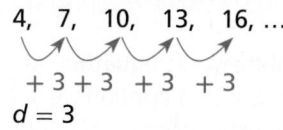

4, 7, 10, 13, 16, …
$+3\ +3\ +3\ +3$
$d = 3$

Associative Property of Addition For all numbers a, b, and c, $(a + b) + c = a + (b + c)$.

Propiedad asociativa de la suma Dados tres números cualesquiera a, b y c, $(a + b) + c = a + (b + c)$.

$(5 + 3) + 7 = 5 + (3 + 7)$

Associative Property of Multiplication For all numbers a, b, and c, $(a \cdot b) \cdot c = a \cdot (b \cdot c)$.

Propiedad asociativa de la multiplicación Dados tres números cualesquiera a, b y c, $(a \cdot b) \cdot c = a \cdot (b \cdot c)$.

$(5 \cdot 3) \cdot 7 = 5 \cdot (3 \cdot 7)$

---

asymptote A line that a graph gets closer to as the value of a variable becomes extremely large or small.

asíntota Línea recta a la cual se aproxima una gráfica a medida que el valor de una variable se hace sumamente grande o pequeño.

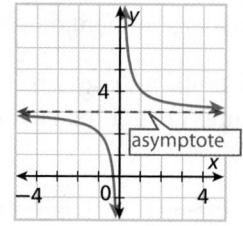

---

average *See* mean.

promedio *Ver* media.

---

axis of a coordinate plane One of two perpendicular number lines, called the *x*-axis and the *y*-axis, used to define the location of a point in a coordinate plane.

eje de un plano cartesiano Una de las dos rectas numéricas perpendiculares, denominadas eje *x* y eje *y*, utilizadas para definir la ubicación de un punto en un plano cartesiano.

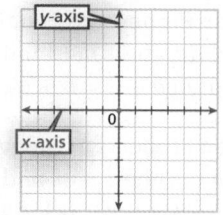

---

axis of symmetry A line that divides a plane figure or a graph into two congruent reflected halves.

eje de simetría Línea que divide una figura plana o una gráfica en dos mitades reflejadas congruentes.

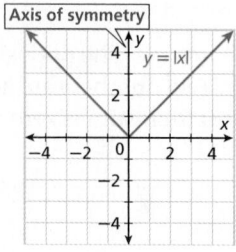

Glossary/Glosario

ENGLISH	SPANISH	EXAMPLES

back-to-back stem-and-leaf plot (A graph used to organize and compare two sets of data so that the frequencies can be compared. *See also* stem-and-leaf plot.

diagrama doble de tallo y hojas Gráfica utilizada para organizar y comparar dos conjuntos de datos para poder comparar las frecuencias. *Ver también* diagrama de tallo y hojas.

Data set A: 9, 12, 14, 16, 23, 27
Data set B: 6, 8, 10, 13, 15, 16, 21

Set A		Set B
9	0	6 8
6 4 2	1	0 3 5 6
7 3	2	1

Key: |2|1 means 21
7|2| means 27

---

bar graph A graph that uses vertical or horizontal bars to display data.

gráfica de barras Gráfica con barras horizontales o verticales para mostrar datos.

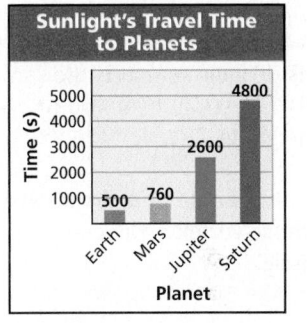

---

base of a power The number in a power that is used as a factor.

base de una potencia Número de una potencia que se utiliza como factor.

$3^4 = 3 \cdot 3 \cdot 3 \cdot 3 = 81$
3 is the base.

---

base of an exponential function The value of b in a function of the form $f(x) = ab^x$, where a and b are real numbers with $a \neq 0$, $b > 0$, and $b \neq 1$.

base de una función exponencial Valor de b en una función del tipo $f(x) = ab^x$, donde a y b son números reales con $a \neq 0$, $b > 0$ y $b \neq 1$.

In the function $f(x) = 5(2)^x$, the base is 2.

---

biased sample A sample that does not fairly represent the population.

muestra no representativa Muestra que no representa adecuadamente una población.

To find out about the exercise habits of average Americans, a fitness magazine surveyed its readers about how often they exercise. The population is all Americans and the sample is readers of the fitness magazine. This sample will likely be biased because readers of fitness magazines may exercise more often than other people do.

---

binomial A polynomial with two terms.

binomio Polinomio con dos términos.

$x + y$
$2a^2 + 3$
$4m^3n^2 + 6mn^4$

---

boundary line A line that divides a coordinate plane into two half-planes.

línea de límite Línea que divide un plano cartesiano en dos semiplanos.

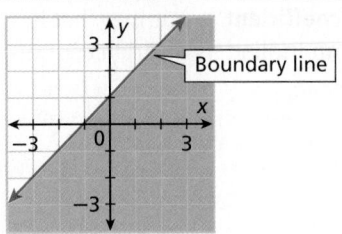

---

box-and-whisker plot A method of showing how data are distributed by using the median, quartiles, and minimum and maximum values; also called a *box plot*.

gráfica de mediana y rango Método para mostrar la distribución de datos utilizando la mediana, los cuartiles y los valores mínimo y máximo; también llamado *gráfica de caja*.

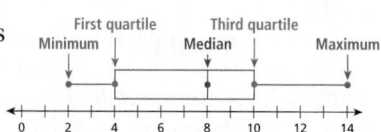

C

Cartesian coordinate system *See* coordinate plane.

sistema de coordenadas cartesianas *Ver* plano cartesiano.

center of a circle The point inside a circle that is the same distance from every point on the circle.

centro de un círculo Punto dentro de un círculo que se encuentra a la misma distancia de todos los puntos del círculo.

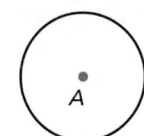

central angle of a circle An angle whose vertex is the center of a circle.

ángulo central de un círculo Ángulo cuyo vértice es el centro de un círculo.

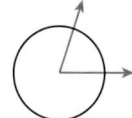

circle The set of points in a plane that are a fixed distance from a given point called the center of the circle.

círculo Conjunto de puntos en un plano que se encuentran a una distancia fija de un punto determinado denominado centro del círculo.

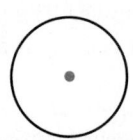

circle graph A way to display data by using a circle divided into non-overlapping sectors.

gráfica circular Forma de mostrar datos mediante un círculo dividido en sectores no superpuestos.

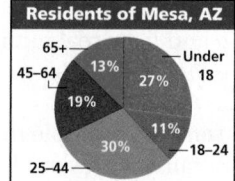

circumference The distance around a circle.

circunferencia Distancia alrededor de un círculo.

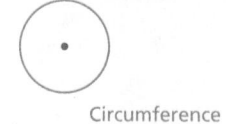

Circumference

closure A set of numbers is said to be closed, or to have closure, under a given operation if the result of the operation on any two numbers in the set is also in the set.

cerradura Se dice que un conjunto de números es cerrado, o tiene cerradura, respecto de una operación determinada, si el resultado de la operación entre dos números cualesquiera del conjunto también está en el conjunto.

The natural numbers are closed under addition because the sum of two natural numbers is always a natural number.

coefficient A number that is multiplied by a variable.

coeficiente Número que se multiplica por una variable.

In the expression $2x + 3y$, 2 is the coefficient of x and 3 is the coefficient of y.

ENGLISH	SPANISH	EXAMPLES
common difference In an arithmetic sequence, the nonzero constant difference of any term and the previous term.	**diferencia común** En una sucesión aritmética, diferencia constante distinta de cero entre cualquier término y el término anterior.	In the arithmetic sequence 3, 5, 7, 9, 11, ..., the common difference is 2.
common factor A factor that is common to all terms of an expression or to two or more expressions.	**factor común** Factor que es común a todos los términos de una expresión o a dos o más expresiones.	Expression: $4x^2 + 16x^3 - 8x$ Common factor: $4x$ Expressions: 12 and 18 Common factors: 2, 3, and 6
common ratio In a geometric sequence, the constant ratio of any term and the previous term.	**razón común** En una sucesión geométrica, la razón constante entre cualquier término y el término anterior.	In the geometric sequence 32, 16, 8, 4, 2, . . ., the common ratio is $\frac{1}{2}$.
Commutative Property of Addition For any two numbers a and b, $a + b = b + a$.	**Propiedad conmutativa de la suma** Dados dos números cualesquiera a y b, $a + b = b + a$.	$3 + 4 = 4 + 3 = 7$
Commutative Property of Multiplication For any two numbers a and b, $a \cdot b = b \cdot a$.	**Propiedad conmutativa de la multiplicación** Dados dos números cualesquiera a y b, $a \cdot b = b \cdot a$.	$3 \cdot 4 = 4 \cdot 3 = 12$
complement of an event The set of all outcomes that are not the event.	**complemento de un suceso** Todos los resultados que no están en el suceso.	In the experiment of rolling a number cube, the complement of rolling a 3 is rolling a 1, 2, 4, 5, or 6.
complementary angles Two angles whose measures have a sum of 90°.	**ángulos complementarios** Dos ángulos cuyas medidas suman 90°.	
completing the square A process used to form a perfect-square trinomial. To complete the square of $x^2 + bx$, add $\left(\frac{b}{2}\right)^2$.	**completar el cuadrado** Proceso utilizado para formar un trinomio cuadrado perfecto. Para completar el cuadrado de $x^2 + bx$, hay que sumar $\left(\frac{b}{2}\right)^2$.	$x^2 + 6x + \blacksquare$ Add $\left(\frac{6}{2}\right)^2 = 9$. $x^2 + 6x + 9$
complex fraction A fraction that contains one or more fractions in the numerator, the denominator, or both.	**fracción compleja** Fracción que contiene una o más fracciones en el numerador, en el denominador, o en ambos.	$\dfrac{\frac{1}{2}}{1 + \frac{2}{3}}$
composite figure A plane figure made up of triangles, rectangles, trapezoids, circles, and other simple shapes, or a three-dimensional figure made up of prisms, cones, pyramids, cylinders, and other simple three-dimensional figures.	**figura compuesta** Figura plana compuesta por triángulos, rectángulos, trapecios, círculos y otras figuras simples, o figura tridimensional compuesta por prismas, conos, pirámides, cilindros y otras figuras tridimensionales simples.	

ENGLISH	SPANISH	EXAMPLES
compound event An event made up of two or more simple events.	**suceso compuesto** Suceso formado por dos o más sucesos simples.	In the experiment of tossing a coin and rolling a number cube, the event of the coin landing heads and the number cube landing on 3.
compound inequality Two inequalities that are combined into one statement by the word *and* or *or*.	**desigualdad compuesta** Dos desigualdades unidas en un enunciado por la palabra *y* u *o*.	$x \geq 2$ AND $x < 7$ (also written $2 \leq x < 7$) $x < 2$ OR $x > 6$
compound interest Interest earned or paid on both the principal and previously earned interest. The formula for compound interest is $A = P\left(1 + \frac{r}{n}\right)^{nt}$, where A is the final amount, P is the principal, r is the interest rate expressed as a decimal, n is the number of times interest is compounded, and t is the time.	**interés compuesto** Intereses ganados o pagados sobre el capital y los intereses ya devengados. La fórmula de interés compuesto es $A = P\left(1 + \frac{r}{n}\right)^{nt}$, donde A es la cantidad final, P es el capital, r es la tasa de interés expresada como un decimal, n es la cantidad de veces que se capitaliza el interés y t es el tiempo.	If \$100 is put into an account with an interest rate of 5% compounded monthly, then after 2 years, the account will have $100\left(1 + \frac{0.05}{12}\right)^{12 \cdot 2} = \$110.49$.
compound statement Two statements that are connected by the word *and* or *or*.	**enunciado compuesto** Dos enunciados unidos por la palabra *y* u *o*.	The sky is blue and the grass is green. I will drive to school or I will take the bus.
cone A three-dimensional figure with a circular base and a curved surface that connects the base to a point called the vertex.	**cono** Figura tridimensional con una base circular y una superficie lateral curva que conecta la base con un punto denominado vértice.	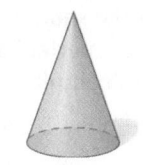
congruent Having the same size and shape, denoted by $\cong$.	**congruente** Que tiene el mismo tamaño y la misma forma, expresado por $\cong$.	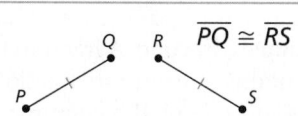
conjugate of an irrational number The conjugate of a number in the form $a + \sqrt{b}$ is $a - \sqrt{b}$.	**conjugado de un número irracional** El conjugado de un número en la forma $a + \sqrt{b}$ es $a - \sqrt{b}$.	The conjugate of $1 + \sqrt{2}$ is $1 - \sqrt{2}$.
consistent system A system of equations or inequalities that has at least one solution.	**sistema consistente** Sistema de ecuaciones o desigualdades que tiene por lo menos una solución.	$\begin{cases} x + y = 6 \\ x - y = 4 \end{cases}$ solution: $(5, 1)$
constant A value that does not change.	**constante** Valor que no cambia.	$3, 0, \pi$

Glossary/Glosario

ENGLISH	SPANISH	EXAMPLES
constant of variation The constant k in direct and inverse variation equations.	**constante de variación** La constante k en ecuaciones de variación directa e inversa.	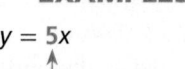$y = 5x$ constant of variation
continuous graph A graph made up of connected lines or curves.	**gráfica continua** Gráfica compuesta por líneas rectas o curvas conectadas.	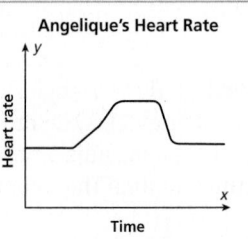
convenience sample A sample based on members of the population that are readily available.	**muestra de conveniencia** Una muestra basada en miembros de la población que están fácilmente disponibles.	A reporter surveys people he personally knows.
conversion factor The ratio of two equal quantities, each measured in different units.	**factor de conversión** Razón entre dos cantidades iguales, cada una medida en unidades diferentes.	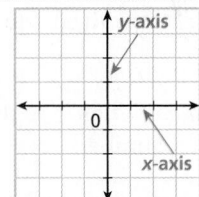$\dfrac{12 \text{ inches}}{1 \text{ foot}}$
coordinate plane A plane that is divided into four regions by a horizontal line called the x-axis and a vertical line called the y-axis.	**plano cartesiano** Plano dividido en cuatro regiones por una línea horizontal denominada eje x y una línea vertical denominada eje y.	
correlation A measure of the strength and direction of the relationship between two variables or data sets.	**correlación** Medida de la fuerza y dirección de la relación entre dos variables o conjuntos de datos.	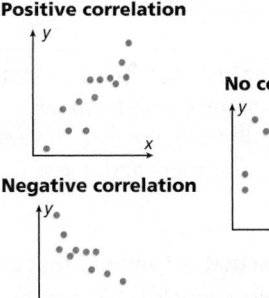
correlation coefficient A number r, where $-1 \le r \le 1$, that describes how closely the points in a scatter plot cluster around the least-squares line.	**coeficiente de correlación** Número r, donde $-1 \le r \le 1$, que describe a qué distancia de la recta de mínimos cuadrados se agrupan los puntos de un diagrama de dispersión.	An r-value close to 1 describes a strong positive correlation. An r-value close to 0 describes a weak correlation or no correlation. An r-value close to -1 describes a strong negative correlation.
corresponding angles of polygons Angles in the same relative position in polygons with an equal number of angles.	**ángulos correspondientes de los polígonos** Ángulos que se ubican en la misma posición relativa en polígonos que tienen el mismo número de ángulos.	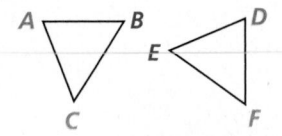 $\angle A$ and $\angle D$ are corresponding angles.

ENGLISH	SPANISH	EXAMPLES
corresponding sides of polygons Sides in the same relative position in polygons with an equal number of sides.	**lados correspondientes de los polígonos** Lados que se ubican en la misma posición relativa en polígonos que tienen el mismo número de lados.	$\overline{AB}$ and $\overline{DE}$ are corresponding sides.
cosine In a right triangle, the cosine of angle A is the ratio of the length of the leg adjacent to angle A to the length of the hypotenuse.	**coseno** En un triángulo rectángulo, el coseno del ángulo A es la razón entre la longitud del cateto adyacente al ángulo A y la longitud de la hipotenusa.	$\cos A = \dfrac{\text{adjacent}}{\text{hypotenuse}}$
cross products In the statement $\frac{a}{b} = \frac{c}{d}$, bc and ad are the cross products.	**productos cruzados** En el enunciado $\frac{a}{b} = \frac{c}{d}$, bc y ad son productos cruzados.	$\dfrac{1}{2} = \dfrac{3}{6}$ Cross products: $2 \cdot 3 = 6$ and $1 \cdot 6 = 6$
Cross Product Property For any real numbers a, b, c, and d, where $b \neq 0$ and $d \neq 0$, if $\frac{a}{b} = \frac{c}{d}$, then $ad = bc$.	**Propiedad de productos cruzados** Dados los números reales a, b, c y d, donde $b \neq 0$ y $d \neq 0$, si $\frac{a}{b} = \frac{c}{d}$, entonces $ad = bc$.	If $\dfrac{4}{6} = \dfrac{10}{x}$, then $4x = 60$, so $x = 15$.
cube A prism with six square faces.	**cubo** Prisma con seis caras cuadradas.	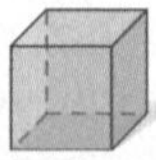
cube in numeration The third power of a number.	**cubo en numeración** Tercera potencia de un número.	8 is the cube of 2.
cube root A number, written as $\sqrt[3]{x}$, whose cube is x.	**raíz cúbica** Número, expresado como $\sqrt[3]{x}$, cuyo cubo es x.	$\sqrt[3]{64} = 4$, because $4^3 = 64$; 4 is the cube root of 64.
cubic equation An equation that can be written in the form $ax^3 + bx^2 + cx + d = 0$, where a, b, c, and d are real numbers and $a \neq 0$.	**ecuación cúbica** Ecuación que se puede expresar como $ax^3 + bx^2 + cx + d = 0$, donde a, b, c, y d son números reales y $a \neq 0$.	$4x^3 + x^2 - 3x - 1 = 0$
cubic function A function that can be written in the form $f(x) = ax^3 + bx^2 + cx + d$, where a, b, c, and d are real numbers and $a \neq 0$.	**función cúbica** Función que se puede expresar como $f(x) = ax^3 + bx^2 + cx + d$, donde a, b, c, y d son números reales y $a \neq 0$.	$f(x) = x^3 + 2x^2 - 6x + 8$
cubic polynomial A polynomial of degree 3.	**polinomio cúbico** Polinomio de grado 3.	$x^3 + 4x^2 - 6x + 2$
cumulative frequency The frequency of all data values that are less than or equal to a given value.	**frecuencia acumulativa** Frecuencia de todos los valores de los datos que son menores que o iguales a un valor dado.	For the data set 2, 2, 3, 5, 5, 6, 7, 7, 8, 8, 8, 9, the cumulative frequency table is shown below.

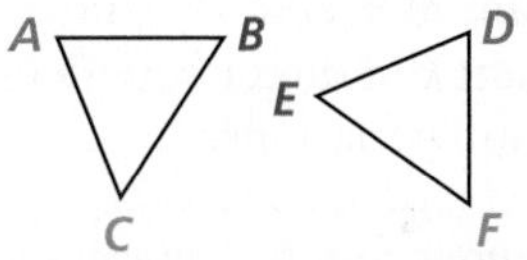

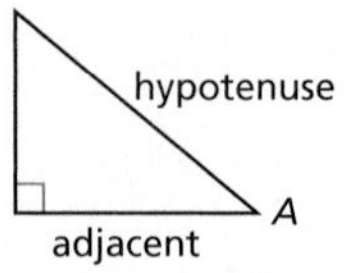

Data	Frequency	Cumulative Frequency
2	2	2
3	1	3
5	2	5
6	1	6
7	2	8
8	3	11
9	1	12

Glossary/Glosario

ENGLISH	SPANISH	EXAMPLES
cylinder A three-dimensional figure with two parallel congruent circular bases and a curved surface that connects the bases.	**cilindro** Figura tridimensional con dos bases circulares congruentes paralelas y una superficie lateral curva que conecta las bases.	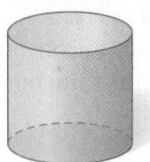

D

ENGLISH	SPANISH	EXAMPLES
data Information gathered from a survey or experiment.	**datos** Información reunida en una encuesta o experimento.	
degree measure of an angle A unit of angle measure; one degree is $\frac{1}{360}$ of a circle.	**medida en grados de un ángulo** Unidad de medida de los ángulos; un grado es $\frac{1}{360}$ de un círculo.	
degree of a monomial The sum of the exponents of the variables in the monomial.	**grado de un monomio** Suma de los exponentes de las variables del monomio.	$4x^2y^5z^3$ Degree: $2 + 5 + 3 = 10$ $5 = 5x^0$ Degree: 0
degree of a polynomial The degree of the term of the polynomial with the greatest degree.	**grado de un polinomio** Grado del término del polinomio con el grado máximo.	$3x^2y^2 + 4xy^5 - 12x^3y^2$ ↑ Degree 4 ↑ Degree 6 ↑ Degree 5 Degree 6
dependent events Events for which the occurrence or nonoccurrence of one event affects the probability of the other event.	**sucesos dependientes** Dos sucesos son dependientes si el hecho de que uno de ellos ocurra o no afecta la probabilidad del otro suceso.	From a bag containing 3 red marbles and 2 blue marbles, draw a red marble, and then draw a blue marble without replacing the first marble.
dependent system A system of equations that has infinitely many solutions.	**sistema dependiente** Sistema de ecuaciones que tiene infinitamente muchas soluciones.	$\begin{cases} x + y = 2 \\ 2x + 2y = 4 \end{cases}$
dependent variable The output of a function; a variable whose value depends on the value of the input, or independent variable.	**variable dependiente** Salida de una función; variable cuyo valor depende del valor de la entrada, o variable independiente.	For $y = 2x + 1$, y is the dependent variable. input: x output: y
diameter A segment that has endpoints on the circle and that passes through the center of the circle; also the length of that segment.	**diámetro** Segmento que atraviesa el centro de un círculo y cuyos extremos están sobre la circunferencia; longitud de dicho segmento.	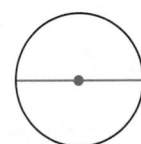
difference of two cubes A polynomial of the form $a^3 - b^3$, which may be written as the product $(a - b)(a^2 + ab + b^2)$.	**diferencia de dos cubos** Polinomio del tipo $a^3 - b^3$, que se puede expresar como el producto $(a - b)(a^2 + ab + b^2)$.	$x^3 - 8 = (x - 2)(x^2 + 2x + 4)$
difference of two squares A polynomial of the form $a^2 - b^2$, which may be written as the product $(a + b)(a - b)$.	**diferencia de dos cuadrados** Polinomio del tipo $a^2 - b^2$, que se puede expresar como el producto $(a + b)(a - b)$.	$x^2 - 4 = (x + 2)(x - 2)$

Glossary/Glosario

Glossary/Glosario

dimensional analysis A process that uses rates to convert measurements from one unit to another.

análisis dimensional Un proceso que utiliza tasas para convertir medidas de unidad a otra.

$$12 \text{ pt} \cdot \frac{1 \text{ qt}}{2 \text{ pt}} = 6 \text{ qt}$$

---

direct variation A linear relationship between two variables, x and y, that can be written in the form $y = kx$, where k is a nonzero constant.

variación directa Relación lineal entre dos variables, x e y, que puede expresarse en la forma $y = kx$, donde k es una constante distinta de cero.

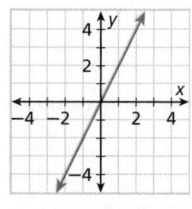

$y = 2x$

---

discontinuous function A function whose graph has one or more jumps, breaks, or holes.

función discontinua Función cuya gráfica tiene uno o más saltos, interrupciones u hoyos.

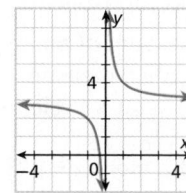

---

discount An amount by which an original price is reduced.

descuento Cantidad por la que se reduce un precio original.

---

discrete graph A graph made up of unconnected points.

gráfica discreta Gráfica compuesta de puntos no conectados.

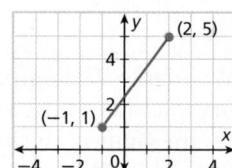

Theme Park Attendance

People / Years

---

discriminant The discriminant of the quadratic equation $ax^2 + bx + c = 0$ is $b^2 - 4ac$.

discriminante El discriminante de la ecuación cuadrática $ax^2 + bx + c = 0$ es $b^2 - 4ac$.

The discriminant of $2x^2 - 5x - 3 = 0$ is $(-5)^2 - 4(2)(-3)$ or 49.

Distance Formula In a coordinate plane, the distance from (x_1, y_1) to (x_2, y_2) is

$$d = \sqrt{(x_2 - x_1)^2 + (y_2 - y_1)^2}.$$

Fórmula de distancia En un plano cartesiano, la distancia desde (x_1, y_1) hasta (x_2, y_2) es

$$d = \sqrt{(x_2 - x_1)^2 + (y_2 - y_1)^2}.$$

The distance from $(2, 5)$ to $(-1, 1)$ is
$$d = \sqrt{(-1 - 2)^2 + (1 - 5)^2}$$
$$= \sqrt{(-3)^2 + (-4)^2}$$
$$= \sqrt{9 + 16} = \sqrt{25} = 5.$$

Distributive Property For all real numbers a, b, and c, $a(b + c) = ab + ac$, and $(b + c)a = ba + ca$.

Propiedad distributiva Dados los números reales a, b y c, $a(b + c) = ab + ac$, y $(b + c)a = ba + ca$.

$$3(4 + 5) = 3 \cdot 4 + 3 \cdot 5$$
$$(4 + 5)3 = 4 \cdot 3 + 5 \cdot 3$$

Division Property of Equality For real numbers a, b, and c, where $c \neq 0$, if $a = b$, then $\frac{a}{c} = \frac{b}{c}$.

Propiedad de igualdad de la división Dados los números reales a, b y c, donde $c \neq 0$, si $a = b$, entonces $\frac{a}{c} = \frac{b}{c}$.

$$4x = 12$$
$$\frac{4x}{4} = \frac{12}{4}$$
$$x = 3$$

Glossary/Glosario

ENGLISH	SPANISH	EXAMPLES
Division Property of Inequality If both sides of an inequality are divided by the same positive quantity, the new inequality will have the same solution set. If both sides of an inequality are divided by the same negative quantity, the new inequality will have the same solution set if the inequality symbol is reversed.	**Propiedad de desigualdad de la división** Cuando ambos lados de una desigualdad se dividen entre el mismo número positivo, la nueva desigualdad tiene el mismo conjunto solución. Cuando ambos lados de una desigualdad se dividen entra el mismo número negativo, la nueva desigualdad tiene el mismo conjunto solución si se invierte el símbolo de desigualdad.	$4x \geq 12$ $\dfrac{4x}{4} \geq \dfrac{12}{4}$ $x \geq 3$ $-4x \geq 12$ $\dfrac{-4x}{-4} \leq \dfrac{12}{-4}$ $x \leq -3$
domain The set of all first coordinates (or x-values) of a relation or function.	**dominio** Conjunto de todos los valores de la primera coordenada (o valores de x) de una función o relación.	The domain of the function $\{(-5, 3), (-3, -2), (-1, -1), (1, 0)\}$ is $\{-5, -3, -1, 1\}$.

E

element Each member in a set or matrix. *See also* entry.	**elemento** Cada miembro en un conjunto o matriz. *Ver también* entrada.	
elimination method A method used to solve systems of equations in which one variable is eliminated by adding or subtracting two equations of the system.	**eliminación** Método utilizado para resolver sistemas de ecuaciones por el cual se elimina una variable sumando o restando dos ecuaciones del sistema.	
empty set A set with no elements.	**conjunto vacío** Conjunto sin elementos.	The solution set of $|x| < 0$ is the empty set, $\{\ \}$, or $\varnothing$.
entry Each value in a matrix; also called an element.	**entrada** Cada valor de una matriz, también denominado elemento.	3 is the entry in the first row and second column of $A = \begin{bmatrix} 2 & 3 \\ 0 & 1 \end{bmatrix}$, denoted a_{12}.
equally likely outcomes Outcomes are equally likely if they have the same probability of occurring. If an experiment has n equally likely outcomes, then the probability of each outcome is $\frac{1}{n}$.	**resultados igualmente probables** Los resultados son igualmente probables si tienen la misma probabilidad de ocurrir. Si un experimento tiene n resultados igualmente probables, entonces la probabilidad de cada resultado es $\frac{1}{n}$.	If a fair coin is tossed, then $P(\text{heads}) = P(\text{tails}) = \frac{1}{2}$. So the outcome "heads" and the outcome "tails" are equally likely.
equation A mathematical statement that two expressions are equivalent.	**ecuación** Enunciado matemático que indica que dos expresiones son equivalentes.	$x + 4 = 7$ $2 + 3 = 6 - 1$ $(x - 1)^2 + (y + 2)^2 = 4$
equilateral triangle A triangle with three congruent sides.	**triángulo equilátero** Triángulo con tres lados congruentes.	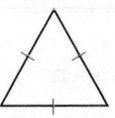
equivalent ratios Ratios that name the same comparison.	**razones equivalentes** Razones que expresan la misma comparación.	$\frac{1}{2}$ and $\frac{2}{4}$ are equivalent ratios.

Glossary/Glosario

ENGLISH	SPANISH	EXAMPLES
evaluate To find the value of an algebraic expression by substituting a number for each variable and simplifying by using the order of operations.	**evaluar** Calcular el valor de una expresión algebraica sustituyendo cada variable por un número y simplificando mediante el orden de las operaciones.	Evaluate $2x + 7$ for $x = 3$. $2x + 7$ $2(3) + 7$ $6 + 7$ 13
event An outcome or set of outcomes of an experiment.	**suceso** Resultado o conjunto de resultados en un experimento.	In the experiment of rolling a number cube, the event "an odd number" consists of the outcomes 1, 3, and 5.
excluded values Values of x for which a function or expression is not defined.	**valores excluidos** Valores de x para los cuales no está definida una función o expresión.	The excluded values of $\dfrac{(x + 2)}{(x - 1)(x + 4)}$ are $x = 1$ and $x = -4$, which would make the denominator equal to 0.
experiment An operation, process, or activity in which outcomes can be used to estimate probability.	**experimento** Una operación, proceso o actividad en la que se usan los resultados para estimar una probabilidad.	Tossing a coin 10 times and noting the number of heads
experimental probability The ratio of the number of times an event occurs to the number of trials, or times, that an activity is performed.	**probabilidad experimental** Razón entre la cantidad de veces que ocurre un suceso y la cantidad de pruebas, o veces, que se realiza una actividad.	Kendra attempted 27 free throws and made 16 of them. The experimental probability that she will make her next free throw is $P(\text{free throw}) = \dfrac{\text{number made}}{\text{number attempted}} = \dfrac{16}{27} \approx 0.59$.
exponent The number that indicates how many times the base in a power is used as a factor.	**exponente** Número que indica la cantidad de veces que la base de una potencia se utiliza como factor.	$3^4 = 3 \cdot 3 \cdot 3 \cdot 3 = 81$ 4 is the exponent.
exponential decay An exponential function of the form $f(x) = ab^x$ in which $0 < b < 1$. If r is the rate of decay, then the function can be written $y = a(1 - r)^t$, where a is the initial amount and t is the time.	**decremento exponencial** Función exponencial del tipo $f(x) = ab^x$ en la cual $0 < b < 1$. Si r es la tasa decremental, entonces la función se puede expresar como $y = a(1 - r)^t$, donde a es la cantidad inicial y t es el tiempo.	$f(x) = 3\left(\dfrac{1}{2}\right)^x$ 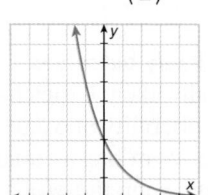
exponential expression An algebraic expression in which the variable is in an exponent with a fixed number as the base.	**expresión exponencial** Expresión algebraica en la que la variable está en un exponente y que tiene un número fijo como base.	2^{x+1}
exponential function A function of the form $f(x) = ab^x$, where a and b are real numbers with $a \neq 0$, $b > 0$, and $b \neq 1$.	**función exponencial** Función del tipo $f(x) = ab^x$, donde a y b son números reales con $a \neq 0$, $b > 0$ y $b \neq 1$.	$f(x) = 3 \cdot 4^x$ 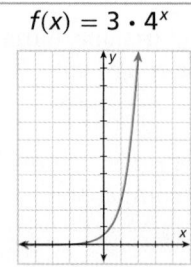

ENGLISH	SPANISH	EXAMPLES
exponential growth An exponential function of the form $f(x) = ab^x$ in which $b > 1$. If r is the rate of growth, then the function can be written $y = a(1 + r)^t$, where a is the initial amount and t is the time.	**crecimiento exponencial** Función exponencial del tipo $f(x) = ab^x$ en la que $b > 1$. Si r es la tasa de crecimiento, entonces la función se puede expresar como $y = a(1 + r)^t$, donde a es la cantidad inicial y t es el tiempo.	$f(x) = 2^x$ 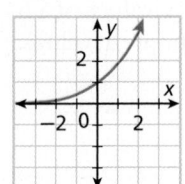
expression A mathematical phrase that contains operations, numbers, and/or variables.	**expresión** Frase matemática que contiene operaciones, números y/o variables.	$6x + 1$
extraneous solution A solution of a derived equation that is not a solution of the original equation.	**solución extraña** Solución de una ecuación derivada que no es una solución de la ecuación original.	To solve $\sqrt{x} = -2$, square both sides; $x = 4$. **Check** $\sqrt{4} = -2$ is false; so 4 is an extraneous solution.

ENGLISH	SPANISH	EXAMPLES
factor A number or expression that is multiplied by another number or expression to get a product. *See also* factoring.	**factor** Número o expresión que se multiplica por otro número o expresión para obtener un producto. *Ver también* factoreo.	$12 = 3 \cdot 4$ 3 and 4 are factors of 12. $x^2 - 1 = (x - 1)(x + 1)$ $(x - 1)$ and $(x + 1)$ are factors of $x^2 - 1$.
factorial If n is a positive integer, then n factorial, written $n!$, is $n \cdot (n - 1) \cdot (n - 2) \cdot \ldots \cdot 2 \cdot 1$. The factorial of 0 is defined to be 1.	**factorial** Si n es un entero positivo, entonces el factorial de n, expresado como $n!$, es $n \cdot (n - 1) \cdot (n - 2) \cdot \ldots \cdot 2 \cdot 1$. Por definición, el factorial de 0 será 1.	$7! = 7 \cdot 6 \cdot 5 \cdot 4 \cdot 3 \cdot 2 \cdot 1$ $= 5040$
factoring The process of writing a number or algebraic expression as a product.	**factorización** Proceso por el que se expresa un número o expresión algebraica como un producto.	$x^2 - 4x - 21 = (x - 7)(x + 3)$
fair When all outcomes of an experiment are equally likely.	**justo** Cuando todos los resultados de un experimento son igualmente probables.	When tossing a fair coin, heads and tails are equally likely. Each has a probability of $\frac{1}{2}$.
family of functions A set of functions whose graphs have basic characteristics in common. Functions in the same family are transformations of their parent function.	**familia de funciones** Conjunto de funciones cuyas gráficas tienen características básicas en común. Las funciones de la misma familia son transformaciones de su función madre.	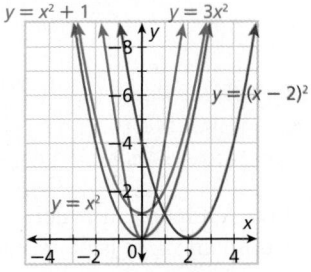

ENGLISH	SPANISH	EXAMPLES

first differences The differences between y-values of a function for evenly spaced x-values.

primeras diferencias Diferencias entre los valores de y de una función para valores de x espaciados uniformemente.

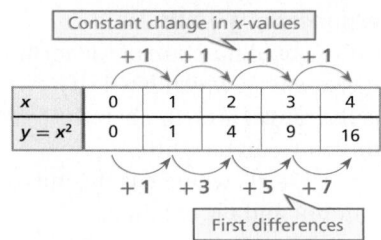

---

first quartile The median of the lower half of a data set, denoted Q_1. Also called *lower quartile*.

primer cuartil Mediana de la mitad inferior de un conjunto de datos, expresada como Q_1. También se llama *cuartil inferior*.

Lower half   Upper half
18, (23), 28,   29, 36, 42
First quartile

FOIL A mnemonic (memory) device for a method of multiplying two binomials:

Multiply the **First** terms.
Multiply the **Outer** terms.
Multiply the **Inner** terms.
Multiply the **Last** terms.

FOIL Regla mnemotécnica para recordar el método de multiplicación de dos binomios:

Multiplicar los términos **Primeros** (*First*).
Multiplicar los términos **Externos** (*Outer*).
Multiplicar los términos **Internos** (*Inner*).
Multiplicar los términos **Últimos** (*Last*).

F   L
$(x + 2)(x - 3) = x^2 - 3x + 2x - 6$
$= x^2 - x - 6$
I
O

---

formula A literal equation that states a rule for a relationship among quantities.

fórmula Ecuación literal que establece una regla para una relación entre cantidades.

$A = \pi r^2$

---

fractional exponent *See* rational exponent.

exponente fraccionario *Ver* exponente racional.

---

frequency The number of times the value appears in the data set.

frecuencia Cantidad de veces que aparece el valor en un conjunto de datos.

In the data set 5, 6, 6, 7, 8, 9, the data value 6 has a frequency of 2.

---

frequency table A table that lists the number of times, or frequency, that each data value occurs.

tabla de frecuencia Tabla que enumera la cantidad de veces que ocurre cada valor de datos, o la frecuencia.

Data set: 1, 1, 2, 2, 3, 4, 5, 5, 5, 6, 6, 6, 6
Frequency table:

Data	Frequency
1	2
2	2
3	1
4	1
5	3
6	4

---

function A relation in which every domain value is paired with exactly one range value.

función Relación en la que a cada valor de dominio corresponde exactamente un valor de rango.

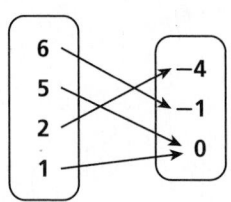

Glossary/Glosario

ENGLISH	SPANISH	EXAMPLES
function notation If x is the independent variable and y is the dependent variable, then the function notation for y is $f(x)$, read "f of x," where f names the function.	**notación de función** Si x es la variable independiente e y es la variable dependiente, entonces la notación de función para y es $f(x)$, que se lee "f de x," donde f nombra la función.	equation: $y = 2x$ function notation: $f(x) = 2x$
function rule An algebraic expression that defines a function.	**regla de función** Expresión algebraica que define una función.	$f(x) = \underline{2x^2 + 3x - 7}$ $\uparrow$ function rule
Fundamental Counting Principle If one event has m possible outcomes and a second event has n possible outcomes after the first event has occurred, then there are mn total possible outcomes for the two events.	**Principio fundamental de conteo** Si un suceso tiene m resultados posibles y otro suceso tiene n resultados posibles después de ocurrido el primer suceso, entonces hay mn resultados posibles en total para los dos sucesos.	If there are 4 colors of shirts, 3 colors of pants, and 2 colors of shoes, then there are $4 \cdot 3 \cdot 2 = 24$ possible outfits.

ENGLISH	SPANISH	EXAMPLES
geometric sequence A sequence in which the ratio of successive terms is a constant r, called the common ratio, where $r \neq 0$ and $r \neq 1$.	**sucesión geométrica** Sucesión en la que la razón de los términos sucesivos es una constante r, denominada razón común, donde $r \neq 0$ y $r \neq 1$.	$1, \quad 2, \quad 4, \quad 8, \quad 16, \ldots$ $\cdot 2 \cdot 2 \cdot 2 \cdot 2 \qquad r = 2$
graph of a function The set of points in a coordinate plane with coordinates (x, y), where x is in the domain of the function f and $y = f(x)$.	**gráfica de una función** Conjunto de los puntos de un plano cartesiano con coordenadas (x, y), donde x está en el dominio de la función f e $y = f(x)$.	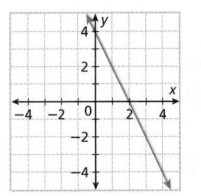 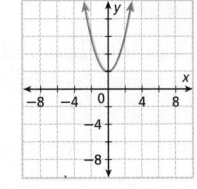
graph of a system of linear inequalities The region in a coordinate plane consisting of points whose coordinates are solutions to all of the inequalities in the system.	**gráfica de un sistema de desigualdades lineales** Región de un plano cartesiano que consta de puntos cuyas coordenadas son soluciones de todas las desigualdades del sistema.	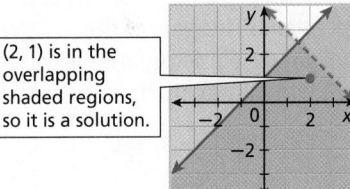 (2, 1) is in the overlapping shaded regions, so it is a solution.
graph of an inequality in one variable The set of points on a number line that are solutions of the inequality.	**gráfica de una desigualdad en una variable** Conjunto de los puntos de una recta numérica que representan soluciones de la desigualdad.	$x \geq 2$ 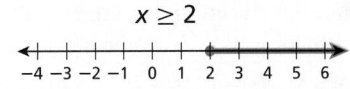
graph of an inequality in two variables The set of points in a coordinate plane whose coordinates (x, y) are solutions of the inequality.	**gráfica de una desigualdad en dos variables** Conjunto de los puntos de un plano cartesiano cuyas coordenadas (x, y) son soluciones de la desigualdad.	$y \leq x + 1$ 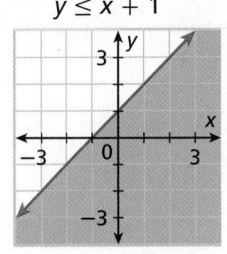

ENGLISH	SPANISH	EXAMPLES

graph of an ordered pair For the ordered pair (x, y), the point in a coordinate plane that is a horizontal distance of x units from the origin and a vertical distance of y units from the origin.

gráfica de un par ordenado Dado el par ordenado (x, y), punto en un plano cartesiano que está a una distancia horizontal de x unidades desde el origen y a una distancia vertical de y unidades desde el origen.

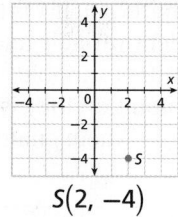

$S(2, -4)$

---

greatest common factor (monomials) (GCF) The product of the greatest integer and the greatest power of each variable that divide evenly into each monomial.

máximo común divisor (monomios) (MCD) Producto del entero mayor y la potencia mayor de cada variable que divide exactamente cada monomio.

The GCF of $4x^3y$ and $6x^2y$ is $2x^2y$.

---

greatest common factor (numbers) (GCF) The largest common factor of two or more given numbers.

máximo común divisor (números) (MCD) El mayor de los factores comunes compartidos por dos o más números dados.

The GCF of 27 and 45 is 9.

---

grouping symbols Symbols such as parentheses ( ), brackets [ ], and braces { } that separate part of an expression. A fraction bar, absolute-value symbols, and radical symbols may also be used as grouping symbols.

símbolos de agrupación Símbolos tales como paréntesis ( ), corchetes [ ] y llaves { } que separan parte de una expresión. La barra de fracciones, los símbolos de valor absoluto y los símbolos de radical también se pueden utilizar como símbolos de agrupación.

$6 + \{3 - [(4 - 3) + 2] + 1\} - 5$
$6 + \{3 - [1 + 2] + 1\} - 5$
$6 + \{3 - 3 + 1\} - 5$
$6 + 1 - 5$
2

---

half-life The half-life of a substance is the time it takes for one-half of the substance to decay into another substance.

vida media La vida media de una sustancia es el tiempo que tarda la mitad de la sustancia en desintegrarse y transformarse en otra sustancia.

Carbon-14 has a half-life of 5730 years, so 5 g of an initial amount of 10 g will remain after 5730 years.

---

half-plane The part of the coordinate plane on one side of a line, which may include the line.

semiplano La parte del plano cartesiano de un lado de una línea, que puede incluir la línea.

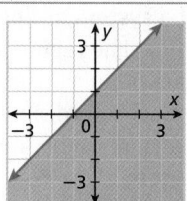

Heron's Formula A triangle with side lengths a, b, and c has area $A = \sqrt{s(s - a)(s - b)(s - c)}$, where s is one-half the perimeter, or $s = \frac{1}{2}(a + b + c)$.

fórmula de Herón Un triángulo con longitudes de lado a, b y c tiene un área $A = \sqrt{s(s - a)(s - b)(s - c)}$, donde s es la mitad del perímetro ó $s = \frac{1}{2}(a + b + c)$.

ENGLISH	SPANISH	EXAMPLES
histogram A bar graph used to display data grouped in intervals.	**histograma** Gráfica de barras utilizada para mostrar datos agrupados en intervalos de clases.	
horizontal line A line described by the equation $y = b$, where b is the y-intercept.	**línea horizontal** Línea descrita por la ecuación $y = b$, donde b es la intersección con el eje y.	$y = 4$ 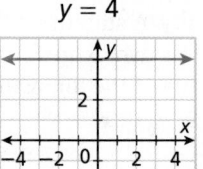
hypotenuse The side opposite the right angle in a right triangle.	**hipotenusa** Lado opuesto al ángulo recto de un triángulo rectángulo.	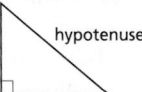

ENGLISH	SPANISH	EXAMPLES
identity An equation that is true for all values of the variables.	**identidad** Ecuación verdadera para todos los valores de las variables.	$3 = 3$ $2(x - 1) = 2x - 2$
inclusive events Events that have one or more outcomes in common.	**sucesos inclusivos** Sucesos que tienen uno o más resultados en común.	In the experiment of rolling a number cube, rolling an even number and rolling a number less than 3 are inclusive events because both contain the outcome 2.
inconsistent system A system of equations or inequalities that has no solution.	**sistema inconsistente** Sistema de ecuaciones o desigualdades que no tiene solución.	$\begin{cases} x + y = 0 \\ x + y = 1 \end{cases}$
independent events Events for which the occurrence or nonoccurrence of one event does not affect the probability of the other event.	**sucesos independientes** Dos sucesos son independientes si el hecho de que se produzca o no uno de ellos no afecta la probabilidad del otro suceso.	From a bag containing 3 red marbles and 2 blue marbles, draw a red marble, replace it, and then draw a blue marble.
independent system A system of equations that has exactly one solution.	**sistema independiente** Sistema de ecuaciones que tiene sólo una solución.	$\begin{cases} x + y = 7 \\ x - y = 1 \end{cases}$ Solution: $(4, 3)$
independent variable The input of a function; a variable whose value determines the value of the output, or dependent variable.	**variable independiente** Entrada de una función; variable cuyo valor determina el valor de la salida, o variable dependiente.	For $y = 2x + 1$, x is the independent variable.

Glossary/Glosario

ENGLISH	SPANISH	EXAMPLES
index In the radical $\sqrt[n]{x}$, which represents the nth root of x, n is the index. In the radical $\sqrt{x}$, the index is understood to be 2.	**índice** En el radical $\sqrt[n]{x}$, que representa la enésima raíz de x, n es el índice. En el radical $\sqrt{x}$, se da por sentado que el índice es 2.	The radical $\sqrt[3]{8}$ has an index of 3.
indirect measurement A method of measurement that uses formulas, similar figures, and/or proportions.	**medición indirecta** Método de medición en el que se usan fórmulas, figuras semejantes y/o proporciones.	
inequality A statement that compares two expressions by using one of the following signs: $<, >, \leq, \geq,$ or $\neq$.	**desigualdad** Enunciado que compara dos expresiones utilizando uno de los siguientes signos: $<, >, \leq, \geq,$ o $\neq$.	$x \geq 2$ ←—┼—┼—┼—┼—┼—┼—┼—┼—┼—┼—→ −4 −3 −2 −1 0 1 2 3 4 5 6
input A value that is substituted for the independent variable in a relation or function.	**entrada** Valor que sustituye a la variable independiente en una relación o función.	For the function $f(x) = x + 5$, the input 3 produces an output of 8.
input-output table A table that displays input values of a function or expression together with the corresponding outputs.	**tabla de entrada y salida** Tabla que muestra los valores de entrada de una función o expresión junto con las correspondientes salidas.	Input x: 1, 2, 3, 4 Output y: 4, 7, 10, 13
integer A member of the set of whole numbers and their opposites.	**entero** Miembro del conjunto de números cabales y sus opuestos.	..., −3, −2, −1, 0, 1, 2, 3, ...
intercept *See x-intercept and y-intercept.*	**intersección** *Ver* intersección con el eje x e intersección con el eje y.	
interest The amount of money charged for borrowing money or the amount of money earned when saving or investing money. *See also* compound interest, simple interest.	**interés** Cantidad de dinero que se cobra por prestar dinero o cantidad de dinero que se gana cuando se ahorra o invierte dinero. *Ver también* interés compuesto, interés simple.	
interquartile range (IQR) The difference of the third (upper) and first (lower) quartiles in a data set, representing the middle half of the data.	**rango entre cuartiles** Diferencia entre el tercer cuartil (superior) y el primer cuartil (inferior) de un conjunto de datos, que representa la mitad central de los datos.	Lower half Upper half 18, (23), 28, | 29, (36), 42 First quartile Third quartile Interquartile range: $36 - 23 = 13$
intersection The intersection of two sets is the set of all elements that are common to both sets, denoted by $\cap$.	**intersección de conjuntos** La intersección de dos conjuntos es el conjunto de todos los elementos que son comunes a ambos conjuntos, expresado por $\cap$.	$A = \{1, 2, 3, 4\}$ $B = \{1, 3, 5, 7, 9\}$ $A \cap B = \{1, 3\}$
inverse operations Operations that undo each other.	**operaciones inversas** Operaciones que se anulan entre sí.	Addition and subtraction of the same quantity are inverse operations: $5 + 3 = 8, 8 - 3 = 5$ Multiplication and division by the same quantity are inverse operations: $2 \cdot 3 = 6, 6 \div 3 = 2$

Glossary/Glosario

ENGLISH	SPANISH	EXAMPLES
inverse variation A relationship between two variables, x and y, that can be written in the form $y = \frac{k}{x}$, where k is a nonzero constant and $x \neq 0$.	**variación inversa** Relación entre dos variables, x e y, que puede expresarse en la forma $y = \frac{k}{x}$, donde k es una constante distinta de cero y $x \neq 0$.	$y = \dfrac{8}{x}$ 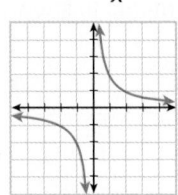
irrational number A real number that cannot be expressed as the ratio of two integers.	**número irracional** Número real que no se puede expresar como una razón de enteros.	$\sqrt{2}, \pi, e$
isolate the variable To isolate a variable in an equation, use inverse operations on both sides until the variable appears by itself on one side of the equation and does not appear on the other side.	**despejar la variable** Para despejar la variable de una ecuación, utiliza operaciones inversas en ambos lados hasta que la variable aparezca sola en uno de los lados de la ecuación y no aparezca en el otro lado.	$$10 = 6 - 2x$$ $$\frac{-6}{4} = \frac{-6}{-2x}$$ $$\frac{4}{-2} = \frac{-2x}{-2}$$ $$-2 = x$$
isosceles triangle A triangle with at least two congruent sides.	**triángulo isósceles** Triángulo que tiene al menos dos lados congruentes.	

leading coefficient The coefficient of the first term of a polynomial in standard form.	**coeficiente principal** Coeficiente del primer término de un polinomio en forma estándar.	$3x^2 + 7x - 2$ Leading coefficient: 3
least common denominator (LCD) The least common multiple of the denominators of two or more given fractions or rational expressions.	**mínimo común denominador (MCD)** Mínimo común múltiplo de los denominadores de dos o más fracciones dadas o expresionnes racionales.	The LCD of $\frac{3}{4}$ and $\frac{5}{6}$ is 12.
least common multiple (monomials) (LCM) The product of the smallest positive number and the lowest power of each variable that divide evenly into each monomial.	**mínimo común múltiplo (monomios) (MCM)** El producto del número positivo más pequeño y la menor potencia de cada variable que divide exactamente cada monomio.	The LCM of $6x^2$ and $4x$ is $12x^2$.
least common multiple (numbers) (LCM) The smallest whole number, other than zero, that is a multiple of two or more given numbers.	**mínimo común múltiplo (números) (MCM)** El menor de los números cabales, distinto de cero, que es múltiplo de dos o más números dados.	The LCM of 10 and 18 is 90.
least-squares line The line of fit for which the sum of the squares of the residuals is as small as possible.	**línea de mínimos cuadrados** La línea de ajuste en que la suma de cuadrados de los residuos es la menor.	

ENGLISH	SPANISH	EXAMPLES
line graph A graph that uses line segments to show how data changes.	**gráfica lineal** Gráfica que se vale de segmentos de recta para mostrar cambios en los datos.	
line of best fit The line that comes closest to all of the points in a data set.	**línea de mejor ajuste** Línea que más se acerca a todos los puntos de un conjunto de datos.	
linear equation in one variable An equation that can be written in the form $ax = b$ where a and b are constants and $a \neq 0$.	**ecuación lineal en una variable** Ecuación que puede expresarse en la forma $ax = b$ donde a y b son constantes y $a \neq 0$.	$x + 1 = 7$
linear equation in two variables An equation that can be written in the form $Ax + By = C$ where A, B, and C are constants and A and B are not both 0.	**ecuación lineal en dos variables** Ecuación que puede expresarse en la forma $Ax + By = C$ donde A, B y C son constantes y A y B no son ambas 0.	$2x + 3y = 6$
linear function A function that can be written in the form $y = mx + b$, where x is the independent variable and m and b are real numbers. Its graph is a line.	**función lineal** Función que puede expresarse en la forma $y = mx + b$, donde x es la variable independiente y m y b son números reales. Su gráfica es una línea.	$y = x - 1$ 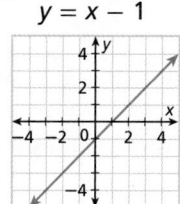
linear inequality in one variable An inequality that can be written in one of the following forms: $ax < b$, $ax > b$, $ax \leq b$, $ax \geq b$, or $ax \neq b$, where a and b are constants and $a \neq 0$.	**desigualdad lineal en una variable** Desigualdad que puede expresarse de una de las siguientes formas: $ax < b$, $ax > b$, $ax \leq b$, $ax \geq b$ o $ax \neq b$, donde a y b son constantes y $a \neq 0$.	$3x - 5 \leq 2(x + 4)$
linear inequality in two variables An inequality that can be written in one of the following forms: $Ax + By < C$, $Ax + By > C$, $Ax + By \leq C$, $Ax + By \geq C$, or $Ax + By \neq C$, where A, B, and C are constants and A and B are not both 0.	**desigualdad lineal en dos variables** Desigualdad que puede expresarse de una de las siguientes formas: $Ax + By < C$, $Ax + By > C$, $Ax + By \leq C$, $Ax + By \geq C$ o $Ax + By \neq C$, donde A, B y C son constantes y A y B no son ambas 0.	$2x + 3y > 6$
linear regression A statistical method used to fit a linear model to a given data set.	**regresión lineal** Método estadístico utilizado para ajustar un modelo lineal a un conjunto de datos determinado.	

Glossary/Glosario

ENGLISH	SPANISH	EXAMPLES
literal equation An equation that contains two or more variables.	**ecuación literal** Ecuación que contiene dos o más variables.	$d = rt$ $A = \frac{1}{2}h(b_1 + b_2)$
lower quartile *See* first quartile.	**cuartil inferior** *Ver* primer cuartil.	

ENGLISH	SPANISH	EXAMPLES
mapping diagram A diagram that shows the relationship of elements in the domain to elements in the range of a relation or function.	**diagrama de correspondencia** Diagrama que muestra la relación entre los elementos del dominio y los elementos del rango de una función.	**Mapping Diagram** 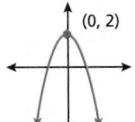
markup The amount by which a wholesale cost is increased.	**margen de ganancia** Cantidad que se agrega a un costo mayorista.	
matrix A rectangular array of numbers.	**matriz** Arreglo rectangular de números.	$\begin{bmatrix} 1 & 0 & 3 \\ -2 & 2 & -5 \\ 7 & -6 & 3 \end{bmatrix}$
maximum of a function The *y*-value of the highest point on the graph of the function.	**máximo de una función** Valor de *y* del punto más alto en la gráfica de la función.	(0, 2) The maximum of the function is 2.
mean The sum of all the values in a data set divided by the number of data values. Also called the *average*.	**media** Suma de todos los valores de un conjunto de datos dividida entre el número de valores de datos. También llamada *promedio*.	Data set: 4, 6, 7, 8, 10 Mean: $\dfrac{4 + 6 + 7 + 8 + 10}{5}$ $= \dfrac{35}{5} = 7$
measure of an angle Angles are measured in degrees. A degree is $\frac{1}{360}$ of a complete circle.	**medida de un ángulo** Los ángulos se miden en grados. Un grado es $\frac{1}{360}$ de un círculo completo.	M 26.8°
measure of central tendency A measure that describes the center of a data set.	**medida de tendencia dominante** Medida que describe el centro de un conjunto de datos.	mean, median, or mode
median For an ordered data set with an odd number of values, the median is the middle value. For an ordered data set with an even number of values, the median is the average of the two middle values.	**mediana** Dado un conjunto de datos ordenado con un número impar de valores, la mediana es el valor medio. Dado un conjunto de datos con un número par de valores, la mediana es el promedio de los dos valores medios.	8, 9, ⑨ 12, 15 Median: 9 4, 6, ⑦ ⑩ 10, 12 Median: $\dfrac{7 + 10}{2} = 8.5$
midpoint The point that divides a segment into two congruent segments.	**punto medio** Punto que divide un segmento en dos segmentos congruentes.	A B C Point B is the midpoint of $\overline{AC}$.

ENGLISH	SPANISH	EXAMPLES
minimum of a function The y-value of the lowest point on the graph of the function.	**mínimo de una función** Valor de y del punto más bajo en la gráfica de la función.	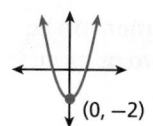 (0, −2) The minimum of the function is −2.
mode The value or values that occur most frequently in a data set; if all values occur with the same frequency, the data set is said to have no mode.	**moda** El valor o los valores que se presentan con mayor frecuencia en un conjunto de datos. Si todos los valores se presentan con la misma frecuencia, se dice que el conjunto de datos no tiene moda.	Data set: 3, 6, 8, 8, 10 Mode: 8 Data set: 2, 5, 5, 7, 7 Modes: 5 and 7 Data set: 2, 3, 6, 9, 11 No mode
monomial A number or a product of numbers and variables with whole-number exponents, or a polynomial with one term.	**monomio** Número o producto de números y variables con exponentes de números cabales, o polinomio con un término.	$3x^2y^4$
Multiplication Property of Equality If a, b, and c are real numbers and $a = b$, then $ac = bc$.	**Propiedad de igualdad de la multiplicación** Si a, b y c son números reales y $a = b$, entonces $ac = bc$.	$\frac{1}{3}x = 7$ $(3)\left(\frac{1}{3}x\right) = (3)(7)$ $x = 21$
Multiplication Property of Inequality If both sides of an inequality are multiplied by the same positive quantity, the new inequality will have the same solution set. If both sides of an inequality are multiplied by the same negative quantity, the new inequality will have the same solution set if the inequality symbol is reversed.	**Propiedad de desigualdad de la multiplicación** Si ambos lados de una desigualdad se multiplican por el mismo número positivo, la nueva desigualdad tendrá el mismo conjunto solución. Si ambos lados de una desigualdad se multiplican por el mismo número negativo, la nueva desigualdad tendrá el mismo conjunto solución si se invierte el símbolo de desigualdad.	$\frac{1}{3}x > 7$ $(3)\left(\frac{1}{3}x\right) > (3)(7)$ $x > 21$ $-x \leq 2$ $(-1)(-x) \geq (-1)(2)$ $x \geq -2$
multiplicative inverse The reciprocal of the number.	**inverso multiplicativo** Recíproco de un número.	The multiplicative inverse of 5 is $\frac{1}{5}$.
mutually exclusive events Two events are mutually exclusive if they cannot both occur in the same trial of an experiment.	**sucesos mutuamente excluyentes** Dos sucesos son mutuamente excluyentes si ambos no pueden ocurrir en la misma prueba de un experimento.	In the experiment of rolling a number cube, rolling a 3 and rolling an even number are mutually exclusive events.

natural number A counting number.	**número natural** Número que se utiliza para contar.	1, 2, 3, 4, 5, 6, ...
negative correlation Two data sets have a negative correlation if one set of data values increases as the other set decreases.	**correlación negativa** Dos conjuntos de datos tienen una correlación negativa si un conjunto de valores de datos aumenta a medida que el otro conjunto disminuye.	

ENGLISH	SPANISH	EXAMPLES
negative exponent For any nonzero real number x and any integer n, $x^{-n} = \frac{1}{x^n}$.	**exponente negativo** Para cualquier número real distinto de cero x y cualquier entero n, $x^{-n} = \frac{1}{x^n}$.	$x^{-2} = \frac{1}{x^2}$; $3^{-2} = \frac{1}{3^2}$
negative number A number that is less than zero. Negative numbers lie to the left of zero on a number line.	**número negativo** Número menor que cero. Los números negativos se ubican a la izquierda del cero en una recta numérica.	-2 is a negative number. 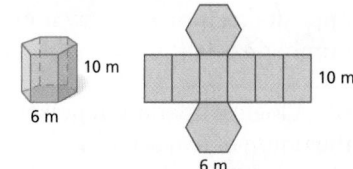
net A diagram of the faces of a three-dimensional figure arranged in such a way that the diagram can be folded to form the three-dimensional figure.	**plantilla** Diagrama de las caras de una figura tridimensional que se puede plegar para formar la figura tridimensional.	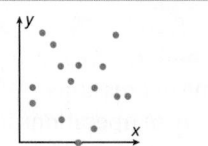
no correlation Two data sets have no correlation if there is no relationship between the sets of values.	**sin correlación** Dos conjuntos de datos no tienen correlación si no existe una relación entre los conjuntos de valores.	
nonlinear system of equations A system in which at least one of the equations is not linear.	**sistema no lineal de ecuaciones** Sistema en el cual por lo menos una de las ecuaciones no es lineal.	A system that contains one quadratic equation and one linear equation is a nonlinear system.
nth root The nth root of a number a, written as $\sqrt[n]{a}$ or $a^{\frac{1}{n}}$, is a number that is equal to a when it is raised to the nth power.	**enésima raíz** La enésima raíz de un número a, que se escribe $\sqrt[n]{a}$ o $a^{\frac{1}{n}}$, es un número igual a a cuando se eleva a la enésima potencia.	$\sqrt[5]{32} = 2$, because $2^5 = 32$.
number line A line used to represent the real numbers.	**recta numérica** Línea utilizada para representar los números reales.	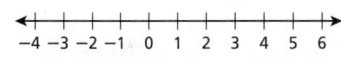

ENGLISH	SPANISH	EXAMPLES
obtuse angle An angle that measures greater than 90° and less than 180°.	**ángulo obtuso** Ángulo que mide más de 90° y menos de 180°.	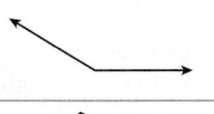
obtuse triangle A triangle with one obtuse angle.	**triángulo obtusángulo** Triángulo con un ángulo obtuso.	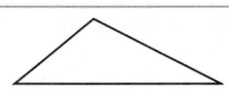
odds A comparison of favorable and unfavorable outcomes. The odds in favor of an event are the ratio of the number of favorable outcomes to the number of unfavorable outcomes. The odds against an event are the ratio of the number of unfavorable outcomes to the number of favorable outcomes.	**probabilidades a favor y en contra** Comparación de los resultados favorables y desfavorables. Las probabilidades a favor de un suceso son la razón entre la cantidad de resultados favorables y la cantidad de resultados desfavorables. Las probabilidades en contra de un suceso son la razón entre la cantidad de resultados desfavorables y la cantidad de resultados favorables.	The odds in favor of rolling a 3 on a number cube are 1:5. The odds against rolling a 3 on a number cube are 5:1.

opposite The opposite of a number a, denoted $-a$, is the number that is the same distance from zero as a, on the opposite side of the number line. The sum of opposites is 0.

opuesto El opuesto de un número a, expresado $-a$, es el número que se encuentra a la misma distancia de cero que a, del lado opuesto de la recta numérica. La suma de los opuestos es 0.

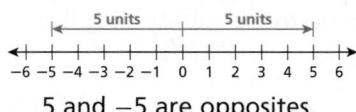

5 and -5 are opposites.

---

opposite reciprocal The opposite of the reciprocal of a number. The opposite reciprocal of any nonzero number a is $-\frac{1}{a}$.

recíproco opuesto Opuesto del recíproco de un número. El recíproco opuesto de a es $-\frac{1}{a}$.

The opposite reciprocal of $\frac{2}{3}$ is $-\frac{3}{2}$.

OR A logical operator representing the union of two sets.

O Operador lógico que representa la unión de dos conjuntos.

$A = \{2, 3, 4, 5\}$ $B = \{1, 3, 5, 7\}$
The set of values that are in A OR B is $A \cup B = \{1, 2, 3, 4, 5, 7\}$.

---

order of operations A process for evaluating expressions:
First, perform operations in parentheses or other grouping symbols.
Second, simplify powers and roots.
Third, perform all multiplication and division from left to right.
Fourth, perform all addition and subtraction from left to right.

orden de las operaciones Regla para evaluar las expresiones:
Primero, realizar las operaciones entre paréntesis u otros símbolos de agrupación.
Segundo, simplificar las potencias y las raíces.
Tercero, realizar todas las multiplicaciones y divisiones de izquierda a derecha.
Cuarto, realizar todas las sumas y restas de izquierda a derecha.

$2 + 3^2 - (7 + 5) \div 4 \cdot 3$	
$2 + 3^2 - 12 \div 4 \cdot 3$	Add inside parentheses.
$2 + 9 - 12 \div 4 \cdot 3$	Simplify the power.
$2 + 9 - 3 \cdot 3$	Divide.
$2 + 9 - 9$	Multiply.
$11 - 9$	Add.
2	Subtract.

---

ordered pair A pair of numbers (x, y) that can be used to locate a point on a coordinate plane. The first number x indicates the distance to the left or right of the origin, and the second number y indicates the distance above or below the origin.

par ordenado Par de números (x, y) que se pueden utilizar para ubicar un punto en un plano cartesiano. El primer número, x, indica la distancia a la izquierda o derecha del origen y el segundo número, y, indica la distancia hacia arriba o hacia abajo del origen.

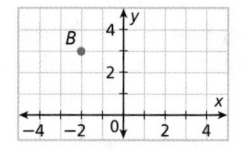

The ordered pair $(-2, 3)$ can be used to locate B.

---

origin The intersection of the x- and y-axes in a coordinate plane. The coordinates of the origin are $(0, 0)$.

origen Intersección de los ejes x e y en un plano cartesiano. Las coordenadas de origen son $(0, 0)$.

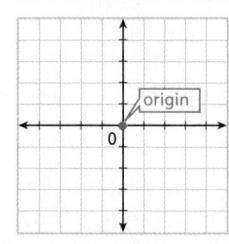

---

outcome A possible result of a probability experiment.

resultado Resultado posible de un experimento de probabilidad.

In the experiment of rolling a number cube, the possible outcomes are 1, 2, 3, 4, 5, and 6.

---

outlier A data value that is far removed from the rest of the data.

valor extremo Valor de datos que está muy alejado del resto de los datos.

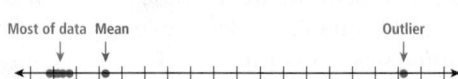

---

output The result of substituting a value for a variable in a function.

salida Resultado de la sustitución de una variable por un valor en una función.

For the function $f(x) = x^2 + 1$, the input 3 produces an output of 10.

Glossary/Glosario

ENGLISH	SPANISH	EXAMPLES

parabola The shape of the graph of a quadratic function. | **parábola** Forma de la gráfica de una función cuadrática. |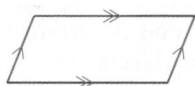

parallel lines Linesin the same plane that do not intersect. | **líneas paralelas** Líneas en el mismo plano que no se cruzan. |
←————→ r

←————→ s

parallelogram A quadrilateral with two pairs of parallel sides. | **paralelogramo** Cuadrilátero con dos pares de lados paralelos. |

parent function The simplest function with the defining characteristics of the family. Functions in the same family are transformations of their parent function. | **función madre** La función más básica que tiene las características distintivas de una familia. Las funciones de la misma familia son transformaciones de su función madre. | $f(x) = x^2$ is the parent function for $g(x) = x^2 + 4$ and $h(x) = (5x + 2)^2 - 3$.

Pascal's triangle A triangular arrangement of numbers in which every rowstarts and ends with 1 and each other number is the sum of the two numbers above it. | **triángulo de Pascal** Arreglo triangular de números en el cual cada fila comienza y termina con 1 y los demás números son la suma de los dos valores que están arriba de cada uno. | 1
1 1
1 2 1
1 3 3 1
1 4 6 4 1

percent A ratio that compares a number to 100. | **porcentaje** Razón que compara un número con 100. | $\dfrac{17}{100} = 17\%$

percent change An increase or decrease given as a percent of the original amount. *See also* percent decrease, percent increase. | **porcentaje de cambio** Incremento o disminución dada como un porcentaje de la cantidad original. *Ver también* porcentaje de disminución, porcentaje de incremento. |

percent decrease A decrease given as a percent of the original amount. | **porcentaje de disminución** Disminución dada como un porcentaje de la cantidad original. | If an item that costs $8.00 is marked down to $6.00, the amount of the decrease is $2.00, so the percent decrease is $\frac{2.00}{8.00} = 0.25 = 25\%$.

percent increase An increase given as a percent of the original amount. | **porcentaje de incremento** Incremento dado como un porcentaje de la cantidad original. | If an item's wholesale cost of $8.00 is marked up to $12.00, the amount of the increase is $4.00, so the percent increase is $\frac{4.00}{8.00} = 0.5 = 50\%$.

perfect square A number whose positive square root is a whole number. | **cuadrado perfecto** Número cuya raíz cuadrada positiva es un número cabal. | 36 is a perfect square because $\sqrt{36} = 6$.

Glossary/Glosario

ENGLISH	SPANISH	EXAMPLES
perfect-square trinomial A trinomial whose factored form is the square of a binomial. A perfect-square trinomial has the form $a^2 - 2ab + b^2 = (a - b)^2$ or $a^2 + 2ab + b^2 = (a + b)^2$.	**trinomio cuadrado perfecto** Trinomio cuya forma factorizada es el cuadrado de un binomio. Un trinomio cuadrado perfecto tiene la forma $a^2 - 2ab + b^2 = (a - b)^2$ o $a^2 + 2ab + b^2 = (a + b)^2$.	$x^2 + 6x + 9$ is a perfect-square trinomial, because $x^2 + 6x + 9 = (x + 3)^2$.
perimeter The sum of the side lengths of a closed plane figure.	**perímetro** Suma de las longitudes de los lados de una figura plana cerrada.	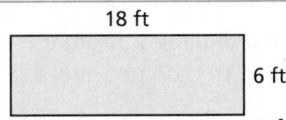 Perimeter = 18 + 6 + 18 + 6 = 48 ft
permutation An arrangement of a group of objects in which order is important.	**permutación** Arreglo de un grupo de objetos en el cual el orden es importante.	For objects A, B, C, and D, there are 12 different permutations of 2 objects. AB, AC, AD, BC, BD, CD BA, CA, DA, CB, DB, DC
perpendicular Intersecting to form 90° angles.	**perpendicular** Que se cruza para formar ángulos de 90°.	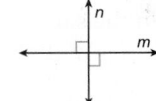
perpendicular lines Lines that intersect at 90° angles.	**líneas perpendiculares** Líneas que se cruzan en ángulos de 90°.	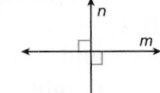
plane A flat surface that has no thickness and extends forever.	**plano** Una superficie plana que no tiene grosor y se extiende infinitamente.	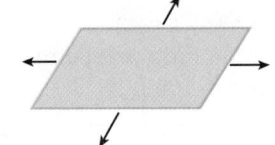
point A location that has no size.	**punto** Ubicación exacta que no tiene ningún tamaño.	P • point P
point-slope form The point-slope form of a linear equation is $y - y_1 = m(x - x_1)$, where m is the slope and (x_1, y_1) is a point on the line.	**forma de punto y pendiente** La forma de punto y pendiente de una ecuación lineal es $y - y_1 = m(x - x_1)$, donde m es la pendiente y (x_1, y_1) es un punto en la línea.	$y - 3 = 2(x - 3)$
polygon A closed plane figure formed by three or more segments such that each segment intersects exactly two other segments only at their endpoints and no two segments with a common endpoint are collinear.	**polígono** Figura plana cerrada formada por tres o más segmentos tal que cada segmento se cruza únicamente con otros dos segmentos sólo en sus extremos y ningún segmento con un extremo común a otro es colineal con éste.	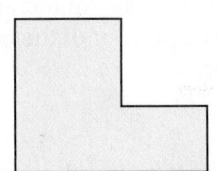
polynomial A monomial or a sum or difference of monomials.	**polinomio** Monomio o suma o diferencia de monomios.	$2x^2 + 3xy - 7y^2$

Glossary/Glosario

ENGLISH	SPANISH	EXAMPLES
polynomial long division A method of dividing one polynomial by another.	**división larga polinomial** Método por el que se divide un polinomio entre otro.	$$\begin{array}{r} x + 1 \\ x+2{\overline{\smash{\big)}\,x^2 + 3x + 5}} \\ \underline{-(x^2 + 2x)} \\ x + 5 \\ \underline{-(x+2)} \\ 3 \end{array}$$ $$\frac{x^2 + 3x + 5}{x+2} = x + 1 + \frac{3}{x+2}$$
population The entire group of objects or individuals considered for a survey.	**población** Grupo completo de objetos o individuos que se desea estudiar.	In a survey about the study habits of high school students, the population is all high school students.
positive correlation Two data sets have a positive correlation if both sets of data values increase.	**correlación positiva** Dos conjuntos de datos tienen correlación positiva si los valores de ambos conjuntos de datos aumentan.	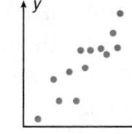
positive number A number greater than zero.	**número positivo** Número mayor que cero.	2 is a positive number. $$\begin{array}{c} \longleftarrow\!\!+\!\!+\!\!+\!\!+\!\!+\!\!+\!\!+\!\!+\!\!+\!\!\longrightarrow \\ {-4}\;{-3}\;{-2}\;{-1}\;\;0\;\;1\;\;2\;\;3\;\;4 \end{array}$$
Power of a Power Property If a is any nonzero real number and m and n are integers, then $(a^m)^n = a^{mn}$.	**Propiedad de la potencia de una potencia** Dado un número real a distinto de cero y los números enteros m y n, entonces $(a^m)^n = a^{mn}$.	$$\begin{aligned}(6^7)^4 &= 6^{7 \cdot 4} \\ &= 6^{28}\end{aligned}$$
Power of a Product Property If a and b are any nonzero real numbers and n is any integer, then $(ab)^n = a^n b^n$.	**Propiedad de la potencia de un producto** Dados los números reales a y b distintos de cero y un número entero n, entonces $(ab)^n = a^n b^n$.	$$\begin{aligned}(2 \cdot 4)^3 &= 2^3 \cdot 4^3 \\ &= 8 \cdot 64 \\ &= 512\end{aligned}$$
Power of a Quotient Property If a and b are any nonzero real numbers and n is an integer, then $\left(\frac{a}{b}\right)^n = \frac{a^n}{b^n}$.	**Propiedad de la potencia de un cociente** Dados los números reales a y b distintos de cero y un número entero n, entonces $\left(\frac{a}{b}\right)^n = \frac{a^n}{b^n}$.	$$\begin{aligned}\left(\frac{3}{5}\right)^4 &= \frac{3}{5} \cdot \frac{3}{5} \cdot \frac{3}{5} \cdot \frac{3}{5} \\ &= \frac{3 \cdot 3 \cdot 3 \cdot 3}{5 \cdot 5 \cdot 5 \cdot 5} \\ &= \frac{3^4}{5^4}\end{aligned}$$
precision The level of detail of a measurement, determined by the unit of measure.	**precisión** Detalle de una medición, determinado por la unidad de medida.	A ruler marked in millimeters has a greater level of precision than a ruler marked in centimeters.
prediction An estimate or guess about something that has not yet happened.	**predicción** Estimación o suposición sobre algo que todavía no ha sucedido.	
prime factorization A representation of a number or a polynomial as a product of primes.	**factorización prima** Representación de un número o de un polinomio como producto de números primos.	The prime factorization of 60 is $2 \cdot 2 \cdot 3 \cdot 5$.

Glossary/Glosario

ENGLISH	SPANISH	EXAMPLES
prime number A whole number greater than 1 that has exactly two positive factors, itself and 1.	**número primo** Número cabal mayor que 1 que es divisible únicamente entre sí mismo y entre 1.	5 is prime because its only positive factors are 5 and 1.
principal An amount of money borrowed or invested.	**capital** Cantidad de dinero que se pide prestado o se invierte.	
prism A polyhedron formed by two parallel congruent polygonal bases connected by faces that are parallelograms.	**prisma** Poliedro formado por dos bases poligonales congruentes y paralelas conectadas por caras laterales que son paralelogramos.	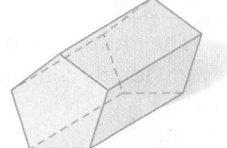
probability A number from 0 to 1 (or 0% to 100%) that is the measure of how likely an event is to occur.	**probabilidad** Número entre 0 y 1 (o entre 0% y 100%) que describe cuán probable es que ocurra un suceso.	A bag contains 3 red marbles and 4 blue marbles. The probability of randomly choosing a red marble is $\frac{3}{7}$.
Product of Powers Property If a is any nonzero real number and m and n are integers, then $a^m \cdot a^n = a^{m+n}$.	**Propiedad del producto de potencias** Dado un número real a distinto de cero y los números enteros m y n, entonces $a^m \cdot a^n = a^{m+n}$.	$6^7 \cdot 6^4 = 6^{7+4}$ $= 6^{11}$
Product Property of Square Roots For $a \geq 0$ and $b \geq 0$, $\sqrt{ab} = \sqrt{a} \cdot \sqrt{b}$.	**Propiedad del producto de raíces cuadradas** Dados $a \geq 0$ y $b \geq 0$, $\sqrt{ab} = \sqrt{a} \cdot \sqrt{b}$.	$\sqrt{9 \cdot 25} = \sqrt{9} \cdot \sqrt{25}$ $= 3 \cdot 5 = 15$
proportion A statement that two ratios are equal; $\frac{a}{b} = \frac{c}{d}$.	**proporción** Ecuación que establece que dos razones son iguales; $\frac{a}{b} = \frac{c}{d}$.	$\frac{2}{3} = \frac{4}{6}$
pyramid A polyhedron formed by a polygonal base and triangular lateral faces that meet at a common vertex.	**pirámide** Poliedro formado por una base poligonal y caras laterales triangulares que se encuentran en un vértice común.	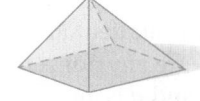
Pythagorean Theorem If a right triangle has legs of lengths a and b and a hypotenuse of length c, then $a^2 + b^2 = c^2$.	**Teorema de Pitágoras** Dado un triángulo rectángulo con catetos de longitudes a y b y una hipotenusa de longitud c, entonces $a^2 + b^2 = c^2$.	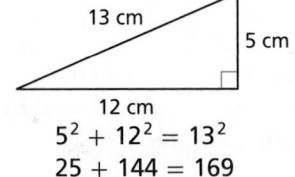 $5^2 + 12^2 = 13^2$ $25 + 144 = 169$
Pythagorean triple A set of three positive integers a, b, and c such that $a^2 + b^2 = c^2$.	**Tripleta de Pitágoras** Conjunto de tres enteros positivos a, b y c tal que $a^2 + b^2 = c^2$.	The numbers 3, 4, and 5 form a Pythagorean triple because $3^2 + 4^2 = 5^2$.

quadrant One of the four regions into which the x- and y-axes divide the coordinate plane.	**cuadrante** Una de las cuatro regiones en las que los ejes x e y dividen el plano cartesiano.	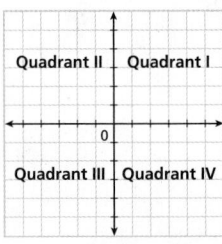

Glossary/Glosario

ENGLISH	SPANISH	EXAMPLES
quadratic equation An equation that can be written in the form $ax^2 + bx + c = 0$, where a, b, and c are real numbers and $a \neq 0$.	**ecuación cuadrática** Ecuación que se puede expresar como $ax^2 + bx + c = 0$, donde a, b y c son números reales y $a \neq 0$.	$x^2 + 3x - 4 = 0$ $x^2 - 9 = 0$
Quadratic Formula The formula $x = \frac{-b \pm \sqrt{b^2 - 4ac}}{2a}$, which gives solutions, or roots, of equations in the form $ax^2 + bx + c = 0$, where $a \neq 0$.	**fórmula cuadrática** La fórmula $x = \frac{-b \pm \sqrt{b^2 - 4ac}}{2a}$, que da soluciones, o raíces, para las ecuaciones del tipo $ax^2 + bx + c = 0$, donde $a \neq 0$.	The solutions of $2x^2 - 5x - 3 = 0$ are given by $$x = \frac{-(-5) \pm \sqrt{(-5)^2 - 4(2)(-3)}}{2(2)}$$ $$= \frac{5 \pm \sqrt{25 + 24}}{4} = \frac{5 \pm 7}{4}$$ $x = 3$ or $x = -\frac{1}{2}$
quadratic function A function that can be written in the form $f(x) = a x^2 + bx + c$, where a, b, and c are real numbers and $a \neq 0$.	**función cuadrática** Función que se puede expresar como $f(x) = ax^2 + bx + c$, donde a, b y c son números reales y $a \neq 0$.	$f(x) = x^2 - 6x + 8$
quadratic polynomial A polynomial of degree 2.	**polinomio cuadrático** Polinomio de grado 2.	$x^2 - 6x + 8$
quartile The median of the upper or lower half of a data set. *See also* first quartile, third quartile.	**cuartil** La mediana de la mitad superior o inferior de un conjunto de datos. *Ver también* primer cuartil, tercer cuartil.	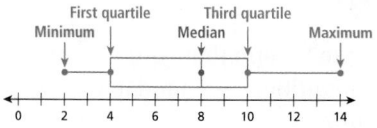
Quotient of Powers Property If a is a nonzero real number and m and n are integers, then $\frac{a^m}{a^n} = a^{m-n}$.	**Propiedad del cociente de potencias** Dado un número real a distinto de cero y los números enteros m y n, entonces $\frac{a^m}{a^n} = a^{m-n}$.	$\frac{6^7}{6^4} = 6^{7-4} = 6^3$
Quotient Property of Square Roots For $a \geq 0$ and $b > 0$, $\sqrt{\frac{a}{b}} = \frac{\sqrt{a}}{\sqrt{b}}$.	**Propiedad del cociente de raíces cuadradas** Dados $a \geq 0$ y $b > 0$, $\sqrt{\frac{a}{b}} = \frac{\sqrt{a}}{\sqrt{b}}$.	$\sqrt{\frac{9}{25}} = \frac{\sqrt{9}}{\sqrt{25}} = \frac{3}{5}$

ENGLISH	SPANISH	EXAMPLES
radical equation An equation that contains a variable within a radical.	**ecuación radical** Ecuación que contiene una variable dentro de un radical.	$\sqrt{x + 3} + 4 = 7$
radical expression An expression that contains a radical sign.	**expresión radical** Expresión que contiene un signo de radical.	$\sqrt{x + 3} + 4$
radical symbol The symbol $\sqrt{}$ used to denote a root. The symbol is used alone to indicate a square root or with an index, $\sqrt[n]{}$, to indicate the nth root.	**símbolo de radical** Símbolo $\sqrt{}$ que se utiliza para expresar una raíz. Puede utilizarse solo para indicar una raíz cuadrada, o con un índice, $\sqrt[n]{}$, para indicar la enésima raíz.	$\sqrt{36} = 6$ $\sqrt[3]{27} = 3$

ENGLISH	SPANISH	EXAMPLES
radicand The expression under a radical sign.	**radicando** Número o expresión debajo del signo de radical.	Expression: $\sqrt{x+3}$ Radicand: $x+3$
radius A segment whose endpoints are the center of a circle and a point on the circle; the distance from the center of a circle to any point on the circle.	**radio** Segmento cuyos extremos son el centro de un círculo y un punto de la circunferencia; distancia desde el centro de un círculo hasta cualquier punto de la circunferencia.	
random sample A sample selected from a population so that each member of the population has an equal chance of being selected.	**muestra aleatoria** Muestra seleccionada de una población tal que cada miembro de ésta tenga igual probabilidad de ser seleccionada.	Mr. Hansen chose a random sample of the class by writing each student's name on a slip of paper, mixing up the slips, and drawing five slips without looking.
range of a data set The difference of the greatest and least values in the data set.	**rango de un conjunto de datos** La diferencia del mayor y menor valor en un conjunto de datos.	The data set {3, 3, 5, 7, 8, 10, 11, 11, 12} has a range of $12 - 3 = 9$.
range of a function or relation The set of all second coordinates (or y-values) of a function or relation.	**rango de una función o relación** Conjunto de todos los valores de la segunda coordenada (o valores de y) de una función o relación.	The range of the function {(−5, 3), (−3, −2), (−1, −1), (1, 0)} is {−2, −1, 0, 3}.
rate A ratio that compares two quantities measured in different units.	**tasa** Razón que compara dos cantidades medidas en diferentes unidades.	$\dfrac{55\text{ miles}}{1\text{ hour}} = 55$ mi/h
rate of change A ratio that compares the amount of change in a dependent variable to the amount of change in an independent variable.	**tasa de cambio** Razón que compara la cantidad de cambio de la variable dependiente con la cantidad de cambio de la variable independiente.	The cost of mailing a letter increased from 22 cents in 1985 to 25 cents in 1988. During this period, the rate of change was $\dfrac{\text{change in cost}}{\text{change in year}} = \dfrac{25-22}{1988-1985} = \dfrac{3}{3}$ $= 1$ cent per year.
ratio A comparison of two quantities by division.	**razón** Comparación de dos cantidades mediante una división.	$\dfrac{1}{2}$ or $1:2$
rational equation An equation that contains one or more rational expressions.	**ecuación racional** Ecuación que contiene una o más expresiones racionales.	$\dfrac{x+2}{x^2+3x-1} = 6$
rational exponent An exponent that can be expressedas $\frac{m}{n}$ such that if m and n are integers, then $b^{\frac{m}{n}} = \sqrt[n]{b^m} = \left(\sqrt[n]{b}\right)^m$.	**exponente racional** Exponente que se puede expresar como $\frac{m}{n}$ tal que si m y n son números enteros, entonces $b^{\frac{m}{n}} = \sqrt[n]{b^m} = \left(\sqrt[n]{b}\right)^m$.	$64^{\frac{1}{6}} = \sqrt[6]{64}$
rational expression An algebraic expression whose numerator and denominator are polynomials and whose denominator has a degree ≥ 1.	**expresión racional** Expresión algebraica cuyo numerador y denominador son polinomios y cuyo denominador tiene un grado ≥ 1.	$\dfrac{x+2}{x^2+3x-1}$

ENGLISH	SPANISH	EXAMPLES
rational function A function whose rule can be written as a rational expression.	**función racional** Función cuya regla se puede expresar como una expresión racional.	$f(x) = \dfrac{x+2}{x^2 + 3x - 1}$
rational number A number that can be written in the form $\frac{a}{b}$, where a and b are integers and $b \neq 0$.	**número racional** Número que se puede expresar como $\frac{a}{b}$, donde a y b son números enteros y $b \neq 0$.	$3,\ 1.75,\ 0.\overline{3},\ -\frac{2}{3},\ 0$
rationalizing the denominator A method of rewriting a fraction by multiplying by another fraction that is equivalent to 1 in order to remove radical terms from the denominator.	**racionalizar el denominador** Método que consiste en escribir nuevamente una fracción multiplicándola por otra fracción equivalente a 1 a fin de eliminar los términos radicales del denominador.	$\dfrac{1}{\sqrt{2}} \cdot \dfrac{\sqrt{2}}{\sqrt{2}} = \dfrac{\sqrt{2}}{2}$
ray A part of a line that starts at an endpoint and extends forever in one direction.	**rayo** Parte de una recta que comienza en un extremo y se extiende infinitamente en una dirección.	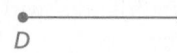
real number A rational or irrational number. Every point on the number line represents a real number.	**número real** Número racional o irracional. Cada punto de la recta numérica representa un número real.	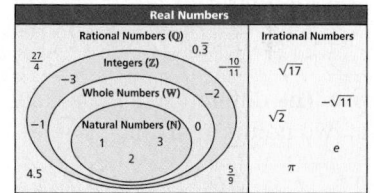
reciprocal For a real number $a \neq 0$, the reciprocal of a is $\frac{1}{a}$. The product of reciprocals is 1.	**recíproco** Dado el número real $a \neq 0$, el recíproco de a es $\frac{1}{a}$. El producto de los recíprocos es 1.	Number / Reciprocal table: 2 → $\frac{1}{2}$ 1 → 1 −1 → −1 0 → No reciprocal
rectangle A quadrilateral with four right angles.	**rectángulo** Cuadrilátero con cuatro ángulos rectos.	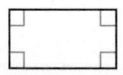
rectangular prism A prism whose bases are rectangles.	**prisma rectangular** Prisma cuyas bases son rectángulos.	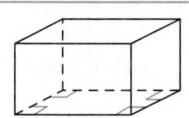
rectangular pyramid A pyramid whose base is a rectangle.	**pirámide rectangular** Pirámide cuya base es un rectángulo.	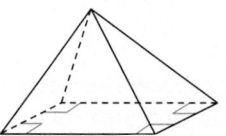
reflection A transformation that reflects, or "flips," a graph or figure across a line, called the line of reflection.	**reflexión** Transformación en la que una gráfica o figura se refleja o se invierte sobre una línea, denominada la línea de reflexión.	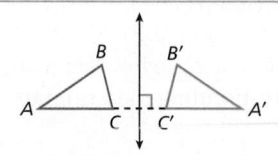
regular polygon A polygon that is both equilateral and equiangular.	**polígono regular** Polígono equilátero de ángulos iguales.	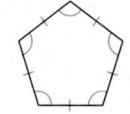

Glossary/Glosario

relation A set of ordered pairs.

relación Conjunto de pares ordenados.

$\{(0, 5), (0, 4), (2, 3), (4, 0)\}$

---

repeating decimal A rational number in decimal form that has a nonzero block of one or more digits that repeat continuously.

decimal periódico Número racional en forma decimal que tiene un bloque de uno o más dígitos que se repite continuamente.

$1.\overline{3}, 0.\overline{6}, 2.\overline{14}, 6.77\overline{3}$

---

replacement set A set of numbers that can be substituted for a variable.

conjunto de reemplazo Conjunto de números que pueden sustituir una variable.

---

residual The signed vertical distance between a data point and a line of fit.

residuo La diferencia vertical entre un dato y una línea de ajuste.

---

rhombus A quadrilateral with four congruent sides.

rombo Cuadrilátero con cuatro lados congruentes.

---

right angle An angle that measures 90°.

ángulo recto Ángulo que mide 90°.

---

rise The difference in the *y*-values of two points on a line.

distancia vertical Diferencia entre los valores de *y* de dos puntos de una línea.

For the points $(3, -1)$ and $(6, 5)$, the rise is $5 - (-1) = 6$.

---

rotation A transformation that rotates or turns a figure about a point called the center of rotation.

rotación Transformación que rota o gira una figura sobre un punto llamado centro de rotación.

---

run The difference in the *x*-values of two points on a line.

distancia horizontal Diferencia entre los valores de *x* de dos puntos de una línea.

For the points $(3, -1)$ and $(6, 5)$, the run is $6 - 3 = 3$.

S

sample A part of the population.

muestra Una parte de la población.

In a survey about the study habits of high school students, a sample is a survey of 100 students.

---

sample space The set of all possible outcomes of a probability experiment.

espacio muestral Conjunto de todos los resultados posibles de un experimento de probabilidad.

In the experiment of rolling a number cube, the sample space is $\{1, 2, 3, 4, 5, 6\}$.

---

scale The ratio between two corresponding measurements.

escala Razón entre dos medidas correspondientes.

1 cm : 5 mi

Glossary/Glosario

ENGLISH	SPANISH	EXAMPLES
scale drawing A drawing that uses a scale to represent an object as smaller or larger than the actual object.	**dibujo a escala** Dibujo que utiliza una escala para representar un objeto como más pequeño o más grande que el objeto original.	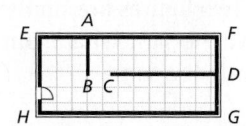 A blueprint is an example of a scale drawing.
scale factor The multiplier used on each dimension to change one figure into a similar figure.	**factor de escala** El multiplicador utilizado en cada dimensión para transformar una figura en una figura semejante.	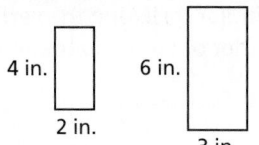 4 in. 2 in. 6 in. 3 in. Scale factor: $\frac{3}{2} = 1.5$
scale model A three-dimensional model that uses a scale to represent an object as smaller or larger than the actual object.	**modelo a escala** Modelo tridimensional que utiliza una escala para representar un objeto como más pequeño o más grande que el objeto real.	
scalene triangle A triangle with no congruent sides.	**triángulo escaleno** Triángulo sin lados congruentes.	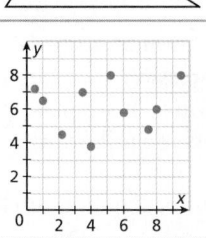
scatter plot A graph with points plotted to show a possible relationship between two sets of data.	**diagrama de dispersión** Gráfica con puntos que se usa para demostrar una relación posible entre dos conjuntos de datos.	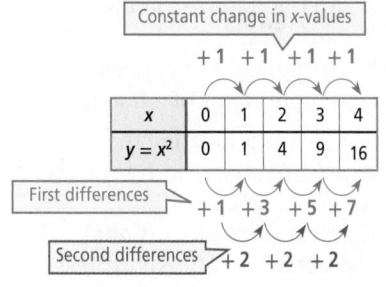
second differences Differences between first differences of a function.	**segundas diferencias** Diferencias entre las primeras diferencias de una función.	Constant change in *x*-values $+1 \ +1 \ +1 \ +1$ 	*x*	0	1	2	3	4	 	$y = x^2$	0	1	4	9	16	 First differences $+1 \ +3 \ +5 \ +7$ Second differences $+2 \ +2 \ +2$
sequence A list of numbers that often form a pattern.	**sucesión** Lista de números que generalmente forman un patrón.	1, 2, 4, 8, 16, …
set A collection of items called elements.	**conjunto** Grupo de componentes denominados elementos.	{1, 2, 3}
set-builder notation A notation for a set that uses a rule to describe the properties of the elements of the set.	**notación de conjuntos** Notación para un conjunto que se vale de una regla para describir las propiedades de los elementos del conjunto.	$\{x \mid x > 3\}$ is read "The set of all *x* such that *x* is greater than 3."

ENGLISH	SPANISH	EXAMPLES
similar Two figures are similar if they have the same shape but not necessarily the same size.	**semejantes** Dos figuras con la misma forma pero no necesariamente del mismo tamaño.	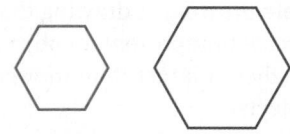
similarity statement A statement that indicates that two polygons are similar by listing the vertices in the order of correspondence.	**enunciado de semejanza** Enunciado que indica que dos polígonos son semejantes enumerando los vértices en orden de correspondencia.	quadrilateral $ABCD \sim$ quadrilateral $EFGH$
simple event An event consisting of only one outcome.	**suceso simple** Suceso que tiene sólo un resultado.	In the experiment of rolling a number cube, the event consisting of the outcome 3 is a simple event.
simple interest A fixed percent of the principal. For principal P, interest rate r, and time t in years, the simple interest is $I = Prt$.	**interés simple** Porcentaje fijo del capital. Dado el capital P, la tasa de interés r y el tiempo t expresado en años, el interés simple es $I = Prt$.	If \$100 is put into an account with a simple interest rate of 5%, then after 2 years, the account will have earned $I = 100 \cdot 0.05 \cdot 2 = \$10$ in interest.
simplest form of a square root expression A square root expression is in simplest form if it meets the following criteria: 1. No perfect squares are in the radicand. 2. No fractions are in the radicand. 3. No square roots appear in the denominator of a fraction. *See also* rationalizing the denominator.	**forma simplificada de una expresión de raíz cuadrada** Una expresión de raíz cuadrada está en forma simplificada si reúne los siguientes requisitos: 1. No hay cuadrados perfectos en el radicando. 2. No hay fracciones en el radicando. 3. No aparecen raíces cuadradas en el denominador de una fracción. *Ver también* racionalizar el denominador.	<table><tr><th>Not Simplest Form</th><th>Simplest Form</th></tr><tr><td>$\sqrt{180}$</td><td>$6\sqrt{5}$</td></tr><tr><td>$\sqrt{216a^2b^2}$</td><td>$6ab\sqrt{6}$</td></tr><tr><td>$\dfrac{\sqrt{7}}{\sqrt{2}}$</td><td>$\dfrac{\sqrt{14}}{2}$</td></tr></table>
simplest form of a rational expression A rational expression is in simplest form if the numerator and denominator have no common factors.	**forma simplificada de una expresión racional** Una expresión racional está en forma simplificada cuando el numerador y el denominador no tienen factores comunes.	$\dfrac{x^2 - 1}{x^2 + x - 2} = \dfrac{(x-1)(x+1)}{(x-1)(x+2)}$ $= \dfrac{x+1}{x+2}$ ↑ Simplest form

ENGLISH	SPANISH	EXAMPLES

simplest form of an exponential expression An exponential expression is in simplest form if it meets the following criteria:

1. There are no negative exponents.
2. The same base does not appear more than once in a product or quotient.
3. No powers, products, or quotients are raised to powers.
4. Numerical coefficients in a quotient do not have any common factor other than 1.

forma simplificada de una expresión exponencial Una expresión exponencial está en forma simplificada si reúne los siguientes requisitos:

1. No hay exponentes negativos.
2. La misma base no aparece más de una vez en un producto o cociente.
3. No se elevan a potencias productos, cocientes ni potencias.
4. Los coeficientes numéricos en un cociente no tienen ningún factor común que no sea 1.

Not Simplest Form	Simplest Form
$7^8 \cdot 7^4$	7^{12}
$(x^2)^{-4} \cdot x^5$	$\dfrac{1}{x^3}$
$\dfrac{a^5 b^9}{(ab)^4}$	ab^5

---

simplify To perform all indicated operations.

simplificar Realizar todas las operaciones indicadas.

$$13 - 20 + 8$$
$$-7 + 8$$
$$1$$

---

simulation A model of an experiment, often one that would be too difficult or time-consuming to actually perform.

simulación Modelo de un experimento; generalmente se recurre a la simulación cuando realizar dicho experimento sería demasiado difícil o llevaría mucho tiempo.

---

sine In a right triangle, the ratio of the length of the leg opposite $\angle A$ to the length of the hypotenuse.

seno En un triángulo rectángulo, razón entre la longitud del cateto opuesto a $\angle A$ y la longitud de la hipotenusa.

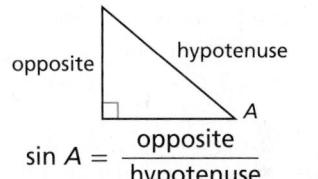

$$\sin A = \frac{\text{opposite}}{\text{hypotenuse}}$$

---

slope A measure of the steepness of a line. If (x_1, y_1) and (x_2, y_2) are any two points on the line, the slope of the line, known as m, is represented by the equation $m = \frac{y_2 - y_1}{x_2 - x_1}$.

pendiente Medida de la inclinación de una línea. Dados dos puntos (x_1, y_1) y (x_2, y_2) en una línea, la pendiente de la línea, denominada m, se representa con la ecuación $m = \frac{y_2 - y_1}{x_2 - x_1}$.

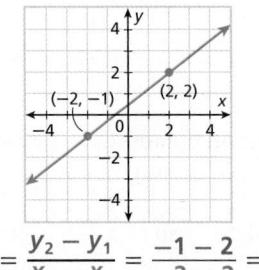

$$m = \frac{y_2 - y_1}{x_2 - x_1} = \frac{-1 - 2}{-2 - 2} = \frac{3}{4}$$

---

slope-intercept form The slope-intercept form of a linear equation is $y = mx + b$, where m is the slope and b is the y-intercept.

forma de pendiente-intersección La forma de pendiente-intersección de una ecuación lineal es $y = mx + b$, donde m es la pendiente y b es la intersección con el eje y.

$y = -2x + 4$
The slope is -2.
The y-intercept is 4.

---

solution of a linear equation in two variables An ordered pair or ordered pairs that make the equation true.

solución de una ecuación lineal en dos variables Un par ordenado o pares ordenados que hacen que la ecuación sea verdadera.

(4, 2) is a solution of
$x + y = 6$.

ENGLISH	SPANISH	EXAMPLES
solution of a linear inequality in two variables An ordered pair or ordered pairs that make the inequality true.	**solución de una desigualdad lineal en dos variables** Un par ordenado o pares ordenados que hacen que la desigualdad sea verdadera.	$(3, 1)$ is a solution of $x + y < 6$.
solution of a system of linear equations Any ordered pair that satisfies all the equations in a system.	**solución de un sistema de ecuaciones lineales** Cualquier par ordenado que resuelva todas las ecuaciones de un sistema.	$\begin{cases} x + y = -1 \\ -x + y = -3 \end{cases}$ Solution: $(1, -2)$
solution of a system of linear inequalities Any ordered pair that satisfies all the inequalities in a system.	**solución de un sistema de desigualdades lineales** Cualquier par ordenado que resuelva todas las desigualdades de un sistema.	$\begin{cases} y \le x + 1 \\ y < -x + 4 \end{cases}$ $(2, 1)$ is in the overlapping shaded regions, so it is a solution.
solution of an equation in one variable A value or values that make the equation true.	**solución de una ecuación en una variable** Valor o valores que hacen que la ecuación sea verdadera.	Equation: $x + 2 = 6$ Solution: $x = 4$
solution of an inequality in one variable A value or values that make the inequality true.	**solución de una desigualdad en una variable** Valor o valores que hacen que la desigualdad sea verdadera.	Inequality: $x + 2 < 6$ Solution: $x < 4$
solution set The set of values that make a statement true.	**conjunto solución** Conjunto de valores que hacen verdadero un enunciado.	Inequality: $x + 3 \ge 5$ Solution set: $\{x \mid x \ge 2\}$
square A quadrilateral with four congruent sides and four right angles.	**cuadrado** Cuadrilátero con cuatro lados congruentes y cuatro ángulos rectos.	
square in numeration The second power of a number.	**cuadrado en numeración** La segunda potencia de un número.	16 is the square of 4.
standard form of a linear equation $Ax + By = C$, where A, B, and C are real numbers and A and B are not both 0.	**forma estándar de una ecuación lineal** $Ax + By = C$, donde A, B y C son números reales y A y B no son ambos cero.	$2x + 3y = 6$
standard form of a polynomial A polynomial in one variable is written in standard form when the terms are in order from greatest degree to least degree.	**forma estándar de un polinomio** Un polinomio de una variable se expresa en forma estándar cuando los términos se ordenan de mayor a menor grado.	$4x^5 - 2x^4 + x^2 - x + 1$

ENGLISH	SPANISH	EXAMPLES
standard form of a quadratic equation $ax^2 + bx + c = 0$, where a, b, and c are real numbers and $a \neq 0$.	**forma estándar de una ecuación cuadrática** $ax^2 + bx + c = 0$, donde a, b y c son números reales y $a \neq 0$.	$2x^2 + 3x - 1 = 0$
stem-and-leaf plot A graph used to organize and display data by dividing each data value into two parts, a stem and a leaf.	**diagrama de tallo y hojas** Gráfica utilizada para organizar y mostrar datos dividiendo cada valor de datos en dos partes, un tallo y una hoja.	Stem | Leaves 3 | 2 3 4 4 7 9 4 | 0 1 5 7 7 7 8 5 | 1 2 2 3 *Key: 3|2 means 3.2*
stratified random sample A sample in which a population is divided into distinct groups and members are selected at random from each group.	**muestra aleatoria estratificada** Muestra en la que la población está dividida en grupos diferenciados y los miembros de cada grupo se seleccionan al azar.	Ms. Carter chose a stratified random sample of her school's student population by randomly selecting 30 students from each grade level.
subset A set that is contained entirely within another set. Set B is a subset of set A if every element of B is contained in A, denoted $B \subset A$.	**subconjunto** Conjunto que se encuentra dentro de otro conjunto. El conjunto B es un subconjunto del conjunto A si todos los elementos de B son elementos de A; se expresa $B \subset A$.	The set of integers is a subset of the set of rational numbers.
substitution method A method used to solve systems of equations by solving an equation for one variable and substituting the resulting expression into the other equation(s).	**sustitución** Método utilizado para resolver sistemas de ecuaciones resolviendo una ecuación para una variable y sustituyendo la expresión resultante en las demás ecuaciones.	
Subtraction Property of Equality If a, b, and c are real numbers and $a = b$, then $a - c = b - c$.	**Propiedad de igualdad de la resta** Si a, b y c son números reales y $a = b$, entonces $a - c = b - c$.	$\begin{aligned} x + 6 &= 8 \\ -6 \quad &-6 \\ \hline x &= 2 \end{aligned}$
Subtraction Property of Inequality For real numbers a, b, and c, if $a < b$, then $a - c < b - c$. Also holds true for $>$, $\leq$, $\geq$, and $\neq$.	**Propiedad de desigualdad de la resta** Dados los números reales a, b y c, si $a < b$, entonces $a - c < b - c$. Es válido también para $>$, $\leq$, $\geq$ y $\neq$.	$\begin{aligned} x + 6 &< 8 \\ -6 \quad &-6 \\ \hline x &< 2 \end{aligned}$
supplementary angles Two angles whose measures have a sum of 180°.	**ángulos suplementarios** Dos ángulos cuyas medidas suman 180°.	30° 150°
surface area The total area of all faces and curved surfaces of a three-dimensional figure.	**área total** Área total de todas las caras y superficies curvas de una figura tridimensional.	12 cm 6 cm 8 cm Surface area $= 2(8)(12) + 2(8)(6) + 2(12)(6)$ $= 432 \text{ cm}^2$

ENGLISH	SPANISH	EXAMPLES
system of linear equations A system of equations in which all of the equations are linear.	**sistema de ecuaciones lineales** Sistema de ecuaciones en el que todas las ecuaciones son lineales.	$\begin{cases} 2x + 3y = -1 \\ x - 3y = 4 \end{cases}$
system of linear inequalities A system of inequalities in which all of the inequalities are linear.	**sistema de desigualdades lineales** Sistema de desigualdades en el que todas las desigualdades son lineales.	$\begin{cases} 2x + 3y > -1 \\ x - 3y \leq 4 \end{cases}$
systematic random sample A sample based on selecting one member of the population at random and then selecting other members by using a pattern.	**muestra sistemática** Muestra en la que se elige a un miembro de la población al azar y luego se elige a otros miembros mediante un patrón.	Mr. Martin chose a systematic random sample of customers visiting a store by selecting one customer at random and then selecting every tenth customer after that.

ENGLISH	SPANISH	EXAMPLES
tangent In a right triangle, the ratio of the length of the leg opposite $\angle A$ to the length of the leg adjacent to $\angle A$.	**tangente** En un triángulo rectángulo, razón entre la longitud del cateto opuesto a $\angle A$ y la longitud del cateto adyacente a $\angle A$.	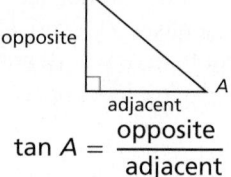 $\tan A = \dfrac{\text{opposite}}{\text{adjacent}}$
term of an expression The parts of the expression that are added or subtracted.	**término de una expresión** Parte de una expresión que debe sumarse o restarse.	$3x^2 + 6x - 8$ Term Term Term
term of a sequence An element or number in the sequence.	**término de una sucesión** Elemento o número de una sucesión.	5 is the third term in the sequence 1, 3, 5, 7, ...
terminating decimal A decimal that ends, or terminates.	**decimal finito** Decimal con un número determinados de posiciones decimales.	1.5, 2.75, 4.0
theoretical probability The ratio of the number of equally likely outcomes in an event to the total number of possible outcomes.	**probabilidad teórica** Razón entre el número de resultados igualmente probables de un suceso y el número total de resultados posibles.	In the experiment of rolling a number cube, the theoretical probability of rolling an odd number is $\frac{3}{6} = \frac{1}{2}$.
third quartile The median of the upper half of a data set. Also called *upper quartile*.	**tercer cuartil** La mediana de la mitad superior de un conjunto de datos. También se llama *cuartil superior*.	Lower half Upper half 18, 23, 28, 29, ⟨36⟩ 42 Third quartile
tolerance The amount by which a measurement is permitted to vary from a specified value.	**tolerancia** La cantidad por que una medida se permite variar de un valor especificado.	
transformation A change in the position, size, or shape of a figure or graph.	**transformación** Cambio en la posición, tamaño o forma de una figura o gráfica.	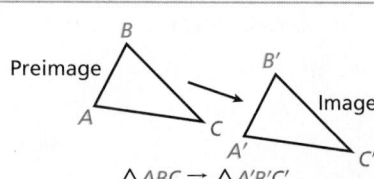 $\triangle ABC \rightarrow \triangle A'B'C'$

Glossary/Glosario

ENGLISH	SPANISH	EXAMPLES

translation A transformation that shifts or slides every point of a figure or graph the same distance in the same direction.

traslación Transformación en la que todos los puntos de una figura o gráfica se mueven la misma distancia en la misma dirección.

trapezoid A quadrilateral with exactly one pair of parallel sides.

trapecio Cuadrilátero con sólo un par de lados paralelos.

tree diagram A branching diagram that shows all possible combinations or outcomes of an experiment.

diagrama de árbol Diagrama con ramificaciones que muestra todas las combinaciones o resultados posibles de un experimento.

The tree diagram shows the possible outcomes when tossing a coin and rolling a number cube.

trend line A line on a scatter plot that helps show the correlation between data sets more clearly.

línea de tendencia Línea en un diagrama de dispersión que sirve para mostrar la correlación entre conjuntos de datos más claramente.

trial Each repetition or observation of an experiment.

prueba Una sola repetición u observación de un experimento.

In the experiment of rolling a number cube, each roll is one trial.

triangle A three-sided polygon.

triángulo Polígono de tres lados.

triangular prism A prism whose bases are triangles.

prisma triangular Prisma cuyas bases son triángulos.

Bases

triangular pyramid A pyramid whose base is a triangle.

pirámide triangular Pirámide cuya base es un triángulo.

trigonometric ratio Ratio of the lengths of two sides of a right triangle.

razón trigonométrica Razón entre dos lados de un triángulo rectángulo.

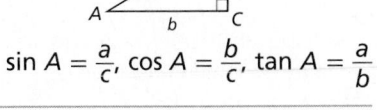

$\sin A = \dfrac{a}{c},\ \cos A = \dfrac{b}{c},\ \tan A = \dfrac{a}{b}$

trinomial A polynomial with three terms.

trinomio Polinomio con tres términos.

$4x^2 + 3xy - 5y^2$

ENGLISH	SPANISH	EXAMPLES

 U

union The union of two sets is the set of all elements that are in either set, denoted by ∪. | **unión** La unión de dos conjuntos es el conjunto de todos los elementos que se encuentran en ambos conjuntos, expresado por ∪. | $A = \{1, 2, 3, 4\}$ $B = \{1, 3, 5, 7, 9\}$ $A \cup B = \{1, 2, 3, 4, 5, 7, 9\}$

unit rate A rate in which the second quantity in the comparison is one unit. | **tasa unitaria** Tasa en la que la segunda cantidad de la comparación es una unidad. | $\dfrac{30 \text{ mi}}{1 \text{ h}} = 30$ mi/h

unlike radicals Radicals with a different quantity under the radical. | **radicales distintos** Radicales con cantidades diferentes debajo del signo de radical. | $2\sqrt{2}$ and $2\sqrt{3}$

unlike terms Terms with different variables or the same variables raised to different powers. | **términos distintos** Términos con variables diferentes o las mismas variables elevadas a potencias diferentes. | $4xy^2$ and $6x^2y$

upper quartile *See* third quartile. | **cuartil superior** *Ver* tercer cuartil. |

V

value of a function The result of replacing the independent variable with a number and simplifying. | **valor de una función** Resultado de reemplazar la variable independiente por un número y luego simplificar. | The value of the function $f(x) = x + 1$ for $x = 3$ is 4.

value of a variable A number used to replace a variable to make an equation true. | **valor de una variable** Número utilizado para reemplazar una variable y hacer que una ecuación sea verdadera. | In the equation $x + 1 = 4$, the value of x is 3.

value of an expression The result of replacing the variables in an expression with numbers and simplifying. | **valor de una expresión** Resultado de reemplazar las variables de una expresión por un número y luego simplificar. | The value of the expression $x + 1$ for $x = 3$ is 4.

variable A symbol used to represent a quantity that can change. | **variable** Símbolo utilizado para representar una cantidad que puede cambiar. | In the expression $2x + 3$, x is the variable.

Venn diagram A diagram used to show relationships between sets. | **diagrama de Venn** Diagrama utilizado para mostrar la relación entre conjuntos. |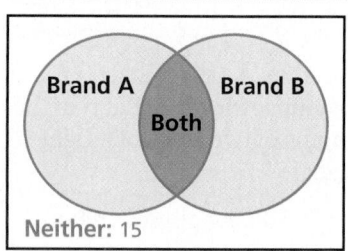

vertex of a parabola The highest or lowest point on the parabola. | **vértice de una parábola** Punto más alto o más bajo de una parábola. | 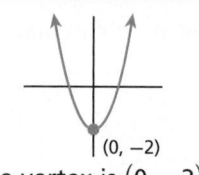 The vertex is $(0, -2)$.

G40 *Glossary/Glosario*

ENGLISH	SPANISH	EXAMPLES
vertex of an absolute-value graph The point on the axis of symmetry of the graph.	**vértice de una gráfica de valor absoluto** Punto en el eje de simetría de la gráfica.	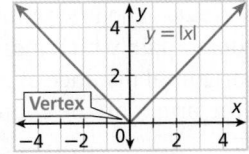
vertical angles The nonadjacent angles formed by two intersecting lines.	**ángulos opuestos por el vértice** Ángulos no adyacentes formados por dos líneas que se cruzan.	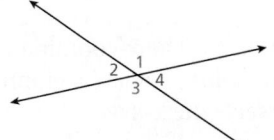 ∠1 and ∠3 are vertical angles. ∠2 and ∠4 are vertical angles.
vertical line A line whose equation is $x = a$, where a is the x-intercept.	**línea vertical** Línea cuya ecuación es $x = a$, donde a es la intersección con el eje x.	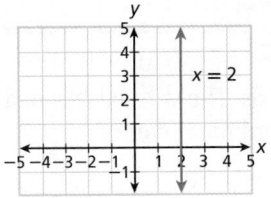
vertical-line test A test used to determine whether a relation is a function. If any vertical line crosses the graph of a relation more than once, the relation is not a function.	**prueba de la línea vertical** Prueba utilizada para determinar si una relación es una función. Si una línea vertical corta la gráfica de una relación más de una vez, la relación no es una función.	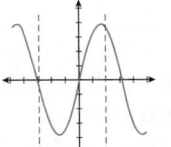 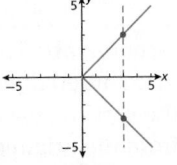 Function Not a function
volume The number of nonoverlapping unit cubes of a given size that will exactly fill the interior of a three-dimensional figure.	**volumen** Cantidad de cubos unitarios no superpuestos de un determinado tamaño que llenan exactamente el interior de una figura tridimensional.	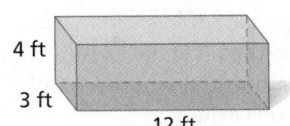 Volume = (3)(4)(12) = 144 ft³
voluntary response sample A sample in which members choose to be in the sample.	**muestra de respuesta voluntaria** Una muestra en la que los miembros eligen participar.	A store provides survey cards for customers who wish to fill them out.

whole number A member of the set of natural numbers and zero.	**número cabal** Miembro del conjunto de los números naturales y cero.	0, 1, 2, 3, 4, 5, …

x-axis The horizontal axis in a coordinate plane.	**eje x** Eje horizontal en un plano cartesiano.	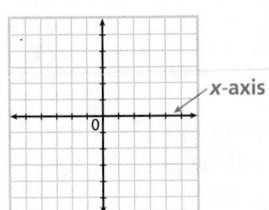

ENGLISH	SPANISH	EXAMPLES
x-coordinate The first number in an ordered pair, which indicates the horizontal distance of a point from the origin on the coordinate plane.	**coordenada x** Primer número de un par ordenado, que indica la distancia horizontal de un punto desde el origen en un plano cartesiano.	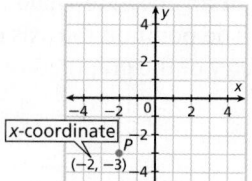
x-intercept The x-coordinate(s) of the point(s) where a graph intersects the x-axis.	**intersección con el eje x** Coordenada(s) x de uno o más puntos donde una gráfica corta el eje x.	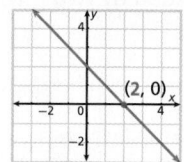 The x-intercept is 2.

ENGLISH	SPANISH	EXAMPLES
y-axis The vertical axis in a coordinate plane.	**eje y** Eje vertical en un plano cartesiano.	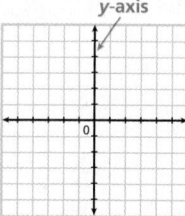
y-coordinate The second number in an ordered pair, which indicates the vertical distance of a point from the origin on the coordinate plane.	**coordenada y** Segundo número de un par ordenado, que indica la distancia vertical de un punto desde el origen en un plano cartesiano.	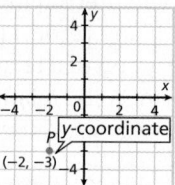
y-intercept The y-coordinate(s) of the point(s) where a graph intersects the y-axis.	**intersección con el eje y** Coordenada(s) y de uno o más puntos donde una gráfica corta el eje y.	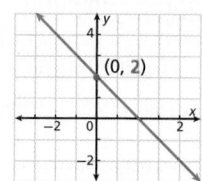 The y-intercept is 2.

Z

ENGLISH	SPANISH	EXAMPLES
zero exponent For any nonzero real number x, $x^0 = 1$.	**exponente cero** Dado un número real distinto de cero x, $x^0 = 1$.	$5^0 = 1$
zero of a function For the function f, any number x such that $f(x) = 0$.	**cero de una función** Dada la función f, todo número x tal que $f(x) = 0$.	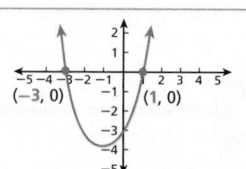 The zeros are −3 and 1.
Zero Product Property For real numbers p and q, if $pq = 0$, then $p = 0$ or $q = 0$.	**Propiedad del producto cero** Dados los números reales p y q, si $pq = 0$, entonces $p = 0$ o $q = 0$.	If $(x - 1)(x + 2) = 0$, then $x - 1 = 0$ or $x + 2 = 0$, so $x = 1$ or $x = -2$.

Index

Index

explain, 8, 20, 22, 28, 35, 44, 45, 51, 52, 56, 58, 65, 67, 73, 104, 105, 109, 110, 115, 116, 129, 131, 132, 139, 140, 147, 166, 172, 174, 176, 182, 184, 190, 191, 201, 202, 209, 210, 236, 251, 258, 264, 265, 298, 299, 304, 331, 332, 334, 341, 347, 348, 349, 356, 357, 363, 366, 371, 372, 396, 403, 408, 410, 411, 418, 428, 438, 439, 459, 460, 466, 468, 469, 475, 477, 485, 486, 495, 502, 503, 541, 542, 543, 549, 550, 558, 565, 571, 573, 580, 588, 589, 622, 623, 638, 639, 654, 692, 693, 694, 697, 699, 700, 705, 718, 719, 720, 729, 738, 739, 745, 746

find, 46, 461, 478, 479, 486, 549

give (an) example(s), 67, 117, 166, 176, 184, 410, 429, 439, 500, 550, 694, 705, 717, 729, 744

identify, 273, 313, 416, 639

list, 371

make, 699, 719

name, 71, 105, 182, 239, 365, 690

Reading and Writing Math, 5, 99, 163, 229, 327, 391, 455, 521, 617, 683, 697, Writing Strategies (*see also* **Reading Math; Reading Strategies; Study Strategies; Writing Math; Writing Strategies**)

show, 20, 21, 22, 28, 29, 44, 66, 68, 109, 110, 117, 299, 402, 468, 478, 485, 502, 528

tell, 27, 30, 43, 58, 146, 168, 259, 313, 363, 528, 537, 548, 578, 628, 731, 737

write, 8, 9, 38, 45, 242, 333, 428, 485, 496, 503, 529, 622, 639

Write About It
  Write About It questions are found in every exercise set. Some examples: 9, 22, 29, 38, 45

Communication, 57, 123

Community, 291

complement of an event, 735

completing the square, 575–578, 586

composite figures, areas of, 23

compound events, 748–749

compound inequalities, 134–137, 142

compound interest, 636

compound statements, 133

cones, 430

Conjecture, making a, 252, 253, 300, 544, 560, 574

Connecting Algebra
  to Data Analysis, 205, 284, 684–685, 722–723
  to Geometry, 14–15, 23, 141, 243, 430, 631
  to Number Theory, 350–351, 497

consistent systems, 352–353

constant
  definition of, 6

in trinomial factoring, 472–474
of variation, 260

constant changes, exploring, 252–253

Construction, 51, 57, 250, 478

Consumer Application, 42, 114, 174, 244, 271

Consumer Economics, 28, 36, 43, 109, 201, 251, 280, 339, 340, 346, 347, 362, 653

contact lenses, 110

contests, 629

continuous graphs, 165

convenience sample, 723

conversion factors, 63, 521

converting between probabilities and odds, 736

convincing arguments/ explanations, writing, 327

coordinate plane, area in, 243

correlation, 196
  causation and, 288

correlation coefficient, 287–288

corresponding angles, 69

corresponding sides, 69

Countdown to Mastery, CC36–CC59

crash test dummies, 410

create a table to evaluate expressions, 12–13

Critical Thinking
  Critical Thinking questions are found in every exercise set. Some examples: 11, 22, 28, 38, 45

cross products, in proportions, 63

Cross Products Property, 63

cubes, difference of, 496

cubic binomials, 443

cubic equations, 601–603

cubic functions, 600–603

cubic polynomials, 407

Culinary Arts major, 132

Cumulative Assessment, 92–93, 158–159, 222–223, 322–323, 384–385, 450–451, 514–515, 612–613, 678–679, 760–761

cumulative frequency, 697

cylinders
  surface area of, 430
  volume of, 430, 573

data
  displaying, 686–690
  distributions, 702–705, 710–711
  graphing, to choose a model, 649–650
  organizing, 686–690

Data Analysis, Connecting Algebra to, 205, 284, 684–685, 722–723

Data Collection Applications, 168, 250, 549

Data Mining major, 282

decay, exponential, 635–638

Decorating, 67

degrees
  of monomials, 406
  of polynomials, 406

Demographics, 595

dependent events, 740–744

dependent systems, 353

dependent variables, 180, 181, 182, 183, 184

Devon Island, 10

diagrams
  ladder, 456
  mapping, 170
  reading and interpreting, 697
  using, 448–449

difference(s)
  of cubes, 496
  first, 522
  second, 522
  of two squares, 435, 492

dimensional analysis, 63

dimensions, changing, 15, 71

direct variation, 260–263

discrete graphs, 165

discriminant, 584
  quadratic formula and, 582–587

displaying data, 686–690

distracters, recognizing, 320–321

distributions, data, 702–705, 710–711

Distributive Property, 463

division
  solving equations by, 24–27
  solving inequalities by, 112–114

Division Property of Equality, 26

Division Property of Inequality, 112, 113

domain(s), 170, 171, 172, 173, 174, 175, 176, 182, 183, 184, 185, 186, 187, 189, 190, 193, 194, 195
  of linear functions, 233
  of quadratic functions, 525
  reasonable, 182, 183, 184, 185, 189, 195, 217, 218, 233, 238, 528

dot plots, 710–711

double-bar graphs, 687

double-line graphs, 688

draw a diagram, PS2

Drum Corps International, 460

earned run average (ERA), 52

Earth Science, 28

Ecology, 201

Ecology Link, 201

Economics, 28, 36, 43, 109, 201, 251, 339, 340, 346, 347, 362, 653

Education, 116, 130

Index

of linear functions, 300
of quadratic functions, 544

Farming, 371

Fibonacci sequence, 210

figures
  composite, 23
  reading and interpreting, 697
  similar, 69

final exam preparation, 683

Finance, 20, 28, 51, 66, 341, 467, 595, 636, 655

find a pattern, PS6

finding a term of an arithmetic sequence, 206–208

finding a term of a geometric sequence, 618–620

first coordinates, 170

first differences, 522

first quartile, 704

Fitness, 19, 273, 333

FOIL method, 423, 472

formula(s), 49
  area
    of composite figures, 23
    in the coordinate plane, 243
    of a rectangle, 23
    of a square, 23
    surface, 403, 430
    of a trapezoid, 566
    of a triangle, 23
  axis of symmetry of a parabola, 533
  compound interest, 636
  distance from a light source, 402
  experimental probability, 728
  exponential decay, 637
  exponential growth, 635
  half-life, 637
  period of a pendulum, 572
  probability of dependent events, 743
  probability of independent events, 741
  Quadratic, 582
  recursive, 647
  remembering, 617
  slope, 254
  solving for a variable, 50
  speed of light, 404
  surface area of a sphere, 403
  term of an arithmetic sequence, 206–207
  term of a geometric sequence, 618
  theoretical probability, 734
  volume of a cylinder, 573

fraction(s)
  as exponents, 398–400
  negative, 276

frequency, 695–697
  cumulative, 697

frequency table, 696

function(s)
  absolute-value, 310–313
  comparing, 660–664
  cubic, 600–603
  definition of, 171

degree of, 406
evaluating, 181
exponential, 624–627, 651, 661
families of, 301, 544
general forms of, 651
graphing, 186–190
identifying, 644–646
linear
  comparing, 660–661
  definition of, 230, 657
  family of, 300
  general form of, 651
  graphing, 232
  identifying, 230–233
  reflections of, 303
  rotations of, 302
  transformations of, 301–304
  vertical translations of, 301
parent
  definition of, 301
  linear, 301
  quadratic, 544, 545
quadratic
  characteristics of, 531–535
  comparing, 662–663
  comparing graphs of, 547
  definition of, 522
  domain of, 525
  in families of functions, 544
  finding zeros of, 531
  general form of, 651
  graphing, 538–541
    using a table of values, 523
  identifying, 522–525
  range of, 525
  transformations of, 545–548
relations and, 170–172
writing, 179–182
zeros of, 531

function notation, 180

function rules, 180, 193

function table, 193

fund-raising, 199

G

Galileo Galilei, 185

gallium, 139

Games, 565

Gardening, 66, 122, 485

GCF (greatest common factor), 457–458
  factoring by, 463–466

general forms of functions, 651

geodes, 356

Geology, 20, 21, 356

Geology Link, 21, 356

geometric models of special products, 433, 435

geometric sequences, 618–620

geometry, 461, 477, 485, 558. *See also* **Applications**

angles
  central, 689
  corresponding, 69
annulus, 469
area
  of composite figures, 23
  in the coordinate plane, 243
  of a rectangle, 23
  of a square, 23
  surface, 403, 430
  of a trapezoid, 566
  of a triangle, 23
changing dimensions, 15, 71
cones
  surface area of, 430
  volume of, 430
Connecting Algebra to, 14–15, 23, 141, 243, 430
coordinate plane
  area in the, 243
corresponding sides, 69
cylinders, 430
dimensions, changing, 15, 71
geometric models
  of special products, 433, 435
half-plane, 360
indirect measurement, 70
perimeter, 14–15
polygons, 14–15
prisms, 430
pyramids, 430
Pythagorean Theorem, 573
rectangles, area of, 23
reflections, 303
rotations, 302
scale, 64
scale drawing, 64
scale factor, 71
scale model, 64
sectors, 688
similar figures, 69
slopes of lines, 293–296
transformations
  of absolute-value functions, 311–313
  of linear functions, 301–304
  of quadratic functions, 545–548
translations, 301
Triangle Inequality, 141
volume, 430

Get Organized. *See* **Graphic Organizers**

glossary, G1–G42

graph(s). *See also* **graphing**
  bar, 684–685, 686
  circle, 684–685, 688
  comparing, of quadratic functions, 547
  connecting to function rules and tables, 193
  continuous, 165
  discrete, 165
  double-bar, 687
  double-line, 688
  finding slope from, 255

real, closure sets of, 431
Number Sense, 460, 461
Number Theory, 210, 566, 572
    Connecting Algebra to, 350–351, 497
Number Theory Link, 210
numerical expressions, 6
Nutrition, 27, 28, 145, 174, 712

Oceanography, 63, 190
ocelots, 201
odds, 736
Online Resources
    Career Resources Online, 46, 132, 334, 479
    Chapter Project Online, 2, 72, 96, 160, 226, 324, 388, 452, 518, 614, 680
    Homework Help Online
        Homework Help Online is available for every lesson. Refer to the box at the beginning of each exercise set. Some examples: 9, 20, 27, 36, 45
    Lab Resources Online, 12, 16, 39, 193, 204, 328, 335, 412, 487, 544, 560
    Parent Resources Online
        Parent Resources Online are available for every lesson. Refer to the box at the beginning of each exercise set. Some examples: 9, 20, 27, 36, 45
    State Test Practice Online, 92, 158, 222, 322, 384, 450, 514, 612, 678, 760
operations, inverse, 17, 24, 32, 40, 49, 106
opposite binomials, 466
    factoring with, 466
opposite coefficients, 343
orangutans, 116
ordered pairs
    identifying exponential functions by using, 522, 650
    identifying linear functions by using, 231, 650
    identifying quadratic functions by using, 625, 650
    showing relations by, 170
organizing data, 686–690
outcome, 727
outliers, 702–703, 715
output, 179

paella, 260
parabola(s)
    axis of symmetry of a, 532–533
    definition of, 523

exploring, 530
    identifying the direction of a, 524
    vertex of a, 524, 533
    vertical translations of a, 547
    width of a, 545
parallel lines, slopes of, 293–296
parent functions
    definition of, 301
    linear, 301
    quadratic, 544, 545
Parent Resources Online
    Parent Resources Online are available for every lesson. Refer to the box at the beginning of each exercise set. Some examples: 9, 20, 27, 36, 45
Pascal, Blaise, 502
Pascal's Triangle, 502
patterns
    in choosing a model, 650
    identifying, 644–645
    in investigating integer exponents, 392
    recursive, 644–645
Pearl, Nancy, 306
pendulum, period of a, 572
perfect-square trinomials, 433, 490
perimeter, 14–15
perpendicular lines, slopes of, 293–296
Personal Finance, 241, 463, 468, 642, 664
Pet Care, 655
Photography, 417, 427
Physical Science, 236, 621, 658
Physics, 408, 467, 485, 501, 548, 550, 566, 572, 585, 593, 628
Pimlico Race Course, 168
point-slope form of linear equations, 275–279
polygons, 14–15
polynomial(s). *See also* **factoring polynomials**
    addition of, 414–416
    closure of sets of, 432
    cubic, 407, 443
    degrees of, 406–407
    leading coefficients of, 407
    multiplication of, 422–426
    quadratic, 407
    standard form of, 407
    subtraction of, 412–416
    unfactorable, 499
Population, 68
positive correlation, 197
positive slope, 246
precision of measurements, 75–78
prediction, 729
preparing for your final exam, 683
prime factorization, 456
prime numbers, 456
prisms, 430

probability
    converting between odds and, 736
    definition of, 727
    of dependent events, 743
    experimental, 727–729
    of inclusive events, 748
    of independent events, 741
    of mutually exclusive events, 748
    theoretical, 734–737
Problem-Solving Applications, 34, 107–108, 189, 278, 331, 435–436, 491–492, 539–540, 577–578, 651–652, 743
Problem-Solving Handbook, PS2–PS11
    draw a diagram, PS2
    find a pattern, PS6
    guess and test, PS4
    make a model, PS3
    make an organized list, PS11
    make a table, PS7
    solve a simpler problem, PS8
    use a Venn diagram, PS10
    use logical reasoning, PS9
    work backward, PS5
properties
    of equality, 19, 26
    of inequality, 106, 112, 113
proportions
    applications of, 69–71
    cross products in, 63
    definition of, 62
    rates, ratios and, 62–65
pyramids, 430
Pythagorean theorem, 573

Qin Jiushao, 348
quadratic equations
    definition of, 554
    discriminant of, 584
    related function of, 554
    roots of, 560–561
    solving
        by completing the square, 576, 586
        by factoring, 562–565, 586
        by graphing, 554–559, 586
        by using square roots, 568–571, 586
        by using the Quadratic Formula, 582–587
    standard form of, 554
quadratic formula
    discriminant and, 583–587
    in estimating solutions, 583–584
    solving quadratic equations by, 582–587
quadratic functions
    characteristics of, 531–535
    comparing, 662–663
    comparing graphs of, 547
    definition of, 522
    domain of, 525

in families of functions, 544
finding zeros of, 531
general form of, 651
graphing, 538–541
    using a table of values, 523
identifying, 522–525
range of, 525
transformations of, 545–548
quadratic models, 649–652
quadratic parent functions, 544, 545
quadratic polynomials, 407
Quality Control, 729

radical symbol, 398, 400
rainbows, 404
random numbers, 733
random samples, 717, 722
range, 22, 170, 171, 172, 173, 174, 175, 176, 182, 183, 184, 185, 190, 194, 195
of linear functions, 233
of quadratic functions, 525
reasonable, 182, 183, 184, 185, 189, 195, 217, 218, 233, 238, 304, 529
range (of a data set), 702, 703
rate of change
constant and variable, 656–657
decrease, 631
definition of, 244, 656
identifying linear and nonlinear functions from, 657–658
increase, 631
slope and, 244–247
rates, 62–65
ratio(s)
equivalent, 62
rates, proportions and, 62–65
rational exponents, 398–400
reading
graphics, 697
the problem, 391
Reading Math, 62, 64, 69, 102, 181, 206, 254, 354, 392, 493, 568, 636, 661, 688, 704, 735, 736
Reading and Writing Math, 5, 99, 163, 229, 327, 391, 455, 521, 617, 683, 697. *See also* **Reading Strategies; Study Strategies; Writing Strategies**
Reading Strategies
Read a Lesson for Understanding, 455
Read and Interpret Graphics, 697
Read and Interpret Math Symbols, 163
Read and Understand the Problem, 391
Use Your Book for Success, 5
Ready to Go On?, 61, 83, 119, 149, 195, 213, 267, 309, 359, 375, 405, 441, 489, 505, 553, 599, 633, 669, 725, 751. *See also* **Assessment**

Real Estate, 73
real numbers, closure of sets of, 431
Real-World Connections, 94–95, 224–225, 386–387, 516–517, 762–763
reasonable answer, 19, 20, 21, 22, 28, 29, 35, 44, 63, 65, 66, 68, 70, 72, 91, 102, 108, 114, 165, 189, 331, 332, 362, 369, 548, 555, 578, 586, 624, 635, 637
reasonable domain, 182, 183, 184, 185, 189, 195, 217, 218, 233, 238, 304, 529
reasonableness, 19, 20, 21, 22, 28, 29, 35, 44, 65, 66, 68, 70, 72, 91, 184, 185, 189, 195, 199, 555
reasonable range, 182, 183, 184, 185, 189, 195, 217, 218, 233, 238, 304, 529
reasoning
explaining your, in extended responses, 610–611
spatial, 676–677
recognizing distracters, 320–321
Recreation, 27, 58, 130, 168, 174, 210, 251, 340, 371, 665, 666
Recreation Link, 130
rectangle model for multiplying polynomials, 424
rectangles, area of, 23
recursive formula, 647
recursive patterns, 644–645
Recycling, 8
reflections, 303
regression, linear, 286–287
relations, functions and, 170–172
relationships
graphing, 164–166
variable, model, 178
Remember!, 50, 55, 120, 135, 144, 232, 233, 294, 301, 344, 367, 392, 398, 406, 407, 414, 422, 436, 456, 472, 481, 539, 545, 570, 577, 582, 590, 591, 592, 602, 650, 662, 686
remembering formulas, 617
Remodeling, 477
replacement set, 8
representations
multiple, 16, 19, 26, 39, 41, 101, 106, 112, 113, 128, 134, 135, 136, 170 248, 193, 229, 254, 268, 293, 295, 335, 392, 412, 413, 420, 421, 433, 435, 462, 470, 471, 473, 490, 492, 524, 532, 533, 545, 560, 561, 562, 568, 574, 575
residual, 285
rise, 245
root(s)
exploring, 560–561
of quadratic equations, 560–561
rotations, 302
run, 245

Safety, 144
samples, random, 717, 722
sample space, 727
Sandia Peak Tramway, 238
scale, 64
scale drawing, 64
scale factor, 71
scale model, 64
scatter plots
interpreting, 204
trend lines and, 196–199, 284
School, 21, 129, 306, 332, 365, 713, 745
School Link, 745
Science, 66, 280, 464, 638
Science Link, 280
Seabiscuit, 168
sea horses, 63
second coordinates, 170
second differences, 522
sectors, 688
Selected Answers, SA2–SA34
sequences
arithmetic, 206–208
definition of, 206
geometric, 618–620
recursive, 644–645
set, 41
set-builder notation, 100
Sheppard, Alfred, 66
Shipping, 209
Short Response, 22, 30, 93, 117, 132, 156–157, 159, 169, 203, 223, 274, 323, 349, 372, 383, 385, 397, 411, 448, 449, 451, 478, 503, 512, 513, 515, 529, 543, 581, 613, 641, 677, 679, 694, 709, 732, 761
Understand Short Response Scores, 156–157
silicon chips, 629
similar figures, 69
simple random sample, 722
simulations, 726
skewed data distributions, 711
slope(s)
comparing, 247
defined, 245
finding, 255–256
formula, 254–257
negative, 246
of parallel lines, 293–296
of perpendicular lines, 293–296
positive, 246
rate of change and, 244–247
of trend lines, 284
undefined, 246
zero, 246
slope formula, 254–257
slope-intercept form of linear equations, 268–271, 274

Index

Index